8th Edition Fundamentals of Business Law: Summarized Cases

Roger LeRoy Miller

Institute for University Studies
Arlington, Texas

Gaylord A. Jentz

Herbert D. Kelleher
Emeritus Professor in Business Law
University of Texas at Austin

SOUTH-WESTERN
CENGAGE Learning

Australia • Brazil • Japan • Korea • Mexico • Singapore • Spain • United Kingdom • United States

SOUTH-WESTERN
CENGAGE Learning™

Fundamentals of Business Law: Summarized Cases
EIGHTH EDITION

Roger LeRoy Miller
Gaylord A. Jentz

Vice President and Editorial Director:
Jack Calhoun

Editor-in-Chief:
Rob Dewey

Acquisitions Editor:
Vicky True

Senior Developmental Editor:
Jan Lamar

Executive Marketing Manager:
Lisa L. Lysne

Marketing Manager:
Jennifer Garamy

Marketing Coordinator:
Gretchen Swann

Marketing Communications Manager:
Sarah Greber

Production Manager:
Bill Stryker

Senior Media Editor:
Kristen Meere

Manufacturing Buyer:
Kevin Kluck

Editorial Assistant:
Krista Kellman

Compositor:
Parkwood Composition Service, Inc.

Senior Art Director:
Michelle Kunkler

Internal Designer:
Bill Stryker

Cover Designer:
Rokusek Design

Cover Image:
© kentoh/Shutterstock

For product information and technology assistance, contact us at
Cengage Learning Academic Resource Center, 1-800-423-0563

For permission to use material from this text or product, submit all requests online at **www.cengage.com/permissions**
Further permissions questions can be emailed to
permissionrequest@cengage.com

ExamView® and ExamView Pro® are registered trademarks of FSCreations, Inc. Windows is a registered trademark of the Microsoft Corporation used herein under license. Macintosh and Power Macintosh are registered trademarks of Apple Computer, Inc., used herein under license.

© 2010, 2007 Cengage Learning. All Rights Reserved.
Cengage Learning WebTutor™ is a trademark of Cengage Learning.

Library of Congress Control Number: 2008939882

ISBN-13: 978-0-324-59573-4
ISBN-10: 0-324-59573-5

SOUTH-WESTERN CENGAGE LEARNING
5191 Natorp Boulevard
Mason, OH 45040
USA

Cengage Learning products are represented in Canada by Nelson Education, Ltd.

For your course and learning solutions, visit **www.cengage.com**

Purchase any of our products at your local college store or at our preferred online store at **www.ichapters.com**

Contents in Brief

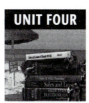

Contents

UNIT 2

**Torts and
Crimes   79**

UNIT 3
Contracts 151

UNIT 6

Debtor-Creditor Relationships 397

UNIT 7

Employment Relations 445

UNIT 8

**Business
Organizations 499**

Preface to the Instructor

Now, more than ever before, a fundamental knowledge of the tenets of business law is crucial for anyone contemplating a career in business. Consequently, we have written *Fundamentals of Business Law: Summarized Cases*, Eighth Edition, with this goal in mind: to present a clear and comprehensive treatment of what every student should know about commercial law. While some of this may change, the fundamentals rarely do—and that's what students reading this text will acquire.

WHAT'S NEW IN THE EIGHTH EDITION

Instructors have come to rely on the up-to-date coverage, accuracy, and applicability of *Fundamentals of Business Law: Summarized Cases*. To make sure that our text engages your students' interests, solidifes their understanding of the legal concepts presented, and provides the best teaching tools available, we now offer the following items in the text.

Practical Elements in Every Chapter

We have added a **special new feature entitled** *Preventing Legal Disputes*. These brief features offer practical guidance on steps that businesspersons can take in their daily transactions to avoid legal disputes and litigation. These features are integrated throughout the text in selected chapters as appropriate to the topics being discussed.

We have also revised the Internet exercises that conclude each chapter to focus on the practical aspects of doing business in today's global legal environment.

Reviewing Features in Every Chapter

For the Eighth Edition of *Fundamentals of Business Law: Summarized Cases*, we have included a special feature at the end of every chapter that helps solidify students' understanding of the chapter materials. Each of these *Reviewing [chapter topic]* features presents a hypothetical scenario and then asks a series of questions that require students to identify the issues and apply the legal concepts discussed in the chapter. These features are designed to help students review the chapter topics in a simple and interesting way and see how the legal principles discussed in the chapter affect the world in which they live. An instructor can use these features as the basis for in-class discussion or encourage students to use them for self-study before completing homework assignments. **Suggested answers to the questions posed in the *Reviewing* features can be found in both the *Instructor's Manual* and the *Answers Manual* that accompany this text.**

Critical Thinking and Legal Reasoning

Today's business leaders are often required to think "outside the box" when making business decisions. For this reason, **we have added a number of critical-thinking elements for the Eighth Edition** that are designed to challenge students' understanding of the materials beyond simple retention. Nearly every feature and every case presented in the text concludes with some type of critical-thinking question. These questions include *For Critical Analysis, What If the Facts Were Different?* and *Why Is This Case Important?*

New Streamlined Organization for the Chapter-Ending *Questions and Case Problems*

We have completely reorganized and streamlined the *Questions and Case Problems* that conclude each chapter. To facilitate assessment, the problems are now divided by sub-headings into the following two categories:

1 Hypothetical Scenarios and Case Problems—We begin with a few hypothetical scenarios, which present simple situations and ask students to apply the legal concepts from the chapter. Included in this group of questions is the new *Hypothetical Question with Sample Answer,*

(for which a sample answer is available in Appendix E of the text and on the Web site). Next are the case problems, which present the facts of recent cases and ask students to analyze how the law applies. These problems include a *Case Problem with Sample Answer* (that is based on an actual case and answered on the text's Web site) and *A Question of Ethics,* most of which are new to this edition.

2 Critical Thinking and Writing Assignments—The second subsection consists of the critical thinking and writing assignments, which are designed to enhance critical-thinking skills and include several types of questions that are new to this edition.

- Selected chapters include a *Critical Legal Thinking* question that requires students to think critically about some aspect of the law discussed in the chapter.

- A number of chapters include a *Critical Thinking and Writing Assignment for Business* question that focuses on critical thinking in a business-oriented context.

- Many chapters also include a special *Video Question* that directs students to the text's Web site (at **www.cengage.com/blaw/fbl**) to access a video relevant to a topic covered in the chapter (a passcode is required—see the discussion of the *Business Law Digital Video Library* later in this preface). The students view the video clip and then answer a series of questions on how the law applies to the situation depicted in the video.

More on the Sarbanes-Oxley Act of 2002

In a number of places in this text, we refer to the Sarbanes-Oxley Act of 2002 and the corporate scandals that led to the passage of that legislation. For example, Chapter 3 mentions how the requirements of the Sarbanes-Oxley Act were intended to deter unethical corporate conduct and make certain corporate acts illegal. In Chapter 27, we discuss this act in the context of securities law and corporate governance and present an exhibit (Exhibit 27–4) containing some of the key provisions of the act relating to corporate accountability in securities transactions. In Chapter 31, we look at provisions of the Sarbanes-Oxley Act as they relate to public accounting firms and accounting practices.

Because the Sarbanes-Oxley Act is a topic of significant concern in today's business climate, for the Eighth Edition, we have added **excerpts and explanatory comments on the Sarbanes-Oxley Act of 2002 as Appendix D.** Students and instructors alike will find it useful to have the provisions of the act immediately available for reference and explained in plain language.

FUNDAMENTALS OF BUSINESS LAW ON THE WEB

For this edition of *Fundamentals of Business Law: Summarized Cases,* we have redesigned and streamlined the text's Web site so that users can easily locate the resources they seek. When you visit our Web site at **www.cengage.com/blaw/fbl**, you will find a broad array of teaching/learning resources, including the following:

- *Relevant Web sites* for all of the *Landmark and Classic Cases* that are presented in this text.

- *Sample Answers* to the *Case Problems with Sample Answers,* which appear at the end of all the chapters, are posted on the student companion Web site. This problem-answer set is designed to help your students learn how to answer case problems by giving them model answers to selected problems. In addition, we post the answers to the *Hypothetical Questions with Sample Answers* on the Web site as well as in the text (Appendix E).

- *Videos* referenced in the *Video Questions* that appear at the ends of selected chapters (available only with a passcode).

- *Practical Internet Exercises* for every chapter in the text (at least two per chapter). The Internet exercises have been refocused to provide more practical information to business law students on topics covered in the chapters and to acquaint students with the legal resources that are available online.

- *Interactive quizzes* for every chapter in this text that include a number of questions related to each chapter's contents.

- *Terms and Concepts* for every chapter in the text.

- *Flashcards* that provide students with an optional study tool to review the key terms in every chapter.

- *Appendix A: How to Brief Cases and Analyze Case Problems* This useful appendix for the book is also posted on the Web site.

- *PowerPoint slides* for this edition.

- *Legal reference materials* including a "Statutes" page that offers links to the full text of selected statutes referenced in the text, a Spanish glossary, the text of the appendices that were removed for the Eighth Edition, and links to other important legal resources available for free on the Web.

- *Online Legal Research Guide* that offers complete yet brief guidance to using the Internet and evaluating information obtained from the Internet. As an online resource, it now includes hyperlinks to the Web sites discussed for click-through convenience.

■ *Court case updates* that present summaries of new cases from around the country that specifically relate to the topics covered in chapters of this text.

Business Law Digital Video Library

For this edition of *Fundamentals of Business Law: Summarized Cases,* we have included special *Video Questions* at the ends of selected chapters. Each of these questions directs students to the text's Web site at www.cengage.com/blaw/fbl. Once there, to view the specific video referenced in the *Video Question,* students click on the "Digital Video Library" link and type in their access code. After viewing the video online, students can return to the text's Web site and click on the relevant chapter's "Video Questions" link to view the series of questions based on the video they have just viewed. (An access code for the videos can be packaged with each new copy of this textbook for no additional charge. If *Business Law Digital Video Library* access did not come packaged with the textbook, it can be purchased online at www.cengage.com/blaw/dvl.)

These videos can be used as homework assignments, discussion starters, or classroom demonstrations. By watching a video and answering the questions, students will gain an understanding of how the legal concepts they have studied in the chapter apply to the real-life situation portrayed in the video. **Suggested answers for all of the *Video Questions* are given in both the *Instructor's Manual* and the *Answers Manual* that accompany this text.** The videos are part of our *Business Law Digital Video Library,* a compendium of more than sixty video scenarios and explanations.

SPECIAL FEATURES AND PEDAGOGY

In addition to the components of the *Fundamentals of Business Law: Summarized Cases* teaching/learning package described above, the Eighth Edition offers a number of special features and pedagogical devices, including those described here.

Adapting the Law to the Online Environment

Several chapters in the Eighth Edition contain one of these special features, which examine cutting-edge cyberlaw issues coming before today's courts. Here are some examples of these features:

■ How the Internet Is Expanding Precedent (Chapter 1)

■ Search Engines versus Copyright Owners (Chapter 5)

■ When Spamming Is a Crime (Chapter 6)

■ Are Online Fantasy Sports Just Another Form of Real-Life Gambling? (Chapter 9)

■ Online Personals—Fraud and Misrepresentation Issues (Chapter 10)

Each feature concludes with a *For Critical Analysis* section that asks the student to think critically about some facet of the issues discussed in the feature. **Suggested answers to these questions are included in both the *Instructor's Manual* and the *Answers Manual* that accompany this text.**

Management Perspective

Each of these features begins with a section titled *Management Faces a Legal Issue* that describes a practical issue facing management (such as whether to include arbitration clauses in employment contracts). Next comes a section titled **What the Courts Say** that discusses what the courts have concluded with respect to this issue. The feature concludes with *Implications for Managers,* a section indicating the importance of the courts' decisions for business management and offering some practical guidance. Some examples of these features in the Eighth Edition include:

■ Protecting Trade Secrets (Chapter 5)

■ Covenants Not to Compete in the Internet Context (Chapter 9)

■ Independent-Contractor Negligence (Chapter 22)

■ Interviewing Job Applicants with Disabilities (Chapter 23)

Preventing Legal Disputes

As already discussed, these new features provide practical information to future businesspersons on how to avoid legal problems. Each chapter includes a *Preventing Legal Disputes* feature, integrated as appropriate with the topics being discussed.

Reviewing . . . Features

As discussed previously, these features present a hypothetical scenario and ask a series of questions that require students to identify the issues and apply the legal concepts discussed in the chapter. Each chapter concludes with one of these features, which are intended to help students review the chapter materials in a simple and interesting way.

Case Presentation and Format

For this edition, we have carefully selected recent cases for each chapter that not only provide on-point illustrations of the legal principles discussed in the chapter but also are of high interest to students. The cases are numbered sequentially for easy referencing in class discussions, homework assignments, and examinations. The vast majority of cases in this text are new to the Eighth Edition.

Each case is presented in a special format, which begins with the case title and citation (including parallel citations). Whenever possible, we also include a URL, just below the case citation, that can be used to access the case online (a footnote to the URL explains how to find the specific case at that Web site). We then briefly outline the facts of the dispute, the legal issue presented, and the court's decision. To enhance student understanding, we paraphrase the reason for the court's decision.

Each case concludes with one of the following:

- *For Critical Analysis* These questions require students to think about the court's holding from a variety of different perspectives. For instance, a student might be asked to consider the ethical or global ramifications of a particular ruling. **Suggested answers to these questions are included in both the *Instructor's Manual* and the *Answers Manual* that accompany this text.**

- *What If the Facts Were Different?* These questions ask the student to decide whether and how a specified change in the facts of the case would alter the outcome of the case. **Suggested answers to these questions are included in both the *Instructor's Manual* and the *Answers Manual* that accompany this text.**

- *Why Is This Case Important?* These discussions, which follow selected cases and are answered in the text, clearly set forth the importance of the court's decision in the specific case in today's legal environment. Some of these features focus specifically on why businesspersons today should heed the court's ruling in a particular case.

- *Impact of This Case on Today's Law* For *Landmark and Classic Cases*, we include these sections to clarify the relevance of the case to modern law. As mentioned earlier, we also have a section titled *Relevant Web Sites* at the conclusion of each *Landmark and Classic Case* that directs students to the Web site for additional online resources.

Other Pedagogical Devices within Each Chapter

- *Learning Objectives* (a series of brief questions at the beginning of each chapter designed to provide a framework for the student as he or she reads through the chapter).

- *Highlighted and numbered examples illustrating legal principles* (we have added more for this edition to better clarify legal concepts).

- *Exhibits.*

Chapter-Ending Pedagogy

- *Terms and Concepts* (with appropriate page references).

- *Chapter Summary* (in graphic format with page references).

- *For Review* (the questions set forth in the chapter-opening *Learning Objectives* section are presented again to aid the student in reviewing the chapter. Answers to the even-numbered questions for each chapter are provided on the text's Web site).

- *Questions and Case Problems* (including two new subsections—*Hypothetical Scenarios and Case Problems* and *Critical Thinking and Writing Assignments*).

- *Hypothetical Question with Sample Answer* (as discussed earlier, each chapter contains one hypothetical factual situation, and we provide a sample answer for students in Appendix E of the text and on the Web site).

- *Case Problem with Sample Answer* (as discussed earlier, each chapter contains one of these case problems, for which the answer has been provided on the text's Web site at **www.cengage.com/blaw/fbl**).

- *A Question of Ethics.*

- *Critical Legal Thinking* (in selected chapters).

- *Critical Thinking and Writing Assignment for Business* (in selected chapters).

- *Video Question* (in selected chapters).

- *Accessing the Internet* (including a list of related Web sites, *Practical Internet Exercises*, and *Interactive Quizzes* for each chapter).

Unit-Ending Pedagogy—Extended Case Studies

At the end of each unit is a two-page feature entitled *Extended Case Study.* This feature focuses on a recent court case relating to a topic covered in the unit. Each feature opens with an introductory section, which discusses the background and significance of the case being presented. Then we present excerpts from the court's majority opinion and from a **dissenting opinion** in the case as well. The feature concludes with *Questions for Analysis*—a series of questions that prompt the student to think critically about the legal, ethical, economic, global, or general business implications of the case. **Suggested answers to these questions are included in both the *Instructor's Manual* and the *Answers Manual.***

Appendices

To help students learn how to find and analyze case law, we have included a special appendix at the end of Chapter 1.

There, your students will find information, including an exhibit, on how to read case citations, how to locate cases in case reporters, and what the different components of URLs (Internet addresses) mean. **The appendix to Chapter 1 also presents an annotated sample court case to help your students understand how to read and understand the cases presented within this text.**

We have included at the end of the book the following set of appendices:

A How to Brief Cases and Analyze Case Problems (also now available on the Web site)

B The Constitution of the United States

C The Uniform Commercial Code (Excerpts)

D The Sarbanes-Oxley Act of 2002 (Excerpts and Explanatory Comments)

E Sample Answers for End-of-Chapter Hypothetical Questions with Sample Answers

Those appendices from the Seventh Edition that we did not include in this edition are now posted on the text's Web site (located at www.cengage.com/blaw/fbl).

SUPPLEMENTAL TEACHING MATERIALS

This edition of *Fundamentals of Business Law: Summarized Cases* is accompanied by an expansive number of teaching and learning supplements. Individually and in conjunction with a number of our colleagues, we have developed supplementary teaching materials that we believe are the best available today. Each component of the supplements package is listed below.

Printed Supplements

- *Instructor's Manual* (Includes **additional cases on point** with at least one such case summary per chapter, answers to all *For Critical Analysis* questions in the features, answers for the *Video Questions* at the ends of selected chapters, and answers to the *Extended Case Study* that concludes each unit. Also available on the *Instructor's Resource CD-ROM*, or IRCD, described below.)

- *Study Guide.*

- A comprehensive *Test Bank* (also available on the IRCD).

- *Answers Manual* (Includes answers to the *Questions and Case Problems*, answers to the *For Critical Analysis* questions in the features and all case-ending questions, answers for the *Video Questions* that conclude selected chapters, and alternate problem sets with answers. Also available on the IRCD.)

Software, Video, and Multimedia Supplements

- *Instructor's Resource CD-ROM (IRCD)*—The IRCD includes the following supplements: *Instructor's Manual, Answers Manual, Test Bank,* Case-Problem Cases, Case Printouts, ExamView, PowerPoint Slides, *Online Legal Research Guide,* transparency masters, *Instructor's Manual* for the *Drama of the Law* video series, *Handbook of Landmark Cases and Statutes in Business Law and the Legal Environment, Handbook on Critical Thinking and Writing in Business Law and the Legal Environment,* and *A Guide to Personal Law.*

- **ExamView Testing Software** (available only on the IRCD).

- **WebTutor**—Features chat, discussion groups, testing, student progress tracking, and business law course materials (available for WebCT and Blackboard).

- **PowerPoint Slides**—Many of which have been revised for the Eighth Edition.

- **Case-Problem Cases** (available only on the IRCD).

- **Transparency Masters** (available only on the IRCD).

- *Business Law Digital Video Library*—This dynamic video library features more than sixty video clips that spark class discussion and clarify core legal principles. Access is available for free as an optional package item with each new text. If *Business Law Digital Video Library* access did not come packaged with the textbook, your students can purchase it online at www.cengage.com/blaw/dvl.

FOR USERS OF THE SEVENTH EDITION

We thought that those of you who have been using *Fundamentals of Business Law: Summarized Cases* would like to know some of the major changes that have been made for the Eighth Edition.

New Features and Special Pedagogy

We have added the following entirely new elements for the Eighth Edition:

- *Preventing Legal Disputes*

- *Reviewing . . .* features

- Reorganized and streamlined chapter-ending *Questions and Case Problems* with labels for different categories and more focus on critical thinking and legal reasoning

- *Hypothetical Question with Sample Answer* (in the *Questions and Case Problems* section)

- *Critical Thinking and Writing Assignments for Business* in selected chapters

Significantly Revised Chapters

Every chapter of the Eighth Edition has been revised as necessary to incorporate new developments in the law or to streamline the presentations. A number of new trends in business law are also addressed in the cases and special features of the Eighth Edition. Other major changes and additions made for this edition include the following:

■ Chapter 2 (Traditional and Online Dispute Resolution)—The section on electronic evidence and discovery issues has been updated to include federal rules that became effective in 2006. To provide greater clarity on important foundational issues, many parts of this chapter were reworked, including the discussions of personal jurisdiction, Internet jurisdiction, standing to sue, and appellate review. A chart was added to illustrate the differences among various methods of alternative dispute resolution, and the discussion of electronic filing systems and online dispute resolution was updated. Features were added to discuss the use of private judges and judicial review in other nations.

■ Chapter 3 (Ethics and Business Decision Making)—At the request of reviewers, we have supplemented our ethics coverage with even more practical elements throughout and have included a section that deals with corporate social responsibility and profit maximization. Recent case examples are provided.

■ Chapter 4 (Torts and Cyber Torts)—The discussion of damages was expanded and enhanced, and the subsections on defamation and privacy were thoroughly updated. The negligence coverage has been simplified for clarity. For this edition, we added a high-interest case involving an online roommate-matching service's immunity under the Communications Decency Act. The section on cyber torts in this chapter now includes a feature discussing cross-border spam and the U.S. Safe Web Act, which was enacted in 2006 to address the problem.

■ Chapter 5 (Intellectual Property and Internet Law)—The materials on intellectual property rights in the online environment have been thoroughly revised and updated with a feature included on search engines and copyright owners. Several recent Supreme Court cases are discussed. The section on patents was expanded, and new examples were added. The discussion of file-sharing was updated. A 2008 United States Supreme Court case is presented on the obviousness requirement and patents. In addition, an entirely new subsection on counterfeit goods was added.

■ Chapters 7 through 13 (the Contracts unit)—Throughout this unit, we have added more examples to clarify and enhance our already superb contract law coverage. We have also included more up-to-date information and new features on topics likely to gain student interest, such as on online gambling (see Chapter 9) and online personals (see Chapter 10).

■ Chapters 14 through 17 (the unit on Sales and Lease Contracts)—We have streamlined and simplified our coverage of the Uniform Commercial Code. We have added numerous new numbered examples throughout the unit to increase student comprehension. Because no state has adopted the 2003 amendments to Articles 2 and 2A, we eliminated the references to these amendments throughout the chapters. We have included a new concept summary to clarify delivery without movement of the goods and have added several new features, such as the one discussing the Statute of Frauds and e-mail confirmations in Chapter 14.

■ Chapter 18 (Negotiability, Transferability, and Liability) and Chapter 19 (Checks and Banking in the Digital Age)—We have updated these chapters to accommodate the reality of digital banking and funds transfers. We have also provided additional numbered examples and exhibits to improve the comprehensibility of the materials.

■ Chapter 21 (Creditor's Rights and Bankruptcy)—This chapter has been completely revamped in light of the passage of bankruptcy reform legislation and includes updated dollar amounts for various provisions of the Bankruptcy Code.

■ Chapter 23 (Employment and Immigration Law)—The materials covering employment law have been thoroughly updated to include discussions of legal issues facing employers today. The chapter now includes an entirely new section on immigration law, a topic of increasing importance to employers. A feature discusses how overtime regulations apply to telecommuters. We also cover the latest developments and United States Supreme Court decisions on constructive discharge and affirmative action. The text discussion of burden of proof in unintentional discrimination cases has been revised and clarified.

■ Chapter 24 (Sole Proprietorships, Partnerships, and Limited Liability Companies)—We have revised and updated this chapter in light of the fact that a majority of states have adopted the revised Uniform Partnership Act. The concept of dissociation is covered, and we clarify how it has replaced dissolution when a partner dies or withdraws from a partnership.

■ Chapters 25 and 26 (covering corporate law)—Chapter 25 now provides an updated and streamlined presentation of issues surrounding corporation formation and termination. We have included several new and updated examples, additional key terms, and a new exhibit. The preincorporation materials have been significantly revised to reflect modern practices, as have the materials on fiduciary duties.

- Chapter 27 (Investor Protection, Insider Trading, and Corporate Governance)—This chapter now includes more discussion of insider trading, a revised section on registration statements, and new numbered examples. The requirement of an intent to deceive (*scienter*) is explored in the text. An entirely new section on corporate governance has been added, with references to the Sarbanes-Oxley Act. We have updated the material on online securities offerings and fraud as well.

New Cases and Case Problems

In addition to the changes noted above, you will find that most of the cases in this edition are new. Nearly every chapter has two new cases, and some chapters have three new cases. We have selected these cases with care, choosing topics that are engaging for today's students. We have also added numerous new *Case Problems* and *Questions of Ethics* based on recent cases. We were also able to add many new 2008 case problems.

ACKNOWLEDGMENTS

Numerous careful and conscientious users of *Fundamentals of Business Law: Summaried Cases* were kind enough to help us revise the book. In addition, the staff at Cengage/ South-Western went out of its way to make sure that this edition came out early and in accurate form. In particular, we wish to thank Rob Dewey and Vicky True for their countless new ideas, many of which have been incorporated into the Eighth Edition. We also extend special thanks to Jan Lamar, our longtime developmental editor, for her many useful suggestions and for her efforts in coordinating reviews and ensuring the timely and accurate publication of all supplemental materials. We are particularly indebted to Jennifer Garamy for her support and excellent marketing advice.

Our production manager and designer, Bill Stryker, made sure that we came out with an error-free, visually attractive edition. We will always be in his debt. We are also indebted to the staff at Parkwood Composition, our compositor. Their ability to generate the pages for this text quickly and accurately made it possible for us to meet our ambitious printing schedule.

We must especially thank Katherine Marie Silsbee and Vickie Reierson for their management of the project, as well as for the application of their superb research and editorial skills. We also wish to thank William Eric Hollowell, co-author of the *Instructor's Manual, Study Guide, Test Bank,* and *Online Legal Research Guide,* for his excellent research efforts. The proofreading by Pat Lewis and Ann Whetstone will not go unnoticed. Thank you to Stephanie Reymann for her indexing expertise. We also thank Lavina Leed Miller and Roxanna Lee for their proofreading and other assistance, which helped to ensure an error-free text. Finally, our appreciation goes to Suzanne Jasin for her many special efforts on the projects.

ACKNOWLEDGMENTS FOR PREVIOUS EDITIONS

Kenneth Anderson
Mott Community College

Leonard Axelrod
Metropolitan State University

Denise A. Bartles
Missouri Western State College

Janie Blankenship
Del Mar College

Daniel R. Cahoy
The Pennsylvania State University

Mikelle Calhoun
Valparaiso University

Len Callahan
Embry-Riddle Aeronautical University

William V. Cheek
Embry-Riddle Aeronautical University

Felipe Chia
Harrisburg Area Community College

Anniken Davenport
Harrisburg Area Community College

Philip E. De Marco
Mission College

Carol Docan
California State University, Northridge

James T. Foster
Florence Darlington Technical College

Frank Giesber
Texas Lutheran University

Thomas F. Goldman
Bucks County Community College

Jacqueline S. Groover
Piedmont College

Edward M. Kissling
Ocean County College

Percy L. Lambert
Borough of Manhattan CC

Daniel A. Levin
University of Colorado, Boulder

Jane A. Malloy
Delaware County Community College

John F. Mastriani
El Paso Community College

Russell A. Meade
Gardner-Webb University

Michael W. Pearson
Arizona State University

Steven M. Platau
The University of Tampa

Lee Ruck
George Mason University

Gayle L. Terry
Mary Washington College

Sheila Vagle
Northwest Technical College

Russell A. Walden
College of the Canyons

Alan L. Weldy
Goshen College

John O. Wheeler
University of Virginia

Stephen J. Willis
Vance-Granville Community College

Paula York
Northern Maine Technical College

Acknowledgments for the Eighth Edition

Jamie Baldwin
Embry Riddle Aeronautical University—Daytona Beach

Peter Dawson
Collin College

Douglas V. Jensen
Pierce College

Edward M. Kissling
Ocean County College

Nancy Lahmers
The Ohio State University

Robert M. Rowlands
Harrisburg Area Community College

John Spengler
University of Florida

Staci L. Thornsbury
York Technical College

Deborah Vinecour
SUNY Rockland Community College

We know that we are not perfect. If you or your students find something you don't like or want us to change, write to us or let us know via e-mail, using the "Talk to Us" feature on this text's Web site. That is how we can make *Fundamentals of Business Law: Summarized Cases* an even better book in the future.

Roger LeRoy Miller
Gaylord A. Jentz

Dedication

To John Orr,
Thanks for your loyalty,
your professionalism,
the countless nights and
weekends of work on my
projects, all with your
endless enthusiasm.

            –R.L.M.

To my wife, JoAnn;
my children,
Kathy, Gary, Lori, and Rory;
and my grandchildren,
Erin, Megan, Eric, Emily, Michelle,
Javier, Carmen, and Steve.

            –G.A.J.

UNIT ONE

The Legal Environment of Business

UNIT CONTENTS

CHAPTER 1
The Legal and Constitutional Environment of Business

LEARNING OBJECTIVES

AFTER READING THIS CHAPTER, YOU SHOULD BE ABLE TO ANSWER THE FOLLOWING QUESTIONS:

1 What is the Uniform Commercial Code?

2 What is the common law tradition?

3 What is a precedent? When might a court depart from precedent?

4 What are some important differences between civil law and criminal law?

5 How does the U.S. Constitution affect business activities in the United States?

T he law is of interest to all persons, not just to lawyers. Those entering the world of business will find themselves subject to numerous laws and government regulations. A basic knowledge of these laws and regulations is beneficial— if not essential—to anyone contemplating a successful career in today's business world.

Although the law has had and will continue to have different definitions, they all are based on the general observation that, at a minimum, **law** consists of *enforceable rules governing relationships among individuals and between individuals and their society.* These "enforceable rules" may consist of unwritten principles of behavior established by a nomadic tribe. They may be set forth in an ancient or a contemporary law code. They may consist of written laws and court decisions created by modern legislative and judicial bodies, as in the United States. Regardless of how such rules are created, they all have one thing in common: they establish rights, duties, and privileges that are consistent with the values and beliefs of their society or its ruling group.

In this introductory chapter, we first look at an important question for any student reading this text: How does the legal environment affect business decision making? We next describe the basic sources of American law, the common law tradition, and some general classifications of law. We conclude the chapter with a discussion of the U.S. Constitution as it affects business.

BUSINESS ACTIVITIES AND THE LEGAL ENVIRONMENT

As those entering the world of business will learn, laws and government regulations affect virtually all business activities—hiring and firing decisions, workplace safety, the manufacturing and marketing of products, and business financing, to name just a few. To make good business decisions, a basic knowledge of the laws and regulations governing these activities is beneficial, if not essential. In today's world, though, a knowledge of "black-letter" law is not enough. Businesspersons are also pressured to make ethical decisions. Thus, the study of business law necessarily involves an ethical dimension.

Many Different Laws May Affect a Single Business Transaction

As you will note, each chapter in this text covers a specific area of the law and shows how the legal rules in that area affect business activities. Although compartmentalizing the law in this fashion facilitates learning, it does not indicate the extent to which many different laws may apply to just one transaction. **■EXAMPLE 1.1** Suppose that you are the president of NetSys, Inc., a company that creates and maintains computer network systems for its clients, including business firms. NetSys also markets software for customers who require an internal computer network. One day, Janet Hernandez, an operations officer for Southwest Distribution Corporation (SDC), contacts you by e-mail about a possible contract involving SDC's computer network. In deciding whether to enter into a contract with SDC, you need to consider, among other things, the legal requirements for an enforceable contract. Are the requirements different for a contract for services and a contract for products? What are your options if SDC **breaches** (breaks, or fails to perform) the contract? The answers to these questions are part of contract law and sales law.

Other questions might concern payment under the contract. How can you guarantee that NetSys will be paid? For example, if SDC pays with a check that is returned for insufficient funds, what are your options? Answers to these questions can be found in the laws that relate to negotiable instruments (such as checks) and creditors' rights. Also, a dispute may arise over the rights to NetSys's software, or there may be a question of liability if the software is defective. There may be an issue as to whether you and Hernandez had the authority to make the deal in the first place, or an accountant's evaluation of the contract may lead to a dispute. Resolutions of these questions may be found in the laws that relate to intellectual property, e-commerce, torts, product liability, agency, business organizations, or professional liability. ▣

Finally, if any dispute cannot be resolved amicably, then the laws and the rules concerning courts and court procedures spell out the steps of a lawsuit. Exhibit 1–1 illustrates the various areas of the law that may influence business decision making.

 **PREVENTING LEGAL DISPUTES**

To prevent potential legal disputes, businesspersons need to be aware of the many different laws that may apply to a single business transaction. It is equally important for businesspersons to understand enough about the law to know when to turn to an expert for advice.

▣

Ethics and Business Decision Making

Merely knowing the areas of law that may affect a business decision is not sufficient in today's business world. Businesspersons must also take ethics into account. As you will learn in Chapter 3, *ethics* is generally defined as the study of what constitutes right or wrong behavior. Today, business decision makers need to consider not just whether a decision is legal, but also whether it is ethical.

EXHIBIT 1–1 Areas of the Law That May Affect Business Decision Making

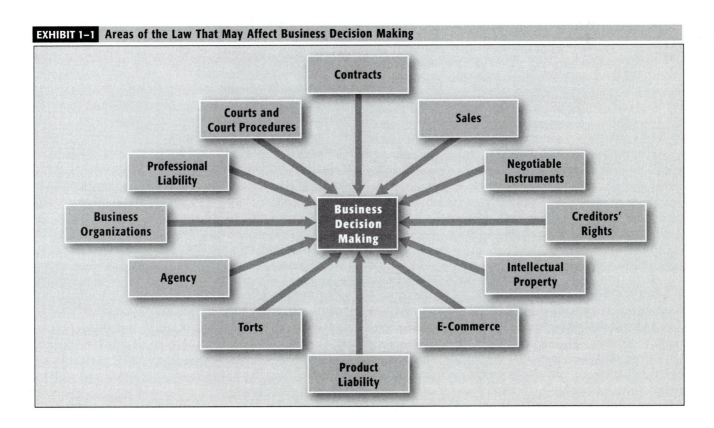

Throughout this text, you will learn about the relationship between the law and ethics, as well as about some of the types of ethical questions that often arise in the business context. Not only is Chapter 3 devoted solely to an examination of the importance of ethical considerations in business decision making, but various other elements in every chapter of this text are designed to help you become aware of the ethical aspects of questions that businesspersons may face. For example, the *Ethical Consideration* questions that follow selected cases in this text explore the ethical dimensions of the case. In addition, the case problems at the end of each chapter include *A Question of Ethics* designed to introduce you to the ethical aspects of a specific case involving a real-life situation.

SOURCES OF AMERICAN LAW

There are numerous sources of American law. **Primary sources of law,** or sources that establish the law, include the following:

1 The U.S. Constitution and the constitutions of the various states.

2 Statutes, or laws, passed by Congress and by state legislatures.

3 Regulations created by administrative agencies, such as the federal Food and Drug Administration.

4 Case law (court decisions).

We describe each of these important primary sources of law in the following pages. (See the appendix at the end of this chapter for a discussion of how to find statutes, regulations, and case law.)

Secondary sources of law are books and articles that summarize and clarify the primary sources of law. Legal encyclopedias, compilations (such as *Restatements of the Law*, which summarize court decisions on a particular topic), official comments to statutes, treatises, articles in law reviews published by law schools, and articles in other legal journals are examples of secondary sources of law. Courts often refer to secondary sources of law for guidance in interpreting and applying the primary sources of law discussed here.

Constitutional Law

The federal government and the states have separate written constitutions that set forth the general organization, powers, and limits of their respective governments. **Constitutional law** is the law as expressed in these constitutions.

The U.S. Constitution is the supreme law of the land. As such, it is the basis of all law in the United States. A law in violation of the Constitution, if challenged, will be declared unconstitutional and will not be enforced no matter what its source. Because of its paramount importance in the American legal system, we discuss the U.S. Constitution at length later in this chapter and present the complete text of the Constitution in Appendix B.

The Tenth Amendment to the U.S. Constitution reserves to the states all powers not granted to the federal government. Each state in the union has its own constitution.

Statutory Law

Laws enacted by legislative bodies at any level of government, such as the statutes passed by Congress or by state legislatures, make up the body of law generally referred to as **statutory law.** When a legislature passes a statute, that statute ultimately is included in the federal code of laws or the relevant state code of laws. Whenever a particular statute is mentioned in this text, we usually provide a footnote showing its **citation** (a reference to a publication in which a legal authority—such as a statute or a court decision—or other source can be found). In the appendix following this chapter, we explain how you can use these citations to find statutory law.

Statutory law also includes local **ordinances**—statutes (laws, rules, or orders) passed by municipal or county governing units to govern matters not covered by federal or state law. Ordinances commonly have to do with city or county land use (zoning ordinances), building and safety codes, and other matters affecting the local governing unit.

A federal statute, of course, applies to all states. A state statute, in contrast, applies only within the state's borders. State laws thus may vary from state to state. No federal statute may violate the U.S. Constitution, and no state statute or local ordinance may violate the U.S. Constitution or the relevant state constitution.

Uniform Laws   During the 1800s, the differences among state laws frequently created difficulties for businesspersons conducting trade and commerce among the states. To counter these problems, a group of legal scholars, judges, and lawyers formed the National Conference of Commissioners on Uniform State Laws (NCCUSL) in 1892 to draft **uniform laws** ("model statutes") for the states to consider adopting. The NCCUSL still exists today and continues to issue new uniform laws and periodic revisions of earlier laws.

Each state has the option of adopting or rejecting a uniform law. *Only if a state legislature adopts a uniform law does that law become part of the statutory law of that state.* Note that a state legislature may adopt all or part of a uniform law as it is written, or the legislature may rewrite the law however the legislature wishes. Hence, even though many states may have adopted a uniform law, those states' laws may not be entirely "uniform."

The earliest uniform law, the Uniform Negotiable Instruments Law, was completed by 1896 and was adopted in every state by the early 1920s (although not all states used exactly the same wording). Over the following decades, other acts were drawn up in a similar manner. In all, the NCCUSL has issued more than two hundred uniform acts since its inception. The most ambitious uniform act of all, however, was the Uniform Commercial Code.

The Uniform Commercial Code (UCC)   The Uniform Commercial Code (UCC), which was created through the joint efforts of the NCCUSL and the American Law Institute,[1] was first issued in 1952. The UCC has been adopted in all fifty states,[2] the District of Columbia, and the Virgin Islands. The UCC facilitates commerce among the states by providing a uniform, yet flexible, set of rules governing commercial transactions. The UCC assures businesspersons that their contracts, if validly entered into, normally will be enforced. Because of its importance in the area of commercial law, we cite the UCC frequently in this text. We also present excerpts of the UCC in Appendix C.

Administrative Law

An increasingly important source of American law is **administrative law,** which consists of the rules, orders, and decisions of administrative agencies. An **administrative agency** is a federal, state, or local government agency established to perform a specific function. Rules issued by various administrative agencies now affect virtually every aspect of a business's operations, including the firm's capital structure and financing, its hiring and firing procedures, its relations with employees and unions, and the way it manufactures and markets its products.

Federal Agencies   At the national level, numerous **executive agencies** exist within the cabinet departments of the executive branch. For example, the Food and Drug Administration is within the U.S. Department of Health and Human Services. Executive agencies are subject to the authority of the president, who has the power to appoint and remove officers of federal agencies. There are also many **independent regulatory agencies** at the federal level, including the Federal Trade Commission, the Securities and Exchange Commission, and the Federal Communications Commission. The president's power is less pronounced in

regard to independent agencies, whose officers serve for fixed terms and cannot be removed without just cause.

State and Local Agencies   There are administrative agencies at the state and local levels as well. Commonly, a state agency (such as a state pollution-control agency) is created as a parallel to a federal agency (such as the Environmental Protection Agency). Just as federal statutes take precedence over conflicting state statutes, so do federal agency regulations take precedence over conflicting state regulations. Because the rules of state and local agencies vary widely, we focus here exclusively on federal administrative law.

Agency Creation   Because Congress cannot possibly oversee the actual implementation of all the laws it enacts, it must delegate such tasks to agencies, especially when the legislation involves highly technical matters, such as air and water pollution. Congress creates an administrative agency by enacting **enabling legislation,** which specifies the name, composition, purpose, and powers of the agency being created.

■EXAMPLE 1.2 The Federal Trade Commission (FTC) was created in 1914 by the Federal Trade Commission Act.[3] This act prohibits unfair and deceptive trade practices. It also describes the procedures the agency must follow to charge persons or organizations with violations of the act, and it provides for judicial review (review by the courts) of agency orders. Other portions of the act grant the agency powers to "make rules and regulations for the purpose of carrying out the Act," to conduct investigations of business practices, to obtain reports from interstate corporations concerning their business practices, to investigate possible violations of the act, to publish findings of its investigations, and to recommend new legislation. The act also empowers the FTC to hold trial-like hearings and to **adjudicate** (resolve judicially) certain kinds of disputes that involve FTC regulations. ■

Note that the powers granted to the FTC incorporate functions associated with the legislative branch of government (rulemaking), the executive branch (investigation and enforcement), and the judicial branch (adjudication). Taken together, these functions constitute **administrative process,** which is the administration of law by administrative agencies.

Case Law and Common Law Doctrines

The rules of law announced in court decisions constitute another basic source of American law. These rules of law include interpretations of constitutional provisions, of statutes enacted by legislatures, and of regulations created by administrative agencies. Today, this body of judge-made law is referred to as **case law.** Case law—the doctrines and principles

---

1. This institute was formed in the 1920s and consists of practicing attorneys, legal scholars, and judges.
2. Louisiana has adopted only Articles 1, 3, 4, 5, 7, 8, and 9.

3. 15 U.S.C. Sections 45–58.

announced in cases—governs all areas not covered by statutory law or administrative law and is part of our common law tradition. We look at the origins and characteristics of the common law tradition in some detail in the pages that follow.

THE COMMON LAW TRADITION

Because of our colonial heritage, much of American law is based on the English legal system. A knowledge of this tradition is crucial to understanding our legal system today because judges in the United States still apply common law principles when deciding cases.

Early English Courts

After the Normans conquered England in 1066, William the Conqueror and his successors began the process of unifying the country under their rule. One of the means they used to do this was the establishment of the king's courts, or *curiae regis*. Before the Norman Conquest, disputes had been settled according to the local legal customs and traditions in various regions of the country. The king's courts sought to establish a uniform set of rules for the country as a whole. What evolved in these courts was the beginning of the **common law**—a body of general rules that applied throughout the entire English realm. Eventually, the common law tradition became part of the heritage of all nations that were once British colonies, including the United States.

Courts developed the common law rules from the principles underlying judges' decisions in actual legal controversies. Judges attempted to be consistent, and whenever possible, they based their decisions on the principles suggested by earlier cases. They sought to decide similar cases in a similar way and considered new cases with care, because they knew that their decisions would make new law. Each interpretation became part of the law on the subject and served as a legal **precedent**—that is, a decision that furnished an example or authority for deciding subsequent cases involving similar legal principles or facts.

In the early years of the common law, there was no single place or publication where court opinions, or written decisions, could be found. Beginning in the late thirteenth and early fourteenth centuries, however, each year portions of significant decisions of that year were gathered together and recorded in *Year Books*. The *Year Books* were useful references for lawyers and judges. In the sixteenth century, the *Year Books* were discontinued, and other reports of cases became available. (See the appendix to this chapter for a discussion of how cases are reported, or published, in the United States today.)

Stare Decisis

The practice of deciding new cases with reference to former decisions, or precedents, eventually became a cornerstone of the English and U.S. judicial systems. The practice forms a doctrine called *stare decisis*[4] ("to stand on decided cases").

The Importance of Precedents in Judicial Decision Making   Under the doctrine of *stare decisis*, once a court has set forth a principle of law as being applicable to a certain set of facts, that court and courts of lower rank must adhere to that principle and apply it in future cases involving similar fact patterns. *Stare decisis* has two aspects: first, that decisions made by a higher court are binding on lower courts; and second, that a court should not overturn its own precedents unless there is a strong reason to do so.

Controlling precedents in a *jurisdiction* (an area in which a court or courts have the power to apply the law—see Chapter 2) are referred to as binding authorities. A **binding authority** is any source of law that a court must follow when deciding a case. Binding authorities include constitutions, statutes, and regulations that govern the issue being decided, as well as court decisions that are controlling precedents within the jurisdiction. United States Supreme Court case decisions, no matter how old, remain controlling until they are overruled by a subsequent decision of the Supreme Court, by a constitutional amendment, or by congressional legislation.

Stare Decisis and Legal Stability   The doctrine of *stare decisis* helps the courts to be more efficient because if other courts have carefully reasoned through a similar case, their legal reasoning and opinions can serve as guides. *Stare decisis* also makes the law more stable and predictable. If the law on a given subject is well settled, someone bringing a case to court can usually rely on the court to make a decision based on what the law has been.

Departures from Precedent   Although courts are obligated to follow precedents, sometimes a court will depart from the rule of precedent if it decides that a given precedent should no longer be followed. If a court decides that a precedent is simply incorrect or that technological or social changes have rendered the precedent inapplicable, the court might rule contrary to the precedent. Cases that overturn precedent often receive a great deal of publicity.

EXAMPLE 1.3   In *Brown v. Board of Education of Topeka*,[5] the United States Supreme Court expressly overturned precedent when it concluded that separate educational facilities for

---

4. Pronounced *stahr*-ee dih-*si*-sis.
5. 347 U.S. 483, 74 S.Ct. 686, 98 L.Ed. 873 (1954). See the appendix at the end of this chapter for an explanation of how to read legal citations.

whites and blacks, which had been upheld as constitutional in numerous previous cases,[6] were inherently unequal. The Supreme Court's departure from precedent in *Brown* received a tremendous amount of publicity as people began to realize the ramifications of this change in the law. ■

When There Is No Precedent At times, a court hears a case for which there are no precedents within its jurisdiction on which to base its decision. When hearing such cases, called "cases of first impression," courts often look at precedents established in other jurisdictions for guidance. Precedents from other jurisdictions, because they are not binding on the court, are referred to as **persuasive authorities**. A court may also consider various other factors, including legal principles and policies underlying previous court decisions or existing statutes, fairness, social values and customs, public policy, and data and concepts drawn from the social sciences.

Can a court consider unpublished decisions as persuasive precedent? See this chapter's *Adapting the Law to the Online Environment* feature on the following page for a discussion of this issue.

Equitable Remedies and Courts of Equity

A **remedy** is the means given to a party to enforce a right or to compensate for the violation of a right. **■EXAMPLE 1.4** If Shem is injured because of Rowan's wrongdoing, a court may order Rowan to compensate Shem for the harm by paying him a certain amount. ■

In the early king's courts of England, the kinds of remedies that could be granted were severely restricted. If one person wronged another, the king's courts could award as compensation either money or property, including land. These courts became known as *courts of law*, and the remedies were called *remedies at law*. Even though this system introduced uniformity in the settling of disputes, when plaintiffs wanted a remedy other than economic compensation, the courts of law could do nothing, so "no remedy, no right."

Remedies in Equity *Equity* refers to a branch of the law, founded in justice and fair dealing, that seeks to supply a fair and adequate remedy when no remedy is available at law. In medieval England, when individuals could not obtain an adequate remedy in a court of law, they petitioned the king for relief. Most of these petitions were decided by an adviser to the king called the *chancellor*. The chancellor was said to be the "keeper of the king's conscience." When the chancellor thought that the claim was a fair one, new and unique

remedies were granted. In this way, a new body of rules and remedies came into being, and eventually formal *chancery courts*, or *courts of equity*, were established. The remedies granted by these courts were called *remedies in equity*. Thus, two distinct court systems were created, each having its own set of judges and its own set of remedies.

Plaintiffs (those bringing lawsuits) had to specify whether they were bringing an "action at law" or an "action in equity," and they chose their courts accordingly. **■EXAMPLE 1.5** A plaintiff might ask a court of equity to order a **defendant** (a person against whom a lawsuit is brought) to perform within the terms of a contract. A court of law could not issue such an order because its remedies were limited to payment of money as compensation for damages. A court of equity, however, could issue a decree for *specific performance*—an order to perform what was promised. A court of equity could also issue an *injunction*, directing a party to do or refrain from doing a particular act. In certain cases, a court of equity could allow for the *rescission* (cancellation) of the contract, thereby returning the parties to the positions that they held prior to the contract's formation. ■ Equitable remedies will be discussed in greater detail in Chapter 12.

The Merging of Law and Equity Today, in most states, the courts of law and equity have merged, and thus the distinction between the two courts has largely disappeared. A plaintiff may now request both legal and equitable remedies in the same action, and the trial court judge may grant either form—or both forms—of relief. The merging of law and equity, however, does not diminish the importance of distinguishing legal remedies from equitable remedies. To request the proper remedy, a businessperson (or her or his attorney) must know what remedies are available for the specific kinds of harms suffered. Today, as a rule, courts will grant an equitable remedy only when the remedy at law (money damages) is inadequate. Exhibit 1–2 on page 9 summarizes the procedural differences (applicable in most states) between an action at law and an action in equity.

CLASSIFICATIONS OF LAW

The huge body of the law may be broken down according to several classification systems. For example, one classification system divides law into **substantive law** (all laws that define, describe, regulate, and create legal rights and obligations) and **procedural law** (all laws that establish the methods of enforcing the rights established by substantive law). Other classification systems divide law into federal law and state law or private law (dealing with relationships between persons) and public law (addressing the relationship between persons and their governments).

---

6. See *Plessy v. Ferguson*, 163 U.S. 537, 16 S.Ct. 1138, 41 L.Ed. 256 (1896).

ADAPTING THE LAW TO THE ONLINE ENVIRONMENT   How the Internet Is Expanding Precedent

T he notion that courts should rely on precedents to decide the outcome of similar cases has long been a cornerstone of U.S. law. Nevertheless, the availability of "unpublished opinions" over the Internet is changing what the law considers to be precedent. An *unpublished opinion* is a decision made by an appellate court that is not intended for publication in a reporter (the bound books that contain court opinions).[a] Courts traditionally have not considered unpublished opinions to be "precedent," binding or persuasive, and attorneys were often not allowed to refer to these decisions in their arguments.

An Increasing Number of Decisions Are Not Published in Case Reporters but Are Available Online

The number of court decisions not published in printed books has risen dramatically in recent years. By some estimates, nearly 80 percent of the decisions of the federal appellate courts are unpublished. The number is equally high in some state court systems. California's intermediate appellate courts, for example, publish only about 7 percent of their decisions.

Even though certain decisions are not intended for publication, they are posted ("published") almost immediately on online legal databases, such as Westlaw and Lexis. With the proliferation of free legal databases and court Web sites, the general public also has almost instant access to the unpublished decisions of most courts. This situation has caused a substantial amount of debate over whether unpublished opinions should be given the same precedential effect as published opinions.

Should Unpublished Decisions Establish Precedent?

Prior to the Internet, one might have been able to justify not considering unpublished decisions to be precedent on the grounds of fairness. How could courts and lawyers be expected to consider the reasoning in unpublished decisions if they were not printed in the case reporters? Now that opin-

ions are so readily available on the Web, however, this justification is no longer valid. Moreover, it now seems unfair not to consider these decisions as precedent to some extent because they are so publicly accessible.

Another argument against allowing unpublished decisions to be precedent concerns the quality of the legal reasoning set forth in these decisions. Staff attorneys and law clerks frequently write unpublished opinions so that judges can spend more time on the opinions intended for publication. Consequently, some claim that allowing unpublished decisions to establish precedent could result in bad precedents because the reasoning may not be up to par. If the decision is regarded merely as persuasive precedent, however, then judges who disagree with the reasoning are free to reject the conclusion.

The United States Supreme Court Changes Federal Rules on Unpublished Opinions as of 2007

In spite of objections from several hundred judges and lawyers, the United States Supreme Court made history in 2006 when it announced that it would allow lawyers to refer to (cite) unpublished decisions in all federal courts. The new rule, Rule 32.1 of the Federal Rules of Appellate Procedure, states that federal courts may not prohibit or restrict the citation of federal judicial opinions that have been designated as "not for publication," "non-precedential," or "not precedent." The rule applies only to federal courts and only to unpublished opinions issued after January 1, 2007. It does not specify the effect that a court must give to one of its unpublished opinions or to an unpublished opinion from another court. Basically, the rule simply makes all the federal courts follow a uniform rule that allows attorneys to cite—and judges to consider as persuasive precedent—unpublished decisions beginning in 2007.

The impact of this new rule remains to be seen. At present, the majority of states do not allow their state courts to consider the rulings in unpublished cases as persuasive precedent, and this rule does not affect the states. The Supreme Court's decision, however, provides an example of how technology—the availability of unpublished opinions over the Internet—has affected the law.

FOR CRITICAL ANALYSIS *Now that the Supreme Court is allowing unpublished decisions to be used as persuasive precedent in federal courts, should state courts follow? Why or why not?*

---

a. Recently decided cases that are not yet published are also sometimes called *unpublished opinions,* but because these decisions will eventually be printed in reporters, we do not include them here.

EXHIBIT 1–2 Procedural Differences between an Action at Law and an Action in Equity

PROCEDURE	ACTION AT LAW	ACTION IN EQUITY
Initiation of lawsuit	By filing a complaint.	By filing a petition.
Decision	By jury or judge.	By judge (no jury).
Result	Judgment.	Decree.
Remedy	Monetary damages.	Injunction, specific performance, or rescission.

Frequently, people use the term **cyberlaw** to refer to the emerging body of law that governs transactions conducted via the Internet. Cyberlaw is not really a classification of law, nor is it a new *type* of law. Rather, it is an informal term used to describe traditional legal principles that have been modified and adapted to fit situations that are unique to the online world. Of course, in some areas new statutes have been enacted, at both the federal and the state levels, to cover specific types of problems stemming from online communications. Throughout this book, you will read how the law in a given area is evolving to govern specific legal issues that arise in the online context.

Civil Law and Criminal Law

Civil law spells out the rights and duties that exist between persons and between persons and their governments, and the relief available when a person's rights are violated. Typically, in a civil case, a private party sues another private party (although the government can also sue a party for a civil law violation) to make that other party comply with a duty or pay for the damage caused by the failure to comply with a duty. **EXAMPLE 1.6** If a seller fails to perform a contract with a buyer, the buyer may bring a lawsuit against the seller. The purpose of the lawsuit will be either to compel the seller to perform as promised or, more commonly, to obtain money damages for the seller's failure to perform. ■

Much of the law that we discuss in this text is civil law. Contract law, for example, which we discuss in Chapters 7 through 13, is civil law. The whole body of tort law (see Chapter 4) is civil law. Note that *civil law* is not the same as a *civil law system*. As you will read shortly, a **civil law system** is a legal system based on a written code of laws.

Criminal law has to do with wrongs committed against society for which society demands redress. Criminal acts are proscribed by local, state, or federal government statutes. Thus, criminal defendants are prosecuted by public officials, such as a district attorney (D.A.), on behalf of the state, not by their victims or other private parties. Whereas in a civil case the object is to obtain remedies (such as money damages) to compensate the injured party, in a criminal case the object is to punish the wrongdoer in an attempt to deter others from similar actions. Penalties for violations of criminal statutes consist of fines and/or imprisonment—and, in some cases, death. We will discuss the differences between civil and criminal law in greater detail in Chapter 6.

National and International Law

Although the focus of this book is U.S. business law, increasingly businesspersons in this country engage in transactions that extend beyond our national borders. In these situations, the laws of other nations or the laws governing relationships among nations may come into play. For this reason, those who pursue a career in business today should have an understanding of the global legal environment.

National Law   The law of a particular nation, such as the United States or Sweden, is **national law.** National law, of course, varies from country to country because each country's law reflects the interests, customs, activities, and values that are unique to that nation's culture. Even though the laws and legal systems of various countries differ substantially, broad similarities do exist.

Two types of legal systems predominate around the globe today. One is the common law system of England and the United States, which we have already discussed. The other system is based on Roman civil law, or "code law."[7] The term *civil law*, as used here, refers not to civil as opposed to criminal law but to codified law—an ordered grouping of legal principles enacted into law by a legislature or governing body. In a civil law system, the primary source of law is a statutory code, and case precedents are not judicially binding, as they normally are in a common law system. Although judges in a civil law system commonly refer to

---

7. A third, less prevalent, legal system is common in Islamic countries, where the law is often influenced by *sharia*, the religious law of Islam. Although *sharia* affects the legal codes of many Muslim countries, the extent of its impact and its interpretation vary widely.

previous decisions as sources of legal guidance, they are not bound by precedent; in other words, the doctrine of *stare decisis* does not apply. Exhibit 1–3 lists some countries that today follow either the common law system or the civil law system.

International Law   In contrast to national law, international law applies to more than one nation. **International law** can be defined as a body of written and unwritten laws observed by independent nations and governing the acts of individuals as well as governments. International law is an intermingling of rules and constraints derived from a variety of sources, including the laws of individual nations, the customs that have evolved among nations in their relations with one another, and treaties and international organizations. In essence, international law is the result of centuries-old attempts to reconcile the traditional need of each nation to be the final authority over its own affairs with the desire of nations to benefit economically from trade and harmonious relations with one another.

The key difference between national law and international law is that government authorities can enforce national law. If a nation violates an international law, however, the most that other countries or international organizations can do (if persuasive tactics fail) is to resort to coercive actions against the violating nation. (See Chapter 32 for a more detailed treatment of international law.)

THE CONSTITUTION AS IT AFFECTS BUSINESS

Each of the sources of law discussed earlier helps to frame the legal environment of business. Because laws that govern business have their origin in the lawmaking authority granted by the U.S. Constitution, we examine that document more closely here. We focus on two areas of the Constitution of particular concern to business—the commerce clause and the Bill of Rights. As mentioned earlier, the Constitution pro-

vides the legal basis for both state and federal (national) powers. It is the supreme law in this country, and any law that conflicts with the Constitution, if challenged in court, will be declared invalid by the court.

The Commerce Clause

To prevent states from establishing laws and regulations that would interfere with trade and commerce among the states, the Constitution expressly delegated to the national government the power to regulate interstate commerce. Article I, Section 8, of the U.S. Constitution expressly permits Congress "[t]o regulate Commerce with foreign Nations, and among the several States, and with the Indian Tribes." This clause, referred to as the **commerce clause,** has had a greater impact on business than any other provision in the Constitution.

Initially, the commerce power was interpreted as being limited to *interstate* commerce (commerce among the states) and not applicable to *intrastate* commerce (commerce within a state). In 1824, however, in the landmark case *Gibbons v. Ogden*,[8] the United States Supreme Court held that commerce within a state could also be regulated by the national government as long as the commerce *substantially affected* commerce involving more than one state.

The Commerce Clause and the Expansion of National Powers   In *Gibbons v. Ogden*, the commerce clause was expanded to regulate activities that "substantially affect interstate commerce." As the nation grew and faced new kinds of problems, the commerce clause became a vehicle for the additional expansion of the national government's regulatory powers. Even activities that seemed purely local came under the regulatory reach of the national government if those activities were deemed to substantially affect interstate commerce. **■EXAMPLE 1.7]** In 1942, in *Wickard v. Filburn*,[9] the

---

8. 22 U.S. (9 Wheat.) 1, 6 L.Ed. 23 (1824).
9. 317 U.S. 111, 63 S.Ct. 82, 87 L.Ed. 122 (1942).

EXHIBIT 1–3 The Legal Systems of Selected Nations			
CIVIL LAW		**COMMON LAW**	
Argentina	Indonesia	Australia	Nigeria
Austria	Iran	Bangladesh	Singapore
Brazil	Italy	Canada	United Kingdom
Chile	Japan	Ghana	United States
China	Mexico	India	Zambia
Egypt	Poland	Israel	
Finland	South Korea	Jamaica	
France	Sweden	Kenya	
Germany	Tunisia	Malaysia	
Greece	Venezuela	New Zealand	

Supreme Court held that wheat production by an individual farmer intended wholly for consumption on his own farm was subject to federal regulation. The Court reasoned that the home consumption of wheat reduced the market demand for wheat and thus could have a substantial effect on interstate commerce. ▣

The following landmark case involved a challenge to the scope of the national government's constitutional authority to regulate local activities.

CASE 1.1 **Heart of Atlanta Motel v. United States**

LANDMARK AND CLASSIC CASES

Supreme Court of the United States, 379 U.S. 241, 85 S.Ct. 348, 13 L.Ed.2d 258 (1964).
www.findlaw.com/casecode/supreme.html[a]

FACTS The owner of the Heart of Atlanta Motel, in violation of the Civil Rights Act of 1964, refused to rent rooms to African Americans. The motel owner brought an action in a federal district court to have the Civil Rights Act declared unconstitutional, alleging that Congress had exceeded its constitutional authority to regulate commerce by enacting the act. The owner argued that his motel was not engaged in interstate commerce but was "of a purely local character." The motel, however, was accessible to state and interstate highways. The owner advertised nationally, maintained billboards throughout the state, and accepted convention trade from outside the state (75 percent of the guests were residents of other states). The court ruled that the act did not violate the Constitution and enjoined (prohibited) the owner from discriminating on the basis of race. The owner appealed. The case ultimately went to the United States Supreme Court.

ISSUE Did Congress exceed its constitutional power to regulate interstate commerce by enacting the Civil Rights Act of 1964?

DECISION No. The United States Supreme Court upheld the constitutionality of the act.

REASON The Court noted that the act was passed to correct "the deprivation of personal dignity" accompanying the denial of equal access to "public establishments." Testimony before

Congress leading to the passage of the act indicated that African Americans in particular experienced substantial discrimination in attempting to secure lodging while traveling. This discrimination impeded interstate travel and thus impeded interstate commerce. As for the owner's argument that his motel was "of a purely local character," the Court said that even if this was true, the motel affected interstate commerce. According to the Court, "if it is interstate commerce that feels the pinch, it does not matter how local the operation that applies the squeeze." Therefore, under the commerce clause, "the power of Congress to promote interstate commerce also includes the power to regulate the local incidents thereof, including local activities."

IMPACT OF THIS CASE ON TODAY'S LAW *If the United States Supreme Court had invalidated the Civil Rights Act of 1964, the legal landscape of the United States would be much different today. The act prohibits discrimination based on race, color, national origin, religion, or gender in all "public accommodations," including hotels and restaurants. The act also prohibits discrimination in employment based on these criteria. Although state laws now prohibit many of these forms of discrimination as well, the protections available vary from state to state—and it is not certain when (and if) such laws would have been passed had the 1964 federal Civil Rights Act been deemed unconstitutional.*

RELEVANT WEB SITES *To locate information on the Web concerning the* Heart of Atlanta Motel *decision, go to this text's Web site at* **www.cengage.com/blaw/fbl**, *select "Chapter 1," and click on "URLs for Landmarks."*

a. Under "Citation Search," type in "379" before "U.S." and then "241." Click "Search" to access this court opinion.

▣

The Commerce Power Today Today, at least theoretically, the power over commerce authorizes the national government to regulate every commercial enterprise in the United States. Federal (national) legislation governs virtually every major activity conducted by businesses—from hiring and firing decisions to workplace safety, competitive practices, and financing. In the last fifteen years, however, the Supreme

Court has begun to curb somewhat the national government's regulatory authority under the commerce clause. In 1995, the Court held—for the first time in sixty years—that Congress had exceeded its regulatory authority under the commerce clause. The Court struck down an act that banned the possession of guns within one thousand feet of any school because the act attempted to regulate an area that had "nothing to do with commerce."[10] Subsequently, the Court invalidated key portions of two other federal acts on the ground that they exceeded Congress's commerce clause authority.[11]

In one notable case, however, the Supreme Court did allow the federal government to regulate noncommercial activities taking place wholly within a state's borders. **■EXAMPLE 1.8** Eleven states, including California, have adopted "medical marijuana" laws that legalize marijuana for medical purposes. Marijuana possession, however, is illegal under the federal Controlled Substances Act (CSA).[12] After the federal government seized the marijuana that two seriously ill California women were using on the advice of their physicians, the women argued that it was unconstitutional for the federal act to prohibit them from using marijuana for medical purposes that were legal within the state. In 2003, the U.S. Court of Appeals for the Ninth Circuit agreed, deciding the case on commerce clause grounds. In 2005, however, the United States Supreme Court held that Congress has the authority to prohibit the *intra*state possession and noncommercial cultivation of marijuana as part of a larger regulatory scheme (the CSA).[13] In other words, state medical marijuana laws do not pose barriers to federal drug enforcement. ■

The Regulatory Powers of the States   As part of their inherent sovereignty, state governments have the authority to regulate affairs within their borders. This authority stems in part from the Tenth Amendment to the Constitution, which reserves to the states all powers not delegated to the national government. State regulatory powers are often referred to as **police powers.** The term encompasses not only the enforcement of criminal law but also the right of state governments to regulate private activities to protect or promote the public order, health, safety, morals, and general welfare. Fire and building codes, antidiscrimination laws, parking regulations, zoning restrictions, licensing requirements, and thousands of other state statutes covering virtually every aspect of life have been enacted pursuant to a state's police powers. Local governments, including cities, also exercise police powers. Generally, state laws enacted pursuant to a state's police powers carry a strong presumption of validity.

The "Dormant" Commerce Clause   The United States Supreme Court has interpreted the commerce clause to mean that the national government has the *exclusive* authority to regulate commerce that substantially affects trade and commerce among the states. This express grant of authority to the national government, which is often referred to as the "positive" aspect of the commerce clause, implies a negative aspect—that the states do *not* have the authority to regulate interstate commerce. This negative aspect of the commerce clause is often referred to as the "dormant" (implied) commerce clause.

The dormant commerce clause comes into play when state regulations affect interstate commerce. In this situation, the courts normally weigh the state's interest in regulating a certain matter against the burden that the state's regulation imposes on interstate commerce. Because courts balance the interests involved, it can be extremely difficult to predict the outcome in a particular case.

■EXAMPLE 1.9 At one time, many states regulated the sale of alcoholic beverages, including wine, through a "three-tier" system. This system required separate licenses for producers, wholesalers, and retailers, subject to a complex set of overlapping regulations that effectively banned direct sales to consumers from out-of-state wineries. In-state wineries, in contrast, could obtain a license for direct sales to consumers. In 2005, the United States Supreme Court ruled that these laws violated the dormant commerce clause. The Court reasoned that by mandating different treatment of in-state and out-of-state economic interests, these laws deprived "citizens of their right to have access to the markets of other states on equal terms."[14] ■

Business and the Bill of Rights

The importance of having a written declaration of the rights of individuals eventually caused the first Congress of the United States to enact twelve amendments to the Constitution and submit them to the states for approval. The first ten of these amendments, commonly known as the **Bill of Rights,** were adopted in 1791 and embody a series of protections for the individual against various types of interference by the federal government.[15] Some constitutional protections apply to business entities as well. For example, corporations exist as separate legal entities, or legal persons, and enjoy many of the same rights and privileges as natural persons do. Summarized here are the protections guaranteed

10. The United States Supreme Court held the Gun-Free School Zones Act of 1990 to be unconstitutional in *United States v. Lopez,* 514 U.S. 549, 115 S.Ct. 1624, 131 L.Ed.2d 626 (1995).
11. See, for example, *Printz v. United States,* 521 U.S. 898, 117 S.Ct. 2365, 138 L.Ed.2d 914 (1997), involving the Brady Handgun Violence Prevention Act of 1993; and *United States v. Morrison,* 529 U.S. 598, 120 S.Ct. 1740, 146 L.Ed.2d 658 (2000), concerning the federal Violence Against Women Act of 1994.
12. 21 U.S.C. Sections 801 *et seq.*
13. *Gonzales v. Raich,* 545 U.S. 1, 125 S.Ct. 2195, 162 L.Ed.2d 1 (2005).
14. *Granholm v. Heald,* 544 U.S. 460, 125 S.Ct. 1885, 161 L.Ed.2d 796 (2005); see also *Cherry Hill Vineyard, LLC v. Baldacci,* 505 F.3d 28 (1st Cir. 2007).
15. One of these proposed amendments was ratified more than two hundred years later (in 1992) and became the Twenty-seventh Amendment to the U.S. Constitution. See Appendix B.

by these ten amendments (see the Constitution in Appendix B for the complete text of each amendment):

1 The First Amendment guarantees the freedoms of religion, speech, and the press and the rights to assemble peaceably and to petition the government.

2 The Second Amendment concerns a well-regulated militia and the right of the people to keep and bear arms.

3 The Third Amendment prohibits, in peacetime, the lodging of soldiers in any house without the owner's consent.

4 The Fourth Amendment prohibits unreasonable searches and seizures of persons or property.

5 The Fifth Amendment guarantees the rights to indictment[16] (formal accusation—see Chapter 6) by grand jury, to due process of law, and to fair payment when private property is taken for public use. The Fifth Amendment also prohibits compulsory self-incrimination and double jeopardy (trial for the same crime twice).

6 The Sixth Amendment guarantees the accused in a criminal case the right to a speedy and public trial by an impartial jury and with counsel. The accused has the right to cross-examine witnesses against him or her and to solicit testimony from witnesses in his or her favor.

7 The Seventh Amendment guarantees the right to a trial by jury in a civil (noncriminal) case involving at least twenty dollars.[17]

8 The Eighth Amendment prohibits excessive bail and fines, as well as cruel and unusual punishment.

9 The Ninth Amendment establishes that the people have rights in addition to those specified in the Constitution.

10 The Tenth Amendment establishes that those powers neither delegated to the federal government nor denied to the states are reserved for the states.

As originally intended, the Bill of Rights limited only the powers of the national government. Over time, however, the Supreme Court "incorporated" most of these rights into the protections against state actions afforded by the Fourteenth Amendment to the Constitution. That amendment, passed in 1868 after the Civil War, provides in part that "[n]o State shall . . . deprive any person of life, liberty, or property, without due process of law." Starting in 1925, the Supreme Court began to define various rights and liberties guaranteed in the national Constitution as constituting "due process of law," which was required of state

governments under the Fourteenth Amendment. Today, most of the rights and liberties set forth in the Bill of Rights apply to state governments as well as the national government.

We will look closely at several of the amendments in the above list in Chapter 6, in the context of criminal law and procedures. Here, we examine two important guarantees of the First Amendment—freedom of speech and freedom of religion—and the Fourth Amendment's prohibition of *unreasonable* searches and seizures. These protections have all been applied to the states through the due process clause of the Fourteenth Amendment. As you read through the following pages, keep in mind that none of these (or other) constitutional freedoms confers an absolute right. Ultimately, it is the United States Supreme Court, as the final interpreter of the Constitution, that gives meaning to these rights and determines their boundaries.

The First Amendment—Freedom of Speech Freedom of speech is the most prized freedom that Americans have. Indeed, it is essential to our democratic form of government, which could not exist if people were not allowed to express their political opinions freely and criticize government actions or policies. Because of its importance, the courts traditionally have protected this right to the fullest extent possible.

Speech often includes not only what we say, but also what we do to express our political, social, and religious views. The courts generally protect **symbolic speech**—gestures, movements, articles of clothing, and other forms of nonverbal expressive conduct. **EXAMPLE 1.10** The burning of the American flag to protest government policies is a constitutionally protected form of expression. Similarly, participating in a hunger strike or wearing a black armband would be protected as symbolic speech. ◼

Reasonable Restrictions. Expression—oral, written, or symbolized by conduct—is subject to reasonable restrictions. A balance must be struck between a government's obligation to protect its citizens and those citizens' exercise of their rights. Reasonableness is analyzed on a case-by-case basis. If a restriction imposed by the government is content neutral, then a court may allow it. To be content neutral, the restriction must be aimed at combating some societal problem, such as crime, and not be aimed at suppressing the expressive conduct or its message. **EXAMPLE 1.11** Courts have often protected nude dancing as a form of symbolic expression. Nevertheless, the courts have also allowed content-neutral laws that ban all public nudity, not just erotic dancing.[18] ◼

---

16. Pronounced in-*dyte*-ment.
17. Twenty dollars was forty days' pay for the average person when the Bill of Rights was written.

18. See, for example, *Rameses, Inc. v. County of Orange*, 481 F.Supp.2d 1305 (M.D.Fla. 2007); and *City of Erie v. Pap's A.M.*, 529 U.S. 277, 120 S.Ct. 1382, 146 L.Ed.2d 265 (2000).

The United States Supreme Court has also held that schools may restrict students' free speech rights at school events. **■EXAMPLE 1.12** In 2007, the Court heard a case involving a high school student who had held up a banner saying "Bong Hits 4 Jesus" at an off-campus but school-sanctioned event. In a split decision, the majority of the Court ruled that school officials did not violate the student's free speech rights when they confiscated the banner and suspended the student for ten days. Because the banner could reasonably be interpreted as promoting the use of marijuana, and because the school had a written policy against illegal drugs, the majority concluded that the school's actions were justified. Several justices disagreed, however, noting that the majority's holding creates a special exception that will allow schools to censor any student speech that mentions drugs.[19] ■

Corporate Political Speech. Political speech by corporations also falls within the protection of the First Amendment. Many years ago, the United States Supreme Court ruled that a Massachusetts statute, which prohibited corporations from making political contributions or expenditures that individuals were permitted to make, was unconstitutional.[20] Although the Supreme Court has reversed this trend somewhat,[21] corporate political speech continues to be given significant protection under the First Amendment. **■EXAMPLE 1.13** In 2003 and again in 2007, the Supreme Court struck down portions of bipartisan campaign-finance reform laws as unconstitu-

tional. The Court found that these provisions constituted unlawful restraints on corporate political speech.[22] ■

Commercial Speech. The courts also give substantial protection to "commercial" speech, which consists of communications—primarily advertising and marketing—made by business firms that involve only their commercial interests. The protection given to commercial speech under the First Amendment is not as extensive as that afforded to noncommercial speech, however. A state may restrict certain kinds of advertising, for example, in the interest of protecting consumers from being misled by the advertising practices. States also have a legitimate interest in the beautification of roadsides, and this interest allows states to place restraints on billboard advertising. **■EXAMPLE 1.14** Café Erotica, a nude-dancing establishment, sued the state after being denied a permit to erect a billboard along an interstate highway in Florida. The state appellate court decided that because the law directly advanced a substantial government interest in highway beautification and safety, it was not an unconstitutional restraint on commercial speech.[23] ■

Generally, a restriction on commercial speech will be considered valid as long as it meets three criteria: (1) it must seek to implement a substantial government interest, (2) it must directly advance that interest, and (3) it must go no further than necessary to accomplish its objective. At issue in the following case was whether a government agency had unconstitutionally restricted commercial speech when it prohibited the inclusion of a certain illustration on beer labels.

---

19. *Morse v. Frederick,* ___ U.S. ___, 127 S.Ct. 2618, 168 L.Ed.2d 290 (2007).
20. *First National Bank of Boston v. Bellotti,* 435 U.S. 765, 98 S.Ct. 1407, 55 L.Ed.2d 707 (1978).
21. See *Austin v. Michigan Chamber of Commerce,* 494 U.S. 652, 110 S.Ct. 1391, 108 L.Ed.2d 652 (1990), in which the Supreme Court upheld a state law prohibiting corporations from using general corporate funds for independent expenditures in state political campaigns.

22. *McConnell v. Federal Election Commission,* 540 U.S. 93, 124 S.Ct. 619, 157 L.Ed.2d 491 (2003); and *Federal Election Commission v. Wisconsin Right to Life, Inc.,* ___U.S. ___, 127 S.Ct. 2652, 168 L.Ed.2d 329 (2007).
23. *Café Erotica v. Florida Department of Transportation,* 830 So.2d 181 (Fla.App. 1 Dist. 2002); review denied, *Café Erotica/We Dare to Bare v. Florida Department of Transportation,* 845 So.2d 888 (Fla. 2003).

CASE 1.2 **Bad Frog Brewery, Inc. v. New York State Liquor Authority**

United States Court of Appeals, Second Circuit, 134 F.3d 87 (1998).
www.findlaw.com/casecode/index.html[a]

FACTS Bad Frog Brewery, Inc., makes and sells alcoholic beverages. Some of the beverages feature labels that display a drawing of a frog making the gesture generally known as "giving the finger." Bad Frog's authorized New York distributor, Renaissance Beer Company, applied to the New York State

Liquor Authority (NYSLA) for brand label approval, as required by state law before the beer could be sold in New York. The NYSLA denied the application, in part, because "the label could appear in grocery and convenience stores, with obvious exposure on the shelf to children of tender age." Bad Frog filed a suit in a federal district court against the NYSLA, asking for, among other things, an injunction against the denial of the application. The court granted summary judgment in favor of the NYSLA. Bad Frog appealed to the U.S. Court of Appeals for the Second Circuit.

---

a. Under the heading "US Court of Appeals," click on "2nd." Enter "Bad Frog Brewery" in the "Party Name Search" box and click on "search." On the resulting page, click on the case name to access the opinion.

ISSUE Was the New York State Liquor Authority's ban of Bad Frog's beer labels a reasonable restriction on commercial speech?

DECISION No. The U.S. Court of Appeals for the Second Circuit reversed the judgment of the district court and remanded the case for judgment to be entered in favor of Bad Frog.

REASON The appellate court held that the NYSLA's denial of Bad Frog's application violated the First Amendment. The ban on the use of the labels lacked a "reasonable fit" with the state's interest in shielding minors from vulgarity, and the NYSLA did not adequately consider alternatives to the ban. The court acknowledged that the NYSLA's interest "in protecting children from vulgar and profane advertising" was "substantial." The question was whether banning Bad Frog's labels "directly advanced" that interest. "In view of the wide currency of vulgar displays throughout contemporary society, including comic books targeted directly at children, barring

such displays from labels for alcoholic beverages cannot realistically be expected to reduce children's exposure to such displays to any significant degree." The court concluded that a "commercial speech limitation" must be "part of a substantial effort to advance a valid state interest, not merely the removal of a few grains of offensive sand from a beach of vulgarity." Finally, as to whether the ban on the labels was more extensive than necessary to serve this interest, the court pointed out that there were "numerous less intrusive alternatives." For example, the NYSLA's "concern could be less intrusively dealt with by placing restrictions on the permissible locations where the appellant's products may be displayed within * * * stores."

WHAT IF THE FACTS WERE DIFFERENT?
If Bad Frog had sought to use the offensive label to market toys instead of beer, would the court's ruling likely have been the same? Explain your answer.

Unprotected Speech. The United States Supreme Court has made it clear that certain types of speech will not be given any protection under the First Amendment. Speech that harms the good reputation of another, or defamatory speech (see Chapter 4), will not be protected. Speech that violates criminal laws (such as threatening speech) is not constitutionally protected. Other unprotected speech includes "fighting words," or words that are likely to incite others to respond violently.

The First Amendment, as interpreted by the Supreme Court, also does not protect obscene speech. Establishing an objective definition of obscene speech has proved difficult, however, and the Court has grappled from time to time with this problem. In a 1973 case, *Miller v. California*,[24] the Supreme Court created a test for legal obscenity, which involved a set of requirements that must be met for material to be legally obscene. Under this test, material is obscene if (1) the average person finds that it violates contemporary community standards; (2) the work taken as a whole appeals to a prurient (arousing or obsessive) interest in sex; (3) the work shows patently offensive sexual conduct; and (4) the work lacks serious redeeming literary, artistic, political, or scientific merit.

Because community standards vary widely, the *Miller* test has had inconsistent application, and obscenity remains a constitutionally unsettled issue. Numerous state and federal

statutes make it a crime to disseminate obscene materials, however, and the Supreme Court has often upheld such laws, including laws prohibiting the sale and possession of child pornography.

Online Obscenity. Congress first attempted to protect minors from pornographic materials on the Internet by passing the Communications Decency Act (CDA) of 1996. The CDA declared it a crime to make available to minors online any "obscene or indecent" message that "depicts or describes, in terms patently offensive as measured by contemporary community standards, sexual or excretory activities or organs."[25] Civil rights groups challenged the act, and ultimately the United States Supreme Court ruled that portions of the act were unconstitutional. The Court held that the terms *indecent* and *patently offensive* covered large amounts of nonpornographic material with serious educational or other value.[26]

A second attempt to protect children from online obscenity, the Child Online Protection Act (COPA) of 1998,[27] met with a similar fate. Although the COPA was more narrowly tailored than its predecessor, the CDA, it still used "contemporary community standards" to define which material was obscene

---

24. 413 U.S. 15, 93 S.Ct. 2607, 37 L.Ed.2d 419 (1973).

25. 47 U.S.C. Section 223(a)(1)(B)(ii).
26. *Reno v. American Civil Liberties Union*, 521 U.S. 844, 117 S.Ct. 2329, 138 L.Ed.2d 874 (1997).
27. 47 U.S.C. Section 231.

and harmful to minors. In 2004, the United States Supreme Court concluded that it was likely that the COPA did violate the right to free speech and prevented enforcement of the act.[28]

In 2000, Congress enacted the Children's Internet Protection Act (CIPA),[29] which requires public schools and libraries to block adult content from access by children by installing **filtering software.** Such software is designed to prevent persons from viewing certain Web sites by responding to a site's Internet address or its meta tags, or key words. The CIPA was also challenged on constitutional grounds, but in 2003 the Supreme Court held that the act did not violate the First Amendment. The Court concluded that because libraries can disable the filters for any patrons who ask, the system is reasonably flexible and does not burden free speech to an unconstitutional extent.[30]

Because of the difficulties of policing the Internet as well as the constitutional complexities of prohibiting online obscenity through legislation, obscenity on the Internet is a continuing problem in the United States (and worldwide). In 2005, the Federal Bureau of Investigation established an anti-porn squad to target and prosecute companies that distribute child pornography in cyberspace. The Federal Communications Commission has also passed new obscenity regulations for television networks.

The First Amendment—Freedom of Religion The First Amendment states that the government may neither establish any religion nor prohibit the free exercise of religious practices. The first part of this constitutional provision is referred to as the **establishment clause,** and the second part is known as the **free exercise clause.** Government action, both federal and state, must be consistent with this constitutional mandate.

The Establishment Clause. The establishment clause prohibits the government from establishing a state-sponsored religion, as well as from passing laws that promote (aid or endorse) religion or that show a preference for one religion over another. The establishment clause does not require a complete separation of church and state, though. On the contrary, it requires the government to accommodate religions.

The establishment clause covers all conflicts about such matters as the legality of state and local government support for a particular religion, government aid to religious organizations and schools, the government's allowing or requiring school prayers, and the teaching of evolution versus fundamentalist theories of creation. For a government law or policy to be constitutional, it must not have the primary effect of advancing or inhibiting religion. Generally, federal or state regulation that does not promote religion or place a significant burden on religion is constitutional even if it has some impact on religion.

Religious displays on public property have often been challenged as violating the establishment clause, and the United States Supreme Court has ruled on a number of such cases. Generally, the Court has focused on the proximity of the religious display to nonreligious symbols, such as reindeer and candy canes, or to symbols from different religions, such as a menorah (a nine-branched candelabrum used in celebrating Hanukkah). **■EXAMPLE 1.15** In 2005, however, the Supreme Court took a slightly different approach. The dispute involved a six-foot-tall monument of the Ten Commandments on the Texas state capitol grounds. The Court held that the monument did not violate the establishment clause because the Ten Commandments had historical as well as religious significance.[31] ■

The Free Exercise Clause. The free exercise clause guarantees that a person can hold any religious belief that she or he wants or can choose to have no religious belief. When religious *practices* work against public policy and the public welfare, however, the government can act. For example, regardless of a child's or parent's religious beliefs, the government can require certain types of vaccinations. Similarly, although children of Jehovah's Witnesses are not required to say the Pledge of Allegiance at school, their parents cannot prevent them from accepting medical treatment (such as blood transfusions) if their lives are in danger. Additionally, public school students can be required to study from textbooks chosen by school authorities.

For business firms, an important issue involves the accommodation that businesses must make for the religious beliefs of their employees. Federal employment laws require business firms to accommodate employees' religious beliefs. If an employee's religion prohibits him or her from working on a certain day of the week or at a certain type of job, the employer must make a reasonable attempt to accommodate these religious requirements. Employers must reasonably accommodate an employee's religious beliefs even if the beliefs are not based on the tenets or dogma of a particular church, sect, or denom-

28. *American Civil Liberties Union v. Ashcroft,* 542 U.S. 656, 124 S.Ct. 2783, 159 L.Ed.2d 690 (2004). See also *Ashcroft v. American Civil Liberties Union,* 535 U.S. 564, 122 S.Ct. 1700, 152 L.Ed.2d 771 (2002); and *American Civil Liberties Union v. Ashcroft,* 322 F.3d 240 (3d Cir. 2003).

29. 17 U.S.C. Sections 1701–1741.

30. *United States v. American Library Association,* 539 U.S. 194, 123 S.Ct. 2297, 156 L.Ed.2d 221 (2003).

31. *Van Orden v. Perry,* 545 U.S. 677, 125 S.Ct. 2854, 162 L.Ed.2d 607 (2005).

ination. The only requirement is that the belief be religious in nature and sincerely held by the employee.

Fourth Amendment—Searches and Seizures The Fourth Amendment protects the "right of the people to be secure in their persons, houses, papers, and effects." Before searching or seizing private property, law enforcement officers must usually obtain a **search warrant**—an order from a judge or other public official authorizing the search or seizure.

Search Warrants and Probable Cause. To obtain a search warrant, law enforcement officers must convince a judge that they have reasonable grounds, or probable cause, to believe a search will reveal evidence of a specific illegality. To establish *probable cause,* the officers must have trustworthy evidence that would convince a reasonable person that the proposed search or seizure is more likely justified than not. Furthermore, the Fourth Amendment prohibits *general* warrants. It requires a particular description of whatever is to be searched or seized. General searches through a person's belongings are impermissible. The search cannot extend beyond what is described in the warrant.

The requirement for a search warrant has several exceptions. One exception applies when the items sought are likely to be removed before a warrant can be obtained. **■EXAMPLE 1.16** During a routine traffic stop, a police officer sees evidence that the car is being used to transport illegal drugs. If the officer has probable cause to believe that an automobile contains evidence of a crime and that the vehicle will likely be unavailable by the time a warrant is obtained, the officer can search the vehicle without a warrant. ■

Searches and Seizures in the Business Context. Constitutional protection against unreasonable searches and seizures is important to businesses and professionals. Equally important is the government's interest in ensuring compliance with federal and state regulations, especially rules meant to protect the safety of employees and the public.

Because of the strong governmental interest in protecting the public, a warrant normally is not required for the seizure of spoiled or contaminated food. In addition, warrants are not required for searches of businesses in such highly regulated industries as liquor, guns, and strip mining. General manufacturing is not considered to be one of these highly regulated industries, however.

Generally, government inspectors do not have the right to search business premises without a warrant, although the standard of probable cause is not the same as that required in nonbusiness contexts. The existence of a general and neutral enforcement plan normally will justify issuance of the warrant. Lawyers and accountants frequently possess the business records of their clients, and inspecting these documents while they are out of the hands of their true owners also requires a warrant.

In the following case, after receiving a report of suspected health-care fraud, state officials entered and searched the office of a licensed physician without obtaining a warrant. The physician claimed that the search was unreasonable and improper.

CASE 1.3 United States v. Moon

United States Court of Appeals, Sixth Circuit, 513 F.3d 527 (2008).
www.ca6.uscourts.gov[a]

FACTS Young Moon was a licensed physician, specializing in oncology and hematology. Moon operated a medical practice in Crossville, Tennessee. As part of her practice, Moon contracted with the state of Tennessee to provide medical treatment to patients pursuant to a state and federally funded health benefit program for the uninsured known as "TennCare." Moon routinely utilized chemotherapy medications in her treatment of cancer patients insured under the program. In March 2001, the Tennessee Bureau of Investigation (TBI) received a complaint from one of Moon's employees alleging that she had administered partial doses of chemotherapy medication while billing the insurance program for full doses. In January 2002, investigating agents conducted an on-site review at Moon's office. The agents identified themselves, informed Moon of a general complaint against her, and requested permission to "scan" particular patient records. Moon agreed. She also provided the agents with a location where they could scan the requested files. Later, Moon attempted to suppress the evidence, arguing that it was obtained without a search warrant. The federal district court sentenced Moon to 188 months in prison, followed by two years of supervised release. She was also ordered to pay restitution of $432,000. She appealed her conviction and sentence to the U.S. Court of Appeals for the Sixth Circuit.

a. Click on "Opinions Search" and in the "Short Title contains" box, type in "Moon." Click on "Submit Query." Under "Published Opinions," select the link to "08a0031p.06" to access the opinion.

CASE 1.3–Continues next page

ISSUE   Can state officials scan a physician's business records without a warrant if the physician agreed to allow the search?

DECISION   Yes. The U.S. Court of Appeals for the Sixth Circuit affirmed the district court's decision.

REASON   The appellate court acknowledged that the Fourth Amendment prohibits the government from conducting unreasonable searches and seizures, but found that in this case an exception applied. "The well-delineated exception at issue here is consent. If an officer obtains consent to search, a warrantless search does not offend the Constitution." Further, "consent is voluntary when it is unequivocal, specific, and intelligently given, uncontaminated by duress or coercion." Moon clearly stated that it would be acceptable for agents to access requested files and that they could "scan whatever they needed to." Because Moon voluntarily allowed the agents to examine her files and to scan them, the resulting evidence did not have to be suppressed. A search warrant was not necessary.

WHAT IF THE FACTS WERE DIFFERENT?   *Assume that Moon had proved that using partial doses of the chemotherapy drugs did not affect the "cure" rate for her cancer patients. Would the court have ruled differently? Why or why not?*

■

Due Process   Both the Fifth and the Fourteenth Amendments provide that no person shall be deprived "of life, liberty, or property, without due process of law." The **due process clause** of each of these constitutional amendments has two aspects—procedural and substantive. Note that the due process clause applies to "legal persons," such as corporations, as well as to individuals.

Procedural Due Process.   Procedural due process requires that any government decision to take life, liberty, or property must be made fairly—that is, the government must give a person proper notice and an opportunity to be heard. Fair procedures must be used in determining whether a person will be subjected to punishment or have some burden imposed on him or her. Fair procedure has been interpreted as requiring that the person have at least an opportunity to object to a proposed action before a fair, neutral decision maker (which need not be a judge). In most states, a driver's license is construed as a property interest. Therefore, the state must provide some sort of opportunity for the driver to object before suspending or terminating the license.

 **PREVENTING LEGAL DISPUTES**   **Many of the constitutional protections discussed in this chapter have become part of our culture in the United States. Due process, especially procedural due process, has become synonymous with what Americans consider "fair." For this reason, businesspersons seeking to avoid legal disputes should consider giving due process to anyone who might object to some business decision or action, whether that person is an employee, a partner, an affiliate, or a customer. For instance, giving ample notice of new policies to all affected persons is a prudent move, as is giving them at least an opportunity to express their opinions on the matter. Providing an opportunity to be heard is often the ideal way to make people feel that they are being treated fairly. If people believe that a businessperson or firm is fair and listens to both sides of an issue, they are less likely to sue that businessperson or firm.**

■

Substantive Due Process.   Substantive due process protects an individual's life, liberty, or property against certain government actions regardless of the fairness of the procedures used to implement them. Substantive due process limits what the government may do in its legislative and executive capacities. Legislation must be fair and reasonable in content and must further a legitimate governmental objective. Only when state conduct is arbitrary, or shocks the conscience, however, will it rise to the level of violating substantive due process.[32]

If a law or other governmental action limits a fundamental right, the state must have a legitimate and compelling interest to justify its action. Fundamental rights include interstate travel, privacy, voting, marriage and family, and all First Amendment rights. Thus, a state must have substantial reason for taking any action that infringes on a person's free speech rights. In situations not involving fundamental rights, a law or action does not violate substantive due process if it rationally relates to any legitimate government purpose. Under this test, virtually any business regulation will be upheld as reasonable. The United States Supreme Court has sustained insurance regulations, price and wage controls, banking limitations, and restrictions on unfair com-

---

32. See, for example, *Breen v. Texas A&M University*, 485 F.3d 325 (5th Cir. 2007).

petition and trade practices against substantive due process challenges.

■EXAMPLE 1.17 If a state legislature enacted a law imposing a fifteen-year term of imprisonment without a trial on all businesspersons who appeared in their own television commercials, the law would be unconstitutional on both substan-

tive and procedural grounds. Substantive review would invalidate the legislation because it infringes on freedom of speech. Procedurally, the law is unfair because it imposes the penalty without giving the accused a chance to defend her or his actions. ■

REVIEWING The Legal and Constitutional Environment of Business

Suppose that the California legislature passes a law that severely restricts carbon dioxide emissions from automobiles in that state. A group of automobile manufacturers files a suit against the state of California to prevent the enforcement of the law. The automakers claim that a federal law already sets fuel economy standards nationwide and that these standards are essentially the same as carbon dioxide emission standards. According to the automobile manufacturers, it is unfair to allow California to impose more stringent regulations than those set by the

federal law. Using the information presented in the chapter, answer the following questions.

1 Who are the parties (the plaintiffs and the defendant) in this lawsuit?

2 Are the plaintiffs seeking a legal remedy or an equitable remedy? Why?

3 What is the primary source of the law that is at issue here?

4 Read through the appendix that follows this chapter, and then answer the following question: Where would you look to find the relevant California and federal laws?

TERMS AND CONCEPTS

adjudicate 5
administrative agency 5
administrative law 5
administrative process 5
Bill of Rights 12
binding authority 6
breach 3
case law 5
citation 4
civil law 9
civil law system 9
commerce clause 10
common law 6
constitutional law 4

criminal law 9
cyberlaw 9
defendant 7
due process clause 18
enabling legislation 5
establishment clause 16
executive agency 5
filtering software 16
free exercise clause 16
independent regulatory agency 5
international law 10
law 2
national law 9
ordinance 4

persuasive authority 7
plaintiff 7
police powers 12
precedent 6
primary source of law 4
procedural law 7
remedy 7
search warrant 17
secondary source of law 4
stare decisis 6
statutory law 4
substantive law 7
symbolic speech 13
uniform law 4

CHAPTER SUMMARY The Legal and Constitutional Environment of Business

Sources of American Law (See pages 4–6.)	1. *Constitutional law*—The law as expressed in the U.S. Constitution and the various state constitutions. The U.S. Constitution is the supreme law of the land. State constitutions are supreme within state borders to the extent that they do not violate the U.S. Constitution or a federal law.

(Continued)

CHAPTER SUMMARY	The Legal and Constitutional Environment of Business—Continued
Sources of American Law— Continued	2. *Statutory law*—Laws or ordinances created by federal, state, and local legislatures and governing bodies. None of these laws can violate the U.S. Constitution or the relevant state constitutions. Uniform laws, when adopted by a state legislature, become statutory law in that state.
	3. *Administrative law*—The rules, orders, and decisions of federal or state government administrative agencies. Federal administrative agencies are created by enabling legislation enacted by the U.S. Congress. Agency functions include rulemaking, investigation and enforcement, and adjudication.
	4. *Case law and common law doctrines*—Judge-made law, including interpretations of constitutional provisions, of statutes enacted by legislatures, and of regulations created by administrative agencies. The common law—the doctrines and principles embodied in case law—governs all areas not covered by statutory law (or agency regulations issued to implement various statutes).
The Common Law Tradition (See pages 6–7.)	1. *Common law*—Law that originated in medieval England with the creation of the king's courts, or *curiae regis,* and the development of a body of rules that were common to (or applied throughout) the land.
	2. *Stare decisis*—A doctrine under which judges "stand on decided cases"—or follow the rule of precedent—in deciding cases. *Stare decisis* is the cornerstone of the common law tradition.
	3. *Remedies*—
	a. Remedies at law—Money or something else of value.
	b. Remedies in equity—Remedies that are granted when the remedies at law are unavailable or inadequate. Equitable remedies include specific performance, an injunction, and contract rescission (cancellation).
Classifications of Law (See pages 7–10.)	The law may be broken down according to several classification systems, such as substantive or procedural law, federal or state law, and private or public law. Two broad classifications are civil and criminal law, and national and international law. Cyberlaw is not really a classification of law but a term that is used for the growing body of case law and statutory law that applies to Internet transactions.
The Constitution as It Affects Business (See pages 10–19.)	1. *Commerce clause*—Expressly permits Congress to regulate commerce. That power authorizes the national government, at least theoretically, to regulate every commercial enterprise in the United States. Under their police powers, state governments may regulate private activities to protect or promote the public order, health, safety, morals, and general welfare.
	2. *Bill of Rights*—The first ten amendments to the U.S. Constitution. They embody a series of protections for individuals—and in some cases, business entities—against various types of interference by the federal government. One of the freedoms guaranteed by the Bill of Rights that affects businesses is the freedom of speech guaranteed by the First Amendment. Also important are the protections of the Fifth and the Fourteenth Amendments, which provide that no person shall be deprived of "life, liberty, or property, without due process of law."

FOR REVIEW

Answers for the even-numbered questions in this **For Review** *section can be found on this text's accompanying Web site at* **www.cengage.com/blaw/fbl**. *Select "Chapter 1" and click on "For Review."*

1 What is the Uniform Commercial Code?

2 What is the common law tradition?

3 What is a precedent? When might a court depart from precedent?

4 What are some important differences between civil law and criminal law?

5 How does the U.S. Constitution affect business activities in the United States?

QUESTIONS AND CASE PROBLEMS

 HYPOTHETICAL SCENARIOS AND CASE PROBLEMS

1.1 Binding versus Persuasive Authority. A county court in Illinois is deciding a case involving an issue that has never been addressed before in that state's courts. The Iowa Supreme Court, however, recently decided a case involving a very similar fact pattern. Is the Illinois court obligated to follow the Iowa Supreme Court's decision on the issue? If the United States Supreme Court had decided a similar case, would that decision be binding on the Illinois court? Explain.

1.2 Hypothetical Question with Sample Answer. This chapter discussed a number of sources of American law. Which source of law takes priority in each of the following situations, and why?

1 A federal statute conflicts with the U.S. Constitution.

2 A federal statute conflicts with a state constitution.

3 A state statute conflicts with the common law of that state.

4 A state constitutional amendment conflicts with the U.S. Constitution.

5 A federal administrative regulation conflicts with a state constitution.

 **For a sample answer to Question 1.2, go to Appendix E at the end of this text.**

1.3 Commerce Clause. Suppose that Georgia enacts a law requiring the use of contoured rear-fender mudguards on trucks and trailers operating within its state lines. The statute further makes it illegal for trucks and trailers to use straight mudguards. In thirty-five other states, straight mudguards are legal. Moreover, in the neighboring state of Florida, straight mudguards are explicitly required by law. There is some evidence suggesting that contoured mudguards might be a little safer than straight mudguards. Discuss whether this Georgia statute would violate the commerce clause of the U.S. Constitution.

1.4 Freedom of Religion. A business has a backlog of orders, and to meet its deadlines, management decides to run the firm seven days a week, eight hours a day. One of the employees, Marjorie Tollens, refuses to work on Saturday on religious grounds. Her refusal to work means that the firm may not meet its production deadlines and may therefore suffer a loss of future business. The firm fires Tollens and replaces her with an employee who is willing to work seven days a week. Tollens claims that in terminating her employment, her employer violated her constitutional right to the free exercise of her religion. Do you agree? Why or why not?

1.5 Reading Citations. Assume that you want to read the court's entire opinion in the case of *Buell-Wilson v. Ford Motor Co.*, 160 Cal.App.4th 1107, 73 Cal.Rptr.3d 277 (2008). The case focuses on whether a punitive damages award was excessive. (Note that this case will be presented in Chapter 4 of this text

as Case 4.1.) Read the section entitled "Finding Case Law" in the appendix that follows this chapter, and then explain specifically where you would find the court's opinion.

1.6 *Stare Decisis.* In the text of this chapter, we stated that the doctrine of *stare decisis* "became a cornerstone of the English and U.S. judicial systems." What does *stare decisis* mean, and why has this doctrine been so fundamental to the development of our legal tradition?

1.7 Case Problem with Sample Answer. For decades, New York City has had to deal with the vandalism and defacement of public property caused by unauthorized graffiti. Among other attempts to stop the damage, in December 2005 the city banned the sale of aerosol spray-paint cans and broad-tipped indelible markers to persons under twenty-one years of age and prohibited them from possessing such items on property other than their own. By May 1, 2006, five people—all under age twenty-one—had been cited for violations of these regulations, while 871 individuals had been arrested for actually making graffiti. Artists who wished to create graffiti on legal surfaces, such as canvas, wood, and clothing, included college student Lindsey Vincenty, who was studying visual arts. Unable to buy her supplies in the city or to carry them in the city if she bought them elsewhere, Vincenty, with others, filed a suit in a federal district court on behalf of themselves and other young artists against Michael Bloomberg, the city's mayor, and others. The plaintiffs claimed that, among other things, the new rules violated their right to freedom of speech. They asked the court to enjoin the enforcement of the rules. Should the court grant this request? Why or why not? [*Vincenty v. Bloomberg*, 476 F.3d 74 (2d Cir. 2007)]

After you have answered Problem 1.7, compare your answer with the sample answer given on the Web site that accompanies this text. Go to www.cengage.com/blaw/fbl, select "Chapter 1," and click on "Case Problem with Sample Answer."

1.8 **A Question of Ethics.** *Aric Toll owns and manages the Balboa Island Village Inn, a restaurant and bar in Newport Beach, California. Anne Lemen owns "Island Cottage," a residence across an alley from the Inn. Lemen often complained to the authorities about excessive noise and the behavior of the Inn's customers, whom she called "drunks" and "whores." Lemen referred to Theresa Toll, Aric's wife, as "Madam Whore." Lemen told the Inn's bartender Ewa Cook that Cook "worked for Satan," was "Satan's wife," and was "going to have Satan's children." She told the Inn's neighbors that it was "a whorehouse" with "prostitution going on inside" and that it sold illegal drugs, sold alcohol to minors, made "sex videos," was involved in child pornography, had "Mafia connections," encouraged "lesbian activity," and stayed open until 6:00 A.M. Lemen also voiced her complaints to potential customers, and* *the Inn's sales dropped more than 20 percent. The Inn filed a suit in a California state court against Lemen, asserting defamation and other claims. [Balboa Island Village Inn, Inc. v. Lemen, 40 Cal.4th 1141, 156 P.3d 339 (2007)]*

1 Are Lemen's statements about the Inn's owners and activities protected by the Constitution? Should they be protected? In whose favor should the court rule? Why?

2 Did Lemen behave unethically in this case? Explain.

CRITICAL THINKING AND WRITING ASSIGNMENTS

1.9   Critical Legal Thinking. John's company is involved in a lawsuit with a customer, Beth. John argues that for fifty years, in cases involving circumstances similar to this case, judges have ruled in a way that indicates that the judge in this case should rule in favor of John's company. Is this a valid argument? If so, must the judge in this case rule as those other judges have? What argument could Beth use to counter John's reasoning?

1.10   Critical Thinking and Writing Assignment for Business. The commerce clause was originally interpreted to regulate only interstate commerce. Over time, however, the United States Supreme Court has made it clear that the commerce clause also applies to commerce that is purely intrastate. Today, the federal government has the power to regulate every commercial enterprise in the United States. What does this mean for commercial businesses that operate only within the borders of one state? Does it promote or discourage intrastate commerce?

ACCESSING THE INTERNET

Today, business law professors and students can go online to access information on almost every topic covered in this text. A good point of departure for online legal research is this text's Web site at

www.cengage.com/blaw/fbl

There, you will find numerous materials relevant to this text and to business law generally, including links to various legal resources on the Web. Additionally, every chapter in this text ends with an *Accessing the Internet* feature that contains selected Web addresses.

You can access many of the sources of law discussed in this chapter at the FindLaw Web site, which is probably the most comprehensive source of free legal information on the Internet. Go to

www.findlaw.com

The Legal Information Institute at Cornell Law School, which offers extensive information about U.S. law, is also a good starting point for legal research. The URL for this site is

www.law.cornell.edu

The Library of Congress offers extensive links to state and federal government resources at

www.loc.gov

For an online version of the U.S. Constitution that provides hypertext links to amendments and other changes, go to

www.law.cornell.edu/constitution/constitution.overview.html

For discussions of current issues involving the rights and liberties contained in the Bill of Rights, go to the Web site of the American Civil Liberties Union at

www.aclu.org

Summaries and the full texts of constitutional law decisions by the United States Supreme Court are included at the Oyez site, which also features audio clips of arguments before the Court. Go to

www.oyez.org

PRACTICAL INTERNET EXERCISES

Go to this text's Web site at **www.cengage.com/blaw/fbl**, select "Chapter 1," and click on "Practical Internet Exercises." There you will find the following Internet research exercises that you can perform to learn more about the topics covered in this chapter.

PRACTICAL INTERNET EXERCISE 1-1   LEGAL PERSPECTIVE—Internet Sources of Law

PRACTICAL INTERNET EXERCISE 1-2   MANAGEMENT PERSPECTIVE—Online Assistance from Government Agencies

PRACTICAL INTERNET EXERCISE 1-3   MANAGEMENT PERSPECTIVE—Commercial Speech

BEFORE THE TEST

Go to this text's Web site at **www.cengage.com/blaw/fbl**, select "Chapter 1," and click on "Interactive Quizzes." You will find a number of interactive questions relating to this chapter.

APPENDIX TO CHAPTER 1

The statutes, agency regulations, and case law referred to in this text establish the rights and duties of businesspersons engaged in various types of activities. The cases presented in the following chapters provide you with concise, real-life illustrations of how the courts interpret and apply these laws. Because of the importance of knowing how to find statutory, administrative, and case law, this appendix offers a brief introduction to how these laws are published and to the legal "shorthand" employed in referencing these legal sources.

FINDING STATUTORY AND ADMINISTRATIVE LAW

When Congress passes laws, they are collected in a publication titled *United States Statutes at Large*. When state legislatures pass laws, they are collected in similar state publications. Most frequently, however, laws are referred to in their codified form—that is, the form in which they appear in the federal and state codes. In these codes, laws are compiled by subject.

United States Code

The *United States Code* (U.S.C.) arranges all existing federal laws of a public and permanent nature by subject. Each of the fifty subjects into which the U.S.C. arranges the laws is given a title and a title number. For example, laws relating to commerce and trade are collected in "Title 15, Commerce and Trade." Titles are subdivided by sections. A citation to the U.S.C. includes title and section numbers. Thus, a reference to "15 U.S.C. Section 1" means that the statute can be found in Section 1 of Title 15. ("Section" may also be designated by the symbol §, and "Sections" by §§.)

Sometimes, a citation includes the abbreviation *et seq.*— as in "15 U.S.C. Sections 1 *et seq.*" The term is an abbreviated form of *et sequitur*, which is Latin for "and the following"; when used in a citation, it refers to sections that concern the same subject as the numbered section and follow it in sequence.

Commercial publications of these laws and regulations are available and are widely used. For example, West Group publishes the *United States Code Annotated* (U.S.C.A.). The U.S.C.A. contains the complete text of laws included in the U.S.C., notes of court decisions that interpret and apply specific sections of the statutes, and the text of presidential proclamations and executive orders. The U.S.C.A. also includes research aids, such as cross-references to related statutes, historical notes, and library references. A citation to the U.S.C.A. is similar to a citation to the U.S.C.: "15 U.S.C.A. Section 1."

State Codes

State codes follow the U.S.C. pattern of arranging law by subject. The state codes may be called codes, revisions, compilations, consolidations, general statutes, or statutes, depending on the preferences of the states. In some codes, subjects are designated by number. In others, they are designated by name. For example, "13 Pennsylvania Consolidated Statutes Section 1101" means that the statute can be found in Title 13, Section 1101, of the Pennsylvania code. "California Commercial Code Section 1101" means the statute can be found in Section 1101 under the subject heading "Commercial Code" of the California code. Abbreviations may be used. For example, "13 Pennsylvania Consolidated Statutes Section 1101" may be abbreviated "13 Pa. C.S. § 1101," and "California Commercial Code Section 1101" may be abbreviated "Cal. Com. Code § 1101."

Administrative Rules

Rules and regulations adopted by federal administrative agencies are compiled in the *Code of Federal Regulations* (C.F.R.). Like the U.S.C., the C.F.R. is divided into fifty titles. Rules within each title are assigned section numbers. A full citation to the C.F.R. includes title and section numbers. For example, a reference to "17 C.F.R. Section 230.504" means that the rule can be found in Section 230.504 of Title 17.

FINDING CASE LAW

Before discussing the case reporting system, we need to look briefly at the court system (which will be discussed in detail in Chapter 2). There are two types of courts in the United States, federal courts and state courts. Both the federal and the state court systems consist of several levels, or tiers, of courts. *Trial courts*, in which evidence is presented and testimony given, are on the bottom tier (which also includes lower courts handling specialized issues). Decisions from a trial court can be appealed to a higher court, which commonly would be an intermediate *court of appeals*, or an *appellate court*. Decisions from these intermediate courts of appeals may be appealed to an even higher court, such as a state supreme court or the United States Supreme Court.

State Court Decisions

Most state trial court decisions are not published. Except in New York and a few other states that publish selected opinions of their trial courts, decisions from state trial courts are merely filed in the office of the clerk of the court, where the decisions are available for public inspection. (Sometimes, they can be found online as well.) Written decisions of the appellate, or reviewing, courts, however, are published and distributed. As you will note, most of the state court cases presented in this book are from state appellate courts. The reported appellate decisions are published in volumes called *reports* or *reporters,* which are numbered consecutively. State appellate court decisions are found in the state reporters of that particular state.

Additionally, state court opinions appear in regional units of the *National Reporter System,* published by West Group. Most lawyers and libraries have the West reporters because they report cases more quickly and are distributed more widely than the state-published reports. In fact, many states have eliminated their own reporters in favor of West's National Reporter System. The National Reporter System divides the states into the following geographic areas: *Atlantic* (A. or A.2d), *North Eastern* (N.E. or N.E.2d), *North Western* (N.W. or N.W.2d), *Pacific* (P., P.2d, or P.3d), *South Eastern* (S.E. or S.E.2d), *South Western* (S.W., S.W.2d, or S.W.3d), and *Southern* (So. or So.2d). (The *2d* and *3d* in the abbreviations refer to *Second Series* and *Third Series,* respectively.) The states included in each of these regional divisions are indicated in Exhibit 1A–1 on the following page, which illustrates West's National Reporter System.

After appellate decisions have been published, they are normally referred to (cited) by the name of the case; the volume, name, and page number of the state's official reporter (if different from West's National Reporter System); the volume, name, and page number of the *National Reporter;* and the volume, name, and page number of any other selected reporter. This information is included in the *citation.* (Citing a reporter by volume number, name, and page number, in that order, is common to all citations.) When more than one reporter is cited for the same case, each reference is called a *parallel citation.* Note that some states have adopted a "public domain citation system" that uses a somewhat different format for the citation. For example, in Wisconsin, a Wisconsin Supreme Court decision might be designated "2008 WI 40," meaning that the case was decided in the year 2008 by the Wisconsin Supreme Court and was the fortieth decision issued by that court during that year. Parallel citations to the *Wisconsin Reports* and West's *North Western Reporter* are still included after the public domain citation.

Consider the following case citation: *Ramirez v. Health Net of Northeast, Inc.,* 285 Conn. 1, 938 A.2d 576 (2008). We see that the opinion in this case can be found in Volume 285 of the official *Connecticut Reports,* which reports only the decisions of the Supreme Court of Connecticut, on page 1. The parallel citation is to Volume 938 of the *Atlantic Reporter, Second Series,* page 576. In presenting opinions in this text, in addition to the reporter, we give the name of the court hearing the case and the year of the court's decision. Sample citations to state court decisions are explained in Exhibit 1A–2 on pages 27–29.

Federal Court Decisions

Federal district court decisions are published unofficially in West's *Federal Supplement* (F.Supp. or F.Supp.2d), and opinions from the circuit courts of appeals (federal reviewing courts) are reported unofficially in West's *Federal Reporter* (F., F.2d, or F.3d). Cases concerning federal bankruptcy law are published unofficially in West's *Bankruptcy Reporter* (Bankr.). The official edition of United States Supreme Court decisions is the *United States Reports* (U.S.), which is published by the federal government. Unofficial editions of Supreme Court cases include West's *Supreme Court Reporter* (S.Ct.) and the *Lawyers' Edition of the Supreme Court Reports* (L.Ed. or L.Ed.2d). Sample citations for federal court decisions are also listed and explained in Exhibit 1A–2.

Unpublished Opinions and Old Cases

Many court opinions that are not yet published or that are not intended for publication can be accessed through Westlaw® (abbreviated in citations as "WL"), an online legal database maintained by Thomson Reuters/West. When no citation to a published reporter is available for cases cited in this text, we give the WL citation (see Exhibit 1A–2 for an example).

On a few occasions, this text cites opinions from old, classic cases dating to the nineteenth century or earlier; some of these are from the English courts. The citations to these cases may not conform to the descriptions given above because the reporters in which they were published have since been replaced.

READING AND UNDERSTANDING CASE LAW

The cases in this text have been condensed from the full text of the courts' opinions. For those wishing to review court cases for future research projects or to gain additional legal information, the following sections will provide useful insights into how to read and understand case law.

Case Titles and Terminology

The title of a case, such as *Adams v. Jones,* indicates the names of the parties to the lawsuit. The *v.* in the case title stands for *versus,* which means "against." In the trial court,

EXHIBIT 1A–1　West's National Reporter System—Regional/Federal

Regional Reporters	Coverage Beginning	Coverage
Atlantic Reporter (A. or A.2d)	1885	Connecticut, Delaware, District of Columbia, Maine, Maryland, New Hampshire, New Jersey, Pennsylvania, Rhode Island, and Vermont.
North Eastern Reporter (N.E. or N.E.2d)	1885	Illinois, Indiana, Massachusetts, New York, and Ohio.
North Western Reporter (N.W. or N.W.2d)	1879	Iowa, Michigan, Minnesota, Nebraska, North Dakota, South Dakota, and Wisconsin.
Pacific Reporter (P., P.2d, or P.3d)	1883	Alaska, Arizona, California, Colorado, Hawaii, Idaho, Kansas, Montana, Nevada, New Mexico, Oklahoma, Oregon, Utah, Washington, and Wyoming.
South Eastern Reporter (S.E. or S.E.2d)	1887	Georgia, North Carolina, South Carolina, Virginia, and West Virginia.
South Western Reporter (S.W., S.W.2d, or S.W.3d)	1886	Arkansas, Kentucky, Missouri, Tennessee, and Texas.
Southern Reporter (So. or So.2d)	1887	Alabama, Florida, Louisiana, and Mississippi.

Federal Reporters		
Federal Reporter (F., F.2d, or F.3d)	1880	U.S. Circuit Courts from 1880 to 1912; U.S. Commerce Court from 1911 to 1913; U.S. District Courts from 1880 to 1932; U.S. Court of Claims (now called U.S. Court of Federal Claims) from 1929 to 1932 and since 1960; U.S. Courts of Appeals since 1891; U.S. Court of Customs and Patent Appeals since 1929; U.S. Emergency Court of Appeals since 1943.
Federal Supplement (F.Supp. or F.Supp.2d)	1932	U.S. Court of Claims from 1932 to 1960; U.S. District Courts since 1932; U.S. Customs Court since 1956.
Federal Rules Decisions (F.R.D.)	1939	U.S. District Courts involving the Federal Rules of Civil Procedure since 1939 and Federal Rules of Criminal Procedure since 1946.
Supreme Court Reporter (S.Ct.)	1882	United States Supreme Court since the October term of 1882.
Bankruptcy Reporter (Bankr.)	1980	Bankruptcy decisions of U.S. Bankruptcy Courts, U.S. District Courts, U.S. Courts of Appeals, and the United States Supreme Court.
Military Justice Reporter (M.J.)	1978	U.S. Court of Military Appeals and Courts of Military Review for the Army, Navy, Air Force, and Coast Guard.

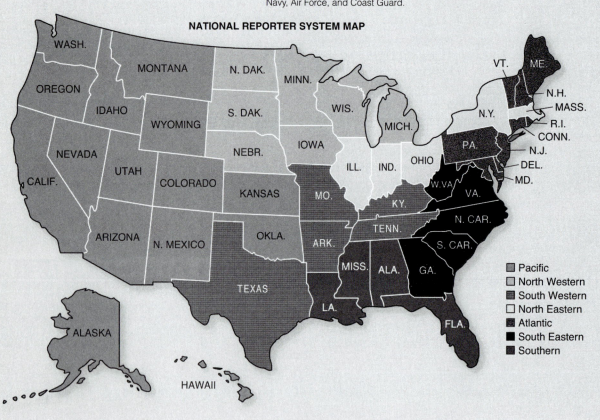

NATIONAL REPORTER SYSTEM MAP

EXHIBIT 1A–2 **How to Read Citations**

STATE COURTS

274 Neb. 796, 743 N.W.2d 632 (2008)[a]

> *N.W.* is the abbreviation for West's publication of state court decisions rendered in the *North Western Reporter* of the National Reporter System. *2d* indicates that this case was included in the *Second Series* of that reporter. The number 743 refers to the volume number of the reporter; the number 632 refers to the page in that volume on which this case begins.

> *Neb.* is an abbreviation for *Nebraska Reports,* Nebraska's official reports of the decisions of its highest court, the Nebraska Supreme Court.

159 Cal.App.4th 1114, 72 Cal.Rptr.3d 81 (2008)

> *Cal.Rptr.* is the abbreviation for West's unofficial reports—titled *California Reporter*— of the decisions of California courts.

8 N.Y.3d 422, 867 N.E.2d 381, 835 N.Y.S.2d 530 (2007)

> *N.Y.S.* is the abbreviation for West's unofficial reports—titled *New York Supplement*—of the decisions of New York courts.

> *N.Y.* is the abbreviation for *New York Reports*, New York's official reports of the decisions of its court of appeals. The New York Court of Appeals is the state's highest court, analogous to other states' supreme courts. In New York, a supreme court is a trial court.

289 Ga.App. 85, 656 S.E.2d 222 (2008)

> *Ga.App.* is the abbreviation for *Georgia Appeals Reports,* Georgia's official reports of the decisions of its court of appeals.

FEDERAL COURTS

___ U.S. ___, 128 S.Ct. 1184, 170 L.Ed.2d 151 (2008)

> *L.Ed.* is an abbreviation for *Lawyers' Edition of the Supreme Court Reports*, an unofficial edition of decisions of the United States Supreme Court.

> *S.Ct.* is the abbreviation for West's unofficial reports—titled *Supreme Court Reporter*—of decisions of the United States Supreme Court.

> *U.S.* is the abbreviation for *United States Reports*, the official edition of the decisions of the United States Supreme Court. The blank lines in this citation (or any other citation) indicate that the appropriate volume of the case reporter has not yet been published and no number is available.

a. The case names have been deleted from these citations to emphasize the publications. It should be kept in mind, however, that the name of a case is as important as the specific page numbers in the volumes in which it is found. If a citation is incorrect, the correct citation may be found in a publication's index of case names. In addition to providing a check on errors in citations, the date of a case is important because the value of a recent case as an authority is likely to be greater than that of older cases from the same court.

(Continued)

| **EXHIBIT 1A–2** | **How to Read Citations–Continued** |

FEDERAL COURTS (Continued)

512 F.3d 582 (9th Cir. 2008)

9th Cir. is an abbreviation denoting that this case was decided in the U.S. Court of Appeals for the Ninth Circuit.

533 F.Supp.2d 740 (W.D.Mich. 2008)

W.D.Mich. is an abbreviation indicating that the U.S. District Court for the Western District of Michigan decided this case.

ENGLISH COURTS

9 Exch. 341, 156 Eng.Rep. 145 (1854)

Eng.Rep. is an abbreviation for *English Reports, Full Reprint,* a series of reports containing selected decisions made in English courts between 1378 and 1865.

Exch. is an abbreviation for *English Exchequer Reports,* which includes the original reports of cases decided in England's Court of Exchequer.

STATUTORY AND OTHER CITATIONS

18 U.S.C. Section 1961(1)(A)

U.S.C. denotes *United States Code,* the codification of *United States Statutes at Large.* The number 18 refers to the statute's U.S.C. title number and 1961 to its section number within that title. The number 1 in parentheses refers to a subsection within the section, and the letter A in parentheses to a subdivision within the subsection.

UCC 2–206(1)(b)

UCC is an abbreviation for *Uniform Commercial Code.* The first number 2 is a reference to an article of the UCC, and 206 to a section within that article. The number 1 in parentheses refers to a subsection within the section, and the letter b in parentheses to a subdivision within the subsection.

Restatement (Second) of Torts, Section 568

Restatement (Second) of Torts refers to the second edition of the American Law Institute's *Restatement of the Law of Torts.* The number 568 refers to a specific section.

17 C.F.R. Section 230.505

C.F.R. is an abbreviation for *Code of Federal Regulations,* a compilation of federal administrative regulations. The number 17 designates the regulation's title number, and 230.505 designates a specific section within that title.

EXHIBIT 1A–2 How to Read Citations—Continued

WESTLAW CITATIONS[b]

2008 WL 427478

WL is an abbreviation for Westlaw. The number 2008 is the year of the document that can be found with this citation in the Westlaw database. The number 427478 is a number assigned to a specific document. A higher number indicates that a document was added to the Westlaw database later in the year.

UNIFORM RESOURCE LOCATORS (URLs)

http://www.westlaw.com[c]

The suffix *com* is the top level domain (TLD) for this Web site. The TLD *com* is an abbreviation for "commercial," which usually means that a for-profit entity hosts (maintains or supports) this Web site.

westlaw is the host name—the part of the domain name selected by the organization that registered the name. In this case, West Group registered the name. This Internet site is the Westlaw database on the Web.

www is an abbreviation for "World Wide Web." The Web is a system of Internet servers that support documents formatted in *HTML* (hypertext markup language). HTML supports links to text, graphics, and audio and video files.

http://www.uscourts.gov

This is "The Federal Judiciary Home Page." The host is the Administrative Office of the U.S. Courts. The TLD *gov* is an abbreviation for "government." This Web site includes information and links from, and about, the federal courts.

http://www.law.cornell.edu/index.html

This part of a URL points to a Web page or file at a specific location within the host's domain. This page is a menu with links to documents within the domain and to other Internet resources.

This is the host name for a Web site that contains the Internet publications of the Legal Information Institute (LII), which is a part of Cornell Law School. The LII site includes a variety of legal materials and links to other legal resources on the Internet. The TLD *edu* is an abbreviation for "educational institution" (a school or a university).

http://www.ipl.org/div/news

This part of the Web site points to a static *news* page at this Web site, which provides links to online newspapers from around the world.

div is an abbreviation for "division," which is the way that the Internet Public Library tags the content on its Web site as relating to a specific topic.

ipl is an abbreviation for "Internet Public Library," which is an online service that provides reference resources and links to other information services on the Web. The IPL is supported chiefly by the School of Information at the University of Michigan. The TLD *org* is an abbreviation for "organization" (normally nonprofit).

b. Many court decisions that are not yet published or that are not intended for publication can be accessed through Westlaw, an online legal database.

c. The basic form for a URL is "service://hostname/path." The Internet service for all of the URLs in this text is *http* (hypertext transfer protocol). Because most Web browsers add this prefix automatically when a user enters a host name or a hostname/path, we have omitted the http:// from the URLs listed in this text.

Adams was the plaintiff—the person who filed the suit. Jones was the defendant. If the case is appealed, however, the appellate court will sometimes place the name of the party appealing the decision first, so the case may be called *Jones v. Adams.* Because some reviewing courts retain the trial court order of names, it is often impossible to distinguish the plaintiff from the defendant in the title of a reported appellate court decision. You must carefully read the facts of each case to identify the parties.

The following terms and phrases are frequently encountered in court opinions and legal publications. Because it is important to understand what these terms and phrases mean, we define and discuss them here.

Plaintiffs and Defendants   As mentioned in Chapter 1, the plaintiff in a lawsuit is the party that initiates the action. The defendant is the party against which a lawsuit is brought. Lawsuits frequently involve more than one plaintiff and/or defendant.

Appellants and Appellees   The *appellant* is the party that appeals a case to another court or jurisdiction from the court or jurisdiction in which the case was originally brought. Sometimes, an appellant is referred to as the *petitioner.* The *appellee* is the party against which the appeal is taken. Sometimes, the appellee is referred to as the *respondent.*

Judges and Justices   The terms *judge* and *justice* are usually synonymous and represent two designations given to judges in various courts. All members of the United States Supreme Court, for example, are referred to as justices. And justice is the formal title usually given to judges of appellate courts, although this is not always the case. In New York, a justice is a judge of the trial court (which is called the Supreme Court), and a member of the Court of Appeals (the state's highest court) is called a judge. The term *justice* is commonly abbreviated to J., and *justices* to JJ. A Supreme Court case might refer to Justice Ginsburg as Ginsburg, J., or to Chief Justice Roberts as Roberts, C.J.

Decisions and Opinions   Most decisions reached by reviewing, or appellate, courts are explained in written *opinions.* The opinion contains the court's reasons for its decision, the rules of law that apply, and the judgment. When all judges or justices unanimously agree on an opinion, the opinion is written for the entire court and can be deemed a *unanimous opinion.* When there is not unanimous agreement, a *majority opinion* is written, outlining the views of the majority of the judges or justices deciding the case.

Often, a judge or justice who feels strongly about making or emphasizing a point that was not made or emphasized in the unanimous or majority opinion will write a *concurring opinion.* That means the judge or justice agrees (concurs) with the judgment given in the unanimous or majority opinion but for different reasons. When there is not a unanimous opinion, a *dissenting opinion* is usually written by a judge or justice who does not agree with the majority. (See the *Extended Case Study* following Chapter 3 on pages 77 and 78 for an example of a dissenting opinion.) The dissenting opinion is important because it may form the basis of the arguments used years later in overruling the precedential majority opinion. Occasionally, a court issues a *per curiam* (Latin for "of the court") opinion, which does not indicate which judge or justice authored the opinion.

A Sample Court Case

Knowing how to read and analyze a court opinion is an essential step in undertaking accurate legal research. A further step involves "briefing" the case. Legal researchers routinely brief cases by summarizing and reducing the texts of the opinions to their essential elements. (For instructions on how to brief a case, go to Appendix A at the end of this text.) The cases contained within the chapters of this text have already been analyzed and partially briefed by the authors, and the essential aspects of each case are presented in a convenient format consisting of four basic sections: *Facts, Issue, Decision,* and *Reason.* Each case is followed by either a brief *For Critical Analysis* section, which presents a question regarding some issue raised by the case; a *Why Is This Case Important?* section, which explains the significance of the case; or a *What If the Facts Were Different?* question, which alters the facts slightly and asks you to consider how this would change the outcome. A section entitled *Impact of This Case on Today's Law* concludes the *Landmark and Classic Cases* that appear throughout the text to indicate the significance of the case for today's legal landscape.

To illustrate the elements in a court opinion, we present an annotated opinion in Exhibit 1A–3 on pages 31 and 32. The opinion is from an actual case that the U.S. Court of Appeals for the Ninth Circuit decided in 2008.

You will note that triple asterisks (* * *) frequently appear in the quoted portions of the opinion. The triple asterisks indicate that we have deleted a few words or sentences from the opinion for the sake of readability or brevity. Additionally, when the opinion cites another case or legal source, the citation to the case or other source has been omitted to save space and to improve the flow of the text. These editorial practices are continued in the other court opinions presented in this book. In addition, whenever we present a court opinion that includes a term or phrase that may not be readily understandable, a bracketed definition or paraphrase has been added.

EXHIBIT 1A–3 **A Sample Court Case**

This section contains the citation—the name of the case, the name of the court that heard the case, the year of the decision, and the reporter in which the court's opinion can be found.

BERGER v. CITY OF SEATTLE

U.S. Court of Appeals, Ninth Circuit, 512 F.3d 582 (2008).

This section identifies the parties and describes the events leading up to the trial and its appeal. The decision of the lower court is included, as well as the issue to be decided by the U.S. Court of Appeals for the Ninth Circuit.

FACTS In the heart of the city of Seattle, Washington, is the Seattle Center, an entertainment zone covering eighty acres of land. Within this area, the city requires that all street performers follow the so-called Campus Rules. One such rule, Rule F.1, requires a permit for street performers and requires badges to be worn during street performances. Michael Berger, a street performer, has been performing there since the 1980s. After the Campus Rules were enacted in 2002, Berger obtained a permit. Thereafter, Seattle Center authorities received numerous publicly filed complaints alleging that Berger had exhibited threatening behavior. Also, the Seattle Center staff reported several rule violations. In 2003, Berger filed a **complaint** seeking damages and **injunctive relief**, alleging that the Campus Rules violated the **First Amendment** to the U.S. Constitution. In 2005, a federal district court granted **summary judgment** to Berger. The city appealed the district court's order of summary judgment to the U.S. Court of Appeals for the Ninth Circuit and sought a reversal with instructions to enter summary judgment in its favor.

A document that, when filed with a court, initiates a lawsuit.

A court decree ordering a person to do or refrain from doing a certain act.

The First Amendment to the Constitution guarantees, among other freedoms, the right of free speech—to express one's views without governmental restrictions.

A judgment that a court enters without beginning or continuing a trial. It can be entered only if no facts are in dispute and the only question is how the law applies.

This section presents the central issue (or issues) to be decided by the court. In this case, the U.S. Court of Appeals for the Ninth Circuit considered whether certain rules imposed on street performers by local government authorities satisfied the requirements for valid restrictions on speech under the First Amendment to the U.S. Constitution.

ISSUE Did the rules issued by the Seattle Center under the city's authority meet the requirements for valid restrictions on speech under the First Amendment?

This section contains the court's decision on the issue or issues before it. An appellate court's decision is often phrased with reference to the decision of the lower court from which the case was appealed. For example, an appellate court may "affirm" or "reverse" (as it did in this case) a lower court's ruling.

DECISION Yes. The U.S. Court of Appeals for the Ninth Circuit reversed the decision of the lower court and **remanded** the case for further proceedings. "Such content neutral and narrowly tailored rules * * * must be upheld."

Sent back.

(Continued)

EXHIBIT 1A–3   A Sample Court Case–Continued

This section indicates the relevant laws and legal principles that the court applied in coming to its conclusion in the case. The relevant law in the *Berger* case included the requirements under the First Amendment for evaluating the purpose and effect of government regulation with respect to expression. This section also explains the court's application of the law to the facts in this case.

REASON The appellate court looked at the rules requiring permits and badges to determine if they were "content neutral." Time, place, and manner restrictions do not violate the First Amendment if they burden all expression equally and do not allow officials to treat messages differently. The court found that the rules in this case met this requirement and did not discriminate based on content. The court also concluded that the rules were "narrowly tailored" to "promote a substantial government interest that would be achieved less effectively" otherwise. With the rules, the city was trying to "reduce territorial disputes among performers, deter patron harassment, and facilitate the identification and apprehension of offending performers." This was pursuant to the valid governmental objective of protecting the safety and convenience of the other performers and the public generally. The public's complaints about Berger and others showed that unregulated street performances posed a threat to the city's interest in maintaining order at the Seattle Center. The court was "satisfied that the city's permit scheme was designed to further valid governmental objectives."

CHAPTER 2
Traditional and Online Dispute Resolution

LEARNING OBJECTIVES

AFTER READING THIS CHAPTER, YOU SHOULD BE ABLE TO ANSWER THE FOLLOWING QUESTIONS:

1 What is judicial review? How and when was the power of judicial review established?

2 Before a court can hear a case, it must have jurisdiction. Over what must it have jurisdiction? How are the courts applying traditional jurisdictional concepts to cases involving Internet transactions?

3 What is the difference between a trial court and an appellate court?

4 In a lawsuit, what are the pleadings? What is discovery, and how does electronic discovery differ from traditional discovery? What is electronic filing?

5 How are online forums being used to resolve disputes?

U ltimately, we are all affected by what the courts say and do. This is particularly true in the business world—nearly every businessperson will face either a potential or an actual lawsuit at some time or another. For this reason, anyone contemplating a career in business will benefit from an understanding of court systems in the United States, including the mechanics of lawsuits.

In this chapter, after examining the judiciary's overall role in the American governmental scheme, we discuss some basic requirements that must be met before a party may bring a lawsuit before a particular court. We then look at the court systems of the United States in some detail and, to clarify judicial procedures, follow a hypothetical case through a state court system. Even though there are fifty-two court systems in the United States—one for each of the fifty states, one for the District of Columbia, plus a federal system—similarities abound. Keep in mind that the federal courts are not superior to the state courts; they are simply an independent system of courts, which derives its authority from Article III, Sections 1 and 2, of the U.S. Constitution. The chapter concludes with an overview of some alternative methods of settling disputes, including methods for settling disputes in online forums.

Note that technological developments are affecting court procedures just as they are affecting all other areas of the law. In this chapter, we also indicate how court doctrines and procedures, as well as alternative methods of dispute settlement, are being adapted to the needs of a cyber age.

THE JUDICIARY'S ROLE IN AMERICAN GOVERNMENT

As you learned in Chapter 1, the body of American law includes the federal and state constitutions, statutes passed by legislative bodies, administrative law, and the case decisions and legal principles that form the common law. These laws would be meaningless, however, without the courts to interpret and apply them. This is the essential role of the judiciary—the courts—in the American governmental system: to interpret and apply the law.

Judicial Review

As the branch of government entrusted with interpreting the laws, the judiciary can decide, among other things, whether the laws or actions of the other two branches are constitutional.

The process for making such a determination is known as **judicial review.** The power of judicial review enables the judicial branch to act as a check on the other two branches of government, in line with the checks-and-balances system established by the U.S. Constitution.

The Origins of Judicial Review in the United States

The power of judicial review was not mentioned in the Constitution, but the concept was not new at the time the nation was founded. Indeed, before 1789 state courts had already overturned state legislative acts that conflicted with state constitutions. The doctrine of judicial review was not legally established, however, until 1803, when the United States Supreme Court rendered its decision in *Marbury v. Madison.*[1] In that case, the Supreme Court stated, "It is emphatically the province and duty of the Judicial Department to say what the law is. . . . If two laws conflict with each other, the courts must decide on the operation of each. . . . So if the law be in opposition to the Constitution . . . [t]he Court must determine which of these conflicting rules governs the case. This is the very essence of judicial duty." Since the *Marbury v. Madison* decision, the power of judicial review has remained unchallenged. Today, this power is exercised by both federal and state courts.

BASIC JUDICIAL REQUIREMENTS

Before a court can hear a lawsuit, certain requirements must first be met. These requirements relate to jurisdiction, venue, and standing to sue. We examine each of these important concepts here.

Jurisdiction

In Latin, *juris* means "law," and *diction* means "to speak." Thus, "the power to speak the law" is the literal meaning of the term **jurisdiction.** Before any court can hear a case, it must have jurisdiction over the person (or company) against whom the suit is brought (the defendant) or over the property involved in the suit. The court must also have jurisdiction over the subject matter.

Jurisdiction over Persons Generally, a court can exercise personal jurisdiction (*in personam* jurisdiction) over any person or business that resides in a certain geographic area. A state trial court, for example, normally has jurisdictional

authority over residents (including businesses) in a particular area of the state, such as a county or district. A state's highest court (often called the state supreme court)[2] has jurisdiction over all residents of that state.

Jurisdiction over Nonresident Defendants. In addition, under the authority of a state **long arm statute,** a court can exercise personal jurisdiction over certain out-of-state defendants based on activities that took place within the state. Before exercising long arm jurisdiction over a nonresident, however, the court must be convinced that the defendant had sufficient contacts, or *minimum contacts*, with the state to justify the jurisdiction.[3] Generally, this means that the defendant must have enough of a connection to the state for the judge to conclude that it is fair for the state to exercise power over the defendant. If an out-of-state defendant caused an automobile accident or sold defective goods within the state, for instance, a court will usually find that minimum contacts exist to exercise jurisdiction over that defendant. Similarly, a state may exercise personal jurisdiction over a nonresident defendant who is sued for breaching a contract that was formed within the state.

Personal Jurisdiction over Corporations. Because corporations are considered legal persons, courts use the same principles to determine whether it is fair to exercise jurisdiction over a corporation.[4] Usually, a corporation has met the minimum-contacts requirement if it does business within the state or has an office or branch within the state. **■EXAMPLE 2.1** Suppose that a business is incorporated under the laws of Maine but has a branch office and manufacturing plant in Georgia. The corporation also advertises and sells its products in Georgia. These activities would likely constitute sufficient contacts with the state of Georgia to allow a Georgia court to exercise jurisdiction over the corporation. ■

Some corporations, however, do not sell or advertise products or place any goods in the stream of commerce. Determining what constitutes minimum contacts in these situations can be more difficult, as the following case—involving a resort hotel in Mexico and a hotel guest from New Jersey—illustrates.

1. 5 U.S. (1 Cranch) 137, 2 L.Ed. 60 (1803).

2. As will be discussed shortly, a state's highest court is frequently referred to as the state supreme court, but there are exceptions. For example, the court that is labeled supreme court in New York is actually a trial court.
3. The minimum-contacts standard was established in *International Shoe Co. v. State of Washington*, 326 U.S. 310, 66 S.Ct. 154, 90 L.Ed. 95 (1945).
4. In the eyes of the law, corporations are "legal persons"—entities that can sue and be sued. See Chapter 25.

CASE 2.1 Mastondrea v. Occidental Hotels Management S.A.

Superior Court of New Jersey, Appellate Division, 391 N.J.Super. 261, 918 A.2d 27 (2007).
lawlibrary.rutgers.edu/search.shtml[a]

FACTS Libgo Travel, Inc., in Ramsey, New Jersey, with Allegro Resorts Management Corporation (ARMC), a marketing agency in Miami, Florida, placed an ad in the *Newark Star Ledger,* a newspaper in Newark, New Jersey, to tout vacation packages for accommodations at the Royal Hideaway Playacar, an all-inclusive resort hotel in Quintana Roo, Mexico. ARMC is part of Occidental Hotels Management, B.V., a Netherlands corporation that owns the hotel with Occidental Hotels Management S.A., a Spanish company. In response to the ad, Amanda Mastondrea, a New Jersey resident, bought one of the packages through Liberty Travel, a chain of travel agencies in the eastern United States that Libgo owns and operates. On June 16, 2003, Mastondrea slipped and fell on a wet staircase at the resort, breaking her ankle. She filed a suit in a New Jersey state court against the hotel, its owners, and others, alleging negligence. The defendants asked the court to dismiss the suit on the ground that it did not have personal jurisdiction over them. The court ruled, in part, that it had jurisdiction over the hotel. The hotel appealed this ruling to a state intermediate appellate court.

ISSUE Could a New Jersey state court exercise personal jurisdiction over a hotel located in Mexico based on the hotel's

a. In the "SEARCH THE N.J. COURTS DECISIONS" section, type "Mastondrea" in the box, and click on "Search!" In the result, click on the case name to access the opinion. Rutgers University Law School in Camden, New Jersey, maintains this Web site.

agreement with a New Jersey travel agency to solicit business for the hotel?

DECISION Yes. The state intermediate appellate court affirmed the lower court's ruling. "This evidence was sufficient to support the assertion of * * * personal jurisdiction over the hotel in this state."

REASON The appellate court noted that the hotel's operations were located entirely in Mexico and that the hotel was not registered, licensed, or otherwise authorized to do business in New Jersey. In spite of the hotel's lack of business presence within the state, the court reasoned that the hotel had minimum contacts because of the "Tour Operators Agreements" in effect between the hotel and Libgo Travel. A specific number of rooms were allotted to Libgo clients at agreed-on rates. Libgo was required to provide the hotel with weekly sales reports. Libgo had to confirm all reservations in writing. Moreover, the hotel "purposely and successfully" sought vacationers from New Jersey, and it derived a profit from them. Finally, the owners of the hotel entered into cooperative marketing agreements with Libgo Travel.

WHAT IF THE FACTS WERE DIFFERENT? *If Mastondrea had not seen Libgo and Allegro's ad, but had bought a Royal Hideaway vacation package on the recommendation of a Liberty Travel agent, is it likely that the result in this case would have been different? Why or why not?*

■

Jurisdiction over Property A court can also exercise jurisdiction over property that is located within its boundaries. This kind of jurisdiction is known as *in rem* jurisdiction, or "jurisdiction over the thing." ■**EXAMPLE 2.2** Suppose that a dispute arises over the ownership of a boat in dry dock in Fort Lauderdale, Florida. The boat is owned by an Ohio resident, over whom a Florida court normally cannot exercise personal jurisdiction. The other party to the dispute is a resident of Nebraska. In this situation, a lawsuit concerning the boat could be brought in a Florida state court on the basis of the court's *in rem* jurisdiction. ■

Jurisdiction over Subject Matter Jurisdiction over subject matter is a limitation on the types of cases a court can hear. In both the federal and state court systems, there are courts of *general* (unlimited) *jurisdiction* and courts of *limited jurisdiction.* An example of a court of general jurisdiction is a state

trial court or a federal district court. An example of a state court of limited jurisdiction is a probate court. **Probate courts** are state courts that handle only matters relating to the transfer of a person's assets and obligations after that person's death, including matters relating to the custody and guardianship of children. An example of a federal court of limited subject-matter jurisdiction is a bankruptcy court. **Bankruptcy courts** handle only bankruptcy proceedings, which are governed by federal bankruptcy law (discussed in Chapter 21). In contrast, a court of general jurisdiction can decide a broad array of cases.

A court's jurisdiction over subject matter is usually defined in the statute or constitution creating the court. In both the federal and state court systems, a court's subject-matter jurisdiction can be limited not only by the subject of the lawsuit but also by the amount in controversy, by whether a case involves a felony (a more serious type of crime) or a misdemeanor (a less serious type of crime), or by whether the proceeding is a trial or an appeal.

Original and Appellate Jurisdiction The distinction between courts of original jurisdiction and courts of appellate jurisdiction normally lies in whether the case is being heard for the first time. Courts having original jurisdiction are courts of the first instance, or trial courts—that is, courts in which lawsuits begin, trials take place, and evidence is presented. In the federal court system, the *district courts* are trial courts. In the various state court systems, the trial courts are known by various names, as will be discussed shortly.

The key point here is that any court having original jurisdiction is normally known as a trial court. Courts having appellate jurisdiction act as reviewing courts, or appellate courts. In general, cases can be brought before appellate courts only on appeal from an order or a judgment of a trial court or other lower court.

Jurisdiction of the Federal Courts Because the federal government is a government of limited powers, the jurisdiction of the federal courts is limited. Article III of the U.S. Constitution establishes the boundaries of federal judicial power. Section 2 of Article III states that "[t]he judicial Power shall extend to all Cases, in Law and Equity, arising under this Constitution, the Laws of the United States, and Treaties made, or which shall be made, under their Authority."

Federal Questions. Whenever a plaintiff's cause of action is based, at least in part, on the U.S. Constitution, a treaty, or a federal law, then a **federal question** arises, and the case comes under the judicial power of the federal courts. Any lawsuit involving a federal question can originate in a federal court. People who claim that their rights under the U.S. Constitution have been violated can begin their suits in a federal court. Note that most cases involving a federal question do not have to be tried in a federal court. The plaintiff can file the action in either a federal court or a state trial court (because the federal and state courts have *concurrent jurisdiction* over many matters, as will be discussed shortly).

Diversity of Citizenship. Federal district courts can also exercise original jurisdiction over cases involving **diversity of citizenship.** Such cases may arise between (1) citizens of different states, (2) a foreign country and citizens of a state or of different states, or (3) citizens of a state and citizens or subjects of a foreign country. The amount in controversy must be more than $75,000 before a federal court can take jurisdiction in such cases. For purposes of diversity jurisdiction, a corporation is a citizen of both the state in which it is incorporated and the state in which its principal place of

business is located. A case involving diversity of citizenship can be filed in the appropriate federal district court, or, if the case starts in a state court, it can sometimes be transferred to a federal court. A large percentage of the cases filed in federal courts each year are based on diversity of citizenship.

Note that in a case based on a federal question, a federal court will apply federal law. In a case based on diversity of citizenship, however, a federal court will apply the relevant state law (which is often the law of the state in which the court sits).

Exclusive versus Concurrent Jurisdiction When both federal and state courts have the power to hear a case, as is true in suits involving diversity of citizenship, **concurrent jurisdiction** exists. When cases can be tried only in federal courts or only in state courts, exclusive jurisdiction exists. Federal courts have **exclusive jurisdiction** in cases involving federal crimes, bankruptcy, patents, and copyrights; in suits against the United States; and in some areas of admiralty law (law governing transportation on ocean waters). States also have exclusive jurisdiction over certain subject matter—for example, divorce and adoption. The concepts of exclusive and concurrent jurisdiction are illustrated in Exhibit 2–1.

When either a federal court or a state court can exercise jurisdiction, a party has a choice of courts in which to bring a suit. The party's lawyer will consider several factors in counseling the party as to which choice is preferable. The lawyer may prefer to litigate the case in a state court because he or she is more familiar with the state court's procedures, or perhaps the attorney believes that the state's judge or jury would be more sympathetic to the client and the case. Alternatively, the lawyer may advise the client to sue in federal court. Perhaps the state court's **docket** (the court's schedule listing the cases to be heard) is crowded, and the case could come to trial sooner in a federal court. Perhaps some feature of federal practice or procedure could offer an advantage in the client's case. Other important considerations include the law in the particular jurisdiction, how that law has been applied in the jurisdiction's courts, and what the results in similar cases have been in that jurisdiction.

Jurisdiction in Cyberspace

The Internet's capacity to bypass political and geographic boundaries undercuts the traditional basic limitations on a court's authority to exercise jurisdiction. These limits include a party's contacts with a court's geographic jurisdiction. As already discussed, for a court to compel a defendant to come before it, there must be at least minimum contacts—the presence of a salesperson within the state, for example. Are there sufficient minimum contacts if the defendant's only connec-

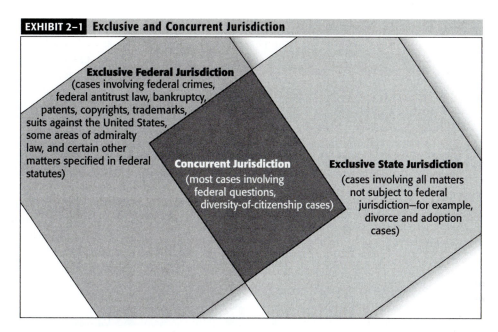

EXHIBIT 2–1 Exclusive and Concurrent Jurisdiction

Exclusive Federal Jurisdiction
(cases involving federal crimes, federal antitrust law, bankruptcy, patents, copyrights, trademarks, suits against the United States, some areas of admiralty law, and certain other matters specified in federal statutes)

Concurrent Jurisdiction
(most cases involving federal questions, diversity-of-citizenship cases)

Exclusive State Jurisdiction
(cases involving all matters not subject to federal jurisdiction—for example, divorce and adoption cases)

tion to a jurisdiction is an ad on the Web originating from a remote location?

The "Sliding-Scale" Standard Gradually, the courts are developing a standard—called a "sliding-scale" standard—for determining when the exercise of jurisdiction over an out-of-state defendant is proper. In developing this standard, the courts have identified three types of Internet business contacts: (1) substantial business conducted over the Internet (with contracts and sales, for example), (2) some interactivity through a Web site, and (3) passive advertising. Jurisdiction is proper for the first category, is improper for the third, and may or may not be appropriate for the second.[5] An Internet communication is typically considered passive if people have to voluntarily access it to read the message and active if it is sent to specific individuals.

In certain situations, even a single contact can satisfy the minimum-contacts requirement. **■EXAMPLE 2.3** A Louisiana resident, Daniel Crummey, purchased a used recreational vehicle (RV) from sellers in Texas after viewing numerous photos of the RV on eBay. The sellers' description of the RV on eBay stated that "everything works great on this RV and will provide comfort and dependability for years to come. This RV will go to Alaska and back without problems!" Crummey picked up the RV in Texas, but on the drive back to Louisiana, the RV quit working. He filed a lawsuit in Louisiana against the sellers alleging that the vehicle was defective. The sellers claimed that the Louisiana court lacked jurisdiction, but the court held that because the sell-

ers had used eBay to market and sell the RV to a Louisiana buyer, jurisdiction was proper.[6] ■

 **PREVENTING LEGAL DISPUTES**

Today's entrepreneurs are often eager to establish Web sites to promote their products and solicit orders. Many of these individuals may not be aware that defendants can be sued in states in which they have never been physically present, provided they have had sufficient contacts with that state's residents over the Internet. Businesspersons who contemplate making their Web sites the least bit interactive should consult an attorney to find out whether by doing so they will be subjecting themselves to jurisdiction in every state. Becoming informed about the extent of potential exposure to lawsuits in various locations is an important part of preventing litigation.

■

International Jurisdictional Issues Because the Internet is international in scope, international jurisdictional issues understandably have come to the fore. What seems to be emerging in the world's courts is a standard that echoes the minimum-contacts requirement applied by the U.S. courts. Most courts are indicating that minimum contacts—doing business within the jurisdiction, for example—are enough to compel a defendant to appear and that a physical presence is not necessary. The effect of this standard is that a business

5. See *Zippo Manufacturing Co. v. Zippo Dot Com, Inc.*, 952 F.Supp. 1119 (W.D.Pa. 1997).

6. *Crummey v. Morgan*, 965 So.2d 497 (La.App. 1st Cir. 2007).

firm has to comply with the laws in any jurisdiction in which it targets customers for its products. This situation is complicated by the fact that many countries' laws on particular issues—free speech, for example—are very different from U.S. laws.

Venue

Jurisdiction has to do with whether a court has authority to hear a case involving specific persons, property, or subject matter. **Venue**[7] is concerned with the most appropriate physical location for a trial. Two state courts (or two federal courts) may have the authority to exercise jurisdiction over a case, but it may be more appropriate or convenient to hear the case in one court than in the other.

Basically, the concept of venue reflects the policy that a court trying a suit should be in the geographic neighborhood (usually the county) where the incident leading to the lawsuit occurred or where the parties involved in the lawsuit reside. Venue in a civil case typically is where the defendant resides, whereas venue in a criminal case normally is where the crime occurred. Pretrial publicity or other factors, though, may require a change of venue to another community, especially in criminal cases when the defendant's right to a fair and impartial jury has been impaired. **■EXAMPLE 2.4** A defendant is charged with sexually abusing several teenagers from the local high school. One of the alleged victims is also the daughter of the city's mayor. The local newspaper publishes many reports about the sexual abuse scandal, some of which are not accurate. In this situation, a court will likely grant a defense request to change venue because the defendant's right to a fair and impartial trial in the local court may be impaired. ■

Standing to Sue

Before a person can bring a lawsuit before a court, the party must have **standing to sue,** or a sufficient "stake" in the matter to justify seeking relief through the court system. In other words, to have standing, a party must have a legally protected and tangible interest at stake in the litigation. The party bringing the lawsuit must have suffered a harm, or have been threatened by a harm, as a result of the action about which she or he has complained. Standing to sue also requires that the controversy at issue be a **justiciable**[8] **controversy**—a controversy that is real and substantial, as opposed to hypothetical or academic.

■EXAMPLE 2.5 To persuade DaimlerChrysler Corporation to build a $1.2 billion Jeep assembly plant in the area, the city

of Toledo, Ohio, gave the company an exemption from local property tax for ten years, as well as a state franchise tax credit. Toledo taxpayers filed a lawsuit in state court claiming that the tax breaks violated the commerce clause in the U.S. Constitution. The taxpayers alleged that the tax exemption and credit injured them because they would have to pay higher taxes to cover the shortfall in tax revenues. The United States Supreme Court ruled that the taxpayers lacked standing to sue over the incentive program because their alleged injury was "conjectural or hypothetical" and, therefore, there was no justiciable controversy.[9] ■

Note that in some situations a person may have standing to sue on behalf of another person, such as a minor or a mentally incompetent person. **■EXAMPLE 2.6** Three-year-old Emma suffers serious injuries as a result of a defectively manufactured toy. Because Emma is a minor, her parent or legal guardian can bring a lawsuit on her behalf. ■

THE STATE AND FEDERAL COURT SYSTEMS

As mentioned earlier in this chapter, each state has its own court system. Additionally, there is a system of federal courts. Although state court systems differ, Exhibit 2–2 illustrates the basic organizational structure characteristic of the court systems in many states. The exhibit also shows how the federal court system is structured. We turn now to an examination of these court systems, beginning with the state courts.

The State Court System

Typically, a state court system will include several levels, or tiers, of courts. As indicated in Exhibit 2–2, state courts may include (1) trial courts of limited jurisdiction, (2) trial courts of general jurisdiction, (3) appellate courts, and (4) the state's highest court (often called the state supreme court). Generally, any person who is a party to a lawsuit has the opportunity to plead the case before a trial court and then, if he or she loses, before at least one level of appellate court. Finally, if the case involves a federal statute or federal constitutional issue, the decision of the state supreme court on that issue may be further appealed to the United States Supreme Court.

The states use various methods to select judges for their courts. Usually, voters elect judges, but sometimes judges are appointed. In Iowa, for example, the governor appoints judges, and then the general population decides whether to confirm their appointment in the next general election. The states usually specify the number of years that the judge will

---

7. Pronounced *ven-yoo.*

8. Pronounced jus-*tish*-uh-bul.

9. *DaimlerChrysler Corp. v. Cuno,* 547 U.S. 332, 126 S.Ct.1854, 164 L.Ed.2d 589 (2006). (In 2007, DaimlerChrysler sold Chrysler to Cerberus Capital Management.)

EXHIBIT 2-2 Federal Court and State Court Systems

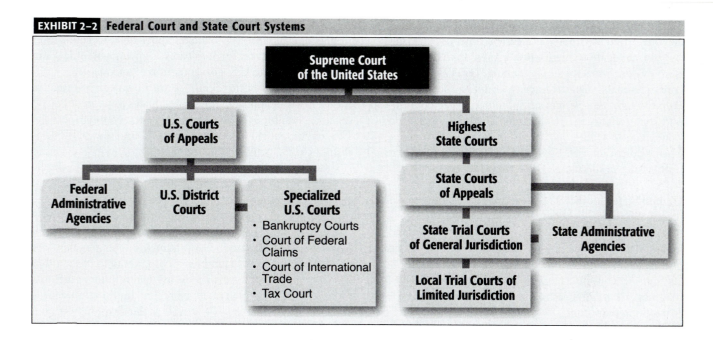

serve. In contrast, as you will read shortly, judges in the federal court system are appointed by the president of the United States and, if they are confirmed by the Senate, hold office for life—unless they engage in blatantly illegal conduct.

Trial Courts Trial courts are exactly what their name implies—courts in which trials are held and testimony taken. State trial courts have either general or limited jurisdiction. Trial courts that have general jurisdiction as to subject matter may be called county, district, superior, or circuit courts.[10] The jurisdiction of these courts is often determined by the size of the county in which the court sits. State trial courts of general jurisdiction have jurisdiction over a wide variety of subjects, including both civil disputes and criminal prosecutions. (In some states, trial courts of general jurisdiction may hear appeals from courts of limited jurisdiction.)

Some courts of limited jurisdiction are called special inferior trial courts or minor judiciary courts. **Small claims courts** are inferior trial courts that hear only civil cases involving claims of less than a certain amount, such as $5,000 (the amount varies from state to state). Suits brought in small claims courts are generally conducted informally, and lawyers are not required (in a few states, lawyers are not even allowed). Another example of an inferior trial court is a local municipal court that hears mainly traffic cases. Decisions of small claims courts and municipal courts may sometimes be appealed to a state trial court of general jurisdiction. Other

courts of limited jurisdiction as to subject matter include domestic relations courts, which handle primarily divorce actions and child-custody disputes, and probate courts, as mentioned earlier.

Appellate, or Reviewing, Courts Every state has at least one court of appeals (appellate court, or reviewing court), which may be an intermediate appellate court or the state's highest court. About three-fourths of the states have intermediate appellate courts. Generally, courts of appeals do not conduct new trials, in which evidence is submitted to the court and witnesses are examined. Rather, an appellate court panel of three or more judges reviews the record of the case on appeal, which includes a transcript of the trial proceedings, and determines whether the trial court committed an error.

Usually, appellate courts focus on questions of law, not questions of fact. A **question of fact** deals with what really happened in regard to the dispute being tried—such as whether a party actually burned a flag. A **question of law** concerns the application or interpretation of the law—such as whether flag-burning is a form of speech protected by the First Amendment to the Constitution. Only a judge, not a jury, can rule on questions of law. Appellate courts normally defer to a trial court's findings on questions of fact because the trial court judge and jury were in a better position to evaluate testimony by directly observing witnesses' gestures, demeanor, and nonverbal behavior during the trial. At the appellate level, the judges review the written transcript of the trial, which does not include these nonverbal elements.

---

10. The name in Ohio and Pennsylvania is court of common pleas; the name in New York is supreme court, trial division.

An appellate court will challenge a trial court's finding of fact only when the finding is clearly erroneous (that is, when it is contrary to the evidence presented at trial) or when there is no evidence to support the finding. **■EXAMPLE 2.7** A jury concludes that a manufacturer's product harmed the plaintiff even though no evidence was submitted to the court to support that conclusion. In this situation, the appellate court would hold that the trial court's decision was erroneous. ■ The options exercised by appellate courts will be discussed further later in this chapter.

Highest State Courts The highest appellate court in a state is usually called the supreme court but may be called by some other name. For example, in both New York and Maryland, the highest state court is called the court of appeals. The decisions of each state's highest court are final on all questions of state law. Only when issues of federal law are involved can a decision made by a state's highest court be overruled by the United States Supreme Court.

The Federal Court System

The federal court system is basically a three-tiered model consisting of (1) U.S. district courts (trial courts of general jurisdiction) and various courts of limited jurisdiction, (2) U.S. courts of appeals (intermediate courts of appeals), and (3) the United States Supreme Court. Unlike state court judges, who are usually elected, federal court judges—including the justices of the Supreme Court—are appointed by the president of the United States and confirmed by the U.S. Senate. All federal judges receive lifetime appointments (because under Article III they "hold their offices during Good Behavior").

U.S. District Courts At the federal level, the equivalent of a state trial court of general jurisdiction is the district court. There is at least one federal district court in every state. The number of judicial districts can vary over time, primarily owing to population changes and corresponding caseloads. Currently, there are ninety-four federal judicial districts.

U.S. district courts have original jurisdiction in federal matters. Federal cases typically originate in district courts. There are other courts with original, but special (or limited), jurisdiction, such as the federal bankruptcy courts and others shown in Exhibit 2–2 on page 39.

U.S. Courts of Appeals In the federal court system, there are thirteen U.S. courts of appeals—also referred to as U.S. circuit courts of appeals. The federal courts of appeals for twelve of the circuits, including the U.S. Court of Appeals for the District of Columbia Circuit, hear appeals from the federal district courts located within their respective judicial circuits. The Court of Appeals for the Thirteenth Circuit, called the Federal Circuit, has national appellate jurisdiction over certain types of cases, such as cases involving patent law and cases in which the U.S. government is a defendant.

The decisions of the circuit courts of appeals are final in most cases, but appeal to the United States Supreme Court is possible. Exhibit 2–3 shows the geographic boundaries of the U.S. circuit courts of appeals and the boundaries of the U.S. district courts within each circuit.

The United States Supreme Court The highest level of the three-tiered model of the federal court system is the United States Supreme Court. According to the language of Article III of the U.S. Constitution, there is only one national Supreme Court. All other courts in the federal system are considered "inferior." Congress is empowered to create other inferior courts as it deems necessary. The inferior courts that Congress has created include the second tier in our model—the U.S. courts of appeals—as well as the district courts and any other courts of limited, or specialized, jurisdiction.

The United States Supreme Court consists of nine justices. Although the Supreme Court has original, or trial, jurisdiction in rare instances (set forth in Article III, Section 2), most of its work is as an appeals court. The Supreme Court can review any case decided by any of the federal courts of appeals, and it also has appellate authority over some cases decided in the state courts.

Appeals to the Supreme Court. To bring a case before the Supreme Court, a party requests that the Court issue a writ of *certiorari.* A **writ of** *certiorari*[11] is an order issued by the Supreme Court to a lower court requiring the latter to send it the record of the case for review. The Court will not issue a writ unless at least four of the nine justices approve of it. This is called the **rule of four.** Whether the Court will issue a writ of *certiorari* is entirely within its discretion. The Court is not required to issue one, and most petitions for writs are denied. (Thousands of cases are filed with the Supreme Court each year; yet it hears, on average, fewer than one hundred of these cases.)[12] A denial is not a decision on the merits of a case, nor does it indicate agreement with the lower court's opinion. Furthermore, a denial of the writ has no value as a precedent.

Petitions Granted by the Court. Typically, the Court grants petitions when cases raise important constitutional questions or

11. Pronounced sur-shee-uh-*rah*-ree.
12. From the mid-1950s through the early 1990s, the United States Supreme Court reviewed more cases per year than it has in the last few years. In the Court's 1982–1983 term, for example, the Court issued opinions in 151 cases. In contrast, in its 2007–2008 term, the Court issued opinions in only 72 cases.

EXHIBIT 2-3 Boundaries of the U.S. Courts of Appeals and U.S. District Courts

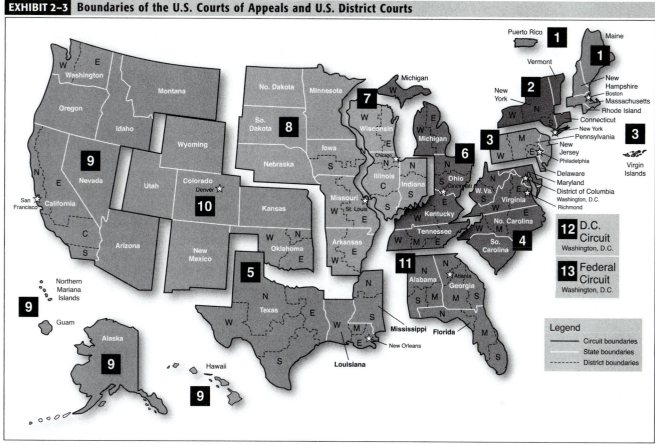

Source: Administrative Office of the United States Courts.

when the lower courts are issuing conflicting decisions on a significant question. The justices, however, never explain their reasons for hearing certain cases and not others, so it is difficult to predict which type of case the Court might select.

FOLLOWING A STATE COURT CASE

To illustrate the procedures that would be followed in a civil lawsuit brought in a state court, we present a hypothetical case and follow it through the state court system. The case involves an automobile accident in which Kevin Anderson, driving a Mercedes, struck Lisa Marconi, driving a Ford Taurus. The accident occurred at the intersection of Wilshire Boulevard and Rodeo Drive in Beverly Hills, California. Marconi suffered personal injuries, incurring medical and hospital expenses as well as lost wages for four months. Anderson and Marconi are unable to agree on a settlement, and Marconi sues Anderson. Marconi is the plaintiff, and Anderson is the defendant. Both are represented by lawyers.

During each phase of the **litigation** (the process of working a lawsuit through the court system), Marconi and

Anderson will have to observe strict procedural requirements. A large body of law—procedural law—establishes the rules and standards for determining disputes in courts. Procedural rules are very complex, and they vary from court to court and from state to state. There is a set of federal rules of procedure as well as various sets of rules for state courts. Additionally, the applicable procedures will depend on whether the case is a civil or criminal proceeding. Generally, the Marconi-Anderson civil lawsuit will involve the procedures discussed in the following subsections. Keep in mind that attempts to settle the case may be ongoing throughout the trial.

The Pleadings

The complaint and answer (and the counterclaim and reply)—all of which are discussed below—taken together are called the **pleadings.** The pleadings inform each party of the other's claims and specify the issues (disputed questions) involved in the case. Because the rules of procedure vary depending on the jurisdiction of the court, the style and form of the pleadings may be quite different in different states.

The Plaintiff's Complaint Marconi's suit against Anderson commences when her lawyer files a **complaint** with the appropriate court. The complaint contains a statement alleging (asserting to the court, in a pleading) the facts necessary for the court to take jurisdiction, a brief summary of the facts necessary to show that the plaintiff is entitled to a remedy, and a statement of the remedy the plaintiff is seeking. Complaints may be lengthy or brief, depending on the complexity of the case and the rules of the jurisdiction.

After the complaint has been filed, the sheriff, a deputy of the county, or another *process server* (one who delivers a complaint and summons) serves a **summons** and a copy of the complaint on defendant Anderson. The summons notifies Anderson that he must file an answer to the complaint with both the court and the plaintiff's attorney within a specified time period (usually twenty to thirty days). The summons also informs Anderson that failure to answer may result in a **default judgment** for the plaintiff, meaning the plaintiff could be awarded the damages alleged in her complaint.

The Defendant's Answer The defendant's **answer** either admits the statements or allegations set forth in the complaint or denies them and outlines any defenses that the defendant may have. If Anderson admits to all of Marconi's allegations in his answer, the court will enter a judgment for Marconi. If Anderson denies any of Marconi's allegations, the litigation will go forward.

Anderson can deny Marconi's allegations and set forth his own claim that Marconi was in fact negligent and therefore owes him compensation for the damage to his Mercedes. This is appropriately called a **counterclaim.** If Anderson files a counterclaim, Marconi will have to answer it with a pleading, normally called a **reply,** which has the same characteristics as an answer.

Anderson can also admit the truth of Marconi's complaint but raise new facts that may result in dismissal of the action. This is called raising an *affirmative defense.* For example, Anderson could assert as an affirmative defense the expiration of the time period under the relevant *statute of limitations* (a state or federal statute that sets the maximum time period during which a certain action can be brought or rights enforced).

Motion to Dismiss A **motion to dismiss** requests the court to dismiss the case for stated reasons. Grounds for dismissal of a case include improper delivery of the complaint and summons, improper venue, and the plaintiff's failure to state a claim for which a court could grant relief (a remedy). For example, if Marconi had suffered no injuries or losses as a result of Anderson's negligence, Anderson could move to have the case dismissed because Marconi had not stated a claim for which relief could be granted.

If the judge grants the motion to dismiss, the plaintiff generally is given time to file an amended complaint. If the judge denies the motion, the suit will go forward, and the defendant must then file an answer. Note that if Marconi wishes to discontinue the suit because, for example, an out-of-court settlement has been reached, she can likewise move for dismissal. The court can also dismiss the case on its own motion.

Pretrial Motions

Either party may attempt to get the case dismissed before trial through the use of various pretrial motions. We have already mentioned the motion to dismiss. Two other important pretrial motions are the motion for judgment on the pleadings and the motion for summary judgment.

At the close of the pleadings, either party may make a **motion for judgment on the pleadings,** or on the merits of the case. The judge will grant the motion only when there is no dispute over the facts of the case and the sole issue to be resolved is a question of law. In deciding on the motion, the judge may consider only the evidence contained in the pleadings.

In contrast, in a **motion for summary judgment,** the court may consider evidence outside the pleadings, such as sworn statements (affidavits) by parties or witnesses, or other documents relating to the case. A motion for summary judgment can be made by either party. As with the motion for judgment on the pleadings, a motion for summary judgment will be granted only if there are no genuine questions of fact and the sole question is a question of law. Pretrial motions, including summary judgment motions and motions for judgment on the pleadings, are listed and described in Exhibit 2–4.

Discovery

Before a trial begins, each party can use a number of procedural devices to obtain information and gather evidence about the case from the other party or from third parties. The process of obtaining such information is known as **discovery.** Discovery includes gaining access to witnesses, documents, records, and other types of evidence.

The Federal Rules of Civil Procedure and similar rules in the states set forth the guidelines for discovery activity. The rules governing discovery are designed to make sure that a witness or a party is not unduly harassed, that privileged material (communications that need not be presented in court) is safeguarded, and that only matters relevant to the case at hand are discoverable. Discovery prevents surprises at trial by giving parties access to evidence that might otherwise be hidden. This allows both parties to learn as much as they can about what to expect at a trial before they reach the courtroom. It also serves to nar-

EXHIBIT 2–4 **Pretrial Motions**

MOTION TO DISMISS

A motion normally filed by the defendant in which the defendant asks the court to dismiss the case for a specified reason, such as improper service, lack of personal jurisdiction, or the plaintiff's failure to state a claim for which relief can be granted.

MOTION TO STRIKE

A motion filed by the defendant in which the defendant asks the court to strike (delete) from the complaint certain paragraphs contained in the complaint. Motions to strike help to clarify the underlying issues that form the basis for the complaint by removing paragraphs that are redundant or irrelevant to the action.

MOTION TO MAKE MORE DEFINITE AND CERTAIN

A motion filed by the defendant to compel the plaintiff to clarify the basis of the plaintiff's cause of action. The motion is filed when the defendant believes that the complaint is too vague or ambiguous for the defendant to respond to it in a meaningful way.

MOTION FOR JUDGMENT ON THE PLEADINGS

A motion that may be filed by either party in which the party asks the court to enter a judgment in his or her favor based on information contained in the pleadings. A judgment on the pleadings will be made only if there are no facts in dispute and the only question is how the law applies to a set of undisputed facts.

MOTION TO COMPEL DISCOVERY

A motion that may be filed by either party in which the party asks the court to compel the other party to comply with a discovery request. If a party refuses to allow the opponent to inspect and copy certain documents, for example, the party requesting the documents may make a motion to compel production of those documents.

MOTION FOR SUMMARY JUDGMENT

A motion that may be filed by either party in which the party asks the court to enter judgment in her or his favor without a trial. Unlike a motion for judgment on the pleadings, a motion for summary judgment can be supported by evidence outside the pleadings, such as witnesses' affidavits, answers to interrogatories, and other evidence obtained prior to or during discovery.

row the issues so that trial time is spent on the main questions in the case.

Depositions and Interrogatories Discovery can involve the use of depositions or interrogatories, or both. A **deposition** is sworn testimony by a party to the lawsuit or any witness. The person being deposed (the deponent) answers questions asked by the attorneys, and the questions and answers are recorded by an authorized court official and sworn to and signed by the deponent. (Occasionally, written depositions are taken when witnesses are unable to appear in person.) The answers given

to depositions will, of course, help the attorneys prepare their cases. They can also be used in court to impeach (challenge the credibility of) a party or a witness who changes his or her testimony at the trial. In addition, the answers given in a deposition can be used as testimony if the witness is not available at trial.

Interrogatories are written questions for which written answers are prepared and then signed under oath. The main difference between interrogatories and written depositions is that interrogatories are directed to a party to the lawsuit (the plaintiff or the defendant), not to a witness, and the party can

ADAPTING THE LAW TO THE ONLINE ENVIRONMENT — Electronic Discovery and Cost-Shifting

Before the computer age, discovery involved searching through paper records—physical evidence. Today, less than 0.5 percent of new information is created on paper. Instead of sending letters and memos, for example, people send e-mails—about 600 billion of them annually in the United States. The all-inclusive nature of electronic information means that electronic discovery (e-discovery) now plays an important role in almost every business lawsuit.

Changes in the Federal Rules of Civil Procedure

As e-discovery has become ubiquitous, the Federal Rules of Civil Procedure (FRCP) have changed to encompass it. Amended Section 26(f) of the FRCP, for example, requires that the parties confer about "preserving discoverable information" and discuss "any issues relating to . . . discovery of electronically stored information, including the electronic forms in which it should be produced."

The most recent amendment to Section 34(a) of the FRCP expressly permits one party to a lawsuit to request that the other produce "electronically stored information—including . . . data compilation stored in any medium from which information can be obtained." The new rule has put in place a two-tiered process for discovery of electronically stored information. Relevant and nonprivileged information that is reasonably

accessible is discoverable as a matter of right. Discovery of less accessible—and therefore more costly to obtain—electronic data may or may not be allowed by the court. The problem of the costs of e-discovery is discussed further below.

The *Ameriwood* Three-Step Process

The new federal rules were applied in *Ameriwood Industries, Inc. v. Liberman*, a major case involving e-discovery in which the court developed a three-step procedure for obtaining electronic data.[a] In the first step, *imaging*, mirror images of a party's hard drives, can be required. The second step involves *recovering* available word-processing documents, e-mails, PowerPoint presentations, spreadsheets, and other files. The final step is *full disclosure*, in which a party sends the other party all responsive and nonprivileged documents and information obtained in the previous two steps.

Limitations on E-Discovery and Cost-Shifting

Complying with requests for electronically discoverable information can cost hundreds of thousands, if not millions, of dollars, especially if a party is a large corporation with thousands of employees creating millions of electronic documents. Consequently, there is a trend toward limiting e-discovery. Under the FRCP, a court can limit electronic discovery (1) when it would be unreasonably cumulative or duplicative, (2) when the requesting party has already had ample opportu-

a. 2007 WL 685623 (E.D.Mo. 2007).

---

prepare answers with the aid of an attorney. The scope of interrogatories is broader because parties are obligated to answer the questions, even if that means disclosing information from their records and files.

Requests for Other Information   A party can serve a written request on the other party for an admission of the truth of matters relating to the trial. Any matter admitted under such a request is conclusively established for the trial. For example, Marconi can ask Anderson to admit that he was driving at a speed of forty-five miles an hour. A request for admission saves time at trial because the parties will not have to spend time proving facts on which they already agree.

A party can also gain access to documents and other items not in her or his possession in order to inspect and examine them. Likewise, a party can gain "entry upon land" to inspect the premises. Anderson's attorney, for example, normally can gain permission to inspect and photocopy Marconi's car repair bills.

When the physical or mental condition of one party is in question, the opposing party can ask the court to order a physical or mental examination. If the court is willing to make the order, which it will do only if the need for the information outweighs the right to privacy of the person to be examined, the opposing party can obtain the results of the examination.

Electronic Discovery   Any relevant material, including information stored electronically, can be the object of a discovery request. The federal rules and most state rules (as well as court decisions) now specifically allow individuals to obtain discovery of electronic "data compilations." Electronic evidence, or **e-evidence**, consists of all computer-generated or electronically recorded information, such as e-mail, voice mail, spreadsheets, word-processing documents, and other data. E-evidence can reveal significant facts that are not discoverable by other means. For example, a computer's hard drive automatically records certain information about each file—such as who created the file and when, and who nity during discovery to obtain the information, or (3) when the burden or expense outweighs the likely benefit.

Many courts are allowing responding parties to object to e-discovery requests on the ground that complying with the request would cause an undue financial burden. In a suit between E*Trade and Deutsche Bank, for example, the court denied E*Trade's request that the defendant produce its hard drives because doing so would create an undue burden.[b]

In addition, sometimes when a court finds that producing the requested information would create an undue financial burden, the court orders the party to comply but shifts the cost to the requesting party (usually the plaintiff). A major case in this area involved Rowe Entertainment and the William Morris Agency. When the e-discovery costs were estimated to be as high as $9 million, the court determined that cost-shifting was warranted.[c] In deciding whether to order cost-shifting, courts increasingly take into account the amount in controversy and each party's ability to pay. Sometimes, a court may require the responding party to restore and produce representative documents from a small sample of the requested medium to verify the relevance of the data before the party incurs significant expenses.[d]

b. *E*Trade Securities, LLC v. Deutsche Bank A.G.,* 230 F.R.D. 582 (D.Minn. 2005). This is a *Federal Rules Decision* not designated for publication in the *Federal Supplement,* citing *Zubulake v. UBS Warburg, LLC,* 2003 WL 21087884 (S.D.N.Y. 2003).

c. *Rowe Entertainment, Inc. v. William Morris Agency, Inc.,* 2002 WL 975713 (S.D.N.Y. 2002).

d. See, for example, *Quinby v. WestLB AG,* 2006 WL 2597900 (S.D.N.Y. 2006).

The Duty to Preserve E-Evidence

Whenever there is a "reasonable anticipation of litigation," all of the relevant documents must be preserved. Preserving e-evidence can be a challenge, particularly for large corporations that have electronic data scattered across multiple networks, servers, desktops, laptops, handheld devices, and even home computers.

The failure to preserve electronic evidence or to comply with electronic discovery requests can lead a court to impose sanctions (such as fines) on one of the parties. This failure can also convince a party to settle the dispute. For instance, Gateway's failure to preserve and produce a single damaging e-mail caused that firm to settle a dispute on the evening before trial.[e]

Businesspersons should also be aware that their computer systems may contain electronic information that they presumed no longer existed. Even though an e-mail is deleted, for example, it is not necessarily eliminated from the hard drive, unless it is completely overwritten by new data. Experts may be able to retrieve this e-mail.

 FOR CRITICAL ANALYSIS *How might a large corporation protect itself from allegations that it intentionally failed to preserve electronic data? Given the significant and often burdensome costs associated with electronic discovery, should courts consider cost-shifting in every case involving electronic discovery? Why or why not?*

e. *Adams v. Gateway, Inc.,* 2006 WL 2563418 (D. Utah 2006).

---

accessed, modified, or transmitted it. This information can be obtained only from the file in its electronic format—not from printed-out versions.

Amendments to the Federal Rules of Civil Procedure that took effect in December 2006 deal specifically with the preservation, retrieval, and production of electronic data. Although traditional means, such as interrogatories and depositions, are still used to find out whether e-evidence exists, a party must usually hire an expert to retrieve the evidence in its electronic format. The expert uses software to reconstruct e-mail exchanges to establish who knew what and when they knew it. The expert can even recover files that the user thought had been deleted from the computer. Reviewing back-up copies of documents and e-mail can provide useful—and often quite damaging—information about how a particular matter progressed over several weeks or months.

Electronic discovery has significant advantages over paper discovery, but it is also time consuming and expensive. For a discussion of how the courts are apportioning the costs asso-

ciated with electronic discovery, see this chapter's *Adapting the Law to the Online Environment* feature.

Pretrial Conference

Either party or the court can request a pretrial conference, or hearing. Usually, the judge and the opposing attorneys meet for an informal discussion after discovery has taken place. The purpose of this conference is to explore the possibility of a settlement without trial and, if this is not possible, to identify the matters that are in dispute and to plan the course of the trial.

Jury Selection

A trial can be held with or without a jury. The Seventh Amendment to the U.S. Constitution guarantees the right to a jury trial for cases in *federal* courts when the amount in controversy exceeds $20, but this guarantee does not apply to state courts. Most states have similar guarantees in their own constitutions (although the threshold dollar amount is higher than $20). The right to a trial by jury does not have to be exercised, and many cases are tried without a jury. In most states and in federal courts, one of the parties must request a jury in a civil case, or the right is presumed to be waived.

Before a jury trial commences, a jury must be selected. The jury selection process is known as *voir dire*.[13] During *voir dire* in most jurisdictions, attorneys for the plaintiff and the defendant ask prospective jurors oral questions to determine whether a potential jury member is biased or has any connection with a party to the action or with a prospective witness. In some jurisdictions, the judge may do all or part of the questioning based on written questions submitted by counsel for the parties.

During *voir dire*, a party may challenge a certain number of prospective jurors *peremptorily*—that is, ask that an individual not be sworn in as a juror without providing any reason. Alternatively, a party may challenge a prospective juror *for cause*—that is, provide a reason why an individual should not be sworn in as a juror. If the judge grants the challenge, the individual is asked to step down. A prospective juror may not be excluded from the jury by the use of discriminatory challenges, however, such as those based on racial criteria or gender.

At the Trial

At the beginning of the trial, the attorneys present their opening arguments, setting forth the facts that they expect to provide during the trial. Then the plaintiff's case is presented. In our hypothetical case, Marconi's lawyer would introduce evidence (relevant documents, exhibits, and the testimony of witnesses) to support Marconi's position. The defendant has the opportunity to challenge any evidence introduced and to cross-examine any of the plaintiff's witnesses.

At the end of the plaintiff's case, the defendant's attorney has the opportunity to ask the judge to direct a verdict for the defendant on the ground that the plaintiff has presented no evidence that would justify the granting of the plaintiff's remedy. This is called a **motion for a directed verdict** (known in federal courts as a *motion for judgment as a matter of law*). If the motion is not granted (it seldom is granted), the defendant's attorney then presents the evidence and witnesses for the defendant's case. At the conclusion of the defendant's case, the defendant's attorney has another opportunity to make a motion for a directed verdict. The plaintiff's attorney can challenge any evidence introduced and cross-examine the defendant's witnesses.

After the defense concludes its presentation, the attorneys present their closing arguments, each urging a verdict in

---

13. Pronounced vwahr-*deehr*.

favor of her or his client. The judge instructs the jury in the law that applies to the case (these instructions are often called *charges*), and the jury retires to the jury room to deliberate a verdict. In the Marconi-Anderson case, the jury will not only decide for the plaintiff or for the defendant but, if it finds for the plaintiff, will also decide on the amount of the **award** (the compensation to be paid to her).

Posttrial Motions

After the jury has rendered its verdict, either party may make a posttrial motion. If Marconi wins and Anderson's attorney has previously moved for a directed verdict, Anderson's attorney may make a **motion for judgment** *n.o.v.* (from the Latin *non obstante veredicto*, which means "notwithstanding the verdict"—called a *motion for judgment as a matter of law* in the federal courts). Such a motion will be granted only if the jury's verdict was unreasonable and erroneous. If the judge grants the motion, the jury's verdict will be set aside, and a judgment will be entered in favor of the opposite party (Anderson).

Alternatively, Anderson could make a **motion for a new trial,** asking the judge to set aside the adverse verdict and to hold a new trial. The motion will be granted if, after looking at all the evidence, the judge is convinced that the jury was in error but does not feel it is appropriate to grant judgment for the other side. A judge can also grant a new trial on the basis of newly discovered evidence, misconduct by the participants or the jury during the trial, or error by the judge.

The Appeal

Assume here that any posttrial motion is denied and that Anderson appeals the case. (If Marconi wins but receives a smaller monetary award than she sought, she can appeal also.) Keep in mind, though, that a party cannot appeal a trial court's decision simply because he or she is dissatisfied with the outcome of the trial. A party must have legitimate grounds to file an appeal; that is, he or she must be able to claim that the lower court committed an error. If Anderson has grounds to appeal the case, a notice of appeal must be filed with the clerk of the trial court within a prescribed time. Anderson now becomes the appellant, or petitioner, and Marconi becomes the appellee, or respondent.

Filing the Appeal   Anderson's attorney files with the appellate court the record on appeal, which includes the pleadings, the trial transcript, the judge's rulings on motions made by the parties, and other trial-related documents. Anderson's attorney will also provide a condensation of the record, known as an *abstract*, which is filed with the reviewing court along with the brief. The **brief** is a formal legal document outlining the facts and issues of the case, the judge's rulings or jury's findings that should be reversed or modified, the applicable law, and arguments on Anderson's behalf (citing applicable statutes and relevant cases as precedents).

Marconi's attorney will file an answering brief. Anderson's attorney can file a reply to Marconi's brief, although it is not required. The reviewing court then considers the case.

Appellate Review   As mentioned earlier, a court of appeals does not hear evidence. Rather, it reviews the record for errors of law. Its decision concerning a case is based on the record on appeal and the briefs and arguments. The attorneys present oral arguments, after which the case is taken under advisement. The court then issues a written opinion. In general, appellate courts do not reverse findings of fact unless the findings are unsupported or contradicted by the evidence.

An appellate court has the following options after reviewing a case:

1 The court can *affirm* the trial court's decision.

2 The court can *reverse* the trial court's judgment if it concludes that the trial court erred or that the jury did not receive proper instructions.

3 The appellate court can *remand* (send back) the case to the trial court for further proceedings consistent with its opinion on the matter.

4 The court might also affirm or reverse a decision *in part*. For example, the court might affirm the jury's finding that Anderson was negligent but remand the case for further proceedings on another issue (such as the extent of Marconi's damages).

5 An appellate court can also *modify* a lower court's decision. If the appellate court decides that the jury awarded an excessive amount in damages, for example, the court might reduce the award to a more appropriate, or fairer, amount.

Appellate courts apply different standards of review depending on the type of issue involved and the lower court's rulings. Generally, these standards require the reviewing court to give a certain amount of deference, or weight, to the findings of lower courts on specific issues. The following case illustrates the importance of standards of review as a means of exercising judicial restraint.

CASE 2.2   **Evans v. Eaton Corp. Long Term Disability Plan**

United States Court of Appeals, Fourth Circuit, 514 F.3d 315 (2008).

FACTS   Eaton Corporation is a multinational manufacturing company that funds and administers a long-term disability benefits plan for its employees. Brenda Evans was an employee at Eaton. In 1998, due to severe rheumatoid arthritis, Evans quit her job at Eaton and filed for disability benefits. Eaton paid disability benefits to Evans without controversy until 2003, but that year, Evans's disability status became questionable. Her physician had prescribed a new medication that had dramatically improved Evans's arthritis. In addition, Evans had injured her spine in a car accident in 2002 and was claiming to be disabled by continuing back problems as well as arthritis. But diagnostic exams during that period indicated that the injuries to Evans's back were not severe, and she could cook, shop, do laundry, wash dishes, and drive about seven miles a day. By 2004, several physicians who reviewed Evans's file had determined that she could work and was no longer totally disabled, and Eaton terminated Evans's disability benefits. Evans filed a complaint in the U.S. District Court for South Carolina alleging violations of the Employee Retirement Income Security Act of 1974 (ERISA—a federal law regulating pension plans that will be discussed in Chapter 23). The district court examined the

evidence in great detail and concluded that Eaton's termination of Evans's benefits was an abuse of discretion because the physicians who testified in Evans's favor were more believable than the reviewing physicians. Eaton appealed to the U.S. Court of Appeals for the Fourth Circuit.

ISSUE   When applying the abuse of discretion standard, should a reviewing court reverse a decision simply because it would have arrived at a different conclusion based on a perceived lack of credibility of witnesses?

DECISION   No. The U.S. Court of Appeals for the Fourth Circuit reversed the district court's award of benefits to Evans and remanded the case with instructions to the district court to enter a judgment in favor of Eaton. The district court incorrectly applied the abuse of discretion standard when reviewing Eaton's termination of Evans's benefits.

REASON   When reviewing a decision for abuse of discretion, a court must give deference, or weight, to the findings of fact made by the trial court—or, in this case, the ERISA plan administrator. The court found that the ERISA plan's language

CASE 2.2–Continues next page

CASE 2.2—Continued

was unambiguous and gave Eaton "discretionary authority to determine eligibility for benefits." It also gave the plan administrator "the power and discretion to determine all questions of fact * * * arising in connection with the administration, interpretation and application of the Plan." The court reasoned that "the abuse of discretion standard requires a reviewing court to show enough deference to a primary decision-maker's judgment that the court does not reverse merely because it would have come to a different result." Moreover, under this standard, a reviewing court must give weight to the administrator's decision "even if another, and

arguably a better, decision-maker might have come to a different, and arguably a better, result."

 FOR CRITICAL ANALYSIS—Ethical Consideration *The appellate court noted that in this case the district court's decision—which granted benefits to Evans—may arguably have been a better decision under the facts. If the court believed the district court's conclusion was right, then why did it reverse the decision? What does this tell you about the standards for review that appellate judges use?*

Appeal to a Higher Appellate Court   If the reviewing court is an intermediate appellate court, the losing party may decide to appeal to the state supreme court (the highest state court). Such a petition corresponds to a petition for a writ of *certiorari* from the United States Supreme Court. Although the losing party has a right to ask (petition) a higher court to review the case, the party does not have a right to have the case heard by the higher appellate court. Appellate courts normally have discretionary power and can accept or reject an appeal. Like the United States Supreme Court, in general state supreme courts deny most appeals. If the appeal is granted, new briefs must be filed before the state supreme court, and the attorneys may be allowed or requested to present oral arguments. Like the intermediate appellate court, the supreme court may reverse or affirm the appellate court's decision or remand the case. At this point, the case typically has reached its end (unless a federal question is at issue and one of the parties has legitimate grounds to seek review by a federal appellate court).

Enforcing the Judgment

The uncertainties of the litigation process are compounded by the lack of guarantees that any judgment will be enforceable. Even if a plaintiff wins an award of damages in court, the defendant may not have sufficient assets or insurance to cover that amount. Usually, one of the factors considered before a lawsuit is initiated is whether the defendant has sufficient assets to cover the amount of damages sought, should the plaintiff win the case.

THE COURTS ADAPT TO THE ONLINE WORLD

We have already mentioned that the courts have attempted to adapt traditional jurisdictional concepts to the online world.

Not surprisingly, the Internet has also brought about changes in court procedures and practices, including new methods for filing pleadings and other documents and issuing decisions and opinions. Some jurisdictions are exploring the possibility of cyber courts, in which legal proceedings could be conducted totally online.

Electronic Filing

The federal court system first experimented with an electronic filing system in January 1996, and its Case Management/Electronic Case Files (CM/ECF) system has now been implemented in nearly all of the federal appellate courts and bankruptcy courts, as well as a majority of the district courts. The CM/ECF system allows federal courts to accept documents filed electronically in PDF format via the Internet. A few federal bankruptcy courts now even *require* some documents to be filed electronically.

Nearly half of the states have some form of electronic filing. These states include Arizona, California, Colorado, Connecticut, Delaware, Georgia, Kansas, Maryland, Michigan, New Hampshire, New Jersey, New Mexico, New York, North Carolina, North Dakota, Ohio, Pennsylvania, Utah, Texas, Virginia, Washington, and Wisconsin, as well as the District of Columbia. Some of these states, including Arizona, California, Colorado, Delaware, and New York, offer statewide e-filing systems. Generally, when electronic filing is made available, it is optional. Nonetheless, some state courts have now made e-filing mandatory in certain types of disputes, such as complex civil litigation.

The expenses associated with an appeal can be considerable, and e-filing can add substantially to the cost. In some cases, appellants who successfully appeal a judgment are entitled to be awarded their costs, including an amount for printing the copies of the record on appeal and the briefs. In other cases, the courts have refused to award e-filing costs to the successful party even though the court encouraged the parties to submit briefs and other documents in an electronic format.[14]

Courts Online

Most courts today have sites on the Web. Of course, each court decides what to make available at its site. Some courts display only the names of court personnel and office phone numbers. Others add court rules and forms. Many appellate court sites include judicial decisions, although the decisions may remain online for only a limited time period. In addition, in some states, such as California and Florida, court clerks offer docket information and other searchable databases online.

Appellate court decisions are often posted online immediately after they are rendered. Recent decisions of the U.S. courts of appeals, for example, are available online at their Web sites. The United States Supreme Court also has an official Web site and publishes its opinions there immediately after they are announced to the public. (Information on accessing federal and state court Web sites is included at the end of this chapter in the *Accessing the Internet* feature.) In fact, even decisions that are designated as unpublished opinions by the appellate courts are often published online (as discussed in the *Adapting the Law to the Online Environment* feature in Chapter 1 on page 8).

Cyber Courts and Proceedings

Someday, litigants may be able to use cyber courts, in which judicial proceedings take place only on the Internet. The parties to a case could meet online to make their arguments and present their evidence. This might be done with e-mail submissions, through video cameras, in designated "chat" rooms, at closed sites, or through the use of other Internet facilities. These courtrooms could be efficient and economical. We might also see the use of virtual lawyers, judges, and juries— and possibly the replacement of court personnel with computer software. Already the state of Michigan has passed legislation creating cyber courts that will hear cases involving technology issues and high-tech businesses. Many lawyers predict that other states will follow suit.

The courts may also use the Internet in other ways. For example, a Florida county court granted "virtual" visitation rights in a couple's divorce proceeding. Although the court granted custody of the couple's ten-year-old daughter to the father, the court also ordered each parent to buy a computer

---

14. See, for example, *Phansalkar v. Andersen Weinroth & Co.*, 356 F.3d 188 (2d Cir. 2004).

and a videoconferencing system so that the mother could "visit" with her child via the Internet at any time.

ALTERNATIVE DISPUTE RESOLUTION

Litigation is expensive. It is also time consuming. Because of the backlog of cases pending in many courts, several years may pass before a case is actually tried. For these and other reasons, more and more businesspersons are turning to **alternative dispute resolution (ADR)** as a means of settling their disputes.

The great advantage of ADR is its flexibility. Methods of ADR range from the parties sitting down together and attempting to work out their differences to multinational corporations agreeing to resolve a dispute through a formal hearing before a panel of experts. Normally, the parties themselves can control how the dispute will be settled, what procedures will be used, whether a neutral third party will be present or make a decision, and whether that decision will be legally binding or nonbinding.

Today, more than 90 percent of cases are settled before trial through some form of ADR. Indeed, most states either require or encourage parties to undertake ADR prior to trial. Many federal courts have instituted ADR programs as well. In the following pages, we examine the basic forms of ADR. Keep in mind, though, that new methods of ADR—and new combinations of existing methods—are constantly being devised and employed.

Negotiation

The simplest form of ADR is **negotiation,** a process in which the parties attempt to settle their dispute informally, with or without attorneys to represent them. Attorneys frequently advise their clients to negotiate a settlement voluntarily before they proceed to trial. Parties may even try to negotiate a settlement during a trial, or after the trial but before an appeal. Negotiation traditionally involves just the parties themselves and (typically) their attorneys. The attorneys, though, are advocates—they are obligated to put their clients' interests first.

Mediation

In **mediation,** a neutral third party acts as a mediator and works with both sides in the dispute to facilitate a resolution. The mediator talks with the parties separately as well as jointly and emphasizes their points of agreement in an attempt to help the parties evaluate their options. Although the mediator may propose a solution (called a mediator's proposal), he or she does not make a decision resolving the matter. States that require parties to undergo ADR before trial often offer mediation as one of the ADR options or (as in Florida) the only option.

One of the biggest advantages of mediation is that it is not as adversarial as litigation. In trials, the parties "do battle" with each other in the courtroom, trying to prove one another wrong, while the judge is usually a passive observer. In mediation, the mediator takes an active role and attempts to bring the parties together so that they can come to a mutually satisfactory resolution. The mediation process tends to reduce the hostility between the disputants, allowing them to resume their former relationship without bad feelings. For this reason, mediation is often the preferred form of ADR for disputes involving business partners, employers and employees, or other parties involved in long-term relationships.

■EXAMPLE 2.8 Two business partners have a dispute over how the profits of their firm should be distributed. If the dispute is litigated, the parties will be adversaries, and their respective attorneys will emphasize how the parties' positions differ, not what they have in common. In contrast, when a dispute is mediated, the mediator emphasizes the common ground shared by the parties and helps them work toward agreement. The business partners can work out the distribution of profits without damaging their continuing relationship as partners. ■

Arbitration

A more formal method of ADR is **arbitration,** in which an arbitrator (a neutral third party or a panel of experts) hears a dispute and imposes a resolution on the parties. Arbitration is unlike other forms of ADR because the third party hearing the dispute makes a decision for the parties. Exhibit 2–5 outlines the basic differences among the three traditional forms of ADR. Usually, the parties in arbitration agree that the third party's decision will be *legally binding,* although the parties can also agree to *nonbinding* arbitration. (Additionally, arbitration that is mandated by the courts often is not binding on the par-

ties.) In nonbinding arbitration, the parties can go forward with a lawsuit if they do not agree with the arbitrator's decision.

In some respects, formal arbitration resembles a trial, although usually the procedural rules are much less restrictive than those governing litigation. In the typical arbitration, the parties present opening arguments and ask for specific remedies. Evidence is then presented, and witnesses may be called and examined by both sides. The arbitrator then renders a decision, which is called an *award.*

An arbitrator's award is usually the final word on the matter. Although the parties may appeal an arbitrator's decision, a court's review of the decision will be much more restricted in scope than an appellate court's review of a trial court's decision. The general view is that because the parties were free to frame the issues and set the powers of the arbitrator at the outset, they cannot complain about the results. The award will be set aside only if the arbitrator's conduct or "bad faith" substantially prejudiced the rights of one of the parties, if the award violates an established public policy, or if the arbitrator exceeded her or his powers (arbitrated issues that the parties did not agree to submit to arbitration).

Arbitration Clauses and Statutes　Virtually any commercial matter can be submitted to arbitration. Frequently, parties include an **arbitration clause** in a contract (a written agreement—see Chapter 7); the clause provides that any dispute that arises under the contract will be resolved through arbitration rather than through the court system. Parties can also agree to arbitrate a dispute after a dispute arises.

Most states have statutes (often based in part on the Uniform Arbitration Act of 1955) under which arbitration clauses will be enforced, and some state statutes compel arbitration of certain types of disputes, such as those involving public employees. At the federal level, the Federal Arbitration Act (FAA), enacted in 1925, enforces arbitration clauses in

EXHIBIT 2–5　**Basic Differences in the Traditional Forms of Alternative Dispute Resolution**

TYPE OF ADR	DESCRIPTION	NEUTRAL THIRD PARTY PRESENT	WHO DECIDES THE RESOLUTION
Negotiation	The parties meet informally with or without their attorneys and attempt to agree on a resolution.	No.	The parties themselves reach a resolution.
Mediation	A neutral third party meets with the parties and emphasizes points of agreement to help them resolve their dispute.	Yes.	The parties, but the mediator may suggest or propose a resolution.
Arbitration	The parties present their arguments and evidence before an arbitrator at a hearing, and the arbitrator renders a decision resolving the parties' dispute.	Yes.	The arbitrator imposes a resolution on the parties that may be either binding or nonbinding.

contracts involving maritime activity and interstate commerce (though its applicability to employment contracts has been controversial, as discussed in a later subsection). Because of the breadth of the commerce clause (see Chapter 1), arbitration agreements involving transactions only slightly connected to the flow of interstate commerce may fall under the FAA.

The Issue of Arbitrability When a dispute arises as to whether the parties have agreed in an arbitration clause to submit a particular matter to arbitration, one party may file a suit to compel arbitration. The court before which the suit is brought will decide *not* the basic controversy but rather the issue of arbitrability—that is, whether the matter is one that must be resolved through arbitration. If the court finds that the subject matter in controversy is covered by the agreement to arbitrate, then a party may be compelled to arbitrate the dispute. Even when a claim involves a violation of a statute passed to protect a certain class of people,

such as employees, a court may determine that the parties must nonetheless abide by their agreement to arbitrate the dispute. Usually, a court will allow the claim to be arbitrated if the court, in interpreting the statute, can find no legislative intent to the contrary. No party, however, will be ordered to submit a particular dispute to arbitration unless the court is convinced that the party consented to do so.

The terms of an arbitration agreement can limit the types of disputes that the parties agree to arbitrate. When the parties do not specify limits, however, disputes can arise as to whether the particular matter is covered by the arbitration agreement, and it is up to the court to resolve the issue of arbitrability. In the following case, the parties had previously agreed to arbitrate disputes involving their contract to develop software, but the dispute involved claims of copyright infringement (see Chapter 5). The question was whether the copyright infringement claims were beyond the scope of the arbitration clause.

CASE 2.3   **NCR Corp. v. Korala Associates, Ltd.**

United States Court of Appeals, Sixth Circuit, 512 F.3d 807 (2008).
www.ca6.uscourts.gov[a]

FACTS In response to a need to upgrade the security of its automated teller machines (ATMs), NCR Corporation developed a software solution to install in all of its machines. At the same time, Korala Associates, Ltd. (KAL), claimed to have developed a similar security upgrade for NCR's ATMs. Indeed, KAL had entered into a contract with NCR in 1998 (the 1998 Agreement) to develop such software. To enable KAL to do so, NCR loaned to KAL a proprietary ATM that contained copyrighted software called APTRA XFS. NCR alleged that KAL "obtained access to, made unauthorized use of, and engaged in unauthorized copying of the APTRA XFS software." By so doing, KAL developed its own version of a security upgrade for NCR's ATMs. When NCR brought a suit against KAL, the latter moved to compel arbitration under the terms of the 1998 Agreement between the two companies. At trial, KAL prevailed. NCR appealed the order compelling arbitration to the U.S. Court of Appeals for the Sixth Circuit.

ISSUE Did the arbitration clause in the parties' agreement regarding software development require the arbitration of a later dispute involving copyright infringement?

a. Click on "Opinions Search" and then on "Short Title;" and type "NCR." Click on "Submit Query." Next, click on the opinion link in the first column of the row corresponding to the name of this case.

DECISION Yes. The U.S. Court of Appeals for the Sixth Circuit affirmed part of the district court's decision. Specifically, it affirmed the judgment compelling arbitration of NCR's claims relating to direct copyright infringement of the APTRA XFS software.

REASON The court first pointed out that the 1998 Agreement clearly provided for arbitration. Then the court turned to the issue of whether NCR's claims fell within the substantive scope of the agreement. "As a matter of Federal law, any doubts concerning the scope of arbitrable issues should be resolved in favor of arbitration." Because the arbitration clause in the 1998 Agreement was so broad, the appellate court reasoned that a trial court should follow the "presumption of arbitration and resolve doubts in favor of arbitration." Consequently, the court found that NCR's copyright infringement claims fell within the scope of the arbitration agreement.

FOR CRITICAL ANALYSIS—Social Consideration *Why do you think that NCR did not want its claims decided by arbitration?*

Mandatory Arbitration in the Employment Context A significant question in the last several years has concerned mandatory arbitration clauses in employment contracts. Many claim that employees' rights are not sufficiently protected when the workers are forced, as a condition of being hired, to agree to arbitrate all disputes and thus waive their rights under statutes specifically designed to protect employees. The United States Supreme Court, however, has generally held that mandatory arbitration clauses in employment contracts are enforceable.

■**EXAMPLE 2.9** In a landmark 1991 decision, *Gilmer v. Interstate/Johnson Lane Corp.*,[15] the Supreme Court held that a claim brought under a federal statute prohibiting age discrimination could be subject to arbitration. The Court concluded that the employee had waived his right to sue when he agreed, as part of a required registration application to be a securities representative with the New York Stock Exchange, to arbitrate "any dispute, claim, or controversy" relating to his employment. ■ (Recently, however, some courts have deemed some notably one-sided arbitration clauses unconscionable and refused to enforce them. See this chapter's *Management Perspective* feature for details.)

Other Types of ADR

The three forms of ADR just discussed are the oldest and traditionally the most commonly used. In recent years, a variety of new types of ADR have emerged. Some parties today are using *assisted negotiation*, in which a third party participates in the negotiation process. The third party may be an expert in the subject matter of the dispute. In *early neutral case evaluation*, the parties explain the situation to the expert, who then assesses the strengths and weaknesses of each party's claims. Another form of assisted negotiation is the *mini-trial*, in which the parties present arguments before the third party (usually an expert), who renders an advisory opinion on how a court would likely decide the issue. This proceeding is designed to assist the parties in determining whether they should settle or take the dispute to court.

Other types of ADR combine characteristics of mediation with those of arbitration. In *binding mediation*, for example, the parties agree that if they cannot resolve the dispute, the mediator can make a legally binding decision on the issue. In *mediation-arbitration*, or "med-arb," the parties agree to first attempt to settle their dispute through mediation. If no settlement is reached, the dispute will be arbitrated.

Today's courts are also experimenting with a variety of ADR alternatives to speed up (and reduce the cost of) justice. Numerous federal courts now hold **summary jury trials (SJTs)**,

in which the parties present their arguments and evidence and the jury renders a verdict. The jury's verdict is not binding, but it does act as a guide to both sides in reaching an agreement during the mandatory negotiations that immediately follow the trial. Other alternatives being employed by the courts include summary procedures for commercial litigation and the appointment of special masters to assist judges in deciding complex issues.

Providers of ADR Services

ADR services are provided by both government agencies and private organizations. A major provider of ADR services is the American Arbitration Association (AAA), which was founded in 1926 and now handles more than 200,000 claims a year in its numerous offices worldwide. Most of the largest U.S. law firms are members of this nonprofit association.

Cases brought before the AAA are heard by an expert or a panel of experts in the area relating to the dispute and are usually settled quickly. Generally, about half of the panel members are lawyers. To cover its costs, the AAA charges a fee, paid by the party filing the claim. In addition, each party to the dispute pays a specified amount for each hearing day, as well as a special additional fee for cases involving personal injuries or property loss. The AAA has a special team devoted to resolving large complex disputes across a wide range of industries.

Hundreds of for-profit firms around the country also provide various forms of dispute-resolution services. Typically, these firms hire retired judges to conduct arbitration hearings or otherwise assist parties in settling their disputes. The judges follow procedures similar to those of the federal courts and use similar rules. Usually, each party to the dispute pays a filing fee and a designated fee for a hearing session or conference.

ONLINE DISPUTE RESOLUTION

An increasing number of companies and organizations offer dispute-resolution services using the Internet. The settlement of disputes in these online forums is known as **online dispute resolution (ODR)**. The disputes resolved in these forums have most commonly involved disagreements over the rights to domain names (Web site addresses—see Chapter 5) or over the quality of goods sold via the Internet, including goods sold through Internet auction sites.

ODR may be best for resolving small- to medium-sized business liability claims, which may not be worth the expense of litigation or traditional ADR. Rules being developed in online forums, however, may ultimately become a code of conduct for everyone who does business in cyberspace. Most online forums do not automatically apply the law of any

---

15. 500 U.S. 20, 111 S.Ct. 1647, 114 L.Ed.2d 26 (1991).

Arbitration Clauses in Employment Contracts

Management Faces a Legal Issue

Arbitration is normally simpler, speedier, and less costly than litigation. For that reason, business owners and managers today often include arbitration clauses in their contracts, including employment contracts. What happens, though, if a job candidate whom you wish to hire (or an existing employee whose contract is being renewed) objects to one or more of the provisions in an arbitration clause? If you insist that signing the agreement to arbitrate future disputes is a mandatory condition of employment, will such a clause be enforceable? Put another way, in which situations might a court invalidate an arbitration agreement because it is considered *unconscionable* (morally unacceptable—shocks the conscience)?

What the Courts Say

The United States Supreme Court has consistently taken the position that because the Federal Arbitration Act (FAA) favors the arbitration of disputes, arbitration clauses in employment contracts should generally be enforced. Nonetheless, some courts have held that arbitration clauses in employment contracts should not be enforced if they are too one sided and unfair to the employee. In one case, for example, the U.S. Court of Appeals for the Ninth Circuit refused to enforce an arbitration clause on the ground that the agreement was unconscionable—so one sided and unfair as to be unenforceable under "ordinary principles of state contract law." The agreement was a standard-form contract drafted by the employer (the party with superior bargaining power), and the employee had to sign it without any modification as a prerequisite to employment. Moreover, only the employees were required to arbitrate their disputes, while the employer remained free to litigate any claims it had against its employees in court. Among other things, the contract also severely limited the relief that was available to employees. For these reasons, the court held the entire arbitration agreement unenforceable.[a] Other courts have cited similar

reasons for deciding not to enforce one-sided arbitration clauses.[b]

In a more recent case, employees of a large California law firm were given copies of that firm's new dispute-resolution program. The program culminated in final binding arbitration for most employment-related claims by and against the firm's employees. The new program became effective three months after it was distributed. After leaving employment at the law firm, an employee filed a lawsuit alleging failure to pay overtime wages. She also claimed that her former employer's dispute-resolution program was unconscionable. The reviewing court found that the dispute-resolution program was presented to the employees on a take-it-or-leave-it basis and was therefore procedurally unconscionable. The court also found that the program was substantively unconscionable because it required employees to waive claims if those employees failed to give the firm notice and demand for mediation within one year from the time when the claim was discovered.[c]

Implications for Managers

Although the United States Supreme Court has made it clear that arbitration clauses in employment contracts are enforceable under the FAA, managers should be careful when drafting such clauses. It is especially important to make sure that the terms of the agreement are not so one sided that a court could declare the entire agreement unconscionable.

Managers should also be aware that the proposed Arbitration Fairness Act might eventually become law. This planned "consumer protection" bill would render unenforceable all predispute mandatory arbitration provisions in consumer, employment, and franchise contracts. It would amend the FAA and seriously restrict the ability of firms to require arbitration.

a. *Circuit City Stores, Inc. v. Adams,* 279 F.3d 889 (9th Cir. 2002). (This was the Ninth Circuit's decision, on remand, after the United States Supreme Court reviewed the case.)

b. See, for example, *Hooters of America, Inc. v. Phillips,* 173 F.3d 933 (4th Cir. 1999); and *Hardwick v. Sherwin Williams Co.,* 2002 WL 31992364 (Ohio App. 8 Dist. 2003).

c. *Davis v. O'Melveny & Myers, LLC,* 485 F.3d 1066 (9th Cir. 2007).

specific jurisdiction. Instead, results are often based on general, universal legal principles. As with most offline methods of dispute resolution, any party may appeal to a court at any time.

Negotiation and Mediation Services

The online negotiation of a dispute is generally simpler and more practical than litigation. Typically, one party files a complaint, and the other party is notified by e-mail. Password-protected access is possible twenty-four hours a day, seven days a week. Fees are generally low (often 2 to 4 percent, or less, of the disputed amount).

CyberSettle.com, National Arbitration and Mediation (NAM), and other Web-based firms offer online forums for negotiating monetary settlements. Even the Better Business Bureau now provides online dispute settlement (**www.bbbonline.org**). The parties to a dispute may agree to submit offers; if the offers fall within a previously agreed-on range, they will end the dispute. Special software keeps secret any offers that are not within the range. If there is no agreed-on range, typically an offer includes a deadline when the offer will expire, and the other party must respond before then. The parties can drop the negotiations at any time.

Mediation providers have also tried resolving disputes online. SquareTrade, for example, provides mediation services for the online auction site eBay as well as other parties. It has resolved more than 2 million disputes between merchants and consumers in 120 countries. SquareTrade uses Web-based software that walks participants through a five-step e-resolution process. Disputing parties first attempt to negotiate directly on a secure page within SquareTrade's Web site. There is no fee for negotiation. If the parties cannot reach an agreement, they can consult with a mediator. The entire process takes as little as ten to fourteen days.

Arbitration Programs

A number of organizations, including the American Arbitration Association, offer online arbitration programs. The Internet Corporation for Assigned Names and Numbers (ICANN), a nonprofit corporation that the federal government set up to oversee the distribution of domain names, has issued special rules for the resolution of domain name disputes.[16] ICANN has also authorized several organizations to arbitrate domain name disputes in accordance with ICANN's rules.

Resolution Forum, Inc. (RFI), a nonprofit organization associated with the Center for Legal Responsibility at South Texas College of Law, offers arbitration services through its CAN-WIN conferencing system. Using standard browser software and an RFI password, the parties to a dispute access an online conference room.

The Virtual Magistrate (VMAG) is a program provided through Chicago-Kent College of Law. VMAG offers arbitration for disputes involving online activities, including torts such as spamming and defamation (discussed in Chapter 4), wrongful messages and postings, and online contract or property disputes. VMAG attempts to resolve a dispute quickly (within seventy-two hours) and inexpensively. A VMAG arbitrator's decision is issued in a written opinion and may be appealed to a court.

---

16. ICANN's Rules for Uniform Domain Name Dispute Resolution Policy are online at **www.icann.org/dndr/udrp/uniform-rules.htm**. Domain names will be discussed in more detail in Chapter 5, in the context of trademark law.

REVIEWING Traditional and Online Dispute Resolution

Stan Garner resides in Illinois and promotes boxing matches for SuperSports, Inc., an Illinois corporation. Garner created the promotional concept of the "Ages" fights—a series of three boxing matches pitting an older fighter (George Foreman) against a younger fighter, such as John Ruiz or Riddick Bowe. The concept included titles for each of the three fights ("Challenge of the Ages," "Battle of the Ages," and "Fight of the Ages"), as well as promotional epithets to characterize the two fighters ("the Foreman Factor"). Garner contacted George Foreman and his manager, who both reside in Texas, to sell the idea, and they arranged a meeting at Caesar's Palace in Las Vegas, Nevada. At some point in the negotiations, Foreman's manager signed a nondisclosure agreement prohibiting him from disclosing Garner's promotional concepts unless they signed a contract. Nevertheless, after negotiations between Garner and Foreman fell through, Foreman used Garner's "Battle of the Ages" concept to promote a subsequent fight. Garner filed a lawsuit against Foreman and his manager in a federal district court located in Illinois, alleging breach of contract. Using the information presented in the chapter, answer the following questions.

1 On what basis might the federal district court in Illinois exercise jurisdiction in this case?

2 Does the federal district court have original or appellate jurisdiction?

3 Suppose that Garner had filed his action in an Illinois state court. Could an Illinois state court exercise personal jurisdiction over Foreman or his manager? Why or why not?

4 Assume that Garner had filed his action in a Nevada state court. Would that court have personal jurisdiction over Foreman or his manager? Explain.

TERMS AND CONCEPTS

alternative dispute
 resolution (ADR) 49
answer 42
arbitration 50
arbitration clause 50
award 46
bankruptcy court 35
brief 46
complaint 42
concurrent jurisdiction 36
counterclaim 42
default judgment 42
deposition 43
discovery 42
diversity of citizenship 36
docket 36

e-evidence 44
exclusive jurisdiction 36
federal question 36
interrogatories 43
judicial review 34
jurisdiction 34
justiciable controversy 38
litigation 41
long arm statute 34
mediation 49
motion for a directed verdict 46
motion for a new trial 46
motion for judgment *n.o.v.* 46
motion for judgment on the
 pleadings 42
motion for summary judgment 42

motion to dismiss 42
negotiation 49
online dispute resolution (ODR) 52
pleadings 41
probate court 35
question of fact 39
question of law 39
reply 42
rule of four 40
small claims court 39
standing to sue 38
summary jury trial (SJT) 52
summons 42
venue 38
voir dire 46
writ of *certiorari* 40

CHAPTER SUMMARY — Traditional and Online Dispute Resolution

The Judiciary's Role in American Government (See pages 33–34.)	The role of the judiciary—the courts—in the American governmental system is to interpret and apply the law. Through the process of judicial review—determining the constitutionality of laws—the judicial branch acts as a check on the executive and legislative branches of government.

Basic Judicial Requirements (See pages 34–38.)	1. *Jurisdiction*—Before a court can hear a case, it must have jurisdiction over the person against whom the suit is brought or the property involved in the suit, as well as jurisdiction over the subject matter.
	
	  a. Limited versus general jurisdiction—Limited jurisdiction exists when a court is limited to a specific subject matter, such as probate or divorce. General jurisdiction exists when a court can hear any kind of case.
	
	  b. Original versus appellate jurisdiction—Original jurisdiction exists when courts have authority to hear a case for the first time (trial courts). Appellate jurisdiction exists with courts of appeals, or reviewing courts; generally, appellate courts do not have original jurisdiction.
	
	  c. Federal jurisdiction—Arises (1) when a federal question is involved (when the plaintiff's cause of action is based, at least in part, on the U.S. Constitution, a treaty, or a federal law) or (2) when a case involves diversity of citizenship (citizens of different states, for example) and the amount in controversy exceeds $75,000.
	
	  d. Concurrent versus exclusive jurisdiction—Concurrent jurisdiction exists when two different courts have authority to hear the same case. Exclusive jurisdiction exists when only state courts or only federal courts have authority to hear a case.
	
	2. *Jurisdiction in cyberspace*—Because the Internet does not have physical boundaries, traditional jurisdictional concepts have been difficult to apply in cases involving activities conducted via

(Continued)

CHAPTER SUMMARY	**Traditional and Online Dispute Resolution–Continued**
Basic Judicial Requirements– Continued	the Web. Gradually, the courts are developing standards to use in determining when jurisdiction over a Web site owner or operator located in another state is proper. 3. *Venue*—Venue has to do with the most appropriate location for a trial, which is usually the geographic area where the event leading to the dispute took place or where the parties reside. 4. *Standing to sue*—A requirement that a party must have a legally protected and tangible interest at stake sufficient to justify seeking relief through the court system. The controversy at issue must also be a justiciable controversy—one that is real and substantial, as opposed to hypothetical or academic.
The State and Federal Court Systems (See pages 38–41.)	1. *Trial courts*—Courts of original jurisdiction, in which legal actions are initiated. a. State—Courts of general jurisdiction can hear any case; courts of limited jurisdiction include domestic relations courts, probate courts, traffic courts, and small claims courts. b. Federal—The federal district court is the equivalent of the state trial court. Federal courts of limited jurisdiction include the U.S. Tax Court, the U.S. Bankruptcy Court, and the U.S. Court of Federal Claims. 2. *Intermediate appellate courts*—Courts of appeals, or reviewing courts; generally without original jurisdiction. Many states have an intermediate appellate court; in the federal court system, the U.S. circuit courts of appeals are the intermediate appellate courts. 3. *Supreme (highest) courts*—Each state has a supreme court, although it may be called by some other name; appeal from the state supreme court to the United States Supreme Court is possible only if the case involves a federal question. The United States Supreme Court is the highest court in the federal court system and the final arbiter of the U.S. Constitution and federal law.
Following a State Court Case (See pages 41–48.)	Rules of procedure prescribe the way in which disputes are handled in the courts. Rules differ from court to court, and separate sets of rules exist for federal and state courts, as well as for criminal and civil cases. A sample civil court case in a state court would involve the following procedures: 1. *The pleadings*— a. Complaint—Filed by the plaintiff with the court to initiate the lawsuit; served with a summons on the defendant. b. Answer—A response to the complaint in which the defendant admits or denies the allegations made by the plaintiff; may assert a counterclaim or an affirmative defense. c. Motion to dismiss—A request to the court to dismiss the case for stated reasons, such as the plaintiff's failure to state a claim for which relief can be granted. 2. *Pretrial motions (in addition to the motion to dismiss)*— a. Motion for judgment on the pleadings—May be made by either party; will be granted if the parties agree on the facts and the only question is how the law applies to the facts. The judge bases the decision solely on the pleadings. b. Motion for summary judgment—May be made by either party; will be granted if the parties agree on the facts. The judge applies the law in rendering a judgment. The judge can consider evidence outside the pleadings when evaluating the motion. 3. *Discovery*—The process of gathering evidence concerning the case. Discovery involves depositions (sworn testimony by a party to the lawsuit or any witness), interrogatories (written questions and answers to these questions made by parties to the action with the aid of their attorneys), and various requests (for admissions, documents, and medical examinations, for example). Discovery may also involve electronically recorded information, such as e-mail, voice

CHAPTER SUMMARY Traditional and Online Dispute Resolution—Continued

Following a State Court Case— Continued	mail, word-processing documents, and other data compilations. Although electronic discovery has significant advantages over paper discovery, it is also more time consuming and expensive and often requires the parties to hire experts.
	
	4. *Pretrial conference*—Either party or the court can request a pretrial conference to identify the matters in dispute after discovery has taken place and to plan the course of the trial.
	
	5. *Trial*—Following jury selection (*voir dire*), the trial begins with opening statements from both parties' attorneys. The following events then occur:
	
	  a. The plaintiff's introduction of evidence (including the testimony of witnesses) supporting the plaintiff's position. The defendant's attorney can challenge evidence and cross-examine witnesses.
	
	  b. The defendant's introduction of evidence (including the testimony of witnesses) supporting the defendant's position. The plaintiff's attorney can challenge evidence and cross-examine witnesses.
	
	  c. Closing arguments by the attorneys in favor of their respective clients, the judge's instructions to the jury, and the jury's verdict.
	
	6. *Posttrial motions*—
	
	  a. Motion for judgment *n.o.v.* ("notwithstanding the verdict")—Will be granted if the judge is convinced that the jury was in error.
	
	  b. Motion for a new trial—Will be granted if the judge is convinced that the jury was in error; can also be granted on the grounds of newly discovered evidence, misconduct by the participants during the trial, or error by the judge.
	
	7. *Appeal*—Either party can appeal the trial court's judgment to an appropriate court of appeals. After reviewing the record on appeal, the abstracts, and the attorneys' briefs, the appellate court holds a hearing and renders its opinion.

The Courts Adapt to the Online World (See pages 48–49.)	A number of state and federal courts now allow parties to file litigation-related documents with the courts via the Internet or other electronic means. Nearly all of the federal appellate courts and bankruptcy courts and a majority of the federal district courts have implemented electronic filing systems. Almost every court now has a Web page offering information about the court and its procedures, and increasingly courts are publishing their opinions online. In the future, we may see "cyber courts," in which all trial proceedings are conducted online.
Alternative Dispute Resolution (See pages 49–52.)	1. *Negotiation*—The parties come together, with or without attorneys to represent them, and try to reach a settlement without the involvement of a third party. 2. *Mediation*—The parties themselves reach an agreement with the help of a neutral third party, called a mediator, who proposes solutions. At the parties' request, a mediator may make a legally binding decision. 3. *Arbitration*—A more formal method of ADR in which the parties submit their dispute to a neutral third party, the arbitrator, who renders a decision. The decision may or may not be legally binding, depending on the circumstances. 4. *Other types of ADR*—These include early neutral case evaluation, mini-trials, and summary jury trials (SJTs); generally, these are forms of "assisted negotiation." 5. *Providers of ADR services*—The leading nonprofit provider of ADR services is the American Arbitration Association. Hundreds of for-profit firms also provide ADR services.
Online Dispute Resolution (See pages 52–54.)	A number of organizations and firms are now offering negotiation, mediation, and arbitration services through online forums. To date, these forums have been a practical alternative for the resolution of domain name disputes and e-commerce disputes in which the amount in controversy is relatively small.

FOR REVIEW

Answers for the even-numbered questions in this For Review section can be found on this text's accompanying Web site at www.cengage.com/blaw/fbl. Select "Chapter 2" and click on "For Review."

1 What is judicial review? How and when was the power of judicial review established?

2 Before a court can hear a case, it must have jurisdiction. Over what must it have jurisdiction? How are the courts applying traditional jurisdictional concepts to cases involving Internet transactions?

3 What is the difference between a trial court and an appellate court?

4 In a lawsuit, what are the pleadings? What is discovery, and how does electronic discovery differ from traditional discovery? What is electronic filing?

5 How are online forums being used to resolve disputes?

QUESTIONS AND CASE PROBLEMS

HYPOTHETICAL SCENARIOS AND CASE PROBLEMS

2.1 Arbitration. In an arbitration proceeding, the arbitrator need not be a judge or even a lawyer. How, then, can the arbitrator's decision have the force of law and be binding on the parties involved?

2.2 Hypothetical Question with Sample Answer. Marya Callais, a citizen of Florida, was walking along a busy street in Tallahassee when a large crate flew off a passing truck and hit her, causing numerous injuries to Callais. She incurred a great deal of pain and suffering plus significant medical expenses, and she could not work for six months. She wishes to sue the trucking firm for $300,000 in damages. The firm's headquarters are in Georgia, although the company does business in Florida. In what court may Callais bring suit—a Florida state court, a Georgia state court, or a federal court? What factors might influence her decision?

For a sample answer to Question 2.2, go to Appendix E at the end of this text.

2.3 Standing to Sue. Lamar Advertising of Penn, LLC, an outdoor advertising business, wanted to erect billboards of varying sizes in a multiphase operation throughout the town of Orchard Park, New York. An Orchard Park ordinance restricted the signs to certain sizes in certain areas, to advertising products and services available for sale only on the premises, and to other limits. Lamar asked Orchard Park for permission to build signs in some areas larger than the ordinance allowed in those locations (but not as large as allowed in other areas). When the town refused, Lamar filed a suit in a federal district court, claiming that the ordinance violated the First Amendment. Did Lamar have standing to challenge the ordinance? If the court could sever the provisions of the ordinance restricting a sign's content from the provisions limiting a sign's size, would your answer be the same? Explain. [*Lamar Advertising of Penn, LLC v. Town of Orchard Park, New York*, 356 F.3d 365 (2d Cir. 2004)]

2.4 E-Jurisdiction. Xcentric Ventures, LLC, is an Arizona firm that operates the Web sites RipOffReport.com and

BadBusinessBureau.com. Visitors to the sites can buy a copy of a book titled *Do-It-Yourself Guide: How to Get Rip-Off Revenge.* The price ($21.95) includes shipping to anywhere in the United States, including Illinois, to which thirteen copies have been shipped. The sites accept donations and feature postings by individuals who claim to have been "ripped off." Some visitors posted comments about George S. May International Co., a management-consulting firm. The postings alleged fraud, larceny, possession of child pornography, and possession of controlled substances (illegal drugs). May filed a suit against Xcentric and others in a federal district court in Illinois, alleging, in part, "false descriptions and representations." The defendants filed a motion to dismiss for lack of jurisdiction. What is the standard for exercising jurisdiction over a party whose only connection to a jurisdiction is over the Web? How would that standard apply in this case? Explain. [*George S. May International Co. v. Xcentric Ventures, LLC*, 409 F.Supp.2d 1052 (N.D.Ill. 2006)]

2.5 Appellate Review. BSH Home Appliances Corp. makes appliances under the Bosch, Siemens, Thermador, and Gaggenau brands. To make and market the "Pro 27 Stainless Steel Range," a restaurant-quality range for home use, BSH gave specifications for its burner to Detroit Radiant Products Co. and requested a price for 30,000 units. Detroit quoted $28.25 per unit, offering to absorb all tooling and research and development costs. In 2001 and 2003, BSH sent Detroit two purchase orders, for 15,000 and 16,000 units, respectively. In 2004, after Detroit had shipped 12,886 units, BSH stopped scheduling deliveries. Detroit filed a suit against BSH, alleging breach of contract. BSH argued, in part, that the second purchase order had not added to the first but had replaced it. After a trial, a federal district court issued its "Findings of Fact and Conclusions of Law." The court found that the two purchase orders "required BSH to purchase 31,000 units of the burner at $28.25 per unit." The court ruled that Detroit was entitled to $418,261 for 18,114 unsold burners. BSH appealed to the U.S. Court of Appeals for the Sixth Circuit. Can an appellate court set aside a trial court's findings of fact? Can an appellate court come to its own conclusions of law? What should the court rule in this case? Explain. [*Detroit Radiant Products Co. v. BSH Home Appliances Corp.*, 473 F.3d 623 (6th Cir. 2007)]

2.6 Case Problem with Sample Answer. Kathleen Lowden sued cellular phone company T-Mobile, claiming that its service agreements were not enforceable under Washington state law. Lowden sued to create a class-action suit, in which her claims would extend to similarly affected customers. She contended that T-Mobile had improperly charged her fees beyond the advertised price of service and charged her for roaming calls that should not have been classified as roaming. T-Mobile moved to force arbitration in accord with the arbitration provision in the service agreement. The arbitration provision was clearly explained in the service agreement. The agreement also specified that no class-action suit could be brought, so T-Mobile asked the court to dismiss the class-action request. Was T-Mobile correct that Lowden's only course of action would be to file arbitration personally? [*Lowden v. T-Mobile USA, Inc.*, 512 F.3d 1213 (9th Cir. 2008)]

 After you have answered Problem 2.6, compare your answer with the sample answer given on the Web site that accompanies this text. Go to www.cengage.com/blaw/fbl, select "Chapter 2," and click on "Case Problem with Sample Answer."

2.7 Jurisdiction. In 2001, Raul Leal, the owner and operator of Texas Labor Contractors in East Texas, contacted Poverty Point Produce, Inc., which operates a sweet potato farm in West Carroll Parish, Louisiana, and offered to provide field workers. Poverty Point accepted the offer. Jeffrey Brown, an owner of, and field manager for, the farm, told Leal the number of workers needed and gave him forms for them to fill out and sign. Leal placed an ad in a newspaper in Brownsville, Texas. Job applicants were directed to Leal's car dealership in Weslaco, Texas, where they were told the details of the work. Leal recruited, among others, Elias Moreno, who lives in the Rio Grande Valley in Texas, and transported Moreno and the others to Poverty Point's farm. At the farm, Leal's brother Jesse oversaw the work with instructions from Brown, lived with the workers in the on-site housing, and gave them their paychecks. When the job was done, the workers were returned to Texas. Moreno and others filed a suit in a federal district court against Poverty Point and others, alleging, in part, violations of Texas state law related to the work. Poverty Point filed a motion to dismiss the suit on

the ground that the court did not have personal jurisdiction. All of the meetings between Poverty Point and the Leals occurred in Louisiana. All of the farmwork was done in Louisiana. Poverty Point has no offices, bank accounts, or phone listings in Texas. It does not advertise or solicit business in Texas. Despite these facts, can the court exercise personal jurisdiction? Explain. [*Moreno v. Poverty Point Produce, Inc.*, 243 F.R.D. 275 (S.D.Tex. 2007)]

2.8 Arbitration. Thomas Baker and others who bought new homes from Osborne Development Corp. sued for multiple defects in the houses they purchased. When Osborne sold the homes, it paid for them to be in a new home warranty program administered by Home Buyers Warranty (HBW). When the company enrolled a home with HBW, it paid a fee and filled out a form that stated the following: "By signing below, you acknowledge that you . . . CONSENT TO THE TERMS OF THESE DOCUMENTS INCLUDING THE BINDING ARBITRATION PROVISION contained therein." HBW then issued warranty booklets to the new homeowners that stated: "Any and all claims, disputes and controversies by or between the Homeowner, the Builder, the Warranty Insurer and/or HBW . . . shall be submitted to arbitration." Would the new homeowners be bound by the arbitration agreement, or could they sue the builder, Osborne, in court? [*Baker v. Osborne Development Corp.*, 159 Cal.App.4th 884, 71 Cal.Rptr.3d 854 (2008)]

2.9 **A Question of Ethics.** *Nellie Lumpkin, who suffered from various illnesses, including dementia, was admitted to the Picayune Convalescent Center, a nursing home. Because of her mental condition, her daughter, Beverly McDaniel, filled out the admissions paperwork and signed the admissions agreement. It included a clause requiring parties to submit to arbitration any disputes that arose. After Lumpkin left the center two years later, she sued, through her husband, for negligent treatment and malpractice during her stay. The center moved to force the matter to arbitration. The trial court held that the arbitration agreement was not enforceable. The center appealed.* [Covenant Health & Rehabilitation of Picayune, LP v. Lumpkin, __ So.2d __ (Miss.App. 2008)]

1 Should a dispute involving medical malpractice be forced into arbitration? This is a claim of negligent care, not a breach of a commercial contract. Is it ethical for medical facilities to impose such a requirement? Is there really any bargaining over such terms?

2 Should a person with limited mental capacity be held to the arbitration clause agreed to by the next-of-kin who signed on behalf of that person?

 CRITICAL THINKING AND WRITING ASSIGNMENTS

2.10 Critical Legal Thinking. Suppose that a state statute requires that all civil lawsuits involving damages of less than $50,000

be arbitrated and allows such a case to be tried in court only if a party is dissatisfied with the arbitrator's decision. Suppose further that the statute also provides that if a trial does not result in an improvement of more than 10 percent in the position of the party who demanded the trial, that party must pay the entire costs of the arbitration proceeding. Would such a statute violate litigants' rights of access to the courts and to trial by jury? Would it matter if the statute was part of a pilot program and affected only a few judicial districts in the state?

2.11  **Video Question.** Go to this text's Web site at **www.cengage.com/blaw/fbl** and select "Chapter 2." Click on "Video Questions" and view the video titled *Jurisdiction in Cyberspace*. Then answer the following questions.

1 What standard would a court apply to determine whether it has jurisdiction over the out-of-state computer firm in the video?

2 What factors is a court likely to consider in assessing whether sufficient contacts exist when the only connection to the jurisdiction is through a Web site?

3 How do you think a court would resolve the issue in this case?

ACCESSING THE INTERNET

For updated links to resources available on the Web, as well as a variety of other materials, visit this text's Web site at

www.cengage.com/blaw/fbl

The Web site for the federal courts offers information on the federal court system and links to all federal courts at

www.uscourts.gov

The National Center for State Courts (NCSC) offers links to the Web pages of all state courts. Go to

www.ncsconline.org

For information on alternative dispute resolution, go to the American Arbitration Association's Web site at

www.adr.org

To learn more about online dispute resolution, go to the following Web sites:

onlineresolution.com
cybersettle.com
SquareTrade.com

PRACTICAL INTERNET EXERCISES

Go to this text's Web site at **www.cengage.com/blaw/fbl**, select "Chapter 2," and click on "Practical Internet Exercises." There you will find the following Internet research exercises that you can perform to learn more about the topics covered in this chapter.

PRACTICAL INTERNET EXERCISE 2-1   LEGAL PERSPECTIVE—The Judiciary's Role in American Government

PRACTICAL INTERNET EXERCISE 2-2   MANAGEMENT PERSPECTIVE—Alternative Dispute Resolution

PRACTICAL INTERNET EXERCISE 2-3   SOCIAL PERSPECTIVE—Resolve a Dispute Online

BEFORE THE TEST

Go to this text's Web site at **www.cengage.com/blaw/fbl**, select "Chapter 2," and click on "Interactive Quizzes." You will find a number of interactive questions relating to this chapter.

CHAPTER 3
Ethics and Business Decision Making

| LEARNING OBJECTIVES |

AFTER READING THIS CHAPTER, YOU SHOULD BE ABLE TO ANSWER THE FOLLOWING QUESTIONS:

1 What is business ethics, and why is it important?

2 How can business leaders encourage their companies to act ethically?

3 How do duty-based ethical standards differ from outcome-based ethical standards?

4 What are six guidelines that an employee can use to evaluate whether his or her actions are ethical?

5 What types of ethical issues might arise in the context of international business transactions?

All of the following businesspersons have been in the news in the past few years:

- Dennis Kozlowski (former chairman and chief executive officer of Tyco International).
- Mark H. Swartz (former chief financial officer of Tyco International).
- Jeffrey Skilling (former chief executive officer of Enron Corporation).
- Bernard Ebbers (former chief executive officer of WorldCom).

What do these individuals have in common? They are all in prison, and some may stay there until they die. They were all convicted of various crimes ranging from overseeing revenue exaggeration in order to increase stock prices to personal use of millions of dollars of public company funds. Not only did they break the law, but they also clearly violated even the minimum ethical principles that a civil society expects to be followed. Other officers and directors of the companies mentioned in the preceding list cost shareholders billions of dollars. In the case of those companies that had to enter bankruptcy, such as Enron Corporation, tens of thousands of employees lost their jobs.

Acting ethically in a business context is not child's play; it can mean billions of dollars—up or down—for corporations, shareholders, and employees. In the wake of these scandals, Congress attempted to prevent similar unethical business behavior in the future by passing stricter legislation in the form of the Sarbanes-Oxley Act of 2002, which will be discussed in detail in Chapters 27 and 31. This act generally imposed more reporting requirements on corporations in an effort to deter unethical behavior and encourage accountability.

BUSINESS ETHICS

As you might imagine, business ethics is derived from the concept of ethics. **Ethics** can be defined as the study of what constitutes right or wrong behavior. It is a branch of philosophy focusing on morality and the way moral principles are derived. Ethics has to do with the fairness, justness, rightness, or wrongness of an action.

What Is Business Ethics?

Business ethics focuses on what is right and wrong behavior in the business world. It has to do with how businesses apply moral and ethical principles to situations that arise in the workplace. Because business decision makers must often address more complex ethical issues in the workplace than they face in their personal lives, business ethics is more complicated than personal ethics.

Why Is Business Ethics Important?

To see why business ethics is so important, reread the first paragraph of this chapter. All of the individuals who are sitting behind bars could have avoided these outcomes. Had they engaged in ethical decision making throughout their business careers, these problems would not have arisen. The corporations, shareholders, and employees who suffered because of those individuals' unethical and criminal behavior certainly paid a high price. Thus, an in-depth understanding of business ethics is important to the long-run viability of any corporation today. It is also important to the well-being of individual officers and directors and to the firm's employees. Finally, unethical corporate decision making can negatively affect suppliers, consumers, the community, and society as a whole.

Common Reasons Why Ethical Problems Occur

Not that many years ago, the popular painkiller Vioxx was recalled because its long-term use increased the risk of heart attack and stroke. Little by little, evidence surfaced that the drug's maker, Merck & Company, had known about these dangers yet had allowed Vioxx to remain on the market. Merck's failure to recall the drug earlier could potentially have adversely affected the health of thousands of patients. In addition, Merck has undergone investigations by both Congress and the U.S. Department of Justice. Merck was facing thousands of lawsuits, years of litigation, and millions of dollars in attorneys' fees and settlements when it agreed, in November 2007, to settle all outstanding cases concerning Vioxx for $4.85 billion. How did a major corporation manage to make so many missteps? The answer is simply that certain officers and employees of Merck felt that it was not necessary to reveal the results of studies that might have decreased sales of Vioxx.

In other words, the common thread among the ethical problems that occur in business is the desire to increase sales (or not lose them), thereby increasing profits and, for the corporation, increasing market value. In most situations, though, ethically wrong behavior by a corporation turns out to be costly to everyone concerned. Just ask the shareholders of Merck (and, of course, Enron, WorldCom, and Tyco).

Short-Run Profit Maximization Some people argue that a corporation's only goal should be profit maximization, which will be reflected in a higher market value. When all firms strictly adhere to the goal of profit maximization, resources tend to flow to where they are most highly valued by society. Ultimately, profit maximization, in theory, leads to the most efficient allocation of scarce resources.

Corporate executives and employees have to distinguish, though, between *short-run* and *long-run* profit maximization. In the short run, the employees of Merck & Company may have increased profits because of the continuing sales of Vioxx. In the long run, however, because of lawsuits, large settlements, and bad publicity, profits have suffered. Thus, business ethics is consistent only with long-run profit maximization.

Determining Society's Rules—The Role of Corporate Influence Another possible cause of bad business ethics has to do with corporations' role in influencing the law. Corporations may use lobbyists to persuade government agencies not to institute new regulations that would increase the corporations' costs and reduce their profits. Once regulatory rules are promulgated, corporations may undertake actions to reduce their impact. One way to do this is to make it known that regulators will always have jobs waiting for them when they leave their regulatory agencies. This revolving door, as it is commonly called, has existed as long as there have been regulatory agencies at the state and federal levels of government.

The Importance of Ethical Leadership

Talking about ethical business decision making is meaningless if management does not set standards. Furthermore, managers must apply the same standards to themselves as they do to the employees of the company.

Attitude of Top Management One of the most important ways to create and maintain an ethical workplace is for top management to demonstrate its commitment to ethical decision making. A manager who is not totally committed to an ethical workplace rarely succeeds in creating one. Management's behavior, more than anything else, sets the ethical tone of a firm. Employees take their cues from management. If a firm's managers adhere to obvious ethical norms in their business dealings, employees will likely follow their example. In contrast, if managers act unethically, employees will see no reason not to do so themselves. **■EXAMPLE 3.1** Kevin observes his manager cheating on her expense account. Kevin quickly understands that such behavior is acceptable. Later, when Kevin is promoted to a managerial position, he "pads" his expense account as well—knowing that he is unlikely to face sanctions for doing so. ■

Managers who set unrealistic production or sales goals increase the probability that employees will act unethically.

If a sales quota can be met only through high-pressure, unethical sales tactics, employees will try to act "in the best interest of the company" and will continue to behave unethically.

A manager who knows about an employee's unethical behavior but looks the other way also sets an example—one indicating that ethical transgressions will be accepted. Managers have found that discharging even one employee for ethical reasons has a tremendous impact as a deterrent to unethical behavior in the workplace.

Behavior of Owners and Managers Business owners and managers sometimes take more active roles in fostering unethical and illegal conduct. This may indicate to their co-owners, co-managers, employees, and others that unethical business behavior will be tolerated. The following case illustrates how business owners' misbehavior can have negative consequences for themselves and their business. Not only can a court sanction the business owners and managers, but it can also issue an injunction that prevents them from engaging in similar patterns of conduct in the future.

CASE 3.1   Baum v. Blue Moon Ventures, LLC

United States Court of Appeals, Fifth Circuit, 513 F.3d 181 (2008).

FACTS Douglas Baum runs an asset recovery business, along with his brother, Brian Baum, and his father, Sheldon Baum (the Baums). The Baums research various unclaimed funds, try to locate the rightful owners, and receive either a finder's fee or the right to some or all of the funds recovered. In 2002, the Baums became involved in a federal district court case by recruiting investors—through misrepresentation—to file a lawsuit against a receiver (a court-appointed person who oversees a business firm's affairs), among others. The district court in that case determined that the Baums' legal allegations were without merit and that their conduct was a malicious attempt to extort funds. The court sanctioned the Baums for wrongfully interfering in the case, wrongfully holding themselves out to be attorneys licensed to practice in Texas, lying to the parties and the court, and generally abusing the judicial system. The district court also issued a permanent injunction against all three Baums to prohibit them from filing claims related to the same case in Texas state courts without the express permission of Judge Lynn Hughes (the district court judge).

In June 2005, the Baums entered an appearance in a bankruptcy proceeding (bankruptcy will be discussed in Chapter 21) involving Danny Hilal and Blue Moon Ventures, LLC. Blue Moon's primary business was purchasing real property at foreclosure sales and leasing those properties to residential tenants. Sheldon Baum claimed to be a creditor in the bankruptcy, but he would not identify his claim. Brian Baum misled the parties and the court about being a licensed attorney in Texas. Douglas Baum participated by posting a fake notice stating that the Internal Revenue Service might foreclose on some property to collect unpaid taxes. The bankruptcy court concluded that this was a continuation of a pattern of malicious conduct and forwarded a memo on the case to the district court that had imposed the sanctions on

the Baums. The district court, after conducting two hearings and listening to testimony from all of the Baums, also found that the Baums had continued in their abusive practices. The district court therefore modified and expanded its injunction to include the filing of any claim in any federal or state court or agency in Texas. Douglas Baum filed an appeal, claiming that the court had exceeded its power and arguing that the injunction would impede his business.

ISSUE Did the district court have the power to modify its prefiling injunction to deter the Baums from filing claims in state and federal courts without the express permission of the judge who ordered it?

DECISION Yes, but the injunction can extend only to actions filed in courts located within the state of Texas. The U.S. Court of Appeals for the Fifth Circuit upheld the modified prefiling injunction as it applied to all filings in Texas state courts, in lower federal courts located in Texas, and in administrative agencies in Texas. In contrast, the court struck down those portions of the injunction that attempted to require the Baums to obtain the district court judge's permission before filing a claim in any court or agency located outside Texas, or before filing in any federal appellate court.

REASON The appellate court accepted that a district court has jurisdiction to impose prefiling injunctions to deter abusive and harassing litigation. "Federal courts have both the inherent power and the Constitutional obligation to protect their jurisdiction from conduct [that] impairs their ability to carry out [their] functions." It further noted that federal courts have the power to prevent plaintiffs from future filings when those plaintiffs consistently abuse the court system and harass their opponents. The reason the appellate court did not

CASE 3.1–Continues next page

CASE 3.1—Continued

uphold the lower court's broad extension of the prefiling injunction was that "those [other] courts or agencies are capable of taking appropriate action on their own."

 FOR CRITICAL ANALYSIS–Ethical Consideration *Are there situations in which a business owner's conduct would be more reprehensible than the Baums' behavior in this case? Explain.*

■

Periodic Evaluation Some companies require their managers to meet individually with employees and to grade them on their ethical (or unethical) behavior. **■EXAMPLE 3.2** Brighton Company asks its employees to fill out ethical checklists each month and return them to their supervisors. This practice serves two purposes: First, it demonstrates to employees that ethics matters. Second, employees have an opportunity to reflect on how well they have measured up in terms of ethical performance. ■

APPROACHES TO ETHICAL REASONING

Each individual, when faced with a particular ethical dilemma, engages in **ethical reasoning**—that is, a reasoning process in which the individual examines the situation at hand in light of his or her moral convictions or ethical standards. Businesspersons do likewise when making decisions with ethical implications.

How do business decision makers decide whether a given action is the "right" one for their firms? What ethical standards should be applied? Broadly speaking, ethical reasoning relating to business traditionally has been characterized by two fundamental approaches. One approach defines ethical behavior in terms of duty, which also implies certain rights. The other approach determines what is ethical in terms of the consequences, or outcome, of any given action. We examine both of these approaches here.

In addition to the two basic ethical approaches, a few theories have been developed that specifically address the social responsibility of corporations. Because these theories also influence today's business decision makers, we conclude this section with a short discussion of the different views of corporate social responsibility.

Duty-Based Ethics

Duty-based ethical standards often are derived from revealed truths, such as religious precepts. They can also be derived through philosophical reasoning.

Religious Ethical Standards In the Judeo-Christian tradition, which is the dominant religious tradition in the United States, the Ten Commandments of the Old Testament establish fundamental rules for moral action. Other religions have their own sources of revealed truth. Religious rules generally are absolute with respect to the behavior of their adherents. **■EXAMPLE 3.3** The commandment "Thou shalt not steal" is an absolute mandate for a person who believes that the Ten Commandments reflect revealed truth. Even a benevolent motive for stealing (such as Robin Hood's) cannot justify the act because the act itself is inherently immoral and thus wrong. ■

Kantian Ethics Duty-based ethical standards may also be derived solely from philosophical reasoning. The German philosopher Immanuel Kant (1724–1804), for example, identified some general guiding principles for moral behavior based on what he believed to be the fundamental nature of human beings. Kant believed that human beings are qualitatively different from other physical objects and are endowed with moral integrity and the capacity to reason and conduct their affairs rationally. Therefore, a person's thoughts and actions should be respected. When human beings are treated merely as a means to an end, they are being treated as the equivalent of objects and are being denied their basic humanity.

A central theme in Kantian ethics is that individuals should evaluate their actions in light of the consequences that would follow if *everyone* in society acted in the same way. This **categorical imperative** can be applied to any action. **■EXAMPLE 3.4** Suppose that you are deciding whether to cheat on an examination. If you have adopted Kant's categorical imperative, you will decide *not* to cheat because if everyone cheated, the examination (and the entire education system) would be meaningless. ■

The Principle of Rights Because a duty cannot exist without a corresponding right, duty-based ethical standards imply that human beings have basic rights. The principle that human beings have certain fundamental rights (to life, freedom, and the pursuit of happiness, for example) is deeply embedded in Western culture as part of the natural law tradition. This tradition embraces the concept that certain actions (such as killing another person) are morally wrong because they are contrary to nature (the natural desire to continue living). Those who adhere to this **principle of rights,** or "rights theory," believe that a key factor in determining whether a business decision is ethical is how that decision affects the rights of others. These others include the firm's owners, its employees, the consumers of its products or services, its suppliers, the community in which it does business, and society as a whole.

A potential dilemma for those who support rights theory, however, is that they may disagree on which rights are most important. Management constantly faces ethical conflicts and trade-offs. When considering all those affected by a business decision, for example, how much weight should be given to employees relative to shareholders, customers relative to the community, or employees relative to society as a whole?

In general, rights theorists believe that whichever right is stronger in a particular circumstance takes precedence. **■EXAMPLE 3.5** A business firm can either keep a plant open, saving the jobs of twelve workers, or shut the plant down and avoid contaminating a river with pollutants that would endanger the health of thousands of people. In this situation, a rights theorist can easily choose which group to favor. (Not all choices are so clear-cut, however.) ■

Outcome-Based Ethics: Utilitarianism

"The greatest good for the greatest number" is a paraphrase of the major premise of the utilitarian approach to ethics. **Utilitarianism** is a philosophical theory developed by Jeremy Bentham (1748–1832) and modified by John Stuart Mill (1806–1873)—both British philosophers. In contrast to duty-based ethics, utilitarianism is outcome oriented. It focuses on the consequences of an action, not on the nature of the action itself or on any set of preestablished moral values or religious beliefs.

Under a utilitarian model of ethics, an action is morally correct, or "right," when, among the people it affects, it produces the greatest amount of good for the greatest number. When an action affects the majority adversely, it is morally wrong. Applying the utilitarian theory thus requires (1) a determination of which individuals will be affected by the action in question; (2) a **cost-benefit analysis,** which involves an assessment of the negative and positive effects of alternative actions on these individuals; and (3) a choice among alternative actions that will produce maximum societal utility (the greatest positive net benefits for the greatest number of individuals).

Corporate Social Responsibility

For many years, groups concerned with civil rights, employee safety and welfare, consumer protection, envi-

ronmental preservation, and other causes have pressured corporate America to behave in a responsible manner with respect to these causes. Thus was born the concept of **corporate social responsibility**—the idea that those who run corporations can and should act ethically and be accountable to society for their actions. Just what constitutes corporate social responsibility has been debated for some time, however, and there are a number of different theories today.

Stakeholder Approach One view of corporate social responsibility stresses that corporations have a duty not just to shareholders, but also to other groups affected by corporate decisions ("stakeholders"). Under this approach, a corporation would consider the impact of its decision on the firm's employees, customers, creditors, suppliers, and the community in which the corporation operates. The reasoning behind this "stakeholder view" is that in some circumstances, one or more of these other groups may have a greater stake in company decisions than the shareholders do. Although this may be true, it is often difficult to decide which group's interests should receive greater weight if the interests conflict.

Corporate Citizenship Another theory of social responsibility argues that corporations should behave as good citizens by promoting goals that society deems worthwhile and taking positive steps toward solving social problems. The idea is that because business controls so much of the wealth and power of this country, business in turn has a responsibility to society to use that wealth and power in socially beneficial ways. Under a corporate citizenship view, companies are judged on how much they donate to social causes, as well as how they conduct their operations with respect to employment discrimination, human rights, environmental concerns, and similar issues.

In the following case, a corporation's board of directors did not seem to doubt the priority of the firm's responsibilities. Focused solely on the profits delivered into the hands of the shareholders, the board failed to check the actions of the firm's chief executive officer (CEO) and, in fact, appeared to condone the CEO's misconduct. If the board had applied a different set of priorities, the shareholders might have been in a better financial position, however. A regulatory agency soon found the situation "troubling" and imposed a restriction on the firm. The board protested. The protest reminded the court of "the old saw about the child who murders his parents and then asks for mercy because he is an orphan."

United States Court of Appeals, District of Columbia Circuit, 474 F.3d 822 (2007).

FACTS The National Association of Securities Dealers (NASD) operates the Nasdaq, an electronic securities exchange, on which Fog Cutter Capital Group was listed.[a] Andrew Wiederhorn had founded Fog Cutter in 1997 to manage a restaurant chain and make other investments. With family members, Wiederhorn controlled more than 50 percent of Fog Cutter's stock. The firm agreed that if Wiederhorn was terminated "for cause," he was entitled only to his salary through the date of termination. If terminated "without cause," he would be owed three times his $350,000 annual salary, three times his largest annual bonus from the previous three years, and any unpaid salary and bonus. "Cause" included the conviction of a felony. In 2001, Wiederhorn became the target of an investigation into the collapse of Capital Consultants, LLC. Fog Cutter then redefined "cause" in his termination agreement to cover only a felony involving Fog Cutter. In June 2004, Wiederhorn agreed to plead guilty to two felonies, serve eighteen months in prison, pay a $25,000 fine, and pay $2 million to Capital Consultants. The day before he entered his plea, Fog Cutter agreed that while he was in prison, he would keep his title, responsibilities, salary, bonuses, and other benefits. It also agreed to a $2 million "leave of absence payment." In July, the NASD delisted Fog Cutter from the Nasdaq. Fog Cutter appealed this decision to the Securities and Exchange Commission (SEC), which dismissed the appeal. Fog Cutter petitioned the U.S. Court of Appeals for the District of Columbia Circuit for review.

ISSUE Was the SEC's action justified?

a. Securities (stocks and bonds) can be bought and sold through national exchanges. Whether a security is listed on an exchange is subject to the discretion of the organization that operates it. The Securities and Exchange Commission oversees the securities exchanges (see Chapter 27).

DECISION Yes. The U.S. Court of Appeals for the District of Columbia Circuit denied the firm's petition for review. The SEC's dismissal was not "arbitrary, capricious, or an abuse of discretion."

REASON Fog Cutter's deals with Wiederhorn indicated that, as the SEC found, he had "thorough control" over the firm. As further evidence in support of the SEC's decision, the court noted that Fog Cutter had done nothing to check Wiederhorn's conduct. In fact, the board's actions only "aggravated the concerns Wiederhorn's conviction and imprisonment raised." In its petition for review of the SEC's dismissal, Fog Cutter claimed that the NASD's decision was unfair. The court pointed out, however, that the decision was in accord with the NASD's rules, which gave it "broad discretion to determine whether the public interest requires delisting securities in light of events at a company." In this case, "Fog Cutter made a deal with Wiederhorn that cost the company $4.75 million in a year in which it reported a $3.93 million net loss. We know as well that Fog Cutter handed Wiederhorn a $2 million bonus right before he went off to prison, a bonus stemming directly from the consequences of Wiederhorn's criminal activity." Fog Cutter knew that Wiederhorn would use this "bonus" to pay Capital Consultants. In its appeal, Fog Cutter also claimed that if it fired Wiederhorn in light of his guilty plea, it would have to pay him $6 million under his termination agreement. But, the court responded, Fog Cutter amended this agreement during the investigation of Wiederhorn "knowing full well" that it would "dramatically" increase the cost of firing him.

 FOR CRITICAL ANALYSIS–Ethical Consideration *Should more consideration have been given to the fact that Fog Cutter was not convicted of a violation of the law? Why or why not?*

Creating Ethical Codes of Conduct

One of the most effective ways to set a tone of ethical behavior within an organization is to create an ethical code of conduct. A well-written code of ethics explicitly states a company's ethical priorities and demonstrates the company's commitment to ethical behavior.

 PREVENTING LEGAL DISPUTES **Business owners wishing to avoid disputes over ethical violations must focus on creating a written ethical code that is clear and understandable (in plain English). The code should establish specific procedures that employees can follow if they have questions or complaints. It should assure employees that their jobs will be secure and that they will not face reprisals if**

they do file a complaint. Business owners should also explain to employees why these ethics policies are important to the company. A well-written code might include examples to clarify what the company considers to be acceptable and unacceptable conduct.

■

Providing Ethics Training to Employees For an ethical code to be effective, its provisions must be clearly communicated to employees. Most large companies have implemented ethics training programs in which management and employees discuss face to face the firm's policies and the importance of ethical conduct. Some firms hold periodic ethics seminars during which employees can openly describe any ethical issues that they may be experiencing and learn how the firm's ethical policies apply to those specific problems. Smaller firms should also offer some form of ethics training to employees, because this is one factor that courts will consider if the firm is later accused of an ethics violation.

The Sarbanes-Oxley Act and Web-Based Reporting Systems The Sarbanes-Oxley Act of 2002[1] requires that companies set up confidential systems so that employees and others can "raise red flags" about suspected illegal or unethical auditing and accounting practices.

Some companies have created online reporting systems to accomplish this goal. In one such system, employees can click on an icon on their computers that anonymously links them with Ethicspoint, an organization based in Portland, Oregon. Through Ethicspoint, employees can report suspicious accounting practices, sexual harassment, and other possibly unethical behavior. Ethicspoint, in turn, alerts management personnel or the audit committee at the designated company to the potential problem. Those who have used the system say that it is less inhibiting than calling a company's toll-free number.

HOW THE LAW INFLUENCES BUSINESS ETHICS

Although business ethics and the law are closely related, they are not always identical. Here, we examine some situations in which what is legal and what is ethical may not be the same.

The Moral Minimum

Compliance with the law is normally regarded as the **moral minimum**—the minimum acceptable standard for ethical

---

1. 15 U.S.C. Sections 7201 *et seq.* This act will be discussed in Chapters 27 and 31.

---

business behavior. In many corporate scandals, had most of the businesspersons involved simply followed the law, they would not have gotten into trouble. Note, though, that in the interest of preserving personal freedom, as well as for practical reasons, the law does not—and cannot—codify all ethical requirements. As they make business decisions, businesspersons must remember that just because an action is legal does not necessarily make it ethical. Look at Exhibit 3–1. Here, you see that there is an intersection between what is ethical and what is legal. Businesspersons should attempt to operate in the area where what is legal and what is ethical intersect.

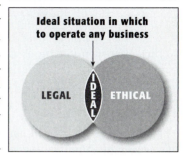

EXHIBIT 3–1 The Intersection of What Is Legal and What Is Ethical

Ideal situation in which to operate any business

LEGAL IDEAL ETHICAL

Excessive Executive Pay As just mentioned, business behavior that is legal may still be unethical. Consider executive pay. There is no law that specifies what public corporations can pay their officers. Consequently, "executive-pay scandals" do not involve executives breaking the law. Rather, the concern is with the ethical underpinnings of executive-pay scales that can exceed millions of dollars. Such high pay for executives may appear unethical when their companies are not making very high profits (or are even suffering losses) and their share prices are falling.

Even this subject, though, does not lend itself to a black-and-white ethical analysis. As with many other things, there is a market for executives that operates according to supply and demand. Sometimes, corporate boards decide to offer executives very large compensation packages to entice them to come to work for the company or to keep them from leaving for another corporation. There is no simple formula for determining the ethical level of compensation for a given executive in a given company. If a law were passed that limited executive compensation to, say, twenty times the salary of the lowest-paid worker in the company, fewer individuals would be willing to undergo the stress and long hours associated with running major companies.

Determining the Legality of a Given Action It may seem that determining the legality of a given action should be simple. Either something is legal or it is not. In fact, one of the major challenges businesspersons face is that the legality of a particular action is not always clear. In part, this is because business is regulated by so many laws that it is possible to violate one of them without realizing it. The law also contains numerous "gray areas," making it difficult to predict with certainty how a court will apply a given law to a particular action.

Determining whether a planned action is legal thus requires that decision makers keep abreast of the law. Normally, large business firms have attorneys on their staffs to assist them in making key decisions. Small firms must also seek legal advice before making important business decisions because the consequences of just one violation of a regulatory rule may be costly.

Ignorance of the law will not excuse a business owner or manager from liability for violating a statute or regulation. **■EXAMPLE 3.6** In one case, Riverdale Mills Corporation was held liable for its employee's attempt to board a plane with two cans of flammable hazardous material from Riverdale in his luggage. The court found that even though the employer was unaware of the employee's actions—and the employee did not know that his actions were illegal—Riverdale had violated Federal Aviation Administration (FAA) regulations.[2] **■**

The Law Cannot Control All Business Behavior

Congress, the regulatory agencies, and state and local governments do not have perfect knowledge. Often they discover the negative impact of corporate activities only after the fact. The same can be true of corporate executives. They do not always know the full impact of their actions. **■EXAMPLE 3.7** In the past, asbestos was used for insulation. At that time, the corporations that supplied the asbestos did not know that it was capable of causing a rare type of cancer. **■**

At other times, though, the law is not ambiguous. Nevertheless, it may still be unable to control business behavior—at least initially.

Breaking the Law—Backdating Stock Options
Sometimes, a practice that is legal, such as granting stock options, is used in an unethical and illegal manner. Stock options are a device that potentially rewards hard work. Publicly held corporations offer stock options to employees at the current price of the company's stock on the day that the options are granted. If at a later time the market price of the stock has gone up, an employee can exercise the stock options and reap the difference between the price of the options and the current market price.

In 2006 and 2007, it was revealed that a number of large corporations had backdated stock options. If stock options are granted and the price of the company's stock subsequently

falls or does not rise very much, the value of the stock options is essentially zero. One way around this problem is to go back and change the date on which the stock options were granted to the employee. In other words, the date of the stock options is simply moved back to a day when the stock had a lower price than it has currently, thereby making the options valuable again.

When Is Backdating Illegal?   Backdating stock options can be legal or illegal, depending on whether the company follows proper accounting procedures and Securities and Exchange Commission (SEC) disclosure rules. Generally, **backdating** stock options is legal if no documents are falsified, the corporation's shareholders are notified of the backdating, and the backdating is properly reflected in the corporation's financial statements and tax returns. If a company fails to meet any of these conditions, then backdating is illegal, and those involved risk prosecution by the SEC or the U.S. Department of Justice.

Even when it is legal, backdating may be unethical because shareholders lose by paying inflated compensation to the persons whose stock options were backdated. A company's shareholders can bring a lawsuit against the company for improper backdating and seek to have the corporation reimbursed for the loss. Many of the companies that the SEC has investigated for backdating (discussed next) have faced civil lawsuits by their shareholders.

The Consequences of Illegal Backdating.   During the past few years, the SEC has prosecuted numerous corporate executives involved in backdating scandals. These include individuals at Apple, Inc., and Monster Worldwide, Inc., among others. The penalties have included restitution of the improper gains, as well as fines and prison sentences. For example, in 2008, Nancy M. Tullos, a former vice president at Broadcom Corporation, agreed to repay more than $1.3 million and to pay a $100,000 fine. As a result of the backdating, Broadcom had to restate its financial results and report an additional $2.2 billion in compensation expenses. In 2007, William W. McGuire, the former chief executive officer (CEO) of UnitedHealth Group, Inc., agreed to a $468 million settlement, the largest to date. Additionally, Gregory L. Reyes, Jr., the former CEO of Brocade Communications Systems, Inc., was sentenced to twenty-one months in prison and ordered to pay a $15 million fine for "tampering" with records of stock option gains.

The backdating scandal is another example of unethical behavior resulting in long-run profit reduction. As of 2009, at least 252 public companies had disclosed that they had undertaken internal investigations to discover if backdating

---

2. *Riverdale Mills Corp. v. U.S. F.A.A.*, 417 F.Supp.2d 167 (D.Mass. 2006).

had occurred. The companies involved face more than 125 shareholder lawsuits and as many SEC investigations, plus fifty-eight U.S. Department of Justice investigations and even six criminal cases.

Misleading Regulators—The Case of OxyContin In 1996, the pharmaceutical company Purdue Pharma, LP, started marketing a "wonder" narcotic painkiller called OxyContin. This powerful, long-lasting drug provides pain relief for twelve hours. Just a few years after its introduction, Purdue Pharma's annual sales of the drug reached $1 billion.

The company's executives initially contended that OxyContin, because of its time-release formulation, posed no risk for serious abuse or addiction. Quickly, though, experienced drug abusers and even teenagers discovered that chewing on an OxyContin tablet or crushing one and snorting the powder produced a powerful high, comparable to that of heroin. By 2000, large parts of the United States were experiencing increases in addiction and crime related to OxyContin.

In reality, the company and three of its executives had fraudulently marketed OxyContin for more than six years as a drug unlikely to lead to abuse. Internal company documents showed that even before OxyContin was marketed, executives recognized that if physicians knew that the drug could be abused and become addictive, they would be less likely to prescribe it. Consequently, the company simply kept the information secret.

In 2007, Purdue Pharma and three former executives pleaded guilty to criminal charges that they had misled regulators, patients, and physicians about OxyContin's risks of addiction. Purdue Pharma agreed to pay $600 million in fines and other payments. The three ex-executives agreed to pay $34.5 million in fines. Once again, company executives resorted to unethical reasoning because they wanted to maximize profits in the short run, rather than engaging in behavior that would lead to profit maximization in the long run.

"Gray Areas" in the Law

In many situations, business firms can predict with a fair amount of certainty whether a given action is legal. For instance, firing an employee solely because of that person's race or gender clearly violates federal laws prohibiting employment discrimination. In some situations, though, the legality of a particular action may be less clear.

EXAMPLE 3.8 Suppose that a business firm decides to launch a new advertising campaign. How far can the firm go in making claims for its products or services? Federal and state laws prohibit firms from engaging in "deceptive advertising." At the federal level, the test for deceptive advertising normally used by the Federal Trade Commission is whether an advertising claim would deceive a "reasonable consumer."[3] At what point, though, would a reasonable consumer be deceived by a particular ad? ■

In addition, many rules of law require a court to determine what is "foreseeable" or "reasonable" in a particular situation. Because a business has no way of predicting how a specific court will decide these issues, decision makers need to proceed with caution and evaluate an action and its consequences from an ethical perspective. The same problem often occurs in cases involving the Internet because it is often unclear how a court will apply existing laws in the context of cyberspace. Generally, if a company can demonstrate that it acted in good faith and responsibly in the circumstances, it has a better chance of successfully defending its action in court or before an administrative law judge.

The following case shows that businesses and their customers have different expectations with respect to the standard of care regarding the handling of personal information. The case also illustrates that the legal standards in this area may be inconsistent and vague.

3. The Federal Trade Commission regulates deceptive trade practices, including misleading advertising.

CASE 3.3 Guin v. Brazos Higher Education Service Corp.

United States District Court, District of Minnesota, __ F.Supp.2d __ (2006).

FACTS Brazos Higher Education Service Corporation, which is based in Waco, Texas, makes and services student loans. Brazos issued a laptop computer to its employee John Wright, who works from an office in his home in Silver Spring, Maryland, analyzing loan information. Wright used the laptop to store borrowers' personal information. In September 2004, Wright's home was burglarized and the laptop was stolen.

Based on Federal Trade Commission (FTC) guidelines and California state law (which requires notice to all resident borrowers), Brazos sent a letter to all of its 550,000 customers. The letter stated that "some personal information associated with your student loan, including your name, address, Social Security number and loan balance, may have been

CASE 3.3–Continues next page

CASE 3.3—Continued

inappropriately accessed by [a] third party." The letter urged borrowers to place "a free 90-day security alert" on their credit bureau files and review FTC consumer assistance materials. Brazos set up a call center to answer further questions and track any reports of identity theft. Stacy Guin, a Brazos customer, filed a suit against Brazos in a federal district court, alleging negligence. Brazos filed a motion for summary judgment.

ISSUE Does a lender that complies with the legal requirements for safeguarding its customers' personal information breach a duty to those customers if the information is inappropriately accessed by a third party?

DECISION No. The district court granted the defendant's motion for summary judgment and dismissed the case. Brazos may have owed Guin a duty of care, but neither Brazos nor Wright breached that duty. Wright had followed Brazos's written security procedures, which was all that the law requires.

REASON The court acknowledged that Brazos had a duty to protect the security and confidentiality of its customers' personal information. Under the Gramm-Leach-Bliley (GLB) Act, a financial institution must "develop, implement, and

maintain a comprehensive written information security program that * * * contains administrative, technical, and physical safeguards that are appropriate to * * * the sensitivity of any customer information." Guin argued that Brazos breached this duty by (1) "providing Wright with [personal information] that he did not need for the task at hand," (2) "permitting Wright to continue keeping [personal information] in an unattended, insecure personal residence," and (3) "allowing Wright to keep [personal information] on his laptop unencrypted." The court disagreed. Brazos had established written security policies and other mandated safeguards for its customers' personal information. Brazos gave Wright access to the information because Wright needed it to analyze loan portfolios. Besides, the GLB Act does not prohibit someone from working with sensitive data on a laptop computer in a home office or require that the data be encrypted.

WHAT IF THE FACTS WERE DIFFERENT? *Suppose that Wright had not been a financial analyst and that his duties for Brazos had not included reviewing confidential loan data. How might the opinion of the court have been different?*

MAKING ETHICAL BUSINESS DECISIONS

As Dean Krehmeyer, executive director of the Business Roundtable's Institute for Corporate Ethics, once said, "Evidence strongly suggests being ethical—doing the right thing—pays." Instilling ethical business decision making into the fabric of a business organization is no small task, even if ethics "pays." The job is to get people to understand that they have to think more broadly about how their decisions will affect employees, shareholders, customers, and even the community. Great companies, such as Enron and the accounting firm Arthur Andersen, were brought down by the unethical behavior of a few. A two-hundred-year-old British investment banking firm, Barings Bank, was destroyed by the actions of one employee and a few of his friends. Clearly, ensuring that all employees get on the ethical business decision-making "bandwagon" is crucial in today's fast-paced world.

The George S. May International Company has provided six basic guidelines to help corporate employees judge their actions. Each employee—no matter what his or her level in the organization—should evaluate his or her actions using the following six guidelines:

1 *The law.* Is the action you are considering legal? If you do not know the laws governing the action, then find out. Ignorance of the law is no excuse.

2 *Rules and procedures.* Are you following the internal rules and procedures that have already been laid out by your company? They have been developed to avoid problems. Is what you are planning to do consistent with your company's policies and procedures? If not, stop.

3 *Values.* Laws and internal company policies reinforce society's values. You might wish to ask yourself whether you are attempting to find a loophole in the law or in your company's policies. Next, you have to ask yourself whether you are following the "spirit" of the law as well as the letter of the law or the internal policy.

4 *Conscience.* If you have any feeling of guilt, let your conscience be your guide. Alternatively, ask yourself whether you would be happy to be interviewed by a national news magazine about the actions you are going to take.

5 *Promises.* Every business organization is based on trust. Your customers believe that your company will do what it is supposed to do. The same is true for your suppliers and employees. Will your actions live up to the commitments

you have made to others, both inside the business and outside?

6 *Heroes.* We all have heroes who are role models for us. Is what you are planning on doing an action that your hero would take? If not, how would your hero act? That is how you should be acting.

BUSINESS ETHICS ON A GLOBAL LEVEL

Given the various cultures and religions throughout the world, conflicts in ethics frequently arise between foreign and U.S. businesspersons. **EXAMPLE 3.9** In certain countries, the consumption of alcohol and specific foods is forbidden for religious reasons. Under such circumstances, it would be thoughtless and imprudent for a U.S. businessperson to invite a local business contact out for a drink. ■ The role played by women in other countries may also present some difficult ethical problems for firms doing business internationally. Equal employment opportunity is a fundamental public policy in the United States, and Title VII of the Civil Rights Act of 1964 prohibits discrimination against women in the employment context (see Chapter 23). Some other countries, however, offer little protection for women against gender discrimination in the workplace, including sexual harassment.

We look here at how the employment practices that affect workers in other countries, particularly developing countries, have created some especially difficult ethical problems for U.S. sellers of goods manufactured in foreign nations. We also examine some of the ethical ramifications of laws prohibiting bribery and the expansion of ethics programs in the global community.

Monitoring the Employment Practices of Foreign Suppliers

Many U.S. businesses now contract with companies in developing nations to produce goods, such as shoes and clothing, because the wage rates in those nations are significantly lower than those in the United States. Yet what if a foreign company hires women and children at below-minimum-wage rates, for example, or requires its employees to work long hours in a workplace full of health hazards? What if the company's supervisors routinely engage in workplace conduct that is offensive to women?

Given today's global communications network, few companies can assume that their actions in other nations will go unnoticed by "corporate watch" groups that discover and publicize unethical corporate behavior. As a result, U.S. businesses today usually take steps to avoid such adverse public-

ity—either by refusing to deal with certain suppliers or by arranging to monitor their suppliers' workplaces to make sure that the employees are not being mistreated.

The Foreign Corrupt Practices Act

Another ethical problem in international business dealings has to do with the legitimacy of certain side payments to government officials. In the United States, the majority of contracts are formed within the private sector. In many foreign countries, however, government officials make the decisions on most major construction and manufacturing contracts because of extensive government regulation and control over trade and industry. Side payments to government officials in exchange for favorable business contracts are not unusual in such countries, nor are they considered to be unethical. In the past, U.S. corporations doing business in these nations largely followed the dictum, "When in Rome, do as the Romans do."

In the 1970s, however, the U.S. media uncovered a number of business scandals involving large side payments by U.S. corporations to foreign representatives for the purpose of securing advantageous international trade contracts. In response to this unethical behavior, in 1977 Congress passed the Foreign Corrupt Practices Act (FCPA), which prohibits U.S. businesspersons from bribing foreign officials to secure beneficial contracts.

Prohibition against the Bribery of Foreign Officials The first part of the FCPA applies to all U.S. companies and their directors, officers, shareholders, employees, and agents. This part prohibits the bribery of most officials of foreign governments if the purpose of the payment is to get the official to act in his or her official capacity to provide business opportunities.

The FCPA does not prohibit payment of substantial sums to minor officials whose duties are ministerial. These payments are often referred to as "grease," or facilitating payments. They are meant to accelerate the performance of administrative services that might otherwise be carried out at a slow pace. Thus, for example, if a firm makes a payment to a minor official to speed up an import licensing process, the firm has not violated the FCPA. Generally, the act, as amended, permits payments to foreign officials if such payments are lawful within the foreign country. The act also does not prohibit payments to private foreign companies or other third parties unless the U.S. firm knows that the payments will be passed on to a foreign government in violation of the FCPA.

Accounting Requirements In the past, bribes were often concealed in corporate financial records. Thus, the second part of the FCPA is directed toward accountants. All companies must keep detailed records that "accurately and fairly" reflect their financial activities. In addition, all companies must have accounting systems that provide "reasonable assurance" that all transactions entered into by the companies are accounted for and legal. These requirements assist in detecting illegal bribes. The FCPA further prohibits any person from making false statements to accountants or false entries in any record or account.

Penalties for Violations   In 1988, the FCPA was amended to provide that business firms that violate the act may be fined up to $2 million. Individual officers or directors who violate the FCPA may be fined up to $100,000 (the fine cannot be paid by the company) and may be imprisoned for up to five years.

REVIEWING Ethics and Business Decision Making

Isabel Arnett was promoted to CEO of Tamik, Inc., a pharmaceutical company that manufactures a vaccine called Kafluk, which supposedly provides some defense against bird flu. The company began marketing Kafluk throughout Asia. After numerous media reports that bird flu could soon become a worldwide epidemic, the demand for Kafluk increased, sales soared, and Tamik earned record profits. Tamik's CEO, Arnett, then began receiving disturbing reports from Southeast Asia that in some patients, Kafluk had caused psychiatric disturbances, including severe hallucinations, and heart and lung problems. Arnett was informed that six children in Japan had committed suicide by jumping out of windows after receiving the vaccine. To cover up the story and prevent negative publicity, Arnett instructed Tamik's partners in Asia to offer cash to the Japanese families whose

children had died in exchange for their silence. Arnett also refused to authorize additional research within the company to study the potential side effects of Kafluk. Using the information presented in the chapter, answer the following questions.

1 This scenario illustrates one of the main reasons why ethical problems occur in business. What is that reason?

2 Would a person who adheres to the principle of rights consider it ethical for Arnett not to disclose potential safety concerns and to refuse to conduct additional research on Kafluk? Why or why not?

3 If Kafluk prevented fifty Asian people who were infected with bird flu from dying, would Arnett's conduct in this situation be ethical under a utilitarian model of ethics? Why or why not?

4 Did Tamik or Arnett violate the Foreign Corrupt Practices Act in this scenario? Why or why not?

TERMS AND CONCEPTS

backdating 68
business ethics 61
categorical imperative 64
corporate social
  responsibility 65

cost-benefit analysis 65
ethical reasoning 64
ethics 61
moral minimum 67
principle of rights 65

utilitarianism 65

CHAPTER SUMMARY Ethics and Business Decision Making

Business Ethics (See pages 61–64.)	Ethics can be defined as the study of what constitutes right or wrong behavior. Business ethics focuses on how moral and ethical principles are applied in the business context.
	1. *Reasons for ethical problems*—One of the most pervasive reasons why ethical breaches occur is the desire to increase sales (or not lose them), thereby increasing profits (and for corporations, market value). Some people believe that a corporation's only goal should be profit maximization. Even if this is true, executives should distinguish between short-run and

CHAPTER SUMMARY Ethics and Business Decision Making—Continued

Business Ethics—Continued	long-run profit goals and focus on maximizing profits over the long run because only long-run profit maximization is consistent with business ethics. 2. *Behavior of owners and managers*—Management's commitment and behavior are essential in creating an ethical workplace. Management's behavior, more than anything else, sets the ethical tone of a firm and influences the behavior of employees.
Approaches to Ethical Reasoning (See pages 64–67.)	1. *Duty-based ethics*—Ethics based on religious beliefs; philosophical reasoning, such as that of Immanuel Kant; and the basic rights of human beings (the principle of rights). A potential problem for those who support this approach is deciding which rights are more important in a given situation. Management constantly faces ethical conflicts and trade-offs when considering all those affected by a business decision. 2. *Outcome-based ethics (utilitarianism)*—Ethics based on philosophical reasoning, such as that of John Stuart Mill. Applying this theory requires a cost-benefit analysis, weighing the negative effects against the positive and deciding which course of conduct produces the best outcome. 3. *Corporate social responsibility*—A number of theories based on the idea that corporations can and should act ethically and be accountable to society for their actions. These include the stakeholder approach and corporate citizenship. 4. *Ethical codes*—Most large firms have ethical codes or policies and training programs to help employees determine whether certain actions are ethical. In addition, the Sarbanes-Oxley Act requires firms to set up confidential systems so that employees and others can report suspected illegal or unethical auditing or accounting practices.
How the Law Influences Business Ethics (See pages 67–70.)	1. *The moral minimum*—Lawful behavior is a moral minimum. The law has its limits, though, and some actions may be legal but not ethical. The law cannot control all business behavior (such as initially failing to prevent the backdating of stock options). 2. *Legal uncertainties*—It may be difficult to predict with certainty whether particular actions are legal, given the numerous and frequent changes in the laws regulating business and the "gray areas" in the law.
Making Ethical Business Decisions (See pages 70–71.)	Although it can be difficult for businesspersons to ensure that all employees make ethical business decisions, it is crucial in today's legal environment. Doing the right thing pays off in the long run, in terms of both increasing profits and avoiding negative publicity and the potential for bankruptcy. Each employee should be taught to evaluate her or his action using guidelines set forth by the company. A set of six guidelines for making ethical business decisions appears on pages 70 and 71.
Business Ethics on a Global Level (See pages 71–72.)	Businesses must take account of the many cultural, religious, and legal differences among nations. Notable differences relate to the role of women in society, employment laws governing workplace conditions, and the practice of giving side payments to foreign officials to secure favorable contracts.

FOR REVIEW

*Answers for the even-numbered questions in this **For Review** section can be found on this text's accompanying Web site at* **www.cengage.com/blaw/fbl**. *Select "Chapter 3" and click on "For Review."*

1 What is business ethics, and why is it important?

2 How can business leaders encourage their companies to act ethically?

3 How do duty-based ethical standards differ from outcome-based ethical standards?

4 What are six guidelines that an employee can use to evaluate whether his or her actions are ethical?

5 What types of ethical issues might arise in the context of international business transactions?

QUESTIONS AND CASE PROBLEMS

 HYPOTHETICAL SCENARIOS AND CASE PROBLEMS

3.1 Business Ethics. Some business ethicists maintain that whereas personal ethics has to do with "right" or "wrong" behavior, business ethics is concerned with "appropriate" behavior. In other words, ethical behavior in business has less to do with moral principles than with what society deems to be appropriate behavior in the business context. Do you agree with this distinction? Do personal and business ethics ever overlap? Should personal ethics play any role in business ethical decision making?

3.2 Hypothetical Question with Sample Answer. If a firm engages in "ethical" behavior solely for the purpose of gaining profits from the goodwill it generates, the "ethical" behavior is essentially a means toward a self-serving end (profits and the accumulation of wealth). In this situation, is the firm acting unethically in any way? Should motive or conduct carry greater weight on the ethical scales in this situation?

 For a sample answer to Question 3.2, go to Appendix E at the end of this text.

3.3 Business Ethics and Public Opinion. Assume that you are a high-level manager for a shoe manufacturer. You know that your firm could increase its profit margin by producing shoes in Indonesia, where you could hire women for $40 a month to assemble them. You also know, however, that human rights advocates recently accused a competing shoe manufacturer of engaging in exploitative labor practices because the manufacturer sold shoes made by Indonesian women working for similarly low wages. You personally do not believe that paying $40 a month to Indonesian women is unethical because you know that in their impoverished country, $40 a month is a better-than-average wage rate. Assuming that the decision is yours to make, should you have the shoes manufactured in Indonesia and make higher profits for your company? Or should you avoid the risk of negative publicity and the consequences of that publicity for the firm's reputation and subsequent profits? Are there other alternatives? Discuss fully.

3.4 Ethical Decision Making. Shokun Steel Co. owns many steel plants. One of its plants is much older than the others. Equipment at the old plant is outdated and inefficient, and the costs of production at that plant are now twice as high as at any of Shokun's other plants. Shokun cannot increase the price of its steel because of competition, both domestic and international. The plant employs more than a thousand workers; it is located in Twin Firs, Pennsylvania, which has a population of about forty-five thousand. Shokun is contemplating whether to close the plant. What factors should the firm consider in making its decision? Will the firm violate any ethical duties if it closes the plant? Analyze these questions from the two basic perspectives on ethical reasoning discussed in this chapter.

3.5 Case Problem with Sample Answer. Eden Electrical, Ltd., owned twenty-five appliance stores throughout Israel, at least some of which sold refrigerators made by Amana Co. Eden bought the appliances from Amana's Israeli distributor, Pan El A/Yesh Shem, which approached Eden about taking over the distributorship. Eden representatives met with Amana executives. The executives made assurances about Amana's good faith, its hope of having a long-term business relationship with Eden, and its willingness to have Eden become its exclusive distributor in Israel. Eden signed a distributorship agreement and paid Amana $2.4 million. Amana failed to deliver this amount in inventory to Eden, continued selling refrigerators to other entities for the Israeli market, and represented to others that it was still looking for a long-term distributor. Less than three months after signing the agreement with Eden, Amana terminated it, without explanation. Eden filed a suit in a federal district court against Amana, alleging fraud. The court awarded Eden $12.1 million in damages. Is this amount warranted? Why or why not? How does this case illustrate why business ethics is important? [*Eden Electrical, Ltd. v. Amana Co.*, 370 F.3d 824 (8th Cir. 2004)]

After you have answered Problem 3.5, compare your answer with the sample answer given on the Web site that accompanies this text. Go to www.cengage.com/blaw/fbl, select "Chapter 3," and click on "Case Problem with Sample Answer."

3.6 Ethical Conduct. Richard Fraser was an "exclusive career insurance agent" under a contract with Nationwide Mutual Insurance Co. Fraser leased computer hardware and software from Nationwide for his business. During a dispute between Nationwide and the Nationwide Insurance Independent Contractors Association, an organization representing Fraser and other exclusive career agents, Fraser prepared a letter to Nationwide's competitors asking whether they were interested in acquiring the represented agents' policyholders. Nationwide obtained a copy of the letter and searched its electronic file server for e-mail indicating that the letter had been sent. It found a stored e-mail that Fraser had sent to a co-worker indicating that the letter had been sent to at least one competitor. The e-mail was retrieved from the co-worker's file of already received and discarded messages stored on the server. When Nationwide canceled its contract with Fraser, he filed a suit in a federal district court against the firm, alleging, among other things, violations of various federal laws that prohibit the interception of electronic communications during transmission. In whose favor should the court rule, and why? Did Nationwide act ethically in retrieving the e-mail? Explain. [*Fraser v. Nationwide Mutual Insurance Co.*, 352 F.3d 107 (3d Cir. 2004)]

3.7 Ethical Conduct. Ernest Price suffered from sickle-cell ane-
mia. In 1997, Price asked Dr. Ann Houston, his physician, to
prescribe OxyContin, a strong narcotic, for the pain. Over
the next several years, Price saw at least ten different physicians at ten different clinics in two cities, and used seven
pharmacies in three cities, to obtain and fill simultaneous
prescriptions for OxyContin. In March 2001, when Houston
learned of these activities, she refused to write more prescriptions for Price. As other physicians became aware of Price's
actions, they also stopped writing his prescriptions. Price
filed a suit in a Mississippi state court against Purdue
Pharma Co. and other producers and distributors of
OxyContin, as well as his physicians and the pharmacies that
had filled the prescriptions. Price alleged negligence, among
other things, claiming that OxyContin's addictive nature
caused him injury and that this was the defendants' fault.
The defendants argued that Price's claim should be dismissed because it arose from his own wrongdoing. Who
should be held *legally* liable? Should any of the parties be
considered *ethically* responsible? Why or why not? [*Price v.
Purdue Pharma Co.*, 920 So.2d 479 (Miss. 2006)]

3.8 Ethical Leadership. In 1999, Andrew Fastow, chief financial
officer of Enron Corp., asked Merrill Lynch, an investment
firm, to participate in a bogus sale of three barges so that
Enron could record earnings of $12.5 million from the sale.
Through a third entity, Fastow bought the barges back within
six months and paid Merrill for its participation. Five Merrill
employees were convicted of conspiracy to commit wire fraud,
in part, on an "honest services" theory. Under this theory, an
employee deprives his or her employer of "honest services"
when the employee promotes his or her own interests, rather
than the interests of the employer. Four of the employees
appealed to the U.S. Court of Appeals for the Fifth Circuit,
arguing that this charge did not apply to the conduct in which
they engaged. The court agreed, reasoning that the barge deal
was conducted to benefit Enron, not to enrich the Merrill
employees at Enron's expense. Meanwhile, Kevin Howard,
chief financial officer of Enron Broadband Services (EBS),
engaged in "Project Braveheart," which enabled EBS to show
earnings of $111 million in 2000 and 2001. Braveheart
involved the sale of an interest in the future revenue of a
video-on-demand venture to nCube, a small technology firm,
which was paid for its help when EBS bought the interest
back. Howard was convicted of wire fraud, in part, on the
"honest services" theory. He filed a motion to vacate his conviction on the same basis that the Merrill employees had

argued. Did Howard act unethically? Explain. Should the
court grant his motion? Discuss. [*United States v. Howard*, 471
F.Supp.2d 772 (S.D.Tex. 2007)]

3.9 **A Question of Ethics.** *Steven Soderbergh is the
Academy Award–winning director of* Traffic, Erin
Brockovich, *and many other films. CleanFlicks, LLC, filed a
suit in a federal district court against Soderbergh, fifteen other
directors, and the Directors Guild of America. The plaintiff
asked the court to rule that it had the right to sell DVDs of
the defendants' films altered without the defendants' consent
to delete scenes of "sex, nudity, profanity and gory violence."
CleanFlicks sold or rented the edited DVDs under the slogan
"It's About Choice" to consumers, sometimes indirectly
through retailers. It would not sell to retailers that made unauthorized copies of the edited films. The defendants, with
DreamWorks, LLC, and seven other movie studios that own
the copyrights to the films, filed a counterclaim against
CleanFlicks and others engaged in the same business, alleging
copyright infringement. Those filing the counterclaim asked
the court to enjoin (prevent) CleanFlicks and the others
from making and marketing altered versions of the films.*
[*CleanFlicks of Colorado, LLC v. Soderbergh*, 433
F.Supp.2d 1236 (D.Colo. 2006)]

1 Movie studios often edit their films to conform to content
and other standards and sell the edited versions to network
television and other commercial buyers. In this case, however, the studios objected when CleanFlicks edited the
films and sold the altered versions directly to consumers.
Similarly, CleanFlicks made unauthorized copies of the
studios' DVDs to edit the films, but objected to others'
making unauthorized copies of the altered versions. Is
there anything unethical about these apparently contradictory positions? Why or why not?

2 CleanFlicks and its competitors asserted, among other
things, that they were making "fair use" of the studios'
copyrighted works. They argued that by their actions "they
are criticizing the objectionable content commonly found
in current movies and that they are providing more
socially acceptable alternatives to enable families to view
the films together, without exposing children to
the presumed harmful effects emanating from the objectionable content." If you were the judge, how would you
view this argument? Is a court the appropriate forum for
making determinations of public or social policy? Explain.

CRITICAL THINKING AND WRITING ASSIGNMENT

3.10 **Video Question.** Go to this text's Web site at **www.
cengage.com/blaw/fbl** and select "Chapter 3." Click
on "Video Questions" and view the video titled *Ethics: Business
Ethics an Oxymoron?* Then answer the following questions.

1 According to the instructor in the video, what is the
primary reason that businesses act ethically?

2 Which of the two approaches to ethical reasoning that
were discussed in the chapter seems to have had more

influence on the instructor in the discussion of how business activities are related to societies? Explain your answer.

3 The instructor asserts that "[i]n the end, it is the unethical behavior that becomes costly, and conversely ethical behavior creates its own competitive advantage." Do you agree with this statement? Why or why not?

ACCESSING THE INTERNET

For updated links to resources available on the Web, as well as a variety of other materials, visit this text's Web site at

www.cengage.com/blaw/fbl

South-Western Legal Studies in Business at Cengage Learning offers an in-depth "Inside Look" at the Enron debacle at

insidelook.westbuslaw.com

You can find articles on issues relating to stakeholders and corporate accountability at the Corporate Governance Web site. Go to

www.corpgov.net

Global Exchange offers information on global business activities, including some of the ethical issues stemming from those activities, at

www.globalexchange.org

PRACTICAL INTERNET EXERCISES

Go to this text's Web site at **www.cengage.com/blaw/fbl**, select "Chapter 3," and click on "Practical Internet Exercises." There you will find the following Internet research exercises that you can perform to learn more about the topics covered in this chapter.

PRACTICAL INTERNET EXERCISE 3-1 LEGAL PERSPECTIVE—Ethics in Business

PRACTICAL INTERNET EXERCISE 3-2 MANAGEMENT PERSPECTIVE—Environmental Self-Audits

BEFORE THE TEST

Go to this text's Web site at **www.cengage.com/blaw/fbl**, select "Chapter 3," and click on "Interactive Quizzes." You will find a number of interactive questions relating to this chapter.

Vo v. City of Garden Grove

As explained in Chapter 1, the First Amendment protects the freedom of speech. This protection is not unlimited, however. Expression—oral, written, or symbolized by conduct—is subject to reasonable restrictions on time, place, and manner. A restriction is valid if it can be justified without reference to the content of the regulated speech. It also must be narrowly tailored (go no further than necessary) to serve a significant governmental interest and leave open ample alternative channels for communication of information. The requirement of narrow tailoring is satisfied as long as the regulation promotes a substantial governmental interest that would be achieved less effectively without the regulation. In this extended case study, we examine Vo v. City of Garden Grove,[1] *a decision in which these principles were applied.*

CASE BACKGROUND   On December 30, 2001, Phong Ly, a minor, was stabbed to death with a screwdriver while standing outside PC Café, a cybercafé in the city of Garden Grove, California. A *cybercafé* is an establishment that provides Internet access to customers for a fee. The number of cybercafés in Garden Grove rose from three to twenty-two between 2000 and 2002. Over the same period, gang-related activities, including violent crime, increased near some of the cybercafés. Within a few days of Ly's murder, on the basis of a report from Joseph Polisar (the city's chief of police) who detailed the accelerating criminal activity,

---

1. 115 Cal.App.4th 425, 9 Cal.Rptr.3d 257 (4 Dist. 2004).

the city enacted a temporary ordinance to halt the establishment of new cybercafés.

In July 2002, on the strength of an updated report from Polisar, the city enacted a permanent ordinance that, as amended the following December, required cybercafé owners to provide security guards and install video surveillance systems, among other things. Minors were prohibited from visiting the cybercafés during school hours unless accompanied by a parent or guardian. Thanh Thuy Vo and four other owners filed a suit in a California state court against the city, alleging, in part, that the ordinance violated their right to freedom of speech. The court agreed with the owners and enjoined the city from enforcing the ordinance. The city appealed to a state intermediate appellate court.

MAJORITY OPINION

IKOLA, J. [Judge]

*   *   *   *

From the information provided [by Chief Polisar], the city concluded that excluding minors from Cybercafes during school hours would advance its significant public interest in their protection and safety. That conclusion is reasonable. Although parents presumably believe their minor children are in school while it is in session, they are not in a position to assert direct supervision and control during school hours. As noted by the chief of police, if Cybercafes allow minor children on the premises during school hours, the potential that gang members will recruit minors is increased, as well as the potential that minors will become witnesses or victims of gang violence. *Thus, the regulation promotes a substantial government interest that would be achieved less effectively absent the regulation.* This is all that is required to meet the narrow tailoring requirement. [Emphasis added.]

Further, the means chosen to advance the city's interest are not substantially broader than necessary. The city perceived that danger to minors existed in the risky environment of the Cybercafes. The daytime curfew is limited to Cybercafes with

their risky environment, and to those times when the students are not under the presumed direct control and supervision of their parents.

Finally, plaintiffs presented no evidence to establish the lack of open ample alternative channels for communication. It is common knowledge that alternative channels for communication over the Internet are abundant. Many have Internet access at home. Schools (where the minors should be in any event) commonly provide Internet access, as do public libraries. And, of course, the Cybercafes themselves are open to minors, even without parental supervision, for seven hours each day.

*   *   *   *

* * * The staffing requirements make no reference to the content of any communication and are thus content neutral. And, as with the daytime curfew, ample alternative channels for communication are available. The remaining question is whether the staffing requirements are narrowly tailored to advance the city's substantial interest in public safety.

*   *   *   *

Given the well-demonstrated criminal activity observed at Cybercafes, and their tendency to attract gang members, the

(Continued)

* * * staffing requirements are * * * narrowly tailored to serve a significant governmental interest. Ample alternative means of communication remain open, and the requirements are not substantially broader than necessary.

* * * *

* * * We are not persuaded the video surveillance system affects First Amendment activity any more than does the presence of an adult employee and/or security guard. The ordinance does not require video surveillance of e-mail or images from the Internet appearing on the customer's computer screens. The ordinance requires only that the system be capable of showing "the activity and physical features of persons or areas within the premises." This is no more than can be observed by employees, security guards, or indeed, other customers. * * * For the reasons discussed * * * in connection with the employee and security guard requirements, the video surveillance requirement is a content-neutral manner restriction, narrowly tailored to advance the city's legitimate interest in public safety and deterrence of gang violence.

* * * *

* * * The court's order * * * enjoining [preventing] the enforcement of * * * [the cybercafé ordinance is] reversed.

DISSENTING OPINION

SILLS, P.J. [Presiding Judge] * * * Dissenting.

I respectfully dissent to the most important part of the majority opinion, in which it holds that Garden Grove may *require* video surveillance in *every* cybercafe in the city, regardless of whether that cybercafe has experienced any gang-related violence, or, indeed, even any problems of the most minor nature.

* * * Only 3 of 22 cybercafes have experienced "gang-related" violence, only 2 more have experienced serious crime of any kind (one of the two was a drug deal), * * * [and] the city's own evidence concerning cybercafes in other cities showed no gang-related crimes at cybercafes outside of Garden Grove. That leaves 17 cybercafes which have experienced no serious problems, a fact which should be enough to require this court to affirm the trial court's injunction * * * .

It is the video surveillance issue, though, that is the most problematic.

* * * *

* * * There are any number of substantial means by which the city's interest in protecting against gang violence could be realized without video surveillance. Police patrols could be increased. Owners could be supplied with a list of gang members who could be refused service. Security guards could be posted at those cybercafes which have already experienced gang-related violence. Yet the majority steadfastly refuse to confront such possibilities, all in the name of deference to " * * * facts" found by the city council. Whatever that is, it isn't trying to minimize any burden on * * * speech to what is reasonably necessary.

* * * *

* * * This is the way Constitutional rights are lost. Not in the thunder of a tyrant's edict, but in the soft judicial whispers of deference.

QUESTIONS FOR ANALYSIS

1 **LAW.** What is the significant, or substantial, governmental interest that is supported by the city ordinance in the Vo case?

2 **LAW.** How exactly does this ordinance implicate First Amendment activities involving "speech"?

3 **ETHICS.** Would an ordinance that allowed city officials to deny a business license to a cybercafé whose "operation does not comport with good morals" be constitutional under the First Amendment?

4 **TECHNOLOGICAL DIMENSIONS.** Why might a cybercafé attract more criminal activity and gang-related violence than other business establishments?

5 **IMPLICATIONS FOR THE BUSINESS MANAGER.** Before installing a video surveillance system, should a business consider any other legal issues besides those relating to freedom of speech?

UNIT TWO Torts and Crimes

UNIT CONTENTS

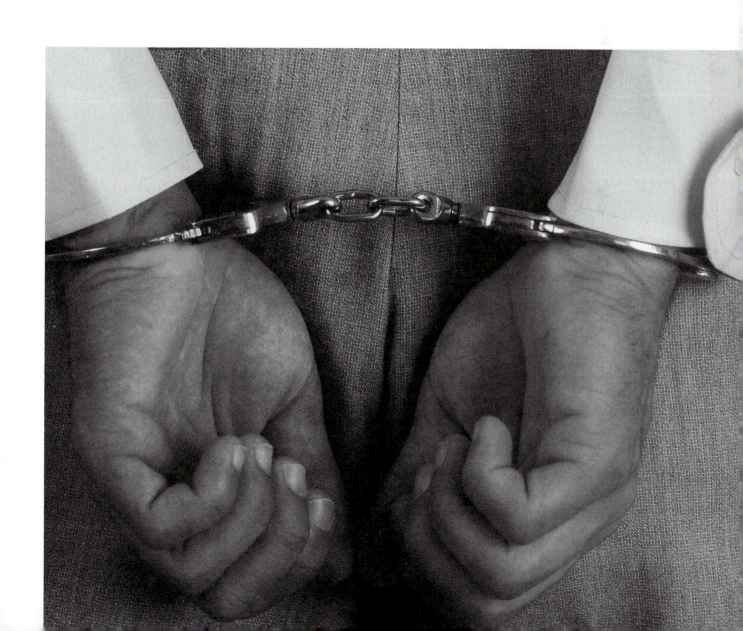

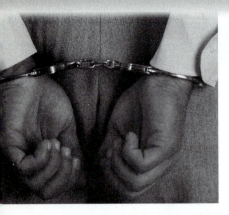

CHAPTER 4
Torts and Cyber Torts

AFTER READING THIS CHAPTER, YOU SHOULD BE ABLE TO ANSWER THE FOLLOWING QUESTIONS:

1 What is a tort?

2 What is the purpose of tort law? What are two basic categories of torts?

3 What are the four elements of negligence?

4 What is meant by strict liability? In what circumstances is strict liability applied?

5 What is a cyber tort, and how are tort theories being applied in cyberspace?

orts are wrongful actions.[1] Through tort law, society compensates those who have suffered injuries as a result of the wrongful conduct of others. Although some torts, such as assault and trespass, originated in the English common law, the field of tort law continues to expand. As new ways to commit wrongs are discovered, such as the use of the Internet to commit wrongful acts, the courts are extending tort law to cover these wrongs.

As you will see in later chapters of this book, many of the lawsuits brought by or against business firms are based on the tort theories discussed in this chapter. Some of the torts examined here can occur in any context, including the business environment. Others, traditionally referred to as **business torts,** involve wrongful interference with the business rights of others. Business torts include such vague concepts as *unfair competition* and *wrongfully interfering with the business relations of another.*

THE BASIS OF TORT LAW

Two notions serve as the basis of all torts: wrongs and compensation. Tort law is designed to compensate those who have suffered a loss or injury due to another person's wrongful act. In a tort action, one person or group brings a personal suit against another person or group to obtain compensation (monetary **damages**) or other relief for the harm suffered.

The Purpose of Tort Law

Generally, the purpose of tort law is to provide remedies for the invasion of various *protected interests.* Society recognizes an interest in personal physical safety, and tort law provides remedies for acts that cause physical injury or interfere with physical security and freedom of movement. Society recognizes an interest in protecting real and personal property, and tort law provides remedies for acts that cause destruction or damage to property. Society also recognizes an interest in protecting certain intangible interests, such as personal privacy, family relations, reputation, and dignity, and tort law provides remedies for invasion of these protected interests.

Damages Available in Tort Actions

Because the purpose of tort law is to compensate the injured party for the damage suffered, it is important to have a basic understanding of the types of damages that plaintiffs seek in tort actions.

Compensatory Damages **Compensatory damages** are intended to compensate or reimburse a plaintiff for actual losses—to make the plaintiff whole and put her or him in the

---

1. The word *tort* is French for "wrong."

same position that she or he would have been in had the tort not occurred. Compensatory damages awards are often broken down into special damages and general damages. *Special damages* compensate the plaintiff for quantifiable monetary losses, such as medical expenses, lost wages and benefits (now and in the future), extra costs, the loss of irreplaceable items, and the costs of repairing or replacing damaged property. *General damages* compensate individuals (not companies) for the nonmonetary aspects of the harm suffered, such as pain and suffering. A court might award general damages for physical or emotional pain and suffering, loss of companionship, loss of *consortium* (losing the emotional and physical benefits of a spousal relationship), disfigurement, loss of reputation, or loss or impairment of mental or physical capacity.

Punitive Damages   Occasionally, the courts may also award **punitive damages** in tort cases to punish the wrongdoer and deter others from similar wrongdoing. Punitive damages are appropriate only when the defendant's conduct was particularly egregious or reprehensible. Usually, this means that punitive damages are available mainly in intentional tort actions and only rarely in negligence lawsuits. They may be awarded, however, in suits involving *gross negligence*, which can be defined as an intentional failure to perform a manifest duty in reckless disregard of the consequences of such a failure for the life or property of another.

Courts exercise restraint in granting punitive damages to plaintiffs in tort actions because punitive damages are subject to the limitations imposed by the due process clause of the U.S. Constitution (discussed in Chapter 1). In *State Farm Mutual Automobile Insurance Co. v. Campbell,*[2] the United States Supreme Court held that to the extent an award of punitive damages is grossly excessive, it furthers no legitimate purpose and violates due process requirements. Although this case dealt with intentional torts (fraud and intentional infliction of emotional distress), the Court's holding applies equally to punitive damages awards in gross negligence cases (as well as to product liability cases).

Although the following case involved a product liability claim (which will be discussed in Chapter 17), the decision illustrates how courts analyze whether punitive damages awards are excessive.

---

2. 538 U.S. 408, 123 S.Ct. 1513, 155 L.Ed.2d 585 (2003).

Court of Appeal of California, Fourth District, 160 Cal.App.4th 1107, 73 Cal.Rptr.3d 277 (2008).

FACTS   Benetta Buell-Wilson was driving her 1997 Ford Explorer when a piece of metal came off another vehicle and headed for her windshield. When she swerved to avoid being hit, she lost control, and her car rolled four and a half times. During the rollover, the roof collapsed almost a foot. The force from the collapsing roof severed her spine, leaving her with no control of her body from the waist down. She had many surgeries and suffers constant pain that is likely to worsen over time. She requires extensive care. Evidence showed the Ford Explorer had two major defects: (1) a design that made it unstable and prone to rollover and (2) an inadequately supported roof likely to collapse on rollover. Records showed that Ford was long aware of these problems. The jury found the defects were substantial factors in causing Buell-Wilson's injuries. She was awarded $4.6 million for economic loss, $105 million for noneconomic losses, and $246 million in punitive damages. Her husband was awarded $13 million in damages for loss of consortium. The trial judge reduced the noneconomic damages to $65 million, the loss of consortium damages to $5 million, and the punitive damages to $75 million. Ford appealed, but the California Supreme Court refused to review the decision. The United States Supreme Court vacated the judgment and remanded the case for reconsideration in light of recent decisions by the Court concerning excessive damages awards.[a]

ISSUE   Is it excessive for a jury to award punitive damages in an amount that is substantially more than the plaintiff requested and more than four times the amount awarded in compensatory damages?

DECISION   Yes. The California appellate court concluded that the jury had acted with passion and prejudice when it imposed noneconomic damages far above those requested by the plaintiff. The court reduced the punitive damages award.

REASON   The court noted that the United States Supreme Court and the California Supreme Court have held that there are three factors to consider in determining whether the amount of a punitive damages award violates the due process clause of the U.S. Constitution: "(1) the degree of

---

a. The Supreme Court of California subsequently granted review of this case and had not yet issued a decision at the time this book went to press (2008 WL 2892940).

CASE 4.1–Continues next page

CASE 4.1—Continued

reprehensibility (wrongfulness) of the defendant's misconduct; (2) the disparity between the . . . harm suffered by the plaintiff and the punitive damages award; and (3) the difference between the punitive damages (and comparable civil penalties where available)." The court reasoned that $65 million in noneconomic damages awarded to a 46-year-old plaintiff who had been healthy prior to the accident was excessive and reduced the amount to $18 million. The court concluded that, "after reducing the noneconomic damage award to Mrs. Wilson to $18 million, the award of punitive damages is excessive and is, therefore, reduced to $55 million, an approximate two-to-one ratio of the total compensatory

damage award ($4.6 million in economic damages + $18 million in noneconomic damages + $5 million in loss of consortium damages = $27.6 million × 2 = $55.2 million)." This is more in line with the guidelines set by the United States Supreme Court regarding punitive damages.

 FOR CRITICAL ANALYSIS—Ethical Consideration *The court stated that punitive damages are designed to punish the defendant for reprehensible behavior. If so, should the punitive damages go to one plaintiff or be shared by all buyers of Ford products or by the general public? Explain your answer.*

■

Classifications of Torts

There are two broad classifications of torts: *intentional torts* and *unintentional torts* (torts involving negligence). The classification of a particular tort depends largely on how the tort occurs (intentionally or negligently) and the surrounding circumstances. In the following pages, you will read about these two classifications of torts.

Torts committed via the Internet are sometimes referred to as **cyber torts.** We will look at how the courts have applied traditional tort law to wrongful actions in the online environment in the concluding pages of this chapter.

INTENTIONAL TORTS AGAINST PERSONS

An **intentional tort,** as the term implies, requires *intent.* The **tortfeasor** (the one committing the tort) must intend to commit an act, the consequences of which interfere with the personal or business interests of another in a way not permitted by law. An evil or harmful motive is not required—in fact, the actor may even have a beneficial motive for committing what turns out to be a tortious act. In tort law, intent means only that the actor intended the consequences of his or her act or knew with substantial certainty that certain consequences would result from the act. The law generally assumes that individuals intend the *normal* consequences of their actions. Thus, forcefully pushing another—even if done in jest and without any evil motive—is an intentional tort (if injury results), because the object of a strong push can ordinarily be expected to fall down.

This section discusses intentional torts against persons, which include assault and battery, false imprisonment, infliction of emotional distress, defamation, invasion of the right to privacy, appropriation, misrepresentation, and wrongful interference.

Assault and Battery

Any intentional, unexcused act that creates in another person a reasonable apprehension of immediate harmful or offensive contact is an **assault.** Apprehension is not the same as fear. If a contact is such that a reasonable person would want to avoid it, and if there is a reasonable basis for believing that the contact will occur, then the plaintiff suffers apprehension whether or not he or she is afraid. The interest protected by tort law concerning assault is the freedom from having to expect harmful or offensive contact. The arousal of apprehension is enough to justify compensation.

The *completion* of the act that caused the apprehension, if it results in harm to the plaintiff, is a **battery,** which is defined as an unexcused and harmful or offensive physical contact *intentionally* performed. Suppose that Ivan threatens Jean with a gun, then shoots her. The pointing of the gun at Jean is an assault; the firing of the gun (if the bullet hits Jean) is a battery. The interest protected by tort law concerning battery is the right to personal security and safety. The contact can be harmful, or it can be merely offensive (such as an unwelcome kiss). Physical injury need not occur. The contact can involve any part of the body or anything attached to it—for example, a hat or other item of clothing, a purse, or a chair or an automobile in which one is sitting. Whether the contact is offensive or not is determined by the *reasonable person standard.*[3] The contact can be made by the defendant or by some force the defendant sets in motion—for example, a rock thrown, food poisoned, or a stick swung.

Compensation If the plaintiff shows that there was contact, and the jury (or judge, if there is no jury) agrees that the con-

---

3. The reasonable person standard is an "objective" test of how a reasonable person would have acted under the same circumstances, as will be discussed later in this chapter.

tact was offensive, the plaintiff has a right to compensation. There is no need to show that the defendant acted out of malice; the person could have just been joking or playing around. The underlying motive does not matter, only the intent to bring about the harmful or offensive contact to the plaintiff. In fact, proving a motive is never necessary (but is sometimes relevant). A plaintiff may be compensated for the emotional harm or loss of reputation resulting from a battery, as well as for physical harm.

Defenses to Assault and Battery A defendant who is sued for assault, battery, or both can raise any of the following legally recognized **defenses** (reasons why plaintiffs should not obtain what they are seeking) :

1 *Consent.* When a person consents to the act that is allegedly tortious, this may be a complete or partial defense to liability (legal responsibility).

2 *Self-defense.* An individual who is defending her or his life or physical well-being can claim self-defense. In situations of both *real* and *apparent* danger, a person may use whatever force is *reasonably* necessary to prevent harmful contact.

3 *Defense of others.* An individual can act in a reasonable manner to protect others who are in real or apparent danger.

4 *Defense of property.* Reasonable force may be used in attempting to remove intruders from one's home, although force that is likely to cause death or great bodily injury can never be used just to protect property.

False Imprisonment

False imprisonment is the intentional confinement or restraint of another person's activities without justification. False imprisonment interferes with the freedom to move without restraint. The confinement can be accomplished through the use of physical barriers, physical restraint, or threats of physical force. Moral pressure or threats of future harm do not constitute false imprisonment. It is essential that the person being restrained not agree to the restraint.

Businesspersons are often confronted with suits for false imprisonment after they have attempted to confine a suspected shoplifter for questioning. Under the "privilege to detain" granted to merchants in some states, a merchant can use the defense of *probable cause* to justify delaying a suspected shoplifter. In this context, probable cause exists when there is sufficient evidence to support the belief that a person is guilty (as you will read in Chapter 6, *probable cause* is defined differently in the context of criminal law). Although laws pertaining to the privilege to detain vary from state to state, generally they

require that any detention be conducted in a *reasonable* manner and for only a *reasonable* length of time.

Intentional Infliction of Emotional Distress

The tort of *intentional infliction of emotional distress* can be defined as an intentional act that amounts to extreme and outrageous conduct resulting in severe emotional distress to another. To be **actionable** (capable of serving as the ground for a lawsuit), the act must be extreme and outrageous to the point that it exceeds the bounds of decency accepted by society. **■EXAMPLE 4.1** A prankster telephones a pregnant woman and says that her husband and two sons have just been killed in a horrible accident (although they have not). As a result, the woman suffers intense mental pain and has a miscarriage. In that situation, the woman would be able to sue for intentional infliction of emotional distress. ■

Courts in most jurisdictions are wary of emotional distress claims and confine them to situations involving truly outrageous behavior. Generally, repeated annoyances (such as those experienced by a person who is being stalked), coupled with threats, are sufficient to support a claim, but acts that cause indignity or annoyance alone usually are not.

Note that when the outrageous conduct consists of speech about a public figure, the First Amendment's guarantee of freedom of speech also limits emotional distress claims. **■EXAMPLE 4.2** *Hustler* magazine once printed a fake advertisement that showed a picture of Reverend Jerry Falwell and described him as having lost his virginity to his mother in an outhouse while he was drunk. Falwell sued the magazine for intentional infliction of emotional distress and won, but the United States Supreme Court overturned the decision. The Court held that creators of parodies of public figures are protected under the First Amendment from intentional infliction of emotional distress claims. (The Court used the same standards that apply to public figures in defamation lawsuits, discussed next.)[4] ■

Defamation

As discussed in Chapter 1, the freedom of speech guaranteed by the First Amendment to the U.S. Constitution is not absolute. In interpreting the First Amendment, the courts must balance free speech rights against other strong social interests, including society's interest in preventing and redressing attacks on reputation.

---

4. *Hustler Magazine, Inc. v. Falwell*, 485 U.S. 46, 108 S.Ct. 876, 99 L.Ed.2d 41 (1988). For another example of how the courts protect parody, see *Busch v. Viacom International, Inc.*, 477 F.Supp.2d 764 (N.D.Tex. 2007), involving a fake endorsement of televangelist Pat Robertson's diet shake.

Defamation of character involves wrongfully hurting a person's good reputation. The law imposes a general duty on all persons to refrain from making *false*, defamatory *statements of fact* about others. Breaching this duty in writing or other permanent form (such as a digital recording) involves the tort of **libel.** Breaching this duty orally involves the tort of **slander.** As you will read later in this chapter, the tort of defamation can also arise when a false statement of fact is made about a person's product, business, or legal ownership rights to property.

Often at issue in defamation lawsuits (including online defamation, discussed later in this chapter) is whether the defendant made a statement of fact or a *statement of opinion.* Statements of opinion normally are not actionable because they are protected under the First Amendment. In other words, making a negative statement about another person is defamation only if the statement is false and represents something as a fact (for example, "Vladik cheats on his taxes") rather than a personal opinion (for example, "Vladik is a jerk").

In the following case, the issue was whether a certain statement was an expression of a person's opinion—and thus protected by the First Amendment—or an unprotected factual assertion.

CASE 4.2   **Lott v. Levitt**

United States District Court, Northern District of Illinois, 469 F.Supp.2d 575 (2007).

FACTS In 2005, economist Steven Levitt and journalist Stephen Dubner co-authored the best-selling book *Freakonomics.* Levitt and Dubner discuss in a single paragraph a theory of fellow economist John Lott, Jr., in which Lott claims that violent crime has decreased in areas where law-abiding citizens are allowed to carry concealed weapons. The paragraph states that the idea is intriguing, but it questions whether Lott's data were valid and implies that other scholars have not been able to replicate Lott's findings—that is, to show that right-to-carry gun laws reduce crime. Economist John McCall sent Levitt an e-mail regarding this paragraph. McCall cited an issue of *The Journal of Law and Economics* in which other scholars claimed to support Lott's research. Levitt responded in an e-mail, "It was not a peer refereed edition of the *Journal.* For $15,000 he was able to buy an issue and put in only work that supported him. My best friend was the editor and was outraged the press let Lott do this." Based in part on this e-mail, Lott filed a suit in a federal district court against Levitt and others, claiming, among other things, defamation. Levitt filed a motion to dismiss, arguing that the First Amendment protects his statements.

ISSUE Did Levitt's statements in the e-mail regarding Lott's theories constitute statements of fact that could form the basis of a defamation lawsuit?

DECISION Yes. The federal district court denied the motion to dismiss Lott's complaint. Levitt could be sued for defamation.

REASON The court explained that the test to determine if a statement is factual is "whether the statement is precise, readily understood, and susceptible of being verified as true or false." Language that is "loose, figurative, or hyperbolic" most likely expresses an opinion. Statements that are subjective, theoretical, or conjectural likewise comprise opinions. Expressions of opinion are protected under the First Amendment. But the statement of a speaker or writer who claims to possess "objectively verifiable facts" may be actionable. Levitt's e-mail was "a string of defamatory assertions * * * that—no matter how rash or short-sighted Levitt was when he made them—cannot be reasonably interpreted as innocent or mere opinion." Therefore, Levitt's e-mail met the test. "First, it would be unreasonable to interpret Levitt's unqualified statement that the journal edition was not 'peer refereed' as Levitt merely giving his opinion on the 'peers' * * * . Second, a reasonable reader would not interpret Levitt's assertion that 'For $15,000, he was able to buy an issue and put in only work that supported him' as simply a statement of Levitt's opinion." Finally, Levitt's assertion that the editor of the *Journal* was "outraged" could be verified by the editor, who might also be able to attest to the truth or falsity of the other statements.

FOR CRITICAL ANALYSIS—Legal Consideration *Did the statements about Lott in the book* Freakonomics *constitute unprotected speech? Why or why not?*

■

The Publication Requirement The basis of the tort of defamation is the publication of a statement or statements that hold an individual up to contempt, ridicule, or hatred. *Publication* here means that the defamatory statements are communicated (either intentionally or accidentally) to persons other than the defamed party. **■EXAMPLE 4.3** If Thompson writes Andrews a private letter accusing him of embezzling funds, the action does not constitute libel. If

Peters falsely states that Gordon is dishonest and incompetent when no one else is around, the action does not constitute slander. In neither instance was the message communicated to a third party. ◼

The courts generally have held that even dictating a letter to a secretary constitutes publication, although the publication may be privileged (privileged communications will be discussed shortly). Moreover, if a third party merely overhears defamatory statements by chance, the courts usually hold that this also constitutes publication. Defamatory statements made via the Internet are also actionable, as you will read later in this chapter. Note further that any individual who republishes or repeats defamatory statements is liable even if that person reveals the source of such statements.

Damages for Libel   Once a defendant's liability for libel is established, *general damages* are presumed as a matter of law. As mentioned earlier, general damages are designed to compensate the plaintiff for nonspecific harms such as disgrace or dishonor in the eyes of the community, humiliation, injured reputation, and emotional distress—harms that are difficult to measure. In other words, to recover damages in a libel case, the plaintiff need not prove that she or he was actually injured in any way as a result of the libelous statement.

Damages for Slander   In contrast to cases alleging libel, in a case alleging slander, the plaintiff must prove *special damages* to establish the defendant's liability. In other words, the plaintiff must show that the slanderous statement caused the plaintiff to suffer actual economic or monetary losses. Unless this initial hurdle of proving special damages is overcome, a plaintiff alleging slander normally cannot go forward with the suit and recover any damages. This requirement is imposed in cases involving slander because slanderous statements have a temporary quality. In contrast, a libelous (written) statement has the quality of permanence, can be circulated widely, and usually results from some degree of deliberation on the part of the author.

Exceptions to the burden of proving special damages in cases alleging slander are made for certain types of slanderous statements. If a false statement constitutes "slander *per se*," no proof of special damages is required for it to be actionable. The following four types of utterances are considered to be slander *per se*:

1 A statement that another has a loathsome disease (historically, leprosy and sexually transmitted diseases, but now also including allegations of mental illness).

2 A statement that another has committed improprieties while engaging in a business, profession, or trade.

3 A statement that another has committed or has been imprisoned for a serious crime.

4 A statement that a person (usually only unmarried persons and sometimes only women) is unchaste or has engaged in serious sexual misconduct.

Defenses against Defamation   Truth is normally an absolute defense against a defamation charge. In other words, if the defendant in a defamation suit can prove that his or her allegedly defamatory statements were true, normally no tort has been committed. Other defenses to defamation may exist if the statement is privileged or concerns a public figure. Note that the majority of defamation actions in the United States are filed in state courts, and the states may differ in how they define both defamation and the particular defenses they allow, such as privilege (discussed next).

Privileged Communications.   In some circumstances, a person will not be liable for defamatory statements because she or he enjoys a **privilege**, or immunity. Privileged communications are of two types: absolute and qualified.[5] Only in judicial proceedings and certain government proceedings is an *absolute* privilege granted. For instance, statements made in the courtroom by attorneys and judges during a trial are absolutely privileged. So are statements made by government officials during legislative debate, even if the officials make such statements maliciously—that is, knowing them to be untrue. An absolute privilege is granted in these situations because government personnel deal with matters that are so much in the public interest that the parties involved should be able to speak out fully and freely without restriction.

In other situations, a person will not be liable for defamatory statements because he or she has a *qualified*, or conditional, privilege. An employer's statements in written evaluations of employees are an example of a qualified privilege. Generally, if the statements are made in good faith and the publication is limited to those who have a legitimate interest in the communication, the statements fall within the area of qualified privilege. ◼**EXAMPLE 4.4**◼ Jorge applies for membership at the local country club. After the country club's board rejects his application, Jorge sues the club's office manager for making allegedly defamatory statements to the board concerning a conversation she had with Jorge. Assuming that the office manager had simply relayed what she thought was her duty to convey to the club's board, her statements would likely be protected by qualified privilege. ◼

The concept of conditional privilege rests on the assumption that in some situations, the right to know or speak is

---

5. Note that the term *privileged communication* in this context is not the same as privileged communication between a professional, such as an attorney, and his or her client. The latter type of privilege will be discussed in Chapter 31, in the context of the liability of professionals.

paramount to the right not to be defamed. Only if the privilege is abused or the statement is knowingly false or malicious will the person be liable for damages.

Public Figures. Public officials who exercise substantial governmental power and any persons in the public limelight are considered *public figures.* In general, public figures are considered fair game, and false and defamatory statements about them that are published in the press will not constitute defamation unless the statements are made with **actual malice.** To be made with actual malice, a statement must be made *with either knowledge of falsity or a reckless disregard of the truth.* Statements made about public figures, especially when the statements are made via a public medium, are usually related to matters of general interest; they are made about people who substantially affect all of us. Furthermore, public figures generally have some access to a public medium for answering disparaging (belittling, discrediting) falsehoods about themselves; private individuals do not. For these reasons, public figures have a greater burden of proof in defamation cases (they must prove actual malice) than do private individuals.

Invasion of the Right to Privacy

A person has a right to solitude and freedom from prying public eyes—in other words, to privacy. Although the U.S. Constitution does not contain an explicit guarantee of a right to privacy, the United States Supreme Court has held that a fundamental right to privacy is also implied by various amendments to the U.S. Constitution. Some state constitutions explicitly provide for privacy rights. In addition, a number of federal and state statutes have been enacted to protect individual rights in specific areas. Tort law also safeguards these rights through the tort *invasion of privacy.* Four acts qualify as an invasion of privacy:

1 *Appropriation of identity.* Under the common law, using a person's name, picture, or other likeness for commercial purposes without permission is a tortious invasion of privacy. Most states today have also enacted statutes prohibiting appropriation (discussed further in the next subsection).

2 *Intrusion into an individual's affairs or seclusion.* For example, invading someone's home or illegally searching someone's briefcase is an invasion of privacy. The tort has been held to extend to eavesdropping by wiretap, the unauthorized scanning of a bank account, compulsory blood testing, and window peeping.

3 *False light.* Publication of information that places a person in a false light is another category of invasion of privacy.

This could be a story attributing to the person ideas not held or actions not taken by the person. (Publishing such a story could involve the tort of defamation as well.)

4 *Public disclosure of private facts.* This type of invasion of privacy occurs when a person publicly discloses private facts about an individual that an ordinary person would find objectionable or embarrassing. A newspaper account of a private citizen's sex life or financial affairs could be an actionable invasion of privacy, even if the information revealed is true, because it is not of public concern.

Appropriation

The use by one person of another person's name, likeness, or other identifying characteristic, without permission and for the benefit of the user, constitutes the tort of **appropriation.** Under the law, an individual's right to privacy normally includes the right to the exclusive use of her or his identity.

■**EXAMPLE 4.5** In one early case, Vanna White, the hostess of the popular television game show *Wheel of Fortune,* brought a case against Samsung Electronics America, Inc. Without White's permission, Samsung included in an advertisement for its videocassette recorders (VCRs) a depiction of a robot dressed in a wig, gown, and jewelry, posed in a scene that resembled the *Wheel of Fortune* set, in a stance for which White is famous. The court held in White's favor, holding that the tort of appropriation does not require the use of a celebrity's name or likeness. The court stated that Samsung's robot ad left "little doubt" as to the identity of the celebrity whom the ad was meant to depict.[6] ■

The common law tort of appropriation in many states has become known as the right of publicity. Rather than being aimed at protecting a person's right to be left alone (privacy), this right aims to protect an individual's pecuniary (financial) interest in the commercial exploitation of his or her identity. Most states have also concluded that the right of publicity is inheritable and survives the death of the person who held the right. Normally, though, the person must provide for the passage of the right to another in her or his will. ■**EXAMPLE 4.6** A case involving Marilyn Monroe's right of publicity came before a federal trial court. The court held that because Marilyn Monroe's will did not specifically state a desire to pass the right to publicity to her heirs, the beneficiaries under her will did not have a right to prevent a company from marketing T-shirts and other merchandise using Monroe's name, picture, and likeness.[7] ■

---

6. *White v. Samsung Electronics America, Inc.,* 971 F.2d 1395 (9th Cir. 1992).
7. *Shaw Family Archives, Ltd. v. CMG Worldwide, Inc.,* 486 F.Supp.2d 309 (S.D.N.Y. 2007).

Fraudulent Misrepresentation

A misrepresentation leads another to believe in a condition that is different from the condition that actually exists. This is often accomplished through a false or incorrect statement. Although persons sometimes make misrepresentations accidentally because they are unaware of the existing facts, the tort of **fraudulent misrepresentation,** or fraud, involves *intentional* deceit for personal gain. The tort includes several elements:

1 The misrepresentation of facts or conditions with knowledge that they are false or with reckless disregard for the truth.

2 An intent to induce another to rely on the misrepresentation.

3 Justifiable reliance by the deceived party.

4 Damage suffered as a result of the reliance.

5 A causal connection between the misrepresentation and the injury suffered.

Fact versus Opinion For fraud to occur, more than mere **puffery,** or *seller's talk,* must be involved. Fraud exists only when a person represents as a fact something she or he knows is untrue. For example, it is fraud to claim that a roof does not leak when one knows it does. Facts are objectively ascertainable, whereas seller's talk is not. "I am the best accountant in town" is seller's talk. The speaker is not trying to represent something as fact because *best* is a subjective, not an objective, term.

Normally, the tort of misrepresentation or fraud occurs only when there is reliance on a *statement of fact.* Sometimes, however, reliance on a *statement of opinion* may involve the tort of misrepresentation if the individual making the statement of opinion has a superior knowledge of the subject matter. For example, when a lawyer makes a statement of opinion about the law in a state in which the lawyer is licensed to practice, a court would construe reliance on such a statement to be equivalent to reliance on a statement of fact.

Negligent Misrepresentation Sometimes, a tort action can arise from misrepresentations that are made negligently rather than intentionally. The key difference between intentional and negligent misrepresentation is whether the person making the misrepresentation had actual knowledge of its falsity. Negligent misrepresentation only requires that the person making the statement or omission did not have a reasonable basis for believing its truthfulness.

Liability for negligent misrepresentation usually arises when the defendant who made the misrepresentation owed a duty of care to the particular plaintiff to supply correct information. Statements or omissions made by attorneys and

accountants to their clients, for example, can lead to liability for negligent misrepresentation, as can statements made by a landlord to a commercial tenant. **■EXAMPLE 4.7** Kelly McClain leased commercial space in a shopping center from Ted and Wanda Charanian to operate her business. The lease described the size of the unit as "approximately 2,624 square feet," and McClain paid $1.45 per square foot per month in rent ($3,804). Moreover, because the unit presumably occupied 23 percent of the shopping center, McClain was responsible for this share of the common expenses. McClain later discovered that the Charanians had exaggerated the size of the unit she was leasing by 186 square feet, or 7.6 percent of its actual size. When McClain sued the Charanians for negligent misrepresentation, she claimed that she had paid more than $90,000 in excess rent during the term of the lease. A California appellate court ruled in her favor.[8] ■

Wrongful Interference

Business torts involving wrongful interference are generally divided into two categories: wrongful interference with a contractual relationship and wrongful interference with a business relationship.

Wrongful Interference with a Contractual Relationship The body of tort law relating to *intentional interference with a contractual relationship* has expanded greatly in recent years. A landmark case involved an opera singer, Joanna Wagner, who was under contract to sing for a man named Lumley for a specified period of years. A man named Gye, who knew of this contract, nonetheless "enticed" Wagner to refuse to carry out the agreement, and Wagner began to sing for Gye. Gye's action constituted a tort because it wrongfully interfered with the contractual relationship between Wagner and Lumley.[9] (Of course, Wagner's refusal to carry out the agreement also entitled Lumley to sue Wagner for breach of contract.)

Three elements are necessary for wrongful interference with a contractual relationship to occur:

1 A valid, enforceable contract must exist between two parties.

2 A third party must know that this contract exists.

3 The third party must *intentionally* induce a party to breach the contract.

In principle, any lawful contract can be the basis for an action of this type. The contract could be between a firm and

---

8. *McClain v. Octagon Plaza, LLC,* 159 Cal.App.4th 784, 71 Cal.Rptr.3d 885 (2008).
9. *Lumley v. Gye,* 118 Eng.Rep. 749 (1853).

its employees or a firm and its customers. Sometimes, a competitor of a firm draws away one of the firm's key employees. Only if the original employer can show that the competitor knew of the contract's existence and intentionally induced the breach can damages be recovered from the competitor.

■EXAMPLE 4.8 Carlin has a contract with Sutter that calls for Sutter to do gardening work on Carlin's large estate every week for fifty-two weeks at a specified price per week. Mellon, who needs gardening services and knows nothing about the Sutter-Carlin contract, contacts Sutter and offers to pay Sutter a wage that is substantially higher than that offered by Carlin. Sutter breaches his contract with Carlin so that he can work for Mellon. Carlin cannot sue Mellon because Mellon knew nothing of the Sutter-Carlin contract and was totally unaware that the higher wage he offered induced Sutter to breach that contract. ■

Wrongful Interference with a Business Relationship Businesspersons devise countless schemes to attract customers, but they are prohibited from unreasonably interfering with another's business in their attempts to gain a share of the market. There is a difference between competitive methods and **predatory behavior**—actions undertaken with the intention of unlawfully driving competitors completely out of the market. The distinction usually depends on whether a business is attempting to attract customers in general or to solicit only those customers who have shown an interest in a similar product or service of a specific competitor.

■EXAMPLE 4.9 A shopping mall contains two athletic shoe stores: Joe's and SneakerSprint. Joe's cannot station an employee at the entrance of SneakerSprint to divert customers to Joe's and tell them that Joe's will beat SneakerSprint's prices. This type of activity constitutes the tort of wrongful interference with a business relationship, which is commonly considered to be an unfair trade practice. If this type of activity were permitted, Joe's would reap the benefits of SneakerSprint's advertising. ■

Defenses to Wrongful Interference A person will not be liable for the tort of wrongful interference with a contractual or business relationship if it can be shown that the interference was justified, or permissible. Bona fide competitive behavior is a permissible interference even if it results in the breaking of a contract. **■EXAMPLE 4.10** If Antonio's Meats advertises so effectively that it induces Sam's Restaurant to break its contract with Burke's Meat Company, Burke's Meat Company will be unable to recover against Antonio's Meats on a wrongful interference theory. After all, the public policy that favors free competition through advertising outweighs any possible instability that such competitive activity might cause in contractual relations. ■ Although luring customers away from a competitor

through aggressive marketing and advertising strategies obviously interferes with the competitor's relationship with its customers, courts typically allow such activities in the spirit of competition.

INTENTIONAL TORTS AGAINST PROPERTY

Intentional torts against property include trespass to land, trespass to personal property, conversion, and disparagement of property. These torts are wrongful actions that interfere with individuals' legally recognized rights with regard to their land or personal property. The law distinguishes real property from personal property (see Chapters 28 and 29). *Real property* is land and things "permanently" attached to the land. *Personal property* consists of all other items, which are basically movable. Thus, a house and lot are real property, whereas the furniture inside a house is personal property. Cash and stocks and bonds are also personal property.

Trespass to Land

A **trespass to land** occurs whenever a person, without permission, enters onto, above, or below the surface of land that is owned by another; causes anything to enter onto the land; remains on the land; or permits anything to remain on it. Actual harm to the land is not an essential element of this tort because the tort is designed to protect the right of an owner to exclusive possession of her or his property. Common types of trespass to land include walking or driving on someone else's land, shooting a gun over the land, throwing rocks at a building that belongs to someone else, building a dam across a river and thereby causing water to back up on someone else's land, and constructing a building so that part of it is on an adjoining landowner's property.

Trespass Criteria, Rights, and Duties Before a person can be a trespasser, the owner of the real property (or other person in actual and exclusive possession of the property) must establish that person as a trespasser. For example, "posted" trespass signs expressly establish as a trespasser a person who ignores these signs and enters onto the property. A guest in your home is not a trespasser—unless she or he has been asked to leave but refuses. Any person who enters onto your property to commit an illegal act (such as a thief entering a lumberyard at night to steal lumber) is established impliedly as a trespasser, without posted signs.

At common law, a trespasser is liable for damages caused to the property and generally cannot hold the owner liable for injuries sustained on the premises. This common law rule is being abandoned in many jurisdictions in favor of a *reasonable duty of care* rule that varies depending on the status of the parties; for example, a landowner may have a duty to post a notice that the property is patrolled by guard dogs. Also, under the *attractive nuisance* doctrine, children do not assume the risks of the premises if they are attracted to the property by some object, such as a swimming pool, an abandoned building, or a sand pile. Trespassers normally can be removed from the premises through the use of reasonable force without the owner's being liable for assault, battery, or false imprisonment.

Defenses against Trespass to Land Trespass to land involves wrongful interference with another person's real property rights. One defense to this claim is to show that the trespass was warranted—for example, that the trespasser entered the property to assist someone in danger. Another defense exists when the trespasser can show that he or she had a license to come onto the land. A *licensee* is one who is invited (or allowed to enter) onto the property of another for the licensee's benefit. A person who enters another's property to read an electric meter, for example, is a licensee. When you purchase a ticket to attend a movie or sporting event, you are licensed to go onto the property of another to view that movie or event. Note that licenses to enter onto another's property are *revocable* by the property owner. If a property owner asks a meter reader to leave and the meter reader refuses to do so, the meter reader at that point becomes a trespasser.

Trespass to Personal Property

Whenever an individual wrongfully takes or harms the personal property of another or otherwise interferes with the lawful owner's possession of personal property, **trespass to personal property** occurs (also called *trespass to chattels* or *trespass to personalty*[10]). In this context, harm means not only destruction of the property, but also anything that diminishes its value, condition, or quality. Trespass to personal property involves intentional meddling with a possessory interest, including barring an owner's access to personal property. **■EXAMPLE 4.11** If Kelly takes Ryan's business law book as a practical joke and hides it so that Ryan is unable to find it for several days prior to the final examination, Kelly has engaged in a trespass to personal property. (Kelly has also committed the tort of *conversion*—to be discussed shortly.) ■

If it can be shown that the trespass to personal property was warranted, then a complete defense exists. Most states, for example, allow automobile repair shops to hold a customer's car (under what is called an *artisan's lien*, discussed in Chapter 21) when the customer refuses to pay for repairs already completed.

Conversion

Whenever a person wrongfully possesses or uses the personal property of another without permission, the tort of **conversion** occurs. Any act that deprives an owner of personal property or of the use of that property without that owner's permission and without just cause can be conversion. Even the taking of electronic records and data can form the basis of a conversion claim.[11] Often, when conversion occurs, a trespass to personal property also occurs because the original taking of the personal property from the owner was a trespass, and wrongfully retaining it is conversion. Conversion is the civil side of crimes related to theft, but it is not limited to theft. Even if the rightful owner consented to the initial taking of the property, so there was no theft or trespass, a failure to return the personal property may still be conversion. **■EXAMPLE 4.12** Chen borrows Marik's iPod to use while traveling home from school for the holidays. When Chen returns to school, Marik asks for his iPod back. Chen tells Marik that she gave it to her little brother for Christmas. In this situation, Marik can sue Chen for conversion, and Chen will have to either return the iPod or pay damages equal to its value. ■

Even if a person mistakenly believed that she or he was entitled to the goods, the tort of conversion may occur. In other words, good intentions are not a defense against conversion; in fact, conversion can be an entirely innocent act. Someone who buys stolen goods, for example, can be liable for conversion even if he or she did not know that the goods were stolen. If the true owner brings a tort action against the buyer, the buyer must either return the property to the owner or pay the owner the full value of the property, despite having already paid the purchase price to the thief.

A successful defense against the charge of conversion is that the purported owner does not, in fact, own the property or does not have a right to possess it that is superior to the right of the holder.

Disparagement of Property

Disparagement of property occurs when economically injurious falsehoods are made about another's product or property, not about another's reputation. Disparagement of property is a general term for torts that can be more specifically referred to as *slander of quality* or *slander of title*.

Slander of Quality Publication of false information about another's product, alleging that it is not what its seller claims, constitutes the tort of **slander of quality,** or **trade libel.** The plaintiff must prove that actual damages proximately resulted

---

10. Pronounced *per-sun-ul-tee.*

11. See, for example, *Thyroff v. Nationwide Mutual Insurance Co.,* 8 N.Y.3d 283, 864 N.E.2d 1272, 832 N.Y.S.2d 873 (2007).

from the slander of quality. In other words, the plaintiff must show not only that a third person refrained from dealing with the plaintiff because of the improper publication but also that there were associated damages. The economic calculation of such damages—they are, after all, conjectural—is often extremely difficult.

An improper publication may be both a slander of quality and defamation of character. For example, a statement that disparages the quality of a product may also, by implication, disparage the character of the person who would sell such a product.

Slander of Title When a publication denies or casts doubt on another's legal ownership of any property, and this results in financial loss to that property's owner, the tort of **slander of title** may exist. Usually, this is an intentional tort in which someone knowingly publishes an untrue statement about property with the intent of discouraging a third person from dealing with the person slandered. For example, it would be difficult for a car dealer to attract customers after competitors published a notice that the dealer's stock consisted of stolen autos.

UNINTENTIONAL TORTS (NEGLIGENCE)

The tort of **negligence** occurs when someone suffers injury because of another's failure to live up to a required *duty of care*. In contrast to intentional torts, in torts involving negligence, the tortfeasor neither wishes to bring about the consequences of the act nor believes that they will occur. The actor's conduct merely creates a *risk* of such consequences. If no risk is created, there is no negligence. Moreover, the risk must be foreseeable—that is, it must be such that a reasonable person engaging in the same activity would anticipate the risk and guard against it. In determining what is reasonable conduct, courts consider the nature of the possible harm.

Many of the actions discussed earlier in the chapter in the section on intentional torts constitute negligence if the element of intent is missing. **EXAMPLE 4.13** Juarez walks up to Natsuyo and intentionally shoves her. Natsuyo falls and breaks an arm as a result. In this situation, Juarez has committed an intentional tort (assault and battery). If Juarez carelessly bumps into Natsuyo, however, and she falls and breaks an arm as a result, Juarez's action will constitute negligence. In either situation, Juarez has committed a tort. ■

To succeed in a negligence action, the plaintiff must prove each of the following:

1 That the defendant owed a duty of care to the plaintiff.

2 That the defendant breached that duty.

3 That the plaintiff suffered a legally recognizable injury.

4 That the defendant's breach caused the plaintiff's injury.

We discuss here each of these four elements of negligence.

The Duty of Care and Its Breach

Central to the tort of negligence is the concept of a **duty of care.** The idea is that if we are to live in society with other people, some actions can be tolerated and some cannot; some actions are right and some are wrong; and some actions are reasonable and some are not. The basic principle underlying the duty of care is that people are free to act as they please so long as their actions do not infringe on the interests of others.

When someone fails to comply with the duty to exercise reasonable care, a potentially tortious act may have been committed. Failure to live up to a standard of care may be an act (setting fire to a building) or an omission (neglecting to put out a campfire). It may be a careless act or a carefully performed but nevertheless dangerous act that results in injury. Courts consider the nature of the act (whether it is outrageous or commonplace), the manner in which the act is performed (cautiously versus heedlessly), and the nature of the injury (whether it is serious or slight) in determining whether the duty of care has been breached.

The Reasonable Person Standard Tort law measures duty by the **reasonable person standard.** In determining whether a duty of care has been breached, the courts ask how a reasonable person would have acted in the same circumstances. The reasonable person standard is said to be (though in an absolute sense it cannot be) objective. It is not necessarily how a particular person would act. It is society's judgment on how people *should* act. If the so-called reasonable person existed, he or she would be careful, conscientious, even tempered, and honest. The courts frequently use this hypothetical reasonable person in decisions relating to other areas of law as well. That individuals are required to exercise a reasonable standard of care in their activities is a pervasive concept in business law, and many of the issues discussed in subsequent chapters of this text have to do with this duty.

In negligence cases, the degree of care to be exercised varies, depending on the defendant's occupation or profession, her or his relationship with the plaintiff, and other factors. Generally, whether an action constitutes a breach of the duty of care is determined on a case-by-case basis. The outcome depends on how the judge (or jury, if it is a jury trial) decides a reasonable person in the position of the defendant would act in the particular circumstances of the case.

The Duty of Landowners Landowners are expected to exercise reasonable care to protect persons coming onto their property from harm. As mentioned earlier, in some jurisdictions, landowners are held to owe a duty to protect even trespassers against certain risks. Landowners who rent or lease premises to tenants (see Chapter 29) are expected to exercise reasonable care to ensure that the tenants and their guests are not harmed in common areas, such as stairways, entryways, and laundry rooms.

Duty to Warn Business Invitees of Risks. Retailers and other firms that explicitly or implicitly invite persons to come onto their premises are usually charged with a duty to exercise reasonable care to protect those persons, who are considered **business invitees.** **■EXAMPLE 4.14** Suppose that you entered a supermarket, slipped on a wet floor, and sustained injuries as a result. The owner of the supermarket would be liable for damages if, when you slipped, there was no sign warning that the floor was wet. A court would hold that the business owner was negligent because the owner failed to exercise a reasonable degree of care in protecting the store's customers against foreseeable risks about which the owner knew or *should have known.* That a patron might slip on the wet floor and be injured as a result was a foreseeable risk, and the owner should have taken care to avoid this risk or to warn the customer of it (by posting a sign or setting out orange cones, for example). **■**

The landowner also has a duty to discover and remove any hidden dangers that might injure a customer or other invitee. Store owners, for example, have a duty to protect customers from potentially slipping and injuring themselves on merchandise that has fallen off the shelves.

Obvious Risks Provide an Exception. Some risks, of course, are so obvious that the owner need not warn of them. For instance, a business owner does not need to warn customers to open a door before attempting to walk through it. Other risks, however, may seem obvious to a business owner but may not be so in the eyes of another, such as a child. **■EXAMPLE 4.15** A hardware store owner may think it is unnecessary to warn customers not to climb a stepladder leaning against the back wall of the store. It is possible, though, that a child could climb up and tip the ladder over and be hurt as a result and that the store could be held liable. Similarly, although wet napkins on the floor of a nightclub might seem obvious as a falling risk, the owner still has a duty to its customers to maintain the premises in a safe condition.[12] **■**

PREVENTING LEGAL DISPUTES **It can sometimes be difficult for business owners to determine whether risks are obvious. Because the law imposes liability on business owners who fail to discover hidden dangers on the premises and protect patrons from being injured, it is advisable to post warnings of any potential risks on the property. Businesspersons should train their employees to be on the lookout for possibly dangerous conditions on the premises at all times and to notify a superior immediately if they notice something. Making the business premises as safe as possible for all persons who might be there, including children, the elderly, and individuals with disabilities, is one of the best ways to prevent potential legal disputes.**

■

The Duty of Professionals If an individual has knowledge, skill, or intelligence superior to that of an ordinary person, the individual's conduct must be consistent with that status. Professionals—including physicians, dentists, architects, engineers, accountants, lawyers, and others—are required to have a standard minimum level of special knowledge and ability. Therefore, in determining whether professionals have exercised reasonable care, their training and expertise are taken into account. In other words, an accountant cannot defend against a lawsuit for negligence by stating, "But I was not familiar with that principle of accounting."

If a professional violates her or his duty of care toward a client, the professional may be sued for **malpractice,** which is essentially professional negligence. For example, a patient might sue a physician for *medical malpractice.* A client might sue an attorney for *legal malpractice.*

The Injury Requirement and Damages

For a tort to have been committed, the plaintiff must have suffered a *legally recognizable* injury. To recover damages (receive compensation), the plaintiff must have suffered some loss, harm, wrong, or invasion of a protected interest. Essentially, the purpose of tort law is to compensate for legally recognized injuries resulting from wrongful acts. If no harm or injury results from a given negligent action, there is nothing to compensate—and no tort exists. **■EXAMPLE 4.16** If you carelessly bump into a passerby, who stumbles and falls as a result, you may be liable in tort if the passerby is injured in the fall. If the person is unharmed, however, there normally could be no suit for damages because no injury was suffered. Although the passerby might be angry and suffer emotional distress, few courts recognize negligently inflicted emotional distress as a tort unless it results in some physical disturbance or dysfunction. **■**

---

12. *Izquierdo v. Gyroscope, Inc.,* 946 So.2d 115 (Fla.App. 4th Dist. 2007).

Compensatory damages are the norm in negligence cases. As noted earlier, a court will award punitive damages only if the defendant's conduct was grossly negligent, reflecting an intentional failure to perform a duty with reckless disregard of the consequences to others.

Causation

Another element necessary to a tort is *causation*. If a person fails in a duty of care and someone suffers an injury, the wrongful activity must have caused the harm for the activity to be considered a tort. In deciding whether there is causation, the court must address two questions:

1 *Is there causation in fact?* Did the injury occur because of the defendant's act, or would it have occurred anyway? If an injury would not have occurred without the defendant's act, then there is causation in fact. **Causation in fact** can usually be determined by the use of the *but for* test: "but for" the wrongful act, the injury would not have occurred. Theoretically, causation in fact is limitless. One could claim, for example, that "but for" the creation of the world, a particular injury would not have occurred. Thus, as a practical matter, the law has to establish limits, and it does so through the concept of proximate cause.

2 *Was the act the proximate cause of the injury?* **Proximate cause,** or legal cause, exists when the connection between an act and an injury is strong enough to justify imposing liability. **■EXAMPLE 4.17** Ackerman carelessly leaves a campfire burning. The fire not only burns down the forest but also sets off an explosion in a nearby chemical plant that spills chemicals into a river, killing all the fish for a hundred miles downstream and ruining the economy of a tourist resort. Should Ackerman be liable to the resort owners? To the tourists whose vacations were ruined? These are questions of proximate cause that a court must decide. **■**

Both questions must be answered in the affirmative for liability in tort to arise. If a defendant's action constitutes causation in fact but a court decides that the action is not the proximate cause of the plaintiff's injury, the causation requirement has not been met—and the defendant normally will not be liable to the plaintiff.

Questions of proximate cause are linked to the concept of foreseeability because it would be unfair to impose liability on a defendant unless the defendant's actions created a foreseeable risk of injury. In determining the issue of proximate cause, the court addressed the following question: Does a defendant's duty of care extend only to those who may be injured as a result of a foreseeable risk, or does it extend also to a person whose injury could not reasonably be foreseen?

Defenses to Negligence

Defendants often defend against negligence claims by asserting that the plaintiffs failed to prove the existence of one or more of the required elements for negligence. Additionally, there are three basic *affirmative* defenses in negligence cases (defenses that a defendant can use to avoid liability even if the facts are as the plaintiff state): (1) assumption of risk, (2) superseding cause, and (3) contributory and comparative negligence.

Assumption of Risk A plaintiff who voluntarily enters into a risky situation, knowing the risk involved, will not be allowed to recover. This is the defense of **assumption of risk.** The requirements of this defense are (1) knowledge of the risk and (2) voluntary assumption of the risk. This defense is frequently asserted when the plaintiff is injured during recreational activities that involve known risk, such as skiing and parachuting.

The risk can be assumed by express agreement, or the assumption of risk can be implied by the plaintiff's knowledge of the risk and subsequent conduct. For example, a driver entering a race knows that there is a risk of being killed or injured in a crash. Of course, the plaintiff does not assume a risk different from or greater than the risk normally carried by the activity. In our example, the race driver would not assume the risk that the banking in the curves of the racetrack will give way during the race because of a construction defect.

Risks are not deemed to be assumed in situations involving emergencies. Neither are they assumed when a statute protects a class of people from harm and a member of the class is injured by the harm. For example, employees are protected by statute from harmful working conditions and therefore do not assume the risks associated with the workplace. An employee who is injured will generally be compensated regardless of fault under state workers' compensation statutes (discussed in Chapter 23).

Superseding Cause An unforeseeable intervening event may break the connection between a wrongful act and an injury to another. If so, the event acts as a *superseding cause*—that is, it relieves a defendant of liability for injuries caused by the intervening event. **■EXAMPLE 4.18** Derrick, while riding his bicycle, negligently hits Julie, who is walking on the sidewalk. As a result of the impact, Julie falls and fractures her hip. While she is waiting for help to arrive, a small aircraft crashes nearby and explodes, and some of the fiery debris hits her, causing her to sustain severe burns. Derrick will be liable for the damages caused by Julie's fractured hip because the risk was foreseeable. Normally, Derrick will not be liable for the burns caused by the plane crash—because the risk of a plane's crashing nearby and injuring Julie was not foreseeable. **■**

Contributory and Comparative Negligence All individuals are expected to exercise a reasonable degree of care in looking out for themselves. In the past, under the common law doctrine of **contributory negligence,** a plaintiff who was also negligent (failed to exercise a reasonable degree of care) could not recover anything from the defendant. Under this rule, no matter how insignificant the plaintiff's negligence was relative to the defendant's negligence, the plaintiff would be precluded from recovering any damages. Today, only a few jurisdictions still hold to this doctrine.

In the majority of states, the doctrine of contributory negligence has been replaced by a **comparative negligence** standard. Under the comparative negligence standard, both the plaintiff's and the defendant's negligence are computed, and the liability for damages is distributed accordingly. Some jurisdictions have adopted a "pure" form of comparative negligence that allows the plaintiff to recover, even if the extent of his or her fault is greater than that of the defendant. For example, if the plaintiff was 80 percent at fault and the defendant 20 percent at fault, the plaintiff may recover 20 percent of his or her damages. Many states' comparative negligence statutes, however, contain a "50 percent" rule under which the plaintiff recovers nothing if she or he was more than 50 percent at fault. Following this rule, a plaintiff who is 35 percent at fault could recover 65 percent of his or her damages, but a plaintiff who is 65 percent (more than 50 percent) at fault could recover nothing.

Special Negligence Doctrines and Statutes

There are a number of special doctrines and statutes relating to negligence. We examine a few of them here.

Res Ipsa Loquitur Generally, in lawsuits involving negligence, the plaintiff has the burden of proving that the defendant was negligent. In certain situations, however, under the doctrine of *res ipsa loquitur*[13] (meaning "the facts speak for themselves"), the courts may infer that negligence has occurred. Then the burden of proof rests on the defendant to prove she or he was *not* negligent. This doctrine is applied only when the event creating the damage or injury is one that ordinarily would occur only as a result of negligence. **■EXAMPLE 4.19** A person undergoes abdominal surgery and following the surgery has nerve damage in her spine near the area of the operation. In this situation, the person can sue the surgeon under a theory of *res ipsa loquitur*, because the injury would never have occurred in the absence of the surgeon's negligence.[14] ■ For the doctrine of *res ipsa loquitur* to apply, the event must have been within the defendant's power to con-

trol, and it must not have been due to any voluntary action or contribution on the part of the plaintiff.

Negligence *Per Se* Certain conduct, whether it consists of an action or a failure to act, may be treated as **negligence *per se*** (*per se* means "in or of itself"). Negligence *per se* may occur if an individual violates a statute or ordinance and thereby causes the kind of harm that the statute was intended to prevent. The injured person must prove (1) that the statute clearly sets out what standard of conduct is expected, when and where it is expected, and of whom it is expected; (2) that he or she is in the class intended to be protected by the statute; and (3) that the statute was designed to prevent the type of injury that he or she suffered. The standard of conduct required by the statute is the duty that the defendant owes to the plaintiff, and a violation of the statute is the breach of that duty. **■EXAMPLE 4.20** A statute provides that anyone who operates a motor vehicle on a public highway and fails to give full time and attention to the operation of that vehicle is guilty of inattentive driving. After an accident involving two motor vehicles, one of the drivers is cited for, and later found guilty of, violating the inattentive driver statute. If the other driver was injured and subsequently files a lawsuit, a court could consider the violation of the statute to constitute negligence *per se*. The statute sets forth a standard of attentive driving specifically to protect the safety of the traveling public.[15] ■

"Danger Invites Rescue" Doctrine Sometimes, a person who is trying to avoid harm ends up causing injury to another as a result. For example, a person swerves to avoid a head-on collision with a drunk driver and, by doing so, hits a cyclist in the bike lane. In those situations, the original wrongdoer (the drunk driver in this scenario) is liable to anyone who is injured, even if the injury actually resulted from another person's attempt to escape harm. The "danger invites rescue" doctrine extends the same protection to a person who is trying to rescue another from harm—the original wrongdoer is liable for injuries to an individual attempting a rescue. The idea is that the rescuer should not be held liable for any damages because he or she did not cause the danger and because danger invites rescue. **■EXAMPLE 4.21** Ludlam, while driving down a street, fails to see a stop sign because he is trying to stop a squabble between his two young children in the car's back seat. Salter, on the curb near the stop sign, realizes that Ludlam is about to hit a pedestrian and runs into the street to push the pedestrian out of the way. If Ludlam's vehicle hits Salter instead, Ludlam will be liable for Salter's injury, as well as for any

---

13. Pronounced *rehz ihp*-suh *low*-kwuh-tuhr.
14. See, for example, *Gubbins v. Hurson*, 885 A.2d 269 (D.C. 2005).

15. See, for example, *Wright v. Moore*, 931 A.2d 405 (Del.Supr. 2007).

injuries the other pedestrian sustained. ■ Rescuers may injure themselves, or the person rescued, or even a stranger, but the original wrongdoer will still be liable.

Special Negligence Statutes A number of states have enacted statutes prescribing duties and responsibilities in certain circumstances. For example, most states now have what are called **Good Samaritan statutes.**[16] Under these statutes, someone who is aided voluntarily by another cannot turn around and sue the "Good Samaritan" for negligence. These laws were passed largely to protect physicians and medical personnel who voluntarily render services in emergency situations to those in need, such as individuals hurt in car accidents.

Many states have also passed **dram shop acts,**[17] under which a tavern owner or bartender may be held liable for injuries caused by a person who became intoxicated while drinking at the bar or who was already intoxicated when served by the bartender. Some states' statutes also impose liability on *social hosts* (persons hosting parties) for injuries caused by guests who became intoxicated at the hosts' homes. Under these statutes, it is unnecessary to prove that the tavern owner, bartender, or social host was negligent.

STRICT LIABILITY

Another category of torts is called **strict liability,** or *liability without fault.* Intentional torts and torts of negligence involve acts that depart from a reasonable standard of care and cause injuries. Under the doctrine of strict liability, liability for injury is imposed for reasons other than fault. Strict liability for damages proximately caused by an abnormally dangerous or exceptional activity is one application of this doctrine. Courts apply the doctrine of strict liability in such cases because of the extreme risk of the activity. Even if blasting with dynamite is performed with all reasonable care, there is still a risk of injury. Balancing that risk against the potential for harm, it seems reasonable to ask the person engaged in the activity to pay for injuries caused by that activity. Although there is no fault, there is still responsibility because of the dangerous nature of the undertaking.

There are other applications of the strict liability principle. Persons who keep dangerous animals, for example, are strictly liable for any harm inflicted by the animals. A significant application of strict liability is in the area of *product*

liability—liability of manufacturers and sellers for harmful or defective products. Liability here is a matter of social policy and is based on two factors: (1) the manufacturer or seller can better bear the cost of injury because it can spread the cost throughout society by increasing prices of goods and services, and (2) the manufacturer or seller is making a profit from its activities and therefore should bear the cost of injury as an operating expense. We will discuss product liability in greater detail in Chapter 17.

CYBER TORTS

Torts can also be committed in the online environment. Torts committed via the Internet are often called *cyber torts.* Over the last ten years, the courts have had to decide how to apply traditional tort law to torts committed in cyberspace. Consider, for example, issues of proof. How can it be proved that an online defamatory remark was "published" (which requires that a third party see or hear it)? How can the identity of the person who made the remark be discovered? Can an Internet service provider (ISP), such as America Online, Inc. (AOL), be forced to reveal the source of an anonymous comment made by one of its subscribers? We explore some of these questions in this section, as well as some of the legal questions that have arisen with respect to bulk e-mail advertising.

Defamation Online

Recall from the discussion of defamation earlier in this chapter that one who repeats or otherwise republishes a defamatory statement can be subject to liability as if she or he had originally published it. Thus, publishers generally can be held liable for defamatory contents in the books and periodicals that they publish. Now consider online forums. These forums allow anyone—customers, employees, or crackpots—to complain about a firm's personnel, policies, practices, or products. Whatever the truth of the complaint is, it might have an impact on the business of the firm. One of the early questions in the online legal arena was whether the providers of such forums could be held liable, as publishers, for defamatory statements made in those forums.

Immunity of Internet Service Providers Newspapers, magazines, and television and radio stations may be held liable for defamatory remarks that they disseminate, even if those remarks are prepared or created by others. Prior to the passage of the Communications Decency Act (CDA) of 1996, the courts grappled on several occasions with the question of whether ISPs should be regarded as publishers and thus be held liable for defamatory messages made by users of their services. The CDA resolved the issue by stating that "[n]o provider or user of an interactive computer service shall

---

16. These laws derive their name from the Good Samaritan story in the Bible. In the story, a traveler who had been robbed and beaten lay along the roadside, ignored by those passing by. Eventually, a man from Samaria (the "Good Samaritan") stopped to render assistance to the injured person.
17. Historically, a *dram* was a small unit of liquid, and distilled spirits (strong alcoholic liquor) were sold in drams. Thus, a dram shop was a place where liquor was sold in drams.

be treated as the publisher or speaker of any information provided by another information content provider."[18] In other words, Internet publishers are treated differently from publishers in print, television, and radio, and are not liable for publishing defamatory statements, provided that the material came from a third party.

■EXAMPLE 4.22 In a leading case on this issue, America Online, Inc. (AOL, now part of Time Warner, Inc.), was not held liable even though it failed to promptly remove defamatory messages of which it had been made aware. In upholding a district court's ruling in AOL's favor, a federal appellate court stated that the CDA "plainly immunizes computer service providers like AOL from liability for information that originates with third parties." The court explained that the

purpose of the statute is "to maintain the robust nature of Internet communication and, accordingly, to keep government interference in the medium to a minimum."[19] ■ The courts have reached similar conclusions in subsequent cases, extending the CDA's immunity to Web message boards, online auction houses, Internet dating services, and any business that provides e-mail and Web browsing services.[20]

In the following case, the court considered the scope of immunity that could be accorded to an online roommate-matching service under the CDA.

---

18. 47 U.S.C. Section 230.

19. *Zeran v. America Online, Inc.*, 129 F.3d 327 (4th Cir. 1997); *cert.* denied, 524 U.S. 937, 118 S.Ct. 2341, 141 L.Ed.2d 712 (1998).
20. See *Universal Communications Systems, Inc. v. Lycos, Inc.*, 478 F.3d 413 (1st Cir. 2007); *Barrett v. Rosenthal*, 40 Cal.4th 33, 51 Cal.Rptr.3d 55 (2006); and *Delfino v. Agilent Technologies, Inc.*, 145 Cal.App. 4th 790, 52 Cal.Rptr.3d 376 (2006).

CASE 4.3   **Fair Housing Council of San Fernando Valley v. Roommate.com, LLC**

United States Court of Appeals, Ninth Circuit, 521 F.3d 1157 (2008).

FACTS Roommate.com, LLC (Roommate), operates an online roommate-matching Web site at **www.roommates.com**. The site helps individuals find roommates based on their descriptions of themselves and their roommate preferences. Roommate has approximately 150,000 active listings and receives about a million user views per day. To become members of Roommate, users respond to a series of online questions, choosing from answers in drop-down and select-a-box menus. Users disclose information about themselves and their roommate preferences based on age, gender, and other characteristics, and on whether children will live in the household. Members can create personal profiles, search lists of compatible roommates, and send "roommail" messages to other members. Roommate also e-mails newsletters to members seeking housing, listing compatible members who have places to rent. The Fair Housing Councils of San Fernando Valley and San Diego, California, filed a suit in a federal district court against Roommate, claiming that the defendant violated the Fair Housing Act (FHA). The court held that the Communications Decency Act (CDA) barred this claim and dismissed it. The Councils appealed to the U.S. Court of Appeals for the Ninth Circuit.

ISSUE Is an online roommate-matching service that asks users to answer questions and then posts the answers to those questions on its Web site immune from liability for the content under the CDA?

DECISION No. The U.S. Court of Appeals for the Ninth Circuit concluded that the CDA does not provide immunity to Roommate for all of the content on its Web site and in its e-mail newsletters. The appellate court reversed the lower court's summary judgment and remanded the case for "a determination of whether [Roommate's] non-immune publication and distribution of information violates the FHA."

REASON The appellate court reasoned that when an Internet service provider becomes an information-content provider, the immunity from liability for content under the CDA no longer applies. Roommate is responsible for the questionnaires that it requires users to fill out to register with the service because it created the forms and the answer choices. Consequently, Roommate must be considered a content provider of these questionnaires. Roommate's search mechanism and e-mail notifications "mean that it is neither a passive pass-through of information provided by others nor merely a facilitator of expression by individuals. By categorizing, channeling, and limiting the distribution of users' profiles, Roommate provides an additional layer of information that it is responsible at least in part for creating or developing."

FOR CRITICAL ANALYSIS—Ethical Consideration *Do Internet service providers have an ethical duty to advise their users if the information that the users provide for distribution through the Internet service providers might violate the law? Explain.*

■

Piercing the Veil of Anonymity A threshold barrier to anyone who seeks to bring an action for online defamation is discovering the identity of the person who posted the defamatory message online. ISPs can disclose personal information about their customers only when ordered to do so by a court. Consequently, businesses and individuals often resort to filing lawsuits against "John Does." Then, using the authority of the courts, they attempt to obtain from the ISPs the identities of the persons responsible for the messages. This strategy has worked in some cases, but not in others.[21] Courts typically are reluctant to deter those who would potentially post messages on the Internet from exercising their First Amendment right to speak anonymously. After all, speaking anonymously is part of the nature of the Internet and helps to make it a useful forum for public discussion.

Spam

Bulk, unsolicited e-mail (junk e-mail) sent to all of the users on a particular e-mailing list is often called **spam**. Typically, spam consists of a product ad sent to all of the users on an e-mailing list or all of the members of a newsgroup. Spam can waste user time and network bandwidth (the amount of data that can be transmitted within a certain time). It also imposes a burden on an ISP's equipment as well as on an e-mail recipient's computer system. Because of the problems associated with spam, a majority of the states now have laws regulating its transmission. In 2003, the U.S. Congress also enacted a law to regulate spam, but the volume of spam has actually increased since the law was enacted.

Before 2006, the Federal Trade Commission (FTC) lacked the authority to investigate cross-border spamming activities and to communicate with foreign nations concerning spam and other deceptive practices conducted via the Internet. In 2006, however, Congress passed the U.S. Safe Web Act (also known as the Undertaking Spam, Spyware, and Fraud Enforcement with Enforcers Beyond Borders Act),[22] which increased the FTC's ability to combat spam on a global level.

---

21. See, for example, *Doe v. Cahill*, 884 A.2d 451 (Del.Suptr. 2005); and *Dendrite International, Inc. v. Doe No. 3*, 342 N.J.Super. 134, 775 A.2d 756 (2001).
22. Pub. L. No. 109-455, 120 Stat. 3372 (December 22, 2006), which enacted 15 U.S.C.A. Sections 57b-2a, 57b-2b, 57c-1, and 57c-2, and amended various other sections of the *United States Code*.

The act allows the FTC to cooperate and share information with foreign agencies in investigating and prosecuting those involved in Internet fraud and deception, including spamming, spyware, and various Internet scams. Although the FTC and foreign agencies can provide investigative assistance to one another, the act exempts foreign agencies from U.S. public disclosure laws. In other words, the activities undertaken by the foreign agency (even if requested by the FTC) will be kept secret.

State Regulation of Spam In an attempt to combat spam, thirty-six states have enacted laws that prohibit or regulate its use. Many state laws regulating spam require the senders of e-mail ads to instruct the recipients on how they can "opt out" of further e-mail ads from the same sources. For instance, in some states an unsolicited e-mail ad must include a toll-free phone number or return e-mail address through which the recipient can contact the sender to request that no more ads be e-mailed. The most stringent state law is California's antispam law, which follows the "opt-in" model favored by consumer groups and antispam advocates. In other words, the law prohibits any person or business from sending e-mail ads to or from any e-mail address in California unless the recipient has expressly agreed to receive e-mails from the sender. An exemption is made for e-mail sent to consumers with whom the advertiser has a "preexisting or current business relationship."

The Federal CAN-SPAM Act In 2003, Congress enacted the Controlling the Assault of Non-Solicited Pornography and Marketing (CAN-SPAM) Act, which applies to any "commercial electronic mail messages" that are sent to promote a commercial product or service. Significantly, the statute preempts state antispam laws except for those provisions in state laws that prohibit false and deceptive e-mailing practices. Generally, the act permits the use of unsolicited commercial e-mail but prohibits certain types of spamming activities, including the use of a false return address and the use of false, misleading, or deceptive information when sending e-mail. The statute also prohibits the use of "dictionary attacks"—sending messages to randomly generated e-mail addresses—and the "harvesting" of e-mail addresses from Web sites through the use of specialized software. Notwithstanding the requirements of the federal act, the reality is that the problem of spam is difficult to address because much of it is funneled through foreign servers.

REVIEWING Torts and Cyber Torts

Two sisters, Darla and Irene, are partners in an import business located in a small town in Rhode Island. Irene is also campaigning to be the mayor of their town. Both sisters travel to other countries to purchase the goods they sell at their retail store. Irene buys Indonesian goods, and Darla buys goods from Africa. After a tsunami (tidal wave) destroys many of the cities in Indonesia to which Irene usually travels, she phones one of her contacts there and asks him to procure some items and ship them to her. He informs her that it will be impossible to buy these items now because the townspeople are being evacuated due to a water shortage. Irene is angry and tells the man that if he cannot purchase the goods, he should just take them without paying for them after the town has been evacuated. Darla overhears her sister's instructions and is outraged. They have a falling-out, and Darla decides that she no longer wishes to be in business with her sister. Using the information presented in the chapter, answer the following questions.

1 Suppose that Darla tells several of her friends about Irene's instructing the man to take goods without paying for them

from the people of Indonesia after the tsunami disaster. If Irene files a tort action against Darla alleging slander, will her suit be successful? Why or why not?

2 Now suppose that Irene wins the election and becomes the city's mayor. Darla then writes a letter to the editor of the local newspaper disclosing Irene's misconduct. If Irene accuses Darla of committing libel, what defenses could Darla assert?

3 If Irene accepts goods shipped from Indonesia that were wrongfully obtained, has she committed an intentional tort against property? Explain.

4 Suppose now that Darla was in the store one day with an elderly customer, Betty Green, who was looking for a unique gift for her granddaughter's graduation present. When the phone rang, Darla left the customer and walked to the counter to answer the phone. Green wandered around the store and eventually went through an open door into the stockroom area, where she fell over some boxes on the floor and fractured her hip. Green files a negligence action against the store. Did Darla breach her duty of care? Why or why not?

TERMS AND CONCEPTS

actionable 83
actual malice 86
appropriation 86
assault 82
assumption of risk 92
battery 82
business invitee 91
business tort 80
causation in fact 92
comparative negligence 93
compensatory damages 80
contributory negligence 93
conversion 89
cyber tort 82
damages 80

defamation 84
defense 83
disparagement of property 89
dram shop act 94
duty of care 90
fraudulent misrepresentation 87
Good Samaritan statute 94
intentional tort 82
libel 84
malpractice 91
negligence 90
negligence *per se* 93
predatory behavior 88
privilege 85
proximate cause 92

puffery 87
punitive damages 81
reasonable person standard 90
res ipsa loquitur 93
slander 84
slander of quality 89
slander of title 90
spam 96
strict liability 94
tort 80
tortfeasor 82
trade libel 89
trespass to land 88
trespass to personal property 89

CHAPTER SUMMARY Torts and Cyber Torts

Intentional Torts against Persons (See pages 82–88.)	1. *Assault and battery*—An assault is an unexcused and intentional act that causes another person to be apprehensive of immediate harm. A battery is an assault that results in physical contact.
	2. *False imprisonment*—The intentional confinement or restraint of another person's movement without justification.

(Continued)

CHAPTER SUMMARY	Torts and Cyber Torts–Continued
Intentional Torts against Persons—Continued	3. *Intentional infliction of emotional distress*—An intentional act that amounts to extreme and outrageous conduct resulting in severe emotional distress to another.
	4. *Defamation (libel or slander)*—A false statement of fact, not made under privilege, that is communicated to a third person and that causes damage to a person's reputation. For public figures, the plaintiff must also prove actual malice.
	5. *Invasion of the right to privacy*—The use of a person's name or likeness for commercial purposes without permission, wrongful intrusion into a person's private activities, publication of information that places a person in a false light, or disclosure of private facts that an ordinary person would find objectionable.
	6. *Appropriation*—The use of another person's name, likeness, or other identifying characteristic, without permission and for the benefit of the user.
	7. *Misrepresentation (fraud)*—A false representation made by one party, through misstatement of facts or through conduct, with the intention of deceiving another and on which the other reasonably relies to his or her detriment.
	8. *Wrongful interference*—The knowing, intentional interference by a third party with an enforceable contractual relationship or an established business relationship between other parties for the purpose of advancing the economic interests of the third party.
Intentional Torts against Property (See pages 88–90.)	1. *Trespass to land*—The invasion of another's real property without consent or privilege. Specific rights and duties apply once a person is expressly or impliedly established as a trespasser.
	2. *Trespass to personal property*—Unlawfully damaging or interfering with the owner's right to use, possess, or enjoy her or his personal property.
	3. *Conversion*—Wrongfully taking personal property from its rightful owner or possessor and placing it in the service of another.
	4. *Disparagement of property*—Any economically injurious falsehood that is made about another's product or property; an inclusive term for the torts of *slander of quality* and *slander of title*.
Unintentional Torts (Negligence) (See pages 90–94.)	1. *Negligence*—The careless performance of a legally required duty or the failure to perform a legally required act. Elements that must be proved are that a legal duty of care exists, that the defendant breached that duty, and that the breach caused damage or injury to another.
	2. *Defenses to negligence*—The basic affirmative defenses in negligence cases are (a) assumption of risk, (b) superseding cause, and (c) contributory or comparative negligence.
	3. *Special negligence doctrines and statutes*—
	a. *Res ipsa loquitur*—A doctrine under which a plaintiff need not prove negligence on the part of the defendant because "the facts speak for themselves."
	b. Negligence *per se*—A type of negligence that may occur if a person violates a statute or an ordinance and the violation causes another to suffer the kind of injury that the statute or ordinance was intended to prevent.
	c. Special negligence statutes—State statutes that prescribe duties and responsibilities in certain circumstances. Dram shop acts and Good Samaritan statutes are examples of special negligence statutes.
Strict Liability (See page 94.)	Under the doctrine of strict liability, a person may be held liable, regardless of the degree of care exercised, for damages or injuries caused by her or his product or activity. Strict liability includes liability for harms caused by abnormally dangerous activities, by dangerous animals, and by defective products (product liability).

CHAPTER SUMMARY   Torts and Cyber Torts–Continued

| Cyber Torts (See pages 94–96.) | General tort principles are being extended to cover cyber torts, or torts that occur in cyberspace, such as online defamation and spamming (which may constitute trespass to personal property). Federal and state statutes may also apply to certain forms of cyber torts. For example, under the federal Communications Decency Act of 1996, Internet service providers are not liable for defamatory messages posted by their subscribers. A majority of the states and the federal government now regulate unwanted e-mail ads (spam). |

FOR REVIEW

Answers for the even-numbered questions in this **For Review** *section can be found on this text's accompanying Web site at* **www.cengage.com/blaw/fbl**. *Select "Chapter 4" and click on "For Review."*

1 What is a tort?

2 What is the purpose of tort law? What are two basic categories of torts?

3 What are the four elements of negligence?

4 What is meant by strict liability? In what circumstances is strict liability applied?

5 What is a cyber tort, and how are tort theories being applied in cyberspace?

QUESTIONS AND CASE PROBLEMS

 HYPOTHETICAL SCENARIOS AND CASE PROBLEMS

4.1 Defenses to Negligence. Corinna was riding her bike on a city street. While she was riding, she frequently looked back to verify that the books that she had fastened to the rear part of her bike were still attached. On one occasion while she was looking behind her, she failed to notice a car that was entering an intersection just as she was crossing it. The car hit her, causing her to sustain numerous injuries. Three eyewitnesses stated that the driver of the car had failed to stop at the stop sign before entering the intersection. Corinna sued the driver of the car for negligence. What defenses might the defendant driver raise in this lawsuit? Discuss fully.

4.2 Hypothetical Question with Sample Answer. In which of the following situations will the acting party be liable for the tort of negligence? Explain fully.

1 Mary goes to the golf course on Sunday morning, eager to try out a new set of golf clubs she has just purchased. As she tees off on the first hole, the head of her club flies off and injures a nearby golfer.

2 Mary's doctor gives her some pain medication and tells her not to drive after she takes it, as the medication induces drowsiness. In spite of the doctor's warning, Mary decides to drive to the store while on the medication. Owing to her lack of alertness, she fails to stop at a traffic light and crashes into another vehicle, injuring a passenger.

 For a sample answer to Question 4.2, go to Appendix E at the end of this text.

4.3 Liability to Business Invitees. Kim went to Ling's Market to pick up a few items for dinner. It was a rainy, windy day, and the wind had blown water through the door of Ling's Market each time the door opened. As Kim entered through the door, she slipped and fell in the approximately one-half inch of rainwater that had accumulated on the floor. The manager knew of the weather conditions but had not posted any sign to warn customers of the water hazard. Kim injured her back as a result of the fall and sued Ling's for damages. Can Ling's be held liable for negligence in this situation? Discuss.

4.4 Defamation. Lydia Hagberg went to her bank, California Federal Bank, FSB, to cash a check made out to her by Smith Barney (SB), an investment-services firm. Nolene Showalter, a bank employee, suspected that the check was counterfeit. Showalter phoned SB and was told that the check was not valid. As she phoned the police, Gary Wood, a bank security officer, contacted SB again and was told that its earlier statement was "erroneous" and that the check was valid. Meanwhile, a police officer arrived, drew Hagberg away from the teller's window, spread her legs, patted her down, and handcuffed her. The officer searched her purse, asked her whether she had any weapons or stolen property and whether she was driving a stolen vehicle, and arrested her. Hagberg filed a suit in a California state court against the bank and others, alleging, among other things, slander. Should the absolute privilege for communications made in judicial or other official proceedings apply to statements made when a citizen contacts the police to report suspected criminal activity? Why or why not? [*Hagberg v. California Federal Bank, FSB*, 32 Cal.4th 350, 81 P.3d 244, 7 Cal.Rptr.3d 803 (2004)]

4.5 Negligence. In July 2004, Emellie Anderson hired Kenneth Whitten, a licensed building contractor, to construct a two-story addition to her home. The bottom floor was to be a garage and the second floor a home office. In August, the parties signed a second contract under which Whitten agreed to rebuild a deck and railing attached to the house and to further improve the office. A later inspection revealed gaps in the siding on the new garage, nails protruding from incomplete framing, improper support for a stairway to the office, and gaps in its plywood flooring. One post supporting the deck was cracked; another was too short. Concrete had not been poured underneath the old posts. A section of railing was missing, and what was installed was warped, with gaps at the joints. Anderson filed a suit in a Connecticut state court against Whitten, alleging that his work was "substandard, not to code, unsafe and not done in a [workmanlike] manner." Anderson claimed that she would have to pay someone else to repair all of the work. Does Whitten's "work" satisfy the requirements for a claim grounded in negligence? Should Anderson's complaint be dismissed, or should she be awarded damages? Explain. [*Anderson v. Whitten*, 100 Conn.App. 730, 918 A.2d 1056 (2007)]

4.6 Case Problem with Sample Answer. Between 1996 and 1998, Donna Swanson received several anonymous, handwritten letters that, among other things, accused her husband, Alan, of infidelity. In 1998, John Grisham, Jr., the author of *The Firm* and many other best-selling novels, received an anonymous letter that appeared to have been written by the same person. Grisham and the Swansons suspected Katherine Almy, who soon filed a suit in a Virginia state court against them, alleging, in part, intentional infliction of emotional distress. According to Almy, Grisham intended to have her "really, really, suffer" for writing the letters, and the three devised a scheme to falsely accuse her. They gave David Liebman, a handwriting analyst, samples of Almy's handwriting. These included copies of confidential documents from her children's files at St. Anne's-Belfield School in Charlottesville, Virginia, where Alan taught and Grisham served on the board of directors. In Almy's view, Grisham influenced Liebman to report that Almy might have written the letters and misrepresented this report as conclusive, which led the police to confront Almy. She claimed that she then suffered severe emotional distress and depression, causing "a complete disintegration of virtually every aspect of her life" and requiring her "to undergo extensive therapy." In response, the defendants asked the court to dismiss the complaint for failure to state a claim. Should the court grant this request? Explain. [*Almy v. Grisham*, 273 Va. 68, 639 S.E.2d 182 (2007)]

After you have answered Problem 4.6, compare your answer with the sample answer given on the Web site that accompanies this text. Go to www.cengage.com/blaw/fbl, select "Chapter 4," and click on "Case Problem with Sample Answer."

4.7 Defenses to Negligence. Neal Peterson's entire family skied, and Peterson started skiing at the age of two. In 2000, at the age of eleven, Peterson was in his fourth year as a member of a ski race team. After a race one morning in February, Peterson continued to practice his skills through the afternoon. Coming down a slope very fast, at a point at which his skis were not touching the ground, Peterson collided with David Donahue. Donahue, a forty-three-year-old advanced skier, was skating (skiing slowly) across the slope toward the parking lot. Peterson and Donahue knew that falls or collisions and accidents and injuries were possible with skiing. Donahue saw Peterson "split seconds" before the impact, which knocked Donahue out of his skis and down the slope ten or twelve feet. When Donahue saw Peterson lying motionless nearby, he immediately sought help. To recover for his injuries, Peterson filed a suit in a Minnesota state court against Donahue, alleging negligence. Based on these facts, which defense to a claim of negligence is Donahue most likely to assert? How is the court likely to apply that defense and rule on Peterson's claim? Why? [*Peterson ex rel. Peterson v. Donahue*, 733 N.W.2d 790 (Minn.App. 2007)]

4.8 A Question of Ethics. *White Plains Coat & Apron Co. is a New York–based linen rental business. Cintas Corp. is a nationwide business that rents similar products. White Plains had five-year exclusive contracts with some of its customers. As a result of Cintas's soliciting of business, dozens of White Plains' customers breached their contracts and entered into rental agreements with Cintas. White Plains demanded that Cintas stop its solicitation of White Plains' customers. Cintas refused. White Plains filed a suit in a federal district court against Cintas, alleging wrongful interference with existing contracts. Cintas argued that it had no knowledge of any contracts with White Plains and had not induced any breach. The court dismissed the suit, ruling that Cintas had a legitimate interest as a competitor to solicit business and make a profit. White Plains appealed to the U.S. Court of Appeals for the Second Circuit.* [*White Plains Coat & Apron Co. v. Cintas Corp.*, 8 N.Y.3d 422, 867 N.E.2d 381 (2007)]

1 What are the two important policy interests at odds in wrongful interference cases? When there is an existing contract, which of these interests should be accorded priority?

2 The U.S. Court of Appeals for the Second Circuit asked the New York Court of Appeals to answer a question: Is a general interest in soliciting business for profit a sufficient defense to a claim of wrongful interference with a contractual relationship? What do you think? Why?

CRITICAL THINKING AND WRITING ASSIGNMENTS

4.9 Critical Legal Thinking. What general principle underlies the common law doctrine that business owners have a duty of care toward their customers? Does the duty of care unfairly burden business owners? Why or why not?

4.10  **Video Question.** Go to this text's Web site at **www.cengage.com/blaw/fbl** and select "Chapter 4." Click on "Video Questions" and view the video titled *Jaws.* Then answer the following questions.

1 In the video, the mayor (Murray Hamilton) and a few other men try to persuade Chief Brody (Roy Scheider) not to close the town's beaches. If Chief Brody keeps the beaches open and a swimmer is injured or killed because he failed to warn swimmers about the potential shark danger, has he committed a tort? If so, what kind of tort (intentional tort against persons, intentional tort against property, or negligence)? Explain your answer.

2 Can Chief Brody be held liable for any injuries or deaths to swimmers under the doctrine of strict liability? Why or why not?

3 Suppose that Chief Brody goes against the mayor's instructions and warns people to stay out of the water. Nevertheless, several swimmers do not heed his warning and are injured as a result. What defense or defenses could Chief Brody raise under these circumstances if he is sued for negligence?

ACCESSING THE INTERNET

For updated links to resources available on the Web, as well as a variety of other materials, visit this text's Web site at

www.cengage.com/blaw/fbl

You can find cases and articles on torts, including business torts, at the Internet Law Library's Web site at

www.lawguru.com/ilawlib/110.htm

For information on the *Restatements of the Law,* including the *Restatement (Second) of Torts* and the *Restatement (Third) of Torts: Products Liability,* go to the Web site of the American Law Institute at

www.ali.org

PRACTICAL INTERNET EXERCISES

Go to this text's Web site at **www.cengage.com/blaw/fbl**, select "Chapter 4," and click on "Practical Internet Exercises." There you will find the following Internet research exercises that you can perform to learn more about the topics covered in this chapter.

PRACTICAL INTERNET EXERCISE 4–1 LEGAL PERSPECTIVE—Online Defamation

PRACTICAL INTERNET EXERCISE 4–2 SOCIAL PERSPECTIVE—Legal and Illegal Uses of Spam

PRACTICAL INTERNET EXERCISE 4–3 MANAGEMENT PERSPECTIVE—The Duty to Warn

BEFORE THE TEST

Go to this text's Web site at **www.cengage.com/blaw/fbl**, select "Chapter 4," and click on "Interactive Quizzes." You will find a number of interactive questions relating to this chapter.

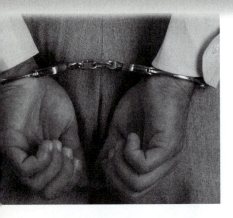

CHAPTER 5
Intellectual Property and Internet Law

LEARNING OBJECTIVES

AFTER READING THIS CHAPTER, YOU SHOULD BE ABLE TO ANSWER THE FOLLOWING QUESTIONS:

1 What is intellectual property?

2 Why are trademarks and patents protected by the law?

3 What laws protect authors' rights in the works they generate?

4 What are trade secrets, and what laws offer protection for this form of intellectual property?

5 What steps have been taken to protect intellectual property rights in today's digital age?

Of significant concern to businesspersons today is the need to protect their rights in intellectual property. **Intellectual property** is any property resulting from intellectual, creative processes—the products of an individual's mind. Although it is an abstract term for an abstract concept, intellectual property is nonetheless familiar to almost everyone. The information contained in books and computer files is intellectual property. The software you use, the movies you see, and the music you listen to are all forms of intellectual property. In fact, in today's information age, it should come as no surprise that the value of the world's intellectual property probably now exceeds the value of physical property, such as machines and houses.

The need to protect creative works was recognized by the framers of the U.S. Constitution more than two hundred years ago: Article I, Section 8, of the Constitution authorized Congress "[t]o promote the Progress of Science and useful Arts, by securing for limited Times to Authors and Inventors the exclusive Right to their respective Writings and Discoveries." Laws protecting patents, trademarks, and copyrights are explicitly designed to protect and reward inventive and artistic creativity. Exhibit 5–1 on page 118 offers a synopsis of these forms of intellectual property, as well as intellectual property that consists of *trade secrets*.

An understanding of intellectual property law is important because intellectual property has taken on increasing significance, not only in the United States but globally as well. Today, the prosperity of many U.S. companies depends more on their ownership rights in intangible intellectual property than on their tangible assets. As you will read in this chapter, protecting these assets in today's online world has proved particularly challenging.

TRADEMARKS AND RELATED PROPERTY

A **trademark** is a distinctive mark, motto, device, or emblem that a manufacturer stamps, prints, or otherwise affixes to the goods it produces so that they may be identified on the market and their origins made known. At common law, the person who used a symbol or mark to identify a business or product was protected in the use of that trademark. Clearly, by using another's trademark, a business could lead consumers to believe that its goods were made by the other business. The law seeks to avoid this kind of confusion. In the following classic case concerning Coca-Cola, the defendants argued that the Coca-Cola trademark was entitled to no protection under the law because the term did not accurately represent the product.

CASE 5.1   **The Coca-Cola Co. v. Koke Co. of America**

LANDMARK AND CLASSIC CASES

Supreme Court of the United States, 254 U.S. 143, 41 S.Ct. 113, 65 L.Ed. 189 (1920).
www.findlaw.com/casecode/supreme.html[a]

FACTS The Coca-Cola Company brought an action in a federal district court to prevent other beverage companies from using the words *Koke* and *Dope* for the defendants' products. The defendants contended that the Coca-Cola trademark was a fraudulent representation and that Coca-Cola was therefore not entitled to any help from the courts. By use of the Coca-Cola name, the defendants alleged, the Coca-Cola Company represented that the beverage contained cocaine (from coca leaves). The district court granted the injunction, but the federal appellate court reversed the lower court's decision. The Coca-Cola Company appealed to the United States Supreme Court.

ISSUE Did the marketing of products called Koke and Dope by the Koke Company of America and other firms constitute an unauthorized use of Coca-Cola's trademark?

DECISION Yes for Koke, but no for Dope. The Court enjoined (prevented) the competing beverage companies from calling their products Koke but did not prevent them from calling their products Dope.

REASON The Court noted that, to be sure, prior to 1900 the Coca-Cola beverage had contained a small amount of cocaine, but this ingredient had been deleted from the formula by 1906 at the latest, and the Coca-Cola Company had advertised to the public that no cocaine was present in its

drink. Coca-Cola was a widely popular drink "to be had at almost any soda fountain." Because of the public's widespread familiarity with Coca-Cola, the retention of the name of the beverage (referring to coca leaves and kola nuts) was not misleading: "Coca-Cola probably means to most persons the plaintiff's familiar product to be had everywhere rather than a compound of particular substances." The name "Coke" was found to be so common a term for the trademarked product Coca-Cola that the defendants' use of the similar-sounding "Koke" as a name for their beverages was disallowed. The Court could find no reason to restrain the defendants from using the name "Dope," however.

WHAT IF THE FACTS WERE DIFFERENT? *Suppose that Coca-Cola had been trying to make the public believe that its product contained cocaine. Would the result in the case likely have been different? Why or why not?*

IMPACT OF THIS CASE ON TODAY'S LAW *In this classic case, the United States Supreme Court made it clear that trademarks and trade names (and nicknames for those marks and names, such as the nickname "Coke" for "Coca-Cola") that are in everyday use receive protection under the common law. This holding is historically significant because the federal statute later passed to protect trademark rights (the Lanham Act of 1946, to be discussed shortly) in many ways represented a codification of common law principles governing trademarks.*

RELEVANT WEB SITES *To locate information on the Web concerning the Coca-Cola Co. decision, go to this text's Web site at* **www.cengage.com/blaw/fbl***, select "Chapter 5," and click on "URLs for Landmark Cases."*

a. This is the "U.S. Supreme Court Opinions" page within the Web site of the "FindLaw Internet Legal Resources" database. This page provides several options for accessing an opinion. Because you know the citation for this case, you can go to the "Citation Search" box, type in the appropriate volume and page numbers for the *United States Reports* ("254" and "143," respectively, for the *Coca-Cola* case), and click on "Get It."

Statutory Protection of Trademarks

Statutory protection of trademarks and related property is provided at the federal level by the Lanham Act of 1946.[1] The Lanham Act was enacted in part to protect manufacturers from losing business to rival companies that used confusingly similar trademarks. The Lanham Act incorporates the common law of trademarks and provides remedies for owners

of trademarks who wish to enforce their claims in federal court. Many states also have trademark statutes.

Trademark Dilution In 1995, Congress amended the Lanham Act by passing the Federal Trademark Dilution Act,[2] which extended the protection available to trademark owners by allowing them to bring a suit in federal court for trademark *dilution*. Until the passage of this amendment,

---

1. 15 U.S.C. Sections 1051–1128.

2. 15 U.S.C. Section 1125.

federal trademark law prohibited only the unauthorized use of the same mark on competing—or on noncompeting but "related"—goods or services when such use would likely confuse consumers as to the origin of those goods and services. Trademark dilution laws protect "distinctive" or "famous" trademarks (such as Jergens, McDonald's, Dell, and Apple) from certain unauthorized uses even when the use is on noncompeting goods or is unlikely to confuse. More than half of the states have also enacted trademark dilution laws.

Use of a Similar Mark May Constitute Trademark Dilution   A famous mark may be diluted not only by the use of an *identical* mark but also by the use of a *similar* mark provided that it reduces the value of the famous mark. A similar mark is more likely to lessen the value of a famous mark when the companies using the marks provide related goods or compete against each other in the same market. **■EXAMPLE 5.1** A woman was operating a coffee shop under the name "Sambuck's Coffeehouse" in Astoria, Oregon, even though she knew that "Starbucks" was one of the largest coffee chains in the nation. When Starbucks Corporation filed a dilution lawsuit, the federal court ruled that use of the "Sambuck's" mark constituted trademark dilution because it created confusion for consumers. Not only was there a "high degree" of similarity between the marks, but also both companies provided coffee-related services and marketed their services through "stand-alone" retail stores. Therefore, the use of the similar mark (Sambuck's) reduced the value of the famous mark (Starbucks).[3] **■**

Note that to establish dilution, it is required that the plaintiff show that the similar (and allegedly infringing) mark actually reduces the value of the famous mark. **■EXAMPLE 5.2** Well-known lingerie maker Victoria's Secret brought a trademark dilution action against "Victor's Little Secret," a small retail store that sold adult videos, lingerie, and other items. Although the lower courts granted Victoria's Secret an injunction prohibiting the adult store from using a similar mark, the United States Supreme Court reversed the decision. According to the Court, the likelihood of dilution is not enough to establish dilution. The plaintiff must present some evidence that the allegedly infringing user's mark actually reduces the value of the famous mark or lessens its capacity to identify goods and services.[4] **■**

Trademark Registration

Trademarks may be registered with the state or with the federal government. To register for protection under federal

trademark law, a person must file an application with the U.S. Patent and Trademark Office in Washington, D.C. Under present law, a mark can be registered (1) if it is currently in commerce or (2) if the applicant intends to put the mark into commerce within six months.

In special circumstances, the six-month period can be extended by thirty months, giving the applicant a total of three years from the date of notice of trademark approval to make use of the mark and file the required use statement. Registration is postponed until the mark is actually used. Nonetheless, during this waiting period, any applicant can legally protect his or her trademark against a third party who previously has neither used the mark nor filed an application for it. Registration is renewable between the fifth and sixth years after the initial registration and every ten years thereafter (every twenty years for trademarks registered before 1990).

Trademark Infringement

Registration of a trademark with the U.S. Patent and Trademark Office gives notice on a nationwide basis that the trademark belongs exclusively to the registrant. The registrant is also allowed to use the symbol ® to indicate that the mark has been registered. Whenever that trademark is copied to a substantial degree or used in its entirety by another, intentionally or unintentionally, the trademark has been *infringed* (used without authorization). When a trademark has been infringed, the owner has a cause of action against the infringer. To succeed in a trademark infringement action, the owner must show that the defendant's use of the mark created a likelihood of confusion about the origin of the defendant's goods or services. The owner need not prove that the infringer acted intentionally or that the trademark was registered (although registration does provide proof of the date of inception of the trademark's use).

The most commonly granted remedy for trademark infringement is an *injunction* to prevent further infringement. Under the Lanham Act, a trademark owner that successfully proves infringement can recover actual damages, plus the profits that the infringer wrongfully received from the unauthorized use of the mark. A court can also order the destruction of any goods bearing the unauthorized trademark. In some situations, the trademark owner may also be able to recover attorneys' fees.

Distinctiveness of Mark

A central objective of the Lanham Act is to reduce the likelihood that consumers will be confused by similar marks. For that reason, only those trademarks that are deemed sufficiently distinct from all competing trademarks will be protected.

---

3. *Starbucks Corp. v. Lundberg*, 2005 WL 3183858 (D.Or. 2005).
4. *Moseley v. V Secret Catalogue, Inc.*, 537 U.S. 418, 123 S.Ct. 1115, 155 L.Ed.2d 1 (2003).

Strong Marks Fanciful, arbitrary, or suggestive trademarks are generally considered to be the most distinctive (strongest) trademarks because they are normally taken from outside the context of the particular product and thus provide the best means of distinguishing one product from another.

■ **EXAMPLE 5.3** Fanciful trademarks include invented words, such as "Xerox" for one manufacturer's copiers and "Kodak" for another company's photographic products. Arbitrary trademarks use common words in a fictitious or arbitrary manner to create a distinctive mark that identifies the source of the product, such as "Dutch Boy" as a name on a can of paint. Suggestive trademarks suggest something about a product without describing the product directly. For instance, "Dairy Queen" suggests an association between its products and milk, but it does not directly describe ice cream. ■

Secondary Meaning Descriptive terms, geographic terms, and personal names are not inherently distinctive and do not receive protection under the law *until* they acquire a secondary meaning. A secondary meaning may arise when customers begin to associate a specific term or phrase, such as "London Fog," with specific trademarked items (coats with "London Fog" labels). Whether a secondary meaning becomes attached to a term or name usually depends on how extensively the product is advertised, the market for the product, the number of sales, and other factors. The United States Supreme Court has held that even a color can qualify for trademark protection.[5] Once a secondary meaning is attached to a term or name, a trademark is considered distinctive and is protected. In one recent case, a federal court ruled that trademark law protects the particular color schemes used by four state university sports teams, including Ohio State University and Louisiana State University.[6]

Generic Terms Generic terms are terms that refer to an entire class of products, such as *bicycle* and *computer*. Generic terms receive no protection, even if they acquire secondary meanings. A particularly thorny problem arises when a trademark acquires generic use. For instance, *aspirin* and *thermos* were originally trademarked products, but today the words are used generically. Other examples are *escalator*, *trampoline*, *raisin bran*, *dry ice*, *lanolin*, *linoleum*, *nylon*, and *corn flakes*.

Sometimes, a company's use of a particular generic phrase or mark becomes so closely associateed with that company that

the firm claims it should be protected under trademark law. ■ **EXAMPLE 5.4** In one case, America Online, Inc. (AOL), sued AT&T Corporation, claiming that AT&T's use of "You Have Mail" on its WorldNet Service infringed AOL's trademark rights in the same phrase. The court ruled, however, that because each of the three words in the phrase was a generic term, the phrase as a whole was generic. Although the phrase had become widely associated with AOL's e-mail notification service, and thus may have acquired a secondary meaning, this issue was of no significance in this case. The court stated that it would not consider whether the mark had acquired any secondary meaning because "generic marks with secondary meaning are still not entitled to protection."[7] ■

Service, Certification, and Collective Marks

A **service mark** is essentially a trademark that is used to distinguish the *services* (rather than the products) of one person or company from those of another. For instance, each airline has a particular mark or symbol associated with its name. Titles and character names used in radio and television are frequently registered as service marks.

Other marks protected by law include certification marks and collective marks. A **certification mark** is used by one or more persons, other than the owner, to certify the region, materials, mode of manufacture, quality, or other characteristic of specific goods or services. ■ **EXAMPLE 5.5** Certification marks include such marks as "Good Housekeeping Seal of Approval" and "UL Tested." ■ When used by members of a cooperative, association, union, or other organization, a certification mark is referred to as a **collective mark**. ■ **EXAMPLE 5.6** Collective marks appear at the ends of the credits of movies to indicate the various associations and organizations that participated in making the movie. The union marks found on the tags of certain products are also collective marks. ■

Trade Dress

The term **trade dress** refers to the image and overall appearance of a product. Trade dress is a broad concept and can include either all or part of the total image or overall impression created by a product or its packaging. ■ **EXAMPLE 5.7** The distinctive decor, menu, layout, and style of service of a particular restaurant may be regarded as the restaurant's trade dress. Similarly, trade dress can include the layout and appearance of a mail-order catalog, the use of a lighthouse as part of the design of a golf hole, the fish shape of a cracker, or the G-shaped design of a Gucci watch. ■ Basically, trade dress is subject to the same protection as trademarks. In cases

---

5. *Qualitex Co. v. Jacobson Products Co.*, 514 U.S. 159, 115 S.Ct. 1300, 131 L.Ed.2d 248 (1995).

6. *Board of Supervisors of LA State University v. Smack Apparel Co.*, 438 F.Supp.2d 653 (E.D.La. 2006).

---

7. *America Online, Inc. v. AT&T Corp.*, 243 F.3d 812 (4th Cir. 2001).

involving trade dress infringement, as in trademark infringement cases, a major consideration is whether consumers are likely to be confused by the allegedly infringing use.

Counterfeit Goods

Counterfeit goods copy or otherwise imitate trademarked goods but are not genuine. The importation of goods that bear a counterfeit (fake) trademark poses a growing problem for U.S. businesses, consumers, and law enforcement. In addition to having negative financial effects on legitimate businesses, sales of certain counterfeit goods, such as pharmaceuticals and nutritional supplements, can present serious public health risks. It is estimated that nearly 7 percent of the goods imported into the United States from abroad are counterfeit.

Stop Counterfeiting in Manufactured Goods Act In 2006, Congress enacted the Stop Counterfeiting in Manufactured Goods Act[8] (SCMGA) to combat the growing problem of counterfeit goods. The act makes it a crime to intentionally traffic in or attempt to traffic in counterfeit goods or services, or to knowingly use a counterfeit mark on or in connection with goods or services. Prior to this act, the law did not prohibit the creation or shipment of counterfeit labels that were not attached to any product.[9] Therefore, counterfeiters would make labels and packaging bearing another's trademark, ship the labels to another location, and then affix them to an inferior product to deceive buyers. The SCMGA has closed this loophole by making it a crime to knowingly traffic in or attempt to traffic in counterfeit labels, stickers, packaging, and the like, regardless of whether the item is attached to any goods.

Penalties for Counterfeiting Persons found guilty of violating the SCMGA may be fined up to $2 million or imprisoned for up to ten years (or more if they are repeat offenders). If a court finds that the statute was violated, it must order the defendant to forfeit the counterfeit products (which are then destroyed), as well as any property used in the commission of the crime. The defendant must also pay restitution to the trademark holder or victim in an amount equal to the victim's actual loss. **■EXAMPLE 5.8** In one case, the defendant pleaded guilty to conspiring with others to import cigarette-rolling papers from Mexico that were falsely marked as "Zig-Zags" and sell them in the United States. The court sentenced the defendant to prison and ordered him to pay $566,267 in restitution. On appeal, the court affirmed the prison sentence but reversed the restitution because the amount exceeded the actual loss suffered by the legitimate sellers of Zig-Zag rolling papers.[10] ■

Trade Names

Trademarks apply to *products*. The term **trade name** is used to indicate part or all of a business's name, whether the business is a sole proprietorship, a partnership, or a corporation. Generally, a trade name is directly related to a business and its goodwill. Trade names may be protected as trademarks if the trade name is the same as the name of the company's trademarked product—for example, Coca-Cola. Unless also used as a trademark or service mark, a trade name cannot be registered with the federal government. Trade names are protected under the common law, however. As with trademarks, words must be unusual or fancifully used if they are to be protected as trade names. The word *Safeway*, for instance, is sufficiently fanciful to obtain protection as a trade name for a grocery chain.

CYBER MARKS

In cyberspace, trademarks are sometimes referred to as **cyber marks**. We turn now to a discussion of trademark-related issues in cyberspace and how new laws and the courts are addressing these issues. One concern relates to the rights of a trademark's owner to use the mark as part of a domain name (Internet address). Other issues have to do with cybersquatting, meta tags, and trademark dilution on the Web. In some instances, licensing can be a way to avoid liability for infringing on another's intellectual property rights in cyberspace.

Domain Names

Conflicts over rights to domain names first emerged as e-commerce expanded on a worldwide scale and have reemerged in the last ten years. By using the same, or a similar, domain name, parties have attempted to profit from the goodwill of a competitor, to sell pornography, to offer for sale another party's domain name, and to otherwise infringe on others' trademarks. A **domain name** is the core part of an Internet address, such as "westlaw.edu." Every domain name ends with a top level domain (TLD), which is the part to the right of the period that indicates the type of entity that operates the site (for example, *edu* is an abbreviation for "educational").

The second level domain (SLD)—the part of the name to the left of the period—is chosen by the business entity or individual registering the domain name. Competition among firms with similar names and products for SLDs has caused numer-

---

8. Pub. L. No. 109-181 (2006), which amended 18 U.S.C. Sections 2318–2320.
9. See, for example, *United States v. Giles*, 213 F.3d 1247 (10th Cir. 2000).
10. For a case discussing the appropriate measure of restitution, see *United States v. Beydoun*, 469 F.3d 102 (5th Cir. 2006).

ous disputes over domain name rights. The Internet Corporation for Assigned Names and Numbers (ICANN), a nonprofit corporation, oversees the distribution of domain names. ICANN also facilitates the settlement of domain name disputes and operates an online arbitration system. Due to the vast number of recent complaints and disputes over domain names, ICANN completely overhauled the domain name distribution system and started selling domain names under a new system in mid-2009. One of the goals of the new system is to alleviate the problem of *cybersquatting*.

Anticybersquatting Legislation

Cybersquatting occurs when a person registers a domain name that is the same as, or confusingly similar to, the trademark of another and then offers to sell the domain name back to the trademark owner. During the 1990s, cybersquatting led to so much litigation that Congress passed the Anticybersquatting Consumer Protection Act of 1999 (ACPA), which amended the Lanham Act—the federal law protecting trademarks discussed earlier.

The ACPA makes it illegal for a person to "register, traffic in, or use" a domain name (1) if the name is identical or confusingly similar to the trademark of another and (2) if the one registering, trafficking in, or using the domain name has a "bad faith intent" to profit from that trademark. The act does not define what constitutes bad faith. Instead, it lists several factors that courts can consider in deciding whether bad faith exists. Some of these factors are whether there is an intent to divert consumers in a way that could harm the goodwill represented by the trademark, whether there is an offer to transfer or sell the domain name to the trademark owner, and whether there is an intent to use the domain name to offer goods and services.

The ACPA applies to all domain name registrations of trademarks, even domain names registered before the passage of the act. Successful plaintiffs in suits brought under the act can collect actual damages and profits or elect to receive statutory damages of $1,000 to $100,000.

Meta Tags

Search engines compile their results by looking through a Web site's key-word field. *Meta tags*, or key words, may be inserted into this field to increase the likelihood that a site will be included in search engine results, even though the site may have nothing to do with the inserted words. Using this same technique, one site may appropriate the key words of other sites with more frequent hits so that the appropriating site appears in the same search engine results as the more popular sites. Using another's trademark in a meta tag without the owner's permission, however, normally constitutes trademark infringement.

Some uses of another's trademark as a meta tag may be permissible if the use is reasonably necessary and does not suggest that the owner authorized or sponsored the use. **■EXAMPLE 5.9** Terri Welles, a former model who had been "Playmate of the Year" in *Playboy* magazine, established a Web site that used the terms *Playboy* and *Playmate* as meta tags. Playboy Enterprises, Inc., which publishes *Playboy*, filed suit seeking to prevent Welles from using these meta tags. The court determined that Welles's use of Playboy's meta tags to direct users to her Web site was permissible because it did not suggest sponsorship and there were no descriptive substitutes for the terms *Playboy* and *Playmate*.[11] **■**

Dilution in the Online World

As discussed earlier, trademark *dilution* occurs when a trademark is used, without authorization, in a way that diminishes the distinctive quality of the mark. Unlike trademark infringement, a claim of dilution does not require proof that consumers are likely to be confused by a connection between the unauthorized use and the mark. For this reason, the products involved do not have to be similar. In the first case alleging dilution on the Web, a court precluded the use of "candyland.com" as the URL for an adult site. The court held that the use of the URL would dilute the value of the "Candyland" mark owned by Hasbro, Inc., the maker of the Candyland children's game.[12]

Licensing

One of the ways to make use of another's trademark or other form of intellectual property, while avoiding litigation, is to obtain a license to do so. A **license** in this context is essentially an agreement permitting the use of a trademark, copyright, patent, or trade secret for certain limited purposes. The party that owns the intellectual property rights and issues the license is the *licensor*, and the party obtaining the license is the *licensee*. A license grants only the rights expressly described in the license agreement. A licensor might, for example, allow the licensee to use the trademark as part of its company name, or as part of its domain name, but not otherwise use the mark on any products or services.

Typically, license agreements are very detailed and should be carefully drafted. Disputes frequently arise over licensing agreements. **■EXAMPLE 5.10** Perry Ellis's products are well known in the apparel industry for their style and quality. Perry Ellis International, Inc. (PEI), owns a family of registered trademarks, including "Perry Ellis America" (the

---

11. *Playboy Enterprises, Inc. v. Welles*, 279 F.3d 796 (9th Cir. 2002).
12. *Hasbro, Inc. v. Internet Entertainment Group, Ltd.*, 1996 WL 84858 (W.D.Wash. 1996).

PEA trademark). The PEA trademark is distinctive and known worldwide as a mark of quality goods. In 2006, PEI entered into a license agreement with URI Corporation, which gave URI an exclusive license to manufacture and distribute footwear using the PEA trademark in Mexico. URI was required to comply with numerous conditions regarding the footwear and agreed to sell the shoes only in certain (listed) high-quality stores. URI was not permitted to authorize any other party to use the PEA trademark. Despite this explicit licensing agreement, PEI discovered that footwear bearing its PEA trademark was being sold in discount stores in Mexico. PEI terminated the licensing agreement and filed a lawsuit in a federal district court against URI. Ultimately, PEI was awarded more than $1 million in damages in the case.[13] ■

PATENTS

A **patent** is a grant from the government that gives an inventor the exclusive right to make, use, and sell an invention for a period of twenty years from the date of filing the application for a patent. Patents for designs, as opposed to inventions, are given for a fourteen-year period. For either a regular patent or a design patent, the applicant must demonstrate to the satisfaction of the U.S. Patent and Trademark Office that the invention, discovery, process, or design is *novel, useful,* and *not obvious* in light of current technology.

In contrast to patent law in many other countries, in the United States the first person to invent a product or process gets the patent rights rather than the first person to file for a patent on that product or process. Because it is difficult to prove who invented an item first, however, the first person to file an application is often deemed the first to invent (unless the inventor has detailed research notes or other evidence showing the date of invention). An inventor can publish the invention or offer it for sale prior to filing a patent application but must apply for a patent within one year of doing so or forfeit the patent rights. The period of patent protection begins on the date the patent application was filed, rather than when it was issued, which can sometimes be years later. After the patent period ends (either fourteen or twenty years later), the product or process enters the public domain, and anyone can make, sell, or use the invention without paying the patent holder.

Searchable Patent Databases

A significant development relating to patents is the availability online of the world's patent databases. The Web site of the U.S. Patent and Trademark Office provides searchable databases covering U.S. patents granted since 1976. The Web site of the European Patent Office provides online access to 50 million patent documents in more than seventy nations through a searchable network of databases. Businesses use these searchable databases in many ways. Because patents are valuable assets, businesses may need to perform patent searches to list or inventory their assets. Patent searches may also be conducted to study trends and patterns in a specific technology or to gather information about competitors in the industry. In addition, a business might search patent databases to develop a business strategy in a particular market or to evaluate a job applicant's contributions to a technology. Although online databases are accessible to anyone, businesspersons might consider hiring a specialist to perform advanced patent searches.

What Is Patentable?

Under federal law, "[w]hoever invents or discovers any new and useful process, machine, manufacture, or composition of matter, or any new and useful improvement thereof, may obtain a patent therefor, subject to the conditions and requirements of this title."[14] Thus, to be patentable, the item must be novel and not obvious.

Almost anything is patentable, except (1) the laws of nature, (2) natural phenomena, and (3) abstract ideas (including algorithms). Even artistic methods, certain works of art, and the structure of storylines are patentable, provided that they are novel and not obvious. Plants that are reproduced asexually (by means other than from seed), such as hybrid or genetically engineered plants, are patentable in the United States, as are genetically engineered (or cloned) microorganisms and animals.

In the following case, the focus was on the application of the test for proving whether a patent claim is "obvious."

---

13. *Perry Ellis International, Inc. v. URI Corp.,* __ F.Supp.2d __ (S.D.Fla. 2007).

14. 35 U.S.C. Section 101.

CASE 5.2	**KSR International Co. v. Teleflex, Inc.**

Supreme Court of the United States, __ U.S. __, 127 S.Ct. 1727, 167 L.Ed.2d 705 (2007).

FACTS Teleflex, Inc., sued KSR International Company for patent infringement. Teleflex holds the exclusive license to a patent for a device developed by Steven J. Engelgau. The patent issued is

CASE 5.2–Continued

entitled "Adjustable Pedal with Electronic Throttle Control." In brief, the Engelgau patent combines an electronic sensor with an adjustable automobile pedal so that the pedal's position can be transmitted to a computer that controls the throttle in the vehicle's engine. KSR contended that the patent in question could not create a claim because the subject matter was obvious. The district court concluded that the Engelgau patent was invalid because it was obvious—several existing patents already covered all of the important aspects of electronic pedal sensors for computer-controlled throttles. On appeal, the U.S. Court of Appeals for the Federal Circuit reversed the district court's ruling. KSR appealed to the United States Supreme Court.

ISSUE Was Teleflex's patent invalid because several existing patents already covered the important aspects of the adjustable automobile pedal with electronic throttle control making its invention obvious?

DECISION Yes. The United States Supreme Court reversed the judgment of the court of appeals and the case was remanded.

REASON The Court pointed out that in many previous decisions it had held "that a patent for a combination which only unites old elements with no change in their respective functions * * * obviously withdraws what is already known into the field of its monopoly and diminishes the resources available to skillful [persons]. * * * If a technique has been used to improve one device, and a person of ordinary skill in the art would recognize that it would improve similar devices in the same way, using the techniques is obvious unless its actual application is beyond his or her skill." In sum, the Court reasoned that there was little difference between what existed in the "teachings" of previously filed patents and the adjustable electronic pedal disclosed in the Engelgau patent.

 FOR CRITICAL ANALYSIS—Ethical Consideration *Based on the Court's reasoning, what other factors should be considered when determining the obviousness of a patent?*

Patent Infringement

If a firm makes, uses, or sells another's patented design, product, or process without the patent owner's permission, it commits the tort of patent infringement. Patent infringement may occur even though the patent owner has not put the patented product in commerce. Patent infringement may also occur even though not all features or parts of an invention are copied. (With respect to a patented process, however, all steps or their equivalent must be copied for infringement to exist.)

Note that, as a general rule, under U.S. law no patent infringement occurs when a patented product is made and sold in another country. **■EXAMPLE 5.11** In 2007, this issue came before the United States Supreme Court in a patent infringement case that AT&T Corporation had brought against Microsoft Corporation. AT&T holds a patent on a device used to digitally encode, compress, and process recorded speech. Microsoft's Windows operating system, as Microsoft admitted, incorporated software code that infringed on AT&T's patent. The only question before the Supreme Court was whether Microsoft's liability extended to computers made in another country. The Court held that it did not. Microsoft was liable only for infringement in the United States and not for the Windows-based computers sold in for-

eign locations. The Court reasoned that Microsoft had not "supplied" the software for the computers but had only electronically transmitted a master copy, which the foreign manufacturers then copied and loaded onto the computers.[15] ■

Remedies for Patent Infringement

If a patent is infringed, the patent holder may sue for relief in federal court. The patent holder can seek an injunction against the infringer and can also request damages for royalties and lost profits. In some cases, the court may grant the winning party reimbursement for attorneys' fees and costs. If the court determines that the infringement was willful, the court can triple the amount of damages awarded (treble damages).

In the past, permanent injunctions were routinely granted to prevent future infringement. In 2006, however, the United States Supreme Court ruled that patent holders are not automatically entitled to a permanent injunction against future infringing activities—the federal courts have discretion to decide whether equity requires it. According to the Supreme Court, a patent holder must prove that it has suffered

---

15. *Microsoft Corp. v. AT&T Corp.,* ___ U.S. ___, 127 S.Ct. 1746, 167 L.Ed.2d 737 (2007).

irreparable injury and that the public interest would not be disserved by a permanent injunction.[16]

This decision gives courts discretion to decide what is equitable in the circumstances and allows them to consider what is in the public interest rather than just the interests of the parties. For example, in the first case applying this rule, a court found that although Microsoft had infringed on the patent of a small software company, the latter was not entitled to an injunction. According to the court, the small company was not irreparably harmed and could be adequately compensated by damages. Also, the public might suffer negative effects from an injunction because the infringement involved part of Microsoft's widely used Office suite software.[17]

 **PREVENTING LEGAL DISPUTES** **Litigation over whether a patent has been infringed is always expensive and often requires a team of experts to investigate and analyze the commercial, technical, and legal aspects of the case. Because of these costs, a businessperson facing patent infringement litigation—either as the patent holder or as the alleged infringer—should carefully evaluate the evidence as well as the various settlement options. If both sides appear to have good arguments, it may be in a firm's best interest to settle the case. This is particularly true if the firm is not certain that the court would grant an injunction. Similarly, if the patented technology is not commercially significant to one's business, it might be best to consider a nonexclusive license as a means of resolving the dispute.**

■

COPYRIGHTS

A **copyright** is an intangible property right granted by federal statute to the author or originator of certain literary or artistic productions. Currently, copyrights are governed by the Copyright Act of 1976,[18] as amended. Works created after January 1, 1978, are automatically given statutory copyright protection for the life of the author plus 70 years. For copyrights owned by publishing houses, the copyright expires 95 years from the date of publication or 120 years from the date of creation, whichever is first. For works by more than one author, the copyright expires 70 years after the death of the last surviving author.

These time periods reflect the extensions of the length of copyright protection enacted by Congress in the Copyright Term Extension Act of 1998.[19] Critics challenged this act as overstepping the bounds of Congress's power and violating the constitutional requirement that copyrights endure for only a limited time. In 2003, however, the United States Supreme Court upheld the act in *Eldred v. Ashcroft*.[20] This ruling obviously favored copyright holders by preventing copyrighted works from the 1920s and 1930s from losing protection and falling into the public domain for an additional two decades.

Copyrights can be registered with the U.S. Copyright Office in Washington, D.C. A copyright owner no longer needs to place a © or *Copr.* or *Copyright* on the work, however, to have the work protected against infringement. Chances are that if somebody created it, somebody owns it.

What Is Protected Expression?

Works that are copyrightable include books, records, films, artworks, architectural plans, menus, music videos, product packaging, and computer software. To be protected, a work must be "fixed in a durable medium" from which it can be perceived, reproduced, or communicated. Protection is automatic. Registration is not required.

To obtain protection under the Copyright Act, a work must be original and fall into one of the following categories:

1 Literary works (including newspaper and magazine articles, computer and training manuals, catalogues, brochures, and print advertisements).

2 Musical works and accompanying words (including advertising jingles).

3 Dramatic works and accompanying music.

4 Pantomimes and choreographic works (including ballets and other forms of dance).

5 Pictorial, graphic, and sculptural works (including cartoons, maps, posters, statues, and even stuffed animals).

6 Motion pictures and other audiovisual works (including multimedia works).

7 Sound recordings.

8 Architectural works.

Section 102 Exclusions Section 102 of the Copyright Act specifically excludes copyright protection for any "idea, procedure, process, system, method of operation, concept, principle, or discovery, regardless of the form in which it is described, explained, illustrated, or embodied." Note that it is

---

16. *eBay, Inc. v. MercExchange, LLC*, 547 U.S. 388, 126 S.Ct. 1837, 164 L.Ed.2d 641 (2006).

17. *z4 Technologies, Inc. v. Microsoft Corp.*, 434 F.Supp.2d 437 (E.D.Tex. 2006). See also *Printguard, Inc. v. Anti-Marking Systems, Inc.*, 535 F.Supp.2d 189 (D.Mass. 2008).

18. 17 U.S.C. Sections 101 *et seq.*

19. 17 U.S.C.A. Section 302.

20. 537 U.S. 186, 123 S.Ct. 769, 154 L.Ed.2d 683 (2003).

not possible to copyright an *idea*. The underlying ideas embodied in a work may be freely used by others. What is copyrightable is the particular way in which an idea is *expressed*. Whenever an idea and an expression are inseparable, the expression cannot be copyrighted. Generally, anything that is not an original expression will not qualify for copyright protection. Facts widely known to the public are not copyrightable. Page numbers are not copyrightable because they follow a sequence known to everyone. Mathematical calculations are not copyrightable.

Compilations of Facts   Unlike ideas, *compilations* of facts are copyrightable. Under Section 103 of the Copyright Act, a compilation is "a work formed by the collection and assembling of preexisting materials or of data that are selected, coordinated, or arranged in such a way that the resulting work as a whole constitutes an original work of authorship." The key requirement for the copyrightability of a compilation is originality. **■EXAMPLE 5.12** The White Pages of a telephone directory do not qualify for copyright protection when the information that makes up the directory (names, addresses, and telephone numbers) is not selected, coordinated, or arranged in an original way. ■

Copyright Infringement

Whenever the form or expression of an idea is copied, an infringement of copyright occurs. The reproduction does not have to be exactly the same as the original, nor does it have to reproduce the original in its entirety. If a substantial part of the original is reproduced, there is copyright infringement.

Damages for Copyright Infringement   Those who infringe copyrights may be liable for damages or criminal penalties. These range from actual damages or statutory damages, imposed at the court's discretion, to criminal proceedings for willful violations. Actual damages are based on the harm caused to the copyright holder by the infringement, while statutory damages, not to exceed $150,000, are provided for under the Copyright Act. In addition, criminal proceedings may result in fines and/or imprisonment.

The "Fair Use" Exception   An exception to liability for copyright infringement is made under the "fair use" doctrine. In certain circumstances, a person or organization can reproduce copyrighted material without paying royalties (fees paid to the copyright holder for the privilege of reproducing the copyrighted material). Section 107 of the Copyright Act provides as follows:

> [T]he fair use of a copyrighted work, including such use by reproduction in copies or phonorecords or by any other means specified by [Section 106 of the Copyright Act,] for purposes such as criticism, comment, news reporting, teaching (including multiple copies for classroom use), scholarship, or research, is not an infringement of copyright. In determining whether the use made of a work in any particular case is a fair use the factors to be considered shall include—
>
> (1) the purpose and character of the use, including whether such use is of a commercial nature or is for nonprofit educational purposes;
> (2) the nature of the copyrighted work;
> (3) the amount and substantiality of the portion used in relation to the copyrighted work as a whole; and
> (4) the effect of the use upon the potential market for or value of the copyrighted work.

Because these guidelines are very broad, the courts determine whether a particular use is fair on a case-by-case basis. Thus, anyone reproducing copyrighted material may be committing a violation. In determining whether a use is fair, courts have often considered the fourth factor to be the most important.

In the following case, the owner of copyrighted music had issued a license to the manufacturer of karaoke devices to reproduce the sound recordings, but had not given its permission to reprint the song lyrics. The issue was whether the manufacturer should pay additional fees to display the lyrics at the same time as the music was playing. The manufacturer claimed, among other things, that its use of the lyrics was educational and therefore did not constitute copyright infringement under the fair use exception.

CASE 5.3   **Leadsinger, Inc. v. BMG Music Publishing**

United States Court of Appeals, Ninth Circuit, 512 F.3d 522 (2008).
www.ca9.uscourts.gov[a]

FACTS   Leadsinger, Inc., manufactures and sells karaoke

devices. Specifically, it sells a microphone that has a chip inside with embedded songs and lyrics that appear at the bottom of a TV screen. This device is similar to those in which

a. Click on "Opinions." When that page opens, click on "2008" and then on "January." Scroll down to "01/02/08." Find the case name and click on it to access the opinion.

CASE 5.3–Continues next page

CASE 5.3–Continued

compact discs and DVDs are inserted to display lyrics on a TV monitor. All karaoke devices necessarily involve copyrighted works. BMG Music Publishing owns and administers copyrights for such music. BMG had issued to Leadsinger the appropriate licenses to copyrighted musical compositions under Section 115 of the Copyright Act. Leadsinger sought a declaration that it was entitled to print or display song lyrics in real time with song recordings without paying any additional fees. In contrast, BMG demanded that Leadsinger and other karaoke companies pay a "lyric reprint" fee and a "synchronization" fee. Leadsinger refused to pay, filing for a declaratory judgment to resolve whether it had the right to display song lyrics in real time with sound recordings without paying any additional fees. The district court concluded that a Section 115 license did not grant Leadsinger the right to display visual images *and* lyrics in real time with music. Leadsinger appealed to the U.S. Court of Appeals for the Ninth Circuit.

ISSUE Was Leadsinger's real-time display of lyrics in a karaoke device educational and therefore not copyright infringement under the fair use exception?

DECISION No. The U.S. Court of Appeals for the Ninth Circuit affirmed the district court's decision dismissing

Leadsinger's request for a declaratory judgment. Leadsinger did not have a right under the fair use doctrine to display lyrics in real time with music without first obtaining a license to do so from the copyright holder.

REASON The court reasoned that a copyright holder has a right to control "the synchronization of musical compositions with the content of audiovisual works." Consequently, courts have required parties to obtain synchronization licenses from copyright holders. Moreover, "lyrics are copyrightable as a literary work and, therefore, enjoy separate protection under the Copyright Act." Leadsinger's microchip that stores visual images and visual representations of lyrics falls within the definition of an audiovisual work. Leadsinger could not avail itself of the fair use doctrine simply by arguing that karaoke devices help teach singing.

 FOR CRITICAL ANALYSIS—Global Consideration *Could Leadsinger have attempted to show that its karaoke programs were used extensively abroad to help others learn English? If successful in this line of reasoning, might Leadsinger have prevailed on appeal? Explain your answer.*

Copyright Protection for Software

In 1980, Congress passed the Computer Software Copyright Act, which amended the Copyright Act of 1976 to include computer programs in the list of creative works protected by federal copyright law. The 1980 statute, which classifies computer programs as "literary works," defines a computer program as a "set of statements or instructions to be used directly or indirectly in a computer in order to bring about a certain result."

Because of the unique nature of computer programs, the courts have had many problems applying and interpreting the 1980 act. Generally, though, the courts have held that copyright protection extends not only to those parts of a computer program that can be read by humans, such as the high-level language of a source code, but also to the binary-language object code of a computer program, which is readable only by the computer. Additionally, such elements as the overall structure, sequence, and organization of a program have been deemed copyrightable. For the most part, however, the courts have not extended copyright protection to the "look and feel"—the general appearance, command structure, video images, menus, windows, and other screen displays—of computer programs.

Copyrights in Digital Information

Copyright law is the most important form of intellectual property protection on the Internet. This is because much of the material on the Internet consists of works of authorship (including multimedia presentations, software, and database information), which are the traditional focus of copyright law. Copyright law is also important because the nature of the Internet requires that data be "copied" to be transferred online. Copies have traditionally been a significant part of the controversies arising in this area of the law.

The Copyright Act of 1976 When Congress drafted the principal U.S. law governing copyrights, the Copyright Act of 1976, cyberspace did not exist for most of us, and the primary threat to copyright owners was from persons making unauthorized *tangible* copies of works. Because of the nature of cyberspace, however, one of the early controversies was determining at what point an intangible, electronic "copy" of a work has been made. The courts held that loading a file or program into a computer's random access memory, or RAM, constitutes the making of a "copy" for purposes of copyright law. RAM is a portion of a computer's memory into which a file, for instance, is loaded so that it can be accessed (read or written over). Thus, a copyright is infringed when a party downloads software into RAM without owning the software or otherwise having a right to download it.

Today, technology has vastly increased the potential for copyright infringement. For a discussion of whether search engines that use thumbnail images of copyrighted materials are liable for infringement, see this chapter's *Adapting the Law to the Online Environment* feature on pages 114 and 115.

Further Developments in Copyright Law Before 1997, criminal penalties under copyright law could be imposed only if unauthorized copies were exchanged for financial gain. Yet much piracy of copyrighted materials was "altruistic" in nature; unauthorized copies were made and distributed not for financial gain but simply for reasons of generosity—to share the copies with others.

To combat altruistic piracy and for other reasons, Congress passed the No Electronic Theft (NET) Act of 1997.[21] This act extends criminal liability for the piracy of copyrighted materials to persons who exchange unauthorized copies of copyrighted works, such as software, even though they realize no profit from the exchange. The act also imposes penalties on those who make unauthorized electronic copies of books, magazines, movies, or music for *personal* use, thus altering the traditional "fair use" doctrine. The criminal penalties for violating the act are steep; they include fines as high as $250,000 and incarceration for up to five years.

In 1998, Congress implemented the provisions of the World Intellectual Property Organization (WIPO) treaty by updating U.S. copyright law. The law—the Digital Millennium Copyright Act of 1998—is a landmark step in the protection of copyright owners and, because of the leading position of the United States in the creative industries, serves as a model for other nations. Among other things, the act established civil and criminal penalties for anyone who circumvents (bypasses—or gets around—through clever maneuvering, for example) encryption software or other technological antipiracy protection. Also prohibited are the manufacture, import, sale, and distribution of devices or services for circumvention.

MP3 and File-Sharing Technology

Soon after the Internet became popular, a few enterprising programmers created software to compress large data files, particularly those associated with music. The reduced file sizes make transmitting music over the Internet feasible. The most widely known compression and decompression system is MP3, which enables music fans to download songs or entire CDs onto their computers or onto a portable listening device, such as an iPod. The MP3 system also made it possible for music fans to access other music fans' files by engaging in file-sharing via the Internet.

File-sharing via the Internet is accomplished through what is called **peer-to-peer (P2P) networking.** The concept is simple. Rather than going through a central Web server, P2P involves numerous personal computers (PCs) that are connected to the Internet. Files stored on one PC can be accessed by other individuals who are members of the same network. Sometimes, this is called a **distributed network.** In other words, parts of the network are distributed all over the country or the world. File-sharing offers an unlimited number of uses for distributed networks. For instance, thousands of researchers allow their home computers' computing power to be simultaneously accessed through file-sharing software so that very large mathematical problems can be solved quickly. Additionally, persons scattered throughout the country or the world can work together on the same project by using file-sharing programs.

Sharing Stored Music Files When file-sharing is used to download others' stored music files, copyright issues arise. Recording artists and their labels stand to lose large amounts of royalties and revenues if relatively few CDs are purchased and then made available on distributed networks, from which everyone can get them for free. The issue of file-sharing infringement has been the subject of an ongoing debate for some time.

■**EXAMPLE 5.13** In the highly publicized case of *A&M Records, Inc. v. Napster, Inc.,*[22] several firms in the recording industry sued Napster, Inc., the owner of the then-popular Napster Web site. The Napster site provided registered users with free software that enabled them to transfer exact copies of the contents of MP3 files from one computer to another via the Internet. Napster also maintained centralized search indices so that users could locate specific titles or artists' recordings on the computers of other members. The firms argued that Napster should be liable for contributory and vicarious[23] (indirect) copyright infringement because it assisted others in obtaining copies of copyrighted music without the copyright owners' permission. Both the federal district court and the U.S. Court of Appeals for the Ninth Circuit agreed and held Napster liable for violating copyright laws. The court reasoned that Napster was liable for its users' infringement because the technology that Napster had used was centralized and gave it "the ability to locate infringing material listed on its search indices and the right to terminate users' access to the system." ■

After the *Napster* decision, the recording industry filed and won numerous lawsuits against companies that distribute

---

21. 17 U.S.C. Sections 2311, 2319, 2319A, 2320; and 28 U.S.C. Sections 994, 1498.

22. 239 F.3d 1004 (9th Cir. 2001).

23. *Vicarious (indirect) liability* exists when one person is subject to liability for another's actions.

ADAPTING THE LAW TO THE ONLINE ENVIRONMENT   Search Engines versus Copyright Owners

Since their humble beginnings more than a decade ago, search engines have become ubiquitous in the e-commerce world. Every day, millions of consumers use search engines to locate various products on the Web. A major legal question arises, however, when the results of a search include copyrighted intellectual property, such as books, downloadable software, movies and other videos, and images. Can the owner of the search engine that returned these results be held liable for copyright infringement?

The Betamax Doctrine

The basic rule that has governed issues relating to the application of new technology for uses that might include copyright infringement was set out more than two decades ago by the United States Supreme Court in the landmark case *Sony Corporation of America v. Universal City Studios*.[a] The case involved the then new technology of the videocassette recorder (VCR), which was available in two formats—VHS and Betamax. Owners of copyrighted television programs, con-

cerned that VCR owners were using the equipment to copy TV programs, brought a suit against a VCR manufacturer, claiming that it was liable for its customers' copyright infringement. The Supreme Court, however, in what became known as the *Betamax doctrine*, held that the manufacturer was not liable for creating a technology that certain customers might use for copyright infringing purposes, as long as that technology was capable of substantial noninfringing uses. Legal scholars believe that the Betamax doctrine has allowed for the development of many other technologies that are capable of both infringing and noninfringing uses—including CD-ROM burners, DVRs, TiVo, Apple's iPod, and even the personal computer.

As discussed later in the text, twenty years after the *Sony* case, organizations and companies in the music and film industry brought a copyright infringement suit against Grokster, Morpheus, and KaZaA, the makers of file-sharing software that allowed millions of individuals to copy copyrighted music. In that case, the Supreme Court did find that there was ample evidence that the software makers had taken steps to promote copyright infringement, but significantly the Court did not overturn the Betamax doctrine. The Court did not specify what steps are necessary to impose liability on the provider of a technology, however.[b]

b. *Metro-Goldwyn-Mayer Studios, Inc. v. Grokster, Ltd.*, 545 U.S. 913, 125 S.Ct. 2764, 162 L.Ed.2d 781 (2005).

a. 464 U.S. 417, 104 S.Ct. 774, 78 L.Ed.2d 574 (1984).

---

online file-sharing software. The courts held these companies liable based on two theories: contributory infringement, which applies if the company had reason to know about a user's infringement and failed to stop it; and vicarious liability, which exists if the company was able to control the users' activities and stood to benefit financially from their infringement.

The Evolution of File-Sharing Technologies In the wake of the *Napster* decision, other companies developed technologies that allow P2P network users to share stored music files, without paying a fee, more quickly and efficiently than ever. Software such as Morpheus, KaZaA, and LimeWire, for example, provides users with an interface that is similar to a Web browser.[24] Instead of the company's locating songs for users on other members' computers, the software automatically annotates files with descriptive information so that the music can easily be categorized and cross-referenced (by artist and title, for instance). When a user

performs a search, the software is able to locate a list of peers that have the file available for downloading. Also, to expedite the P2P transfer, the software distributes the download task over the entire list of peers simultaneously. By downloading even one file, the user becomes a point of distribution for that file, which is then automatically shared with others on the network.

Because the file-sharing software was decentralized and did not use search indices that would enable the companies to locate infringing material, the companies had no ability to supervise or control which music (or other media files) their users exchanged. In addition, it was difficult for courts to apply the traditional doctrines of contributory and vicarious liability to these new technologies.

The Supreme Court's *Grokster* Decision In 2005, the United States Supreme Court expanded the liability of file-sharing companies in its decision in *Metro-Goldwyn-Mayer Studios, Inc. v. Grokster, Ltd.*[25] In that case, organizations in

---

24. Note that in 2005, KaZaA entered into a settlement agreement with four major music companies that had alleged copyright infringement. KaZaA agreed to offer only legitimate, fee-based music downloads in the future.

25. 545 U.S. 913, 125 S.Ct. 2764, 162 L.Ed.2d 781 (2005).

Does Providing Thumbnail Images Violate Copyright Law?

Just as VCRs and file-sharing technology raised new issues of copyright infringement, so does today's search engine technology. In response to a search request, numerous search engines show thumbnail images of books, album covers, and copyrighted photographs. Arriba Soft Corporation (now ditto.com), for example, operated a search engine that displayed its results in the form of thumbnail pictures. It obtained its database of photographs by copying images from other Web sites. When professional photographer Leslie Kelly discovered that his copyrighted photographs were part of Arriba's database, he brought a suit for copyright infringement. Arriba prevailed, as the Ninth Circuit Court of Appeals ruled that its thumbnails were a fair use under the Copyright Act.[c]

A recent innovation enables search engines to search specifically for images. Google Image Search, for example, stores thumbnail images of its search results on Google's servers. The thumbnail images are reduced, lower-resolution versions of full-size images stored on third party computers. In 2005, *Perfect 10*, a men's magazine that features high-resolution photographs of topless and nude women, brought a suit to enjoin Google from caching and displaying its photographs as thumbnails. *Perfect 10* argued that because Google "created the audience" for its sites and indexes, Google should be liable for whatever infringements occurred

on those sites. The magazine also contended that Google had directly infringed *Perfect 10's* copyrights by in-line linking and framing images published on other sites. (The case was combined with a similar suit brought against Amazon.com for its A9 search engine.) Once again, however, as in its *Arriba* decision, the Ninth Circuit Court of Appeals held that the thumbnails constituted a fair use. Pointing out the public benefit that search engines provide, the court said that until *Perfect 10* gave Google specific URLs for infringing images, Google had no duty to act and could not be held liable. The court further held that Google could not "supervise or control" the third party Web sites linked to its search results.[d] In sum, the court refused to hold the creators of image search technology liable for users' infringement because the technology is capable of both infringing and noninfringing uses—just as the Betamax doctrine protected VCR manufacturers from liability for users' infringement.

FOR CRITICAL ANALYSIS *What has changed in the world of technology since the Betamax doctrine was enunciated? Does the fact that more and more intellectual property is being digitized and made available online alter the reasoning underlying the Betamax doctrine?*

c. *Kelly v. Arriba Soft Corporation*, 336 F.3d 811 (9th Cir. 2003).

d. *Perfect 10, Inc. v. Amazon.com, Inc.*, 487 F.3d 701 (9th Cir. 2007).

the music and film industry (the plaintiffs) sued several companies that distribute file-sharing software used in P2P networks, including Grokster, Ltd., and StreamCast Networks, Inc. (the defendants). The plaintiffs claimed that the companies were contributorily and vicariously liable for the infringement of their end users. The Supreme Court held that "one who distributes a device [software] with the object of promoting its use to infringe the copyright, as shown by clear expression or other affirmative steps taken to foster infringement, is liable for the resulting acts of infringement by third parties."

Although the Supreme Court did not specify what kind of affirmative steps are necessary to establish liability, it did note that there was ample evidence that the defendants had acted with the intent to cause copyright violations. (Grokster later settled this dispute out of court and stopped distributing its software.) Essentially, this means that file-sharing companies that have taken affirmative steps to promote copyright infringement can be held secondarily liable for millions of infringing acts that their users commit daily. Because the Court did not define exactly what is necessary to impose liability, however, a substantial amount of legal

uncertainty remains concerning this issue. Although some file-sharing companies have been shut down, illegal file-sharing—and lawsuits against file-sharing companies and the individuals who use them—has continued in the years since this decision.[26]

TRADE SECRETS

The law of trade secrets protects some business processes and information that are not or cannot be patented, copyrighted, or trademarked against appropriation by a competitor. **Trade secrets** include customer lists, plans, research and development, pricing information, marketing techniques, production methods, and generally anything that makes an individual company unique and that would have value to a competitor.

Unlike copyright and trademark protection, protection of trade secrets extends both to ideas and to their expression.

26. See, for example, *Sony BMG Music Entertainment v. Villarreal*, __ F.Supp2d __ (D.Ga. 2007).

(For this reason, and because a trade secret involves no filing requirements, trade secret protection may be well suited for software.) Of course, the secret formula, method, or other information must be disclosed to some persons, particularly to key employees. Businesses generally attempt to protect their trade secrets by having all employees who use the process or information agree in their contracts, or in confidentiality agreements, never to divulge it. See this chapter's *Management Perspective* feature for more advice on how a business can protect its trade secrets.

State and Federal Law on Trade Secrets

Under Section 757 of the *Restatement of Torts*, those who disclose or use another's trade secret, without authorization, are liable to that other party if (1) they discovered the secret by improper means or (2) their disclosure or use constitutes a breach of a duty owed to the other party. The theft of confidential business data by industrial espionage, as when a business taps into a competitor's computer, is a theft of trade secrets without any contractual violation and is actionable in itself.

Until nearly thirty years ago, virtually all law with respect to trade secrets was common law. In an effort to reduce the unpredictability of the common law in this area, a model act, the Uniform Trade Secrets Act, was presented to the states for adoption in 1979. Parts of this act have been adopted in more than thirty states. Typically, a state that has adopted parts of the act has adopted only those parts that encompass its own existing common law. Additionally, in 1996 Congress passed the Economic Espionage Act, which made the theft of trade secrets a federal crime. We will examine the provisions and significance of this act in Chapter 6, in the context of crimes related to business.

Trade Secrets in Cyberspace

The nature of computer technology undercuts a business firm's ability to protect its confidential information, including trade secrets. For instance, a dishonest employee could e-mail trade secrets in a company's computer to a competitor or a future employer. If e-mail is not an option, the employee might walk out with the information on a portable device, such as a flash drive. For an overall summary of trade secrets and other forms of intellectual property, see Exhibit 5–1 on page 118.

INTERNATIONAL PROTECTION FOR INTELLECTUAL PROPERTY

For many years, the United States has been a party to various international agreements relating to intellectual property rights. For example, the Paris Convention of 1883, to which

about 172 countries are signatory, allows parties in one country to file for patent and trademark protection in any of the other member countries. Other international agreements include the Berne Convention and the Trade-Related Aspects of Intellectual Property Rights, or, more simply, TRIPS agreement.

The Berne Convention

Under the Berne Convention of 1886, an international copyright agreement, if a U.S. citizen writes a book, every country that has signed the convention must recognize the U.S. author's copyright in the book. Also, if a citizen of a country that has not signed the convention first publishes a book in one of the 170 countries that have signed, all other countries that have signed the convention must recognize that author's copyright. Copyright notice is not needed to gain protection under the Berne Convention for works published after March 1, 1989.

This convention and other international agreements have given some protection to intellectual property on a worldwide level. None of them, however, has been as significant and far reaching in scope as the agreement discussed next.

The TRIPS Agreement

Representatives from more than one hundred nations signed the TRIPS agreement in 1994. The agreement established, for the first time, standards for the international protection of intellectual property rights, including patents, trademarks, and copyrights for movies, computer programs, books, and music. The TRIPS agreement provides that each member country must include in its domestic laws broad intellectual property rights and effective remedies (including civil and criminal penalties) for violations of those rights.

Members Cannot Discriminate against Foreign Intellectual Property Owners Generally, the TRIPS agreement forbids member nations from discriminating against foreign owners of intellectual property rights (in the administration, regulation, or adjudication of such rights). In other words, a member nation cannot give its own nationals (citizens) favorable treatment without offering the same treatment to nationals of all member countries. **EXAMPLE 5.14** A U.S. software manufacturer brings a lawsuit in Germany for the infringement of intellectual property rights under Germany's national laws. Because Germany is a member nation, the U.S. manufacturer is entitled to receive the same treatment as a German manufacturer. ■ Each member nation must also ensure that legal procedures are available for parties who wish to bring actions for infringement of intellectual property rights. Additionally, a related document

MANAGEMENT PERSPECTIVE — Protecting Trade Secrets

Management Faces a Legal Issue

Most successful businesses have trade secrets. The law protects trade secrets indefinitely provided that the information is not

generally known, is kept secret, and has commercial value. Sometimes, of course, a business needs to disclose secret information to a party in the course of conducting business. For example, a company may engage a consultant to revamp a computer system or hire a marketing firm to implement a sales program. In addition, the company may wish to expand its operations and will need a foreign agent or distributor. All of these individuals or firms may need access to some of the company's trade secrets. One way to protect against the unauthorized disclosure of such information is through *confidentiality agreements.* In such an agreement, one party promises not to divulge information about the other party's activities to anyone else and not to use the other party's confidential information for his or her own benefit. Most confidentiality agreements are included in licensing and employment contracts. The legal question is whether the courts will uphold such an agreement if a business claims it has been violated.

What the Courts Say

The courts are divided on the validity of confidentiality agreements, particularly in employment contracts. Often, the issue is whether the trade secrets described in the agreement are truly "secrets." If they are generally known outside the employer's business, the courts normally will not enforce the agreement. When the employer can demonstrate that such secrets are truly secret, a court usually will enforce a confidentiality agreement. For example, an insurance company employee signed both a confidentiality agreement and a *noncompete* clause (see Chapter 9). Just before quitting, that employee copied her employer's proprietary sales, marketing, and product information sheets. She then

used them while working for her new employer. She also solicited former clients to move their business to her new employer's firm. An appellate court upheld an injunction preventing this employee from using, divulging, disclosing, or communicating trade secrets and confidential information derived from her former employer.[a]

Confidentiality agreements are often used in the technology sector for obvious reasons. One case involved a complicated system for testing flash memory cards, like those used in digital cameras and MP3 music players. An employee copied project documents he had authored and transmitted them to a third party so that he could use them to launch his own independent business. This employee had signed an explicit confidentiality agreement. At trial, one of his defenses was that his former employer had not used reasonable efforts to maintain secrecy because some employees were uncertain how to apply the company's procedures for handling trade secrets. The court was unimpressed. The former employee was prevented from using those trade secrets.[b]

Employers often attempt to protect trade secrets by requiring potential employees to sign noncompete agreements. If the employer would suffer irreparable harm from the former employee's accepting employment with a competitor, a court will often uphold such an agreement.[c]

Implications for Managers

Most companies should require their employees to sign confidentiality agreements. That is not enough to protect trade secrets, though. A company should have formal written procedures that apply to the selection and retention of documents relating to valuable trade secrets. If these documents exist only on hard drives, the firm should put an encryption system in place and limit access to the files that contain trade secrets.

a. *Freeman v. Brown Hiller, Inc.,* 102 Ark.App. 76, ___ S.W.3d ___ (2008).
b. *Verigy US, Inc. v. Mayder,* ___ F.Supp.2d ___, 2008 WL 564634 (N.D.Cal. 2008).
c. *Gleeson v. Preferred Sourcing, LLC,* 883 N.E.2d 164 (Ind.App. 2008).

established a mechanism for settling disputes among member nations.

Covers All Types of Intellectual Property Particular provisions of the TRIPS agreement relate to patent, trademark, and copyright protection for intellectual property. The agree-

ment specifically provides copyright protection for computer programs by stating that compilations of data, databases, or other materials are "intellectual creations" and that they are to be protected as copyrightable works. Other provisions relate to trade secrets and the rental of computer programs and cinematographic works.

EXHIBIT 5–1 **Forms of Intellectual Property**

	DEFINITION	HOW ACQUIRED	DURATION	REMEDY FOR INFRINGEMENT
Patent	A grant from the government that gives an inventor exclusive rights to an invention.	By filing a patent application with the U.S. Patent and Trademark Office and receiving its approval.	Twenty years from the date of the application; for design patents, fourteen years.	Monetary damages, including royalties and lost profits, *plus* attorneys' fees. Damages may be tripled for intentional infringements.
Copyright	The right of an author or originator of a literary or artistic work, or other production that falls within a specified category, to have the exclusive use of that work for a given period of time.	Automatic (once the work or creation is put in tangible form). Only the *expression* of an idea (and not the idea itself) can be protected by copyright.	For authors: the life of the author plus 70 years. For publishers: 95 years after the date of publication or 120 years after creation.	Actual damages plus profits received by the party who infringed *or* statutory damages under the Copyright Act, *plus* costs and attorneys' fees in either situation.
Trademark (service mark and trade dress)	Any distinctive word, name, symbol, or device (image or appearance), or combination thereof, that an entity uses to distinguish its goods or services from those of others. The owner has the exclusive right to use that mark or trade dress.	1. At common law, ownership created by use of the mark. 2. Registration with the appropriate federal or state office gives notice and is permitted if the mark is currently in use or will be within the next six months.	Unlimited, as long as it is in use. To continue notice by registration, the owner must renew by filing between the fifth and sixth years, and thereafter, every ten years.	1. Injunction prohibiting the future use of the mark. 2. Actual damages plus profits received by the party who infringed (can be increased under the Lanham Act). 3. Destruction of articles that infringed. 4. *Plus* costs and attorneys' fees.
Trade secret	Any information that a business possesses and that gives the business an advantage over competitors (including formulas, lists, patterns, plans, processes, and programs).	Through the originality and development of the information and processes that constitute the business secret and are unknown to others.	Unlimited, so long as not revealed to others. Once revealed to others, it is no longer a trade secret.	Monetary damages for misappropriation (the Uniform Trade Secrets Act also permits punitive damages if willful), *plus* costs and attorneys' fees.

The Madrid Protocol

In the past, one of the difficulties in protecting U.S. trademarks internationally was that applying for trademark registration in foreign countries was time consuming and expensive. The filing fees and procedures for trademark registration vary significantly among individual countries. The Madrid Protocol, however, which President George W. Bush signed into law in the fall of 2003, may help to resolve these problems. The Madrid Protocol is an international treaty that has been signed by sixty-eight countries. Under its provisions, a U.S. company wishing to register its trademark abroad can submit a single application and designate other member countries in which it would like to register the mark. The treaty is designed to reduce the costs of obtaining international trademark protection by more than 60 percent, according to proponents.

Although the Madrid Protocol may simplify and reduce the cost of trademark registration in foreign nations, it remains to be seen whether it will provide significant benefits to trademark owners. Even with an easier registration process, the issue of whether member countries will enforce the law and protect the mark still remains.

REVIEWING Intellectual Property and Internet Law

Two computer science majors, Trent and Xavier, have an idea for a new video game, which they propose to call "Hallowed." They form a business and begin developing their idea. Several months later, Trent and Xavier run into a problem with their design and consult with a friend, Brad, who is an expert in creating computer source codes. After the software is completed but before Hallowed is marketed, a video game called Halo 2 is released for both the Xbox and Game Cube systems. Halo 2 uses source codes similar to those of Hallowed and imitates Hallowed's overall look and feel, although not all the features are alike. Using the information presented in the chapter, answer the following questions.

1 Would the name "Hallowed" receive protection as a trademark or as trade dress?

2 If Trent and Xavier had obtained a business process patent on Hallowed, would the release of Halo 2 infringe on their patent? Why or why not?

3 Based only on the facts described above, could Trent and Xavier sue the makers of Halo 2 for copyright infringement? Why or why not?

4 Suppose that Trent and Xavier discover that Brad took the idea of Hallowed and sold it to the company that produced Halo 2. Which type of intellectual property issue does this raise?

TERMS AND CONCEPTS

certification mark 105
collective mark 105
copyright 110
cyber mark 106
cybersquatting 107
distributed network 113

domain name 106
intellectual property 102
license 107
patent 108
peer-to-peer (P2P)
    networking 113

service mark 105
trade dress 105
trade name 106
trade secret 115
trademark 102

CHAPTER SUMMARY Intellectual Property and Internet Law

Trademarks and Related Property (See pages 102–106.)	1. A *trademark* is a distinctive mark, motto, device, or emblem that a manufacturer stamps, prints, or otherwise affixes to the goods it produces so that they may be identified on the market and their origin vouched for.
	2. The major federal statutes protecting trademarks and related property are the Lanham Act of 1946 and the Federal Trademark Dilution Act of 1995. Generally, to be protected, a trademark must be sufficiently distinctive from all competing trademarks.
	3. *Trademark infringement* occurs when one uses a mark that is the same as, or confusingly similar to, the protected trademark, service mark, trade name, or trade dress of another without permission when marketing goods or services.
Cyber Marks (See pages 106–108.)	A *cyber mark* is a trademark in cyberspace. Trademark infringement in cyberspace occurs when one person uses, in a domain name or in meta tags, a name that is the same as, or confusingly similar to, the protected mark of another.

(Continued)

CHAPTER SUMMARY	Intellectual Property and Internet Law–Continued
Patents (See pages 108–110.)	1. A *patent* is a grant from the government that gives an inventor the exclusive right to make, use, and sell an invention for a period of twenty years (fourteen years for a design patent) from the date of filing the application for a patent. To be patentable, an invention (or a discovery, process, or design) must be genuine, novel, useful, and not obvious in light of current technology. 2. Almost anything is patentable, except (1) the laws of nature, (2) natural phenomena, and (3) abstract ideas (including algorithms). 3. *Patent infringement* occurs when one uses or sells another's patented design, product, or process without the patent owner's permission. The patent holder can sue the infringer in federal court and request an injunction, but must prove irreparable injury to obtain a permanent injunction against the infringer. The patent holder can also request damages and attorneys' fees; if the infringement was willful, the court can grant treble damages.
Copyrights (See pages 110–115.)	1. A *copyright* is an intangible property right granted by federal statute to the author or originator of certain literary or artistic productions. Computer software may be copyrighted. 2. *Copyright infringement* occurs whenever the form or expression of an idea is copied without the permission of the copyright holder. An exception applies if the copying is deemed a "fair use." 3. Copyrights are governed by the Copyright Act of 1976, as amended. To protect copyrights in digital information, Congress passed the No Electronic Theft Act of 1997 and the Digital Millennium Copyright Act of 1998. 4. Technology that allows users to share files via the Internet on distributed networks often raises copyright infringement issues. 5. The United States Supreme Court has ruled that companies that provide file-sharing software to users can be held liable for contributory and vicarious copyright liability if they take affirmative steps to promote copyright infringement.
Trade Secrets (See pages 115–116.)	*Trade secrets* include customer lists, plans, research and development, and pricing information, for example. Trade secrets are protected under the common law and, in some states, under statutory law against misappropriation by competitors. The Economic Espionage Act of 1996 made the theft of trade secrets a federal crime (see Chapter 6).
International Protection for Intellectual Property (See pages 116–119.)	Various international agreements provide international protection for intellectual property. A landmark agreement is the 1994 agreement on Trade-Related Aspects of Intellectual Property Rights (TRIPS), which provides for enforcement procedures in all countries signatory to the agreement.

FOR REVIEW

Answers for the even-numbered questions in this **For Review** *section can be found on this text's accompanying Web site at* www.cengage.com/blaw/fbl. *Select "Chapter 5" and click on "For Review."*

1 What is intellectual property?

2 Why are trademarks and patents protected by the law?

3 What laws protect authors' rights in the works they generate?

4 What are trade secrets, and what laws offer protection for this form of intellectual property?

5 What steps have been taken to protect intellectual property rights in today's digital age?

HYPOTHETICAL SCENARIOS AND CASE PROBLEMS

5.1 Copyright Infringement. Professor Wise is teaching a summer seminar in business torts at State University. Several times during the course, he makes copies of relevant sections from business law texts and distributes them to his students. Wise does not realize that the daughter of one of the textbook authors is a member of his seminar. She tells her father about Wise's copying activities, which have taken place without her father's or his publisher's permission. Her father sues Wise for copyright infringement. Wise claims protection under the fair use doctrine. Who will prevail? Explain.

5.2 Hypothetical Question with Sample Answer. In which of the following situations would a court likely hold Maruta liable for copyright infringement?

  1 At the library, Maruta photocopies ten pages from a scholarly journal relating to a topic on which she is writing a term paper.

  2 Maruta makes leather handbags and sells them in her small leather shop. She advertises her handbags as "Vutton handbags," hoping that customers might mistakenly assume that they were made by Vuitton, the well-known maker of high-quality luggage and handbags.

  3 Maruta owns a video store. She purchases one copy of several popular movie DVDs from various distributors. Then, using blank DVDs, she burns copies of the movies to rent or sell to her customers.

  4 Maruta teaches Latin American history at a small university. She has a DVR (digital video recorder) and frequently records television programs relating to Latin America. She then copies the programs to DVDs and takes them to her classroom so that her students can watch them.

 For a sample answer to Question 5.2, go to Appendix E at the end of this text.

5.3 Domain Name Disputes. In 1999, Steve and Pierce Thumann and their father, Fred, created Spider Webs, Ltd., a partnership, to, according to Steve, "develop Internet address names." Spider Webs registered nearly two thousand Internet domain names at an average cost of $70 each, including the names of cities, the names of buildings, names related to a business or trade (such as air-conditioning or plumbing), and the names of famous companies. It offered many of the names for sale on its Web site and through eBay.com. Spider Webs registered the domain name "ERNESTANDJULIOGALLO.COM" in Spider Webs' name. E. & J. Gallo Winery filed a suit against Spider Webs, alleging, in part, violations of the Anticybersquatting Consumer Protection Act (ACPA). Gallo asked the court for, among other things, statutory damages. Gallo also sought to have the domain name at issue transferred to Gallo. During the suit, Spider Webs published anti-

corporate articles and negative opinions about Gallo, as well as discussions of the suit and of the risks associated with alcohol use, at the URL ERNESTANDJULIOGALLO.COM. Should the court rule in Gallo's favor? Why or why not? [*E. & J. Gallo Winery v. Spider Webs, Ltd.*, 129 F.Supp.2d 1033 (S.D.Tex. 2001)]

5.4 Patent Infringement. As a cattle rancher in Nebraska, Gerald Gohl used handheld searchlights to find and help calving animals (animals giving birth) in harsh blizzard conditions. Gohl thought that it would be more helpful to have a portable searchlight mounted on the outside of a vehicle and remotely controlled. He and Al Gebhardt developed and patented practical applications of this idea—the Golight and the wireless, remote-controlled Radio Ray, which could rotate 360 degrees—and formed Golight, Inc., to make and market these products. In 1997, Wal-Mart Stores, Inc., began selling a portable, wireless, remote-controlled searchlight that was identical to the Radio Ray except for a stop piece that prevented the light from rotating more than 351 degrees. Golight sent Wal-Mart a letter, claiming that its device infringed Golight's patent. Wal-Mart sold its remaining inventory of the devices and stopped carrying the product. Golight filed a suit in a federal district court against Wal-Mart, alleging patent infringement. How should the court rule? Explain. [*Golight, Inc. v. Wal-Mart Stores, Inc.*, 355 F.3d 1327 (Fed. Cir. 2004)]

5.5 Trade Dress. Gateway, Inc., sells computers, computer products, computer peripherals, and computer accessories throughout the world. By 1988, Gateway had begun its first national advertising campaign using black-and-white cows and black-and-white cow spots. By 1991, black-and-white cows and spots had become Gateway's symbol. The next year, Gateway registered a black-and-white cow-spots design in association with computers and computer peripherals as its trademark. Companion Products, Inc. (CPI), sells stuffed animals trademarked as "Stretch Pets." Stretch Pets have an animal's head and an elastic body that can wrap around the edges of computer monitors, computer cases, or televisions. CPI produces sixteen Stretch Pets, including a polar bear, a moose, several dogs, and a penguin. One of CPI's top-selling products is a black-and-white cow that CPI identifies as "Cody Cow," which was first sold in 1999. Gateway filed a suit in a federal district court against CPI, alleging trade dress infringement and related claims. What is "trade dress"? What is the major factor in cases involving trade dress infringement? Does that factor exist in this case? Explain. [*Gateway, Inc. v. Companion Products, Inc.*, 384 F.3d 503 (8th Cir. 2004)]

5.6 Case Problem with Sample Answer. Briefing.com offers Internet-based analyses of investment opportunities to investors. Richard Green is the company's president. One of Briefing.com's competitors is StreetAccount, LLC (limited liability company), whose owners include Gregory Jones and Cynthia Dietzmann. Jones worked for Briefing.com for six years until he quit in March 2003, and he was a member of its board of directors until April 2003. Dietzmann worked for Briefing.com for seven years until she quit in March 2003. As Briefing.com employees, Jones and Dietzmann had access to confidential business data. For instance, Dietzmann developed a list of contacts through which Briefing.com obtained market information to display online. When Dietzmann quit, however, she did not return all of the contact information to the company. Briefing.com and Green filed a suit in a federal district court against Jones, Dietzmann, and StreetAccount, alleging that they appropriated these data and other "trade secrets" to form a competing business. What are trade secrets? Why are they protected? Under what circumstances is a party liable at common law for their appropriation? How should these principles apply in this case? [*Briefing.com v. Jones*, 2006 WY 16, 126 P.3d 928 (2006)]

 After you have answered Problem 5.6, compare your answer with the sample answer given on the Web site that accompanies this text. Go to www.cengage.com/blaw/fbl, select "Chapter 5," and click on "Case Problem with Sample Answer."

5.7 Trademarks. In 1969, Jack Masquelier, a professor of pharmacology, discovered a chemical antioxidant made from the bark of a French pine tree. The substance supposedly assists in nutritional distribution and blood circulation. Horphag Research, Ltd., began to sell the product under the name Pycnogenol, which Horphag registered as a trademark in 1993. Pycnogenol became one of the fifteen best-selling herbal supplements in the United States. In 1999, through the Web site **healthierlife.com**, Larry Garcia began to sell Masquelier's Original OPCs, a supplement derived from grape pits. Claiming that this product was the "true Pycnogenol," Garcia used the mark as a meta tag and a generic term, attributing the results of research on Horphag's product to Masquelier's and altering quotes in scientific literature to substitute the name of Masquelier's product for Horphag's.

Customers contacted Horphag, after buying Garcia's product, to learn that it was not Horphag's product. Others called Horphag to ask whether Garcia "was selling . . . real Pycnogenol." Horphag filed a suit in a federal district court against Garcia, alleging, in part, that he was diluting Horphag's mark. What is trademark dilution? Did it occur here? Explain. [*Horphag Research, Ltd. v. Garcia*, 475 F.3d 1029 (9th Cir. 2007)]

5.8 🌐 **A Question of Ethics.** *Custom Copies, Inc., in Gainesville, Florida, is a copy shop, reproducing and distributing, for profit, on request, material published and owned by others. One of the copy shop's primary activities is the preparation and sale of coursepacks, which contain compilations of readings for college courses. For a particular coursepack, a teacher selects the readings and delivers a syllabus to the copy shop, which obtains the materials from a library and copies them, and then binds and sells the copies. Blackwell Publishing, Inc., in Malden, Massachusetts, publishes books and journals in medicine and other fields and owns the copyrights to these publications. Blackwell and others filed a suit in a federal district court against Custom Copies, alleging copyright infringement for its "routine and systematic reproduction of materials from plaintiffs' publications, without seeking permission," to compile coursepacks for classes at the University of Florida. The plaintiffs asked the court to issue an injunction and award them damages, as well as the profit from the infringement. The defendant filed a motion to dismiss the complaint.* [Blackwell Publishing, Inc. v. Custom Copies, Inc., __ F.Supp.2d __ (N.D.Fla. 2007)]

1 Custom Copies argued, among other things, that it did not "distribute" the coursepacks. Does a copy shop violate copyright law if it only copies materials for coursepacks? Does the copying fall under the "fair use" exception? Should the court grant the defendants' motion? Why or why not?

2 What is the potential impact if copies of a book or journal are created and sold without the permission of, and the payment of royalties or a fee to, the copyright owner? Explain.

CRITICAL THINKING AND WRITING ASSIGNMENTS

5.9 Critical Thinking and Writing Assignment for Business. Delta Computers, Inc., makes computer-related products under the brand name "Delta," which the company registers as a trademark. Without Delta's permission, E-Product Corp. embeds the Delta mark in E-Product's Web site, in black type on a blue background. This tag causes the E-Product site to be returned at the top of the list of results on a search engine query for "Delta." Does E-Product's use of the Delta mark as a meta tag without Delta's permission constitute trademark infringement? Explain.

5.10 🎬 **Video Question.** Go to this text's Web site at **www.cengage.com/blaw/fbl** and select "Chapter 5." Click on "Video Questions" and view the video titled *The Jerk.* Then answer the following questions.

1 In the video, Navin (Steve Martin) creates a special handle for Fox's (Bill Macy's) glasses. Can Navin obtain a patent or a copyright protecting his invention? Explain your answer.

2 Suppose that after Navin legally protects his idea, Fox steals it and decides to develop it for himself, without Navin's permission. Has Fox committed infringement? If so, what kind: trademark, patent, or copyright?

3 Suppose that after Navin legally protects his idea, he realizes he doesn't have the funds to mass-produce the special

handle. Navin therefore agrees to allow Fox to manufacture the product. Has Navin granted Fox a license? Explain.

4 Assume that Navin is able to manufacture his invention. What might Navin do to ensure that his product is identifiable and can be distinguished from other products on the market?

ACCESSING THE INTERNET

For updated links to resources available on the Web, as well as a variety of other materials, visit this text's Web site at

www.cengage.com/blaw/fbl

An excellent overview of the laws governing various forms of intellectual property is available at FindLaw's Web site. Go to

profs.lp.findlaw.com

You can find answers to common questions about trademark and patent law—and links to registration forms, statutes, international patent and trademark offices, and numerous other related materials—at the Web site of the U.S. Patent and Trademark Office. Go to

www.uspto.gov

For information on copyrights, go to the U.S. Copyright Office at

www.loc.gov/copyright

You can find extensive information on copyright law—including United States Supreme Court decisions in this area—at the Web site of the Legal Information Institute at Cornell University's School of Law. Go to

www.law.cornell.edu/topics/copyright.html

PRACTICAL INTERNET EXERCISES

Go to this text's Web site at **www.cengage.com/blaw/fbl**, select "Chapter 5," and click on "Practical Internet Exercises." There you will find the following Internet research exercises that you can perform to learn more about the topics covered in this chapter.

PRACTICAL INTERNET EXERCISE 5–1 LEGAL PERSPECTIVE—Unwarranted Legal Threats

PRACTICAL INTERNET EXERCISE 5–2 TECHNOLOGICAL PERSPECTIVE—File-Sharing

PRACTICAL INTERNET EXERCISE 5–3 MANAGEMENT PERSPECTIVE—Protecting Intellectual Property across Borders

BEFORE THE TEST

Go to this text's Web site at **www.cengage.com/blaw/fbl**, select "Chapter 5," and click on "Interactive Quizzes." You will find a number of interactive questions relating to this chapter.

CHAPTER 6
Criminal Law and Cyber Crime

LEARNING OBJECTIVES

AFTER READING THIS CHAPTER, YOU SHOULD BE ABLE TO ANSWER THE FOLLOWING QUESTIONS:

1 What two elements must exist before a person can be held liable for a crime? Can a corporation commit crimes?

2 What are five broad categories of crimes? What is white-collar crime?

3 What defenses might be raised by criminal defendants to avoid liability for criminal acts?

4 What constitutional safeguards exist to protect persons accused of crimes? What are the basic steps in the criminal process?

5 What is cyber crime? What laws apply to crimes committed in cyberspace?

The law imposes various sanctions to help ensure that individuals engaging in business in our society can compete and flourish. These sanctions include damages for various types of tortious conduct (as discussed in Chapter 4), damages for breach of contract (to be discussed in Chapter 12), and the equitable remedies discussed in Chapter 1. Additional sanctions are imposed under criminal law. Many statutes regulating business provide for criminal as well as civil sanctions. Therefore, criminal law joins civil law as an important element in the legal environment of business.

In this chapter, following a brief summary of the major differences between criminal and civil law, we look at how crimes are classified and what elements must be present for criminal liability to exist. We then examine various categories of crimes, the defenses that can be raised to avoid liability for criminal actions, and the rules of criminal procedure. These rules ensure that a criminal defendant's right to "due process of law" is enforced. This right is guaranteed by the Fourteenth Amendment to the U.S. Constitution. We conclude the chapter with a discussion of crime that occurs in cyberspace, often referred to as *cyber crime*. Generally, cyber crime refers more to the way particular crimes are committed than to a specific category of crime.

CIVIL LAW AND CRIMINAL LAW

Remember from Chapter 1 that *civil law* spells out the duties that exist between persons or between persons and their governments, excluding the duty not to commit crimes. Contract law, for example, is part of civil law. The whole body of tort law, which deals with the infringement by one person on the legally recognized rights of another, is also an area of civil law.

Criminal law, in contrast, has to do with crime. A **crime** can be defined as a wrong against society proclaimed in a statute and, if committed, punishable by society through fines and/or imprisonment—and, in some cases, death. As mentioned in Chapter 1, because crimes are *offenses against society as a whole*, they are prosecuted by a public official, such as a district attorney (D.A.) or an attorney general (A.G.), not by victims. Often, a case begins when a victim reports a crime to the police, but it is ultimately the D.A.'s office that decides whether to file criminal charges and to what extent to pursue the prosecution or carry out additional investigation.

Key Differences between Civil Law and Criminal Law

Because the state has extensive resources at its disposal when prosecuting criminal cases, there are numerous procedural safeguards to protect the rights of defendants. We look here at one of these safeguards—the higher burden of proof that applies in a criminal case—as well as the harsher sanctions for criminal acts compared with those for civil wrongs. Exhibit 6–1 summarizes these and other key differences between civil law and criminal law.

Burden of Proof In a civil case, the plaintiff usually must prove his or her case by a *preponderance of the evidence.* Under this standard, the plaintiff must convince the court that, based on the evidence presented by both parties, it is more likely than not that the plaintiff's allegation is true.

In a criminal case, in contrast, the state must prove its case **beyond a reasonable doubt.** If the jury views the evidence in the case as reasonably permitting either a guilty or a not guilty verdict, then the jury's verdict must be *not* guilty. In other words, the government (prosecutor) must prove beyond a reasonable doubt that the defendant has committed every essential element of the offense with which she or he is charged. If the jurors are not convinced of the defendant's guilt beyond a reasonable doubt, they must find the defendant not guilty. Note also that in a criminal case, the jury's verdict normally must be unanimous—agreed to by all members of the jury—to convict the defendant. (In a civil trial by jury, in contrast, typically only three-fourths of the jurors need to agree.)

The higher burden of proof in criminal cases reflects a fundamental social value—the belief that it is worse to con-vict an innocent individual than to let a guilty person go free. We will look at other safeguards later in the chapter, in the context of criminal procedure.

Criminal Sanctions The sanctions imposed on criminal wrongdoers are also harsher than those that are applied in civil cases. Remember from Chapter 4 that the purpose of tort law is to allow persons harmed by the wrongful acts of others to obtain compensation from the wrongdoer rather than to punish the wrongdoer. In contrast, criminal sanctions are designed to pun-ish those who commit crimes and to deter others from commit-ting similar acts in the future. Criminal sanctions include fines as well as the much harsher penalty of the loss of one's liberty by incarceration in a jail or prison. Sanctions may also include probation, community work service, completion of an educa-tional or treatment program, and payment of restitution. The harshest criminal sanction is, of course, the death penalty.

Civil Liability for Criminal Acts

Some torts, such as assault and battery, provide a basis for a criminal prosecution as well as a tort action. **■EXAMPLE 6.1** Joe is walking down the street, minding his own business, when suddenly a person attacks him. In the ensuing struggle, the attacker stabs Joe several times, seriously injuring him. A police officer restrains and arrests the wrongdoer. In this situ-ation, the attacker may be subject both to criminal prosecu-tion by the state and to a tort lawsuit brought by Joe. ■ Exhibit 6–2 on the next page illustrates how the same act can result in both a tort action and a criminal action against the wrongdoer.

CRIMINAL LIABILITY

Two elements must exist simultaneously for a person to be convicted of a crime: (1) the performance of a prohibited act

EXHIBIT 6–1 Key Differences between Civil Law and Criminal Law		
ISSUE	**CIVIL LAW**	**CRIMINAL LAW**
Party who brings suit	The person who suffered harm.	The state.
Wrongful act	Causing harm to a person or to a person's property.	Violating a statute that prohibits some type of activity.
Burden of proof	Preponderance of the evidence.	Beyond a reasonable doubt.
Verdict	Three-fourths majority (typically).	Unanimous.
Remedy	Damages to compensate for the harm or a decree to achieve an equitable result.	Punishment (fine, imprisonment, or death).

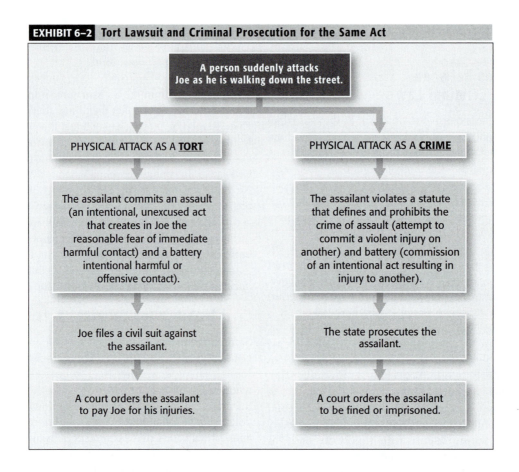

EXHIBIT 6–2 Tort Lawsuit and Criminal Prosecution for the Same Act

and (2) a specified state of mind or intent on the part of the actor. Additionally, to establish criminal liability, there must be a *concurrence* between the act and the intent. In other words, these two elements must occur together.

The Criminal Act

Every criminal statute prohibits certain behavior. Most crimes require an act of *commission*; that is, a person must *do* something in order to be accused of a crime. In criminal law, a prohibited act is referred to as the *actus reus,*[1] or guilty act. In some situations, an act of *omission* can be a crime, but only when a person has a legal duty to perform the omitted act, such as failing to file a tax return. For instance, in 2005 the federal government brought criminal charges against a winner of the reality TV show *Survivor* for failing to report more than $1 million in winnings to the Internal Revenue Service.

The *guilty act* requirement is based on one of the premises of criminal law—that a person is punished for harm done to society. For a crime to exist, the guilty act must cause some harm to a person or to property. Thinking about killing someone or about stealing a car may be wrong, but the thoughts do no harm until they are translated into action. Of course, a person can be punished for attempting murder or robbery, but normally only if he or she took substantial steps toward the criminal objective.

State of Mind

A wrongful mental state (*mens rea*)[2] is generally required to establish criminal liability. What constitutes such a mental state varies according to the wrongful action. For murder, the act is the taking of a life, and the mental state is the intent to take a life. For theft, the guilty act is the taking of another person's property, and the mental state involves both the knowledge that the property belongs to another and the intent to deprive the owner of it.

A guilty mental state can be attributed to acts of negligence or recklessness as well. *Criminal negligence* involves the mental state in which the defendant takes an unjustified, substantial, and foreseeable risk that results in harm. Under the Model Penal Code (on which many states base their

1. Pronounced *ak*-tuhs *ray*-uhs.

2. Pronounced *mehns ray*-uh.

criminal laws), a defendant is negligent even if she or he was not actually aware of the risk but *should have been aware* of it.[3] A defendant is criminally reckless if he or she consciously disregards a substantial and unjustifiable risk.

CORPORATE CRIMINAL LIABILITY

As will be discussed in Chapter 25, a *corporation* is a legal entity created under the laws of a state. Both the corporation as an entity and the individual directors and officers of the corporation are potentially subject to liability for criminal acts.

Liability of the Corporate Entity

At one time, it was thought that a corporation could not incur criminal liability because, although a corporation is a legal person, it can act only through its agents (corporate directors, officers, and employees). Therefore, the corporate entity itself could not "intend" to commit a crime. Under modern criminal law, however, a corporation may be held liable for crimes. Obviously, corporations cannot be imprisoned, but they can be fined or denied certain legal privileges (such as a license).

Today, corporations are normally liable for the crimes committed by their agents and employees within the course and scope of their employment.[4] For such criminal liability to be imposed, the prosecutor normally must show that the corporation could have prevented the act or that there was authorized consent to, or knowledge of, the act by persons in supervisory positions within the corporation. In addition, corporations can be criminally liable for failing to perform specific duties imposed by law (such as duties under environmental laws or securities laws).

Liability of Corporate Officers and Directors

Corporate directors and officers are personally liable for the crimes they commit, regardless of whether the crimes were committed for their personal benefit or on the corporation's behalf. Additionally, corporate directors and officers may be held liable for the actions of employees under their supervision. Under the *responsible corporate officer doctrine*, a court may impose criminal liability on a corporate officer regardless of whether she or he participated in, directed, or even knew about a given criminal violation.

■EXAMPLE 6.2 In *United States v. Park*,[5] the chief executive officer of a national supermarket chain was held personally liable for sanitation violations in corporate warehouses in

which the food was exposed to contamination by rodents. The United States Supreme Court upheld the imposition of personal liability on the corporate officer not because he intended the crime or even knew about it but because he was in a "responsible relationship" to the corporation and had the power to prevent the violation. ■ Since the *Park* decision, courts have applied the responsible corporate officer doctrine on a number of occasions to hold corporate officers liable for their employees' statutory violations.

 **PREVENTING LEGAL DISPUTES** **Because corporate officers and directors can be held liable for the crimes of their subordinates, the former should always be aware of any criminal statutes relevant to their particular industry or trade. In addition, firms should train their employees to comply with all applicable laws, particularly environmental laws and health and safety regulations, which frequently involve criminal sanctions.**

■

TYPES OF CRIMES

The number of acts that are defined as criminal is nearly endless. Federal, state, and local laws provide for the classification and punishment of hundreds of thousands of different criminal acts. Traditionally, though, crimes have been grouped into five broad categories, or types: violent crime (crimes against persons), property crime, public order crime, white-collar crime, and organized crime. Within each of these categories, crimes may also be separated into more than one classification. Cyber crime—crime committed in cyberspace through the use of computers—is, as mentioned earlier in this chapter, less a category of crime than a new way to commit crime. We will examine cyber crime later in this chapter.

Violent Crime

Crimes against persons, because they cause others to suffer harm or death, are referred to as *violent crimes*. Murder is a violent crime. So is sexual assault, or rape. Assault and battery, which were discussed in Chapter 4 in the context of tort law, are also classified as violent crimes. **Robbery**—defined as the taking of cash, personal property, or any other article of value from a person by means of force or fear—is another violent crime. Typically, states have more severe penalties for *aggravated robbery*—robbery with the use of a deadly weapon.

Each of these violent crimes is further classified by degree, depending on the circumstances surrounding the criminal act. These circumstances include the intent of the person

---

3. Model Penal Code Section 2.02(2)(d).

4. See Model Penal Code Section 2.07.

5. 421 U.S. 658, 95 S.Ct. 1903, 44 L.Ed.2d 489 (1975).

committing the crime, whether a weapon was used, and (in cases other than murder) the level of pain and suffering experienced by the victim.

Property Crime

The most common type of criminal activity is property crime—crimes in which the goal of the offender is to obtain some form of economic gain or to damage property. Robbery is a form of property crime, as well as a violent crime, because the offender seeks to obtain the property of another. We look here at a number of other crimes that fall within the general category of property crime.

Burglary Traditionally, **burglary** was defined under the common law as breaking and entering the dwelling of another at night with the intent to commit a felony. Originally, the definition was aimed at protecting an individual's home and its occupants. Most state statutes have eliminated some of the requirements found in the common law definition. The time of day at which the breaking and entering occurs, for example, is usually immaterial. State statutes frequently omit the element of breaking, and some states do not require that the building be a dwelling. When a deadly weapon is used in a burglary, the perpetrator can be charged with *aggravated burglary* and punished more severely.

Larceny Under the common law, the crime of **larceny** involved the unlawful taking and carrying away of someone else's personal property with the intent to permanently deprive the owner of possession. Put simply, larceny is stealing or theft. Whereas robbery involves force or fear, larceny does not. Therefore, picking pockets is larceny. Similarly, taking company products and supplies home for personal use, if one is not authorized to do so, is larceny. (Note that a person who commits larceny generally can also be sued under tort law because the act of taking possession of another's property involves a trespass to personal property.)

Most states have expanded the definition of property that is subject to larceny statutes. Stealing computer programs may constitute larceny even though the "property" consists of magnetic impulses. Stealing computer time can also constitute larceny. So, too, can the theft of natural gas or Internet and television cable service. Trade secrets can be subject to larceny statutes.

The common law distinguished between grand and petit larceny depending on the value of the property taken. Many states have abolished this distinction, but in those that have not, grand larceny (or theft) is a felony and petit larceny (or theft) is a misdemeanor. As will be discussed later in this chapter, a *felony* is a more serious crime than a misdemeanor.

Obtaining Goods by False Pretenses It is a criminal act to obtain goods by means of false pretenses, such as buying groceries with a check knowing that one has insufficient funds to cover it or offering to sell someone a digital camera knowing that one does not actually own the camera. Statutes dealing with such illegal activities vary widely from state to state.

Receiving Stolen Goods It is a crime to receive (acquire or buy) stolen goods. The recipient of such goods need not know the true identity of the owner or the thief. All that is necessary is that the recipient knows or should have known that the goods are stolen, which implies an intent to deprive the owner of those goods.

Arson The willful and malicious burning of a building (and, in some states, personal property) owned by another is the crime of **arson.** At common law, arson traditionally applied only to burning down another person's house. The law was designed to protect human life. Today, arson statutes have been extended to cover the destruction of any building, regardless of ownership, by fire or explosion.

Every state has a special statute that covers the act of burning a building for the purpose of collecting insurance. **EXAMPLE 6.3** Smith owns an insured apartment building that is falling apart. If he sets fire to it himself or pays someone else to do so, he is guilty not only of arson but also of defrauding the insurer, which is attempted larceny. ■ Of course, the insurer need not pay the claim when insurance fraud is proved.

Forgery The fraudulent making or altering of any writing (including electronic records) in a way that changes the legal rights and liabilities of another is **forgery.** **EXAMPLE 6.4** Without authorization, Severson signs Bennett's name to the back of a check made out to Bennett and attempts to cash it. Severson has committed the crime of forgery. ■ Forgery also includes changing trademarks, falsifying public records, counterfeiting, and altering a legal document.

Public Order Crime

Historically, societies have always outlawed activities that are considered to be contrary to public values and morals. Today, the most common public order crimes include public drunkenness, prostitution, pornography, gambling, and illegal drug use. These crimes are sometimes referred to as victimless crimes because they normally harm only the offender. From a broader perspective, however, they are deemed detrimental to society as a whole because they may create an environment that gives rise to property and violent crimes.

White-Collar Crime

Crimes that typically occur only in the business context are popularly referred to as **white-collar crimes.** Although there is no official definition of white-collar crime, the term is commonly used to mean an illegal act or series of acts committed by an individual or business entity using some nonviolent means. Usually, this kind of crime is committed in the course of a legitimate occupation. Corporate crimes fall into this category. In addition, certain property crimes, such as larceny and forgery, may also be white-collar crimes if they occur within the business context.

Embezzlement When a person who is entrusted with another person's property or money fraudulently appropriates it, **embezzlement** occurs. Typically, embezzlement is carried out by an employee who steals funds. Banks are particularly prone to this problem, but embezzlement can occur in any firm. In a number of businesses, corporate officers or accountants have fraudulently converted funds for their own benefit and then "fixed" the books to cover up their crime. Embezzlement is not larceny, because the wrongdoer does not physically take the property from the possession of another, and it is not robbery, because force or fear is not used.

It does not matter whether the accused takes the funds from the victim or from a third person. If the financial officer of a large corporation pockets checks from third parties that were given to her to deposit into the corporate account, she is embezzling. Frequently, an embezzler takes only a small amount at one time but does so repeatedly over a long period. This might be done by underreporting income or deposits and embezzling the remaining amount, for example, or by creating fictitious persons or accounts and writing checks to them from the corporate account.

Practically speaking, an embezzler who returns what has been taken might not be prosecuted because the owner is unwilling to take the time to make a complaint, cooperate with the state's investigative efforts, and appear in court. Also, the owner may not want the crime to become public knowledge. Nevertheless, the intent to return the embezzled property is not a defense to the crime of embezzlement.

Does an employer's failure to remit to the state the withholding taxes that he collected from his employees constitute a form of embezzlement? This was the primary issue in the following case.

CASE 6.1   George v. Commonwealth of Virginia

Court of Appeals of Virginia, 51 Va.App. 137, 655 S.E.2d 43 (2008).
www.courts.state.va.us/wpcap.htm[a]

FACTS Dr. Francis H. George owned and operated a medical practice in Luray, Virginia. From 2001 to 2004, George employed numerous individuals, including nursing assistants, nurse practitioners, and a pediatrician. George withheld funds from his employees' salaries—funds that represented state income taxes owed to the commonwealth[b] of Virginia. George placed these funds in the same banking account that he used to pay his personal and business expenses. During this period, George failed to file withholding tax returns as required by state law. Moreover, he did not remit the withheld funds to the state. At trial, a jury convicted George on four counts of embezzlement. George appealed to the state intermediate appellate court, claiming, among other things, that the evidence was insufficient to sustain the convictions because the state had not proved that he was entrusted with the property of another.

ISSUE Is it embezzlement for an employer to not pay the state funds that he withheld from his employees' salaries for tax purposes?

DECISION Yes. The Court of Appeals of Virginia denied George's appeal to set aside his conviction.

REASON The court found that the evidence clearly established that George was guilty of embezzlement because he used the funds that he held in trust for the state for his own benefit. "To sustain a conviction of embezzlement, the Commonwealth must prove that the accused wrongfully appropriated to his or her own benefit property entrusted or delivered to the accused with the intent to deprive the owner thereof." George contended that the withheld funds amounted to nothing more than a debt he owed the commonwealth; therefore, he did not commit embezzlement. The appellate court reasoned that the withholding taxes that George had collected and maintained in his possession were in fact in trust for the commonwealth. George "neither remitted the withheld funds to the Commonwealth nor maintained them

---

a. Scroll down and click on case "0332064" for January 15, 2008, to access this opinion.
b. In addition to Virginia, three other states designate themselves as commonwealths—Kentucky, Massachusetts, and Pennsylvania. The term *commonwealth* dates to the fifteenth century, when it meant "common well-being."

CASE 6.1–Continues next page

for its benefit. In fact, [George] continued to use the money as though it were his own."

 WHAT IF THE FACTS WERE DIFFERENT? *Assume that George had kept a separate account for taxes withheld from his employees' salaries, but had simply*

failed to remit them to the state. Would the court have ruled differently? If so, in what way?

■

Bribery Basically, three types of bribery are considered crimes: bribery of public officials, commercial bribery, and bribery of foreign officials. The attempt to influence a public official to act in a way that serves a private interest is a crime. As an element of this crime, intent must be present and proved. The bribe can be anything the recipient considers to be valuable. Realize that *the crime of bribery occurs when the bribe is offered.* It does not matter whether the person to whom the bribe is offered accepts the bribe or agrees to perform whatever action is desired by the person offering the bribe. *Accepting a bribe* is a separate crime.

Bribing foreign officials to obtain favorable business contracts is a crime. The Foreign Corrupt Practices Act of 1977, which was discussed in Chapter 3, was passed to curb the use of bribery by U.S. businesspersons in securing foreign contracts.

Bankruptcy Fraud Federal bankruptcy law (see Chapter 21) allows individuals and businesses to be relieved of oppressive debt through bankruptcy proceedings. Numerous white-collar crimes may be committed during the many phases of a bankruptcy proceeding. A creditor, for example, may file a false claim against the debtor, which is a crime. Also, a debtor may fraudulently transfer assets to favored parties before or after the petition for bankruptcy is filed. For example, a company-owned automobile may be "sold" at a bargain price to a trusted friend or relative. Closely related to the crime of fraudulent transfer of property is the crime of fraudulent concealment of property, such as hiding gold coins.

The Theft of Trade Secrets As discussed in Chapter 5, trade secrets constitute a form of intellectual property that for many businesses can be extremely valuable. The Economic Espionage Act of 1996[6] made the theft of trade secrets a federal crime. The act also made it a federal crime to buy or possess trade secrets of another person, knowing that the trade secrets were stolen or otherwise acquired without the owner's authorization.

Violations of the act can result in steep penalties. An individual who violates the act can be imprisoned for up to ten years and fined up to $500,000. If a corporation or other organization violates the act, it can be fined up to $5 million. Additionally, the law provides that any property acquired as a result of the violation, such as airplanes and automobiles, and any property used in the commission of the violation, such as computers and other electronic devices, are subject to criminal *forfeiture*—meaning that the government can take the property. A theft of trade secrets conducted via the Internet, for example, could result in the forfeiture of every computer or other device used in the commission of the crime, as well as any assets gained from the stolen trade secrets.

Insider Trading An individual who obtains "inside information" about the plans of a publicly listed corporation can often make stock-trading profits by purchasing or selling corporate securities based on the information. **Insider trading** is a violation of securities law and will be considered more fully in Chapter 27. Generally, the rule is that a person who possesses inside information and has a duty not to disclose it to outsiders may not profit from the purchase or sale of securities based on that information until the information is made available to the public.

Mail and Wire Fraud One of the most potent weapons against white-collar criminals is the Mail Fraud Act of 1990.[7] Under this act, it is a federal crime (mail fraud) to use the mails to defraud the public. Illegal use of the mails must involve (1) mailing or causing someone else to mail a writing—something written, printed, or photocopied—for the purpose of executing a scheme to defraud and (2) a contemplated or an organized scheme to defraud by false pretenses. If, for example, Johnson advertises by mail the sale of a cure for cancer that he knows to be fraudulent because it has no medical validity, he can be prosecuted for fraudulent use of the mails.

6. 18 U.S.C. Sections 1831–1839.

7. 18 U.S.C. Sections 1341–1342.

Federal law also makes it a crime to use wire (for example, the telephone), radio, or television transmissions to defraud.[8] Violators may be fined up to $1,000, imprisoned for up to five years, or both. If the violation affects a financial institu-

tion, the violator may be fined up to $1 million, imprisoned for up to thirty years, or both.

The following case involved charges of mail fraud in which funds misrepresented to support charities were acquired through telemarketing. The question was whether the prosecution could offer proof of the telemarketers' commission rate when no one had lied about it.

---
8. 18 U.S.C. Section 1343.

CASE 6.2 **United States v. Lyons**

United States Court of Appeals, Ninth Circuit, 472 F.3d 1055 (2007).

FACTS In 1994, in California, Gabriel Sanchez formed the First Church of Life (FCL), which had no congregation, services, or place of worship. Sanchez's friend Timothy Lyons formed a fundraising company called North American Acquisitions (NAA). Through FCL, Sanchez and Lyons set up six charities—AIDS Research Association, Children's Assistance Foundation, Cops and Sheriffs of America, Handicapped Youth Services, U.S. Firefighters, and U.S. Veterans League. NAA hired telemarketers to solicit donations on the charities' behalf. Over time, more than $6 million was raised, of which less than $5,000 was actually spent on charitable causes. The telemarketers kept 80 percent of the donated funds as commissions, and NAA took 10 percent. Most of the rest of the funds went to Sanchez, who spent it on himself. In 2002, Lyons and Sanchez were charged in a federal district court with mail fraud and other crimes. Throughout the trial, the prosecution referred to the high commissions paid to the telemarketers. The defendants were convicted, and each was sentenced to fifteen years' imprisonment. They asked the U.S. Court of Appeals for the Ninth Circuit to overturn their convictions, asserting that the prosecution had used the high cost of fundraising as evidence of fraud even though the defendants had not lied about the cost.

ISSUE Could evidence of the commissions paid to the telemarketers be introduced when those from whom the funds were solicited were not lied to about the commissions?

DECISION Yes. The U.S. Court of Appeals for the Ninth Circuit upheld the convictions. The defendants' "undoing was not that the commissions were large but that their charitable web

was a scam. Donors were told their contributions went to specific charitable activities when, in reality, almost no money did."

REASON The court acknowledged that a failure to reveal the high cost of fundraising to potential donors does not establish fraud. "The mere fact that a telemarketer keeps [80 percent] of contributions it solicits cannot be the basis of a fraud conviction, and neither can the fact that a telemarketer fails to volunteer this information to would-be donors." But when "nondisclosure is accompanied by intentionally misleading statements designed to deceive the listener," the high cost of fundraising may be introduced as evidence of fraud. "The State may vigorously enforce its antifraud laws to prohibit professional fundraisers from obtaining money on false pretenses or by making false statements." Here, in addition to the proof of the telemarketers' commissions, the prosecution offered evidence of Lyons and Sanchez's specific misrepresentations and omissions regarding the defendants' use of the donated funds. All of this "evidence underscored the fact that virtually none of the money that ended up in the bank accounts of the six FCL charities went to any charitable activities at all, let alone the specific charitable activities mentioned in the telemarketers' calls. * * * Admission of evidence regarding the fundraising costs was essential to understanding the overall scheme and the shell game of the multiple charities."

FOR CRITICAL ANALYSIS—Ethical Consideration *It may have been legal in this case, but was it ethical for the prosecution to repeatedly empha-size the size of the telemarketers' commissions? Why or why not?*

■

Organized Crime

As mentioned, white-collar crime takes place within the confines of the legitimate business world. *Organized crime*, in contrast, operates *illegitimately* by, among other things, pro-

viding illegal goods and services. For organized crime, the traditional preferred markets are gambling, prostitution, illegal narcotics, and loan sharking (lending at higher- than-legal interest rates), along with more recent ventures into counterfeiting and credit-card scams.

Money Laundering The profits from organized crime and illegal activities amount to billions of dollars a year, particularly the profits from illegal drug transactions and, to a lesser extent, from racketeering, prostitution, and gambling. Under federal law, banks, savings and loan associations, and other financial institutions are required to report currency transactions involving more than $10,000. Consequently, those who engage in illegal activities face difficulties in depositing their cash profits from illegal transactions.

As an alternative to simply storing cash from illegal transactions in a safe-deposit box, wrongdoers and racketeers have invented ways to launder "dirty" money to make it "clean." This **money laundering** is done through legitimate businesses.

■**EXAMPLE 6.5** Matt, a successful drug dealer, becomes a partner with a restaurateur. Little by little, the restaurant shows increasing profits. As a partner in the restaurant, Matt is able to report the "profits" of the restaurant as legitimate income on which he pays federal and state taxes. He can then spend those funds without worrying that his lifestyle may exceed the level possible with his reported income. ■

The Racketeer Influenced and Corrupt Organizations Act (RICO) In 1970, in an effort to curb the apparently increasing entry of organized crime into the legitimate business world, Congress passed the Racketeer Influenced and Corrupt Organizations Act (RICO).[9] The statute, which is part of the Organized Crime Control Act, makes it a federal crime to (1) use income obtained from racketeering activity to purchase any interest in an enterprise, (2) acquire or maintain an interest in an enterprise through racketeering activity, (3) conduct or participate in the affairs of an enterprise through racketeering activity, or (4) conspire to do any of the preceding activities.

RICO incorporates by reference twenty-six separate types of federal crimes and nine types of state felonies[10] and declares that if a person commits two of these offenses, he or she is guilty of "racketeering activity." Under the criminal provisions of RICO, any individual found guilty is subject to a fine of up to $25,000 per violation, imprisonment for up to twenty years, or both. Additionally, the statute provides that those who violate RICO may be required to forfeit (give up) any assets, in the form of property or cash, that were acquired as a result of the illegal activity or that were "involved in" or an "instrumentality of" the activity.

The broad language of RICO has allowed it to be applied in cases that have little or nothing to do with organized crime. In fact, today the statute is more often used to attack white-collar crimes than organized crime. In addition, RICO creates civil as well as criminal liability. The government can seek civil penalties, including the divestiture of a defendant's interest in a business (called forfeiture) or the dissolution of the business. Moreover, in some cases, the statute allows private individuals to sue violators and potentially recover three times their actual losses (treble damages), plus attorneys' fees, for business injuries caused by a violation of the statute. This is perhaps the most controversial aspect of RICO and one that continues to cause debate in the nation's federal courts.

(See Exhibit 6–3 for an overview of the types of crimes.)

Classification of Crimes

Depending on their degree of seriousness, crimes typically are classified as felonies or misdemeanors. **Felonies** are serious crimes punishable by death or by imprisonment for more than a year. **Misdemeanors** are less serious crimes, punishable by a fine or by confinement for up to a year. In most jurisdictions, **petty offenses** are considered to be a subset of misdemeanors. Petty offenses are minor violations, such as jaywalking or violations of building codes. Even for petty offenses, however, a guilty party can be put in jail for a few days, fined, or both, depending on state or local law.

Whether a crime is a felony or a misdemeanor can determine in which court the case is tried and, in some states, whether the defendant has a right to a jury trial. Many states also define different degrees of felony offenses (first, second, and third degree murder, for example) and vary the punishment according to the degree. Some states also have different classes (degrees) of misdemeanors.

DEFENSES TO CRIMINAL LIABILITY

In certain circumstances, the law may allow a person to be excused from criminal liability because she or he lacks the required mental state. Criminal defendants may also be relieved of criminal liability if they can show that their criminal actions were justified, given the circumstances. Among the most important defenses to criminal liability are infancy, intoxication, insanity, mistake, consent, duress, justifiable use of force, entrapment, and the statute of limitations. Also, in some cases, defendants are given immunity and thus relieved, at least in part, of criminal liability for crimes they committed. We look at each of these defenses here.

Note that procedural violations, such as obtaining evidence without a valid search warrant, may operate as defenses also. As you will read later in this chapter, evidence obtained in violation of a defendant's constitutional rights normally may not be admitted in court. If the evidence is suppressed, then there may be no basis for prosecuting the defendant.

---

9. 18 U.S.C. Sections 1961–1968.
10. See 18 U.S.C. Section 1961(1)(A).

EXHIBIT 6–3 Types of Crimes	
CRIME CATEGORY	**DEFINITION AND EXAMPLES**
Violent Crime	*Definition*—Crimes that cause others to suffer harm or death. *Examples*—Murder, assault and battery, sexual assault (rape), and robbery.
Property Crime	*Definition*—Crimes in which the goal of the offender is to obtain some form of economic gain or to damage property; the most common form of crime. *Examples*—Burglary, larceny, obtaining goods by false pretenses, receiving stolen goods, arson, and forgery.
Public Order Crime	*Definition*—Crimes contrary to public values and morals. *Examples*—Public drunkenness, prostitution, pornography, gambling, and illegal drug use.
White-Collar Crime	*Definition*—An illegal act or series of acts committed by an individual or business entity using some nonviolent means to obtain a personal or business advantage; usually committed in the course of a legitimate occupation. *Examples*—Embezzlement, mail and wire fraud, bribery, bankruptcy fraud, the theft of trade secrets, and insider trading.
Organized Crime	*Definition*—A form of crime conducted by groups operating illegitimately to satisfy the public's demand for illegal goods and services (such as gambling or illegal narcotics). *Examples*— 1. Money laundering—The establishment of legitimate enterprises through which "dirty" money (obtained through criminal activities, such as organized crime) can be "laundered" (made to appear to be legitimate income). 2. RICO—The Racketeer Influenced and Corrupt Organizations Act (RICO) of 1970 makes it a federal crime to (a) use income obtained from racketeering activity to purchase any interest in an enterprise, (b) acquire or maintain an interest in an enterprise through racketeering activity, (c) conduct or participate in the affairs of an enterprise through racketeering activity, or (d) conspire to do any of the preceding activities. RICO provides for both civil and criminal liability.

Infancy

The term *infant*, as used in the law, refers to any person who has not yet reached the age of majority. At common law, children under the age of seven could not commit a crime. It was presumed that children between the ages of seven and fourteen were incapable of committing crimes, but this presumption could be disproved by evidence that the child knew that the act was wrong. Today, most state courts no longer presume that children are incapable of criminal conduct, but may evaluate the particular child's state of mind. In all states, certain courts handle cases involving children who allegedly have violated the law. Courts that handle juvenile cases may also have jurisdiction over additional matters. In most states, a child may be treated as an adult and tried in a regular court if she or he is above a certain age (usually fourteen) and is charged with a felony, such as rape or murder.

Intoxication

The law recognizes two types of intoxication, whether from drugs or from alcohol: *involuntary* and *voluntary*. Involuntary intoxication occurs when a person either is physically forced to ingest or inject an intoxicating substance or is unaware that a substance contains drugs or alcohol. Involuntary intoxication is a defense to a crime if its effect was to make a person incapable of obeying the law or of understanding that the act committed was wrong. Voluntary intoxication is rarely a defense, but it may be effective in cases in which the defendant was so *extremely* intoxicated as to negate the state of mind that a crime requires.

Insanity

Just as a child is often judged to be incapable of the state of mind required to commit a crime, so also may someone suffering from a mental illness. Thus, insanity may be a defense to a criminal charge. The courts have had difficulty deciding what the test for legal insanity should be, however, and psychiatrists as well as lawyers are critical of the tests used. Almost all federal courts and some states use the relatively liberal standard set forth in the Model Penal Code:

> A person is not responsible for criminal conduct if at the time of such conduct as a result of mental disease or defect he [or she] lacks substantial capacity either to appreciate the wrongfulness of his [or her] conduct or to conform his [or her] conduct to the requirements of the law.

Some states use the *M'Naghten* test,[11] under which a criminal defendant is not responsible if, at the time of the offense, he or she did not know the nature and quality of the act or did not know that the act was wrong. Other states use the irresistible-impulse test. A person operating under an irresistible impulse may know an act is wrong but cannot refrain from doing it. Under any of these tests, proving insanity is extremely difficult. For this reason, the insanity defense is rarely used and usually is not successful.

Mistake

Everyone has heard the saying "Ignorance of the law is no excuse." Ordinarily, ignorance of the law or a mistaken idea about what the law requires is not a valid defense. In some states, however, that rule has been modified. Criminal defendants who claim that they honestly did not know that they were breaking a law may have a valid defense if (1) the law was not published or reasonably made known to the public or (2) the defendant relied on an official statement of the law that was erroneous.

A *mistake of fact*, as opposed to a *mistake of law*, operates as a defense if it negates the mental state necessary to commit a crime. **■EXAMPLE 6.6** If Oliver Wheaton mistakenly walks off with Julie Tyson's briefcase because he thinks it is his, there is no theft. Theft requires knowledge that the property belongs to another. (If Wheaton's act causes Tyson to incur damages, however, Wheaton may be subject to liability for trespass to personal property or conversion, torts that were discussed in Chapter 4.) **■**

Consent

What if a victim consents to a crime or even encourages the person intending a criminal act to commit it? Ordinarily, **consent** does not operate as a bar to criminal liability. In some rare circumstances, however, the law may allow consent to be used as a defense. In each case, the question is whether the law forbids an act that was committed against the victim's will or forbids the act without regard to the victim's wish. The law forbids murder, prostitution, and drug use regardless of whether the victim consents to it. Also, if the act causes harm to a third person who has not consented, there is no escape from criminal liability. Consent or forgiveness given after a crime has been committed is not really a defense, though it can affect the likelihood of prosecution or the severity of the sentence. Consent operates most successfully as a defense in crimes against property.

■EXAMPLE 6.7 Barry gives Phong permission to stay in Barry's lakeside cabin and hunt for deer on the adjoining land. After observing Phong carrying a gun into the cabin at night, a neighbor calls the police, and an officer subsequently arrests Phong. If charged with burglary (or aggravated burglary, because he had a weapon), Phong can assert the defense of consent. He had obtained Barry's consent to enter the premises. **■**

Duress

Duress exists when one person's *wrongful threat* induces another person to perform an act that he or she would not otherwise have performed. In such a situation, duress is said to negate the mental state necessary to commit a crime because the perpetrator was forced or compelled to commit the act. Duress can be used as a defense to most crimes except murder.

Duress excuses a crime only when another's unlawful threat of serious bodily injury or death reasonably caused the perpetrator to commit the criminal act. In addition, there must have been no opportunity for the person to escape or avoid the threatened danger.[12] Essentially, to successfully assert duress as a defense, a defendant must have believed in the immediate danger, and the jury (or judge) must conclude that the defendant's belief was reasonable.

Justifiable Use of Force

Self-defense is probably the best-known defense to criminal liability. Other situations, however, also justify the use of force: the defense of one's dwelling, the defense of other property, and the prevention of a crime. In all of these situations, it is important to distinguish between deadly and nondeadly force. *Deadly force* is likely to result in death or serious bodily harm. *Nondeadly force* is force that reasonably appears necessary to prevent the imminent use of criminal force.

Generally speaking, people can use the amount of nondeadly force that seems necessary to protect themselves, their

---

11. A rule derived from *M'Naghten's* Case, 8 Eng.Rep. 718 (1843).

12. See, for example, *State v. Heinemann*, 282 Conn. 281, 920 A.2d 278 (2007).

dwellings, or other property or to prevent the commission of a crime. Deadly force can be used in self-defense if the defender *reasonably believes* that imminent death or grievous bodily harm will otherwise result, if the attacker is using unlawful force (an example of lawful force is that exerted by a police officer), and if the defender has not initiated or provoked the attack. Deadly force normally can be used to defend a dwelling only if the unlawful entry is violent and the person believes deadly force is necessary to prevent imminent death or great bodily harm or—in some jurisdictions—if the person believes deadly force is necessary to prevent a felony (such as arson) from occurring in the dwelling. See this chapter's *Management Perspective* feature on the following page for a discussion of how some states may allow the use of deadly force to prevent the commission of a crime on business premises.

Entrapment

Entrapment is a defense designed to prevent police officers or other government agents from enticing persons to commit crimes in order to later prosecute them for criminal acts. In the typical entrapment case, an undercover agent *suggests* that a crime be committed and somehow pressures or induces an individual to commit it. The agent then arrests the individual for the crime.

For entrapment to be considered a defense, both the suggestion and the inducement must take place. The defense is intended not to prevent law enforcement agents from setting a trap for an unwary criminal but rather to prevent them from pushing the individual into it. The crucial issue is whether the person who committed a crime was predisposed to commit the illegal act or did so because the agent induced it.

Statute of Limitations

With some exceptions, such as for the crime of murder, statutes of limitations apply to crimes just as they do to civil wrongs. In other words, the state must initiate criminal prosecution within a certain number of years. If a criminal action is brought after the statutory time period has expired, the defendant can raise the statute of limitations as a defense.

Immunity

At times, the state may wish to obtain information from a person accused of a crime. Accused persons are understandably reluctant to give information if it will be used to prosecute them, and they cannot be forced to do so. The privilege against **self-incrimination** is granted by the Fifth Amendment to the U.S. Constitution, which reads, in part, "nor shall [any person] be compelled in any criminal case to be a witness against himself." In cases in which the state wishes to obtain

information from a person accused of a crime, the state can grant *immunity* from prosecution or agree to prosecute for a less serious offense in exchange for the information. Once immunity is given, the person can no longer refuse to testify on Fifth Amendment grounds because he or she now has an absolute privilege against self-incrimination.

Often, a grant of immunity from prosecution for a serious crime is part of the **plea bargaining** between the defendant and the prosecuting attorney. The defendant may be convicted of a lesser offense, while the state uses the defendant's testimony to prosecute accomplices for serious crimes carrying heavy penalties.

CONSTITUTIONAL SAFEGUARDS AND CRIMINAL PROCEDURES

Criminal law brings the power of the state, with all its resources, to bear against the individual. Criminal procedures are designed to protect the constitutional rights of individuals and to prevent the arbitrary use of power on the part of the government.

The U.S. Constitution provides specific safeguards for those accused of crimes. Most of these safeguards protect individuals against state government actions, as well as federal government actions, by virtue of the due process clause of the Fourteenth Amendment. These protections are set forth in the Fourth, Fifth, Sixth, and Eighth Amendments.

Fourth Amendment Protections

The Fourth Amendment protects the "right of the people to be secure in their persons, houses, papers, and effects." Before searching or seizing private property, law enforcement officers must obtain a **search warrant**—an order from a judge or other public official authorizing the search or seizure. To obtain a search warrant, the officers must convince a judge that they have reasonable grounds, or **probable cause,** to believe a search will reveal a specific illegality. In addition, the Fourth Amendment prohibits general warrants and requires a precise description of what is to be searched or seized. General searches through a person's belongings are impermissible. The search cannot extend beyond what is described in the warrant. Although search warrants require specificity, if a search warrant is issued for a person's residence, items in that residence may be searched even if they do not belong to that individual.

■**EXAMPLE 6.8** Paycom Billing Services, Inc., facilitates payments from Internet users to its client Web sites and stores vast amounts of credit-card information in the process. Three partners at Paycom received a letter from an employee, Christopher Adjani, threatening to sell Paycom's confidential

MANAGEMENT PERSPECTIVE

Can a Businessperson Use Deadly Force to Prevent a Crime on the Premises?

Management Faces a Legal Issue

Traditionally, the justifiable use of force, or self-defense, doctrine required prosecutors to distinguish between deadly and nondeadly force. In general, state laws have allowed individuals to use the amount of *nondeadly force* that is reasonably necessary to protect themselves, or their dwellings, businesses, or other property. Most states have allowed a person to use *deadly force* only when the person reasonably believed that imminent death or bodily harm would otherwise result. Additionally, the attacker had to be using unlawful force, and the defender had to have no other possible response or alternative way out of the life-threatening situation.

What the Courts Say

Today, many states still have "duty-to-retreat" laws. Under these laws, when a person's home is invaded or an assailant approaches, the person is required to retreat and cannot use deadly force unless her or his life is in danger.[a] Other states, however, are taking a very different approach and expanding the occasions when deadly force can be used in self-defense. Because such laws allow or even encourage the defender to stay and use force, they are known as "stand-your-ground" laws.

Florida, for example, enacted a statute in 2005 that allows the use of deadly force to prevent the commission of a "forcible felony," including not only murder but also such crimes as robbery, carjacking, and sexual battery.[b] Under this

a. See, for example, *State v. Sandoval*, 342 Or. 506, 156 P.3d 60 (2007).
b. Florida Statutes Section 776.012.

law, a Florida resident has a right to shoot an intruder in his or her home or a would-be carjacker even if there is no physical threat to the owner's safety. Similar laws eliminating the duty to retreat have been passed in at least fourteen other states, including Arizona, Georgia, Idaho, Indiana, Kansas, Kentucky, Louisiana, Michigan, Oklahoma, South Carolina, South Dakota, Tennessee, and Texas.

In a number of states, a person may use deadly force to prevent someone from breaking into his or her home, car, or place of business. For example, courts in Louisiana now allow a person to use deadly force to repel an attack while he or she is lawfully in a home, car, or place of business without imposing any duty to retreat.[c] Courts in Connecticut allow the use of deadly force not only to prevent a person from unlawful entry, but also when reasonably necessary to prevent arson or some other violent crime from being committed on the premises.[d]

Implications for Managers

The stand-your-ground laws that many states have enacted often include places of business as well as homes and vehicles. Consequently, businesspersons in those states can be less concerned about the duty-to-retreat doctrine. In addition, business liability insurance often costs less in states without a duty to retreat, because many statutes provide that the business owner is not liable in a civil action for injuries to the attacker. Even in states that impose a duty to retreat, there is no duty to retreat if doing so would increase rather than diminish the danger. Nevertheless, business owners should use deadly force only as a last resort to prevent the commission of crime on their business premises.

c. See, for example, *State v. Johnson*, 948 So.2d 1229 (La.App. 3d Cir. 2007); and Lousiana Statutes Annotated Section 14:20.
d. See, for example, *State v. Terwilliger*, 105 Conn.App. 219, 937 A.2d 735 (2008); and Connecticut General Statutes Section 53a-20.

client information if the company did not pay him $3 million. Pursuant to an investigation, the Federal Bureau of Investigation (FBI) obtained a search warrant to search Adjani's person, automobile, and residence, including computer equipment. When the FBI agents served the warrant, they discovered evidence of the criminal scheme in the e-mail communications on a computer in the residence. The computer belonged to Adjani's live-in girlfriend. Adjani filed a motion to suppress this evidence, claiming that because he did not own the computer, it was beyond the scope of the

warrant. Although the federal trial court granted the defendant's motion and suppressed the incriminating e-mails, in 2006 the U.S. Court of Appeals for the Ninth Circuit reversed. According to the appellate court, despite the novel Fourth Amendment issues raised in the case, the search of the computer was proper given the alleged involvement of computers in the crime.[13] ■

---

13. *United States v. Adjani*, 452 F.3d 1140 (9th Cir. 2006).

As noted in Chapter 1, the standard of probable cause is less stringent in a business context than in nonbusiness contexts. The existence of a general and neutral plan of enforcing government regulations normally will justify the issuance of a search warrant. Moreover, warrants are not required for searches of businesses in highly regulated industries such as liquor, guns, and strip mining.

Fifth Amendment Protections

The Fifth Amendment offers significant protections for accused persons. One is the guarantee that no one can be deprived of "life, liberty, or property without due process of law." Two other important Fifth Amendment provisions protect persons against double jeopardy and self-incrimination.

Due Process of Law Remember from Chapter 1 that *due process of law* has both procedural and substantive aspects. Procedural due process requirements underlie criminal procedures. Basically, the law must be carried out in a fair and orderly way. In criminal cases, due process means that defendants should have an opportunity to object to the charges against them before a fair, neutral decision maker, such as a judge. Defendants must also be given the opportunity to confront and cross-examine witnesses and accusers and to present their own witnesses.

Double Jeopardy The Fifth Amendment also protects persons from **double jeopardy** (being tried twice for the same criminal offense). The prohibition against double jeopardy means that once a criminal defendant is acquitted (found "not guilty") of a particular crime, the government may not retry him or her for the same crime.

The prohibition against double jeopardy does not preclude the crime victim from bringing a civil suit against that same person to recover damages, however. Additionally, a state's prosecution of a crime will not prevent a separate federal prosecution relating to the same activity, and vice versa. **■EXAMPLE 6.9** A person found "not guilty" of assault and battery in a criminal case may be sued by the victim in a civil tort case for damages. A person who is prosecuted for assault and battery in a state court may be prosecuted in a federal court for civil rights violations resulting from the same action. ■

Self-Incrimination As explained earlier, the Fifth Amendment grants a privilege against self-incrimination. Thus, in any criminal proceeding, an accused person cannot be compelled to give testimony that might subject her or him to any criminal prosecution.

The Fifth Amendment's guarantee against self-incrimination extends only to natural persons. Because a corporation is a legal entity and not a natural person, the privilege against self-incrimination does not apply to it. Similarly, the business records of a partnership normally do not receive Fifth Amendment protection. When a partnership is required to produce these records, it must do so even if the information incriminates the persons who constitute the business entity. Sole proprietors and sole practitioners (those who fully own their businesses) who have not incorporated normally cannot be compelled to produce their business records. These individuals have full protection against self-incrimination because they function in only one capacity; there is no separate business entity.

Protections under the Sixth and Eighth Amendments

The Sixth Amendment guarantees several important rights for criminal defendants: the right to a speedy trial, the right to a jury trial, the right to a public trial, the right to confront witnesses, and the right to counsel. **■EXAMPLE 6.10** Law enforcement officers in Nebraska obtained an arrest warrant for John Fellers based on his involvement in distributing methamphetamine (meth) with four other individuals. Two police officers went to Fellers's home to arrest him, showed him the warrant, and asked him about the other persons involved. Fellers responded that he knew the individuals and had used meth with them. After that, the officers arrested Fellers and took him to jail, where they informed him of his right to counsel for the first time. He waived his right and repeated what he had told the officers at his home. After being convicted on drug charges, Fellers appealed, claiming that his incriminating statements to the officers should have been excluded because he was not informed of his right to counsel. Ultimately, the United States Supreme Court agreed. Because Fellers was not informed of his right to counsel and had not waived this right when he first made the statements at his home, the statements he repeated after his arrest should have been excluded (under the "fruit of the poisonous tree" doctrine, which will be discussed shortly).[14] ■

The Eighth Amendment prohibits excessive bail and fines, as well as cruel and unusual punishment. Under this amendment, prison officials are required to provide humane conditions of confinement, including adequate food, clothing, shelter, and medical care. If a prisoner has a serious medical problem, for instance, and a corrections officer is deliberately indifferent to it, a court could find that the prisoner's Eighth Amendment rights have been violated.

Critics of the death penalty claim that it constitutes cruel and unusual punishment. In 2008, the United States

---

14. *Fellers v. United States*, 540 U.S. 519, 124 S.Ct. 1019, 157 L.Ed.2d 1016 (2004).

Supreme Court heard a case challenging the use of a three-drug protocol (used in many states) in carrying out the death penalty. Two death-row inmates argued that if the first drug—an anesthetic—does not work for some reason, then the combination of the other two drugs might cause excruciating pain. Although a majority of the Court concluded that this method of lethal injection did not violate the Eighth Amendment, the justices each applied different reasoning.[15] Rather than settling the issue, this case may perhaps pave the way for more litigation on whether the death penalty violates the Constitution.

The Exclusionary Rule and the *Miranda* Rule

Two other procedural protections for criminal defendants are the exclusionary rule and the *Miranda* rule.

The Exclusionary Rule Under what is known as the **exclusionary rule,** all evidence obtained in violation of the constitutional rights spelled out in the Fourth, Fifth, and Sixth Amendments, as well as all evidence derived from illegally obtained evidence, normally must be excluded from the trial. Evidence derived from illegally obtained evidence is known as the "fruit of the poisonous tree." For example, if a confession is obtained after an illegal arrest, the arrest is "the

poisonous tree," and the confession, if "tainted" by the arrest, is the "fruit."

The purpose of the exclusionary rule is to deter police from conducting warrantless searches and engaging in other misconduct. The rule is sometimes criticized because it can lead to injustice. Many a defendant has "gotten off on a technicality" because law enforcement personnel failed to observe procedural requirements. Even though a defendant may be obviously guilty, if the evidence of that guilt was obtained improperly (without a valid search warrant, for example), it normally cannot be used against the defendant in court.

The *Miranda* Rule In regard to criminal procedure, one of the questions many courts faced in the 1950s and 1960s was not whether suspects had constitutional rights—that was not in doubt—but how and when those rights could be exercised. Could the right to be silent (under the Fifth Amendment's prohibition against self-incrimination) be exercised during pretrial interrogation proceedings or only during the trial? Were confessions obtained from suspects admissible in court if the suspects had not been advised of their right to remain silent and other constitutional rights?

To clarify these issues, the United States Supreme Court issued a landmark decision in 1966 in *Miranda v. Arizona,* which we present here. Today, the procedural rights required by the Court in this case are familiar to virtually every American.

---

15. *Baze v. Rees,* ___ U.S. ___, 128 S.Ct. 1520, 170 L.Ed.2d 420 (2008).

CASE 6.3 **Miranda v. Arizona**

LANDMARK AND CLASSIC CASES Supreme Court of the United States, 384 U.S. 436, 86 S.Ct. 1602, 16 L.Ed.2d 694 (1966).

FACTS On March 13, 1963, Ernesto Miranda was arrested at his home for the kidnapping and rape of an eighteen-year-old woman. Miranda was taken to a Phoenix, Arizona, police station and questioned by two officers. Two hours later, the officers emerged from the interrogation room with a written confession signed by Miranda. A paragraph at the top of the confession stated that the confession had been made voluntarily, without threats or promises of immunity, and "with full knowledge of my legal rights, understanding any statement I make may be used against me." Miranda was at no time advised that he had a right to remain silent and a right to have a lawyer present. The confession was admitted into evidence at the trial, and Miranda was convicted and sentenced to prison for twenty to thirty years. Miranda appealed the decision, claiming that he had not been informed of his constitutional rights. The Supreme Court of Arizona held that Miranda's constitutional rights had not been violated and

affirmed his conviction. The *Miranda* case was subsequently reviewed by the United States Supreme Court.

ISSUE Can a confession that was obtained from a person in custody who had not previously been informed of his or her constitutional rights be used as evidence against the person?

DECISION No. The United States Supreme Court held that the defendant Miranda could not be convicted of the crime on the basis of his confession. The confession was inadmissible as evidence because the defendant had not been informed of his constitutional rights to remain silent and to have counsel present prior to police interrogation.

REASON For any statement made by the defendant to be admissible, the defendant must be informed of certain constitutional rights before police interrogation. If, after being informed of these rights, the accused waives the right to remain silent and to have counsel present, the government must demonstrate that the waiver was made knowingly, voluntarily, and intelligently. The Court reasoned that because Miranda had not been explicitly informed of his constitutional rights prior to the police questioning, his confession could not be admitted into evidence. The paragraph on the written confession form was insufficient to show that he knowingly and voluntarily waived these rights before his confession.

IMPACT OF THIS CASE ON TODAY'S LAW *Police officers routinely advise suspects of their "Miranda rights" on arrest. When Ernesto Miranda himself was later murdered, the*

suspected murderer was read his Miranda *rights. Despite significant criticisms and later attempts to overrule the* Miranda *decision through legislation, the requirements stated in this case continue to provide the benchmark by which criminal procedures are judged today.*

RELEVANT WEB SITES *To locate information on the Web concerning the* Miranda *decision, go to this text's Web site at* **www.cengage.com/blaw/fbl***, select "Chapter 6," and click on "URLs for Landmarks."*

■

CRIMINAL PROCESS

As mentioned, a criminal prosecution differs significantly from a civil case in several respects. These differences reflect the desire to safeguard the rights of the individual against the state. Exhibit 6–4 on the next page summarizes the major procedural steps in a criminal case. Here we discuss three phases of the criminal process—arrest, indictment or information, and trial—in more detail.

Arrest

Before a warrant for arrest can be issued, there must be probable cause for believing that the individual in question has committed a crime. As discussed earlier, *probable cause* can be defined as a substantial likelihood that the person has committed or is about to commit a crime. Note that probable cause involves a likelihood, not just a possibility. An arrest may sometimes be made without a warrant if there is no time to get one, as when a police officer observes a crime taking place, but the action of the arresting officer is still judged by the standard of probable cause.

Indictment or Information

Individuals must be formally charged with having committed specific crimes before they can be brought to trial. If issued by a grand jury, this charge is called an **indictment**.[16] A **grand jury** usually consists of more jurors than the ordinary trial jury. A grand jury does not determine the guilt or innocence of an accused party; rather, its function is to hear the state's evidence and determine whether a reasonable basis (probable cause) exists for believing that a crime has been committed and that a trial ought to be held.

Usually, grand juries are used in cases involving serious crimes, such as murder. For lesser crimes, an individual may be formally charged with a crime by what is called an **information,** or criminal complaint. An information will be issued by a government prosecutor if the prosecutor determines that there is sufficient evidence to justify bringing the individual to trial.

Trial

At a criminal trial, the accused person does not have to prove anything; the entire burden of proof is on the prosecutor (the state). As mentioned earlier, the prosecution must show that, based on all the evidence presented, the defendant's guilt is established *beyond a reasonable doubt.* If there is a reasonable doubt as to whether a criminal defendant did, in fact, commit the crime with which she or he has been charged, then the verdict must be "not guilty." Note that giving a verdict of "not guilty" is not the same as stating that the defendant is innocent. Such a verdict merely means that not enough evidence was properly presented to the court to prove guilt beyond a reasonable doubt.

Courts have complex rules about what types of evidence may be presented and how the evidence may be brought out in criminal cases. These rules are designed to ensure that evidence in trials is relevant, reliable, and not prejudicial toward the defendant. For example, under the Sixth Amendment, persons accused of a crime have the right to confront the witnesses against them in open court. If the prosecutor wishes to present a witness's testimony by means of a document obtained in an *ex parte* examination, the prosecutor must show that the witness is unavailable to testify in court and that the defendant had a prior opportunity to cross-examine her or him. (In this context, an *ex parte* examination is a proceeding for the benefit of the prosecution without notice to the defendant.)

---

16. Pronounced in-*dyte*-ment.

EXHIBIT 6–4 **Major Procedural Steps in a Criminal Case**

ARREST
Police officer takes suspect into custody. Most arrests are made without a warrant. After the arrest, the officer searches the suspect, who is then taken to the police station.

BOOKING
At the police station, the suspect is searched again, photographed, fingerprinted, and allowed at least one telephone call. After the booking, charges are reviewed, and if they are not dropped, a complaint is filed and a magistrate (judge) reviews the case for probable cause.

INITIAL APPEARANCE
The defendant appears before the judge, who informs the defendant of the charges and of his or her rights. If the defendant requests a lawyer and cannot afford one, a lawyer is appointed. The judge sets bail (conditions under which a suspect can obtain release pending disposition of the case).

GRAND JURY
A grand jury determines if there is probable cause to believe that the defendant committed the crime. The federal government and about half of the states require grand jury indictments for at least some felonies.

PRELIMINARY HEARING
In a court proceeding, a prosecutor presents evidence, and the judge determines if there is probable cause to hold the defendant over for trial.

INDICTMENT
An *indictment* is a written document issued by the grand jury to formally charge the defendant with a crime.

INFORMATION
An *information* is a formal criminal charge made by the prosecutor.

ARRAIGNMENT
The defendant is brought before the court, informed of the charges, and asked to enter a plea.

PLEA BARGAIN
A plea bargain is a prosecutor's promise to make concessions (or promise to seek concessions) in return for a defendant's guilty plea. Concessions may include a reduced charge or a lesser sentence.

GUILTY PLEA
In many jurisdictions, most cases that reach the arraignment stage do not go to trial but are resolved by a guilty plea, often as a result of a plea bargain. The judge sets the case for sentencing.

TRIAL
Trials can be either jury trials or bench trials. (In a bench trial, there is no jury, and the judge decides questions of fact as well as questions of law.) If the verdict is "guilty," the judge sets a date for the sentencing. Everyone convicted of a crime has the right to an appeal.

Sentencing Guidelines

In 1984, Congress passed the Sentencing Reform Act and created the U.S. Sentencing Commission in an attempt to standardize sentences for federal crimes. The commission's guidelines, which became effective in 1987, established a range of possible penalties for each federal crime and required the judge to select a sentence from within that range. The system was mandatory in that judges were not allowed to deviate from the specified sentencing range. Some federal judges felt uneasy about imposing long prison sentences on certain defendants, particularly first-time offenders and those convicted of crimes involving small quantities of illegal drugs.[17]

In 2005, the Supreme Court held that certain provisions of the federal sentencing guidelines were unconstitutional.[18] The case involved Freddie Booker, who was arrested with 92.5 grams of crack cocaine in his possession. During questioning by police, he signed a written statement in which he admitted to selling an additional quantity—566 grams of crack cocaine—elsewhere. The additional 566 grams of crack were not brought up at trial. Nevertheless, under the federal sentencing guidelines the judge was required to sentence Booker to twenty-two years in prison. Ultimately, the Supreme Court ruled that this sentence was unconstitutional because a jury did not find beyond a reasonable doubt that Booker had possessed the additional 566 grams of crack.

The Supreme Court's ruling in 2005 essentially changed the federal sentencing guidelines from mandatory to advisory. Depending on the circumstances of the case, a federal trial judge may now depart from the guidelines if he or she believes that it is reasonable to do so. Note, however, that the sentencing guidelines still exist and provide for enhanced punishment for certain types of crimes, including white-collar crimes, violations of the Sarbanes-Oxley Act (see Chapter 3), and violations of securities laws (see Chapter 27).

CYBER CRIME

Some years ago, the American Bar Association defined **computer crime** as any act that is directed against computers and computer parts, that uses computers as instruments of crime, or that involves computers and constitutes abuse. Today, because much of the crime committed with the use of computers occurs in cyberspace, many computer crimes fall under the broad label of **cyber crime**. Here, we look at sev-

eral types of activity that constitute cyber crimes against persons or property. Other cyber crimes will be discussed in later chapters of this text as they relate to particular topics, such as banking or consumer law. For a discussion of how some states are passing laws making spamming a crime, see this chapter's *Adapting the Law to the Online Environment* feature on the following page.

Cyber Theft

In cyberspace, thieves are not subject to the physical limitations of the "real" world. A thief can steal data stored in a networked computer with Internet access from anywhere on the globe. Only the speed of the connection and the thief's computer equipment limit the quantity of data that can be stolen.

Financial Crimes Computer networks provide opportunities for employees to commit crimes that can involve serious economic losses. For example, employees of a company's accounting department can transfer funds among accounts with little effort and often with less risk than would be involved in transactions evidenced by paperwork.

Generally, the dependence of businesses on computer operations has left firms vulnerable to sabotage, fraud, embezzlement, and the theft of proprietary data, such as trade secrets or other intellectual property. As noted in Chapter 5, the piracy of intellectual property via the Internet is one of the most serious legal challenges facing lawmakers and the courts today.

Identity Theft A form of cyber theft that has become particularly troublesome in recent years is **identity theft.** Identity theft occurs when the wrongdoer steals a form of identification—such as a name, date of birth, or Social Security number—and uses the information to access the victim's financial resources. This crime existed to a certain extent before the widespread use of the Internet. Thieves would "steal" calling-card numbers by watching people using public telephones, or they would rifle through garbage to find bank account or credit-card numbers. The identity thieves would then use the calling-card or credit-card numbers or would withdraw funds from the victims' accounts. The Internet, however, has turned identity theft into perhaps the fastest-growing financial crime in the United States.

Three federal statutes deal specifically with identity theft. The Identity Theft and Assumption Deterrence Act of 1998[19] made identity theft a federal crime and directed the U.S. Sentencing Commission to incorporate the crime into its sentencing guidelines. The Fair and Accurate Credit Transactions Act of 2003[20] gives victims of identity theft certain rights in

---

17. See, for example, *United States v. Angelos,* 345 F.Supp.2d 1227 (D. Utah 2004).

18. *United States v. Booker,* 543 U.S. 220, 125 S.Ct. 738, 160 L.Ed.2d 621 (2005).

19. 18 U.S.C. Section 1028.

20. 15 U.S.C. Sections 1681 *et seq.*

When Spamming Is a Crime

A significant issue today is whether persons who send spam (bulk unsolicited e-mail) over the Internet can be charged with a crime. As discussed in Chapter 4, spamming has become a major problem for businesses. At the time the federal CAN-SPAM Act was passed in 2003, the U.S. Senate found that spam constituted more than half of all e-mail traffic and projected that it would cost corporations more than $113 billion by 2009. By all accounts, though, the amount of spam has actually increased since the federal CAN-SPAM Act was enacted. Given that the CAN-SPAM Act has failed to reduce the amount of spam, some states have taken matters into their own hands and have now passed laws making spamming a crime.

A Few States Have Enacted Criminal Spamming Statutes

A few states, such as Maryland and Virginia, have passed groundbreaking laws that make spamming a crime.[a] Under the Virginia Computer Crimes Act (VCCA), it is a crime against property to use a computer or computer network "with the intent to falsify or forge electronic mail transmission information or other routing information in any manner." The law further provides that attempting to send spam to more than 2,500 recipients in any twenty-four-hour period is a felony. The VCCA also includes provisions allowing authorities to seize the assets or proceeds obtained through an illegal spamming operation.

Maryland's antispamming law similarly prohibits sending commercial e-mail to recipients using false information about the identity of the sender, the origin, transmission path, or subject of the message. Under the Maryland law, however, the number of spam messages required to convict a person of the offense is much lower. Sending ten illegal messages in twenty-four hours violates the statute, and the more spam sent, the more severe the punishment will be, up to a maximum of ten years in prison and a $25,000 fine.

a. See, for example, Maryland Code, Criminal Law, Section 3-805.1; and Virginia Code Annotated Sections 18.2–152.3:1.

America's First Conviction for Felony Spamming

In the most significant case on criminal spamming to date, the Supreme Court of Virginia in 2008 upheld the conviction of Jeremy Jaynes, a resident of North Carolina who had sent some of his junk messages through servers in Virginia. One of the world's most prolific spammers, Jaynes had accumulated $24 million by spamming get-rich-quick schemes, pornography, and sham products and services. At his residence, police found a CD containing at least 176 million e-mail addresses and more than 1.3 billion user names. Jaynes also had a DVD containing e-mail addresses and other personal account information for millions of individuals, all of which had been stolen from America Online.

Jaynes was convicted of three counts of felony spamming based on the fact that he had sent more than ten thousand pieces of spam per day on three separate days, using false Internet addresses and aliases. The jury sentenced him to nine years in prison. On appeal, Jaynes argued that Virginia did not have jurisdiction over him and that the state's criminal spamming statute violated his First Amendment rights to free speech. The state appellate court found that jurisdiction was proper because Jaynes had utilized servers within the state and concluded that the statute did not violate the First Amendment.[b] Jaynes appealed to the state's highest court, which ultimately upheld his conviction.[c] This was the first felony conviction for spamming in the United States.

 FOR CRITICAL ANALYSIS *How might criminal spamming statutes, which are likely to vary among the states, affect legitimate businesspersons who advertise on the Internet? If a business discovers that a spammer is using the business's name in connection with spam, what recourse does that business have?*

b. *Jaynes v. Commonwealth of Virginia,* 48 Va.App. 673, 634 S.E.2d 357 (2006).
c. *Jaynes v. Commonwealth of Virginia,* 275 Va. 341, 657 S.E.2d 478 (2008); rehearing granted in part and order clarified by 666 S.E.2d 502 (2008).

working with creditors and credit bureaus to remove negative information from their credit reports. The Identity Theft Penalty Enhancement Act of 2004[21] authorized more severe penalties in aggravated cases in which the identity theft was committed in connection with the thief's employment or with other serious crimes (such as terrorism or firearms or immigration offenses).

21. 18 U.S.C. Section 1028A.

Hacking and Cyberterrorism

Persons who use one computer to break into another are sometimes referred to as **hackers.** Hackers who break into computers without authorization often commit cyber theft. Sometimes, however, their principal aim is to prove how smart they are by gaining access to others' password-protected computers and causing random data errors or making telephone calls for free.[22] **Cyberterrorists** are hackers who, rather than trying to gain attention, strive to remain undetected so that they can exploit computers for a serious impact. Just as "real" terrorists destroyed the World Trade Center towers and a portion of the Pentagon in September 2001, cyberterrorists might explode "logic bombs" to shut down central computers. Such activities can pose a danger to national security.

Businesses may be targeted by cyberterrorists as well as hackers. The goals of a hacking operation might include a wholesale theft of data, such as a merchant's customer files, or the monitoring of a computer to discover a business firm's plans and transactions. A cyberterrorist might also want to insert false codes or data. For example, the processing control system of a food manufacturer could be changed to alter the levels of ingredients so that consumers of the food would become ill.

A cyberterrorist attack on a major financial institution such as the New York Stock Exchange or a large bank could leave securities or money markets in flux and seriously affect the daily lives of millions of citizens. Similarly, any prolonged disruption of computer, cable, satellite, or telecommunications systems due to the actions of expert hackers would have serious repercussions on business operations—and national security—on a global level. Computer viruses are another tool that can be used by cyberterrorists to cripple communications networks.

Prosecuting Cyber Crimes

The "location" of cyber crime (cyberspace) has raised new issues in the investigation of crimes and the prosecution of offenders. A threshold issue is, of course, jurisdiction. A person who commits an act against a business in California, where the act is a cyber crime, might never have set foot in California but might instead reside in New York, or even in Canada, where the act may not be a crime. If the crime was committed via e-mail, the question arises as to whether the

---

22. The total cost of crime on the Internet is estimated to be many billions of dollars annually, but two-thirds of that total is said to consist of unpaid-for long distance calls.

e-mail would constitute sufficient "minimum contacts" (see Chapter 1) for the victim's state to exercise jurisdiction over the perpetrator.

Identifying the wrongdoer can also be difficult. Cyber criminals do not leave physical traces, such as fingerprints or DNA samples, as evidence of their crimes. Even electronic "footprints" can be hard to find and follow. For example, e-mail may be sent through a remailer, an online service that guarantees that a message cannot be traced to its source.

For these reasons, laws written to protect physical property are difficult to apply in cyberspace. Nonetheless, governments at both the state and federal levels have taken significant steps toward controlling cyber crime, both by applying existing criminal statutes and by enacting new laws that specifically address wrongs committed in cyberspace.

The Computer Fraud and Abuse Act

Perhaps the most significant federal statute specifically addressing cyber crime is the Counterfeit Access Device and Computer Fraud and Abuse Act of 1984 (commonly known as the Computer Fraud and Abuse Act, or CFAA). This act, as amended by the National Information Infrastructure Protection Act of 1996,[23] provides, among other things, that a person who accesses a computer online, without authority, to obtain classified, restricted, or protected data, or attempts to do so, is subject to criminal prosecution. Such data could include financial and credit records, medical records, legal files, military and national security files, and other confidential information in government or private computers. The crime has two elements: accessing a computer without authority and taking the data.

This theft is a felony if it is committed for a commercial purpose or for private financial gain, or if the value of the stolen data (or computer time) exceeds $5,000. Penalties include fines and imprisonment for up to twenty years. A victim of computer theft can also bring a civil suit against the violator to obtain damages, an injunction, and other relief.

---

23. 18 U.S.C. Section 1030.

Edward Hanousek worked for Pacific & Arctic Railway and Navigation Company (P&A) as a roadmaster of the White Pass & Yukon Railroad in Alaska. As an officer of

the corporation, Hanousek was responsible "for every detail of the safe and efficient maintenance and construction of track, structures, and marine facilities of the entire railroad," including special projects. One project was a rock quarry, known as "6-mile," above the Skagway River. Next to the quarry, and just beneath the surface, ran a high-pressure oil pipeline owned by

Pacific & Arctic Pipeline, Inc., P&A's sister company. When the quarry's backhoe operator punctured the pipeline, an estimated 1,000 to 5,000 gallons of oil were discharged into the river. Hanousek was charged with negligently discharging a harmful quantity of oil into a navigable water of the United States in violation of the criminal provisions of the Clean Water Act (CWA). Using the information presented in the chapter, answer the following questions.

1 Did Hanousek have the required mental state (*mens rea*) to be convicted of a crime? Why or why not?

2 Which theory discussed in the chapter would enable a court to hold Hanousek criminally liable for violating the statute regardless of whether he participated in, directed, or even knew about the specific violation?

3 Could the quarry's backhoe operator who punctured the pipeline also be charged with a crime in this situation? Explain.

4 Suppose that at trial, Hanousek argued that he could not be convicted because he was not aware of the requirements of the CWA. Would this defense be successful? Why or why not?

TERMS AND CONCEPTS

actus reus 126
arson 128
beyond a reasonable doubt 125
burglary 128
computer crime 141
consent 134
crime 124
cyber crime 141
cyberterrorist 143
double jeopardy 137
duress 134
embezzlement 129

entrapment 135
exclusionary rule 138
felony 132
forgery 128
grand jury 139
hacker 142
identity theft 141
indictment 139
information 139
insider trading 130
larceny 128
mens rea 126

misdemeanor 132
money laundering 132
petty offense 132
plea bargaining 135
probable cause 135
robbery 127
search warrant 135
self-defense 134
self-incrimination 135
white-collar crime 129

CHAPTER SUMMARY   Criminal Law and Cyber Crime

Civil Law and Criminal Law (See pages 124–125.)	1. *Civil law*—Spells out the duties that exist between persons or between citizens and their governments, excluding the duty not to commit crimes. 2. *Criminal law*—Has to do with crimes, which are defined as wrongs against society proclaimed in statutes and punishable by society through fines and/or imprisonment—and, in some cases, death. Because crimes are *offenses against society as a whole,* they are prosecuted by a public official, not by victims. 3. *Key differences*—An important difference between civil and criminal law is that the standard of proof is higher in criminal cases. See Exhibit 6–1 on page 125 for other differences between civil and criminal law. 4. *Civil liability for criminal acts*—A criminal act may give rise to both criminal liability and tort liability. See Exhibit 6–2 on page 126 for an example of criminal and tort liability for the same act.
Criminal Liability (See pages 125–127.)	1. *Guilty act*—In general, some form of harmful act must be committed for a crime to exist. 2. *Intent*—An intent to commit a crime, or a wrongful mental state, is generally required for a crime to exist.
Corporate Criminal Liability (See page 127.)	1. *Liability of corporations*—Corporations normally are liable for the crimes committed by their agents and employees within the course and scope of their employment. Corporations cannot be imprisoned, but they can be fined or denied certain legal privileges.

CHAPTER SUMMARY	Criminal Law and Cyber Crime—Continued
Corporate Criminal Liability—Continued	2. *Liability of corporate officers and directors*—Corporate directors and officers are personally liable for the crimes they commit and may be held liable for the actions of employees under their supervision.
Types of Crimes (See pages 127–132.)	Crimes fall into five general categories: violent crime, property crime, public order crime, white-collar crime, and organized crime. See Exhibit 6–3 on page 133 for definitions and examples of these categories.
Defenses to Criminal Liability (See pages 132–135.)	Defenses to criminal liability include infancy, intoxication, insanity, mistake, consent, duress, justifiable use of force, entrapment, and the statute of limitations. Also, in some cases defendants may be relieved of criminal liability, at least in part, if they are given immunity.
Constitutional Safeguards and Criminal Procedures (See pages 135–139.)	1. *Fourth Amendment*—Provides protection against unreasonable searches and seizures and requires that probable cause exist before a warrant for a search or an arrest can be issued.
	2. *Fifth Amendment*—Requires due process of law, prohibits double jeopardy, and protects against self-incrimination.
	3. *Sixth Amendment*—Provides guarantees of a speedy trial, a trial by jury, a public trial, the right to confront witnesses, and the right to counsel.
	4. *Eighth Amendment*—Prohibits excessive bail and fines, and cruel and unusual punishment.
	5. *Exclusionary rule*—A rule of criminal procedure that prohibits the introduction at trial of all evidence obtained in violation of constitutional rights, as well as any evidence derived from the illegally obtained evidence.
	6. *Miranda rule*—A rule set forth by the Supreme Court in *Miranda v. Arizona* holding that individuals who are arrested must be informed of certain constitutional rights, including their right to counsel.
Criminal Process (See pages 139–141.)	1. *Arrest, indictment, and trial*—Procedures governing arrest, indictment, and trial for a crime are designed to safeguard the rights of the individual against the state. See Exhibit 6–4 on page 140 for a summary of the procedural steps involved in prosecuting a criminal case.
	2. *Sentencing guidelines*—The federal government has established sentencing laws or guidelines. The federal sentencing guidelines indicate a range of penalties for each federal crime; federal judges consider these guidelines when imposing sentences on those convicted of federal crimes.
Cyber Crime (See pages 141–143.)	Cyber crime occurs in cyberspace. Examples include cyber theft (financial crimes committed with the aid of computers, as well as identity theft), hacking, and cyberterrorism. The Computer Fraud and Abuse Act of 1984, as amended by the National Information Infrastructure Protection Act of 1996, is a significant federal statute that addresses cyber crime.

FOR REVIEW

Answers for the even-numbered questions in this For Review *section can be found on this text's accompanying Web site at* www.cengage.com/blaw/fbl. *Select "Chapter 6" and click on "For Review."*

1 What two elements must exist before a person can be held liable for a crime? Can a corporation commit crimes?

2 What are five broad categories of crimes? What is white-collar crime?

3 What defenses might be raised by criminal defendants to avoid liability for criminal acts?

4 What constitutional safeguards exist to protect persons accused of crimes? What are the basic steps in the criminal process?

5 What is cyber crime? What laws apply to crimes committed in cyberspace?

QUESTIONS AND CASE PROBLEMS

HYPOTHETICAL SCENARIOS AND CASE PROBLEMS

6.1 Criminal versus Civil Trials. In criminal trials, the defendant must be proved guilty beyond a reasonable doubt, whereas in civil trials, the defendant need only be proved guilty by a preponderance of the evidence. Discuss why a higher standard of proof is required in criminal trials.

6.2 Hypothetical Question with Sample Answer. The following situations are similar (all involve the theft of Makoto's laptop computer), yet they represent three different crimes. Identify the three crimes, noting the differences among them.

 1 While passing Makoto's house one night, Sarah sees a laptop computer left unattended on Makoto's porch. Sarah takes the computer, carries it home, and tells everyone she owns it.

 2 While passing Makoto's house one night, Sarah sees Makoto outside with a laptop computer. Holding Makoto at gunpoint, Sarah forces him to give up the computer. Then Sarah runs away with it.

 3 While passing Makoto's house one night, Sarah sees a laptop computer on a desk near a window. Sarah breaks the lock on the front door, enters, and leaves with the computer.

 For a sample answer to Question 6.2, go to Appendix E at the end of this text.

6.3 Double Jeopardy. Armington, while robbing a drugstore, shot and seriously injured Jennings, a drugstore clerk. Armington was subsequently convicted of armed robbery and assault and battery in a criminal trial. Jennings later brought a civil tort suit against Armington for damages. Armington contended that he could not be tried again for the same crime, as that would constitute double jeopardy, which is prohibited by the Fifth Amendment to the U.S. Constitution. Is Armington correct? Explain.

6.4 Larceny. In February 2001, a homeowner hired Jimmy Smith, a contractor claiming to employ a crew of thirty workers, to build a garage. The homeowner paid Smith $7,950 and agreed to make additional payments as needed to complete the project, up to $15,900. Smith promised to start the next day and finish within eight weeks. Nearly a month passed with no work, while Smith lied to the homeowner that materials were on "back order." During a second month, footings were created for the foundation, and a subcontractor poured the concrete slab, but Smith did not return the homeowner's phone calls. After eight weeks, the homeowner confronted Smith, who promised to complete the job, worked on the site that day until lunch, and never returned. Three months later, the homeowner again confronted Smith, who promised to "pay [him] off" later that day but did not do so. In March 2002, the state of Georgia filed criminal charges

against Smith. While his trial was pending, he promised to pay the homeowner "next week," but again failed to refund any money. The value of the labor performed before Smith abandoned the project was between $800 and $1,000, the value of the materials was $367, and the subcontractor was paid $2,270. Did Smith commit larceny? Explain. [*Smith v. State of Georgia*, 265 Ga.App.57, 592 S.E.2d 871 (2004)]

6.5 Trial. Robert Michels met Allison Formal through an online dating Web site in 2002. Michels represented himself as the retired chief executive officer of a large company that he had sold for millions of dollars. In January 2003, Michels proposed that he and Formal create a limited liability company (a special form of business organization discussed in Chapter 24)—Formal Properties Trust, LLC—to "channel their investments in real estate." Formal agreed to contribute $100,000 to the company and wrote two $50,000 checks to "Michels and Associates, LLC." Six months later, Michels told Formal that their LLC had been formed in Delaware. Later, Formal asked Michels about her investments. He responded evasively, and she demanded that an independent accountant review the firm's records. Michels refused. Formal contacted the police. Michels was charged in a Virginia state court with obtaining money by false pretenses. The Delaware secretary of state verified, in two certified documents, that "Formal Properties Trust, L.L.C." and "Michels and Associates, L.L.C." did not exist in Delaware. Did the admission of the Delaware secretary of state's certified documents at Michels's trial violate his rights under the Sixth Amendment? Why or why not? [*Michels v. Commonwealth of Virginia*, 47 Va.App. 461, 624 S.E.2d 675 (2006)]

6.6 Case Problem with Sample Answer. Helm Instruction Co. in Maumee, Ohio, makes custom electrical control systems. Helm hired Patrick Walsh in September 1998 to work as comptroller. Walsh soon developed a close relationship with Richard Wilhelm, Helm's president, who granted Walsh's request to hire Shari Price as Walsh's assistant. Wilhelm was not aware that Walsh and Price were engaged in an extramarital affair. Over the next five years, Walsh and Price spent more than $200,000 of Helm's funds on themselves. Among other things, Walsh drew unauthorized checks on Helm's accounts to pay his personal credit-card bills and issued to Price and himself unauthorized salary increases, overtime payments, and tuition reimbursement payments, altering Helm's records to hide the payments. After an investigation, Helm officials confronted Walsh. He denied the affair with Price, claimed that his unauthorized use of Helm's funds was an "interest-free loan" and argued that it was less of a burden on the company to pay his credit-card bills than to give him the salary increases to which he felt he was entitled. Did

Walsh commit a crime? If so, what crime did he commit? Discuss. [*State v. Walsh*, 113 Ohio App.3d 1515, 866 N.E.2d 513 (6 Dist. 2007)]

 After you have answered Problem 6.6, compare your answer with the sample answer given on the Web site that accompanies this text. Go to www.cengage.com/blaw/fbl, select "Chapter 6," and click on "Case Problem with Sample Answer."

6.7 **A Question of Ethics.** *A troublesome issue concerning the constitutional privilege against self-incrimination has to do with the extent to which trickery by law enforcement officers during an interrogation may overwhelm a suspect's will to avoid self-incrimination. For example, in one case two officers questioned Charles McFarland, who was incarcerated in a state prison, about his connection to a handgun that had been used to shoot two other officers. McFarland was advised of his* rights *but was not asked whether he was willing to waive those rights. Instead, to induce McFarland to speak, the officers deceived him into believing that "[n]obody is going to give you charges," and he made incriminating admissions. He was indicted for possessing a handgun as a convicted felon.* [United States v. McFarland, *424 F.Supp.2d 427 (N.D.N.Y. 2006)]*

1 Review Case 6.3, *Miranda v. Arizona*, on pages 138–139. Should McFarland's statements be suppressed—that is, not be admissible at trial—because he was not asked whether he was willing to waive his rights before he made his self-incriminating statements? Does *Miranda* apply to McFarland's situation?

2 Do you think that it is fair for the police to resort to trickery and deception to bring those who may have committed crimes to justice? Why or why not? What rights or public policies must be balanced in deciding this issue?

CRITICAL THINKING AND WRITING ASSIGNMENTS

6.8 For Critical Analysis. Do you think that criminal procedure in this country is weighted too heavily in favor of accused persons? Can you think of a fairer way to balance the constitutional rights of accused persons against the right of society to be protected against criminal behavior? Should different criminal procedures be used when terrorism is involved? Explain.

6.9 **Video Question.** Go to this text's Web site at **www. cengage.com/blaw/fbl** and select "Chapter 6." Click on "Video Questions" and view the video titled *Casino*. Then answer the following questions.

1 In the video, a casino manager, Ace (Robert De Niro), discusses how politicians "won their 'comp life' when they got elected." "Comps" are the free gifts that casinos give to high-stakes gamblers to keep their business. If an elected official accepts comps, is he or she committing a crime? If so, what type of crime? Explain your answers.

2 Assume that Ace committed a crime by giving politicians comps. Can the casino, Tangiers Corp. be held liable for that crime? Why or why not? How could a court punish the corporation?

3 Suppose that the Federal Bureau of Investigation wants to search the premises of the Tangiers for evidence of criminal activity. If casino management refuses to consent to the search, what constitutional safeguards and criminal procedures, if any, protect the Tangiers?

ACCESSING THE INTERNET

For updated links to resources available on the Web, as well as a variety of other materials, visit this text's Web site at

www.cengage.com/blaw/fbl

The Bureau of Justice Statistics in the U.S. Department of Justice offers an impressive collection of statistics on crime at the following Web site:

www.ojp.usdoj.gov/bjs

For summaries and information on famous criminal cases and trials, go to either Court TV's Web site or a Web site maintained by the University of Missouri–Kansas City School of Law, respectively at

www.courttv.com/index.html
www.law.umkc.edu/faculty/projects/ftrials/ftrials.html

Many criminal codes are now online. To find your state's code, go to

www.findlaw.com

and select "State" under the link to "Laws: Cases and Codes."

To learn more about criminal procedures, go to the following interactive Web site on "Anatomy of a Murder: A Trip through Our Nation's Legal Justice System":

library.thinkquest.org/2760/home.htm

The U.S. Sentencing Guidelines can be found online at

www.ussc.gov

PRACTICAL INTERNET EXERCISES

Go to this text's Web site at **www.cengage.com/blaw/fbl**, select "Chapter 6," and click on "Practical Internet Exercises." There you will find the following Internet research exercises that you can perform to learn more about the topics covered in this chapter.

PRACTICAL INTERNET EXERCISE 6-1   LEGAL PERSPECTIVE—Revisiting *Miranda*

PRACTICAL INTERNET EXERCISE 6-2   MANAGEMENT PERSPECTIVE—Hackers

PRACTICAL INTERNET EXERCISE 6-3   INTERNATIONAL PERSPECTIVE—Fighting Cyber Crime Worldwide

BEFORE THE TEST

Go to this text's Web site at **www.cengage.com/blaw/fbl**, select "Chapter 6," and click on "Interactive Quizzes." You will find a number of interactive questions relating to this chapter.

UNIT TWO   EXTENDED CASE STUDY

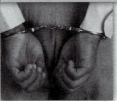

MedImmune, Inc. v. Genentech, Inc.

As explained in Chapter 1, under Article III of the U.S. Constitution, the jurisdiction of the federal courts is limited to actual "Cases" or "Controversies." The Declaratory Judgment Act also requires the existence of an "actual controversy" before a court can act.[1] As you read in Chapter 5 on intellectual property, a license agreement permits the use of a trademark, copyright, patent, or trade secret for certain purposes. In this extended case study, we look at MedImmune, Inc. v. Genentech, Inc.,[2] a case involving a dispute between the holder of a patent license and the owner of the patent over the patent's validity. The petitioner in this case is seeking a declaratory judgment, which is a court ruling that establishes the rights and obligations of the parties but does not include any provisions to enforce those rights or obligations. Is this an "actual controversy" on which a court can issue a declaratory judgment? Or does the licensee first have to breach the license agreement and subject itself to a possible suit for patent infringement, with a potential assessment of treble (triple) damages and a loss of the license?

CASE BACKGROUND   MedImmune, Inc., makes and sells Synagis, a drug to prevent respiratory disease in children. In 1997, MedImmune entered into a license agreement with Genentech, Inc. The license covered a patent relating to the production of "chimeric antibodies"

and a pending patent application relating to "the coexpression of immunoglobulin chains in recombinant host cells." MedImmune agreed to pay royalties on sales of

---

1. 28 U.S.C. Section 2201(a).

2. 549 U.S. 118, 127 S.Ct. 764, 166 L.Ed.2d 604 (2007). This opinion can be read online at **www.findlaw.com/casecode/supreme.html**. In the "Browsing" section, click on "2007 Decisions." On the resulting page, click on the name of the case to access the opinion.

"Licensed Products," which the agreement defined as a specified antibody, "the manufacture, use or sale of which * * * would, if not licensed * * * infringe [the covered patents]."

In December 2001, the "coexpression" application became the "Cabilly II" patent. Genentech contended that the Cabilly II patent covered Synagis and demanded the payment of royalties. MedImmune believed that the patent was invalid, but considered Genentech's demand a threat to terminate the license agreement and sue for patent infringement if MedImmune did not pay. In such a suit, MedImmune could be ordered to pay treble damages and be enjoined from selling Synagis, which accounted for more than 80 percent of its revenue. Unwilling to take this risk, MedImmune paid the royalties and filed a suit in a federal district court against Genentech, seeking a declaratory judgment. The court dismissed the suit, and MedImmune appealed to the U.S. Court of Appeals for the Federal Circuit, which affirmed the dismissal. MedImmune appealed to the United States Supreme Court.

MAJORITY OPINION

Justice *SCALIA* delivered the opinion of the Court.

* * * *

The Declaratory Judgment Act provides that, "in a case of actual controversy within its jurisdiction * * * any court of the United States * * * may declare the rights and other legal relations of any interested party seeking such declaration, whether or not further relief is or could be sought." * * * [T]he phrase "case of actual controversy" in the Act refers to the type of "Cases" and "Controversies" that are justiciable [real issues able to be resolved by a court] under Article III.

* * * *Basically, the question in each case is whether the facts alleged, under all the circumstances, show that there is a substantial controversy, between parties having adverse legal interests, of sufficient immediacy and reality to warrant the issuance of a declaratory judgment.* [Emphasis added.]

There is no dispute that these standards would have been satisfied if petitioner [MedImmune] had taken the final step of refusing to make royalty payments under the 1997 license agreement. * * * Petitioner's own acts, in other words, eliminate the imminent threat of harm. The question before us is whether this causes the dispute no longer to be a case or controversy within the meaning of Article III.

Our analysis must begin with the recognition that, where threatened action by government is concerned, we do not require a plaintiff to expose himself to liability before bringing suit to challenge the basis for the threat—for example, the constitutionality of a law threatened to be enforced. The plaintiff's own action (or inaction) in failing to violate the law eliminates the imminent threat of prosecution, but nonetheless does not eliminate Article III jurisdiction. * * * *Simply not doing what [a plaintiff] claim[s] the right to do * * ** [does] not preclude subject-matter jurisdiction because the threat-eliminating behavior [is] effectively coerced. The dilemma posed by that coercion—putting the challenger to the choice between abandoning his rights or risking prosecution—is a dilemma that it was the very purpose of the Declaratory Judgment Act to ameliorate. [Emphasis added.]

[United States] Supreme Court jurisprudence is more rare regarding application of the Declaratory Judgment Act to situations in which the plaintiff's self-avoidance of imminent injury is coerced by threatened enforcement action of a private party rather than the government. Lower federal courts, however (and state courts interpreting [state] declaratory judgment Acts requiring "actual controversy"), have long accepted jurisdiction in such cases.

The only Supreme Court decision in point is, fortuitously, close on its facts to the case before us. * * * [In that case] royalties were being paid under protest and under the compulsion of an injunction decree, and unless the injunction decree [was] modified, the only other course of action was to defy it, and to risk not only actual but treble damages in infringement suits. We concluded that "the requirements of a case or controversy are met where payment of a claim is demanded as of right and where payment is made, but where the involuntary or coercive nature of the exaction preserves the right to recover the sums paid or to challenge the legality of the claim."

* * * *

We hold that petitioner was not required, insofar as Article III is concerned, to break or terminate its 1997 license agreement before seeking a declaratory judgment in federal court that the underlying patent is invalid, unenforceable, or not infringed. *The Court of Appeals erred in affirming the dismissal of this action for lack of subject-matter jurisdiction.* [Emphasis added.]

The judgment of the Court of Appeals is reversed, and the cause is remanded for proceedings consistent with this opinion.

It is so ordered.

(Continued)

DISSENTING OPINION

Justice *THOMAS*, dissenting.

We granted *certiorari* in this case to determine whether a patent licensee in good standing must breach its license prior to challenging the validity of the underlying patent * * * . The answer to that question is yes. We have consistently held that parties do not have standing to obtain rulings on matters that remain hypothetical or conjectural. We have also held that the declaratory judgment procedure cannot be used to obtain advance rulings on matters that would be addressed in a future case of actual controversy. MedImmune has sought a declaratory judgment for precisely that purpose, and I would therefore affirm the Court of Appeals' holding that there is no Article III jurisdiction over MedImmune's claim. The Court reaches the opposite result * * * . I respectfully dissent.

* * * *

Article III of the Constitution limits the judicial power to the adjudication of "Cases" or "Controversies." * * * In the constitutional sense, a "Controversy" is distinguished from a difference or dispute of a hypothetical or abstract character; from one that is academic or moot. The controversy must be definite and concrete, touching the legal relations of parties having adverse legal interests. * * * It must be a real and substantial controversy * * * , as distinguished from an opinion advising what the law would be upon a hypothetical state of facts.

* * * *

The facts before us present no case or controversy under Article III. * * * MedImmune's actions in entering into and continuing to comply with the license agreement deprived Genentech of any cause of action against MedImmune. Additionally, MedImmune had no cause of action against Genentech. * * *

* * * MedImmune wants to know whether, if it decides to breach its license agreement with Genentech, and if Genentech sues it for patent infringement, it will have a successful affirmative defense. Presumably, upon a favorable determination, MedImmune would then stop making royalty payments, knowing in advance that the federal courts stand behind its decision. * * * MedImmune has therefore asked the courts to render an opinion advising what the law would be upon a hypothetical state of facts. A federal court cannot, consistent with Article III, provide MedImmune with such an opinion.

* * * To hold a patent valid if it is not infringed is to decide a hypothetical case. Of course, MedImmune presents exactly that case. * * * [Thus] I would hold that this case presents no actual case or controversy.

 QUESTIONS FOR ANALYSIS

1 LAW. What was the majority's decision on the principal question before the Court in this case? What were the reasons for this decision?

2 LAW. How did the dissent interpret the issue before the Court? What were the reasons for this interpretation?

3 ETHICS. Suppose that either or both of the parties in this case had asserted their respective positions only to increase their profits. Would this have been unethical? Explain.

4 ECONOMIC DIMENSIONS. This case resolved what seems to be a technical question in a dispute between a pharmaceutical maker and a biotechnology firm. What is the practical importance of the ruling?

5 IMPLICATIONS FOR THE BUSINESSPERSON. What does the outcome of this case suggest to the smaller start-up company that relies on a license to obtain patented technology?

UNIT THREE Contracts

UNIT CONTENTS

CHAPTER 7
Nature and Classification

LEARNING OBJECTIVES

AFTER READING THIS CHAPTER, YOU SHOULD BE ABLE TO ANSWER THE FOLLOWING QUESTIONS:

1 What is a contract? What is the objective theory of contracts?

2 What are the four basic elements necessary to the formation of a valid contract?

3 What is the difference between an implied-in-fact contract and an implied-in-law contract (quasi contract)?

4 How does a void contract differ from a voidable contract? What is an unenforceable contract?

5 Why have plain language laws been enacted? What rules guide the courts in interpreting contracts?

C ontract law deals with, among other things, the formation and keeping of promises. A **promise** is an assertion that something either will or will not happen in the future.

Like other types of law, contract law reflects our social values, interests, and expectations at a given point in time. It shows, for example, what kinds of promises our society thinks should be legally binding. It distinguishes between promises that create only *moral* obligations (such as a promise to take a friend to lunch) and promises that are legally binding (such as a promise to pay for merchandise purchased). Contract law also demonstrates what excuses our society accepts for breaking certain types of promises. In addition, it shows what promises are considered to be contrary to public policy—against the interests of society as a whole—and therefore legally invalid. When the person making a promise is a child or is mentally incompetent, for example, a question will arise as to whether the promise should be enforced. Resolving such questions is the essence of contract law.

AN OVERVIEW OF CONTRACT LAW

Before we look at the numerous rules that courts use to determine whether a particular promise will be enforced, it is necessary to understand some fundamental concepts of contract

law. In this section, we describe the sources and general function of contract law. We also provide the definition of a contract and introduce the objective theory of contracts.

Sources of Contract Law

The common law governs all contracts except when it has been modified or replaced by statutory law, such as the Uniform Commercial Code (UCC),[1] or by administrative agency regulations. Contracts relating to services, real estate, employment, and insurance, for example, generally are governed by the common law of contracts.

Contracts for the sale and lease of goods, however, are governed by the UCC—to the extent that the UCC has modified general contract law. The relationship between general contract law and the law governing sales and leases of goods will be explored in detail in Chapter 14. In this unit covering the common law of contracts (Chapters 7 through 13), we indicate briefly in footnotes the areas in which the UCC has significantly altered common law contract principles.

---

1. See Chapter 1 and Chapter 14 for further discussions of the significance and coverage of the Uniform Commercial Code (UCC). Excerpts from the UCC are presented in Appendix C at the end of this book.

The Function of Contracts

No aspect of modern life is entirely free of contractual relationships. You acquire rights and obligations, for example, when you borrow funds, when you buy or lease a house, when you obtain insurance, when you form a business, and when you purchase goods or services. Contract law is designed to provide stability and predictability for both buyers and sellers in the marketplace.

Contract law assures the parties to private agreements that the promises they make will be enforceable. Clearly, many promises are kept because the parties involved feel a moral obligation to do so or because keeping a promise is in their mutual self-interest. The **promisor** (the person making the promise) and the **promisee** (the person to whom the promise is made) may decide to honor their agreement for other reasons. Nevertheless, the rules of contract law are often followed in business agreements to avoid potential problems.

By supplying procedures for enforcing private agreements, contract law provides an essential condition for the existence of a market economy. Without a legal framework of reasonably assured expectations within which to plan and venture, businesspersons would be able to rely only on the good faith of others. Duty and good faith are usually sufficient, but when dramatic price changes or adverse economic conditions make it costly to comply with a promise, these elements may not be enough. Contract law is necessary to ensure compliance with a promise or to entitle the innocent party to some form of relief.

Definition of a Contract

A **contract** is an agreement that can be enforced in court. It is formed by two or more parties who agree to perform or to refrain from performing some act now or in the future. Generally, contract disputes arise when there is a promise of future performance. If the contractual promise is not fulfilled, the party who made it is subject to the sanctions of a court (see Chapter 12). That party may be required to pay monetary damages for failing to perform the contractual promise; in limited instances, the party may be required to perform the promised act.

The Objective Theory of Contracts

In determining whether a contract has been formed, the element of intent is of prime importance. In contract law, intent is determined by what is referred to as the **objective theory of contracts,** not by the personal or subjective intent, or belief, of a party. The theory is that a party's intention to enter into a contract is judged by outward, objective facts as interpreted by a *reasonable person*, rather than by the party's own secret, sub-

jective intentions. Objective facts include (1) what the party said when entering into the contract, (2) how the party acted or appeared, and (3) the circumstances surrounding the transaction. As will be discussed later in this chapter, in the section on express versus implied contracts, intent to form a contract may be manifested by conduct, as well as by words, oral or written.

Freedom of Contract and Freedom from Contract

As a general rule, the law recognizes everyone's ability to enter freely into contractual arrangements. This recognition is called *freedom of contract*, a freedom protected by the U.S. Constitution in Article I, Section 10. Because freedom of contract is a fundamental public policy of the United States, courts rarely interfere with contracts that have been voluntarily made.

Of course, as in other areas of the law, there are many exceptions to the general rule that contracts voluntarily negotiated will be enforced. For example, illegal bargains, agreements that unreasonably restrain trade, and certain unfair contracts made between one party with a great amount of bargaining power and another with little power are generally not enforced. In addition, as you will read in Chapter 10, certain contracts and clauses may not be enforceable if they are contrary to public policy, fairness, and justice. These exceptions provide *freedom from contract* for persons who may have been pressured into making contracts unfavorable to themselves.

ELEMENTS OF A CONTRACT

The many topics that will be discussed in the following chapters on contract law require an understanding of the basic elements of a valid contract and the way in which the contract was created. The topics to be covered in this unit on contracts also require an understanding of the types of circumstances in which even legally valid contracts will not be enforced.

Requirements of a Valid Contract

The following list briefly describes the four requirements that must be met for a valid contract to exist. If any of these elements is lacking, no contract will have been formed. (Each item will be explained more fully in subsequent chapters.)

1 *Agreement.* An agreement to form a contract includes an *offer* and an *acceptance*. One party must offer to enter into a legal agreement, and another party must accept the terms of the offer (see Chapter 8).

2 *Consideration.* Any promises made by parties must be supported by legally sufficient and bargained-for consideration (something of value received or promised to convince a person to make a deal) (see Chapter 8).

3 *Contractual capacity.* Both parties entering into the contract must have the contractual capacity to do so; the law must recognize them as possessing characteristics that qualify them as competent parties (see Chapter 9).

4 *Legality.* The contract's purpose must be to accomplish some goal that is legal and not against public policy (see Chapter 9).

Defenses to the Enforceability of a Contract

Even if all of the elements of a valid contract are present, a contract may be unenforceable if the following requirements are not met.

1 *Genuineness of assent, or voluntary consent.* The consent of both parties must be genuine. For example, if a contract was formed as a result of fraud, mistake, or duress, the contract may not be enforceable.

2 *Form.* The contract must be in whatever form the law requires; for example, some contracts must be in writing to be enforceable.

The failure to fulfill either requirement may be raised as a *defense* to the enforceability of an otherwise valid contract. Both requirements will be explained in more detail in Chapter 10.

TYPES OF CONTRACTS

There are numerous types of contracts. They are categorized based on legal distinctions as to their formation, performance, and enforceability.

Contract Formation

As you can see in Exhibit 7–1, three classifications, or categories, of contracts are based on how and when a contract is formed. The best way to explain each type of contract is to compare one type with another, as we do in the following pages.

Bilateral versus Unilateral Contracts Every contract involves at least two parties. The **offeror** is the party making the offer. The **offeree** is the party to whom the offer is made. The offeror always promises to do or not to do something and thus is also a promisor. Whether the contract is classified as *bilateral* or *unilateral* depends on what the offeree must do to accept the offer and bind the offeror to a contract.

Bilateral Contracts. If the offeree can accept the offer simply by promising to perform, the contract is a **bilateral contract.** Hence, a bilateral contract is a "promise for a promise." An example of a bilateral contract is a contract in which one person agrees to buy another person's automobile for a specified price. No performance, such as the payment of funds or delivery of goods, need take place for a bilateral contract to be formed. The contract comes into existence at the moment the promises are exchanged.

■**EXAMPLE 7.1** Jeff offers to buy Ann's digital camera for $200. Jeff tells Ann that he will give her the cash for the camera on the following Friday when he gets paid. Ann accepts Jeff's offer and promises to give him the camera when he pays her on Friday. Jeff and Ann have formed a bilateral contract. ■

Unilateral Contracts. If the offer is phrased so that the offeree can accept only by completing the contract performance, the contract is a **unilateral contract.** Hence, a unilateral contract is a "promise for an act." In other words, the

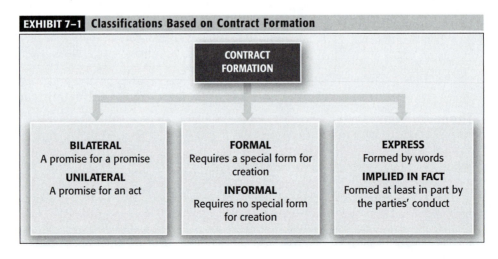

EXHIBIT 7–1 Classifications Based on Contract Formation

CONTRACT FORMATION

BILATERAL
A promise for a promise
UNILATERAL
A promise for an act

FORMAL
Requires a special form for creation
INFORMAL
Requires no special form for creation

EXPRESS
Formed by words
IMPLIED IN FACT
Formed at least in part by the parties' conduct

contract is formed not at the moment when promises are exchanged but rather when the contract is *performed.*
■EXAMPLE 7.2 Reese says to Celia, "If you drive my car from New York to Los Angeles, I'll give you $1,000." Only on Celia's completion of the act—bringing the car to Los Angeles—does she fully accept Reese's offer to pay $1,000. If she chooses not to accept the offer to drive the car to Los Angeles, there are no legal consequences. **■**

Contests, lotteries, and other competitions offering prizes are also examples of offers for unilateral contracts. If a person complies with the rules of the contest—such as by submitting the right lottery number at the right place and time—a unilateral contract is formed, binding the organization offering the prize to a contract to perform as promised in the offer.

Can a school's, or an employer's, letter of tentative acceptance to a prospective student, or a possible employee, qualify as a unilateral contract? That was the issue in the following case.

CASE 7.1 **Ardito v. City of Providence**

United States District Court, District of Rhode Island, 263 F.Supp.2d 358 (2003).

FACTS In 2001, the city of Providence, Rhode Island, decided to begin hiring police officers to fill vacancies in its police department. Because only individuals who had graduated from the Providence Police Academy were eligible, the city also decided to conduct two training sessions, the "60th and 61st Police Academies." To be admitted, an applicant had to pass a series of tests and be deemed qualified by members of the department after an interview. The applicants judged most qualified were sent a letter informing them that they had been selected to attend the academy if they successfully completed a medical checkup and a psychological examination. The letter for the applicants to the 61st Academy, dated October 15, stated that it was "a conditional offer of employment." Meanwhile, a new chief of police, Dean Esserman, decided to revise the selection process, which caused some of those who had received the letter to be rejected. Derek Ardito and thirteen other newly rejected applicants filed a suit in a federal district court against the city, seeking a halt to the 61st Academy unless they were allowed to attend. They alleged, among other things, that the city was in breach of contract.

ISSUE Was the October 15 letter a unilateral offer that the plaintiffs had accepted by passing the required medical and psychological examinations?

DECISION Yes. The court issued an injunction to prohibit the city from conducting the 61st Police Academy unless the plaintiffs were included.

REASON The court found the October 15 letter to be "a classic example of an offer to enter into a unilateral contract. The October 15 letter expressly stated that it was a 'conditional offer of employment' and the message that it conveyed was that the recipient would be admitted into the 61st Academy if he or she successfully completed the medical and psychological examinations." The court contrasted the letter with "notices sent to applicants by the City at earlier stages of the selection process. Those notices merely informed applicants that they had completed a step in the process and remained eligible to be considered for admission into the Academy. Unlike the October 15 letter, the prior notices did not purport to extend a 'conditional offer' of admission." The court concluded that "[t]he plaintiffs accepted the City's offer of admission into the Academy by satisfying the specified conditions. Each of the plaintiffs submitted to and passed lengthy and intrusive medical and psychological examinations."

WHAT IF THE FACTS WERE DIFFERENT? *Suppose that the October 15 letter had used the phrase* potential offer of employment *rather than the word* conditional. *Would the court in this case still have considered the letter to be a unilateral contract?*

■

Revocation of Offers for Unilateral Contracts. A problem arises in unilateral contracts when the promisor attempts to *revoke* (cancel) the offer after the promisee has begun performance but before the act has been completed.
■EXAMPLE 7.3 Roberta offers to buy Ed's sailboat, moored in San Francisco, on delivery of the boat to Roberta's dock in Newport Beach, three hundred miles south of San Francisco. Ed rigs the boat and sets sail. Shortly before his arrival at Newport Beach, Ed receives a radio message from Roberta withdrawing her offer. Roberta's offer is to form a unilateral contract, and only Ed's delivery of the sailboat at her dock is an acceptance. **■**

In contract law, offers are normally *revocable* (capable of being taken back, or canceled) until accepted. Under the traditional view of unilateral contracts, Roberta's revocation would terminate the offer. Because of the harsh effect on the offeree of the revocation of an offer to form a unilateral contract, the modern-day view is that once performance has been *substantially* undertaken, the offeror cannot revoke the offer. Thus, in our example, even though Ed has not yet accepted the offer by complete performance, Roberta is prohibited from revoking it. Ed can deliver the boat and bind Roberta to the contract.

Formal versus Informal Contracts Another classification system divides contracts into formal contracts and informal contracts. **Formal contracts** are contracts that require a special form or method of creation (formation) to be enforceable.[2] *Contracts under seal* are a type of formal contract that involves a formalized writing with a special seal attached.[3] In the past, the seals were often made of wax and impressed on the paper document. Today, the significance of the seal in contract law has lessened, though standard-form contracts still sometimes include a place for a seal next to the signature lines. Letters of credit, which are frequently used in international sales contracts, are another type of formal contract. As will be discussed in Chapter 32, letters of credit are agreements to pay contingent on the purchaser's receipt of invoices and bills of lading (documents evidencing receipt of, and title to, goods shipped).

    Informal contracts (also called *simple contracts*) include all other contracts. No special form is required (except for certain types of contracts that must be in writing), as the contracts are usually based on their substance rather than their form. Typically, businesspersons put their contracts in writing to ensure that there is some proof of a contract's existence should problems arise.

Express versus Implied Contracts Contracts may also be formed and categorized as express or implied by the conduct of the parties. We look here at the differences between these two types of contracts.

Express Contracts. In an **express contract,** the terms of the agreement are fully and explicitly stated in words, oral or

written. A signed lease for an apartment or a house is an express written contract. If a classmate accepts your offer to sell your textbooks from last semester for $300, an express oral contract has been made.

Implied Contracts. A contract that is implied from the conduct of the parties is called an **implied-in-fact contract,** or an implied contract. This type of contract differs from an express contract in that the *conduct* of the parties, rather than their words, creates and defines at least some of the terms of the contract.

Requirements for an Implied-in-Fact Contract. For an implied-in-fact contract to arise, certain requirements must be met. Normally, if the following conditions exist, a court will hold that an implied contract was formed:

1 The plaintiff furnished some service or property.

2 The plaintiff expected to be paid for that service or property, and the defendant knew or should have known that payment was expected (by using the objective-theory-of-contracts test discussed on page 153).

3 The defendant had a chance to reject the services or property and did not.

■**EXAMPLE 7.4** Suppose that you need an accountant to fill out your tax return this year. You look through the Yellow Pages and find an accounting firm located in your neighborhood. You drop by the firm's office, explain your problem to an accountant, and learn what fees will be charged. The next day you return and give the receptionist all of the necessary information and documents, such as canceled checks and W-2 forms. Then you walk out the door without saying anything expressly to the accountant.

    In this situation, you have entered into an implied-in-fact contract to pay the accountant the usual and reasonable fees for her accounting services. The contract is implied by your conduct and by hers. She expects to be paid for completing your tax return. By bringing in the records she will need to do the work, you have implied an intent to pay for her services. ■

    Note that a contract can be a mixture of an express contract and an implied-in-fact contract. In other words, a contract may contain some express terms, while others are implied. During the construction of a home, the homeowner often requests that the builder make changes in the original specifications. When do these changes form part of an implied-in-fact contract that makes the homeowner liable to the builder for any extra expenses? That was the issue in the following case.

---

2. See *Restatement (Second) of Contracts,* Section 6, which explains that formal contracts include (1) contracts under seal, (2) recognizances, (3) negotiable instruments, and (4) letters of credit. As mentioned in Chapter 1, *Restatements of the Law* are books that summarize court decisions on a particular topic and that courts often refer to for guidance.

3. A seal may be actual (made of wax or some other durable substance), impressed on the paper, or indicated simply by the word *seal* or the letters *L.S.* at the end of the document. *L.S.* stands for *locus sigilli,* which means "the place for the seal."

CASE 7.2 Uhrhahn Construction & Design, Inc. v. Hopkins

Court of Appeals of Utah, 179 P.3d 808 (2008).

FACTS Uhrhahn Construction was hired by Lamar Hopkins (Hopkins) and his wife, Joan, for several projects in the building of their home. Each project was based on a cost estimate and specifications. Each of the proposals accepted by Hopkins said that any changes in the signed contracts would be made only "upon written orders." When work was in progress, Hopkins made several requests for changes. There was no written record of these changes, but Uhrhahn performed the work and Hopkins paid for it. A dispute arose after Hopkins requested that Uhrhahn use Durisol blocks rather than cinder blocks in some construction. The original proposal specified cinder blocks, but Hopkins told Uhrhahn that the change should be made because Durisol was "easier to install than traditional cinder block and would take half the time." Hopkins said the total cost would be the same. Uhrhahn orally agreed to the change, but demanded extra payment after discovering that Durisol blocks were more complicated to use than cinder blocks. Hopkins refused to pay, claiming that the cost should be the same. Uhrhahn sued. The trial court held for Uhrhahn, finding that the Durisol blocks were more costly to install. The homeowners appealed.

ISSUE Did the homeowners and the builder have an implied-in-fact contract regarding the substitution of Durisol blocks for the cinder blocks specified in the contract?

DECISION Yes. The Utah appeals court affirmed the decision of the trial court, finding that there was a valid contract between the parties and that both parties had agreed to oral changes in the contract. The changes created an implied-in-fact contract by which the builder agreed to provide extra work in exchange for additional compensation from the homeowners.

REASON The court found that the elements of a contract were present—offer and acceptance, competent parties, and consideration. The terms were clearly specified in the proposals accepted by Hopkins. Uhrhahn promised to perform work in exchange for payment. Although the contract stated that any changes would be in writing, both parties waived that term in the contract when they orally agreed on some changes in the work performed. As often happens in construction, changes were requested that were outside the contract. The builder did the work, and the buyer accepted the work. Such oral modification of the original contract creates an enforceable contract, and payment is due for the extra work. This is an implied-in-fact contract. Hopkins requested Uhrhahn to perform certain work. Uhrhahn expected to be compensated for the work, and Hopkins knew or should have known that Uhrhahn would expect to be paid for work that was outside the specifications of the original contract.

FOR CRITICAL ANALYSIS—Technological Consideration *Would the outcome of this case have been different if the parties had communicated by e-mail for all details regarding changes in the work performed? Why or why not?*

■

Contract Performance

Contracts are also classified according to their state of performance. A contract that has been fully performed on both sides is called an **executed contract.** A contract that has not been fully performed on either side is called an **executory contract.** If one party has fully performed but the other has not, the contract is said to be executed on the one side and executory on the other, but the contract is still classified as executory.

■**EXAMPLE 7.5** Assume that you agree to buy ten tons of coal from Western Coal Company. Further assume that Western has delivered the coal to your steel mill, where it is now being burned. At this point, the contract is an executory contract—it is executed on the part of Western and executory on your part. After you pay Western for the coal, the contract will be executed on both sides. ■

Contract Enforceability

A **valid contract** has the four elements necessary for contract formation: (1) an agreement (offer and acceptance) (2) supported by legally sufficient consideration (3) for a legal purpose and (4) made by parties who have the legal capacity to enter into the contract. As mentioned, we will discuss each of these elements in the following chapters. As you can see in Exhibit 7–2 on the next page, valid contracts may be enforceable, voidable, or unenforceable. Additionally, a contract may be referred to as a *void contract*. We look next at the meaning of the terms *voidable, unenforceable,* and *void* in relation to contract enforceability.

Voidable Contracts A **voidable contract** is a *valid* contract but one that can be avoided at the option of one or both of

EXHIBIT 7–2 Enforceable, Voidable, Unenforceable, and Void Contracts

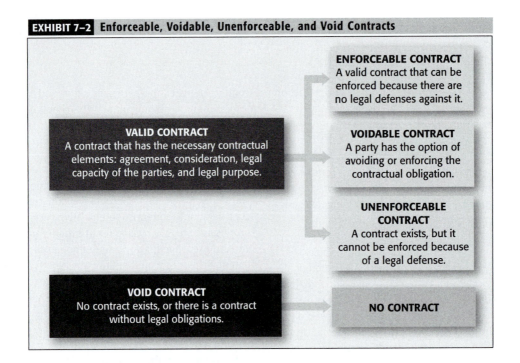

the parties. The party having the option can elect either to avoid any duty to perform or to *ratify* (make valid) the contract. If the contract is avoided, both parties are released from it. If it is ratified, both parties must fully perform their respective legal obligations.

As you will read in Chapter 9, contracts made by minors, insane persons, and intoxicated persons may be voidable. As a general rule, for example, contracts made by minors are voidable at the option of the minor. Additionally, contracts entered into under fraudulent conditions are voidable at the option of the defrauded party. Contracts entered into under legally defined duress or undue influence are voidable (see Chapter 10).

Unenforceable Contracts An **unenforceable contract** is one that cannot be enforced because of certain legal defenses against it. It is not unenforceable because a party failed to satisfy a legal requirement of the contract; rather, it is a valid contract rendered unenforceable by some statute or law. For example, some contracts must be in writing (see Chapter 10), and if they are not, they will not be enforceable except in certain exceptional circumstances.

Void Contracts A **void contract** is no contract at all. The terms *void* and *contract* are contradictory. None of the parties has any legal obligations if a contract is void. A contract can be void because, for example, one of the parties was previously determined by a court to be legally insane (and thus

lacked the legal capacity to enter into a contract) or because the purpose of the contract was illegal.

QUASI CONTRACTS

Quasi contracts, or contracts *implied in law,* are wholly different from actual contracts. Express contracts and implied-in-fact contracts are actual or true contracts formed by the words or actions of the parties. The word *quasi* is Latin for "as if" or "analogous to." Quasi contracts are not true contracts because they do not arise from any agreement, express or implied, between the parties themselves. Rather, quasi contracts are fictional contracts that courts can impose on the parties "as if" the parties had entered into an actual contract. They are equitable rather than legal contracts. Usually, quasi contracts are imposed to avoid the *unjust enrichment* of one party at the expense of another. The doctrine of unjust enrichment is based on the theory that individuals should not be allowed to profit or enrich themselves inequitably at the expense of others.

■EXAMPLE 7.6 A vacationing physician is driving down the highway and finds Emerson lying unconscious on the side of the road. The physician renders medical aid that saves Emerson's life. Although the injured, unconscious Emerson did not solicit the medical aid and was not aware that the aid had been rendered, Emerson received a valuable benefit, and the requirements for a quasi contract were fulfilled. In such a situation, the law normally will impose a quasi contract, and Emerson will have to pay the physician for the reasonable value of the medical services provided. ■

Limitations on Quasi-Contractual Recovery

Although quasi contracts exist to prevent unjust enrichment, the party who obtains a benefit is not liable for the fair value in some situations. Basically, a party who has conferred a benefit on someone else unnecessarily or as a result of misconduct or negligence cannot invoke the doctrine of quasi contract. The enrichment in those situations will not be considered "unjust."

■**EXAMPLE 7.7** You take your car to the local car wash and ask to have it run through the washer and to have the gas tank filled. While your car is being washed, you go to a nearby shopping center for two hours. In the meantime, one of the workers at the car wash mistakenly assumes that your car is the one that he is supposed to hand wax. When you come back, you are presented with a bill for a full tank of gas, a wash job, and a hand wax. Clearly, a benefit has been conferred on you. But this benefit occurred because of a mistake by the car wash employee. You have not been *unjustly* enriched under these circumstances. People normally cannot be forced to pay for benefits "thrust" on them. ■

When an Actual Contract Exists

The doctrine of quasi contract generally cannot be used when an actual contract covers the area in controversy. This is because a remedy already exists if a party is unjustly enriched as a result of a breach of contract: the nonbreaching party can sue the breaching party for breach of contract. In this instance, a court does not need to impose a quasi contract to achieve justice. ■**EXAMPLE 7.8** Fung contracts with Cameron to deliver a furnace to a building owned by

Bateman. Fung delivers the furnace, but Cameron never pays Fung. Bateman has been unjustly enriched in this situation, to be sure. Nevertheless, Fung cannot recover from Bateman in quasi contract because Fung had an actual contract with Cameron. Fung already has a remedy—he can sue for breach of contract to recover the price of the furnace from Cameron. No quasi contract need be imposed by the court in this situation to achieve justice. ■

INTERPRETATION OF CONTRACTS

Sometimes, parties agree that a contract has been formed but disagree on its meaning or legal effect. One reason that this may happen is that one of the parties is not familiar with the legal terminology used in the contract. To an extent, *plain language laws* have helped to avoid this difficulty. Sometimes, though, a dispute may still arise over the meaning of a contract simply because the rights or obligations under the contract are not expressed clearly—no matter how "plain" the language used.

In this section, we look at some common law rules of contract interpretation. These rules, including the *plain meaning rule* and various other rules that have evolved over time, provide the courts with guidelines for deciding disputes over how contract terms or provisions should be interpreted. Exhibit 7–3 provides a brief graphic summary of how these rules are applied.

PREVENTING LEGAL DISPUTES To avoid disputes over contract interpretation, make sure that your intentions are clearly expressed in the contracts. Careful drafting of contracts not only helps prevent potential disputes over the meaning of certain

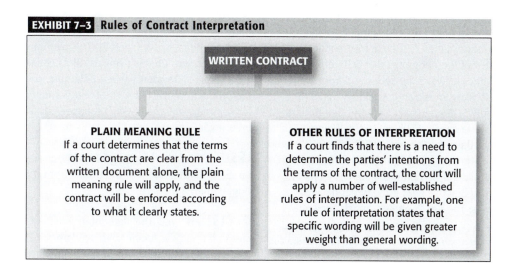

EXHIBIT 7–3 Rules of Contract Interpretation

WRITTEN CONTRACT

PLAIN MEANING RULE
If a court determines that the terms of the contract are clear from the written document alone, the plain meaning rule will apply, and the contract will be enforced according to what it clearly states.

OTHER RULES OF INTERPRETATION
If a court finds that there is a need to determine the parties' intentions from the terms of the contract, the court will apply a number of well-established rules of interpretation. For example, one rule of interpretation states that specific wording will be given greater weight than general wording.

terms but may also be crucial if your firm brings or needs to defend against a lawsuit for breach of contract. By using simple, clear language and avoiding legalese, you take a major step toward avoiding contract disputes.

■

Plain Language Laws

Today, the federal government and a majority of the states have enacted plain language laws to regulate legal writing. All federal agencies are required to use plain language in most of their forms and written communications. Plain language requirements have been extended to agency rulemaking as well.

At the state level, plain language laws frequently apply to consumer contracts that are primarily for personal, family, or household purposes. For example, a New York law requires residential leases and other consumer contracts to be (1) "written in a clear and coherent manner using words with common and everyday meanings" and (2) "appropriately divided and captioned by [the] various sections."[4] If a party to a contract, such as an insurance company, violates a plain language statute, a consumer can sue that party for damages if she or he suffers harm (unless the party can show that it

---

4. New York General Obligations Law Section 5-702.

made a good faith effort to comply with the statute). Some state statutes even allow parties to submit proposed contracts to the state attorney general, whose approval then eliminates any liability for damages because of a supposed violation of the plain language statute.

The legal profession is also moving toward plain English, and court rules in many jurisdictions require attorneys to use plain language in court documents. At times, judges have refused to accept motions that are incoherent due to their highly technical legal language. A number of states have also rewritten their jury instructions. Generally, the revised instructions are phrased in simpler language, use the active voice more often, and avoid "legalese" to the extent that it is possible to do so.

The Plain Meaning Rule

When a contract's writing is clear and unequivocal, a court will enforce it according to its obvious terms. The meaning of the terms must be determined from the *face of the instrument*—from the written document alone. This is sometimes referred to as the *plain meaning rule*.

Under this rule, if a contract's words appear to be clear and unambiguous, a court cannot consider *extrinsic evidence*, which is any evidence not contained in the document itself. Admissibility of extrinsic evidence can significantly affect how a court interprets ambiguous contractual provisions and thus can affect the outcome of litigation. The following case illustrates these points.

CASE 7.3   **Wagner v. Columbia Pictures Industries, Inc.**

California Court of Appeal, Second District, 146 Cal.App.4th 586, 52 Cal.Rptr.3d 898 (2007).

FACTS Actor Robert Wagner entered into an agreement with Spelling-Goldberg Productions (SGP) "relating to Charlie's Angels (herein called the 'series')." The contract entitled Wagner to 50 percent of the net profits that SGP received "for the right to exhibit photoplays of the series and from the exploitation of all ancillary, music and subsidiary rights in connection therewith." SGP hired Ivan Goff and Ben Roberts to write the series, under a contract subject to the Writers Guild of America Minimum Basic Agreement (MBA).[a] The MBA stipulates that the writer of a television show retains the right to make and market films based on the material, subject to the producer's right to buy this right if the writer decides to sell it within five years. The first "Charlie's Angels" episode

---

a. The Writers Guild of America is an association of screen and television writers that negotiates industrywide agreements with motion picture and television producers to cover the rights of its members.

aired in 1976. In 1982, SGP sold its rights to the series to Columbia Pictures Industries, Inc. Thirteen years later, Columbia bought the movie rights to the material from Goff's and Roberts's heirs. In 2000 and 2003, Columbia produced and distributed two "Charlie's Angels" films. Wagner filed a suit in a California state court against Columbia, claiming a share of the profits from the films. The court granted Columbia's motion for summary judgment. Wagner appealed to a state intermediate appellate court.

ISSUE Does the language of the Wagner contract with SGP entitle Columbia to all of the profits from the two "Charlie's Angels" films?

DECISION Yes. The state intermediate appellate court affirmed the lower court's judgment. The contract "unambiguously" stated the conditions under which the parties were to share the films' profits, and those conditions had not occurred.

REASON Wagner offered evidence to show that a previous contract with SGP had been intended to give him half of the net profits from a property titled "Love Song" that were received from all sources without limitation as to source or time. Wagner argued that the "Charlie's Angels" agreement used identical language in its profits provision, which thus should be interpreted to give him the same share. The court stated that an "agreement is the writing itself." Extrinsic evidence is not admissible "to show intention independent of an unambiguous written instrument." In this case, even if the parties intended Wagner to share in the profits from all sources, "they did not say so in their contract." Under the language of the contract, Wagner was entitled to share in the

profits from the exercise of the movie rights to "Charlie's Angels" if those rights were exploited as "ancillary" or "subsidiary" to the primary "right to exhibit photoplays of the series," but not if those rights were acquired separately. SGP's contract with Goff and Roberts was subject to the MBA, under which the writers kept the movie rights, which the producer could buy if the writers opted to sell them within five years. SGP did not acquire the movie rights to "Charlie's Angels" by exercising this right within the five-year period. Columbia obtained those rights independently more than five years later.

 FOR CRITICAL ANALYSIS–Legal Consideration *How might the result in this case have been different if the court had allowed Wagner's extrinsic evidence of the prior contract regarding "Love Song" to be used as evidence in this dispute?*

Other Rules of Interpretation

Generally, a court will interpret the language to give effect to the parties' intent *as expressed in their contract*. This is the primary purpose of the rules of interpretation—to determine the parties' intent from the language used in their agreement and to give effect to that intent. A court normally will not make or remake a contract, nor will it normally interpret the language according to what the parties *claim* their intent was when they made the contract.[5] The courts use the following rules in interpreting contractual terms:

1 Insofar as possible, a reasonable, lawful, and effective meaning will be given to all of a contract's terms.

2 A contract will be interpreted as a whole; individual, specific clauses will be considered subordinate to the contract's general intent. All writings that are a part of the same transaction will be interpreted together.

3 Terms that were the subject of separate negotiation will be given greater consideration than standardized terms and terms that were not negotiated separately.

4 A word will be given its ordinary, commonly accepted meaning, and a technical word or term will be given its technical meaning, unless the parties clearly intended something else.

5 Specific and exact wording will be given greater consideration than general language.

6 Written or typewritten terms prevail over preprinted terms.

7 Because a contract should be drafted in clear and unambiguous language, a party that uses ambiguous expressions is held to be responsible for the ambiguities. Thus, when the language has more than one meaning, it will be interpreted *against* the party that drafted the contract.

8 Evidence of *trade usage, prior dealing,* and *course of performance* may be admitted to clarify the meaning of an ambiguously worded contract. (We define and discuss these terms in Chapter 14.) What each of the parties does pursuant to the contract will be interpreted as consistent with what the other does and with any relevant usage of trade and course of dealing or performance. Express terms (terms expressly stated in the contract) are given the greatest weight, followed by course of performance, course of dealing, and custom and usage of trade—in that order. When considering custom and usage, a court will look at the trade customs and usage common to the particular business or industry and to the locale in which the contract was made or is to be performed.

---

5. Nevertheless, if a court finds that, even after applying the rules of interpretation, the terms are susceptible to more than one meaning, the court may permit extrinsic evidence to prove what the parties intended. See, for example, *Langdon v. United Restaurants, Inc.*, 105 S.W.3d 882 (Mo.Ct.App. 2003).

REVIEWING Nature and Classification

Grant Borman, who was engaged in a construction project, leased a crane from Allied Equipment and hired Crosstown Trucking Company to deliver the crane to the construction site. Crosstown, while the crane was in its possession and without permission from either Borman or Allied Equipment, used the crane to install a transformer for a utility company, which paid Crosstown for the job. Crosstown then delivered the crane to Borman's construction site at the appointed time of delivery. When Allied Equipment learned of the unauthorized use of the crane by Crosstown, it sued Crosstown for damages, seeking to recover the rental value of

Crosstown's use of the crane. Using the information presented in the chapter, answer the following questions.

1 What are the four requirements of a valid contract?

2 Did Crosstown have a valid contract with Borman concerning the use of the crane? If so, was it a bilateral or unilateral contract? Explain.

3 Can Allied Equipment obtain damages from Crosstown based on an implied-in-fact contract? Why or why not?

4 Should a court impose a quasi contract on the parties in this situation to allow Allied to recover damages from Crosstown? Why or why not?

TERMS AND CONCEPTS

bilateral contract 154
contract 153
executed contract 157
executory contract 157
express contract 156
formal contract 156
implied-in-fact contract 156

informal contract 156
objective theory of contracts 153
offeree 154
offeror 154
promise 152
promisee 153
promisor 153

quasi contract 158
unenforceable contract 158
unilateral contract 154
valid contract 157
void contract 158
voidable contract 157

CHAPTER SUMMARY Nature and Classification

An Overview of Contract Law (See pages 152–153.)	1. *Sources of contract law*—The common law governs all contracts except when it has been modified or replaced by statutory law, such as the Uniform Commercial Code (UCC), or by administrative agency regulations. The UCC governs contracts for the sale or lease of goods (see Chapter 14).
	2. *The function of contracts*—Contract law establishes what kinds of promises will be legally binding and supplies procedures for enforcing legally binding promises, or agreements.
	3. *The definition of a contract*—A contract is an agreement that can be enforced in court. It is formed by two or more competent parties who agree to perform or to refrain from performing some act now or in the future.
	4. *Objective theory of contracts*—In contract law, intent is determined by objective facts, not by the personal or subjective intent, or belief, of a party.
Elements of a Contract (See pages 153–154.)	1. *Requirements of a valid contract*—The four requirements of a valid contract are agreement, consideration, contractual capacity, and legality.
	2. *Defenses to the enforceability of a contract*—Even if the four requirements of a valid contract are met, a contract may be unenforceable if it lacks genuineness of assent or is not in the required form.
Types of Contracts (See pages 154–158.)	1. *Bilateral*—A promise for a promise.
	2. *Unilateral*—A promise for an act (acceptance is the completed—or substantial—performance of the contract by the offeree).

CHAPTER SUMMARY	**Nature and Classification—Continued**
Types of Contracts--Continued	3. *Formal*—Requires a special form for contract formation.
	4. *Informal*—Requires no special form for contract formation.
	5. *Express*—Formed by words (oral, written, or a combination).
	6. *Implied in fact*—Formed at least in part by the conduct of the parties.
	7. *Executed*—A fully performed contract.
	8. *Executory*—A contract not yet fully performed.
	9. *Valid*—A contract that has the necessary contractual elements of offer and acceptance, consideration, parties with legal capacity, and a legal purpose.
	10. *Voidable*—A contract that a party has the option of avoiding or enforcing.
	11. *Unenforceable*—A valid contract that cannot be enforced because of a legal defense.
	12. *Void*—No contract exists, or there is a contract without legal obligations.
Quasi Contracts (See pages 158–159.)	A quasi contract, or a contract implied in law, is a contract that is imposed by law to prevent unjust enrichment.
Interpretation of Contracts (See pages 159–161.)	Increasingly, plain language laws are requiring private contracts to be written in plain language so that the terms are clear and understandable to the parties. Under the plain meaning rule, a court will enforce the contract according to its plain terms, the meaning of which must be determined from the written document alone. Other rules applied by the courts when interpreting contracts include the following:
	1. A reasonable, lawful, and effective meaning will be given to all contract terms.
	2. A contract will be interpreted as a whole, specific clauses will be considered subordinate to the contract's general intent, and all writings that are a part of the same transaction will be interpreted together.
	3. Terms that were negotiated separately will be given greater consideration than standardized terms and terms not negotiated separately.
	4. Words will be given their commonly accepted meanings and technical words their technical meanings, unless the parties clearly intended otherwise.
	5. Specific wording will be given greater consideration than general language.
	6. Written or typewritten terms prevail over preprinted terms.
	7. A party that uses ambiguous expressions is held to be responsible for the ambiguities.
	8. Evidence of prior dealing, course of performance, or usage of trade is admissible to clarify an ambiguously worded contract.

FOR REVIEW

Answers for the even-numbered questions in this **For Review** *section can be found on this text's accompanying Web site at* **www.cengage.com/blaw/fbl**. *Select "Chapter 7" and click on "For Review."*

1 What is a contract? What is the objective theory of contracts?

2 What are the four basic elements necessary to the formation of a valid contract?

3 What is the difference between an implied-in-fact contract and an implied-in-law contract (quasi contract)?

4 How does a void contract differ from a voidable contract? What is an unenforceable contract?

5 Why have plain language laws been enacted? What rules guide the courts in interpreting contracts?

QUESTIONS AND CASE PROBLEMS

HYPOTHETICAL SCENARIOS AND CASE PROBLEMS

7.1 Express versus Implied Contracts. Suppose that a local businessperson, McDougal, is a good friend of Krunch, the owner of a local candy store. Every day on his lunch hour McDougal goes into Krunch's candy store and spends about five minutes looking at the candy. After examining Krunch's candy and talking with Krunch, McDougal usually buys one or two candy bars. One afternoon, McDougal goes into Krunch's candy shop, looks at the candy, and picks up a $1 candy bar. Seeing that Krunch is very busy, he catches Krunch's eye, waves the candy bar at Krunch without saying a word, and walks out. Is there a contract? If so, classify it within the categories presented in this chapter.

7.2 Hypothetical Question with Sample Answer. Janine was hospitalized with severe abdominal pain and placed in an intensive care unit. Her doctor told the hospital personnel to order around-the-clock nursing care for Janine. At the hospital's request, a nursing services firm, Nursing Services Unlimited, provided two weeks of in-hospital care and, after Janine was sent home, an additional two weeks of at-home care. During the at-home period of care, Janine was fully aware that she was receiving the benefit of the nursing services. Nursing Services later billed Janine $4,000 for the nursing care, but Janine refused to pay on the ground that she had never contracted for the services, either orally or in writing. In view of the fact that no express contract was ever formed, can Nursing Services recover the $4,000 from Janine? If so, under what legal theory? Discuss.

 For a sample answer to Question 7.2, go to Appendix E at the end of this text.

7.3 Contract Classification. High-Flying Advertising, Inc., contracted with Big Burger Restaurants to fly an advertisement above the Connecticut beaches. The advertisement offered $5,000 to any person who could swim from the Connecticut beaches to Long Island across the Long Island Sound in less than a day. McElfresh saw the streamer and accepted the challenge. He started his marathon swim that same day at 10 A.M. After he had been swimming for four hours and was about halfway across the sound, McElfresh saw another plane pulling a streamer that read, "Big Burger revokes." Is there a contract between McElfresh and Big Burger? If there is a contract, what type(s) of contract is (are) formed?

7.4 Implied Contract. Thomas Rinks and Joseph Shields developed Psycho Chihuahua, a caricature of a Chihuahua dog with a "do-not-back-down" attitude. They promoted and marketed the character through their company, Wrench, L.L.C. Ed Alfaro and Rudy Pollak, representatives of Taco Bell Corp., learned of Psycho Chihuahua and met with Rinks and Shields to talk about using the character as a Taco Bell "icon." Wrench sent artwork, merchandise, and marketing ideas to Alfaro, who promoted the character within Taco Bell. Alfaro asked Wrench to propose terms for Taco Bell's use of Psycho Chihuahua. Taco Bell did not accept Wrench's terms, but Alfaro continued to promote the character within the company. Meanwhile, Taco Bell hired a new advertising agency, which proposed an advertising campaign involving a Chihuahua. When Alfaro learned of this proposal, he sent the Psycho Chihuahua materials to the agency. Taco Bell made a Chihuahua the focus of its marketing but paid nothing to Wrench. Wrench filed a suit against Taco Bell in a federal district court, claiming in part that it had an implied contract with Taco Bell, which the latter breached. Do these facts satisfy the requirements for an implied contract? Why or why not? [*Wrench, L.L.C. v. Taco Bell Corp.*, 256 F.3d 446 (6th Cir.2001), *cert. denied*, 534 U.S. 1114, 122 S.Ct. 921, 151 L.Ed.2d 885 (2002)]

7.5 Interpretation of Contracts. East Mill Associates (EMA) was developing residential "units" in East Brunswick, New Jersey, within the service area of the East Brunswick Sewerage Authority (EBSA). The sewer system required an upgrade to the Ryder's Lane Pumping Station to accommodate the new units. EMA agreed to pay "fifty-five percent (55%) of the total cost" of the upgrade. At the time, the estimated cost to EMA was $150,000 to $200,000. Impediments to the project arose, however, substantially increasing the cost. Among other things, the pumping station had to be moved to accommodate a widened road nearby. The upgrade was delayed for almost three years. When it was completed, EBSA asked EMA for $340,022.12, which represented 55 percent of the total cost. EMA did not pay. EBSA filed a suit in a New Jersey state court against EMA for breach of contract. What rule should the court apply to interpret the parties' contract? How should that rule be applied? Why? [*East Brunswick Sewerage Authority v. East Mill Associates, Inc.*, 365 N.J.Super. 120, 838 A.2d 494 (A.D. 2004)]

7.6 Case Problem with Sample Answer. In December 2000, Nextel South Corp., a communications firm, contacted R. A. Clark Consulting, Ltd., an executive search firm, about finding an employment manager for Nextel's call center in Atlanta, Georgia. Over the next six months, Clark screened, evaluated, and interviewed more than three hundred candidates. Clark provided Nextel with more than fifteen candidate summaries, including one for Dan Sax. Nextel hired Sax for the position at an annual salary of $75,000. Sax started work on June 25, 2001, took two weeks' vacation, and quit on July 31 in the middle of a project. Clark spent the next six weeks looking for a replacement, until Nextel asked Clark to stop. Clark billed Nextel for its service, but Nextel refused to pay, asserting in part that the parties had not signed an agreement. Nextel's typical agreement specified payment to an employment agency of 20 percent of an employee's salary. Clark filed a suit in a Georgia state court against Nextel to recover the reasonable value of its services. What is a quasi contract? What would Clark have to show to recover on this basis? Should the court rule in Clark's favor? Explain. [*Nextel South Corp. v. R. A. Clark Consulting, Ltd.*, 266 Ga.App. 85, 596 S.E.2d 416 (2004)]

 After you have answered Problem 7.6, compare your answer with the sample answer given on the Web site that accompanies this text. Go to www.cengage.com/blaw/fbl, select "Chapter 7," and click on "Case Problem with Sample Answer."

7.7 Contract Enforceability. California's Subdivision Map Act (SMA) prohibits the sale of real property until a map of its subdivision is filed with, and approved by, the appropriate state agency. In 2004, Black Hills Investments, Inc., entered into two contracts with Albertson's, Inc., to buy two parcels of property in a shopping center development. Each contract required that "all governmental approvals relating to any lot split [or] subdivision" be obtained before the sale but permitted Albertson's to waive this condition. Black Hills made a $133,000 deposit on the purchase. A few weeks later, before the sales were complete, Albertson's filed with a local state agency a map that subdivided the shopping center into four parcels, including the two that Black Hills had agreed to buy. In 2005, Black Hills objected to concessions that Albertson's had made to a buyer of one of the other parcels, terminated its deal, and asked for its deposit. Albertson's refused. Black Hills filed a suit against Albertson's, arguing that the contracts were void. Are these contracts valid, voidable, unenforceable, or void? Explain. [*Black Hills Investments, Inc. v. Albertson's, Inc.*, 146 Cal.App.4th 883, 53 Cal.Rptr.3d 263 (4 Dist. 2007)]

7.8 **A Question of Ethics.** *International Business Machines Corp. (IBM) hired Niels Jensen as a software sales rep-*

resentative. In 2001, IBM presented a new "Software Sales Incentive Plan" (SIP) at a conference for its sales employees. A brochure stated, "[T]here are no caps to your earnings; the more you sell, . . . the more earnings for you." The brochure outlined how the plan worked and referred the employees to the "Sales Incentives" section of IBM's corporate intranet for more details. Jensen was given a "quota letter" that said he would be paid $75,000 as a base salary and, if he attained his quota, an additional $75,000 as incentive pay. In September, Jensen closed a deal with the U.S. Department of the Treasury's Internal Revenue Service worth more than $24 million to IBM. Relying on the SIP brochure, Jensen estimated his commission to be $2.6 million. IBM paid him less than $500,000, however. Jensen filed a suit against IBM, contending the SIP brochure and quota letter constituted a unilateral offer that became a binding contract when Jensen closed the sale. Consider the following questions. [Jensen v. International Business Machines Corp., 454 F.3d 382 (4th Cir. 2006)]

1 Is it fair to the employer to hold that the SIP brochure and quota letter created a unilateral contract if IBM did not *intend* to create such a contract? Is it fair to the employee to hold that *no* contract was created? Explain.

2 The "Sales Incentives" section of IBM's intranet included a clause providing that "[m]anagement will decide if an adjustment to the payment is appropriate" when an employee closes a large transaction. Jensen's quota letter stated, "[The SIP] program does not constitute a promise by IBM to make any distributions under it. IBM reserves the right to adjust the program terms or to cancel or otherwise modify the program at any time." How do these statements affect your answers to the above questions? From an ethical perspective, would it be fair to hold that a contract exists despite these statements?

CRITICAL THINKING AND WRITING ASSIGNMENTS

7.9 Critical Legal Thinking. Review the list of basic requirements for contract formation. Then analyze the relationship entered into when a student enrolls in a college or university. Has a bilateral contract or a unilateral contract been formed? Discuss.

7.10 **Video Question.** Go to this text's Web site at **www.cengage.com/blaw/fbl** and select "Chapter 7." Click on "Video Questions" and view the video titled *Bowfinger*. Then answer the following questions.

1 In the video, Renfro (Robert Downey, Jr.) says to Bowfinger (Steve Martin), "You bring me this script and

Kit Ramsey and you've got yourself a 'go' picture." Assume that their agreement is a contract. Is the contract bilateral or unilateral? Is it express or implied? Is it formal or informal? Is it executed or executory? Explain.

2 What criteria would a court rely on to interpret the terms of the contract?

3 Recall from the video that the contract between Bowfinger and the producer was oral. Suppose that a statute requires contracts of this type to be in writing. In that situation would the contract be void, voidable, or unenforceable? Explain.

ACCESSING THE INTERNET

For updated links to resources available on the Web, as well as a variety of other materials, visit this text's Web site at

www.cengage.com/blaw/fbl

The 'Lectric Law Library provides information on contract law, including a definition of a contract and the elements required for a contract. Go to

www.lectlaw.com/lay.html

and scroll down to "Contracts."

For easy-to-understand definitions of legal terms and concepts, including terms and concepts relating to contract law, go to the following Web site and key in a term, such as *contract* or *consideration:*

dictionary.law.com

PRACTICAL INTERNET EXERCISES

Go to this text's Web site at **www.cengage.com/blaw/fbl**, select "Chapter 7," and click on "Practical Internet Exercises." There you will find the following Internet research exercises that you can perform to learn more about the topics covered in this chapter.

PRACTICAL INTERNET EXERCISE 7–1   LEGAL PERSPECTIVE—Contracts and Contract Provisions

PRACTICAL INTERNET EXERCISE 7–2   MANAGEMENT PERSPECTIVE—Implied Employment Contracts

PRACTICAL INTERNET EXERCISE 7–3   HISTORICAL PERSPECTIVE—Contracts in Ancient Mesopotamia

BEFORE THE TEST

Go to this text's Web site at **www.cengage.com/blaw/fbl**, select "Chapter 7," and click on "Interactive Quizzes." You will find a number of interactive questions relating to this chapter.

CHAPTER 8
Agreement and Consideration

LEARNING OBJECTIVES

AFTER READING THIS CHAPTER, YOU SHOULD BE ABLE TO ANSWER THE FOLLOWING QUESTIONS:

1 What elements are necessary for an effective offer? What are some examples of nonoffers?

2 In what circumstances will an offer be irrevocable?

3 What are the elements that are necessary for an effective acceptance?

4 What is consideration? What is required for consideration to be legally sufficient?

5 In what circumstances might a promise be enforced despite a lack of consideration?

In Chapter 7, we pointed out that promises and agreements, and the knowledge that some of those promises and agreements will be legally enforced, are essential to civilized society. The homes we live in, the food we eat, the clothes we wear, the cars we drive, the books we read, the concerts and professional sporting events we attend—all of these have been purchased through contractual agreements. Contract law developed over time, through the common law tradition, to meet society's need to know with certainty what kinds of promises, or contracts, will be enforced and the point at which a valid and binding contract is formed.

For a contract to be considered valid and enforceable, the requirements listed in Chapter 7 must be met. In this chapter, we look closely at two of these requirements, *agreement* and *consideration*. As you read through this chapter, keep in mind that the requirements of agreement and consideration apply to all contracts, regardless of how they are formed. Many contracts continue to be formed in the traditional way—through the exchange of paper documents. Increasingly, though, contracts are also being formed online—through the exchange of electronic messages or documents. We discuss online contracts to a limited extent in this chapter and will look at them more closely in Chapter 13.

AGREEMENT

An essential element for contract formation is **agreement**— the parties must agree on the terms of the contract. Ordinarily, agreement is evidenced by two events: an *offer* and an *acceptance*. One party offers a certain bargain to another party, who then accepts that bargain.

Because words often fail to convey the precise meaning intended, the law of contracts generally adheres to the *objective theory of contracts*, as discussed in Chapter 7. Under this theory, a party's words and conduct are held to mean whatever a reasonable person in the offeree's position would think they meant.

Requirements of the Offer

An **offer** is a promise or commitment to perform or refrain from performing some specified act in the future. As discussed in Chapter 7, the party making an offer is called the *offeror*, and the party to whom the offer is made is called the *offeree*.

Three elements are necessary for an offer to be effective:

1 There must be a serious, objective intention by the offeror.

2 The terms of the offer must be reasonably certain, or definite, so that the parties and the court can ascertain the terms of the contract.

3 The offer must be communicated to the offeree.

Once an effective offer has been made, the offeree's acceptance of that offer creates a legally binding contract (providing the other essential elements for a valid and enforceable contract are present).

In today's e-commerce world, offers are frequently made online. Essentially, the requirements for traditional offers apply to online offers as well, as you will read in Chapter 13.

Intention   The first requirement for an effective offer to exist is a serious, objective intention on the part of the offeror. Intent is not determined by the *subjective* intentions, beliefs, or assumptions of the offeror. Rather, it is determined by what a reasonable person in the offeree's position would conclude the offeror's words and actions meant. Offers made in obvious anger, jest, or undue excitement do not meet the serious-and-objective-intent test. Because these offers are not effective, an offeree's acceptance does not create an agreement.

■EXAMPLE 8.1   You and three classmates ride to school each day in Julio's new automobile, which has a market value of $18,000. One cold morning, the four of you get into the car, but Julio cannot get it started. He yells in anger, "I'll sell this car to anyone for $500!" You drop $500 in his lap. A reasonable person, taking into consideration Julio's frustration and the obvious difference in value between the car's market price and the purchase price, would declare that Julio's offer was not made with serious and objective intent and that you do not have an agreement. ■

In the subsections that follow, we examine the concept of intention further as we look at the distinctions between offers and nonoffers. In the following classic case in the area of contractual agreement, the court had to decide whether an offer was intended when boasts, brags, and dares "after a few drinks" resulted in a contract to sell certain property.

| CASE 8.1 | **Lucy v. Zehmer** |

LANDMARK AND CLASSIC CASES

Supreme Court of Appeals of Virginia, 196 Va. 493, 84 S.E.2d 516 (1954).

FACTS   Lucy and Zehmer had known each other for fifteen to twenty years. For some time, Lucy had been wanting to buy Zehmer's farm. Zehmer had always told Lucy that he was not interested in selling. One night, Lucy stopped in to visit with the Zehmers at a restaurant they operated. Lucy said to Zehmer, "I bet you wouldn't take $50,000 for that place." Zehmer replied, "Yes, I would, too; you wouldn't give fifty." Throughout the evening, the conversation returned to the sale of the farm. At the same time, the parties were drinking whiskey. Eventually, Zehmer wrote up an agreement, on the back of a restaurant check, for the sale of the farm, and he asked his wife to sign it—which she did. When Lucy brought an action in a Virginia state court to enforce the agreement, Zehmer argued that he had been "high as a Georgia pine" at the time and that the offer had been made in jest: "two doggoned drunks bluffing to see who could talk the biggest and say the most." Lucy claimed that he had not been intoxicated and did not think Zehmer had been, either, given the way Zehmer handled the transaction. The trial court ruled in favor of the Zehmers, and Lucy appealed.

ISSUE   Can the agreement between the parties be avoided on the basis of intoxication?

DECISION   No. The agreement to sell the farm was binding.

REASON   The court held that the evidence given about the nature of the conversation, the appearance and completeness of the agreement, and the signing all tended to show that a serious business transaction, not a casual jest, was intended. The court had to look into the objective meaning of the words and acts of the Zehmers: "An agreement or mutual assent is of course essential to a valid contract, but the law imputes to a person an intention corresponding to the reasonable meaning of his words and acts. If his words and acts, judged by a reasonable standard, manifest an intention to agree, it is immaterial what may be the real but unexpressed state of mind."

 WHAT IF THE FACTS WERE DIFFERENT?   *Suppose that the day after Lucy signed the real estate sales agreement, he decided that he did not want the farm after all, and Zehmer sued Lucy to perform the contract. Would this change in the facts alter the court's decision that Lucy and Zehmer had created an enforceable contract? Why or why not?*

IMPACT OF THIS CASE ON TODAY'S LAW   *This is a classic case in contract law because it so clearly illustrates the objective theory of contracts with respect to determining*

CASE 8.1—Continued

whether an offer was intended. Today, the objective theory of contracts continues to be applied by the courts, and Lucy v. Zehmer *is routinely cited as a significant precedent in this area.*

RELEVANT WEB SITES *To locate information on the Web concerning the* Lucy v. Zehmer *decision, go to this text's Web site at* **www.cengage.com/blaw/fbl**, *select "Chapter 8," and click on "URLs for Landmarks."*

■

Expressions of Opinion. An expression of opinion is not an offer. It does not demonstrate an intention to enter into a binding agreement. **■EXAMPLE 8.2** In *Hawkins v. McGee,*[1] Hawkins took his son to McGee, a physician, and asked McGee to operate on the son's hand. McGee said that the boy would be in the hospital three or four days and that the hand would *probably* heal a few days later. The son's hand did not heal for a month, but nonetheless the father did not win a suit for breach of contract. The court held that McGee did not make an offer to heal the son's hand in three or four days. He merely expressed an opinion as to when the hand would heal. ■

Statements of Future Intent. A statement of an *intention* to do something in the future is not an offer. **■EXAMPLE 8.3** If Ari says, "I *plan* to sell my stock in Novation, Inc., for $150 per share," a contract is not created if John "accepts" and tenders $150 per share for the stock. Ari has merely expressed his intention to enter into a future contract for the sale of the stock. If John accepts and tenders the $150 per share, no contract is formed, because a reasonable person would conclude that Ari was only *thinking about* selling his stock, not promising to sell it. ■

Preliminary Negotiations. A request or invitation to negotiate is not an offer; it only expresses a willingness to discuss the possibility of entering into a contract. Examples are statements such as "Will you sell Forest Acres?" and "I wouldn't sell my car for less than $8,000." A reasonable person in the offeree's position would not conclude that such a statement indicated an intention to enter into a binding obligation. Likewise, when the government and private firms need to have construction work done, they invite contractors to submit bids. The *invitation* to submit bids is not an offer, and a contractor does not bind the government or private firm by submitting a bid. (The bids that the contractors submit are offers, however, and the government or private firm can bind the contractor by accepting the bid.)

Advertisements, Catalogues, and Circulars. In general, advertisements, mail-order catalogues, price lists, and circular letters (meant for the general public) are treated as invitations to negotiate, not as offers to form a contract.[2] **■EXAMPLE 8.4** You put an ad in the classified section of your local newspaper offering to sell your guitar for $275. Seven people call and "accept" your "offer" before you can remove the ad from the newspaper. If the ad were truly an offer, you would be bound by seven contracts to sell your guitar. Because *initial* advertisements are treated as *invitations* to make offers rather than offers, however, you will have seven offers to choose from, and you can accept the best one without incurring any liability for the six you reject. ■ On some occasions, though, courts have construed advertisements to be offers because the ads contained definite terms that invited acceptance (such as an ad offering a reward for the return of a lost dog).[3]

Price lists are another form of invitation to negotiate or trade. A seller's price list is not an offer to sell at that price; it merely invites the buyer to offer to buy at that price. In fact, the seller usually puts "prices subject to change" on the price list. Only in rare circumstances will a price quotation be construed as an offer.

Auctions. In an auction, a seller "offers" goods for sale through an auctioneer, but this is not an offer to form a contract. Rather, it is an invitation asking bidders to submit offers. In the context of an auction, a bidder is the offeror, and the auctioneer is the offeree. The offer is accepted when the auctioneer strikes the hammer. Before the fall of the hammer, a bidder may revoke (take back) her or his bid, or the auctioneer may reject that bid or all bids. Typically, an auctioneer will reject a bid that is below the price the seller is willing to accept.

When the auctioneer accepts a higher bid, he or she rejects all previous bids. Because rejection terminates an offer (as will be discussed later), those bids represent offers that have been terminated. Thus, if the highest bidder withdraws his or her bid before the hammer falls, none of the previous bids is reinstated. If the bid is not withdrawn or rejected, the contract is formed when the auctioneer announces, "Going once, going twice, sold!" (or something similar) and lets the hammer fall.

---

1. 84 N.H. 114, 146 A. 641 (1929).

2. *Restatement (Second) of Contracts,* Section 26, Comment b.
3. The classic example is *Lefkowitz v. Great Minneapolis Surplus Store, Inc.,* 251 Minn. 188, 86 N.W.2d 689 (1957).

Traditionally, auctions have been either "with reserve" or "without reserve." In an auction with reserve, the seller (through the auctioneer) may withdraw the goods at any time before the auctioneer closes the sale by announcement or by the fall of the hammer. All auctions are assumed to be auctions with reserve unless the terms of the auction are explicitly stated to be *without reserve*. In an auction without reserve, the goods cannot be withdrawn by the seller and must be sold to the highest bidder. In auctions with reserve, the seller may reserve the right to confirm or reject the sale even after "the hammer has fallen." In this situation, the seller is obligated to notify those attending the auction that sales of goods made during the auction are not final until confirmed by the seller.

Agreements to Agree. Traditionally, agreements to agree—that is, agreements to agree to the material terms of a contract at some future date—were not considered to be binding contracts. The modern view, however, is that agreements to agree may be enforceable agreements (contracts) if it is clear that the parties intend to be bound by the agreements. In other words, under the modern view the emphasis is on the parties' intent rather than on form.

■EXAMPLE 8.5 After a patron was injured and nearly drowned on a water ride at Six Flags Amusement Park, Six Flags, Inc., filed a lawsuit against the manufacturer that had designed the ride. The defendant manufacturer claimed that there was no binding contract between the parties, only preliminary negotiations that were never formalized into a contract to construct the ride. The court, however, held that a faxed document specifying the details of the water ride, along with the parties' subsequent actions (beginning construction and handwriting notes on the fax), was sufficient to show an intent to be bound. Because of the court's finding, the manufacturer was required to provide insurance for the water ride at Six Flags, and its insurer was required to defend Six Flags in the personal-injury lawsuit that arose out of the incident.[4] ■

Increasingly, the courts are holding that a preliminary agreement constitutes a binding contract if the parties have agreed on all essential terms and no disputed issues remain to be resolved.[5] In contrast, if the parties agree on certain major terms but leave other terms open for further negotiation, a preliminary agreement is binding only in the sense that the parties have committed themselves to negotiate the undecided terms in good faith in an effort to reach a final agreement.[6]

In the following case, the dispute was over an agreement to settle a case during a trial. One party claimed that the agreement formed via e-mail was binding, and the other party claimed it was merely an agreement to agree or to work out the terms of a settlement in the future. Can an exchange of e-mails create a complete and unambiguous agreement?

---

4. *Six Flags, Inc. v. Steadfast Insurance Co.*, 474 F.Supp.2d 201 (D.Mass. 2007).
5. See, for example, *Tractebel Energy Marketing, Inc. v. AEP Power Marketing, Inc.*, 487 F.3d 89 (2d Cir. 2007); and *Fluorine On Call, Ltd. v. Fluorogas Limited*, No. 01-CV-186 (W.D.Tex. 2002), contract issue affirmed on appeal at 380 F.3d 849 (5th Cir. 2004).
6. See, for example, *MBH, Inc. v. John Otte Oil & Propane, Inc.*, 727 N.W.2d 238 (Neb.App. 2007); and *Barrand v. Whataburger, Inc.*, 214 S.W.3d 122 (Tex.App.—Corpus Christi 2006).

CASE 8.2   **Basis Technology Corp. v. Amazon.com, Inc.**

Appeals Court of Massachusetts, 71 Mass.App.Ct. 29, 878 N.E.2d 952 (2008).
www.malawyersweekly.com/macoa.cfm [a]

FACTS Basis Technology Corporation created software and provided technical services for Amazon.com, Inc.'s, Japanese-language Web site. The agreement between the two companies allowed for separately negotiated contracts for additional services that Basis might provide to Amazon. At the end of 1999, Basis and Amazon entered into stock-purchase agreements. Later, Amazon objected to certain actions related to the securities that Basis sold. Basis sued Amazon for various claims involving these securities and for failing to pay for services performed by Basis that were not included in the original agreement. During the trial, the two parties appeared to reach an agreement to settle out of court via a series of e-mail exchanges outlining the settlement. When Amazon reneged, Basis served a motion to enforce the proposed settlement. The trial judge entered a judgment against Amazon, which appealed.

ISSUE Was the agreement that was entered into via e-mail by the two parties involved in the litigation a binding settlement contract?

DECISION Yes. The Appeals Court of Massachusetts affirmed the trial court's finding that Amazon intended to be bound by the terms of the e-mail exchanges.

REASON The court examined the evidence consisting of e-mails between the two parties. It pointed out that in open court and on the record, counsel "reported the result of the

---

a. In the search box on the right, enter "71 Mass.App.Ct. 29," and click on "Search." On the resulting page, click on the case name.

CASE 8.2–Continued

settlement without specification of the terms." Amazon claimed that the e-mail terms were not complete and definite enough to form an agreement. The court noted, nonetheless, that "provisions are not ambiguous simply because the parties have developed different interpretations of them." In the exchange of e-mails, the essential business terms were indeed resolved. Afterwards, the parties were simply proceeding to record the settlement terms, not to create them. The e-mails constituted a complete and unambiguous statement of the parties' desire to be bound by the settlement terms.

 WHAT IF THE FACTS WERE DIFFERENT? *Assume that the attorneys for both sides had simply had a phone conversation that included all of the terms to which they actually agreed in their e-mail exchanges. Would the court have ruled differently? Why or why not?*

■

Definiteness The second requirement for an effective offer involves the definiteness of its terms. An offer must have reasonably definite terms so that a court can determine if a breach has occurred and give an appropriate remedy.[7]

An offer may invite an acceptance to be worded in such specific terms that the contract is made definite. **■EXAMPLE 8.6** Marcus Business Machines contacts your corporation and offers to sell "from one to ten MacCool copying machines for $1,600 each; state number desired in acceptance." Your corporation agrees to buy two copiers. Because the quantity is specified in the acceptance, the terms are definite, and the contract is enforceable. ■

Communication A third requirement for an effective offer is communication—the offer must be communicated to the offeree. **■EXAMPLE 8.7** Tolson advertises a reward for the return of her lost cat. Dirlik, not knowing of the reward, finds the cat and returns it to Tolson. Ordinarily, Dirlik cannot recover the reward because an essential element of a reward contract is that the one who claims the reward must have known it was offered. A few states would allow recovery of the reward, but not on contract principles—Dirlik would be allowed to recover on the basis that it would be unfair to deny him the reward just because he did not know about it. ■

Termination of the Offer

The communication of an effective offer to an offeree gives the offeree the power to transform the offer into a binding, legal obligation (a contract) by an acceptance. This power of acceptance does not continue forever, though. It can be terminated by action of the parties or by operation of law.

Termination by Action of the Parties An offer can be terminated by the action of the parties in any of three ways: by revocation, by rejection, or by counteroffer.

Revocation of the Offer. The offeror's act of withdrawing an offer is referred to as **revocation.** Unless an offer is irrevocable, the offeror usually can revoke the offer (even if he or she has promised to keep the offer open), as long as the revocation is communicated to the offeree before the offeree accepts. Revocation may be accomplished by an express repudiation of the offer (for example, with a statement such as "I withdraw my previous offer of October 17") or by the performance of acts that are inconsistent with the existence of the offer and that are made known to the offeree.

■EXAMPLE 8.8 Geraldine offers to sell some land to Gary. A week passes, and Gary, who has not yet accepted the offer, learns from his friend Konstantine that Geraldine has in the meantime sold the property to Nunan. Gary's knowledge of Geraldine's sale of the land to Nunan, even though he learned of it through a third party, effectively revokes Geraldine's offer to sell the land to Gary. Geraldine's sale of the land to Nunan is inconsistent with the continued existence of the offer to Gary, and thus the offer to Gary is revoked. ■

The general rule followed by most states is that a revocation becomes effective when the offeree or the offeree's agent (a person who acts on behalf of another) actually receives it. Therefore, a letter of revocation mailed on April 1 and delivered at the offeree's residence or place of business on April 3 becomes effective on April 3.

An offer made to the general public can be revoked in the same manner in which the offer was originally communicated. **■EXAMPLE 8.9** A department store offers a $10,000 reward to anyone providing information leading to the apprehension of the persons who burglarized its downtown store. The offer is published in three local papers and in four papers in neighboring communities. To revoke the offer, the store must publish the revocation in all seven papers for the same number of days it published the offer. The revocation is then accessible to the general public, and the offer is revoked even if some particular offeree does not know about the revocation. ■

Irrevocable Offers. Although most offers are revocable, some can be made irrevocable. Increasingly, courts refuse to allow an

---

7. *Restatement (Second) of Contracts,* Section 33. The Uniform Commercial Code (UCC) has relaxed the requirements regarding the definiteness of terms in contracts for the sale of goods. See UCC 2–204(3).

offeror to revoke an offer when the offeree has changed position because of justifiable reliance on the offer (under the doctrine of *detrimental reliance*, or *promissory estoppel*, discussed later in this chapter). In some circumstances, "firm offers" made by merchants may also be considered irrevocable. We will discuss these offers in Chapter 14.

Another form of irrevocable offer is an option contract. An **option contract** is created when an offeror promises to hold an offer open for a specified period of time in return for a payment (consideration) given by the offeree. An option contract takes away the offeror's power to revoke an offer for the period of time specified in the option. If no time is specified, then a reasonable period of time is implied. **■EXAMPLE 8.10** Suppose that you are in the business of writing movie scripts. Your agent contacts the head of development at New Line Cinema and offers to sell New Line your new movie script. New Line likes your script and agrees to pay you $25,000 for a six-month option. In this situation, you (through your agent) are the offeror, and New Line is the offeree. You cannot revoke your offer to sell New Line your script for the next six months. After six months, if no contract has been formed, New Line loses the $25,000, and you are free to sell your script to another movie studio. ■

Option contracts are also frequently used in conjunction with the sale of real estate. **■EXAMPLE 8.11** You agree with a landowner to lease a house and include in the lease contract a clause stating that you will pay $15,000 for an option to purchase the property within a specified period of time. If you decide not to purchase the home after the specified period has lapsed, you lose the $15,000, and the landlord is free to sell the property to another buyer. ■

Rejection of the Offer by the Offeree. If the offeree rejects the offer, the offer is terminated. Any subsequent attempt by the offeree to accept will be construed as a new offer, giving the original offeror (now the offeree) the power of acceptance. A rejection is ordinarily accomplished by words or by conduct indicating an intent not to accept the offer.

As with a revocation, a rejection of an offer is effective only when it is actually received by the offeror or the offeror's agent. **■EXAMPLE 8.12** Growgood Farms mails a letter to Smith Soup Company offering to sell carrots at ten cents a pound. (Of course, today, such offers tend to be sent electronically rather than by mail, as will be discussed in Chapter 13.) Smith Soup Company could reject the offer either by sending or faxing a letter to Growgood Farms expressly rejecting the offer or by mailing the offer back to Growgood, indicating an intent to reject it. Alternatively, Smith could offer to buy the carrots at eight cents per pound (a counteroffer), necessarily rejecting the original offer. ■

Merely inquiring about an offer does not constitute rejection. **■EXAMPLE 8.13** A friend offers to buy your DVD movie collection for $300. You respond, "Is this your best offer?" or "Will you pay me $375 for it?" A reasonable person would conclude that you did not reject the offer but merely made an inquiry for further consideration of the offer. You can still accept and bind your friend to the $300 purchase price. When the offeree merely inquires as to the firmness of the offer, there is no reason to presume that she or he intends to reject it. ■

Counteroffer by the Offeree. A **counteroffer** is a rejection of the original offer and the simultaneous making of a new offer. **■EXAMPLE 8.14** Burke offers to sell his home to Lang for $270,000. Lang responds, "Your price is too high. I'll offer to purchase your house for $250,000." Lang's response is called a counteroffer because it rejects Burke's offer to sell at $270,000 and creates a new offer by Lang to purchase the home at a price of $250,000. ■

At common law, the **mirror image rule** requires that the offeree's acceptance match the offeror's offer exactly. In other words, the terms of the acceptance must "mirror" those of the offer. If the acceptance materially changes or adds to the terms of the original offer, it will be considered not an acceptance but a counteroffer—which, of course, need not be accepted. The original offeror can, however, accept the terms of the counteroffer and create a valid contract.[8]

Termination by Operation of Law   The offeree's power to transform an offer into a binding, legal obligation can be terminated by operation of law if any of four conditions occur: lapse of time, destruction of the specific subject matter, death or incompetence of the offeror or offeree, or supervening illegality of the proposed contract.

Lapse of Time. An offer terminates automatically by law when the period of time *specified in the offer* has passed. If the offer states that it will be left open until a particular date, then the offer will terminate at midnight on that day. If the offer states that it will be left open for a number of days, such as ten days, this time period normally begins to run when the offer is actually received by the offeree, not when it is formed or sent. When the offer is delayed (through the misdelivery of mail, for example), the period begins to run from the date the offeree would have received the offer, but only if the offeree knows or should know that the offer is delayed.[9]

---

8. The mirror image rule has been greatly modified in regard to sales contracts. Section 2–207 of the UCC provides that a contract is formed if the offeree makes a definite expression of acceptance (such as signing the form in the appropriate location), even though the terms of the acceptance modify or add to the terms of the original offer (see Chapter 14).

9. *Restatement (Second) of Contracts*, Section 49.

EXAMPLE 8.15 Beth offers to sell her boat to Jonah, stating that the offer will remain open until May 20. Unless Jonah accepts the offer by midnight on May 20, the offer will lapse (terminate). Now suppose that Beth writes a letter to Jonah, offering to sell him her boat if Jonah accepts the offer within twenty days of the letter's date, which is May 1. Jonah must accept within twenty days after May 1, or the offer will terminate. Suppose that instead of including the date May 1 in her letter, Beth had simply written to Jonah offering to sell him her boat if Jonah accepted within twenty days. In this instance, Jonah must accept within twenty days of receiving the letter. The same rule would apply if Beth used insufficient postage and Jonah received the letter ten days late without knowing that it had been delayed. If, however, Jonah knew that the letter was delayed, the offer would lapse twenty days after the day he ordinarily would have received the offer had Beth used sufficient postage. ■

If the offer does not specify a time for acceptance, the offer terminates at the end of a *reasonable* period of time. A reasonable period of time is determined by the subject matter of the contract, business and market conditions, and other relevant circumstances. An offer to sell farm produce, for example, will terminate sooner than an offer to sell farm equipment because farm produce is perishable and subject to greater fluctuations in market value.

Destruction of the Subject Matter. An offer is automatically terminated if the specific subject matter of the offer is destroyed before the offer is accepted. For example, if Bekins offers to sell his prize cow to Yatsen, but the cow is struck by lightning and dies before Yatsen can accept, the offer is automatically terminated. (Note that if Yatsen accepted the offer just before lightning struck the cow, a contract would have been formed, but, because of the cow's death, a court would likely excuse Bekins's obligation to perform the contract on the basis of impossibility of performance—see Chapter 11.)

Death or Incompetence of the Offeror or Offeree. An offeree's power of acceptance is terminated when the offeror or offeree dies or is deprived of legal capacity to enter into the proposed contract, *unless the offer is irrevocable.*[10] A revocable offer is personal to both parties and normally cannot pass to a decedent's heirs or estate or to the guardian of a mentally incompetent person. This rule applies whether or not one party had notice of the death or incompetence of the other party. **EXAMPLE 8.16** Kapola, who is quite ill, writes to her friend Amanda, offering to sell Amanda her grand piano for only $400. That night, Kapola dies. The next day, Amanda, not knowing of Kapola's death, writes a letter to Kapola, accepting the offer and enclosing a check for $400. Is there a contract? No. There is no contract because the offer automatically terminated on Kapola's death. ■

Supervening Illegality of the Proposed Contract. A statute or court decision that makes an offer illegal automatically terminates the offer. **EXAMPLE 8.17** Acme Finance Corporation offers to lend Jack $20,000 at 15 percent interest annually, but before Jack can accept, the state legislature enacts a statute prohibiting loans at interest rates greater than 12 percent. In this situation, the offer is automatically terminated. (If the statute is enacted after Jack accepts the offer, a valid contract is formed, but the contract may still be unenforceable—see Chapter 9.) ■

Acceptance

An **acceptance** is a voluntary act by the offeree that shows assent, or agreement, to the terms of an offer. The offeree's act may consist of words or conduct. The acceptance must be unequivocal and must be communicated to the offeror.

Who Can Accept? Generally, a third person cannot substitute for the offeree and effectively accept the offer. After all, the identity of the offeree is as much a condition of a bargaining offer as any other term contained therein. Thus, except in special circumstances, only the person to whom the offer is made or that person's agent can accept the offer and create a binding contract. For example, Lottie makes an offer to Paul. Paul is not interested, but his friend José accepts the offer. No contract is formed.

Unequivocal Acceptance To exercise the power of acceptance effectively, the offeree must accept unequivocally. This is the *mirror image rule* previously discussed. If the acceptance is subject to new conditions or if the terms of the acceptance materially change the original offer, the acceptance may be deemed a counteroffer that implicitly rejects the original offer.

Certain terms, when added to an acceptance, will not qualify the acceptance sufficiently to constitute rejection of the offer. **EXAMPLE 8.18** Suppose that in response to a person offering to sell a painting by a well-known artist, the offeree replies, "I accept; please send a written contract." The offeree is requesting a written contract but is not making it a condition for acceptance. Therefore, the acceptance is effective without the written contract. In contrast, if the offeree replies, "I accept *if* you send a written contract," the acceptance is expressly conditioned on the request for a writing, and the

---

10. *Restatement (Second) of Contracts*, Section 48. If the offer is irrevocable, it is not terminated when the offeror dies.

statement is not an acceptance but a counteroffer. (Notice how important each word is!)[11] ∎

Silence as Acceptance Ordinarily, silence cannot constitute acceptance, even if the offeror states, "By your silence and inaction, you will be deemed to have accepted this offer." This general rule applies because an offeree should not be put under a burden of liability to act affirmatively in order to reject an offer. No consideration—that is, nothing of value—has passed to the offeree to impose such a liability.

In some instances, however, the offeree does have a duty to speak; if so, his or her silence or inaction will operate as an acceptance. Silence may be an acceptance when an offeree takes the benefit of offered services even though he or she had an opportunity to reject them and knew that they were offered with the expectation of compensation. **■EXAMPLE 8.19** Suppose that John, a college student who earns extra income by washing store windows, taps on the window of a store and catches the attention of the store's manager. John points to the window and raises his cleaner, signaling that he will be washing the window. The manager does nothing to stop him. Here, the store manager's silence constitutes an acceptance, and an implied-in-fact contract is created. The store is bound to pay a reasonable value for John's work. ∎

Silence can also operate as an acceptance when the offeree has had prior dealings with the offeror. If a merchant, for example, routinely receives shipments from a supplier and in the past has always notified the supplier when defective goods are rejected, then silence constitutes acceptance. Also, if a buyer solicits an offer specifying that certain terms and conditions are acceptable, and the seller makes the offer in response to the solicitation, the buyer has a duty to reject—that is, a duty to tell the seller that the offer is not acceptable. Failure to reject (silence) will operate as an acceptance.

Communication of Acceptance Whether the offeror must be notified of the acceptance depends on the nature of the contract. In a bilateral contract, communication of acceptance is necessary because acceptance is in the form of a promise (not performance), and the contract is formed when the promise is made (rather than when the act is performed). Communication of acceptance is not necessary, however, if the offer dispenses with the requirement. Also, if the offer can be accepted by silence, no communication is necessary.

Because a unilateral contract calls for the full performance of some act, acceptance is usually evident, and notification is unnecessary. Nevertheless, exceptions do exist, such as when

the offeror requests notice of acceptance or has no way of determining whether the requested act has been performed. In addition, sometimes the law (such as Article 2 of the Uniform Commercial Code—UCC) requires notice of acceptance, and thus notice is necessary.

Mode and Timeliness of Acceptance Acceptance in bilateral contracts must be timely. The general rule is that acceptance in a bilateral contract is timely if it is made before the offer is terminated. Problems may arise, though, when the parties involved are not dealing face to face. In such situations, the offeree should use an authorized mode of communication.

The Mailbox Rule. Acceptance takes effect, thus completing formation of the contract, at the time the offeree sends or delivers the communication via the mode expressly or impliedly authorized by the offeror. This is the so-called **mailbox rule,** also called the *deposited acceptance rule,* which the majority of courts uphold. Under this rule, if the authorized mode of communication is the mail, then an acceptance becomes valid when it is dispatched (placed in the control of the U.S. Postal Service)—*not* when it is received by the offeror.

The mailbox rule was formed to prevent the confusion that arises when an offeror sends a letter of revocation but, before it arrives, the offeree sends a letter of acceptance. Thus, whereas a revocation becomes effective only when it is *received* by the offeree, an acceptance becomes effective on *dispatch* (when sent, even if it is never received), provided that an *authorized* means of communication is used.

The mailbox rule does not apply to instantaneous forms of communication, such as when the parties are dealing face to face, by telephone, or by fax. There is still some uncertainty in the courts as to whether e-mail should be considered an instantaneous form of communication to which the mailbox rule does not apply. If the parties have agreed to conduct transactions electronically and if the Uniform Electronic Transactions Act (to be discussed in Chapter 13) applies, then e-mail is considered sent when it either leaves the control of the sender or is received by the recipient. This rule takes the place of the mailbox rule when the Uniform Electronic Transactions Act applies but essentially allows an e-mail acceptance to become effective when sent (as it would if sent by U.S. mail).

Authorized Means of Acceptance. A means of communicating acceptance can be expressly authorized by the offeror or impliedly authorized by the surrounding facts and circumstances. If an offer stipulates an authorized mode of acceptance (such as by overnight delivery), then the contract is formed at the moment the offeree accepts the offer using the authorized means. **■EXAMPLE 8.20** Sam Perkins, a dealer in Massachusetts, offers to sell a container of antiques to Leaham's Antiques in Colorado. The offer states that

---

11. As noted in footnote 8, in regard to sales contracts, the UCC provides that an acceptance may still be effective even if some terms are added. The new terms are simply treated as proposals for additions to the contract, unless both parties are merchants. If the parties are merchants, the additional terms (with some exceptions) become part of the contract [UCC 2–207(2)].

Leaham's must accept the offer via FedEx overnight delivery. The acceptance is effective (and a binding contract is formed) the moment that Leaham's gives the overnight envelope containing the acceptance to the FedEx driver. ■

If the offeror does not expressly authorize a certain mode of acceptance, then acceptance can be made by any reasonable means. Courts look at the prevailing business usages and the surrounding circumstances in determining whether the mode of acceptance used was reasonable. Usually, the offeror's choice of a particular means in making the offer implies that the offeree can use the *same or a faster* means for acceptance. Thus, if the offer is made via priority mail, it would be reasonable to accept the offer via priority mail or by a faster method, such as by fax.

If the offeror authorizes a particular method of acceptance, but the offeree accepts by a different means, the acceptance may still be effective if the substituted method serves the same purpose as the authorized means. The use of a substitute method of acceptance is not effective on dispatch, though, and no contract will be formed until the acceptance is received by the offeror. Thus, if an offer specifies FedEx overnight delivery but the offeree accepts by overnight delivery from another carrier, such as UPS or DHL, the acceptance will still be effective, but not until the offeror receives it.

 **An effective way to avoid legal disputes over contracts is to communicate your intentions clearly to the other party and express every detail in writing, even when a written contract is not legally required. If you are the offeror, be explicit in your offer about how long the offer will remain open and stipulate the authorized means of communicating the acceptance. If you are the offeree, make sure that the language you use for any counteroffer, negotiation, or acceptance is absolutely clear and unambiguous. A simple "I accept" is best in most situations. Communicate your acceptance by the means authorized by the offeror or, if none is authorized, by the same method used to convey the offer. This can lessen the potential for problems arising due to revocation or lost communications.**

■

CONSIDERATION AND ITS REQUIREMENTS

In every legal system, some promises will be enforced, and other promises will not be enforced. The simple fact that a party has made a promise, then, does not mean the promise is enforceable. Under the common law, a primary basis for the enforcement of promises is consideration. **Consideration** is usually defined as the value given in return for a promise. We look here at the basic elements of consideration and then at some other contract doctrines relating to consideration.

Elements of Consideration

Often, consideration is broken down into two parts: (1) something of *legally sufficient value* must be given in exchange for the promise, and (2) there must be a *bargained-for exchange*.

Legal Value The "something of legally sufficient value" may consist of (1) a promise to do something that one has no prior legal duty to do (to pay on receipt of certain goods, for example), (2) the performance of an action that one is otherwise not obligated to undertake (such as providing accounting services), or (3) the refraining from an action that one has a legal right to undertake (called a **forbearance**).

Consideration in bilateral contracts normally consists of a promise in return for a promise, as explained in Chapter 7. **■EXAMPLE 8.21** In a contract for the sale of goods, the seller promises to ship specific goods to the buyer, and the buyer promises to pay for those goods when they are received. Each of these promises constitutes consideration for the contract. ■ In contrast, unilateral contracts involve a promise in return for a performance. **■EXAMPLE 8.22** Anita says to her neighbor, "If you paint my garage, I will pay you $800." Anita's neighbor paints the garage. The act of painting the garage is the consideration that creates Anita's contractual obligation to pay her neighbor $800. ■

What if, in return for a promise to pay, a person refrains from pursuing harmful habits, such as the use of tobacco and alcohol? Does such forbearance create consideration for the contract? Normally yes, refraining from doing what one has a legal right to do can constitute consideration.

Bargained-for Exchange The second element of consideration is that it must provide the basis for the bargain struck between the contracting parties. The promise given by the promisor must induce the promisee to incur a legal detriment either now or in the future, and the detriment incurred must induce the promisor to make the promise. This element of bargained-for exchange distinguishes contracts from gifts. **■EXAMPLE 8.23** Roberto says to his son, "In consideration of the fact that you are not as wealthy as your brothers, I will pay you $5,000." This promise is not enforceable because Roberto's son has not given any return consideration for the $5,000 promised. The son (the promisee) incurs no legal detriment; he does not have to promise anything or undertake (or refrain from undertaking) any action to receive the $5,000. Here, Roberto has simply stated his motive for giving his son a gift. The fact that the word *consideration* is used does not, by itself, mean that consideration has been given. ■

Legal Sufficiency and Adequacy of Consideration

Legal sufficiency of consideration involves the requirement that consideration be something of value in the eyes of the law. Adequacy of consideration involves "how much" consideration is given. Essentially, adequacy of consideration concerns the fairness of the bargain. On the surface, fairness would appear to be an issue when the items exchanged are of unequal value. In general, however, courts do not question the adequacy of consideration if the consideration is legally sufficient. Under the doctrine of freedom of contract, parties are usually free to bargain as they wish. If people could sue merely because they had entered into an unwise contract, the courts would be overloaded with frivolous suits.

Nevertheless, in rare situations a court will consider whether the amount or value of the consideration is adequate. This is because apparently inadequate consideration can indicate that fraud, duress, or undue influence was involved (if an elderly person sells her $50,000 car to her neighbor for $5,000, for example). When the consideration is grossly inadequate, a court may declare the contract unenforceable on the ground that it is *unconscionable*,[12] meaning that, generally speaking, it is so one sided under the circumstances as to be clearly unfair. (*Unconscionability* will be discussed further in Chapter 9.)

The determination of whether consideration exists does not depend on the comparative value of the things exchanged. Something need not be of direct economic or financial value to be considered legally sufficient consideration. In many situations, the exchange of promises and potential benefits is deemed sufficient as consideration.

AGREEMENTS THAT LACK CONSIDERATION

Sometimes, one or both of the parties to a contract may think that they have exchanged consideration when in fact they have not. Here we look at some situations in which the parties' promises or actions do not qualify as contractual consideration.

Preexisting Duty

Under most circumstances, a promise to do what one already has a legal duty to do does not constitute legally sufficient consideration because no legal detriment is incurred. The preexisting legal duty may be imposed by law or may arise out of a previous contract. A sheriff, for example, cannot collect a reward for information leading to the capture of a criminal if the sheriff already has a legal duty to capture the criminal. Likewise, if a party is already bound by contract to perform a

certain duty, that duty cannot serve as consideration for a second contract.

EXAMPLE 8.24 Bauman-Bache, Inc., begins construction on a seven-story office building and after three months demands an extra $75,000 on its contract. If the extra $75,000 is not paid, the firm will stop working. The owner of the land, finding no one else to complete construction, agrees to pay the extra $75,000. The agreement is not enforceable because it is not supported by legally sufficient consideration; Bauman-Bache had a preexisting contractual duty to complete the building. ■

Unforeseen Difficulties The rule regarding preexisting duty is meant to prevent extortion and the so-called holdup game. What happens, though, when an honest contractor, who has contracted with a landowner to build a house, runs into extraordinary difficulties that were totally unforeseen at the time the contract was formed? In the interests of fairness and equity, the courts sometimes allow exceptions to the preexisting duty rule. In the example just mentioned, if the landowner agrees to pay extra compensation to the contractor for overcoming the unforeseen difficulties (such as having to use dynamite and special equipment to remove an unexpected rock formation to excavate for a basement), the court may refrain from applying the preexisting duty rule and enforce the agreement. When the "unforeseen difficulties" that give rise to a contract modification are the types of risks ordinarily assumed in business, however, the courts will usually assert the preexisting duty rule.[13]

Rescission and New Contract The law recognizes that two parties can mutually agree to rescind their contract, at least to the extent that it is executory (still to be carried out). **Rescission**[14] is the unmaking of a contract so as to return the parties to the positions they occupied before the contract was made. Sometimes, parties rescind a contract and make a new contract at the same time. When this occurs, it is often difficult to determine whether there was consideration for the new contract or whether the parties had a preexisting duty under the previous contract. If a court finds there was a preexisting duty, then the new contract will be invalid because there was no consideration.

Past Consideration

Promises made in return for actions or events that have already taken place are unenforceable. These promises lack consideration in that the element of bargained-for exchange is missing. In short, you can bargain for something to take place

---

12. Pronounced un-*kon*-shun-uh-bul.

13. Note that under the UCC, any agreement modifying a contract within Article 2 on sales needs no consideration to be binding. See UCC 2–209(1).
14. Pronounced reh-*sih*-zhen.

now or in the future but not for something that has already taken place. Therefore, **past consideration** is no consideration.

■EXAMPLE 8.25 Elsie, a real estate agent, does her friend Judy a favor by selling Judy's house and not charging any commission. Later, Judy says to Elsie, "In return for your generous act, I will pay you $6,000." This promise is made in return for past consideration and is thus unenforceable; in effect, Judy is stating her intention to give Elsie a gift. ■

An employer will often ask an employee to sign a noncompete agreement, also called a covenant not to compete, by which the employee agrees not to work for competitors of the employer for a certain period of time after the employment relationship ends. (*Noncompete agreements* will be discussed further in Chapter 9.) In the following case, the court had to decide if continued employment constituted valid consideration for a noncompete ageement or if it was past consideration.

CASE 8.3 **Access Organics, Inc. v. Hernandez**

Supreme Court of Montana, 341 Mont. 73, 175 P.3d 899 (2008).

FACTS Bonnie Poux hired Andy Hernandez to sell organic produce for her sole proprietorship, Access Organics, Inc. Four months later, he was promoted to sales manager. Soon after, he signed a noncompete agreement in which he agreed "not to directly or indirectly compete with the business . . . for a period of two years following termination of employment." Later, the business encountered financial difficulties. Hernandez left and went into business with another former employee to compete with Access Organics in the sale of produce in the same part of Montana. Poux then sued to enforce the noncompete agreement. The trial court found that Hernandez was in direct competition with Access Organics and was contacting former customers. That was held to be a violation of the noncompete agreement. The agreement was upheld as valid because it was supported by consideration, which was continued employment at Access Organics at the time the agreement was signed. The court ordered Hernandez not to compete directly with Access Organics for the two-year period called for in the agreement. Hernandez appealed.

ISSUE Is continued employment valid consideration to support a noncompete agreement that an employee signed shortly after being hired by an employer?

DECISION No. Montana's highest court held that the noncompete agreement between the employer and the

employee was invalid because it was not supported by consideration. Because no contract had been formed, the court reversed the trial court's order that enforced the agreement.

REASON The court noted that although covenants not to compete are restraints of trade and therefore disfavored, they are upheld in some circumstances if supported by consideration. Consideration exists if the employee enters into the noncompete agreement at the time of hiring because then the agreement is part of a bargained-for exchange. In this case, however, Hernandez signed the agreement more than four months after accepting his initial employment. Hernandez was simply told to sign the agreement when he was already working for Access Organics. His prior employment was not consideration because past consideration is insufficient to support a promise. This was an "afterthought agreement" that could have been valid had it been supported by a pay increase or some other new benefit, but it was not. Because the agreement was unsupported by consideration, it did not create an enforceable contract.

 FOR CRITICAL ANALYSIS—Ethical Consideration *How could Access Organics have obtained a noncompete agreement from Hernandez that would have been enforced?*

■

Illusory Promises

If the terms of the contract express such uncertainty of performance that the promisor has not definitely promised to do anything, the promise is said to be *illusory*—without consideration and unenforceable. **■EXAMPLE 8.26** The president of Tuscan Corporation says to his employees, "All of you have worked hard, and if profits remain high, a 10 percent bonus at the end of the year will be given—if management thinks it is

warranted." This is an *illusory promise*, or no promise at all, because performance depends solely on the discretion of the president (the management). There is no bargained-for consideration. The statement declares merely that management may or may not do something in the future. ■

Option-to-cancel clauses in contracts for specified time periods sometimes present problems in regard to consideration. **■EXAMPLE 8.27** Abe contracts to hire Chris for one year at $5,000 per month, reserving the right to cancel the contract at any time. On close examination of these words, you can see that Abe has not actually agreed to hire Chris, as Abe could cancel without liability before Chris started performance. Abe has not given up the opportunity of hiring someone else. This contract is therefore illusory. Now suppose that Abe contracts to hire Chris for a one-year period at $5,000 per month, reserving the right to cancel the contract at any time after Chris has begun performance by giving Chris thirty days' notice. Abe, by saying that he will give Chris thirty days' notice, is relinquishing the opportunity (legal right) to hire someone else instead of Chris for a thirty-day period. If Chris works for one month, at the end of which Abe gives him thirty days' notice, Chris has a valid and enforceable contractual claim for $10,000 in salary. ■

SETTLEMENT OF CLAIMS

Businesspersons or others can settle legal claims in several ways. It is important to understand the nature of the consideration given in these settlement agreements, or contracts. Claims are commonly settled through an *accord and satisfaction*, in which a debtor offers to pay a lesser amount than the creditor purports is owed. Two other methods that are also often used to settle claims are the *release* and the *covenant not to sue*.

Accord and Satisfaction

In an **accord and satisfaction,** a debtor offers to pay, and a creditor accepts, a lesser amount than the creditor originally claimed was owed. Thus, in an accord and satisfaction, the debtor attempts to terminate an existing obligation. The *accord* is the settlement agreement. In an accord, the debtor offers to give or perform something less than the parties originally agreed on, and the creditor accepts that offer in satisfaction of the claim. *Satisfaction* is the performance (usually payment), which takes place after the accord is executed. A basic rule is that there can be no satisfaction unless there is first an accord.

For accord and satisfaction to occur, the amount of the debt *must be in dispute*. If it is a **liquidated debt,** then accord and satisfaction cannot take place. A debt is liquidated if its amount has been ascertained, fixed, agreed on, settled, or exactly determined. An example of a liquidated debt is a loan contract in which the borrower agrees to pay a stipulated amount every month until the amount of the loan is paid. In the majority of states, acceptance of (an accord for) a lesser sum than the entire amount of a liquidated debt is not satisfaction, and the balance of the debt is still legally owed. The rationale for this rule is that the debtor has given no consideration to satisfy the obligation of paying the balance to the creditor—because the debtor has a preexisting legal obligation to pay the entire debt.

An *unliquidated debt* is the opposite of a liquidated debt. Here, reasonable persons may differ over the amount owed. It is *not* settled, fixed, agreed on, ascertained, or determined. In these circumstances, acceptance of payment of the lesser sum operates as a satisfaction, or discharge, of the debt. One argument to support this rule is that the parties give up a legal right to contest the amount in dispute, and thus consideration is given.

Release

A **release** is a contract in which one party forfeits the right to pursue a legal claim against the other party. Releases will generally be binding if they are (1) given in good faith, (2) stated in a signed writing (required by many states), and (3) accompanied by consideration.[15] Clearly, parties are better off if they know the extent of their injuries or damages before signing releases.

■**EXAMPLE 8.28** Suppose that you are involved in an automobile accident caused by Raoul's negligence. Raoul offers to give you $2,000 if you will release him from further liability resulting from the accident. You believe that this amount will cover your damage, so you agree to and sign the release. Later you discover that the repairs to your car will cost $4,200. Can you collect the balance from Raoul? The answer is normally no; you are limited to the $2,000 in the release. Why? The reason is that a valid contract existed. You and Raoul both assented to the bargain (hence, agreement existed), and sufficient consideration was present. Your consideration for the contract was the legal detriment you suffered (by releasing Raoul from liability, you forfeited your right to sue to recover damages, should they be more than $2,000). This legal detriment was induced by Raoul's promise to give you the $2,000. Raoul's promise was, in turn, induced by your promise not to pursue your legal right to sue him for damages. ■

Covenant Not to Sue

Unlike a release, a **covenant not to sue** does not always bar further recovery. The parties simply substitute a contractual obligation for some other type of legal action based on a valid claim. Suppose (following the earlier example) that you agree with Raoul not to sue for damages in a tort action if he will pay for the damage to your car. If Raoul fails to pay, you can bring an action for breach of contract.

---

15. Under the UCC, a written, signed waiver or renunciation by an aggrieved party discharges any further liability for a breach, even without consideration [UCC 1–107].

PROMISSORY ESTOPPEL

Sometimes, individuals rely on promises, and such reliance may form a basis for contract rights and duties. Under the doctrine of **promissory estoppel** (also called *detrimental reliance*), a person who has reasonably relied on the promise of another can often obtain some measure of recovery. When the doctrine of promissory estoppel is applied, the promisor (the offeror) is **estopped** (barred or impeded) from revoking the promise. For the doctrine of promissory estoppel to be applied, the following elements are required:

1 There must be a clear and definite promise.

2 The promisee must justifiably rely on the promise.

3 The reliance normally must be of a substantial and definite character.

4 Justice will be better served by the enforcement of the promise.

■**EXAMPLE 8.29** Your uncle tells you, "I'll pay you $1,500 a week so that you won't have to work anymore." In reliance on your uncle's promise, you quit your job, but your uncle refuses to pay you. Under the doctrine of promissory estoppel, you may be able to enforce his promise.[16] Now your uncle makes a promise to give you $20,000 to buy a car. If you buy the car with your own funds and he does not pay you, you may once again be able to enforce the promise under this doctrine. ■

---

16. A classic example is *Ricketts v. Scothorn*, 57 Neb. 51, 77 N.W. 365 (1898).

REVIEWING Agreement and Consideration

Shane Durbin wanted to have a recording studio custom built in his home. He sent invitations to a number of local contractors to submit bids on the project. Rory Amstel submitted the lowest bid, which was $20,000 less than any of the other bids Durbin received. Durbin then called Amstel to ascertain the type and quality of the materials that were included in the bid and to find out if he could substitute a superior brand of acoustic tiles for the same bid price. Amstel said he would have to check into the price difference. The parties also discussed a possible start date for construction. Two weeks later, Durbin changed his mind and decided not to go forward with his plan to build a recording studio. Amstel filed a suit against Durbin for breach of contract. Using the information presented in the chapter, answer the following questions.

1 Did Amstel's bid meet the requirements of an offer? Explain.

2 Was there an acceptance of the offer? Why or why not?

3 Suppose that the court determines that the parties did not reach an agreement. Further suppose that Amstel, in anticipation of building Durbin's studio, had purchased materials and refused other jobs so that he would have time in his schedule for Durbin's project. Under what theory discussed in the chapter might Amstel attempt to recover these costs?

4 Now suppose that Durbin had gone forward with his plan to build the studio and immediately accepted Amstel's bid without discussing the type or quality of materials. After Amstel began construction, Durbin asked Amstel to substitute a superior brand of acoustic tiles for the tiles that Amstel had intended to use at the time that he bid on the project. Amstel installed the tiles, then asked Durbin to pay the difference in price, but Durbin refused. Can Amstel sue to obtain the price differential from Durbin in this situation? Why or why not?

TERMS AND CONCEPTS

CHAPTER SUMMARY	Agreement and Consideration
Requirements of the Offer (See pages 167–171.)	1. *Intent*—There must be a serious, objective intention by the offeror to become bound by the offer. Nonoffer situations include (a) expressions of opinion; (b) statements of intention; (c) preliminary negotiations; (d) generally, advertisements, catalogues, price lists, and circulars; (e) solicitations for bids made by an auctioneer; and (f) traditionally, agreements to agree in the future. 2. *Definiteness*—The terms of the offer must be sufficiently definite to be ascertainable by the parties or by a court. 3. *Communication*—The offer must be communicated to the offeree.

Termination of the Offer (See pages 171–173.)	1. *By action of the parties*—
	
	  a. Revocation—Unless the offer is irrevocable, it can be revoked at any time before acceptance without liability. Revocation is not effective until received by the offeree or the offeree's agent. Some offers, such as a merchant's firm offer and option contracts, are irrevocable.
	
	  b. Rejection—Accomplished by words or actions that demonstrate a clear intent not to accept the offer; not effective until received by the offeror or the offeror's agent.
	
	  c. Counteroffer—A rejection of the original offer and the making of a new offer.
	
	2. *By operation of law*—
	
	  a. Lapse of time—The offer terminates (1) at the end of the time period specified in the offer or (2) if no time period is stated in the offer, at the end of a reasonable time period.
	
	  b. Destruction of the specific subject matter of the offer—Automatically terminates the offer.
	
	  c. Death or incompetence of the offeror or offeree—Terminates the offer unless the offer is irrevocable.
	
	  d. Illegality—Supervening illegality terminates the offer.

Acceptance (See pages 173–175.)	1. Can be made only by the offeree or the offeree's agent.
	
	2. Must be unequivocal. Under the common law (mirror image rule), if new terms or conditions are added to the acceptance, it will be considered a counteroffer.
	
	3. Acceptance of a unilateral offer is effective on full performance of the requested act. Generally, no communication is necessary.
	
	4. Acceptance of a bilateral offer can be communicated by the offeree by any authorized mode of communication and is effective on dispatch. Unless the offeror expressly specifies the mode of communication, the following methods are impliedly authorized:
	
	  a. The same mode used by the offeror or a faster mode.
	
	  b. Mail, when the two parties are at a distance.
	
	  c. In sales contracts, by any reasonable medium.

Elements of Consideration (See page 175.)	Consideration is broken down into two parts: (1) something of *legally sufficient value* must be given in exchange for the promise, and (2) there must be a *bargained-for exchange*.
Legal Sufficiency and Adequacy of Consideration (See page 176.)	Legal sufficiency of consideration relates to the first element of consideration—something of legal value must be given in exchange for a promise. Adequacy of consideration relates to "how much" consideration is given and whether a fair bargain was reached. Courts will inquire into the adequacy of consideration (whether the consideration is legally sufficient) only when fraud, undue influence, duress, or unconscionability may be involved.

CHAPTER SUMMARY	Agreement and Consideration–Continued
Agreements That Lack Consideration (See pages 176–178.)	Consideration is lacking in the following situations: 1. *Preexisting duty*—Consideration is not legally sufficient if one is either by law or by contract under a *preexisting duty* to perform the action being offered as consideration for a new contract. 2. *Past consideration*—Actions or events that have already taken place do not constitute legally sufficient consideration. 3. *Illusory promises*—When the nature or extent of performance is too uncertain, the promise is rendered illusory (without consideration and unenforceable).
Settlement of Claims (See page 178.)	1. *Accord and satisfaction*—An *accord* is an agreement in which a debtor offers to pay a lesser amount than the creditor claims is owed. *Satisfaction* may take place when the accord is executed. 2. *Release*—An agreement in which, for consideration, a party forfeits the right to seek further recovery beyond the terms specified in the release. 3. *Covenant not to sue*—An agreement not to sue on a present, valid claim.
Promissory Estoppel (See page 179.)	The equitable doctrine of promissory estoppel applies when a promisor reasonably expects a promise to induce definite and substantial action or forbearance by the promisee, and the promisee does act in reliance on the promise. Such a promise is binding if injustice can be avoided only by enforcement of the promise. Also known as the doctrine of *detrimental reliance*.

FOR REVIEW

Answers for the even-numbered questions in this For Review *section can be found on this text's accompanying Web site at* **www.cengage.com/blaw/fbl**. *Select "Chapter 8" and click on "For Review."*

1 What elements are necessary for an effective offer? What are some examples of nonoffers?

2 In what circumstances will an offer be irrevocable?

3 What are the elements that are necessary for an effective acceptance?

4 What is consideration? What is required for consideration to be legally sufficient?

5 In what circumstances might a promise be enforced despite a lack of consideration?

QUESTIONS AND CASE PROBLEMS

 ## HYPOTHETICAL SCENARIOS AND CASE PROBLEMS

8.1 Agreement. Ball writes to Sullivan and inquires how much Sullivan is asking for a specific forty-acre tract of land Sullivan owns. In a letter received by Ball, Sullivan states, "I will not take less than $60,000 for the forty-acre tract as specified." Ball immediately sends Sullivan a telegram stating, "I accept your offer for $60,000 for the forty-acre tract as specified." Discuss whether Ball can hold Sullivan to a contract for sale of the land.

8.2 Hypothetical Question with Sample Answer. Chernek, the sole owner of a small business, has a large piece of used farm equipment for sale. He offers to sell the equipment to Bollow for $10,000. Discuss the legal effects of the following events on the offer:

1 Chernek dies prior to Bollow's acceptance, and at the time she accepts, Bollow is unaware of Chernek's death.

2 The night before Bollow accepts, a fire destroys the equipment.

3 Bollow pays $100 for a thirty-day option to purchase the equipment. During this period, Chernek dies, and Bollow accepts the offer, knowing of Chernek's death.

4 Bollow pays $100 for a thirty-day option to purchase the equipment. During this period, Bollow dies, and Bollow's estate accepts Chernek's offer within the stipulated time period.

For a sample answer to Question 8.2, go to Appendix E at the end of this text.

8.3 Consideration. Daniel, a recent college graduate, is on his way home for the Christmas holidays from his new job. He gets caught in a snowstorm and is taken in by an elderly couple, who provide him with food and shelter. After the snowplows have cleared the road, Daniel proceeds home. Daniel's father, Fred, is most appreciative of the elderly couple's action and in a letter promises to pay them $500. The elderly couple, in need of funds, accept Fred's offer. Then, because of a dispute with Daniel, Fred refuses to pay the elderly couple the $500. Discuss whether the couple can hold Fred liable in contract for the services rendered to Daniel.

8.4 Intention. Music that is distributed on compact discs and similar media generates income in the form of "mechanical" royalties. Music that is publicly performed, such as when a song is played on the radio, included in a movie or commercial, or sampled in another song, produces "performance" royalties. Both types of royalties are divided between the songwriter and the song's publisher. Vincent Cusano is a musician and songwriter who performed under the name "Vinnie Vincent" as a guitarist with the group KISS in the early 1980s. Cusano co-wrote three songs entitled "Killer," "I Love It Loud," and "I Still Love You," which KISS recorded and released in 1982 on an album titled *Creatures of the Night*. Cusano left KISS in 1984. Eight years later, Cusano sold to Horipro Entertainment Group "one hundred (100%) percent undivided interest" of his rights in the songs "other than Songwriter's share of performance income." Later, Cusano filed a suit in a federal district court against Horipro, claiming in part that he never intended to sell the writer's share of the mechanical royalties. Horipro filed a motion for summary judgment. Should the court grant the motion? Explain. [*Cusano v. Horipro Entertainment Group*, 301 F.Supp.2d 272 (S.D.N.Y. 2004)]

8.5 Consideration. As a child, Martha Carr once visited her mother's 108-acre tract of unimproved land in Richland County, South Carolina. In 1968, Betty and Raymond Campbell leased the land. Carr, a resident of New York, was diagnosed as having schizophrenia and depression in 1986, was hospitalized five or six times, and takes prescription drugs for the illnesses. In 1996, Carr inherited the Richland property and, two years later, contacted the Campbells about selling the land. Carr asked Betty about the value of the land, and Betty said that the county tax assessor had determined that the land's *agricultural value* was $54,000. The Campbells knew at the time that the county had assessed the total property value at $103,700 for tax purposes. On August 6, Carr signed a contract to sell the land to the Campbells for

$54,000. Believing the price to be unfair, however, Carr did not deliver the deed. The Campbells filed a suit in a South Carolina state court against Carr, seeking specific performance of the contract. At trial, an expert real estate appraiser testified that the *real market value* of the property was $162,000 at the time of the contract. Under what circumstances will a court examine the adequacy of consideration? Are those circumstances present in this case? Should the court enforce the contract between Carr and the Campbells? Explain. [*Campbell v. Carr*, 361 S.C. 258, 603 S.E.2d 625 (2004)]

8.6 Case Problem with Sample Answer. In 2000, David and Sandra Harless leased 2.3 acres of real property at 2801 River Road S.E. in Winnabow, North Carolina, to their son-in-law and daughter, Tony and Jeanie Connor. The Connors planned to operate a "general store/variety store" on the premises. They agreed to lease the property for sixty months with an option to renew for an additional sixty months. The lease included an option to buy the property for "fair market value at the time of such purchase (based on at least two appraisals)." In March 2003, Tony told David that the Connors wanted to buy the property. In May, Tony gave David an appraisal that estimated the property's value at $140,000. In July, the Connors presented a second appraisal that put the value at $160,000. The Connors offered $150,000. The Harlesses replied that "under no circumstances would they ever agree to sell their old store building and approximately 2.5 acres to their daughter . . . and their son-in-law." The Connors filed a suit in a North Carolina state court against the Harlesses, alleging breach of contract. Did these parties have a contract to sell the property? If so, what were its terms? If not, why not? [*Connor v. Harless*, 176 N.C.App. 402, 626 S.E.2d 755 (2006)]

After you have answered Problem 8.6, compare your answer with the sample answer given on the Web site that accompanies this text. Go to www.cengage.com/blaw/fbl, select "Chapter 8," and click on "Case Problem with Sample Answer."

8.7 Offer. In August 2000, in California, Terry Reigelsperger sought treatment for pain in his lower back from chiropractor James Siller. Reigelsperger felt better after the treatment and did not intend to return for more, although he did not mention this to Siller. Before leaving the office, Reigelsperger signed an "informed consent" form that read, in part, "I intend this consent form to cover the entire course of treatment for my present condition and for any future condition(s) for which I seek treatment." He also signed an agreement that required the parties to submit to arbitration "any dispute as to medical malpractice. . . .This agreement is intended to bind the patient and the health care provider . . . who now or in the future treat[s] the patient." Two years later, Reigelsperger sought treatment from Siller for a different condition relating to his cervical spine and shoulder. Claiming malpractice with respect to the second treatment, Reigelsperger filed a suit in a California state court against

Siller. Siller asked the court to order the submission of the dispute to arbitration. Does Reigelsperger's lack of intent to return to Siller after his first treatment affect the enforceability of the arbitration agreement and consent form? Why or why not? [*Reigelsperger v. Siller*, 40 Cal.4th 574, 53 Cal.Rptr.3d 887, 150 P.3d 764 (2007)]

8.8 **A Question of Ethics.** *John Sasson and Emily Springer met in January 2002. John worked for the U.S. Army as an engineer. Emily was an attorney with a law firm. When, six months later, John bought a townhouse in Randolph, New Jersey, he asked Emily to live with him. She agreed, but retained the ownership of her home in Monmouth Beach. John paid the mortgage and the other expenses on the townhouse. He urged Emily to quit her job and work from "our house." In May 2003, Emily took John's advice and started her own law practice. In December, John made her the beneficiary of his $150,000 individual retirement account (IRA) and said that he would give her his 2002 BMW M3 car before the end of the next year. He proposed to her in September 2004, giving her a diamond engagement ring and promising to "take care*

*of her" for the rest of her life. Less than a month later, John was critically injured by an accidental blow to his head during a basketball game and died. On behalf of John's estate, which was valued at $1.1 million, his brother Steven filed a complaint in a New Jersey state court to have Emily evicted from the townhouse. Given these facts, consider the following questions. [*In re Estate of Sasson*, 387 N.J.Super. 459, 904 A.2d 769 (App.Div. 2006)]*

1 Based on John's promise to "take care of her" for the rest of her life, Emily claimed that she was entitled to the townhouse, the BMW, and an additional portion of John's estate. Under what circumstances would such a promise constitute a valid, enforceable contract? Does John's promise meet these requirements? Why or why not?

2 Whether or not John's promise is legally binding, is there an ethical basis on which it should be enforced? Is there an ethical basis for *not* enforcing it? Are there any circumstances under which a promise of support should be—or should *not* be—enforced? Discuss.

CRITICAL THINKING AND WRITING ASSIGNMENTS

8.9 Critical Legal Thinking. Under what circumstances should courts examine the adequacy of consideration?

8.10 Video Question. Go to this text's Web site at **www.cengage.com/blaw/fbl** and select "Chapter 8." Click on "Video Questions" and view the video titled *Offer and Acceptance*. Then answer the following questions.

1 On the video, Vinny indicates that he can't sell his car to Oscar for four thousand dollars; then he says, "maybe

five . . . ." Discuss whether Vinny has made an offer or a counteroffer.

2 Oscar then says to Vinny, "Okay, I'll take it. But you gotta let me pay you four thousand now and the other thousand in two weeks." According to the chapter, do Oscar and Vinny have an agreement? Why or why not?

3 When Maria later says to Vinny, "I'll take it," has she accepted an offer? Why or why not?

ACCESSING THE INTERNET

For updated links to resources available on the Web, as well as a variety of other materials, visit this text's Web site at

www.cengage.com/blaw/fbl

You can read an overview of contract law and access contracts cases decided by the United States Supreme Court and federal appellate courts (as well as federal statutory law on contracts) at Cornell University's School of Law site:

topics.law.cornell.edu/wex/Contracts

To view the terms of a sample contract, go to the "forms" pages of the 'Lectric Law Library at

www.lectlaw.com/formb.htm

and select one of the types of contracts listed there to review.

FindLaw offers a collection of sample contracts from U.S. companies that you can explore at

contracts.corporate.findlaw.com/index.html

The *New Hampshire Consumer's Sourcebook* provides information on contract law from a consumer's perspective. You can access this book online at

doj.nh.gov/consumer/index.html

PRACTICAL INTERNET EXERCISES

Go to this text's Web site at **www.cengage.com/blaw/fbl**, select "Chapter 8," and click on "Practical Internet Exercises." There you will find the following Internet research exercises that you can perform to learn more about the topics covered in this chapter.

PRACTICAL INTERNET EXERCISE 8–1   LEGAL PERSPECTIVE—Contract Terms

PRACTICAL INTERNET EXERCISE 8–2   ETHICAL PERSPECTIVE—Offers and Advertisements

PRACTICAL INTERNET EXERCISE 8–3   MANAGEMENT PERSPECTIVE—Promissory Estoppel

BEFORE THE TEST

Go to this text's Web site at **www.cengage.com/blaw/fbl**, select "Chapter 8," and click on "Interactive Quizzes." You will find a number of interactive questions relating to this chapter.

CHAPTER 9
Capacity and Legality

LEARNING OBJECTIVES

AFTER READING THIS CHAPTER, YOU SHOULD BE ABLE TO ANSWER THE FOLLOWING QUESTIONS:

1 What are some exceptions to the rule that a minor can disaffirm (avoid) any contract?

2 Does an intoxicated person have the capacity to enter into an enforceable contract?

3 Does the mental incompetence of one party necessarily make a contract void?

4 Under what circumstances will a covenant not to compete be enforceable? When will such covenants not be enforced?

5 What is an exculpatory clause? In what circumstances might exculpatory clauses be enforced? When will they not be enforced?

C ourts generally want contracts to be enforceable, and much of the law is devoted to aiding the enforceability of contracts. Nonetheless, not all people can make legally binding contracts at all times. Contracts entered into by persons lacking the capacity to do so may be voidable. Similarly, contracts calling for the performance of an illegal act are illegal and thus void—they are not contracts at all. In this chapter, we examine contractual capacity and some aspects of illegal bargains.

CONTRACTUAL CAPACITY

Contractual capacity is the legal ability to enter into a contractual relationship. Courts generally presume the existence of contractual capacity, but in some situations, capacity is lacking or may be questionable. A person who has been determined by a court to be mentally incompetent, for example, cannot form a legally binding contract with another party. In other situations, a party may have the capacity to enter into a valid contract but may also have the right to avoid liability under it. For example, minors—or *infants*, as they are commonly referred to in the law—usually are not legally bound by contracts. In this section, we look at the effect of

youth, intoxication, and mental incompetence on contractual capacity.

Minors

Today, in virtually all states, the *age of majority* (when a person is no longer a minor) for contractual purposes is eighteen years—the so-called coming of age. (The age of majority may still be twenty-one for other purposes, however, such as the purchase and consumption of alcohol.) In addition, some states provide for the termination of minority on marriage. Minority status may also be terminated by a minor's **emancipation,** which occurs when a child's parent or legal guardian relinquishes the legal right to exercise control over the child. Normally, minors who leave home to support themselves are considered emancipated. Several jurisdictions permit minors to petition a court for emancipation themselves. For business purposes, a minor may petition a court to be treated as an adult.

The general rule is that a minor can enter into any contract an adult can, provided that the contract is not one prohibited by law for minors (for example, the sale of alcoholic beverages or tobacco). A contract entered into by a minor, however, is voidable at the option of that minor, subject to certain exceptions (to be discussed shortly). To exercise the option to avoid a contract, a minor need only manifest an intention not to be bound by it. The minor "avoids" the contract by disaffirming it.

Disaffirmance The legal avoidance, or setting aside, of a contractual obligation is referred to as **disaffirmance.** To disaffirm, a minor must express, through words or conduct, his or her intent not to be bound to the contract. The minor must disaffirm the entire contract, not merely a portion of it. For instance, a minor cannot decide to keep part of the goods purchased under a contract and return the remaining goods. When a minor disaffirms a contract, the minor can recover any property that she or he transferred to the adult as consideration for the contract, even if it is then in the possession of a third party.[1]

A contract can ordinarily be disaffirmed at any time during minority[2] or for a reasonable time after the minor comes of age. What constitutes a "reasonable" time may vary. Two months would probably be considered reasonable, but except in unusual circumstances, a court may not find it reasonable to wait a year or more after coming of age to disaffirm. If an individual fails to disaffirm an executed contract within a reasonable time after reaching the age of majority, a court will likely hold that the contract has been ratified (*ratification* will be discussed shortly).

Note that an adult who enters into a contract with a minor cannot avoid his or her contractual duties on the ground that the minor can do so. Unless the minor exercises the option to disaffirm the contract, the adult party normally is bound by it.

A Minor's Obligations on Disaffirmance Although all states' laws permit minors to disaffirm contracts (with certain exceptions), including executed contracts, state laws differ on the extent of a minor's obligations on disaffirmance.

Majority Rule. Courts in a majority of states hold that the minor need only return the goods (or other consideration) subject to the contract, provided the goods are in the minor's possession or control. **■EXAMPLE 9.1** Jim Garrison, a seventeen-year-old, purchases a computer from Radio Shack. While transporting the computer to his home, Garrison, through no fault of his own, is involved in a car accident. As a result of the accident, the plastic casing of the computer is broken. The next day, he returns the computer to Radio Shack and disaffirms the contract. Under the majority view,

this return fulfills Garrison's duty even though the computer is now damaged. Garrison is entitled to receive a refund of the purchase price (if paid in cash) or to be relieved of any further obligations under an agreement to purchase the computer on credit. ■

Minority Rule. A growing number of states, either by statute or by court decision, place an additional duty on the minor—the duty to restore the adult party to the position she or he held before the contract was made. **■EXAMPLE 9.2** Sixteen-year-old Joseph Dodson bought a pickup truck for $4,900 from a used-car dealer. Although the truck developed mechanical problems nine months later, Dodson continued to drive it until the engine blew up and it stopped running. Then Dodson disaffirmed the contract and attempted to return the truck to the dealer for a refund of the full purchase price. The dealer refused to accept the pickup or refund the money. Dodson filed suit. Ultimately, the Tennessee Supreme Court allowed Dodson to disaffirm the contract but required him to compensate the seller for the depreciated value—not the purchase price—of the pickup.[3] ■ This example illustrates the trend among today's courts to hold a minor responsible for damage, ordinary wear and tear, and depreciation of goods that the minor used prior to disaffirmance.

Exceptions to the Minor's Right to Disaffirm State courts and legislatures have carved out several exceptions to the minor's right to disaffirm. Some contracts cannot be avoided simply as a matter of law, on the ground of public policy. For example, marriage contracts and contracts to enlist in the armed services fall into this category. Other contracts may not be disaffirmed for different reasons, including those discussed here.

Misrepresentation of Age. Suppose that a minor tells a seller she is twenty-one years old when she is really seventeen. Ordinarily, the minor can disaffirm the contract even though she has misrepresented her age. Moreover, in some jurisdictions the minor is not liable for the tort of fraudulent misrepresentation, the rationale being that such a tort judgment might indirectly force the minor to perform the contract.

In many jurisdictions, however, a minor who has misrepresented his or her age can be bound by a contract under certain circumstances. First, several states have enacted statutes for precisely this purpose. In these states, misrepresentation of age is enough to prohibit disaffirmance. Other statutes prohibit disaffirmance by a minor who has engaged in business

---

1. The Uniform Commercial Code (UCC), in Section 2–403(1), allows an exception if the third party is a "good faith purchaser for value." See Chapter 15.
2. In some states, however, a minor who enters into a contract for the sale of land cannot disaffirm the contract until she or he reaches the age of majority.

3. *Dodson v. Shrader,* 824 S.W.2d 545 (Tenn. 1992). See also *Restatement (Third) of Restitution,* Sections 16 and 33 (2004).

as an adult. Second, some courts refuse to allow minors to disaffirm executed (fully performed) contracts unless they can return the consideration received. The combination of the minors' misrepresentations and their unjust enrichment has persuaded these courts to *estop* (prevent) the minors from asserting contractual incapacity.

Contracts for Necessaries. A minor who enters into a contract for necessaries may disaffirm the contract but remains liable for the reasonable value of the goods used. **Necessaries** are basic needs, such as food, clothing, shelter, and medical services, at a level of value required to maintain the minor's standard of living or financial and social status. Thus, what will be considered a necessary for one person may be a luxury for another. Additionally, what is considered a necessary depends on whether the minor is under the care or control of his or her parents, who are required by law to provide necessaries for the minor. If a minor's parents provide the minor with shelter, for example, then a contract to lease shelter (such as an apartment) normally will not be regarded as a contract for necessaries.

Generally, then, to qualify as a contract for necessaries, (1) the item contracted for must be necessary to the minor's existence, (2) the value of the necessary item may be up to a level required to maintain the minor's standard of living or financial and social status, and (3) the minor must not be under the care of a parent or guardian who is required to supply this item. Unless these three criteria are met, the minor can normally disaffirm the contract *without* being liable for the reasonable value of the goods used.

Insurance and Loans. Traditionally, insurance has not been viewed as a necessary, so minors can ordinarily disaffirm their insurance contracts and recover all premiums paid. Nevertheless, some jurisdictions prohibit disaffirming insurance contracts—for example, when minors contract for life insurance on their own lives. Financial loans are seldom considered to be necessaries, even if the minor spends the borrowed funds on necessaries. If, however, a lender makes a loan to a minor for the express purpose of enabling the minor to purchase necessaries, and the lender personally makes sure the funds are so spent, the minor normally is obligated to repay the loan.

Ratification In contract law, **ratification** is the act of accepting and giving legal force to an obligation that previously was not enforceable. A minor who has reached the age of majority can ratify a contract expressly or impliedly. *Express* ratification occurs when the individual, on reaching the age of majority, states orally or in writing that she or he intends to be bound by the contract. *Implied* ratification

takes place when the minor, on reaching the age of majority, indicates an intent to abide by the contract.

■**EXAMPLE 9.3** Lin enters a contract to sell her laptop to Arturo, a minor. If Arturo does not disaffirm the contract and, on reaching the age of majority, writes a letter to Lin stating that he still agrees to buy the laptop, he has expressly ratified the contract. If, instead, Arturo takes possession of the laptop as a minor and continues to use it well after reaching the age of majority, he has impliedly ratified the contract. ■

If a minor fails to disaffirm a contract within a reasonable time after reaching the age of majority, then a court must determine whether the conduct constitutes implied ratification or disaffirmance. Generally, courts presume that a contract that is *executed* (fully performed by both sides) was ratified. A contract that is still *executory* (not yet performed by both parties) is normally considered to be disaffirmed.

Parents' Liability As a general rule, parents are not liable for the contracts made by minor children acting on their own, except contracts for necessaries, which the parents are legally required to provide. This is why businesses ordinarily require parents to cosign any contract made with a minor. The parents then become personally obligated to perform the conditions of the contract, even if their child avoids liability.

Normally, minors are personally liable for their own torts. The parents of the minor can *also* be held liable in certain situations. In some states, parents may be liable if they failed to exercise proper parental control when they knew or should have known that this lack of control posed an unreasonable risk of harm to others. ■**EXAMPLE 9.4** An eleven-year-old's parents allow him to drive a car on public roads. If the child drives negligently and causes someone else to be injured, the parents may be held liable for the minor's tort (negligence). ■ Other states have enacted statutes that impose liability on parents for certain kinds of tortious acts committed by their children, such as those that are willful and malicious.

Intoxicated Persons

Contractual capacity also becomes an issue when a party to a contract was intoxicated at the time the contract was made. Intoxication is a condition in which a person's normal capacity to act or think is inhibited by alcohol or some other drug. If the person was sufficiently intoxicated to lack mental capacity, the contract may be voidable even if the intoxication was purely voluntary. For the contract to be voidable, however, the person must prove that the intoxication impaired her or his reason and judgment so severely that she or he did not comprehend the legal consequences of entering into the contract. In addition, to avoid the contract in the majority of states, the person claiming intoxication must be able to return all consideration received.

If, despite intoxication, the person understood the legal consequences of the agreement, the contract is enforceable. The fact that the terms of the contract are foolish or obviously favor the other party does not make the contract voidable (unless the other party fraudulently induced the person to become intoxicated). As a practical matter, courts rarely permit contracts to be avoided on the ground of intoxication, because it is difficult to determine whether a party was sufficiently intoxicated to avoid legal duties. Rather than inquire into the intoxicated person's mental state, many courts instead focus on objective indications of capacity to determine whether the contract is voidable owing to intoxication.[4]

Mentally Incompetent Persons

Contracts made by mentally incompetent persons can be void, voidable, or valid. We look here at the circumstances that determine when these classifications apply.

When the Contract Will Be Void If a court has previously determined that a person is mentally incompetent and has appointed a guardian to represent the person, any contract made by that mentally incompetent person is *void*—no contract exists. Only the guardian can enter into a binding contract on behalf of the mentally incompetent person.

When the Contract Will Be Voidable If a court has not previously judged a person to be mentally incompetent but in fact the person was incompetent at the time, the contract may be *voidable*. A contract is voidable if the person did not know he or she was entering into the contract or lacked the mental capacity to comprehend its nature, purpose, and consequences. In such situations, the contract is voidable at the option of the mentally incompetent person but not the other party. The contract may then be disaffirmed or ratified (if the person regains mental competence). Like intoxicated persons, mentally incompetent persons must return any consideration and pay for the reasonable value of any necessaries they receive.

■**EXAMPLE 9.5** Milo, a mentally incompetent man who had not been previously declared incompetent by a judge, agrees to sell twenty lots in a prime residential neighborhood to Anastof. At the time of entering the contract, Milo is confused over which lots he is selling and how much they are worth. As a result, he contracts to sell the properties for substantially less than their market value. If the court finds that Milo was unable

to understand the nature and consequences of the contract, the contract is voidable. Milo can avoid the sale, provided that he returns any consideration he received. ■

When the Contract Will Be Valid A contract entered into by a mentally incompetent person (whom a court has not previously declared incompetent) may also be *valid* if the person had capacity *at the time the contract was formed*. For instance, a person may be able to understand the nature and effect of entering into a certain contract yet simultaneously lack capacity to engage in other activities. In such cases, the contract ordinarily will be valid because the person is not legally mentally incompetent for contractual purposes.[5] Similarly, an otherwise mentally incompetent person may have a *lucid interval*—a temporary restoration of sufficient intelligence, judgment, and will to enter into contracts—during which she or he will be considered to have full legal capacity.

LEGALITY

To this point, we have discussed three of the requirements for a valid contract to exist—agreement, consideration, and contractual capacity. Now we examine the fourth—legality. For a contract to be valid and enforceable, it must be formed for a legal purpose. A contract to do something that is prohibited by federal or state statutory law is illegal and, as such, void from the outset and thus unenforceable. Additionally, a contract to commit a tortious act or to commit an action that is contrary to public policy is illegal and unenforceable.

Contracts Contrary to Statute

Statutes often set forth rules specifying which terms and clauses may be included in contracts and which are prohibited. We examine here several ways in which contracts may be contrary to a statute and thus illegal.

Contracts to Commit a Crime Any contract to commit a crime is a contract in violation of a statute. Thus, a contract to sell an illegal drug (the sale of which is prohibited by statute) is not enforceable. If the object or performance of the contract is rendered illegal by statute *after* the contract has been entered into, the contract is considered to be discharged by law. (See the discussion of *impossibility of performance* in Chapter 11.)

---

4. See, for example, the court's decision in *Lucy v. Zehmer,* presented as Case 8.1 in Chapter 8 on pages 168 and 169.

5. Modern courts no longer require a person to be completely irrational to disaffirm contracts on the basis of mental incompetence. A contract may be voidable if, by reason of a mental illness or defect, an individual was unable to act reasonably with respect to the transaction and the other party had reason to know of the condition.

Usury Virtually every state has a statute that sets the maximum rate of interest that can be charged for different types of transactions, including ordinary loans. A lender who makes a loan at an interest rate above the lawful maximum commits **usury.** The maximum rate of interest varies from state to state, as do the consequences for lenders who make usurious loans. Some states allow the lender to recover only the principal of a loan along with interest up to the legal maximum. In effect, the lender is denied recovery of the excess interest. In other states, the lender can recover the principal amount of the loan but no interest.

Although usury statutes place a ceiling on allowable rates of interest, exceptions are made to facilitate business transactions. For example, many states exempt corporate loans from the usury laws. In addition, almost all states have special statutes allowing much higher interest rates on small loans to help those borrowers who need funds and could not otherwise obtain loans.

Gambling All states have statutes that regulate gambling—defined as any scheme that involves the distribution of property by chance among persons who have paid valuable consideration for the opportunity (chance) to receive the property. Gambling is the creation of risk for the purpose of assuming it. Traditionally, the states have deemed gambling contracts illegal and thus void.

In several states, however, including Louisiana, Michigan, Nevada, and New Jersey, casino gambling is legal. In other states, certain forms of gambling are legal. California, for example, has not defined draw poker as a crime, although criminal statutes prohibit numerous other types of gambling games. A number of states allow gambling on horse races, and the majority of states have legalized state-operated lotteries, as well as lotteries (such as bingo) conducted for charitable purposes. Many states also allow gambling on Indian reservations.

Sometimes, it is difficult to distinguish a gambling contract from the risk sharing inherent in almost all contracts. **■EXAMPLE 9.6** In one case, five co-workers each received some free lottery tickets from a customer and agreed to split the winnings if one of the tickets turned out to be the winner. At first glance, this may seem entirely legal. The court, however, noted that the oral contract in this case "was an exchange of promises to share winnings from the parties' individually owned lottery tickets upon the happening of the uncertain event" that one of the tickets would win. Consequently, concluded the court, the agreement at issue was "founded on a gambling consideration" and therefore was void.[6] ■

Online Gambling A significant issue today is how gambling laws can be applied in the Internet context. Because state laws pertaining to gambling differ, online gambling raises a number of unique issues. For example, in those states that do not allow casino gambling or offtrack betting, what can a state government do if residents of the state place bets online? Also, where does the actual act of gambling occur? Suppose that a resident of New York places bets via the Internet at a gambling site located in Antigua. Is the actual act of "gambling" taking place in New York or in Antigua? According to a New York court in one case, "if the person engaged in gambling is located in New York, then New York is the location where the gambling occurred."[7] Courts of other states may take a different view, however.

Another issue that is being debated is whether entering contracts that involve gambling on sports teams that do not really exist—fantasy sports—is a form of gambling. For a discussion of this issue, see this chapter's *Adapting the Law to the Online Environment* feature on the following page.

Sabbath (Sunday) Laws Statutes referred to as Sabbath (Sunday) laws prohibit the formation or performance of certain contracts on a Sunday. These laws, which date back to colonial times, are often called **blue laws.** Blue laws get their name from the blue paper on which New Haven, Connecticut, printed its town ordinance in 1781 that prohibited work and required businesses to close on Sunday. According to a few state and local laws, all contracts entered into on a Sunday are illegal. Laws in other states or municipalities prohibit only the sale of certain types of merchandise, such as alcoholic beverages, on a Sunday.

In most states with such statutes, contracts that were entered into on a Sunday can be ratified during a weekday. Also, if a contract that was entered into on a Sunday has been fully performed (executed), normally it cannot be rescinded (canceled). Exceptions to Sunday laws permit contracts for necessities (such as food) and works of charity. Many states do not enforce Sunday laws, and some state courts have held these laws to be unconstitutional because they interfere with the freedom of religion.

Licensing Statutes All states require that members of certain professions obtain licenses allowing them to practice. Physicians, lawyers, real estate brokers, architects, electricians, and stockbrokers are but a few of the people who must be licensed. Some licenses are obtained only after extensive schooling and examinations, which indicate to the public that a special skill has been acquired. Others require only that the particular person be of good moral character and pay a fee.

---

6. *Dickerson v. Deno,* 770 So.2d 63 (Ala. 2000).

7. *United States v. Cohen,* 260 F.3d 68 (2d Cir. 2001).

ADAPTING THE LAW TO THE ONLINE ENVIRONMENT

Are Online Fantasy Sports Just Another Form of Real-Life Gambling?

As many as 20 million adults in the United States play some form of fantasy sports via the Internet. A fantasy sport is a game in which participants, often called owners, build teams composed of real-life players from different real-life teams. Each fantasy team competes against the fantasy teams belonging to other owners. At the end of each week, the statistical performances of all the real-life players are translated into points, and the points of all the players on an owner's fantasy team are totaled. Although a wide variety of fantasy games are available, most participants play fantasy football. On many fantasy sports sites, participants pay a fee in order to play and use the site's facilities, such as statistical tracking and message boards. At the end of the season, prizes ranging from T-shirts to flat-screen televisions are awarded to the winners.

In other instances, the participants in fantasy sports gamble directly on the outcome. In a fantasy football league, for example, each participant-owner adds a given amount to the pot and then "drafts" his or her fantasy team from actual National Football League players. At the end of the football season, each owner's points are totaled, and the owner with the most points wins the pot.

Congress Weighs In

As online gambling has expanded, Congress has attempted to regulate it. In late 2006, a federal law went into effect that makes it illegal for credit-card companies and banks to engage in transactions with Internet gambling companies.[a] Although the law does not prohibit individuals from placing online bets, in effect it makes it almost impossible for them to do so by preventing them from obtaining financing for online gambling. At first glance, the legislation appears comprehensive, but it specifically exempts Internet wagers on horse racing, state lotteries, and fantasy sports. Hence, one could argue that Congress has determined that fantasy sports do not constitute a prohibited Internet gambling activity.

Testing the Gambling Aspect in Court

Thus far, the courts have had the opportunity to rule only on whether the pay-to-play fantasy sports sites that charge an entrance fee and offer prizes to the winners are running gambling operations. Charles Humphrey brought a lawsuit against Viacom, ESPN, *The Sporting News*, and other hosts of such fantasy sports sites under a New Jersey statute that allows the recovery of gambling losses. Humphrey claimed that the fantasy sports leagues were games of chance, not games of skill, because events beyond the participants' control could determine the outcome—for example, a star quarterback might be injured. He also pointed out that in the offline world, federal law prohibits any games of chance, such as sweepstakes or drawings, that require entrants to submit consideration in order to play. *Consideration* has been defined as the purchase of a product or the payment of money. For these reasons, he argued, the entrance fees constituted gambling losses that could be recovered.

The federal district court that heard the case ruled against Humphrey, mostly on procedural grounds, but the court did conclude that as a matter of law the entrance fees did not constitute "bets" or "wagers" because the fees are paid unconditionally, the prizes offered are for a fixed amount and certain to be awarded, and the defendants do not compete for the prizes.[b] The court also observed that if a combination of entrance fees and prizes constituted gambling, a host of contests ranging from golf tournaments to track meets to spelling bees and beauty contests would be gambling operations—a conclusion that the court deemed "patently absurd."[c] Note, however, that the case involved only pay-to-play sites. The court did not have to address the question of whether fantasy sports sites that enable participants to contribute to a pot in the hopes of winning it at the end of the season constitute gambling sites.

 FOR CRITICAL ANALYSIS *What arguments can be used to support the idea that playing fantasy sports requires skill?*

a. Security and Accountability for Every Port Act, Public L. No. 109-347, Sections 5361–5367, 120 Stat. 1884 (2006). (A version of the Unlawful Internet Gambling Enforcement Act of 2006 was incorporated into this statute as Title VIII.)

b. *Humphrey v. Viacom, Inc.,* 2007 WL1797648 (D.N.J. 2007).
c. In reaching this conclusion, the federal district court cited portions of an Arizona Supreme Court ruling, *State v. American Holiday Association, Inc.,* 151 Ariz. 312, 727 P.2d 807 (1986).

The Purpose of Licensing Statutes. Generally, business licenses provide a means of regulating and taxing certain businesses and protecting the public against actions that could threaten the general welfare. For example, in nearly all states, a stockbroker must be licensed and must file a bond with the state to protect the public from fraudulent transactions in stocks. Similarly, a plumber must be licensed and bonded to protect the public against incompetent plumbers and to protect the public health. Only persons or businesses possessing the qualifications and complying with the conditions required by statute are entitled to licenses. For instance, the owner of a bar can be required to sell food as a condition of obtaining a license to serve liquor.

Contracts with Unlicensed Practitioners. A contract with an unlicensed practitioner may still be enforceable, depending on the nature of the licensing statute. Some states expressly provide that the lack of a license in certain occupations bars the enforcement of work-related contracts. If the statute does not expressly state this, one must look to the underlying purpose of the licensing requirements for a particular occupation. If the purpose is to protect the public from unauthorized practitioners, a contract involving an unlicensed individual is illegal and unenforceable. If, however, the underlying purpose of the statute is to raise government revenues, a contract with an unlicensed practitioner is enforceable—although the unlicensed person is usually fined.

Contracts Contrary to Public Policy

Although contracts involve private parties, some are not enforceable because of the negative impact they would have on society. These contracts are said to be *contrary to public policy*. Examples include a contract to commit an immoral act, such as selling a child, and a contract that prohibits marriage. **■EXAMPLE 9.7** Everett offers a young man $10,000 if he refrains from marrying Everett's daughter. If the young man accepts, no contract is formed (the contract is void) because it is contrary to public policy. Thus, if the man marries Everett's daughter, Everett cannot sue him for breach of contract. ■ Business contracts that may be contrary to public policy include contracts in restraint of trade and unconscionable contracts or clauses.

Contracts in Restraint of Trade Contracts in restraint of trade (anticompetitive agreements) usually adversely affect the public policy that favors competition in the economy. Typically, such contracts also violate one or more federal or state statutes.[8] An exception is recognized when the restraint

is reasonable and is part of, or supplemental to, a contract for the sale of a business or an **employment contract** (a contract stating the terms and conditions of employment). Many such exceptions involve a type of restraint called a **covenant not to compete**, or a restrictive covenant.

Covenants Not to Compete and the Sale of an Ongoing Business. Covenants (promises) not to compete are often contained as ancillary (secondary, or subordinate) clauses in contracts concerning the sale of an ongoing business. A covenant not to compete is created when a seller agrees not to open a new store in a certain geographic area surrounding the old store. Such agreements enable the seller to sell, and the purchaser to buy, the goodwill and reputation of an ongoing business. If, for example, a well-known merchant sells his or her store and opens a competing business a block away, many of the merchant's customers will likely do business at the new store. This renders less valuable the good name and reputation sold to the other merchant for a price. If a covenant not to compete is not ancillary to a sales agreement, however, it will be void because it unreasonably restrains trade and is contrary to public policy.

Covenants Not to Compete in Employment Contracts. Agreements not to compete, or *noncompete agreements*, can also be contained in employment contracts. People in middle- or upper-level management positions commonly agree not to work for competitors or not to start competing businesses for a specified period of time after termination of employment. Such agreements are legal in most states so long as the specified period of time (of restraint) is not excessive in duration and the geographic restriction is reasonable. What constitutes a reasonable time period may be shorter in the online environment than in conventional employment contracts because the restrictions apply worldwide. (For a further discussion of this issue, see this chapter's *Management Perspective* feature on page 193.)

To be reasonable, a restriction on competition must protect a legitimate business interest and must not be any greater than necessary to protect that interest.[9] In the following case, the court had to decide whether it was reasonable for an employer's noncompete agreement to restrict a former employee from competing "in any area of business" in which the employer was engaged.

---

8. Federal statutes prohibiting anticompetitive agreements include the Sherman Antitrust Act, the Clayton Act, and the Federal Trade Commission Act.

---

9. See, for example, *Gould & Lamb, LLC v. D'Alusio,* 949 So.2d 1212 (Fla.App. 2007). See also *Moore v. Midwest Distribution, Inc.,* 76 Ark.App. 397, 65 S.W.3d 490 (2002).

Court of Appeals of Georgia, 285 Ga.App. 799, 648 S.E.2d 129 (2007).

FACTS Safety and Compliance Management, Inc. (S&C), in Rossville, Georgia, provides alcohol- and drug-testing services in multiple states. In February 2002, S&C hired Angela Burgess. Her job duties included providing customer service, ensuring that specimens were properly retrieved from clients and transported to the testing lab, contacting clients, and managing the office. Burgess signed a covenant not to compete "in any area of business conducted by Safety and Compliance Management . . . for a two-year period . . . beginning at the termination of employment." In May 2004, Burgess quit her job to work at Rossville Medical Center (RMC) as a medical assistant. RMC provides medical services, including occupational medicine, medical physicals, and workers' compensation injury treatment. RMC also offers alcohol- and drug-testing services. Burgess's duties included setting patient appointments, taking patient medical histories, checking vital signs, performing urinalysis testing, administering injections, conducting alcohol-breath tests, and collecting specimens for drug testing. S&C filed a suit in a Georgia state court against Burgess and others (including a defendant named Stultz), alleging, among other things, that she had violated the noncompete agreement. The court issued a summary judgment in S&C's favor. Burgess appealed to a state intermediate appellate court.

ISSUE Was a two-year noncompete clause that prevented a former employee from working in "any area of business" conducted by the employer a reasonable restraint?

DECISION No. The appellate court reversed the judgment of the lower court, finding that the noncompete clause was unreasonable as to the scope of the activity prohibited and was therefore unenforceable.

REASON The court pointed out that noncompete clauses in employment contracts cannot impose an unreasonable restraint of trade. "A three-element test of duration, territorial coverage, and scope of activity has evolved as a helpful tool in examining the reasonableness of the particular factual setting to which it is applied." The noncompete clause in Angela Burgess's employment contract stated that she would "not compete in any area of business conducted by [her employer]." This agreement, the court reasoned, was intended to prevent any type of competing activity whatsoever. Therefore, the covenant not to compete was "overly broad and indefinite."

FOR CRITICAL ANALYSIS–Global Consideration *Should an employer be permitted to restrict a former employee from engaging in a competing business on a global level? Why or why not?*

Enforcement Problems. The laws governing the enforceability of covenants not to compete vary significantly from state to state. In some states, such as Texas, such a covenant will not be enforced unless the employee has received some benefit in return for signing the noncompete agreement. This is true even if the covenant is reasonable as to time and area. If the employee receives no benefit, the covenant will be deemed void. California prohibits the enforcement of covenants not to compete altogether.

Occasionally, depending on the jurisdiction, courts will *reform* covenants not to compete. If a covenant is found to be unreasonable in time or geographic area, the court may convert the terms into reasonable ones and then enforce the reformed covenant. This presents a problem, however, in that the judge has implicitly become a party to the contract. Consequently, courts usually resort to contract **reformation** only when necessary to prevent undue burdens or hardships.

Unconscionable Contracts or Clauses Ordinarily, a court does not look at the fairness or equity of a contract; for example, a court normally will not inquire into the adequacy of consideration. Persons are assumed to be reasonably intelligent, and the court does not come to their aid just because they have made unwise or foolish bargains. In certain circumstances, however, bargains are so oppressive that the courts relieve innocent parties of part or all of their duties. Such a bargain is called an **unconscionable contract** (or **unconscionable clause**). Both the Uniform Commercial Code (UCC) and the Uniform Consumer Credit Code (UCCC) embody the unconscionability concept—the former with regard to the sale of goods and the latter with regard to consumer loans and the waiver of rights.[10] A contract can be unconscionable on either procedural or substantive grounds, as discussed in the follow-

---

10. See, for example, UCC 2–302 and 2–719, and UCCC 5–108 and 1–107.

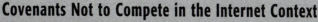

Covenants Not to Compete in the Internet Context

Management Faces a Legal Issue

For some companies, particularly those in high-tech industries, trade secrets are their most valuable assets. Often, to prevent departing employees from disclosing trade secrets to competing employers, a company asks its key employees to sign *covenants not to compete,* in which they agree not to set up a competing business or work for a competitor in a specified geographic area for a certain period of time. Generally, the time and geographic restrictions must be reasonable. A serious issue facing management today is whether time and space restrictions that have been deemed reasonable in the past will be considered reasonable in today's changing legal landscape, which includes the Internet environment.

What the Courts Say

There is little case law to guide management on this issue. One case involved Mark Schlack, who worked as a Web site manager for EarthWeb, Inc., in New York. Schlack signed a covenant stating that, on termination of his employment, he would not work for any competing company for one year. When he resigned and accepted an offer from a company in Massachusetts to design a Web site, EarthWeb sued to enforce the covenant not to compete. The court refused to enforce the covenant, in part, because there was no evidence that Schlack had misappropriated any of EarthWeb's trade secrets or clients. The court also stated that because the Internet lacks physical borders, a covenant prohibiting an employee from working for a competitor anywhere in the world for one year is excessive in duration.[a]

In a later case, a federal district court enforced a one-year noncompete agreement against the founder of a law-related Web site business even though no geographic restriction was included in the agreement. According to the court, "Although there is no geographic limitation on the provision, this is nonetheless reasonable in light of the national, and indeed international, nature of Internet business."[b]

The sale of an Internet-only business involves literally the full worldwide scope of the Internet itself. In a recent case, a company selling vitamins over the Internet was sold for more than $2 million. The purchase agreement contained a noncompete clause that prohibited the seller from engaging in the sale of nutritional and health products via the Internet for four years. Despite the noncompete agreement, after the sale, the seller created at least two Internet sites from which he sold health products and vitamins. When the buyer sued to enforce the noncompete agreement, the court held for the buyer and enjoined (prevented) the seller from violating the agreement.[c] The court pointed out that the seller could still engage in his former business by using non-Internet markets. The seller also remained free to sell other types of products on the Internet.

Implications for Managers

Management in high-tech companies should avoid overreaching in terms of time and geographic restrictions in noncompete agreements. Additionally, when considering whether time and place restrictions are reasonable, the courts tend to balance time restrictions against other factors, such as geographic restrictions. Because for Web-based work the geographic restriction can be worldwide, the time restriction should be narrowed considerably to compensate for the extensive geographic restriction.

a. *EarthWeb, Inc. v. Schlack,* 71 F.Supp.2d 299 (S.D.N.Y. 1999).

b. *West Publishing Corp. v. Stanley,* 2004 WL 73590 (D.N.D. 2004).
c. *MyVitaNet.com v. Kowalski,* __ F.Supp.2d __ , 2008 WL 203008 (S.D. Ohio 2008).

---

ing subsections and illustrated graphically in Exhibit 9–1 on the next page.

Procedural Unconscionability. Procedural unconscionability has to do with how a term becomes part of a contract and relates to factors bearing on a party's lack of knowledge or understanding of the contract terms because of inconspicuous print, unintelligible language ("legalese"), lack of opportunity to read the contract, lack of opportunity to ask questions about the contract's meaning, and other factors. Procedural unconscionability sometimes relates to purported lack of voluntariness because of a disparity in bargaining power between the two parties. Contracts entered into because of one party's vastly superior bargaining power may be deemed unconscionable. Such contracts are often referred to as **adhesion contracts.** An adhesion contract is written exclusively by one party (the dominant party, usually the seller or creditor) and presented to the other (the

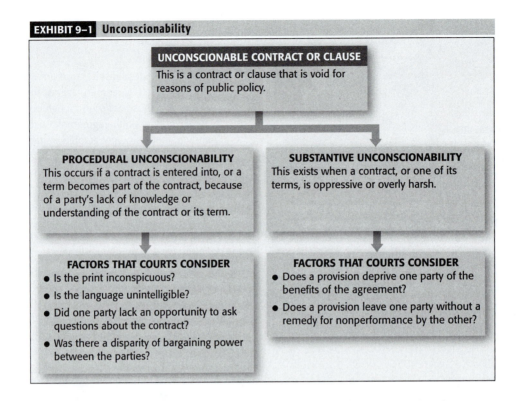

EXHIBIT 9–1 Unconscionability

adhering party, usually the buyer or borrower) on a take-it-or-leave-it basis. In other words, the adhering party has no opportunity to negotiate the terms of the contract.

Substantive Unconscionability. *Substantive* unconscionability characterizes those contracts, or portions of contracts, that are oppressive or overly harsh. Courts generally focus on provisions that deprive one party of the benefits of the agreement or leave that party without remedy for nonperformance by the other. **■EXAMPLE 9.8** A person with little income and only a fourth-grade education agrees to purchase a refrigerator for $4,000 and signs a two-year installment contract. The same type of refrigerator usually sells for $900 on the market. Some courts have held that this type of contract is unconscionable because the contract terms are so oppressive as to "shock the conscience" of the court.[11] **■**

Substantive unconscionability can arise in a wide variety of business contexts. For example, a contract clause that gives the business entity free access to the courts but requires the other party to arbitrate any dispute with the firm may be unconscionable.[12] Similarly, an arbitration clause in a credit-card agreement that prevents credit cardholders from obtaining relief for abusive debt-collection practices under consumer law may be unconscionable.[13] Contracts drafted by insurance companies and cell phone providers have been struck down as substantively unconscionable when they included provisions that were overly harsh or one sided.[14]

Exculpatory Clauses Closely related to the concept of unconscionability are **exculpatory clauses**—clauses that release a party from liability in the event of monetary or physical injury *no matter who is at fault*. Indeed, courts sometimes refuse to enforce such clauses on the ground that they are unconscionable. **■EXAMPLE 9.9** An employer requires its employees to sign a contract containing a provision that shields the employer from liability for any injuries to those employees. In that situation, a court would usually hold the exculpatory clause to be contrary to public policy. **■** Exculpatory clauses found in rental agreements for commercial property are fre-

11. See, for example, *Jones v. Star Credit Corp.*, 59 Misc.2d 189, 298 N.Y.S.2d 264 (1969). This case will be presented in Chapter 14 as Case 14.3.
12. See, for example, *Wisconsin Auto Loans, Inc. v. Jones*, 290 Wis.2d 514, 714 N.W.2d 155 (2006).
13. See, for example, *Coady v. Cross County Bank*, 2007 WI App 26, 299 Wis.2d 420, 729 N.W.2d 732 (2007).
14. See, for example, *Gatton v. T-Mobile USA, Inc.*, 152 Cal.App.4th 571, 61 Cal.Rptr.3d 344 (2007); *Kinkel v. Cingular Wireless, LLC*, 223 Ill.2d 1, 857 N.E.2d 250, 306 Ill.Dec. 157 (2006); and *Aul v. Golden Rule Insurance Co.*, 2007 WI App 165, 737 N.W.2d 24 (2007).

quently held to be contrary to public policy, and such clauses are almost always unenforceable in residential property leases.

Although courts view exculpatory clauses with disfavor, they do enforce such clauses when they do not contravene public policy, are not ambiguous, and do not claim to protect parties from liability for intentional misconduct. Businesses such as health clubs, racetracks, amusement parks, skiing facilities, horse-rental operations, golf-cart concessions, and skydiving organizations frequently use exculpatory clauses to limit their liability for patrons' injuries. Because these services are not essential, the firms offering them are sometimes

considered to have no relative advantage in bargaining strength, and anyone contracting for their services is considered to do so voluntarily.

Sometimes, a company includes an indemnification provision in its contracts with *independent contractors* (see Chapter 22). Such a provision, or clause, removes any responsibility on the company's part for accidents that happen to the independent contractor while working for the company. When is such a provision against public policy? This was the main question in the following case.

CASE 9.2   Speedway SuperAmerica, LLC v. Erwin

Court of Appeals of Kentucky, 250 S.W.3d 339 (2008).

FACTS Speedway SuperAmerica, LLC, hired Sebert Erwin to provide "General Contracting" for five years, but reserved the right to end the contract at any time. The contract contained an *indemnification* clause. Under that clause, Erwin promised to "hold harmless" Speedway for anything that happened to him while working for the company. One day, Erwin was told to report to a Speedway gas station in another city and help remove a walk-in freezer. When he was helping load it on a truck, he fell and was injured. Erwin sued Speedway for damages resulting from the injury he had suffered. Speedway counterclaimed, seeking enforcement of the contract's indemnification clause. Erwin moved to dismiss the counterclaim on the ground that the indemnification clause was invalid because it was against public policy. The trial court held for Erwin. Speedway appealed.

ISSUE Was the indemnification (exculpatory) clause that Erwin signed agreeing not to hold Speedway liable for any injuries he might receive while working for it contrary to public policy?

DECISION Yes. The Kentucky appellate court affirmed the trial court's ruling, holding that the indemnification clause was contrary to public policy and could not be enforced.

REASON The court noted, "The predominant fact of this case is the disparity in bargaining power existing between these two parties." The contract was one sided because it was between a chain of convenience stores and a single worker. While such contracts are not always against public policy, they are when there is no bargaining between parties of similar strength. Here, the situation involved one worker with an eighth-grade education contracting with a large company; the bargaining powers were clearly unequal. Erwin was called an independent contractor despite not having control over his work. The contract stated that he agreed to defend the owner and hold it harmless in the event of any negligence. As an independent contractor (rather than an employee), Erwin had no right to workers' compensation or other benefits that normally would be due to an employee. The court reasoned that the contract was the equivalent of an exculpatory clause, releasing the employer from any liability regardless of fault.

WHAT IF THE FACTS WERE DIFFERENT? *Suppose that Erwin worked for another company as a mover and his employer had sent him to help Speedway move the freezer. Suppose further that the indemnification clause was in a contract signed between Speedway and Erwin's employer. Would that clause be valid? Explain your answer.*

■

THE EFFECT OF ILLEGALITY

In general, an illegal contract is void: the contract is deemed never to have existed, and the courts will not aid either party. In most illegal contracts, both parties are considered to be equally at fault—*in pari delicto*. If the contract is

executory (not yet fulfilled), neither party can enforce it. If it has been executed, there can be neither contractual nor quasi-contractual recovery.

That one wrongdoer in an illegal contract is unjustly enriched at the expense of the other is of no concern to the law—except under certain circumstances (to be discussed shortly). The major justification for this hands-off attitude is that it is improper to place the machinery of justice at the disposal of a plaintiff who has broken the law by entering into an illegal bargain. Another justification is the hoped-for deterrent effect of this general rule. A plaintiff who suffers a loss because of an illegal bargain will presumably be deterred from entering into similar illegal bargains in the future.

There are exceptions to the general rule that neither party to an illegal bargain can sue for breach and neither party can recover for performance rendered. We look at these exceptions here.

Justifiable Ignorance of the Facts

When one of the parties to a contract is relatively innocent (has no reason to know that the contract is illegal), that party can often recover any benefits conferred in a partially executed contract. In this situation, the courts will not enforce the contract but will allow the parties to return to their original positions.

A court may sometimes permit an innocent party who has fully performed under a contract to enforce the contract against the guilty party. **EXAMPLE 9.10** A trucking company contracts with Gillespie to carry crated goods to a specific destination for a normal fee of $5,000. The trucker delivers the crates and later finds out that they contained illegal goods. Although the shipment, use, and sale of the goods are illegal under the law, the trucker, being an innocent party, normally can still legally collect the $5,000 from Gillespie. ■

Members of Protected Classes

When a statute protects a certain class of people, a member of that class can enforce an illegal contract even though the other party cannot. **EXAMPLE 9.11** Statutes prohibit certain employees (such as flight attendants) from working more than a specified number of hours per month. These employees thus constitute a class protected by statute. An employee who is required to work more than the maximum can recover for those extra hours of service. ■

Other examples of statutes designed to protect a particular class of people are **blue sky laws**—state laws that regulate the offering and sale of securities for the protection of the public (see Chapter 27)—and state statutes regulating the sale of insurance. If an insurance company violates a statute when selling insurance, the purchaser can nevertheless enforce the policy and recover from the insurer.

Withdrawal from an Illegal Agreement

If the illegal part of a bargain has not yet been performed, the party rendering performance can withdraw from the contract and recover the performance or its value. **EXAMPLE 9.12** Marta and Amil decide to wager (illegally) on the outcome of a boxing match. Each deposits funds with a stakeholder, who agrees to pay the winner of the bet. At this point, each party has performed part of the agreement, but the illegal part of the agreement will not occur until the funds are paid to the winner. Before such payment occurs, either party is entitled to withdraw from the agreement by giving notice to the stakeholder of his or her withdrawal. ■

Severable, or Divisible, Contracts

A contract that is *severable*, or divisible, consists of distinct parts that can be performed separately, with separate consideration provided for each part. With an *indivisible* contract, in contrast, the parties intended that complete performance by each party would be essential, even if the contract contains a number of seemingly separate provisions.

If a contract is divisible into legal and illegal portions, a court may enforce the legal portion but not the illegal one, so long as the illegal portion does not affect the essence of the bargain. This approach is consistent with the basic policy of enforcing the legal intentions of the contracting parties whenever possible. **EXAMPLE 9.13** Cole signs an employment contract that includes an overly broad and thus illegal covenant not to compete. In this situation, the court may allow the employment contract to be enforceable but reform the unreasonably broad covenant by converting its terms into reasonable ones. Alternatively, the court could declare the covenant illegal (and thus void) and enforce the remaining employment terms. ■

Contracts Illegal through Fraud, Duress, or Undue Influence

Often, one party to an illegal contract is more at fault than the other. When a party has been induced to enter into an illegal bargain through fraud, duress, or undue influence on the part of the other party to the agreement, the first party will be allowed to recover for the performance or its value.

REVIEWING Capacity and Legality

Renee Beaver started racing go-karts competitively in 2007, when she was fourteen. Many of the races required her to sign an exculpatory clause to participate, which she or her parents regularly signed. In 2010, right before her birthday, she participated in the annual Elkhart Grand Prix, a series of races in Elkhart, Indiana. During the event in which she drove, a piece of foam padding used as a course barrier was torn from its base and ended up on the track. A portion of the padding struck Beaver in the head, and another portion was thrown into oncoming traffic, causing a multikart collision during which she sustained severe injuries. Beaver filed an action against the race organizers for negligence. The organizers could not locate the exculpatory clause that Beaver was supposed to have signed. Race organizers argued that she must have signed one to enter the race, but even if she had not signed one, her actions showed her intent to be bound by its terms. Using the information presented in the chapter, answer the following questions.

1 Did Beaver have the contractual capacity to enter a contract with an exculpatory clause? Why or why not?

2 Assuming that Beaver did, in fact, sign the exculpatory clause, did she later disaffirm or ratify the contract? Explain.

3 Now assume that Beaver had stated that she was eighteen years old at the time that she signed the exculpatory clause. How might this affect Beaver's ability to disaffirm or ratify the contract?

4 If Beaver did not actually sign the exculpatory clause, could a court conclude that she impliedly accepted its terms by participating in the race? Why or why not?

TERMS AND CONCEPTS

adhesion contract 193
blue laws 189
blue sky laws 196
contractual capacity 185
covenant not to compete 191

disaffirmance 186
emancipation 185
employment contract 191
exculpatory clause 194
necessaries 187

ratification 187
reformation 192
unconscionable contract or clause 192
usury 189

CHAPTER SUMMARY Capacity and Legality

CONTRACTUAL CAPACITY

Minors
(See pages 185–187.)

A minor is a person who has not yet reached the age of majority. In most states, the age of majority is eighteen for contract purposes. Contracts with minors are voidable at the option of the minor.

1. *Disaffirmance*—The legal avoidance of a contractual obligation.

   a. Disaffirmance can take place (in most states) at any time during minority and within a reasonable time after the minor has reached the age of majority.

   b. If a minor disaffirms part of a contract, the entire contract must be disaffirmed.

   c. When disaffirming executed contracts, the minor has a duty to return received goods if they are still in the minor's control or (in some states) to pay their reasonable value.

   d. A minor who has committed an act of fraud (such as misrepresentation of age) will be denied the right to disaffirm by some courts.

(Continued)

CHAPTER SUMMARY	Capacity and Legality—Continued

Minors—Continued	e. A minor may disaffirm a contract for necessaries but remains liable for the reasonable value of the goods.
	2. *Ratification*—The acceptance, or affirmation, of a legal obligation; may be express or implied.
	   a. Express ratification—Exists when the minor, through a writing or an oral agreement, explicitly assumes the obligations imposed by the contract.
	   b. Implied ratification—Exists when the conduct of the minor is inconsistent with disaffirmance or when the minor fails to disaffirm an executed contract within a reasonable time after reaching the age of majority.
	3. *Parents' liability*—Generally, except for contracts for necessaries, parents are not liable for the contracts made by minor children acting on their own, nor are parents liable for minors' torts except in certain circumstances.
	4. *Emancipation*—Occurs when a child's parent or legal guardian relinquishes the legal right to exercise control over the child. Normally, a minor who leaves home to support himself or herself is considered emancipated. In some jurisdictions, minors themselves are permitted to petition for emancipation for limited purposes.

Intoxicated Persons (See pages 187–188.)	1. A contract entered into by an intoxicated person is voidable at the option of the intoxicated person if the person was sufficiently intoxicated to lack mental capacity, even if the intoxication was voluntary. 2. A contract with an intoxicated person is enforceable if, despite being intoxicated, the person understood the legal consequences of entering into the contract.
Mentally Incompetent Persons (See page 188.)	1. A contract made by a person previously judged by a court to be mentally incompetent is void. 2. A contract made by a mentally incompetent person whom a court has not previously declared to be mentally incompetent is voidable at the option of the mentally incompetent person.
	LEGALITY
Contracts Contrary to Statute (See pages 188–191.)	1. *Usury*—Usury occurs when a lender makes a loan at an interest rate above the lawful maximum. The maximum rate of interest varies from state to state. 2. *Gambling*—Gambling contracts that contravene (go against) state statutes are deemed illegal and thus void. 3. *Sabbath (Sunday) laws*—These laws prohibit the formation or performance of certain contracts on Sunday. Such laws vary widely from state to state, and many states do not enforce them. 4. *Licensing statutes*—Contracts entered into by persons who do not have a license, when one is required by statute, will not be enforceable *unless* the underlying purpose of the statute is to raise government revenues (and not to protect the public from unauthorized practitioners).
Contracts Contrary to Public Policy (See pages 191–195.)	1. *Contracts in restraint of trade*—Contracts to reduce or restrain free competition are illegal and prohibited by statutes. An exception is a *covenant not to compete*. It is usually enforced by the courts if the terms are secondary to a contract (such as a contract for the sale of a business or an employment contract) and are reasonable as to time and area of restraint. Courts tend to scrutinize covenants not to compete closely and, at times, may reform them if they are overbroad rather than declaring the entire covenant unenforceable. 2. *Unconscionable contracts and clauses*—When a contract or contract clause is so unfair that it is oppressive to one party, it may be deemed unconscionable; as such, it is illegal and cannot be enforced. 3. *Exculpatory clauses*—An exculpatory clause is a clause that releases a party from liability in the event of monetary or physical injury, no matter who is at fault. In certain situations, exculpatory clauses may be contrary to public policy and thus unenforceable.

CHAPTER SUMMARY Capacity and Legality–Continued

THE EFFECT OF ILLEGALITY

General Rule (See pages 195–196.)	In general, an illegal contract is void, and the courts will not aid either party when both parties are considered to be equally at fault (*in pari delicto*). If the contract is executory, neither party can enforce it. If the contract is executed, there can be neither contractual nor quasi-contractual recovery.
Exceptions (See page 196.)	Several exceptions exist to the general rule that neither party to an illegal bargain will be able to recover. In the following situations, the court may grant recovery: 1. *Justifiable ignorance of the facts*—When one party to the contract is relatively innocent. 2. *Members of protected classes*—When one party to the contract is a member of a group of persons protected by statute, such as certain employees. 3. *Withdrawal from an illegal agreement*—When either party seeks to recover consideration given for an illegal contract before the illegal act is performed. 4. *Severable, or divisible, contracts*—When the court can divide the contract into illegal and legal portions and the illegal portion is not essential to the bargain. 5. *Fraud, duress, or undue influence*—When one party was induced to enter into an illegal bargain through fraud, duress, or undue influence.

FOR REVIEW

Answers for the even-numbered questions in this **For Review** *section can be found on this text's accompanying Web site at* **www.cengage.com/blaw/fbl**. *Select "Chapter 9" and click on "For Review."*

1 What are some exceptions to the rule that a minor can disaffirm (avoid) any contract?

2 Does an intoxicated person have the capacity to enter into an enforceable contract?

3 Does the mental incompetence of one party necessarily make a contract void?

4 Under what circumstances will a covenant not to compete be enforceable? When will such covenants not be enforced?

5 What is an exculpatory clause? In what circumstances might exculpatory clauses be enforced? When will they not be enforced?

QUESTIONS AND CASE PROBLEMS

 ## HYPOTHETICAL SCENARIOS AND CASE PROBLEMS

9.1 Contracts by Minors. Kalen is a seventeen-year-old minor who has just graduated from high school. He is attending a university two hundred miles from home and has contracted to rent an apartment near the university for one year at $500 per month. He is working at a convenience store to earn enough income to be self-supporting. After living in the apartment and paying monthly rent for four months, he becomes involved in a dispute with his landlord. Kalen, still a minor, moves out and returns the key to the landlord. The landlord wants to hold Kalen liable for the balance of the payments due under the lease. Discuss fully Kalen's liability in this situation.

9.2 Hypothetical Question with Sample Answer. A famous New York City hotel, Hotel Lux, is noted for its food as well as its luxury accommodations. Hotel Lux contracts with a famous chef, Chef Perlee, to become its head chef at $6,000 per month. The contract states that should Perlee leave the employment of Hotel Lux for any reason, he will not work as a chef for any hotel or restaurant in New York, New Jersey, or Pennsylvania for a period of one year. During the first six months of the contract, Hotel Lux extensively advertises Perlee as its head chef, and business at the hotel is excellent. Then a dispute arises between the hotel management and

Perlee, and Perlee terminates his employment. One month later, he is hired by a famous New Jersey restaurant just across the New York state line. Hotel Lux learns of Perlee's employment through a large advertisement in a New York City newspaper. It seeks to enjoin (prevent) Perlee from working in that restaurant as a chef for one year. Discuss how successful Hotel Lux will be in its action.

For a sample answer to Question 9.2, go to Appendix E at the end of this text.

9.3 Mental Incompetence. Joanne is a seventy-five-year-old widow who survives on her husband's small pension. Joanne has become increasingly forgetful, and her family worries that she may have Alzheimer's disease (a brain disorder that seriously affects a person's ability to carry out daily activities). No physician has diagnosed her, however, and no court has ruled on Joanne's legal competence. One day while out shopping, Joanne stops by a store that is having a sale on pianos and enters into a fifteen-year installment contract to buy a grand piano. When the piano arrives the next day, Joanne seems confused and repeatedly asks the delivery-person why a piano is being delivered. Joanne claims that she does not recall buying a piano. Explain whether this contract is void, voidable, or valid. Can Joanne avoid her contractual obligation to buy the piano? If so, how?

9.4 Covenants Not to Compete. In 1993, Mutual Service Casualty Insurance Co. and its affiliates (collectively, MSI) hired Thomas Brass as an insurance agent. Three years later, Brass entered into a career agent's contract with MSI. This contract contained provisions regarding Brass's activities after termination. These provisions stated that, for a period of not less than one year, Brass could not solicit any MSI customers to "lapse, cancel, or replace" any insurance contract in force with MSI in an effort to take that business to a competitor. If he did, MSI could at any time refuse to pay the commissions that it otherwise owed him. The contract also restricted Brass from working for American National Insurance Co. for three years after termination. In 1998, Brass quit MSI and immediately went to work for American National, soliciting MSI customers. MSI filed a suit in a Wisconsin state court against Brass, claiming that he had violated the noncompete terms of his MSI contract. Should the court enforce the covenant not to compete? Why or why not? [*Mutual Service Casualty Insurance Co. v. Brass*, 242 Wis.2d 733, 625 N.W.2d 648 (App. 2001)]

9.5 Misrepresentation of Age. Millennium Club, Inc., operates a tavern in South Bend, Indiana. In January 2003, Pamela Avila and other minors gained admission by misrepresenting that they were at least twenty-one years old. According to Millennium's representatives, the minors used false driver's licenses, "fraudulent transfer of a stamp used to gain admission by another patron or other means of false identification." To gain access, the minors also signed affidavits falsely attesting that they were twenty-one or older. When the state filed criminal charges against the Millennium Club, Millennium

filed a suit in an Indiana state court against Avila and more than two hundred others, seeking damages of $3,000 each for misrepresenting their ages. The minors filed a motion to dismiss the complaint. Should the court grant the motion? What are the competing policy interests in this case? If the Millennium Club was not careful in checking the minors' identification, should it be allowed to recover? If Millennium Club reasonably relied on the minors' representations, should the minors be allowed to avoid liability? Discuss. [*Millennium Club, Inc. v. Avila*, 809 N.E.2d 906 (Ind.App. 2004)]

9.6 Case Problem with Sample Answer. Gary Forsee was an executive officer with responsibility for the U.S. operations of BellSouth Corp., a company providing global telecommunications services. Under a covenant not to compete, Forsee agreed that for a period of eighteen months after termination from employment, he would not provide services in competition with BellSouth "to any person or entity which provides products or services identical or similar to products and services provided by [BellSouth]" within the territory. *Territory* was defined to include the geographic area in which Forsee provided services to BellSouth. The *services* included "management, strategic planning, business planning, administration, or other participation in or providing advice with respect to the communications services business." Forsee announced his intent to resign and accept a position as chief executive officer of Sprint Corp., a competitor of BellSouth. BellSouth filed a suit in a Georgia state court against Forsee, claiming, in part, that his acceptance of employment with Sprint would violate the covenant not to compete. Is the covenant legal? Should it be enforced? Why or why not? [*BellSouth Corp. v. Forsee*, 265 Ga.App. 589, 595 S.E.2d 99 (2004)]

After you have answered Problem 9.6, compare your answer with the sample answer given on the Web site that accompanies this text. Go to www.cengage.com/blaw/fbl, select "Chapter 9," and click on "Case Problem with Sample Answer."

9.7 Licensing Statutes. Under California law, a contract to manage a professional boxer must be in writing and the manager must be licensed by the state athletic commission. Marco Antonio Barrera is a professional boxer and two-time world champion. In May 2003, Jose Castillo, who was not licensed by the state, orally agreed to assume Barrera's management. He "understood" that he would be paid in accord with the "practice in the professional boxing industry, but in no case less than ten percent (10%) of the gross revenue" that Barrera generated as a boxer and through endorsements. Among other accomplishments, Castillo negotiated an exclusive promotion contract for Barrera with Golden Boy Promotions, Inc., which is owned and operated by Oscar De La Hoya. Castillo also helped Barrera settle three lawsuits and resolve unrelated tax problems so that Barrera could continue boxing. Castillo did not train Barrera, pick his opponents, or arrange his fights, however. When Barrera abruptly stopped communicating with Castillo, the latter filed a suit in a California state court against Barrera and others, alleging breach of contract. Under what circumstances is a contract with an unlicensed practitioner enforceable? Is the alleged contract in this case enforceable? Why or why not? [*Castillo v. Barrera*, 146 Cal.App.4th 1317, 53 Cal.Rptr.3d 494 (2 Dist. 2007)]

9.8 **A Question of Ethics.** *Dow AgroSciences, LLC (DAS), makes and sells agricultural seed products. In 2000, Timothy Glenn, a DAS sales manager, signed a covenant not to compete. He agreed that for two years from the date of his termination, he would not "engage in or contribute my knowledge to any work or activity involving an area of technology or business that is then competitive with a technology or business with respect to which I had access to Confidential Information during the five years immediately prior to such termination." Working with DAS business, operations, and research and development personnel, and being a member of high-level*

teams, Glenn had access to confidential DAS information, including agreements with DAS's business partners, marketing plans, litigation details, product secrets, new product development, future plans, and pricing strategies. In 2006, Glenn resigned to work for Pioneer Hi-Bred International, Inc., a DAS competitor. DAS filed a suit in an Indiana state court against Glenn, asking that he be enjoined from accepting any "position that would call on him to use confidential DAS information." [Glenn v. Dow AgroSciences, LLC, 861 N.E.2d 1 (Ind.App. 2007)]

1 Generally, what interests are served by enforcing covenants not to compete? What interests are served by refusing to enforce them?

2 What argument could be made in support of reforming (and then enforcing) illegal covenants not to compete? What argument could be made against this practice?

3 How should the court rule in this case? Why?

CRITICAL THINKING AND WRITING ASSIGNMENTS

9.9 **Critical Legal Thinking.** Are legalized forms of gambling, such as state-operated lotteries, consistent with a continuing public policy against the enforcement of gambling contracts? Why or why not?

9.10 **Video Question.** Go to this text's Web site at **www.cengage.com/blaw/fbl** and select "Chapter 9." Click on "Video Questions" and view the video titled *The Money Pit.* Then answer the following questions.

1 Assume that a valid contract exists between Walter (Tom Hanks) and the plumber. Recall from the video that the plumber had at least two drinks before agreeing to take on the plumbing job. If the plumber was intoxicated, is the contract voidable? Why or why not?

2 Suppose that state law requires plumbers in Walter's state to have a plumber's license and that this plumber does not have a license. Would the contract be enforceable? Why or why not?

3 In the video, the plumber suggests that Walter has been "turned down by every other plumber in the valley." Although the plumber does not even look at the house's plumbing, he agrees to do the repairs if Walter gives him a check for $5,000 right then "before he changes his mind." If Walter later seeks to void the contract because it is contrary to public policy, what should he argue?

ACCESSING THE INTERNET

For updated links to resources available on the Web, as well as a variety of other materials, visit this text's Web site at

www.cengage.com/blaw/fbl

To find your state's statutes governing the emancipation of minors, visit the Legal Information Institute's Web site at

www.law.cornell.edu/topics/Table_Emancipation.htm

For a brief covering contractual capacity and mentally incompetent persons, go to

www.zlawyer2b.com/Contract-4-brief.html

For more information on restrictive covenants in employment contracts, you can access an article written by attorneys at Loose Brown & Associates, P.C., at

www.loosebrown.com/articles/art009.pdf

PRACTICAL INTERNET EXERCISES

Go to this text's Web site at **www.cengage.com/blaw/fbl**, select "Chapter 9," and click on "Practical Internet Exercises." There you will find the following Internet research exercises that you can perform to learn more about the topics covered in this chapter.

PRACTICAL INTERNET EXERCISE 9–1   MANAGEMENT PERSPECTIVE—Minors and the Law

PRACTICAL INTERNET EXERCISE 9–2   SOCIAL PERSPECTIVE—Online Gambling

PRACTICAL INTERNET EXERCISE 9–3   LEGAL PERSPECTIVE—Covenants Not to Compete

BEFORE THE TEST

Go to this text's Web site at **www.cengage.com/blaw/fbl**, select "Chapter 9," and click on "Interactive Quizzes." You will find a number of interactive questions relating to this chapter.

CHAPTER 10
Defenses to Contract Enforceability

LEARNING OBJECTIVES

AFTER READING THIS CHAPTER, YOU SHOULD BE ABLE TO ANSWER THE FOLLOWING QUESTIONS:

1 In what types of situations might genuineness of assent to a contract's terms be lacking?

2 What is the difference between a mistake of value or quality and a mistake of fact?

3 What elements must exist for fraudulent misrepresentation to occur?

4 What contracts must be in writing to be enforceable?

5 What is parol evidence? When is it admissible to clarify the terms of a written contract?

An otherwise valid contract may still be unenforceable if the parties have not genuinely assented to its terms. As mentioned in Chapter 7, lack of genuine assent is a *defense* to the enforcement of a contract. If the law were to enforce contracts not genuinely assented to by the contracting parties, injustice would result. The first part of this chapter focuses on the kinds of factors that indicate that genuineness of assent to a contract may be lacking.

A contract that is otherwise valid may also be unenforceable if it is not in the proper form. For example, if a contract is required by law to be in writing and there is no written evidence of the contract, it may not be enforceable. In the second part of this chapter, we examine the kinds of contracts that require a writing under what is called the *Statute of Frauds*. The chapter concludes with a discussion of the parol evidence rule, under which courts determine the admissibility at trial of evidence extraneous (external) to written contracts.

GENUINENESS OF ASSENT

Genuineness of assent may be lacking because of mistake, fraudulent misrepresentation, undue influence, or duress. Generally, a party who demonstrates that he or she did not

genuinely assent (agree) to the terms of a contract can choose either to carry out the contract or to rescind (cancel) it and thus avoid the entire transaction.

Mistakes

We all make mistakes, so it is not surprising that mistakes are made when contracts are created. In certain circumstances, contract law allows a contract to be avoided on the basis of mistake. It is important to distinguish between *mistakes of fact* and *mistakes of value or quality*. Only a mistake of fact makes a contract voidable.

■EXAMPLE 10.1 Paco buys a violin from Beverly for $250. Although the violin is very old, neither party believes that it is extremely valuable. Later, however, an antiques dealer informs the parties that the violin is rare and worth thousands of dollars. Here, both parties were mistaken, but the mistake is a mistake of *value* rather than a mistake of *fact* that warrants contract rescision. Therefore, Beverly cannot rescind the contract. **■**

Mistakes of fact occur in two forms—*unilateral* and *bilateral (mutual)*. A unilateral mistake is made by only one of the contracting parties; a mutual mistake is made by both. We look next at these two types of mistakes and illustrate them graphically in Exhibit 10–1 on the following page.

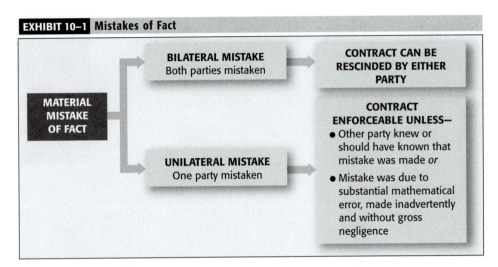

EXHIBIT 10–1 Mistakes of Fact

Unilateral Mistakes   A **unilateral mistake** occurs when only one party is mistaken as to a *material fact*—that is, a fact important to the subject matter of the contract. Generally, a unilateral mistake does not give the mistaken party any right to relief from the contract. In other words, the contract normally is enforceable against the mistaken party. **■EXAMPLE 10.2** Elena intends to sell her motor home for $32,500. When she learns that Chin is interested in buying a used motor home, she sends a fax offering to sell the vehicle to him. When typing the fax, however, she mistakenly keys in the price of $23,500. Chin immediately sends Elena a fax accepting her offer. Even though Elena intended to sell her motor home for $32,500, she has made a unilateral mistake and is bound by contract to sell the vehicle to Chin for $23,500. **■**

There are at least two exceptions to this rule.[1] First, if the *other* party to the contract knows or should have known that a mistake of fact was made, the contract may not be enforceable. **■EXAMPLE 10.3** In the above example, if Chin knew that Elena intended to sell her motor home for $32,500, then Elena's unilateral mistake (stating $23,500 in her offer) may render the resulting contract unenforceable. **■** The second exception arises when a unilateral mistake of fact was due to a mathematical mistake in addition, subtraction, division, or multiplication and was made inadvertently and without gross (extreme) negligence. If a contractor's bid was significantly low because he or she made a mistake in addition when totaling the estimated costs, any contract resulting from the bid normally may be rescinded. Of course, in both situations, the mistake must still involve some *material fact*.

Bilateral (Mutual) Mistakes   When both parties are mistaken about the same material fact, it is a **bilateral mistake**.

When a bilateral mistake occurs, the contract can be rescinded by either party.[2] Note that, as with unilateral mistakes, the mistake must be about a *material fact* (one that is important and central to the contract). **■EXAMPLE 10.4** Keeley buys a landscape painting from Umberto's art gallery. Both Umberto and Keeley believe that the painting is by the artist Vincent van Gogh. Later, Keeley discovers that the painting is a very clever fake. Because neither Umberto nor Keeley was aware of this fact when they made their deal, Keeley can rescind the contract and recover the purchase price of the painting. **■**

A word or term in a contract may be subject to more than one reasonable interpretation. In that situation, if the parties to the contract attach materially different meanings to the term, their mutual misunderstanding may allow the contract to be rescinded. **■EXAMPLE 10.5** In a classic case, *Raffles v. Wichelhaus*,[3] Wichelhaus purchased a shipment of cotton from Raffles to arrive on a ship called the *Peerless* from Bombay, India. Wichelhaus meant a ship called *Peerless* sailing from Bombay in October; Raffles meant a different ship called *Peerless* sailing from Bombay in December. When the goods arrived on the December *Peerless* and Raffles tried to deliver them, Wichelhaus refused to accept them. The British court held for Wichelhaus, concluding that no mutual assent existed because the parties had attached materially different meanings to an essential term of the contract (which ship *Peerless* was to transport the goods). **■**

In the following case, the court had to grapple with the question of whether a mutual mistake of fact had occurred.

---

1. The *Restatement (Second) of Contracts*, Section 153, liberalizes the general rule to take into account the modern trend of allowing avoidance in some circumstances even though only one party has been mistaken.

---

2. *Restatement (Second) of Contracts*, Section 152.

3. 159 Eng.Rep. 375 (1864).

CASE 10.1   **Inkel v. Pride Chevrolet-Pontiac, Inc.**

Supreme Court of Vermont, 945 A.2d 855 (2008).

FACTS The Inkels, who live in Vermont, called Pride Chevrolet-Pontiac, Inc., in Boston about buying a new Chevy Tahoe. They said that they would trade in a high-mileage vehicle they leased. The sales representative told them that the high-mileage penalty would probably not apply as the lease was from a bank, not a dealership. When the Inkels took delivery of the new Tahoe and left their old vehicle at Pride, the price on the contract was $41,200. In small print on the back of the agreement was a provision that the buyer was responsible for any problems with the trade-in vehicle. A month after the sale, Pride told the Inkels they owed another $16,435 because there was a misunderstanding with the leasing company about the high-mileage charge. The Inkels refused to pay. Pride demanded that they return the Tahoe and wanted to cancel the deal; the Inkels refused. The Inkels then sued Pride for breach of contract and other claims. A Vermont superior court held that a mutual mistake had been made in the contract and that the Inkels should have agreed to undo the deal. The court granted summary judgment for Pride and ordered the Inkels to pay damages. They appealed.

ISSUE Was the parties' misunderstanding about whether a high-mileage penalty would be assessed on the trade-in vehicle a mutual mistake of fact?

DECISION The Supreme Court of Vermont reversed the lower court's summary judgment in favor of Pride and remanded the case back to the trial court for further proceedings. It was unclear whether there had been a mutual mistake, and the court was concerned that Pride may have engaged in consumer fraud.

REASON For a court to find that a mutual mistake occurred, evidence would have to be produced at trial to show that both parties had been mistaken about the same material fact. Pride knew about the terms of its contract, and the Inkels knew their vehicle was high mileage. It appears that either Pride was hiding the truth about what would happen due to the high mileage on the trade-in car, or the Inkels were trying to take advantage of Pride's ignorance about the extra payoff needed to their bank for their high-mileage vehicle. Even if there was a mutual mistake, which should be determined at trial, it was not clear that Pride offered to rescind the contract when it said the Inkels could return the vehicle. The terms of a return were never clarified.

FOR CRITICAL ANALYSIS–Ethical Consideration *If a Pride sales representative led the Inkels to believe that the dealership did not care about the excessive miles on the trade-in vehicle, should Pride be willing to incur the loss? Why or why not?*

Fraudulent Misrepresentation

Although fraud is a tort, the presence of fraud also affects the genuineness of the innocent party's consent to a contract. When an innocent party consents to a contract with fraudulent terms, the contract usually can be avoided because she or he has not *voluntarily* consented to the terms.[4] Normally, the innocent party can either rescind (cancel) the contract and be restored to her or his original position or enforce the contract and seek damages for injuries resulting from the fraud.

Typically, fraud involves three elements:

1 A misrepresentation of a material fact must occur.
2 There must be an intent to deceive.
3 The innocent party must justifiably rely on the misrepresentation.

Additionally, to collect damages, a party must have been injured as a result of the misrepresentation.

Fraudulent misrepresentation can also occur in the online environment. For a case involving allegations that Yahoo fraudulently posted online personal ads, see this chapter's *Adapting the Law to the Online Environment* feature on the following page.

Misrepresentation Must Occur The first element of proving fraud is to show that misrepresentation of a material fact has occurred. This misrepresentation can take the form of words or actions. For example, an art gallery owner's statement, "This painting is a Picasso" is a misrepresentation of fact if the painting was done by another artist.

A statement of opinion is generally not subject to a claim of fraud. For example, claims such as "This computer will never break down" and "This car will last for years and years" are statements of opinion, not fact, and contracting parties should recognize them as such and not rely on them. A fact is

---

4. *Restatement (Second) of Contracts*, Sections 163 and 164.

Online Personals—Fraud and Misrepresentation Issues

Keying the words *online personals* into the Google search engine will return more than 35 million hits, including Match.com, Chanceforlove.com, Widowsorwidowers.com, Makefriendsonline.com, and Yahoo! Personals. Yahoo! Personals, which calls itself the "top online dating site," offers two options. One is for people looking for casual dates. It allows users to create their own profiles, browse member profiles, and exchange e-mail or instant messages. The second option, called Yahoo! Personals Primer, is for people who want serious relationships. Users must take a relationship test. Then they can use Yahoo's computerized matching system to "zero in on marriage material." With this service, users can chat on the phone, as well as exchange e-mail.

The Thorny Problem of Misrepresentation

When singles (and others) create their profiles for online dating services, they tend to exaggerate their more appealing features and downplay or omit their less attractive attributes. All users of such services are aware that the profiles may not correspond exactly with reality, but they do assume that the profiles are not complete misrepresentations. In 2006, however, Robert Anthony, individually and on behalf of others, brought a suit against Yahoo in federal district court, alleging fraud and negligent misrepresentation, among other things.

In his complaint, Anthony claimed that Yahoo was not just posting fictitious or exaggerated profiles submitted by users but was deliberately and intentionally originating, creating, and perpetuating false and/or nonexistent profiles. According to Anthony, many profiles used the exact same phrases "with such unique dictation and vernacular [language] that such a random occurrence would not be possible." Anthony also argued that some photo images had multiple identities—that is, the same photo appeared in several different profiles. He also alleged that Yahoo continued to circulate profiles of "actual, legitimate former subscribers whose subscriptions had

expired." Finally, Anthony claimed that when a subscription neared its end date, Yahoo would send the subscriber a fake profile, heralding it as a "potential 'new match.'"

Did Yahoo Have Immunity?

Yahoo asked the court to dismiss the complaint on the grounds that the lawsuit was barred by the Communications Decency Act (CDA) of 1996.[a] As discussed in Chapter 4, the CDA shields Internet service providers (ISPs) from liability for any information submitted by another information content provider. In other words, an interactive computer service cannot be held liable under state law as a publisher of information that originates from a third party information content provider. The CDA defines an information content provider as "any person or entity that is responsible, in whole or in part, for the creation or development of information provided through the Internet or any other interactive computer service."[b]

The court rejected Yahoo's claim that it had immunity under the CDA and held that Yahoo had become an information content provider itself when it created bogus user profiles. The court observed that "no case of which this court is aware has immunized a defendant from allegations that *it* created tortious content."[c] Thus, the court denied Yahoo's motion to dismiss and allowed Anthony's claims of fraud and negligent misrepresentation to proceed to trial.[d]

 FOR CRITICAL ANALYSIS *Assume that Anthony had contacted various users of Yahoo's online dating service only to discover that each user's profile exaggerated the person's physical appearance, intelligence, and occupation. Would Anthony prevail if he brought a lawsuit for fraudulent misrepresentation against Yahoo in that situation? Why or why not?*

a. 47 U.S.C. Section 230.
b. 47 U.S.C. Section 230(f)(3).
c. For an example of the type of cases that have been brought against Internet dating services, see *Carafano v. Metrosplash.com, Inc.,* 339 F.3d 1119 (9th Cir. 2003).
d. *Anthony v. Yahoo!, Inc.,* 421 F.Supp.2d 1257 (N.D.Cal. 2006). See also *Doe v. SexSearch.com,* 502 F.Supp.2d 719 (N.D. Ohio 2007).

objective and verifiable; an opinion is usually subject to debate. Therefore, a seller is allowed to "huff and puff his [or her] wares" without being liable for fraud. In certain cases, however, particularly when a naïve purchaser relies on an expert's opinion, the innocent party may be entitled to *rescission* (cancellation) or *reformation* (an equitable remedy

granted by a court in which the terms of a contract are altered to reflect the true intentions of the parties).

Misrepresentation by Conduct. Misrepresentation can occur by conduct, as well as through express oral or written statements. For example, if a seller, by her or his actions, prevents a buyer from learning of some fact that is material to the contract, such behavior constitutes misrepresentation by conduct.[5] **■EXAMPLE 10.6** Cummings contracts to purchase a racehorse from Garner. The horse is blind in one eye, but when Garner shows the horse, he skillfully conceals this fact by keeping the horse's head turned so that Cummings does not see the defect. The concealment constitutes fraud. ■ Another example of misrepresentation by conduct is the untruthful denial of knowledge or information concerning facts that are material to the contract when such knowledge or information is requested.

Misrepresentation of Law. Misrepresentation of law *ordinarily* does not entitle a party to be relieved of a contract. **■EXAMPLE 10.7** Debbie has a parcel of property that she is trying to sell to Barry. Debbie knows that a local ordinance prohibits building anything higher than three stories on the property. Nonetheless, she tells Barry, "You can build a condominium one hundred stories high if you want to." Barry buys the land and later discovers that Debbie's statement is false. Normally, Barry cannot avoid the contract because under the common law, people are assumed to know state and local laws. ■ Exceptions to this rule occur, however, when the misrepresenting party is in a profession known to require greater knowledge of the law than the average citizen possesses.

Misrepresentation by Silence. Ordinarily, neither party to a contract has a duty to come forward and disclose facts, and a contract normally will not be set aside because certain pertinent information has not been volunteered. **■EXAMPLE 10.8** You are selling a car that has been in an accident and has been repaired. You do not need to volunteer this information to a potential buyer. If, however, the purchaser asks you if the car has had extensive bodywork and you lie, you have committed a fraudulent misrepresentation. ■

Generally, if the seller knows of a serious defect or a serious potential problem about which the buyer cannot reasonably be expected to know, the seller may have a duty to speak. Normally, the seller must disclose only "latent" defects—that is, defects that could not readily be discovered. Thus, termites in a house may not be a latent defect because a buyer could normally discover their presence through a termite inspection. Also, when the parties are in a *fiduciary relationship* (one of trust, such as partners, physician and patient, or attorney and client), there is a duty to disclose material facts; failure to do so may constitute fraud.

Intent to Deceive The second element of fraud is knowledge on the part of the misrepresenting party that facts have

been misrepresented. This element, usually called **scienter,**[6] or "guilty knowledge," generally signifies that there was an intent to deceive. *Scienter* clearly exists if a party knows that a fact is not as stated. *Scienter* also exists if a party makes a statement that he or she believes not to be true or makes a statement recklessly, without regard to whether it is true or false. Finally, this element is met if a party says or implies that a statement is made on some basis, such as personal knowledge or personal investigation, when it is not.

■EXAMPLE 10.9 A convicted felon, Robert Sarvis, applied for a position as an adjunct professor two weeks after his release from prison. On his résumé, he lied about his past work history by representing that he had been the president of a corporation for fourteen years and had taught business law at another college. At his interview, Sarvis stated that he was "well equipped to teach" business law and ethics and that he had "a great interest and knowledge of business law." After he was hired and began working, Sarvis's probation officer alerted the school to his criminal history. The school immediately fired Sarvis, and he brought a lawsuit against the school for breaching his employment contract. The school claimed that it was not liable for the breach because of Sarvis's fraudulent misrepresentations during the hiring process. The court agreed. Sarvis had not fully disclosed his personal history, he clearly had an intent to deceive, and the school had justifiably relied on his misrepresentations. Therefore, the school could rescind Sarvis's employment contract.[7] ■

Reliance on the Misrepresentation The third element of fraud is *justifiable reliance* on the misrepresentation of fact. The deceived party must have a justifiable reason for relying on the misrepresentation, and the misrepresentation must be an important factor (but not necessarily the sole factor) in inducing the party to enter into the contract.

Reliance is not justified if the innocent party knows the true facts or, alternatively, relies on obviously extravagant statements. **■EXAMPLE 10.10** If a used-car dealer tells you, "This old Cadillac will get over sixty miles to the gallon," you normally would not be justified in relying on this statement. Suppose, however, that Merkel, a bank director, induces O'Connell, a co-director, to sign a statement that the bank has sufficient assets to meet its liabilities by telling O'Connell, "We have plenty of assets to satisfy our creditors." This statement is false. If O'Connell knows the true facts or, as a bank director, should know the true facts, he is not justified in relying on Merkel's statement. If O'Connell does not know the true facts, however, *and has no way of finding them out*, he may be justified in relying on the statement. ■

---

5. *Restatement (Second) of Contracts*, Section 160.

6. Pronounced sy-*en*-ter.

7. *Sarvis v. Vermont State Colleges*, 172 Vt. 76, 772 A.2d 494 (2001).

Employers sometimes run into problems by exaggerating their companies' future prospects or financial health when they are interviewing prospective employees. Obviously, an employer wants to paint the future as bright, but should be careful to avoid making representations that an interviewee may rely on to her or his detriment. **■EXAMPLE 10.11** In one case, an employee accepted a job with a brokerage firm, relying on assurances that the firm was not about to be sold. In fact, as the employee was able to prove in his later lawsuit against the firm for fraud, negotiations to sell the firm were under way at the time he was hired. The trial court awarded the employee more than $6 million in damages, a decision that was affirmed on appeal.[8] ■ Generally, employers must be truthful during their hiring procedures to avoid possible lawsuits for fraudulent misrepresentation.

Injury to the Innocent Party Most courts do not require a showing of injury when the action is to rescind (cancel) the contract—these courts hold that because rescission returns the parties to the positions they held before the contract was made, a showing of injury to the innocent party is unnecessary.

To recover damages caused by fraud, however, proof of an injury is universally required. The measure of damages is ordinarily equal to the property's value had it been delivered as represented, less the actual price paid for the property. In actions based on fraud, courts often award *punitive,* or *exemplary, damages,* which are granted to a plaintiff over and above the compensation for the actual loss. As pointed out in Chapter 4, punitive damages are based on the public-policy consideration of punishing the defendant or setting an example to deter similar wrongdoing by others.

PREVENTING LEGAL DISPUTES To avoid making comments that might later be construed as a misrepresentation of material fact, be careful what you say to clients and customers. Those in the business of selling products or services should assume that all customers are naïve and are relying on the seller's representations. Instruct employees to phrase their comments so that customers understand that any statements that are not factual are the employee's opinion. If someone asks a question that is beyond the employee's knowledge, it is better to say that he or she does not know than to guess and have the customer rely on a representation that turns out to be false. This can be particularly important when the questions concern topics such as compatibility or speed of electronic and digital goods, software, or related services.

Also be prudent about what you say when interviewing potential employees. Do not speculate on the financial health of the firm or exaggerate the company's future prospects. Exercising caution in your statements to others in a business context is the best way to avoid potential legal actions for fraudulent misrepresentation.

■

Undue Influence

Undue influence arises from special kinds of relationships in which one party can greatly influence another party, thus overcoming that party's free will. A contract entered into under excessive or undue influence lacks voluntary assent and is therefore voidable.

There are various types of relationships in which one party may dominate another party, thus unfairly influencing him or her. Minors and elderly people, for example, are often under the influence of guardians (persons who are legally responsible for others). If a guardian induces a young or elderly ward (the person whom the guardian looks after) to enter into a contract that benefits the guardian, undue influence may have been exerted. Undue influence can arise from a number of confidential or fiduciary relationships: attorney-client, physician-patient, guardian-ward, parent-child, husband-wife, or trustee-beneficiary.

The essential feature of undue influence is that the party being taken advantage of does not, in reality, exercise free will in entering into a contract. It is not enough that a person is elderly or suffers from some mental or physical impairment. There must be clear and convincing evidence that the person did not act out of her or his free will.

Duress

Assent to the terms of a contract is not genuine if one of the parties is forced into the agreement. Forcing a party to enter into a contract because of the fear created by threats is referred to as **duress.**[9] Inducing consent to a contract through blackmail or extortion also constitutes duress. Duress is both a defense to the enforcement of a contract and a ground for rescission of a contract. Therefore, a party who signs a contract under duress can choose to carry out the contract or to avoid the entire transaction. (The wronged party usually has this choice in cases in which assent is not real or genuine.)

Economic need is generally not sufficient to constitute duress, even when one party exacts a very high price for an

8. *McConkey v. AON Corp.,* 354 N.J.Super. 25, 804 A.2d 572 (A.D. 2002).

9. *Restatement (Second) of Contracts,* Sections 174 and 175.

item the other party needs. If the party exacting the price also creates the need, however, economic duress may be found.

■EXAMPLE 10.12 The Internal Revenue Service (IRS) assessed a large tax and penalty against Weller. Weller retained Eyman to contest the assessment. Two days before the deadline for filing a reply with the IRS, Eyman declined to represent Weller unless he agreed to pay a very high fee for Eyman's services. The agreement was held to be unenforceable.[10] Although Eyman had threatened only to withdraw his services, something that he was legally entitled to do, he was responsible for delaying his withdrawal until just before the deadline. Because Weller was forced into either signing the contract or losing his right to challenge the IRS assessment, the agreement was secured under duress. ■

THE STATUTE OF FRAUDS— REQUIREMENT OF A WRITING

Today, every state has a statute that stipulates what types of contracts must be in writing or be evidenced by a record. In this text, we refer to such a statute as the **Statute of Frauds.** The primary purpose of the statute is to ensure that, for certain types of contracts, there is reliable evidence of the contracts and their terms. These types of contracts are those historically deemed to be important or complex. Although the statutes vary slightly from state to state, the following types of contracts are normally required to be in writing or evidenced by a written memorandum:

1 Contracts involving interests in land.

2 Contracts that cannot by their terms be performed within one year from the date of formation.

3 Collateral contracts, such as promises to answer for the debt or duty of another.

4 Promises made in consideration of marriage.

5 Contracts for the sale of goods priced at $500 or more (under the Uniform Commercial Code, or UCC—see Chapter 14).

Agreements or promises that fit into one or more of these categories are said to "fall under" or "fall within" the Statute of Frauds. (Certain exceptions are made to the Statute of Frauds, however, as you will read later in this section.)

The actual name of the Statute of Frauds is misleading because it does not apply to fraud. Rather, the statute denies enforceability to certain contracts that do not comply with its requirements.

Contracts Involving Interests in Land

Land is a form of *real property*, or real estate, which includes not only land but all physical objects that are permanently attached to the soil, such as buildings, plants, trees, and the soil itself. Under the Statute of Frauds, a contract involving an interest in land must be evidenced by a writing to be enforceable.[11]

■EXAMPLE 10.13 If Carol contracts orally to sell Seaside Shelter to Axel but later decides not to sell, Axel cannot enforce the contract. Similarly, if Axel refuses to close the deal, Carol cannot force Axel to pay for the land by bringing a lawsuit. The Statute of Frauds is a *defense* to the enforcement of this type of oral contract. ■

A contract for the sale of land ordinarily involves the entire interest in the real property, including buildings, growing crops, vegetation, minerals, timber, and anything else affixed to the land. Therefore, a *fixture* (personal property so affixed or so used as to become a part of the realty—see Chapter 29) is treated as real property.

The Statute of Frauds requires written contracts not just for the sale of land but also for the transfer of other interests in land, such as mortgages and leases. We will describe these other interests in Chapter 29.

The One-Year Rule

Contracts that cannot, *by their own terms*, be performed within one year *from the day after* the contract is formed must be in writing to be enforceable. Because disputes over such contracts are unlikely to occur until some time after the contracts are made, resolution of these disputes is difficult unless the contract terms have been put in writing. The one-year period begins to run *the day after the contract is made.*

■EXAMPLE 10.14 Superior University forms a contract with Kimi San stating that San will teach three courses in history during the coming academic year (September 15 through June 15). If the contract is formed in March, it must be in writing to be enforceable—because it cannot be performed within one year. If the contract is not formed until July, however, it will not have to be in writing to be enforceable—because it can be performed within one year. ■ Exhibit 10–2 on the next page graphically illustrates the one-year rule.

Normally, the test for determining whether an oral contract is enforceable under the one-year rule of the Statute of Frauds is whether performance is *possible* within one year from the day after the date of contract formation—not whether the agreement is *likely* to be performed within one year. When

---

10. *Thompson Crane & Trucking Co. v. Eyman*, 123 Cal.App.2d 904, 267 P.2d 1043 (1954).

11. In some states, the contract will be enforced if each party admits to the existence of the oral contract in court or admits to its existence during discovery before trial (see Chapter 2).

EXHIBIT 10-2 The One-Year Rule

Under the Statute of Frauds, contracts that by their terms are impossible to perform within one year from the day after the date of contract formation must be in writing to be enforceable. Put another way, if it is at all possible to perform an oral contract within one year from the day after the contract is made, the contract will fall outside the Statute of Frauds and be enforceable.

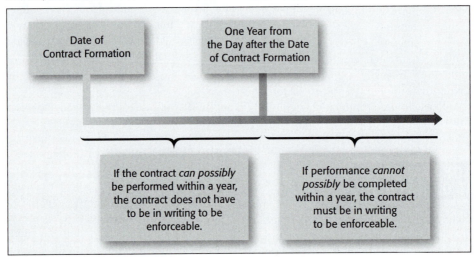

performance of a contract is objectively impossible during the one-year period, the oral contract will be unenforceable.

Collateral Promises

A **collateral promise**, or secondary promise, is one that is ancillary (subsidiary) to a principal transaction or primary contractual relationship. In other words, a collateral promise is one made by a third party to assume the debts or obligations of a primary party to a contract if that party does not perform. Any collateral promise of this nature falls under the Statute of Frauds and therefore must be in writing to be enforceable. To understand this concept, it is important to distinguish between primary and secondary promises and obligations.

Primary versus Secondary Obligations   A contract in which a party assumes a primary obligation normally does not need to be in writing to be enforceable. **■EXAMPLE 10.15** Kenneth orally contracts with Joanne's Floral Boutique to send his mother a dozen roses for Mother's Day. Kenneth promises to pay the boutique when he receives the bill for the flowers. Kenneth is a direct party to this contract and has incurred a *primary* obligation under the contract. Because he is a party to the contract and has a primary obligation to Joanne's Floral Boutique, this contract does not fall under the Statute of Frauds and does not have to be in writing to be enforceable. If Kenneth fails to pay the florist and the florist

sues him for payment, Kenneth cannot raise the Statute of Frauds as a defense. He cannot claim that the contract is unenforceable because it was not in writing. ■

In contrast, a contract in which a party assumes a secondary obligation does have to be in writing to be enforceable. **■EXAMPLE 10.16** Kenneth's mother borrows $10,000 from the Medford Trust Company on a promissory note payable six months later. Kenneth promises the bank officer handling the loan that he will pay the $10,000 *if his mother does not pay the loan on time.* Kenneth, in this situation, becomes what is known as a *guarantor* on the loan. He is guaranteeing to the bank (the creditor) that he will pay the loan if his mother fails to do so. This kind of collateral promise, in which the guarantor states that he or she will become responsible only if the primary party does not perform, must be in writing to be enforceable. ■ We return to the concept of guaranty and the distinction between primary and secondary obligations in Chapter 21, in the context of creditors' rights.

An Exception—The "Main Purpose" Rule   An oral promise to answer for the debt of another is covered by the Statute of Frauds *unless* the guarantor's purpose in accepting secondary liability is to secure a personal benefit. Under the "main purpose" rule, this type of contract need not be in writing.[12] The assumption is that a court can infer from the circum-

---

12. *Restatement (Second) of Contracts*, Section 116.

stances of a case whether a "leading objective" of the promisor was to secure a personal benefit.

■**EXAMPLE 10.17** Carrie Oswald contracts with Machine Manufacturing Company to have some machines custom made for her factory. To ensure that Machine Manufacturing will have the supplies it needs to make the machines, Oswald promises Allrite Materials Supply Company, Machine Manufacturing's supplier, that if Allrite continues to deliver materials to Machine Manufacturing, she will guarantee payment. This promise need not be in writing, even though the effect may be to pay the debt of another, because Oswald's main purpose is to secure a benefit for herself. ■

Another typical application of the so-called main purpose doctrine occurs when one creditor guarantees the debtor's debt to another creditor to forestall litigation. This allows the debtor to remain in business long enough to generate profits sufficient to pay *both* creditors. In this situation, the guaranty does not need to be in writing to be enforceable.

Promises Made in Consideration of Marriage

A unilateral promise to make a monetary payment or to give property in consideration of marriage must be in writing. If Mr. Baumann promises to pay Joe Villard $10,000 if Villard marries Baumann's daughter, the promise must be in writing to be enforceable. The same rule applies to **prenuptial agreements**—agreements made before marriage (also called *antenuptial agreements*) that define each partner's ownership rights in the other partner's property. A prospective wife or husband may wish to limit the amount the prospective spouse can obtain if the marriage ends in divorce. Prenuptial agreements made in consideration of marriage must be in writing to be enforceable.

Generally, courts tend to give more credence to prenuptial agreements that are accompanied by consideration. ■**EXAMPLE 10.18** Maureen, who is not wealthy, marries Kaiser, who has a net worth of $300 million. Kaiser has several children, and he wants them to receive most of his wealth on his death. Prior to their marriage, Maureen and Kaiser draft and sign a prenuptial agreement in which Kaiser promises to give Maureen $100,000 per year for the rest of her life if they divorce. As consideration for consenting to this amount, Kaiser offers Maureen $1 million. If Maureen consents to the agreement and accepts the $1 million, very likely a court would hold that this prenuptial agreement is valid, should it ever be contested. ■

Contracts for the Sale of Goods

The Uniform Commercial Code (UCC) includes Statute of Frauds provisions that require written evidence of a

contract. Section 2–201 contains the major provision, which generally requires a writing or memorandum for the sale of goods priced at $500 or more under the UCC (see Chapter 14). A writing that will satisfy the UCC requirement need only state the quantity term; other terms agreed on need not be stated "accurately" in the writing, as long as they adequately reflect both parties' intentions. The contract will not be enforceable, however, for any quantity greater than that set forth in the writing. In addition, the writing must be signed by the person against whom enforcement is sought. Beyond these two requirements, the writing need not designate the buyer or the seller, the terms of payment, or the price.

Exceptions to the Statute of Frauds

Exceptions to the applicability of the Statute of Frauds are made in certain situations. We describe those situations here.

Partial Performance In cases involving oral contracts for the transfer of interests in land, if the purchaser has paid part of the price, taken possession, and made valuable improvements to the property, and if the parties cannot be returned to their positions prior to the contract, a court may grant *specific performance* (performance of the contract according to its precise terms). Whether a court will enforce an oral contract for an interest in land when partial performance has taken place is usually determined by the degree of injury that would be suffered if the court chose *not* to enforce the oral contract. In some states, mere reliance on certain types of oral contracts is enough to remove them from the Statute of Frauds.

Under the UCC, an oral contract for goods priced at $500 or more is enforceable to the extent that a seller accepts payment or a buyer accepts delivery of the goods.[13] ■**EXAMPLE 10.19** If the president of Ajax Corporation orders by telephone thirty crates of bleach from Cloney, Inc., and repudiates the contract after ten crates have been delivered and accepted, Cloney can enforce the contract to the extent of the ten crates accepted by Ajax. ■

The existence and extent of a contract to supply computer kiosks for use in school cafeterias was in dispute in the following case.

---

13. UCC 2–201(3)(c). See Chapter 14.

CASE 10.2   School-Link Technologies, Inc. v. Applied Resources, Inc.

United States District Court, District of Kansas, 471 F.Supp.2d 1101 (2007).

FACTS Applied Resources, Inc. (ARI), makes computer hardware for point-of-sale systems: kiosks that consist of computers encased in chassis on which card readers or other payment devices are mounted. School-Link Technologies, Inc. (SLT), sells food-service technology to schools. In August 2003, the New York City Department of Education (NYCDOE) asked SLT to propose a cafeteria payment system that included kiosks. SLT asked ARI to participate in a pilot project, orally promising ARI that it would be the exclusive supplier of as many as 1,500 kiosks if the NYCDOE awarded the contract to SLT. ARI agreed. SLT intended to cut ARI out of the deal, however, and told the NYCDOE that SLT would be making its own kiosks. Meanwhile, SLT paid ARI in advance for a certain number of goods, but insisted on onerous terms for a written contract to which ARI would not agree. ARI suspended production of the prepaid items and refused to refund over $55,000 of SLT's funds. SLT filed a suit in a federal district court against ARI. ARI responded in part with a counterclaim for breach of contract, asserting that SLT failed to use ARI as an exclusive supplier as promised. ARI sought the expenses it incurred for the pilot project and the amount of profit that it would have realized on the entire deal. SLT filed a motion for summary judgment on this claim.

ISSUE Was the oral agreement for the kiosks enforceable to the extent to which it had been performed?

DECISION Yes. The court denied SLT's motion for summary judgment on ARI's counterclaim for breach of contract "with respect to goods which SLT already received and accepted, i.e., the goods for the pilot program with the NYCDOE."

REASON The court acknowledged that, according to the Uniform Commercial Code, a contract for a sale of goods for a price of $500 or more generally must be in writing and must be signed by the party against whom enforcement is sought. The court reasoned that "because the NYCDOE contract undisputedly involved the sale of goods in excess of $500, the parties' oral contract that ARI would be the exclusive supplier of kiosks for the project is not enforceable in the absence of an applicable exception to this general rule." Under the partial performance exception to the rule, an oral contract for a sale of goods over $500 that would otherwise be unenforceable for the lack of a writing is enforceable to the extent that the seller delivers the goods and the buyer accepts them. In that situation, the performance serves as a substitute for the required writing. Thus, in this case, the court concluded that the alleged oral contract between SLT and ARI, to the effect that ARI would be the exclusive supplier of kiosks for SLT's contract with the NYCDOE, was enforceable to the extent that ARI had delivered the kiosks for the pilot project and SLT had accepted them. The court added, however, that "the remaining aspect of that claim is barred by the Statute of Frauds."

FOR CRITICAL ANALYSIS–Social Consideration *Could ARI successfully assert a claim against SLT based on fraudulent misrepresentation? Explain.*

■

Admissions   In some states, if a party against whom enforcement of an oral contract is sought admits in pleadings, testimony, or otherwise in court proceedings that a contract for sale was made, the contract will be enforceable.[14] A contract subject to the UCC will be enforceable, but only to the extent of the quantity admitted.[15] **EXAMPLE 10.20** Suppose that the president of Ajax Corporation in the previous example admits under oath that an oral agreement was made with Cloney, Inc., for twenty crates of bleach. In this situation, even if Cloney, Inc., claims that Ajax had contracted for thirty crates, the agreement will be enforceable only to the extent admitted (for twenty rather than thirty crates of bleach). ■

Promissory Estoppel   In some states, an oral contract that would otherwise be unenforceable under the Statute of Frauds may be enforced under the doctrine of promissory estoppel, or detrimental reliance. Recall from Chapter 8 that if a promisor makes a promise on which the promisee justifiably relies to her or his detriment, a court may *estop* (prevent) the promisor from denying that a contract exists. Section 139 of the *Restatement (Second) of Contracts* provides that in these circumstances, an oral promise can be enforceable, notwithstanding the Statute of Frauds, if the reliance was foreseeable to the person making the promise and if injustice can be avoided only by enforcing the promise.

Special Exceptions under the UCC   Special exceptions to the applicability of the Statute of Frauds exist for sales con-

---

14. *Restatement (Second) of Contracts*, Section 133.
15. UCC 2–201(3)(b). See Chapter 14.

tracts. Oral contracts for customized goods may be enforced in certain circumstances. Another exception has to do with oral contracts between merchants that have been confirmed in writing. We will examine these exceptions in Chapter 14. Exhibit 10–3 graphically summarizes the types of contracts that fall under the Statute of Frauds and the various exceptions that apply.

THE STATUTE OF FRAUDS—SUFFICIENCY OF THE WRITING

A written contract will satisfy the writing requirement of the Statute of Frauds. A *written memorandum* (written evidence of the oral contract) signed by the party against whom enforcement is sought will also satisfy the writing requirement.[16] The signature need not be placed at the end of the document but can be anywhere in the writing; it can even be initials rather than the full name.

A significant issue in today's business world has to do with how "signatures" can be created and verified on electronic contracts and other documents. We will examine electronic signatures in Chapter 13.

What Constitutes a Writing?

A writing can consist of any confirmation, invoice, sales slip, check, fax, or e-mail—or such items in combination. The written contract need not consist of a single document to constitute an enforceable contract. One document may incorpo-

___
16. As mentioned earlier, under the UCC's Statute of Frauds, a writing is required only for contracts for the sale of goods priced at $500 or more (see Chapter 14).

rate another document by expressly referring to it. Several documents may form a single contract if they are physically attached, such as by staple, paper clip, or glue. Several documents may form a single contract even if they are only placed in the same envelope.

    ■**EXAMPLE 10.21** Sam orally agrees to sell some land next to a shopping mall to Terry. Sam gives Terry an unsigned memo that contains a legal description of the property, and Terry gives Sam an unsigned first draft of their contract. Sam sends Terry a signed letter that refers to the memo and to the first and final drafts of the contract. Terry sends Sam an unsigned copy of the final draft of the contract with a signed check stapled to it. Together, the documents can constitute a writing sufficient to satisfy the Statute of Frauds and bind both parties to the terms of the contract as evidenced by the writings. ■

What Must Be Contained in the Writing?

A memorandum evidencing the oral contract need only contain the essential terms of the contract. Under most provisions of the Statute of Frauds, the writing must name the parties and identify the subject matter, consideration, and quantity. With respect to contracts for the sale of land, some states require that the memorandum also set forth the essential terms of the contract, such as location and price, with sufficient clarity to allow the terms to be determined from the memo itself, without reference to any outside sources. Under the UCC, in regard to the sale of goods, the writing need only state the quantity and be signed by the party against whom enforcement is sought.

    Because only the party against whom enforcement is sought must have signed the writing, a contract may be

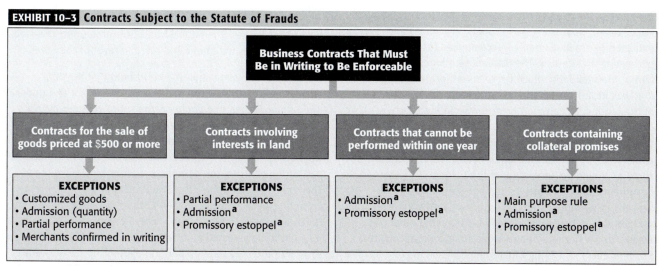

EXHIBIT 10–3 Contracts Subject to the Statute of Frauds

Business Contracts That Must Be in Writing to Be Enforceable

Contracts for the sale of goods priced at $500 or more	Contracts involving interests in land	Contracts that cannot be performed within one year	Contracts containing collateral promises
EXCEPTIONS • Customized goods • Admission (quantity) • Partial performance • Merchants confirmed in writing	**EXCEPTIONS** • Partial performance • Admission[a] • Promissory estoppel[a]	**EXCEPTIONS** • Admission[a] • Promissory estoppel[a]	**EXCEPTIONS** • Main purpose rule • Admission[a] • Promissory estoppel[a]

a. Some states follow Section 133 (on admissions) and Section 139 (on promissory estoppel) of the *Restatement (Second) of Contracts.*

enforceable by one of its parties but not by the other. **■EXAMPLE 10.22** Rock orally agrees to buy Betty Devlin's lake house and lot for $350,000. Devlin writes Rock a letter confirming the sale by identifying the parties and the essential terms of the sales contract—price, method of payment, and legal address—and signs the letter. Devlin has made a written memorandum of the oral land contract. Because she signed the letter, she normally can be held to the oral contract by Rock. Rock, however, because he has not signed or entered into a written contract or memorandum, can plead the Statute of Frauds as a defense, and Devlin cannot enforce the contract against him. ■

THE PAROL EVIDENCE RULE

Sometimes, a written contract does not include—or contradicts—an oral understanding reached by the parties before or at the time of contracting. For example, suppose a person signs a lease agreement that says no pets are allowed because the landlord orally represented at the time of the lease contract that tenants were allowed to have cats. Can the tenant have a cat despite what the lease agreement says? In determining the outcome of such disputes, the courts look to a common law rule governing the admissibility in court of oral evidence, or *parol evidence*.

Under the **parol evidence rule,** if a court finds that a written contract represents the complete and final statement of the parties' agreement, then it will not allow either party to present parol evidence (testimony or other evidence of communications between the parties that are not contained in the contract itself). In other words, a party cannot introduce in court evidence of the parties' prior negotiations, prior agreements, or contemporaneous oral agreements if that evidence contradicts or varies the terms of the parties' written contract.[17]

Does a football team's agreement with its fans to sell "stadium builder licenses" (SBLs) for seats represent the parties' entire contract, or can an SBL brochure explain or vary the agreement? That was the question in the following case.

---

17. *Restatement (Second) of Contracts*, Section 213.

CASE 10.3 **Yocca v. Pittsburgh Steelers Sports, Inc.**

Supreme Court of Pennsylvania, 578 Pa. 479, 854 A.2d 425 (2004).

FACTS In October 1998, Pittsburgh Steelers Sports, Inc., and others (collectively, the Steelers) sent Ronald Yocca a brochure that advertised a new stadium to be built for the Pittsburgh Steelers football team. The brochure publicized the opportunity to buy stadium builder licenses (SBLs), which grant the right to buy annual season tickets to the games. Prices varied, depending on the seats' locations, which were indicated by small diagrams. Yocca applied for an SBL, listing his seating preferences. The Steelers sent him a letter notifying him of the section in which his seat was located. A diagram that was included with the letter showed different parameters of the seating section than were shown in the brochure's diagrams. The Steelers also sent Yocca documents setting out the terms of the SBL and requiring his signature. These documents included a clause that read, "This Agreement contains the entire agreement of the parties." Yocca signed the documents, and the Steelers told him the specific location of his seat. When he arrived at the stadium, however, the seat was not where he expected it to be. Yocca and other SBL buyers filed a suit in a Pennsylvania state court against the Steelers, alleging, among other things, breach of contract. The court ordered the dismissal of the complaint. The plaintiffs

appealed to a state intermediate appellate court, which reversed this order. The defendants appealed to the state supreme court.

ISSUE Did the documents that the Steelers sent to Yocca setting forth the terms of the SBL constitute the parties' entire agreement and preclude the introduction of parol evidence?

DECISION Yes. The Pennsylvania Supreme Court reversed the lower court's judgment and ruled in favor of the Steelers.

REASON The state supreme court held that the SBL documents constituted the parties' entire contract and under the parol evidence rule could not be supplemented by previous negotiations or agreements. Because the plaintiffs' complaint was based on the claim that the defendants violated the terms of the brochure, and the brochure was not part of the contract, the complaint was properly dismissed. The court explained that "the SBL Brochure did not represent a promise by the Steelers to sell SBLs to Appellees. Rather, the Brochure was merely an offer by the Steelers to sell Appellees the right to be assigned an unspecified seat in an unspecified section of the new stadium and the right to receive a contract to buy an SBL for that later-assigned seat. *   *   * The SBL

CASE 10.3—Continued

Agreement clearly represented the parties' contract concerning the sale of SBLs. Unlike the SBL Brochure, the SBL Agreement reflected a promise by the Steelers to actually sell Appellees a specific number of SBL seats in a specified section. Furthermore, the SBL Agreement * * * explicitly stated that it represented the parties' entire contract regarding the sale of SBLs."

WHAT IF THE FACTS WERE DIFFERENT?
Suppose that the Steelers had not sent Yocca a diagram with the letter notifying him of his seat's section and that the SBL documents had not included a clause stating that the documents contained the entire agreement of the parties. Would the result have been different? Why or why not?

■

Exceptions to the Parol Evidence Rule

Because of the rigidity of the parol evidence rule, courts make several exceptions. These exceptions include the following:

1 Evidence of a *subsequent modification* of a written contract can be introduced in court. Keep in mind that the oral modifications may not be enforceable if they come under the Statute of Frauds—for example, if they increase the price of the goods for sale to $500 or more or increase the term for performance to more than one year. Also, oral modifications will not be enforceable if the original contract provides that any modification must be in writing.[18]

2 Oral evidence can be introduced in all cases to show that the contract was voidable or void (for example, induced by mistake, fraud, or misrepresentation). In this situation, if deception led one of the parties to agree to the terms of a written contract, oral evidence indicating fraud should not be excluded. Courts frown on bad faith and are quick to allow the introduction at trial of parol evidence when it establishes fraud.

3 When the terms of a written contract are ambiguous, evidence is admissible to show the meaning of the terms.

4 Evidence is admissible when the written contract is incomplete in that it lacks one or more of the essential terms. The courts allow evidence to "fill in the gaps" in the contract.

5 Under the UCC, evidence can be introduced to explain or supplement a written contract by showing a prior dealing, course of performance, or usage of trade.[19] We will discuss these terms in further detail in Chapter 14, in the context of sales contracts. Here, it is sufficient to say that when buyers and sellers deal with each other over extended periods of time, certain customary practices develop. These practices are often overlooked in the writing of the contract, so courts allow the introduction of evidence to show how the parties have acted in the past. Usage of trade—practices and customs generally followed in a particular industry—can also shed light on the meaning of certain contract provisions, and thus evidence of trade usage may be admissible.

6 The parol evidence rule does not apply if the existence of the entire written contract is subject to an orally agreed-on condition. Proof of the condition does not alter or modify the written terms but affects the *enforceability* of the written contract. **■EXAMPLE 10.23** Jelek orally agrees to purchase Armand's car for $8,000, but only if Jelek's mechanic, Frank, inspects the car and approves of the purchase. Frank cannot do an inspection for another week, and Armand is leaving town for the weekend. Jelek wants to use the car right away, so he drafts a contract of sale that does not include the agreed-on condition of a mechanical inspection. Both parties sign the contract. The following week Frank, the mechanic, inspects the car but does not recommend its purchase. When Jelek does not buy the car, Armand sues him for breach of contract. In this case, Jelek's oral agreement did not alter or modify the terms of the written agreement but concerned whether the contract existed at all. Therefore, the parol evidence rule does not apply. ■

7 When an *obvious* or *gross* clerical (or typographic) error exists that clearly would not represent the agreement of the parties, parol evidence is admissible to correct the error. **■EXAMPLE 10.24** Sempter agrees to lease 1,000 square feet of office space from Stone Enterprises at the current monthly rate of $3 per square foot. The signed written lease provides for a monthly lease payment of $300 rather than the $3,000 agreed to by the parties. Because the error is obvious, Stone Enterprises would be allowed to admit parol evidence to correct the mistake. ■

Integrated Contracts

The determination of whether evidence will be allowed basically depends on whether the written contract is intended to be a complete and final statement of the terms of the

---

18. UCC 2–209(2), (3). See Chapter 14.
19. UCC 1–205, 2–202. See Chapter 14.

agreement. If it is so intended, it is referred to as an **integrated contract,** and extraneous evidence (evidence from outside the contract) is excluded.

An integrated contract can be either completely or partially integrated. If it contains all of the terms of the parties' agreement, then it is completely integrated. If it contains only some of the terms that the parties agreed on and not others, it is partially integrated. If the contract is only partially integrated, evidence of consistent additional terms is admissi-

ble to supplement the written agreement.[20] Note that for both completely and partially integrated contracts, courts exclude any evidence that *contradicts* the writing and allow parol evidence only to add to the terms of a partially integrated contract. Exhibit 10–4 illustrates the relationship between integrated contracts and the parol evidence rule.

---

20. *Restatement (Second) of Contracts,* Section 216.

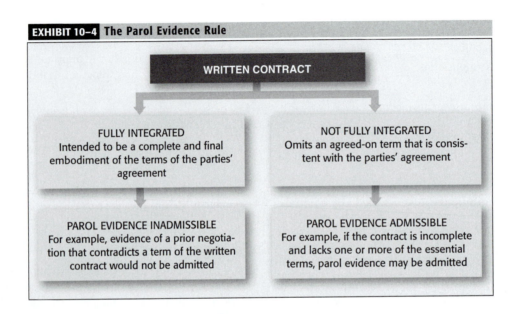

EXHIBIT 10–4 The Parol Evidence Rule

WRITTEN CONTRACT

FULLY INTEGRATED
Intended to be a complete and final embodiment of the terms of the parties' agreement

NOT FULLY INTEGRATED
Omits an agreed-on term that is consistent with the parties' agreement

PAROL EVIDENCE INADMISSIBLE
For example, evidence of a prior negotiation that contradicts a term of the written contract would not be admitted

PAROL EVIDENCE ADMISSIBLE
For example, if the contract is incomplete and lacks one or more of the essential terms, parol evidence may be admitted

---

REVIEWING Defenses to Contract Enforceability

Charter Golf, Inc., manufactures and sells golf apparel and supplies. Ken Odin had worked as a Charter sales representative for six months when he was offered a position with a competing firm. Charter's president, Jerry Montieth, offered Odin a 10 percent commission "for the rest of his life" if Ken would turn down the offer and stay on with Charter. He also promised that Odin would not be fired unless he was dishonest. Odin turned down the competitor's offer and stayed with Charter. Three years later, Charter fired Odin for no reason. Odin sued, alleging breach of contract. Using the information presented in the chapter, answer the following questions.

1 Would a court likely decide that Odin's employment contract falls within the Statute of Frauds? Why or why not?

2 Assume that the court does find that the contract falls within the Statute of Frauds and that the state in which the court sits recognizes every exception to the Statute of Frauds discussed in the chapter. What exception provides Odin with the best chance of enforcing the oral contract in this situation?

3 Now suppose that Montieth had taken out a pencil, written "10 percent for life" on the back of a register receipt, and handed it to Odin. Would this satisfy the Statute of Frauds? Why or why not?

4 Assume that Odin had signed a written employment contract at the time he was hired to work for Charter, but it was not completely integrated. Would a court allow Odin to present parol evidence of Montieth's subsequent promises?

TERMS AND CONCEPTS

bilateral mistake 204	integrated contract 216	*scienter* 207
collateral promise 210	parol evidence rule 214	Statute of Frauds 209
duress 208	prenuptial agreement 211	unilateral mistake 204

CHAPTER SUMMARY Defenses to Contract Enforceability

GENUINENESS OF ASSENT

Mistakes
(See pages 203–205.)

1. *Unilateral*—Generally, the mistaken party is bound by the contract *unless* (a) the other party knows or should have known of the mistake or (b) the mistake is an inadvertent mathematical error—such as an error in addition or subtraction—committed without gross negligence.

2. *Bilateral (mutual)*—When both parties are mistaken about the same material fact, such as identity, either party can avoid the contract.

Fraudulent Misrepresentation
(See pages 205–208.)

When fraud occurs, usually the innocent party can enforce or avoid the contract. The elements necessary to establish fraud are as follows:

1. A misrepresentation of a material fact must occur.

2. There must be an intent to deceive.

3. The innocent party must justifiably rely on the misrepresentation.

Undue Influence
(See page 208.)

Undue influence arises from special relationships, such as fiduciary or confidential relationships, in which one party's free will has been overcome by the undue influence exerted by the other party. Usually, the contract is voidable.

Duress
(See pages 208–209.)

Duress is the tactic of forcing a party to enter a contract under the fear of a threat—for example, the threat of violence or serious economic loss. The party forced to enter the contract can rescind the contract.

FORM

The Statute of Frauds—Requirement of a Writing
(See pages 209–213.)

1. *Applicability*—The following types of contracts fall under the Statute of Frauds and must be in writing to be enforceable:

   a. Contracts involving interests in land—The statute applies to any contract for an interest in realty, such as a sale, a lease, or a mortgage.

   b. Contracts that cannot by their terms be performed within one year—The statute applies only to contracts that are objectively impossible to perform fully within one year from (the day after) the contract's formation.

   c. Collateral promises—The statute applies only to express contracts made between the guarantor and the creditor that make the guarantor secondarily liable. Exception: the main purpose rule.

   d. Promises made in consideration of marriage—The statute applies to promises to make a monetary payment or give property in consideration of a promise to marry and to prenuptial agreements made in consideration of marriage.

   e. Contracts for the sale of goods priced at $500 or more—See the Statute of Frauds provision in Section 2–201 of the Uniform Commercial Code (UCC).

2. *Exceptions*—Partial performance, admissions, and promissory estoppel.

(Continued)

CHAPTER SUMMARY   Defenses to Contract Enforceability–Continued

The Statute of Frauds–Sufficiency of the Writing (See pages 213–214.)	To constitute an enforceable contract under the Statute of Frauds, a writing must be signed by the party against whom enforcement is sought, name the parties, identify the subject matter, and state with reasonable certainty the essential terms of the contract. In a sale of land, the price and a description of the property may need to be stated with sufficient clarity to allow them to be determined without reference to outside sources. Under the UCC, a contract for a sale of goods is not enforceable beyond the quantity of goods shown in the contract.
The Parol Evidence Rule (See pages 214–216.)	The parol evidence rule prohibits the introduction at trial of evidence of the parties' prior negotiations, prior agreements, or contemporaneous oral agreements that contradicts or varies the terms of the parties' written contract. The written contract is assumed to be the complete embodiment of the parties' agreement. Exceptions are made in the following circumstances:

1. To show that the contract was subsequently modified.

2. To show that the contract was voidable or void.

3. To clarify the meaning of ambiguous terms.

4. To clarify the terms of the contract when the written contract lacks one or more of its essential terms.

5. Under the UCC, to explain the meaning of contract terms in light of a prior dealing, course of performance, or usage of trade.

6. To show that the entire contract is subject to an orally agreed-on condition.

7. When an obvious clerical or typographic error was made.

FOR REVIEW

Answers for the even-numbered questions in this **For Review** *section can be found on this text's accompanying Web site at* **www.cengage.com/blaw/fbl**. *Select "Chapter 10" and click on "For Review."*

1 In what types of situations might genuineness of assent to a contract's terms be lacking?

2 What is the difference between a mistake of value or quality and a mistake of fact?

3 What elements must exist for fraudulent misrepresentation to occur?

4 What contracts must be in writing to be enforceable?

5 What is parol evidence? When is it admissible to clarify the terms of a written contract?

QUESTIONS AND CASE PROBLEMS

 HYPOTHETICAL SCENARIOS AND CASE PROBLEMS

10.1 Genuineness of Assent. Jerome is an elderly man who lives with his nephew, Philip. Jerome is totally dependent on Philip's support. Philip tells Jerome that unless Jerome transfers a tract of land he owns to Philip for a price 30 percent below market value, Philip will no longer support and take care of him. Jerome enters into the contract. Discuss fully whether Jerome can set aside this contract.

10.2 Hypothetical Question with Sample Answer. Gemma promises a local hardware store that she will pay for a lawn mower that her brother is purchasing on credit if the brother fails to pay

the debt. Must this promise be in writing to be enforceable? Why or why not?

 For a sample answer to Question 10.2, go to Appendix E at the end of this text.

10.3 Fraudulent Misrepresentation. Larry offered to sell Stanley his car and told Stanley that the car had been driven only 25,000 miles and had never been in an accident. Stanley hired Cohen, a mechanic, to appraise the condition of the car, and Cohen said that the car probably had at least 50,000 miles on it and probably had been in an accident. In spite of this information, Stanley still thought the car would be a good buy for the price, so he purchased it. Later, when the car developed numerous mechanical problems, Stanley sought to rescind the contract on the basis of Larry's fraudulent misrepresentation of the auto's condition. Will Stanley be able to rescind his contract? Discuss.

10.4 Statute of Frauds. Sierra Bravo, Inc., and Shelby's, Inc., entered into a written "Waste Disposal Agreement" under which Shelby's allowed Sierra to deposit on Shelby's land waste products, deleterious (harmful) materials, and debris removed by Sierra in the construction of a highway. Later, Shelby's asked Sierra why it had not constructed a waterway and a building pad suitable for a commercial building on the property, as they had orally agreed. Sierra denied any such agreement. Shelby's filed a suit in a Missouri state court against Sierra, alleging breach of contract. Sierra contended that any oral agreement was unenforceable under the Statute of Frauds. Sierra argued that because the right to remove minerals from land is considered a contract for the sale of an interest in land to which the Statute of Frauds applies, the Statute of Frauds should apply to the right to deposit soil on another person's property. How should the court rule, and why? [*Shelby's, Inc. v. Sierra Bravo, Inc.*, 68 S.W.3d 604 (Mo.App. S.D. 2002)]

10.5 The Parol Evidence Rule. Novell, Inc., owned the source code for DR DOS, a computer operating system that Microsoft Corp. targeted with anticompetitive practices in the early 1990s. Novell worried that if it filed a suit, Microsoft would retaliate with further unfair practices. Consequently, Novell sold DR DOS to Caldera, Inc., the predecessor in interest to Canopy Group. The purposes of the sale were to obligate Canopy to bring an action against Microsoft and to allow Novell to share in the recovery without revealing its role. Novell and Canopy signed two documents: a contract of sale, obligating Canopy to pay $400,000 for rights to the source code, and a temporary license, obligating Canopy to pay at least $600,000 in royalties, which included a percentage of any recovery from the suit. Canopy settled the dispute with Microsoft, deducted its expenses, and paid Novell its percentage. Novell filed a suit in a Utah state court against Canopy, alleging breach of contract for Canopy's deduction of expenses. Canopy responded that it could show that the parties had an oral agreement on this point. On what basis might the court refuse to consider this evidence? Is that the appropriate course in this case? Explain. [*Novell, Inc. v. Canopy Group, Inc.*, 2004 UT App. 162, 92 P.3d 768 (2004)]

10.6 The Parol Evidence Rule. Carlin Krieg owned a dairy farm in St. Joe, Indiana, that was appraised at $154,000 in December 1997. In August 1999, Krieg told Donald Hieber that he intended to sell the farm for $106,000. Hieber offered to buy it. Krieg also told Hieber that he wanted to retain a "right of residency" for life in the farm. In October, Krieg and Hieber executed a "Purchase Agreement" that provided that Krieg "shall transfer full and complete possession" of the farm "subject to [his] right of residency." The agreement also con-

tained an integration clause that stated "there are no conditions, representations, warranties, or agreements not stated in this instrument." In November 2000, the house was burned in a fire, rendering it unlivable. Hieber filed an insurance claim for the damage and received the proceeds, but he did not fix the house. Krieg filed a suit in an Indiana state court against Hieber, alleging breach of contract. Is there any basis on which the court can consider evidence regarding the parties' negotiations prior to their agreement for the sale of the farm? Explain. [*Krieg v. Hieber*, 802 N.E.2d 938 (Ind.App. 2004)]

10.7 Case Problem with Sample Answer. According to the student handbook at Cleveland Chiropractic College (CCC) in Missouri, *academic misconduct* includes "selling . . . any copy of any material intended to be used as an instrument of academic evaluation in advance of its initial administration." Leonard Verni was enrolled at CCC in Dr. Aleksandr Makarov's dermatology class. Before the first examination, Verni was reported to be selling copies of the test. CCC investigated and concluded that Verni had committed academic misconduct. Verni was dismissed from CCC, which informed him of his right to an appeal. According to the handbook, at the hearing on appeal a student could have an attorney or other adviser, present witnesses' testimony and other evidence, and "question any testimony . . . against him/her." At his hearing, however, Verni did not bring his attorney, present evidence on his behalf, or question any adverse witnesses. When the dismissal was upheld, Verni filed a suit in a Missouri state court against CCC and others, claiming, in part, fraudulent misrepresentation. Verni argued that because he "relied" on the handbook's "representation" that CCC would follow its appeal procedure, he was unable to properly refute the charges against him. Can Verni succeed with this argument? Explain. [*Verni v. Cleveland Chiropractic College*, 212 S.W.3d 150 (Mo. 2007)]

After you have answered Problem 10.7, compare your answer with the sample answer given on the Web site that accompanies this text. Go to www.cengage.com/blaw/fbl, select "Chapter 10," and click on "Case Problem with Sample Answer."

10.8 Contract for a Sale of Goods. Milton Blankenship agreed in writing to buy 15 acres of Ella Mae Henry's junkyard property for $15,000 per acre with a ten-year option to buy the remaining 28.32 acres. Blankenship orally agreed to (1) begin operating a car skeleton processing plant within six to fifteen months; (2) buy as many car skeletons generated by the yard as Clifford Henry wanted to sell him, at a certain premium over the market price; and (3) allow all junk vehicles on the property to remain until they were processed at the new plant. Blankenship never operated such a plant, never bought any vehicles from the yard, and demanded that all vehicles be removed from the property. To obtain the remaining 28.32 acres, Blankenship filed a suit in a Georgia state court against Henry, who responded with a counter-claim for breach of contract. Under oath during discovery,

Henry testified that their oral agreement allowed him to sell "as many of the car skeletons generated by the Henry junkyard" as he wished, and Blankenship testified that he had agreed to buy as many skeletons as Henry was willing to sell. Does the Statute of Frauds undercut or support Henry's counterclaim? Explain. [*Henry v. Blankenship*, 284 Ga.App. 578, 644 S.E.2d 419 (2007)]

10.9 **A Question of Ethics.** *On behalf of BRJM, LLC, Nicolas Kepple offered Howard Engelsen $210,000 for a parcel of land known as lot five on the north side of Barnes Road in Stonington, Connecticut. Engelsen's company, Output Systems, Inc., owned the land. Engelsen had the lot surveyed and obtained an appraisal. The appraiser valued the property at $277,000, after determining that it was 3.0 acres and thus could not be subdivided because it did not meet the town's minimum legal requirement of 3.7 acres for subdivision. Engelsen responded to Kepple's offer with a counteroffer of $230,000, which Kepple accepted. On May 3, 2002, the parties signed a contract. When Engelsen*

refused to go through with the deal, BRJM filed a suit in a Connecticut state court against Output, seeking specific performance and other relief. The defendant asserted the defense of mutual mistake on at least two grounds. [*BRJM, LLC v. Output Systems, Inc.*, 100 Conn.App. 143, 917 A.2d 605 (2007)]

1 In the counteroffer, Engelsen asked Kepple to remove from their contract a clause requiring written confirmation of the availability of a "free split," which meant that the property could be subdivided without the town's prior approval. Kepple agreed. After signing the contract, Kepple learned that the property was not entitled to a free split. Would this circumstance qualify as a mistake on which the defendant could avoid the contract? Why or why not?

2 After signing the contract, Engelsen obtained a second appraisal that established the size of lot five as 3.71 acres, which meant that it could be subdivided, and valued the property at $490,000. Can the defendant avoid the contract on the basis of a mistake in the first appraisal? Explain.

CRITICAL THINKING AND WRITING ASSIGNMENTS

10.10 Critical Legal Thinking. Describe the types of individuals who might be capable of exerting undue influence on others.

10.11 **Video Question.** Go to this text's Web site at **www.cengage.com/blaw/fbl** and select "Chapter 10." Click on "Video Questions" and view the video titled *Mistake.* Then answer the following questions.

1 What kind of mistake is involved in the dispute shown in the video (bilateral or unilateral, mistake of fact or mistake of value)?

2 According to the chapter, in what two situations would the supermarket be able to rescind a contract to sell peppers to Melnick at the incorrectly advertised price?

3 Does it matter if the price that was advertised was a reasonable price for the peppers? Why or why not?

For updated links to resources available on the Web, as well as a variety of other materials, visit this text's Web site at

www.cengage.com/blaw/fbl

For information on the *Restatements of the Law,* including the *Restatement (Second) of Contracts,* go to the American Law Institute's Web site at

www.ali.org

The online version of UCC Section 2–201 on the Statute of Frauds includes links to definitions of certain terms used in the section. To access this site, go to

www.law.cornell.edu/ucc/2/2-201.html

For an interesting discussion of the history and current applicability of the Statute of Frauds, both internationally and in the United States, go to

en.wikipedia.org/wiki/Statute_of_frauds

To read more about contesting contracts on the grounds of fraud and duress, go to

www.lawyers.com/index.php

PRACTICAL INTERNET EXERCISES

Go to this text's Web site at **www.cengage.com/blaw/fbl**, select "Chapter 10," and click on "Practical Internet Exercises." There you will find the following Internet research exercises that you can perform to learn more about the topics covered in this chapter.

PRACTICAL INTERNET EXERCISE 10–1   LEGAL PERSPECTIVE—Promissory Estoppel and the Statute of Frauds

PRACTICAL INTERNET EXERCISE 10–2   MANAGEMENT PERSPECTIVE—Fraudulent Misrepresentation

PRACTICAL INTERNET EXERCISE 10–3   ECONOMIC PERSPECTIVE—Economic Duress

BEFORE THE TEST

Go to this text's Web site at **www.cengage.com/blaw/fbl**, select "Chapter 10," and click on "Interactive Quizzes." You will find a number of interactive questions relating to this chapter.

CHAPTER 11
Third Party Rights and Discharge

AFTER READING THIS CHAPTER, YOU SHOULD BE ABLE TO ANSWER THE FOLLOWING QUESTIONS:

1 What is the difference between an assignment and a delegation?

2 What rights can be assigned despite a contract clause expressly prohibiting assignment?

3 What factors indicate that a third party beneficiary is an intended beneficiary?

4 How are most contracts discharged?

5 What is a contractual condition, and how might a condition affect contractual obligations?

Because a contract is a private agreement between the parties who have entered into it, it is fitting that these parties alone should have rights and liabilities under the contract. This concept is referred to as **privity of contract,** and it establishes the basic principle that third parties have no rights in contracts to which they are not parties.

You may be convinced by now that for every rule of contract law, there is an exception. When justice cannot be served by adherence to a rule of law, exceptions to the rule must be made. In this chapter, we look at some exceptions to the rule of privity of contract. These exceptions include *assignments* and *delegations,* as well as *third party beneficiary contracts.* We also examine how contractual obligations can be *discharged.* Normally, contract discharge is accomplished by both parties performing the acts promised in the contract. In the latter part of this chapter, we look at the degree of performance required to discharge a contractual obligation, as well as at some other ways in which contract discharge can occur.

ASSIGNMENTS

In a bilateral contract, the two parties have corresponding rights and duties. One party has a *right* to require the other to perform some task, and the other has a *duty* to perform it. Sometimes, though, a party will transfer her or his rights under the contract to someone else. The transfer of contract *rights* to

a third person is known as an **assignment.** (The transfer of contract duties is a *delegation,* as discussed later in this chapter.)

Assignments are important because they are utilized in much business financing. Lending institutions, such as banks, frequently assign the rights to receive payments under their loan contracts to other firms, which pay for those rights. If you obtain a loan from your local bank to purchase a car, you may later receive in the mail a notice stating that your bank has transferred (assigned) its rights to receive payments on the loan to another firm and that, when the time comes to repay your loan, you must make the payments to that other firm.

Lenders that make *mortgage loans* (loans to allow prospective home buyers to purchase land or a home) often assign their rights to collect the mortgage payments to a third party, such as GMAC Mortgage Corporation. Following an assignment, the home buyer is notified that future payments must be made to the third party, rather than to the original lender. Billions of dollars change hands daily in the business world in the form of assignments of rights in contracts.

Effect of an Assignment

In an assignment, the party assigning the rights to a third party is known as the **assignor,**[1] and the party receiving the rights is the **assignee.** Other traditional terminology used to describe

---

1. Pronounced uh-*sye*-nore.

EXHIBIT 11–1 Assignment Relationships

In the assignment relationship illustrated here, Alex assigns his *rights* under a contract that he made with Brent to a third party, Carmen. Alex thus becomes the *assignor* and Carmen the *assignee* of the contractual rights. Brent, the *obligor* (the party owing performance under the contract), now owes performance to Carmen instead of Alex. Alex's original contract rights are extinguished after assignment.

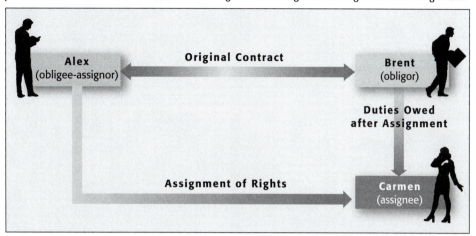

the parties in assignment relationships are the **obligee**[2] (the person to whom a duty, or obligation, is owed) and the **obligor** (the person who is obligated to perform the duty).

When rights under a contract are assigned unconditionally, the rights of the *assignor* (the party making the assignment) are extinguished. The third party (the *assignee*, or the party receiving the assignment) has a right to demand performance from the other original party to the contract (the *obligor*, the person who is obligated to perform). **■EXAMPLE 11.1** Brent (the obligor) owes Alex $1,000, and Alex, the obligee, assigns to Carmen the right to receive the $1,000 (thus, Alex is now the assignor). Here, a valid assignment of a debt exists. Carmen, the assignee, can enforce the contract against Brent, the obligor, if Brent fails to perform (pay the $1,000). **■** Exhibit 11–1 illustrates assignment relationships.

The assignee obtains only those rights that the assignor originally had. Also, the assignee's rights are subject to the defenses

2. Pronounced ä-ble-*gee.*

that the obligor has against the assignor. **■EXAMPLE 11.2** Brent owes Alex $1,000 under a contract in which Brent agreed to buy Alex's MacBook Pro laptop. Alex assigns his right to receive the $1,000 to Carmen. Brent, in deciding to purchase the laptop, relied on Alex's fraudulent misrepresentation that the computer had 2 gigabytes of memory. When Brent discovers that the computer has only 1 gigabyte of memory, he tells Alex that he is going to return the laptop and cancel the contract. Even though Alex has assigned his "right" to receive the $1,000 to Carmen, Brent need not pay Carmen the $1,000— Brent can raise the defense of Alex's fraudulent misrepresentation to avoid payment. **■**

In general, an assignment can take any form, oral or written (except when another law requires it to be in writing, such as assignments of real property interests). Problems can arise with proving oral assignments, however, especially when two parties claim to be the assignee, as the next case illustrates. In addition, like other contracts, assignments must be supported by consideration.

CASE 11.1 | **Martha Graham School and Dance Foundation, Inc. v. Martha Graham Center of Contemporary Dance, Inc.**

United States Court of Appeals, Second Circuit, 380 F.3d 624 (2004).

FACTS Martha Graham's career as a dancer, dance instructor, and choreographer began in the first third of the twentieth century. In the 1920s, she started a dance company and a dance school and choreographed works on commission.

In the 1940s, she funded the Martha Graham Center of Contemporary Dance, Inc. (the Center). She sold her school to the Martha Graham School of Contemporary Dance, Inc. (the

CASE 11.1–Continues next page

CASE 11.1—Continued

School), in 1956. By 1980, the Center encompassed the School. In 1989, two years before her death, Graham executed a will in which she gave Ronald Protas, the Center's general director, "any rights or interests" in "dance works, musical scores [and] scenery sets." After her death, Protas asserted ownership of all of Graham's dances and related property. In 1999, the Center's board removed Protas and, due to financial problems, suspended operations. Meanwhile, Protas founded the Martha Graham School and Dance Foundation, Inc., and began licensing Graham's dances. When the School reopened in 2001, Protas and his foundation filed a suit in a federal district court against the Center and others to enjoin their use of, among other things, seventy of the dances. The Center responded, in part, that Graham had assigned the dances to it. The court ruled that twenty-one of the dances had been assigned to the Center. The plaintiffs appealed to the U.S. Court of Appeals for the Second Circuit.

ISSUE Did Martha Graham orally assign her interest in the dances to the Center before she executed a will leaving the Center's director, Protas, any rights or interests in her dance works?

DECISION Yes. The U.S. Court of Appeals for the Second Circuit affirmed the lower court's judgment on this issue. The oral assignment of certain dances to the Center was valid.

REASON The appellate court found that although the assignment had been oral, it had been reliably proven by written testimony and supported by consideration—that is, Graham had benefited by being relieved of various administrative duties at the time of the assignment. Evidence that Graham had assigned all of her pre-1956 dances to the Center were two letters from Lee Leatherman, the Center's executive administrator at the time. The letters, written in 1968 and 1971, indicated that "recently Miss Graham assigned performing rights to all of her works to the Martha Graham Center of Contemporary Dance, Inc.," and that "Martha has assigned all rights to all of her works to the Martha Graham Center, Inc." In addition, Jeannette Roosevelt, former president of the Center's board of directors, testified that Graham had given the dances to the Center prior to 1965 or 1966, when she joined the board. There was additional evidence that the Center had acted as the owner of the dances by entering into contracts with other parties, and that Graham was aware of this and did not object. Other evidence showed that the Center received royalties for the dances and treated them as its assets.

 WHAT IF THE FACTS WERE DIFFERENT? *Suppose that Graham had not benefited from the Center's assumption of the duties associated with her choreography. Would the alleged assignment have been valid? Why or why not?*

■

Rights That Cannot Be Assigned

As a general rule, all rights can be assigned. Exceptions are made, however, in the following special circumstances.

When a Statute Expressly Prohibits Assignment If a statute expressly prohibits assignment, the particular right in question cannot be assigned. **■EXAMPLE 11.3** Marn is a new employee of CompuFuture, Inc. CompuFuture is an employer under workers' compensation statutes (see Chapter 23) in this state, so Marn is a covered employee. Marn has a relatively high-risk job. In need of a loan, she borrows from Stark, assigning to Stark all workers' compensation benefits due her should she be injured on the job. A state statute prohibits the assignment of *future* workers' compensation benefits, and thus such rights cannot be assigned. ■

When a Contract Is Personal in Nature When a contract is for personal services, the rights under the contract normally cannot be assigned unless all that remains is a monetary payment. **■EXAMPLE 11.4** Brent signs a contract to be a tutor for

Alex's children. Alex then attempts to assign to Carmen his right to Brent's services. Carmen cannot enforce the contract against Brent. Brent may not like Carmen's children or for some other reason may not want to tutor them. Because personal services are unique to the person rendering them, rights to receive personal services cannot be assigned. ■

When an Assignment Will Significantly Change the Risk or Duties of the Obligor A right cannot be assigned if assignment will significantly increase or alter the risks or the duties of the obligor (the party owing performance under the contract).[3] **■EXAMPLE 11.5** Alex has a hotel, and to insure it, he takes out a policy with Northwest Insurance Company. The policy insures against fire, theft, floods, and vandalism. Alex attempts to assign the insurance policy to Carmen, who also owns a hotel. The assignment is ineffective because it may substantially alter the insurance company's duty of performance and the risk that the company undertakes. An insurance company evaluates the particular risk of a certain party

---

3. See Section 2–210(2) of the Uniform Commercial Code (UCC).

and tailors its policy to fit that risk. If the policy is assigned to a third party, the insurance risk is materially altered. ▪

When the Contract Prohibits Assignment If a contract stipulates that the right cannot be assigned, then *ordinarily* it cannot be assigned. ▪**EXAMPLE 11.6** Brent agrees to build a house for Alex. The contract between Brent and Alex states, "This contract cannot be assigned by Alex without Brent's consent. Any assignment without such consent renders this contract void, and all rights hereunder will thereupon terminate." Alex then assigns his rights to Carmen, without first obtaining Brent's consent. Carmen cannot enforce the contract against Brent. ▪ This rule has several exceptions:

1 A contract cannot prevent an assignment of the right to receive funds. This exception exists to encourage the free flow of funds and credit in modern business settings.

2 The assignment of ownership rights in real estate often cannot be prohibited because such a prohibition is contrary to public policy in most states. Prohibitions of this kind are called restraints against **alienation** (the voluntary transfer of land ownership).

3 The assignment of negotiable instruments (see Chapter 18) cannot be prohibited.

4 In a contract for the sale of goods, the right to receive damages for breach of contract or for payment of an account owed may be assigned even though the sales contract prohibits such an assignment.[4]

Notice of Assignment

Once a valid assignment of rights has been made to a third party, the third party should notify the obligor of the assignment (for example, in Exhibit 11–1 on page 223, Carmen should notify Brent). Giving notice is not legally necessary to establish the validity of the assignment because an assignment is effective immediately, whether or not notice is given. Two major problems arise, however, when notice of the assignment is *not* given to the obligor:

1 If the assignor assigns the same right to two different persons, the question arises as to which one has priority—that is, which one has the right to the performance by the obligor. Although the rule most often observed in the United States is that the first assignment in time is the first in right, some states follow the English rule, which basically gives priority to the first assignee who gives notice. ▪**EXAMPLE 11.7** Brent owes Alex $5,000 on a contractual obligation. On May 1, Alex assigns this

monetary claim to Carmen, but she does not give notice of the assignment to Brent. On June 1, for services Dorman has rendered to Alex, Alex assigns the same monetary claim (to collect $5,000 from Brent) to Dorman. Dorman immediately notifies Brent of the assignment. In the majority of states, Carmen would have priority because the assignment to her was first in time. In some states, however, Dorman would have priority because he gave first notice. ▪

2 Until the obligor has notice of an assignment, the obligor can discharge his or her obligation by performance to the assignor, and this performance constitutes a discharge to the assignee. Once the obligor receives proper notice, only performance to the assignee can discharge the obligor's obligations. ▪**EXAMPLE 11.8** Suppose that Alex, in the above example, assigns to Carmen his right to collect $5,000 from Brent, and Carmen does not give notice to Brent. Brent subsequently pays Alex the $5,000. Although the assignment was valid, Brent's payment to Alex is a discharge of the debt, and Carmen's failure to notify Brent of the assignment causes her to lose the right to collect the $5,000 from Brent. (Note that Carmen still has a claim against Alex for the $5,000.) If Carmen had given Brent notice of the assignment, however, Brent's payment to Alex would not have discharged the debt. ▪

PREVENTING LEGAL DISPUTES Providing notice of assignment, though not legally required, is one of the best ways to avoid potential legal disputes over assignments. Whether you are the assignee or the assignor, you should inform the obligor of the assignment. An assignee who does not give notice may lose the right to performance, but failure to notify the obligor may have repercussions for the assignor as well. If no notice is given and the obligor performs the duty for the assignor, the assignee, to whom the right to receive performance was assigned, can sue the assignor for breach of contract. Litigation may also ensue if the assignor has assigned a right to two different parties, which can happen when assigning rights that overlap somewhat (such as rights to receive profits from a specific enterprise).

▪

DELEGATIONS

Just as an individual party can transfer rights to a third party through an assignment, that party can also transfer duties. Duties are not assigned, however; they are *delegated*.

---
4. UCC 2–210(2).

Normally, a **delegation of duties** does not relieve the party making the delegation (the **delegator**) of the obligation to perform in the event that the party to whom the duty has been delegated (the **delegatee**) fails to perform. No special form is required to create a valid delegation of duties. As long as the delegator expresses an intention to make the delegation, it is effective; the delegator need not even use the word *delegate*. Exhibit 11–2 graphically illustrates delegation relationships.

Duties That Cannot Be Delegated

As a general rule, any duty can be delegated. This rule has some exceptions, however. Delegation is prohibited in the following circumstances:

1 When performance depends on the personal skill or talents of the obligor.

2 When special trust has been placed in the obligor.

3 When performance by a third party will vary materially from that expected by the obligee (the one to whom performance is owed) under the contract.

4 When the contract expressly prohibits delegation.

The following examples will help to clarify the kinds of duties that can and cannot be delegated:

1 Brent contracts with Alex to tutor Alex in various aspects of financial underwriting and investment banking. Brent, an experienced businessperson known for his expertise in finance, delegates his duties to a third party, Carmen. This delegation is ineffective because Brent contracted to render a service that is founded on Brent's *expertise* and Alex placed *special trust* in Brent's teaching ability. The delegation changes Alex's expectancy under the contract.

2 Brent, a famous musician, contracts with Alex to *personally* perform at a concert. Then Brent receives a better offer elsewhere and delegates his duty to perform to another musician, Miles. Regardless of Miles's exceptional musical talents, the delegation is not effective without Alex's consent because the contract was for *personal* performance.

3 Brent, an accountant, contracts to perform annual audits of Alex's business records for the next five years. The contract states that Brent must provide the services himself and cannot delegate these duties to another. Two years later, Brent is busy on other projects and delegates his obligations to perform Alex's audit to Arianna, who is a certified public accountant at the same firm. This delegation is not effective because the contract *expressly prohibited* delegation.

4 Alex is a wealthy philanthropist who just created a charitable foundation. Alex has known Brent for twenty years and knows that Brent shares his beliefs on many humanitarian issues. He contracts with Brent to be in charge of allocating funds among various charitable causes. Six months later, Brent is experiencing health problems and delegates his duties to Drew. Alex does not approve of Drew as a replacement. In this situation, Alex can claim the delegation was not effective because it *materially altered his*

EXHIBIT 11–2 Delegation Relationships

In the delegation relationship illustrated here, Brent delegates his *duties* under a contract that he made with Alex to a third party, Carmen. Brent thus becomes the *delegator* and Carmen the *delegatee* of the contractual duties. Carmen now owes performance of the contractual duties to Alex. Note that a delegation of duties normally does not relieve the delegator (Brent) of liability if the delegatee (Carmen) fails to perform the contractual duties.

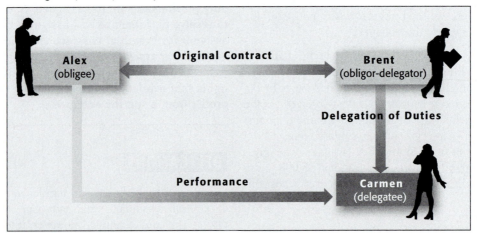

expectations under the contract. Alex had reasonable expectations about the types of charities to which Brent would give the foundation's funds, and substituting Drew's performance materially changes those expectations.

5 Brent contracts with Alex to pick up and deliver heavy construction machinery to Alex's property. Brent delegates this duty to Carmen, who is in the business of delivering heavy machinery. This delegation is effective. The performance required is of a routine and nonpersonal nature, and the delegation does not change Alex's expectations under the contract.

Effect of a Delegation

If a delegation of duties is enforceable, the *obligee* (the one to whom performance is owed) must accept performance from the delegatee (the one to whom the duties are delegated). **■EXAMPLE 11.9** In the fifth example in the above list, Brent delegates his duty (to pick up and deliver heavy construction machinery to Alex's property) to Carmen. In that situation, Alex (the obligee) must accept performance from Carmen (the delegatee) because the delegation was effective. The obligee can legally refuse performance from the delegatee only if the duty is one that cannot be delegated. ■

A valid delegation of duties does not relieve the delegator of obligations under the contract. In the above example, if Carmen (the delegatee) fails to perform, Brent (the delegator) is still liable to Alex (the obligee). The obligee can also hold the delegatee liable if the delegatee made a promise of performance that will directly benefit the obligee. In this situation, there is an "assumption of duty" on the part of the delegatee, and breach of this duty makes the delegatee liable to the obligee. For example, if Carmen (the delegatee) promises Brent (the delegator), in a contract, to pick up and deliver the construction equipment to Alex's property but fails to do so, Alex (the obligee) can sue Brent, Carmen, or both. Although there are many exceptions, the general rule today is that the obligee can sue both the delegatee and the delegator.

Exhibit 11–3 summarizes the basic principles of the laws governing assignments and delegations.

"Assignment of All Rights"

Sometimes, a contract provides for an "assignment of all rights." The traditional view was that under this type of assignment, the assignee did not assume any duties. This view was based on the theory that the assignee's agreement to accept the benefits of the contract was not sufficient to imply a promise to assume the duties of the contract.

EXHIBIT 11–3 Assignments and Delegations		
Which rights can be assigned, and which duties can be delegated?	**All rights can be assigned *unless:*** 1. A statute expressly prohibits assignment. 2. The assignment will materially alter the obligor's risk or duties. 3. The contract is for personal services. 4. The contract prohibits assignment.	**All duties can be delegated *unless:*** 1. Performance depends on the obligor's personal skills or talents. 2. Special trust has been placed in the obligor. 3. Performance by a third party will materially vary from that expected by the obligee. 4. The contract prohibits delegation.
What if the contract prohibits assignment or delegation?	**No rights can be assigned *except:*** 1. Rights to receive money. 2. Ownership rights in real estate. 3. Rights to negotiable instruments. 4. Rights to payments under a sales contract or damages for breach of a sales contract.	**No duties can be delegated.**
What is the effect on the original party's rights?	On a valid assignment, effective immediately, the original party (assignor) no longer has any rights under the contract.	On a valid delegation, if the delegatee fails to perform, the original party (delegator) is liable to the obligee (who may also hold the delegatee liable).

Modern authorities, however, take the view that the probable intent in using such general words is to create both an assignment of rights and an assumption of duties.[5] Therefore, when general words are used (for example, "I assign the contract" or "all my rights under the contract"), the contract is construed as implying both an assignment of rights and an assumption of duties.

THIRD PARTY BENEFICIARIES

As mentioned earlier in this chapter, to have contractual rights, a person normally must be a party to the contract. In other words, privity of contract must exist. An exception to the doctrine of privity exists when the original parties to the contract intend, at the time of contracting, that the contract performance directly benefit a third person. In this situation, the third person becomes a **third party beneficiary** of the contract. As an **intended beneficiary** of the contract, the third party has legal rights and can sue the promisor directly for breach of the contract.

Who, though, is the promisor? In bilateral contracts, both parties to the contract are promisors because they both make promises that can be enforced. In third party beneficiary contracts, courts determine the identity of the promisor by asking which party made the promise that benefits the third party—that person is the promisor. Allowing the third party to sue the promisor directly in effect circumvents the "middle person" (the promisee) and thus reduces the burden on the courts. Otherwise, the third party would sue the promisee, who would then sue the promisor.

A classic case in the area of third party beneficiary contracts is *Lawrence v. Fox*[6]—a case decided in 1859. In that case, the court set aside the traditional requirement of privity and allowed a third party to bring a suit directly against the promisor.

Types of Intended Beneficiaries

The law distinguishes between *intended* beneficiaries and *incidental* beneficiaries. Only intended beneficiaries acquire legal rights in a contract. One type of intended beneficiary is a *creditor beneficiary*. Like the plaintiff in *Lawerence v. Fox*, a creditor beneficiary benefits from a contract in which one party (the promisor) promises another party (the promisee) to pay a debt that the promisee owes to a third party (the creditor beneficiary). As an intended beneficiary, the creditor beneficiary can sue the promisor directly to enforce the contract.

Another type of intended beneficiary is a *donee beneficiary*. When a contract is made for the express purpose of giving a *gift* to a third party, the third party (the donee beneficiary) can sue the promisor directly to enforce the promise.[7] The most common donee beneficiary contract is a life insurance contract. ■**EXAMPLE 11.10** Akins (the promisee) pays premiums to Standard Life, a life insurance company, and Standard Life (the promisor) promises to pay a certain amount on Akins's death to anyone Akins designates as a beneficiary. The designated beneficiary is a donee beneficiary under the life insurance policy and can enforce the promise made by the insurance company to pay her or him on Akins's death. ■

As the law concerning third party beneficiaries evolved, numerous cases arose in which the third party beneficiary did not fit readily into either the creditor beneficiary or the donee beneficiary category. Thus, the modern view, and the one adopted by the *Restatement (Second) of Contracts*, does not draw such clear lines and distinguishes only between intended beneficiaries (who can sue to enforce contracts made for their benefit) and incidental beneficiaries (who cannot sue, as will be discussed shortly).

When the Rights of an Intended Beneficiary Vest

An intended third party beneficiary cannot enforce a contract against the original parties until the rights of the third party have *vested*, meaning that the rights have taken effect and cannot be taken away. Until these rights have vested, the original parties to the contract—the promisor and the promisee—can modify or rescind the contract without the consent of the third party. When do the rights of third parties vest? Generally, the rights vest when one of the following occurs:

1 When the third party demonstrates manifest assent to the contract, such as sending a letter or note acknowledging awareness of and consent to a contract formed for her or his benefit.

2 When the third party materially alters his or her position in detrimental reliance on the contract, such as when a donee beneficiary contracts to have a home built in reliance on the receipt of funds promised to him or her in a donee beneficiary contract.

3 When the conditions for vesting are satisfied. For example, the rights of a beneficiary under a life insurance policy vest when the insured person dies.

If the contract expressly reserves to the contracting parties the right to cancel, rescind, or modify the contract, the rights

---

5. See UCC 2–210(1), (4); and *Restatement (Second) of Contracts*, Section 328.
6. 20 N.Y. 268 (1859).

7. This principle was first enunciated in *Seaver v. Ransom*, 224 N.Y. 233, 120 N.E. 639 (1918).

of the third party beneficiary are subject to any changes that result. In such a situation, the vesting of the third party's rights does not terminate the power of the original contracting parties to alter their legal relationships.[8]

Incidental Beneficiaries

The benefit that an **incidental beneficiary** receives from a contract between two parties is unintentional. Therefore, an incidental beneficiary cannot enforce a contract to which he or she is not a party.

■**EXAMPLE 11.11** In one case, spectators at a Mike Tyson boxing match in which Tyson was disqualified for biting his opponent's ear sued Tyson and the fight's promoters for a refund of their money on the basis of breach of contract. The spectators claimed that they had standing to sue the defen-

dants as third party beneficiaries of the contract between Tyson and the fight's promoters. The court, however, held that the spectators did not have standing to sue because they were not in contractual privity with any of the defendants. Furthermore, any benefits they received from the contract were incidental to the contract. The court noted that the spectators got what they paid for: "the right to view whatever event transpired."[9] ■

In the following case, a national beauty pageant organization and one of its state affiliates agreed that the national organization would accept the winner of the state contest as a competitor in the national pageant. When the state winner was asked to resign her title, she filed a suit to enforce the agreement to have herself declared a contestant in the national pageant. The national organization argued that she was an incidental, not an intended, beneficiary of the agreement.

---

8. Defenses raised against third party beneficiaries are given in the *Restatement (Second) of Contracts*, Section 309.

9. *Castillo v. Tyson*, 268 A.D.2d 336, 701 N.Y.S.2d 423 (Sup.Ct.App.Div. 2000).

CASE 11.2 **Revels v. Miss America Organization**

Court of Appeals of North Carolina, 182 N.C.App. 334, 641 S.E.2d 721 (2007).
www.aoc.state.nc.us/www/public/html/opinions.htm[a]

FACTS The Miss North Carolina Pageant Organization, Inc. (MNCPO), is a franchisee of the Miss America Organization (MAO). Under the "Miss America Organization Official Franchise Agreement," the MNCPO conducts a public contest (the State Finals) to select Miss North Carolina and to prepare Miss North Carolina for participation in the Miss America pageant (the National Finals).[b] In return, the MAO "accept[s] the winner of the State Finals . . . as a contestant in the National Finals." On June 22, 2002, the MNCPO designated Rebekah Revels "Miss North Carolina 2002." On July 19, the MAO received an anonymous e-mail (which was later determined to have been sent by Revels's ex-boyfriend), implying that she had formerly cohabited with a "male non-relative" and that nude photos of her existed. Revels confirmed the existence of the photos. On July 22, the MAO and the MNCPO asked Revels to resign as Miss North Carolina and told her that if she refused, she would be excluded from competing in the National Finals. On July 23, she resigned. She

then filed a suit in a North Carolina state court against the MAO, the MNCPO, and others, asserting, among other things, breach of contract. The court issued a summary judgment in the MAO's favor. Revels appealed this judgment to a state intermediate appellate court.

ISSUE Was Revels an intended beneficiary of the contract between the MAO and the MNCPO?

DECISION No. The state appellate court affirmed the lower court's judgment in favor of the MAO. Revels was an incidental rather than an intended beneficiary.

REASON The reviewing court held that "in order to establish a claim as a third-party beneficiary, plaintiff must show (1) that a contract exists between two persons or entities; (2) that the contract is valid and enforceable; and (3) that the contract was executed for the direct, and not intentional, benefit of the third party." The court pointed out that under that test, Revels was an incidental beneficiary of the agreement between the MAO and the MNCPO. Although the agreement provided that the MAO would accept the winner of the State Finals as a contestant in the National Finals, this did not establish that the two organizations intended to make the winner a direct beneficiary of the agreement. Thus, Revels was an incidental

---

a. In the "Court of Appeals Opinions" section, click on "2007." In the result, scroll to the "20 March 2007" section and click on the name of the case to access the opinion. The North Carolina Administrative Office of the Courts maintains this Web site.

b. A *franchise* is an arrangement by which the owner of a trademark, or other intellectual property, licenses the use of the mark to another party under specific conditions.

CASE 11.2–Continues next page

CASE 11.2–Continued
beneficiary and could not maintain an action against the MAO based on the agreement.

FOR CRITICAL ANALYSIS–Technological Consideration *How might Revels's third party*

status with respect to the agreement between the MAO and the MNCPO have been affected if the contracting parties had conducted their business online? Explain.

■

Intended versus Incidental Beneficiaries

In determining whether a third party beneficiary is an intended or an incidental beneficiary, the courts generally use the *reasonable person* test. Under this test, a beneficiary will be considered an intended beneficiary if a reasonable person in the position of the beneficiary would believe that the promisor *intended* to confer on the beneficiary the right to bring suit to enforce the contract.

In determining whether a party is an intended or an incidental beneficiary, the courts also look at a number of other factors. As you can see in Exhibit 11–4, which graphically illustrates the distinction between intended and incidental beneficiaries, the presence of one or more of the following factors strongly indicates that the third party is an intended (rather than an incidental) beneficiary to the contract:

1 Performance is rendered directly to the third party.
2 The third party has the right to control the details of performance.

3 The third party is expressly designated as a beneficiary in the contract.

CONTRACT DISCHARGE

The most common way to **discharge**, or terminate, one's contractual duties is by the **performance** of those duties. The duty to perform under a contract may be *conditioned* on the occurrence or nonoccurrence of a certain event, or the duty may be *absolute*. As shown in Exhibit 11–5, in addition to performance, a contract can be discharged in numerous other ways, including discharge by agreement of the parties and discharge by operation of law.

Conditions of Performance

In most contracts, promises of performance are not expressly conditioned or qualified. Instead, they are *absolute promises*. They must be performed, or the party promising the act will

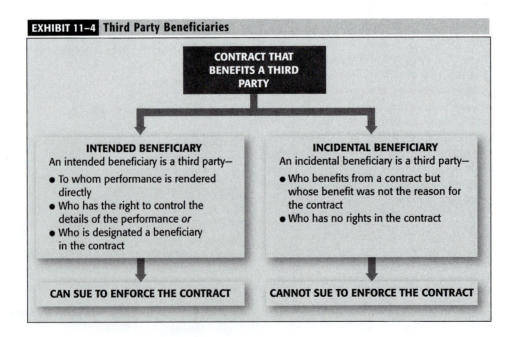

EXHIBIT 11–4 Third Party Beneficiaries

EXHIBIT 11–5 Contract Discharge

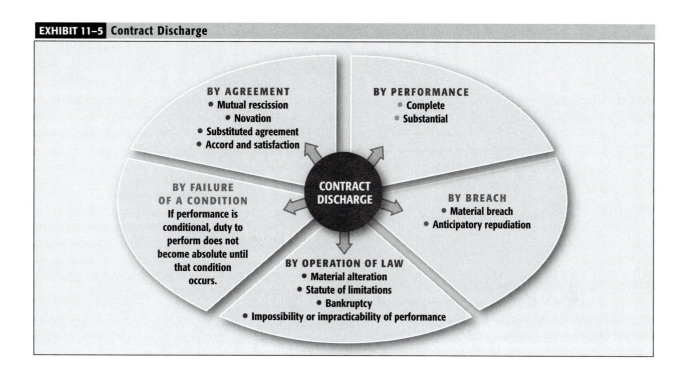

be in breach of contract. **EXAMPLE 11.12** JoAnne contracts to sell Alfonso a painting for $10,000. The parties' promises are unconditional: JoAnne's transfer of the painting to Alfonso and Alfonso's payment of $10,000 to JoAnne. The payment does not have to be made if the painting is not transferred. ■

In some situations, however, contractual promises are conditioned. A **condition** is a possible future event, the occurrence or nonoccurrence of which will trigger the performance of a legal obligation or terminate an existing obligation under a contract. If the condition is not satisfied, the obligations of the parties are discharged. **EXAMPLE 11.13** Suppose that Alfonso, in the above example, offers to purchase JoAnne's painting only if an independent appraisal indicates that it is worth at least $10,000. JoAnne accepts Alfonso's offer. Their obligations (promises) are conditioned on the outcome of the appraisal. Should this condition not be satisfied (for example, if the appraiser deems the value of the painting to be only $5,000), their obligations to each other are discharged and cannot be enforced. ■

We look here at three types of conditions that can be present in any given contract: *conditions precedent, conditions subsequent,* and *concurrent conditions.*

Conditions Precedent   A condition that must be fulfilled before a party's promise becomes absolute is called a **condition precedent.** The condition precedes the absolute duty to perform, as in the JoAnne-Alfonso example just given. Real estate contracts frequently are conditioned on the

buyer's ability to obtain financing. **EXAMPLE 11.14** Fisher promises to buy Calvin's house if Salvation Bank approves Fisher's mortgage application. The Fisher-Calvin contract is therefore subject to a condition precedent—the bank's approval of Fisher's mortgage application. If the bank does not approve the application, the contract will fail because the condition precedent was not met. ■ Insurance contracts frequently specify that certain conditions, such as passing a physical examination, must be met before the insurance company will be obligated to perform under the contract.

Conditions Subsequent   When a condition operates to terminate a party's absolute promise to perform, it is called a **condition subsequent.** The condition follows, or is subsequent to, the absolute duty to perform. If the condition occurs, the party need not perform any further. **EXAMPLE 11.15** A law firm hires Julia Darby, a recent law school graduate and a newly licensed attorney. Their contract provides that the firm's obligation to continue employing Darby is discharged if she fails to maintain her license to practice law. This is a condition subsequent because a failure to maintain the license will discharge a duty that has already arisen. ■

Generally, conditions precedent are common, and conditions subsequent are rare. The *Restatement (Second) of Contracts* deletes the terms *condition subsequent* and *condition precedent* and refers to both simply as "conditions."[10]

_____
10. *Restatement (Second) of Contracts,* Section 224.

Concurrent Conditions When each party's absolute duty to perform is conditioned on the other party's absolute duty to perform, **concurrent conditions** are present. These conditions exist only when the parties expressly or impliedly are to perform their respective duties *simultaneously*. ■EXAMPLE 11.16 If a buyer promises to pay for goods when they are delivered by the seller, each party's absolute duty to perform is conditioned on the other party's absolute duty to perform. The buyer's duty to pay for the goods does not become absolute until the seller either delivers or attempts to deliver the goods. Likewise, the seller's duty to deliver the goods does not become absolute until the buyer pays or attempts to pay for the goods. Therefore, neither can recover from the other for breach without first tendering performance. ■

Discharge by Performance

The contract comes to an end when both parties fulfill their respective duties by performing the acts they have promised. Performance can also be accomplished by tender. **Tender** is an unconditional offer to perform by a person who is ready, willing, and able to do so. Therefore, a seller who places goods at the disposal of a buyer has tendered delivery and can demand payment according to the terms of the agreement. A buyer who offers to pay for goods has tendered payment and can demand delivery of the goods.

Once performance has been tendered, the party making the tender has done everything possible to carry out the terms of the contract. If the other party then refuses to perform, the party making the tender can consider the duty discharged and sue for breach of contract.

Complete Performance When a party performs exactly as agreed, there is no question as to whether the contract has been performed. When a party's performance is perfect, it is said to be complete.

Normally, conditions expressly stated in the contract must fully occur in all aspects for complete performance (strict performance) of the contract to take place. Any deviation breaches the contract and discharges the other party's obligations to perform. For example, most construction contracts require the builder to meet certain specifications. If the specifications are conditions, complete performance is required to avoid material breach. (*Material breach* will be discussed shortly.) If the conditions are met, the other party to the contract must then fulfill her or his obligation to pay the builder. If the specifications are not conditions and if the builder, without the other party's permission, fails to meet the specifications, performance is not complete. What effect does such a failure have on the other party's obligation to pay? The answer is part of the doctrine of *substantial performance*.

Substantial Performance A party who in good faith performs substantially all of the terms of a contract can enforce the contract against the other party under the doctrine of substantial performance. Note that good faith is required. Intentionally failing to comply with the terms is a breach of the contract.

To qualify as *substantial performance*, the performance must not vary greatly from the performance promised in the contract, and it must create substantially the same benefits as those promised in the contract. If the omission, variance, or defect in performance is unimportant and can easily be compensated for by awarding damages, a court is likely to hold that the contract has been substantially performed. Courts decide whether the performance was substantial on a case-by-case basis, examining all of the facts of the particular situation. If performance is substantial, the other party's duty to perform remains absolute (except that the party can sue for damages due to the minor deviations).

■EXAMPLE 11.17 A couple contracts with a construction company to build a house. The contract specifies that Brand X plasterboard be used for the walls. The builder cannot obtain Brand X plasterboard, and the buyers are on holiday in the mountains of Peru and virtually unreachable. The builder decides to install Brand Y instead, which he knows is identical in quality and durability to Brand X plasterboard. All other aspects of construction conform to the contract. In this situation, a court will likely hold that the builder had substantially performed his end of the bargain, and therefore the couple will be obligated to pay the builder. The court might, however, award the couple damages for the use of a different brand of plasterboard, but the couple would still have to pay the contractor the contract price, less the amount of damages. ■

Performance to the Satisfaction of Another Contracts often state that completed work must personally satisfy one of the parties or a third person. The question is whether this satisfaction becomes a condition precedent, requiring actual personal satisfaction or approval for discharge, or whether the test of satisfaction is performance that would satisfy a *reasonable person* (substantial performance).

When the subject matter of the contract is *personal*, a contract to be performed to the satisfaction of one of the parties is conditioned, and performance must actually satisfy that party. For example, contracts for portraits, works of art, and tailoring are considered personal. Therefore, only the personal satisfaction of the party fulfills the condition—unless a court finds the party is expressing dissatisfaction only to avoid payment or otherwise is not acting in good faith.

Most other contracts need to be performed only to the satisfaction of a reasonable person unless they *expressly state otherwise.* When such contracts require performance to the satisfaction of a third party (for example, "to the satisfaction of Robert Ames, the supervising engineer"), the courts are divided. A majority of courts require the work to be satisfactory to a reasonable person, but some courts hold that the personal satisfaction of the third party designated in the contract (Robert Ames, in this example) must be met. Again, the personal judgment must be made honestly, or the condition will be excused.

Material Breach of Contract A **breach of contract** is the nonperformance of a contractual duty. A breach is *material* when performance is not at least substantial. If there is a material breach, the nonbreaching party is excused from the performance of contractual duties and can sue for damages caused by the breach. If the breach is *minor* (not material), the nonbreaching party's duty to perform may sometimes be suspended until the breach is remedied, but the duty is not entirely excused. Once the minor breach is cured, the nonbreaching party must resume performance of the contractual obligations that had been undertaken.

Any breach entitles the nonbreaching party to sue for damages, but only a material breach discharges the nonbreaching party from the contract. The policy underlying these rules is that contracts should go forward when only minor problems occur, but contracts should be terminated if major problems arise.

Anticipatory Repudiation of a Contract Before either party to a contract has a duty to perform, one of the parties may refuse to perform her or his contractual obligations. This is called **anticipatory repudiation.**[11] When anticipatory repudiation occurs, it is treated as a material breach of contract, and the nonbreaching party is permitted to bring an action for damages immediately, even though the scheduled time for performance under the contract may still be in the future.[12] Until the nonbreaching party treats this early repudiation as a breach, however, the breaching party can retract the anticipatory repudiation by proper notice and restore the parties to their original obligations.[13]

An anticipatory repudiation is treated as a present, material breach for two reasons. First, the nonbreaching party should not be required to remain ready and willing to perform when the other party has already repudiated the con-

tract. Second, the nonbreaching party should have the opportunity to seek a similar contract elsewhere and may have the duty to do so to minimize his or her loss.

Quite often, an anticipatory repudiation occurs when a sharp fluctuation in market prices creates a situation in which performance of the contract would be extremely unfavorable to one of the parties. **■EXAMPLE 11.18** Martin Corporation contracts to manufacture and sell ten thousand personal computers to ComAge, a retailer of computer equipment that has five hundred outlet stores. Delivery is to be made six months from the date of the contract. The contract price is based on Martin's present costs of purchasing inventory parts from others. One month later, three suppliers of computer parts raise their prices to Martin. Because of these higher prices, Martin stands to lose $500,000 if it sells the computers to ComAge at the contract price. Martin writes to ComAge, stating that it cannot deliver the ten thousand computers at the contract price. Martin's letter is an anticipatory repudiation of the contract. ComAge has the option of treating the repudiation as a material breach and proceeding immediately to pursue remedies, even though the contract delivery date is still five months away. ■

Discharge by Agreement

Any contract can be discharged by agreement of the parties. The agreement can be contained in the original contract, or the parties can form a new contract for the express purpose of discharging the original contract.

Discharge by Rescission As mentioned in previous chapters, rescission is the process in which the parties cancel the contract and are returned to the positions they occupied prior to the contract's formation. For *mutual rescission* to take place, the parties must make another agreement that also satisfies the legal requirements for a contract—there must be an *offer*, an *acceptance*, and *consideration.* Ordinarily, if the parties agree to rescind the original contract, their promises not to perform those acts promised in the original contract will be legal consideration for the second contract.

Mutual rescission can occur in this manner when the original contract is executory on both sides (that is, neither party has completed performance). Agreements to rescind most executory contracts (with the exception of real estate contracts) are enforceable even if they are made orally and even if the original agreement was in writing.[14] When one party has fully performed, however, an agreement to rescind

---

11. *Restatement (Second) of Contracts*, Section 253; and UCC 2–610 and 2–611.
12. The doctrine of anticipatory repudiation first arose in the landmark case of *Hochster v. De La Tour,* 2 Ellis and Blackburn Reports 678 (1853), when an English court recognized the delay and expense inherent in a rule requiring a nonbreaching party to wait until the time of performance before suing on an anticipatory repudiation.
13. See UCC 2–611.

---

14. Agreements to rescind contracts involving transfers of realty, however, must be evidenced by a writing. Another exception has to do with the sale of goods under the UCC, when the sales contract requires written rescission.

the original contract usually is not enforceable unless additional consideration or restitution is made.[15]

Discharge by Novation   The process of **novation** substitutes a third party for one of the original parties. Essentially, the parties to the original contract and one or more new parties all get together and agree to the substitution. The requirements of a novation are as follows:

1 The existence of a previous, valid obligation.
2 Agreement by all of the parties to a new contract.
3 The extinguishing of the old obligation (discharge of the prior party).
4 A new, valid contract.

A novation may appear to be similar to an assignment or delegation. Nevertheless, there is an important distinction: a novation involves a new contract, and an assignment or delegation involves the old contract.

■EXAMPLE 11.19 Union Corporation contracts to sell its pharmaceutical division to British Pharmaceuticals, Ltd. Before the transfer is completed, Union, British Pharmaceuticals, and a third company, Otis Chemicals, execute a new agreement to transfer all of British Pharmaceutical's rights and duties in the transaction to Otis Chemicals. As long as the new contract is supported by consideration, the novation will discharge the original contract (between Union and British Pharmaceuticals) and replace it with the new contract (between Union and Otis Chemicals). ■

Discharge by Accord and Satisfaction   As Chapter 8 explained, in an *accord and satisfaction*, the parties agree to accept performance different from the performance originally promised. An *accord* is an executory contract (one that has not yet been performed) to perform some act to satisfy an existing contractual duty that is not yet discharged. A *satisfaction* is the performance of the accord agreement. An *accord* and its *satisfaction* discharge the original contractual obligation.

Once the accord has been made, the original obligation is merely suspended until the accord agreement is fully performed. If it is not performed, the party to whom performance is owed can bring an action on the original obligation or for breach of the accord. **■EXAMPLE 11.20** Shea obtains a judgment against Marla for $8,000. Later, both parties agree that the judgment can be satisfied by Marla's transfer of her automobile to Shea. This agreement to accept the auto in lieu of $8,000 in cash is the accord. If Marla transfers her

automobile to Shea, the accord agreement is fully performed, and the $8,000 debt is discharged. If Marla refuses to transfer her car, the accord is breached. Because the original obligation is merely suspended, Shea can sue to enforce the judgment for $8,000 in cash or bring an action for breach of the accord. ■

Discharge by Operation of Law

Under some circumstances, contractual duties may be discharged by operation of law. These circumstances include material alteration of the contract, the running of the relevant statute of limitations, bankruptcy, and impossibility of performance.

Contract Alteration   To discourage parties from altering written contracts, the law allows an innocent party to be discharged when one party has materially altered a written contract without the knowledge or consent of the other party. For example, if a party alters a material term of the contract—such as the quantity term or the price term—without the knowledge or consent of the other party, the party who was unaware of the alteration can treat the contract as discharged or terminated.

Statutes of Limitations   As mentioned earlier in this text, statutes of limitations limit the period during which a party can sue on a particular cause of action. After the applicable limitations period has passed, a suit can no longer be brought. For example, the limitations period for bringing lawsuits for breach of oral contracts is usually two to three years; for written contracts, four to five years; and for recovery of amounts awarded in judgment, ten to twenty years, depending on state law. Lawsuits for breach of a contract for the sale of goods must be brought within four years after the cause of action has accrued. By original agreement, the parties can agree to reduce this four-year period to not less than a one-year period. They cannot, however, agree to extend it beyond the four-year limitations period.

Bankruptcy   A proceeding in bankruptcy attempts to allocate the debtor's assets to the creditors in a fair and equitable fashion. Once the assets have been allocated, the debtor receives a *discharge in bankruptcy* (see Chapter 21). A discharge in bankruptcy ordinarily bars the creditors from enforcing most of the debtor's contracts.

When Performance Is Impossible   After a contract has been made, performance may become impossible in an objective sense. This is known as **impossibility of performance** and may discharge the contract. Performance may also become so

15. Under UCC 2–209(1), however, no consideration is needed to modify a contract for a sale of goods; see also UCC 1–107. See Chapter 14 for an extended discussion of the UCC.

difficult or costly due to some unforeseen event that a court will consider it commercially unfeasible, or impracticable, as will be discussed later in the chapter.

Objective Impossibility. Objective impossibility ("It can't be done") must be distinguished from subjective impossibility ("I'm sorry, I simply can't do it"). An example of subjective impossibility is the inability to pay funds on time because the bank is closed.[16] In effect, the nonperforming party is saying, "It is impossible for *me* to perform," rather than "It is impossible for *anyone* to perform." Accordingly, such excuses do not discharge a contract, and the nonperforming party is normally held in breach of contract. Three basic types of situations will generally qualify as grounds for the discharge of contractual obligations based on impossibility of performance:[17]

1 *When a party whose personal performance is essential to the completion of the contract dies or becomes incapacitated prior to performance.* ■EXAMPLE 11.21 Fred, a famous dancer, contracts with Ethereal Dancing Guild to play a leading role in its new ballet. Before the ballet can be performed, Fred becomes ill and dies. His personal performance was essential to the completion of the contract. Thus, his death discharges the contract and his estate's liability for his nonperformance. ■

2 *When the specific subject matter of the contract is destroyed.* ■EXAMPLE 11.22 A-1 Farm Equipment agrees to sell Gudgel the green tractor on its lot and promises to have the tractor ready for Gudgel to pick up on Saturday. On Friday night, however, a truck veers off the nearby highway and smashes into the tractor, destroying it beyond repair. Because the contract was for this specific tractor, A-1's performance is rendered impossible owing to the accident. ■

3 *When a change in the law renders performance illegal.* ■EXAMPLE 11.23 A contract to build an apartment building becomes impossible to perform when the zoning laws are changed to prohibit the construction of residential rental property at the planned location. A contract to paint a bridge using lead paint becomes impossible when the government passes new regulations forbidding the use of lead paint on bridges.[18] ■

Temporary Impossibility. An occurrence or event that makes performance temporarily impossible operates to suspend performance until the impossibility ceases. Then, ordinarily, the parties must perform the contract as originally

planned. ■EXAMPLE 11.24 On August 22, 2005, Keefe Hurwitz contracted to sell his home in Madisonville, Louisiana, to Wesley and Gwendolyn Payne for a price of $241,500. On August 26—just four days after the parties signed the contract—Hurricane Katrina made landfall and caused extensive property damage to the house. The cost of repairs was estimated at $60,000 and Hurwitz would have to make the repairs before the *closing date* (see Chapter 29). Hurwitz did not have the funds and refused to pay $60,000 for the repairs only to sell the property to the Paynes for the previously agreed-on price of $241,500. The Paynes filed a lawsuit to enforce the contract. Hurwitz claimed that Hurricane Katrina had made it impossible for him to perform and had discharged his duties under the contract. The court, however, ruled that Hurricane Katrina had caused only a temporary impossibility. Hurwitz was required to pay for the necessary repairs and to perform the contract as written. In other words, he could not obtain a higher purchase price to offset the cost of the repairs.[19] ■

In contrast, if the lapse of time and the change in circumstances surrounding the contract make it substantially more burdensome for the parties to perform the promised acts, the contract is discharged. A leading case on the subject, *Autry v. Republic Productions,*[20] involved an actor who was drafted into the army in 1942. Being drafted rendered the actor's contract temporarily impossible to perform, and it was suspended until the end of the war. When the actor got out of the army, the purchasing power of the dollar had so diminished that performance of the contract would have been substantially burdensome to him. Therefore, the contract was discharged.

Commercial Impracticability Courts may excuse parties from their performance obligations when the performance becomes much more difficult or expensive than originally contemplated at the time the contract was formed. For someone to invoke the doctrine of **commercial impracticability** successfully, however, the anticipated performance must become *extremely* difficult or costly.[21]

The added burden of performing not only must be extreme but also *must not have been known by the parties when the contract was made.* For example, in one case, a court held that a contract could be discharged because a party would have to pay ten times more than the original estimate to excavate a certain amount of gravel.[22] In another case, the court allowed a party to rescind a contract for the sale of land because of a potential problem with contaminated groundwater under the

16. *Ingham Lumber Co. v. Ingersoll & Co.,* 93 Ark. 447, 125 S.W. 139 (1910).
17. *Restatement (Second) of Contracts,* Sections 262–266; and UCC 2–615.
18. *M. J. Paquet, Inc. v. New Jersey Department of Transportation,* 171 N.J. 378, 794 A.2d 141 (2002).

19. *Payne v. Hurwitz,* 978 So.2d 1000 (La.App. 1st Cir. 2008).
20. 30 Cal.2d 144, 180 P.2d 888 (1947).
21. *Restatement (Second) of Contracts,* Section 264.
22. *Mineral Park Land Co. v. Howard,* 172 Cal. 289, 156 P. 458 (1916).

land. The court found that "the potential for substantial and unbargained-for" liability made contract performance economically impracticable. Interestingly, the court in that case also noted that the possibility of "environmental degradation with consequences extending well beyond the parties' land sale" was just as important to its decision as the economic considerations.[23]

23. *Cape-France Enterprises v. Estate of Peed*, 305 Mont. 513, 29 P.3d 1011 (2001).

The contract dispute in the following case arose out of the cancellation of a wedding reception due to a power failure. Is a power failure sufficient to invoke the doctrine of commercial impracticability?

CASE 11.3 **Facto v. Pantagis**

Superior Court of New Jersey, Appellate Division, 390 N.J.Super. 227, 915 A.2d 59 (2007).
lawlibrary.rutgers.edu/search.shtml[a]

FACTS Leo and Elizabeth Facto contracted with Snuffy Pantagis Enterprise, Inc., for the use of Pantagis Renaissance, a banquet hall in Scotch Plains, New Jersey, for a wedding reception in August 2002. The Factos paid the $10,578 price in advance. The contract excused Pantagis from performance "if it is prevented from doing so by an act of God [such as a flood or a power failure], or other unforeseen events or circumstances." Soon after the reception began, there was a power failure. The lights and the air conditioning shut off. The band hired for the reception refused to play without electricity to power their instruments, and the lack of lighting prevented the photographer and videographer from taking pictures. The temperature was in the 90s, the humidity was high, and the guests quickly became uncomfortable. Three hours later, after a fight between a guest and a Pantagis employee, the emergency lights began to fade, and the police evacuated the hall. The Factos filed a suit in a New Jersey state court against Pantagis, alleging breach of contract, among other things. The Factos sought to recover their prepayment, plus amounts paid to the band, the photographer, and the videographer. The court concluded that Pantagis did not breach the contract and dismissed the complaint. The Factos appealed to a state intermediate appellate court.

ISSUE Can a power failure constitute the kind of unexpected occurrence that relieves a party of the duty to perform a contract?

DECISION Yes. The state intermediate appellate court agreed that the power failure relieved Pantagis of its

a. In the "Search for Cases by Party Name" section, select the "Appellate Division," type "Pantagis" in the "First Name:" box, and click on "Submit Form." In the result, click on the "click here to get this case" link to access the opinion. The Rutgers University School of Law in Camden, New Jersey, maintains this Web site.

contractual obligation, but held that Pantagis's inability to perform also relieved the Factos of their obligation. The court reversed the dismissal and remanded the case for an award to the Factos of the amount of their prepayment less the value of the services they received.

REASON The appellate court did not attribute any significance to the contract's reference to a power failure as "an act of God." The court reasoned that "even if a power failure caused by circumstances other than a natural event [was] not considered to be 'an act of God,' it still would constitute an unforeseen event or circumstance that would excuse performance." Of course, a power failure is not absolutely unforeseeable during hot summer months. But "absolute unforeseeability of a condition is not a prerequisite to the defense of impracticability." It is "the destruction or * * * deterioration of a specific thing necessary for the performance of the contract [that] makes performance impracticable." In this case, the power failure was area-wide and beyond the control of Pantagis, which was prevented from performing its contract. Because Pantagis was not in breach, however, did not mean that the Factos could not recover the amount they prepaid for the reception. When "one party to a contract is excused from performance as a result of an unforeseen event that makes performance impracticable, the other party is also generally excused from performance." Therefore, the power failure that relieved Pantagis of its obligation to the Factos also relieved the Factos of their obligation to Pantagis.

FOR CRITICAL ANALYSIS—Social Consideration *If Pantagis offered to reschedule the reception, should it be absolved of the obligation to refund the Factos' prepayment? Explain.*

Frustration of Purpose   Closely allied with the doctrine of commercial impracticability is the doctrine of **frustration of purpose**. In principle, a contract will be discharged if supervening circumstances make it impossible to attain the purpose both parties had in mind when making the contract. As with commercial impracticability, the supervening event must not have been foreseeable at the time of the contracting.

REVIEWING Third Party Rights and Discharge

Val's Foods signs a contract to buy 1,500 pounds of basil from Sun Farms, a small organic herb grower, as long as an independent organization inspects and certifies that the crop contains no pesticide or herbicide residue. Val's has a contract with several restaurant chains to supply pesto and intends to use Sun Farms' basil in the pesto to fulfill these contracts. When Sun Farms is preparing to harvest the basil, an unexpected hailstorm destroys half the crop. Sun Farms attempts to purchase additional basil from other farms, but it is late in the season and the price is twice the normal market price. Sun Farms is too small to absorb this cost and immediately notifies Val's that it will not fulfill the contract. Using the information presented in the chapter, answer the following questions.

1 Suppose that the basil does not pass the chemical-residue inspection. Which concept discussed in the chapter might allow Val's to refuse to perform the contract in this situation?

2 Under which legal theory or theories might Sun Farms claim that its obligation under the contract has been discharged by operation of law? Discuss fully.

3 Suppose that Sun Farms contacts every basil grower in the country and buys the last remaining chemical-free basil anywhere. Nevertheless, Sun Farms is able to ship only 1,475 pounds to Val's. Would this fulfill Sun Farms' obligations to Val's? Why or why not?

4 Now suppose that Sun Farms sells its operations to Happy Valley Farms. As a part of the sale, all three parties agree that Happy Valley will provide the basil as stated under the original contract. What is this type of agreement called?

TERMS AND CONCEPTS

alienation 225
anticipatory repudiation 233
assignee 222
assignment 222
assignor 222
breach of contract 233
commercial impracticability 235
concurrent conditions 232
condition 231

condition precedent 231
condition subsequent 231
delegatee 226
delegation of duties 226
delegator 226
discharge 230
frustration of purpose 237
impossibility of performance 234
incidental beneficiary 229

intended beneficiary 228
novation 234
obligee 223
obligor 223
performance 230
privity of contract 222
tender 232
third party beneficiary 228

CHAPTER SUMMARY Third Party Rights and Discharge

THIRD PARTY RIGHTS

Assignments
(See pages 222–225.)

1. An assignment is the transfer of rights under a contract to a third party. The person assigning the rights is the *assignor,* and the party to whom the rights are assigned is the *assignee.* The assignee has a right to demand performance from the other original party to the contract.

2. Generally, all rights can be assigned, except in the following circumstances:

   a. When assignment is expressly prohibited by statute (for example, workers' compensation benefits).

(Continued)

CHAPTER SUMMARY	**Third Party Rights and Discharge–Continued**
Assignments— Continued	b. When a contract calls for the performance of personal services.
	c. When the assignment will materially increase or alter the risks or duties of the *obligor* (the party that is obligated to perform).
	d. When the contract itself stipulates that the rights cannot be assigned (with some exceptions).
	3. The assignee should notify the obligor of the assignment. Although not legally required, notification avoids two potential problems:
	a. If the assignor assigns the same right to two different persons, generally the first assignment in time is the first in right, but in some states the first assignee to give notice takes priority.
	b. Until the obligor is notified of the assignment, the obligor can tender performance to the assignor. If the assignor accepts the performance, the obligor's duties under the contract are discharged without benefit to the assignee.
Delegations (See pages 225–228.)	1. A delegation is the transfer of duties under a contract to a third party (the *delegatee*), who then assumes the obligation of performing the contractual duties previously held by the one making the delegation (the *delegator*).
	2. As a general rule, any duty can be delegated, except in the following circumstances:
	a. When performance depends on the personal skill or talents of the obligor.
	b. When special trust has been placed in the obligor.
	c. When performance by a third party will vary materially from that expected by the obligee (the one to whom the duty is owed) under the contract.
	d. When the contract expressly prohibits delegation.
	3. A valid delegation of duties does not relieve the delegator of obligations under the contract. If the delegatee fails to perform, the delegator is still liable to the obligee.
	4. An "assignment of all rights" or an "assignment of the contract" is often construed to mean that both the rights and the duties arising under the contract are transferred to a third party.
Third Party Beneficiaries (See pages 228–230.)	A third party beneficiary contract is one made for the purpose of benefiting a third party.
	1. *Intended beneficiary*—One for whose benefit a contract is created. When the promisor (the one making the contractual promise that benefits a third party) fails to perform as promised, the third party can sue the promisor directly. Examples of third party beneficiaries are creditor and donee beneficiaries.
	2. *Incidental beneficiary*—A third party who indirectly (incidentally) benefits from a contract but for whose benefit the contract was not specifically intended. Incidental beneficiaries have no rights to the benefits received and cannot sue to have the contract enforced.
	CONTRACT DISCHARGE
Conditions of Performance (See pages 230–232.)	Contract obligations may be subject to the following types of conditions:
	1. *Condition precedent*—A condition that must be fulfilled before a party's promise becomes absolute.
	2. *Condition subsequent*—A condition that operates to terminate a party's absolute promise to perform.
	3. *Concurrent conditions*—Conditions that must be performed simultaneously. Each party's absolute duty to perform is conditioned on the other party's absolute duty to perform.
Discharge by Performance (See pages 232–233.)	A contract may be discharged by complete (strict) performance or by substantial performance. In some instances, performance must be to the satisfaction of another. Totally inadequate performance constitutes a material breach of the contract. An anticipatory repudiation of a contract allows the other party to sue immediately for breach of contract.

CHAPTER SUMMARY Third Party Rights and Discharge—Continued

Discharge by Agreement (See pages 233–234.)	Parties may agree to discharge their contractual obligations in several ways: 1. *By rescission*—The parties mutually agree to rescind (cancel) the contract. 2. *By novation*—A new party is substituted for one of the primary parties to a contract. 3. *By accord and satisfaction*—The parties agree to render and accept performance different from that on which they originally agreed.
Discharge by Operation of Law (See pages 234–237.)	Parties' obligations under contracts may be discharged by operation of law owing to one of the following: 1. Contract alteration. 2. Statutes of limitations. 3. Bankruptcy. 4. Impossibility of performance. 5. Impracticability of performance. 6. Frustration of purpose.

FOR REVIEW

*Answers for the even-numbered questions in this **For Review** section can be found on this text's accompanying Web site at* **www.cengage.com/blaw/fbl**. *Select "Chapter 11" and click on "For Review."*

1 What is the difference between an assignment and a delegation?

2 What rights can be assigned despite a contract clause expressly prohibiting assignment?

3 What factors indicate that a third party beneficiary is an intended beneficiary?

4 How are most contracts discharged?

5 What is a contractual condition, and how might a condition affect contractual obligations?

QUESTIONS AND CASE PROBLEMS

HYPOTHETICAL SCENARIOS AND CASE PROBLEMS

11.1 Third Party Beneficiaries. Wilken owes Rivera $2,000. Howie promises Wilken that he will pay Rivera the $2,000 in return for Wilken's promise to give Howie's children guitar lessons. Is Rivera an intended beneficiary of the Howie-Wilken contract? Explain.

11.2 Anticipatory Repudiation. ABC Clothiers, Inc., has a contract with Taylor & Sons, a retailer, to deliver one thousand summer suits to Taylor's place of business on or before May 1. On April 1, Taylor senior receives a letter from ABC informing him that ABC will not be able to make the delivery as scheduled. Taylor is very upset, as he had planned a big ad campaign. He wants to file a suit against ABC immediately (April 2). Taylor's son, Tom, tells his father that filing a lawsuit is not proper until ABC actually fails to deliver the suits on May 1. Discuss fully who is correct, Taylor senior or Tom.

11.3 Hypothetical Question with Sample Answer. Aron, a college student, signs a one-year lease agreement that runs from September 1 to August 31. The lease agreement specifies that the lease cannot be assigned without the landlord's consent. In late May, Aron decides not to go to summer school and assigns the balance of the lease (three months) to a close friend, Erica. The landlord objects to the assignment and denies Erica access to the apartment. Aron claims that Erica is financially sound and should be allowed the full rights and privileges of an assignee. Discuss fully whether the landlord or Aron is correct.

 For a sample answer to Question 11.3, go to Appendix E at the end of this text.

11.4 Third Party Beneficiary. The National Collegiate Athletic Association (NCAA) regulates intercollegiate amateur athletics among more than 1,200 colleges and universities with which it contracts. Among other things, the NCAA maintains rules of eligibility for student participation in intercollegiate athletic events. Jeremy Bloom, a high school football and track star, was recruited to play football at the University of Colorado (CU). Before enrolling, he competed in Olympic and professional World Cup skiing events, becoming the World Cup champion in freestyle moguls. During the Olympics, Bloom appeared on MTV and was offered other paid entertainment opportunities, including a chance to host a show on Nickelodeon. Bloom was also paid to endorse certain ski equipment and contracted to model clothing for Tommy Hilfiger. On Bloom's behalf, CU asked the NCAA to waive its rules restricting student-athlete endorsement and media activities. The NCAA refused, and Bloom quit the activities to play football for CU. He filed a suit in a Colorado state court against the NCAA, however, asserting breach of contract on the ground that its rules permitted these activities if they were needed to support a professional athletic career. The NCAA responded that Bloom did not have standing to pursue this claim. What contract has allegedly been breached in this case? Is Bloom a party to this contract? If not, is he a third party beneficiary of it, and if so, is his status intended or incidental? Explain. [*Bloom v. National Collegiate Athletic Association*, 93 P.3d 621 (Colo.App. 2004)]

11.5 Discharge by Operation of Law. Train operators and other railroad personnel use signaling systems to ensure safe train travel. Reading Blue Mountain & Northern Railroad Co. (RBMN) and Norfolk Southern Railway Co. entered into a contract for the maintenance of a signaling system that serviced a stretch of track near Jim Thorpe, Pennsylvania. The system included a series of poles, similar to telephone poles, suspending wires above the tracks. The contract provided that "the intent of the parties is to maintain the existing . . . facilities" and split the cost equally. In December 2002, a severe storm severed the wires and destroyed most of the poles. RBMN and Norfolk discussed replacing the old system, which they agreed was antiquated, inefficient, dangerous to rebuild, and expensive, but they could not agree on an alternative. Norfolk installed an entirely new system and filed a suit in a federal district court against RBMN to recover half of the cost. RBMN filed a motion for summary judgment, asserting, in part, the doctrine of frustration of purpose. What is this doctrine? Does it apply in this case? How should the court rule on RBMN's motion? Explain. [*Norfolk Southern Railway Co. v. Reading Blue Mountain & Northern Railroad Co.*, 346 F.Supp.2d 720 (M.D.Pa. 2004)]

11.6 Case Problem with Sample Answer. National Association for Stock Car Auto Racing, Inc. (NASCAR), sanctions stock car races. NASCAR and Sprint Nextel Corp. agreed that Sprint would become the Official Series Sponsor of the NASCAR NEXTEL Cup Series. The agreement granted sponsorship exclusivity to Sprint and contained a list of "Competitors" that were barred from sponsoring Series events. Excepted were existing sponsorships: in "Driver and Car Owner Agreements" between NASCAR and the cars' owners, NASCAR promised to "preserve" those sponsorships, which could continue and be renewed despite Sprint's exclusivity. RCR Team #31 owns the #31 Car. Cingular Wireless, LLC (a Sprint competitor) had been #31 Car's primary sponsor

since 2001. In 2007, Cingular changed its name to AT&T Mobility and proposed a new paint scheme for the #31 Car that called for the Cingular logo to remain on the hood while the AT&T logo would be added. NASCAR rejected the proposal. AT&T filed a suit against NASCAR, claiming that NASCAR was in breach of its "Driver and Car Owner Agreement." Can AT&T maintain an action against NASCAR based on this agreement? Explain. [*AT&T Mobility, LLC v. National Association for Stock Car Auto Racing, Inc.*, 494 F.3d 1356 (11th Cir. 2007)]

After you have answered Problem 11.6, compare your answer with the sample answer given on the Web site that accompanies this text. Go to www.cengage.com/blaw/fbl, select "Chapter 11," and click on "Case Problem with Sample Answer."

11.7 Material Breach. Kermit Johnson formed FB & I Building Products, Inc., in Watertown, South Dakota, to sell building materials. In December 1998, FB & I contracted with Superior Truss & Components in Minneota, Minnesota, "to exclusively sell Superior's open-faced wall panels, floor panels, roof trusses and other miscellaneous products." In March 2000, FB & I agreed to exclusively sell Component Manufacturing Co.'s building products in Colorado. Two months later, Superior learned of FB & I's deal with Component and terminated its contract with FB & I. That contract provided that on cancellation, "FB & I will be entitled to retain the customers that they continue to sell and service with Superior products." Superior refused to honor this provision. Between the cancellation of FB & I's contract and 2004, Superior made $2,327,528 in sales to FB & I customers without paying a commission. FB & I filed a suit in a South Dakota state court against Superior, alleging in part, breach of contract and seeking the unpaid commissions. Superior insisted that FB & I had materially breached their contract, excusing Superior from performing. In whose favor should the court rule and why? [*FB & I Building Products, Inc. v. Superior Truss & Components, a Division of Banks Lumber, Inc.*, 727 N.W.2d 474 (S.D. 2007)]

11.8 A Question of Ethics. King County, Washington, hired Frank Coluccio Construction Co. (FCCC) to act as general contractor for a public works project involving the construction of a small utility tunnel under the Duwamish Waterway. FCCC hired Donald B. Murphy Contractors, Inc. (DBM), as a subcontractor. DBM was responsible for constructing an access shaft at the eastern end of the tunnel. Problems arose during construction, including a "blow in" of the access shaft when it filled with water, soil, and debris. FCCC and DBM incurred substantial expenses from the repairs and delays. Under the project contract, King County was supposed to buy an insurance policy to "insure against physical loss or damage by perils included under an 'All Risk' Builder's Risk policy." Any claim under this policy was to be filed through the insured. King County, which had general property damage insurance, did not obtain an all-risk builder's risk policy. For the losses attributable to the blow-in, FCCC and DBM submitted builder's risk claims, which the county *denied. FCCC filed a suit in a Washington state court against King County, alleging, among other claims, breach of contract. [Frank Coluccio Construction Co. v. King County, 136 Wash.App. 751, 150 P.3d 1147 (Div. 1 2007)]*

1 King County's property damage policy specifically excluded, at the county's request, coverage of tunnels. The county drafted its contract with FCCC to require the all-risk builder's risk policy and authorize itself to "sponsor" claims. When FCCC and DBM filed their claims, the county secretly colluded with its property damage insurer to deny payment. What do these facts indicate about the county's ethics and legal liability in this situation?

2 Could DBM, as a third party to the contract between King County and FCCC, maintain an action on the contract against King County? Discuss.

3 All-risk insurance is a promise to pay on the "fortuitous" happening of a loss or damage from any cause except those that are specifically excluded. Payment is not usually made on a loss that, at the time the insurance was obtained, the claimant subjectively knew would occur. If a loss results from faulty workmanship on the part of a contractor, should the obligation to pay under an all-risk policy be discharged? Explain.

CRITICAL THINKING AND WRITING ASSIGNMENTS

11.9 **Critical Legal Thinking.** The concept of substantial performance permits a party to be discharged from a contract even though the party has not fully performed her or his obligations according to the contract's terms. Is this fair? What policy interests are at issue here?

11.10 **Video Question.** Go to this text's Web site at **www. cengage.com/blaw/fbl** and select "Chapter 11." Click on "Video Questions" and view the video titled *Third Party Beneficiaries*. Then answer the following questions.

1 Discuss whether a valid contract was formed when Oscar and Vinny bet on the outcome of a football game. Would Vinny be able to enforce the contract in court?

2 Is the Fresh Air Fund an incidental or an intended beneficiary? Why?

3 Can Maria sue to enforce Vinny's promise to donate Oscar's winnings to the Fresh Air Fund?

ACCESSING THE INTERNET

For updated links to resources available on the Web, as well as a variety of other materials, visit this text's Web site at

> **www.cengage.com/blaw/fbl**

You can find a number of forms that can be used in the assignment of different types of contracts at

> **www.ilrg.com/forms/#transfers**

A *New York Law Journal* article discussing leading decisions from the New York Court of Appeals on third party rights in contracts is online at

> **www.courts.state.ny.us/history/elecbook/thereshallbe/pg51.htm**

PRACTICAL INTERNET EXERCISES

Go to this text's Web site at **www.cengage.com/blaw/fbl**, select "Chapter 11," and click on "Practical Internet Exercises." There you will find the following Internet research exercises that you can perform to learn more about the topics covered in this chapter.

PRACTICAL INTERNET EXERCISE 11–1 LEGAL PERSPECTIVE—Anticipatory Repudiation

PRACTICAL INTERNET EXERCISE 11–2 MANAGEMENT PERSPECTIVE—Commercial Impracticability

BEFORE THE TEST

Go to this text's Web site at **www.cengage.com/blaw/fbl**, select "Chapter 11," and click on "Interactive Quizzes." You will find a number of interactive questions relating to this chapter.

CHAPTER 12
Breach and Remedies

AFTER READING THIS CHAPTER, YOU SHOULD BE ABLE TO ANSWER THE FOLLOWING QUESTIONS:

1 What is the difference between compensatory damages and consequential damages? What are nominal damages, and when do courts award nominal damages?

2 What is the standard measure of compensatory damages when a contract is breached? How are damages computed differently in construction contracts?

3 Under what circumstances is the remedy of rescission and restitution available?

4 When do courts grant specific performance as a remedy?

5 What is the rationale underlying the doctrine of election of remedies?

As the Athenian political leader Solon instructed centuries ago, a contract will not be broken so long as "it is to the advantage of both" parties to fulfill their contractual obligations. Normally, a person enters into a contract with another to secure an advantage. When it is no longer advantageous for a party to fulfill her or his contractual obligations, that party may breach the contract. As noted in Chapter 11, a *breach of contract* occurs when a party fails to perform part or all of the required duties under a contract.[1] Once a party fails to perform or performs inadequately, the other party—the nonbreaching party—can choose one or more of several remedies.

The most common remedies available to a nonbreaching party under contract law include damages, rescission and restitution, specific performance, and reformation. As discussed in Chapter 1, courts distinguish between *remedies at law* and *remedies in equity*. Today, the remedy at law is normally monetary damages. We discuss this remedy in the first part of this chapter. Equitable remedies include rescission and restitution, specific performance, and reformation, all of which we will examine later in the chapter. Usually, a court will not award an equitable remedy unless the remedy at law is inadequate. In the final pages of this chapter, we will look at some special legal doctrines and concepts relating to remedies.

DAMAGES

A breach of contract entitles the nonbreaching party to sue for monetary damages. As you read in Chapter 4, damages are designed to compensate a party for harm suffered as a result of another's wrongful act. In the context of contract law, damages are designed to compensate the nonbreaching party for the loss of the bargain. Often, courts say that innocent parties are to be placed in the position they would have occupied had the contract been fully performed.[2]

Types of Damages

There are basically four broad categories of damages:

1 Compensatory (to cover direct losses and costs).

2 Consequential (to cover indirect and foreseeable losses).

3 Punitive (to punish and deter wrongdoing).

---

1. *Restatement (Second) of Contracts*, Section 235(2).

2. *Restatement (Second) of Contracts*, Section 347; and Section 1–106(1) of the Uniform Commercial Code (UCC).

4 Nominal (to recognize wrongdoing when no monetary loss is shown).

Compensatory and punitive damages were discussed in Chapter 4 in the context of tort law. Here, we look at these types of damages, as well as consequential and nominal damages, in the context of contract law.

Compensatory Damages   Damages compensating the non-breaching party for the *loss of the bargain* are known as *compensatory damages*. These damages compensate the injured party only for damages actually sustained and proved to have arisen directly from the loss of the bargain caused by the breach of contract. They simply replace what was lost because of the wrong or damage.

The standard measure of compensatory damages is the difference between the value of the breaching party's promised performance under the contract and the value of her or his actual performance. This amount is reduced by any loss that the injured party has avoided.

■EXAMPLE 12.1 You contract with Marinot Industries to perform certain personal services exclusively for Marinot during August for a payment of $4,000. Marinot cancels the contract and is in breach. You are able to find another job during August but can earn only $3,000. You normally can sue Marinot for breach and recover $1,000 as compensatory damages. You may also recover from Marinot the amount that you spent to find the other job. ■ Expenses that are directly incurred because of a breach of contract—such as those incurred to obtain performance from another source—are called **incidental damages.**

The measurement of compensatory damages varies by type of contract. Certain types of contracts deserve special mention—contracts for the sale of goods, contracts for the sale of land, and construction contracts.

Sale of Goods.   In a contract for the sale of goods, the usual measure of compensatory damages is the difference between the contract price and the market price.[3] ■EXAMPLE 12.2 MediQuick Laboratories contracts with Cal Computer Industries to purchase ten model UTS network servers for $8,000 each. If Cal Computer fails to deliver the ten servers, and the current market price of the servers is $8,950, MediQuick's measure of damages is $9,500 (10 × $950), plus any incidental damages (expenses) caused by the breach. ■ If the buyer breaches and the seller has not yet produced the goods, compensatory damages normally equal the seller's lost profits on the sale, rather than the difference between the contract price and the market price.

Sale of Land.   Ordinarily, because each parcel of land is unique, the remedy for a seller's breach of a contract for a sale of real estate is specific performance—that is, the buyer is awarded the parcel of property for which he or she bargained (*specific performance* will be discussed more fully later in this chapter). When this remedy is unavailable (because the property has been sold, for example) or when the buyer is the party in breach, the measure of damages is typically the difference between the contract price and the market price of the land. The majority of states follow this rule.

Construction Contracts.   The measure of damages in a building or construction contract varies depending on which party breaches and when the breach occurs. The owner can breach at three different stages of the construction:

1 Before performance has begun.

2 During performance.

3 After performance has been completed.

If the owner breaches *before performance has begun*, the contractor can recover only the profits that would have been made on the contract (that is, the total contract price less the cost of materials and labor). If the owner breaches *during performance*, the contractor can recover the profits plus the costs incurred in partially constructing the building. If the owner breaches *after the construction has been completed*, the contractor can recover the entire contract price plus interest.

When the contractor breaches the construction contract—either by failing to begin construction or by stopping work partway through the project—the measure of damages is the cost of completion, which includes reasonable compensation for any delay in performance. If the contractor finishes late, the measure of damages is the loss of use.

Consequential Damages   Foreseeable damages that result from a party's breach of contract are referred to as **consequential damages,** or *special damages*. Consequential damages differ from compensatory damages in that they are caused by special circumstances beyond the contract itself. They flow from the consequences, or results, of a breach. When a seller fails to deliver goods, knowing that the buyer is planning to use or resell those goods immediately, consequential damages are awarded for the loss of profits from the planned resale.

■EXAMPLE 12.3 Gilmore contracts to have a specific item shipped to her—one that she desperately needs to repair her printing press. In her contract with the shipper, Gilmore states that she must receive the item by Monday, or she will not be able to print her paper and will lose $3,000. If the shipper is late, Gilmore normally can recover the

---

3. This is the difference between the contract price and the market price at the time and place at which the goods were to be delivered or tendered. [See UCC 2–708, 2–713, and 2–715(1), discussed in Chapter 15.]

consequential damages caused by the delay—that is, the $3,000 in losses. ■ To recover consequential damages, the breaching party must know (or have reason to know) that special circumstances will cause the nonbreaching party to suffer an additional loss.[4]

PREVENTING LEGAL DISPUTES Sometimes, it is impossible to prevent contract disputes. You should understand that collecting damages through a court judgment requires litigation, which can be expensive and time consuming. Furthermore, court judgments are often difficult to enforce, particularly if the breaching party does not have sufficient assets to pay the damages awarded.[5] For these reasons, parties generally choose to settle their contract disputes before trial rather than litigate in hopes of being awarded—and being able to collect—damages (or other remedies). In sum, there is wisdom in the old saying, "a bird in the hand is worth two in the bush."

■

Punitive Damages Recall from Chapter 4 that punitive damages are designed to punish a wrongdoer and to set an example to deter similar conduct in the future. Punitive damages, or *exemplary damages*, generally are not awarded in an action for breach of contract. Such damages have no legitimate place in contract law because they are, in essence, penalties, and a breach of contract is not unlawful in a criminal sense. A contract is simply a civil relationship between the parties. The law may compensate one party for the loss of the bargain—no more and no less.

In a few situations, a person's actions can cause both a breach of contract and a tort. **■EXAMPLE 12.4** Two parties establish by contract a certain reasonable standard or duty of care. Failure to live up to that standard is a breach of the contract. The same act that breached the contract may also constitute negligence, or it may be an intentional tort if, for example, the breaching party committed fraud. In such a situation, it is possible for the nonbreaching party to recover punitive damages for the tort in addition to compensatory and consequential damages for the breach of contract. ■

4. UCC 2–715(2). See Chapter 16.
5. Courts dispose of cases, after trials, by entering judgments. A judgment may order the losing party to pay monetary damages to the winning party. Collecting a judgment, however, can pose problems. For example, the judgment debtor may be insolvent (unable to pay his or her bills when they come due) or have only a small net worth, or exemption laws may prevent a creditor from seizing the debtor's assets to satisfy a debt (see Chapter 21).

Nominal Damages When no actual damage or financial loss results from a breach of contract and only a technical injury is involved, the court may award **nominal damages** to the innocent party. Nominal damages awards are often small, such as one dollar, but they do establish that the defendant acted wrongfully. Most lawsuits for nominal damages are brought as a matter of principle under the theory that a breach has occurred and some damages must be imposed regardless of actual loss.

■EXAMPLE 12.5 Hernandez contracts to buy potatoes at fifty cents a pound from Lentz. Lentz breaches the contract and does not deliver the potatoes. Meanwhile, the price of potatoes falls. Hernandez is able to buy them in the open market at half the price he agreed to pay Lentz. Hernandez is clearly better off because of Lentz's breach. Thus, in a suit for breach of contract, Hernandez may be awarded only nominal damages for the technical injury he sustained, as no monetary loss was involved. ■

Mitigation of Damages

In most situations, when a breach of contract occurs, the injured party is held to a duty to mitigate, or reduce, the damages that he or she suffers. Under this doctrine of **mitigation of damages,** the required action depends on the nature of the situation.

■EXAMPLE 12.6 Some states require a landlord to use reasonable means to find a new tenant if a tenant abandons the premises and fails to pay rent. If an acceptable tenant is found, the landlord is required to lease the premises to this tenant to mitigate the damages recoverable from the former tenant. The former tenant is still liable for the difference between the amount of the rent under the original lease and the rent received from the new tenant. If the landlord has not taken the reasonable steps necessary to find a new tenant, a court will likely reduce any award by the amount of rent the landlord could have received had such reasonable means been used. ■

In the majority of states, a person whose employment has been wrongfully terminated has a duty to mitigate damages incurred because of the employer's breach of the employment contract. In other words, a wrongfully terminated employee has a duty to take a similar job if one is available. If the employee fails to do this, the damages awarded will be equivalent to the employee's salary less the income he or she would have received in a similar job obtained by reasonable means. The employer has the burden of proving that such jobs existed and that the employee could have been hired. Normally, the employee is under no duty to take a job that is not of the same type and rank.

Whether a tenant farmer acceptably attempted to mitigate his damages on his landlord's breach of their lease was at issue in the following case.

CASE 12.1 Hanson v. Boeder

Supreme Court of North Dakota, 2007 ND 20, 727 N.W.2d 280 (2007).
www.ndcourts.com/court/opinions.htm[a]

FACTS In 1998, Paul Hanson signed a five-year lease to farm 1,350 acres of Donald Boeder's land in Steele County, North Dakota, for $50 per acre beginning with the 1999 crop year. Under the lease, Hanson could use grain bins with a capacity of 93,000 bushels and two machine sheds on the property. The rent was $67,515 per year, with half due on April 1 and the balance due on November 1. In 2003, Boeder and Hanson renewed the lease for a second five-year period. During both terms, Boeder and Hanson disagreed about Hanson's farming practices, but during the second term, their disagreement escalated. In August 2005, Boeder told Hanson that their lease was over. Boeder also told Hanson not to till the land in the fall because it had been leased to a new tenant who wanted to do it himself. Hanson continued to work Boeder's land, however, while running ads in the local newspapers for other farmland to rent. Unable to find other land, Hanson filed a suit in a North Dakota state court against Boeder for breach of contract, asking the court to assess damages. The court awarded Hanson $315,194.26 to cover his lost profits, the lost use of the bins and sheds, and the value of the fall tillage. Boeder appealed to the North Dakota Supreme Court, arguing, among other things, that Hanson failed to mitigate his damages.

ISSUE Did Hanson take appropriate steps to mitigate his damages?

a. Click on the "By ND citation" link. In the result, click on "2007" and then the name of the case to access the opinion. The North Dakota Supreme Court maintains this Web site.

DECISION Yes. The Supreme Court of North Dakota affirmed the lower court's award of damages to Hanson.

REASON The state supreme court explained that normally, "for the breach of an obligation arising from contract, the measure of damages . . . is the amount which will compensate the party aggrieved for all the detriment proximately caused thereby or which in the ordinary course of things would be likely to result therefrom." The court recognized that "a person injured by the wrongful acts of another has a duty to mitigate or minimize the damages and must protect himself if he can do so with reasonable exertion or at trifling expense, and can recover from the delinquent party only such damages as he could not, with reasonable effort, have avoided." In this case, Hanson had not been aware of any farmland available for lease, and he had run ads in the local newspapers seeking other farmland to rent. That Hanson was unsuccessful affected the amount of his recovery, but it did not point to a failure to mitigate his damages.

FOR CRITICAL ANALYSIS–Social Consideration *During the trial, Boeder tried to retract his repudiation of the lease to allow Hanson to continue farming for the rest of the lease term. Should the court have considered this an acceptable way for Hanson to mitigate his damages?*

Liquidated Damages versus Penalties

A **liquidated damages** provision in a contract specifies that a certain dollar amount is to be paid in the event of a future default or breach of contract. (*Liquidated* means determined, settled, or fixed.) For example, a provision requiring a construction contractor to pay $300 for every day he or she is late in completing the project is a liquidated damages provision. Liquidated damages differ from penalties. A **penalty** specifies a certain amount to be paid in the event of a default or breach of contract and is designed to penalize the breaching party. Liquidated damages provisions normally are enforceable. In contrast, if a court finds that a provision calls for a penalty, the agreement as to the amount will not be enforced, and recovery will be limited to actual damages.[6]

To determine whether a particular provision is for liquidated damages or for a penalty, the court must answer two questions:

1 At the time the contract was formed, was it apparent that damages would be difficult to estimate in the event of a breach?

2 Was the amount set as damages a reasonable estimate of those potential damages and not excessive?[7]

---

6. This is also the rule under the UCC. See UCC 2–718(1).

7. *Restatement (Second) of Contracts*, Section 356(1).

If the answers to both questions are yes, the provision normally will be enforced. If either answer is no, the provision normally will not be enforced. Liquidated damages provisions are frequently used in construction contracts because it is difficult to estimate the amount of damages that would be caused by a delay in completing the work.

EQUITABLE REMEDIES

In some situations, damages are an inadequate remedy for a breach of contract. In these cases, the nonbreaching party may ask the court for an equitable remedy. Equitable remedies include rescission and restitution, specific performance, and reformation.

Rescission and Restitution

As discussed in Chapter 11, *rescission* is essentially an action to undo, or cancel, a contract—to return nonbreaching parties to the positions that they occupied prior to the transaction. When fraud, mistake, duress, or failure of consideration is present, rescission is available. The failure of one party to perform under a contract entitles the other party to rescind the contract.[8] The rescinding party must give prompt notice to the breaching party.

Restitution To rescind a contract, both parties generally must make **restitution** to each other by returning goods, property, or funds previously conveyed.[9] If the physical property or goods can be returned, they must be. If the property or goods have been consumed, restitution must be made in an equivalent dollar amount.

Essentially, restitution involves the recapture of a benefit conferred on the defendant that has unjustly enriched her or him. **EXAMPLE 12.7** Andrea pays $32,000 to Myles in return for his promise to design a house for her. The next day, Myles calls Andrea and tells her that he has taken a position with a large architectural firm in another state and cannot design the house. Andrea decides to hire another architect that afternoon. Andrea can require restitution of $32,000 because Myles has received an unjust benefit of $32,000. ■

Restitution Is Not Limited to Rescission Cases Restitution may be required when a contract is rescinded, but the right to restitution is not limited to rescission cases.

Restitution may be sought in actions for breach of contract, tort actions, and other actions at law or in equity. Usually, restitution can be obtained when funds or property has been transferred by mistake or because of fraud. An award in a case may include restitution of funds or property obtained through embezzlement, conversion, theft, copyright infringement, or misconduct by a party in a confidential or other special relationship.

Specific Performance

The equitable remedy of **specific performance** calls for the performance of the act promised in the contract. This remedy is often attractive to a nonbreaching party because it provides the exact bargain promised in the contract. It also avoids some of the problems inherent in a suit for monetary damages. First, the nonbreaching party need not worry about collecting the judgment. Second, the nonbreaching party need not look around for another contract. Third, the actual performance may be more valuable than the monetary damages.

Normally, however, specific performance will not be granted unless the party's legal remedy (monetary damages) is inadequate.[10] For this reason, contracts for the sale of goods rarely qualify for specific performance. Monetary damages ordinarily are adequate in such situations because substantially identical goods can be bought or sold in the market. Only if the goods are unique will a court grant specific performance. For instance, paintings, sculptures, and rare books and coins are often unique, and monetary damages will not enable a buyer to obtain substantially identical substitutes in the market.

Sale of Land A court will grant specific performance to a buyer in an action for a breach of contract involving the sale of land. In this situation, the legal remedy of monetary damages will not compensate the buyer adequately because every parcel of land is unique; obviously, the buyer cannot obtain the same land in the same location elsewhere. Only when specific performance is unavailable (for example, when the seller has sold the property to someone else) will damages be awarded instead.

Is specific performance warranted when one of the parties has substantially—but not *fully*—performed under the contract? That was the question in the following case.

---

8. The rescission discussed here refers to *unilateral* rescission, in which only one party wants to undo the contract. In *mutual* rescission, both parties agree to undo the contract. Mutual rescission discharges the contract; unilateral rescission is generally available as a remedy for breach of contract.

9. *Restatement (Second) of Contracts*, Section 370.

10. *Restatement (Second) of Contracts*, Section 359.

CASE 12.2 Stainbrook v. Low

Court of Appeals of Indiana, 842 N.E.2d 386 (2006).

FACTS In April 2004, Howard Stainbrook agreed to sell to Trent Low forty acres of land in Jennings County, Indiana, for $45,000. Thirty-two of the acres were wooded and eight were tillable. Under the agreement, Low was to pay for a survey of the property and other costs, including a tax payment due in November. Low gave Stainbrook a check for $1,000 to show his intent to fulfill the contract. They agreed to close the deal on May 11, and Low made financial arrangements to meet his obligations. On May 8, a tractor rolled over on Stainbrook, and he died. Stainbrook's son David became the executor of his father's estate. David asked Low to withdraw his offer to buy the forty acres. Low refused and filed a suit in an Indiana state court against David, seeking to enforce the contract. The court ordered specific performance. David appealed to a state intermediate appellate court, arguing, among other things, that his father's contract with Low was "ambiguous and inequitable."

ISSUE Is complete performance of a contract required for the party to be entitled to the remedy of specific performance?

DECISION No. A party who has substantially performed or offered to perform his or her obligations under a contract is entitled to pursue specific performance as a remedy. The state intermediate appellate court held that specific performance was an appropriate remedy in this case and affirmed the lower court's order.

REASON The appellate court explained that a contracting party's substantial performance is sufficient to support a court's order for specific performance. Here, "Low both offered to perform and substantially performed his contractual obligations." The appellate court found that Low had offered to make the tax payment that was due, but Stainbrook's estate refused the offer. Also, Low had obtained financing before the closing date, and there was nothing to indicate that he was not prepared to meet his financial obligations and go forward with the sale. Moreover, although the survey had not yet been arranged, there was no evidence that Low would not have paid for the survey of the land as required by the contract. Because Low had substantially performed under the terms of the contract, the court held that Low was entitled to the remedy of specific performance.

WHY IS THIS CASE IMPORTANT? *The court reaffirmed the principle that "specific performance is a matter of course when it involves contracts to purchase real estate." The court also emphasized that "a party seeking specific performance of a real estate contract must prove that he has substantially performed his contract obligations or offered to do so." The court's reasoning underscores the importance of focusing on the elements of a principle to resolve a case fairly.*

Contracts for Personal Services Personal-service contracts require one party to work personally for another party. Courts normally refuse to grant specific performance of contracts for personal services. This is because to order a party to perform personal services against his or her will amounts to a type of involuntary servitude, which is contrary to the public policy expressed in the Thirteenth Amendment to the U.S. Constitution. Moreover, the courts do not want to monitor contracts for personal services.

■EXAMPLE 12.8 If you contract with a brain surgeon to perform brain surgery on you and the surgeon refuses to perform, the court will not compel (and you certainly would not want) the surgeon to perform under these circumstances. There is no way the court can assure meaningful performance in such a situation.[11] ■

Reformation

Reformation is an equitable remedy used when the parties have *imperfectly* expressed their agreement in writing. Reformation allows a court to rewrite the contract to reflect the parties' true intentions. Courts order reformation most often when fraud or mutual mistake is present. **■EXAMPLE 12.9** If Keshan contracts to buy a forklift from Shelley but the written contract refers to a crane, a mutual mistake has occurred. Accordingly, a court could reform the contract so that the writing conforms to the parties' original intention as to which piece of equipment is being sold. ■

Courts frequently reform contracts in two other situations. The first occurs when two parties who have made a binding oral contract agree to put the oral contract in writing but, in doing so, make an error in stating the terms. Universally, the courts allow into evidence the correct terms of the oral contract, thereby reforming the written contract. The second situation occurs when the parties have executed a written

---

11. Similarly, courts often refuse to order specific performance of construction contracts because courts are not set up to operate as construction supervisors or engineers.

covenant not to compete (see Chapter 9). If the covenant not to compete is for a valid and legitimate purpose (such as the sale of a business) but the area or time restraints are unreasonable, some courts will reform the restraints by making them reasonable and will enforce the entire contract as reformed. Other courts, however, will throw the entire restrictive covenant out as illegal. Exhibit 12–1 graphically presents the remedies, including reformation, that are available to the nonbreaching party.

RECOVERY BASED ON QUASI CONTRACT

Recall from Chapter 7 that a quasi contract is not a true contract but rather a fictional contract that is imposed on the parties to prevent unjust enrichment. Hence, a quasi contract provides a basis for relief when no enforceable contract exists. The legal obligation arises because the law considers that the party accepting the benefits has made an implied promise to pay for them. Generally, when one party confers a benefit on another party, justice requires that the party receiving the benefit pay a reasonable value for it.

When Quasi Contracts Are Used

Quasi contract is a legal theory under which an obligation is imposed in the absence of an agreement. It allows the courts to act as if a contract exists when there is no actual contract or agreement between the parties. The courts can also use this theory when the parties have a contract, but it is unenforceable for some reason.

Quasi-contractual recovery is often granted when one party has partially performed under a contract that is unenforceable. It provides an alternative to suing for damages and allows the party to recover the reasonable value of the partial performance. **■EXAMPLE 12.10** Ericson contracts to build two oil derricks for Petro Industries. The derricks are to be built

over a period of three years, but the parties do not create a written contract. Therefore, the Statute of Frauds will bar the enforcement of the contract.[12] After Ericson completes one derrick, Petro Industries informs him that it will not pay for the derrick. Ericson can sue Petro Industries under the theory of quasi contract. ■

The Requirements of Quasi Contract

To recover on a quasi contract theory, the party seeking recovery must show the following:

1 The party conferred a benefit on the other party.

2 The party conferred the benefit with the reasonable expectation of being paid.

3 The party did not act as a volunteer in conferring the benefit.

4 The party receiving the benefit would be unjustly enriched by retaining the benefit without paying for it.

■EXAMPLE 12.11 In Example 12.10, Ericson can sue in quasi contract because all of the conditions for quasi-contractual recovery have been fulfilled. Ericson built the oil derrick with the expectation of being paid. The derrick conferred an obvious benefit on Petro Industries, and Petro Industries would be unjustly enriched if it was allowed to keep the derrick without paying Ericson for the work. Therefore, Ericson should be able to recover the reasonable value of the oil derrick that was built (under the theory of *quantum meruit*[13]—"as much as he or she deserves"). The reasonable value is ordinarily equal to the fair market value. ■

---

12. Contracts that by their terms cannot be performed within one year from the day after the date of contract formation must be in writing to be enforceable (see Chapter 10).

13. Pronounced *kwahn*-tuhm *mehr*-oo-wuht.

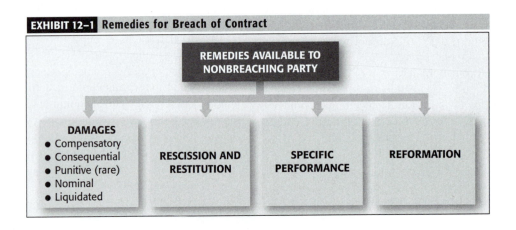

EXHIBIT 12–1 **Remedies for Breach of Contract**

REMEDIES AVAILABLE TO NONBREACHING PARTY

DAMAGES
● Compensatory
● Consequential
● Punitive (rare)
● Nominal
● Liquidated

RESCISSION AND RESTITUTION

SPECIFIC PERFORMANCE

REFORMATION

CONTRACT PROVISIONS LIMITING REMEDIES

A contract may include provisions stating that no damages can be recovered for certain types of breaches or that damages will be limited to a maximum amount. The contract may also provide that the only remedy for breach is replacement, repair, or refund of the purchase price. Provisions stating that no damages can be recovered are called *exculpatory clauses* (see Chapter 9). Provisions that affect the availability of certain remedies are called *limitation-of-liability clauses.*

Whether these contract provisions and clauses will be enforced depends on the type of breach that is excused by the provision. For example, a clause excluding liability for negligence may be enforced in some cases. When an exculpatory

clause for negligence is contained in a contract made between parties who have roughly equal bargaining power, the clause usually will be enforced. The Uniform Commercial Code (UCC) specifically allows limitation-of-liability clauses to be included in contracts for the sale of goods, as will be discussed in detail in Chapter 16.[14] A provision excluding liability for fraudulent or intentional injury, however, will not be enforced. Likewise, a clause excluding liability for illegal acts or violations of the law will not be enforced.

At issue in the following case was the enforceability of a limitation-of-liability clause in a home-inspection contract.

---

14. UCC 2–719.

CASE 12.3   Lucier v. Williams

Superior Court of New Jersey, Appellate Division, 366 N.J.Super. 485, 841 A.2d 907 (2004).
lawlibrary.rutgers.edu/search.shtml[a]

FACTS Eric Lucier and Karen Haley, first-time home buyers, contracted to buy a single-family home for $128,500 from James and Angela Williams in Berlin Township, New Jersey. The buyers asked Cambridge Associates, Limited (CAL), to perform a home inspection. CAL presented the buyers with a contract that limited CAL's liability to "$500, or 50% of fees actually paid to CAL by Client, whichever sum is smaller. Such causes include, but are not limited to, CAL's negligence, errors, omissions, * * * [or] breach of contract." Lucier reluctantly signed the contract. On CAL's behalf, Al Vasys performed the inspection and issued a report. The buyers paid CAL $385. Shortly after Lucier and Haley moved into the house, they noticed leaks, which required roof repairs estimated to cost $8,000 to $10,000. They filed a suit in a New Jersey state court against CAL and others, seeking damages for the loss. CAL filed a motion for summary judgment, claiming that under the limitation-of-liability clause, its liability, if any, was limited to one-half of the contract price, or $192.50. The court granted the motion. The plaintiffs appealed to a state intermediate appellate court.

ISSUE Did the limitation-of-liability clause in the CAL contract limit the plaintiffs' recovery?

DECISION No. The state intermediate appellate court held that the provision was unenforceable. The court reversed the

ruling of the lower court and remanded the case for further proceedings.

REASON The appellate court held that the limitation-of-liability clause was unenforceable for three reasons: (1) the contract was an adhesion contract prepared by the home inspector (an *adhesion contract* is a standard-form contract presented on a take-it-or-leave-it basis—see Chapter 9); (2) the parties had grossly unequal bargaining power; and (3) the provision undermined the fundamental purpose of the contract, having "the practical effect of avoiding almost all responsibility for the professional's negligence." Additionally, the court explained that limiting liability in home-inspection contracts is contrary to the state's public policy of requiring "reliable evaluation of a home's fitness for purchase and holding professionals to certain industry standards." The court added that "the foisting [forcing] of a contract of this type in this setting on an inexperienced consumer clearly demonstrates a lack of fair dealing by the professional. * * * If, upon the occasional dereliction, the home inspector's only consequence is the obligation to refund a few hundred dollars (the smaller of 50 percent of the inspection contract price or $500), there is no meaningful incentive to act diligently in the performance of home inspection contracts."

FOR CRITICAL ANALYSIS—Social Consideration *What is the difference between the limitation-of-liability clause in this case and an exculpatory clause (discussed in Chapter 9)?*

---

a. Click on the link to "Search by party name." Select "Appellate Division," and type "Lucier" in the first box and "Williams" in the second box. Click on "Submit Form" to access the opinion. Rutgers University School of Law in Camden, New Jersey, maintains this Web site.

■

ELECTION OF REMEDIES

In many cases, a nonbreaching party has several remedies available. Because the remedies may be inconsistent with one another, the common law of contracts requires the party to choose which remedy to pursue. This is called *election of remedies*. The purpose of the doctrine of election of remedies is to prevent double recovery. **■EXAMPLE 12.12** Jefferson agrees to sell his land to Adams. Then Jefferson changes his mind and repudiates the contract. Adams can sue for compensatory damages or for specific performance. If Adams receives damages as a result of the breach, she should not also be granted specific performance of the sales contract because that would mean she would unfairly end up with both the land and the damages. The doctrine of election of remedies requires Adams to choose the remedy she wants, and it eliminates any possibility of double recovery. ■

In contrast, remedies under the UCC are cumulative. They include all of the remedies available under the UCC for breach of a sales or lease contract.[15] We will examine the UCC provisions on limited remedies in Chapter 16, in the context of the remedies available on the breach of a contract for the sale or lease of goods.

---

15. See UCC 2–703 and 2–711.

REVIEWING Breach and Remedies

Kyle Bruno enters into a contract with X Entertainment to be a stuntman in a movie that X Entertainment is producing. Bruno is widely known as the best motorcycle stuntman in the business, and the movie, *Xtreme Riders,* has numerous scenes involving high-speed freestyle street-bike stunts. Filming is set to begin August 1 and end by December 1 so that the film can be released the following summer. Both parties to the contract have stipulated that the filming must end on time in order to capture the profits from the summer movie market. The contract states that Bruno will be paid 10 percent of the net proceeds from the movie for his stunts. The contract also includes a liquidated damages provision, which specifies that if Bruno breaches the contract, he will owe X Entertainment $1 million. In addition, the contract includes a limitation-of-liability clause stating that if Bruno is injured during filming, X Entertainment's liability is limited to nominal damages. Using the information presented in the chapter, answer the following questions.

1 One day, while Bruno is preparing for a difficult stunt, he gets into an argument with the director and refuses to perform any stunts. Can X Entertainment seek specific performance of the contract? Why or why not?

2 Suppose that while performing a high-speed wheelie on a motorcycle, Bruno is injured by an intentionally reckless act of an X Entertainment employee. Will a court be likely to enforce the limitation-of-liability clause? Why or why not?

3 What factors would a court consider to determine if the $1 million liquidated damages clause is valid or is a penalty?

4 Suppose that there was no liquidated damages clause (or the court refused to enforce it) and X Entertainment breached the contract. The breach caused the release of the film to be delayed until after summer. Could Bruno seek consequential (special) damages for lost profits from the summer movie market in that situation? Explain.

TERMS AND CONCEPTS

consequential damages 243
incidental damages 243
liquidated damages 245

mitigation of damages 244
nominal damages 244
penalty 245

restitution 246
specific performance 246

CHAPTER SUMMARY Breach and Remedies

COMMON REMEDIES AVAILABLE TO NONBREACHING PARTY	
Damages (See pages 242–246.)	The legal remedy designed to compensate the nonbreaching party for the loss of the bargain. By awarding monetary damages, the court tries to place the parties in the positions that they would

CHAPTER SUMMARY	Breach and Remedies—Continued

Damages—Continued	have occupied had the contract been fully performed. The nonbreaching party frequently has a duty to *mitigate* (lessen or reduce) the damages incurred as a result of the contract's breach. Damages can be classified in the following broad categories:
	
	 1. *Compensatory damages*—Damages that compensate the nonbreaching party for injuries actually sustained and proved to have arisen directly from the loss of the bargain resulting from the breach of contract.
	
	     a. In breached contracts for the sale of goods, the usual measure of compensatory damages is the difference between the contract price and the market price.
	
	     b. In breached contracts for the sale of land, the measure of damages is ordinarily the same as in contracts for the sale of goods.
	
	     c. In breached construction contracts, the measure of damages depends on which party breaches and at what stage of construction the breach occurs.
	
	 2. *Consequential damages*—Damages resulting from special circumstances beyond the contract itself; the damages flow only from the consequences of a breach. For a party to recover consequential damages, the damages must be the foreseeable result of a breach of contract, and the breaching party must have known at the time the contract was formed that special circumstances existed that would cause the nonbreaching party to incur additional loss on breach of the contract. Also called *special damages.*
	
	 3. *Punitive damages*—Damages awarded to punish the breaching party. Usually not awarded in an action for breach of contract unless a tort is involved.
	
	 4. *Nominal damages*—Damages small in amount (such as one dollar) that are awarded when a breach has occurred but no actual injury has been suffered. Awarded only to establish that the defendant acted wrongfully.
	
	 5. *Liquidated damages*—Damages that may be specified in a contract as the amount to be paid to the nonbreaching party in the event the contract is breached in the future. Clauses providing for liquidated damages are enforced if the damages were difficult to estimate at the time the contract was formed and if the amount stipulated is reasonable. If the amount is construed to be a penalty, the clause will not be enforced.

Rescission and Restitution (See page 246.)	1. *Rescission*—A remedy whereby a contract is canceled and the parties are restored to the original positions that they occupied prior to the transaction. Available when fraud, a mistake, duress, or failure of consideration is present. The rescinding party must give prompt notice of the rescission to the breaching party. 2. *Restitution*—When a contract is rescinded, both parties must make restitution to each other by returning the goods, property, or funds previously conveyed. Restitution prevents the unjust enrichment of the parties.
Specific Performance (See pages 246–247.)	An equitable remedy calling for the performance of the act promised in the contract. This remedy is available only in special situations—such as those involving contracts for the sale of unique goods or land—and when monetary damages would be an inadequate remedy. Specific performance is not available as a remedy for breached contracts for personal services.
Reformation (See pages 247–248.)	An equitable remedy allowing a contract to be "reformed," or rewritten, to reflect the parties' true intentions. Available when an agreement is imperfectly expressed in writing.
Recovery Based on Quasi Contract (See page 248.)	An equitable theory imposed by the courts to obtain justice and prevent unjust enrichment in a situation in which no enforceable contract exists. The party seeking recovery must show the following:

(Continued)

CHAPTER SUMMARY	Breach and Remedies–Continued
Recovery Based on Quasi Contract– Continued	1. A benefit was conferred on the other party. 2. The party conferring the benefit did so with the expectation of being paid. 3. The benefit was not volunteered. 4. Retaining the benefit without paying for it would result in the unjust enrichment of the party receiving the benefit.
	CONTRACT DOCTRINES RELATING TO REMEDIES
Contract Provisions Limiting Remedies (See page 249.)	A contract may provide that no damages (or only a limited amount of damages) can be recovered in the event the contract is breached. Clauses excluding liability for fraudulent or intentional injury or for illegal acts cannot be enforced. Clauses excluding liability for negligence may be enforced if both parties hold roughly equal bargaining power. Under the Uniform Commercial Code (UCC), remedies may be limited in contracts for the sale of goods.
Election of Remedies (See page 250.)	A common law doctrine under which a nonbreaching party must choose one remedy from those available. This doctrine prevents double recovery. Under the UCC, remedies are cumulative for the breach of a contract for the sale of goods.

FOR REVIEW

Answers for the even-numbered questions in this **For Review** *section can be found on this text's accompanying Web site at* **www.cengage.com/blaw/fbl**. *Select "Chapter 12" and click on "For Review."*

1 What is the difference between compensatory damages and consequential damages? What are nominal damages, and when do courts award nominal damages?

2 What is the standard measure of compensatory damages when a contract is breached? How are damages computed differently in construction contracts?

3 Under what circumstances is the remedy of rescission and restitution available?

4 When do courts grant specific performance as a remedy?

5 What is the rationale underlying the doctrine of election of remedies?

QUESTIONS AND CASE PROBLEMS

HYPOTHETICAL SCENARIOS AND CASE PROBLEMS

12.1 Liquidated Damages. Carnack contracts to sell his house and lot to Willard for $100,000. The terms of the contract call for Willard to pay 10 percent of the purchase price as a deposit toward the purchase price, or as a down payment. The terms further stipulate that should the buyer breach the contract, Carnack will retain the deposit as liquidated damages. Willard pays the deposit, but because her expected financing of the $90,000 balance falls through, she breaches the contract. Two weeks later, Carnack sells the house and lot to Balkova for $105,000. Willard demands her $10,000 back, but Carnack refuses, claiming that Willard's breach and the contract terms entitle him to keep the deposit. Discuss who is correct.

12.2 Hypothetical Question with Sample Answer. In which of the following situations might a court grant specific performance as a remedy for the breach of the contract?

1 Tarrington contracts to sell her house and lot to Rainier. Then, on finding another buyer willing to pay a higher purchase price, she refuses to deed the property to Rainier.

2 Marita contracts to sing and dance in Horace's nightclub for one month, beginning June 1. She then refuses to perform.

3 Juan contracts to purchase a rare coin from Edmund, who is breaking up his coin collection. At the last minute, Edmund decides to keep his coin collection intact and refuses to deliver the coin to Juan.

4 Astro Computer Corp. has three shareholders: Coase, who owns 48 percent of the stock; De Valle, who owns 48 percent; and Cary, who owns 4 percent. Cary contracts to sell his 4 percent to De Valle but later refuses to transfer the shares to him.

For a sample answer to Question 12.2, go to Appendix E at the end of this text.

12.3 Measure of Damages. Johnson contracted to lease a house to Fox for $700 a month, beginning October 1. Fox stipulated in the contract that before he moved in, the interior of the house had to be completely repainted. On September 9, Johnson hired Keever to do the required painting for $1,000. He told Keever that the painting had to be finished by October 1 but did not explain why. On September 28, Keever quit for no reason, having completed approximately 80 percent of the work. Johnson then paid Sam $300 to finish the painting, but Sam did not finish until October 4. When Fox found that the painting had not been completed as stipulated in his contract with Johnson, he leased another home. Johnson found another tenant who would lease the property at $700 a month, beginning October 15. Johnson then sued Keever for breach of contract, claiming damages of $650. This amount included the $300 Johnson paid Sam to finish the painting and $350 for rent for the first half of October, which Johnson had lost as a result of Keever's breach. Johnson had not yet paid Keever anything for Keever's work. Can Johnson collect the $650 from Keever? Explain.

12.4 Waiver of Breach. In May 1998, RDP Royal Palm Hotel, L.P., contracted with Clark Construction Group, Inc., to build the Royal Palms Crowne Plaza Resort in Miami Beach, Florida. The deadline for "substantial completion" was February 28, 2000, but RDP could ask for changes, and the date would be adjusted accordingly. During construction, Clark faced many setbacks, including a buried seawall, contaminated soil, the unforeseen deterioration of the existing hotel, and RDP's issue of hundreds of change orders. Clark requested extensions of the deadline, and RDP agreed, but the parties never specified a date. After the original deadline passed, RDP continued to issue change orders, Clark continued to perform, and RDP accepted the work. In March 2002, when the resort was substantially complete, RDP stopped paying Clark. Clark stopped working. RDP hired another contractor to finish the resort, which opened in May. RDP filed a suit in a federal district court against Clark, alleging, among other things, breach of contract for the two-year delay in the resort's completion. In whose favor should the court rule, and why? Discuss. [*RDP Royal Palm Hotel, L.P. v. Clark Construction Group, Inc.,* __ F.3d __ (11th Cir. 2006)]

12.5 Case Problem with Sample Answer. Tyna Ek met Russell Peterson in Seattle, Washington. Peterson persuaded Ek to buy a boat that he had once owned, the *O'Hana Kai,* which was in Juneau, Alaska. Ek paid the boat's current owner $43,000 for the boat, and in January 2000, she and Peterson entered into a contract, under which Peterson agreed to

make the vessel seaworthy so that within one month it could be transported to Seattle, where he would pay its moorage costs. He would renovate the boat at his own expense in return for a portion of the profit on its resale in 2001. On the sale, Ek would recover her costs, and then Peterson would be reimbursed for his. Ek loaned Peterson her cell phone so that they could communicate while he prepared the vessel for the trip to Seattle. In March, Peterson, who was still in Alaska, borrowed $4,000 from Ek. Two months later, Ek began to receive unanticipated, unauthorized bills for vessel parts and moorage, the use of her phone, and charges on her credit card. She went to Juneau to take possession of the boat. Peterson moved it to Petersburg, Alaska, where he registered it under a false name, and then to Taku Harbor, where the police seized it. Ek filed a suit in an Alaska state court against Peterson, alleging breach of contract and seeking damages. If the court finds in Ek's favor, what should her damages include? Discuss. [*Peterson v. Ek,* 93 P.3d 458 (Alaska 2004)]

After you have answered Problem 12.5, compare your answer with the sample answer given on the Web site that accompanies this text. Go to www.cengage.com/blaw/fbl, select "Chapter 12," and click on "Case Problem with Sample Answer."

12.6 Remedies. On July 7, 2000, Frances Morelli agreed to sell to Judith Bucklin a house at 126 Lakedell Drive in Warwick, Rhode Island, for $77,000. Bucklin made a deposit on the house. The closing at which the parties would exchange the deed for the price was scheduled for September 1. The agreement did not state that "time is of the essence," but it did provide, in "Paragraph 10" that "[i]f Seller is unable to [convey good, clear, insurable, and marketable title], Buyer shall have the option to: (a) accept such title as Seller is able to convey without abatement or reduction of the Purchase Price, or (b) cancel this Agreement and receive a return of all Deposits." An examination of the public records revealed that the house did not have marketable title. Wishing to be flexible, Bucklin offered Morelli time to resolve the problem, and the closing did not occur as scheduled. Morelli decided "the deal is over" and offered to return the deposit. Bucklin refused and, in mid-October, decided to exercise her option under Paragraph 10(a). She notified Morelli, who did not respond. Bucklin filed a suit in a Rhode Island state court against Morelli. In whose favor should the court rule? Should damages be awarded? If not, what is the appropriate remedy? Why? [*Bucklin v. Morelli,* 912 A.2d 931 (R.I. 2007)]

12.7 Contract Limits on Damages. David Hanson was flying on American West Airlines. In his carry-on duffel bag, he carried a robotic head that was worth about $750,000. (This head was used in making movies.) When he transferred to another plane, he forgot about his duffel bag, which he had stored above his seat. When he got to his final destination, he reported the loss and was told that the airline had retrieved the bag and its contents and that the airlines would send it to him. But it never arrived. Hanson sued for damages for breach of contract. The airline requested a summary judgment. The ticket Hanson had purchased stated that there was a $2,800 damage limit for checked baggage, per passenger, and that there was no liability for items passengers carry on board a plane. Is this sort of damage restriction by American West Airlines reasonable? Why or why not? [*Hanson v. American West Airlines*, 544 F.Supp.2d 1038 (C.D. Cal. 2008)]

12.8 **A Question of Ethics.** *In 2004, Tamara Cohen, a real estate broker, began showing property in Manhattan to Steven Galistinos, who represented comedian Jerry Seinfeld and his wife, Jessica. According to Cohen, she told Galistinos that her commission would be 5 or 6 percent, and he agreed. According to Galistinos, there was no such agreement. Cohen spoke with Maximillan Sanchez, another broker, about a townhouse owned by Ray and Harriet Mayeri. According to Cohen, Sanchez said that the commission would be 6 percent, which they agreed to split equally. Sanchez later acknowledged that they agreed to split the fee, but claimed that they did not discuss a specific amount. On a Friday in February 2005, Cohen showed the townhouse to Jessica. According to Cohen, she told Jessica that the commission would be 6 percent, with the Seinfelds paying half, and Jessica agreed. According to Jessica, there was no such conversation. Later that day, Galistinos asked Cohen to arrange for the Seinfelds*

to see the premises again. Cohen told Galistinos that her religious beliefs prevented her from showing property on Friday evenings or Saturdays before sundown. She suggested the following Monday or Tuesday, but Galistinos said that Jerry would not be available and asked her to contact Carolyn Liebling, Jerry's business manager. Cohen left Liebling a message. Over the weekend, the Seinfelds toured the building on their own and agreed to buy the property for $3.95 million. Despite repeated attempts, they were unable to contact Cohen. [*Cohen v. Seinfeld*, 15 Misc.3d 1118(A), 839 N.Y.S.2d 432 (Sup. 2007)]

1 The contract between the Seinfelds and the Mayeris stated that the sellers would pay Sanchez's fee and the "buyers will pay buyer's real estate broker's fees." The Mayeris paid Sanchez $118,500, which is 3 percent of $3.95 million. The Seinfelds refused to pay Cohen. She filed a suit in a New York state court against them, asserting, among other things, breach of contract. Should the court order the Seinfelds to pay Cohen? If so, is she entitled to a full commission even though she was not available to show the townhouse when the Seinfelds wanted to see it? Explain.

2 What obligation do parties involved in business deals owe to each other with respect to their religious beliefs? How might the situation in this case have been avoided?

CRITICAL THINKING AND WRITING ASSIGNMENTS

12.9 **Critical Legal Thinking.** Review the discussion of the doctrine of election of remedies in this chapter. What are some of the advantages and disadvantages of this doctrine?

12.10 **Video Question.** Go to this text's Web site at **www.cengage.com/blaw/fbl** and select "Chapter 12." Click on "Video Questions" and view the video titled *Midnight Run*. Then answer the following questions.

1 In the video, Eddie (Joe Pantoliano) and Jack (Robert De Niro) negotiate a contract for Jack to find "the Duke," a mob accountant who embezzled funds, and bring him back

for trial. Assume that the contract is valid. If Jack breaches the contract by failing to bring in the Duke, what kinds of remedies, if any, can Eddie seek? Explain your answer.

2 Would the equitable remedy of specific performance be available to either Jack or Eddie in the event of a breach? Why or why not?

3 Now assume that the contract between Eddie and Jack is unenforceable. Nevertheless, Jack performs his side of the bargain by bringing in the Duke. Does Jack have any legal recourse in this situation? Explain.

ACCESSING THE INTERNET

For updated links to resources available on the Web, as well as a variety of other materials, visit this text's Web site at

www.cengage.com/blaw/fbl

The following site offers a brief summary of and several related articles on breach of contract:

www.legalmatch.com/law-library/article/breach-of-contract.html

PRACTICAL INTERNET EXERCISES

Go to this text's Web site at **www.cengage.com/blaw/fbl**, select "Chapter 12," and click on "Practical Internet Exercises." There you will find the following Internet research exercises that you can perform to learn more about the topics covered in this chapter.

PRACTICAL INTERNET EXERCISE 12–1   LEGAL PERSPECTIVE—Contract Damages and Contract Theory

PRACTICAL INTERNET EXERCISE 12–2   MANAGEMENT PERSPECTIVE—The Duty to Mitigate

BEFORE THE TEST

Go to this text's Web site at **www.cengage.com/blaw/fbl**, select "Chapter 12," and click on "Interactive Quizzes." You will find a number of interactive questions relating to this chapter.

CHAPTER 13
E-Contracts and E-Signatures

LEARNING OBJECTIVES

AFTER READING THIS CHAPTER, YOU SHOULD BE ABLE TO ANSWER THE FOLLOWING QUESTIONS:

1 What are some important clauses to include when making offers to form electronic contracts, or e-contracts?

2 How do shrink-wrap and click-on agreements differ from other contracts? How have traditional laws been applied to these agreements?

3 What is an electronic signature? Are electronic signatures valid?

4 What is a partnering agreement? What purpose does it serve?

5 What is the Uniform Electronic Transactions Act (UETA)? What are some of its major provisions?

E lectronic technology offers businesses several advantages, including speed, efficiency, and lower costs. In the 1990s, many observers argued that the development of cyberspace was revolutionary. Therefore, new legal theories, and new laws, would be needed to govern **e-contracts,** or contracts entered into electronically. To date, however, most courts have simply adapted traditional contract law principles and, when applicable, provisions of the Uniform Commercial Code to cases involving e-contract disputes.

In the first part of this chapter, we look at how traditional laws are being applied to contracts formed online. We then examine some new laws that have been created to apply in situations in which traditional laws governing contracts have sometimes been thought inadequate. For example, traditional laws governing signature and writing requirements are not easily adapted to contracts formed in the online environment. Thus, new laws have been created to address these issues.

FORMING CONTRACTS ONLINE

Numerous contracts are formed online. Although the medium through which these contracts are generated has changed, the age-old problems attending contract formation have not. Disputes concerning contracts formed online con-

tinue to center on contract terms and whether the parties voluntarily assented to those terms.

Note that online contracts may be formed not only for the sale of goods and services but also for *licensing*. The "sale" of software generally involves a license, or a right to use the software, rather than the passage of title (ownership rights) from the seller to the buyer. **■EXAMPLE 13.1** Galynn wants to obtain software that will allow her to work on spreadsheets on her BlackBerry. She goes online and purchases GridMagic. During the transaction, she has to click on several on-screen "I agree" boxes to indicate that she understands that she is purchasing only the right to use the software and will not obtain any ownership rights. After she agrees to these terms (the licensing agreement), she can download the software to her computer. ■

As you read through the following pages, keep in mind that although we typically refer to the offeror and the offeree as a *seller* and a *buyer*, in many transactions these parties would be more accurately described as a *licensor* and a *licensee*.

Online Offers

Sellers doing business via the Internet can protect themselves against contract disputes and legal liability by creating offers that clearly spell out the terms that will govern their transac-

256

tions if the offers are accepted. All important terms should be conspicuous and easy to view.

Displaying the Offer   The seller's Web site should include a hypertext link to a page containing the full contract so that potential buyers are made aware of the terms to which they are assenting. The contract generally must be displayed online in a readable format, such as a twelve-point typeface. All provisions should be reasonably clear.   **■EXAMPLE 13.2** Netquip sells a variety of heavy equipment, such as trucks and trailers, online at its Web site. Because Netquip's pricing schedule is very complex, the schedule must be fully provided and explained on the Web site. In addition, the terms of the sale (such as any warranties and the refund policy) must be fully disclosed. **■**

Is an online contract enforceable if the offeror requires an offeree to scroll down or print the contract to read its terms, which are otherwise readily accessible and clear? That was the question in the following case.

CASE 13.1   **Feldman v. Google, Inc.**

United States District Court, Eastern District of Pennsylvania, 513 F.Supp.2d 229 (2007).

FACTS   In Google, Inc.'s AdWords program, when an Internet user searches on **www.google.com** using key words that an advertiser has identified, an ad appears. If the user clicks on it, Google charges the advertiser. Google requires an advertiser to agree to certain terms before placing an ad. These terms—set out in a preamble and seven paragraphs—are displayed online in a window with a scroll bar. A link to a printer-friendly version of the terms is at the top of the window. At the bottom of the page, viewable without scrolling, are the words, "Yes, I agree to the above terms and conditions," and a box on which an advertiser must click to proceed. Among the terms, a forum-selection clause provides that any dispute over the program is to be "adjudicated in Santa Clara County, California." Lawrence Feldman, a lawyer, participated in the program by selecting key words, including "Vioxx," "Bextra," and "Celebrex," to trigger a showing of his ad to potential clients. In a subsequent suit between Feldman and Google in a federal district court in Pennsylvania, Feldman claimed that at least 20 percent of the clicks for which he was charged $100,000 between January 2003 and January 2006 were fraudulent.[a] Feldman filed a motion for summary judgment. Google asked the court to transfer the case to a court in Santa Clara County, California.

a. Feldman was alleging that *click fraud* had taken place. Click fraud occurs when someone, such as a competitor or a prankster with no interest in an advertiser's goods or services, clicks repeatedly on an ad, driving up the ad's cost to the advertiser without generating a sale.

ISSUE   Was the online contract between Feldman and Google enforceable?

DECISION   Yes. The court denied Feldman's motion for summary judgment and granted Google's motion to transfer the case.

REASON   The court held that "the requirements of an express contract for reasonable notice of terms and mutual assent are satisfied" in this situation. Feldman and Google were bound to the terms. The court pointed out that the contract at issue was a click-wrap agreement (or *click-on agreement,* to be discussed shortly in this chapter) that appeared on an Internet Web page. "Even though they are electronic, click-wrap agreements are considered to be writings because they are printable and storable. * * * Absent a showing of fraud, failure to read an enforceable click-wrap agreement, as with any binding contract, will not excuse compliance with its terms." By clicking "Yes," Feldman agreed to all of the terms. Without clicking the "Yes" button, Feldman could not have engaged in an agreement with the defendant.

   FOR CRITICAL ANALYSIS—Technological Consideration   *Under what different facts might the court have held that the plaintiff did not have reasonable notice of the terms of the agreement and thus did not assent to them?*

■

Provisions to Include   An important rule to keep in mind is that the offeror controls the offer and thus the resulting contract. The seller should therefore anticipate the terms he or she wants to include in a contract and provide for them in the offer. In some instances, a standardized contract form may suffice. At a minimum, an online offer should include the following provisions:

1   A clause that clearly indicates what constitutes the buyer's agreement to the terms of the offer, such as a box containing the words "I accept" that the buyer can click on to indicate acceptance. (Mechanisms for accepting online offers will be discussed in detail later in the chapter.)

2 A provision specifying how payment for the goods (including any applicable taxes) must be made.

3 A statement of the seller's refund and return policies.

4 Disclaimers of liability for certain uses of the goods. For example, an online seller of business forms may add a disclaimer that the seller does not accept responsibility for the buyer's reliance on the forms rather than on an attorney's advice.

5 A provision specifying the remedies available to the buyer if the goods are found to be defective or if the contract is otherwise breached. Any limitation of remedies should be clearly spelled out.

6 A statement indicating how the seller will use the information gathered about the buyer.

7 Provisions relating to dispute settlement, such as an arbitration clause, a choice-of-law clause (see Chapter 32), or a *forum-selection clause* (discussed next).

Dispute-Settlement Provisions Online offers frequently include provisions relating to dispute settlement. For example, the offer might include an arbitration clause specifying that any dispute arising under the contract will be arbitrated in a designated forum.

Many online contracts also contain a **forum-selection clause** (indicating the forum, or location, for the resolution of any dispute arising under the contract). As discussed in Chapter 2, significant jurisdictional issues may occur when parties are at a great distance, as they often are when they form contracts via the Internet. A forum-selection clause will help to avert future jurisdictional problems and also help to ensure that the seller will not be required to appear in court in a distant state.

Online Acceptances

The *Restatement (Second) of Contracts*—a compilation of common law contract principles—states that parties may agree to a contract "by written or spoken words or by other action or by failure to act."[1] The Uniform Commercial Code (UCC), which governs sales contracts, has a similar provision. Section 2–204 of the UCC states that any contract for the sale of goods "may be made in any manner sufficient to show agreement, including conduct by both parties which recognizes the existence of such a contract."

Click-On Agreements The courts have used these provisions to conclude that a binding contract can be created by conduct, including the act of clicking on a box indicating "I accept" or "I agree" to accept an online offer. When an online buyer indicates his or her assent to be bound by the terms of the offer by clicking on some on-screen prompt, a **click-on agreement** (sometimes referred to as a *click-on license* or *click-wrap agreement*) is formed. Exhibit 13–1 shows a portion of a click-on agreement that accompanies a package of software made and marketed by Microsoft.

Generally, the law does not require that all of the parties to a contract must actually have read all of its terms for the contract to be effective. Therefore, clicking on a button or box that states "I agree" to certain terms can be enough. The terms may be contained on a Web site through which the buyer is obtaining goods or services, or they may appear on a computer screen when software is loaded from a CD-ROM or DVD or downloaded from the Internet.

In the following case, the court considered the enforceability of a click-on (click-wrap) software licensing agreement that included a forum-selection clause.

---

1. *Restatement (Second) of Contracts*, Section 19.

CASE 13.2 **Mortgage Plus, Inc. v. DocMagic, Inc.**

United States District Court, District of Kansas, __ F.Supp.2d __ (2004).

FACTS In 1997, Mortgage Plus, Inc., a mortgage lender in Kansas, asked DocMagic, Inc., a California firm, for software to prepare and manage loan documents, and for document-preparation services. DocMagic sent Mortgage Plus a CD-ROM containing the software, which had to be loaded onto a computer. Before the software could be installed, a window displayed a "Software License and User Agreement" on the screen. The agreement asked, "Do you accept all terms of the preceding License Agreement? If you choose No, Setup will close." A click on a "Yes" button was needed to continue. The agreement also included a clause designating California as the venue for the resolution of any disputes. To prepare loan documents, the software asked for certain information, which it used to create a worksheet. The worksheet was e-mailed to DocMagic, which completed the documents and returned

CASE 13.2—Continued

them via e-mail. Over the next six years, people who had obtained loans from Mortgage Plus filed claims against the firm, charging it with mistakes, which cost $150,000 to resolve. Mortgage Plus filed a suit in a federal district court against DocMagic, alleging that its software failed to produce documents meeting certain legal requirements. The defendant filed a motion to transfer the suit to a federal court in California based on the clause in the click-on agreement.

ISSUE Is a forum-selection clause contained in a click-on software licensing agreement enforceable?

DECISION Yes. The court concluded that the software licensing agreement was a valid contract because a user had to agree to its terms before the software could be installed and used. Hence, the forum-selection clause was enforceable, and the court ordered the suit to be transferred to a federal district court in California.

REASON Mortgage Plus argued that the parties had negotiated and entered into a contract before DocMagic

shipped the software and that the forum-selection clause was a later, improper attempt to modify this contract. The court, however, found no evidence of this purported "original contractual agreement." Mortgage Plus also argued that it was not aware of, and thus did not accept, the licensing agreement, declaring that "a click-wrap agreement consisting of a window entitled 'Software Licensing Agreement' appearing prior to installation of software cannot be construed as a legally binding contract." The court, however, explained that "the software required users to accept the terms by clicking through a series of screens before they could access and subsequently install the software." Because Mortgage Plus had a choice as to whether to install the software and utilize the related services, "installation and use of the software with the attached license constituted an affirmative acceptance of the license terms."

WHAT IF THE FACTS WERE DIFFERENT?
Suppose that the individual who clicked on the "Yes" button and installed the software was not authorized to do this. Would the result have been different? Why or why not?

◼

Shrink-Wrap Agreements In many ways, click-on agreements are the Internet equivalents of *shrink-wrap agreements* (or *shrink-wrap licenses,* as they are sometimes called). A **shrink-wrap agreement** is an agreement whose terms are expressed inside a box in which the goods are packaged. (The term *shrink-wrap* refers to the plastic that covers the box.) Usually, the party who opens the box is told that she or he agrees to the terms by keeping whatever is in the box.

Similarly, when the purchaser opens a software package, he or she agrees to abide by the terms of the limited license agreement.

◼EXAMPLE 13.3 John orders a new computer from a national company, which ships the computer to him. Along with the computer, the box contains an agreement setting forth the terms of the sale, including what remedies are available. The document also states that John's retention of the computer for longer than thirty days will be construed as an acceptance of the terms. ◼

In most instances, a shrink-wrap agreement is not between a retailer and a buyer, but between the manufacturer of the hardware or software and the ultimate buyer-user of the product. The terms generally concern warranties, remedies, and other issues associated with the use of the product.

Shrink-Wrap Agreements and Enforceable Contract Terms. In many cases, the courts have enforced the terms of shrink-wrap agreements in the same way as the terms of other contracts. Some courts have reasoned that by including the terms with the product, the seller proposed a contract that the buyer could accept by using the product after having an opportunity to read the terms. Thus, a buyer's failure to object to terms contained within a shrink-wrapped software package may constitute an acceptance of the terms by conduct. Also, it seems practical from a business's point of view to enclose a full statement of the legal terms of a sale with the

EXHIBIT 13–1 A Click-On Agreement

This exhibit illustrates an online offer to form a contract. To accept the offer, the user simply scrolls down the page and clicks on the "Accept" box.

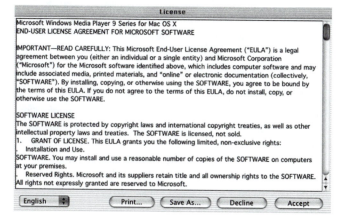

product rather than to read the statement over the phone, for example, when a buyer calls to order the product.

Shrink-Wrap Terms That May Not Be Enforced. Nevertheless, the courts have not enforced all of the terms included in shrink-wrap agreements. One important consideration is whether the parties form their contract before or after the seller communicates the terms of the shrink-wrap agreement to the buyer. If a buyer learned of the shrink-wrap terms *after* the parties entered into a contract, a court may conclude that those terms were proposals for additional terms and were not part of the contract unless the buyer expressly agreed to them.

Browse-Wrap Terms   Like the terms of a click-on agreement, **browse-wrap terms** can occur in a transaction conducted over the Internet. Unlike a click-on agreement, however, browse-wrap terms do not require an Internet user

to assent to the terms before, say, downloading or using certain software. In other words, a person can install the software without clicking "I agree" to the terms of a license. Offerors of browse-wrap terms generally assert that the terms are binding without the user's active consent.

Critics contend that browse-wrap terms are not enforceable because they do not satisfy the basic elements of contract formation. Some argue that a user must at least be presented with the terms before indicating agreement in order to form a valid online contract. With respect to a browse-wrap term, this would require that a user navigate past it and agree to it before being able to obtain whatever is being sold.

The following case involved the enforceability of a clause in an agreement that the court characterized as a browse-wrap license.

CASE 13.3   **Specht v. Netscape Communications Corp.**

United States Court of Appeals, Second Circuit, 306 F.3d 17 (2002).

FACTS Netscape Communications Corporation's "SmartDownload" software makes it easier for users to download files from the Internet without losing progress if they pause to do some other task or if their Internet connection is interrupted. Netscape offers SmartDownload free of charge on its Web site to those who indicate, by clicking on a designated box, that they wish to obtain it. John Gibson clicked on the box and downloaded the software. On the Web site's download page is a reference to a license agreement that is visible only by scrolling to the next screen. Affirmatively indicating assent to the agreement is not required to download the software. The agreement provides that any disputes arising from use of the software are to be submitted to arbitration in California. Believing that the use of SmartDownload transmits private information about its users, Gibson and others filed a suit in a federal district court in New York against Netscape, alleging violations of federal law. Netscape asked the court to order the parties to arbitration in California, according to the license agreement.

ISSUE Was the arbitration clause in the license agreement enforceable?

DECISION No. The court denied the motion to compel arbitration.

REASON The court applied Article 2 of the Uniform Commercial Code because "although in this case the product

was provided free of charge, the roles are essentially the same as when an individual uses the Internet to purchase software from a company: here, the Plaintiff requested Defendant's product by clicking on an icon marked 'Download,' and Defendant then tendered the product." The court emphasized that unless the plaintiffs agreed to the license contract, they could not be bound by the arbitration clause. After discussing the forms of license agreements that accompany sales of software (shrink-wrap, click-on, and browse-wrap licenses) and their enforceability, the court characterized Netscape's license in this case as a browse-wrap license. According to the court, Netscape's SmartDownload "allows a user to download and use the software without taking any action that plainly manifests assent to the terms of the associated license or indicates an understanding that a contract is being formed." The court pointed out that "the individual obtaining SmartDownload is not made aware that he is entering into a contract * * * . The user need not view any license agreement terms or even any reference to a license agreement, and need not do anything to manifest assent." The court reasoned that the plaintiffs did not assent to the license agreement and thus were not subject to the arbitration clause.

WHY IS THIS CASE IMPORTANT? *The ruling in this case is significant because it marks an application of traditional contract principles to a type of dispute that can arise only in the online context. In the case, the court clearly applied a long-standing principle of contract law: a person will not be bound to an agreement to which he or she did not assent.*

E-SIGNATURES

In many instances, a contract cannot be enforced unless it is signed by the party against whom enforcement is sought. In the days when many people could not write, they signed documents with an "X." Then handwritten signatures became common, followed by typed signatures, printed signatures, and, most recently, digital signatures that are transmitted electronically. Throughout the evolution of signature technology, the question of what constitutes a valid signature has arisen again and again, and with good reason—without some consensus on what constitutes a valid signature, less business and legal work could be accomplished. In this section, we look at how electronic signatures, or *e-signatures*, can be created and verified on e-contracts, as well as how the parties can enter into agreements that prevent disputes concerning e-signatures.

E-Signature Technologies

Today, numerous technologies allow electronic documents to be signed. An **e-signature** has been defined as "an electronic sound, symbol, or process attached to or logically associated with a record and executed or adopted by a person with the intent to sign the record."[2] Thus, e-signatures include encrypted digital signatures, names (intended as signatures) at the ends of e-mail messages, and "clicks" on a Web page if the click includes the identification of the person. The technologies for creating e-signatures generally fall into one of two categories, *digitized handwritten signatures* and *public-key infrastructure–based digital signatures*. A digitized signature is a graphical image of a handwritten signature that is often created using a digital pen and pad, such as an ePad, and special software. For security reasons, the strokes of a person's signature can be measured by software to authenticate the person signing (this is referred to as *signature dynamics*).

In a public-key infrastructure (such as an *asymmetric cryptosystem*), two mathematically linked but different keys are generated—a private signing key and a public validation key. A digital signature is created when the signer uses the private key to create a unique mark on an electronic document. The appropriate software enables the recipient of the document to use the public key to verify the identity of the signer. A **cybernotary,** or legally recognized certification authority, issues the key pair, identifies the owner of the keys, and certifies the validity of the public key. The cybernotary also serves as a repository for public keys.

State Laws Governing E-Signatures

Most states have laws governing e-signatures. The problem is that the state e-signature laws are not uniform. Some states—California is a notable example—do not allow many types of documents to be signed with e-signatures, whereas other states are more permissive. Additionally, some states recognize only digital signatures as valid, while others permit other types of e-signatures.

The National Conference of Commissioners on Uniform State Laws, in an attempt to create more uniformity among the states, promulgated the Uniform Electronic Transactions Act (UETA) in 1999. To date, the UETA has been adopted, at least in part, by forty-eight states. Most states have also included a similar provision in their version of the UCC. Among other things, the UETA provides that a signature may not be denied legal effect or enforceability solely because it is in electronic form. (Other aspects of the UETA will be discussed shortly.)

Federal Law on E-Signatures and E-Documents

In 2000, Congress enacted the Electronic Signatures in Global and National Commerce Act (E-SIGN Act)[3] to provide that no contract, record, or signature may be "denied legal effect" solely because it is in an electronic form. In other words, under this law, an electronic signature is as valid as a signature on paper, and an electronic document can be as enforceable as a paper one.

For an electronic signature to be enforceable, the contracting parties must have agreed to use e-signatures. For an electronic document to be valid, it must be in a form that can be retained and accurately reproduced.

The E-SIGN Act does not apply to all types of documents, however. Contracts and documents that are exempt include court papers, divorce decrees, evictions, foreclosures, health-insurance terminations, prenuptial agreements, and wills. Also, the only agreements governed by the UCC that fall under this law are those covered by Articles 2 and 2A and UCC 1–107 and 1–206. Despite these limitations, the E-SIGN Act greatly expanded the possibilities for contracting online.

PARTNERING AGREEMENTS

One way that online sellers and buyers can prevent disputes over signatures in their e-contracts, as well as disputes over the terms and conditions of those contracts, is to form partnering agreements. In a **partnering agreement,** a seller and

2. This definition is from the Uniform Electronic Transactions Act, which will be discussed later in this chapter.

3. 15 U.S.C. Sections 7001 *et seq.*

a buyer who frequently do business with each other agree in advance on the terms and conditions that will apply to all transactions subsequently conducted electronically. The partnering agreement can also establish special access and identification codes to be used by the parties when transacting business electronically.

A partnering agreement reduces the likelihood that disputes will arise under the contract because the buyer and the seller have agreed in advance to the terms and conditions that will accompany each sale. Furthermore, if a dispute does arise, a court or arbitration forum will be able to refer to the partnering agreement when determining the parties' intent with respect to subsequent contracts. Of course, even with a partnering agreement fraud remains a possibility. If an unauthorized person uses a purchaser's designated access number and identification code, it may be some time before the problem is discovered.[4]

 **If you are contemplating an extended contractual relationship with another party, enter into a partnering agreement—particularly if any aspect of the contract involves foreign parties or international deliveries. Partnering agreements offer an efficient way to establish the standards between contracting parties by addressing what type of e-signature will be acceptable, who will be authorized to sign or modify the contract on behalf of the parties, and what security methods will be used. The contract should also outline the parties' understanding as to the effect of any errors, indicate which state's or nation's laws will apply, and specify how any disputes that arise will be resolved.**

■

THE UNIFORM ELECTRONIC TRANSACTIONS ACT (UETA)

As noted earlier, the Uniform Electronic Transactions Act (UETA) was set forth in 1999. It represents one of the first comprehensive efforts to create uniform laws pertaining to e-commerce.

The primary purpose of the UETA is to remove barriers to e-commerce by establishing that electronic records and signatures have the same legal effect as paper documents and signatures. As mentioned earlier, the UETA broadly defines an *e-signature* as "an electronic sound, symbol, or process attached

to or logically associated with a record and executed or adopted by a person with the intent to sign the record."[5] A **record** is "information that is inscribed on a tangible medium or that is stored in an electronic or other medium and is retrievable in perceivable [visual] form."[6]

The Scope and Applicability of the UETA

The UETA does not create new rules for electronic contracts but rather establishes that records, signatures, and contracts may not be denied enforceability solely due to their electronic form. The UETA does not apply to all writings and signatures but only to electronic records and electronic signatures *relating to a transaction*. A *transaction* is defined as an interaction between two or more people relating to business, commercial, or governmental activities.[7] The act specifically does not apply to wills or testamentary trusts or to transactions governed by the UCC (other than those covered by Articles 2 and 2A).[8] In addition, the provisions of the UETA allow the states to exclude its application to other areas of law. As described earlier, Congress passed the E-SIGN Act in 2000, a year after the UETA was presented to the states for adoption. Thus, a significant issue is whether and to what extent the federal E-SIGN Act preempts the UETA as adopted by the states.

The Federal E-SIGN Act and the UETA

The E-SIGN Act of 2002[9] refers explicitly to the UETA and provides that if a state has enacted the uniform version of the UETA, it is not preempted by the E-SIGN Act. In other words, if the state has enacted the UETA without modification, state law will govern. The problem is that many states have enacted nonuniform (modified) versions of the UETA, largely for the purpose of excluding other areas of state law from the UETA's terms. The E-SIGN Act specifies that those exclusions will be preempted to the extent that they are inconsistent with the E-SIGN Act's provisions.

The E-SIGN Act, however, explicitly allows the states to enact alternative requirements for the use of electronic records or electronic signatures. Generally, however, the requirements must be consistent with the provisions of the E-SIGN Act, and the state must not give greater legal status or effect to one specific type of technology. Additionally, if a state has enacted alternative requirements *after* the E-SIGN Act was adopted, the state law must specifically

4. See, for example, *AET, Inc. v. C5 Communications, LLC,* ___ F.Supp.2d ___ (S.D.Tex. 2007).

5. UETA 102(8).
6. UETA 102(15).
7. UETA 2(12) and 3.
8. UETA 3(b).
9. 15 U.S.C. Section 7002(2)(A)(i).

refer to the E-SIGN Act. The relationship between the UETA and the E-SIGN Act is illustrated in Exhibit 13–2.

Highlights of the UETA

We look next at selected provisions of the UETA. Our discussion is, of course, based on the act's uniform provisions. Keep in mind that the states that have enacted the UETA may have adopted slightly different versions.

The Parties Must Agree to Conduct Transactions Electronically The UETA will not apply to a transaction unless each of the parties has previously agreed to conduct transactions by electronic means. The agreement need not be explicit, however, and it may be implied by the conduct of the parties and the surrounding circumstances.[10] In the comments that accompany the UETA, the drafters stated that it may be reasonable to infer that a person who gives out a business card with an e-mail address on it has consented to transact business electronically.[11] The party's agreement may also be inferred from a letter or other writing, as well as from some verbal communication. Nothing in the UETA requires that the agreement to conduct transactions electronically be made electronically.

Note, however, that some courts have required that the parties' agreement to conduct transactions electronically be clear and unambiguous. For example, in one Louisiana case,

---

10. UETA 5(b).
11. UETA 5, Comment 4B.

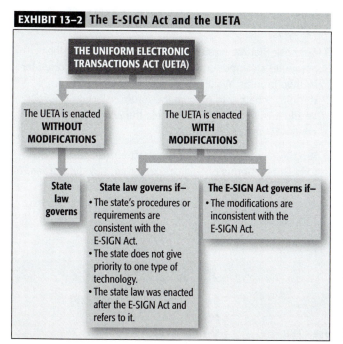

EXHIBIT 13–2 The E-SIGN Act and the UETA

the fact that the parties had *negotiated* the terms of previous contracts via e-mail was not sufficient evidence (by itself) to show that the parties had *agreed* to transact business electronically.[12]

A person who has previously agreed to an electronic transaction can withdraw his or her consent and refuse to conduct further business electronically. Additionally, the act expressly gives parties the power to vary the UETA's provisions by contract. In other words, *parties can opt out of some or all of the terms of the UETA*. If the parties do not opt out of the terms of the UETA, however, the UETA will govern their electronic transactions.

Attribution In the context of electronic transactions, the term *attribution* refers to the procedures that may be used to ensure that the person sending an electronic record is the same person whose e-signature accompanies the record. Under the UETA, if an electronic record or signature is the act of a particular person, the record or signature may be attributed to that person. If a person types her or his name at the bottom of an e-mail purchase order, that name would qualify as a "signature" and be attributed to the person whose name appeared. Just as in paper contracts, one may use any relevant evidence to prove that the record or signature is or is not the act of the person.[13]

Note that even if an individual's name does not appear on a record, the UETA states that the effect of the record is to be determined from the context and surrounding circumstances. In other words, a record may have legal effect even if no one has signed it. **■EXAMPLE 13.4** Darby sends a fax to Corina. The fax contains a letterhead identifying Darby as the sender, but Darby's signature does not appear on the faxed document. Depending on the circumstances, the fax may be attributed to Darby. **■**

The UETA does not contain any express provisions about what constitutes fraud or whether an agent (a person who acts on behalf of another—see Chapter 22) is authorized to enter a contract. Under the UETA, other state laws control if any issues relating to agency, authority, forgery, or contract formation arise.

Notarization If existing state law requires a document to be notarized, the UETA provides that this requirement is satisfied by the electronic signature of a notary public or other person authorized to verify signatures. **■EXAMPLE 13.5** Joel receives an offer to purchase real estate and wants to send his acceptance via e-mail. The state in which Joel resides requires his acceptance to be notarized. Under the UETA, the requirement is

---

12. See *EPCO Carbondioxide Products, Inc. v. Bank One, N.A.*, ___ F.Supp.2d ___ (W.D.La. 2007).
13. UETA 9.

satisfied if a notary public is present to verify Joel's identity and affix an e-signature to his e-mail acceptance. ∎

The Effect of Errors   Section 10 of the UETA encourages, but does not require, the use of security procedures (such as encryption) to verify changes to electronic documents and to correct errors. If the parties have agreed to a security procedure and one party does not detect an error because of failure to follow the procedure, the other party can legally avoid the effect of the change or error. If the parties have not agreed to use a security procedure, then other state laws (including contract law governing mistakes—see Chapter 10) will determine the effect of the error on the parties' agreement. To avoid the effect of errors, a party must promptly notify the other party of the error and of her or his intent not to be bound by the error. In addition, the party must take reasonable steps to return any benefit or consideration received. Parties cannot avoid a transaction from which they have benefited.

Timing   The UETA's provisions relating to the sending and receiving of electronic records apply unless the parties agree to different terms. Under Section 15, an electronic record is considered *sent* when it is properly directed to the intended recipient in a form readable by the recipient's computer system. Once the electronic record leaves the control of the sender or comes under the control of the recipient, the UETA deems it to have been sent. An electronic record is considered *received* when it enters the recipient's processing system in a readable form—*even if no individual is aware of its receipt.*

Additionally, the UETA provides that, unless otherwise agreed, an electronic record is to be sent from or received at the party's principal place of business. If a party has no place of business, the provision then authorizes the place of sending or receipt to be the party's residence. If a party has multiple places of business, the record should be sent from or received at the location that has the closest relationship to the underlying transaction.

REVIEWING E-Contracts and E-Signatures

Ted and Betty Hyatt live in California, a state that has extensive statutory protection for consumers. The Hyatts decided to buy a computer so that they could use e-mail to stay in touch with their grandchildren, who live in another state. Over the phone, they ordered a computer from CompuEdge, Inc. When the box arrived, it was sealed with a brightly colored sticker warning that the terms enclosed within the box would govern the sale unless the computer was returned within thirty days. Among those terms was a clause that required any disputes to be resolved in Tennessee state courts. The Hyatts then signed up for Internet service through CyberTool, an Internet service provider. They downloaded CyberTool's software and clicked on the "quick install" box that allowed them to bypass CyberTool's "Terms of Service" page. It was possible to read this page by scrolling to the next screen, but the Hyatts did not realize this. The terms included a clause stating that all disputes were to be submitted to a Virginia state court. As soon as the Hyatts attempted to e-mail their grandchildren, they experienced problems using CyberTool's e-mail service, which continually

stated that the network was busy. They also were unable to receive the photos sent by their grandchildren. Using the information presented in the chapter, answer the following questions.

1 Did the Hyatts accept the list of contract terms included in the computer box? Why or why not? What is the name used for this type of e-contract?

2 What type of agreement did the Hyatts form with CyberTool?

3 Suppose that the Hyatts experienced trouble with the computer's components after they had used the computer for two months. What factors will a court consider in deciding whether to enforce the forum-selection clause? Would a court be likely to enforce the clause in this contract? Why or why not?

4 Are the Hyatts bound by the contract terms specified on CyberTool's "Terms of Service" page that they did not read? Which of the required elements for contract formation might the Hyatts' claim lack? How might a court rule on this issue?

TERMS AND CONCEPTS

browse-wrap terms 260
click-on agreement 258
cybernotary 261

e-contract 256
e-signature 261
forum-selection clause 258

partnering agreement 261
record 262
shrink-wrap agreement 259

CHAPTER SUMMARY E-Contracts and E-Signatures

Online Offers (See pages 256–258.)	The terms of contract offers presented via the Internet should be as inclusive as the terms in an offer made in a written (paper) document. The offer should be displayed in an easily readable format and should include some mechanism, such as an "I accept" box, by which the customer may accept the offer. Because jurisdictional issues frequently arise with online transactions, the offer should include dispute-settlement provisions, as well as a forum-selection clause.

Online Acceptances
(See pages 258–260.)
	1. *Click-on agreement*—
	  a. Definition—An agreement created when a buyer, completing a transaction on a computer, is required to indicate her or his assent to be bound by the terms of an offer by clicking on a box that says, for example, "I agree." The terms of the agreement may appear on the Web site through which the buyer is obtaining goods or services, or they may appear on a computer screen when software is downloaded.
	  b. Enforceability—The courts have enforced click-on agreements, holding that by clicking on "I agree," the offeree has indicated acceptance by conduct. Browse-wrap terms (terms in a license that an Internet user does not have to read prior to downloading the product, such as software), however, may not be enforced on the ground that the user is not made aware that he or she is entering into a contract.
	2. *Shrink-wrap agreement*—
	  a. Definition—An agreement whose terms are expressed inside a box in which the goods are packaged. The party who opens the box is informed that, by keeping the goods that are in the box, he or she agrees to the terms of the shrink-wrap agreement.
	  b. Enforceability—The courts have often enforced shrink-wrap agreements, even if the purchaser-user of the goods did not read the terms of the agreement. A court may deem a shrink-wrap agreement unenforceable, however, if the buyer learns of the shrink-wrap terms *after* the parties entered into the agreement.

E-Signatures (See page 261.)	The Uniform Electronic Transactions Act (UETA) defines an *e-signature* as "an electronic sound, symbol, or process attached to or logically associated with a record and executed or adopted by a person with the intent to sign the record." 1. *E-signature technologies*—The two main categories of technology include digitized handwritten signatures and public-key infrastructure–based digital signatures. 2. *State laws governing e-signatures*—Although most states have laws governing e-signatures, these laws are not uniform. The UETA provides for the validity of e-signatures and may ultimately create more uniformity among the states in this respect. 3. *Federal law on e-signatures and e-documents*—The Electronic Signatures in Global and National Commerce Act (E-SIGN Act) of 2000 gave validity to e-signatures by providing that no contract, record, or signature may be "denied legal effect" solely because it is in an electronic form.
Partnering Agreements (See pages 261–262.)	To reduce the likelihood that disputes will arise under their e-contracts, parties who frequently do business with each other online may form a partnering agreement, setting out the terms and conditions that will apply to all their subsequent electronic transactions. The agreement may also establish access and identification codes to be used by the parties when transacting business electronically.
The Uniform Electronic Transactions Act (UETA) (See pages 262–264.)	This uniform act, which has been adopted at least in part by most states, was created by the National Conference of Commissioners on Uniform State Laws to provide rules to support the enforcement of e-contracts. Under the UETA, contracts entered into online, as well as other documents, are presumed to be valid. The UETA does not apply to certain transactions governed by the UCC or to wills or testamentary trusts.

FOR REVIEW

Answers for the even-numbered questions in this **For Review** *section can be found on this text's accompanying Web site at* **www.cengage.com/blaw/fbl**. *Select "Chapter 13" and click on "For Review."*

1   What are some important clauses to include when making offers to form electronic contracts, or e-contracts?

2   How do shrink-wrap and click-on agreements differ from other contracts? How have traditional laws been applied to these agreements?

3   What is an electronic signature? Are electronic signatures valid?

4   What is a partnering agreement? What purpose does it serve?

5   What is the Uniform Electronic Transactions Act (UETA)? What are some of its major provisions?

QUESTIONS AND CASE PROBLEMS

 HYPOTHETICAL SCENARIOS AND CASE PROBLEMS

13.1   Click-On Agreements.   Paul is a financial analyst for King Investments, Inc., a brokerage firm. He uses the Internet to find information about companies that might be good investments for King's customers. While visiting the Web site of Business Research, Inc., Paul sees on his screen a message that reads, "Welcome to businessresearch.com. By visiting our site, you have been entered as a subscriber to our e-publication, *Companies Unlimited.* This publication will be sent to you daily at a cost of $7.50 per week. An invoice will be included with *Companies Unlimited* every four weeks. You may cancel your subscription at any time." Has Paul entered into an enforceable contract to pay for *Companies Unlimited?* Why or why not?

13.2   Hypothetical Question with Sample Answer.   Anne is a reporter for *Daily Business Journal,* a print publication consulted by investors and other businesspersons. She often uses the Internet to perform research for the articles that she writes for the publication. While visiting the Web site of Cyberspace Investments Corp., Anne reads a pop-up window that states, "Our business newsletter, *E-Commerce Weekly,* is available at a one-year subscription rate of $5 per issue. To subscribe, enter your e-mail address below and click 'SUBSCRIBE.' By subscribing, you agree to the terms of the subscriber's agreement. To read this agreement, click 'AGREEMENT.'" Anne enters her e-mail address, but does not click on "AGREEMENT" to read the terms. Has Anne entered into an enforceable contract to pay for *E-Commerce Weekly?* Explain.

 For a sample answer to Question 13.2, go to Appendix E at the end of this text.

13.3   Online Acceptance.   Bob, a sales representative for Central Computer Co., occasionally uses the Internet to obtain information about his customers and to look for new sales leads.

While visiting the Web site of Marketing World, Inc., Bob is presented with an on-screen message that offers, "To improve your ability to make deals, read our monthly online magazine, *Sales Genius,* available at a subscription rate of $15 a month. To subscribe, fill in your name, company name, and e-mail address below, and click 'YES!' By clicking 'YES!' you agree to the terms of the subscription contract. To read this contract, click 'TERMS.'" Among those terms is a clause that allows Marketing World to charge interest for subscription bills not paid within a certain time. The terms also prohibit subscribers from copying or distributing part or all of *Sales Genius* in any form. Bob subscribes without reading the terms. Marketing World later files a suit against Bob, based on his failure to pay for his subscription. Should the court hold that Bob is obligated to pay interest on the amount? Explain.

13.4   Click-On Agreements.   America Online, Inc. (AOL), provided e-mail service to Walter Hughes and other members under a click-on agreement titled "Terms of Service." This agreement consisted of three parts: a "Member Agreement," "Community Guidelines," and a "Privacy Policy." The "Member Agreement" included a forum-selection clause that read, "You expressly agree that exclusive jurisdiction for any claim or dispute with AOL or relating in any way to your membership or your use of AOL resides in the courts of Virginia." When Officer Thomas McMenamon of the Methuen, Massachusetts, Police Department received threatening e-mail sent from an AOL account, he requested and obtained from AOL Hughes's name and other personal information. Hughes filed a suit in a federal district court against AOL, which filed a motion to dismiss on the basis of the forum-selection clause. Considering that the clause was a click-on provision, is it enforceable? Explain. [*Hughes v. McMenamon,* 204 F.Supp.2d 178 (D.Mass. 2002)]

13.5 Shrink-Wrap Agreements/Browse-Wrap Terms. Mary DeFontes bought a computer and a service contract from Dell Computers Corp. DeFontes was charged $950.51, of which $13.51 was identified on the invoice as "tax." This amount was paid to the state of Rhode Island. DeFontes and other Dell customers filed a suit in a Rhode Island state court against Dell, claiming that Dell was overcharging its customers by collecting a tax on service contracts and transportation costs. Dell asked the court to order DeFontes to submit the dispute to arbitration. Dell cited its "Terms and Conditions Agreement," which provides, in part, that by accepting delivery of Dell's products or services, a customer agrees to submit any dispute to arbitration. Customers can view this agreement through an *inconspicuous* link at the bottom of Dell's Web site, and Dell encloses a copy with an order when it is shipped. Dell argued that DeFontes accepted these terms by failing to return her purchase within thirty days, although the agreement did not state this. Is DeFontes bound to the "Terms and Conditions Agreement"? Should the court grant Dell's request? Why or why not? [*DeFontes v. Dell Computers Corp.,* __ A.2d __ (R.I. 2004)]

13.6 Case Problem with Sample Answer. Stewart Lamle invented "Farook," a board game similar to Tic Tac Toe. In May 1996, Lamle began negotiating with Mattel, Inc., to license Farook for distribution outside the United States. On June 11, 1997, the parties met and agreed on many terms, including a three-year duration, the geographic scope, a schedule for payment, and a royalty percentage. On June 26, Mike Bucher, a Mattel employee, sent Lamle an e-mail titled "Farook Deal" that repeated these terms and added that they "ha[ve] been agreed [to] . . . by . . . Mattel subject to contract. . . . Best regards Mike Bucher." Lamle faxed Mattel a more formal draft of the terms, but Mattel did not sign it. Mattel displayed Farook at its "Pre-Toy Fair" in August. After the fair, Mattel sent Lamle a fax saying that it no longer wished to license his game. Lamle filed a suit in a federal district court against Mattel, asserting, in part, breach of contract. One of the issues was whether the parties had entered into a contract. Could Bucher's name on the June 26 e-mail be considered a valid signature under the Uniform Electronic Transactions Act (UETA)? Could it be considered a valid signature outside the UETA? Why or why not? [*Lamle v. Mattel, Inc.,* 394 F.3d 1355 (Fed.Cir. 2005)]

After you have answered Problem 13.6, compare your answer with the sample answer given on the Web site that accompanies this text. Go to www.cengage.com/blaw/fbl, select "Chapter 13," and click on "Case Problem with Sample Answer."

13.7 Online Acceptances. Internet Archive (IA) is devoted to preserving a record of resources on the Internet for future generations. IA uses the "Wayback Machine" to automatically browse Web sites and reproduce their contents in an archive. IA does not ask the owners' permission before copying their material but will remove it on request. Suzanne Shell, a resident of Colorado, owns **www.profane-justice.org**, which is dedicated to providing information to individuals accused of child abuse or neglect. The site warns, "IF YOU COPY OR DISTRIBUTE ANYTHING ON THIS SITE, YOU ARE ENTERING INTO A CONTRACT." The terms, which can be accessed only by clicking on a link, include, among other charges, a fee of $5,000 for each page copied "in advance of printing." Neither the warning nor the terms require a user to indicate assent. When Shell discovered that the Wayback Machine had copied the contents of her site—approximately eighty-seven times between May 1999 and October 2004—she asked IA to remove the copies from its archive and pay her $100,000. IA removed the copies and filed a suit in a federal district court against Shell, who responded, in part, with a counterclaim for breach of contract. IA filed a motion to dismiss this claim. Did IA contract with Shell? Explain. [*Internet Archive v. Shell,* __ F.Supp.2d __ (D.Colo. 2007)]

13.8 A Question of Ethics. *In 2000 and 2001, Dewayne Hubbert, Elden Craft, Chris Grout, and Rhonda Byington bought computers from Dell Corp. through its Web site. Before buying, Hubbert and the others configured their own computers. To make a purchase, each buyer completed forms on five Web pages. On each page, Dell's "Terms and Conditions of Sale" were accessible by clicking on a blue hyperlink. A statement on three of the pages read, "All sales are subject to Dell's Term[s] and Conditions of Sale," but a buyer was not required to click an assent to the terms to complete a purchase. The terms were also printed on the backs of the invoices and on separate documents contained in the shipping boxes with the computers. Among those terms was a "Binding Arbitration" clause. The computers contained Pentium 4 microprocessors, which Dell advertised as the fastest, most powerful Intel Pentium processor available. In 2002, Hubbert and the others filed a suit in an Illinois state court against Dell, alleging that this marketing was false, misleading, and deceptive. The plaintiffs claimed that the Pentium 4 microprocessor was slower and less powerful, and provided less performance, than either a Pentium III or an AMD Athlon, and at a greater cost. Dell asked the court to compel arbitration. [Hubbert v. Dell Corp., 359 Ill.App.3d 976, 835 N.E.2d 113, 296 Ill.Dec. 258 (5 Dist. 2005)]*

1 Should the court enforce the arbitration clause in this case? If you were the judge, how would you rule on this issue?

2 In your opinion, do shrink-wrap, click-on, and browse-wrap terms impose too great a burden on purchasers? Why or why not?

3 An ongoing complaint about shrink-wrap, click-on, and browse-wrap terms is that sellers (often large corporations) draft them and buyers (typically individual consumers) do not read them. Should purchasers be bound in contract by terms that they have not even read? Why or why not?

CRITICAL THINKING AND WRITING ASSIGNMENTS

13.9 **Critical Thinking and Writing Assignment for Business.** Delta Co. buys accounting software from Omega Corp. On the outside of the software box, on the inside cover of the instruction manual, and on the first screen that appears each time the program is accessed is a license that claims to cover the use of the product. The license also includes a limitation on Omega's liability arising from the use of the software. One year later, Delta discovers that the software contains a bug that has caused Delta to incur a financial loss. Delta files a lawsuit against Omega. Is the limitation-of-liability clause enforceable?

13.10  **Video Question.** Go to this text's Web site at **www.cengage.com/blaw/fbl** and select "Chapter 13." Click on "Video Questions" and view the video titled *E-Contracts: Agreeing Online.* Then answer the following questions.

1 According to the instructor in the video, what is the key factor in determining whether a particular term in an online agreement is enforceable?

2 Suppose that you click on "I accept" in order to download software from the Internet. You do not read the terms of the agreement before accepting it, even though you know that such agreements often contain forum-selection and arbitration clauses. The software later causes irreparable harm to your computer system, and you want to sue. When you go to the Web site and view the agreement, however, you discover that a choice-of-law clause in the contract specified that the law of Nigeria controls. Is this term enforceable? Is it a term that should reasonably be expected in an online contract?

3 Does it matter what the term actually says if it is a type of term that one could reasonably expect to be in the contract? What arguments can be made for and against enforcing a choice-of-law clause in an online contract?

ACCESSING THE INTERNET

For updated links to resources available on the Web, as well as a variety of other materials, visit this text's Web site at

www.cengage.com/blaw/fbl

The Web site of the National Conference of Commissioners on Uniform State Laws (NCCUSL) includes questions and answers about the UCC, UETA, and more. Go to

www.nccusl.org

You can access the Uniform Commercial Code, including Article 2, at the Web site of the University of Pennsylvania Law School. Go to

www.law.upenn.edu/bll/ulc/ulc.htm

You can find many good resources online about the E-SIGN Act of 2000, including articles available at

archives.cnn.com/2000/ALLPOLITICS/stories/06/30/clinton.e.signatures.04/index.html

PRACTICAL INTERNET EXERCISES

Go to this text's Web site at **www.cengage.com/blaw/fbl**, select "Chapter 13," and click on "Practical Internet Exercises." There you will find the following Internet research exercises that you can perform to learn more about the topics covered in this chapter.

PRACTICAL INTERNET EXERCISE 13-1 LEGAL PERSPECTIVE—E-Contract Formation

PRACTICAL INTERNET EXERCISE 13-2 MANAGEMENT PERSPECTIVE—E-Signatures

BEFORE THE TEST

Go to this text's Web site at **www.cengage.com/blaw/fbl**, select "Chapter 13," and click on "Interactive Quizzes." You will find a number of interactive questions relating to this chapter.

Friezo v. Friezo

Prenuptial agreements were mentioned in Chapter 10 in the discussion of the Statute of Frauds. A prenuptial, or premarital, agreement can be entered into before marriage to delineate each partner's rights to the other's property. To be enforceable, a prenuptial agreement must satisfy the same requirements as any other contract. Under the Statute of Frauds, a prenuptial agreement must be in writing. Because, in a prenuptial agreement, a party typically waives rights that he or she might otherwise assert in a dissolution proceeding, some states impose additional requirements. For example, many jurisdictions mandate a "fair and reasonable" disclosure of each party's finances. In this extended case study, we look at Friezo v. Friezo,[1] a case considering the enforceability of a prenuptial agreement. The question before the court was whether one spouse had provided a "fair and reasonable" disclosure.

CASE BACKGROUND   Victoria Wood, a citizen of the United Kingdom, began working in London, England, for Bankers Trust as a trader's assistant and personal aide in 1994. She worked under the direction of David Friezo, an American, whom she began dating within a week. Less than three months later, they were living together in his apartment.

They were in Westport, Connecticut, in 1998 when David proposed marriage. He asked Victoria to sign a prenuptial agreement that included nineteen "articles," or sections, on twenty-one pages with two attached financial-disclosure "schedules." Victoria consulted an attorney who, at Victoria's request, obtained some changes to the docu-

1. 281 Conn. 166, 914 A.2d 533 (2007).

ment through David's attorney. Less than a week after seeing the first draft, Victoria was given a copy of the final draft. On schedule "B," she specified a total of $22,000 in asset value. On schedule "A," David listed assets with a total value of $6,576,000. Victoria signed the agreement. Twenty-four hours later, they married.

By 2002, when Victoria filed for dissolution of the marriage in a Connecticut state court, David's net worth was estimated to be more than $22 million. Under the prenuptial agreement, Victoria was entitled to $400,000, plus "a residence" for herself and the couple's child. The court concluded that the agreement was unenforceable. David's appeal to a state intermediate appellate court was transferred to the Supreme Court of Connecticut.

MAJORITY OPINION

ZARELLA, J. [Justice]

* * * *

Prenuptial agreements in Connecticut have been governed since October 1, 1995, by the Connecticut Premarital Agreement Act. [The act] provides: "A premarital agreement or amendment shall not be enforceable if the party against whom enforcement is sought proves that * * * before execution of the agreement, such party was not provided a fair and reasonable disclosure of the amount, character and value of property, financial obligations and income of the other party * * * ."

Although the act does not expressly define "fair and reasonable" financial disclosure, a plain reading of the statute indicates that the term was intended to be understood in the context of the phrase that directly follows, namely, "the amount, character and value of property, financial obligations and income of the other party * * * ." Accordingly, "fair and reasonable" disclosure refers to the nature, extent and accuracy of the information to be disclosed, and not to extraneous factors such as the timing of the disclosure.

* * * *

* * * The purpose of disclosure is to ensure that each party has sufficient knowledge of the other party's financial

circumstances to understand the nature of the legal rights being waived. In other words, a party cannot know what is being waived unless he or she is privy to all of the relevant facts, in particular, the financial status of the other party. * * * Financial disclosure * * * must be understood as a burden to inform borne solely by the disclosing party. Accordingly, the court's examination of whether proper disclosure has been made must focus on the actions of the disclosing party rather than on the party to whom disclosure is made. [Also] "full" financial disclosure is required in a prenuptial agreement only if the party to whom disclosure is made does not have independent knowledge of the other party's financial circumstances.

* * * *

The overwhelming majority of jurisdictions that apply this standard do not require financial disclosure to be exact or precise. We agree with the majority of jurisdictions that *a fair and reasonable financial disclosure requires each contracting party to provide the other with a general approximation of their income, assets and liabilities, and that a written schedule appended to the agreement itself, although not absolutely necessary, is the most effective method of satisfying the statutory obligation in most circumstances.* [Emphasis added.]

In the present case, the defendant's [David's] disclosure was more than adequate to ensure that the plaintiff [Victoria]

(Continued)

would be able to make an intelligent waiver of her statutory rights. Article ten of the agreement provided that the defendant's gross income from all sources for 1997, excluding capital gains, was $2,300,000. In addition, schedule A set forth a list of the defendant's assets and liabilities, most of which were valued individually, for a total net worth of $6,576,000. These assets * * * included money market accounts, mutual funds, checking accounts, investments, real and personal property, stocks, various employee and equity participation plans, United States savings bonds, and four frequent flier accounts, all identified by account numbers, where applicable.

Moreover, the plaintiff acknowledged in article eleven of the agreement that she had examined the list of assets and liabilities provided in schedule A and clearly understood and consented to all of the agreement's terms. * * * We therefore conclude that the defendant's disclosure was "fair and reasonable" because it provided the plaintiff with an accurate representation, in writing, of his income and financial assets at the time the agreement was executed.

* * * *

* * * We conclude that * * * the agreement must be enforced and the assets distributed according to its terms.

The judgment is reversed and the case is remanded for further proceedings according to law.

DISSENTING OPINION

NORCOTT, J. [Justice], dissenting.

I disagree with the majority's conclusion that the trial court improperly determined that the parties' prenuptial agreement * * * was unenforceable.

* * * *

* * * [The trial court found] that the plaintiff "was not provided a fair and reasonable disclosure of the amount, character and value of property, financial obligations, and income of the [defendant] * * * ."

* * * *

The financial disclosure document attached to the agreement lists several assets that purportedly comprised the defendant's property. It does so, however, in cursory terms that fail to describe the nature of the property in any way whatsoever. As the trial court noted, the disclosure document simply lists thirty-one ambiguously labeled assets, giving no indication of how they were valued or, in some cases, what they truly are. * * * The disclosure document is similarly vague with regard to the defendant's liabilities.

Furthermore, although the final agreement signed by the plaintiff listed the defendant's income for the year 1997 as $2,300,000, the [first] draft * * * did not contain any statement regarding the defendant's income. Additionally, the income stated on the final agreement was not itemized, and provided the plaintiff with no way of assessing its source or consistency. To the extent that the agreement can be construed as having disclosed the defendant's income, it did so only twenty-four hours before the wedding took place, leaving the plaintiff little time to evaluate that disclosure or take any other action to protect her interest.

Additionally, the trial court made significant findings regarding the plaintiff's financial inexperience. Specifically, the trial court found that the plaintiff possessed only a high school education, "had no knowledge of Connecticut marriage and divorce laws, * * * etc." The trial court further found that the parties "kept their finances completely separated," and "did not talk of money issues."

* * * Accordingly, given the trial court's findings, the scope and timing of the disclosure raise serious doubts that the parties were aware of their legal rights and their respective assets and liabilities, and proceeded by the agreement to alter those rights in a fair and voluntary manner.

QUESTIONS FOR ANALYSIS

1 **LAW.** What was the majority's conclusion on the issue before the court in this case? What was the reasoning to support this conclusion?

2 **LAW.** On what points did the dissent disagree with the majority? Why?

3 **ETHICS.** At David's suggestion, before signing the prenuptial agreement, Victoria consulted an attorney who was an associate of the same law firm as David's sister-in-law. David paid his attorney more than $5,000 for working on the agreement. Victoria sent her attorney, again at David's suggestion, two bottles of wine as compensation. How do you interpret these circumstances?

4 **CULTURAL DIMENSIONS.** What does this case indicate about the status of women?

5 **IMPLICATIONS FOR THE INVESTOR.** Litigating a dispute through a trial and an appeal is expensive. How might a party in David's position avoid the cost?

UNIT CONTENTS

CHAPTER 14
The Formation of
Sales and Lease Contracts

AFTER READING THIS CHAPTER, YOU SHOULD BE ABLE TO ANSWER THE FOLLOWING QUESTIONS:

1 How do Article 2 and Article 2A of the UCC differ? What types of transactions does each article cover?

2 What is a merchant's firm offer?

3 If an offeree includes additional or different terms in an acceptance, will a contract result? If so, what happens to these terms?

4 Article 2 and Article 2A of the UCC both define several exceptions to the writing requirements of the Statute of Frauds. What are these exceptions?

5 What law governs contracts for the international sale of goods?

It is often said that the object of the law is to encourage commerce. This is particularly true with respect to the Uniform Commercial Code (UCC). The UCC facilitates commercial transactions by making the laws governing sales and lease contracts uniform, clearer, simpler, and more readily applicable to the numerous difficulties that can arise during such transactions. Recall from Chapter 1 that the UCC is one of many uniform (model) acts drafted by the National Conference of Commissioners on Uniform State Laws and submitted to the states for adoption. Once a state legislature has adopted a uniform act, the act becomes statutory law in that state. Thus, when we turn to sales and lease contracts, we move away from common law principles and into the area of statutory law.

We open this chapter with a discussion of the general coverage of the UCC and its significance as a legal landmark. We then look at the scope of the UCC's Article 2 (on sales) and Article 2A (on leases) as a background to the focus of this chapter, which is the formation of contracts for the sale and lease of goods. Because international sales transactions are increasingly commonplace in the business world, we conclude this chapter with an examination of the United Nations Convention on Contracts for the International Sale of Goods (CISG), which governs international sales contracts.

THE SCOPE OF THE UCC

The UCC attempts to provide a consistent and integrated framework of rules to deal with all phases ordinarily arising in a commercial sales or lease transaction from start to finish. For example, consider the following events, all of which may occur during a single transaction:

1 *A contract for the sale or lease of goods is formed and executed.* Article 2 and Article 2A of the UCC provide rules governing all aspects of this transaction.

2 *The transaction may involve a payment—by check, electronic fund transfer, or other means.* Article 3 (on negotiable instruments), Article 4 (on bank deposits and collections), Article 4A (on fund transfers), and Article 5 (on letters of credit) cover this part of the transaction.

3 *The transaction may involve a bill of lading or a warehouse receipt that covers goods when they are shipped or stored.* Article 7 (on documents of title) deals with this subject.

4 *The transaction may involve a demand by the seller or lender for some form of security for the remaining balance owed.* Article 9 (on secured transactions) covers this part of the transaction.

The UCC has been adopted in whole or in part by all of the states.[1]

THE SCOPE OF ARTICLE 2—SALES

Article 2 of the UCC governs **sales contracts,** or contracts for the sale of goods. To facilitate commercial transactions, Article 2 modifies some of the common law contract requirements that were summarized in Chapter 7 and discussed in detail in Chapters 8 through 12. To the extent that it has not been modified by the UCC, however, the common law of contracts also applies to sales contracts. In general, the rule is that when a UCC provision addresses a certain issue, the UCC governs; when the UCC is silent, the common law governs.

In regard to Article 2, keep two points in mind. First, Article 2 deals with the sale of *goods;* it does not deal with real property (real estate), services, or intangible property such as stocks and bonds. Thus, if a dispute involves goods, the UCC governs. If it involves real estate or services, the common law applies. The relationship between general contract law and the law governing sales of goods is illustrated in Exhibit 14–1. Second, in some instances, the rules may vary quite a bit, depending on whether the buyer or the seller is a merchant. We look now at how the UCC defines three important terms: *sale, goods,* and *merchant status.*

1. Louisiana has not adopted Articles 2 and 2A, however.

EXHIBIT 14–1 **The Law Governing Contracts**

This exhibit graphically illustrates the relationship between general contract law and statutory law (UCC Articles 2 and 2A) governing contracts for the sale and lease of goods. Sales contracts are not governed exclusively by Article 2 of the UCC but are also governed by general contract law whenever it is relevant and has not been modified by the UCC.

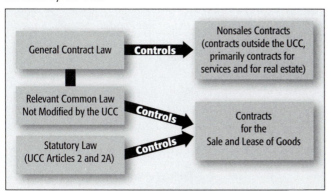

What Is a Sale?

The UCC defines a **sale** as "the passing of title [evidence of ownership] from the seller to the buyer for a price" [UCC 2–106(1)]. The price may be payable in cash (or its equivalent) or in other goods or services.

What Are Goods?

To be characterized as a *good,* the item of property must be *tangible,* and it must be *movable.* **Tangible property** has physical existence—it can be touched or seen. **Intangible property**—such as corporate stocks and bonds, patents and copyrights, and ordinary contract rights—has only conceptual existence and thus does not come under Article 2. A movable item can be carried from place to place. Hence, real estate is excluded from Article 2.

Two issues often give rise to disputes in determining whether the object of a contract is goods and thus whether Article 2 is applicable. One problem has to do with *goods associated with real estate,* such as crops or timber, and the other concerns contracts involving a combination of *goods and services.*

Goods Associated with Real Estate Goods associated with real estate often fall within the scope of Article 2. Section 2–107 provides the following rules:

1 A contract for the sale of minerals or the like (including oil and gas) or a structure (such as a building) is a contract for the sale of goods if *severance,* or *separation,* is to be made by the *seller.* If the *buyer* is to sever (separate) the minerals or structure from the land, the contract is considered to be a sale of real estate governed by the principles of real property law, not the UCC.

2 A sale of growing crops (such as potatoes, carrots, wheat, and the like) or timber to be cut is considered to be a contract for the sale of goods *regardless of who severs them.*

3 Other "things attached" to realty but capable of severance without material harm to the land are considered goods *regardless of who severs them.*[2] "Things attached" that are severable without harm to realty could include such items as a portable heater, a window air conditioner in a house, and stools in a restaurant. Thus, removal of one of these things would be considered a sale of goods. The test is whether removal will cause substantial harm to the real property to which the item is attached.

2. The UCC avoids the term *fixtures* here because the word has numerous definitions. A fixture is anything so firmly or permanently attached to land or to a building as to become a part of it. Once personal property becomes a fixture, it is governed by real estate law. See Chapter 29.

Goods and Services Combined In cases involving contracts in which goods and services are combined, courts have reached different results. For instance, is providing blood to a patient during an operation a "sale of goods" or the "performance of a medical service"? Some courts say it is a good; others say it is a service. Because the UCC does not provide the answers to such questions, the courts generally use the **predominant-factor test** to determine whether a contract is primarily for the sale of goods or for the sale of services.[3] This determination is important because the UCC will apply to

services provided under a mixed contract that is predominantly for goods, even though the majority of courts treat services as being excluded by the UCC. In other words, if a court decides that a mixed contract is primarily a goods contract, *any* dispute, even a dispute over the services portion, will be decided under the UCC. Likewise, any disagreement over a predominantly services contract will not be decided using the UCC, even if the dispute involves the goods portion of the contract.

If an entire business, including a truck and its equipment, is sold, but the contract does not specify what portion of the sale price relates to the goods, does Article 2 of the UCC still apply to the transaction? That was the main issue in the following case.

---

3. UCC 2–314(1) does stipulate that serving food or drinks is a "sale of goods" for purposes of the implied warranty of merchantability, as will be discussed in Chapter 17. The UCC also specifies that selling unborn animals and rare coins qualifies as a "sale of goods."

CASE 14.1   **Jannusch v. Naffziger**

Appellate Court of Illinois, Fourth District, 379 Ill.App.3d 381, 883 N.E.2d 711 (2008).

FACTS Gene and Martha Jannusch ran Festival Foods, which provided concessions at events around Illinois and Indiana. They owned a truck, a trailer, freezers, roasters, chairs, tables, a fountain service, signs, and lighting. Lindsey and Louann Naffziger were interested in buying the concessions business. They met with the Jannusches and orally agreed to a price of $150,000. The Naffzigers paid $10,000 down with the balance to come from a bank loan. They took possession of the equipment and began to use it immediately in Festival Foods operations at various events, even though Gene Jannusch kept the titles to the truck and trailer in his name. Gene Jannusch was paid to attend two events with the Naffzigers to provide advice about running the operation. After six events, and at the end of the outdoor season, the Naffzigers returned the truck and all the equipment to its storage location and wanted out of the deal. They said the business did not generate as much income as they had expected. The Jannusches sued the Naffzigers for the balance due on the purchase price. The trial court held that the Uniform Commercial Code (UCC) governed the case but that there was not enough evidence to show that the parties had a sufficient meeting of the minds to form a contract. The Jannusches appealed.

ISSUE Were the goods the predominant factor in the sale of this business?

DECISION Yes. The appeals court reversed the decision of the trial court, finding that there was a contract formed under the UCC and that the Naffzigers had breached it.

REASON The oral agreement for the sale of the business was predominantly one for the sale of goods and therefore was within Article 2 of the UCC. The oral agreement was sufficiently definite to form a sales contract, even though it did not specify the price of each item being sold or distinguish between the value of the equipment and the value of the goodwill of the business. The Naffzigers made a payment, took possession of the business, and operated it as their own. While some terms of the contract were missing, it was definite enough to be enforced. The fact that it was not in writing does not preclude enforcement of a specific promise.

FOR CRITICAL ANALYSIS—Ethical Consideration *Given that the business was not what the Naffzigers expected it to be, and that they returned everything, was it fair for the Jannusches to demand full payment? Explain your answer.*

■

Who Is a Merchant?

Article 2 governs the sale of goods in general. It applies to sales transactions between all buyers and sellers. In a limited number of instances, however, the UCC presumes that certain special business standards ought to be imposed on merchants because they possess a relatively high degree of

commercial expertise.[4] Such standards do not apply to the casual or inexperienced seller or buyer (a "consumer").

---

4. The provisions that apply only to merchants deal principally with the Statute of Frauds, firm offers, confirmatory memorandums, warranties, and contract modifications. These special rules reflect expedient business practices commonly known to merchants in the commercial setting. They will be discussed later in this chapter.

Section 2–104 sets out three ways in which merchant status can arise:

1 A merchant is a person who *deals in goods of the kind* involved in the sales contract. Thus, a retailer, a wholesaler, or a manufacturer is a merchant of those goods sold in the business. A merchant for one type of goods is not necessarily a merchant for another type. For example, a sporting equipment retailer is a merchant when selling tennis rackets but not when selling a used computer.

2 A merchant is a person who, *by occupation, holds himself or herself out as having knowledge and skill unique to the practices or goods* involved in the transaction. Note that this broad definition may include banks or universities as merchants.

3 A person who *employs a merchant as a broker, agent, or other intermediary* has the status of merchant in that transaction. Hence, if a "gentleman farmer" who ordinarily does not run the farm hires a broker to purchase or sell livestock, the farmer is considered a merchant in the transaction.

In summary, a person is a **merchant** when she or he, acting in a mercantile capacity, possesses or uses an expertise specifically related to the goods being sold. Nevertheless, the distinction between merchants and nonmerchants is not always clear-cut. For example, state courts appear to be split on whether farmers should be considered merchants.[5] In some states, farmers are considered merchants because they sell products or livestock on a regular basis. In other states, courts have held that the drafters of the UCC did not intend to include farmers as merchants.

THE SCOPE OF ARTICLE 2A–LEASES

In the past few decades, leases of personal property (goods) have become increasingly common. In this context, a **lease** is a transfer of the right to possess and use goods for a period of time in exchange for payment. Article 2A of the UCC was created to fill the need for uniform guidelines in this area. Article 2A covers any transaction that creates a lease of goods, as well as subleases of goods [UCC 2A–102, 2A–103(1)(k)]. Except that it applies to leases, rather than sales, of goods, Article 2A is essentially a repetition of Article 2 and varies only to reflect differences between sales and lease transactions. (Note that Article 2A is not concerned with leases of real property, such as land or buildings. The laws governing these types of transactions will be examined in Chapter 29.)

5. See the court's discussion of this issue in *R. F. Cunningham & Co. v. Driscoll*, 7 Misc.3d 234, 790 N.Y.S.2d 368 (2005).

Definition of a Lease Agreement

Article 2A defines a **lease agreement** as a lessor and lessee's bargain with respect to the lease of goods, as found in their language and as implied by other circumstances, including course of dealing and usage of trade or course of performance [UCC 2A–103(1)(k)]. A **lessor** is one who transfers the right to the possession and use of goods under a lease [UCC 2A–103(1)(p)]. A **lessee** is one who acquires the right to the temporary possession and use of goods under a lease [UCC 2A–103(1)(o)]. In other words, the lessee is the party who is leasing the goods from the lessor. Article 2A applies to all types of leases of goods, including commercial leases and consumer leases. Special rules apply to certain types of leases, however, including consumer leases and finance leases.

Consumer Leases

A *consumer lease* involves three elements: (1) a lessor who regularly engages in the business of leasing or selling; (2) a lessee (except an organization) who leases the goods "primarily for a personal, family, or household purpose"; and (3) total lease payments that are less than a dollar amount set by state statute [UCC 2A–103(1)(e)]. To ensure special protection for consumers, certain provisions of Article 2A apply only to consumer leases. For example, one provision states that a consumer may recover attorneys' fees if a court finds that a term in a consumer lease contract is unconscionable [UCC 2A–108(4)(a)].

Finance Leases

A *finance lease* involves a lessor, a lessee, and a supplier. The lessor buys or leases goods from the supplier and leases or subleases them to the lessee [UCC 2A–103(1)(g)]. Typically, in a finance lease, the lessor is simply financing the transaction.
■EXAMPLE 14.1 Marlin Corporation wants to lease a crane for use in its construction business. Marlin's bank agrees to purchase the equipment from Jennco, Inc., and lease the equipment to Marlin. In this situation, the bank is the lessor-financer, Marlin is the lessee, and Jennco is the supplier. ■

Article 2A, unlike ordinary contract law, makes the lessee's obligations under a commercial finance lease irrevocable and independent from the financer's obligations [UCC 2A–407]. In other words, the lessee must perform and continue to make lease payments even if the leased equipment turns out to be defective. The lessee must look almost entirely to the supplier for warranties.

THE FORMATION OF SALES AND LEASE CONTRACTS

In regard to the formation of sales and lease contracts, Article 2 and Article 2A of the UCC modify common law contract rules in several ways. Remember, though, that parties to sales contracts are free to establish whatever terms they wish. The UCC comes into play only when the parties have failed to provide in their contract for a contingency that later gives rise to a dispute. The UCC makes this clear time and again by using such phrases as "unless the parties otherwise agree" or "absent a contrary agreement by the parties."

Offer

In general contract law, the moment a definite offer is met by an unqualified acceptance, a binding contract is formed. In commercial sales transactions, the verbal exchanges, correspondence, and actions of the parties may not reveal exactly when a binding contractual obligation arises. The UCC states that an agreement sufficient to constitute a contract can exist even if the moment of its making is undetermined [UCC 2–204(2), 2A–204(2)].

Open Terms Remember from Chapter 8 that under the common law of contracts, an offer must be definite enough for the parties (and the courts) to ascertain its essential terms when it is accepted. In contrast, the UCC states that a sales or lease contract will not fail for indefiniteness even if one or more terms are left open as long as (1) the parties intended to make a contract and (2) there is a reasonably certain basis for the court to grant an appropriate remedy [UCC 2–204(3), 2A–204(3)].

■EXAMPLE 14.2 Mike agrees to lease from CompuQuik a highly specialized computer work station. Mike and one of CompuQuik's sales representatives sign a lease agreement that leaves some of the details blank, to be "worked out" the following week, when the leasing manager will be back from her vacation. In the meantime, CompuQuik obtains the necessary equipment from one of its suppliers and spends several days modifying the equipment to suit Mike's needs. When the leasing manager returns, she calls Mike and tells him that his work station is ready. Mike says he is no longer interested in the work station, as he has arranged to lease the same type of equipment for a lower price from another firm. CompuQuik sues Mike to recover its costs in obtaining and modifying the equipment, and one of the issues before the court is whether the parties had an enforceable contract. The court will likely hold that they did, based on their intent and conduct, despite the "blanks" in their written agreement. **■**

Relative to the common law of contracts, the UCC has radically lessened the requirement of definiteness of terms. Keep in mind, though, that the more terms left open, the less likely it is that a court will find that the parties intended to form a contract.

Open Price Term. If the parties have not agreed on a price, the court will determine a "reasonable price at the time for delivery" [UCC 2–305(1)]. If either the buyer or the seller is to determine the price, the price is to be fixed (set) in good faith [UCC 2–305(2)]. Under the UCC, *good faith* means honesty in fact and the observance of reasonable commercial standards of fair dealing in the trade [UCC 2–103(1)(b)]. The concepts of *good faith* and *commercial reasonableness* permeate the UCC. Sometimes, the price fails to be fixed through the fault of one of the parties. In that situation, the other party can treat the contract as canceled or fix a reasonable price. **■EXAMPLE 14.3** Perez and Merrick enter into a contract for the sale of unfinished doors and agree that Perez will determine the price. Perez refuses to specify the price. Merrick can either treat the contract as canceled or set a reasonable price [UCC 2–305(3)]. **■**

Open Payment Term. When parties do not specify payment terms, payment is due at the time and place at which the buyer is to receive the goods [UCC 2–310(a)]. The buyer can tender payment using any commercially normal or acceptable means, such as a check or credit card. If the seller demands payment in cash, however, the buyer must be given a reasonable time to obtain it [UCC 2–511(2)]. This is especially important when the contract states a definite and final time for performance.

Open Delivery Term. When no delivery terms are specified, the buyer normally takes delivery at the seller's place of business [UCC 2–308(a)]. If the seller has no place of business, the seller's residence is used. When goods are located in some other place and both parties know it, delivery is made there. If the time for shipment or delivery is not clearly specified in the sales contract, the court will infer a "reasonable" time for performance [UCC 2–309(1)].

Duration of an Ongoing Contract. A single contract might specify successive performances but not indicate how long the parties are required to deal with each other. In this situation, either party may terminate the ongoing contractual relationship. Principles of good faith and sound commercial practice call for reasonable notification before termination, however, to give the other party reasonable time to seek a substitute arrangement [UCC 2–309(2), (3)].

Options and Cooperation Regarding Performance. When the contract contemplates shipment of the goods but does not specify the shipping arrangements, the *seller* has the right to make these arrangements in good faith, using commercial reasonableness in the situation [UCC 2–311].

When a sales contract omits terms relating to the assortment of goods, the *buyer* can specify the assortment. **■EXAMPLE 14.4** Petry Drugs, Inc., agrees to purchase one thousand toothbrushes from Marconi's Dental Supply. The toothbrushes come in a variety of colors, but the contract does not specify color. Petry, the buyer, has the right to take six hundred blue toothbrushes and four hundred green ones if it wishes. Petry, however, must exercise good faith and commercial reasonableness in making its selection [UCC 2–311]. ■

Open Quantity Term. Normally, if the parties do not specify a quantity, a court will have no basis for determining a remedy. This is because there is almost no way to determine objectively what is a reasonable quantity of goods for someone to buy (whereas a court can objectively determine a reasonable price for particular goods by looking at the market). Nevertheless, the UCC recognizes two exceptions involving requirements and output contracts [UCC 2–306(1)].

In a **requirements contract,** the buyer agrees to purchase and the seller agrees to sell all or up to a stated amount of what the buyer *needs* or *requires*. ■**EXAMPLE 14.5** Umpqua Cannery forms a contract with Al Garcia. The cannery agrees to purchase from Garcia, and Garcia agrees to sell to the cannery, all of the green beans that the cannery needs or requires during the summer of 2010. ■ There is implicit consideration in a requirements contract because the buyer (the cannery, in this situation) gives up the right to buy green beans from any other seller, and this forfeited right creates a legal detriment (that is, consideration). Requirements contracts are common in the business world and are normally enforceable. In contrast, if the buyer promises to purchase only if the buyer *wishes* to do so, or if the buyer reserves the right to buy the goods from someone other than the seller, the promise is illusory (without consideration) and unenforceable by either party.[6]

In an **output contract,** the seller agrees to sell and the buyer agrees to buy all or up to a stated amount of what the seller *produces*. ■**EXAMPLE 14.6** Al Garcia forms a contract with Umpqua Cannery. Garcia agrees to sell to the cannery, and the cannery agrees to purchase from Garcia, all of the beans that Garcia produces on his farm during the summer of 2010. ■ Again, because the seller essentially forfeits the right to sell goods to another buyer, there is implicit consideration in an output contract.

The UCC imposes a *good faith limitation* on requirements and output contracts. The quantity under such contracts is the amount of requirements or the amount of output that occurs during a *normal* production year. The actual quantity purchased or sold cannot be unreasonably disproportionate to normal or comparable prior requirements or output [UCC 2–306].

If you leave certain terms of a sales or lease contract open, the UCC allows a court to supply the missing terms. Although this can sometimes be advantageous (to establish that a contract existed, for instance), it can also be a major disadvantage. If you fail to state a price in your contract offer, for example, a court will impose a reasonable price by looking at the market price of similar goods *at the time of delivery*. Thus, instead of receiving your standard price for the goods, you will receive what a court considers a reasonable price when the goods are delivered. When drafting contracts for the sale or lease of goods, make sure that the contract clearly states any terms that are essential to the bargain, particularly price. It is often better to establish the terms of your own contracts rather than to leave it up to a court to determine what terms are reasonable after a dispute has arisen.

■

Merchant's Firm Offer Under common law contract principles, an offer can be revoked at any time before acceptance. The major common law exception is an *option contract* (discussed in Chapter 8), in which the offeree pays consideration for the offeror's irrevocable promise to keep the offer open for a stated period. The UCC creates a second exception for firm offers made by a merchant to sell, buy, or lease goods.

A **firm offer** arises when a merchant-offeror gives *assurances* in a *signed writing* that the offer will remain open. The merchant's firm offer is irrevocable without the necessity of consideration[7] for the stated period or, if no definite period is stated, a reasonable period (neither period to exceed three months) [UCC 2–205, 2A–205]. ■**EXAMPLE 14.7** Osaka, a used-car dealer, writes a letter to Saucedo on January 1 stating, "I have a used 2009 Suzuki SX4 on the lot that I'll sell you for $11,000 any time between now and January 31." This writing creates a firm offer, and Osaka will be liable for breach if he sells the Suzuki SX4 to someone other than Saucedo before January 31. ■

It is necessary that the offer be both *written* and *signed* by the offeror.[8] When a firm offer is contained in a form contract prepared by the offeree, the offeror must also sign a separate assurance of the firm offer. This requirement ensures

---

6. See, for example, *In re Anchor Glass Container Corp.*, 345 Bankr. 765 (M.D.Fla. 2006).

7. If the offeree pays consideration, then an option contract (not a merchant's firm offer) is formed.

8. *Signed* includes any symbol executed or adopted by a party with a present intention to authenticate a writing [UCC 1–201(39)]. A complete signature is not required. Therefore, initials, a thumbprint, a trade name, or any mark used in lieu of a written signature will suffice, regardless of its location on the document.

that the offeror is aware of the offer. For instance, an offeree might respond to an initial offer by sending its own form contract containing a clause stating that the offer will remain open for three months. If the firm offer is buried amid copious language in one of the pages of the offeree's form contract, the offeror may inadvertently sign the contract without realizing that it contains a firm offer, thus defeating the purpose of the rule—which is to give effect to a merchant's deliberate intent to be bound to a firm offer.

Acceptance

The following subsections examine the UCC's provisions governing acceptance. As you will see, acceptance of an offer to buy, sell, or lease goods generally may be made in any reasonable manner and by any reasonable means.

Methods of Acceptance   The general common law rule is that an offeror can specify, or authorize, a particular means of acceptance, making that method the only one effective for contract formation. Even an unauthorized means of communication is effective, however, as long as the acceptance is received by the specified deadline.   **EXAMPLE 14.8** Janel offers to sell her Hummer H2 to Arik for $24,000. The offer states, "Answer by fax within five days." If Arik sends a letter, and Janel receives it within five days, a valid contract is formed, nonetheless. ■

Any Reasonable Means.   When the offeror does not specify a means of acceptance, the UCC provides that acceptance can be made by any means of communication that is reasonable under the circumstances [UCC 2–206(1), 2A–206(1)]. This broadens the common law rules concerning authorized means of acceptance. (For a review of the requirements relating to mode and timeliness of acceptance, see Chapter 8.)   **EXAMPLE 14.9** Anodyne Corporation sends Bethlehem Industries a letter offering to lease $1,000 worth of postage meters. The offer states that Anodyne will keep the offer open for only ten days from the date of the letter. Before the ten days elapse, Bethlehem sends Anodyne an acceptance by fax. Is a valid contract formed? The answer is yes, because acceptance by fax is a commercially reasonable medium of acceptance under the circumstances. Acceptance is effective on Bethlehem's transmission of the fax, which occurred before the offer lapsed. ■

Promise to Ship or Prompt Shipment.   The UCC permits a seller to accept an offer to buy goods "either by a prompt *promise* to ship or by the prompt or current shipment of conforming or nonconforming goods" [UCC 2–206(1)(b)]. *Conforming* goods are goods that accord with the contract's terms; *nonconforming* goods do not. The seller's prompt ship-

ment of nonconforming goods in response to the offer constitutes both an acceptance (a contract) and a *breach* of that contract.

This rule does not apply if the seller **seasonably** (within a reasonable amount of time) notifies the buyer that the nonconforming shipment is offered only as an *accommodation*, or as a favor. The notice of accommodation must clearly indicate to the buyer that the shipment does not constitute an acceptance and that, therefore, no contract has been formed.   **EXAMPLE 14.10** McFarrell Pharmacy orders five cases of Johnson & Johnson 3-by-5-inch gauze pads from Halderson Medical Supply, Inc. If Halderson ships five cases of Xeroform 3-by-5-inch gauze pads instead, the shipment acts as both an acceptance of McFarrell's offer and a *breach* of the resulting contract. McFarrell may sue Halderson for any appropriate damages. If, however, Halderson notifies McFarrell that the Xeroform gauze pads are being shipped *as an accommodation*—because Halderson has only Xeroform pads in stock—the shipment will constitute a counteroffer, not an acceptance. A contract will be formed only if McFarrell accepts the Xeroform gauze pads. ■

Communication of Acceptance   Under the common law, because a unilateral offer invites acceptance by a performance, the offeree need not notify the offeror of performance unless the offeror would not otherwise know about it. In other words, beginning the requested performance is an implied acceptance. The UCC is more stringent than the common law in this regard. Under the UCC, if the offeror is not notified within a reasonable time that the offeree has accepted the contract by beginning performance, then the offeror can treat the offer as having lapsed before acceptance [UCC 2–206(2), 2A–206(2)].   **EXAMPLE 14.11** Lee writes to Pickwick Bookstore on Monday, "Please send me a copy of *Webster's New College Dictionary* for $25.55, C.O.D.," and signs it, "Lee." Pickwick receives the request but does not ship the book for four weeks. When the book arrives, Lee rejects it, claiming that it has arrived too late to be of value. In this situation, because Lee had heard nothing from Pickwick for a month, he was justified in assuming that the store did not intend to deliver the book. Lee could consider that the offer had lapsed because of the length of time Pickwick delayed shipment. ■

Additional Terms   Under the common law, if Alderman makes an offer to Beale, and Beale in turn accepts but in the acceptance makes some slight modification to the terms of the offer, there is no contract. Recall from Chapter 8 that the so-called *mirror image rule* requires that the terms of the acceptance exactly match those of the offer. The UCC dispenses with the mirror image rule. Generally, the UCC takes the position that if the offeree's response indicates a *definite* acceptance of the offer, a contract is formed *even if the acceptance includes additional or different terms from those contained in the offer* [UCC 2–207(1)]. What happens to these additional terms? The answer to this question depends, in part, on whether the parties are nonmerchants or merchants.

Rules When One Party or Both Parties Are Nonmerchants. If one (or both) of the parties is a *nonmerchant*, the contract is formed according to the terms of the original offer submitted by the original offeror and not according to the additional terms of the acceptance [UCC 2–207(2)]. ■**EXAMPLE 14.12** Tolsen offers in writing to sell his laptop computer and printer to Valdez for $650. Valdez faxes a reply to Tolsen stating, "I accept your offer to purchase your laptop and printer for $650. I *would like* a box of laser printer paper and two extra toner cartridges to be included in the purchase price." Valdez has given Tolsen a definite expression of acceptance (creating a contract), even though the acceptance also *suggests* an added term for the offer. Because Tolsen is not a merchant, the additional term is merely a proposal (suggestion), and Tolsen is not legally obligated to comply with that term. ■

Rules When Both Parties Are Merchants. In contracts *between merchants*, the additional terms automatically become part of the contract unless (1) the original offer expressly limits acceptance to the terms of the offer, (2) the new or changed terms *materially* alter the contract, or (3) the offeror objects to the new or changed terms within a reasonable period of time [UCC 2–207(2)].

What constitutes a material alteration is frequently a question that only a court can decide. Generally, if the modification involves no unreasonable element of surprise or hardship for the offeror, the court will hold that the modification did not materially alter the contract. ■**EXAMPLE 14.13** Woolf has ordered meat from Tupman sixty-four times over a two-year period. Each time, Woolf placed the order over the phone, and Tupman mailed a confirmation form, and then an invoice, to Woolf. Tupman's confirmation form and invoice have always included an arbitration clause. If Woolf places another order and fails to pay for the meat, the court will likely hold that the additional term—the arbitration provision—did not materially alter the contract because Woolf should not have been surprised by the term. ■

In the following case, the court explains the significant change in contract law caused by the UCC's principles on additional terms.

CASE 14.2   **Sun Coast Merchandise Corp. v. Myron Corp.**

Superior Court of New Jersey, Appellate Division, 393 N.J.Super. 55, 922 A.2d 782 (2007).
lawlibrary.rutgers.edu/search.shtml[a]

FACTS Sun Coast Merchandise Corporation, a California firm, designs and sells products that businesses distribute as promotional items. Myron Corporation, a New Jersey firm, asked Sun about a flip-top calculator on which Myron could engrave the names of its customers. In December 2000, Myron began to submit purchase orders for about 400,000 of what the parties referred to as "Version I" calculators. In April 2001, Sun redesigned the flip-top. Over the next few weeks, the parties discussed terms for making and shipping 4 million of the "Version II" calculators before the Christmas season. By May 27, Myron had faxed four orders with specific delivery dates. Two days later, Sun announced a delayed schedule and asked Myron to submit revised orders. Unwilling to agree to the new dates, Myron did not honor this request. The parties attempted to negotiate the issue but were unsuccessful. Finally, Sun filed a suit in a New Jersey state court against

Myron, claiming, among other things, breach of contract. The court entered a judgment in Sun's favor. On appeal to a state intermediate appellate court, Myron argued, among other things, that the judge's instructions to the jury regarding Sun's claim was inadequate.

ISSUE Were the judge's instructions to the trial jury regarding Sun's claim of breach of contract inadequate?

DECISION Yes. The state intermediate appellate court reversed the lower court's judgment and remanded the case for a new trial.

REASON The court pointed out that "no longer are communicating parties left to debate whether an acceptance perfectly meets the terms of an offer, but instead the existence of a binding contract may be based on words or conduct, which need not mirror an offer, so long as they reveal the parties' intention to be bound." Thus, the jury could have found that a contract was formed. Nonetheless, the court

---

a. In the "SEARCH THE N.J. COURTS DECISIONS" section, type "Sun Coast" in the box, and click on "Search!" In the result, click on the case name to access the opinion.

CASE 14.2—Continues next page

CASE 14.2—Continued

accepted the possibility that the jury could also have found that the parties' "inability to agree on certain terms reveals the lack of an intent to be bound; in other words, that their communications constituted new negotiations that never ripened into a contract." Therefore, the reviewing court concluded that the trial judge's instructions to the jury with respect to the question of whether Sun and Myron had

formed a contract were "fundamentally flawed" and "provided insufficient guidance for the jury's resolution of the issues."

 FOR CRITICAL ANALYSIS—Ethical Consideration *How does the UCC's obligation of good faith relate to the application of the principles concerning additional terms?*

■

Conditioned on Offeror's Assent.   Regardless of merchant status, the UCC provides that the offeree's expression cannot be construed as an acceptance if it contains additional or different terms that are explicitly conditioned on the offeror's assent to those terms [UCC 2–207(1)]. **■EXAMPLE 14.14** Philips offers to sell Hundert 650 pounds of turkey thighs at a specified price and with specified delivery terms. Hundert responds, "I accept your offer for 650 pounds of turkey thighs *on the condition that you give me ninety days to pay for them.*" Hundert's response will be construed not as an acceptance but as a counteroffer, which Philips may or may not accept. ■

Additional Terms May Be Stricken.   The UCC provides yet another option for dealing with conflicting terms in the parties' writings. Section 2–207(3) states that conduct by both parties that recognizes the existence of a contract is sufficient to establish a contract for the sale of goods even though the writings of the parties do not otherwise establish a contract. In this situation, "the terms of the particular contract will consist of those terms on which the writings of the parties agree, together with any supplementary terms incorporated under any other provisions of this Act." In a dispute over contract terms, this provision allows a court simply to strike from the contract those terms on which the parties do not agree.

■EXAMPLE 14.15 SMT Marketing orders goods over the phone from Brigg Sales, Inc., which ships the goods with an acknowledgment form (confirming the order) to SMT. SMT accepts and pays for the goods. The parties' writings do not establish a contract, but there is no question that a contract exists. If a dispute arises over the terms, such as the extent of any warranties, UCC 2–207(3) provides the governing rule. ■

The fact that a merchant's acceptance frequently contains additional terms or even terms that conflict with those of the offer is often referred to as the "battle of the forms." Although the drafters of UCC 2–207 tried to eliminate this battle, the problem of differing contract terms still arises in commercial settings, particularly when contracts are based on the merchants' forms, such as order forms and confirmation forms.

Consideration

The common law rule that a contract requires consideration also applies to sales and lease contracts. Unlike the common law, however, the UCC does not require a contract modification to be supported by new consideration. An agreement modifying a contract for the sale or lease of goods "needs no consideration to be binding" [UCC 2–209(1), 2A–208(1)].

Modifications Must Be Made in Good Faith   Of course, a contract modification must be sought in good faith [UCC 1–203]. **■EXAMPLE 14.16** Allied, Inc., agrees to lease a new recreational vehicle (RV) to Louise for a stated monthly payment. Subsequently, a sudden shift in the market makes it difficult for Allied to lease the new RV to Louise at the contract price without suffering a loss. Allied tells Louise of the situation, and she agrees to pay an additional sum for the lease of the RV. Later Louise reconsiders and refuses to pay more than the original price. Under the UCC, Louise's promise to modify the contract needs no consideration to be binding. Hence, she is bound by the modified contract. ■

In this example, a shift in the market is a *good faith* reason for contract modification. What if there really was no shift in the market, however, and Allied knew that Louise needed to lease the new RV immediately but refused to deliver it unless she agreed to pay a higher price? This attempt at extortion through modification without a legitimate commercial reason would be ineffective because it would violate the duty of good faith. Allied would not be permitted to enforce the higher price.

When Modification without Consideration Requires a Writing   In some situations, an agreement to modify a sales or lease contract without consideration must be in writing to be enforceable. If the contract itself prohibits any changes to the contract unless they are in a signed writing, for instance, then only those changes agreed to in a signed writing are enforceable. If a consumer (nonmerchant buyer) is dealing with a merchant and the merchant supplies the form that contains a prohibition against oral modification, the consumer must sign a separate acknowledgment of such a clause [UCC 2–209(2), 2A–208(2)].

Also, under Article 2, any modification that brings a sales contract under the Statute of Frauds must usually be in writing to be enforceable. Thus, if an oral contract for the sale of goods priced at $400 is modified so that the contract goods are now priced at $600, the modification must be in writing to be enforceable [UCC 2–209(3)]. (This is because the UCC's Statute of Frauds provision, as you will read shortly, requires a written record of sales contracts for goods priced at $500 or more.) If, however, the buyer accepts delivery of the goods after the modification, he or she is bound to the $600 price [UCC 2–201(3)(c)]. (Unlike Article 2, Article 2A does not say whether a lease as modified needs to satisfy the Statute of Frauds.)

The Statute of Frauds

The UCC contains Statute of Frauds provisions covering sales and lease contracts. Under these provisions, sales contracts for goods priced at $500 or more and lease contracts requiring payments of $1,000 or more must be in writing to be enforceable [UCC 2–201(1), 2A–201(1)]. (Note that these low threshold amounts may eventually be raised.)

Sufficiency of the Writing   The UCC has greatly relaxed the requirements for the sufficiency of a writing to satisfy the Statute of Frauds. A writing or a memorandum will be sufficient as long as it indicates that the parties intended to form a contract and as long as it is signed by the party (or agent of the party—see Chapter 22) against whom enforcement is sought. The contract normally will not be enforceable beyond the quantity of goods shown in the writing, however. All other terms can be proved in court by oral testimony. For leases, the writing must reasonably identify and describe the goods leased and the lease term.

Special Rules for Contracts between Merchants   Once again, the UCC provides a special rule for merchants.[9] Merchants can satisfy the requirements of a writing for the Statute of Frauds if, after the parties have agreed orally, one of the merchants sends a signed written confirmation to the other merchant. The communication must indicate the terms of the agreement, and the merchant receiving the confirmation must have reason to know of its contents. Unless the merchant who receives the confirmation gives written

notice of objection to its contents within ten days after receipt, the writing is sufficient against the receiving merchant, even though she or he has not signed anything [UCC 2–201(2)].

■**EXAMPLE 14.17** Alfonso is a merchant-buyer in Cleveland. He contracts over the telephone to purchase $6,000 worth of spare aircraft parts from Goldstein, a merchant-seller in New York City. Two days later, Goldstein sends a written confirmation detailing the terms of the oral contract, and Alfonso subsequently receives it. If Alfonso does not notify Goldstein in writing of his objection to the contents of the confirmation within ten days of receipt, Alfonso cannot raise the Statute of Frauds as a defense against the enforcement of the oral contract. ■

Note that the written confirmation need not be a traditional paper document with a handwritten signature. Courts have held that an e-mail confirming the order and including the company's typed name was sufficient to satisfy the UCC's Statute of Frauds. For a discussion of a case involving this issue, see this chapter's *Adapting the Law to the Online Environment* feature on the following page.

Exceptions   In addition to the special rules for merchants, the UCC defines three exceptions to the writing requirements of the Statute of Frauds. An oral contract for the sale of goods priced at $500 or more or the lease of goods involving total payments of $1,000 or more will be enforceable despite the absence of a writing in the circumstances discussed in the following subsections [UCC 2–201(3), 2A–201(4)]. These exceptions and other ways in which sales law differs from general contract law are summarized in Exhibit 14–2 on page 283.

Specially Manufactured Goods.   An oral contract is enforceable if (1) it is for goods that are specially manufactured for a particular buyer or specially manufactured or obtained for a particular lessee, (2) these goods are not suitable for resale or lease to others in the ordinary course of the seller's or lessor's business, and (3) the seller or lessor has substantially started to manufacture the goods or has made commitments for their manufacture or procurement. In this situation, once the seller or lessor has taken action, the buyer or lessee cannot repudiate the agreement claiming the Statute of Frauds as a defense.

■**EXAMPLE 14.18** Womach orders custom-made draperies for her new boutique. The price is $6,000, and the contract is oral. When the merchant-seller manufactures the draperies and tenders delivery to Womach, she refuses to pay for them even though the job has been completed on time. Womach claims that she is not liable because the contract was oral. Clearly, if the unique style and color of the draperies make it improbable that the seller can find another buyer, Womach is liable to the seller. Note that the seller must have made a

---

9. Note that this rule applies only to sales (under Article 2); there is no corresponding rule that applies to leases (under Article 2A). According to the comments accompanying UCC 2A–201 (Article 2A's Statute of Frauds), the "between merchants" provision was not included because "the number of such transactions involving leases, as opposed to sales, was thought to be modest."

Applying the Statute of Frauds to E-Mail Confirmations

Many contracts require a writing to satisfy the Statute of Frauds. As more and more contracts are negotiated orally or through e-mail, the question arises as to whether e-mail communications can fulfill the writing requirement. This issue was at the heart of a case involving a textile merchandising company and its supplier.

Was There an Enforceable Contract?

Bazak International Corporation contracted to buy numerous pairs of jeans from Tarrant Apparel Group for a total price of around $2 million. After a series of disputes between the companies, Tarrant sold the jeans to a third party at a higher price. Bazak sued for breach of contract. Tarrant claimed that the contract was not enforceable because there was no signed writing.

Although the parties never drew up a written contract, they did engage in a series of e-mail transmissions. In one, Bazak provided details of the purchase and attached a letter on its own company stationery. Bazak claimed that this e-mail constituted a written confirmation that satisfied the Statute of Frauds. Tarrant disagreed, arguing that (1) because an e-mail transmission is electronic, it cannot qualify as a written confirmation of the agreement; (2) the e-mail was not a written memorandum between merchants because it was not signed; and (3) using e-mail was not an appropriate means of communication in the apparel industry.

The Court Rules in Favor of E-Mail Communications

The court ruled against all of Tarrant's arguments. Even though the e-mails were "intangible messages," they still qualified as writings. The court pointed out that faxes, telexes, and telegrams are all intangible forms of communication while they are being transmitted. Whether an e-mail is printed on paper or saved on a server, it remains "an objectively observable and tangible record that such a confirmation exists." Additionally, a signed writing does not necessarily mean a piece of paper to which a signature is physically applied. In this case, the e-mail attachment, consisting of a letter on company letterhead with the company president's typed "signature," was sufficient. Finally, stating that e-mail was an inappropriate method of communication meant very little. Tarrant would have to prove that the parties' prior course of dealing and trade usage in the apparel industry rarely involved e-mails. The court found that there was evidence to the contrary.[a]

Indeed, a court in a subsequent case involving the apparel industry applied the same reasoning to allow a breach of contract claim to go forward based on an e-mail confirmation. Great White Bear, LLC, a clothing maker, alleged that Mervyns, LLC, had agreed to purchase $11.7 million in clothing from the company. After placing only $2.3 million in orders, Mervyns informed Great White Bear that it would not place any more orders. Great White Bear filed a lawsuit, claiming that an e-mail confirmation between the two merchants was sufficient to satisfy the Statute of Frauds. The court agreed, noting that "there are no rigid requirements as to the form or content of a confirmatory writing."[b]

FOR CRITICAL ANALYSIS *Are there any trades or industries in today's environment for which e-mail confirmation would be inappropriate? Explain.*

---

a. *Bazak International Corp. v. Tarrant Apparel Group,* 378 F.Supp.2d 377 (S.D.N.Y. 2005).
b. *Great White Bear, LLC v. Mervyns, LLC,* __ F.Supp.2d __, 2007 WL 1295747 (S.D.N.Y. 2007).

---

substantial beginning in manufacturing the specialized item prior to the buyer's repudiation. (Here, the manufacture was completed.) Of course, the court must still be convinced by evidence of the terms of the oral contract. ∎

Admissions. An oral contract for the sale or lease of goods is enforceable if the party against whom enforcement of the contract is sought admits in pleadings, testimony, or other court proceedings that a contract for sale was made. In this situation, the contract will be enforceable even though it was oral, but enforceability will be limited to the quantity of goods admitted.

■EXAMPLE 14.19 Lane and Byron negotiate an agreement over the telephone. During the negotiations, Lane requests a delivery price for five hundred gallons of gasoline and a separate price for seven hundred gallons of gasoline. Byron replies that the price would be the same, $3.50 per gallon. Lane orally orders five hundred gallons. Byron honestly believes that Lane ordered seven hundred gallons and tenders that amount. Lane refuses the shipment of seven hundred gallons,

EXHIBIT 14–2 Major Differences between Contract Law and Sales Law

	CONTRACT LAW	SALES LAW
Contract Terms	Contract must contain all material terms.	Open terms are acceptable, if parties intended to form a contract, but the contract is not enforceable beyond quantity term.
Acceptance	Mirror image rule applies. If additional terms are added in acceptance, counteroffer is created.	Additional terms will not negate acceptance unless acceptance is made expressly conditional on assent to the additional terms.
Contract Modification	Modification requires consideration.	Modification does not require consideration.
Irrevocable Offers	Option contracts (with consideration).	Merchants' firm offers (without consideration).
Statute of Frauds Requirements	All material terms must be included in the writing.	Writing is required only for the sale of goods of $500 or more, but contract is not enforceable beyond quantity specified. Merchants can satisfy the requirement by a confirmatory memorandum evidencing their agreement. *Exceptions:* 1. Specially manufactured goods. 2. Admissions by party against whom enforcement is sought. 3. Partial performance.

and Byron sues for breach. In his pleadings and testimony, Lane admits that an oral contract was made, but only for five hundred gallons. Because Lane admits the existence of the oral contract, Lane cannot plead the Statute of Frauds as a defense. The contract is enforceable, however, only to the extent of the quantity admitted (five hundred gallons). ■

Partial Performance.   An oral contract for the sale or lease of goods is enforceable if payment has been made and accepted or goods have been received and accepted. This is the "partial performance" exception. The oral contract will be enforced at least to the extent that performance *actually* took place.

■EXAMPLE 14.20 Allan orally contracts to lease to Opus Enterprises a thousand chairs at $2 each to be used during a one-day concert. Before delivery, Opus sends Allan a check for $1,000, which Allan cashes. Later, when Allan attempts to deliver the chairs, Opus refuses delivery, claiming the Statute of Frauds as a defense, and demands the return of its $1,000. Under the UCC's partial performance rule, Allan can enforce the oral contract by tender of delivery of five hundred chairs for the $1,000 accepted. Similarly, if Opus had made no payment but had accepted the delivery of five hundred chairs from Allan, the oral contract would have been enforceable against Opus for $1,000, the lease payment due for the five hundred chairs delivered. ■

The Parol Evidence Rule

If the parties intended the terms set forth in the contract as a complete and final expression of their agreement, then the terms of the contract cannot be contradicted by evidence of any prior agreements or contemporaneous oral agreements. As discussed in Chapter 10, this principle of law is known as the *parol evidence rule.* If, however, the writing contains only some of the terms that the parties agreed on and not others, then the contract is not fully integrated.

When a court finds that the terms of the agreement are not fully integrated, then the court may allow evidence of *consistent additional terms* to explain or supplement the terms stated in the contract. The court may also allow the parties to submit evidence of *course of dealing, usage of trade,* and *course of performance* when the contract was only partially integrated [UCC 2–202, 2A–202]. A court will not under any circumstances allow the parties to submit evidence that contradicts the stated terms (this is also the rule under the common law of contracts).

Course of Dealing and Usage of Trade Under the UCC, the meaning of any agreement, evidenced by the language of the parties and by their actions, must be interpreted in light of commercial practices and other surrounding circumstances. In interpreting a commercial agreement, the court will assume that the course of prior dealing between the parties and the general usage of trade were taken into account when the agreement was phrased.

A **course of dealing** is a sequence of previous actions and communications between the parties to a particular transaction that establishes a common basis for their understanding [UCC 1–205(1)]. A course of dealing is restricted to the sequence of conduct between the parties in their transactions previous to the agreement.

Usage of trade is defined as any practice or method of dealing having such regularity of observance in a place, vocation, or trade as to justify an expectation that it will be observed with respect to the transaction in question [UCC 1–205(2)]. The express terms of an agreement and an applicable course of dealing or usage of trade will be construed to be consistent with each other whenever reasonable. When such a construction is *unreasonable*, however, the express terms in the agreement will prevail [UCC 1–205(4)].

Course of Performance A **course of performance** is the conduct that occurs under the terms of a particular agreement. Presumably, the parties themselves know best what they meant by their words, and the course of performance actually undertaken under their agreement is the best indication of what they meant [UCC 2–208(1), 2A–207(1)].

■EXAMPLE 14.21 Janson's Lumber Company contracts with Barrymore to sell Barrymore a specified number of "two-by-fours." The lumber in fact does not measure 2 inches by 4 inches but rather 1⅞ inches by 3¾ inches. Janson's agrees to deliver the lumber in five deliveries, and Barrymore, without objection, accepts the lumber in the first three deliveries. On the fourth delivery, however, Barrymore objects that the two-by-fours do not measure 2 inches by 4 inches. The course of performance in this transaction—that is, the fact that Barrymore accepted three deliveries without objection under the agreement—is relevant in determining that here the term *two-by-four* actually means "1⅞ by 3¾." Janson's can also prove that two-by-fours need not be exactly 2 inches by 4 inches by applying usage of trade, course of prior dealing, or both. Janson's can, for example, show that in previous transactions, Barrymore took 1⅞-by-3¾-inch lumber without objection. In addition, Janson's can show that in the lumber trade, two-by-fours are commonly 1⅞ inches by 3¾ inches. ■

Rules of Construction The UCC provides *rules of construction* for interpreting contracts. Express terms, course of performance, course of dealing, and usage of trade are to be construed together when they do not contradict one another. When such a construction is unreasonable, however, the following order of priority controls: (1) express terms, (2) course of performance, (3) course of dealing, and (4) usage of trade [UCC 1–205(4), 2–208(2), 2A–207(2)].

Unconscionability

As discussed in Chapter 9, an unconscionable contract is one that is so unfair and one sided that it would be unreasonable to enforce it. The UCC allows the court to evaluate a contract or any clause in a contract, and if the court deems it to have been unconscionable at the time it was made, the court can (1) refuse to enforce the contract, (2) enforce the remainder of the contract without the unconscionable clause, or (3) limit the application of any unconscionable clauses to avoid an unconscionable result [UCC 2–302, 2A–108]. The following landmark case illustrates an early application of the UCC's unconscionability provisions.

CASE 14.3	**Jones v. Star Credit Corp.**

LANDMARK AND CLASSIC CASES

Supreme Court of New York, Nassau County, 59 Misc.2d 189, 298 N.Y.S.2d 264 (1969).

FACTS The Joneses, the plaintiffs, agreed to purchase a freezer for $900 as the result of a salesperson's visit to their home. Tax and financing charges raised the total price to $1,439.69. At trial, the freezer was found to have a maximum retail value of approximately $300. The plaintiffs, who had made payments totaling $619.88, brought a suit in a New York state court to have the purchase contract declared unconscionable under the UCC.

ISSUE Can this contract be denied enforcement on the ground of unconscionability?

DECISION Yes. The court held that the contract was not enforceable as it stood, and the contract was reformed so that no further payments were required.

REASON The court relied on UCC 2–302(1), which states that if "the court as a matter of law finds the contract or any clause of the contract to have been unconscionable at the time

CASE 14.3–Continued

it was made, the court may * * * so limit the application of any unconscionable clause as to avoid any unconscionable result." The court then examined the disparity between the $900 purchase price and the $300 retail value, as well as the fact that the credit charges alone exceeded the retail value. These excessive charges were exacted despite the seller's knowledge of the plaintiffs' limited resources. The court reformed the contract so that the plaintiffs' payments, amounting to more than $600, were regarded as payment in full.

 FOR CRITICAL ANALYSIS–Legal Consideration *Why didn't the court rule that the Joneses, as adults, had made a decision of their own free will and therefore were bound by the terms of the contract, regardless of the difference between the freezer's contract price and its retail value?*

IMPACT OF THIS CASE ON TODAY'S LAW
Classical contract theory holds that a contract is a bargain in which the terms have been worked out freely between the parties. In many modern commercial transactions, this may not have happened. For example, standard-form contracts and leases are often signed by consumer-buyers who understand few of the terms used and who often do not even read them. The inclusion of Sections 2–302 and 2A–108 in the UCC gave the courts a means of policing such transactions, and the courts continue to use this means to prevent injustice.

RELEVANT WEB SITES *To locate information on the Web concerning* Jones v. Star Credit Corp., *go to this text's Web site at* **www.cengage.com/blaw/fbl**, *select "Chapter 14," and click on "URLs for Landmark Cases."*

■

CONTRACTS FOR THE INTERNATIONAL SALE OF GOODS

International sales contracts between firms or individuals located in different countries are governed by the 1980 United Nations Convention on Contracts for the International Sale of Goods (CISG). The CISG governs international contracts only if the countries of the parties to the contract have ratified the CISG and if the parties have not agreed that some other law will govern their contract. As of 2009, the CISG had been adopted by seventy countries, including the United States, Canada, Mexico, some Central and South American countries, and most European nations. This means that the CISG is the uniform international sales law of countries accounting for more than two-thirds of all global trade.

Applicability of the CISG

Essentially, the CISG is to international sales contracts what Article 2 of the UCC is to domestic sales contracts. As discussed in this chapter, in domestic transactions the UCC applies when the parties to a contract for a sale of goods have failed to specify in writing some important term concerning price, delivery, or the like. Similarly, whenever the parties subject to the CISG have failed to specify in writing the precise terms of a contract for the international sale of goods, the CISG will be applied. Unlike the UCC, *the CISG does not apply to consumer sales*, and neither the UCC nor the CISG applies to contracts for services.

Businesspersons must take special care when drafting international sales contracts to avoid problems caused by distance, including language differences and varying national laws. There are many special terms and clauses that are typically contained in international contracts for the sale of goods. (See Chapter 32 for a discussion of other laws that frame global business transactions.)

A Comparison of CISG and UCC Provisions

The provisions of the CISG, although similar for the most part to those of the UCC, differ from them in certain respects. Under Article 11 of the CISG, an international sales contract does not need to be evidenced by a writing or to be in any particular form. We look here at some differences between the UCC and the CISG with respect to contract formation. In the following chapters, we will continue to point out differences between the CISG and the UCC as they relate to the topics covered. These topics include risk of loss, performance, remedies, and warranties.

Offers Some differences between the UCC and the CISG have to do with offers. For instance, the UCC provides that a merchant's firm offer is irrevocable, even without consideration, if the merchant gives assurances in a signed writing. In contrast, under the CISG, an offer can become irrevocable without a signed writing. Article 16(2) of the CISG provides that an offer will be irrevocable if the merchant-offeror simply states orally that the offer is irrevocable or if the offeree reasonably relies on the offer as being irrevocable. In both of these situations, the offer will be irrevocable even without a writing and without consideration.

Another difference is that, under the UCC, if the price term is left open, the court will determine "a reasonable price at the time for delivery" [UCC 2–305(1)]. Under the CISG, however, the price term must be specified, or at least provisions for its specification must be included in the agreement; otherwise, normally no contract will exist.

Acceptances Like UCC 2–207, the CISG provides that a contract can be formed even though the acceptance contains additional terms, unless the additional terms materially alter the contract. Under the CISG, however, the definition of a "material alteration" includes virtually any change in the terms. If an additional term relates to payment, quality, quantity, price, time and place of delivery, extent of one party's liability to the other, or the settlement of disputes, the CISG considers the added term a "material alteration." In effect, then, the CISG requires that the terms of the acceptance mirror those of the offer.

Additionally, under the UCC, an acceptance is effective on dispatch. Under the CISG, however, a contract is not created until the offeror receives the acceptance. (The offer becomes irrevocable, however, when the acceptance is sent.) Also, in contrast to the UCC, the CISG provides that acceptance by performance does not require that the offeror be notified of the performance.

REVIEWING The Formation of Sales and Lease Contracts

Guy Holcomb owns and operates Oasis Goodtime Emporium, an adult entertainment establishment. Holcomb wanted to create an adult Internet system for Oasis that would offer customers adult theme videos and "live" chat room programs using performers at the club. On May 10, Holcomb signed a work order authorizing Crossroads Consulting Group (CCG) "to deliver a working prototype of a customer chat system, demonstrating the integration of live video and chatting in a Web browser." In exchange for creating the prototype, Holcomb agreed to pay CCG $64,697. On May 20, Holcomb signed an additional work order in the amount of $12,943 for CCG to install a customized firewall system. The work orders stated that Holcomb would make monthly installment payments to CCG, and both parties expected the work would be finished by September. Due to unforeseen problems largely attributable to system configuration and software incompatibility, completion of the project required more time than anticipated. By the end of the summer, the Web site was still not ready, and Holcomb had fallen behind in the payments to CCG. CCG was threatening to cease work and file a suit for breach of contract unless the bill was paid. Rather than make further payments, Holcomb wanted to abandon the Web site project. Using the information presented in the chapter, answer the following questions.

1 Would a court be likely to decide that the transaction between Holcomb and CCG was covered by the Uniform Commercial Code (UCC)? Why or why not?

2 Would a court be likely to consider Holcomb a merchant under the UCC? Why or why not?

3 Did the parties have a valid contract under the UCC? Explain.

4 Suppose that Holcomb and CCG meet in October in an attempt to resolve their problems. At that time, the parties reach an oral agreement that CCG will continue to work without demanding full payment of the past-due amounts and Holcomb will pay CCG $5,000 per week. Assuming that the contract falls under the UCC, is the oral agreement enforceable? Why or why not?

TERMS AND CONCEPTS

course of dealing 284
course of performance 284
firm offer 277
intangible property 273
lease 275
lease agreement 275

lessee 275
lessor 275
merchant 275
output contract 277
predominant-factor test 274
requirements contract 277

sale 273
sales contract 273
seasonably 278
tangible property 273
usage of trade 284

CHAPTER SUMMARY — The Formation of Sales and Lease Contracts

The Scope of the UCC (See pages 272–273.)	The UCC attempts to provide a consistent, uniform, and integrated framework of rules to deal with all phases *ordinarily arising* in a commercial sales or lease transaction, including contract formation, passage of title and risk of loss, performance, remedies, payment for goods, warehoused goods, and secured transactions.
The Scope of Article 2—Sales (See pages 273–275.)	Article 2 governs contracts for the sale of goods (tangible, movable personal property). The common law of contracts also applies to sales contracts to the extent that the common law has not been modified by the UCC. If there is a conflict between a common law rule and the UCC, the UCC controls.
The Scope of Article 2A—Leases (See page 275.)	Article 2A governs contracts for the lease of goods. Except that it applies to leases, instead of sales, of goods, Article 2A is essentially a repetition of Article 2 and varies only to reflect differences between sales and lease transactions.
The Formation of Sales and Lease Contracts—Offer and Acceptance (See pages 275–280.)	1. *Offer—* a. Not all terms have to be included for a contract to be formed (only the subject matter and quantity term must be specified). b. The price does not have to be included for a contract to be formed. c. Particulars of performance can be left open. d. A written and signed offer by a *merchant,* covering a period of three months or less, is irrevocable without payment of consideration. 2. *Acceptance—* a. Acceptance may be made by any reasonable means of communication; it is effective when dispatched. b. An offer can be accepted by a promise to ship or by prompt shipment of conforming goods, or by prompt shipment of nonconforming goods if not accompanied by a notice of accommodation. c. Acceptance by performance requires notice within a reasonable time; otherwise, the offer can be treated as lapsed. d. A definite expression of acceptance creates a contract even if the terms of the acceptance vary from those of the offer, unless the varied terms in the acceptance are expressly conditioned on the offeror's assent to those terms.
Consideration (See pages 280–281.)	A modification of a contract for the sale of goods does not require consideration.
The Statute of Frauds (See pages 281–283.)	1. All contracts for the sale of goods priced at $500 or more must be in writing. A writing is sufficient as long as it indicates a contract between the parties and is signed by the party against whom enforcement is sought. A contract is not enforceable beyond the quantity shown in the writing. 2. When written confirmation of an oral contract *between merchants* is not objected to in writing by the receiver within ten days, the contract is enforceable. 3. Exceptions to the requirement of a writing exist in the following situations: a. When the oral contract is for specially manufactured goods not suitable for resale to others, and the seller has substantially started to manufacture the goods. b. When the defendant admits in pleadings, testimony, or other court proceedings that an oral contract for the sale of goods was made. In this case, the contract will be enforceable to the extent of the quantity of goods admitted.

(Continued)

CHAPTER SUMMARY	The Formation of Sales and Lease Contracts—Continued
The Statute of Frauds—Continued	c. The oral agreement will be enforceable to the extent that payment has been received and accepted by the seller or to the extent that the goods have been received and accepted by the buyer.

The Parol Evidence Rule (See pages 283–284.)	1. The terms of a clearly and completely worded written contract cannot be contradicted by evidence of prior agreements or contemporaneous oral agreements.
	2. Evidence is admissible to clarify the terms of a writing in the following situations:
	  a. If the contract terms are ambiguous.
	  b. If evidence of course of dealing, usage of trade, or course of performance is necessary to learn or to clarify the intentions of the parties to the contract.

Unconscionability (See pages 284–285.)	An unconscionable contract is one that is so unfair and one sided that it would be unreasonable to enforce it. If the court deems a contract to have been unconscionable at the time it was made, the court can (1) refuse to enforce the contract, (2) refuse to enforce the unconscionable clause of the contract, or (3) limit the application of any unconscionable clauses to avoid an unconscionable result.
Contracts for the International Sale of Goods (See pages 285–286.)	International sales contracts are governed by the United Nations Convention on Contracts for the International Sale of Goods (CISG)—if the countries of the parties to the contract have ratified the CISG (and if the parties have not agreed that some other law will govern their contract). Essentially, the CISG is to international sales contracts what Article 2 of the UCC is to domestic sales contracts. Whenever parties who are subject to the CISG have failed to specify in writing the precise terms of a contract for the international sale of goods, the CISG will be applied.

FOR REVIEW

Answers for the even-numbered questions in this **For Review** *section can be found on this text's accompanying Web site at* **www.cengage.com/blaw/fbl**. *Select "Chapter 14" and click on "For Review."*

1 How do Article 2 and Article 2A of the UCC differ? What types of transactions does each article cover?

2 What is a merchant's firm offer?

3 If an offeree includes additional or different terms in an acceptance, will a contract result? If so, what happens to these terms?

4 Article 2 and Article 2A of the UCC both define several exceptions to the writing requirements of the Statute of Frauds. What are these exceptions?

5 What law governs contracts for the international sale of goods?

QUESTIONS AND CASE PROBLEMS

 ## HYPOTHETICAL SCENARIOS AND CASE PROBLEMS

14.1 Statute of Frauds. Fresher Foods, Inc., orally agreed to purchase from Dale Vernon, a farmer, one thousand bushels of corn for $1.25 per bushel. Fresher Foods paid $125 down and agreed to pay the remainder of the purchase price on delivery, which was scheduled for one week later. When Fresher Foods tendered the balance of $1,125 on the scheduled day of delivery and requested the corn, Vernon refused to deliver it. Fresher Foods sued Vernon for damages, claiming that Vernon had breached their oral contract. Can Fresher Foods recover? If so, to what extent?

14.2 Hypothetical Question with Sample Answer. M. M. Salinger, Inc., a retailer of television sets, orders one hundred model Color-X sets from manufacturer Fulsom. The order specifies the price and that the television sets are to be shipped via Interamerican Freightways on or before October 30. Fulsom receives the order on October 5. On October 8, Fulsom writes Salinger a letter indicating that it has received the order and that it will ship the sets as directed, at the specified price. Salinger receives this letter on October 10. On October 28, Fulsom, in preparing the shipment, discovers it has only ninety Color-X sets in stock. Fulsom ships the ninety Color-X sets and ten television sets of a different model, stating clearly on the invoice that the ten sets are being shipped only as an accommodation. Salinger claims that Fulsom is in breach of contract. Fulsom claims that there was not an acceptance and, therefore, no contract was formed. Explain who is correct, and why.

For a sample answer to Question 14.2, go to Appendix E at the end of this text.

14.3 Statute of Frauds. Quality Pork International is a Nebraska firm that makes and sells custom pork products. Rupari Food Services, Inc., buys food products and sells them to retail operations and food brokers. In November 1999, Midwest Brokerage arranged an oral contract between Quality and Rupari, under which Quality would ship three orders to Star Food Processing, Inc., and Rupari would pay for the products. Quality shipped the goods to Star and sent invoices to Rupari. In turn, Rupari billed Star for all three orders but paid Quality only for the first two (for $43,736.84 and $47,467.80, respectively), not for the third. Quality filed a suit in a Nebraska state court against Rupari, alleging breach of contract, to recover $44,051.98, the cost of the third order. Rupari argued that there was nothing in writing, as required by Section 2–201 of the Uniform Commercial Code (UCC), and thus there was no contract. What are the exceptions to the UCC's writing requirement? Do any of those exceptions apply here? Explain. [*Quality Pork International v. Rupari Food Services, Inc.*, 267 Neb. 474, 675 N.W.2d 642 (2004)]

14.4 Offer. In 1998, Johnson Controls, Inc. (JCI), began buying auto parts from Q. C. Onics Ventures, LP. For each part, JCI would inform Onics of its need and ask the price. Onics would analyze the specifications, contact its suppliers, and respond with a formal quotation. A quote listed a part's number and description, the price per unit, and an estimate of units available for a given year. A quote did not state payment terms, an acceptance date, the time of performance, warranties, or quantities. JCI would select a supplier and issue a purchase order for a part. The purchase order required the seller to supply all of JCI's requirements for the part but gave the buyer the right to end the deal at any time. Using this procedure, JCI issued hundreds of purchase orders. In July 2001, JCI terminated its relationship with Onics and began buying parts through another supplier. Onics filed a suit in a federal district court against Johnson, alleging breach of contract. Which documents—the price quotations or the purchase orders—constituted offers?

Which were acceptances? What effect would the answers to these questions have on the result in this case? Explain. [*Q. C. Onics Ventures, LP. v. Johnson Controls, Inc.*, __ F.Supp.2d __ (N.D.Ind. 2006)]

14.5 Case Problem with Sample Answer. Propulsion Technologies, Inc., a Louisiana firm doing business as (dba) PowerTech Marine Propellers, markets small steel boat propellers that are made by a unique tooling technique. Attwood Corp., a Michigan firm, operated a foundry (a place where metal is cast) in Mexico. In 1996, Attwood offered to produce castings of the propellers. Attwood promised to maintain quality, warrant the castings against defects, and obtain insurance to cover liability. In January 1997, the parties signed a letter that expressed these and other terms—Attwood was to be paid per casting, and twelve months' notice was required to terminate the deal—but the letter did not state a quantity. PowerTech provided the tooling. Attwood produced rough castings, which PowerTech refined by checking each propeller's pitch, machining its interior, grinding, balancing, polishing, and adding serial numbers and a rubber clutch. In October, Attwood told PowerTech that the foundry was closing. PowerTech filed a suit in a federal district court against Attwood, alleging, in part, breach of contract. One of the issues was whether their deal was subject to Article 2 of the Uniform Commercial Code. What type of transactions does Article 2 cover? Does the arrangement between PowerTech and Attwood qualify? Explain. [*Propulsion Technologies, Inc. v. Attwood Corp.*, 369 F.3d 896 (5th Cir. 2004)]

After you have answered Problem 14.5, compare your answer with the sample answer given on the Web site that accompanies this text. Go to www.cengage.com/blaw/fbl, select "Chapter 14," and click on "Case Problem with Sample Answer."

14.6 Parol Evidence. Clear Lakes Trout Co. operates a fish hatchery in Idaho. Rodney and Carla Griffith are trout growers. Clear Lakes agreed to sell "small trout" to the Griffiths, who agreed to sell the trout back when they had grown to "market size." At the time, in the trade "market size" referred to fish approximating one-pound live weight. The parties did business without a written agreement until September 1998, when they executed a contract with a six-year duration. The contract did not define "market size." All went well until September 2001, after which there was a demand for larger fish. Clear Lakes began taking deliveries later and in smaller loads, leaving the Griffiths with overcrowded ponds and other problems. In 2003, the Griffiths refused to accept more fish and filed a suit in an Idaho state court against Clear Lakes, alleging breach of contract. Clear Lakes argued that there was no contract because the parties had different interpretations of "market size." Clear Lakes claimed that "market size" varied according to whatever its customers demanded. The Griffiths asserted that the term referred to fish of about one-pound live weight. Is outside evidence admissible to explain the terms of a contract? Are there any exceptions that could apply in this case? If so, what is the likely result?

Explain. [*Griffith v. Clear Lakes Trout Co.*, 143 Idaho 733, 152 P.3d 604 (2007)]

14.7 **A Question of Ethics.** *Daniel Fox owned Fox & Lamberth Enterprises, Inc., a kitchen and bath remodeling business, in Dayton, Ohio. Fox leased a building from Carl and Bellulah Hussong. Craftsmen Home Improvement, Inc., also remodeled baths and kitchens. When Fox planned to close his business, Craftsmen expressed an interest in buying his showroom assets. Fox set a price of $50,000. Craftsmen's owners agreed and gave Fox a list of the desired items and "A Bill of Sale" that set the terms for payment. The parties did not discuss Fox's arrangement with the Hussongs, but Craftsmen expected to negotiate a new lease and extensively modified the premises, including removing some of the displays to its own showroom. When the Hussongs and Craftsmen could not agree on new terms, Craftsmen told Fox*

that the deal was off. [Fox & Lamberth Enterprises, Inc. v. Craftsmen Home Improvement, Inc., __ N.E.2d __ (Ohio App., 2 Dist. 2006)]

1 In Fox's suit in an Ohio state court for breach of contract, Craftsmen raised the Statute of Frauds as a defense. What are the requirements of the Statute of Frauds? Did the deal between Fox and Craftsmen meet these requirements? Did it fall under one of the exceptions? Explain.

2 Craftsmen also claimed that the "predominant factor" of its agreement with Fox was a lease for the Hussongs' building. What is the predominant-factor test? Does it apply here? In any event, is it fair to hold a party to a contract to buy a business's assets when the buyer is unable to negotiate a favorable lease of the premises on which the assets are located? Discuss.

CRITICAL THINKING AND WRITING ASSIGNMENTS

14.8 Critical Legal Thinking. Why is the designation *merchant* or *nonmerchant* important?

14.9 **Video Question.** Go to this text's Web site at **www.cengage.com/blaw/fbl** and select "Chapter 14." Click on "Video Questions" and view the video titled *Sales and Lease Contracts: Price as a Term.* Then answer the following questions.

1 Is Anna correct in assuming that a contract can exist even though the sales price for the computer equipment was not specified? Explain.

2 According to the Uniform Commercial Code (UCC), what conditions must be satisfied in order for a contract to be formed when certain terms are left open? What terms (in addition to price) can be left open?

3 Are the e-mail messages that Anna refers to sufficient proof of the contract?

4 Would parol evidence be admissible?

ACCESSING THE INTERNET

For updated links to resources available on the Web, as well as a variety of other materials, visit this text's Web site at

www.cengage.com/blaw/fbl

For information on proposed amendments to Articles 2 and 2A of the Uniform Commercial Code (UCC), go to the Web site of the National Conference of Commissioners on Uniform State Laws (NCCUSL) at

www.nccusl.org

The full text of the Contracts for the International Sale of Goods (CISG) is available online at the Pace University School of Law's Institute of International Commercial Law. Go to

cisgw3.law.pace.edu/cisg/text/treaty.html

To read an in-depth article comparing the provisions of the CISG and the UCC, go to

cisgw3.law.pace.edu/cisg/thesis/Oberman.html

PRACTICAL INTERNET EXERCISES

Go to this text's Web site at **www.cengage.com/blaw/fbl**, select "Chapter 14," and click on "Practical Internet Exercises." There you will find the following Internet research exercises that you can perform to learn more about the topics covered in this chapter.

PRACTICAL INTERNET EXERCISE 14–1 LEGAL PERSPECTIVE—Is It a Contract?

PRACTICAL INTERNET EXERCISE 14–2 MANAGEMENT PERSPECTIVE—A Checklist for Sales Contracts

BEFORE THE TEST

Go to this text's Web site at **www.cengage.com/blaw/fbl**, select "Chapter 14," and click on "Interactive Quizzes." You will find a number of interactive questions relating to this chapter.

CHAPTER 15
Title and Risk of Loss

LEARNING OBJECTIVES

AFTER READING THIS CHAPTER, YOU SHOULD BE ABLE TO ANSWER THE FOLLOWING QUESTIONS:

1 What is the significance of identifying goods to a contract?

2 If the parties to a contract do not expressly agree on when title to goods passes, what determines when title passes?

3 Risk of loss does not necessarily pass with title. If the parties to a contract do not expressly agree when risk passes and the goods are to be delivered without movement by the seller, when does risk pass?

4 Under what circumstances will the seller's title to goods being sold be void? When does a seller have voidable title?

5 At what point does the buyer acquire an insurable interest in goods subject to a sales contract? Can both the buyer and the seller have an insurable interest in the goods simultaneously?

A sale of goods transfers ownership rights in (title to) the goods from the seller to the buyer. Often, a sales contract is signed before the actual goods are available. For example, a sales contract for oranges might be signed in May, but the oranges may not be ready for picking and shipment until October. Any number of things can happen between the time the sales contract is signed and the time the goods are actually transferred into the buyer's possession. Fire, flood, or frost may destroy the orange groves, or the oranges may be lost or damaged in transit. The same problems may occur under a lease contract. Because of these possibilities, it is important to know the rights and liabilities of the parties between the time the contract is formed and the time the goods are actually received by the buyer or lessee.

Before the creation of the Uniform Commercial Code (UCC), *title*—the right of ownership—was the central concept in sales law, controlling all issues of rights and remedies of the parties to a sales contract. In some situations, title is still relevant under the UCC, and the UCC has special rules for determining who has title. These rules will be discussed in the sections that follow. In most situations, however, the UCC has replaced the concept of title with three other con-

cepts: (1) identification, (2) risk of loss, and (3) insurable interest. By breaking down the transfer of ownership into these three components, the drafters of the UCC have created greater precision in the law governing sales—leaving as few points of law as possible "to the decision of the judges."

In lease contracts, of course, the lessor-owner of the goods retains title. Hence, the UCC's provisions relating to passage of title do not apply to leased goods. Other concepts discussed in this chapter, though, including identification, risk of loss, and insurable interest, relate to lease contracts as well as to sales contracts.

IDENTIFICATION

Before any interest in specific goods can pass from the seller or lessor to the buyer or lessee, the goods must be (1) in existence and (2) identified as the specific goods designated in the contract. **Identification** takes place when specific goods are designated as the subject matter of a sales or lease contract. Title and risk of loss cannot pass from seller to buyer unless the goods are identified to the contract. (As mentioned, title to leased goods remains with the lessor—or, if the owner is a third party, with that party. The lessee does not acquire title to leased goods.) Identification is significant because it gives the buyer or lessee the right to insure (or to have an insurable interest in) the goods and the right to recover from third parties who damage the goods.

In their contract, the parties can agree on when identification will take place, but identification is effective to pass title and risk of loss to the buyer only *after* the goods are considered to be in existence. If the parties do not so specify, however, the UCC provisions discussed here determine when identification takes place [UCC 2–501(1), 2A–217].

Existing Goods

If the contract calls for the sale or lease of specific and ascertained goods that are already in existence, identification takes place at the time the contract is made. For example, you contract to purchase or lease a fleet of five cars by the vehicle identification numbers of the cars.

Future Goods

If a sale involves unborn animals to be born within twelve months after contracting, identification takes place when the animals are conceived. If a lease involves any unborn animals, identification occurs when the animals are conceived. If a sale involves crops that are to be harvested within twelve months (or the next harvest season occurring after contracting, whichever is longer), identification takes place when the crops are planted; otherwise, identification takes place when they begin to grow. In a sale or lease of any other future goods, identification occurs when the goods are shipped, marked, or otherwise designated by the seller or lessor as the goods to which the contract refers.

Goods That Are Part of a Larger Mass

As a general rule, goods that are part of a larger mass are identified when the goods are marked, shipped, or somehow designated by the seller or lessor as the particular goods that are the subject of the contract. **■EXAMPLE 15.1** A buyer orders 1,000 cases of beans from a 10,000-case lot. Until the seller separates the 1,000 cases of beans from the 10,000-case lot, title and risk of loss remain with the seller. ■

A common exception to this rule involves fungible goods. **Fungible goods** are goods that are alike by physical nature, by agreement, or by trade usage. Typical examples are specific grades or types of wheat, oil, and wine, usually stored in large containers. If these goods are held or intended to be held by owners as tenants in common (owners having jointly owned shares undivided from the entire mass), a seller-owner

can pass title and risk of loss to the buyer without an actual separation. The buyer replaces the seller as an owner in common [UCC 2–105(4)].

■EXAMPLE 15.2 Alvarez, Braudel, and Carpenter are farmers. They deposit, respectively, 5,000 bushels, 3,000 bushels, and 2,000 bushels of grain of the same grade and quality in a grain elevator. The three become owners in common, with Alvarez owning 50 percent of the 10,000 bushels, Braudel 30 percent, and Carpenter 20 percent. Alvarez contracts to sell her 5,000 bushels of grain to Tamur; because the goods are fungible, she can pass title and risk of loss to Tamur without physically separating the 5,000 bushels. Tamur now becomes an owner in common with Braudel and Carpenter. ■

PASSAGE OF TITLE

Once goods exist and are identified, the provisions of UCC 2–401 apply to the passage of title. In virtually all subsections of UCC 2–401, the words "unless otherwise explicitly agreed" appear, meaning that any explicit understanding between the buyer and the seller determines when title passes. Without an explicit agreement to the contrary, title passes to the buyer at the time and the place the seller performs by delivering the goods [UCC 2–401(2)]. For example, if a person buys cattle at a livestock auction, title will pass to the buyer when the cattle are physically delivered to him or her (unless, of course, the parties agree otherwise).[1]

Shipment and Destination Contracts

Unless otherwise agreed, delivery arrangements can determine when title passes from the seller to the buyer. In a **shipment contract,** the seller is required or authorized to ship goods by carrier, such as a trucking company. Under a shipment contract, the seller is required only to deliver conforming goods into the hands of a carrier, and title passes to the buyer at the time and place of shipment [UCC 2–401(2)(a)]. Generally, *all contracts are assumed to be shipment contracts if nothing to the contrary is stated in the contract.*

In a **destination contract,** the seller is required to deliver the goods to a particular destination, usually directly to the buyer, but sometimes to another party designated by the buyer. Title passes to the buyer when the goods are *tendered* at that destination [UCC 2–401(2)(b)]. As you will read in Chapter 16, *tender of delivery* occurs when the seller places or holds conforming goods at the buyer's disposal (with any necessary notice), enabling the buyer to take possession [UCC 2–503(1)].

---

1. See, for example, *In re Stewart,* 274 Bankr. 503 (W.D.Ark. 2002).

Delivery without Movement of the Goods

When the sales contract does not call for the seller to ship or deliver the goods (when the buyer is to pick up the goods), the passage of title depends on whether the seller must deliver a **document of title,** such as a bill of lading or a warehouse receipt, to the buyer. A *bill of lading* is a receipt for goods that is signed by a carrier and serves as a contract for the transportation of the goods. A *warehouse receipt* is a receipt issued by a warehouser for goods stored in a warehouse.

When a document of title is required, title passes to the buyer *when and where the document is delivered.* Thus, if the goods are stored in a warehouse, title passes to the buyer when the appropriate documents are delivered to the buyer. The goods never move. In fact, the buyer can choose to leave the goods at the same warehouse for a period of time, and the buyer's title to those goods will be unaffected.

When no documents of title are required and delivery is made without moving the goods, title passes at the time and place the sales contract is made, if the goods have already been identified. If the goods have not been identified, title does not pass until identification occurs. **■EXAMPLE 15.3** Juan sells lumber to Bodan. They agree that Bodan will pick up the lumber at the lumberyard. If the lumber has been identified (segregated, marked, or in any other way distinguished from all other lumber), title passes to Bodan when the contract is signed. If the lumber is still in large storage bins at the lumberyard, title does not pass to Bodan until the particular pieces of lumber to be sold under this contract are identified [UCC 2–401(3)]. ■

Sales or Leases by Nonowners

Problems occur when persons who acquire goods with *imperfect* titles attempt to sell or lease them. Sections 2–402 and 2–403 of the UCC deal with the rights of two parties who lay claim to the same goods, sold with imperfect titles. Generally, a buyer acquires at least whatever title the seller has to the goods sold.

The UCC also protects a person who leases such goods from the buyer. Of course, a lessee does not acquire whatever title the lessor has to the goods. A lessee acquires a right to possess and use the goods—that is, a *leasehold interest.* A lessee acquires whatever leasehold interest the lessor has or has

the power to transfer, subject to the lease contract [UCC 2A–303, 2A–304, 2A–305].

Void Title A buyer may unknowingly purchase goods from a seller who is not the owner of the goods. If the seller is a thief, the seller's title is *void*—legally, no title exists. Thus, the buyer acquires no title, and the real owner can reclaim the goods from the buyer. If the goods were only leased, the same result would occur because the lessor has no leasehold interest to transfer.

 ■EXAMPLE 15.4 If Saki steals diamonds owned by Maren, Saki has a *void title* to those diamonds. If Saki sells the diamonds to Shannon, Maren can reclaim them from Shannon even though Shannon acted in good faith and honestly was not aware that the goods were stolen. ■ (Article 2A contains similar provisions for leases.)

Voidable Title A seller has *voidable title* if the goods that she or he is selling were obtained by fraud, paid for with a check that is later dishonored, purchased from a minor, or purchased on credit when the seller was insolvent. (Under the UCC, a person is **insolvent** when that person ceases to "pay his [or her] debts in the ordinary course of business or cannot pay his [or her] debts as they become due or is insolvent within the meaning of federal bankruptcy law" [UCC 1–201(23)].)

Good Faith Purchasers. In contrast to a seller with *void title,* a seller with *voidable title* has the power to transfer good title to a good faith purchaser for value. A **good faith purchaser** is one who buys without knowledge of circumstances that would make a person of ordinary prudence inquire about the validity of the seller's title to the goods. One who purchases *for value* gives legally sufficient consideration (value) for the goods purchased. The real, or original, owner cannot recover goods from a good faith purchaser for value [UCC 2–403(1)].[2] If the buyer of the goods is not a good faith purchaser for value, then the actual owner of the goods can reclaim them from the buyer (or from the seller, if the goods are still in the seller's possession).

The dispute in the following case arose from the transfer of a car without its document of title to a third party who never suspected that the seller would turn out to be a thief.

---

2. The real owner could, of course, sue the person who initially obtained voidable title to the goods.

CASE 15.1 **Empire Fire and Marine Insurance Co. v. Banc Auto, Inc.**

Pennsylvania Superior Court, 897 A.2d 1247 (2006).

FACTS In July 2001, Euro Motorcars, an auto dealership in Bethesda, Maryland, agreed to sell a used 2000 Mercedes-Benz S430 for $56,500 to an intermediary, Patrick Figueroa,

CASE 15.1—Continued

whose job was to buy and sell cars among dealers. The parties understood that Euro would turn over a document of title to the Mercedes when the price was paid. Banc Auto, Inc., a dealer in Manheim, Pennsylvania, agreed to buy the car from Figueroa for $56,500, plus a percentage of Banc's profit in reselling the vehicle. Banc issued a check to Figueroa. Figueroa cashed the check but did not pay Euro. Consequently, Euro refused to deliver the document of title. Figueroa was convicted of stealing the check and paid Banc $10,000 in restitution. Empire Fire and Marine Insurance Company, Banc's insurer, filed a suit in a Pennsylvania state court against Banc and Euro, asking the court to determine Empire's obligation to its insured. The court ordered the Mercedes to be sold and awarded Banc the $40,000 in proceeds. Euro appealed to a state intermediate appellate court, asserting that Banc was not entitled to the funds because Euro still possessed the document of title.

ISSUE Did Euro's possession of the document of title affect Banc's award?

DECISION No. The state intermediate appellate court held that because Euro had given possession of the Mercedes to Figueroa with the intent of later providing the document of title, Figueroa had obtained voidable title to the car. Because Figueroa had a voidable title when he transferred the car to Banc, Banc was a good faith purchaser and was entitled to the damages awarded. The court affirmed the lower court's ruling in Banc's favor.

REASON The state intermediate appellate court pointed out that under UCC 2–401(2), "title passes to the buyer at the time and place at which the seller completes his performance with reference to the physical delivery of the goods * * * even though a document of title is to be delivered at a different time." Under UCC 2–403, "a person with voidable title has power to transfer a good title to a good faith purchaser for value * * * even though * * * the delivery was procured through fraud punishable as larcenous [theft] under the criminal law." Applying these principles to the case, the court concluded that when Euro delivered the Mercedes to Figueroa, he obtained voidable title to the car and was free to sell it to Banc or any other buyer in good faith. The court noted that a person who obtains goods through the assent of the original owner obtains a voidable title, whereas a person who obtains the goods without the original owner's consent has a void title. It was immaterial that Figueroa obtained the car through criminal fraud, because there was no evidence that Banc knew or had any reason to suspect Figueroa of fraud in the transaction.

 FOR CRITICAL ANALYSIS—Ethical Consideration *Given that Euro Motorcars had had prior dealings with Figueroa on a number of occasions and did not suspect that Figueroa would commit theft, was the result in this case fair? Why or why not?*

Voidable Title and Leases. The same rules apply in circumstances involving leases. A lessor with voidable title has the power to transfer a valid leasehold interest to a good faith lessee for value. The real owner cannot recover the goods, except as permitted by the terms of the lease. The real owner can, however, receive all proceeds arising from the lease, as well as a transfer of all rights, title, and interest as lessor under the lease, including the lessor's interest in the return of the goods when the lease expires [UCC 2A–305(1)].

The Entrustment Rule According to UCC 2–403(2), entrusting goods to a merchant *who deals in goods of that kind* gives the merchant the power to transfer all rights to *a buyer in the ordinary course of business.* This is known as the **entrustment rule.** A buyer in the ordinary course of business is a person who—in good faith and without knowledge that the sale violates the rights of another party—buys goods in the ordinary course from a merchant (other than a pawnbro-

ker) in the business of selling goods of that kind [UCC 1–201(9)].

The entrustment rule basically allows innocent buyers to obtain legitimate title to goods purchased from merchants even if the merchants do not have good title. ▪**EXAMPLE 15.5** Jan leaves her watch with a jeweler to be repaired. The jeweler sells both new and used watches. The jeweler sells Jan's watch to Kim, a customer who does not know that the jeweler has no right to sell it. Kim, as a good faith buyer, gets good title against Jan's claim of ownership.[3]

Note, however, that Kim obtains only those rights held by the person entrusting the goods (here, Jan). Suppose instead that Jan had stolen the watch from Greg and then left it with the jeweler to be repaired. The jeweler then sold it to Kim.

---

3. Jan, of course, can sue the jeweler for the tort of conversion (or trespass to personal property) to obtain damages equivalent to the cash value of the watch (see Chapter 4).

Kim would obtain good title against Jan, who entrusted the watch to the jeweler, but not against Greg (the real owner), who neither entrusted the watch to Jan nor authorized Jan to entrust it. ■

Red Elvis, an artwork by Andy Warhol, was at the center of the dispute over title in the following case.

CASE 15.2 **Lindholm v. Brant**

Supreme Court of Connecticut, 283 Conn. 65, 925 A.2d 1048 (2007).

FACTS In 1987, Kerstin Lindholm of Greenwich, Connecticut, bought a silkscreen by Andy Warhol titled *Red Elvis* from Anders Malmberg, a Swedish art dealer, for $300,000. In 1998, Lindholm loaned *Red Elvis* to the Guggenheim Museum in New York City for an exhibition to tour Europe. Peter Brant, who was on the museum's board of trustees and also a Greenwich resident, believed that Lindholm was the owner. Stellan Holm, a Swedish art dealer who had bought and sold other Warhol works with Brant, told him, however, that Malmberg had bought it and would sell it for $2.9 million. Malmberg refused Brant's request to provide a copy of an invoice between Lindholm and himself on the ground that such documents normally and customarily are not disclosed in art deals. To determine whether Malmberg had good title, Brant hired an attorney to search the Art Loss Register (an international database of stolen and missing artworks) and other sources. No problems were found, but Brant was cautioned that this provided only "minimal assurances." Brant's attorney drafted a formal contract, which conditioned payment on the delivery of *Red Elvis* to a warehouse in Denmark. The exchange took place in April 2000.[a] Lindholm filed a suit in a Connecticut state court against Brant, alleging conversion,

among other things. The court issued a judgment in Brant's favor. Lindholm appealed to the Connecticut Supreme Court.

ISSUE Was Brant a buyer in the ordinary course of business when he purchased *Red Elvis*?

DECISION Yes. The Connecticut Supreme Court affirmed the judgment of the lower court concluding that Brant was a buyer in the ordinary course of business and therefore took all rights to *Red Elvis* under UCC 2–403(2).

REASON The appellate court pointed out that "a person buys goods in good faith if there is honesty in fact and the observance of reasonable commercial standards of fair dealing in the conduct or transaction concerned." In most art transactions, the buyer has no reason for concern about the seller's ability to convey good title; such transactions are completed by a handshake and an invoice exchange. Sophisticated buyers and sellers normally do not obtain signed invoices from the original seller to the dealer prior to a transaction. "Nor is it an ordinary or customary practice to request the underlying invoice corroborating [substantiating] information as to a dealer's authority to convey title." In sum, it is customary to rely on representations made by "respected dealers regarding their authority to sell works of art."

 FOR CRITICAL ANALYSIS—Global Consideration *Considering the international locales in this case, why was Lindholm able to bring an action against Brant in Connecticut?*

---

a. Unaware of this deal, Lindholm accepted a Japanese buyer's offer of $4.6 million for *Red Elvis*. The funds were wired to Malmberg, who kept them. Lindholm filed a criminal complaint against Malmberg in Sweden. In 2003, a Swedish court convicted Malmberg of "gross fraud embezzlement." The court awarded Lindholm $4.6 million and other relief.

■

RISK OF LOSS

Under the UCC, risk of loss does not necessarily pass with title. When risk of loss passes from a seller or lessor to a buyer or lessee is generally determined by the contract between the parties. Sometimes, the contract states expressly when the risk of loss passes. At other times, it does not, and a court must interpret the performance and delivery terms of the contract to determine whether the risk has passed.

Delivery with Movement of the Goods—Carrier Cases

When the agreement does not state when risk of loss passes, the courts apply the following rules to cases involving movement of the goods (carrier cases).

Contract Terms Specific delivery terms in the contract can determine when risk of loss passes to the buyer. The terms that have traditionally been used in contracts within the United States are listed and defined in Exhibit 15–1 on the next page. *Unless the parties agree otherwise,* these terms determine which party will pay the costs of delivering the goods and who bears the risk of loss.

Shipment Contracts   In a shipment contract, if the seller or lessor is required or authorized to ship goods by carrier (but is not required to deliver them to a particular final destination), risk of loss passes to the buyer or lessee when the goods are duly delivered to the carrier [UCC 2–319(1)(a), 2–509(1)(a), 2A–219(2)(a)].

■**EXAMPLE 15.6** A seller in Texas sells five hundred cases of grapefruit to a buyer in New York, F.O.B. Houston (free on board in Houston—that is, the buyer pays the transportation charges from Houston). The contract authorizes shipment by carrier; it does not require that the seller tender the grapefruit in New York. Risk passes to the buyer when conforming goods are properly placed in the possession of the carrier. If the goods are damaged in transit, the loss is the buyer's. (Actually, buyers have recourse against carriers, subject to certain limitations, and buyers usually insure the goods from the time the goods leave the seller.) ■

The following case illustrates how the application of a contract's delivery term can affect a buyer's recovery for goods damaged in transit.

CASE 15.3   **Spray-Tek, Inc. v. Robbins Motor Transportation, Inc.**

United States District Court, Western District of Wisconsin, 426 F.Supp.2d 875 (2006).

FACTS Spray-Tek, Inc., is engaged in the business of commercial dehydration of food-flavoring, pharmaceutical, and chemical products. In 2003, Spray-Tek contracted with Niro, Inc., for the design and manufacture of a customized dryer for $1,161,500. Niro agreed to ship the dryer "F.O.B. points of manufacture in the U.S.A." from its facility in Hudson, Wisconsin, to Spray-Tek's facility in Bethlehem, Pennsylvania. Niro arranged for Robbins Motor Transportation, Inc., to pick up the dryer on October 18, 2004. Robbins acknowledged in the bill of lading that it received the dryer "in apparent good order." On October 28, while in transit through Baltimore, Maryland, the dryer struck an overpass and fell off Robbins's truck. It was declared a total loss. Niro made a replacement, delivered it, and billed Spray-Tek an additional $233,100. Spray-Tek filed a suit in a federal district court against Robbins under a federal statute known as the "Carmack Amendment"[a] to recover the replacement cost and other expenses. A plaintiff must show three elements to recover under the Carmack Amendment: (1) delivery of goods to a carrier in good condition, (2) their arrival in damaged condition, and (3) proof of the amount of damages. Spray-Tek filed a motion for summary judgment. Robbins argued, among other things, that Spray-Tek was not entitled to recovery because it did not own the dryer during its transport.

ISSUE Does a contract that provides for the delivery of goods "F.O.B. points of manufacture in the U.S.A." mean that the goods become the buyer's property when placed in the possession of a carrier?

DECISION Yes. The court issued a summary judgment in Spray-Tek's favor on this issue. "The drying chamber became plaintiff's property once it was placed on board the delivery truck at its point of manufacture in Hudson, Wisconsin." The court concluded, however, that other issues, including a possible contractual limitation on the amount of damages, involved genuine questions of material fact to be resolved at trial.

REASON The court determined that there was no dispute as to the first and second elements required for recovery under the Carmack Amendment: the dryer was delivered in good condition to Robbins, and on its "arrival," it was damaged. The question was whether, at the time the damage occurred, the title and the risk of loss had passed to Spray-Tek. The court held that the contract between Spray-Tek and Niro established Spray-Tek as the owner of the dryer when it was damaged. One clause in the contract provided that Spray-Tek would bear the risk of loss of the dryer after its delivery to the shipping point if delivery "F.O.B. shipping point" was specified. Another of the contract's terms of sale specified "F.O.B. points of manufacture in the U.S.A." Thus, "here the shipping point and the manufacturing point were identical. Accordingly, the F.O.B. points of manufacture language contained within plaintiff's contract demonstrates that plaintiff bore the risk of

---

a. The Carmack Amendment is part of the Interstate Commerce Act and can be found at 49 U.S.C. Section 14706. Its purpose is to remove some of the uncertainty surrounding a carrier's liability when an interstate shipment of goods is damaged.

CASE 15.3–Continues next page

CASE 15.3–Continued

loss once the drying chamber departed from Niro's Hudson, Wisconsin facility." Although Robbins argued that Spray-Tek had not satisfied the third element, failing to show what "it is obligated to pay for the dryer," the court pointed out that Niro's invoice for the replacement dryer established the amount of damages.

WHAT IF THE FACTS WERE DIFFERENT?
Would the outcome of this case have been different if the contract between Spray-Tek and Niro had specified "F.O.B. Bethlehem, Pennsylvania"? Explain.

■

Destination Contracts In a destination contract, the risk of loss passes to the buyer or lessee when the goods are tendered to the buyer or lessee at the specified destination [UCC 2–319(1)(b), 2–509(1)(b), 2A–219(2)(b)]. In Example 15.6, if the contract had been F.O.B. New York, the risk of loss during transit to New York would have been the seller's.

Delivery without Movement of the Goods

The UCC also addresses situations in which the seller or lessor is required neither to ship nor to deliver the goods. Frequently, the buyer or lessee is to pick up the goods from the seller or lessor, or the goods are held by a bailee. Under the UCC, a **bailee** is a party who, by a bill of lading, warehouse receipt, or other document of title, acknowledges possession of goods and/or contracts to deliver them. A warehousing company, for example, or a trucking company that normally issues documents of title for the goods it receives is a bailee.[4]

Goods Held by the Seller If the goods are held by the seller, a document of title usually is not used. If the seller is not a merchant, the risk of loss to goods held by the seller passes to the buyer on *tender of delivery* [UCC 2–509(3)]. If the seller is a merchant, risk of loss to goods held by the seller passes to the buyer when the buyer *actually takes physical possession of the goods* [UCC 2–509(3)]. **■EXAMPLE 15.7** Henry Ganno purchases lumber at a lumberyard, and an employee at the lumberyard loads it onto Ganno's truck with a forklift. Once the truck is loaded, the risk of loss passes to Ganno because he has taken physical possession of the goods. In the event that Ganno suffers a loss driving away from the lumberyard, he—not the lumberyard—will bear the burden of that loss.[5] ■

In respect to leases, the risk of loss passes to the lessee on the lessee's receipt of the goods if the lessor—or supplier, in a finance lease (see Chapter 14)—is a merchant. Otherwise, the risk passes to the lessee on tender of delivery [UCC

---

4. Bailments will be discussed in detail in Chapter 28.

5. *Ganno v. Lanoga Corp.*, 119 Wash.App. 310, 80 P.3d 180 (2003).

EXHIBIT 15–1 Contract Terms–Definitions

The contract terms listed and defined in this exhibit help to determine which party will bear the costs of delivery and when risk of loss will pass from the seller to the buyer.

F.O.B. (free on board)—Indicates that the selling price of goods includes transportation costs to the specific F.O.B. place named in the contract. The seller pays the expenses and carries the risk of loss to the F.O.B. place named [UCC 2–319(1)]. If the named place is the place from which the goods are shipped (for example, the seller's city or place of business), the contract is a shipment contract. If the named place is the place to which the goods are to be shipped (for example, the buyer's city or place of business), the contract is a destination contract.

F.A.S. (free alongside)—Requires that the seller, at his or her own expense and risk, deliver the goods alongside the carrier before risk passes to the buyer [UCC 2–319(2)].

C.I.F. or **C.&F.** (cost, insurance, and freight or just cost and freight)—Requires, among other things, that the seller "put the goods in the possession of a carrier" before risk passes to the buyer [UCC 2–320(2)]. (These are basically pricing terms, and the contracts remain shipment contracts, not destination contracts.)

Delivery ex-ship (delivery from the carrying vessel)—Means that risk of loss does not pass to the buyer until the goods are properly unloaded from the ship or other carrier [UCC 2–322].

2A–219(c)]. ■**EXAMPLE 15.8** Erikson Crane leases a helicopter from Jevis, Ltd., which is in the business of renting aircraft. While Erikson's pilot is on the way to Idaho to pick up the particular helicopter, the helicopter is damaged during an unexpected storm. In this situation, Jevis is a merchant-lessor, so it bears the risk of loss to the leased helicopter until Erikson takes possession of the helicopter. ■

Goods Held by a Bailee When a bailee is holding goods for a person who has contracted to sell them and the goods are to be delivered without being moved, the goods are usually represented by a negotiable or nonnegotiable document of title (a bill of lading or a warehouse receipt). Risk of loss passes to the buyer when (1) the buyer receives a negotiable document of title for the goods, (2) the bailee acknowledges the buyer's right to possess the goods, or (3) the buyer receives a nonnegotiable document of title or a writing (record) directing the bailee to deliver the goods *and* has had a *reasonable time* to present the document to the bailee and demand the goods. Obviously, if the bailee refuses to honor the document, the risk of loss remains with the seller [UCC 2–503(4)(b), 2–509(2)].

With respect to leases, if goods held by a bailee are to be delivered without being moved, the risk of loss passes to the lessee on acknowledgment by the bailee of the lessee's right to possession of the goods [UCC 2A–219(2)(b)]. These rules are summarized in Exhibit 15–2.

Conditional Sales

Buyers and sellers sometimes form sales contracts that are conditioned either on the buyer's approval of the goods or on the buyer's resale of the goods. Under such contracts, the buyer is in possession of the goods. Sometimes, however, questions arise as to whether the buyer or seller should bear the loss if, for example, the goods are damaged or stolen while in the possession of the buyer.

Sale-or-Return Contracts A **sale or return** is a type of contract by which the buyer (usually a merchant) purchases goods primarily for resale, but has the right to return part or all of the goods (undo the sale) in lieu of payment if the goods fail to be resold. Basically, a sale or return is a sale of goods in the present, which may be undone at the buyer's option within a specified time period. When the buyer receives possession at the time of the sale, title and risk of loss pass to the buyer. Title and risk of loss remain with the buyer until the buyer returns the goods to the seller within the time period specified. If the buyer fails to return the goods within this time period, the sale is finalized. The return of the goods is made at the buyer's risk and expense. Goods held under a sale-or-return contract are subject to the claims of the buyer's creditors while they are in the buyer's possession.

The UCC treats a **consignment** as a sale or return. Under a consignment, the owner of goods (the *consignor*) delivers them

---

EXHIBIT 15–2 **Delivery without Movement of the Goods**

CONCEPT	DESCRIPTION
Goods Not Represented by a Document of Title	Unless otherwise agreed, if the goods are not represented by a document of title, title and risk pass as follows: 1. Title passes on the formation of the contract [UCC 2–401(3)(b)]. 2. If the seller or lessor (or supplier, in a finance lease) is a merchant, risk passes to the buyer or lessee on the buyer's or lessee's receipt of the goods. If the seller or lessor is a nonmerchant, risk passes to the buyer or lessee on the seller's or lessor's *tender* of delivery of the goods [UCC 2–509(3), 2A–219(c)].
Goods Represented by a Document of Title	Unless otherwise agreed, if the goods are represented by a document of title, title and risk pass to the buyer when: 1. The buyer receives a negotiable document of title for the goods, or 2. The bailee acknowledges the buyer's right to possess the goods, or 3. The buyer receives a nonnegotiable document of title and has had a reasonable time to present the document to the bailee and demand the goods [UCC 2–503(4)(b), 2–509(2)].
Leased Goods Held by a Bailee	If leased goods held by a bailee are to be delivered without being moved, the risk of loss passes to the lessee on acknowledgment by the bailee of the lessee's right to possession of the goods [UCC 2A–219(2)(b)].

to another (the *consignee*) for the consignee to sell. If the consignee sells the goods, the consignee must pay the consignor for them. If the consignee does not sell the goods, they may simply be returned to the consignor. While the goods are in the possession of the consignee, the consignee holds title to them, and creditors of the consignee will prevail over the consignor in any action to repossess the goods [UCC 2–326(3)].

Sale-on-Approval Contracts   When a seller offers to sell goods to a buyer and permits the buyer to take the goods on a trial basis, a **sale on approval** is usually made. The term *sale* here is a misnomer, as only an *offer* to sell has been made, along with a *bailment* created by the buyer's possession. (A bailment is a temporary delivery of personal property into the care of another—see Chapter 28.)

Therefore, title and risk of loss (from causes beyond the buyer's control) remain with the seller until the buyer accepts (approves) the offer. Acceptance can be made expressly, by any act inconsistent with the trial purpose or the seller's ownership, or by the buyer's election not to return the goods within the trial period. If the buyer does not wish to accept, the buyer may notify the seller of that fact within the trial period, and the return is made at the seller's expense and risk [UCC 2–327(1)]. Goods held on approval are not subject to the claims of the buyer's creditors until acceptance.

It is often difficult to determine whether a particular transaction involves a contract for a sale on approval, a contract for a sale or return, or a contract for sale. The UCC states that (unless otherwise agreed) "if the goods are delivered primarily for use," the transaction is a sale on approval; "if the goods are delivered primarily for resale," the transaction is a sale or return [UCC 2–326(1)].

Risk of Loss When a Sales or Lease Contract Is Breached

A sales or lease contract can be breached in many ways, and the transfer of risk operates differently depending on which party breaches. Generally, the party in breach bears the risk of loss.

When the Seller or Lessor Breaches   If the goods are so nonconforming that the buyer has the right to reject them, the risk of loss does not pass to the buyer until the defects are **cured** (that is, until the goods are repaired, replaced, or discounted in price by the seller) or until the buyer accepts the goods in spite of their defects (thus waiving the right to reject). ■**EXAMPLE 15.9** A buyer orders ten white refrigerators from a seller, F.O.B. the seller's plant. The seller ships amber refrigerators instead. The amber refrigerators (nonconforming goods)

are damaged in transit. The risk of loss falls on the seller. Had the seller shipped white refrigerators (conforming goods) instead, the risk would have fallen on the buyer [UCC 2–510(1)]. ■

If a buyer accepts a shipment of goods and later discovers a defect, acceptance can be revoked. Revocation allows the buyer to pass the risk of loss back to the seller, at least to the extent that the buyer's insurance does not cover the loss [UCC 2–510(2)].

In regard to leases, Article 2A states a similar rule. If the lessor or supplier tenders goods that are so nonconforming that the lessee has the right to reject them, the risk of loss remains with the lessor or the supplier until cure or acceptance [UCC 2A–220(1)(a)]. If the lessee, after acceptance, revokes his or her acceptance of nonconforming goods, the revocation passes the risk of loss back to the seller or supplier, to the extent that the lessee's insurance does not cover the loss [UCC 2A–220(1)(b)].

When the Buyer or Lessee Breaches   The general rule is that when a buyer or lessee breaches a contract, the risk of loss immediately shifts to the buyer or lessee. This rule has three important limitations:

1 The seller or lessor must already have identified the contract goods.

2 The buyer or lessee bears the risk for only a *commercially reasonable* time after the seller or lessor has learned of the breach.

3 The buyer or lessee is liable only to the extent of any deficiency in the seller's insurance coverage [UCC 2–510(3), 2A–220(2)].

INSURABLE INTEREST

Parties to sales and lease contracts often obtain insurance coverage to protect against damage, loss, or destruction of goods. Any party purchasing insurance, however, must have a sufficient interest in the insured item to obtain a valid policy. Insurance laws—not the UCC—determine sufficiency. The UCC is helpful, however, because it contains certain rules regarding insurable interests in goods.

Insurable Interest of the Buyer or Lessee

A buyer or lessee has an **insurable interest** in identified goods. The moment the contract goods are identified by the seller or lessor, the buyer or lessee has a special property interest that allows the buyer or lessee to obtain necessary insurance coverage for those goods even before the risk of loss has passed [UCC 2–501(1), 2A–218(1)].

Under the rule stated in UCC 2–501(1)(c), buyers obtain an insurable interest in crops by identification, which occurs when the crops are planted or otherwise become growing crops, provided that the contract is for "the sale of crops to be harvested within twelve months or the next normal harvest season after contracting, whichever is longer." ■EXAMPLE 15.10 In March, a farmer sells a cotton crop that he hopes to harvest in October. When the crop is planted, the buyer acquires an insurable interest in it because those goods (the cotton crop) are identified to the sales contract between the seller and the buyer. ■

Insurable Interest of the Seller or Lessor

A seller has an insurable interest in goods if she or he retains title to the goods. Even after title passes to the buyer, a seller who has a security interest in the goods (a right to secure payment—see Chapter 20) still has an insurable interest and can insure the goods [UCC 2–501(2)]. Hence, both a buyer and a seller can have an insurable interest in identical goods at the same time. Of course, the buyer or seller must sustain an actual loss to have the right to recover from an insurance company. In regard to leases, the lessor retains an insurable interest in leased goods until the lessee exercises an option to buy and the risk of loss has passed to the lessee [UCC 2A–218(3)].

 **PREVENTING LEGAL DISPUTES**

Sellers frequently retain a security interest in goods because the buyer has not yet paid for the goods at the time of delivery. A seller who has a security interest in goods can still insure those goods, even though title has passed to the buyer. A business that sells and ships goods should usually maintain adequate insurance on all goods sold at least until it is assured that the buyer will pay for the goods. Remember that losses can still occur after the goods have been delivered to the buyer. Do not assume that the buyer's insurance will pay for losses the seller sustains. Insurance is essential to protect against loss.

REVIEWING Title and Risk of Loss

In December, Mendoza agreed to buy the broccoli grown on one hundred acres of Willow Glen's one-thousand-acre broccoli farm. The sales contract specified F.O.B. Willow Glen's field by Falcon Trucking. The broccoli was to be planted in February and harvested in March of the following year. Using the information presented in the chapter, answer the following questions.

1 At what point is a crop of broccoli identified to the contract under the UCC? Explain. Why is identification significant?

2 When does title to the broccoli pass from Willow Glen to Mendoza under the terms of this contract? Why?

3 Suppose that while in transit, Falcon's truck overturned and spilled the entire load. Who bears the loss, Mendoza or Willow Glen?

4 Suppose that instead of buying fresh broccoli, Mendoza had contracted with Willow Glen to purchase one thousand cases of frozen broccoli from Willow Glen's processing plant. The highest grade of broccoli is packaged under the "FreshBest" label, and everything else is packaged under the "FamilyPac" label. Although the contract specified that Mendoza was to receive FreshBest broccoli, Falcon Trucking delivered FamilyPac broccoli to Mendoza. If Mendoza refuses to accept the broccoli, who bears the loss?

TERMS AND CONCEPTS

bailee 298
consignment 299
cure 300
destination contract 293
document of title 294

entrustment rule 295
fungible goods 293
good faith purchaser 294
identification 292
insolvent 294

insurable interest 300
sale on approval 300
sale or return 299
shipment contract 293

CHAPTER SUMMARY　Title and Risk of Loss

Shipment Contracts (See page 293.)	In the absence of an agreement, title and risk pass on the seller's or lessor's delivery of conforming goods to the carrier [UCC 2–319(1)(a), 2–401(2)(a), 2–509(1)(a), 2A–219(2)(a)].
Destination Contracts (See page 293.)	In the absence of an agreement, title and risk pass on the seller's or lessor's *tender* of delivery of conforming goods to the buyer or lessee at the point of destination [UCC 2–319(1)(b), 2–401(2)(b), 2–509(1)(b), 2A–219(2)(b)].
Delivery without Movement of the Goods (See page 294.)	In the absence of an agreement, if the goods are not represented by a document of title, title passes on the formation of the contract, and risk passes when the goods are delivered to a merchant or when the seller or lessor tenders delivery to a nonmerchant. See Exhibit 15–2 on page 299 for the detailed rules stated in the UCC.
Sales or Leases by Nonowners (See pages 294–296.)	Between the owner and a good faith purchaser or between the lessee and a sublessee: 1. *Void title*—Owner prevails [UCC 2–403(1)]. 2. *Voidable title*—Buyer prevails [UCC 2–403(1)]. 3. *Entrusting to a merchant*—Buyer or sublessee prevails [UCC 2–403(2), (3); 2A–305(2)].
Sale-or-Return Contracts (See page 299.)	When the buyer receives possession of the goods, title and risk of loss pass to the buyer, but the buyer has the option of returning the goods to the seller. If the buyer returns the goods to the seller, title and risk of loss pass back to the seller [UCC 2–326(3)].
Sale-on-Approval Contracts (See page 300.)	Title and risk of loss (from causes beyond the buyer's control) remain with the seller until the buyer approves (accepts) the offer [UCC 2–327(1)].
Risk of Loss When a Sales or Lease Contract Is Breached (See page 300.)	1. If the seller or lessor breaches by tendering nonconforming goods that are rejected by the buyer or lessee, the risk of loss does not pass to the buyer or lessee until the defects are cured (unless the buyer or lessee accepts the goods in spite of their defects, thus waiving the right to reject) [UCC 2–510(1), 2A–220(1)]. 2. If the buyer or lessee breaches the contract, the risk of loss immediately shifts to the buyer or lessee. Limitations to this rule are as follows [UCC 2–510(3), 2A–220(2)]: a. The seller or lessor must already have identified the contract goods. b. The buyer or lessee bears the risk for only a commercially reasonable time after the seller or lessor has learned of the breach. c. The buyer or lessee is liable only to the extent of any deficiency in the seller's or lessor's insurance coverage.
Insurable Interest (See pages 300–301.)	1. Buyers and lessees have an insurable interest in goods the moment the goods are identified to the contract by the seller or the lessor [UCC 2–501(1), 2A–218(1)]. 2. Sellers have an insurable interest in goods as long as they have (a) title to the goods or (b) a security interest in the goods [UCC 2–501(2)]. Lessors have an insurable interest in leased goods until the lessee exercises an option to buy and the risk of loss has passed to the lessee [UCC 2A–218(3)].

FOR REVIEW

Answers for the even-numbered questions in this **For Review** *section can be found on this text's accompanying Web site at* **www.cengage.com/blaw/fbl**. *Select "Chapter 15" and click on "For Review."*

1 What is the significance of identifying goods to a contract?

2 If the parties to a contract do not expressly agree on when title to goods passes, what determines when title passes?

3 Risk of loss does not necessarily pass with title. If the parties to a contract do not expressly agree when risk passes and the goods are to be delivered without movement by the seller, when does risk pass?

4 Under what circumstances will the seller's title to goods being sold be void? When does a seller have voidable title?

5 At what point does the buyer acquire an insurable interest in goods subject to a sales contract? Can both the buyer and the seller have an insurable interest in the goods simultaneously?

QUESTIONS AND CASE PROBLEMS

 HYPOTHETICAL SCENARIOS AND CASE PROBLEMS

15.1 Sales by Nonowners. In the following situations, two parties lay claim to the same goods sold. Explain which party would prevail in each situation.

1 Terry steals Dom's iPod and sells it to Blake, an innocent purchaser, for value. Dom learns that Blake has the iPod and demands its return.

2 Karlin takes her laptop computer for repair to Orken, a merchant who sells new and used computers. By accident, one of Orken's employees sells Karlin's laptop computer to Grady, an innocent purchaser-customer, who takes possession. Karlin wants her laptop back from Grady.

15.2 Hypothetical Question with Sample Answer. When will risk of loss pass from the seller to the buyer under each of the following contracts, assuming the parties have not expressly agreed on when risk of loss will pass?

1 A New York seller contracts with a San Francisco buyer to ship goods to the buyer F.O.B. San Francisco.

2 A New York seller contracts with a San Francisco buyer to ship goods to the buyer in San Francisco. There is no indication as to whether the shipment will be F.O.B. New York or F.O.B. San Francisco.

3 A seller contracts with a buyer to sell goods located on the seller's premises. The buyer pays for the goods and arranges to pick them up the next week at the seller's place of business.

4 A seller contracts with a buyer to sell goods located in a warehouse.

For a sample answer to Question 15.2, go to Appendix E at the end of this text.

15.3 Sales by Nonowners. Julian Makepeace, who had been declared mentally incompetent by a court, sold his diamond ring to Golding for value. Golding later sold the ring to Carmichael for value. Neither Golding nor Carmichael knew that Makepeace had been adjudged mentally incompetent by a court. Farrel, who had been appointed as Makepeace's guardian, subsequently learned that the diamond ring was in Carmichael's possession and demanded its return from Carmichael. Who has legal ownership of the ring? Why?

15.4 Case Problem with Sample Answer. William Bisby gave an all-terrain vehicle (ATV) to Del City Cycle in Enid, Oklahoma, to sell on his behalf. Joseph Maddox bought the ATV, but paid for it with a check written on a closed checking account. The bank refused to honor the check. Before Del City or Bisby could reclaim the ATV, however, Maddox sold it to Aaron Jordan, who sold it to Shannon Skaggs. In 2003, the Enid police seized the ATV from Skaggs. Bisby filed a suit in a state court against the state and Skaggs, claiming that he was the owner of the ATV and asking the court to return it to him. Skaggs objected. Is there a distinction between the ownership interests of a party who steals an item and a party who acquires the item with a dishonored check? What was the status of Skaggs's title, if any, to the ATV? Which of the many parties involved in this case should the court rule has "good" title to the ATV? [*State v. Skaggs*, 140 P.3d 576 (Okla.Civ.App. Div. 3 2006)]

After you have answered Problem 15.4, compare your answer with the sample answer given on the Web site that accompanies this text. Go to www.cengage.com/blaw/fbl, select "Chapter 15," and click on "Case Problem with Sample Answer."

15.5 Shipment and Destination Contracts. In 2003, Karen Pearson and Steve and Tara Carlson agreed to buy a 2004 Dynasty recreational vehicle (RV) from DeMartini's RV Sales in Grass Valley, California. On September 29, Pearson, the Carlsons, and DeMartini's signed a contract providing that "seller agrees to deliver the vehicle to you on the date this contract is signed." The buyers made a payment of $145,000 on the total price of $356,416 the next day, when they also signed a form acknowledging that the RV had been inspected and accepted. They agreed to return later to have the RV transported out of state for delivery (to avoid paying state sales tax on the purchase). On October 7 Steve Carlson returned to DeMartini's to ride with the seller's driver to Nevada to consummate the out-of-state delivery. When the RV developed problems, Pearson and the Carlsons filed a suit in a federal district court against the RV's manufacturer, Monaco Coach Corp., alleging, breach of warranty under state law. The applicable statute is expressly limited to goods sold in California. Monaco argued that this RV had been sold in Nevada. How does the UCC define a sale? What does the

UCC provide with respect to the passage of title? How do these provisions apply here? Discuss. [*Carlson v. Monaco Coach Corp.*, 486 F.Supp.2d 1127 (E.D.Cal. 2007)]

15.6 **A Question of Ethics.** *Kenneth West agreed to sell his car, a 1975 Corvette, to a man representing himself as Robert Wilson. In exchange for a cashier's check, West signed over the Corvette's title to Wilson and gave him the car. Ten days later, when West learned that the cashier's check was a forgery, he filed a stolen vehicle report with the police. The police could not immediately locate Wilson or the Corvette, however, and the case grew cold. Nearly two and a half years later, the police found the Corvette in the possession of Tammy Roberts, who also had the certificate of title. She said that she had bought the car from her brother, who had obtained it through an ad in the newspaper. West filed a suit in a Colorado state court against Roberts to reclaim the car.*

The court applied Colorado Revised Statutes Section 4-2-403 (Colorado's version of Section 2–403 of the Uniform Commercial Code) to determine the vehicle's rightful owner. [West v. Roberts, 143 P.3d 1037 (Colo. 2006)]

1 Under UCC 2–403, what title, if any, to the Corvette did "Wilson" acquire? What was the status of Roberts's title, if any, assuming that she bought the car without knowledge of circumstances that would make a person of ordinary prudence inquire about the validity of the seller's title? In whose favor should the court rule? Explain.

2 Should the original owner of a vehicle that he or she relinquished due to fraud be allowed to recover the vehicle from a good faith purchaser? If not, whom might the original owner sue for recovery? What is the ethical principle underlying your answer to these questions? Discuss.

CRITICAL THINKING AND WRITING ASSIGNMENT

15.7 **Video Question.** Go to this text's Web site at **www.cengage.com/blaw/fbl** and select "Chapter 15." Click on "Video Questions" and view the video titled *Risk of Loss.* Then answer the following questions.

1 Does Oscar have a right to refuse the shipment because the lettuce is wilted? Why or why not? What type of contract is involved in this video?

2 Does Oscar have a right to refuse the shipment because the lettuce is not organic butter crunch lettuce? Why or why not?

3 Assume that you are in Oscar's position—that is, you are buying produce for a supermarket. What different approaches might you take to avoid having to pay for a delivery of wilted produce?

ACCESSING THE INTERNET

For updated links to resources available on the Web, as well as a variety of other materials, visit this text's Web site at

www.cengage.com/blaw/fbl

For a brief historical review of commercial law, go to

www.answers.com/topic/commercial-law

For an overview of bills of lading, go to

www.law.cornell.edu/ucc/7/overview.html

PRACTICAL INTERNET EXERCISES

Go to this text's Web site at **www.cengage.com/blaw/fbl**, select "Chapter 15," and click on "Practical Internet Exercises." There you will find the following Internet research exercises that you can perform to learn more about the topics covered in this chapter.

PRACTICAL INTERNET EXERCISE 15-1 LEGAL PERSPECTIVE—The Entrustment Rule

PRACTICAL INTERNET EXERCISE 15-2 MANAGEMENT PERSPECTIVE—Passage of Title

BEFORE THE TEST

Go to this text's Web site at **www.cengage.com/blaw/fbl**, select "Chapter 15," and click on "Interactive Quizzes." You will find a number of interactive questions relating to this chapter.

CHAPTER 16
Performance and Breach of Sales and Lease Contracts

LEARNING OBJECTIVES

AFTER READING THIS CHAPTER, YOU SHOULD BE ABLE TO ANSWER THE FOLLOWING QUESTIONS:

1 What are the respective obligations of the parties under a contract for the sale or lease of goods?

2 What is the perfect tender rule? What are some important exceptions to this rule that apply to sales and lease contracts?

3 What options are available to the nonbreaching party when the other party to a sales or lease contract repudiates the contract prior to the time for performance?

4 What remedies are available to a seller or lessor when the buyer or lessee breaches the contract? What remedies are available to a buyer or lessee if the seller or lessor breaches the contract?

5 In contracts subject to the UCC, are parties free to limit the remedies available to the nonbreaching party on a breach of contract? If so, in what ways?

he performance that is required of the parties under a sales or lease contract consists of the duties and obligations each party has under the terms of the contract. Keep in mind that "duties and obligations" under the terms of the contract include those specified by the agreement, by custom, and by the Uniform Commercial Code (UCC). In this chapter, we examine the basic performance obligations of the parties under a sales or lease contract.

Sometimes, when circumstances make it difficult for a person to carry out the promised performance, the contract may be breached. When breach occurs, the aggrieved party looks for remedies—which we discuss in the second half of the chapter.

PERFORMANCE OBLIGATIONS

As discussed in previous chapters, the standards of good faith and commercial reasonableness are read into every contract. These standards provide a framework in which the parties can specify particulars of performance. Thus, when one party delays specifying particulars of performance for an unreasonable period of time or fails to cooperate with the other party,

the innocent party is excused from any resulting delay in performance. The innocent party can proceed to perform in any reasonable manner, and the other party's failure to specify particulars or to cooperate can be treated as a breach of contract. Good faith is a question of fact for the jury.

In the performance of a sales or lease contract, the basic obligation of the seller or lessor is to *transfer and deliver conforming goods*. The basic obligation of the buyer or lessee is to *accept and pay for conforming goods* in accordance with the contract [UCC 2–301, 2A–516(1)]. Overall performance of a sales or lease contract is controlled by the agreement between the parties. When the contract is unclear and disputes arise, the courts look to the UCC and impose standards of good faith and commercial reasonableness. For a discussion of the importance of good faith in contract performance, see this chapter's *Management Perspective* feature on the following page.

OBLIGATIONS OF THE SELLER OR LESSOR

The major obligation of the seller or lessor under a sales or lease contract is to tender conforming goods to the buyer or lessee.

MANAGEMENT PERSPECTIVE
Good Faith and Fair Dealing

Management Faces a Legal Issue

As discussed elsewhere, all contracts governed by the Uniform Commercial Code (UCC) must meet the requirements of good faith and fair dealing. Yet do these requirements supersede the written terms of a contract? In other words, if a party adheres strictly to the express, written terms of a contract, can that party nonetheless face liability for breaching the UCC's good faith requirements?

What the Courts Say

Generally, the courts take the good faith provisions of the UCC very seriously. Some courts have held that good faith can be breached even when the parties have equal bargaining power. In one case, for example, the court held that, although the plaintiffs were sophisticated businesspersons who had the assistance of highly competent counsel, they could still maintain an action for breach of good faith and fair dealing. The court reasoned that "the presence of bad faith is to be found in the eye of the beholder or, more to the point, in the eye of the trier of fact," indicating that it was up to a jury to determine whether the parties had performed in good faith.[a]

a. *Seidenberg v. Summit Bank,* 348 N.J.Super. 243, 791 A.2d 1068 (2002).

Courts have also applied the requirements of good faith and fair dealing to individuals who form partnerships. In one case involving a dispute between two individuals who had jointly bought properties for development over a ten-year period, the reviewing court stated that the "implied covenant of good faith and fair dealing is present in every contract." Further, "the duty imposed by this covenant prohibits either party from doing anything that would have the effect of injuring the other party's right to receive the fruits of the contract." Hence, juries are entitled to afford great weight to the conduct of the parties when determining the meaning of a contract.[b]

Implications for Managers

The message for business owners and managers involved in sales contracts (and even other contracts) is clear: compliance with the literal terms of a contract is not enough—the standards of good faith and fair dealing must also be met. Although the specific standards of good faith performance are still evolving, the overriding principle is that a party to a contract should do nothing to injure or destroy the rights of the other party to receive the fruits of the contract.

b. *Stankovits v. Schrager,* 2007 WL 4410247 (N.J.Super.A.D. 2007).

Tender of Delivery

Goods that conform to the contract description in every way are called **conforming goods.** To fulfill the contract, the seller or lessor must either deliver or tender delivery of conforming goods to the buyer or lessee. **Tender of delivery** occurs when the seller or lessor makes conforming goods available to the buyer or lessee and gives the buyer or lessee whatever notification is reasonably necessary to enable the buyer or lessee to take delivery [UCC 2–503(1), 2A–508(1)].

Tender must occur at a *reasonable hour* and in a *reasonable manner.* Thus, a seller cannot call the buyer at 2:00 A.M. and say, "The goods are ready. I'll give you twenty minutes to get them." Unless the parties have agreed otherwise, the goods must be tendered for delivery at a reasonable hour and kept available for a reasonable period of time to enable the buyer to take possession of them [UCC 2–503(1)(a)].

Normally, all goods called for by a contract must be tendered in a single delivery—unless the parties have agreed that the goods may be delivered in several lots or *installments* (to be discussed shortly) [UCC 2–307, 2–612, 2A–510]. Hence, an order for 1,000 shirts cannot be delivered two shirts at a time. If, however, the parties agree that the shirts will be delivered in four orders of 250 each as they are produced (for summer, fall, winter, and spring stock), then tender of delivery may occur in this manner.

Place of Delivery

The buyer and seller (or lessor and lessee) may agree that the goods will be delivered to a particular destination where the buyer or lessee will take possession. If the contract does not designate the place of delivery, then the goods must be made available to the buyer at the *seller's place of business* or, if the seller has none, at the *seller's residence* [UCC 2–308]. If, at the time of contracting, the parties know that the goods identified to the contract are located somewhere other than the seller's business, then the *location of the goods* is the place for their delivery [UCC 2–308].

■EXAMPLE 16.1 Li Wan and Boyd both live in San Francisco. In San Francisco, Li Wan contracts to sell Boyd five used trucks, which both parties know are located in a Chicago warehouse. If nothing more is specified in the contract, the place of delivery for the trucks is Chicago. Li Wan may tender delivery either by giving Boyd a negotiable or nonnegotiable document of title or by obtaining the bailee's (warehouser's) acknowledgment that the buyer is entitled to possession.[1] ■

Delivery via Carrier

In many instances, attendant circumstances or delivery terms in the contract (such as F.O.B. or F.A.S. terms, shown in Exhibit 15–1 on page 298) make it apparent that the parties intend that a carrier be used to move the goods. In contracts involving a carrier, a seller can complete performance of the obligation to deliver the goods in two ways—through a shipment contract or through a destination contract.

Shipment Contracts Recall from Chapter 15 that a *shipment contract* requires or authorizes the seller to ship goods by a carrier. The contract does not require the seller to deliver the goods at a particular destination [UCC 2–319, 2–509]. Unless otherwise agreed, the seller must do the following:

1 Place the goods into the hands of the carrier.

2 Make a contract for their transportation that is reasonable according to the nature of the goods and their value. (For example, certain types of goods need refrigeration in transit.)

3 Obtain and promptly deliver or tender to the buyer any documents necessary to enable the buyer to obtain possession of the goods from the carrier.

4 Promptly notify the buyer that shipment has been made [UCC 2–504].

If the seller does not make a reasonable contract for transportation or fails to notify the buyer of the shipment, the buyer can reject the goods, but only if a *material loss* of the

goods or a significant *delay* results. Suppose that a contract involves the shipment of fresh fruit, such as strawberries, but the seller does not arrange for refrigerated transportation. If the fruit spoils during transport, a material loss would likely result. (Of course, the parties are free to make agreements that alter the UCC's rules and allow the buyer to reject goods for other reasons.)

Destination Contracts In a *destination contract*, the seller agrees to deliver conforming goods to the buyer at a particular destination. The goods must be tendered at a reasonable hour and held at the buyer's disposal for a reasonable length of time. The seller must also give the buyer appropriate notice. In addition, the seller must provide the buyer with any documents of title necessary to enable the buyer to obtain delivery from the carrier. Sellers often do this by tendering the documents through ordinary banking channels [UCC 2–503].

The Perfect Tender Rule

As previously noted, the seller or lessor has an obligation to ship or tender *conforming goods*, and the buyer or lessee is required to accept and pay for the goods according to the terms of the contract. Under the common law, the seller was obligated to deliver goods in conformity with the terms of the contract in every detail. This was called the *perfect tender* doctrine. The UCC preserves the perfect tender doctrine by stating that if goods or tender of delivery fails *in any respect* to conform to the contract, the buyer or lessee has the right to accept the goods, reject the entire shipment, or accept part and reject part [UCC 2–601, 2A–509].

■EXAMPLE 16.2 A lessor contracts to lease fifty Vericlear monitors to be delivered at the lessee's place of business on or before October 1. On September 28, the lessor discovers that it has only thirty Vericlear monitors in inventory, but that it will have another forty Vericlear monitors within the next two weeks. The lessor tenders delivery of the thirty Vericlear monitors on October 1, with the promise that the other monitors will be delivered within two weeks. Because the lessor failed to make a perfect tender of fifty Vericlear monitors, the lessee has the right to reject the entire shipment and hold the lessor in breach. ■

Exceptions to Perfect Tender

Because of the rigidity of the perfect tender rule, several exceptions to the rule have been created, some of which are discussed here.

Agreement of the Parties Exceptions to the perfect tender rule may be established by agreement. If the parties have

---

1. If the seller delivers a nonnegotiable document of title or merely instructs the bailee in a writing (record) to release the goods to the buyer without the bailee's acknowledgment of the buyer's rights, this is also a sufficient tender, unless the buyer objects [UCC 2–503(4)]. Risk of loss, however, does not pass until the buyer has had a reasonable amount of time in which to present the document or the instructions. See Chapter 15.

agreed, for example, that defective goods or parts will not be rejected if the seller or lessor is able to repair or replace them within a reasonable period of time, the perfect tender rule does not apply.

Cure The UCC does not specifically define the term *cure*, but it refers to the right of the seller or lessor to repair, adjust, or replace defective or nonconforming goods [UCC 2–508, 2A–513]. When any delivery is rejected because of nonconforming goods and the time for performance has not yet expired, the seller or lessor can attempt to "cure" the defect *within the contract time for performance* [UCC 2–508(1), 2A–513(1)]. Once the time for performance has expired, the seller or lessor can still, for a reasonable time, exercise the right to cure with respect to the rejected goods if he or she had, at the time of delivery, *reasonable grounds to believe that the nonconforming tender would be acceptable to the buyer or lessee* [UCC 2–508(2), 2A–513(2)].

■EXAMPLE 16.3 If in the past a buyer frequently accepted a particular substitute for a good when the good ordered was not available, the seller has reasonable grounds to believe the buyer will again accept the substitute. Even if the buyer rejects the substitute good on a particular occasion, the seller nonetheless had reasonable grounds to believe that the substitute would be acceptable. A seller or lessor will sometimes tender nonconforming goods with some type of price allowance, which can serve as the "reasonable grounds" to believe the buyer or lessee will accept the nonconforming tender. ■

The right to cure means that, to reject goods, the buyer or lessee must give notice to the seller or lessor of a particular defect. For example, if a lessee refuses a tender of goods as nonconforming but does not disclose the nature of the defect to the lessor, the lessee cannot later assert the defect as a defense if the defect is one that the lessor could have cured. Generally, buyers and lessees must act in good faith and state specific reasons for refusing to accept goods [UCC 2–605, 2A–514].

Substitution of Carriers When an agreed-on manner of delivery (such as which carrier will be used to transport the goods) becomes impracticable or unavailable through no fault of either party, but a commercially reasonable substitute is available, the seller must use this substitute performance, which is sufficient tender to the buyer [UCC 2–614(1)]. ■EXAMPLE 16.4 A sales contract calls for the delivery of a large generator to be shipped by Roadway Trucking Corporation on or before June 1. The contract terms clearly state the importance of the delivery date. The employees of Roadway Trucking go on strike. The seller must make a reasonable substitute tender, perhaps by another trucking firm or by rail if that is available. Note that the seller will nor-

mally be responsible for any additional shipping costs, unless other arrangements have been made in the sales contract. ■

Installment Contracts An **installment contract** is a single contract that requires or authorizes delivery in two or more separate lots to be accepted and paid for separately. With an installment contract, a buyer or lessee can reject an installment *only if the nonconformity substantially impairs the value* of the installment and cannot be cured [UCC 2–307, 2–612(2), 2A–510(1)]. If the buyer or lessee subsequently accepts a nonconforming installment and fails to notify the seller or lessor of cancellation, however, the contract is reinstated [UCC 2–612(3), 2A–510(2)].

The entire installment contract is breached only when one or more nonconforming installments *substantially* impair the value of the *whole contract*. The UCC strictly limits its rejection to cases of *substantial* nonconformity. ■EXAMPLE 16.5 An installment contract involves parts of a machine. The first part is necessary for the machine to operate, but when it is delivered, it is irreparably defective. The failure of this first installment is a breach of the whole contract because the machine will not operate without the first part. The situation would likely be different, however, if the contract had called for twenty carloads of plywood and only 9 percent of one carload had deviated from the thickness specifications in the contract. ■

The point to remember is that the UCC significantly alters the right of the buyer or lessee to reject the entire contract if the contract requires delivery to be made in several installments. The UCC strictly limits rejection to cases of *substantial* nonconformity (unless the parties agree that breach of an installment constitutes a breach of the entire contract).

Commercial Impracticability As mentioned in Chapter 11, occurrences unforeseen by either party when a contract was made may make performance commercially impracticable. When this occurs, the rule of perfect tender no longer holds. According to UCC 2–615(a) and 2A–405(a), a delay in delivery or nondelivery in whole or in part is not a breach when performance has been made impracticable "by the occurrence of a contingency the nonoccurrence of which was a basic assumption on which the contract was made." The seller or lessor must, however, notify the buyer or lessee as soon as practicable that there will be a delay or nondelivery.

Foreseeable versus Unforeseeable Contingencies. The doctrine of commercial impracticability extends only to problems that could not have been foreseen. ■EXAMPLE 16.6 A major oil company that receives its supplies from the Middle East has a contract to supply a buyer with 100,000 gallons of oil. Because of an oil embargo by the Organization of Petroleum Exporting Countries (OPEC), the seller is prevented from securing oil to meet the terms of the contract. Because of the same embargo, the seller cannot secure oil from any other source. This situation comes fully under the commercial impracticability exception to the perfect tender doctrine. In contrast, an increase in cost resulting from inflation does not in and of itself excuse performance as this kind of risk is ordinarily assumed by a seller or lessor conducting business. ■

Can unanticipated increases in a seller's costs, which make performance "impracticable," constitute a valid defense to performance on the basis of commercial impracticability? The court dealt with this question in the following case.

CASE 16.1 **Maple Farms, Inc. v. City School District of Elmira**

LANDMARK AND CLASSIC CASES

Supreme Court of New York, 76 Misc.2d 1080, 352 N.Y.S.2d 784 (1974).

FACTS On June 15, 1973, Maple Farms, Inc., formed an agreement with the city school district of Elmira, New York, to supply the school district with milk for the 1973–1974 school year. The agreement was in the form of a requirements contract, under which Maple Farms would sell to the school district all the milk the district required at a fixed price—which was the June market price of milk. By December 1973, the price of raw milk had increased by 23 percent over the price specified in the contract. This meant that if the terms of the contract were fulfilled, Maple Farms would lose $7,350. Because it had similar contracts with other school districts, Maple Farms stood to lose a great deal if it was held to the price stated in the contracts. When the school district would not agree to release Maple Farms from its contract, Maple Farms brought an action in a New York state court for a declaratory judgment (a determination of the parties' rights under a contract). Maple Farms contended that the substantial increase in the price of raw milk was an event not contemplated by the parties when the contract was formed and that, given the increased price, performance of the contract was commercially impracticable.

ISSUE Can Maple Farms be released from the contract on the ground of commercial impracticability?

DECISION No. The court ruled that performance in this case was not impracticable.

REASON The court reasoned that commercial impracticability arises when an event occurs that is totally unexpected and unforeseeable by the parties. The increased price of raw milk was not totally unexpected, given that in the previous year the price of milk had risen 10 percent and that the price of milk had traditionally varied. Additionally, the general inflation of prices in the United States should have been anticipated. Maple Farms had reason to know these facts and could have included a clause in its contract with the school district to protect itself from its present situation. The court also noted that the primary purpose of the contract, on the part of the school district, was to protect itself (for budgeting purposes) against price fluctuations.

WHAT IF THE FACTS WERE DIFFERENT? *Suppose that the court had ruled in the plaintiff's favor. How might that ruling have affected the plaintiff's contracts with other parties?*

IMPACT OF THIS CASE ON TODAY'S LAW *This case is a classic illustration of the UCC's commercial impracticability doctrine. Under this doctrine, parties who freely enter into contracts normally will not be excused from their contractual obligations simply because changed circumstances make performance difficult or unprofitable. Rather, to be excused from performance, a party must show that the changed circumstances were impossible to foresee at the time the contract was formed. This principle continues to be applied today.*

RELEVANT WEB SITES *To locate information on the Web concerning the* Maple Farms, Inc. v. City School District of Elmira *decision, go to this text's Web site at* **www.cengage.com/blaw/fbl**, *select "Chapter 16," and click on "URLs for Landmarks."*

■

Partial Performance. Sometimes, an unforeseen event only *partially* affects the capacity of the seller or lessor to perform, and the seller or lessor is thus able to fulfill the contract *partially* but cannot tender total performance. In this event, the seller or lessor is required to allocate in a fair and reasonable manner any remaining production and deliveries among those to whom it is contractually obligated to deliver the goods, and this allocation may take into account its regular customers [UCC 2–615(b), 2A–405(b)]. The buyer or lessee must receive notice of the allocation and has the right to accept or reject the allocation [UCC 2–615(c), 2A–405(c)].

■EXAMPLE 16.7 A Florida orange grower, Best Citrus, Inc., contracts to sell this season's crop to a number of customers, including Martin's grocery chain. Martin's contracts to purchase two thousand crates of oranges. Best Citrus has sprayed some of its orange groves with a chemical called Karmoxin. The Department of Agriculture discovers that persons who eat products sprayed with Karmoxin may develop cancer. The department issues an order prohibiting the sale of these products. Best Citrus picks all of the oranges not sprayed with Karmoxin, but the quantity does not fully meet all the contracted-for deliveries. In this situation, Best Citrus is required to allocate its production, and it notifies Martin's that it cannot deliver the full quantity agreed on in the contract and specifies the amount it will be able to deliver under the circumstances. Martin's can either accept or reject the allocation, but Best Citrus has no further contractual liability. ■

Destruction of Identified Goods The UCC provides that when an unexpected event, such as a fire, totally destroys *goods identified at the time the contract is formed* through no fault of either party and *before risk passes to the buyer or lessee*, the parties are excused from performance [UCC 2–613, 2A–221]. If the goods are only partially destroyed, however, the buyer or lessee can inspect them and either treat the contract as void or accept the goods with a reduction of the contract price.

■EXAMPLE 16.8 Atlas Sporting Equipment agrees to lease to River Bicycles sixty bicycles of a particular model that has been discontinued. No other bicycles of that model are available. River specifies that it needs the bicycles to rent to tourists. Before Atlas can deliver the bicycles, they are destroyed by a fire. In this situation, Atlas is not liable to River for failing to deliver the bicycles. The goods were destroyed through no fault of either party, before the risk of loss passed to the lessee. The loss was total, so the contract is avoided. Clearly, Atlas has no obligation to tender the bicycles, and River has no obligation to pay for them. ■

Assurance and Cooperation Two other exceptions to the perfect tender doctrine apply equally to parties to sales and lease contracts: the right of assurance and the duty of cooperation.

The Right of Assurance. The UCC provides that if one party to a contract has "reasonable grounds" to believe that the other party will not perform as contracted, he or she may *in writing* "demand adequate assurance of due performance" from the other party. Until such assurance is received, he or she may "suspend" further performance (such as payments due under

the contract) without liability. What constitutes "reasonable grounds" is determined by commercial standards. If such assurances are not forthcoming within a reasonable time (not to exceed thirty days), the failure to respond may be treated as a *repudiation* of the contract [UCC 2–609, 2A–401].

■EXAMPLE 16.9 Two companies that make road-surfacing materials, LLM Company and Shore Seal, Inc., enter into a contract. LLM obtains a license to use Novachip, a special material made by Shore, and Shore agrees to buy all of its asphalt from LLM for the next seven years. A few years into the contract term, Shore notifies LLM that it is planning to sell its assets to Asphalt Paving Systems, Inc. LLM demands assurances that Asphalt Paving will continue the deal, but Shore refuses to provide assurances. In this situation, LLM can treat Shore's failure to give assurances as a repudiation and file a suit against Shore for breach of contract. ■

PREVENTING LEGAL DISPUTES

The UCC comes to the aid of a party who has reasonable grounds to suspect that the other party to a contract will not perform as promised. Rather than having to "wait and see" (and possibly incur significant losses as a result), the party with such suspicions may seek adequate assurance of performance from the other party. The failure to give such assurance can be treated as an anticipatory repudiation (breach) of the contract, thus entitling the nonbreaching party to seek damages. Perhaps more important, this failure allows the nonbreaching party to suspend its performance, which can save a business from sustaining substantial losses that could be recovered only through litigation. Ultimately, it may be better to withdraw from a deal when the other party will not provide assurances of performance.

■

The Duty of Cooperation. Sometimes, the performance of one party depends on the cooperation of the other. The UCC provides that when such cooperation is not forthcoming, the other party can suspend her or his own performance without liability and hold the uncooperative party in breach or proceed to perform the contract in any reasonable manner [UCC 2–311(3)(b)].

■EXAMPLE 16.10 Aman is required by contract to deliver 1,200 model HE washing machines to various locations in California. Deliveries are to be made on or before October 1, and the locations are to be specified later by Farrell. Aman has repeatedly requested the delivery locations, but Farrell has not responded. On October 1, the washing machines are ready to be shipped, but Farrell still refuses to give Aman the delivery locations. Aman does not ship on October 1. Can Aman be held liable? The answer is no. Aman is excused for any resulting delay of performance because of Farrell's failure to cooperate. ◾

OBLIGATIONS OF THE BUYER OR LESSEE

The main obligation of the buyer or lessee under a sales or lease contract is to pay for the goods tendered in accordance with the contract. Once the seller or lessor has adequately tendered delivery, the buyer or lessee is obligated to accept the goods and pay for them according to the terms of the contract.

Payment

In the absence of any specific agreements, the buyer or lessee must make payment at the time and place the goods are received, even if the place of shipment is the place of delivery [UCC 2–310(a), 2A–516(1)]. Payment can be made by any means agreed on by the parties—cash or any other method generally acceptable in the commercial world. If the seller demands cash when the buyer offers a check, credit card, or the like, the seller must permit the buyer reasonable time to obtain legal tender [UCC 2–511].

Right of Inspection

The buyer or lessee has an absolute right to inspect the goods unless the parties have agreed otherwise. This right allows the buyer or lessee to verify, before making payment, that the goods tendered or delivered are what were contracted for or ordered. If the goods are not what were ordered, the buyer or lessee has no duty to pay. *An opportunity for inspection is therefore a condition precedent to the right of the seller or lessor to enforce payment* [UCC 2–513(1), 2A–515(1)].

Inspection can take place at any reasonable place and time and in any reasonable manner. Generally, what is reasonable is determined by custom of the trade, past practices of the parties, and the like. The buyer bears the costs of inspecting the goods (unless otherwise agreed), but if the goods are rejected because they are not conforming, the buyer can recover the costs of inspection from the seller [UCC 2–513(2)].

Acceptance

A buyer or lessee can manifest assent to the delivered goods in the following ways, each of which constitutes acceptance:

1 If, after having had a reasonable opportunity to inspect the goods, the buyer or lessee signifies to the seller or lessor

that the goods either are conforming or are acceptable in spite of their nonconformity [UCC 2–606(1)(a), 2A–515(1)(a)].

2 If the buyer or lessee has had a reasonable opportunity to inspect the goods and has failed to reject them within a reasonable period of time, then acceptance is presumed [UCC 2–602(1), 2–606(1)(b), 2A–515(1)(b)].

3 In sales contracts, if the buyer performs any act inconsistent with the seller's ownership, then the buyer will be deemed to have accepted the goods. For example, any use or resale of the goods—except for the limited purpose of testing or inspecting the goods—generally constitutes an acceptance [UCC 2–606(1)(c)].

If some of the goods delivered do not conform to the contract and the seller or lessor has failed to cure, the buyer or lessee can make a *partial* acceptance [UCC 2–601(c), 2A–509(1)]. The same is true if the nonconformity was not reasonably discoverable before acceptance. (In the latter situation, the buyer or lessee may be able to revoke the acceptance, as will be discussed later in this chapter.)

A buyer or lessee cannot accept less than a single commercial unit, however. The UCC defines a *commercial unit* as a unit of goods that, by commercial usage, is viewed as a "single whole" for purposes of sale, and its division would materially impair the character of the unit, its market value, or its use [UCC 2–105(6), 2A–103(1)(c)]. A commercial unit can be a single article (such as a machine), a set of articles (such as a suite of furniture or an assortment of sizes), a quantity (such as a bale, a gross, or a carload), or any other unit treated in the trade as a single whole.

ANTICIPATORY REPUDIATION

What if, before the time for contract performance, one party clearly communicates to the other the intention not to perform? As discussed in Chapter 11, such an action is a breach of the contract by *anticipatory repudiation*.[2] When anticipatory repudiation occurs, the nonbreaching party has a choice of two responses. One option is to treat the repudiation as a final breach by pursuing a remedy; the other is to wait and hope that the repudiating party will decide to honor the obligations required by the contract despite the avowed intention to renege [UCC 2–610, 2A–402]. (In either situation, the nonbreaching party may suspend performance.)

Should the second option be pursued, the UCC permits the breaching party (subject to some limitations) to "retract" his or her repudiation. This can be done by any method that

---

2. This doctrine was first enunciated in an English case decided in 1853, *Hochster v. De La Tour,* 2 Ellis and Blackburn Reports 678 (1853).

clearly indicates an intent to perform. Once retraction is made, the rights of the repudiating party under the contract are reinstated [UCC 2–611, 2A–403].

EXAMPLE 16.11 Cora, who owns a small inn, purchases a suite of furniture from Horton's Furniture Warehouse on April 1. The contract states, "delivery must be made on or before May 1." On April 10, Horton informs Cora that he cannot make delivery until May 10 and asks her to consent to the modified delivery date. In this situation, Cora has the option of either treating Horton's notice of late delivery as a final breach of contract and pursuing a remedy or agreeing to the later delivery date. Suppose that Cora does neither for two weeks. On April 24, Horton informs Cora that he will be able to deliver the furniture by May 1, after all. In effect, Horton has retracted his repudiation, reinstating the rights and obligations of the parties under the original contract. Note that if Cora had indicated after Horton's repudiation that she was canceling the contract, Horton would not have been able to retract his repudiation. ■

REMEDIES OF THE SELLER OR LESSOR

When the buyer or lessee is in breach, the seller or lessor has numerous remedies available under the UCC. Generally, the remedies available to the seller or lessor depend on the circumstances at the time of the breach, such as which party has possession of the goods, whether the goods are in transit, and whether the buyer or lessee has rejected or accepted the goods.

When the Goods Are in the Possession of the Seller or Lessor

Under the UCC, if the buyer or lessee breaches the contract before the goods have been delivered to her or him, the seller or lessor has the right to pursue the remedies discussed here.

The Right to Cancel the Contract One of the options available to a seller or lessor when the buyer or lessee breaches the contract is simply to cancel (rescind) the contract [UCC 2–703(f), 2A–523(1)(a)]. The seller must notify the buyer or lessee of the cancellation, and at that point all remaining obligations of the seller or lessor are discharged. The buyer or lessee is not discharged from all remaining obligations, however; he or she is in breach, and the seller or lessor can pursue remedies available under the UCC for breach.

The Right to Withhold Delivery In general, sellers and lessors can withhold or discontinue performance of their obligations under sales or lease contracts when the buyers or lessees are in breach. If a buyer or lessee has wrongfully rejected or revoked acceptance of contract goods (rejection and revocation of acceptance will be discussed later), failed to make proper and timely payment, or repudiated a part of the contract, the seller or lessor can withhold delivery of the goods in question [UCC 2–703(a), 2A–523(1)(c)]. If the breach results from the buyer's or the lessee's insolvency (inability to pay debts as they become due), the seller or lessor can refuse to deliver the goods unless the buyer or lessee pays in cash [UCC 2–702(1), 2A–525(1)].

The Right to Resell or Dispose of the Goods When a buyer or lessee breaches or repudiates a sales contract while the seller or lessor is still in possession of the goods, the seller or lessor can resell or dispose of the goods. The seller can retain any profits made as a result of the sale and can hold the buyer or lessee liable for any loss [UCC 2–703(d), 2–706(1), 2A–523(1)(e), 2A–527(1)].

When the goods contracted for are unfinished at the time of breach, the seller or lessor can do one of two things: (1) cease manufacturing the goods and resell them for scrap or salvage value or (2) complete the manufacture and resell or dispose of them, holding the buyer or lessee liable for any deficiency. In choosing between these two alternatives, the seller or lessor must exercise reasonable commercial judgment to mitigate the loss and obtain maximum value from the unfinished goods [UCC 2–704(2), 2A–524(2)]. Any resale of the goods must be made in good faith and in a commercially reasonable manner.

In sales transactions, the seller can recover any deficiency between the resale price and the contract price, along with **incidental damages,** defined as the costs resulting from the breach [UCC 2–706(1), 2–710]. The resale can be private or public, and the goods can be sold as a unit or in parcels. The seller must give the original buyer reasonable notice of the resale, unless the goods are perishable or will rapidly decline in value [UCC 2–706(2), (3)]. A good faith purchaser in a resale takes the goods free of any of the rights of the original buyer, even if the seller fails to comply with these requirements of the UCC [UCC 2–706(5)].

In lease transactions, the lessor may lease the goods to another party and recover from the original lessee, as damages, any unpaid lease payments up to the beginning date of the lease term under the new lease. The lessor can also recover any deficiency between the lease payments due under the original lease contract and those due under the new lease contract, along with incidental damages [UCC 2A–527(2)].

The Right to Recover the Purchase Price or the Lease Payments Due Under the UCC, an unpaid seller or lessor can bring an action to recover the purchase price or payments due under the lease contract, plus incidental damages, if the seller or lessor is unable to resell or dispose of the goods [UCC 2–709(1), 2A–529(1)].

■EXAMPLE 16.12 Southern Realty contracts with Gem Point, Inc., to purchase one thousand pens with Southern Realty's name inscribed on them. Gem Point tenders delivery of the one thousand pens, but Southern Realty wrongfully refuses to accept them. Gem Point obviously cannot sell to anyone else the pens inscribed with the buyer's business name, so this situation falls under UCC 2–709. Gem Point's remedy is to bring an action for the purchase price. ■

If a seller or lessor is unable to resell or dispose of goods and sues for the contract price or lease payments due, the goods must be held for the buyer or lessee. The seller or lessor can resell or dispose of the goods at any time prior to collection (of the judgment) from the buyer or lessee, but must credit the net proceeds from the sale to the buyer or lessee. This is an example of the duty to mitigate damages.

The Right to Recover Damages   If a buyer or lessee repudiates a contract or wrongfully refuses to accept the goods, a seller or lessor can maintain an action to recover the damages that were sustained. Ordinarily, the amount of damages equals the difference between the contract price or lease payments and the market price or lease payments (at the time and place of tender of the goods), plus incidental damages [UCC 2–708(1), 2A–528(1)]. The time and place of tender are frequently given by such terms as F.O.B., F.A.S., and C.I.F., which determine whether there is a shipment or destination contract.[3]

When the Goods Are in Transit

When the seller or lessor has delivered the goods to a carrier or a bailee but the buyer or lessee has not yet received them, the goods are said to be *in transit*. If, while the goods are in transit, the seller or lessor learns that the buyer or lessee is insolvent, the seller or lessor can stop the carrier or bailee from delivering the goods, regardless of the quantity of goods shipped. If the buyer or lessee is in breach but is not insolvent, the seller or lessor can stop the goods in transit only if the quantity shipped is at least a carload, a truckload, a planeload, or a larger shipment [UCC 2–705(1), 2A–526(1)].

To stop delivery, the seller or lessor must *timely notify* the carrier or other bailee that the goods are to be returned or held for the seller or lessor. If the carrier has sufficient time to stop delivery, the goods must be held and delivered according to the instructions of the seller or lessor, who is liable to the carrier for any additional costs incurred [UCC 2–705(3), 2A–526(3)].

The seller or lessor has the right to stop delivery of the goods under UCC 2–705(2) and 2A–526(2) until the time when:

1 The buyer or lessee receives the goods.

2 The carrier or the bailee acknowledges the rights of the buyer or lessee in the goods (by reshipping or holding the goods for the buyer or lessee, for example).

3 A negotiable document of title covering the goods has been properly transferred to the buyer in a sales transaction, giving the buyer ownership rights in the goods [UCC 2–705(2)].

Once the seller or lessor reclaims the goods in transit, she or he can pursue the remedies allowed to sellers and lessors when the goods are in their possession.

When the Goods Are in the Possession of the Buyer or Lessee

When the buyer or lessee has breached a sales or lease contract and the goods are in his or her possession, the seller or lessor can sue to recover the purchase price of the goods or the lease payments due, plus incidental damages [UCC 2–709(1), 2A–529(1)]. In some situations, a seller may also have a right to reclaim the goods from the buyer. For example, in a sales contract, if the buyer has received the goods on credit and the seller discovers that the buyer is insolvent, the seller can demand return of the goods [UCC 2–702(2)]. Ordinarily, the demand must be made within ten days of the buyer's receipt of the goods.[4] The seller's right to reclaim the goods is subject to the rights of a good faith purchaser or other subsequent buyer in the ordinary course of business who purchases the goods from the buyer before the seller reclaims them.

In regard to lease contracts, if the lessee is in default (fails to make payments that are due, for example), the lessor may reclaim the leased goods that are in the lessee's possession [UCC 2A–525(2)].

REMEDIES OF THE BUYER OR LESSEE

When the seller or lessor breaches the contract, the buyer or lessee has numerous remedies available under the UCC in addition to recovery of as much of the price as has been paid. Like the remedies available to sellers and lessors, the remedies of buyers and lessees depend on the circumstances existing at the time of the breach.

---

3. See Exhibit 15–1 on page 298 for definitions of these contract terms.

4. The seller can demand and reclaim the goods at any time, though, if the buyer misrepresented his or her solvency in writing within three months prior to the delivery of the goods.

When the Seller or Lessor Refuses to Deliver the Goods

If the seller or lessor refuses to deliver the goods or the buyer or lessee has rejected the goods, the remedies available to the buyer or lessee include those discussed here.

The Right to Cancel the Contract When a seller or lessor fails to make proper delivery or repudiates the contract, the buyer or lessee can cancel, or rescind, the contract. The buyer or lessee is relieved of any further obligations under the contract but retains all rights to other remedies against the seller [UCC 2–711(1), 2A–508(1)(a)].

The Right to Recover the Goods If a buyer or lessee has made a partial or full payment for goods that remain in the possession of the seller or lessor, the buyer or lessee can recover the goods if the seller or lessor is insolvent or becomes insolvent within ten days after receiving the first payment and if the goods are identified to the contract. To exercise this right, the buyer or lessee must tender to the seller any unpaid balance of the purchase price [UCC 2–502, 2A–522].

The Right to Obtain Specific Performance A buyer or lessee can obtain specific performance if the goods are unique and the remedy at law (monetary damages) is inadequate [UCC 2–716(1), 2A–521(1)]. Ordinarily, a successful suit for monetary damages is sufficient to place a buyer or lessee in the position he or she would have occupied if the seller or lessor had fully performed. When the contract is for the purchase of a particular work of art or a similarly unique item, however, monetary damages may not be sufficient. Under these circumstances, equity will require that the seller or lessor perform exactly by delivering the particular goods identified to the contract (a remedy of specific performance).

The Right of Cover In certain situations, buyers and lessees can protect themselves by obtaining **cover**—that is, by purchasing or leasing other goods to substitute for those due under the contract. This option is available when the seller or lessor repudiates the contract or fails to deliver the goods, or when a buyer or lessee has rightfully rejected goods or revoked acceptance.

In obtaining cover, the buyer or lessee must act in good faith and without unreasonable delay [UCC 2–712, 2A–518]. After purchasing or leasing substitute goods, the buyer or lessee can recover from the seller or lessor the difference between the cost of cover and the contract price (or lease payments), plus incidental and consequential damages, less the

expenses (such as delivery costs) that were saved as a result of the breach [UCC 2–712, 2–715, 2A–518]. Consequential damages are any losses suffered by the buyer or lessee that the seller or lessor had reason to know about at the time of contract formation and any injury to the buyer's or lessee's person or property proximately resulting from the contract's breach [UCC 2–715(2), 2A–520(2)].

Buyers and lessees are not required to cover, and failure to do so will not bar them from using any other remedies available under the UCC. A buyer or lessee who fails to cover, however, may *not* be able to collect consequential damages that could have been avoided by purchasing or leasing substitute goods.

The Right to Replevy Goods Buyers and lessees also have the right to replevy goods. **Replevin**[5] is an action to recover specific goods in the hands of a party who is wrongfully withholding them from the other party. Outside the UCC, the term *replevin* refers to a *prejudgment process* (a proceeding that takes place prior to a court's judgment) that permits the seizure of specific personal property in which a party claims a right or an interest. Under the UCC, the buyer or lessee can replevy goods subject to the contract if the seller or lessor has repudiated or breached the contract. To maintain an action to replevy goods, usually buyers and lessees must show that they made a reasonable effort to cover for the goods but were unable to do so [UCC 2–716(3), 2A–521(3)].

The Right to Recover Damages If a seller or lessor repudiates the sales contract or fails to deliver the goods, or the buyer or lessee has rightfully rejected or revoked acceptance of the goods, the buyer or lessee can sue for damages. The measure of recovery is the difference between the contract price (or lease payments) and the market price of (or lease payments that could be obtained for) the goods at the time the buyer (or lessee) *learned* of the breach. The market price or market lease payments are determined at the place where the seller or lessor was supposed to deliver the goods. The buyer or lessee can also recover incidental and consequential damages, less the expenses that were saved as a result of the breach [UCC 2–713, 2A–519].

■**EXAMPLE 16.13** Schilling orders ten thousand bushels of wheat from Valdone for $25 a bushel, with delivery due on June 14 and payment due on June 20. Valdone does not deliver on June 14. On June 14, the market price of wheat is $25.50 per bushel. Schilling chooses to do without the wheat. He sues Valdone for damages for nondelivery. Schilling can

---

5. Pronounced ruh-*pleh*-vun.

recover $0.50 × 10,000, or $5,000, plus any expenses the breach may have caused him. The measure of damages is the market price less the contract price on the day Schilling was to have received delivery. Any expenses Schilling saved by the breach would be deducted from the damages. ■

When the Seller or Lessor Delivers Nonconforming Goods

When the seller or lessor delivers nonconforming goods, the buyer or lessee has several remedies available under the UCC.

The Right to Reject the Goods If either the goods or the tender of the goods by the seller or lessor fails to conform to

the contract *in any respect*, the buyer or lessee can reject the goods in whole or in part [UCC 2–601, 2A–509]. If the buyer or lessee rejects the goods, she or he may then obtain cover, cancel the contract, or sue for damages for breach of contract, just as if the seller or lessor had refused to deliver the goods (see the earlier discussion of these remedies).

In the following case, the buyer of a piano that was represented to be new rejected the instrument on its delivery in an "unacceptable" condition and brought an action against the seller, seeking damages.

CASE 16.2 **Jauregui v. Bobb's Piano Sales & Service, Inc.**

District Court of Appeal of Florida, Third District, 922 So.2d 303 (2006).

FACTS In November 2001, Jorge Jauregui contracted to buy a Kawai RX5 piano—"Serial No. 2392719a"—for $24,282 from Bobb's Piano Sales and Service, Inc., in Miami, Florida. The piano was represented to be in new condition and to qualify for the manufacturer's "new piano" warranty. Bobb's did not mention that the piano had been in storage for almost a year and had been moved at least six times. The piano was delivered with "unacceptable damage," according to Jauregui, who videotaped its condition. He sent a letter of complaint to the state department of consumer services, identifying at least four "necessary repairs." He then filed a suit in a Florida state court against Bobb's, claiming breach of contract. Bobb's admitted that the piano needed repair. The court concluded that Bobb's was in breach of the parties' contract and that specific performance was not possible, but ruled that Jauregui "takes nothing in damages." Jauregui appealed to a state intermediate appellate court.

ISSUE On a seller's delivery of nonconforming goods in breach of a sales contract and a buyer's rejection of the goods, is the buyer entitled to obtain damages?

DECISION Yes. The state intermediate appellate court agreed with the lower court's conclusion that the defendant had breached the parties' contract but not with the ruling that

the plaintiff should not obtain damages. The appellate court awarded Jauregui the contract price with interest, the amounts of the sales tax and delivery charge, and attorneys' fees. The court also ordered Bobb's to remove the piano.

REASON The appellate court stated that the lower court's ruling was "erroneous as a matter of law." The lower court had reasoned that even in a defective condition, the piano as delivered was worth as much or more than Jauregui had paid for it, and thus no damages had been sustained. The appellate court explained, however, that "in a case such as this one, the purchaser of non-conforming goods like the offending piano retains the option to claim either the difference in value or, as plaintiff clearly did in this case, in effect, to cancel the deal and get his money back. This principle is based on the common sense idea that the purchaser is entitled to receive what he wanted to buy and pay for and that the seller is not free to supply any non-conforming item [he or] she wishes just so long as the deviant goods are worth just as much."

 FOR CRITICAL ANALYSIS—Social Consideration *If the defendant had delivered the piano in new condition and the plaintiff had refused to pay for it only out of "buyer's remorse," what might the court have ruled in this case?*

■

Timeliness and Reason for Rejection Required. The buyer or lessee must reject the goods within a reasonable amount of time and must notify the seller or lessor *seasonably*—that is, in a timely fashion or at the proper time [UCC 2–602(1),

2A–509(2)]. If the buyer or lessee fails to reject the goods within a reasonable amount of time, acceptance will be presumed.

Note that when rejecting goods, the buyer or lessee must designate defects that would have been apparent to the seller or lessor on reasonable inspection. If the buyer or lessee fails to state the particular defects, he or she may not use such defects to justify rejection or to establish breach when the seller could have cured the defects if it had been notified about them in a timely fashion [UCC 2–605, 2A–514].

Duties of Merchant Buyers and Lessees When Goods Are Rejected. Suppose that a *merchant buyer* or *lessee* rightfully rejects goods and the seller or lessor has no agent or business at the place of rejection. What should the buyer or lessee do in that situation? Under the UCC, the merchant buyer or lessee has a good faith obligation to follow any reasonable instructions received from the seller or lessor with respect to the goods [UCC 2–603, 2A–511]. The buyer or lessee is entitled to be reimbursed for the care and cost entailed in following the instructions. The same requirements hold if the buyer or lessee rightfully revokes his or her acceptance of the goods at some later time [UCC 2–608(3), 2A–517(5)].

If no instructions are forthcoming and the goods are perishable or threaten to decline in value quickly, the buyer can resell the goods in good faith, taking the appropriate reimbursement from the proceeds. In addition, the buyer is entitled to a selling commission (not to exceed 10 percent of the gross proceeds) [UCC 2–603(1), (2); 2A–511(1)]. If the goods are not perishable, the buyer or lessee may store them for the seller or lessor or reship them to the seller or lessor [UCC 2–604, 2A–512].

Revocation of Acceptance Acceptance of the goods precludes the buyer or lessee from exercising the right of rejection, but it does not necessarily prevent the buyer or lessee from pursuing other remedies. Additionally, in certain circumstances, a buyer or lessee is permitted to *revoke* her or his acceptance of the goods. Acceptance of a lot or a commercial unit can be revoked if the nonconformity *substantially* impairs the value of the lot or unit and if one of the following factors is present:

1 If acceptance was predicated on the reasonable assumption that the nonconformity would be cured, and it has not been cured within a reasonable period of time [UCC 2–608(1)(a), 2A–517(1)(a)].

2 If the buyer or lessee did not discover the nonconformity before acceptance, either because it was difficult to discover before acceptance or because assurances made by the seller or lessor that the goods were conforming kept the buyer or lessee from inspecting the goods [UCC 2–608(1)(b), 2A–517(1)(b)].

Revocation of acceptance is not effective until the seller or lessor is notified, which must occur within a reasonable time after the buyer or lessee either discovers or *should have discovered* the grounds for revocation. Additionally, revocation must occur before the goods have undergone any substantial change (such as spoilage) not caused by their own defects [UCC 2–608(2), 2A–517(4)].

The Right to Recover Damages for Accepted Goods A buyer or lessee who has accepted nonconforming goods may also keep the goods and recover damages caused by the breach. The buyer or lessee, however, must notify the seller or lessor of the breach within a reasonable time after the defect was or should have been discovered. Failure to give notice of the defects (breach) to the seller or lessor bars the buyer or lessee from pursuing any remedy [UCC 2–607(3), 2A–516(3)]. In addition, the parties to a sales or lease contract can insert a provision requiring the buyer or lessee to give notice of any defects in the goods within a set period.

When the goods delivered and accepted are not as promised, the measure of damages equals the difference between the value of the goods as accepted and their value if they had been delivered as warranted, plus incidental and consequential damages if appropriate [UCC 2–714(2), 2A–519(4)]. For this and other types of breaches in which the buyer or lessee has accepted the goods, the buyer or lessee is entitled to incidental and consequential damages [UCC 2–714(3), 2A–519]. The UCC also permits the buyer or lessee, with proper notice to the seller or lessor, to deduct all or any part of the damages from the price or lease payments still due and payable to the seller or lessor [UCC 2–717, 2A–516(1)].

Is two years after a sale of goods a reasonable time period in which to discover a defect in those goods and notify the seller or lessor of a breach? That was the question in the following case.

CASE 16.3 **Fitl v. Strek**

Supreme Court of Nebraska, 269 Neb. 51, 690 N.W.2d 605 (2005).
www.findlaw.com/11stategov/ne/neca.html[a]

FACTS Over the Labor Day weekend in 1995, James Fitl attended a sports-card show in San Francisco, California, where he met Mark Strek, doing business as Star Cards of San Francisco, an exhibitor at the show. Later, on Strek's representation that a certain 1952 Mickey Mantle Topps baseball card was in near-mint condition, Fitl bought the card

a. In the "Supreme Court Opinions" section, in the "2005" row, click on "January." In the result, click on the appropriate link next to the name of the case to access the opinion.

CASE 16.3—Continued

from Strek for $17,750. Strek delivered it to Fitl in Omaha, Nebraska, and Fitl placed it in a safe-deposit box. In May 1997, Fitl sent the card to Professional Sports Authenticators (PSA), a sports-card grading service. PSA told Fitl that the card was ungradable because it had been discolored and doctored. Fitl complained to Strek, who replied that Fitl should have initiated a return of the card within "a typical grace period for the unconditional return of a card, * * * 7 days to 1 month" of its receipt. In August, Fitl sent the card to ASA Accugrade, Inc. (ASA), another grading service, for a second opinion of the value. ASA also concluded that the card had been refinished and trimmed. Fitl filed a suit in a Nebraska state court against Strek, seeking damages. The court awarded Fitl $17,750, plus his court costs. Strek appealed to the Nebraska Supreme Court.

ISSUE Is two years after a sale of goods a reasonable time to discover a defect in those goods and notify the seller or lessor of a breach?

DECISION Yes. The state supreme court affirmed the decision of the lower court.

REASON UCC 2–607(3)(a) states, "Where a tender has been accepted * * * the buyer must within a reasonable time after he discovers or should have discovered any breach notify the seller of breach or be barred from any remedy." Under UCC 1–204(2), "what is a reasonable time for taking any action depends on the nature, purpose and circumstances of such action." The state supreme court concluded here that the buyer (Fitl) had reasonably relied on the seller's (Strek's) representation that the goods were "authentic," which they were not, and when their defects were discovered, Fitl had given a timely notice. The court reasoned that "the policies behind the notice requirement, to allow the seller to correct a defect, to prepare for negotiation and litigation, and to protect against stale claims at a time beyond which an investigation can be completed, were not unfairly prejudiced by the lack of an earlier notice to Strek. Any problem Strek may have had with the party from whom he obtained the baseball card was a separate matter from his transaction with Fitl, and an investigation into the source of the altered card would not have minimized Fitl's damages."

WHAT IF THE FACTS WERE DIFFERENT? *Suppose that Fitl and Strek had included in their deal a written clause requiring Fitl to give notice of any defect in the card within "7 days to 1 month" of its receipt. Would the result have been different? Why or why not?*

LIMITATION OF REMEDIES

The parties to a sales or lease contract can vary their respective rights and obligations by contractual agreement. For example, a seller and buyer can expressly provide for remedies in addition to those provided in the UCC. They can also provide remedies in lieu of those provided in the UCC, or they can change the measure of damages. The seller can provide that the buyer's only remedy on breach of warranty will be repair or replacement of the item, or the seller can limit the buyer's remedy to return of the goods and refund of the purchase price. In sales and lease contracts, an agreed-on remedy is in addition to those provided in the UCC unless the parties expressly agree that the remedy is exclusive of all others [UCC 2–719(1), 2A–503(1)].

Exclusive Remedies

If the parties state that a remedy is exclusive, then it is the sole remedy. **■EXAMPLE 16.14** Standard Tool Company agrees to sell a pipe-cutting machine to United Pipe & Tubing Corporation. The contract limits United's remedy exclusively to repair or replacement of any defective parts. Thus, repair or replacement of defective parts is the buyer's exclusive remedy under this contract. ■

When circumstances cause an exclusive remedy to fail in its essential purpose, however, it is no longer exclusive, and the buyer or lessee may pursue other remedies available under the UCC [UCC 2–719(2), 2A–503(2)]. **■EXAMPLE 16.15** In the example just given, suppose that Standard Tool Company was unable to repair a defective part, and no replacement parts were available. In this situation, because the exclusive remedy failed in its essential purpose, the buyer normally is entitled to seek other remedies provided to a buyer by the UCC. ■

Limitations on Consequential Damages

As discussed in Chapter 12, *consequential damages* are special damages that compensate for indirect losses (such as lost profits) resulting from a breach of contract that were reasonably foreseeable. Under the UCC, parties to a contract can limit or exclude consequential damages, provided the limitation is not unconscionable. When the buyer or lessee is a consumer, any limitation of consequential damages for personal injuries resulting from consumer goods is *prima facie* (presumptively) unconscionable. The limitation of consequential damages is not necessarily unconscionable when the loss is commercial in nature—for example, lost profits and property damage [UCC 2–719(3), 2A–503(3)].

Statute of Limitations

An action for breach of contract under the UCC must be commenced *within four years after the cause of action accrues*—that is, within four years after the breach occurs [UCC 2–725(1)]. In addition to filing suit within the four-year period, a buyer or lessee who has accepted nonconforming

goods usually must notify the breaching party of the breach within a reasonable time, or the aggrieved party is barred from pursuing any remedy [UCC 2–607(3)(a), 2A–516(3)]. The parties can agree in their contract to reduce this period to not less than one year, but cannot extend it beyond four years [UCC 2–725(1), 2A–506(1)]. A cause of action accrues for breach of warranty when the seller or lessor tenders delivery. This is the rule even if the aggrieved party is unaware that the cause of action has accrued [UCC 2–725(2), 2A–506(2)].

REVIEWING Performance and Breach of Sales and Lease Contracts

GFI, Inc., a Hong Kong company, makes audio decoder chips, one of the essential components used in the manufacture of MP3 players. Egan Electronics contracts with GFI to buy 10,000 chips on an installment contract, with 2,500 chips to be shipped every three months, F.O.B. Hong Kong via Air Express. At the time for the first delivery, GFI delivers only 2,400 chips but explains to Egan that while the shipment is less than 5 percent short, the chips are of a higher quality than those specified in the contract and are worth 5 percent more than the contract price. Egan accepts the shipment and pays GFI the contract price. At the time for the second shipment, GFI makes a shipment identical to the first. Egan again accepts and pays for the chips. At the time for the third shipment, GFI ships 2,400 of the same chips, but this time GFI sends them via Hong Kong Air instead of Air Express.

While in transit, the chips are destroyed. When it is time for the fourth shipment, GFI again sends 2,400 chips, but this time Egan rejects the chips without explanation. Using the information presented in the chapter, answer the following questions.

1 Did GFI have a legitimate reason to expect that Egan would accept the fourth shipment? Why or why not?

2 Does the substitution of carriers in the third shipment constitute a breach of the contract by GFI? Explain.

3 Suppose that the silicon used for the chips becomes unavailable for a period of time and that GFI cannot manufacture enough chips to fulfill the contract, but does ship as many as it can to Egan. Under what doctrine might a court release GFI from further performance of the contract?

4 Under the UCC, does Egan have a right to reject the fourth shipment? Why or why not?

TERMS AND CONCEPTS

conforming goods 306	**incidental damages 312**	**replevin 314**
cover 314	**installment contract 308**	**tender of delivery 306**

CHAPTER SUMMARY Performance and Breach of Sales and Lease Contracts

REQUIREMENTS OF PERFORMANCE

Obligations of the Seller or Lessor (See pages 305–311.)	1. The seller or lessor must tender *conforming* goods to the buyer or lessee. Tender must take place at a *reasonable hour* and in a *reasonable manner.* Under the perfect tender doctrine, the seller or lessor must tender goods that conform exactly to the terms of the contract [UCC 2–503(1), 2A–508(1)]. 2. If the seller or lessor tenders nonconforming goods prior to the performance date and the buyer or lessee rejects them, the seller or lessor may *cure* (repair or replace the goods) within the contract time for performance [UCC 2–508(1), 2A–513(1)]. If the seller or lessor has reasonable grounds to believe that the buyer or lessee would accept the tendered goods, on the buyer's or lessee's rejection the seller or lessor has a reasonable time to substitute conforming goods without liability [UCC 2–508(2), 2A–513(2)].

CHAPTER SUMMARY Performance and Breach of Sales and Lease Contracts–Continued

Obligations of the Seller or Lessor— Continued	3. If the agreed-on means of delivery becomes impracticable or unavailable, the seller must substitute an alternative means (such as a different carrier) if one is available [UCC 2–614(1)]. 4. If a seller or lessor tenders nonconforming goods in any one installment under an installment contract, the buyer or lessee may reject the installment only if its value is substantially impaired and cannot be cured. The entire installment contract is breached when one or more nonconforming installments *substantially* impair the value of the *whole* contract [UCC 2–612, 2A–510]. 5. When performance becomes commercially impracticable owing to circumstances that were not foreseeable when the contract was formed, the perfect tender rule no longer holds [UCC 2–615, 2A–405].
Obligations of the Buyer or Lessee (See page 311.)	1. On tender of delivery by the seller or lessor, the buyer or lessee must pay for the goods at the time and place the buyer or lessee *receives* the goods, even if the place of shipment is the place of delivery. Payment may be made by any method generally acceptable in the commercial world unless the seller demands cash [UCC 2–310, 2–511]. 2. Unless otherwise agreed, the buyer or lessee has an absolute right to inspect the goods before acceptance [UCC 2–513(1), 2A–515(1)]. 3. The buyer or lessee can manifest acceptance of delivered goods expressly in words or by conduct or by failing to reject the goods after a reasonable period of time following inspection or after having had a reasonable opportunity to inspect them [UCC 2–606(1), 2A–515(1)]. A buyer will be deemed to have accepted goods if he or she performs any act inconsistent with the seller's ownership [UCC 2–606(1)(c)].
Anticipatory Repudiation (See pages 311–312.)	If, before the time for performance, either party clearly indicates to the other an intention not to perform, under UCC 2–610 and 2A–402 the aggrieved party may do the following: 1. Await performance by the repudiating party for a commercially reasonable time. 2. Resort to any remedy for breach. 3. In either situation, suspend performance.
	REMEDIES FOR BREACH OF CONTRACT

Remedies of the Seller or Lessor (See pages 312–313.)	1. *When the goods are in the possession of the seller or lessor*—The seller or lessor may do the following:
	
	  a. Cancel the contract [UCC 2–703(f), 2A–523(1)(a)].
	  b. Withhold delivery [UCC 2–703(a), 2A–523(1)(c)].
	  c. Resell or dispose of the goods [UCC 2–703(d), 2–706(1), 2A–523(1)(e), 2A–527(1)].
	  d. Sue to recover the purchase price or lease payments due [UCC 2–709(1), 2A–529(1)].
	  e. Sue to recover damages [UCC 2–703(e), 2–708, 2A–528].
	
	2. *When the goods are in transit*—The seller or lessor may stop the carrier or bailee from delivering the goods [UCC 2–705, 2A–526].
	
	3. *When the goods are in the possession of the buyer or lessee*—The seller or lessor may do the following:
	
	  a. Sue to recover the purchase price or lease payments due [UCC 2–709(1), 2A–529(1)].
	  b. Reclaim the goods. A seller may reclaim goods received by an insolvent buyer if the demand is made within ten days of receipt (reclaiming goods excludes all other remedies) [UCC 2–702]; a lessor may repossess goods if the lessee is in default [UCC 2A–525(2)].

(Continued)

CHAPTER SUMMARY	Performance and Breach of Sales and Lease Contracts–Continued

Remedies of the Buyer or Lessee (See pages 313–317.)	1. *When the seller or lessor refuses to deliver the goods*—The buyer or lessee may do the following:
	a. Cancel the contract [UCC 2–711(1), 2A–508(1)(a)].
	b. Recover the goods if the seller or lessor becomes insolvent within ten days after receiving the first payment and the goods are identified to the contract [UCC 2–502, 2A–522].
	c. Obtain specific performance (when the goods are unique and when the remedy at law is inadequate) [UCC 2–716(1), 2A–521(1)].
	d. Obtain cover [UCC 2–712, 2A–518].
	e. Replevy the goods (if cover is unavailable) [UCC 2–716(3), 2A–521(3)].
	f. Sue to recover damages [UCC 2–713, 2A–519].
	
	2. *When the seller or lessor delivers or tenders delivery of nonconforming goods*—The buyer or lessee may do the following:
	a. Reject the goods [UCC 2–601, 2A–509].
	b. Revoke acceptance if the nonconformity *substantially* impairs the value of the unit or lot and if one of the following factors is present:
	   (1) Acceptance was predicated on the reasonable assumption that the nonconformity would be cured and it was not cured within a reasonable time [UCC 2–608(1)(a), 2A–517(1)(a)].
	   (2) The buyer or lessee did not discover the nonconformity before acceptance, either because it was difficult to discover before acceptance or because the seller's or lessor's assurance that the goods were conforming kept the buyer or lessee from inspecting the goods [UCC 2–608(1)(b), 2A–517(1)(b)].
	c. Accept the goods and recover damages [UCC 2–607, 2–714, 2–717, 2A–519].

Limitation of Remedies (See pages 317–318.)	Remedies may be limited in sales or lease contracts by agreement of the parties. If the contract states that a remedy is exclusive, then that is the sole remedy unless the remedy fails in its essential purpose. Sellers and lessors can also limit the rights of buyers and lessees to consequential damages unless the limitation is unconscionable [UCC 2–719, 2A–503].
Statute of Limitations (See page 318.)	The UCC has a four-year statute of limitations for actions involving breach of contract. By agreement, the parties to a sales or lease contract can reduce this period to not less than one year, but they cannot extend it beyond four years [UCC 2–725(1), 2A–506(1)].

FOR REVIEW

Answers for the even-numbered questions in this **For Review** *section can be found on this text's accompanying Web site at* **www.cengage.com/blaw/fbl**. *Select "Chapter 16" and click on "For Review."*

1 What are the respective obligations of the parties under a contract for the sale or lease of goods?

2 What is the perfect tender rule? What are some important exceptions to this rule that apply to sales and lease contracts?

3 What options are available to the nonbreaching party when the other party to a sales or lease contract repudiates the contract prior to the time for performance?

4 What remedies are available to a seller or lessor when the buyer or lessee breaches the contract? What remedies are available to a buyer or lessee if the seller or lessor breaches the contract?

5 In contracts subject to the UCC, are parties free to limit the remedies available to the nonbreaching party on a breach of contract? If so, in what ways?

QUESTIONS AND CASE PROBLEMS

 HYPOTHETICAL SCENARIOS AND CASE PROBLEMS

16.1 Remedies. Genix, Inc., has contracted to sell Larson five hundred washing machines of a certain model at list price. Genix is to ship the goods on or before December 1. Genix produces one thousand washing machines of this model but has not yet prepared Larson's shipment. On November 1, Larson repudiates the contract. Discuss the remedies available to Genix in this situation.

16.2 Hypothetical Question with Sample Answer. Cummings ordered two model X Super Fidelity speakers from Jamestown Wholesale Electronics, Inc. Jamestown shipped the speakers via United Parcel Service, C.O.D. (collect on delivery), although Cummings had not requested or agreed to a C.O.D. shipment of the goods. When the speakers were delivered, Cummings refused to accept them because he would not be able to inspect them before payment. Jamestown claimed that it had shipped conforming goods and that Cummings had breached their contract. Had Cummings breached the contract? Explain.

 For a sample answer to Question 16.2, go to Appendix E at the end of this text.

16.3 Right of Assurance. Advanced Polymer Sciences, Inc. (APS), based in Ohio, makes polymers and resins for use as protective coatings in industrial applications. APS also owns the technology for equipment used to make certain composite fibers. *SAVA gumarska in kemijska industria d.d.* (SAVA), based in Slovenia, makes rubber goods. In 1999, SAVA and APS contracted to form *SAVA Advanced Polymers proizvodno podjetje d.o.o.* (SAVA AP) to make and distribute APS products in Eastern Europe. Their contract provided for, among other things, the alteration of a facility to make the products using specially made equipment to be sold by APS to SAVA. Disputes arose between the parties, and in August 2000, SAVA stopped work on the new facility. APS then notified SAVA that it was stopping the manufacture of the equipment and "insist[ed] on knowing what is SAVA's intention towards this venture." In October, SAVA told APS that it was canceling their contract. In subsequent litigation, SAVA claimed that APS had repudiated the contract when it stopped making the equipment. What might APS assert in its defense? How should the court rule? Explain. [*SAVA gumarska in kemijska industria d.d. v. Advanced Polymer Sciences, Inc.*, 128 S.W.3d 304 (Tex.App.—Dallas 2004)]

16.4 Case Problem with Sample Answer. Eaton Corp. bought four air-conditioning units from Trane Co. The contract stated in part, "Neither party shall be liable for . . . consequential damages." Trane was responsible for servicing the units. In March 2003, Trane's employees serviced and inspected the units and made a material list for repairs. On April 3, a fire occurred at Eaton's facility, extensively damaging the units and the facility.

Alleging that the fire started in the electric motor of one of the units, and that Trane's faulty servicing of the units caused the fire, Eaton filed a suit against Trane. Eaton asserted breach of contract, among other claims, seeking consequential damages. Trane filed a motion for summary judgment, based on the limitation-of-remedies clause. What are consequential damages? Can these be limited in some circumstances? Is the clause valid in this case? Explain. [*Eaton Corp. v. Trane Carolina Plains*, 350 F.Supp.2d 699 (D.S.C. 2004)]

 After you have answered Problem 16.4, compare your answer with the sample answer given on the Web site that accompanies this text. Go to www.cengage.com/blaw/fbl, select "Chapter 16," and click on "Case Problem with Sample Answer."

16.5 Remedies of the Buyer. L.V.R.V., Inc., sells recreational vehicles (RVs) in Nevada, as Wheeler's Las Vegas RV. In 1997, Wheeler's sold a Santara RV to Arthur and Roswitha Waddell. The Waddells hoped to spend two or three years driving around the country, but almost immediately—and repeatedly—they experienced problems with the RV. Its entry door popped open. Its cooling and heating systems did not work properly. Its batteries did not maintain a charge. Most significantly, its engine overheated when ascending a moderate grade. The Waddells brought it to Wheeler's for repairs. Over the next year and a half, the RV spent more than seven months at Wheeler's. In 1999, the Waddells filed a complaint against the dealer to revoke their acceptance of the RV. What are the requirements for a buyer's revocation of acceptance? Were the requirements met in this case? In whose favor should the court rule? Why? [*Waddell v. L.V.R.V., Inc.*, 122 Nev. 125, 125 P.3d 1160 (2006)]

16.6 Additional Provisions Affecting Remedies. Nomo Agroindustrial Sa De CV is a company based in Mexico that grows vegetables to sell in the United States. In the early 2000s, Nomo had problems when its tomato plants contracted a disease: tomato spotted wilt virus (TSWV). To obtain a crop that was resistant to TSWV, Nomo contacted Enza Zaden North America, Inc., an international corporation that manufactures seeds. Enza's brochures advertised—and Enza told Nomo—that its Caiman variety was resistant to TSWV. Based on these assurances, Nomo bought Caiman seeds. The invoice, which Nomo's representative signed, limited any damages to the purchase price. The plants germinated from the Caiman seeds contracted TSWV, destroying Nomo's entire tomato crop. Nomo filed a suit against Enza, seeking to recover for the loss. Enza argued that any damages were limited to the price of the seeds. Can parties agree to limit their remedies under the UCC? If so, what are Nomo's best arguments against the enforcement of the limitations clause in Enza's invoice? What should the court rule on this issue? Why? [*Nomo Agroindustrial Sa De CV v. Enza Zaden North America, Inc.*, 492 F.Supp.2d 1175 (D.Ariz. 2007)]

16.7 **A Question of Ethics.** *Scotwood Industries, Inc., sells calcium chloride flake for use in ice melt products. Between July and September 2004, Scotwood delivered thirty-seven shipments of flake to Frank Miller & Sons, Inc. After each delivery, Scotwood billed Miller, which paid thirty-five of the invoices and processed 30 to 50 percent of the flake. In August, Miller began complaining about the quality. Scotwood assured Miller that it would remedy the situation. Finally, Miller told Scotwood, "[T]his is totally unacceptable. We are willing to discuss Scotwood picking up the material." Miller claimed that the flake was substantially defective because it*

was chunked. Calcium chloride maintains its purity for up to five years but chunks if it is exposed to and absorbs moisture, making it unusable. In response to Scotwood's suit to collect payment on the unpaid invoices, Miller filed a counterclaim for breach of contract, seeking to recover based on revocation of acceptance. [Scotwood Industries, Inc. v. Frank Miller & Sons, Inc., 435 F.Supp.2d 1160 (D.Kan. 2006)]

1 What is revocation of acceptance? Do the facts support this theory as a ground for Miller to recover damages? Why or why not?

2 Is there an ethical basis for allowing a buyer to revoke acceptance of goods and recover damages? If so, is there an ethical limit to this right? Discuss.

CRITICAL THINKING AND WRITING ASSIGNMENTS

16.8 Critical Legal Thinking. Under what circumstances should courts not allow fully informed contracting parties to agree to limit remedies?

16.9 Critical Thinking and Writing Assignment for Business. Suppose that you own antique cars and you need spare parts for a 1938 engine, which are scarce. You discover that Beem has the spare parts. To get the contract with Beem, you agree to

pay 50 percent of the purchase price in advance. You send the payment on May 1, and Beem receives it on May 2. On May 3, Beem, having found another buyer willing to pay substantially more for the parts, informs you that he will not deliver as contracted. That same day, you learn that Beem is insolvent. Discuss fully any possible remedies that would enable you to take possession of these parts.

ACCESSING THE INTERNET

For updated links to resources available on the Web, as well as a variety of other materials, visit this text's Web site at

www.cengage.com/blaw/fbl

To view the UCC provisions discussed in this chapter, go to

www.law.cornell.edu/ucc/ucc.table.html

PRACTICAL INTERNET EXERCISES

Go to this text's Web site at **www.cengage.com/blaw/fbl**, select "Chapter 16," and click on "Practical Internet Exercises." There you will find the following Internet research exercises that you can perform to learn more about the topics covered in this chapter.

PRACTICAL INTERNET EXERCISE 16–1 MANAGEMENT PERSPECTIVE—The Right to Reject Goods

PRACTICAL INTERNET EXERCISE 16–2 LEGAL PERSPECTIVE—International Performance Requirements

BEFORE THE TEST

Go to this text's Web site at **www.cengage.com/blaw/fbl**, select "Chapter 16," and click on "Interactive Quizzes." You will find a number of interactive questions relating to this chapter.

CHAPTER 17
Warranties and Product Liability

LEARNING OBJECTIVES

AFTER READING THIS CHAPTER, YOU SHOULD BE ABLE TO ANSWER THE FOLLOWING QUESTIONS:

1 What factors determine whether a seller's or lessor's statement constitutes an express warranty or mere *puffery?*

2 What implied warranties arise under the UCC?

3 Can a manufacturer be held liable to any person who suffers an injury proximately caused by the manufacturer's negligently made product?

4 What are the elements of a cause of action in strict product liability?

5 What defenses to liability can be raised in a product liability lawsuit?

Warranty is an age-old concept. In sales and lease law, a warranty is an assurance by one party of the existence of a fact on which the other party can rely. Sellers and lessors warrant to those who purchase or lease their goods that the goods are as represented or will be as promised.

The Uniform Commercial Code (UCC) has numerous rules governing product warranties as they occur in sales and lease contracts. Those rules are the subject matter of the first part of this chapter. A natural addition to the discussion is *product liability:* Who is liable to consumers, users, and bystanders for physical harm and property damage caused by a particular good or its use? Product liability encompasses the contract theory of warranty, as well as the tort theories of negligence and strict liability (discussed in Chapter 4).

WARRANTIES

Most goods are covered by some type of warranty designed to protect buyers. Article 2 (on sales) and Article 2A (on leases) of the UCC designate several types of warranties that can arise in a sales or lease contract, including warranties of title, express warranties, and implied warranties. We discuss these types of warranties in the following subsections, as well as a federal statute that is designed to prevent deception and make warranties more understandable.

Warranties of Title

Title warranty arises automatically in most sales contracts. The UCC imposes three types of warranties of title.

Good Title In most sales, sellers warrant that they have good and valid title to the goods sold and that transfer of the title is rightful [UCC 2–312(1)(a)]. **■EXAMPLE 17.1** Sharon steals goods from Miguel and sells them to Carrie, who does not know that the goods are stolen. If Miguel reclaims the goods from Carrie, which he has a right to do, Carrie can then sue Sharon for breach of warranty. When Sharon sold Carrie the goods, Sharon *automatically* warranted to her that the title conveyed was valid and that its transfer was rightful. Because this was not in fact the case, Sharon breached the warranty of title imposed by UCC 2–312(1)(a) and became liable to the buyer for the appropriate damages. ■

No Liens   A second warranty of title protects buyers who are *unaware* of any encumbrances, or **liens** (claims, charges, or liabilities—see Chapter 21), against the goods at the time the contract is made [UCC 2–312(1)(b)]. This warranty protects buyers who, for example, unknowingly purchase goods that are subject to a creditor's security interest (an interest in the goods that secures payment or performance, to be discussed in Chapter 20). If a creditor legally repossesses the goods from a buyer *who had no actual knowledge of the security interest*, the buyer can recover from the seller for breach of warranty. (A buyer who actually knows that a security interest exists has no recourse against the seller.)

Article 2A affords similar protection for lessees. Section 2A–211(1) provides that during the term of the lease, no claim of any third party will interfere with the lessee's enjoyment of the leasehold interest.

No Infringements   A merchant-seller is also deemed to warrant that the goods delivered are free from any copyright, trademark, or patent claims of a third person [UCC 2–312(3), 2A–211(2)].[1] If this warranty is breached and the buyer is sued by the party holding copyright, trademark, or patent rights in the goods, the buyer must notify the seller of the litigation within a reasonable time to enable the seller to decide whether to defend the lawsuit. If the seller states in a writing (or record) that she or he has decided to defend and agrees to bear all expenses, then the buyer must turn over control of the litigation to the seller; otherwise, the buyer is barred from any remedy against the seller for liability established by the litigation [UCC 2–607(3)(b), 2–607(5)(b)].

In situations that involve leases rather than sales, Article 2A requires the same notice of infringement litigation [UCC 2A–516(3)(b), 2A–516(4)(b)]. There is an exception for leases to individual consumers for personal, family, or household purposes. A consumer who fails to notify the lessor within a reasonable time does not lose his or her remedy against the lessor for whatever liability is established in the litigation [UCC 2A–516(3)(b)].

Disclaimer of Title Warranty   In an ordinary sales transaction, the title warranty can be disclaimed or modified only by *specific language* in the contract [UCC 2–312(2)]. For example, sellers can assert that they are transferring only such rights, title, and interest as they have in the goods. In a lease transaction, the disclaimer must be specific, be in a writing (or record), and be conspicuous [UCC 2A–214(4)].

---

1. Recall from Chapter 14 that a *merchant* is defined in UCC 2–104(1) as a person who deals in goods of the kind involved in the sales contract or who, by occupation, presents himself or herself as having knowledge or skill peculiar to the goods involved in the transaction.

Express Warranties

A seller or lessor can create an **express warranty** by making representations concerning the quality, condition, description, or performance potential of the goods. Under UCC 2–313 and 2A–210, express warranties arise when a seller or lessor indicates any of the following:

1 That the goods conform to any *affirmation* (declaration that something is true) or *promise* of fact that the seller or lessor makes to the buyer or lessee about the goods. Such affirmations or promises are usually made during the bargaining process. Statements such as "these drill bits will penetrate stainless steel—and without dulling" are express warranties.

2 That the goods conform to any *description* of them. For example, a label that reads "Crate contains one 150-horsepower diesel engine" or a contract that calls for the delivery of a "camel's-hair coat" creates an express warranty.

3 That the goods conform to any *sample or model* of the goods shown to the buyer or lessee.

Basis of the Bargain   To create an express warranty, a seller or lessor does not have to use formal words such as *warrant* or *guarantee* [UCC 2–313(2), 2A–210(2)]. It is only necessary that a reasonable buyer or lessee would regard the representation of fact as part of the basis of the bargain [UCC 2–313(1), 2A–210(1)]. Just what constitutes the basis of the bargain is hard to say. The UCC does not define the concept, and it is a question of fact in each case whether a representation was made at such a time and in such a way that it induced the buyer or lessee to enter into the contract.

PREVENTING LEGAL DISPUTES

Be careful about the words you use with customers, in writing and orally. Express warranties can be found in a seller's or lessor's advertisement, brochure, or promotional materials, in addition to being made orally or in an express warranty provision in a contract. Avoiding unintended warranties is crucial in preventing legal disputes, and all employees should be instructed on how the promises they make to buyers during a sale can create warranties.

Statements of Opinion and Value   Only statements of fact create express warranties. If the seller or lessor makes a statement that relates to the supposed value or worth of the goods, or makes a statement of opinion or recommendation about the goods, the seller or lessor is not creating an express warranty [UCC 2–313(2), 2A–210(2)].

■EXAMPLE 17.2 A seller claims that "this is the best used car to come along in years; it has four new tires and a 250-horsepower engine just rebuilt this year." The seller has made several *affirmations of fact* that can create a warranty: the automobile has an engine; it has a 250-horsepower engine; it was rebuilt this year; there are four tires on the automobile; and the tires are new. The seller's *opinion* that the vehicle is "the best used car to come along in years," however, is known as "puffery" and creates no warranty. (*Puffery* is the expression of opinion by a seller or lessor that is not made as a representation of fact.) **■**

A statement relating to the value of the goods, such as "this is worth a fortune" or "anywhere else you'd pay $10,000 for it," usually does not create a warranty. If the seller or lessor is an expert and gives an opinion as an expert to a layperson, though, then a warranty may be created.

It is not always easy to determine whether a statement constitutes an express warranty or puffery. The reasonableness of the buyer's or lessee's reliance appears to be the controlling criterion in many cases. For example, a salesperson's statements that a ladder "will never break" and will "last a lifetime" are so clearly improbable that no reasonable buyer should rely on them. Additionally, the context in which a statement is made might be relevant in determining the reasonableness of the buyer's or lessee's reliance. For example, a reasonable person is more likely to rely on a written statement made in an advertisement than on a statement made orally by a salesperson.

Implied Warranties

An **implied warranty** is one that *the law derives* by implication or inference because of the circumstances of a sale, rather than by the seller's express promise. In an action based on breach of implied warranty, it is necessary to show that an implied warranty existed and that the breach of the warranty proximately caused[2] the damage sustained. We look here at some of the implied warranties that arise under the UCC.

Implied Warranty of Merchantability   Every sale or lease of goods made *by a merchant who deals in goods of the kind sold or leased* automatically gives rise to an **implied warranty of merchantability** [UCC 2–314, 2A–212]. **■EXAMPLE 17.3** A merchant who is in the business of selling ski equipment, for instance, makes an implied warranty of merchantability every time she sells a pair of skis. A neighbor selling his skis at a garage sale does not (because he is not in the business of selling goods of this type). **■**

Merchantable Goods.   Goods that are *merchantable* are "reasonably fit for the ordinary purposes for which such goods are used." They must be of at least average, fair, or medium-grade quality. The quality must be comparable to a level that will pass without objection in the trade or market for goods of the same description. To be merchantable, the goods must also be adequately packaged and labeled, and they must conform to the promises or affirmations of fact made on the container or label, if any.

It makes no difference whether the merchant knew or could have discovered that a product was defective (not merchantable). Of course, merchants are not absolute insurers against all accidents arising in connection with the goods. For example, a bar of soap is not unmerchantable merely because a user could slip and fall by stepping on it.

If the buyer of a product that requires a significant number of repairs sells the item before filing a complaint against its manufacturer, is the sale evidence of the product's merchantability? That was the question in the following case.

---

2. Proximate, or legal, cause exists when the connection between an act and an injury is strong enough to justify imposing liability—see Chapter 4.

CASE 17.1   **Shoop v. DaimlerChrysler Corp.**

Appellate Court of Illinois, First District, 371 Ill.App.3d 1058, 864 N.E.2d 785, 309 Ill.Dec. 544 (2007).

FACTS   In April 2002, Darrell Shoop bought a 2002 Dodge Dakota truck for $28,000 from Dempsey Dodge in Chicago, Illinois. DaimlerChrysler Corporation had manufactured the Dakota. Problems with the truck arose almost immediately. Defects in the engine, suspension, steering, transmission, and other components required repairs twelve times within the first eighteen months, including at least five times for the same defect, which remained uncorrected. In May 2005, after having driven the Dakota 39,000 miles, Shoop accepted $16,500 for the trade-in value of the truck as part of a purchase of a new vehicle. At the time, a comparable vehicle in average condition would have had an average trade-in value of $14,425 and an average retail value of $17,225. Shoop filed a suit in an Illinois state court against DaimlerChrysler, alleging, among other things, a breach of the implied warranty of merchantability.

CASE 17.1–Continues next page

CASE 17.1—Continued

DaimlerChrysler countered, in part, that Shoop's sale of the Dakota was evidence of its merchantability. The court issued a summary judgment in DaimlerChrysler's favor. Shoop appealed to a state intermediate appellate court.

ISSUE Was there sufficient evidence that DaimlerChrysler breached the implied warranty of merchantability?

DECISION Yes. The state appellate court reversed the lower court's summary judgment and remanded the case for trial.

REASON For automobiles, fitness for the ordinary purpose of driving implies that the vehicle should be in safe condition and free from defects. The reviewing court stated that, in addition, "breach of an implied warranty of merchantability

may also occur when the warrantor has unsuccessfully attempted to repair or replace defective parts. Whether an implied warranty has been breached is a question of fact." The facts in this case were clear: the plaintiff was required to take the truck to the Chrysler dealership twelve times within eighteen months. The dealership was unable to cure the defects after a reasonable number of attempts. The state appellate court concluded that "a genuine issue of material fact existed as to whether Chrysler breached the implied warranty of merchantability."

 FOR CRITICAL ANALYSIS—Legal Consideration *If Shoop is allowed to recover damages for breach of warranty, what should be the measure of those damages?*

■

Merchantable Food. The UCC recognizes the serving of food or drink to be consumed on or off the premises as a sale of goods subject to the implied warranty of merchantability [UCC 2–314(1)]. "Merchantable" food means food that is fit to eat. Courts generally determine whether food is fit to eat on the basis of consumer expectations. The courts assume that consumers should reasonably expect on occasion to find bones in fish fillets, cherry pits in cherry pie, or a nutshell in a package of shelled nuts, for example—because such substances are natural incidents of the food. In contrast, consumers would not reasonably expect to find an inchworm in a can of peas or a piece of glass in a soft drink—because these substances are not natural to the food product.[3] In the following classic case, the court had to determine whether a fish bone was a substance that one should reasonably expect to find in fish chowder.

---

3. See, for example, *Ruvolo v. Homovich,* 149 Ohio App.3d 701, 778 N.E.2d 661 (2002).

CASE 17.2	**Webster v. Blue Ship Tea Room, Inc.**

LANDMARK AND CLASSIC CASES

Supreme Judicial Court of Massachusetts, 347 Mass. 421, 198 N.E.2d 309 (1964).

FACTS Blue Ship Tea Room, Inc., was located in Boston in an old building overlooking the ocean. Priscilla Webster, who had been born and raised in New England, went to the restaurant and ordered fish chowder. The chowder was milky in color. After three or four spoonfuls, she felt something lodged in her throat. As a result, she underwent two esophagoscopies; in the second esophagoscopy, a fish bone was found and removed. Webster filed a lawsuit against the restaurant in a Massachusetts state court for breach of the implied warranty of merchantability. The jury rendered a verdict for Webster, and the restaurant appealed to the state's highest court.

ISSUE Does serving fish chowder that contains a bone constitute a breach of an implied warranty of merchantability on the part of the restaurant?

DECISION No. The Supreme Judicial Court of Massachusetts held that Webster could not recover against Blue Ship Tea Room because no breach of warranty had occurred.

REASON The court, citing UCC Section 2–314, stated that "a warranty that goods shall be merchantable is implied in a contract for their sale if the seller is a merchant with respect to goods of that kind. Under this section the serving for value of food or drink to be consumed either on the premises or elsewhere is a sale. * * * Goods to be merchantable must at least be * * * fit for the ordinary purposes for which such goods are used." The question here was whether a fish bone made the chowder unfit for eating. In the judge's opinion, "the joys of life in New England include the ready availability of fresh fish chowder. We should be prepared to cope with the hazards of fish bones, the occasional presence of which in

CASE 17.2–Continued

chowders is, it seems to us, to be anticipated, and which, in the light of a hallowed tradition, do not impair their fitness or merchantability."

 FOR CRITICAL ANALYSIS—Technological Consideration *If Webster had made the chowder herself from a recipe that she had found on the Internet, could she have successfully brought an action against its author for a breach of the implied warranty of merchantability? Explain your answer.*

IMPACT OF THIS CASE ON TODAY'S LAW *This classic case, phrased in memorable language, was an early*

application of the UCC's implied warranty of merchantability to food products. The case established the rule that consumers should expect to find, on occasion, elements of food products that are natural to the product (such as fish bones in fish chowder). Courts today still apply this rule.

RELEVANT WEB SITES *To locate information on the Web concerning the* Webster v. Blue Ship Tea Room, Inc., *decision, go to this text's Web site at* **www.cengage.com/blaw/fbl**, *select "Chapter 17," and click on "URLs for Landmarks."*

■

Implied Warranty of Fitness for a Particular Purpose The **implied warranty of fitness for a particular purpose** arises when any seller or lessor (merchant or nonmerchant) knows the particular purpose for which a buyer or lessee will use the goods *and* knows that the buyer or lessee is relying on the skill and judgment of the seller or lessor to select suitable goods [UCC 2–315, 2A–213].

Particular versus Ordinary Purpose. A "particular purpose" of the buyer or lessee differs from the "ordinary purpose for which goods are used" (merchantability). Goods can be merchantable but unfit for a particular purpose. **■EXAMPLE 17.4** Suppose that you need a gallon of paint to match the color of your living room walls—a light shade somewhere between coral and peach. You take a sample to your local hardware store and request a gallon of paint of that color. Instead, you are given a gallon of bright blue paint. Here, the salesperson has not breached any warranty of implied merchantability—the bright blue paint is of high quality and suitable for interior walls—but he or she has breached an implied warranty of fitness for a particular purpose. ■

Knowledge and Reliance Requirements. A seller or lessor is not required to have actual knowledge of the buyer's or lessee's particular purpose, so long as the seller or lessor "has reason to know" the purpose. For an implied warranty to be created, however, the buyer or lessee must have *relied* on the skill or judgment of the seller or lessor in selecting or furnishing suitable goods.

■EXAMPLE 17.5 Bloomberg leases a computer from Future Tech, a lessor of technical business equipment. Bloomberg tells the clerk that she wants a computer that will run a complicated new engineering graphics program at a realistic speed. Future Tech leases Bloomberg an Architex One computer

with a CPU speed of only 2.4 gigahertz, even though a speed of at least 3.8 gigahertz would be required to run Bloomberg's graphics program at a "realistic speed." Bloomberg, after discovering that it takes forever to run her program, wants her money back. Here, because Future Tech has breached the implied warranty of fitness for a particular purpose, Bloomberg normally will be able to recover. The clerk knew specifically that Bloomberg wanted a computer with enough speed to run certain software. Furthermore, Bloomberg relied on the clerk to furnish a computer that would fulfill this purpose. Because Future Tech did not do so, the warranty was breached. ■

Warranties Implied from Prior Dealings or Trade Custom Implied warranties can also arise (or be excluded or modified) as a result of course of dealing or usage of trade [UCC 2–314(3), 2A–212(3)]. In the absence of evidence to the contrary, when both parties to a sales or lease contract have knowledge of a well-recognized trade custom, the courts will infer that both parties intended for that trade custom to apply to their contract. **■EXAMPLE 17.6** Suppose that it is an industry-wide custom to lubricate new cars before the cars are delivered to a buyer. Latoya buys a new car from Bender Chevrolet. After the purchase, Latoya discovers that Bender failed to lubricate the car before delivering it to her. In this situation, Latoya can hold the dealer liable for damages resulting from the breach of an implied warranty. (This, of course, would also be negligence on the part of the dealer.) ■

Overlapping Warranties

Sometimes, two or more warranties are made in a single transaction. An implied warranty of merchantability, an implied warranty of fitness for a particular purpose, or both can exist in addition to an express warranty. For example, when a sales contract for a new car states that "this car engine is warranted to be free from defects for 36,000 miles or thirty-six months, whichever occurs first," there is an express warranty against all defects and an implied warranty that the car will be fit for normal use.

The rule under the UCC is that express and implied warranties are construed as *cumulative* if they are consistent with one another [UCC 2–317, 2A–215]. In other words, courts interpret two or more warranties as being in agreement with each other unless this construction is unreasonable. If it is unreasonable, then a court will hold that the warranties are inconsistent and apply the following rules to interpret which warranty is most important:

1 *Express* warranties displace inconsistent *implied* warranties, except for implied warranties of fitness for a particular purpose.

2 Samples take precedence over inconsistent general descriptions.

3 Exact or technical specifications displace inconsistent samples or general descriptions.

■EXAMPLE 17.7 Suppose that when Bloomberg leases the computer from Future Tech in Example 17.5, the contract contains an express warranty concerning the speed of the CPU and the application programs that the computer is capable of running. Bloomberg does not realize that the speed expressly warranted in the contract is insufficient for her needs. Bloomberg later claims that Future Tech has breached the implied warranty of fitness for a particular purpose because she made it clear that she was leasing the computer to perform certain tasks. In this situation, Bloomberg has a good claim for the breach of implied warranty of fitness for a particular purpose, because she had discussed with Future Tech the specific tasks that she needed the computer to perform. Although the express warranty on CPU speed takes precedence over the implied warranty of merchantability, it normally does not take precedence over an implied warranty of fitness for a particular purpose. Bloomberg normally will prevail. ■

Warranty Disclaimers

The UCC generally permits warranties to be disclaimed or limited by specific and unambiguous language, provided that this is done in a manner that protects the buyer or lessee from surprise. Because each type of warranty is created in a special way, the manner in which a seller or lessor can disclaim warranties varies depending on the type of warranty.

Express Warranties As already stated, any affirmation of fact or promise, description of the goods, or use of samples or models by a seller or lessor creates an express warranty. Obviously, then, express warranties can be excluded if the seller or lessor carefully refrains from making any promise or affirmation of fact relating to the goods, describing the goods, or using a sample or model.

In addition, a written (or recorded) disclaimer in language that is clear and conspicuous, and called to a buyer's or lessee's attention, can negate all oral express warranties not included in the sales or lease contract [UCC 2–316(1), 2A–214(1)]. This allows the seller or lessor to avoid false allegations that oral warranties were made, and it ensures that only representations made by properly authorized individuals are included in the bargain.

Note, however, that a buyer or lessee must be made aware of any warranty disclaimers or modifications *at the time the contract is formed.* In other words, any oral or written warranties—or disclaimers—made during the bargaining process as part of a contract's formation cannot be modified at a later time by the seller or lessor.

Implied Warranties Generally speaking, implied warranties are much easier for a seller or lessor to disclaim. Under the UCC, unless circumstances indicate otherwise, all implied warranties are disclaimed by the expressions "as is," "with all faults," and other similar language that in common understanding call the buyer's or lessee's attention to the fact that there are no implied warranties [UCC 2–316(3)(a), 2A–214(3)(a)]. (Note, however, that some states have passed consumer protection statutes forbidding "as is" sales or making it illegal to disclaim warranties of merchantability on consumer goods.)

■EXAMPLE 17.8 Sue Hallett saw an advertisement offering a "lovely, eleven-year-old mare" with extensive jumping ability for sale. After visiting Mandy Morningstar's ranch and examining the horse twice, Hallett contracted to buy it for $2,950. The contract she signed described the horse as an eleven-year-old mare, but indicated that the horse was being sold "as is." Shortly after the purchase, a veterinarian determined that the horse was actually sixteen years old and in no condition for jumping. Hallett immediately notified her bank and stopped payment on the check she had written to pay for the horse. Hallett also tried to return the horse and cancel the contract with Morningstar, but Morningstar refused and filed a suit against Hallett, claiming breach of contract. The trial court found in favor of Morningstar because Hallett had examined the horse and was satisfied with its condition at the time she signed the "as is" sales contract. The appellate court reversed, however, finding that the statement in the contract describing the horse as eleven years old constituted an express warranty, which Morningstar breached. The appellate court reasoned that although the "as is" clause effectively disclaimed any implied warranties (of merchantability and fitness for a particular purpose, such as jumping), it did not disclaim the express warranty concerning the horse's age.[4] ◼

Disclaimer of the Implied Warranty of Merchantability. The UCC also permits a seller or lessor to specifically disclaim an implied warranty of merchantability [UCC 2–316(2), 2A–214(2)]. A merchantability disclaimer must specifically mention the word *merchantability*. The disclaimer need not be written, but if it is, the writing (or record) must be conspicuous [UCC 2–316(2), 2A–214(4)]. Under the UCC, a term or clause is conspicuous when it is written or displayed in such a way that a reasonable person would notice it. Conspicuous terms include words set in capital letters, in a larger font size, or in a different color so as to be set off from the surrounding text.

◼**EXAMPLE 17.9** Forbes, a merchant, sells Maves a particular lawn mower selected by Forbes with the characteristics clearly requested by Maves. At the time of the sale, Forbes orally tells Maves that he does not warrant the merchantability of the mower, as it is last year's model and has been used for demonstration purposes. If the mower proves to be defective and does not work, Maves can hold Forbes liable for breach of the warranty of fitness for a particular purpose but not for breach of the warranty of merchantability. Forbes's oral disclaimer mentioning the word *merchantability* is a proper disclaimer. ◼

Disclaimer of the Implied Warranty of Fitness. To specifically disclaim an implied warranty of fitness for a particular purpose, the disclaimer *must* be in a writing (or record) and must be conspicuous. The word *fitness* does not have to be mentioned; it is sufficient if, for example, the disclaimer states, "THERE ARE NO WARRANTIES THAT EXTEND BEYOND THE DESCRIPTION ON THE FACE HEREOF."

Buyer's or Lessee's Examination or Refusal to Inspect If a buyer or lessee actually examines the goods (or a sample or model) as fully as desired before entering into a contract, or if the buyer or lessee refuses to examine the goods on the seller's or lessor's request that he or she do so, *there is no implied warranty with respect to defects that a reasonable examination would reveal or defects that are actually found* [UCC 2–316(3)(b), 2A–214(2)(b)].

◼**EXAMPLE 17.10** Joplin buys a lamp at Gershwin's Home Store. No express warranties are made. Gershwin requests that Joplin inspect the lamp before buying it, but she refuses. Had Joplin inspected the lamp, she would have noticed that the base of the lamp was obviously cracked and the electrical cord was loose. If the lamp later cracks or starts a fire in Joplin's home and she is injured, she normally will not be able to hold Gershwin's liable for breach of the warranty of merchantability. Because Joplin refused to examine the lamp when asked by Gershwin, Joplin will be deemed to have assumed the risk that it was defective. ◼

Warranty Disclaimers and Unconscionability The UCC sections dealing with warranty disclaimers do not refer specifically to unconscionability as a factor. Ultimately, however, the courts will test warranty disclaimers with reference to the UCC's unconscionability standards [UCC 2–302, 2A–108]. Such things as lack of bargaining position, "take-it-or-leave-it" choices, and a buyer's or lessee's failure to understand or know of a warranty disclaimer will become relevant to the issue of unconscionability.

Magnuson-Moss Warranty Act

The Magnuson-Moss Warranty Act of 1975[5] was designed to prevent deception in warranties by making them easier to understand. The Federal Trade Commission (FTC) is the main agency that enforces this federal law. Additionally, the attorney general or a consumer who has been injured can bring an action to enforce the act if informal procedures for settling disputes prove to be ineffective. The act modifies UCC warranty rules to some extent when consumer transactions are involved. The UCC, however, remains the primary codification of warranty rules for commercial transactions.

Under the Magnuson-Moss Act, no seller or lessor is required to give an express written warranty for consumer goods sold. If a seller or lessor chooses to make an express written warranty, however, and the goods are priced at more than $25, the warranty must be labeled as "full" or "limited." In addition, the warrantor must make certain disclosures fully and conspicuously in a single document in "readily understood language." This disclosure must state the names and addresses of the warrantor(s), what specifically is warranted, procedures for enforcing the warranty, any limitations on warranty relief, and that the buyer has legal rights.

Full Warranty Although a *full warranty* may not cover every aspect of the consumer product sold, what it does cover ensures some type of consumer satisfaction in the event that the product is defective. A full warranty requires free repair or replacement of any defective part; if the product cannot be repaired within a reasonable time, the consumer has the choice of a refund or a replacement without charge.

---

4. *Morningstar v. Hallett*, 858 A.2d 125 (Pa.Super.Ct. 2004).

5. 15 U.S.C. Sections 2301–2312.

Frequently, there is no time limit on a full warranty. Any limitation on consequential damages must be *conspicuously* stated. Additionally, the warrantor need not perform warranty services if the problem with the product was caused by the consumer's unreasonable use of the product.

Limited Warranty   A *limited warranty* arises when the written warranty fails to meet one of the minimum requirements of a full warranty. The fact that only a limited warranty is being given must be conspicuously stated. If the only distinction between a limited warranty and a full warranty is a time limitation, the Magnuson-Moss Warranty Act allows the warrantor to identify the warranty as a full warranty by such language as "full twelve-month warranty."

Implied Warranties   Implied warranties do not arise under the Magnuson-Moss Warranty Act; they continue to be created according to UCC provisions. Implied warranties may not be disclaimed under the Magnuson-Moss Warranty Act, however. Although a warrantor can impose a time limit on the duration of an implied warranty, it must correspond to the duration of the express warranty.[6]

LEMON LAWS

Some purchasers of defective automobiles—called "lemons"—found that the remedies provided by the UCC were inadequate due to limitations imposed by the seller. In response to the frustrations of these buyers, all of the states have enacted *lemon laws.*

Coverage of Lemon Laws

Basically, state lemon laws provide remedies to consumers who buy automobiles that repeatedly fail to meet standards of quality and performance because they are "lemons." Although lemon laws vary by state, typically they apply to automobiles under warranty that are defective in a way that significantly affects the vehicle's value or use. Lemon laws do not necessarily cover used-car purchases (unless the car is covered by a manufacturer's extended warranty) or vehicles that are leased. (Note that in some states, such as California, these laws may extend beyond automobile purchases and apply to other consumer goods.) Generally, the seller or manufacturer is given a number of opportunities to remedy the defect (usually four). If the seller fails to cure the problem despite a reasonable number of attempts (as specified by state law), the buyer is entitled to a new car, replacement of defec-

tive parts, or return of all consideration paid. Buyers who prevail in a lemon law dispute may also be entitled to reimbursement for their attorneys' fees.

Arbitration Is Typical Procedure

In most states, lemon laws require an aggrieved new-car owner to notify the dealer or manufacturer of the problem and to provide the dealer or manufacturer with an opportunity to solve it. If the problem persists, the owner must then submit complaints to the arbitration program specified in the manufacturer's warranty before taking the case to court. Decisions by arbitration panels are binding on the manufacturer (that is, cannot be appealed by the manufacturer to the courts) but usually are not binding on the purchaser.

Most major automobile companies use their own arbitration panels. Some companies, however, subscribe to independent arbitration services, such as those provided by the Better Business Bureau. Although arbitration boards must meet state and/or federal standards of impartiality, industry-sponsored arbitration boards have been criticized for not being truly impartial. In response to this criticism, some states have established mandatory, government-sponsored arbitration programs for lemon-law disputes.

PRODUCT LIABILITY

Those who make, sell, or lease goods can be held liable for physical harm or property damage caused by those goods to a consumer, user, or bystander. This is called **product liability.** Product liability claims may be based on the warranty theories just discussed, as well as on the theories of negligence, misrepresentation, and strict liability. We look here at product liability based on negligence and misrepresentation.

Negligence

Chapter 4 defined *negligence* as the failure to exercise the degree of care that a reasonable, prudent person would have exercised under the circumstances. If a manufacturer fails to exercise "due care" to make a product safe, a person who is injured by the product may sue the manufacturer for negligence.

Due Care Must Be Exercised   The manufacturer must exercise due care in designing the product, selecting the materials, using the appropriate production process, assembling the product, and placing adequate warnings on the label informing the user of dangers of which an ordinary person might not be aware. The duty of care also extends to the inspection and testing of any purchased products that are used in the final product sold by the manufacturer.

---

6. The time limit on an implied warranty occurring by virtue of the warrantor's express warranty must, of course, be reasonable, conscionable, and set forth in clear and conspicuous language on the face of the warranty.

Privity of Contract Not Required A product liability action based on negligence does not require the injured plaintiff and the negligent defendant-manufacturer to be in *privity of contract* (see Chapter 11). In other words, the plaintiff and the defendant need not be directly involved in a contractual relationship—that is, in privity. Thus, any person who is injured by a product may bring a negligence suit even though he or she was not the one who actually purchased the product. A manufacturer, seller, or lessor is liable for failure to exercise due care to *any person* who sustains an injury proximately caused by a negligently made (defective) product. Relative to the long history of the common law, this exception to the privity requirement is a fairly recent development, dating to the early part of the twentieth century.[7]

Misrepresentation

When a fraudulent misrepresentation has been made to a user or consumer, and that misrepresentation ultimately results in an injury, the basis of liability may be the tort of fraud. For example, the intentional mislabeling of packaged cosmetics or the intentional concealment of a product's defects would constitute fraudulent misrepresentation. The misrepresentation must be of a material fact, and the seller must have had the intent to induce the buyer's reliance on the misrepresentation. Misrepresentation on a label or advertisement is enough to show an intent to induce the reliance of anyone who may use the product. In addition, the buyer must have relied on the misrepresentation.

STRICT PRODUCT LIABILITY

Under the doctrine of strict liability (discussed in Chapter 4), parties may be liable for the results of their acts regardless of their intentions or their exercise of reasonable care. In addition, liability does not depend on privity of contract. The injured party does not have to be the buyer or a third party beneficiary (see Chapter 11), as required under contract warranty theory. In the 1960s, courts applied the doctrine of strict liability in several landmark cases involving manufactured goods, and it has since become a common method of holding manufacturers liable.

Strict Product Liability and Public Policy

The law imposes strict product liability as a matter of public policy. This public policy rests on the threefold assumption that (1) consumers should be protected against unsafe products; (2) manufacturers and distributors should not escape

liability for faulty products simply because they are not in privity of contract with the ultimate user of those products; and (3) manufacturers, sellers, and lessors of products are generally in a better position than consumers to bear the costs associated with injuries caused by their products—costs that they can ultimately pass on to all consumers in the form of higher prices.

California was the first state to impose strict product liability in tort on manufacturers. In a landmark 1963 decision, *Greenman v. Yuba Power Products, Inc.*,[8] the California Supreme Court set out the reason for applying tort law rather than contract law in cases involving consumers injured by defective products. According to the court, the "purpose of such liability is to [e]nsure that the costs of injuries resulting from defective products are borne by the manufacturers . . . rather than by the injured persons who are powerless to protect themselves."

Requirements for Strict Product Liability

Section 402A of the *Restatement (Second) of Torts* indicates how the drafters envisioned that the doctrine of strict product liability should be applied. The *Restatement* was issued in 1964, and during the next decade, Section 402A became a widely accepted statement of the liabilities of sellers of goods (including manufacturers, processors, assemblers, packagers, bottlers, wholesalers, distributors, retailers, and lessors).

The bases for an action in strict product liability as set forth in Section 402A of the *Restatement (Second) of Torts*, and as the doctrine came to be commonly applied, can be summarized as a series of six requirements, which are listed here. Depending on the jurisdiction, if these requirements are met, a manufacturer's liability to an injured party can be virtually unlimited.

1 The product must be in a *defective condition* when the defendant sells it.

2 The defendant normally must be engaged in the *business of selling* (or otherwise distributing) that product.

3 The product must be *unreasonably dangerous* to the user or consumer because of its defective condition (in most states).

4 The plaintiff must incur *physical harm* to self or property by use or consumption of the product.

5 The defective condition must be the *proximate cause* of the injury or damage.

6 The *goods must not have been substantially changed* from the time the product was sold to the time the injury was sustained.

---

7. A landmark case in this respect is *MacPherson v. Buick Motor Co.*, 217 N.Y. 382, 111 N.E. 1050 (1916).

8. 59 Cal.2d 57, 377 P.2d 897, 27 Cal.Rptr. 697 (1963).

Proving a Defective Condition   Under these requirements, in any action against a manufacturer, seller, or lessor, the plaintiff does not have to show why or in what manner the product became defective. The plaintiff does, however, have to prove that the product was defective at the time it left the hands of the seller or lessor and that this defective condition made it "unreasonably dangerous" to the user or consumer. Unless evidence can be presented that will support the conclusion that the product was defective when it was sold or leased, the plaintiff normally will not succeed. If the product was delivered in a safe condition and subsequent mishandling made it harmful to the user, the seller or lessor normally is not strictly liable.

Unreasonably Dangerous Products   The *Restatement* recognizes that many products cannot possibly be made entirely safe for all consumption, and thus holds sellers or lessors liable only for products that are *unreasonably* dangerous. A court may consider a product so defective as to be an **unreasonably dangerous product** in either of the following situations.

1 The product is dangerous beyond the expectation of the ordinary consumer.

2 A less dangerous alternative was economically feasible for the manufacturer, but the manufacturer failed to produce it.

As will be discussed next, a product may be unreasonably dangerous due to a flaw in the manufacturing process, a design defect, or an inadequate warning.

Product Defects—*Restatement (Third) of Torts*

Because Section 402A of the *Restatement (Second) of Torts* did not clearly define such terms as "defective" and "unreasonably dangerous," they were interpreted differently by different courts. In 1997, to address these concerns, the American Law Institute issued the *Restatement (Third) of Torts: Products Liability*. This *Restatement* defines the three types of product defects that have traditionally been recognized in product liability law—manufacturing defects, design defects, and inadequate warnings.

Manufacturing Defects   According to Section 2(a) of the *Restatement (Third) of Torts: Products Liability*, a product "contains a manufacturing defect when the product departs from its intended design even though all possible care was exercised in the preparation and marketing of the product." Basically, a manufacturing defect is a departure from a product's design specifications, which results in products that are physically flawed, damaged, or incorrectly assembled. A glass bottle that is made too thin and explodes in a consumer's face is an example of a product with a manufacturing defect.

Liability is imposed on the manufacturer (and on the wholesaler and retailer) regardless of whether the manufacturer's quality control efforts were "reasonable." The idea behind holding defendants strictly liable for manufacturing defects is to encourage greater investment in product safety and stringent quality control standards.

Cases involving allegations of manufacturing defects are often decided based on the opinions and testimony of experts.[9] **EXAMPLE 17.11** Kevin Schmude had just purchased an eight-foot stepladder that he was using to install radio-frequency shielding in a hospital room. While Schmude was standing on the ladder, it collapsed, and he was seriously injured. He filed a lawsuit against the ladder's maker, Tricam Industries, Inc., alleging a manufacturing defect. Experts testified that when the ladder was assembled, the preexisting holes in the top cap did not properly line up with the holes in the rear right rail and backing plate. As a result of the misalignment, the rivet at the rear legs of the ladder was more likely to fail. In 2008, a jury concluded that this manufacturing defect made the ladder unreasonably dangerous and awarded Schmude more than $677,000 in damages.[10] ◼

Design Defects   In contrast to a manufacturing defect, which is a failure of a product to meet the manufacturer's design specifications, a design defect is a flaw in the product's actual design that causes the product to create an unreasonable risk to the user. A product "is defective in design when the foreseeable risks of harm posed by the product could have been reduced or avoided by the adoption of a reasonable alternative design by the seller or other distributor, or a predecessor in the commercial chain of distribution, and the omission of the alternative design renders the product not reasonably safe."[11]

Test for Design Defects.   To successfully assert a design defect, a plaintiff has to show that a reasonable alternative design was available and that the defendant's failure to adopt the alternative design rendered the product unreasonably dangerous. In other words, a manufacturer or other defendant is liable only when the harm was reasonably preventable. **EXAMPLE 17.12** Gillespie, who cut off several of his fingers while operating a table saw, filed a lawsuit against the maker of the table saw. Gillespie alleged that the blade guards on the saw were defectively designed. At trial, however, an expert testified that the alternative design for blade

---

9. See, for example, *DeRienzo v. Trek Bicycle Corp.*, 376 F.Supp.2d 537 (S.D.N.Y. 2005).

10. *Schmude v. Tricam Industries, Inc.*, 550 F.Supp.2d 846 (E.D.Wis. 2008).

11. *Restatement (Third) of Torts: Products Liability*, Section 2(b).

guards used for table saws could not have been used for the particular cut that Gillespie was performing at the time he was injured. The court found that Gillespie's claim about defective blade guards failed because there was no proof that the "better" design would have prevented his injury.[12] ■

Factors to Be Considered. According to the Official Comments accompanying the *Restatement (Third) of Torts*, a court can consider a broad range of factors in deciding claims of design defects. These factors include the magnitude and probability of the foreseeable risks, as well as the relative advantages and disadvantages of the product as designed and as it alternatively could have been designed.

■ **EXAMPLE 17.13** A nine-year-old child finds rat poison in a cupboard at the local boys' club and eats it, thinking that it is

_____
12. *Gillespie v. Sears, Roebuck & Co.*, 386 F.3d 21 (1st Cir. 2004).

candy. The child dies, and his parents file a suit against the manufacturer alleging that the rat poison was defectively designed because it looked like candy and was supposed to be placed in cupboards. In this situation, a court would probably consider factors such as the foreseeability that a child would think the rat poison was candy, the gravity of the potential harm from consumption, the availability of an alternative design, and the usefulness of the product. If the parents could offer sufficient evidence for a reasonable person to conclude that the harm was reasonably preventable, then the manufacturer could be held liable. ■

In the following case, a smoker who developed lung cancer sued a cigarette manufacturer claiming, among other things, that there was a defect in the design of its cigarettes. The jury instruction given by the trial court and quoted by the appellate court shows the numerous factors that judges and juries consider in determining design defects.

CASE 17.3   **Bullock v. Philip Morris USA, Inc.**

Court of Appeal of California, Second District, 159 Cal.App.4th 655, 71 Cal.Rptr.3d 775 (2008).

FACTS Jodie Bullock smoked cigarettes manufactured by Philip Morris for forty-five years—from 1956, when she was seventeen years old, until she was diagnosed with lung cancer in 2001. By the late 1950s, scientific professionals in the United States had proved that cigarette smoking caused lung cancer. Nonetheless, Philip Morris issued full-page announcements stating that there was no proof that cigarette smoking caused cancer and that "numerous scientists" questioned "the validity of the statistics themselves." In 1971, Philip Morris's chief executive officer stated on a television news program, "We do not believe that cigarettes are hazardous; we don't accept that." Bullock sued Philip Morris in April 2001 seeking to recover damages for personal injuries based on product liability, among other claims. At trial, the jury found that there was a defect in the design of the cigarettes and that they had been negligently designed. It awarded Bullock $850,000 in compensatory damages, including $100,000 in noneconomic damages for pain and suffering, and later awarded her $28 million in punitive damages. Philip Morris appealed.

ISSUE Was Philip Morris liable to Bullock because of a design defect in its cigarettes?

DECISION Yes. The California Court of Appeal for the Second District affirmed the trial court's judgment as to the finding of liability.

REASON At trial, Philip Morris contended that there was no evidence showing that a design defect existed because there was no evidence that a safer alternative cigarette design had been available. The reviewing court pointed out that "a product is defective in design for purposes of tort liability if the benefits of the design do not outweigh the risk of danger inherent in the design, or if the product, used in an intended or reasonably foreseeable manner, failed to perform as safely as an ordinary consumer would expect." In this case, the jury instructions were broad ranging. The jury was instructed to consider the gravity of the danger posed by the design, as well as the likelihood that the danger would cause damage. Philip Morris failed to show any error with respect to its liability based on a design defect.

WHAT IF THE FACTS WERE DIFFERENT? *Assume that Philip Morris had never publicly denied the scientific link between smoking and lung cancer. In other words, the company simply sold cigarettes without saying anything about the medical consequences of smoking. Do you think the jury award would have been the same? Explain your answer.*

■

Inadequate Warnings A product may also be deemed defective because of inadequate instructions or warnings. A product will be considered defective "when the foreseeable risks of harm posed by the product could have been reduced or avoided by the provision of reasonable instructions or warnings by the seller or other distributor, or a predecessor in the commercial chain of distribution, and the omission of the instructions or warnings renders the product not reasonably safe."[13] Generally, a seller must warn those who purchase its product of the harm that can result from the *foreseeable misuse* of the product as well.

Important factors for a court to consider under the *Restatement (Third) of Torts* include the risks of a product, the "content and comprehensibility" and "intensity of expression" of warnings and instructions, and the "characteristics of expected user groups."[14] A "reasonableness" test is applied to determine if the warnings adequately alert consumers to the product's risks. For example, children will likely respond more readily to bright, bold, simple warning labels, while educated adults might need more detailed information.

There is no duty to warn about risks that are obvious or commonly known. Warnings about such risks do not add to the safety of a product and could even detract from it by making other warnings seem less significant. The obviousness of a risk and a user's decision to proceed in the face of that risk may be a defense in a product liability suit based on a warning defect. (This defense and other defenses in product liability suits will be discussed shortly.)

Market-Share Liability

Ordinarily, a plaintiff must prove that the defective product that caused his or her injury was the product of a specific defendant. In a few situations, however, courts have dropped this requirement when plaintiffs could not prove which of many distributors of a harmful product supplied the particular product that caused the injuries. Under the theory of **market-share liability,** all firms that manufactured and distributed the product during the period in question are held liable for the plaintiff's injuries in proportion to the firms' respective shares of the market for that product during that period. ■EXAMPLE 17.14 In one case a plaintiff who was a hemophiliac received injections of a blood protein known as antihemophiliac factor (AHF) concentrate. The plaintiff later tested positive for the AIDS (acquired immune deficiency syndrome) virus. Because it was not known which manufacturer was responsible for the particular AHF received by the plaintiff, the court held that all of the manu-

facturers of AHF could be held liable under the theory of market-share liability.[15] ■

Courts in many jurisdictions do not recognize this theory of liability, believing that it deviates too significantly from traditional legal principles.[16] In jurisdictions that do recognize market-share liability, it is usually applied in cases involving drugs or chemicals, when it is difficult or impossible to determine which company made a particular product.

Other Applications of Strict Product Liability

Virtually all courts extend the strict liability of manufacturers and other sellers to injured bystanders. Thus, if a defective forklift that will not go into reverse injures a passerby, that individual can sue the manufacturer for product liability (and possibly bring a negligence action against the forklift operator as well).

Strict product liability also applies to suppliers of component parts. ■EXAMPLE 17.15 General Motors buys brake pads from a subcontractor and puts them in Chevrolets without changing their composition. If those pads are defective, both the supplier of the brake pads and General Motors will be held strictly liable for the damages caused by the defects. ■

DEFENSES TO PRODUCT LIABILITY

Defendants in product liability suits can raise a number of defenses. One defense, of course, is to show that there is no basis for the plaintiff's claim. For example, in a product liability case based on negligence, if a defendant can show that the plaintiff has *not* met the requirements (such as causation) for an action in negligence, generally the defendant will not be liable. In regard to strict product liability, a defendant can claim that the plaintiff failed to meet one of the requirements for an action in strict liability. For instance, if the defendant establishes that the goods have been altered, normally the defendant will not be held liable.[17] A defendant may also assert that the *statute of limitations*[18] for a product liability claim has lapsed. Several other defenses may also be avail-

13. *Restatement (Third) of Torts: Products Liability*, Section 2(c).
14. *Restatement (Third) of Torts: Products Liability*, Section 2, Comment h.
15. *Smith v. Cutter Biological, Inc.*, 72 Haw. 416, 823 P.2d 717 (1991); *Sutowski v. Eli Lilly & Co.*, 82 Ohio St.3d 347, 696 N.E.2d 187 (1998); and *In re Methyl Tertiary Butyl Ether ("MTBE") Products Liability Litigation*, 447 F.Supp.2d 289 (S.D.N.Y. 2006).
16. For the Illinois Supreme Court's position on market-share liability, see *Smith v. Eli Lilly & Co.*, 137 Ill.2d 222, 560 N.E.2d 324 (1990). Pennsylvania law also does not recognize market-share liability. See *Bortell v. Eli Lilly & Co.*, 406 F.Supp.2d 1 (D.D.C. 2005).
17. See, for example, *Edmondson v. Macclesfield L-P Gas Co.*, 642 S.E.2d 265 (N.C.App. 2007); and *Pichardo v. C. S. Brown Co.*, 35 A.D.3d 303, 827 N.Y.S.2d 131 (N.Y.App. 2006).
18. Similar state statutes, called *statutes of repose*, place *outer* time limits on product liability actions.

able to defendants, as discussed below. Today, some defendants are raising the defense of preemption—that government regulations preempt claims for product liability.

Preemption

In today's world, the federal government has instituted numerous regulations that attempt to ensure the safety of products distributed to the public. Before 2008, a person who was injured by a product could assert a product liability claim regardless of whether the product was subject to government regulations. Today, however, under the United States Supreme Court's decision in *Riegel v. Medtronic, Inc.*,[19] the injured party may *not* be able to sue the manufacturer of defective products that are subject to federal regulatory schemes.

In the *Medtronic* case, the Court observed that the Medical Device Amendments of 1976 (MDA) created a comprehensive scheme of federal safety oversight for medical devices. The MDA requires the federal Food and Drug Administration (FDA) to review the design, labeling, and manufacturing of these devices before they are marketed to make sure that they are safe and effective. The Court reasoned that because premarket approval is a "rigorous process," it preempts all common law claims challenging the safety or effectiveness of a medical device that has been approved. Therefore, a man who was injured by an approved medical device (in this case, a balloon catheter) could not sue its maker for negligence or strict product liability or claim that the device was defectively designed.

Is it fair to deny an injured party relief from the company that made a defective product simply because the federal government was supposed to ensure the product's safety? Many believe that it is not. Nonetheless, courts are extending the preemption defense in the *Medtronic* case to other product liability actions. For example, surviving family members of consumers who had committed suicide after taking the prescription antidepressants Paxil and Zoloft brought product liability actions against the drugs' makers for failing to warn of an increased tendency to commit suicide. Because the FDA has detailed regulations regarding drug labels and these product labels had been approved, a federal appellate court concluded that the families' failure-to-warn claims were preempted by the FDA's regulatory actions.[20]

Assumption of Risk

Assumption of risk can sometimes be used as a defense in a product liability action. For example, if a buyer fails to heed a product recall by the seller, a court might conclude that the buyer assumed the risk caused by the defect that led to the recall. To establish such a defense, the defendant must show that (1) the plaintiff knew and appreciated the risk created by the product defect and (2) the plaintiff voluntarily assumed the risk, even though it was unreasonable to do so. (See Chapter 4 for more on assumption of risk.)

Product Misuse

Similar to the defense of voluntary assumption of risk is that of *product misuse*, which occurs when a product is used for a purpose for which it was not intended. Here, in contrast to assumption of risk, the injured party *does not know that the product is dangerous for a particular use.* The courts have severely limited this defense, however. Even if the injured party does not know about the inherent danger of using the product in a wrong way, if the misuse is reasonably foreseeable, the seller must take measures to guard against it.

Comparative Negligence (Fault)

Developments in the area of comparative negligence, or fault (discussed in Chapter 4), have also affected the doctrine of strict liability. In the past, the plaintiff's conduct was never a defense to liability for a defective product. Today, courts in many jurisdictions consider the negligent or intentional actions of both the plaintiff and the defendant when apportioning liability and damages.[21] This means that a defendant may be able to limit at least some of its liability if it can show that the plaintiff's misuse of the product contributed to his or her injuries. When proved, comparative negligence does not completely absolve the defendant of liability (as do other defenses), but it can reduce the total amount of damages that will be awarded to the plaintiff.

Note that some jurisdictions allow only intentional conduct to affect a plaintiff's recovery, whereas other states allow ordinary negligence to be used as a defense to product liability. **■EXAMPLE 17.16** Dan Smith, a mechanic in Alaska, was not wearing a hard hat at work when he was asked to start the diesel engine of an air compressor. Because the compressor was an older model, he had to prop open a door to start it. When Smith got the engine started, the door fell from its position and hit his head. The injury caused him to suffer from seizures and epilepsy. Smith sued the manufacturer, claiming that the engine was defectively designed. The manufacturer contended that Smith had been negligent by failing to wear a hard hat and propping open the door in an unsafe manner. Smith's attorney argued that ordinary

19. ___ U.S. ___, 128 S.Ct. 999, 169 L.Ed.2d 892 (2008).
20. *Colacicco v. Apotex Inc.*, 521 F.3d 253 (3d Cir. 2008).

21. See, for example, *State Farm Insurance Companies v. Premier Manufactured Systems, Inc.*, 213 Ariz. 419, 142 P.3d 1232 (2006); and *Ready v. United/Goedecke Services, Inc.*, 367 Ill.App.3d 272, 854 N.E.2d 758 (2006).

negligence could not be used as a defense in product liability cases. The Alaska Supreme Court ruled that defendants in product liability actions can raise the plaintiff's ordinary negligence to reduce their liability proportionately.[22] ■

Commonly Known Dangers

The dangers associated with certain products (such as sharp knives and guns) are so commonly known that manufacturers need not warn users of those dangers. If a defendant succeeds in convincing the court that a plaintiff's injury resulted from a *commonly known danger*, the defendant normally will not be liable.

■EXAMPLE 17.17 A classic case on this issue involved a plaintiff who was injured when an elastic exercise rope that she had purchased slipped off her foot and struck her in the eye, causing a detachment of the retina. The plaintiff claimed that the manufacturer should be liable because it

had failed to warn users that the exerciser might slip off a foot in such a manner. The court stated that to hold the manufacturer liable in these circumstances "would go beyond the reasonable dictates of justice in fixing the liabilities of manufacturers." After all, stated the court, "[a]lmost every physical object can be inherently dangerous or potentially dangerous in a sense. . . . A manufacturer cannot manufacture a knife that will not cut or a hammer that will not mash a thumb or a stove that will not burn a finger. The law does not require [manufacturers] to warn of such common dangers."[23] ■

A related defense is the *knowledgeable user* defense. If a particular danger (such as electrical shock) is or should be commonly known by particular users of the product (such as electricians), the manufacturer of electrical equipment need not warn these users of the danger.

---

22. *Smith v. Ingersoll-Rand Co.*, 14 P.3d 990 (Alaska 2000).

23. *Jamieson v. Woodward & Lothrop*, 247 F.2d 23, 101 D.C.App. 32 (1957).

REVIEWING Warranties and Product Liability

Shalene Kolchek bought a Great Lakes Spa from Val Porter, a dealer who was selling spas at the state fair. Porter told Kolchek that Great Lakes spas are "top of the line" and "the Cadillac of spas" and indicated that the spa she was buying was "fully warranted for three years." Kolchek signed an installment sale contract; then Porter handed her the manufacturer's paperwork and arranged for the spa to be delivered and installed for Kolchek. Three months later, Kolchek noticed that one corner of the spa was leaking onto her new deck and causing damage. She complained to Porter, but he did nothing about the problem. Kolchek's family continued to use the spa. Using the information presented in the chapter, answer the following questions.

1 Did Porter's statement that the spa was "top of the line" and "the Cadillac of spas" create any type of warranty? Why or why not?

2 Did Porter breach the implied warranty of merchantability? Why or why not?

3 One night, Kolchek's six-year-old daughter, Litisha, was in the spa with her mother. Litisha's hair became entangled in the spa's drain, and she was sucked down and held under water for a prolonged period, causing her to suffer brain damage. Under which theory or theories of product liability can Kolchek sue Porter to recover for Litisha's injuries?

4 If Kolchek had negligently left Litisha alone in the spa prior to the incident described in the previous question, what defense to liability might Porter assert?

TERMS AND CONCEPTS

express warranty   324
implied warranty   325
implied warranty of fitness for a
    particular purpose   327

implied warranty
    of merchantability   325
lien   324
market-share liability   334

product liability   330
unreasonably dangerous
    product   332

CHAPTER SUMMARY	**Warranties and Product Liability**

WARRANTIES

Warranties of Title (See pages 323–324.)	The UCC provides for the following warranties of title [UCC 2–312, 2A–211]: 1. *Good title*—A seller warrants that he or she has the right to pass good and rightful title to the goods. 2. *No liens*—A seller warrants that the goods sold are free of any encumbrances (claims, charges, or liabilities—usually called *liens*). A lessor warrants that the lessee will not be disturbed in her or his possession of the goods by the claims of a third party. 3. *No infringements*—A merchant-seller warrants that the goods are free of infringement claims (claims that a patent, trademark, or copyright has been infringed) by third parties. Lessors make similar warranties.

Express Warranties
(See pages 324–325.)
	1. *Under the UCC*—An express warranty arises under the UCC when a seller or lessor indicates, as part of the basis of the bargain, any of the following [UCC 2–313, 2A–210]:
	
	   a. An affirmation or promise of fact.
	   b. A description of the goods.
	   c. A sample shown as conforming to the contract goods.
	
	2. *Under the Magnuson-Moss Warranty Act*—Express written warranties covering consumer goods priced at more than $25, *if made,* must be labeled as one of the following:
	
	   a. Full warranty—Free repair or replacement of defective parts; refund or replacement for goods if they cannot be repaired in a reasonable time.
	   b. Limited warranty—When less than a full warranty is being offered.

Implied Warranty of Merchantability (See pages 325–327.)	When a seller or lessor is a merchant who deals in goods of the kind sold or leased, the seller or lessor warrants that the goods sold or leased are properly packaged and labeled, are of proper quality, and are reasonably fit for the ordinary purposes for which such goods are used [UCC 2–314, 2A–212].
Implied Warranty of Fitness for a Particular Purpose (See page 327.)	Arises when the buyer's or lessee's purpose or use is expressly or impliedly known by the seller or lessor, and the buyer or lessee purchases or leases the goods in reliance on the seller's or lessor's selection [UCC 2–315, 2A–213].
Other Implied Warranties (See page 327.)	Other implied warranties can arise as a result of course of dealing or usage of trade [UCC 2–314(3), 2A–212(3)].
Overlapping Warranties (See pages 327–328.)	The UCC construes warranties as cumulative if they are consistent with each other. If warranties are inconsistent, then express warranties take precedence over implied warranties, except for the implied warranty of fitness for a particular purpose. Also, samples take precedence over general descriptions, and exact or technical specifications displace inconsistent samples or general descriptions.
Warranty Disclaimers (See pages 328–329.)	Express warranties can be disclaimed in language that is clear and conspicuous and called to the buyer's attention when the contract is formed. A disclaimer of the implied warranty of merchantability must specifically mention the word *merchantability*. The disclaimer need not be in writing, but if it is written, it must be conspicuous. A disclaimer of the implied warranty of fitness *must* be in writing and be conspicuous, though it need not mention the word *fitness*.

(Continued)

CHAPTER SUMMARY **Warranties and Product Liability—Continued**

PRODUCT LIABILITY

Product Liability Based on Negligence (See pages 330–331.)	1. The manufacturer must use due care in designing the product, selecting materials, using the appropriate production process, assembling and testing the product, and placing adequate warnings on the label or product.
	2. Privity of contract is not required. A manufacturer is liable for failure to exercise due care to any person who sustains an injury proximately caused by a negligently made (defective) product.
Product Liability Based on Misrepresentation (See page 331.)	Fraudulent misrepresentation of a product may result in product liability based on the tort of fraud.
Strict Product Liability— Requirements (See pages 331–332.)	1. The defendant must sell the product in a defective condition.
	2. The defendant normally must be engaged in the business of selling that product.
	3. The product must be *unreasonably dangerous* to the consumer because of its defective condition (in most states).
	4. The plaintiff must incur physical harm to self or property by use or consumption of the product.
	5. The defective condition must be the proximate cause of the injury or damage.
	6. The goods must not have been substantially changed from the time the product was sold to the time the injury was sustained.
Strict Product Liability— Product Defects (See pages 332–334.)	A product may be defective in three basic ways:
	1. In its manufacture.
	2. In its design.
	3. In the instructions or warnings that come with it.
Market-Share Liability (See page 334.)	When plaintiffs cannot prove which of many distributors of a defective product supplied the particular product that caused the plaintiffs' injuries, some courts apply market-share liability. All firms that manufactured and distributed the harmful product during the period in question are then held liable for the plaintiffs' injuries in proportion to the firms' respective shares of the market, as directed by the court.
Other Applications of Strict Product Liability (See page 334.)	1. Manufacturers and other sellers are liable for harms suffered by bystanders as a result of defective products.
	2. Suppliers of component parts are strictly liable for defective parts that, when incorporated into a product, cause injuries to users.
Defenses to Product Liability (See pages 334–336.)	1. *Preemption*—Under a 2008 United States Supreme Court ruling, consumers' claims under state law may be preempted if the product is subject to a federal regulatory scheme.
	2. *Assumption of risk*—The user or consumer knew of the risk of harm and voluntarily assumed it.
	3. *Product misuse*—The user or consumer misused the product in a way unforeseeable by the manufacturer.
	4. *Comparative negligence and liability*—Liability may be distributed between the plaintiff and the defendant under the doctrine of comparative negligence if the plaintiff's misuse of the product contributed to the risk of injury.
	5. *Commonly known dangers*—If a defendant succeeds in convincing the court that a plaintiff's injury resulted from a commonly known danger, such as the danger associated with using a sharp knife, the defendant will not be liable.

FOR REVIEW

Answers for the even-numbered questions in this **For Review** *section can be found on this text's accompanying Web site at* **www.cengage.com/blaw/fbl**. *Select "Chapter 17" and click on "For Review."*

1 What factors determine whether a seller's or lessor's statement constitutes an express warranty or mere *puffery?*

2 What implied warranties arise under the UCC?

3 Can a manufacturer be held liable to any person who suffers an injury proximately caused by the manufacturer's negligently made product?

4 What are the elements of a cause of action in strict product liability?

5 What defenses to liability can be raised in a product liability lawsuit?

QUESTIONS AND CASE PROBLEMS

HYPOTHETICAL SCENARIOS AND CASE PROBLEMS

17.1 Product Liability. Under what contract theory can a seller be held liable to a consumer for physical harm or property damage that is caused by the goods sold? Under what tort theories can the seller be held liable?

17.2 Hypothetical Question with Sample Answer. Tandy purchased a washing machine from Marshall Appliances. The sales contract included a provision explicitly disclaiming all express or implied warranties, including the implied warranty of merchantability. The disclaimer was printed in the same size and color as the rest of the contract. The machine turned out to be a "lemon" and never functioned properly. Tandy sought a refund of the purchase price, claiming that Marshall had breached the implied warranty of merchantability. Can Tandy recover her money, notwithstanding the warranty disclaimer in the contract? Explain.

> For a sample answer to Question 17.2, go to Appendix E at the end of this text.

17.3 Implied Warranties. Sam, a farmer, needs to install a piece of equipment in his barn. The equipment, which weighs two thousand pounds, must be lifted thirty feet into a hayloft. Sam goes to Durham Hardware and tells Durham that he needs some heavy-duty rope to be used on his farm. Durham recommends a one-inch-thick nylon rope, and Sam purchases two hundred feet of it. Sam ties the rope around the piece of equipment, puts the rope through a pulley, and with the aid of a tractor lifts the equipment off the ground. Suddenly, the rope breaks. The equipment crashes to the ground and is extensively damaged. Sam files a suit against Durham for breach of the implied warranty of fitness for a particular purpose. Discuss how successful Sam will be with his suit.

17.4 Case Problem with Sample Answer. Mary Jane Boerner began smoking in 1945 at the age of fifteen. For a short time, she smoked Lucky Strike–brand cigarettes before switching to the Pall Mall brand, which she smoked until she quit altogether

in 1981. Pall Malls had higher levels of carcinogenic tar than other cigarettes and lacked effective filters, which would have reduced the amount of tar inhaled into the lungs. In 1996, Mary Jane developed lung cancer. She and Henry Boerner, her husband, filed a suit in a federal district court against Brown & Williamson Tobacco Co., the maker of Pall Malls. The Boerners claimed, among other things, that Pall Malls contained a design defect. Mary Jane died in 1999. According to Dr. Peter Marvin, her treating physician, she died from the effects of cigarette smoke. Henry continued the suit, offering evidence that Pall Malls featured a filter that actually increased the amount of tar taken into the body. When is a product defective in design? Does this product meet the requirements? Why or why not? [*Boerner v. Brown & Williamson Tobacco Co.,* 394 F.3d 594 (8th Cir. 2005)]

> After you have answered Problem 17.4, compare your answer with the sample answer given on the Web site that accompanies this text. Go to **www.cengage.com/blaw/fbl**, select "Chapter 17," and click on "Case Problem with Sample Answer."

17.5 Product Liability. Bret D'Auguste was an experienced skier when he rented equipment to ski at Hunter Mountain Ski Bowl, Inc., owned by Shanty Hollow Corp., in New York. The adjustable retention/release value for the bindings on the rented equipment was set at a level that, according to skiing industry standards, was too low—meaning that the skis would be released too easily—given D'Auguste's height, weight, and ability. When D'Auguste entered a "double black diamond," or extremely difficult, trail, he noticed immediately that the surface consisted of ice and virtually no snow. He tried to exit the steeply declining trail by making a sharp right turn, but in the attempt, his left ski snapped off. D'Auguste lost his balance, fell, and slid down the mountain, striking his face and head against a fence along the trail. According to a report by a rental shop employee, one of the bindings on D'Auguste's skis had a "cracked heel housing." D'Auguste filed a suit in a New York state court against Shanty Hollow and others, including the bindings' manufacturer, on a theory of strict product liability. The manufacturer filed a motion for summary judgment. On what basis might the court grant the motion? On what basis might the court deny the motion? How should the court rule? Explain. [*D'Auguste v. Shanty Hollow Corp.*, 26 A.D.3d 403, 809 N.Y.S.2d 555 (2 Dept. 2006)]

17.6 **Implied Warranties.** Peter and Tanya Rothing operate Diamond R Stables near Belgrade, Montana, where they bred, trained, and sold horses. Arnold Kallestad owns a ranch in Gallatin County, Montana, where he grows hay and grain, and raises Red Angus cattle. For more than twenty years, Kallestad has sold between three hundred and one thousand tons of hay annually, sometimes advertising it for sale in the *Bozeman Daily Chronicle*. In 2001, the Rothings bought hay from Kallestad for $90 a ton. They received delivery on April 23. In less than two weeks, at least nine of the Rothings' horses exhibited symptoms of poisoning that was diagnosed as botulism. Before the outbreak was over, nineteen animals died. Robert Whitlock, associate professor of medicine and the director of the Botulism Laboratory at the University of Pennsylvania, concluded that Kallestad's hay was the source. The Rothings filed a suit in a Montana state court against Kallestad, claiming, in part, breach of the implied warranty of merchantability. Kallestad asked the court to dismiss this claim on the ground that, if botulism had been present, it had been in no way foreseeable. Should the court grant this request? Why or why not? [*Rothing v. Kallestad*, 337 Mont. 193, 159 P.3d 222 (2007)]

17.7 **Implied Warranty.** Robert and Beverly Speight bought a home in 2000 from a homeowner. Walters Development Co. had built the home in 1995. After the Speights bought the home, they noticed water damage and mold. A home inspection determined that the damage came from a defectively constructed room and rain gutters. The Speights sued Walters in 2005 for breach of the implied warranty of workmanlike construction. (This is similar to an implied warranty of merchantability.) The district court held for Walters due to the five-year statute of limitations and because Iowa does not recognize the implied warranty of workmanlike construction. The Speights appealed. Would

such an implied warranty be reasonable? Could this warranty apply after such a long time to people who did not buy the house from the builder? [*Speight v. Walters Development Co.*, 744 N.W.2d 108 (Sup.Ct. Iowa 2008)]

17.8 **A Question of Ethics.** *Susan Calles lived with her four daughters, Amanda, age eleven; Victoria, age five; and Jenna and Jillian, age three. In March 1998, Calles bought an Aim N Flame utility lighter, which she stored on the top shelf of her kitchen cabinet. A trigger can ignite the Aim N Flame after an "ON/OFF" switch is slid to the "on" position. On the night of March 31, Calles and Victoria left to get videos. Jenna and Jillian were in bed, and Amanda was watching television. Calles returned to find fire trucks and emergency vehicles around her home. Robert Finn, a fire investigator, determined that Jenna had started a fire using the lighter. Jillian suffered smoke inhalation, was hospitalized, and died on April 21. Calles filed a suit in an Illinois state court against Scripto-Tokai Corp., which distributed the Aim N Flame, and others. In her suit, which was grounded, in part, in strict liability claims, Calles alleged that the lighter was an "unreasonably dangerous product." Scripto filed a motion for summary judgment. [Calles v. Scripto-Tokai Corp., 224 Ill.2d 247, 864 N.E.2d 249, 309 Ill.Dec. 383 (2007)]*

1 A product is "unreasonably dangerous" when it is dangerous beyond the expectation of the ordinary consumer. Whose expectation—Calles's or Jenna's—applies here? Why? Does the lighter pass this test? Explain.

2 A product is also "unreasonably dangerous" when a less dangerous alternative was economically feasible for its maker, who failed to produce it. Scripto contended that because its product was "simple" and the danger was "obvious," it should be excepted from this test. Do you agree? Why or why not?

3 Calles presented evidence as to the likelihood and seriousness of injury from lighters that do not have child-safety devices. Scripto argued that the Aim N Flame is a useful, inexpensive, alternative source of fire and is safer than a match. Calles admitted that she was aware of the dangers presented by lighters in the hands of children. Scripto admitted that it had been a defendant in at least twenty-five suits for injuries that occurred under similar circumstances. With these factors in mind, how should the court rule? Why?

 CRITICAL THINKING AND WRITING ASSIGNMENTS

17.9 **Critical Legal Thinking.** The United States has the strictest product liability laws in the world today. Why do you think many other countries, particularly developing countries, are more lax with respect to holding manufacturers liable for product defects?

17.10 **Video Question.** Go to this text's Web site at **www.cengage.com/blaw/fbl** and select "Chapter 17." Click on "Video Questions" and view the video titled *Warranties*. Then answer the following questions.

1 Discuss whether the grocery store's label of a "Party Platter for Twenty" creates an express warranty under the Uniform Commercial Code that the platter will actually serve twenty people.

2 List and describe any implied warranties discussed in the chapter that apply to this scenario.

3 How would a court determine whether Oscar had breached any express or implied warranties concerning the quantity of food on the platter?

ACCESSING THE INTERNET

For updated links to resources available on the Web, as well as a variety of other materials, visit this text's Web site at

www.cengage.com/blaw/fbl

For an example of a warranty disclaimer, go to

www.bizguardian.com/terms.php

The Lemon Law Office Web site provides a variety of information on lemon laws. Take a look at the "Hot Lemon Tips" and "Lemon Wisdom" pages. Go to

www.lemonlawoffice.com

For articles explaining product liability, go to FindLaw for Business at

smallbusiness.findlaw.com/business-operations/insurance.html

For information on product liability litigation against tobacco companies, including defenses raised by tobacco manufacturers in trial-related documents, go to the State Tobacco Information Center's Web site at

stic.neu.edu/index.html

PRACTICAL INTERNET EXERCISES

Go to this text's Web site at **www.cengage.com/blaw/fbl**, select "Chapter 17," and click on "Practical Internet Exercises." There you will find the following Internet research exercises that you can perform to learn more about the topics covered in this chapter.

PRACTICAL INTERNET EXERCISE 17-1 LEGAL PERSPECTIVE—Product Liability Litigation

PRACTICAL INTERNET EXERCISE 17-2 MANAGEMENT PERSPECTIVE—Warranties

PRACTICAL INTERNET EXERCISE 17-3 SOCIAL PERSPECTIVE—Lemon Laws

BEFORE THE TEST

Go to this text's Web site at **www.cengage.com/blaw/fbl**, select "Chapter 17," and click on "Interactive Quizzes." You will find a number of interactive questions relating to this chapter.

Greene v. A. P. Products, Ltd.

In Chapter 17, we discussed product liability, which can arise from a manufacturer's or a seller's failure to fulfill a duty to warn of risks associated with a product. One defense that may be raised in an action based on failure to warn is that the plaintiff's injury resulted from a commonly known danger, which may consist of a risk that is perceived as obvious. The extent of the duty to warn and the effect of the defense are questions for each state's legislature and courts.

In this extended case study, we examine Greene v. A. P. Products, Ltd.,[1] a decision of the Michigan Supreme Court considering the scope of a manufacturer's statutory duty to warn of a material risk that is or should be obvious to a reasonably prudent product user.

CASE BACKGROUND   A. P. Products, Ltd., packaged African Pride Ginseng Miracle Wonder 8 Oil, Hair and Body Mist-Captivate with a nonaerosol pump actuator. Wonder 8 was marketed principally to African Americans as a hair and body moisturizer, containing "eight natural oils."

At Pro Care Beauty Supply in Detroit, Michigan, in April 1999, Cheryce Greene read the label on a bottle of Wonder 8. There was a caution to consumers not to spray the oil near sparks or an open flame, but no warning that the oil should be kept out of reach of children or that it could be fatal if swallowed. Greene decided to try it and bought the bottle.

At home, Greene's eleven-month-old son, Keimer Easley, momentarily unattended, obtained the bottle of Wonder 8. He drank and inhaled the contents. The oil clogged the child's lungs, causing respiratory failure, and he died about one month later from multisystem organ failure.

Greene filed a suit in a Michigan state court against A. P. Products and others, alleging a breach of a duty to warn. The court granted the defendants' motion for summary judgment. On Greene's appeal, a state intermediate appellate court reversed this judgment. The defendants appealed to the Michigan Supreme Court.

1. 475 Mich. 502, 717 N.W.2d 855 (2006).

MAJORITY OPINION

CORRIGAN, J. [Justice]

* * * *

* * * [Michigan Compiled Laws (MCL) Section] 600.2948 * * * governs a defendant's duty to warn of an obvious danger in a product-liability action. It states, in relevant part:

A defendant is not liable for failure to warn of a material risk that is or should be obvious to a reasonably prudent product user * * * .

* * * *

Under the plain language of MCL [Section] 600.2948, *a manufacturer has no duty to warn of a material risk associated with the use of a product if the risk * * * is obvious, or should be obvious, to a reasonably prudent product user * * * . Accordingly, this statute, by looking to the reasonably prudent product user * * * establishes an objective standard.* [Emphasis added.]

* * * Our research reveals that the term "material risk" has no prior peculiar and appropriate meaning in the law. It is thus not a term of art. When considering a word or phrase that has not been given prior legal meaning, resort to a lay dictionary such as *Webster's* is appropriate. *Random House Webster's College Dictionary* (1997) defines "material," in relevant part,

as "important: to make a material difference; pertinent: a material question." *Random House Webster's College Dictionary* (1997) defines "risk" as "exposure to the chance of injury or loss." *We thus conclude that a "material risk" is an important or significant exposure to the chance of injury or loss.* [Emphasis added.]

Finally, regarding the meaning of the statute, we conclude that the [Michigan] Legislature has imposed no duty to warn beyond obvious material risks. The statute does not impose a duty to warn of a specific type of injury that could result from a risk.

* * * *

Here, tragically, plaintiff's 11-month-old son died after ingesting and inhaling Wonder 8 Hair Oil. Under the law, however, defendants owed no duty to warn of specific injuries or losses, no matter how severe, if it is or should have been obvious to a reasonably prudent product user that ingesting or inhaling Wonder 8 Hair Oil involved a material risk. We conclude that it is obvious to a reasonably prudent product user that a material risk is involved with ingesting and inhaling Wonder 8 Hair Oil.

The product, as plaintiff concedes, was not marketed as safe for human consumption or ingestion. Rather, the label clearly states that the product is intended for use as a hair and body oil. Although subjective awareness is not the standard, we find it noteworthy that plaintiff herself demonstrated an understanding that Wonder 8 Hair Oil posed a material risk if ingested. We believe it would also be obvious to a reasonably prudent user that ingestion and inhalation of the product poses a material risk. The ingredient label's inclusion of eight natural oils has no bearing on our conclusion. Many, if not all, oils are natural. It should be obvious to a reasonably prudent product user that many oils, although natural, pose a material risk if ingested or inhaled.

Additionally, the product label on Wonder 8 Hair Oil does not state that it contains only natural oils. Indeed, it lists numerous other ingredients, many of which would be unfamiliar to the average product user, such as isopropryl

myristate, fragrance, and azulene. Given such unfamiliar ingredients, a reasonably prudent product user would be, or should be, loath [unwilling] to ingest it.

Accordingly, we hold that defendants owed no duty to warn plaintiff that her son's ingestion and inhalation of the Wonder 8 Hair Oil posed a material risk. Moreover, defendants owed no duty to warn of the potential injuries that could arise from ingesting and inhaling the product.

* * * *

We conclude that the Court of Appeals erroneously reversed the trial court's grant of summary disposition to defendants * * * .

DISSENTING OPINION

CAVANAGH, J. [Justice], dissenting.

* * * *

To determine in what instances a manufacturer will have no duty to place a warning on its product and what exactly it must warn about, it must first be determined what the "material risk" is alleged to be. * * * Otherwise, there is no way to determine whether the risk is obvious and no way to determine whether it would make some material difference.

* * * *

By * * * failing to identify the material risk at issue in this case * * * , the majority prevents the statute from operating as the Legislature intended and deprives Michigan consumers of their right to assess levels of risk when making purchasing decisions. * * *

* * * *

This leads to another of the majority opinion's shortcomings: its assumption that knowledge of one risk is

knowledge of all. * * * If a risk, such as illness, is "material," and if someone knows or should know that risk, then that person need not be warned of it. But that says nothing regarding whether that person knows of a different risk, here, the risk of death. Defendants did not need to warn of the risk of death only if a reasonably prudent product user would have already known of it because a person need not be told what he or she already knows.

* * * Even assuming that a reasonably prudent product user would or should have known that inhaling or ingesting Wonder 8 Hair Oil posed a risk of illness, plaintiff raised a genuine issue of material fact regarding whether the user would have known that inhaling or ingesting Wonder 8 Hair Oil posed the risk of death and whether the same was common knowledge. * * *

* * * *

For these reasons, * * * I respectfully dissent.

QUESTIONS FOR ANALYSIS

1 LAW. What did the majority hold in this case? What was the majority's rationale for this decision?

2 LAW. How did the dissent view the majority's reasoning and conclusion? On what points did the two opinions differ?

3 ETHICS. Does a manufacturer have an ethical duty to warn of an obvious, material risk associated with the use of its product? Why or why not?

4 ECONOMIC DIMENSIONS. What are some of the likely motivations behind the enactment of the statute at the center of this case?

5 IMPLICATIONS FOR THE MANUFACTURER. What should a manufacturer do to avoid litigation on issues such as the one that arose here?

UNIT FIVE — Negotiable Instruments

UNIT CONTENTS

CHAPTER 18
Negotiability, Transferability, and Liability

LEARNING OBJECTIVES

AFTER READING THIS CHAPTER, YOU SHOULD BE ABLE TO ANSWER THE FOLLOWING QUESTIONS:

1 What requirements must an instrument meet to be negotiable?

2 What are the requirements for attaining the status of a holder in due course (HDC)?

3 What is the key to liability on a negotiable instrument? What is the difference between signature liability and warranty liability?

4 Certain defenses are valid against all holders, including HDCs. What are these defenses called? Name four defenses that fall within this category.

5 Certain defenses can be used to avoid payment to an ordinary holder of a negotiable instrument but are not effective against an HDC. What are these defenses called? Name four defenses that fall within this category.

Most commercial transactions would be inconceivable without negotiable instruments. A **negotiable instrument** is a signed writing (or record) that contains an unconditional promise or order to pay an exact sum on demand or at a specified future time to a specific person or order, or to bearer. Most negotiable instruments are paper documents, which is why they are sometimes referred to as *commercial paper*. The checks you write to pay for groceries, rent, your monthly car payment, insurance premiums, and other items are negotiable instruments.

A negotiable instrument can function as a substitute for cash or as an extension of credit. When a buyer writes a check to pay for goods, the check serves as a substitute for cash. When a buyer gives a seller a promissory note in which the buyer promises to pay the seller the purchase price within sixty days, the seller has essentially extended credit to the buyer for a sixty-day period. For a negotiable instrument to operate *practically* as either a substitute for cash or a credit device, or both, it is essential that the instrument be *easily transferable without danger of being uncollectible.* Each rule described in the following pages can be examined in light of this essential function of negotiable instruments.

It took hundreds of years for paper to become an acceptable substitute for gold or silver. In the medieval world, merchants engaging in foreign trade used negotiable instruments to finance and conduct their affairs, rather than risk transporting gold or coins. Because the English king's courts of those times did not recognize the validity of negotiable instruments, however, the merchants developed their own set of rules, which were enforced by "fair" or "borough" courts. Eventually, the decisions of these courts formed a distinct set of laws that became known as the *Lex Mercatoria* (Law Merchant). The Law Merchant was codified in England in the Bills of Exchange Act of 1882. In 1896, in the United States, the National Conference of Commissioners on Uniform State Laws (NCCUSL) drafted the Uniform Negotiable Instruments Law. This law was the forerunner of Article 3 of the Uniform Commercial Code (UCC).

ARTICLES 3 AND 4 OF THE UCC

Negotiable instruments must meet special requirements relating to form and content. These requirements, which are imposed by Article 3 of the UCC, will be discussed at length in this chapter. Article 3 also governs the process of *negotiation* (transferring an instrument from one party to another), as will be discussed. Note that UCC 3–104(b) defines *instrument* as a "negotiable instrument." For that reason, whenever the term *instrument* is used in this book, it refers to a negotiable instrument.

The 1990 Revision of Articles 3 and 4

In 1990, a revised version of Article 3 was issued for adoption by the states. Many of the changes to Article 3 simply clarified old sections, but some significantly altered the former provisions. As of this writing, nearly every state has adopted the revised article. Therefore, all references to Article 3 in this chapter and in the following chapter are to the *revised* Article 3.

Article 4 of the UCC, which governs bank deposits and collections (to be discussed in Chapter 19), was also revised in 1990. In part, these changes were necessary to reflect changes in Article 3 that affect Article 4 provisions. Excerpts from the revised Articles 3 and 4 are included in Appendix C.

The 2002 Amendments to Articles 3 and 4

In 2002, the NCCUSL and the American Law Institute approved a number of amendments to Articles 3 and 4 of the UCC. One of the purposes of these amendments was to update the law with respect to e-commerce. For example, the amended versions of the articles implement the policy of the Uniform Electronic Transactions Act (see Chapter 13) by removing

unnecessary obstacles to electronic communications. Additionally, the term *record* replaces the word *writing* throughout the articles. Other amendments relate to such topics as telephone-generated checks and the payment and discharge of negotiable instruments.

To date, only a handful of states have adopted these amendments. Therefore, in this text we provide footnotes to the amendments only if they will significantly alter existing law. Keep in mind, however, that even when the changes are not substantive, some of the section numbers may change slightly once a state has adopted the amendments to Article 3 (subpart 9 may become subpart 12, for example).

TYPES OF INSTRUMENTS

The UCC specifies four types of negotiable instruments: *drafts*, *checks*, *promissory notes*, and *certificates of deposit* (CDs). These instruments are frequently divided into *orders to pay* (drafts and checks) and *promises to pay* (promissory notes and CDs), as shown in Exhibit 18–1 and discussed in the following subsections.

Negotiable instruments may also be classified as either demand instruments or time instruments. A *demand instrument* is payable on demand—that is, it is payable immediately after it is issued and thereafter for a reasonable period of time. All checks are demand instruments because, by definition, they must be payable on demand. A *time instrument* is payable at a future date.

EXHIBIT 18–1 Basic Types of Negotiable Instruments

INSTRUMENTS	CHARACTERISTICS	PARTIES
ORDERS TO PAY		
Draft	An order by one person to another person or to bearer [UCC 3–104(e)].	Drawer—The person who signs or makes the order to pay [UCC 3–103(a)(3)].
Check	A draft drawn on a bank and payable on demand [UCC 3–104(f)].[a] (With certain types of checks, such as cashier's checks, the bank is both the drawer and the drawee—see Chapter 19 for details.)	Drawee—The person to whom the order to pay is made [UCC 3–103(a)(2)]. Payee—The person to whom payment is ordered.
PROMISES TO PAY		
Promissory note	A promise by one party to pay money to another party or to bearer [UCC 3–104(e)].	Maker—The person who promises to pay [UCC 3–103(a)(5)]. Payee—The person to whom the promise is made.
Certificate of deposit	A note issued by a bank acknowledging a deposit of funds made payable to the holder of the note [UCC 3–104(j)].	

a. Under UCC 4–105(1), banks include savings banks, savings and loan associations, credit unions, and trust companies.

Drafts and Checks (Orders to Pay)

A **draft** is an unconditional written order to pay rather than a promise to pay. Drafts involve three parties. The party creating the draft (the **drawer**) orders another party (the **drawee**) to pay money, usually to a third party (the **payee**). The most common type of draft is a check, but drafts other than checks may be used in commercial transactions.

Time Drafts and Sight Drafts A *time draft* is payable at a definite future time. A *sight draft* (or demand draft) is payable on sight—that is, when it is presented to the drawee (usually a bank or financial institution) for payment. A sight draft may be payable on acceptance. **Acceptance** is the drawee's written promise to pay the draft when it comes due. Usually, an instrument is accepted by writing the word *accepted* across its face, followed by the date of acceptance and the signature of the drawee. A draft can be both a time and a sight draft; such a draft is payable at a stated time after sight (a draft that states it is payable ninety days after sight, for instance).

Exhibit 18–2 shows a typical time draft. For the drawee to be obligated to honor the order, the drawee must be obligated to the drawer either by agreement or through a debtor-creditor relationship. **■EXAMPLE 18.1** On January 16, Ourtown Real Estate Company orders $1,000 worth of office supplies from Eastman Supply Company, with payment due in ninety days. Also on January 16, Ourtown sends Eastman a draft drawn on its account with the First National Bank of Whiteacre as payment. In this scenario, the drawer is Ourtown, the drawee is Ourtown's bank (First National Bank of Whiteacre), and the payee is Eastman Supply Company. **■**

Trade Acceptances A *trade acceptance* is a draft that is commonly used in the sale of goods. In this type of draft, the seller is both the drawer and the payee. The buyer to whom credit is extended is the drawee. **■EXAMPLE 18.2** Jackson Street Bistro buys its restaurant supplies from Osaka Industries. When Jackson requests supplies, Osaka creates a draft ordering Jackson to pay Osaka for the supplies within ninety days. Jackson accepts the draft by signing its face and is then obligated to make the payment. If Osaka is in need of cash, it can sell the trade acceptance to a third party in the commercial money market (the market for short-term borrowing that businesses use) before the payment is due. **■** (If the draft orders the buyer's bank to pay, it is called a *banker's acceptance*.)

Checks As mentioned, the most commonly used type of draft is a **check.** The writer of the check is the drawer, the bank on which the check is drawn is the drawee, and the person to whom the check is payable is the payee. As mentioned earlier, checks are demand instruments because they are payable on demand.

Checks will be discussed more fully in Chapter 19, but it should be noted here that with certain types of checks, such as *cashier's checks,* the bank is both the drawer and the drawee. The bank customer purchases a cashier's check from the bank—that is, pays the bank the amount of the check—and indicates to whom the check should be made payable. The bank, not the customer, is the drawer of the check, as well as the drawee. The idea behind a cashier's check is that it functions the same as cash, so there is no question about whether the check will be paid—the bank has committed itself to paying the stated amount on demand.

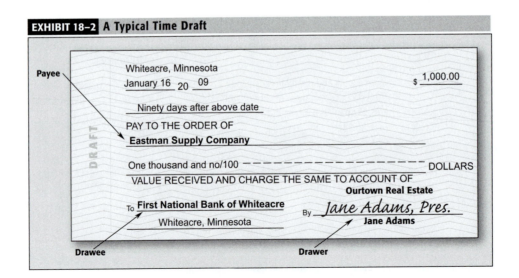

EXHIBIT 18–2 A Typical Time Draft

Promissory Notes and Certificates of Deposit (Promises to Pay)

A **promissory note** is a written promise made by one person (the **maker** of the promise to pay) to another (usually a payee). A promissory note, which is often referred to simply as a *note*, can be made payable at a definite time or on demand. It can name a specific payee or merely be payable to bearer (bearer instruments will be discussed later in this chapter). ■**EXAMPLE 18.3** On April 30, Laurence and Margaret Roberts sign a writing unconditionally promising to pay "to the order of" the First National Bank of Whiteacre $3,000 (with 8 percent interest) on or before June 29. This writing is a promissory note. ■ A typical promissory note is shown in Exhibit 18–3.

Types of Promissory Notes Notes are used in a variety of credit transactions and often carry the name of the transaction involved. For example, a note that is secured by personal property, such as an automobile, is called a *collateral note*, because the property pledged as security for the satisfaction of the debt is called collateral (see Chapter 20). A note secured by real estate is called a *mortgage note*. A note payable in installments, such as for payment for a suite of furniture over a twelve-month period, is called an *installment note*.

Certificate of Deposit A **certificate of deposit (CD)** is a type of note. A CD is issued when a party deposits funds with a bank that the bank promises to repay, with interest, on a certain date [UCC 3–104(j)]. The bank is the maker of the note, and the depositor is the payee. ■**EXAMPLE 18.4** On February 15, Sara Levin deposits $5,000 with the First National Bank of Whiteacre. The bank issues a CD, in which it promises to repay the $5,000, plus 5 percent annual interest, on August 15. ■

Certificates of deposit in small denominations (for amounts up to $100,000) are often sold by savings and loan associations, savings banks, commercial banks, and credit unions. Certificates of deposit for amounts over $100,000 are called large or jumbo CDs. Exhibit 18–4 on the next page shows a typical small CD.

Because CDs are time deposits, the purchaser-payee typically is not allowed to withdraw the funds prior to the date of maturity (except in limited circumstances, such as disability or death). If a payee wants to access the funds prior to the maturity date, he or she can sell (negotiate) the CD to a third party.

REQUIREMENTS FOR NEGOTIABILITY

For an instrument to be negotiable, it must meet the following requirements:

1 Be in writing.
2 Be signed by the maker or the drawer.
3 Be an unconditional promise or order to pay.
4 State a fixed amount of money.
5 Be payable on demand or at a definite time.
6 Be payable to order or to bearer, unless it is a check.

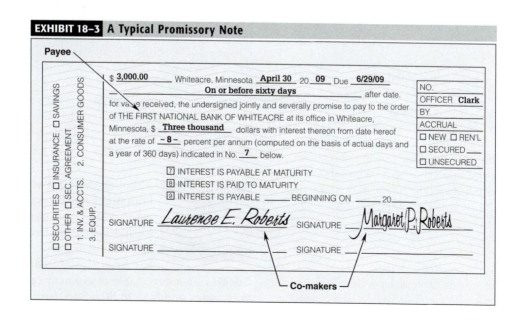

EXHIBIT 18–3 A Typical Promissory Note

EXHIBIT 18–4 A Typical Small CD

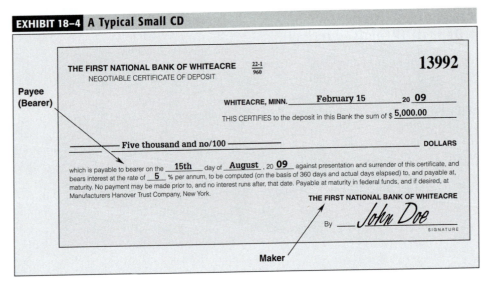

Payee (Bearer)

THE FIRST NATIONAL BANK OF WHITEACRE $\frac{22-1}{960}$ **13992**
NEGOTIABLE CERTIFICATE OF DEPOSIT

WHITEACRE, MINN. ___February 15___ 20 09

THIS CERTIFIES to the deposit in this Bank the sum of $ 5,000.00

_____ Five thousand and no/100 _____ DOLLARS

which is payable to bearer on the __15th__ day of __August__, 20 09 against presentation and surrender of this certificate, and bears interest at the rate of __5__ % per annum, to be computed (on the basis of 360 days and actual days elapsed) to, and payable at, maturity. No payment may be made prior to, and no interest runs after, that date. Payable at maturity in federal funds, and if desired, at Manufacturers Hanover Trust Company, New York.

THE FIRST NATIONAL BANK OF WHITEACRE

By ___*John Doe*___
SIGNATURE

Maker

Written Form

Negotiable instruments normally must be in written form [UCC 3–103(a)(6), (9)]. This is because negotiable instruments must possess the quality of certainty that only formal, written expression can give. The writing must have the following qualities:

1 The writing must be on material that lends itself to *permanence.* Promises carved in blocks of ice or inscribed in sand or on other impermanent surfaces will not qualify as negotiable instruments. Thus, if Suzanne writes in the sand, "I promise to pay $500 to the order of Jack," this cannot be a negotiable instrument because, although it is in writing, it lacks permanence. The UCC nevertheless gives considerable leeway as to what can be a negotiable instrument. Checks and notes have been written on napkins, menus, tablecloths, shirts, and a variety of other materials.

2 The writing must also have *portability.* Although the UCC does not explicitly state this requirement, if an instrument is not movable, it obviously cannot meet the requirement that it be freely transferable. For example, Charles writes on the side of a cow, "I promise to pay $500 to the order of Jason." Technically, this would meet the requirements of a negotiable instrument—except for portability. A cow cannot easily be transferred in the ordinary course of business; thus, the "instrument" is nonnegotiable.

Signatures

For an instrument to be negotiable, it must be signed by (1) the maker, if it is a note or a certificate of deposit, or (2) the drawer, if it is a draft or a check [UCC 3–103(a)(3)]. If a person signs

an instrument as an authorized agent of the maker or drawer, the maker or drawer has effectively signed the instrument. (Agents' signatures will be discussed later in this chapter.)

The UCC grants extreme latitude in regard to what constitutes a signature. UCC 1–201(39) provides that a **signature** may include "any symbol executed or adopted by a party with a present intention to authenticate a writing." UCC 3–401(b) expands on this by stating that a "signature may be made (i) manually or by means of a device or machine, and (ii) by the use of any name, including a trade or assumed name, or by a word, mark, or symbol executed or adopted by a person with present intention to authenticate a writing." Thus, initials, an X (if the writing is signed by a witness), or a thumbprint will normally suffice as a signature. A trade name or an assumed name is also sufficient. Signatures that are placed onto instruments by means of rubber stamps are permitted and frequently used in the business world. If necessary, *parol evidence* (discussed in Chapter 10) is admissible to identify the signer. When the signer is identified, the signature becomes effective.

The location of the signature on the document is unimportant, although the usual place is the lower right-hand corner. A *handwritten* statement on the body of the instrument, such as "I, Jerome Garcia, promise to pay Elena Greer," is sufficient to act as a signature.

PREVENTING LEGAL DISPUTES

Although there are virtually no limitations on the manner in which a signature can be made, businesspersons should be careful about receiving an instrument that has been signed in an unusual way. Oddities on a negotiable instrument can open the door to disputes and lead to litigation. Furthermore, an

unusual signature clearly decreases the *marketability* of an instrument because it creates uncertainty.

◼

Unconditional Promise or Order to Pay

For an instrument to be negotiable, it must contain an express order or promise to pay. If a buyer executes a promissory note using the words "I promise to pay Jonas $1,000 on demand for the purchase of these goods," then this requirement for a negotiable instrument is satisfied. A mere acknowledgment of the debt, such as an I.O.U. ("I owe you"), might logically *imply* a promise, but it is not sufficient under the UCC. This is because the promise must be an affirmative (express) undertaking [UCC 3–103(a)(9)]. If such words as "to be paid on demand" or "due on demand" are added to an I.O.U., however, the need for an express promise to pay is satisfied.[1]

An *order* is associated with three-party instruments, such as checks, drafts, and trade acceptances. An order directs a third party to pay the instrument as drawn. In the typical check, for example, the word *pay* (to the order of a payee) is a command to the drawee bank to pay the check when presented; thus, the check is an order. A command, such as "pay," is mandatory even if it is accompanied by courteous words as in "Please pay" or "Kindly pay." Stating "I wish you would pay" does not fulfill this requirement. An order may be addressed to one party or to more than one party, either jointly ("to A *and* B") or alternatively ("to A *or* B") [UCC 3–103(a)(6)].

A promise or order is conditional (and *not* negotiable) if it states (1) an express condition to payment, (2) that the promise or order is subject to or governed by another writing, or (3) that the rights or obligations with respect to the promise or order are stated in another writing. A mere reference to another writing, however, does not of itself make the promise or order conditional [UCC 3–106(a)]. For example, the words "As per contract" or "This debt arises from the sale of goods X and Y" do not render an instrument nonnegotiable. Similarly, a statement in the instrument that payment can be made only out of a particular fund or source will not render the instrument nonnegotiable [UCC 3–106(b)(ii)]. **◼EXAMPLE 18.5** A note's terms include the statement that payment will be made out of the proceeds of next year's cotton crop. This does not make the note nonnegotiable—although the payee of the note may find it commercially unacceptable and refuse to take it. ◼

---

1. A certificate of deposit (CD) is an exception in this respect. A CD does not have to contain an express promise because the bank's acknowledgment of the deposit and the other terms of the instrument clearly indicate a promise by the bank to repay the sum of money [UCC 3–104(j)].

A Fixed Amount of Money

The term *fixed amount* means that the amount must be ascertainable from the face of the instrument. Interest may be stated as a fixed or variable rate. A demand note payable with 8 percent interest meets the requirement of a fixed amount because its amount can be determined at the time it is payable or at any time thereafter [UCC 3–104(a)].

The rate of interest may also be determined with reference to information that is not contained in the instrument if that information is readily ascertainable by reference to a formula or a source described in the instrument [UCC 3–112(b)]. For instance, an instrument that is payable at the *legal rate of interest* (a rate of interest fixed by statute) is negotiable. Mortgage notes tied to a variable rate of interest (a rate that fluctuates as a result of financial market conditions) are also negotiable.

UCC 3–104(a) provides that a fixed amount is to be *payable in money*. The UCC defines money as "a medium of exchange authorized or adopted by a domestic or foreign government as a part of its currency" [UCC 1–201(24)]. **◼EXAMPLE 18.6** The maker of a note promises "to pay on demand $1,000 in U.S. gold." Because gold is not a medium of exchange adopted by the U.S. government, the note is not payable in money. The same result would occur if the maker promises "to pay $1,000 and fifty bottles of 1990 Château Lafite-Rothschild wine," because the instrument is not payable *entirely* in money. An instrument payable in government bonds or in shares of IBM stock is not negotiable because neither is a medium of exchange recognized by the U.S. government. ◼ Any instrument payable in the United States with a face amount stated in a foreign currency, however, is negotiable and can be paid in the foreign money or in the equivalent in U.S. dollars [UCC 3–107].

Payable on Demand or at a Definite Time

Instruments that are payable on demand include those that contain the words "Payable at sight" or "Payable upon presentment." When a person brings the instrument to the appropriate party for payment or acceptance, *presentment* occurs. **Presentment** means a demand made by or on behalf of a person entitled to enforce an instrument to either pay or accept the instrument [UCC 3-501].

The very nature of the instrument may indicate that it is payable on demand. For instance, a check, by definition, is payable on demand [UCC 3–104(f)]. If no time for payment is specified and the person responsible for payment must pay on the instrument's presentment, the instrument is payable on demand [UCC 3–108(a)].

If an instrument is not payable on demand, to be negotiable it must be payable at a definite time. An instrument is payable at a definite time if it states that it is payable (1) on a specified date, (2) within a definite period of time (such as thirty days) after being presented for payment, or (3) on a date or time readily ascertainable at the time the promise or order is issued [UCC 3–108(b)]. The maker or drawee in a time draft, for example, is under no obligation to pay until the specified time. When an instrument is payable by the maker or drawer on or before a stated date, it is clearly payable at a definite time. ■**EXAMPLE 18.7** Levine gives Hirsch an instrument dated November 1, 2009, which indicates on its face that it is payable *on or before* November 1, 2010. This instrument satisfies the definite-time requirement. ■

Acceleration Clause An **acceleration clause** allows a payee or other holder of a time instrument to demand payment of the entire amount due, with interest, if a certain event occurs, such as a default in payment of an installment when due. (Under the UCC, a **holder** is any person in possession of a negotiable instrument that is payable either to the bearer or to an identified person that is the person in possession [UCC 1–201(20)].)

Under the UCC, instruments that include acceleration clauses are negotiable, regardless of the reason for the acceleration, because (1) the exact value of the instrument can be ascertained and (2) the instrument will be payable on a specified date if the event allowing acceleration does not occur [UCC 3–108(b)(ii)]. Thus, the specified date is the outside limit used to determine the value of the instrument.

In the following case, the question was whether a party entitled to installment payments on a promissory note that contained an acceleration clause waived the right to exercise this provision when the party accepted late payments from the maker.

CASE 18.1 **Foundation Property Investments, LLC v. CTP, LLC**

Court of Appeals of Kansas, 37 Kan.App.2d 890, 159 P.3d 1042 (2007).
www.kscourts.org/Cases-and-Opinions/opinions[a]

FACTS In April 2004, CTP, LLC, bought a truck stop in South Hutchinson, Kansas. As part of the deal, CTP borrowed $96,000 from Foundation Property Investments, LLC. The loan was evidenced by a promissory note, which provided that CTP was to make monthly payments of $673.54 between June 1, 2004, and June 1, 2009. The note stated that on default in any payment, "the whole amount then unpaid shall become immediately due and payable at the option of the holder without notice." CTP paid the first four installments on or before the due dates, but beginning in October 2004, CTP paid the next ten installments late. In July 2005, citing the late payments, Foundation demanded full payment of the note by the end of the month. CTP responded that the parties' course of dealing permitted payments to be made beyond their due dates. Foundation filed a suit in a Kansas state court against CTP to collect the note's full amount. CTP asserted that Foundation had waived its right to accelerate the note by its acceptance of late payments. The court determined that Foundation was entitled to payment of the note in full, plus interest and

attorneys' fees and costs, for a total of $110,975.58, and issued a summary judgment in Foundation's favor. CTP appealed to a state intermediate appellate court.

ISSUE Does a party that repeatedly accepts late payments on a promissory note waive the right to enforce the note's acceleration clause for failure to make timely payments?

DECISION Yes. The state intermediate appellate court reversed the lower court's ruling and remanded the case with instructions to enter a judgment in CTP's favor.

REASON The court looked at the plaintiff's actions to determine whether it had relinquished its right to accelerate. *Course of dealing* is defined as "a sequence of previous conduct between the parties to a particular transaction which is fairly to be regarded as a establishing a common basis of understanding for interpreting their expressions and other conduct." The reviewing court pointed out that Foundation never objected to CTP's late payments during the nine-month period. The action of accepting late payments "was inconsistent with [Foundation's] claim or right to receive prompt payments. Accordingly, the trial court incorrectly determined that Foundation's conduct did not constitute a waiver of its right of acceleration." The acceptance of late payments did constitute a waiver. CTP was not required to pay the note in full, plus interest and attorneys' fees and costs.

a. In the menu at the left, click on "Search by Docket Number." In the result, in the right column, click on "96000–96999." On the next page, scroll to "96697" and click on the number to access the opinion. The Kansas courts, Washburn University School of Law Library, and University of Kansas School of Law Library maintain this Web site.

FOR CRITICAL ANALYSIS—Global Consideration *Suppose that Foundation was an entity based outside the United States. Could it have*

successfully claimed, in attempting to enforce the acceleration clause, that it had not given CTP notice because it had not been aware of Kansas law? Discuss.

■

Extension Clause The reverse of an acceleration clause is an **extension clause,** which allows the date of maturity to be extended into the future [UCC 3–108(b)(iii), (iv)]. To keep the instrument negotiable, the interval of the extension must be specified if the right to extend the time of payment is given to the maker or drawer of the instrument. If, however, the holder of the instrument can extend the time of payment, the extended maturity date does not have to be specified.

■EXAMPLE 18.8 Alek executes a note that reads, "The maker has the right to postpone the time of payment of this note beyond its definite maturity date of January 1, 2010. This extension, however, shall be for no more than a reasonable time." A note with this language is not negotiable because it does not satisfy the definite-time requirement. The right to extend is the maker's, and Alek has not indicated when the note will become due after the extension. Suppose instead that Alek's note reads, "The holder of this note at the date of maturity, January 1, 2010, can extend the time of payment until the following June 1 or later, if the holder so wishes." This note is a negotiable instrument. The length of the extension does not have to be specified because the option to extend is solely that of the holder. After January 1, 2010, the note is, in effect, a demand instrument. ■

Payable to Order or to Bearer

An **order instrument** is an instrument that is payable (1) "to the order of an identified person" or (2) "to an identified person or order" [UCC 3–109(b)]. An identified person is the person "to whom the instrument is initially payable" as determined by the intent of the maker or drawer [UCC 3–110(a)]. The identified person, in turn, may transfer the instrument to whomever he or she wishes. Thus, the maker or drawer is agreeing to pay either the person specified on the instrument or whomever that person might designate. In this way, the instrument retains its transferability. **■EXAMPLE 18.9** An instrument states, "Payable to the order of Kako Yung" or "Pay to Kako Yung or order." Clearly, the maker or drawer has indicated that a payment will be made to Yung or to whomever Yung designates. The instrument is therefore negotiable. ■

A **bearer instrument** is an instrument that does not designate a specific payee [UCC 3–109(a)]. The term **bearer** refers to a person in possession of an instrument that is payable to bearer or indorsed in blank (with a signature only, as will be discussed shortly) [UCC 1–201(5), 3–109(a),

3–109(c)]. This means that the maker or drawer agrees to pay anyone who presents the instrument for payment. Any instrument containing terms such as "Payable to Kathy Esposito or bearer" or "Pay to the order of cash" is a bearer instrument. In addition, an instrument that "indicates that it is not payable to an identified person" is a bearer instrument [UCC 3–109(a)(3)]. Thus, an instrument "payable to X" or "payable to Batman" can be negotiated as a bearer instrument, as though it were payable to cash. The UCC does not accept an instrument issued to a nonexistent *organization* as payable to bearer, however [UCC 3–109, Comment 2].

FACTORS THAT DO NOT AFFECT NEGOTIABILITY

Certain ambiguities or omissions will not affect the negotiability of an instrument. The UCC provides the following rules for dealing with ambiguous terms:

1 Unless the date of an instrument is necessary to determine a definite time for payment, the fact that an instrument is undated does not affect its negotiability. For example, an undated check is still negotiable.

2 Antedating or postdating an instrument does not affect the instrument's negotiability [UCC 3–113(a)]. *Antedating* occurs when a party puts a date on the instrument that is before the actual date; *postdating* occurs when a party puts a date on an instrument that is after the actual date. **■EXAMPLE 18.10** On May 1, Avery draws a check on her account with First State Bank made payable to Consumer Credit Corporation. Avery postdates the check "May 15." Consumer Credit can negotiate the check, and, unless Avery tells First State otherwise, the bank can charge the amount of the check to Avery's account before May 15 [UCC 4–401(c)]. ■

3 Handwritten terms outweigh typewritten and printed terms (preprinted terms on forms, for example), and typewritten terms outweigh printed terms [UCC 3–114]. **■EXAMPLE 18.11** Suppose that your check, like most checks, is printed "Pay to the order of" with a blank next to it. In handwriting, you insert in the blank, "Anita Delgado or bearer." The handwritten terms outweigh the printed form (an order instrument), and the check is a bearer instrument. ■

4 Words outweigh figures unless the words are ambiguous [UCC 3–114]. This rule is important when the numerical amount and the written amount on a check differ. **EXAMPLE 18.12** Rob issues a check payable to Standard Appliance Company. For the amount, he fills in the numbers "$100" and writes in the words "One thousand and 00/100" dollars. The check is payable in the amount of $1,000. ■

5 When an instrument does not specify a particular interest rate but simply states "with interest," the interest rate is the *judgment rate of interest* (a rate of interest fixed by statute that is applied to a monetary judgment awarded by a court until the judgment is paid or terminated) [UCC 3–112(b)].

6 A check is negotiable even if there is a notation on it stating that it is "nonnegotiable" or "not governed by Article 3." Any other instrument, in contrast, can be made nonnegotiable by the maker's or drawer's conspicuously noting on it that it is "nonnegotiable" or "not governed by Article 3" [UCC 3–104(d)].

TRANSFER OF INSTRUMENTS

Once issued, a negotiable instrument can be transferred by *assignment* or by *negotiation*. Only a transfer by negotiation can result in the party obtaining the instrument receiving the rights of a holder, as discussed next.

Transfer by Assignment

Recall from Chapter 11 that an assignment is a transfer of rights under a contract. Under general contract principles, a transfer by assignment to an assignee gives the assignee only those rights that the assignor possessed. Any defenses that can be raised against an assignor can normally be raised against the assignee. This same principle applies when a negotiable instrument, such as a promissory note, is transferred by assignment. The transferee is then an *assignee* rather than a *holder*. Sometimes, a transfer fails to qualify as a negotiation because it fails to meet one or more of the requirements of a negotiable instrument, discussed above. When this occurs, the transfer becomes an assignment.

Transfer by Negotiation

Negotiation is the transfer of an instrument in such form that the transferee (the person to whom the instrument is transferred) becomes a holder [UCC 3–201(a)]. Under UCC principles, a transfer by negotiation creates a holder who, at the very least, receives the rights of the previous possessor [UCC 3–203(b)]. Unlike an assignment, a transfer by negotiation can make it possible for a holder to receive more rights

in the instrument than the prior possessor had [UCC 3–202(b), 3–305, 3–306]. A holder who receives greater rights is known as a *holder in due course*, a concept we will discuss later in this chapter.

There are two methods of negotiating an instrument so that the receiver becomes a holder: by *indorsement and delivery* and by *delivery only*. The method used depends on whether the instrument is order paper or bearer paper. An **indorsement** is a signature placed on an instrument, such as the back of a check, for the purpose of transferring one's ownership rights in the instrument.[2]

Negotiating Order Instruments   An order instrument contains the name of a payee capable of indorsing it, as in "Pay to the order of Lloyd Sorenson." If the instrument is an order instrument, it is negotiated by delivery with any necessary indorsements. **EXAMPLE 18.13** National Express Corporation issues a payroll check "to the order of Lloyd Sorenson." Sorenson takes the check to the bank, signs his name on the back (an indorsement), gives it to the teller (a delivery), and receives cash. Sorenson has *negotiated* the check to the bank [UCC 3–201(b)]. ■ Types of indorsements and their effects are listed in Exhibit 18–5.

Negotiating order instruments requires both delivery and indorsement. If Sorenson had taken the check to the bank and delivered it to the teller without signing it, the transfer would not qualify as a negotiation. In that situation, the transfer would be treated as an assignment, and the bank would become an assignee rather than a holder.

Negotiating Bearer Instruments   If an instrument is payable to bearer, it is negotiated by delivery—that is, by transfer into another person's possession. Indorsement is not necessary [UCC 3–201(b)]. The use of bearer instruments thus involves more risk through loss or theft than the use of order instruments.

EXAMPLE 18.14 Richard Kray writes a check "payable to cash" and hands it to Jessie Arnold (a delivery). Kray has issued the check (a bearer instrument) to Arnold. Arnold places the check in her wallet, which is subsequently stolen. The thief has possession of the check. At this point, the thief has no rights to the check. If the thief "delivers" the check to an innocent third person, however, negotiation will be complete. All rights to the check will be passed absolutely to that third person, and Arnold will lose all rights to recover the proceeds of the check from that person [UCC 3–306]. Of course, Arnold could attempt to recover the amount from the thief if the thief can be found. ■

---

2. Because the UCC uses the spelling *indorse* (*indorsement*, and so forth), rather than *endorse* (*endorsement*, and so forth), we adopt that spelling here and in other chapters in the text.

EXHIBIT 18–5 Types of Indorsements and their Consequences

WORDS CONSTITUTING THE INDORSEMENT	TYPE OF INDORSEMENT	INDORSER'S SIGNATURE LIABILITY[a]
"Rosemary White"	Blank	Unqualified signature liability on proper presentment and notice of dishonor.[b]
"Pay to Sam Wilson, Rosemary White"	Special	Unqualified signature liability on proper presentment and notice of dishonor.
"Without recourse, Rosemary White"	Qualified (blank for further negotiation)	No signature liability. Transfer warranty liability if breach occurs.[c]
"Pay to Sam Wilson, without recourse, Rosemary White"	Qualified (special for further negotiation)	No signature liability. Transfer warranty liability if breach occurs.
"Pay to Sam Wilson on condition he completes painting my house at 23 Elm Street by 9/1/07, Rosemary White"	Restrictive—conditional (special for further negotiation)	Signature liability only if condition is met. If condition is met, signature liability on proper presentment and notice of dishonor.
"Pay to Sam Wilson only, Rosemary White"	Restrictive—prohibitive (special for further negotiation)	Signature liability only on Sam Wilson's receiving payment. If Wilson receives payment, signature liability on proper presentment and notice of dishonor.
"For deposit, Rosemary White"	Restrictive—for deposit (blank for further negotiation)	Signature liability only on White having amount deposited in her account. If deposit is made, signature liability on proper presentment and notice of dishonor.
"Pay to Ann South in trust for John North, Rosemary White"	Restrictive—trust (special for further negotiation)	Signature liability only on payment to Ann South for John North's benefit. If restriction is met, signature liability on proper presentment and notice of dishonor.

a. *Signature liability* refers to the liability of a party who signs an instrument, as will be discussed later in this chapter. The basic questions include whether there is any liability and, if so, whether it is unqualified or restricted.

b. When an instrument is dishonored—such as when a drawer's bank refuses to cash the drawer's check on proper presentment—an indorser of the check may be liable on it if she or he is given proper *notice of dishonor.*

c. The transferor of an instrument makes certain warranties to the transferee and subsequent holders, and thus, even if the transferor's signature does not render him or her liable on the instrument, he or she may be liable for breach of a transfer warranty. Transfer warranties will be discussed later in this chapter.

HOLDER IN DUE COURSE (HDC)

Often, whether a holder of an instrument is entitled to obtain payment will depend on whether the holder is an ordinary holder or a *holder in due course.* An ordinary holder obtains only those rights that the transferor had in the instrument. In this respect, a holder has the same status as an assignee (see Chapter 11). Like an assignee, a holder normally is subject to the same defenses that could be asserted against the transferor.

In contrast, a **holder in due course (HDC)** is a holder who, by meeting certain acquisition requirements (to be dis-

cussed shortly), takes the instrument *free* of most of the defenses and claims that could be asserted against the transferor. Stated another way, an HDC can normally acquire a higher level of immunity than can an ordinary holder in regard to defenses against payment on the instrument or ownership claims to the instrument by other parties.

■EXAMPLE 18.15 Marcia Cambry signs a $1,000 note payable to Alex Jerrod in payment for some ancient Roman coins. Jerrod negotiates the note to Alicia Larson, who promises to pay Jerrod for it in thirty days. During the next month, Larson learns that Jerrod has breached his contract with Cambry by delivering coins that were not from the Roman era, as promised, and that for this reason Cambry will not honor the $1,000 note. Whether Larson can hold Cambry liable on the note depends on whether Larson has met the requirements for HDC status. If Larson has met these requirements and thus has HDC status, Larson is entitled to payment on the note. If Larson has not met these requirements, she has the status of an ordinary holder, and Cambry's defense of breach of contract against payment to Jerrod will also be effective against Larson. ▪

REQUIREMENTS FOR HDC STATUS

The basic requirements for attaining HDC status are set forth in UCC 3–302. A holder of a negotiable instrument is an HDC if she or he takes the instrument (1) for value; (2) in good faith; and (3) without notice that it is overdue, that it has been dishonored, that any person has a defense against it or a claim to it, or that the instrument contains unauthorized signatures, contains alterations, or is so irregular or incomplete as to call into question its authenticity. We now examine each of these requirements.

Taking for Value

An HDC must have given *value* for the instrument [UCC 3–302(a)(2)(i)]. A person who receives an instrument as a gift or inherits it has not met the requirement of value. In these situations, the person becomes an ordinary holder and does not possess the rights of an HDC.

How an Instrument Is Taken for Value Under UCC 3–303(a), a holder takes an instrument for value if the holder has done any of the following:

1 Performed the promise for which the instrument was issued or transferred.

2 Acquired a security interest or other lien in the instrument, excluding a lien obtained by a judicial proceeding. (Security interests and liens will be discussed in Chapters 20 and 21.)

3 Taken the instrument in payment of, or as security for, a preexisting claim. **■EXAMPLE 18.16** Zon owes Dwyer $2,000 on a past-due account. If Zon negotiates a $2,000 note signed by Gordon to Dwyer and Dwyer accepts it to discharge the overdue account balance, Dwyer has given value for the instrument. ▪

4 Given a negotiable instrument as payment for the instrument. **■EXAMPLE 18.17** Martin has issued a $500 negotiable promissory note to Paulene. The note is due six months from the date issued. Paulene needs cash and does not want to wait for the maturity date to collect. She negotiates the note to her friend Kristen, who pays her $200 in cash and writes her a check—a negotiable instrument—for the balance of $300. Kristen has given full value for the note by paying $200 in cash and issuing Paulene the check for $300. ▪

5 Given an irrevocable commitment (such as a letter of credit) as payment for the instrument.

The Concept of Value in Negotiable Instruments Law The concept of value in the law of negotiable instruments is not the same as the concept of *consideration* in the law of contracts. A promise to give value in the future is clearly sufficient consideration to support a contract [UCC 1–201(44)]. A promise to give value in the future, however, normally does not constitute value sufficient to make one an HDC. A holder takes an instrument for value only to the extent that the promise has been performed [UCC 3–303(a)(1)]. Therefore, if the holder plans to pay for the instrument later or plans to perform the required services at some future date, the holder has not yet given value. In that situation, the holder is not yet an HDC.

In the Larson-Cambry example presented earlier as Example 18.15 on the previous page, Larson is not an HDC because she did not take the instrument (Cambry's note) for value—she has not yet paid Jerrod for the note. Thus, Cambry's defense of breach of contract is valid not only against Jerrod but also against Larson. If Larson had paid Jerrod for the note at the time of transfer (which would mean she had given value for the instrument), she would be an HDC. As an HDC, she could hold Cambry liable on the note even though Cambry has a valid defense against Jerrod on the basis of breach of contract. Exhibit 18–6 illustrates these concepts.

Taking in Good Faith

The second requirement for HDC status is that the holder take the instrument in *good faith* [UCC 3–302(a)(2)(ii)]. Under Article 3, *good faith* is defined as "honesty in fact and the observance of reasonable commercial standards of fair dealing" [UCC 3–103(a)(4)].[3] The good faith requirement applies only to the *holder*. It is immaterial whether the transferor acted in good faith. Thus, a person who in good faith takes a negotiable instrument from a thief may become an HDC.

The good faith requirement means that the purchaser, when acquiring the instrument, must honestly believe that it is not defective. If a person purchases a $10,000 note for $300 from a stranger on a street corner, the issue of good faith can be raised on the grounds of both the suspicious circumstances and the grossly inadequate consideration (value). In the following case, the court had to deal with the meaning of accepting a check in good faith.

---

3. Before the revision of Article 3, the applicable definition of *good faith* was "honesty in fact in the conduct or transaction concerned" [UCC 1–201(19)].

CASE 18.2 Georg v. Metro Fixtures Contractors, Inc.

Supreme Court of Colorado, 178 P.3d 1209 (2008).

FACTS Clinton Georg employed Cassandra Demery as a bookkeeper at his business, Freestyle, until he discovered she had embezzled more than $200,000 and had failed to pay $240,000 in state and federal taxes owed by Freestyle. Georg fired Demery and said that if she did not repay the embezzled funds, he would notify the authorities. Demery went to work for Metro Fixtures, a company owned by her parents, as a bookkeeper. She wrote a check to Freestyle for $189,000 out of Metro's account and deposited it to Freestyle's checking account. She told Georg it was a loan to her from her family to repay him. Georg used the funds to pay his back taxes. Two years later, Metro discovered Demery's theft and sued Georg and Freestyle for *conversion* (see Chapter 4), as Demery had no authority to take the funds. The trial court held that Freestyle was a holder in due course and granted summary judgment. Metro appealed. The appeals court reversed, holding that because Demery deposited the check directly into Freestyle's account, Freestyle could not have been a holder in due course as it never had actual possession of the check. Georg and Freestyle appealed.

ISSUE Did Freestyle take the check that Demery wrote from Metro's account in good faith and therefore become a holder in due course?

DECISION Yes. The Colorado Supreme Court reversed the ruling of the appellate court and found that the payee, Freestyle, was a holder in due course based on its constructive possession of the check.

REASON The court reasoned that Demery was the wrongdoer in this case, and either Metro or Freestyle would have to absorb the loss. Even though Metro did not authorize Demery to issue the check for $189,000, she had the authority to issue checks for Metro. Georg had no reason to know that Demery had lied when she said her parents, who owned the company, had loaned her the funds. Because Demery deposited the check into Freestyle's account, Freestyle clearly had constructive possession of it, and this was sufficient under the circumstances. Therefore, Freestyle took the check in good faith. The UCC intends to protect the party least able to protect itself. Metro gave Demery authority to write checks on its account, so it bears the loss.

WHAT IF THE FACTS WERE DIFFERENT? *Suppose that Demery had gone to work for a company with which she had no relationship and had stolen funds from it to pay Georg. Would Georg then be the more innocent party? Why or why not?*

Taking without Notice

The final requirement for HDC status concerns notice of defects. A person cannot be an HDC if she or he knows or has reason to know that the instrument is defective in any one of the following ways [UCC 3–302(a)]:

1 It is overdue.

2 It has been dishonored.

3 It is part of a series of which at least one instrument has an uncured (uncorrected) default.

EXHIBIT 18–6 Taking for Value

By exchanging defective goods for the note, Jerrod breached his contract with Cambry. Cambry could assert this defense if Jerrod presented the note to her for payment. Jerrod exchanged the note for Larson's promise to pay in thirty days, however. Because Larson did not take the note for value, she is not a holder in due course. Thus, Cambry can assert against Larson the defense of Jerrod's breach when Larson submits the note to Cambry for payment. In contrast, if Larson had taken the note for value, Cambry could not assert that defense and would be liable to pay the note.

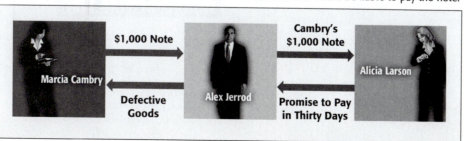

4 The instrument contains an unauthorized signature or has been altered.

5 There is a defense against the instrument or a claim to the instrument.

6 The instrument is so incomplete or irregular as to call into question its authenticity.

What Constitutes Notice? Notice of a defective instrument is given whenever the holder (1) has actual knowledge of the defect; (2) has received a notice of the defect (such as a letter from a bank identifying the serial numbers of stolen checks); or (3) has reason to know that a defect exists, given all the facts and circumstances known at the time in question [UCC 1–201(25)]. The holder must also have received the notice "at a time and in a manner that gives a reasonable opportunity to act on it" [UCC 3–302(f)]. A purchaser's knowledge of certain facts, such as insolvency proceedings against the maker or drawer of the instrument, does not constitute notice that the instrument is defective [UCC 3–302(b)].

Overdue Instruments What constitutes notice that an instrument is overdue depends on whether it is a demand instrument (payable on demand) or a time instrument (payable at a definite time). A purchaser has notice that a *demand instrument* is overdue if he or she either takes the instrument knowing that demand has been made or takes the instrument an unreasonable length of time after its date. For a check, a "reasonable time" is ninety days after the date of the check. For all other demand instruments, what will be considered a reasonable time depends on the circumstances [UCC 3–304(a)].

Normally, a *time instrument* is overdue on the day after its due date; hence, anyone who takes a time instrument after the due date is on notice that it is overdue [UCC 3–304(b)].[4] Thus, if a promissory note due on May 15 is purchased on May 16, the purchaser will be an ordinary holder, not an HDC. If an instrument states that it is "Payable in thirty days," counting begins the day after the instrument is dated. For example, a note dated December 1 that is payable in thirty days is due by midnight on December 31. If the payment date falls on a Sunday or holiday, the instrument is payable on the next business day.

If the principal is to be paid in installments or through a series of notes, the default or nonpayment of any one installment of principal or on any one note in the series will provide notice to prospective purchasers that the instrument is overdue [UCC 3–304(b)(1). The instrument will remain overdue until the default is cured [UCC 3–304(b)(1)]. An instrument does not become overdue if there is a default on a payment of interest only [UCC 3–304(c)].

HOLDER THROUGH AN HDC

A person who does not qualify as an HDC but who derives his or her title through an HDC can acquire the rights and privileges of an HDC. This rule, which is sometimes called the **shelter principle,** is set out in UCC 3–203(b):

Transfer of an instrument, whether or not the transfer is a negotiation, vests in the transferee any right of the transferor to enforce the instrument, including any right as a holder in due course, but the transferee cannot acquire rights of a holder in due course by a transfer, directly or indirectly, from a holder in due course if the transferee engaged in fraud or illegality affecting the instrument.

The shelter principle extends the benefits of HDC status and is designed to aid the HDC in readily disposing of the instrument. Under this rule, anyone—no matter how far removed from an HDC—who can ultimately trace his or her title back to an HDC may acquire the rights of an HDC. By extending the benefits of HDC status, the shelter principle promotes the marketability and free transferability of negotiable instruments.

There are some limitations on the shelter principle, though. Certain persons who formerly held instruments cannot improve their positions by later reacquiring the instruments from HDCs [UCC 3–203(b)]. If a holder participated in fraud or illegality affecting the instrument, or had notice of a claim or defense against an instrument, that holder is not allowed to improve her or his status by repurchasing the instrument from a later HDC. **■EXAMPLE 18.18** Matt and Carla collaborate to defraud Lorena. Lorena is induced to give Carla a negotiable note payable to Carla's order. Carla then specially indorses the note for value to Larry, an HDC. Matt and Carla split the proceeds. Larry negotiates the note to Stuart, another HDC. Stuart then negotiates the note for value to Matt. Even though Matt obtained the note through an HDC, he does not have the rights of an HDC—and can never acquire HDC rights in this note—because he participated in the original fraud. ■

SIGNATURE LIABILITY

The key to liability on a negotiable instrument is a *signature.* The general rule is as follows: Every party, except a qualified indorser,[5] who signs a negotiable instrument is either prima-

---

4. A time instrument also becomes overdue the day after an accelerated due date, unless the purchaser has no reason to know that the due date has been accelerated [UCC 3–302(a)(2)(iii), 3–304(b)(3)].

5. A qualified indorser—one who indorses "without recourse"—undertakes no contractual obligation to pay. A qualified indorser merely assumes warranty liability, which will be discussed later in this chapter.

rily or secondarily liable for payment of that instrument when it comes due. The following subsections discuss these two types of liability, as well as the conditions that must be met before liability can arise.

Primary Liability

A person who is primarily liable on a negotiable instrument is absolutely required to pay the instrument—unless, of course, he or she has a valid defense to payment [UCC 3–305]. Only *makers* and *acceptors* of instruments are primarily liable.

The maker of a promissory note promises to pay the note. It is the maker's promise to pay that makes the note a negotiable instrument. The words "I promise to pay" embody the maker's obligation to pay the instrument according to the terms as written at the time of the signing. If the instrument was incomplete when the maker signed it, the maker is obligated to pay it according to its stated terms or according to terms that were agreed on and later filled in to complete the instrument [UCC 3–115, 3–407(a), 3–412].

An **acceptor** is a drawee that promises to pay an instrument when it is presented for payment. Once a drawee indicates acceptance by signing the draft, the drawee becomes an acceptor and is obligated to pay the draft when it is presented for payment [UCC 3–409(a)]. A drawee that refuses to accept a draft that *requires* the drawee's acceptance (such as a trade acceptance) has dishonored the instrument. Acceptance of a check is called *certification* (certified checks will be discussed in Chapter 19). Certification is not necessary on checks, and a bank is under no obligation to certify checks. On certification, however, the drawee bank occupies the position of an acceptor and is primarily liable on the check to any holder [UCC 3–409(d)].

Secondary Liability

Drawers and *indorsers* are secondarily liable. On a negotiable instrument, secondary liability is similar to the liability of a guarantor in a simple contract (see Chapter 11) in the sense that it is *contingent liability*. In other words, a drawer or an indorser will be liable only if the party that is responsible for paying the instrument refuses to do so (dishonors the instrument). In regard to drafts and checks, the drawer's secondary liability does not arise until the drawee fails to pay or to accept the instrument, whichever is required [UCC 3–412, 3–415].

Dishonor of an instrument thus triggers the liability of parties who are secondarily liable on the instrument—that is, the drawer and *unqualified* indorsers. **■EXAMPLE 18.19** Nina Lee writes a check on her account at Universal Bank payable to the order of Stephen Miller. Universal Bank refuses to pay the check when Miller presents it for payment, thus dishon-

oring the check. In this situation, Lee will be liable to Miller on the basis of her secondary liability. ■ Drawers are secondarily liable on drafts unless they disclaim their liability by drawing the instruments "without recourse" (if the draft is a check, however, a drawer cannot disclaim liability) [UCC 3–414(e)].

Parties who are secondarily liable on a negotiable instrument promise to pay on that instrument only if the following events occur:[6]

1 The instrument is properly and timely presented.

2 The instrument is dishonored.

3 Timely notice of dishonor is given to the secondarily liable party.

Proper Presentment   *Presentment* is the formal production of a negotiable instrument for acceptance or payment. The UCC requires that a holder present the instrument to the appropriate party, in a timely fashion, and give reasonable identification if demanded [UCC 3–414(f), 3–415(e), 3–501]. The party to whom the instrument must be presented depends on the type of instrument involved. A note or certificate of deposit (CD) must be presented to the maker for payment. A draft is presented to the drawee for acceptance, payment, or both. A check is presented to the drawee for payment [UCC 3–501(a), 3–502(b)].

Presentment can be made by any commercially reasonable means, including oral, written, or electronic communication [UCC 3–501(b)]. It is ordinarily effective when the demand for payment or acceptance is received (unless presentment takes place after an established cutoff hour, in which case it may be treated as occurring the next business day).

Timely Presentment   One of the most crucial criteria for proper presentment is timeliness [UCC 3–414(f), 3–415(e), 3–501(b)(4)]. Failure to present an instrument on time is the most common reason for improper presentment and leads to unqualified indorsers being discharged from secondary liability. Under the UCC, the holder of a domestic check must present that check for payment or collection within thirty days of its *date* to hold the drawer secondarily liable, and within thirty days after its indorsement to hold the indorser secondarily liable. Failure to meet that deadline results in a discharge of secondary liability. The time for proper presentment for different types of instruments is shown in Exhibit 18–7 on the next page.

---

6. These requirements are necessary for a secondarily liable party to have signature liability on a negotiable instrument, but they are not necessary for a secondarily liable party to have warranty liability (to be discussed later in the chapter).

EXHIBIT 18–7 **Time for Proper Presentment**

TYPE OF INSTRUMENT	FOR ACCEPTANCE	FOR PAYMENT
Time	On or before due date.	On due date.
Demand	Within a reasonable time (after date of issue or after secondary party becomes liable on the instrument).	Within a reasonable time.
Check	Not applicable.	Within thirty days of its date, to hold drawer secondarily liable. Within thirty days of indorsement, to hold indorser secondarily liable.

Dishonor As mentioned previously, an instrument is **dishonored** when the required acceptance or payment is refused or cannot be obtained within the prescribed time. An instrument is also dishonored when the required presentment is excused (as it would be, for example, if the maker had died) and the instrument is not properly accepted or paid [UCC 3–502(e), 3–504].

In certain situations, a postponement of payment or a refusal to pay an instrument will *not* dishonor the instrument. When presentment is made after an established cutoff hour (not earlier than 2:00 P.M.), for instance, a bank can postpone payment until the following business day without dishonoring the instrument. In addition, when the holder refuses to exhibit the instrument, to give reasonable identification, or to sign a receipt for the payment on the instrument, a bank's refusal to pay does not dishonor the instrument.

Proper Notice Once an instrument has been dishonored, proper notice must be given to secondary parties (drawers and indorsers) for them to be held contractually liable. Notice may be given in any reasonable manner, including an oral, written, or electronic communication, as well as notice written or stamped on the instrument itself. The bank must give any necessary notice before its midnight deadline (midnight of the next banking day after receipt). Notice by any party other than a bank must be given within thirty days following the day of dishonor or the day on which the person who is secondarily liable receives notice of dishonor [UCC 3–503].

Unauthorized Signatures

Unauthorized signatures arise in two situations—when a person forges another person's name on a negotiable instrument and when an *agent* (see Chapter 22) who lacks the authority signs an instrument on behalf of a principal. The general rule is that an unauthorized signature is wholly inoperative and will

not bind the person whose name is signed or forged. **■EXAMPLE 18.20** Parra finds Dolby's checkbook lying in the street, writes out a check to himself, and forges Dolby's signature. If a bank fails to determine that Dolby's signature is not genuine (which banks normally have a duty to do) and cashes the check for Parra, the bank will generally be liable to Dolby for the amount. ■ (The liability of banks for paying checks with forged signatures will be discussed further in Chapter 19.)

If an agent lacks the authority to sign the principal's name or has exceeded the authority given by the principal, the signature does not bind the principal but will bind the "unauthorized signer" [UCC 3–403(a)].

There are two exceptions to the general rule that an unauthorized signature will not bind the person whose name is signed:

1 When the person whose name is signed ratifies (affirms) the signature, he or she will be bound [UCC 3–403(a)]. A principal can ratify an unauthorized signature made by an agent, either expressly, by affirming the validity of the signature, or impliedly, by other conduct, such as keeping any benefits received in the transaction or failing to repudiate the signature. The parties involved need not be principal and agent. **■EXAMPLE 18.21** Allison Malone steals several checks from her mother, Brenda Malone; makes them out to herself; and signs "Brenda Malone." Brenda, the mother, may ratify her daughter's signature so that Allison will not be prosecuted for forgery. ■

2 When the negligence of the person whose name was forged substantially contributed to the forgery, a court may not allow the person to deny the effectiveness of an unauthorized signature [UCC 3–115, 3–406, 4–401(d)(2)]. **■EXAMPLE 18.22** Rob, the owner of a business, leaves his signature stamp and a blank check on an office counter. An employee, using the stamp, fills in and cashes the check. Rob can be estopped (prevented), on the basis of negligence, from denying liability for payment of the check. Whatever loss occurs may be allocated, however, between certain parties on the basis of comparative negligence [UCC 3–406(b)]. For example, if Rob can demonstrate that the bank was negligent in paying the check, the bank may bear a portion of the loss. ◾

A person who forges a check can be held personally liable for payment by an HDC [UCC 3–403(a)]. This is true even if the name of the person signing the instrument without authorization does not appear on the instrument.

Special Rules for Unauthorized Indorsements

Generally, when an indorsement is forged or unauthorized, the burden of loss falls on the first party to take the instrument with the forged or unauthorized indorsement. This general rule is premised on the concept that the first party to take an instrument is in the best position to prevent the loss.

There are two important exceptions to this general rule. These exceptions arise when an indorsement is made by an imposter or by a fictitious payee. In these situations, as discussed next, the loss falls on the maker or drawer.

Imposter Rule An **imposter** is one who, by her or his personal appearance or use of the mails, Internet, telephone, or other communication, induces a maker or drawer to issue an instrument in the name of an impersonated payee. If the maker or drawer believes the imposter to be the named payee at the time of issue, the indorsement by the imposter is not treated as unauthorized when the instrument is transferred to an innocent party. This is because the maker or drawer *intended* the imposter to receive the instrument. In this situation, under the UCC's *imposter rule*, the imposter's indorsement will be effective—that is, not considered a forgery—insofar as the drawer or maker is concerned [UCC 3–404(a)]. **EXAMPLE 18.23** Carol impersonates Donna and induces Edward to write a check payable to the order of Donna. Carol, continuing to impersonate Donna, negotiates the check to First National Bank as payment on her loan there. As the drawer of the check, Edward is liable for its amount to First National. ◾

Fictitious Payee Rule When a person causes an instrument to be issued to a payee who will have *no interest* in the instrument, the payee is referred to as a **fictitious payee**. A fictitious payee can be a person or firm that does not truly exist, or it may be an identifiable party that will not acquire any interest in the instrument. Under the UCC's *fictitious payee rule*, the payee's indorsement is not treated as a forgery, and an innocent holder can hold the maker or drawer liable on the instrument [UCC 3–404(b), 3–405].

Situations involving fictitious payees most often arise when (1) a dishonest employee deceives the employer into signing an instrument payable to a party with no right to receive payment on the instrument or (2) a dishonest employee or agent has the authority to issue an instrument on behalf of the employer.

EXAMPLE 18.24 Blair Industries, Inc., gives its bookkeeper, Axel Ford, general authority to issue company checks drawn on First State Bank so that Ford can pay employees' wages and other corporate bills. Ford decides to cheat Blair Industries out of $10,000 by issuing a check payable to Erica Nied, an old acquaintance. Neither Blair nor Ford intends Nied to receive any of the funds, and Nied is not an employee or creditor of the company. Ford indorses the check in Nied's name, naming himself as indorsee. He then cashes the check at a local bank, which collects payment from the drawee bank, First State Bank. First State Bank charges the Blair Industries account $10,000. Blair Industries discovers the fraud and demands that the account be recredited. Under UCC 3–404(b)(2), neither the local bank that first accepted the check nor First State Bank is liable. Because Ford's indorsement in the name of a payee with no interest in the instrument is "effective," there is no "forgery." Hence, the collecting bank is protected in paying on the check, and the drawee bank is protected in charging Blair's account. Thus, the employer-drawer, Blair Industries, will bear the loss. Of course, Blair Industries has recourse against Axel Ford, if Ford has not absconded with the funds. ◾

Regardless of whether a dishonest employee actually signs the check or merely supplies his or her employer with names of fictitious creditors (or with true names of creditors having fictitious debts), the result is the same under the UCC.

WARRANTY LIABILITY

In addition to the signature liability discussed in the preceding pages, transferors make certain implied warranties regarding the instruments that they are negotiating. Liability under these warranties is not subject to the conditions of proper presentment, dishonor, or notice of dishonor. These warranties arise even when a transferor does not indorse the instrument (as in the delivery of a bearer instrument) [UCC 3–416, 3–417]. Warranty liability is particularly important when a holder cannot hold a party liable on her or his signature.

Warranties fall into two categories: those that arise on the *transfer* of a negotiable instrument and those that arise on *presentment*. Both transfer and presentment warranties attempt to shift liability back to a wrongdoer or to the person who dealt face to face with the wrongdoer and thus was in the best position to prevent the wrongdoing.

Transfer Warranties

The UCC describes five **transfer warranties** [UCC 3–416]. For transfer warranties to arise, an instrument *must be transferred for consideration*. One who transfers an instrument for consideration makes the following warranties to all subsequent transferees and holders who take the instrument in good faith (with some exceptions, as will be noted shortly):

1 The transferor is entitled to enforce the instrument.

2 All signatures are authentic and authorized.

3 The instrument has not been altered.

4 The instrument is not subject to a defense or claim of any party that can be asserted against the transferor.

5 The transferor has no knowledge of any insolvency (bankruptcy) proceedings against the maker, the acceptor, or the drawer of the instrument.[7]

Parties to Whom Warranty Liability Extends The manner of transfer and the negotiation that is used determine how far and to whom a transfer warranty will run. Transfer of order paper, for consideration, by indorsement and delivery extends warranty liability to any subsequent holder who takes the instrument in good faith. The warranties of a person who transfers *without indorsement* (by the delivery of a bearer instrument), however, will extend the transferor's warranties only to the immediate transferee [UCC 3–416(a)].

EXAMPLE 18.25 Wylie forges Peter's name as a maker of a promissory note. The note is made payable to Wylie. Wylie indorses the note in blank, negotiates it to Carla, and then leaves the country. Carla, without indorsement, delivers the note to Frank for consideration. Frank in turn, without indorsement, delivers the note to Ricardo for consideration. On Ricardo's presentment of the note to Peter, the forgery is discovered. Ricardo can hold Frank (the immediate transferor) liable for breach of the transfer warranty that all signatures are genuine. Ricardo cannot hold Carla liable because the transfer warranties made by Carla, who negotiated the bearer instrument by delivery only, extend solely to Frank, the immediate transferee. ■

Note that if Wylie had added a special indorsement ("Payable to Carla") instead of a blank indorsement, the instrument would have remained an order instrument. In that situation, to negotiate the instrument to Frank, Carla would have had to indorse the instrument, and her transfer warranties would extend to all subsequent holders, including Ricardo. This example shows the importance of the distinction between a transfer by indorsement and delivery (of an order instrument) and a transfer by delivery only, without indorsement (of a bearer instrument).

Recovery for Breach of Warranty A transferee or holder who takes an instrument in good faith can sue on the basis of a breach of warranty as soon as he or she has reason to know of the breach [UCC 3–416(d)]. Notice of a claim for breach of warranty must be given to the warrantor within thirty days after the transferee or holder has reason to know of the breach and the identity of the warrantor, or the warrantor is not liable for any loss caused by a delay [UCC 3–416(c)]. The transferee or holder can recover damages for the breach in an amount equal to the loss suffered (but not more than the amount of the instrument), plus expenses and any loss of interest caused by the breach [UCC 3–416(b)].

These warranties can be disclaimed with respect to any instrument except a check [UCC 3–416(c)]. In the check-collection process, banks rely on these warranties. For all other instruments, the immediate parties can agree to a disclaimer, and an indorser can disclaim by including in the indorsement such words as "without warranties."

Presentment Warranties

Any person who presents an instrument for payment or acceptance makes the following **presentment warranties** to any other person who in good faith pays or accepts the instrument [UCC 3–417(a), 3–417(d)]:

1 The person obtaining payment or acceptance is entitled to enforce the instrument or is authorized to obtain payment or acceptance on behalf of a person who is entitled to enforce the instrument. (This is, in effect, a warranty that there are no missing or unauthorized indorsements.)

2 The instrument has not been altered.

3 The person obtaining payment or acceptance has no knowledge that the signature of the issuer of the instrument is unauthorized.[8]

These warranties are referred to as presentment warranties because they protect the person to whom the instrument is

---

7. A 2002 amendment to UCC 3–416(a) adds a sixth warranty: "with respect to a remotely created consumer item, that the person on whose account the item is drawn authorized the issuance of the item in the amount for which the item is drawn." UCC 3–103(16) defines a "remotely created consumer item" as an item, such as a check, drawn on a consumer account, which is not created by the payor bank and does not contain the drawer's handwritten signature. For example, a telemarketer submits an instrument to a bank for payment, claiming that the consumer on whose account the instrument purports to be drawn authorized it over the phone. Under this amendment, a bank that accepts and pays the instrument warrants to the next bank in the collection chain that the consumer authorized the item in that amount.

8. As discussed in footnote 7, the 2002 amendments to Article 3 of the UCC provide additional protection for "remotely created" consumer items [see Amended UCC 3–417(a)(4)].

presented. The second and third warranties do not apply to makers, acceptors, and drawers. It is assumed, for example, that a drawer or a maker will recognize his or her own signature and that a maker or an acceptor will recognize whether an instrument has been materially altered.

DEFENSES, LIMITATIONS, AND DISCHARGE

Persons who would otherwise be liable on negotiable instruments may be able to avoid liability by raising certain defenses. There are two general categories of defenses—*universal defenses* and *personal defenses*—which are discussed below and summarized in Exhibit 18–8.

Universal Defenses

Universal defenses (also called *real defenses*) are valid against *all* holders, including HDCs and holders who take through an HDC. Universal defenses include those described here.

Forgery Forgery of a maker's or drawer's signature cannot bind the person whose name is used unless that person ratifies (approves or validates) the signature or is barred from denying it (because the forgery was made possible by the maker's or drawer's negligence, for example) [UCC 3–403(a)]. Thus, when a person forges an instrument, the person whose name is forged normally has no liability to pay any holder or any HDC the value of the forged instrument.

Fraud in the Execution If a person is deceived into signing a negotiable instrument, believing that she or he is signing something other than a negotiable instrument (such as a receipt), *fraud in the execution*, or fraud in the inception, is committed against the signer [UCC 3–305(a)(1)].
■EXAMPLE 18.26 Gerard, a salesperson, asks Javier, a customer, to sign a paper, which Gerard says is a receipt for the delivery of goods that Javier is picking up from the store. In fact, the paper is a promissory note, but Javier is unfamiliar with the English language and does not realize this. In this situation, even if the note is negotiated to an HDC, Javier has a valid defense against payment. ■

The defense of fraud in the execution cannot be raised, however, if a reasonable inquiry would have revealed the nature and terms of the instrument. Thus, the signer's age, experience, and intelligence are relevant because they frequently determine whether the signer should have known the nature of the transaction before signing.

Material Alteration An alteration is *material* if it changes the contract terms between two parties *in any way*. Examples of material alterations include completing an instrument, adding words or numbers, or making any other unauthorized change that relates to a party's obligation [UCC 3–407(a)]. Any change in the amount, the date, or the rate of interest—even if the change is only one penny, one day, or 1 percent—is material. It is not a material alteration, however, to correct the maker's address, to draw a red line across the instrument to indicate that an auditor has checked it, or to correct the total final payment due when a mathematical error is discovered in the original computation. If the alteration is not material, any holder is entitled to enforce the instrument according to its original terms.

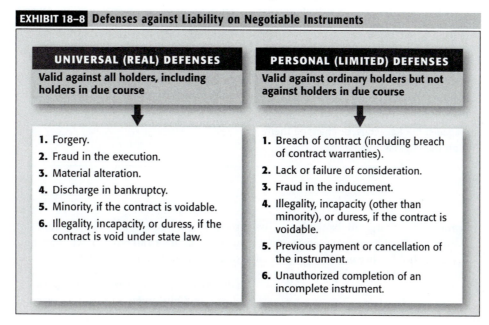

EXHIBIT 18–8 Defenses against Liability on Negotiable Instruments

UNIVERSAL (REAL) DEFENSES	PERSONAL (LIMITED) DEFENSES
Valid against all holders, including holders in due course	Valid against ordinary holders but not against holders in due course
1. Forgery. 2. Fraud in the execution. 3. Material alteration. 4. Discharge in bankruptcy. 5. Minority, if the contract is voidable. 6. Illegality, incapacity, or duress, if the contract is void under state law.	1. Breach of contract (including breach of contract warranties). 2. Lack or failure of consideration. 3. Fraud in the inducement. 4. Illegality, incapacity (other than minority), or duress, if the contract is voidable. 5. Previous payment or cancellation of the instrument. 6. Unauthorized completion of an incomplete instrument.

Material alteration is a *complete defense* against an ordinary holder but only a *partial defense* against an HDC. An ordinary holder can recover nothing on an instrument that has been materially altered [UCC 3–407(b)]. In contrast, when the holder is an HDC and an original term, such as the monetary amount payable, has been *altered*, the HDC can enforce the instrument against the maker or drawer according to the original terms but not for the altered amount [UCC 3–407(c)(i)]. If the instrument was originally incomplete and was later completed in an unauthorized manner, alteration can no longer be claimed as a defense against an HDC, and the HDC can enforce the instrument as completed [UCC 3–407(b), (c)]. This is because a drawer or maker who has issued an incomplete instrument normally will be held responsible for such an alteration, which could have been avoided by the exercise of greater care. If the alteration is readily apparent (such as a number changed on the face of a check), then obviously the holder has notice of some defect or defense and therefore cannot be an HDC [UCC 3–302(a)(1), (2)(iv)].

Is a note that allows for an extension of the time for payment materially altered when, on its expiration, its maker and payee execute a second note that the payee insists is only an extension of the time for payment but that in reality increases the balance due? That was the question in the following case.

CASE 18.3   Keesling v. T.E.K. Partners, LLC

Indiana Court of Appeals, 861 N.E.2d 1246 (2007).

FACTS In January 1998, two separate entities formed Heritage/M.G., LLC, in order to develop a residential neighborhood. A year and a half later, Heritage/M.G. borrowed $300,000 to partially finance the development. Final payment on the note was due on June 1, 2001. The signatories included Thomas McMullen, on behalf of Heritage/M.G., and Larry and Vivian Keesling. Heritage/M.G. did not complete the payments by the original deadline. By January 3, 2002, the balance was just below $50,000. Without the knowledge or consent of the Keeslings, Heritage/M.G. borrowed another $102,000 on which no payments were ever made. The original lenders assigned both the first and the second note to T.E.K. Partners, LLC. The trial court concluded that T.E.K. Partners was entitled to a judgment of $375,905.07. The Keeslings appealed.

ISSUE Does the issuance of a second promissory note that effectively increases the balance due on a first note constitute a material alteration?

DECISION Yes. The Indiana Court of Appeals reversed the trial court's judgment against the Keeslings, discharging them from personal liability on the original note.

REASON The reviewing court noted that a guarantee is a promise to answer for the debt, default, or miscarriage of another person. Therefore, the Keeslings were guarantors on the original note. Under Indiana law, "when parties cause material alteration of an underlying obligation without the consent of the guarantor, the guarantor is discharged from future liability." In this case, the change increased the risk of loss to the guarantor. Initially, the Keeslings guaranteed the original note; they were accommodation parties. McMullen, on behalf of Heritatge/M.G., executed the second note for $102,000 without consulting the accommodation parties (the Keeslings). The "second note not only added new debt but increased the total principle draws beyond the $300,000 face amount of the original note." Because the second note constituted a material alteration of the original obligation, the Keeslings were discharged from liability on it.

 FOR CRITICAL ANALYSIS—Legal Consideration *What might the parties who executed the second note have done at the time to avoid the outcome in this case?*

Discharge in Bankruptcy Discharge in bankruptcy (see Chapter 21) is an absolute defense on any instrument, regardless of the status of the holder, because the purpose of bankruptcy is to settle finally all of the insolvent party's debts [UCC 3–305(a)(1)].

Minority Minority, or infancy, is a universal defense only to the extent that state law recognizes it as a defense to a simple contract (see Chapter 11). Because state laws on minority vary, so do determinations of whether minority is a universal defense against an HDC [UCC 3–305(a)(1)(i)].

Illegality Certain types of illegality constitute universal defenses. Other types constitute personal defenses—that is, defenses that are effective against ordinary holders but not against HDCs. If a statute provides that an illegal transaction is void, then the defense is universal—that is, absolute against both an ordinary holder and an HDC. If the law merely makes the instrument voidable, then the illegality is still a personal defense against an ordinary holder but not against an HDC [UCC 3–305(a)(1)(ii)].

Mental Incapacity If a person has been declared by a court to be mentally incompetent, then any instrument issued thereafter by that person is void. The instrument is void *ab initio* (from the beginning) and unenforceable by any holder or HDC [UCC 3–305(a)(1)(ii)]. Mental incapacity in these circumstances is thus a universal defense. If a court has not declared a person to be mentally incompetent, then mental incapacity operates as a defense against an ordinary holder but not against an HDC.

Extreme Duress When a person signs and issues a negotiable instrument under such extreme duress as an immediate threat of force or violence (for example, at gunpoint), the instrument is void and unenforceable by any holder or HDC [UCC 3–305(a)(1)(ii)]. (Ordinary duress is a defense against ordinary holders but not against HDCs.)

Personal Defenses

Personal defenses (sometimes called *limited defenses*), such as those described here, can be used to avoid payment to an ordinary holder of a negotiable instrument, but not to an HDC or a holder with the rights of an HDC.

Breach of Contract or Breach of Warranty When there is a breach of the underlying contract for which the negotiable instrument was issued, the maker of a note can refuse to pay it, or the drawer of a check can order his or her bank to stop payment on the check. Breach of warranty can also be claimed as a defense to liability on the instrument.

■**EXAMPLE 18.27** Rhoda agrees to purchase several sets of imported china from Livingston. The china is to be delivered in four weeks. Rhoda gives Livingston a promissory note for $2,000, which is the price of the china. The china arrives, but many of the pieces are broken, and several others are chipped or cracked. Rhoda refuses to pay the note on the basis of breach of contract and breach of warranty. (Recall from Chapter 17 that a seller impliedly promises that the goods are at least merchantable.) Livingston cannot enforce payment on the note because of the breach of contract and breach of warranty. If Livingston has negotiated the note to a third party, however, and the third party is an HDC, Rhoda will not be able to use breach of contract or warranty as a defense against liability on the note. ■

Lack or Failure of Consideration The absence of consideration (value) may be a successful personal defense in some instances [UCC 3–303(b), 3–305(a)(2)]. ■**EXAMPLE 18.28** Tara gives Clem, as a gift, a note that states, "I promise to pay you $100,000." Clem accepts the note. Because there is no consideration for Tara's promise, a court will not enforce the promise. ■

Fraud in the Inducement (Ordinary Fraud) A person who issues a negotiable instrument based on false statements by the other party will be able to avoid payment on that instrument, unless the holder is an HDC. ■**EXAMPLE 18.29** Jerry agrees to purchase Howard's used tractor for $26,500. Howard, knowing his statements to be false, tells Jerry that the tractor is in good working order, that it has been used for only one harvest, and that he owns the tractor free and clear of all claims. Jerry pays Howard $4,500 in cash and issues a negotiable promissory note for the balance. As it turns out, Howard still owes the original seller $10,000 on the purchase of the tractor. In addition, the tractor is three years old and has been used in three harvests. Jerry can refuse to pay the note if it is held by an ordinary holder. If Howard has negotiated the note to an HDC, however, Jerry must pay the HDC. (Of course, Jerry can then sue Howard to recover the funds paid.) ■

Illegality As mentioned, if a statute provides that an illegal transaction is void, a universal defense exists. If, however, the statute provides that an illegal transaction is voidable, the defense is personal.

Mental Incapacity As mentioned, if a maker or drawer has been declared by a court to be mentally incompetent, any instrument issued by the maker or drawer is void. In that situation, mental incapacity is a universal defense [UCC 3–305(a)(1)(ii)]. If a maker or drawer issues a negotiable instrument while mentally incompetent but before a formal court hearing has declared him or her to be so, however, the instrument is voidable. In this situation, mental incapacity can serve only as a personal defense.

Other Personal Defenses Other personal defenses that can be used to avoid payment to an ordinary holder of a negotiable instrument include the following:

1 Discharge by payment or cancellation [UCC 3–601(b), 3–602(a), 3–603, 3–604].

2 Unauthorized completion of an incomplete instrument [UCC 3–115, 3–302, 3–407, 4–401(d)(2)].

3 Nondelivery of the instrument [UCC 1–201(14), 3–105(b), 3–305(a)(2)].

4 Ordinary duress or undue influence rendering the contract voidable [UCC 3–305(a)(1)(ii)].

Discharge from Liability

Discharge from liability on an instrument can occur in several ways. The liability of all parties to an instrument is discharged when the party primarily liable on it pays to the holder the amount due in full [UCC 3–602, 3–603]. Payment by any other party discharges only the liability of that party and subsequent parties.

Intentional cancellation of an instrument discharges the liability of all parties [UCC 3–604]. Intentionally writing "Paid" across the face of an instrument cancels it, as does intentionally tearing up the instrument. If a holder intentionally crosses out a party's signature, that party's liability and the liability of subsequent indorsers who have already indorsed the instrument are discharged. Materially altering an instrument may discharge the liability of any party affected by the alteration, as previously discussed [UCC 3–407(b)]. (An HDC may be able to enforce a materially altered instrument against its maker or drawer according to the instrument's original terms, however.)

Discharge of liability can also occur when a party's right of recourse is impaired [UCC 3–605]. A *right of recourse* is a right to seek reimbursement. Ordinarily, when a holder collects the amount of an instrument from an indorser, the indorser has a right of recourse against prior indorsers, the maker or drawer, and accommodation parties. If the holder has adversely affected the indorser's right to seek reimbursement from these other parties, however, the indorser is not liable on the instrument. This occurs when, for example, the holder releases or agrees not to sue a party against whom the indorser has a right of recourse.

REVIEWING **Negotiability, Transferability, and Liability**

Robert Durbin, a student, borrowed funds from a bank for his education and signed a promissory note for its repayment. The bank lent the funds under a federal program designed to assist students at postsecondary institutions. Under this program, repayment ordinarily begins nine to twelve months after the student borrower fails to carry at least one-half of the normal full-time course load at his or her school. The federal government guarantees that the note will be fully repaid. If the student defaults on the repayment, the lender presents the current balance—principal, interest, and costs—to the government. When the government pays the balance, it becomes the lender, and the borrower owes the government directly. After Durbin defaulted on his note, the government paid the lender the balance due and took possession of the note. Durbin then refused to pay the government, claiming that the government was not the holder of the note. The government filed a suit in a federal district court against Durbin to collect the amount due. Using the information presented in the chapter, answer the following questions.

1 Using the categories discussed in the chapter, what type of negotiable instrument was the note that Durbin signed (an order to pay or a promise to pay)? Explain.

2 Suppose that the note did not state a specific interest rate but instead referred to a statute that established the maximum interest rate for government-guaranteed school loans. Would the note fail to meet the requirements for negotiability in that situation? Why or why not?

3 How does a party who is not named by a negotiable instrument (in this situation the government) obtain a right to enforce the instrument?

4 Suppose that in court, Durbin argues that because the school closed down before he could finish his education, there was a failure of consideration: he did not get something of value in exchange for his promise to pay. Assuming that the government is a holder of the promissory note, would this argument likely be successful against it? Why or why not?

TERMS AND CONCEPTS

acceleration clause 352	check 348	fictitious payee 361
acceptance 348	dishonor 360	holder 352
acceptor 359	draft 348	holder in due course (HDC) 355
bearer 353	drawee 348	imposter 361
bearer instrument 353	drawer 348	indorsement 354
certificate of deposit (CD) 349	extension clause 353	maker 349

CHAPTER SUMMARY	Negotiability, Transferability, and Liability
Articles 3 and 4 of the UCC (See pages 346–347.)	Article 3 of the Uniform Commercial Code (UCC) governs the negotiability and transferability of negotiable instruments. Article 3 was significantly revised in 1990. Almost all of the states have adopted the revised article.
Types of Instruments (See pages 347–349.)	The UCC specifies four types of negotiable instruments: drafts, checks, promissory notes, and certificates of deposit (CDs). These instruments fall into two basic classifications: 1. *Demand instruments versus time instruments*—A demand instrument is payable on demand (when the holder presents it to the maker or drawer). A time instrument is payable at a future date. 2. *Orders to pay versus promises to pay*—Checks and drafts are *orders* to pay. Promissory notes and CDs are *promises* to pay.
Requirements for Negotiability (See pages 349–353.)	To be negotiable, an instrument must meet the following requirements: 1. Be in writing [UCC 3–103(a)(6), (9)]. 2. Be signed by the maker or the drawer [UCC 1–201(39)]. 3. Be an unconditional promise or order to pay [UCC 3–106]. 4. State a fixed amount of money [UCC 3–104(a), 3–112(b)]. 5. Be payable on demand or at a definite time [UCC 3–104(a)(2), 3–108(a), (b), (c)]. 6. Be payable to order or to bearer [UCC 3–104(a)(1), (c)].
Factors That Do Not Affect Negotiability (See pages 353–354.)	1. The fact that an instrument is undated does not affect its negotiability unless the date is necessary to determine a definite time for payment. 2. Postdating or antedating an instrument does not affect its negotiability. 3. Handwritten terms take priority over typewritten and printed terms. 4. Words outweigh figures unless the words are ambiguous. 5. An instrument that states "with interest" but does not state the interest rate is payable at the judgment rate of interest.
Transfer of Instruments (See pages 354–355.)	1. *Transfer by assignment*—A transfer by assignment to an assignee gives the assignee only those rights that the assignor possessed. Any defenses against payment that can be raised against an assignor can normally be raised against the assignee. 2. *Transfer by negotiation*—An order instrument is negotiated by indorsement and delivery; a bearer instrument is negotiated by delivery only.
Holder in Due Course (HDC) (See pages 355–356.)	1. *Holder*—A person in the possession of an instrument drawn, issued, or indorsed to him or her, to his or her order, to bearer, or in blank. A holder obtains only those rights that the transferor had in the instrument. 2. *Holder in due course (HDC)*—A holder who, by meeting certain acquisition requirements (summarized next), takes the instrument free of most defenses and claims to which the transferor was subject.

(Continued)

CHAPTER SUMMARY	Negotiability, Transferability, and Liability—Continued

Requirements for HDC Status (See pages 356–358.)	To be an HDC, a holder must take the instrument:
	
	1. *For value*—A holder can take an instrument for value in one of five ways [UCC 3–303]:
	  a. By the complete or partial performance of the promise for which the instrument was issued or transferred.
	  b. By acquiring a security interest or other lien in the instrument, excluding a lien obtained by a judicial proceeding.
	  c. By taking an instrument in payment of (or as security for) a preexisting debt.
	  d. By giving a negotiable instrument as payment.
	  e. By giving an irrevocable commitment as payment.
	
	2. *In good faith*—Good faith is defined as "honesty in fact and the observance of reasonable commercial standards of fair dealing" [UCC 3–103(a)(4)].
	
	3. *Without notice*—To be an HDC, a holder must not be on notice that the instrument is defective in any of the following ways [UCC 3–302, 3–304]:
	  a. The instrument is overdue.
	  b. The instrument has been dishonored.
	  c. The instrument is part of a series of which at least one instrument has an uncured (uncorrected) default.
	  d. The instrument contains an unauthorized signature or has been altered.
	  e. There is a defense against the instrument or a claim to the instrument.
	  f. The instrument is so irregular or incomplete as to call into question its authenticity.

Holder through an HDC (See page 358.)	A holder who cannot qualify as an HDC has the *rights* of an HDC if he or she derives title through an HDC, unless the holder engaged in fraud or illegality affecting the instrument [UCC 3–203(b)]. This is known as the shelter principle.

Signature Liability (See pages 358–361.)	Every party (except a qualified indorser) who signs a negotiable instrument is either primarily or secondarily liable for payment of the instrument when it comes due.
	
	1. *Primary liability*—Makers and acceptors are primarily liable (an *acceptor* is a drawee that promises in writing to pay an instrument when it is presented for payment at a later time) [UCC 3–115, 3–407, 3–409, 3–412].
	
	2. *Secondary liability*—Drawers and indorsers are secondarily liable [UCC 3–412, 3–414, 3–415, 3–501, 3–502, 3–503]. Parties who are secondarily liable on an instrument promise to pay on that instrument if the following events occur:
	  a. The instrument is properly and timely presented.
	  b. The instrument is dishonored.
	  c. Timely notice of dishonor is given to the secondarily liable party.
	
	3. *Unauthorized signatures*—An unauthorized signature is wholly inoperative *unless:*
	  a. The person whose name is signed ratifies (affirms) it or is precluded from denying it [UCC 3–115, 3–403, 3–406, 4–401(d)(2)].
	  b. The instrument has been negotiated to an HDC [UCC 3–403].
	
	4. *Special rules for unauthorized indorsements*—An unauthorized indorsement will not bind the maker or drawer except in the following circumstances:
	  a. When an imposter induces the maker or drawer of an instrument to issue it to the imposter (imposter rule) [UCC 3–404(a)].

CHAPTER SUMMARY	Negotiability, Transferability, and Liability–Continued
Signature Liability—Continued	b. When a person signs as or on behalf of a maker or drawer, intending that the payee will have no interest in the instrument, or when an agent or employee of the maker or drawer has supplied him or her with the name of the payee, also intending the payee to have no such interest (fictitious payee rule) [UCC 3–404(b), 3–405].
Warranty Liability (See pages 361–363.)	1. *Transfer warranties*—Any person who transfers an instrument for consideration makes the following warranties to all subsequent transferees and holders who take the instrument in good faith (but when a bearer instrument is transferred by delivery only, the transferor's warranties extend only to the immediate transferee) [UCC 3–416]: a. The transferor is entitled to enforce the instrument. b. All signatures are authentic and authorized. c. The instrument has not been altered. d. The instrument is not subject to a defense or claim of any party that can be asserted against the transferor. e. The transferor has no knowledge of any insolvency proceedings against the maker, the acceptor, or the drawer of the instrument. 2. *Presentment warranties*—Any person who presents an instrument for payment or acceptance makes the following warranties to any other person who in good faith pays or accepts the instrument [UCC 3–417(a), 3–417(d)]: a. The person obtaining payment or acceptance is entitled to enforce the instrument or is authorized to obtain payment or acceptance on behalf of a person who is entitled to enforce the instrument. (This is, in effect, a warranty that there are no missing or unauthorized indorsements.) b. The instrument has not been altered. c. The person obtaining payment or acceptance has no knowledge that the signature of the drawer of the instrument is unauthorized.
Defenses, Limitations, and Discharge (See pages 363–366.)	1. *Universal (real) defenses*—See Exhibit 18–8 on page 363 for a list of the defenses that are valid against all holders, including HDCs and holders with the rights of HDCs. 2. *Personal (limited) defenses*—See Exhibit 18–8 on page 363 for a list of the defenses that are valid against ordinary holders but *not* against HDCs or holders with the rights of HDCs. 3. *Discharge from liability*—All parties to a negotiable instrument will be discharged when the party primarily liable on it pays to a holder the amount due in full. Discharge can also occur in other circumstances (if the instrument has been canceled or materially altered, for example) [UCC 3–601 through 3–605].

FOR REVIEW

Answers for the even-numbered questions in this **For Review** *section can be found on this text's accompanying Web site at* **www.cengage.com/blaw/fbl**. *Select "Chapter 18" and click on "For Review."*

1 What requirements must an instrument meet to be negotiable?

2 What are the requirements for attaining the status of a holder in due course (HDC)?

3 What is the key to liability on a negotiable instrument? What is the difference between signature liability and warranty liability?

4 Certain defenses are valid against all holders, including HDCs. What are these defenses called? Name four defenses that fall within this category.

5 Certain defenses can be used to avoid payment to an ordinary holder of a negotiable instrument but are not effective against an HDC. What are these defenses called? Name four defenses that fall within this category.

QUESTIONS AND CASE PROBLEMS

HYPOTHETICAL SCENARIOS AND CASE PROBLEMS

18.1 Negotiability. Muriel Evans writes the following note on the back of an envelope: "I, Muriel Evans, promise to pay Karen Marvin or bearer $100 on demand." Is this a negotiable instrument? Discuss fully.

18.2 Hypothetical Question with Sample Answer. Williams purchased a used car from Stein for $1,000. Williams paid for the car with a check, written in pencil, payable to Stein for $1,000. Stein, through careful erasures and alterations, changed the amount on the check to read $10,000 and negotiated the check to Boz. Boz took the check for value, in good faith, and without notice of the alteration and thus met the Uniform Commercial Code's requirements for holder in due course status. Can Williams successfully raise the universal (real) defense of material alteration to avoid payment on the check? Explain.

For a sample answer to Question 18.2, go to Appendix E at the end of this text.

18.3 Holder in Due Course. Deola Bishop sold her home in Cameron County, Texas, to Cristobal and Juana Elisa Gonzalez in 1998. The Gonzalezes signed a note for $76,500 payable to Bishop. In January 2000, Bishop saw a newspaper ad in which American Notice Investments, Inc. (ANI), was soliciting such notes (ANI was in the business of buying notes at a discount). Bishop responded to the ad. ANI contacted First National Acceptance Co. (FNAC) to borrow the funds to make the purchase. FNAC approved the deal. ANI sent the note to FNAC, which authorized payment to Bishop on the note. ANI did not pay Bishop, however, before it ceased doing business. FNAC also did not pay Bishop, refused to return the note, and told the Gonzalezes to make their payments on the note to FNAC. Bishop and the Gonzalezes filed a suit in a Texas state court against FNAC, contending, in part, that Bishop was entitled to the note. FNAC asserted that it was a holder in due course (HDC). What is the reason for the HDC doctrine? What are the requirements for HDC status? Does FNAC qualify? Discuss. [*First National Acceptance Co. v. Bishop*, 187 S.W.3d 710 (Tex.App.—Corpus Christi 2006)]

18.4 Holder in Due Course. Robert Triffin bought a number of dishonored checks from McCall's Liquor Corp., Community Check Cashing II, LLC (CCC), and other licensed check-cashing businesses in New Jersey. Seventeen of the checks had been dishonored as counterfeit. In an attempt to recover on the items, Triffin met with the drawer, Automatic Data Processing, Inc. (ADP). At the meeting, Triffin said that he knew the checks were counterfeit. When ADP refused to pay, Triffin filed suits in New Jersey state courts to collect, asserting claims totaling $11,021.33. With each complaint were copies of assignment agreements corresponding to each check. Each agreement stated, among other things, that the seller was a holder in due course (HDC) and had assigned its rights in the check to Triffin. ADP had not previously seen these agreements. A private investigator determined that the forms attached to the McCall's and CCC checks had not been signed by their sellers but that Triffin had scanned the signatures into his computer and pasted them onto the agreements. ADP claimed fraud. Does Triffin qualify as an HDC? If not, did he acquire the rights of an HDC under the shelter principle? As for the fraud claim, which element of fraud would ADP be least likely to prove? [*Triffin v. Automatic Data Processing, Inc.*, 394 N.J.Super. 237, 926 A.2d 362 (App.Div. 2007)]

18.5 Case Problem with Sample Answer. In September 2001, Cory Babcock and Honest Air Conditioning & Heating, Inc., bought a new 2001 Chevrolet Corvette from Cox Chevrolet in Sarasota, Florida. Their retail installment sales contract (RISC) required monthly payments until $52,516.20 was paid. The RISC imposed many other conditions on the buyers and seller with respect to the payment for, and handling of, the Corvette. Cox assigned the RISC to General Motors Acceptance Corp. (GMAC). In August 2002, the buyers sold the car to Florida Auto Brokers, which agreed to pay the balance due on the RISC. The check to GMAC for this amount was dishonored for insufficient funds, however, after the vehicle's title had been forwarded. GMAC filed a suit in a Florida state court against Honest Air and Babcock, seeking $35,815.26 as damages for breach of contract. The defendants argued that the RISC was a negotiable instrument. A ruling in their favor on this point would reduce any damages due GMAC to less than the Corvette's current value. What are the requirements for an instrument to be negotiable? Does the

RISC qualify? Explain. [*General Motors Acceptance Corp. v. Honest Air Conditioning & Heating, Inc.*, 933 So.2d 34 (Fla.App. 2 Dist. 2006)]

After you have answered Problem 18.5, compare your answer with the sample answer given on the Web site that accompanies this text. Go to www.cengage.com/blaw/fbl, select "Chapter 18," and click on "Case Problem with Sample Answer."

18.6 Holder in Due Course. American International Group, Inc. (AIG), an insurance company, issued a check to Jermielem Merriwether in connection with a personal injury matter. Merriwether presented the check to A-1 Check Cashing Emporium (A-1) for payment. A-1's clerk forgot to have Merriwether sign the check. When he could not reach Merriwether to come back to A-1 to sign the check, he printed Merriwether's name on the back and deposited it for collection. When the check was not paid, A-1 sold it to Robert Triffin, who is in the business of buying dishonored checks. When Triffin could not get the check honored, he sued AIG, contending that he, through A-1, had the right to collect on the check as the holder in due course. The trial court rejected that claim. Triffin appealed. On what basis could he claim holder in due course status? [*Triffin v. American International Group, Inc.*, ___ A.2d ___ (N.J.Super. 2008)]

18.7 A Question of Ethics. *Clarence Morgan, Jr., owned Easy Way Automotive, a car dealership in D'Lo, Mississippi. Easy Way sold a truck to Loyd Barnard, who signed a note for the amount of the price payable to*

Trustmark National Bank in six months. Before the note came due, Barnard returned the truck to Easy Way, which sold it to another buyer. Using some of the proceeds from the second sale, Easy Way sent a check to Trustmark to pay Barnard's note. Meanwhile, Barnard obtained another truck from Easy Way financed through another six-month note payable to Trustmark. After eight of these deals, some of which involved more than one truck, an Easy Way check to Trustmark was dishonored. In a suit in a Mississippi state court, Trustmark sought to recover the amounts of two of the notes from Barnard. Trustmark had not secured titles to two of the trucks covered by the notes, however, and this complicated Barnard's efforts to reclaim the vehicles from the later buyers. [*Trustmark National Bank v. Barnard*, 930 So.2d 1281 (Miss.App. 2006)]

1 On what basis might Barnard be liable on the Trustmark notes? Would he be primarily or secondarily liable? Could this liability be discharged on the theory that Barnard's right of recourse had been impaired when Trustmark did not secure titles to the trucks covered by the notes? Explain.

2 Easy Way's account had been subject to other recent overdrafts, and a week after the check to Trustmark was returned for insufficient funds, Morgan committed suicide. At the same time, Barnard was unable to obtain a mortgage because the unpaid notes affected his credit rating. How do the circumstances of this case underscore the importance of practicing business ethics?

CRITICAL THINKING AND WRITING ASSIGNMENTS

18.8 Critical Legal Thinking. The Uniform Commercial Code (UCC) generally sets forth strict requirements for negotiable instruments. In regard to what constitutes a signature on an instrument, however, the UCC grants extreme latitude— X marks, initials, and rubber-stamped signatures are all permitted. Given the potential for forgery of these kinds of signatures, why does the UCC permit them?

18.9 Critical Thinking and Writing Assignment for Business. Karen Thorpe is a purchasing agent for GymNast, Inc., a manufacturer of sports equipment. Karen has authority to sign checks in payment for purchases made by GymNast. Karen makes out three checks to suppliers and signs each one differently, as follows:

1 GymNast, Inc., by Karen Thorpe, purchasing agent.

2 Karen Thorpe, purchasing agent.

3 Karen Thorpe.

Discuss whether Karen is personally liable on each signature and whether the principal, GymNast, can be held liable.

18.10 **Video Question.** Go to this text's Web site at **www. cengage.com/blaw/fbl** and select "Chapter 18." Click on "Video Questions" and view the video titled *Negotiable Instruments.* Then answer the following questions.

1 Who is the maker of the promissory note discussed in the video?

2 Is the note in the video payable on demand or at a definite time?

3 Does the note contain an unconditional promise or order to pay?

4 If the note does not meet the requirements of negotiability, can Onyx assign the note (assignment was discussed in Chapter 11) to the bank in exchange for cash?

For updated links to resources available on the Web, as well as a variety of other materials, visit this text's Web site at

www.cengage.com/blaw/fbl

The National Conference of Commissioners on Uniform State Laws, in association with the University of Pennsylvania Law School, now offers an official site for final drafts of uniform and model acts. For an index of final acts, including UCC Articles 3 and 4, go to

www.law.upenn.edu/bll/ulc/ulc_final.htm

Cornell University's Legal Information Institute offers online access to the UCC, as well as to UCC articles as enacted by particular states and proposed revisions to articles, at

www.law.cornell.edu/ucc/ucc.table.html

PRACTICAL INTERNET EXERCISES

Go to this text's Web site at **www.cengage.com/blaw/fbl**, select "Chapter 18," and click on "Practical Internet Exercises." There you will find the following Internet research exercises that you can perform to learn more about the topics covered in this chapter.

PRACTICAL INTERNET EXERCISE 18-1 LEGAL PERSPECTIVE—Overview of Negotiable Instruments

PRACTICAL INTERNET EXERCISE 18-2 MANAGEMENT PERSPECTIVE—Holder in Due Course

PRACTICAL INTERNET EXERCISE 18-3 TECHNOLOGICAL PERSPECTIVE—Electronic Negotiable Instruments

BEFORE THE TEST

Go to this text's Web site at **www.cengage.com/blaw/fbl**, select "Chapter 18," and click on "Interactive Quizzes." You will find a number of interactive questions relating to this chapter.

CHAPTER 19
Checks and Banking in the Digital Age

LEARNING OBJECTIVES

AFTER READING THIS CHAPTER, YOU SHOULD BE ABLE TO ANSWER THE FOLLOWING QUESTIONS:

1 On what type of check does a bank agree in advance to accept when the check is presented for payment?

2 When may a bank properly dishonor a customer's check without the bank being liable to the customer? What happens if a bank wrongfully dishonors a customer's check?

3 What duties does the Uniform Commercial Code impose on a bank's customers with regard to forged and altered checks? What are the consequences of a customer's negligence in performing those duties?

4 What are the four most common types of electronic fund transfers?

5 What is e-money, and how is it stored and used? What laws apply to e-money transactions and online banking services?

C hecks are the most common type of negotiable instruments regulated by the Uniform Commercial Code (UCC). Checks are convenient to use because they serve as a substitute for cash. As Henry Ford once said, checks help us to "keep tally." To be sure, most students today tend to use debit cards rather than checks for many retail transactions. Indeed, debit cards now account for more retail payments than checks. Nonetheless, commercial checks remain an integral part of the U.S. economic system.

Issues relating to checks are governed by Articles 3 and 4 of the UCC. Recall from Chapter 18 that Article 3 establishes the requirements that all negotiable instruments, including checks, must meet. Article 3 also sets forth the rights and liabilities of parties to negotiable instruments. Article 4 of the UCC governs bank deposits and collections as well as bank-customer relationships. Article 4 regulates the relationships of banks with one another as they process checks for payment, and it establishes a framework for deposit and checking agreements between a bank and its customers. A check therefore may fall within the scope of Article 3 and yet be subject to the provisions of Article 4 while in the course of collection. If a conflict between Article 3 and Article 4 arises, Article 4 controls [UCC 4–102(a)].

In this chapter, we first identify the legal characteristics of checks and the legal duties and liabilities that arise when a check is issued. Then we examine the collection process. Increasingly, credit cards, debit cards, and other devices and methods of transferring funds electronically are being used to pay for goods and services. In the latter part of this chapter, we look at the law governing electronic fund transfers.

CHECKS

A **check** is a special type of draft that is drawn on a bank, ordering the bank to pay a fixed amount of money on demand [UCC 3–104(f)]. Article 4 defines a bank as "a person engaged in the business of banking, including a savings bank, savings and loan association, credit union or trust company" [UCC 4–105(1)]. If any other institution (such as a brokerage firm) handles a check for payment or for collection, the check is *not* covered by Article 4.

Recall from the preceding chapter that a person who writes a check is called the *drawer*. The drawer is a depositor in the bank on which the check is drawn. The person to whom the check is payable is the *payee*. The bank or financial institution on which the check is drawn is the *drawee*.

■EXAMPLE 19.1 Anita Cruzak writes a check from her checking account to pay her college tuition. In that situation, Anita is the drawer, her bank is the drawee, and her college is the payee. ■ We now look at some special types of checks.

Cashier's Checks

Checks are usually three-party instruments, but on certain types of checks, the bank can serve as both the drawer and the drawee. For example, when a bank draws a check on itself, the check is called a **cashier's check** and is a negotiable instrument on issue (see Exhibit 19–1) [UCC 3–104(g)]. Normally, a cashier's check indicates a specific payee. In effect, with a cashier's check, the bank assumes responsibility for paying the check, thus making the check more readily acceptable as a substitute for cash.

■EXAMPLE 19.2 Kramer needs to pay a moving company $8,000 for moving his household goods to a new home in another state. The moving company requests payment in the form of a cashier's check. Kramer goes to a bank (he does not need to have an account at the bank) and purchases a cashier's check, payable to the moving company, in the amount of $8,000. Kramer has to pay the bank the $8,000 for the check, plus a small service fee. He then gives the check to the moving company. ■

Cashier's checks are sometimes used in the business community as nearly the equivalent of cash. Except in very limited circumstances, the issuing bank must honor its cashier's checks when they are presented for payment. If a bank wrongfully dishonors a cashier's check, a holder can recover from the bank all expenses incurred, interest, and consequential damages [UCC 3–411]. This same rule applies if a bank wrongfully dishonors a certified check (to be discussed shortly) or a teller's check. (A *teller's check* is a check drawn by a bank on another bank or, when drawn on a nonbank, payable at or through a bank [UCC 3–104(h)]. For example, when a credit union issues a check to withdraw funds from its account at another financial institution, and the teller at the credit union signs the check, it is a teller's check.)

Traveler's Checks

A **traveler's check** is an instrument that is payable on demand, drawn on or payable at or through a financial institution (such as a bank), and designated as a traveler's check. The institution is directly obligated to accept and pay its traveler's check according to the check's terms. Traveler's checks are designed as a safe substitute for cash for vacationers and travelers and are issued for a fixed amount, such as $20, $50, or $100. The purchaser must sign the check at the time it is bought and again when it is used [UCC 3–104(i)]. Exhibit 19–2 shows an example of a traveler's check.

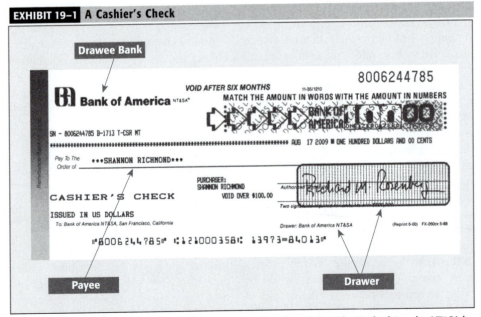

EXHIBIT 19–1 A Cashier's Check

*The abbreviation *NT&SA* stands for National Trust and Savings Association. The Bank of America NT&SA is a subsidiary of Bank of America Corporation, which is engaged in financial services, insurance, investment management, and other businesses.

EXHIBIT 19–2 A Traveler's Check

Certified Checks

A **certified check** is a check that has been *accepted* in writing by the bank on which it is drawn [UCC 3–409(d)]. When a drawee bank *certifies* (accepts) a check, it immediately charges the drawer's account with the amount of the check and transfers those funds to its own certified check account. In effect, the bank is agreeing in advance to accept that check when it is presented for payment and to make payment from those funds reserved in the certified check account. Essentially, certification prevents the bank from denying liability. It is a promise that sufficient funds are on deposit and *have been set aside* to cover the check.

To certify a check, the bank writes or stamps the word *certified* on the face of the check and typically writes the amount that it will pay.[1] Either the drawer or the holder (payee) of a check can request certification, but the drawee bank is not required to certify a check. A bank's refusal to certify a check is not a dishonor of the check [UCC 3–409(d)]. Once a check is certified, the drawer and any prior indorsers are completely discharged from liability on the check [UCC 3–414(c), 3–415(d)]. Only the certifying bank is required to pay the instrument.

THE BANK-CUSTOMER RELATIONSHIP

The bank-customer relationship begins when the customer opens a checking account and deposits funds that the bank will use to pay for checks written by the customer. Essentially, three types of relationships come into being, as discussed next.

---

1. If the certification does not state an amount, and the amount is later increased and the instrument negotiated to a holder in due course (HDC), the obligation of the certifying bank is the amount of the instrument when it was taken by the HDC [UCC 3–413(b)].

Creditor-Debtor Relationship

A creditor-debtor relationship is created between a customer and a bank when the customer makes deposits into a checking account. When a customer makes a deposit, the customer becomes a creditor, and the bank a debtor, for the amount deposited.

Agency Relationship

An agency relationship (see Chapter 22) also arises between the customer and the bank when the customer writes a check on his or her account. In effect, the customer is ordering the bank to pay the amount specified on the check to the holder when the holder presents the check to the bank for payment. In this situation, the bank becomes the customer's agent and is obligated to honor the customer's request. Similarly, if the customer deposits a check into her or his account, the bank, as the customer's agent, is obligated to collect payment on the check from the bank on which the check was drawn. To transfer checkbook funds among different banks, each bank acts as the agent of collection for its customer [UCC 4–201(a)].

Contractual Relationship

Whenever a bank-customer relationship is established, certain contractual rights and duties arise. The specific rights and duties of the bank and its customer depend on the nature of the transaction, as we discuss in detail in the following pages.

BANK'S DUTY TO HONOR CHECKS

When a banking institution provides checking services, it agrees to honor the checks written by its customers, with the usual stipulation that the account must have sufficient funds available to pay each check [UCC 4–401(a)]. When a drawee bank *wrongfully* fails to honor a check, it is liable to its customer for damages resulting from its refusal to pay. The customer does not have to prove that the bank breached its contractual commitment, slandered the customer's credit, or was negligent [UCC 4–402(b)].

The customer's agreement with the bank includes a general obligation to keep sufficient funds on deposit to cover all checks written. The customer is liable to the payee or to the holder of a check in a civil suit if a check is dishonored for insufficient funds. If intent to defraud can be proved, the customer can also be subject to criminal prosecution.

When the bank properly dishonors a check for insufficient funds, it has no liability to the customer. The bank may rightfully refuse to pay a customer's check in other circumstances as well. We look here at specific situations involving the bank and its customers.

Overdrafts

When the bank receives an item properly payable from its customer's checking account but the account contains insufficient funds to cover the amount of the check, the bank has two options. It can either (1) dishonor the item or (2) pay the item and charge the customer's account, thus creating an **overdraft**, providing that the customer has authorized the payment and the payment does not violate any bank-customer agreement [UCC 4–401(a)].[2] The bank can subtract the difference (plus a service charge) from the customer's next deposit or other customer funds because the check carries with it an enforceable implied promise to reimburse the bank.

A bank can expressly agree with a customer to accept overdrafts through what is sometimes called an "overdraft protection agreement." If such an agreement is formed, any failure of the bank to honor a check because it would create an overdraft breaches this agreement and is treated as a wrongful dishonor [UCC 4–402(a)].

When a check "bounces," a holder can resubmit the check, hoping that at a later date sufficient funds will be available to pay it. The holder must notify any indorsers on the check of the first dishonor, however; otherwise, they will be discharged from their signature liability (see Chapter 18).

Postdated Checks

A bank may also charge a postdated check against a customer's account, unless the customer notifies the bank not to pay the check until the stated date. This notice must be given in time to allow the bank to act on the notice before committing itself to pay on the check. The UCC states that the bank should treat a notice of postdating the same as a stop-payment order—to be discussed shortly. If the bank fails to act on the customer's notice and charges the customer's account before the date on the postdated check, the bank may be liable for any damages incurred by the customer [UCC 4–401(c)].[3]

Stale Checks

Commercial banking practice regards a check that is presented for payment more than six months from its date as a **stale check**. A bank is not obligated to pay an uncertified check presented more than six months from its date [UCC 4–404]. When receiving a stale check for payment, the bank has the option of paying or not paying the check. The bank may consult the customer before paying the check. If a bank pays a stale check in good faith without consulting the customer, however, the bank has the right to charge the customer's account for the amount of the check.

Stop-Payment Orders

A **stop-payment order** is an order by a customer to his or her bank not to pay or certify a certain check. Only a customer or a person authorized to draw on the account can order the bank not to pay the check when it is presented for payment [UCC 4–403(a)].[4] A customer has no right to stop payment on a check that has been certified or accepted by a bank, however. The customer must issue the stop-payment order within a reasonable time and in a reasonable manner to permit the bank to act on it [UCC 4–403(a)]. Although a stop-payment order can be given orally, usually by phone, it is binding on the bank for only fourteen calendar days unless confirmed in writing.[5] A written stop-payment order (the bank typically provides a preprinted form) or an oral order confirmed in writing is effective for six months and then must be renewed in writing [UCC 4–403(b)].

Bank's Liability for Wrongful Payment   If the bank pays the check in spite of a stop-payment order, the bank will be obligated to recredit the customer's account. In addition, if

---

2. With a joint account, the bank cannot hold the nonsigning customer liable for payment of an overdraft unless that person benefited from its proceeds [UCC 4–401(b)].

3. Under the UCC, postdating does not affect the negotiability of a check. In fact, under the automated check-collection system now in use, the bank can ignore the date on the check (treat it as a demand instrument) unless it has received notice from the customer that the check was postdated.

4. For a deceased customer, any person claiming a legitimate interest in the account may issue a stop-payment order [UCC 4–405].

5. Some states do not recognize oral stop-payment orders; they must be in writing.

the bank's payment over a stop-payment order causes subsequent checks written on the drawer's account to "bounce," the bank will be liable for the resultant costs the drawer incurs. The bank is liable only for the amount of the actual damages suffered by the drawer, however [UCC 4–403(c)].
■EXAMPLE 19.3 Toshio Murano orders six bamboo palms from a local nursery at $50 each and gives the nursery a check for $300. Later that day, the nursery tells Murano that it will not deliver the palms as arranged. Murano immediately calls his bank and stops payment on the check. If the bank nonetheless honors the check, the bank will be liable to Murano for the full $300. The result would be different, however, if the nursery had delivered five palms. In that situation, Murano would owe the nursery $250 for the delivered palms, and his actual losses would be only $50. Consequently, the bank would be liable to Murano for only $50. ■

Customer's Liability for Wrongful Stop-Payment Order

A stop-payment order has its risks for a customer. The customer-drawer must have a *valid legal ground* for issuing such an order; otherwise, the holder can sue the drawer for payment. Moreover, defenses sufficient to refuse payment against a payee may not be valid grounds to prevent payment against a subsequent holder in due course [UCC 3–305, 3–306]. A person who wrongfully stops payment on a check is liable to the payee for the amount of the check and can also be liable for consequential damages incurred by the payee.

Death or Incompetence of a Customer

Neither the death nor the incompetence of a customer revokes a bank's authority to pay an item until the bank is informed of the situation and has had reasonable time to act on the notice. Thus, if a bank is unaware that the customer who wrote a check has been declared incompetent or has died, the bank can pay the item without incurring liability [UCC 4–405]. Even when a bank knows of the death of its customer, for ten days after the *date of death*, it can pay or certify checks drawn on or before the date of death. An exception to this rule is made if a person claiming an interest in that account, such as an heir, orders the bank to stop payment. Without this provision, banks would constantly be required to verify the continued life and competence of their drawers.

Checks Bearing Forged Drawers' Signatures

When a bank pays a check on which the drawer's signature is forged, generally the bank is liable. The bank may be able to

recover at least some of the loss from the customer, however, if her or his negligence contributed to the making of the forgery. The bank may also obtain partial recovery from the forger (if he or she can be found) or from the holder who presented the check for payment (if the holder knew that the signature was forged).

The General Rule A forged signature on a check has no legal effect as the signature of a drawer [UCC 3–403(a)]. For this reason, banks require a signature card from each customer who opens a checking account. Signature cards allow the bank to verify whether the signatures on their customers' checks are genuine. The general rule is that the bank must recredit the customer's account when it pays a check with a forged signature. (Note that banks today normally verify signatures only on checks that exceed a certain threshold, such as $1,000, $2,500, or some higher amount. Even though a bank sometimes incurs liability costs when it has paid forged checks, the costs involved in verifying every check's signature would be much higher.)

Customer Negligence When the customer's negligence substantially contributes to the forgery, the bank normally will not be obligated to recredit the customer's account for the amount of the check [UCC 3–406]. The customer's liability may be reduced, however, by the amount of loss caused by negligence on the part of the bank (or other "person") paying the instrument or taking it for value if the negligence substantially contributed to the loss [UCC 3–406(b)].
■EXAMPLE 19.4 Gemco Corporation uses special check-writing equipment to write its payroll and business checks. Gemco discovers that one of its employees used the equipment to write himself a check for $10,000 and that the bank subsequently honored it. Gemco asks the bank to recredit $10,000 to its account for improperly paying the forged check. If the bank can show that Gemco failed to take reasonable care in controlling access to the check-writing equipment, the bank will not be required to recredit Gemco's account for the amount of the forged check. If Gemco can show that negligence on the part of the bank contributed substantially to the loss, however, then Gemco's liability may be reduced proportionally. ■

In the following case, an employee opened a bogus bank account and fraudulently deposited his employer's checks in it for years. The court had to determine if the bank should have requested written authorization from the company before opening the account.

CASE 19.1   Auto-Owners Insurance Co. v. Bank One

Supreme Court of Indiana, 879 N.E.2d 1086 (2008).

FACTS Kenneth Wulf worked in the claims department of Auto-Owners Insurance Company for ten years. When the department received checks, a staff member would note it in the file and send it on to headquarters. Wulf opened a checking account at Bank One in the name of "Auto-Owners, Kenneth B. Wulf." Over a period of eight years, he deposited $546,000 worth of checks that he had stolen from Auto-Owners and had endorsed with a stamp that read "Auto-Owners Insurance Deposit Only." When the scam was finally discovered, Auto-Owners sued Bank One, contending that it had failed to exercise ordinary care in opening the account because it had not asked for documentation to show that Wulf was authorized to open an account in the name of Auto-Owners. The lower courts rejected that argument and granted summary judgment for Bank One. Auto-Owners appealed.

ISSUE Did the bank's failure to request proof from Wulf that he was authorized to deposit checks made out to Auto-Owners substantially contribute to the loss?

DECISION No. The state supreme court affirmed the decision of the lower courts, finding that Bank One's conduct

did not "substantially contribute" to bringing about the losses suffered by Auto-Owners.

REASON The court reasoned that UCC 3–405(b) makes no mention of a bank's responsibilities when opening an account for a new customer. Rather, subsection (b) requires ordinary care from a bank in the "paying" or "taking" of an instrument. Therefore, the bank did not breach any duty to the insurance company by opening Wulf's checking account. In such cases, the courts consider all of the facts surrounding the transactions that occurred. Here, the major reason for the losses suffered by Auto-Owners was its weak internal monitoring of its own files and the lack of controls in the handling of company checks. The bank did not worsen the situation by allowing Wulf to have a checking account.

 FOR CRITICAL ANALYSIS—Management Consideration *What reasonable steps could Auto-Owners have taken to prevent such internal fraud?*

■

Timely Examination of Bank Statements Required. Banks typically send or make available to their customers monthly statements detailing activity in their checking accounts. A bank is not obligated to include the canceled checks themselves (or photocopies of them) with the statement. It must, however, provide the customer with information (check number, amount, and date of payment) on the statement that will allow the customer to reasonably identify the checks that the bank has paid [UCC 4–406(a), (b)]. If the bank retains the canceled checks, it must keep the checks—or legible copies—for seven years [UCC4–406(b)]. The customer may obtain a canceled check (or a copy of the check) during this time.

The customer has a duty to promptly examine bank statements (and canceled checks or photocopies, if they are included with the statements) with reasonable care when the statements are received or made available to determine whether any payment was not authorized [UCC 4–406(c)]. The customer must report any alterations or forged signatures, including forged signatures of indorsers if discovered

(to be discussed later). If the customer fails to fulfill this duty and the bank suffers a loss as a result, the customer will be liable for the loss [UCC 4–406(d)].

Consequences of Failing to Detect Forgeries. When the same wrongdoer has committed a series of forgeries, the UCC provides that the customer, to recover for all the forged items, must discover and report the *first* forged check to the bank within thirty calendar days of the receipt of the bank statement (and canceled checks or copies, if they are included) [UCC 4–406(d)(2)]. Failure to notify the bank within this period of time discharges the bank's liability for all forged checks that it pays prior to notification.

When the Bank Is Also Negligent. In one situation, a bank customer can escape liability, at least in part, for failing to notify the bank of forged or altered checks promptly or within the required thirty-day period. If the customer can prove that the bank was also negligent—that is, that the bank failed to exercise ordinary care—then the bank will also be liable, and the loss will be allocated between the bank and the customer on the basis of comparative negligence [UCC 4–406(e)]. In other words, even though a customer may have been negligent, the bank may still have to recredit the customer's account for a portion of the loss if the bank failed to exercise ordinary care.

The UCC defines *ordinary care* as the "observance of reasonable commercial standards, prevailing in the area in which [a] person is located, with respect to the business in which that person is engaged" [UCC 3–103]. As mentioned earlier, it is customary in the banking industry to manually examine signatures only on checks over a certain amount (such as $1,000, $2,500, or some higher amount). Thus, if a bank, in accordance with prevailing banking standards, fails to examine a signature on a particular check, the bank has not necessarily breached its duty to exercise ordinary care.

Regardless of the degree of care exercised by the customer or the bank, the UCC places an absolute time limit on the liability of a bank for paying a check with a forged customer signature. A customer who fails to report a forged signature within one year from the date that the statement was made available for inspection loses the legal right to have the bank recredit his or her account [UCC 4–406(f)].

 **PREVENTING LEGAL DISPUTES** Checks forged by employees and embezzlement of company funds are disturbingly common in today's business world. To avoid significant losses due to forgery or embezzlement and to prevent litigation over a bank's liability for forged items, keep a watchful eye on business accounts. Limit access to your business's bank accounts. Never leave company checkbooks or signature stamps in unsecured areas. Use passwords to limit access to computerized check-writing software.

Examine bank statements in a timely fashion and be on the lookout for suspicious transactions. Remember that if forgeries are not reported within thirty days of the first statement in which a forged item appears, the account holder normally loses the right to hold the bank liable. Be careful not to do anything that could be construed as negligence contributing to a forgery (or to a subsequent alteration of a check, to be discussed shortly). Be diligent about reviewing bank statements and reporting discrepancies to the bank.

■

Checks Bearing Forged Indorsements

A bank that pays a customer's check bearing a forged indorsement must recredit the customer's account or be liable to the customer-drawer for breach of contract. **■EXAMPLE 19.5** Simon issues a $500 check "to the order of Antonio." Juan steals the check, forges Antonio's indorsement, and cashes the check. When the check reaches Simon's bank, the bank pays it and debits Simon's account. The bank must recredit the $500 to Simon's account because it failed to carry out Simon's order to pay "to the order of Antonio" [UCC 4–401(a)]. Of course, Simon's bank can in turn recover—for breach of warranty (see Chapter 18)—from the bank that cashed the check when Juan presented it [UCC 4–207(a)(2)]. ■

Eventually, the loss usually falls on the first party to take the instrument bearing the forged indorsement because, as discussed in Chapter 18, a forged indorsement does not transfer title. Thus, whoever takes an instrument with a forged indorsement cannot become a holder.

The customer, in any event, has a duty to report forged indorsements promptly. Failure to report forged indorsements, whether discovered or not, within three years after the forged items have been made available to the customer relieves the bank of liability [UCC 4–111].

Altered Checks

The customer's instruction to the bank is to pay the exact amount on the face of the check to the holder. The bank has a duty to examine each check before making final payment. If it fails to detect an alteration, it is liable to its customer for the loss because it did not pay as the customer ordered. The loss is the difference between the original amount of the check and the amount actually paid [UCC 4–401(d)(1)]. **■EXAMPLE 19.6** Suppose that a check written for $11 is raised to $111. The customer's account will be charged $11 (the amount the customer ordered the bank to pay). The bank will normally be responsible for the $100. ■

Customer Negligence As in a situation involving a forged drawer's signature, a customer's negligence can shift the loss when payment is made on an altered check (unless the bank was also negligent). A common example occurs when a person carelessly writes a check and leaves large gaps around the numbers and words where additional numbers and words can be inserted (see Exhibit 19–3 on the next page).

Similarly, a person who signs a check and leaves the dollar amount for someone else to fill in is barred from protesting when the bank unknowingly and in good faith pays whatever amount is shown [UCC 4–401(d)(2)]. Finally, if the bank can trace its loss on successive altered checks to the customer's failure to discover the initial alteration, then the bank can reduce its liability for reimbursing the customer's account [UCC 4–406]. The law governing the customer's duty to examine monthly statements and canceled checks,

EXHIBIT 19–3 **A Poorly Filled-Out Check**

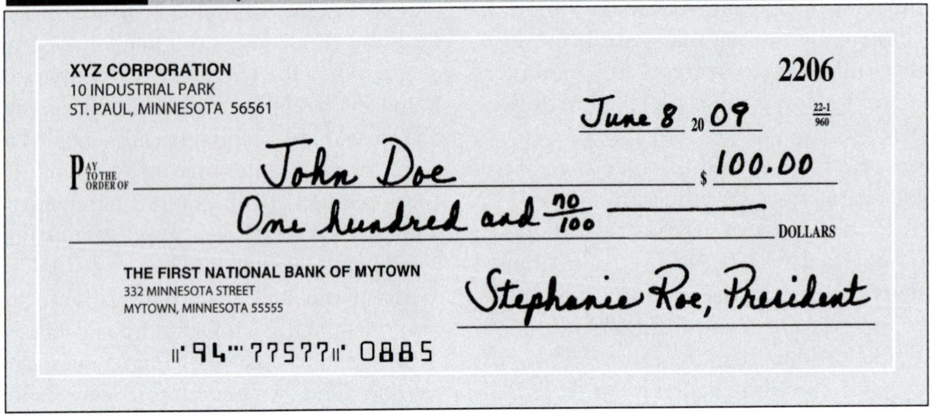

```
XYZ CORPORATION                                              2206
10 INDUSTRIAL PARK
ST. PAUL, MINNESOTA 56561                                    22-1
                                          June 8  20 09       960

PAY                                                  $ 100.00
TO THE        John Doe
ORDER OF
              One hundred and 00/100                         DOLLARS

    THE FIRST NATIONAL BANK OF MYTOWN
    332 MINNESOTA STREET                  Stephanie Roe, President
    MYTOWN, MINNESOTA 55555

         ⑈94⑈ 77577⑈ 0885
```

and to discover and report alterations to the bank, is the same as that applied to a forged drawer's signature.

In every situation involving a forged drawer's signature or an alteration, a bank must observe reasonable commercial standards of care in paying on a customer's checks [UCC 4–406(e)]. The customer's negligence can be used as a defense only if the bank has exercised ordinary care.

Other Parties from Whom the Bank May Recover The bank is entitled to recover the amount of loss from the transferor who, by presenting the check for payment, warrants that the check has not been materially altered. This rule has two exceptions, though. If the bank is the drawer (as it is on a cashier's check and a teller's check), it cannot recover from the presenting party if the party is a holder in due course (HDC) acting in good faith [UCC 3–417(a)(2), 4–208(a)(2)]. The reason is that an instrument's drawer is in a better position than an HDC to know whether the instrument has been altered.

Similarly, an HDC who presents a certified check for payment in good faith will not be held liable under warranty principles if the check was altered before the HDC acquired it [UCC 3–417(a)(2), 4–207(a)(2)]. ■**EXAMPLE 19.7** Jordan draws a check for $500 payable to Deffen. Deffen alters the amount to $5,000. The drawee bank, First National, certifies the check for $5,000. Deffen negotiates the check to Ethan, an HDC. The drawee bank pays Ethan $5,000. On discovering the mistake, the bank cannot recover from Ethan the $4,500 paid by mistake, even though the bank was not in a superior position to detect the alteration. This is in accord with the purpose of certification, which is to obtain the definite obligation of a bank to honor a definite instrument. ■

BANK'S DUTY TO ACCEPT DEPOSITS

A bank has a duty to its customer to accept the customer's deposits of cash and checks. When checks are deposited, the bank must make the funds represented by those checks available within certain time frames. A bank also has a duty to collect payment on any checks payable or indorsed to its customers and deposited by them into their accounts. Cash deposits made in U.S. currency are received into customers' accounts without being subject to further collection procedures.

Availability Schedule for Deposited Checks

The Expedited Funds Availability Act of 1987[6] and Regulation CC,[7] which was issued by the Federal Reserve Board of Governors (the *Federal Reserve System* will be discussed shortly) to implement the act, require that any local check deposited must be available for withdrawal by check or as cash within one business day from the date of deposit. A check is classified as a local check if the first bank to receive the check for payment and the bank on which the check is drawn are located in the same check-processing region (check-processing regions are designated by the Federal Reserve Board of Governors). For nonlocal checks, the funds must be available for withdrawal within not more than five business days. Note that under the Check Clearing in the 21st Century Act[8] (Check 21), a bank now must credit a cus-

---

6. 12 U.S.C. Sections 4001–4010.
7. 12 C.F.R. Sections 229.1–229.42.
8. 12 U.S.C. Sections 5001–5018.

tomer's account as soon as the bank receives the funds. (Check 21 will be discussed later in this chapter.)

In addition, the Expedited Funds Availability Act requires the following:

1 That funds be available on the next business day for cash deposits and wire transfers, government checks, the first $100 of a day's check deposits, cashier's checks, certified checks, and checks for which the depositary and payor banks are branches of the same institution (*depositary* and *payor banks* will be discussed shortly).

2 That the first $100 of any deposit be available for cash withdrawal on the opening of the next business day after deposit. If a local check is deposited, the next $400 is to be available for withdrawal by no later than 5:00 P.M. the next business day. If, for example, you deposit a local check for $500 on Monday, you can withdraw $100 in cash at the opening of the business day on Tuesday, and an additional $400 must be available for withdrawal by no later than 5:00 P.M. on Wednesday.

A different availability schedule applies to deposits made at *nonproprietary* automated teller machines (ATMs). These are ATMs that are not owned or operated by the bank receiving the deposits. Basically, a five-day hold is permitted on all deposits, including cash deposits, made at nonproprietary ATMs. Other exceptions also exist. A depository institution has eight days to make funds available in new accounts (those open less than thirty days) and has an extra four days on deposits that exceed $5,000 (except deposits of government and cashier's checks).

The Traditional Collection Process

Usually, deposited checks involve parties that do business at different banks, but sometimes checks are written between customers of the same bank. Either situation brings into play the bank collection process as it operates within the statutory framework of Article 4 of the UCC. Note that the check-collection process described in the following subsections will be modified in the future as the banking industry implements the Check 21 Act (to be discussed shortly).

Designations of Banks Involved in the Collection Process The first bank to receive a check for payment is the **depositary bank**.[9] For example, when a person deposits an IRS tax-refund check into a personal checking account at the

local bank, that bank is the depositary bank. The bank on which a check is drawn (the drawee bank) is called the **payor bank**. Any bank except the payor bank that handles a check during some phase of the collection process is a **collecting bank**. Any bank except the payor bank or the depositary bank to which an item is transferred in the course of this collection process is called an **intermediary bank**.

During the collection process, any bank can take on one or more of the various roles of depositary, payor, collecting, and intermediary bank. ■**EXAMPLE 19.8** A buyer in New York writes a check on her New York bank and sends it to a seller in San Francisco. The seller deposits the check in her San Francisco bank account. The seller's bank is both a *depositary bank* and a *collecting bank*. The buyer's bank in New York is the *payor bank*. As the check travels from San Francisco to New York, any collecting bank handling the item in the collection process (other than the depositary bank and the payor bank) is also called an *intermediary bank*. Exhibit 19–4 on the following page illustrates how various banks function in the collection process in the context of this example. ■

Check Collection between Customers of the Same Bank An item that is payable by the depositary bank (also the payor bank) that receives it is called an "on-us item." If the bank does not dishonor the check by the opening of the second banking day following its receipt, the check is considered paid [UCC 4–215(e)(2)]. ■**EXAMPLE 19.9** Oswald and Merkowitz both have checking accounts at State Bank. On Monday morning, Merkowitz deposits into his own checking account a $300 check drawn by Oswald. That same day, State Bank issues Merkowitz a "provisional credit" for $300. When the bank opens on Wednesday, Oswald's check is considered honored, and Merkowitz's provisional credit becomes final. ■

Check Collection between Customers of Different Banks Once a depositary bank receives a check, it must arrange to present it either directly or through intermediary banks to the appropriate payor bank. Each bank in the collection chain must pass the check on before midnight of the next banking day following its receipt [UCC 4–202(b)].[10] A "banking day" is any part of a day that the bank is open to carry on substantially all of its banking functions. Thus, if a bank has only its drive-through facilities open, a check deposited on Saturday would not trigger a bank's midnight deadline until the following Monday. When the check reaches the payor bank, that bank is liable for the face amount of the check, unless the

---

9. All definitions in this section are found in UCC 4–105. The terms *depositary* and *depository* have different meanings in the banking context. A depository bank refers to a *physical place* (a bank or other institution) in which deposits or funds are held or stored.

10. A bank may take a "reasonably longer time," such as when the bank's computer system is down due to a power failure, but the bank must show that its action is still timely [UCC 4–202(b)].

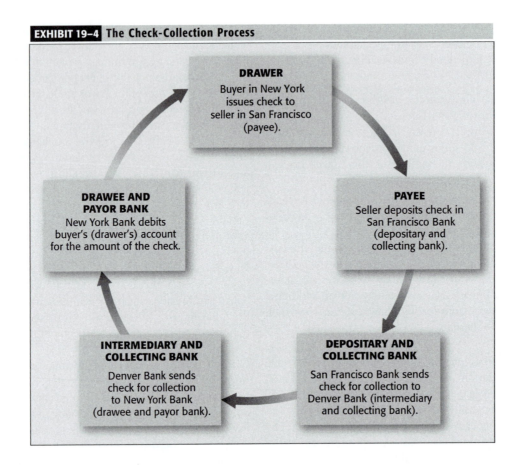

EXHIBIT 19–4 The Check-Collection Process

DRAWER
Buyer in New York
issues check to
seller in San Francisco
(payee).

PAYEE
Seller deposits check in
San Francisco Bank
(depositary and
collecting bank).

**DEPOSITARY AND
COLLECTING BANK**
San Francisco Bank sends
check for collection to
Denver Bank (intermediary
and collecting bank).

**INTERMEDIARY AND
COLLECTING BANK**
Denver Bank sends
check for collection
to New York Bank
(drawee and payor bank).

**DRAWEE AND
PAYOR BANK**
New York Bank debits
buyer's (drawer's) account
for the amount of the check.

payor bank dishonors the check or returns it by midnight on the next banking day following receipt [UCC 4–302].[11]

Because of this deadline and because banks need to maintain an even work flow in the many items they handle daily, the UCC permits what is called *deferred posting*. According to UCC 4–108, "a bank may fix an afternoon hour of 2:00 P.M. or later as a cutoff hour for the handling of money and items and the making of entries on its books." Any checks received after that hour "may be treated as being received at the opening of the next banking day." Thus, if a bank's "cutoff hour" is 3:00 P.M., a check received by a payor bank at 4:00 P.M. on Monday would be deferred for posting until Tuesday. In this situation, the payor bank's deadline would be midnight Wednesday.

Does a delay of more than one month in a bank's notice to its customer that a check deposited in his account is counterfeit reduce the customer's liability for overdrafts in his account? That was the customer's contention in the following case.

---

11. Most checks are cleared by a computerized process, and communication and computer facilities may fail because of electrical outages, equipment malfunction, or other conditions. If such conditions arise and a bank fails to meet its midnight deadline, the bank is "excused" from liability if the bank has exercised "such diligence as the circumstances require" [UCC 4–109(d)].

CASE 19.2   **Bank One, N.A. v. Dunn**

Court of Appeal of Louisiana, Second Circuit, 927 So.2d 645 (2006).

FACTS Floyd Dunn, a U.S. citizen, was hired to lobby in the United States for Zaire (now the Democratic Republic of the Congo). After three years of efforts on Zaire's behalf, Dunn submitted a bill for $500,000. Instead of paying, Zaire agreed to trade computers to Dunn, who was to sell them to Nigeria for $32,100,000. "Senator Frank," who claimed to be from Nigeria, told Dunn that he would receive the $32,100,000 after he paid alleged "back taxes" to that country. Frank offered to facilitate the payments. Dunn gave Frank the number of his

CASE 19.2—Continued

account at Bank One, N.A., in Shreveport, Louisiana. As part of the deal, on August 1, 2001, a check in the amount of $315,000 drawn on the account of Argenbright Security, Inc., at First Union National Bank of Georgia was deposited into Dunn's account—which had never held more than $5,000—and sent out for collection. Because the check contained an incorrect routing number, its processing was delayed. Meanwhile, on Frank's instructions, Dunn wired $277,000 to an account at a Virginia bank. On September 24, the $315,000 check was returned to Bank One as counterfeit. Bank One filed a suit in a Louisiana state court against Dunn, alleging that he owed $281,019.11, the amount by which his account was overdrawn. The court issued a summary judgment in Bank One's favor. Dunn appealed to a state intermediate appellate court.

ISSUE Is a bank liable to its customer for a delay in determining the counterfeit nature of a check?

DECISION No. The state intermediate appellate court affirmed the lower court's judgment.

REASON In the collection process, a bank is required to pass on a check before midnight of the next banking day following the check's receipt. The appellate court acknowledged that under UCC 4–202, the bank must "exercise

ordinary care in sending a notice of dishonor after learning that the item has not been paid or accepted." The court explained that "[n]otifying the customer of dishonor after the bank's midnight deadline may constitute the exercise of ordinary care if the bank took proper action within a reasonably longer time." Of course, the bank is liable for its failure to exercise ordinary care. In that situation, the measure of damages is the amount of the check "reduced by an amount that could not have been realized by the exercise of ordinary care." In other words, if a check could not have been collected even by the use of ordinary care, the recovery for a failure to exercise ordinary care is reduced by the amount of the uncollectible check. Thus, in this case, "Dunn's liability is not diminished because of Bank One's delay in notifying Dunn that the check was counterfeit. Even if Dunn had received earlier notice from Bank One that the check was counterfeit, he still had no recourse against Argenbright Security. The $315,000 was uncollectible against Argenbright Security."

 FOR CRITICAL ANALYSIS—Ethical Consideration *Does a bank have a duty to protect its customers from their own naïveté, as exemplified in this case by Dunn's giving his bank account information to someone he did not know? Why or why not?*

■

How the Federal Reserve System Clears Checks The **Federal Reserve System** is a network of twelve district banks, which are located around the country and headed by the Federal Reserve Board of Governors. Most banks in the United States have Federal Reserve accounts. The Federal Reserve System has greatly simplified the check-collection process by acting as a **clearinghouse**—a system or a place where banks exchange checks and drafts drawn on each other and settle daily balances.

■EXAMPLE 19.10 Pamela Moy of Philadelphia writes a check to Jeanne Sutton in San Francisco. When Sutton receives the check in the mail, she deposits it in her bank. Her bank then deposits the check in the Federal Reserve Bank of San Francisco, which transfers it to the Federal Reserve Bank of Philadelphia. That Federal Reserve bank then sends the check to Moy's bank, which deducts the amount of the check from Moy's account. Exhibit 19–5 on the following page illustrates this process. ■

Electronic Check Presentment In the past, most checks were processed manually—the employees of each bank in the collection chain would physically handle each check

that passed through the bank for collection or payment. Today, however, most checks are processed electronically. In contrast to manual check processing, which can take days, *electronic check presentment* can be done on the day of deposit. With electronic check presentment, items may be encoded with information (such as the amount of the check) that is read and processed by other banks' computers. In some situations, a check may be retained at its place of deposit, and only its image or description is presented for payment under an electronic presentment agreement [UCC 4–110].[12]

A person who encodes information on an item warrants to any subsequent bank or payor that the encoded information is correct [UCC 4–209]. This is also true for a person who retains an item while transmitting its image or information describing it as presentation for payment. This person warrants that the retention and presentment of the item comply with the electronic presentment agreement.

---

12. This section of the UCC assumes that no bank will participate in an electronic presentment program without an express agreement (which is no longer true since Check 21). See Comment 2 to UCC 4–110.

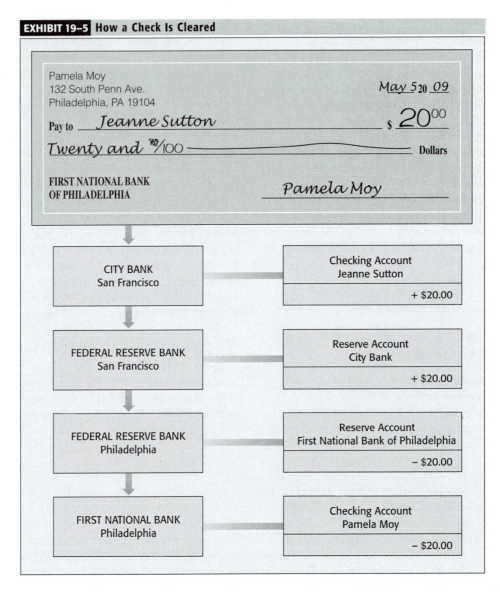

EXHIBIT 19–5 How a Check Is Cleared

Regulation CC provides that a returned check must be encoded with the routing number of the depositary bank, the amount of the check, and other information and adds that this "does not affect a paying bank's responsibility to return a check within the deadlines required by the U.C.C." Under UCC 4–301(d)(2), an item is returned "when it is sent or delivered to the bank's customer or transferor or pursuant to his [or her] instructions."

Check Clearing in the 21st Century Act (Check 21)

In the traditional collection process, paper checks had to be physically transported before they could be cleared. To streamline this costly and time-consuming process and to improve the overall efficiency of the nation's payment system, Congress passed the Check Clearing in the 21st Century Act (Check 21).

Before the implementation of Check 21, banks had to present the original paper check for payment in the absence of an agreement for presentment in some other form. Although the UCC authorizes banks to use other means of presentment, such as electronic presentment, a broad-based system of electronic presentment failed to develop because it required agreements among individual banks.

Check 21 has changed this situation by creating a new negotiable instrument called a *substitute check*. Although the act did not require any bank to change its current check-collection practices, the creation of substitute checks will certainly facilitate the use of electronic check processing over time.

What Is a Substitute Check? A substitute check is a paper reproduction of the front and back of an original check that contains all of the same information required on checks for automated processing. Banks create a substitute check from a digital image of an original check. Every substitute check must include the following statement somewhere on it: "This is a legal copy of your check. You can use it in the same way you would use the original check."

In essence, those financial institutions that exchange digital images of checks do not have to send the original paper checks. They can simply transmit the information electronically and replace the original checks with the paper reproductions—the substitute checks. Banks that do not exchange checks electronically are required to accept substitute checks in the same way that they accept original checks.

The Gradual Elimination of Paper Checks Because financial institutions must accept substitute checks as if they were original checks, the original checks will no longer be needed and will probably be destroyed after their digital images are created. By eliminating the original check after a substitute check is created, the financial system can prevent the check from being paid twice. Also, eliminating original checks and retaining only digital images will reduce the expense of storage and retrieval. Nevertheless, at least for quite a while, not all checks will be converted to substitute checks. That means that if a bank returns canceled checks to deposit holders at the end of each month, some of those returned checks may be substitute checks, and some may be original canceled paper checks.

Since the passage of Check 21, financial institution customers cannot demand an original canceled check. Check 21 is a federal law and applies to all financial institutions, other businesses, and individuals in the United States. In other words, no customers can opt out of Check 21 and demand that their original canceled checks be returned with their monthly statements. Also, businesses and individuals must accept a substitute check as proof of payment because it is the legal equivalent of the original check.

Reduced "Float" Time Sometimes, individuals and businesses write checks even though they have insufficient funds in their accounts to cover those checks. Such check writers are relying on "float," or the time between when a check is written and when the amount is actually deducted from their account. When all checks had to be physically transported, the float time could be several days, but as Check 21 is implemented, the time required to process checks will be substantially reduced—and so will float time. Thus, account holders

who plan to cover their checks after writing them may experience unexpected overdrafts.

Though consumers and businesses will no longer be able to rely on float time, they may benefit in another way from Check 21. The Expedited Funds Availability Act (mentioned earlier in this chapter) requires that the Federal Reserve Board revise the availability schedule for funds from deposited checks to correspond to reductions in check-processing time. Therefore, as the speed of check processing increases under Check 21, the Federal Reserve Board will reduce the maximum time that a bank can hold funds from deposited checks before making them available to the depositor. Thus, account holders will have faster access to their deposited funds.

ELECTRONIC FUND TRANSFERS

The application of computer technology to banking, in the form of electronic fund transfer systems, has helped to relieve banking institutions of the burden of having to move mountains of paperwork to process fund transfers. An **electronic fund transfer** (EFT) is a transfer of funds through the use of an electronic terminal, a telephone, a computer, or magnetic tape. The law governing EFTs depends on the type of transfer involved. Consumer fund transfers are governed by the Electronic Fund Transfer Act (EFTA) of 1978.[13] Commercial fund transfers are governed by Article 4A of the UCC.

Although electronic banking offers many benefits, it also poses difficulties on occasion. It is difficult to issue stop-payment orders with electronic banking. Also, fewer records are available to prove or disprove that a transaction took place. The possibilities for tampering with a person's private banking information have also increased.

Types of EFT Systems

Most banks today offer EFT services to their customers. The following are the four most common types of EFT systems used by bank customers:

1 *Automated teller machines* (ATMs)—The machines are connected online to the bank's computers. A customer inserts a plastic card (called an *ATM* or *debit card*) issued by the bank and keys in a *personal identification number* (PIN) to access her or his accounts and conduct banking transactions.

2 *Point-of-sale systems*—Online terminals allow consumers to transfer funds to merchants to pay for purchases using a debit card.

3 *Direct deposits and withdrawals*—Customers can authorize the bank to allow another party—such as the government or

---

13. 15 U.S.C. Sections 1693–1693r. The EFTA amended Title IX of the Consumer Credit Protection Act.

an employer—to make direct deposits into their accounts. Similarly, customers can request the bank to make automatic payments to a third party at regular, recurrent intervals from the customer's funds (insurance premiums or loan payments, for example).

4 *Internet payment systems*—Many financial institutions permit their customers to access the institution's computer system via the Internet and direct a transfer of funds between accounts or pay a particular bill, such as a utility bill, for example.

Consumer Fund Transfers

The Electronic Fund Transfer Act (EFTA) provides a basic framework for the rights, liabilities, and responsibilities of users of EFT systems. Additionally, the act gave the Federal Reserve Board authority to issue rules and regulations to help implement the act's provisions. The Federal Reserve Board's implemental regulation is called **Regulation E.**

The EFTA governs financial institutions that offer electronic fund transfers involving consumer accounts. The types of accounts covered include checking accounts, savings accounts, and any other asset accounts established for personal, family, or household purposes. Telephone transfers are covered by the EFTA only if they are made in accordance with a prearranged plan under which periodic or recurring transfers are contemplated.

Disclosure Requirements   The EFTA is essentially a disclosure law benefiting consumers. The act requires financial institutions to inform consumers of their rights and responsibilities, including those listed here, with respect to EFT systems.

1 If a customer's debit card is lost or stolen and used without his or her permission, the customer may be required to pay no more than $50. The customer, however, must notify the bank of the loss or theft within two days of learning about it. Otherwise, the liability increases to $500. The customer may be liable for more than $500 if he or she does not report the unauthorized use within sixty days after it appears on the customer's statement. (If a customer voluntarily gives her or his debit card to another, who then uses it improperly, the protections just mentioned do not apply.)

2 The customer must discover any error on the monthly statement within sixty days and must notify the bank. The bank then has ten days to investigate and must report its conclusions to the customer in writing. If the bank takes longer than ten days, it must return the disputed amount to the customer's account until it finds the error. If there is no error, the customer has to return the disputed funds to the bank.

3 The bank must furnish receipts for transactions made through computer terminals, but it is not obligated to do so for telephone transfers.

4 The bank must provide a monthly statement for every month in which there is an electronic transfer of funds. Otherwise, the bank must provide statements every quarter. The statement must show the amount and date of the transfer, the names of the retailers or other third parties involved, the location or identification of the terminal, and the fees. Additionally, the statement must give an address and a phone number for inquiries and error notices.

5 Any preauthorized payment for utility bills and insurance premiums can be stopped three days before the scheduled transfer if the customer notifies the financial institution orally or in writing. (The institution may require the customer to provide written confirmation within fourteen days of an oral notification.)

Unauthorized Transfers   Because of the vulnerability of EFT systems to fraudulent activities, the EFTA clearly defined what constitutes an unauthorized transfer. Under the act, a transfer is unauthorized if (1) it is initiated by a person other than the consumer who has no actual authority to initiate the transfer; (2) the consumer receives no benefit from it; and (3) the consumer did not furnish the person "with the card, code, or other means of access" to her or his account. Unauthorized access to an EFT system constitutes a federal felony, and those convicted may be fined up to $10,000 and sentenced to as long as ten years in prison.

Violations and Damages   Banks must strictly comply with the terms of the EFTA. If they fail to adhere to the letter of the law of the EFTA, they will be held liable for violation. For a bank's violation of the EFTA, a consumer may recover both actual damages (including attorneys' fees and costs) and punitive damages of not less than $100 and not more than $1,000. (Unlike actual damages, *punitive damages* are assessed to punish a defendant or to deter similar wrongdoers.) Failure to investigate an error in good faith makes the bank liable for treble damages (three times the amount of damages). Even when a customer has sustained no actual damage, the bank may be liable for legal costs and punitive damages if it fails to follow the proper procedures outlined by the EFTA in regard to error resolution.

Commercial Transfers

Funds are also transferred electronically "by wire" between commercial parties. In fact, the dollar volume of payments by wire transfer is more than $1 trillion a day—an amount that far exceeds the dollar volume of payments made by other means. The two major wire payment systems are the Federal Reserve's wire transfer network (Fedwire) and the New York Clearing House Interbank Payments Systems.

Commercial wire transfers are governed by Article 4A of the UCC, which has been adopted by most states. The following example illustrates the type of fund transfer covered by Article 4A. **■EXAMPLE 19.11** Jellux, Inc., owes $5 million to Perot Corporation. Instead of sending Perot a check or some other instrument that would enable Perot to obtain payment, Jellux tells its bank, East Bank, to credit $5 million to Perot's account in West Bank. East Bank debits Jellux's East Bank account and wires $5 million to Perot's West Bank account. In more complex transactions, additional banks would be involved. ■

E-MONEY AND ONLINE BANKING

New forms of electronic payments (e-payments) have the potential to replace *physical* cash—coins and paper currency—with *virtual* cash in the form of electronic impulses. This is the unique promise of **digital cash,** which consists of funds stored on microchips and on other computer storage devices. Online banking has also become a reality in today's world. In a few minutes, anybody with the proper software can access his or her account, transfer funds, write "checks," pay bills, and often even buy and sell stocks.

Various forms of electronic money, or **e-money,** are emerging. The simplest kind of e-money system uses **stored-value cards.** These are plastic cards embossed with magnetic strips containing magnetically encoded data. In some applications, a stored-value card can be used only to purchase specific goods and services offered by the card issuer. Another form of e-money is the smart card. **Smart cards** are plastic cards containing computer microchips that can hold more information than a magnetic strip. A smart card carries and processes security programming. This capability gives smart cards a technical advantage over stored-value cards. The microprocessors on smart cards can also authenticate the validity of transactions. Retailers can program electronic cash registers to confirm the authenticity of a smart card by examining a unique digital signature stored on its microchip. (Digital signatures were discussed in Chapter 13.)

Online Banking Services

Most online bank customers use three kinds of services. One of the most popular is bill consolidation and payment. Another is transferring funds among accounts. These online services are now offered via the Internet as well as by phone. The third is applying for loans, which many banks permit customers to do over the Internet. Customers typically have to appear in person to finalize the terms of a loan.

Two important banking activities generally are not yet available online: depositing and withdrawing funds. With smart cards, people could transfer funds on the Internet, thereby effectively transforming their personal computers into ATMs. Many observers believe that online banking is the way to introduce people to e-money and smart cards.

Since the late 1990s, several banks have operated exclusively on the Internet. These "virtual banks" have no physical branch offices. Because few people are equipped to send funds to virtual banks via smart-card technology, deposits are made through physical delivery systems, such as the U.S. Postal Service or Federal Express.

Regulatory Compliance

Banks have an interest in seeing the widespread use of online banking because of its significant potential for reducing costs. As in other areas of cyberspace, however, determining how laws apply to online banking activities can be difficult. The Home Mortgage Disclosure Act[14] and the Community Reinvestment Act (CRA) of 1977,[15] for example, require a bank to define its market area and also to provide information to regulators about its deposits and loans. Under the CRA, banks establish market areas in communities next to their branch offices. The banks map these areas, using boundaries defined by counties or standard metropolitan areas; they annually review these maps. These requirements are intended to prevent discrimination in lending practices.

But how does a successful "cyberbank" delineate its community? Does it even have a physical community? Will regulators simply allow a written description of a cybercommunity for Internet customers? Such regulatory issues are new, challenging, and certain to become more complicated as Internet banking widens its scope internationally.

Privacy Protection

At the present time, it is not clear which, if any, laws apply to the security of e-money payment information and e-money issuers' financial records. This is partly because it is not clear whether e-money issuers fit within the traditional definition of a financial institution.

E-Money Payment Information The Federal Reserve has decided not to impose Regulation E, which governs certain electronic fund transfers, on e-money transactions. Federal laws prohibiting unauthorized access to electronic communications might apply, however. For example, the Electronic Communications Privacy Act of 1986[16] prohibits any person

14. 12 U.S.C. Sections 2801–2810.
15. 12 U.S.C. Sections 2901–2908.
16. 18 U.S.C. Sections 2510–2521.

from knowingly divulging to any other person the contents of an electronic communication while that communication is in transmission or in electronic storage.

E-Money Issuers' Financial Records   Under the Right to Financial Privacy Act of 1978,[17] before a financial institution may give financial information about you to a federal agency, you must explicitly consent. If you do not, a federal agency wishing to access your financial records must obtain a warrant. A digital cash issuer may be subject to this act if that issuer is deemed to be (1) a bank by virtue of its holding customer funds or (2) any entity that issues a physical card similar to a credit or debit card.

Consumer Financial Data   In 1999, Congress passed the Financial Services Modernization Act,[18] also known as the Gramm-Leach-Bliley Act, in an attempt to delineate how financial institutions can treat customer data. In general, the act and its rules[19] place restrictions and obligations on financial institutions to protect consumer data and privacy. Every financial institution must provide its customers with information on its privacy policies and practices. No financial institution can disclose nonpublic personal information about a consumer to an unaffiliated third party unless the act's disclosure and opt-out requirements are met.

18. 12 U.S.C. Sections 24a, 248b, 1820a, 1828b, 1831v–1831y, 1848a, 2908, 4809; 15 U.S.C. Sections 80b–10a, 6701, 6711–6717, 6731–6735, 6751–6766, 6781, 6801–6809, 6821–6827, 6901–6910; and others.

19. 12 C.F.R. Part 40.

17. 12 U.S.C. Sections 3401 *et seq.*

REVIEWING   Checks and Banking in the Digital Age

RPM Pizza, Inc., issued a check for $96,000 to Systems Marketing for an advertising campaign. A few days later, RPM decided not to go through with the deal and placed a written stop-payment order on the check. RPM and Systems had no further contact for many months. Three weeks after the stop-payment order expired, however, Toby Rierson, an employee at Systems, cashed the check. Bank One Cambridge, RPM's bank, paid the check with funds from RPM's account. Because the check was more than six months old, it was stale, and thus, according to standard banking procedures as well as Bank One's own policies, the signature on the check should have been specially verified, but it was not. RPM filed a suit in

a federal district court against Bank One to recover the amount of the check. Using the information presented in the chapter, answer the following questions.

1   How long is a written stop-payment order effective? What could RPM have done to further prevent this check from being cashed?

2   What would happen if it turned out that RPM did not have a legitimate reason for stopping payment on the check?

3   What are a bank's obligations with respect to stale checks?

4   Would a court be likely to hold the bank liable for the amount of the check because it failed to verify the signature on the check? Why or why not?

TERMS AND CONCEPTS

cashier's check 374
certified check 375
check 373
clearinghouse 383
collecting bank 381
depositary bank 381
digital cash 387

electronic fund transfer (EFT) 385
e-money 387
Federal Reserve System 383
intermediary bank 381
overdraft 376
payor bank 381
Regulation E 386

smart card 387
stale check 376
stop-payment order 376
stored-value card 387
traveler's check 374

CHAPTER SUMMARY   Checks and Banking in the Digital Age

Checks
(See pages 373–375.)

1. *Cashier's check*—A check drawn by a bank on itself (the bank is both the drawer and the drawee) and purchased by a customer. In effect, the bank assumes responsibility for paying the check, thus making the check nearly the equivalent of cash.

CHAPTER SUMMARY	Checks and Banking in the Digital Age–Continued
Checks—Continued	2. *Traveler's check*—An instrument on which a financial institution is both the drawer and the drawee. The purchaser must provide his or her signature as a countersignature for a traveler's check to become a negotiable instrument.
	3. *Certified check*—A check for which the drawee bank certifies in writing that it has set aside funds from the drawer's account to ensure payment on presentation. On certification, the drawer and all prior indorsers are completely discharged from liability on the check.
The Bank-Customer Relationship (See page 375.)	1. *Creditor-debtor relationship*—The bank and its customer have a creditor-debtor relationship (the bank is the debtor because it holds the customer's funds on deposit).
	2. *Agency relationship*—Because a bank must act in accordance with the customer's orders in regard to the customer's deposited money, an agency relationship also arises—the bank is the agent for the customer, who is the principal.
	3. *Contractual relationship*—The bank's relationship with its customer is also contractual; the bank and the customer assume certain contractual duties when a customer opens an account.
Bank's Duty to Honor Checks (See pages 375–380.)	Generally, a bank has a duty to honor its customers' checks, provided that the customers have sufficient funds on deposit to cover the checks [UCC 4–401(a)]. The bank is liable to its customers for actual damages proved to be due to wrongful dishonor. The bank's duty to honor its customers' checks is not absolute. The following list summarizes the rights and liabilities of the bank and the customer in various situations:
	1. *Wrongful dishonor*—The bank is liable to its customer for actual damages proved if it wrongfully dishonors a check due to mistake [UCC 4–402]. When the bank properly dishonors a check (for insufficient funds or because of a stop-payment order, for example), it has no liability to the customer.
	2. *Overdraft*—The bank has a right to charge a customer's account for any item properly payable, even if the charge results in an overdraft [UCC 4–401].
	3. *Postdated check*—The bank may charge a postdated check against a customer's account, unless the customer notifies the bank of the postdating in time to allow the bank to act on the customer's notice and verify the date has passed before the bank commits itself to pay on the check [UCC 4–401].
	4. *Stale check*—The bank is not obligated to pay an uncertified check presented more than six months after its date, but the bank may do so in good faith without liability [UCC 4–404].
	5. *Stop-payment order*—The customer (or a "person authorized to draw on the account") must make a stop-payment order in time for the bank to have a reasonable opportunity to act. Oral orders are binding for only fourteen days unless they are confirmed in writing. Written orders are effective for only six months unless renewed in writing. The bank is liable for wrongful payment over a timely stop-payment order to the extent that the customer suffers a loss [UCC 4–403]. A customer has no right to stop payment on a check that has been certified or accepted by a bank, however. A payee can hold a person liable for actual and consequential damages if that person stopped payment on a check without a valid legal ground.
	6. *Death or incompetence of a customer*—So long as the bank does not know of the death or incompetence of a customer, the bank can pay an item without liability. Even with knowledge of a customer's death, a bank can honor or certify checks (in the absence of a stop-payment order) for ten days after the date of the customer's death [UCC 4–405].
	7. *Forged signature or alteration*—The customer has a duty to examine account statements with reasonable care on receipt and to notify the bank promptly of any forged signatures or alterations. On a series of forged signatures or alterations by the same wrongdoer, examination and report must be made within thirty calendar days of receipt of the first statement

(Continued)

CHAPTER SUMMARY	**Checks and Banking in the Digital Age—Continued**

Bank's Duty to Honor Checks—Continued

containing a forged or altered item. The customer's failure to comply with these rules releases the bank from liability unless the bank failed to exercise reasonable care; in that event, liability may be apportioned according to a comparative negligence standard. Regardless of care or lack of care, the customer is barred from holding the bank liable after one year for forged customer signatures or alterations and after three years for forged indorsements [UCC 3–403, 4–111, 4–406].

Bank's Duty to Accept Deposits
(See pages 380–385.)

A bank has a duty to accept deposits made by its customers into their accounts. Funds represented by checks deposited must be made available to customers. A bank also has a duty to collect payment on any checks deposited by its customers. When checks deposited by customers are drawn on other banks, the check-collection process comes into play.

1. *Definitions of banks—*
   a. Depository bank—The first bank to accept a check for payment.
   b. Payor bank—The bank on which a check is drawn.
   c. Collecting bank—Any bank except the payor bank that handles a check during the collection process.
   d. Intermediary bank—Any bank except the payor bank or the depositary bank to which an item is transferred in the course of the collection process.

2. *Check collection between customers of the same bank—*A check payable by the depositary bank that receives it is an "on-us item"; if the bank does not dishonor the check by the opening of the second banking day following its receipt, the check is considered paid [UCC 4–215(e)(2)].

3. *Check collection between customers of different banks—*Each bank in the collection process must pass the check on to the next appropriate bank before midnight of the next banking day following its receipt [UCC 4–108, 4–202(b), 4–302].

4. *How the Federal Reserve System clears checks—*The Federal Reserve System facilitates the check-clearing process by serving as a clearinghouse for checks.

5. *Electronic check presentment—*When checks are presented electronically, items may be encoded with information (such as the amount of the check) that is read and processed by other banks' computers. In some situations, a check may be retained at its place of deposit, and only its image or information describing it is presented for payment under a Federal Reserve agreement, clearinghouse rule, or other agreement [UCC 4–110].

6. *Check Clearing in the 21st Century Act (Check 21)—*Check 21 changes the traditional paper check–collection process by creating a new negotiable instrument called a *substitute check,* thus gradually reducing the number of paper checks and the length of float time. Additionally, banks will eventually have less time to hold funds from deposited checks before making them available, allowing account holders quicker access to those funds.

Electronic Fund Transfers
(See pages 385–387.)

1. *Types of EFT systems—*
   a. Automated teller machines (ATMs).
   b. Point-of-sale systems.
   c. Direct deposits and withdrawals.
   d. Internet payment systems.

2. *Consumer fund transfers—*Consumer fund transfers are governed by the Electronic Fund Transfer Act (EFTA) of 1978. The EFTA is basically a disclosure law that sets forth the rights and duties of the bank and the customer with respect to EFT systems. Banks must comply strictly with EFTA requirements.

3. *Commercial transfers—*Article 4A of the UCC, which has been adopted by almost all of the states, governs fund transfers not subject to the EFTA or other federal or state statutes.

CHAPTER SUMMARY	Checks and Banking in the Digital Age–Continued

E-Money and Online Banking (See pages 387–388.)	1. *New forms of e-payments*—These include stored-value cards and smart cards.
	
	2. *Current online banking services*—
	  a. Bill consolidation and payment.
	  b. Transferring funds among accounts.
	  c. Applying for loans.
	
	3. *Regulatory compliance*—Banks must define their market areas, in communities situated next to their branch offices. It is not clear how an online bank would define its market area or its community.
	
	4. *Privacy protection*—It is not entirely clear which, if any, laws apply to e-money and online banking. The Financial Services Modernization Act outlines how financial institutions can treat consumer data and privacy in general. The Right to Financial Privacy Act may also apply.

FOR REVIEW

*Answers for the even-numbered questions in this **For Review** section can be found on this text's accompanying Web site at* www.cengage.com/blaw/fbl. *Select "Chapter 19" and click on "For Review."*

1 On what type of check does a bank agree in advance to accept when the check is presented for payment?

2 When may a bank properly dishonor a customer's check without the bank being liable to the customer? What happens if a bank wrongfully dishonors a customer's check?

3 What duties does the Uniform Commercial Code impose on a bank's customers with regard to forged and altered checks? What are the consequences of a customer's negligence in performing those duties?

4 What are the four most common types of electronic fund transfers?

5 What is e-money, and how is it stored and used? What laws apply to e-money transactions and online banking services?

QUESTIONS AND CASE PROBLEMS

 HYPOTHETICAL SCENARIOS AND CASE PROBLEMS

19.1 Forged Checks. Roy Supply, Inc., and R. M. R. Drywall, Inc., had checking accounts at Wells Fargo Bank. Both accounts required all checks to carry two signatures—that of Edward Roy and that of Twila June Moore, both of whom were executive officers of both companies. Between January 1989 and March 1991, the bank honored hundreds of checks on which Roy's signature was forged by Moore. On January 31, 1992, Roy and the two corporations notified the bank of the forgeries and then filed a suit in a California state court against the bank, alleging negligence. Who is liable for the amounts of the forged checks? Why?

19.2 Hypothetical Question with Sample Answer. First Internet Bank operates exclusively on the Web with no physical branch offices. Although some of First Internet's business is transacted with smart-card technology, most of its business with its customers is conducted through the mail. First Internet offers free checking, no-fee money market accounts, mortgage refinancing, and other services. With

what regulation covering banks might First Internet find it difficult to comply, and what is the difficulty?

 For a sample answer to Question 19.2, go to Appendix E at the end of this text.

19.3 Check Collection. Robert Santoro was the manager of City Check Cashing, Inc., a check-cashing service in New Jersey, and Peggyann Slansky was the clerk. On July 14, Misir Koci presented Santoro with a $290,000 check signed by Melvin Green and drawn on Manufacturers Hanover Trust Co. (a bank). The check was stamped with a Manufacturers certification stamp. The date on the check had clearly been changed from August 8 to July 7. Slansky called the bank to verify the check and was told that the serial number "did not sound like one belonging to the bank." Slansky faxed a copy of the check to the bank with a query about the date, but she received no reply. Slansky also called Green, who stated that the date on the check was altered before it was certified.

Check Cashing cashed and deposited the check within two hours. The drawee bank found the check to be invalid and timely returned it unpaid. Check Cashing filed a suit against Manufacturers and others, asserting that the bank should have responded to the fax before the midnight deadline in UCC Section 4–302. Did the bank violate the midnight deadline rule? Explain. [*City Check Cashing, Inc. v. Manufacturers Hanover Trust Co.*, 166 N.J. 49, 764 A.2d 411 (2001)]

19.4 Forged Indorsement. Visiting Nurses Association of Telfair County, Inc. (VNA), maintained a checking account at Security State Bank in Valdosta, Georgia. Wanda Williamson, a VNA clerk, was responsible for making VNA bank deposits, but she was not a signatory on the association's account. Over a four-year period, Williamson embezzled more than $250,000 from VNA by forging its indorsement on checks, cashing them at the bank, and keeping a portion of the proceeds. Williamson was arrested, convicted, sentenced to a prison term, and ordered to pay restitution. VNA filed a suit in a Georgia state court against the bank, alleging, among other things, negligence. The bank filed a motion for summary judgment on the ground that VNA was precluded by Section 4–406(f) of the Uniform Commercial Code from recovering on checks with forged indorsements. Should the court grant the motion? Explain. [*Security State Bank v. Visiting Nurses Association of Telfair County, Inc.*, 568 S.E.2d 491 (Ga.App. 2002)]

19.5 Forged Signatures. Cynthia Stafford worked as an administrative professional at Gerber & Gerber, P.C. (professional corporation), for more than two years. During that time, she stole ten checks payable to Gerber & Gerber (G&G), which she indorsed in blank by forging one of the attorney's signatures. She then indorsed the forged checks in her name and deposited them in her account at Regions Bank. Over the same period, G&G deposited in its accounts at Regions Bank thousands of checks amounting to $300 million to $400 million. Each G&G check was indorsed with a rubber stamp for deposit into the G&G account. The thefts were made possible in part because G&G kept unindorsed checks in an open file accessible to all employees and Stafford was sometimes the person assigned to stamp the checks. When the thefts were discovered, G&G filed a suit against Regions Bank to recover the stolen funds, alleging negligence. Regions Bank filed a motion for summary judgment. What principles apply to attribute liability between these parties? How should the court rule on the bank's motion? Explain. [*Gerber & Gerber, P.C. v. Regions Bank*, 596 S.E.2d 174 (Ga.App. 2004)]

19.6 Case Problem with Sample Answer. In December 1999, Jenny Triplett applied for a bookkeeping position with Spacemakers of America, Inc., in Atlanta, Georgia. Spacemakers hired Triplett and delegated to her all responsibility for maintaining the company checkbook and reconciling it with the monthly statements from SunTrust Bank. Triplett also handled invoices from vendors. Spacemakers'

president, Dennis Rose, reviewed the invoices and signed the checks to pay them, but no other employee checked Triplett's work. By the end of her first full month of employment, Triplett had forged six checks totaling more than $22,000, all payable to Triple M Entertainment, which was not a Spacemakers vendor. By October 2000, Triplett had forged fifty-nine more checks, totaling more than $475,000. A SunTrust employee became suspicious of an item that required sight inspection under the bank's fraud detection standards, which exceeded those of other banks in the area. Triplett was arrested. Spacemakers filed a suit against SunTrust. The bank filed a motion for summary judgment. On what basis could the bank avoid liability? [*Spacemakers of America, Inc. v. SunTrust Bank*, 271 Ga.App. 335, 609 S.E.2d 683 (2005)]

After you have answered Problem 19.6, compare your answer with the sample answer given on the Web site that accompanies this text. Go to www.cengage.com/blaw/fbl, select "Chapter 19," and click on "Case Problem with Sample Answer."

19.7 Forged Indorsements. In 1994, Brian and Penny Grieme bought a house in Mandan, North Dakota. They borrowed for the purchase through a loan program financed by the North Dakota Housing Finance Agency (NDHFA). The Griemes obtained insurance for the house from Center Mutual Insurance Co. When a hailstorm damaged the house in 2001, Center Mutual determined that the loss was $4,378 and issued a check for that amount, drawn on Bremer Bank, N.A. The check's payees included Brian Grieme and the NDHFA. Grieme presented the check for payment to Wells Fargo Bank of Tempe, Arizona. The back of the check bore his signature and in hand-printed block letters the words "ND Housing Finance." The check was processed for collection and paid, and the canceled check was returned to Center Mutual. By the time the insurer learned that NDHFA's indorsement had been forged, the Griemes had canceled their policy, defaulted on their loan, and filed for bankruptcy. The NDHFA filed a suit in a North Dakota state court against Center Mutual for the amount of the check. Who is most likely to suffer the loss in this case? Why? [*State ex rel. North Dakota Housing Finance Agency v. Center Mutual Insurance Co.*, 720 N.W.2d 425 (N.Dak. 2006)]

19.8 **A Question of Ethics.** *From the 1960s, James Johnson served as Bradley Union's personal caretaker and assistant, and was authorized by Union to handle his banking transactions. Louise Johnson, James's wife, wrote checks on Union's checking account to pay his bills, normally signing the checks "Brad Union." Branch Banking & Trust Co. (BB&T) managed Union's account. In December 2000, on the basis of Union's deteriorating mental and physical condition, a North Carolina state court declared him incompetent. Douglas Maxwell was appointed as Union's guardian. Maxwell "froze" Union's checking account and asked BB&T for copies of the canceled checks, which were provided by*

July 2001. Maxwell believed that Union's signature on the checks had been forged. In August 2002, Maxwell contacted BB&T, which refused to recredit Union's account. Maxwell filed a suit on Union's behalf in a North Carolina state court against BB&T. [Union v. Branch Banking & Trust Co., 176 N.C.App. 711, 627 S.E.2d 276 (2006)]

1 Before Maxwell's appointment, BB&T sent monthly statements and canceled checks to Union, and Johnson reviewed them, but no unauthorized signatures were ever reported. On whom can liability be imposed in the case of a forged drawer's signature on a check? What are the limits set by Section 4–406(f) of the Uniform Commercial Code? Should Johnson's position, Union's incompetence, or Maxwell's appointment affect the application of these principles? Explain.

2 Why was this suit brought against BB&T? Is BB&T liable? If not, who is? Why? Did anyone act unethically in this case? If so, who and why?

CRITICAL THINKING AND WRITING ASSIGNMENT

19.9 Critical Legal Thinking. Under the 1990 revision of Article 4, a bank is not required to include the customer's canceled checks when it sends monthly statements to the customer. Banks may simply itemize the checks (by number, date, and amount) or, in addition to this itemization, also provide photocopies of the checks. What implications do the revised rules have for bank customers in terms of liability for unauthorized signatures and indorsements?

ACCESSING THE INTERNET

For updated links to resources available on the Web, as well as a variety of other materials, visit this text's Web site at

www.cengage.com/blaw/fbl

You can obtain information about banking regulation from the Federal Deposit Insurance Corporation (FDIC) at

www.fdic.gov

Cornell University's Legal Information Institute provides an overview of banking, as well as a "menu of sources" of federal and state statutes and court decisions relating to banking transactions. To access this information, go to

www.law.cornell.edu/topics/banking.html

You can obtain extensive information about the Federal Reserve System by accessing "the Fed's" home page at

www.federalreserve.gov

You can find a series of articles on smart cards at the following Web site:

users.aol.com/pjsmart/index.htm

PRACTICAL INTERNET EXERCISES

Go to this text's Web site at **www.cengage.com/blaw/fbl**, select "Chapter 19," and click on "Practical Internet Exercises." There you will find the following Internet research exercises that you can perform to learn more about the topics covered in this chapter.

PRACTICAL INTERNET EXERCISE 19-1 MANAGEMENT PERSPECTIVE—Check Fraud

PRACTICAL INTERNET EXERCISE 19-2 LEGAL PERSPECTIVE—Smart Cards

BEFORE THE TEST

Go to this text's Web site at **www.cengage.com/blaw/fbl**, select "Chapter 19," and click on "Interactive Quizzes." You will find a number of interactive questions relating to this chapter.

Prestridge v. Bank of Jena

In Chapters 18 and 19, we reviewed some of the laws that govern checks and the banking system, explaining the rights, duties, and liabilities of banks and their customers. We discussed those concepts as they apply under Articles 3 and 4 of the Uniform Commercial Code (UCC). In this extended case study, we examine Prestridge v. Bank of Jena,[1] a decision focusing on the parties' obligations under the UCC with respect to a series of forged checks. A bank is generally liable if it pays a check over the forged signature of its customer, but to enforce this liability, the customer must report a forgery within thirty days of receiving his or her account statement on which the check amount appears. How do these principles apply when neither the bank nor the customer verifies the signatures on the checks?

CASE BACKGROUND   In October 2002, sisters Glynda and Vera Prestridge opened a checking account at Bank of Jena in Libuse, Rapides Parish, Louisiana. Each sister signed a signature card. Vera's name was included on the account only so that it could be accessed, if necessary, while Glynda and her husband were traveling. Vera did not make a deposit into the account, write a check on it, or receive correspondence regarding it.

Over the next seven months, Marye Prestridge, Glynda's daughter-in-law, obtained blank checks on the account. Marye forged Glynda's name on the checks to steal more than $60,000 from the account. In April 2003, Glynda dis-

covered that the balance was significantly lower than she expected. She learned of Marye's withdrawals and froze the account, but was able to recover only $5,700. Marye and Glynda's son Larry were soon divorced.

Glynda and Vera filed a suit in a Louisiana state court against the bank, claiming that it should reimburse them for the missing funds because it had been negligent in paying on the forged checks. The court awarded the plaintiffs $37,450, the amount that Marye took before January 22. The court ruled that after that date, the plaintiffs were negligent in not checking their account statements. Both parties appealed to a state intermediate appellate court.

---

1. 924 So.2d 1266 (La.App. 3 Cir. 2006).

MAJORITY OPINION

GENOVESE, Judge.

* * * *

On appeal, both parties have asserted the provisions of La.R.S. 10:4-406 [Louisiana's version of UCC 4–406] in support of their respective positions. Bank of Jena asserts that the Plaintiffs should be precluded from recovery because they also failed to exercise reasonable care after the forgeries had been committed. Bank of Jena argues that Glynda had a duty to examine the monthly account statements sent to her, and that she failed * * * to examine them * * * before April 2003. The Plaintiffs, however, assert that Bank of Jena improperly paid on the instruments because it failed to verify the signatures on any of the checks at the time they were paid. * * *

* * * *

Our review of the evidence supports a determination that Bank of Jena made statements available to the Plaintiffs by sending Glynda the account information monthly. Further, the record supports a finding that * * * Glynda had not examined the statements that were sent to her * * * .

* * * *

In support of their [argument] that Bank of Jena failed to exercise ordinary care, and that apportionment of fault is

therefore appropriate, the Plaintiffs point out that the signatures which appear on the signature lines of the forged checks clearly do not match Glynda's signature as it appears on the signature card that she signed with Bank of Jena when she opened the account. * * * The Plaintiffs contend that this failure to verify Glynda's signature was below the level of ordinary care and substantially contributed to their loss.

* * * *

Our review of the record in the instant case [the case now before the court] reveals that Bank of Jena had adopted an automated means of clearing its checks, by sending them to Computer Services, Inc ("CSI") [which] clears checks for Bank of Jena as well as more than five hundred other banks nationally. * * * CSI * * * electronically photographed the checks and kept the original paper checks for ninety days before destroying them. * * * Bank of Jena never sees the paper check[s] and can only view the checks electronically.

* * * *

After review, we do not find that overall the record supports a determination that the Plaintiffs have proven that Bank of Jena failed to adhere to a reasonable commercial standard, prevailing in the area, when paying on the instruments at issue. * * * Other area community banks use data processing companies like CSI to process their checks using a similar check-clearing process. Accordingly, because the Plaintiffs have not proven that Bank of Jena failed overall to exercise ordinary care, * * * the loss due to the forgeries should not be allocated between the parties.

* * * *

* * * La.R.S. 10:4-406(d)(2) allow[s] Plaintiffs a thirty-day period from the issuance of their monthly account statement to identify any forged instrument and notify the bank accordingly. * * * Therefore, Bank of Jena is liable unto Plaintiffs for paying on fraudulent instruments up through December 22, 2002, which is thirty days after * * * the first bank statement [was] issued. The trial court judgment is affirmed in that regard, but amended to allow Plaintiffs to recover only for forged

instruments up through thirty days after the first bank statement, i.e., December 22, 2002, and no further. [Emphasis added.]

* * * Because we cannot determine from the record the exact amount of the forgeries up through December 22, 2002, we remand this matter to the trial court for a hearing to determine said amount * * * .

* * * *

For the foregoing reasons, the judgment of the trial court in favor of the Plaintiffs, Glynda Prestridge and Vera Prestridge, is affirmed in part as amended, reversed in part, and remanded to the trial court * * * .

DISSENTING OPINION

AMY, J. [Judge], dissenting.

I respectfully dissent from the majority opinion. Chiefly, I disagree that the plaintiffs are entitled to any recovery given the present circumstances.

The evidence supports a determination that Bank of Jena made monthly statements available to the plaintiffs * * * .

* * * La.R.S. 10:4-406(c) * * * states that "the customer must exercise reasonable promptness in examining the statement * * * to determine whether any payment was not authorized because of an alteration of an item or because a purported signature by or on behalf of the customer was not authorized." It further provides that, if an authorized payment should have been discovered, "the customer must promptly notify the bank of the relevant facts." As the plaintiffs failed to do so within the period of "reasonable promptness," required by La.R.S. 10:4-406(c) * * * , the plaintiffs cannot recover for the initial forgeries.

With regard to subsequent forgeries, La.R.S. 10:4-406 provides:

(d) If the bank proves that the customer failed, with respect to an item, to comply with the duties imposed on the customer by Subsection (c), the customer is precluded from asserting against the bank: * * *

(2) the customer's unauthorized signature or alteration by the same wrongdoer on any other item paid in good faith by the bank if the payment was made before the bank received notice from the customer of the unauthorized signature or alteration and after the customer had been afforded a reasonable period of time, not exceeding thirty days, in which to examine the item or statement of account and notify the bank.

Again, the plaintiffs failed to notify the bank of the irregularities within this time frame.

In short, I conclude that the trial court erred in allowing the plaintiffs to recover any funds paid by the Bank of Jena on the checks forged by Marye Prestridge.

QUESTIONS FOR ANALYSIS

1   LAW. How did the majority in this case respond to the question stated at the beginning of this feature? What was the reasoning behind the response?

2   LAW. Did the dissent agree with the majority's application of UCC 4–406? With what part of the majority's ruling did the dissent disagree? Why?

3   ETHICS. Should a bank that uses outsourced check-collection procedures be absolved of responsibility for verifying the signatures of its customers on items drawn on the bank?

4   TECHNOLOGICAL DIMENSIONS. How has electronic banking affected the relationship between a bank and its customer?

5   IMPLICATIONS FOR THE BUSINESS OWNER. What is the significance of the outcome in this case to a business?

UNIT SIX

Debtor-Creditor Relationships

UNIT CONTENTS

CHAPTER 20
Security Interests in Personal Property

AFTER READING THIS CHAPTER, YOU SHOULD BE ABLE TO ANSWER THE FOLLOWING QUESTIONS:

1 What is a security interest? Who is a secured party? What is a security agreement? What is a financing statement?

2 What three requirements must be met to create an enforceable security interest?

3 What is the most common method of perfecting a security interest under Article 9?

4 If two secured parties have perfected security interests in the collateral of the debtor, which party has priority to the collateral on the debtor's default?

5 What rights does a secured creditor have on the debtor's default?

Whenever the payment of a debt is guaranteed, or *secured*, by personal property owned by the debtor or in which the debtor has a legal interest, the transaction becomes known as a **secured transaction.** The concept of the secured transaction is as basic to modern business practice as the concept of credit. Logically, sellers and lenders do not want to risk nonpayment, so they usually will not sell goods or lend funds unless the payment is somehow guaranteed. Indeed, business as we know it could not exist without laws permitting and governing secured transactions.

Article 9 of the Uniform Commercial Code (UCC) governs secured transactions as applied to personal property, *fixtures* (certain property that is attached to land—see Chapter 29), accounts, instruments, commercial assignments of $1,000 or more, *chattel paper* (any writing evidencing a debt secured by personal property), agricultural liens, and what are called general intangibles (such as patents and copyrights). Article 9 does not cover other creditor devices, such as liens and real estate mortgages, which will be discussed in Chapter 21.

In this chapter, we first look at the terminology of secured transactions. We then discuss how the rights and duties of creditors and debtors are created and enforced under Article 9. As

will become evident, the law of secured transactions tends to favor the rights of creditors; but, to a lesser extent, it offers debtors some protections, too.

THE TERMINOLOGY OF SECURED TRANSACTIONS

The UCC's terminology is now uniformly adopted in all documents used in situations involving secured transactions. A brief summary of the UCC's definitions of terms relating to secured transactions follows.

1 A **secured party** is any creditor who has a *security interest* in the *debtor's collateral*. This creditor can be a seller, a lender, a cosigner, or even a buyer of accounts or chattel paper [UCC 9–102(a)(72)].

2 A **debtor** is the "person" who *owes payment* or other performance of a secured obligation [UCC 9–102(a)(28)].

3 A **security interest** is the *interest* in the collateral (such as personal property or fixtures) that *secures payment or performance of an obligation* [UCC 1–201(37)].

4 A **security agreement** is an *agreement* that *creates* or provides for a *security interest* [UCC 9–102(a)(73)].

5 **Collateral** is the *subject* of the *security interest* [UCC 9–102(a)(12)].

6 A **financing statement**—referred to as the UCC-1 form—is the *instrument normally filed* to give *public notice* to *third parties* of the *secured party's security interest* [UCC 9–102(a)(39)].

Together, these definitions form the concept by which a debtor-creditor relationship becomes a secured transaction relationship (see Exhibit 20–1).

CREATING A SECURITY INTEREST

A creditor has two main concerns if the debtor **defaults** (fails to pay the debt as promised): (1) Can the debt be satisfied through the possession and (usually) sale of the collateral? (2) Will the creditor have priority over any other creditors or buyers who may have rights in the same collateral? These two concerns are met through the creation and perfection of a security interest. We begin by examining how a security interest is created.

To become a secured party, the creditor must obtain a security interest in the collateral of the debtor. Three requirements must be met for a creditor to have an enforceable security interest:

1 Either (a) the collateral must be in the possession of the secured party in accordance with an agreement, or (b) there must be a written or authenticated security agreement that describes the collateral subject to the security interest and is signed or authenticated by the debtor.

2 The secured party must give something of value to the debtor.

EXHIBIT 20–1 Secured Transactions–Concept and Terminology

In a security agreement, a debtor and a creditor agree that the creditor will have a security interest in collateral in which the debtor has rights. In essence, the collateral secures the loan and ensures the creditor of payment should the debtor default.

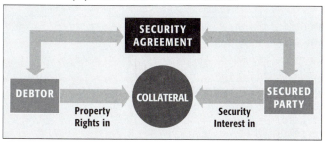

3 The debtor must have "rights" in the collateral.

Once these requirements have been met, the creditor's rights are said to attach to the collateral. **Attachment** gives the creditor an enforceable security interest in the collateral [UCC 9–203].[1]

Written or Authenticated Security Agreement

When the collateral is *not* in the possession of the secured party, the security agreement must be either written or authenticated, and it must describe the collateral. Note here that *authentication* means to sign, execute, or adopt any symbol on an electronic record that verifies the person signing has the intent to adopt or accept the record [UCC 9–102(a)(7)(69)]. If the security agreement is in writing or authenticated, *only the debtor's signature or authentication* is required to create the security interest. The reason authentication is acceptable is to provide for electronic filing (the filing process will be discussed later).

A security agreement must contain a description of the collateral that reasonably identifies it. Generally, such phrases as "all the debtor's personal property" or "all the debtor's assets" would *not* constitute a sufficient description [UCC 9–108(c)].

Secured Party Must Give Value

The secured party must give to the debtor something of value. Some examples would be a binding commitment to extend credit or consideration to support a simple contract [UCC 1–201(44)]. Normally, the value given by a secured party is in the form of a direct loan or a commitment to sell goods on credit.

Debtor Must Have Rights in the Collateral

The debtor must have rights in the collateral; that is, the debtor must have some ownership interest in or right to obtain possession of that collateral. The debtor's rights can represent either a current or a future legal interest in the collateral. For example, a retail seller-debtor can give a secured party a security interest not only in existing inventory owned by the retailer but also in *future* inventory to be acquired by the retailer.

One common misconception about having rights in the collateral is that the debtor must have title. This is not a requirement. A beneficial interest in a trust (*trusts* will be discussed in Chapter 30), when the trustee holds title to the trust

---

1. Note that in the context of judicial liens, to be discussed in Chapter 21, the term *attachment* has a different meaning. In that context, it refers to a court-ordered seizure and taking into custody of property before the securing of a court judgment for a past-due debt.

property, can be the subject of a security interest for a loan that a creditor makes to the beneficiary.

PERFECTING A SECURITY INTEREST

Perfection is the legal process by which secured parties protect themselves against the claims of third parties who may wish to have their debts satisfied out of the same collateral. Whether a secured party's security interest is perfected or unperfected may have serious consequences for the secured party if, for example, the debtor defaults on the debt or files for bankruptcy. What if the debtor has borrowed from two different creditors, using the same property as collateral for both loans? If the debtor defaults on both loans, which of the two creditors has first rights to the collateral? In this situation, the creditor with a perfected security interest will prevail.

Usually, perfection is accomplished by filing a financing statement, but in some circumstances, a security interest becomes perfected without the filing of a financing statement. Where or how a security interest is perfected sometimes depends on the type of collateral. Collateral is generally divided into two classifications: *tangible collateral* (collateral that can be seen, felt, and touched) and *intangible*

collateral (collateral that consists of or generates rights). Exhibit 20–2 summarizes the various classifications of collateral and the methods of perfecting a security interest in collateral falling within each of these classifications.[2]

Perfection by Filing

The most common means of perfection is by filing a *financing statement*—a document that gives public notice to third parties of the secured party's security interest—with the office of the appropriate government official. The security agreement itself can also be filed to perfect the security interest. The financing statement must provide the names of the debtor and the secured party and must indicate the collateral covered by the financing statement.[3]

Communication of the financing statement to the appropriate filing office, together with the correct filing fee, or the acceptance of the financing statement by the filing officer

---

2. There are additional classifications, such as agricultural liens, investment property, and commercial tort claims. For definitions of these types of collateral, see UCC 9–102(a)(5), (a)(13), and (a)(49).
3. To view a sample uniform financing statement, go to **www.sos.nh.gov/ucc/ucc1.pdf**.

EXHIBIT 20–2 Types of Collateral and Methods of Perfection

TANGIBLE COLLATERAL		METHOD OF PERFECTION
All things that are movable at the time the security interest attaches (such as livestock) or that are attached to the land, including timber to be cut and growing crops.		
1. Consumer Goods [UCC 9–301, 9–303, 9–309(1), 9–310(a), 9–313(a)]	Goods used or bought primarily for personal, family, or household purposes—for example, household furniture [UCC 9–102(a)(23)].	For purchase-money security interest, attachment (that is, the creation of a security interest) is sufficient; for boats, motor vehicles, and trailers, filing or compliance with a certificate-of-title statute is required; for other consumer goods, general rules of filing or possession apply.
2. Equipment [UCC 9–301, 9–310(a), 9–313(a)]	Goods bought for or used primarily in business (and not part of inventory or farm products)—for example, a delivery truck [UCC 9–102(a)(33)].	Filing or (rarely) possession by secured party.
3. Farm Products [UCC 9–301, 9–310(a), 9–313(a)]	Crops (including aquatic goods), livestock, or supplies produced in a farming operation—for example, ginned cotton, milk, eggs, and maple syrup [UCC 9–102(a)(34)].	Filing or (rarely) possession by secured party.
4. Inventory [UCC 9–301, 9–310(a), 9–313(a)]	Goods held by a person for sale or under a contract of service or lease; raw materials held for production and work in progress [UCC 9–102(a)(48)].	Filing or (rarely) possession by secured party.
5. Accessions [UCC 9–301, 9–310(a), 9–313(a)]	Personal property that is so attached, installed, or fixed to other personal property (goods) that it becomes a part of these goods—for example, a DVD player installed in an automobile [UCC 9–102(a)(1)].	Filing or (rarely) possession by secured party (same as personal property being attached).

EXHIBIT 20–2 Types of Collateral and Methods of Perfection–Continued

INTANGIBLE COLLATERAL		METHOD OF PERFECTION
Nonphysical property that exists only in connection with something else.		
1. Chattel Paper [UCC 9–301, 9–310(a), 9–312(a), 9–313(a), 9–314(a)]	A writing or writings (records) that evidence both a monetary obligation and a security interest in goods and software used in goods–for example, a security agreement or a security agreement and promissory note. *Note:* If the record or records consist of information stored in an electronic medium, the collateral is called *electronic chattel paper.* If the information is inscribed on a tangible medium, it is called *tangible chattel paper* [UCC 9–102(a)(11), (a)(31), and (a)(78)].	Filing or possession or control by secured party.
2. Instruments [UCC 9–301, 9–309(4), 9–310 (a), 9–312(a) and (e), 9–313(a)]	A negotiable instrument, such as a check, note, certificate of deposit, or draft, or other writing that evidences a right to the payment of money and is not a security agreement or lease but rather a type that can ordinarily be transferred (after indorsement, if necessary) by delivery [UCC 9–102(a)(47)].	Except for temporary perfected status, filing or possession. For the sale of promissory notes, perfection can be by attachment (automatically on the creation of the security interest).
3. Accounts [UCC 9–301, 9–309(2) and (5), 9–310(a)]	Any right to receive payment for the following: (a) any property, real or personal, sold, leased, licensed, assigned, or otherwise disposed of, including intellectual licensed property; (b) services rendered or to be rendered, such as contract rights; (c) policies of insurance; (d) secondary obligations incurred; (e) use of a credit card; (f) winnings of a government-sponsored or government-authorized lottery or other game of chance; and (g) health-care insurance receivables, defined as an interest or claim under a policy of insurance to payment for health-care goods or services provided [UCC 9–102(a)(2) and (a)(46)].	Filing required except for certain assignments that can be perfected by attachment (automatically on the creation of the security interest).
4. Deposit Accounts [UCC 9–104, 9–304, 9–312(b), 9–314(a)]	Any demand, time, savings, passbook, or similar account maintained with a bank [UCC 9–102(a)(29)].	Perfection by control, such as when the secured party is the bank in which the account is maintained or when the parties have agreed that the secured party can direct the disposition of funds in a particular account.
5. General Intangibles [UCC 9–301, 9–309(3), 9–310(a) and (b)(8)]	Any personal property (or debtor's obligation to make payments on such) other than that defined above [UCC 9–102(a)(42)], including software that is independent from a computer or other good [UCC 9–102(a)(44), (a)(61), and (a)(75)].	Filing only (for copyrights, with the U.S. Copyright Office), except a sale of a payment intangible by attachment (automatically on the creation of the security interest).

constitutes a filing [UCC 9–516(a)]. The word *communication* means that the filing can be accomplished electronically [UCC 9–102(a)(18)]. Once completed, filings are indexed in the name of the debtor so that they can be located by subsequent searchers. A financing statement may be filed even before a security agreement is made or a security interest attaches [UCC 9–502(d)].

The Debtor's Name The UCC requires that a financing statement be filed under the name of the debtor [UCC 9–502(a)(1)]. Slight variations in names normally will not be considered misleading if a search of the records, using a stan-

dard computer search engine routinely used by that filing office, would disclose the filings [UCC 9–506(c)].[4] If the debtor is identified by the correct name at the time the financing statement is filed, the secured party's interest retains its priority even if the debtor later changes his or her name. Because most states use electronic filing systems,

---

4. If the name listed in the financing statement is so inaccurate that a search using the standard search engine will not disclose the debtor's name, then it is deemed seriously misleading under UCC 9–506. This may also occur when a debtor changes names after the financing statement is filed. See also UCC 9–507, which governs the effectiveness of financing statements found to be seriously misleading.

UCC 9–503 sets out rules for determining when the debtor's name as it appears on a financing statement is sufficient.

Specific Types of Debtors. For corporations, which are organizations that have registered with the state, the debtor's name on the financing statement must be "the name of the debtor indicated on the public record of the debtor's jurisdiction of organization" [UCC 9–503(a)(1)]. If the debtor is a trust or a trustee with respect to property held in trust, the filed financing statement must disclose this information and must provide the trust's name as specified in its official documents [UCC 9–503(a)(3)]. For all others, the filed financing statement must disclose "the individual or organizational name of the debtor" [UCC 9–503(a)(4)(A)]. As used here, the word *organization* includes unincorporated associations, such as clubs and some churches, as well as joint ventures and general partnerships. If an organizational debtor does not have a group name, the names of the individuals in the group must be listed.

Trade Names. Providing only the debtor's trade name (or a fictitious name) in a financing statement is *not* sufficient for perfection [UCC 9–503(c)]. **■EXAMPLE 20.1** A loan is being made to a sole proprietorship owned by Peter Jones. The trade, or fictitious, name is Pete's Plumbing. A financing statement filed in the trade name Pete's Plumbing would not be sufficient because it does not identify Peter Jones as the debtor. The financing statement must be filed under the name of the actual debtor—in this instance, Peter Jones. ■ The reason for this rule is to ensure that the debtor's name on a financing statement is one that prospective lenders can locate and recognize in future searches.

 **PREVENTING LEGAL DISPUTES** **Debtors frequently change their trade names. This can make it difficult to find out whether the debtor's collateral is subject to a prior perfected security interest. Keep this in mind when extending credit to a customer. Find out if the prospective debtor has used any other names and include those former names when you search the records. When perfecting a security interest, make sure that the financing statement adequately notifies other potential creditors that a security interest exists. If a search using the debtor's correct name would disclose the interest, the filing generally is sufficient. Making sure that no other creditor has a prior interest in the property being used as collateral, and filing the financing statement under the correct name, are basic steps that can prevent disputes.**

Description of the Collateral The UCC requires that both the security agreement and the financing statement contain a description of the collateral in which the secured party has a security interest. The security agreement must describe the collateral because no security interest in goods can exist unless the parties agree on which goods are subject to the security interest. The financing statement must also describe the collateral because the purpose of filing the statement is to give public notice of the fact that certain goods of the debtor are subject to a security interest. Other parties who might later wish to lend funds to the debtor or buy the collateral can thus learn of the security interest by checking with the state or local office in which a financing statement for that type of collateral would be filed. For land-related security interests, a legal description of the realty is also required [UCC 9–502(b)].

Sometimes, the descriptions in the two documents vary, with the description in the security agreement being more precise than the description in the financing statement, which is allowed to be more general. **■EXAMPLE 20.2** A security agreement for a commercial loan to a manufacturer may list all of the manufacturer's equipment subject to the loan by serial number, whereas the financing statement may simply state "all equipment owned or hereafter acquired." ■ The UCC permits broad, general descriptions in the financing statement, such as "all assets" or "all personal property." Generally, whenever the description in a financing statement accurately describes the agreement between the secured party and the debtor, the description is sufficient [UCC 9–504].

Where to File In most states, a financing statement must be filed centrally in the appropriate state office, such as the office of the secretary of state, in the state where the debtor is located. Filing in the county where the collateral is located is required only when the collateral consists of timber to be cut, fixtures, or collateral to be extracted—such as oil, coal, gas, and minerals [UCC 9–301(3) and (4), 9–502(b)].

The state office in which a financing statement should be filed depends on the *debtor's location*, not the location of the collateral [UCC 9–301]. The debtor's location is determined as follows [UCC 9–307]:

1 For *individual debtors*, it is the state of the debtor's principal residence.

2 For an organization that is registered with the state, it is the state in which the organization is registered. For example, if a debtor is incorporated in Maryland and has its chief executive office in New York, a secured party would file the financing statement in Maryland because that is where the debtor's business is registered.

3 For all other entities, it is the state in which the business is located or, if the debtor has more than one office, the

place from which the debtor manages its business operations and affairs (its chief executive offices).

Consequences of an Improper Filing   Any improper filing renders the security interest unperfected and reduces the secured party's claim in bankruptcy to that of an unsecured creditor. For instance, if the debtor's name on the financing statement is seriously misleading or if the collateral is not sufficiently described in the financing statement, the filing may not be effective. The following case provides an illustration.

CASE 20.1   **Corona Fruits & Veggies, Inc. v. Frozsun Foods, Inc.**

Court of Appeal of California, Second District, 143 Cal.App.4th 319, 48 Cal.Rptr.3d 868 (2006).

FACTS   In July 2001, Corona Fruits & Veggies, Inc., and Corona Marketing Company sublet farmland in Santa Barbara County, California, to Armando Munoz Juarez, a strawberry farmer. The Corona companies also loaned funds to Juarez for payroll and production expenses. The sublease and other documents involved in the transaction set out Juarez's full name, but Juarez generally went by the name "Munoz" and signed the sublease "Armando Munoz." The Coronas filed UCC-1 financing statements that identified the debtor as "Armando Munoz." In December, Juarez contracted to sell strawberries to Frozsun Foods, Inc., which advanced funds secured by a financing statement that identified the debtor as "Armando Juarez." By the next July, Juarez owed the Coronas $230,482.52 and Frozsun $19,648.52. When Juarez did not repay the Coronas, they took possession of the farmland, harvested and sold the strawberries, and kept the proceeds. The Coronas and Frozsun filed a suit in a California state court against Juarez to collect the rest of his debt. The court ruled that Frozsun's interest took priority because only its financing statement was recorded properly. The Coronas appealed to a state intermediate appellate court.

ISSUE   Does a creditor fail to perfect a security interest if a financing statement lists a debtor's name incorrectly?

DECISION   Yes. The state intermediate appellate court affirmed the lower court's ruling. "Shakespeare asked, 'What's in a name?' We supply an answer * * * : Everything when the last name is true and nothing when the last name is false."

REASON   The appellate court recognized that "minor errors in a UCC financing statement do not affect the effectiveness of the financing statement." It is only when "errors render the document seriously misleading to other creditors" that the effectiveness of a statement is undercut. "When a creditor files a UCC-1 financing statement, the debtor's true last name is crucial because the financing statements are indexed by last names. A subsequent creditor who loans [funds] to a debtor with the same name is put on notice that its lien is secondary." In this case, Juarez's identification cards and tax returns stated his true, full name, and the Coronas identified him by this name in their contracts, business records, and checks, and even in their pleadings filed with the court. The Coronas could have used this name in their financing statements, too, to protect the priority of their security interests, but they did not. Frozsun searched the UCC records under the name "Juarez" and did not find the Coronas' statements. For these reasons, Frozsun's interest was superior.

 FOR CRITICAL ANALYSIS—Technological Consideration   *Under what circumstances might a financing statement be considered effective even if it does not identify the debtor correctly?*

■

Perfection without Filing

In two types of situations, security interests can be perfected without filing a financing statement. The first occurs when the collateral is transferred into the possession of the secured party. The second occurs when the security interest is one of a limited number (thirteen) under the UCC that can be perfected on attachment (without a filing and without having to possess the goods) [UCC 9–309]. The phrase *perfected on attachment* means that these security interests are automatically perfected at the time of their creation. Two of the more common security interests that are perfected on attachment are a *purchase-money security interest* in consumer goods (defined and explained below) and an assignment of a beneficial interest in a decedent's estate [UCC 9–309(1), (13)].

Perfection by Possession In the past, one of the most common means of obtaining financing was to **pledge** certain collateral as security for the debt and transfer the collateral into the creditor's possession. When the debt was paid, the collateral was returned to the debtor. Although the debtor usually entered into a written security agreement, an oral security agreement was also enforceable as long as the secured party possessed the collateral. Article 9 of the UCC retained the common law pledge and the principle that the security agreement need not be in writing to be enforceable if the collateral is transferred to the secured party [UCC 9–310, 9–312(b), 9–313].

For most collateral, possession by the secured party is impractical because it denies the debtor the right to use or derive income from the property to pay off the debt. **■EXAMPLE 20.3** A farmer takes out a loan to finance the purchase of a piece of heavy farm equipment needed to harvest crops and uses the equipment as collateral. Clearly, the purpose of the purchase would be defeated if the farmer transferred the collateral into the creditor's possession. ■ Certain items, however, such as stocks, bonds, negotiable instruments, and jewelry, are commonly transferred into the creditor's possession when they are used as collateral for loans.

Perfection by Attachment Under the UCC, thirteen types of security interests are perfected automatically at the time they are created [UCC 9–309]. The most common of these is the **purchase-money security interest (PMSI)** in consumer goods (items bought primarily for personal, family, or household purposes). A PMSI in consumer goods is created when a person buys goods and the seller or lender agrees to extend credit for part or all of the purchase price of the goods. The entity that extends the credit and obtains the PMSI can be either the seller (a store, for example) or a financial institution that lends the buyer the funds with which to purchase the goods [UCC 9–102(a)(2)].

Automatic Perfection. A PMSI in consumer goods is perfected automatically at the time of a credit sale—that is, at the time the PMSI is created. The seller need do nothing more to perfect her or his interest. **■EXAMPLE 20.4** Jamie wants to purchase a new television from Link Television, Inc. The purchase price is $2,500. Not being able to pay the entire amount in cash, Jamie signs a purchase agreement to pay $1,000 down and $100 per month until the balance plus interest is fully paid. Link is to retain a security interest in the purchased goods until full payment has been made. Because the security interest was created as part of the purchase agreement, it is a PMSI in consumer goods. Link does not need to do anything else to perfect its security interest. ■

Exceptions to the Rule of Automatic Perfection. There are exceptions to the rule of automatic perfection. First, certain types of security interests that are subject to other federal or state laws may require additional steps to be perfected [UCC 9–311]. For example, most states have certificate-of-title statutes that establish perfection requirements for specific goods, such as automobiles, trailers, boats, mobile homes, and farm tractors. If a consumer in these jurisdictions purchases a boat, for example, the secured party will need to file a certificate of title with the appropriate state official to perfect the PMSI. A second exception involves PMSIs in nonconsumer goods, such as livestock or a business's inventory, which are not automatically perfected (these types of PMSIs will be discussed later in this chapter in the context of priorities).

Effective Time Duration of Perfection

A financing statement is effective for five years from the date of filing [UCC 9–515]. If a **continuation statement** is filed within six months *prior to* the expiration date, the effectiveness of the original statement is continued for another five years, starting with the expiration date of the first five-year period [UCC 9–515(d), (e)]. The effectiveness of the statement can be continued in the same manner indefinitely. Any attempt to file a continuation statement outside the six-month window will render the continuation ineffective, and the perfection will lapse at the end of the five-year period.

If a financing statement lapses, the security interest that had been perfected by the filing now becomes unperfected. A purchaser for value can acquire the collateral as if the security interest had never been perfected as against a purchaser for value [UCC 9–515(c)].

THE SCOPE OF A SECURITY INTEREST

In addition to covering collateral already in the debtor's possession, a security agreement can cover various other types of property, including the proceeds of the sale of collateral, after-acquired property, and future advances.

Proceeds

Proceeds are whatever cash or property is received when collateral is sold or disposed of in some other way [UCC 9–102(a)(64)]. A security interest in the collateral gives the secured party a security interest in the proceeds acquired from the sale of that collateral. **■EXAMPLE 20.5** A bank has a perfected security interest in the inventory of a retail seller of heavy farm machinery. The retailer sells a tractor out of this inventory to a farmer, who is by definition a *buyer in the* *ordinary course of business* (this term will be discussed later in the chapter). The farmer agrees, in a security agreement, to make monthly payments to the retailer for a period of twenty-four months. If the retailer goes into default on the loan from the bank, the bank is entitled to the remaining payments the farmer owes to the retailer as proceeds. ▪

A security interest in proceeds perfects automatically on the *perfection* of the secured party's security interest in the original collateral and remains perfected for twenty days after the debtor receives the proceeds. One way to extend the twenty-day automatic perfection period is to provide for such extended coverage in the original security agreement [UCC 9–315(c), (d)]. This is typically done when the collateral is the type that is likely to be sold, such as a retailer's inventory—for example, of computers or DVD players. The UCC also permits a security interest in identifiable cash proceeds to remain perfected after twenty days [UCC 9–315(d)(2)].

After-Acquired Property

After-acquired property is property that the debtor acquired after the execution of the security agreement. The security agreement may provide for a security interest in after-acquired property [UCC 9–204(1)]. This is particularly useful for inventory financing arrangements because a secured party whose security interest is in existing inventory knows that the debtor will sell that inventory, thereby reducing the collateral subject to the security interest.

Generally, the debtor will purchase new inventory to replace the inventory sold. The secured party wants this newly acquired inventory to be subject to the original security interest. Thus, the after-acquired property clause continues the secured party's claim to any inventory acquired thereafter. (This is not to say that the original security interest will take priority over the rights of all other creditors with regard to this after-acquired inventory, as will be discussed later.)

▪**EXAMPLE 20.6** Amato buys factory equipment from Bronson on credit, giving as security an interest in all of her equipment—both what she is buying and what she already owns. The security interest with Bronson contains an after-acquired property clause. Six months later, Amato pays cash to another seller of factory equipment for more equipment. Six months after that, Amato goes out of business before she has paid off her debt to Bronson. Bronson has a security interest in all of Amato's equipment, even the equipment bought from the other seller. ▪

Future Advances

Often, a debtor will arrange with a bank to have a *continuing line of credit* under which the debtor can borrow funds intermittently. Advances against lines of credit can be sub-

ject to a properly perfected security interest in certain collateral. The security agreement may provide that any future advances made against that line of credit are also subject to the security interest in the same collateral [UCC 9–204(c)]. Future advances do not have to be of the same type or otherwise related to the original advance to benefit from this type of **cross-collateralization.**[5] Cross-collateralization occurs when an asset that is not the subject of a loan is used to secure that loan.

▪**EXAMPLE 20.7** Stroh is the owner of a small manufacturing plant with equipment valued at $1 million. He has an immediate need for $50,000 of working capital, so he obtains a loan from Midwestern Bank and signs a security agreement, putting up all of his equipment as security. The bank properly perfects its security interest. The security agreement provides that Stroh can borrow up to $500,000 in the future, using the same equipment as collateral for any future advances. In this situation, Midwestern Bank does not have to execute a new security agreement and perfect a security interest in the collateral each time an advance is made, up to a cumulative total of $500,000. For priority purposes, each advance is perfected as of the date of the *original* perfection. ▪

The Floating-Lien Concept

A security agreement that provides for a security interest in proceeds, in after-acquired property, or in collateral subject to future advances by the secured party (or in all three) is often characterized as a **floating lien.** This type of security interest continues in the collateral or proceeds even if the collateral is sold, exchanged, or disposed of in some other way.

A Floating Lien in Inventory Floating liens commonly arise in the financing of inventories. A creditor is not interested in specific pieces of inventory, which are constantly changing, so the lien "floats" from one item to another, as the inventory changes.

▪**EXAMPLE 20.8** Cascade Sports, Inc., is an Oregon corporation that operates as a cross-country ski dealer and has a line of credit with Portland First Bank to finance its inventory of cross-country skis. Cascade and Portland First enter into a security agreement that provides for coverage of proceeds, after-acquired inventory, present inventory, and future advances. Portland First perfects its security interest in the inventory by filing centrally with the office of the secretary of state in Oregon. One day, Cascade sells a new pair of the latest cross-country skis and receives a used pair in trade. That same day, Cascade purchases two new pairs of cross-country skis from a local manufacturer for cash. Later that day, to

5. See official Comment 5 to UCC 9–204.

meet its payroll, Cascade borrows $8,000 from Portland First Bank under the security agreement.

Portland First gets a perfected security interest in the used pair of skis under the proceeds clause, has a perfected security interest in the two new pairs of skis purchased from the local manufacturer under the after-acquired property clause, and has the new amount of funds advanced to Cascade secured on all of the above collateral by the future-advances clause. All of this is accomplished under the original perfected security interest. The various items in the inventory have changed, but Portland First still has a perfected security interest in Cascade's inventory. Hence, it has a floating lien on the inventory. ■

A Floating Lien in a Shifting Stock of Goods The concept of the floating lien can also apply to a shifting stock of goods. The lien can start with raw materials; follow them as they become finished goods and inventories; and continue as the goods are sold and are turned into accounts receivable, chattel paper, or cash.

PRIORITIES

When more than one party claims an interest in the same collateral, which has priority? The UCC sets out detailed rules to answer this question. Although in many situations the party who has a perfected security interest will have priority, there are exceptions that give priority rights to another party, such as a buyer in the ordinary course of business.

General Rules of Priority

The basic rule is that when more than one security interest has been perfected in the same collateral, the first security interest to be perfected (or filed) has priority over any security interests that are perfected later. If only one of the conflicting security interests has been perfected, then that security interest has priority. If none of the security interests have been perfected, then the first security interest that attaches has priority. The UCC's rules of priority can be summarized as follows:

1 A *perfected security interest has priority over unsecured creditors and unperfected security interests.* When two or more parties have claims to the same collateral, a perfected secured party's interest has priority over the interests of most other parties [UCC 9–322(a)(2)]. This includes priority to the proceeds from a sale of collateral resulting from a bankruptcy (giving the perfected secured party rights superior to those of the bankruptcy trustee as will be discussed in Chapter 21).

2 *Conflicting perfected security interests.* When two or more secured parties have perfected security interests in the same collateral, generally the first to perfect (by filing or taking possession of the collateral) has priority [UCC 9–322(a)(1)].

3 *Conflicting unperfected security interests.* When two conflicting security interests are unperfected, the first to attach (be created) has priority [UCC 9–322(a)(3)]. This is sometimes called the "first-in-time" rule.

Exceptions to the General Rule

Under some circumstances, on the debtor's default, the perfection of a security interest will not protect a secured party against certain other third parties having claims to the collateral. For example, the UCC provides that in some instances a PMSI, properly perfected,[6] will prevail over another security interest in after-acquired collateral, even though the other was perfected first. We discuss several significant exceptions to the general rules of priority in the following subsections.

Buyers in the Ordinary Course of Business Under the UCC, a person who buys "in the ordinary course of business" takes the goods free from any security interest created by the seller *even if the security interest is perfected and the buyer knows of its existence* [UCC 9–320(a)]. In other words, a buyer in the ordinary course will have priority even if a previously perfected security interest exists as to the goods. The rationale for this rule is obvious: if buyers could not obtain the goods free and clear of any security interest the merchant had created, for example, in inventory, the unfettered flow of goods in the marketplace would be hindered. Note that the buyer can know about the existence of a perfected security interest, so long as he or she does not know that buying the goods violates the rights of any third party.

The UCC defines a *buyer in the ordinary course of business* as any person who in good faith, and without knowledge that the sale violates the rights of another in the goods, buys in ordinary course from a person in the business of selling goods of that kind [UCC 1–201(9)]. ■**EXAMPLE 20.9** On August 1, West Bank perfects a security interest in all of Best Television's existing inventory and any inventory thereafter acquired. On September 1, Carla, a student at Central University, purchases one of the television sets in Best's inventory. If, on December 1, Best goes into default, can West Bank repossess the television set sold to Carla? The

---

6. Recall that, with some exceptions (such as motor vehicles), a PMSI in *consumer goods* is automatically perfected—no filing is necessary. A PMSI that is *not* in consumer goods must still be perfected, however.

answer is no, because Carla is a buyer in the ordinary course of business (Best is in the business of selling goods of that kind) and takes the television free and clear of West Bank's perfected security interest. This is true even if Carla knew that West Bank had a security interest in Best's inventory when she purchased the TV. ■

PMSI in Goods Other Than Inventory and Livestock An important exception to the first-in-time rule involves certain types of collateral, such as equipment, that is not inventory (or livestock) and in which one of the secured parties has a perfected PMSI [UCC 9–324(a)]. **■EXAMPLE 20.10** Sandoval borrows funds from West Bank, signing a security agreement in which she puts up all of her present and after-acquired equipment as security. On May 1, West Bank perfects this security interest (which is not a PMSI). On July 1, Sandoval purchases a new piece of equipment from Zylex Company on credit, signing a security agreement. The delivery date for the new equipment is August 1.

Zylex thus has a PMSI in the new equipment (that is not part of its inventory), but the PMSI is not in consumer goods and thus is not automatically perfected. If Sandoval defaults on her payments to both West Bank and Zylex, which of them has priority with regard to the new piece of equipment? Generally, West Bank would have priority because its interest perfected first in time. In this situation, however, Zylex has a PMSI, and provided that Zylex perfected its interest in the equipment within twenty days after Sandoval took possession on August 1, Zylex has priority. ■

PMSI in Inventory Another important exception to the first-in-time rule has to do with security interests in inventory [UCC 9–324(b)]. **■EXAMPLE 20.11** On May 1, SNS Television borrows funds from West Bank. SNS signs a security agreement, putting up all of its present inventory and any inventory thereafter acquired as collateral. West Bank perfects its interest (not a PMSI) on that date. On June 10, SNS buys new inventory from Martin, Inc., a manufacturer, to use for its Fourth of July sale. SNS makes a down payment for the new inventory and signs a security agreement giving Martin a PMSI in the new inventory as collateral for the remaining debt. Martin delivers the inventory to SNS on June 28. Because of a hurricane in the area, SNS's Fourth of July sale is a disaster, and most of its inventory remains unsold. In August, SNS defaults on its payments to both West Bank and Martin.

Does West Bank or Martin have priority with respect to the new inventory delivered to SNS on June 28? If Martin has not perfected its security interest by June 28, West Bank's after-acquired collateral clause has priority because it was the first to be perfected. If, however, Martin has perfected and

gives proper notice of its security interest to West Bank before SNS takes possession of the goods on June 28, Martin has priority. ■

Buyers of the Collateral The UCC recognizes that there are certain types of buyers whose interest in purchased goods could conflict with those of a perfected secured party on the debtor's default. These include buyers in the ordinary course of business (as discussed), as well as buyers of farm products, instruments, documents, or securities. The UCC sets down special rules of priority for these types of buyers. Exhibit 20–3 on the following page describes the various rules regarding the priority of claims to a debtor's collateral.

RIGHTS AND DUTIES OF DEBTORS AND CREDITORS

The security agreement itself determines most of the rights and duties of the debtor and the secured party. The UCC, however, imposes some rights and duties that are applicable in the absence of a valid security agreement that states the contrary.

Information Requests

Under UCC 9–523(a), a secured party has the option, when making the filing, of furnishing a *copy* of the financing statement being filed to the filing officer and requesting that the filing officer make a note of the file number, the date, and the hour of the original filing on the copy. The filing officer must send this copy to the person designated by the secured party or to the debtor, if the debtor makes the request. Under UCC 9–523(c) and (d), a filing officer must also give information to a person who is contemplating obtaining a security interest from a prospective debtor. The filing officer must issue a certificate that provides information on possible perfected financing statements with respect to the named debtor. The filing officer will charge a fee for the certification and for any information copies provided [UCC 9–525(d)].

Release, Assignment, and Amendment

A secured party can release all or part of any collateral described in the financing statement, thereby terminating its security interest in that collateral. The release is recorded by filing a uniform amendment form [UCC 9–512, 9–521(b)]. A secured party can also assign all or part of the security interest to a third party (the assignee). The assignee becomes the secured party of record if the assignment is filed by use of a uniform amendment form [UCC 9–514, 9–521(a)].

EXHIBIT 20–3 Priority of Claims to a Debtor's Collateral

PARTIES	PRIORITY
Perfected Secured Party versus Unsecured Parties/ Creditors	A perfected secured party's interest has priority over the interests of most other parties, including unsecured creditors, unperfected secured parties, subsequent lien creditors, trustees in bankruptcy, and buyers who do not purchase the collateral in the ordinary course of business.
Perfected Secured Party versus Perfected Secured Party	Between two perfected secured parties in the same collateral, the general rule is that the first in time of perfection is the first in right to the collateral [UCC 9–322(a)(1)].
Perfected Secured Party versus Perfected PMSI	A PMSI, even if second in time of perfection, has priority providing that the following conditions are met: 1. *Other collateral*–A PMSI has priority, providing it is perfected within twenty days after the debtor takes possession [UCC 9–324(a)]. 2. *Inventory*–A PMSI has priority if it is perfected and proper written or authenticated notice is given to the other security-interest holder *on* or *before* the time the debtor takes possession [UCC 9–324(b)]. 3. *Software*–Applies to a PMSI in software only if used in goods subject to a PMSI. If the goods are inventory, priority is determined the same as for inventory; if they are not, priority is determined as for goods other than inventory [UCC 9–103(c), 9–324(f)].

Perfected Secured Party versus Purchaser of Debtor's Collateral	1. *Buyer of goods in the ordinary course of the seller's business*–Buyer prevails over a secured party's security interest, even if perfected and even if the buyer knows of the security interest [UCC 9–320(a)].
	2. *Buyer of consumer goods purchased outside the ordinary course of business*–Buyer prevails over a secured party's interest, even if perfected by attachment, providing the buyer purchased as follows:
	  a. For value.
	  b. Without actual knowledge of the security interest.
	  c. For use as a consumer good.
	  d. Prior to the secured party's perfection by *filing* [UCC 9–320(b)].
	3. *Buyer of chattel paper*–Buyer prevails if the buyer:
	  a. Gave new value in making the purchase.
	  b. Took possession in the ordinary course of the buyer's business.
	  c. Took without knowledge of the security interest [UCC 9–330].
	4. *Buyer of instruments, documents, or securities*–Buyer who is a holder in due course, a holder to whom negotiable documents have been duly negotiated, or a bona fide purchaser of securities has priority over a previously perfected security interest [UCC 9–330(d), 9–331(a)].
	5. *Buyer of farm products*–Buyer from a farmer takes free and clear of perfected security interests unless, where permitted, a secured party files centrally an effective financing statement (EFS) or the buyer receives proper notice of the security interest before the sale.

Unperfected Secured Party versus Unsecured Creditor	An unperfected secured party prevails over unsecured creditors and creditors who have obtained judgments against the debtor but who have not begun the legal process to collect on those judgments [UCC 9–201(a)].

If the debtor and the secured party agree, they can amend the financing statement—by adding new collateral if authorized by the debtor, for example—by filing a uniform amendment form that indicates the file number of the initial financing statement [UCC 9–512(a)]. The amendment does not extend the time period of perfection, but if collateral is added, the perfection date (for priority purposes) for the new collateral begins on the date the amendment is filed [UCC 9–512(b), (c)].

Confirmation or Accounting Request by Debtor

If the debtor believes that the amount of the unpaid debt or the listing of the collateral subject to the security interest is inaccurate, the debtor has the right to request a confirmation of his or her view of the unpaid debt or listing of collateral. The secured party must either approve or correct this confirmation request [UCC 9–210].

The secured party must comply with the debtor's confirmation request by authenticating and sending to the debtor an accounting within fourteen days after the request is received. Otherwise, the secured party will be held liable for any loss suffered by the debtor, plus $500 [UCC 9–210, 9–625(f)]. The debtor is entitled to one request without charge every six months. For any additional requests, the secured party is entitled to be paid a statutory fee of up to $25 per request [UCC 9–210(f)].

Termination Statement

When the debtor has fully paid the debt, if the secured party perfected the security interest by filing, the debtor is entitled to have a termination statement filed. Such a statement demonstrates to the public that the filed perfected security interest has been terminated [UCC 9–513].

Whenever consumer goods are involved, the secured party *must* file a termination statement (or, alternatively, a release) within one month of the final payment or within twenty days of receiving the debtor's authenticated demand, whichever is earlier [UCC 9–513(b)]. When the collateral is other than consumer goods, on an authenticated demand by the debtor, the secured party must either send a termination statement to the debtor or file such a statement within twenty days [UCC 9–513(c)]. Otherwise, the secured party is not required to file or send a termination statement. Whenever a secured party fails to file or send the termination statement as requested, the debtor can recover $500 plus any additional loss suffered [UCC 9–625(e)(4), (f)].

DEFAULT

Article 9 defines the rights, duties, and remedies of the secured party and of the debtor on the debtor's default. Should the secured party fail to comply with her or his duties, the debtor is afforded particular rights and remedies.

The topic of default is one of great concern to secured lenders and to the lawyers who draft security agreements. What constitutes default is not always clear. In fact, Article 9 does not define the term. Consequently, parties are encouraged in practice—and by the UCC—to include in their security agreements certain standards to be applied in determining when default has actually occurred. In so doing, the parties can stipulate the conditions that will constitute a default [UCC 9–601, 9–603]. Often, these critical terms are shaped by the creditor in an attempt to provide the maximum protection possible. The ultimate terms, however, are not allowed to go beyond the limitations imposed by the good faith requirement and the unconscionability provisions of the UCC.

Any breach of the terms of the security agreement can constitute default. Nevertheless, default occurs most commonly when the debtor fails to meet the scheduled payments that the parties have agreed on or when the debtor becomes bankrupt.

Basic Remedies

The rights and remedies under UCC 9–601(a),(b) are *cumulative* [UCC 9–601(c)]. Therefore, if a creditor is unsuccessful in enforcing rights by one method, he or she can pursue another method. Generally, a secured party's remedies can be divided into the two basic categories discussed next.

Repossession of the Collateral On the debtor's default, a secured party can take peaceful possession of the collateral without the use of judicial process [UCC 9–609(b)]. This provision is often referred to as the "self-help" provision of Article 9. The UCC does not define *peaceful possession*, however. The general rule is that the collateral has been taken peacefully if the secured party can take possession without committing (1) trespass onto land, (2) assault and/or battery, or (3) breaking and entering. On taking possession, the secured party may either retain the collateral for satisfaction of the debt [UCC 9–620] or resell the goods and apply the proceeds toward the debt [UCC 9–610].

Judicial Remedies Alternatively, a secured party can relinquish the security interest and use any judicial remedy available, such as obtaining a judgment on the underlying debt, followed by execution and levy. (**Execution** is the implementation of a court's decree or judgment. **Levy** is the obtaining of funds by legal process through the seizure and sale of non-secured property, usually done after a writ of execution has been issued.) Execution and levy are rarely undertaken unless the collateral is no longer in existence or has declined so much in value that it is worth substantially less than the amount of the debt and the debtor has other assets available that may be legally seized to satisfy the debt [UCC 9–601(a)].[7]

If a customer finances a purchase through a bank loan, returns the item, and refuses to make the loan payments, what are the rights of the secured party (the bank)? That was one of the issues in the following case.

7. Some assets are exempt from creditors' claims—see Chapter 21.

CASE 20.2 | **First National Bank of Litchfield v. Miller**

Supreme Court of Connecticut, 285 Conn. 294, 939 A.2d 572 (2008).

FACTS The Millers wanted to buy a boat from Norwest Marine, so they made a deposit and signed a form contract. Title and ownership would pass when the Millers made full payment, although delivery would occur earlier. The agreement stated that the Millers had inspected and accepted the boat and that the document constituted the entire agreement between the parties. The Millers needed financing and contacted First National Bank of Litchfield to begin the loan process. The Millers signed a loan agreement with the bank, which sent Norwest full payment for the boat. When the Millers took delivery of the boat, it did not run properly, so they returned it to Norwest for repairs. After the repairs were completed, the Millers refused to accept the boat, claiming that it was not satisfactory. They told the bank that they did not want the boat, and they stopped making loan payments. The bank sued, contending that the Millers had breached the retail contract by refusing to make monthly payments. The Millers filed claims against the bank and Norwest asserting that they had committed fraud. The trial court held for the bank, awarding it the full amount owed under the loan contract, plus attorneys' fees. The Millers appealed, and the appellate court reversed and remanded. The case was certified to the state's highest court for review.

ISSUE Were the Millers released from making loan payments on the boat they had purchased because they had returned it to the seller?

DECISION No. The state supreme court reinstated the verdict of the trial court, holding that the Millers had accepted delivery of the boat under the UCC and were required to pay under the financing agreement.

REASON The court noted that the Millers had signed a purchase agreement that stated they had inspected the boat and were satisfied with it. Additionally, they had signed a retail installment contract with the bank stating that they had already accepted delivery of the boat, and it was registered in their names. Norwest acted in good faith by performing warranty repair work on the boat that solved the mechanical problem. Norwest also installed some equipment on the boat specifically requested by the Millers. The Millers could not claim they had never taken delivery of the boat, and they were therefore responsible for the loan they had accepted.

 FOR CRITICAL ANALYSIS—Legal Consideration *How could Norwest and the bank have avoided the problem that arose in this case?*

Disposition of Collateral

Once default has occurred and the secured party has obtained possession of the collateral, the secured party may either retain the collateral in full satisfaction of the debt or sell, lease, or otherwise dispose of the collateral in any commercially reasonable manner and apply the proceeds toward satisfaction of the debt [UCC 9–602(7), 9–603, 9–610(a), 9–620]. Any sale is always subject to procedures established by state law.

Retention of Collateral by the Secured Party The UCC acknowledges that parties are sometimes better off if they do not sell the collateral. Therefore, a secured party may retain the collateral unless it consists of consumer goods and the debtor has paid 60 percent or more of the purchase price in a PMSI or debt in a non-PMSI—as will be discussed shortly [UCC 9–620(e)].

This general right, however, is subject to several conditions. The secured party must send notice of the proposal to the debtor if the debtor has not signed a statement renouncing or modifying her or his rights *after default* [UCC 9–620(a), 9–621]. If the collateral is consumer goods, the secured party does not need to give any other notice. In all other situations, the secured party must send notice to any other secured party from whom the secured party has received written or authenticated notice of a claim of interest in the collateral in question. The secured party must also send notice to any other **junior lienholder** (one holding a lien that is subordinate to one or more other liens on the same property) who has filed a statutory lien (such as a *mechanic's lien*—see Chapter 21) or a security interest in the collateral ten days before the debtor consented to the retention [UCC 9–621].

If, within twenty days after the notice is sent, the secured party receives an objection sent by a person entitled to receive notification, the secured party must sell or otherwise dispose of the collateral. The collateral must be disposed of in accordance with the provisions of UCC 9–602, 9–603, 9–610, and 9–613 (disposition procedures will be discussed shortly). If no such written objection is forthcoming, the secured party may retain the collateral in full or partial satisfaction of the debtor's obligation [UCC 9–620(a), 9–621].

Consumer Goods When the collateral is consumer goods and the debtor has paid 60 percent or more of the purchase price on a PMSI or 60 percent of the debt on a non-PMSI, the secured party must sell or otherwise dispose of the repossessed collateral within ninety days [UCC 9–620(e), (f)]. Failure to comply opens the secured party to an action for conversion or other liability under UCC 9–625(b) and (c) unless the consumer-debtor signed a written statement *after default* renouncing or modifying the right to demand the sale of the goods [UCC 9–624].

Disposition Procedures A secured party who does not choose to retain the collateral or who is required to sell it must resort to the disposition procedures prescribed under UCC 9–602(7), 9–603, 9–610(a), and 9–613. The UCC allows a great deal of flexibility with regard to disposition. UCC 9–610(a) states that after default, a secured party may sell, lease, license, or otherwise dispose of any or all of the collateral in its present condition or following any commercially reasonable preparation or processing. The secured party may purchase the collateral at a public sale, but not at a private sale—unless the collateral is of a kind customarily sold on a recognized market or is the subject of widely distributed standard price quotations [UCC 9–610(c)].

One of the major limitations on the disposition of the collateral is that it must be accomplished in a commercially reasonable manner. UCC 9–610(b) states as follows:

> Every aspect of a disposition of collateral, including the method, manner, time, place, and other terms, must be commercially reasonable. If commercially reasonable, a secured party may dispose of collateral by public or private proceedings, by one or more contracts, as a unit or in parcels, and at any time and place and on any terms.

Whenever the secured party fails to conduct a disposition in a commercially reasonable manner or to give proper notice, the deficiency of the debtor is reduced to the extent that such failure affected the price received at the disposition [UCC 9–626(a)(3)].

Unless the collateral is perishable or will decline rapidly in value or is a type customarily sold on a recognized market, a secured party must send to the debtor and other identified persons "a reasonable authenticated notification of disposition" [UCC 9–611(b), (c)]. The debtor may waive the right to receive this notice, but only after default [UCC 9–624(a)].

Proceeds from the Disposition Proceeds from the disposition of collateral after default on the underlying debt are distributed in the following order:

1 Expenses incurred by the secured party in repossessing, storing, and reselling the collateral.
2 Balance of the debt owed to the secured party.
3 Junior lienholders who have made written or authenticated demands.
4 Unless the collateral consists of accounts, payment intangibles, promissory notes, or chattel paper, any surplus goes to the debtor [UCC 9–608(a); 9–615(a), (e)].

Noncash Proceeds Whenever the secured party receives noncash proceeds from the disposition of collateral after default, the secured party must make a value determination and apply this value in a commercially reasonable manner [UCC 9–608(a)(3), 9–615(c)].

Deficiency Judgment Often, after proper disposition of the collateral, the secured party has not collected all that the debtor still owes. Unless otherwise agreed, the debtor is liable for any deficiency, and the creditor can obtain a **deficiency judgment** from a court to collect the deficiency. Note, however, that if the underlying transaction was, for example, a sale of accounts or of chattel paper, the debtor is entitled to any surplus or is liable for any deficiency only if the security agreement so provides [UCC 9–615(d), (e)].

Redemption Rights At any time before the secured party disposes of the collateral or enters into a contract for its disposition, or before the debtor's obligation has been discharged through the secured party's retention of the collateral, the debtor or any other secured party can exercise the right of *redemption* of the collateral. The debtor or other secured party can do this by tendering performance of all obligations secured by the collateral and by paying the expenses reasonably incurred by the secured party in retaking and maintaining the collateral [UCC 9–623].

REVIEWING Security Interests in Personal Property

Paul Barton owned a small property-management company, doing business as Brighton Homes. In October, Barton went on a spending spree. First, he bought a Bose surround-sound system for his home from KDM Electronics. The next day, he purchased a Wilderness Systems kayak from Outdoor Outfitters, and the day after that he bought a new Toyota 4-Runner financed through Bridgeport Auto. Two weeks later, Barton purchased six new iMac computers for his office, also from KDM Electronics. Barton bought each of these items under installment sales contracts. Six months later, Barton's property-management business was failing, and he could not make the payments due on any of these purchases and thus defaulted on the loans. Using the information presented in the chapter, answer the following questions.

1 For which of Barton's purchases (the surround-sound system, the kayak, the 4-Runner, and the six iMacs) would the creditor need to file a financing statement to perfect its security interest?

2 Suppose that Barton's contract for the office computers mentioned only the name *Brighton Homes.* What would be the consequences if KDM Electronics filed a financing statement that listed only Brighton Homes as the debtor's name?

3 Which of these purchases would qualify as a PMSI in consumer goods?

4 Suppose that after KDM Electronics repossesses the surround-sound system, it decides to keep the system rather than sell it. Can KDM do this under Article 9? Why or why not?

TERMS AND CONCEPTS

after-acquired property 405
attachment 399
collateral 399
continuation statement 404
cross-collateralization 405
debtor 398
default 399
deficiency judgment 411

execution 409
financing statement 399
floating lien 405
junior lienholder 410
levy 409
perfection 400
pledge 404
proceeds 404

purchase-money security
   interest (PMSI) 404
secured party 398
secured transaction 398
security agreement 399
security interest 398

CHAPTER SUMMARY Security Interests in Personal Property

Creating a Security Interest (See pages 399–400.)	1. Unless the creditor has possession of the collateral, there must be a written or authenticated security agreement that is signed or authenticated by the debtor and describes the collateral subject to the security interest.
	2. The secured party must give value to the debtor.
	3. The debtor must have rights in the collateral—some ownership interest in or right to obtain possession of the specified collateral.
Perfecting a Security Interest (See pages 400–404.)	1. *Perfection by filing*—The most common method of perfection is by filing a financing statement containing the names of the secured party and the debtor and indicating the collateral covered by the financing statement.
	a. Communication of the financing statement to the appropriate filing office, together with the correct filing fee, constitutes a filing.
	b. The financing statement must be filed under the name of the debtor; fictitious (trade) names normally are not accepted.
	c. The classification of collateral determines whether filing is necessary and, if it is, where to file (see Exhibit 20–2 on pages 400 and 401).

CHAPTER SUMMARY	Security Interests in Personal Property–Continued

Perfecting a Security Interest– Continued	2. *Perfection without filing*—
	
	  a. By transfer of collateral—The debtor can transfer possession of the collateral to the secured party. A *pledge* is an example of this type of transfer.
	  b. By attachment, such as the attachment of a purchase-money security interest (PMSI) in consumer goods—If the secured party has a PMSI in consumer goods (goods bought or used by the debtor for personal, family, or household purposes), the secured party's security interest is perfected automatically.

The Scope of a Security Interest (See pages 404–406.)	A security agreement can cover the following types of property: 1. *Collateral in the present possession or control of the debtor.* 2. *Proceeds from a sale, exchange, or disposition of secured collateral.* 3. *After-acquired property*—A security agreement may provide that property acquired after the execution of the security agreement will also be secured by the agreement. This provision often accompanies security agreements covering a debtor's inventory. 4. *Future advances*—A security agreement may provide that any future advances made against a line of credit will be subject to the initial security interest in the same collateral.
Priorities (See pages 406–407.)	See Exhibit 20–3 on page 408.
Rights and Duties of Debtors and Creditors (See pages 407–409.)	1. *Information request*—On request by any person, the filing officer must send a statement listing the file number, the date, and the hour of the filing of financing statements and other documents covering collateral of a particular debtor; a fee is charged. 2. *Release, assignment, and amendment*—A secured party may (a) release part or all of the collateral described in a filed financing statement, (b) assign part or all of the security interest to another party, and (c) amend a filed financing statement. 3. *Confirmation or accounting request by debtor*—The debtor has the right to request a confirmation of his or her view of the unpaid debt or listing of collateral. The secured party must authenticate and send to the debtor an accounting within fourteen days after the request is received. 4. *Termination statement*—When a debt is paid, the secured party generally must send a termination statement to the debtor or file such a statement. Failure to comply results in the secured party's liability to the debtor for $500, plus any loss suffered by the debtor.

Default (See pages 409–411.)	On the debtor's default, the secured party may do either of the following:
	
	1. Take possession (peacefully or by court order) of the collateral covered by the security agreement and then pursue one of two alternatives:
	
	  a. Retain the collateral (unless the secured party has a PMSI in consumer goods and the debtor has paid 60 percent or more of the selling price or loan). The secured party may be required to give notice to the debtor and to other secured parties with interests in the collateral.
	
	  b. Dispose of the collateral in accordance with the requirements of UCC 9–602(7), 9–603, 9–610(a), and 9–613. The disposition must be carried out in a commercially reasonable manner; unless the collateral is perishable, notice of the disposition must be given to the debtor and other identified persons. The proceeds are applied in the following order:
	
	    (1) Expenses incurred by the secured party in repossessing, storing, and reselling the collateral.
	    (2) The balance of the debt owed to the secured party.

(Continued)

CHAPTER SUMMARY Security Interests in Personal Property–Continued

Default–Continued	(3) Junior lienholders who have made written or authenticated demands. (4) Surplus to the debtor (unless the collateral consists of accounts, payment intangibles, promissory notes, or chattel paper). 2. Relinquish the security interest and use any judicial remedy available, such as proceeding to judgment on the underlying debt, followed by execution and levy on the nonexempt assets of the debtor.

FOR REVIEW

Answers for the even-numbered questions in this **For Review** *section can be found on this text's accompanying Web site at* **www.cengage.com/blaw/fbl**. *Select "Chapter 20" and click on "For Review."*

1 What is a security interest? Who is a secured party? What is a security agreement? What is a financing statement?

2 What three requirements must be met to create an enforceable security interest?

3 What is the most common method of perfecting a security interest under Article 9?

4 If two secured parties have perfected security interests in the collateral of the debtor, which party has priority to the collateral on the debtor's default?

5 What rights does a secured creditor have on the debtor's default?

QUESTIONS AND CASE PROBLEMS

HYPOTHETICAL SCENARIOS AND CASE PROBLEMS

20.1 Priority Disputes. Redford is a seller of electric generators. He purchases a large quantity of generators from a manufacturer, Mallon Corp., by making a down payment and signing an agreement to pay the balance over a period of time. The agreement gives Mallon Corp. a security interest in the generators and the proceeds. Mallon Corp. properly files a financing statement on its security interest. Redford receives the generators and immediately sells one of them to Garfield on an installment contract with payment to be made in twelve equal installments. At the time of the sale, Garfield knows of Mallon's security interest. Two months later, Redford goes into default on his payments to Mallon. Discuss Mallon's rights against purchaser Garfield in this situation.

20.2 Hypothetical Question with Sample Answer. Marsh has a prize horse named Arabian Knight. Marsh is in need of working capital. She borrows $5,000 from Mendez, who takes possession of Arabian Knight as security for the loan. No written agreement is signed. Discuss whether, in the absence of a written agreement, Mendez has a security interest in Arabian Knight. If Mendez does have a security interest, is it a perfected security interest? Explain.

For a sample answer to Question 20.2, go to Appendix E at the end of this text.

20.3 The Scope of a Security Interest. Edward owned a retail sporting goods shop. A new ski resort was being created in his area, and to take advantage of the potential business, Edward decided to expand his operations. He borrowed a large sum from his bank, which took a security interest in his present inventory and any after-acquired inventory as collateral for the loan. The bank properly perfected the security interest by filing a financing statement. Edward's business was profitable, so he doubled his inventory. A year later, just a few months after the ski resort had opened, an avalanche destroyed the ski slope and lodge. Edward's business consequently took a turn for the worse, and he defaulted on his debt to the bank. The bank then sought possession of his entire inventory, even though the inventory was now twice as large as it had been when the loan was made. Edward claimed that the bank had rights to only half of his inventory. Is Edward correct? Explain.

20.4 Purchase-Money Security Interest. When a customer opens a credit-card account with Sears, Roebuck & Co., the customer fills out an application and sends it to Sears for review; if the application is approved, the customer receives a Sears card. The application contains a security agreement, a copy of which is also sent with the card. When a customer buys an item using the card, the customer signs a sales receipt that describes the merchandise and contains language granting Sears a purchase-money security interest (PMSI) in the merchandise. Dayna Conry bought a variety of consumer goods from Sears on her card. When she did not make payments on her account, Sears filed a suit against her in an Illinois state court to repossess the goods. Conry filed for bankruptcy and was granted a discharge. Sears then filed a suit against her to obtain possession of the goods through its PMSI, but it could not find Conry's credit-card application to offer into evidence. Is a signed Sears sales receipt sufficient proof of its security interest? In whose favor should the court rule? Explain. [*Sears, Roebuck & Co. v. Conry*, 321 Ill.App.3d 997, 748 N.E.2d 1248 (3 Dist. 2001)]

20.5 Case Problem with Sample Answer. In St. Louis, Missouri, in 2000, Richard Miller orally agreed to loan Jeff Miller $35,000 in exchange for a security interest in a Kodiak dump truck. The Millers did not put anything in writing concerning the loan, its repayment terms, or Richard's security interest or rights in the truck. Jeff used the amount of the loan to buy the truck, which he kept in his possession. In 2004, Jeff filed a petition to obtain a discharge of his debts in bankruptcy. Richard claimed that he had a security interest in the truck and thus was entitled to any proceeds from its sale. What are a creditor's main concerns on a debtor's default? How does a creditor satisfy these concerns? What are the requirements for a creditor to have an enforceable security interest? Considering these points, what is the court likely to rule with respect to Richard's claim? [*In re Miller*, 320 Bankr. 911 (E.D.Mo. 2005)]

 After you have answered Problem 20.5, compare your answer with the sample answer given on the Web site that accompanies this text. Go to **www.cengage.com/blaw/fbl**, select "Chapter 20," and click on "Case Problem with Sample Answer."

20.6 Creating a Security Interest. In 2002, Michael Sabol, doing business in the recording industry as Sound Farm Productions, applied to Morton Community Bank in Bloomington, Illinois, for a $58,000 loan to expand his business. Besides the loan application, Sabol signed a promissory note that referred to the bank's rights in "any collateral." Sabol also signed a letter that stated, "the undersigned does hereby authorize Morton Community Bank to execute, file and record all financing statements, amendments, termination statements and all other statements authorized by Article 9 of the Illinois Uniform Commercial

Code, as to any security interest." Sabol did not sign any other documents, including the financing statement, which contained a description of the collateral. Less than three years later, without having repaid the loan, Sabol filed for bankruptcy. The bank claimed a security interest in Sabol's sound equipment. What are the elements of an enforceable security interest? What are the requirements of each of those elements? Does the bank have a valid security interest in this case? Explain. [*In re Sabol*, 337 Bankr. 195 (C.D.Ill. 2006)]

20.7 **A Question of Ethics.** *In 1995, Mark Denton cosigned a $101,250 loan that the First Interstate Bank (FIB) in Missoula, Montana, issued to Denton's friend Eric Anderson. Denton's business assets—a mini-warehouse operation—secured the loan. On his own, Anderson obtained a $260,000 U.S. Small Business Administration (SBA) loan from FIB at the same time. The purpose of both loans was to buy logging equipment with which Anderson could start a business. In 1997, the business failed. As a consequence, FIB repossessed and sold the equipment and applied the proceeds to the SBA loan. FIB then asked Denton to pay the other loan's outstanding balance ($98,460). When Denton refused, FIB initiated proceedings to obtain his business assets. Denton filed a suit against FIB, claiming, in part, that Anderson's equipment was the collateral for the loan that FIB was attempting to collect from Denton. [Denton v. First Interstate Bank of Commerce, 2006 MT 193, 333 Mont. 169, 142 P.3d 797 (2006)]*

1 Denton's assets served as the security for Anderson's loan because Anderson had nothing to offer. When the loan was obtained, Dean Gillmore, FIB's loan officer, explained to them that if Anderson defaulted, the proceeds from the sale of the logging equipment would be applied to the SBA loan first. Under these circumstances, is it fair to hold Denton liable for the unpaid balance of Anderson's loan? Why or why not?

2 Denton argued that the loan contract was unconscionable and constituted a "contract of adhesion." What makes a contract unconscionable? Did the transaction in this case qualify? What is a "contract of adhesion"? Was this deal unenforceable on that basis? Explain.

CRITICAL THINKING AND WRITING ASSIGNMENTS

20.8 Critical Legal Thinking. Review the three requirements for an enforceable security interest. Why is each of these requirements necessary?

20.9 Video Question. Go to this text's Web site at **www.cengage.com/blaw/fbl** and select "Chapter 20." Click

on "Video Questions" and view the video titled *Secured Transactions*. Then answer the following questions.

1 This chapter lists three requirements for creating a security interest. In the video, which requirement does Laura assert has not been met?

2 What, if anything, must the bank have done to perfect its interest in the editing equipment?

3 If the bank exercises its self-help remedy to repossess Onyx's editing equipment, does Laura have any chance of getting it back? Explain.

4 Assume that the bank had a perfected security interest and repossessed the editing equipment. Also assume that the purchase price (and the loan amount) for the equipment was $100,000, of which Onyx has paid $65,000. Discuss the rights and duties of the bank with regard to the collateral in this situation.

ACCESSING THE INTERNET

For updated links to resources available on the Web, as well as a variety of other materials, visit this text's Web site at

www.cengage.com/blaw/fbl

To find Article 9 of the UCC as modified by a particular state on adoption, go to

www.law.cornell.edu/ucc/ucc.table.html

For an overview of secured transactions law and links to UCC provisions and case law on this topic, go to

www.law.cornell.edu/topics/secured_transactions.hml

PRACTICAL INTERNET EXERCISES

Go to this text's Web site at **www.cengage.com/blaw/fbl**, select "Chapter 20," and click on "Practical Internet Exercises." There you will find the following Internet research exercises that you can perform to learn more about the topics covered in this chapter.

PRACTICAL INTERNET EXERCISE 20-1 LEGAL PERSPECTIVE—Repossession

PRACTICAL INTERNET EXERCISE 20-2 MANAGEMENT PERSPECTIVE—Filing Financial Statements

BEFORE THE TEST

Go to this text's Web site at **www.cengage.com/blaw/fbl**, select "Chapter 20," and click on "Interactive Quizzes." You will find a number of interactive questions relating to this chapter.

CHAPTER 21
Creditors' Rights and Bankruptcy

LEARNING OBJECTIVES

AFTER READING THIS CHAPTER, YOU SHOULD BE ABLE TO ANSWER THE FOLLOWING QUESTIONS:

1 What is a prejudgment attachment? What is a writ of execution? How does a creditor use these remedies?

2 What is garnishment? When might a creditor undertake a garnishment proceeding?

3 In a bankruptcy proceeding, what constitutes the debtor's estate in property? What property is exempt from the estate under federal bankruptcy law?

4 What is the difference between an exception to discharge and an objection to discharge?

5 In a Chapter 11 reorganization, what is the role of the debtor in possession?

H istorically, debtors and their families were subjected to punishment, including involuntary servitude and imprisonment, for their inability to pay debts. The modern legal system, however, has moved away from a punishment philosophy in dealing with debtors. In fact, until reforms were passed in 2005, many observers argued that it had moved too far in the other direction, to the detriment of creditors.

Normally, creditors have no problem collecting the debts owed to them. When disputes arise over the amount owed, however, or when the debtor simply cannot or will not pay, what happens? What remedies are available to creditors when debtors default? We have already discussed, in Chapter 20, the remedies available to secured creditors under Article 9 of the Uniform Commercial Code (UCC). In the first part of this chapter, we focus on some basic laws that assist the debtor and creditor in resolving their dispute. We then examine the process of bankruptcy as a last resort in resolving debtor-creditor problems. We specifically include changes resulting from the 2005 Bankruptcy Reform Act.

LAWS ASSISTING CREDITORS

Both the common law and statutory laws other than Article 9 of the UCC create various rights and remedies for creditors. Here we discuss some of these rights and remedies.

Liens

As mentioned in Chapter 17, a *lien* is an encumbrance on (claim against) property to satisfy a debt or protect a claim for the payment of a debt. Creditors' liens may arise under the common law or under statutory law. Statutory liens include *mechanic's liens*, whereas *artisan's liens* were recognized at common law. *Judicial liens* reflect a creditor's efforts to collect on a debt before or after a judgment is entered by a court.

Generally, a lien creditor has priority over an unperfected secured party but not over a perfected secured party. In other words, if a person becomes a lien creditor *before* another party perfects a security interest in the same property, the lienholder has priority. If a lien is obtained *after* another's security interest in the property is perfected, the lienholder does not have priority. This is true for all liens except mechanic's and artisan's liens, which normally have priority over perfected security interests—unless a statute provides otherwise.

Mechanic's Lien   When a person contracts for labor, services, or materials to be furnished for the purpose of making improvements on real property (land and things attached to the land, such as buildings and trees—see Chapter 29) but does not immediately pay for the improvements, the creditor can file a **mechanic's lien** on the property. This creates a special type of debtor-creditor relationship in which the real estate itself becomes security for the debt.

■EXAMPLE 21.1 A painter agrees to paint a house for a homeowner for an agreed-on price to cover labor and materials. If the homeowner refuses to pay for the work or pays only a portion of the charges, a mechanic's lien against the property can be created. The painter is the lienholder, and the real property is encumbered (burdened) with a mechanic's lien for the amount owed. If the homeowner does not pay the lien, the property can be sold to satisfy the debt. Notice of the foreclosure (the process by which the creditor deprives the debtor of his or her property) and sale must be given to the debtor in advance, however. ■

Note that state law governs the procedures that must be followed to create a mechanic's lien. Generally, the lienholder must file a written notice of lien against the particular property involved. The notice of lien must be filed within a specific time period, normally measured from the last date on which materials or labor were provided (usually within 60 to 120 days). If the property owner fails to pay the debt, the lienholder is entitled to foreclose on the real estate on which the work or materials were provided and to sell it to satisfy the amount of the debt.

Artisan's Lien An **artisan's lien** is a security device created at common law through which a creditor can recover payment from a debtor for labor and materials furnished for the repair or improvement of personal property. In contrast to a mechanic's lien, an artisan's lien is *possessory*—that is, the lienholder ordinarily must have retained possession of the property and have expressly or impliedly agreed to provide the services on a cash, not a credit, basis. The lien remains in existence as long as the lienholder maintains possession, and the lien is terminated once possession is voluntarily surrendered—unless the surrender is only temporary.

■EXAMPLE 21.2 Tenetia leaves her diamond ring at the jeweler's to be repaired and to have her initials engraved on the band. In the absence of an agreement, the jeweler can keep the ring until Tenetia pays for the services. Should Tenetia fail to pay, the jeweler has a lien on Tenetia's ring for the amount of the bill and normally can sell the ring in satisfaction of the lien. ■

Modern statutes permit the holder of an artisan's lien to foreclose and sell the property subject to the lien to satisfy payment of the debt. As with a mechanic's lien, the holder of an artisan's lien is required to give notice to the owner of the property prior to foreclosure and sale. The sale proceeds are used to pay the debt and the costs of the legal proceedings, and the surplus, if any, is paid to the former owner.

Judicial Liens When a debt is past due, a creditor can bring a legal action against the debtor to collect the debt. If the creditor is successful in the action, the court awards the creditor a judgment against the debtor (usually for the amount of the debt plus any interest and legal costs incurred in obtaining the judgment). Frequently, however, the creditor is unable to collect the awarded amount.

To ensure that a judgment in the creditor's favor will be collectible, the creditor is permitted to request that certain nonexempt property of the debtor be seized to satisfy the debt. (As will be discussed later in this chapter, under state or federal statutes, certain property is exempt from attachment by creditors.) If the court orders the debtor's property to be seized prior to a judgment in the creditor's favor, the court's order is referred to as a *writ of attachment*. If the court orders the debtor's property to be seized following a judgment in the creditor's favor, the court's order is referred to as a *writ of execution.*

Writ of Attachment. Recall from Chapter 20 that *attachment*, in the context of secured transactions, refers to the process through which a security interest in a debtor's collateral becomes enforceable. In the context of judicial liens, this word has another meaning: **attachment** is a court-ordered seizure and taking into custody of property prior to the securing of a judgment for a past-due debt. Attachment rights are created by state statutes. Normally, attachment is a *prejudgment* remedy occurring either at the time a lawsuit is filed or immediately afterward. To attach before judgment, a creditor must comply with the specific state's statutory restrictions and requirements. The due process clause of the Fourteenth Amendment to the U.S. Constitution also applies and requires that the debtor be given notice and an opportunity to be heard (see Chapter 1).

The creditor must have an enforceable right to payment of the debt under law and must follow certain procedures. Otherwise, the creditor can be liable for damages for wrongful attachment. She or he must file with the court an *affidavit* (a written or printed statement, made under oath or sworn to) stating that the debtor is in default and indicating the statutory grounds under which attachment is sought. The creditor must also post a bond to cover at least the court costs, the value of the loss of use of the property suffered by the debtor, and the value of the property attached. When the court is satisfied that all the requirements have been met, it issues a **writ of attachment,** which directs the sheriff or other public officer to seize nonexempt property. If the creditor prevails at trial, the seized property can be sold to satisfy the judgment.

Writ of Execution. If the creditor wins and the debtor will not or cannot pay the judgment, the creditor is entitled to go back to the court and request a **writ of execution.** This writ is a court order directing the sheriff to seize (levy) and sell any of the debtor's nonexempt real or personal property that is within the court's geographic jurisdiction (usually the county in which the courthouse is located). The proceeds of the sale are used to pay off the judgment, accrued interest, and the costs of the sale. Any excess is paid to the debtor. The debtor can pay the judgment and redeem the nonexempt property any time before the sale takes place. (Because of exemption laws and bankruptcy laws, however, many judgments are virtually uncollectible.)

Garnishment

An order for **garnishment** permits a creditor to collect a debt by seizing property of the debtor that is being held by a third party. In a garnishment proceeding, the third party—the person or entity that the court is ordering to garnish an individual's property—is called the *garnishee.* Frequently, a garnishee is the debtor's employer. A creditor may seek a garnishment judgment against the debtor's employer so that part of the debtor's usual paycheck will be paid to the creditor. In some situations, however, the garnishee is a third party that holds funds belonging to the debtor (such as a bank) or has possession of, or exercises control over, other types of property belonging to the debtor. Almost all types of property can be garnished, including tax refunds, pensions, and trust funds—as long as the property is not exempt from garnishment and is in the possession of a third party.

Garnishment Proceedings The legal proceeding for a garnishment action is governed by state law, and garnishment operates differently from state to state. As a result of a garnishment proceeding, as noted, the court orders a third party (such as the debtor's employer) to turn over property owned by the debtor (such as wages) to pay the debt. Garnishment can be a prejudgment remedy, requiring a hearing before a court, but is most often a postjudgment remedy. According to the laws in some states, the creditor needs to obtain only one order of garnishment, which will then apply continuously to the debtor's wages until the entire debt is paid. In other states, the judgment creditor must go back to court for a separate order of garnishment for each pay period.

Laws Limiting the Amount of Wages Subject to Garnishment Both federal and state laws limit the amount that can be taken from a debtor's weekly take-home pay through garnishment proceedings.[1] Federal law provides a framework to protect debtors from suffering unduly when

paying judgment debts.[2] State laws also provide dollar exemptions, and these amounts are often larger than those provided by federal law. Under federal law, an employer cannot dismiss an employee because his or her wages are being garnished.

Creditors' Composition Agreements

Creditors may contract with the debtor for discharge of the debtor's liquidated debts (debts that are definite, or fixed, in amount) on payment of a sum less than that owed. These agreements are called **creditors' composition agreements,** or simply *composition agreements,* and are usually held to be enforceable.

Mortgage Foreclosure

A **mortgage** is a written instrument giving a creditor an interest in (lien on) the debtor's real property as security for the payment of a debt. Financial institutions grant mortgage loans for the purchase of property—usually a dwelling and the land on which it sits (*real property* will be discussed in Chapter 29). Given the relatively large sums that many individuals borrow to purchase a home, defaults are not uncommon.

Mortgage holders have the right to foreclose on mortgaged property in the event of a debtor's default. The usual method of foreclosure is by judicial sale of the property, although the statutory methods of foreclosure vary from state to state. If the proceeds of the foreclosure sale are sufficient to cover both the costs of the foreclosure and the mortgaged debt, the debtor receives any surplus. If the sale proceeds are insufficient to cover the foreclosure costs and the mortgaged debt, however, the **mortgagee** (the creditor-lender) can seek to recover the difference from the **mortgagor** (the debtor) by obtaining a deficiency judgment representing the difference between the mortgaged debt and the amount actually received from the proceeds of the foreclosure sale.

The mortgagee obtains a deficiency judgment in a separate legal action pursued subsequent to the foreclosure action. The deficiency judgment entitles the mortgagee to recover the amount of the deficiency from other property owned by the debtor.

Mortgage-Lending Practices and High-Risk Borrowers Mortgage lenders extend credit to high-risk borrowers at higher-than-normal interest rates (called subprime mortgages) or through adjustable-rate mortgages (ARMs). The

---

1. Some states (for example, Texas) do not permit garnishment of wages by private parties except under a child-support order.

2. For example, the federal Consumer Credit Protection Act of 1968, 15 U.S.C. Sections 1601–1693r, provides that a debtor can retain either 75 percent of the disposable earnings per week or a sum equivalent to thirty hours of work paid at federal minimum-wage rates, whichever is greater.

recent widespread use of subprime mortgages and ARMs resulted in many borrowers who were unable to make their loan payments on time. In addition, U.S. housing prices dropped, and some borrowers could not sell their homes for the amount they owed on their mortgages. Consequently, the number of home foreclosures increased dramatically in 2008, prompting significant debate. Some claimed that the mortgage lenders were responsible for the problem because they sometimes encouraged people to borrow more than they could afford. Others argued that it is ultimately the borrowers' responsibility to understand the terms and decide if they are able to repay the mortgage loan.

2008 Housing Reform Bill Congress responded by passing the Foreclosure Prevention Act of 2008[3] to help some troubled borrowers refinance their mortgage loans and to prohibit certain mortgage-lending practices. The law raised the national debt ceiling to $10.6 trillion (an increase of $800 billion) to fund the bailout of two government-sponsored mortgage industry giants (Fannie Mae and Freddie Mac—taken over in September 2008). The law also expanded the Federal Housing Administration's loan guarantee program to $300 billion. If existing mortgage lenders agree to write down loan balances to 90 percent of the homes' current appraised value, the government will guarantee a new fixed-rate loan. Nevertheless, this legislation helped only a small percentage of the estimated 3 million homeowners who likely lost their homes to foreclosure by the end of 2009.

Suretyship and Guaranty

When a third person promises to pay a debt owed by another in the event the debtor does not pay, either a *suretyship* or a *guaranty* relationship is created. Suretyship and guaranty provide creditors with the right to seek payment from the third party if the primary debtor defaults on her or his obligations. Exhibit 21–1 illustrates the relationship between a suretyship or guaranty party and the creditor. At common law, there were significant differences in the liability of a *surety* and a *guarantor*, as will be discussed in the following subsections. Today, however, the distinctions outlined here have been abolished in some states.

Surety A contract of strict **suretyship** is a promise made by a third person to be responsible for the debtor's obligation. It is an express contract between the **surety** (the third party) and the creditor. The surety in the strictest sense is primarily liable for the debt of the principal. The creditor need not

exhaust all legal remedies against the principal debtor before holding the surety responsible for payment. The creditor can demand payment from the surety from the moment the debt is due.

■EXAMPLE 21.3 Roberto Delmar wants to borrow from the bank to buy a used car. Because Roberto is still in college, the bank will not lend him the funds unless his father, José Delmar, who has dealt with the bank before, will cosign the note (add his signature to the note, thereby becoming a surety and thus jointly liable for payment of the debt). When José Delmar cosigns the note, he becomes primarily liable to the bank. On the note's due date, the bank can seek payment from either Roberto or José Delmar, or both jointly. **■**

Guaranty With a suretyship arrangement, the surety is *primarily* liable for the debtor's obligation. With a guaranty arrangement, the **guarantor**—the third person making the guaranty—is *secondarily* liable. The guarantor can be required to pay the obligation *only after the principal debtor defaults*, and default usually takes place only after the creditor has made an attempt to collect from the debtor.

■EXAMPLE 21.4 A small corporation, BX Enterprises, needs to borrow funds to meet its payroll. The bank is skeptical about the creditworthiness of BX and requires Dawson, its president, who is a wealthy businessperson and the owner of 70 percent of BX Enterprises, to sign an agreement making himself personally liable for payment if BX does not pay off the loan. As a guarantor of the loan, Dawson cannot be held liable until BX Enterprises is in default. **■**

EXHIBIT 21–1 Suretyship and Guaranty Parties

In a suretyship or guaranty arrangement, a third party promises to be responsible for a debtor's obligations. A third party who agrees to be responsible for the debt even if the primary debtor does not default is known as a *surety;* a third party who agrees to be *secondarily* responsible for the debt—that is, responsible only if the primary debtor defaults—is known as a *guarantor.* As noted in Chapter 10, normally a promise of guaranty (a collateral, or secondary, promise) must be in writing to be enforceable.

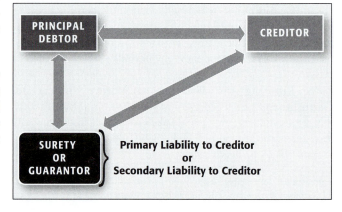

---

3. The Foreclosure Prevention Act of 2008, Pub. L. No. 110-289, 122 Stat. 2830; see 12 U.S.C. Sections 1701, 1706f, 1708, 1715z-24, and 15 U.S.C. Section 1639a.

The Statute of Frauds (see Chapter 10) requires that a guaranty contract between the guarantor and the creditor must be in writing to be enforceable unless the *main purpose* exception applies. Under this exception, if the main purpose of the guaranty agreement is to benefit the guarantor, then the contract need not be in writing to be enforceable. A suretyship agreement, by contrast, need never be in writing to be enforceable. In other words, surety agreements can be oral, whereas guaranty contracts generally must be written.

In the following case, the issue was whether a guaranty form for a partnership's debt was actually made out in the guarantors' names and whether the guarantors signed this form.

CASE 21.1   **Capital Color Printing, Inc. v. Ahern**

 Court of Appeals of Georgia, 291 Ga.App. 101, 661 S.E.2d 578 (2008).

FACTS Quality Printing is a printing broker that sells printing services to customers, but subcontracts the printing work to third parties. It contacted Capital Color Printing, Inc. (CCP), about doing some work. The credit manager at CCP said that Jason Ahern and Todd Heflin, the owners of Quality, would have to execute personal guaranties before CCP would do any work. Quality sent CCP a credit application, which contained a guaranty. The names "Ahern" and "Heflin" appeared on the "Your Name" line. Quality's name, address, tax number, and other information were provided in the "Customer" box on the form. Ahern and Heflin stated that they were partners who owned Quality. Below the signature line was the following statement: "The undersigned guarantees payment of any and all invoices for services rendered to customer." Ahern and Heflin did not sign on the signature line, but their names were signed where printed names were requested. The back of the form stated that the guarantors agreed to be liable for any unpaid bills. When Quality did not pay CCP $76,000 for work it had done, CCP sued Ahern, Heflin, and Quality. Ahern and Heflin moved for summary judgment as to CCP's claims against them, contending that the guaranty failed to specifically identify the principal debtor (Quality) and thus was unenforceable as a matter of law because it violated the Statute of Frauds. Ahern claimed that he was not liable because he had stopped working with Heflin and Heflin had put his name on the guaranty without his permission. The trial court agreed with the defendants and dismissed the claim. CCP appealed.

ISSUE Does the preprinted credit form that identified Quality Printing as the "customer" and included a guaranty and what appeared to be the signatures of Ahern and Heflin satisfy the requirements of the Statute of Frauds?

DECISION Yes. The appeals court reversed the lower court, holding that CCP was entitled to summary judgment against Heflin as guarantor of payment for services performed for Quality. The court remanded the case for a trial to determine if Ahern was liable on the debt or if Heflin had forged his name on the guaranty.

REASON The owners (Ahern and Heflin) claimed that the Statute of Frauds was violated because the guaranty did not specify the name of the principal debtor, Quality. That would be true if the document failed to identify Quality at all, but the form identified Quality as the customer, and that would, taken as a whole, sufficiently identify Quality as the principal debtor. The law does not require a specific format for such forms, only the ability to identify the roles of the parties named in the document. While the signature lines on the form were left blank, the evidence indicated that Heflin filled in both his and Ahern's name as guarantors, even though the signatures were in the wrong place on the form. Ahern claimed that his signature was a forgery and that he had ended his business dealings with Heflin. On remand, a jury could explore the details of the business relationship. If Ahern's signature was forged, only Heflin might be liable. If Heflin had apparent authority (to be discussed in Chapter 22) to bind Ahern to the contract with CCP, which performed $76,000 in printing services for Quality, then Ahern would also be liable on the guaranty.

FOR CRITICAL ANALYSIS–Global Consideration *If a firm was attempting to obtain a guaranty from third parties to a contract with a company in another country, what steps might be taken?*

Defenses of the Surety and the Guarantor   The defenses of the surety and the guarantor are basically the same. Therefore, the following discussion applies to both, although it refers only to the surety.

Actions Releasing the Surety.   Certain actions will release the surety from the obligation. For example, making any material modification in the terms of the original contract between the principal debtor and the creditor—including a binding extension of time for payment—without first obtaining the consent of the surety will discharge a gratuitous surety completely. (A *gratuitous surety* is one who receives no consideration in return for acting as a surety, such as a father who agrees to assume responsibility for his daughter's obligation.) A surety who is compensated (such as a venture capitalist who will profit from a loan made to the principal debtor) will be discharged to the extent that the surety suffers a loss. Naturally, if the principal obligation is paid by the debtor or by another person on behalf of the debtor, the surety is discharged from the obligation. Similarly, if valid tender of payment is made, and the creditor rejects it with knowledge of the surety's existence, the surety is released from any obligation on the debt.

In addition, if a creditor surrenders the collateral to the debtor or impairs the collateral while knowing of the surety and without the surety's consent, the surety is released to the extent of any loss suffered as a result of the creditor's actions. The primary reason for this requirement is to protect a surety who agreed to become obligated only because the debtor's collateral was in the possession of the creditor.

Defenses of the Principal Debtor. Generally, the surety can use any defenses available to a principal debtor to avoid liability on the obligation to the creditor. The ability of the surety to assert any defenses the debtor may have against the creditor is the most important concept in suretyship. A few exceptions do exist, however. The surety cannot assert the principal debtor's incapacity or bankruptcy as a defense, nor can the surety assert the statute of limitations as a defense.

Obviously, a surety may also have his or her own defenses—for instance, his or her own incapacity or bankruptcy. If the creditor fraudulently induced the surety to guarantee the debt of the debtor, the surety can assert fraud as a defense. In most states, the creditor has a legal duty to inform the surety, prior to the formation of the suretyship contract, of material facts known by the creditor that would substantially increase the surety's risk. Failure to so inform may constitute fraud and makes the suretyship obligation voidable.

Rights of the Surety and the Guarantor Generally, when the surety or guarantor pays the debt owed to the creditor, the surety or guarantor is entitled to certain rights. Because the rights of the surety and guarantor are basically the same, the following discussion applies to both.

The Right of Subrogation. The surety has the legal **right of subrogation.** Simply stated, this means that any right the creditor had against the debtor now becomes the right of the surety. Included are creditor rights in bankruptcy and rights to judgments secured by the creditor. In short, the surety now stands in the shoes of the creditor and may pursue any remedies that were available to the creditor against the debtor.

The Right of Reimbursement. The surety has a **right of reimbursement** from the debtor. Basically, the surety is entitled to receive from the debtor all outlays made on behalf of the suretyship arrangement. Such outlays can include expenses incurred as well as the actual amount of the debt paid to the creditor.

The Right of Contribution. In a situation involving **co-sureties** (two or more sureties on the same obligation owed by the debtor), a surety who pays more than her or his proportionate share on a debtor's default is entitled to recover from the co-sureties the amount paid above the surety's obligation. This is the **right of contribution.** Generally, a co-surety's liability either is determined by agreement between the co-sureties or, in the absence of an agreement, can be specified in the suretyship contract itself.

EXAMPLE 21.5 Two co-sureties are obligated under a suretyship contract to guarantee the debt of a debtor. Together, the sureties' maximum liability is $25,000. As specified in the suretyship contract, surety A's maximum liability is $15,000, and surety B's is $10,000. The debtor owes $10,000 and is in default. Surety A pays the creditor the entire $10,000. In the absence of any agreement between the two co-sureties, surety A can recover $4,000 from surety B ($10,000/$25,000 × $10,000 = $4,000). ■

PREVENTING LEGAL DISPUTES

Be careful when signing guaranty contracts and explicitly indicate if you are signing on behalf of a company rather than personally. For example, if you are a corporate officer and you sign your name on a guaranty for a third party without indicating that you are signing as a representative of the corporation, you might be held personally liable as the guarantor. Although a guaranty contract may be preferable to a suretyship contract because it creates secondary rather than primary liability, a guaranty still involves substantial risk. Depending on the wording used in a guaranty contract, the extent of the guarantor's liability may be unlimited. Be absolutely clear about the potential liability before agreeing to serve as a guarantor, and contact an attorney for guidance.

■

LAWS ASSISTING DEBTORS

The law protects debtors as well as creditors. Certain property of the debtor, for example, is exempt from creditors' actions. Probably the most familiar exemption is the **homestead exemption.** Each state permits the debtor to retain the family home, either in its entirety or up to a specified dollar amount, free from the claims of unsecured creditors or trustees in bankruptcy (a *bankruptcy trustee* is appointed by the court to hold and protect the debtor's property, as will be discussed later in this chapter). The purpose of the homestead exemption is to ensure that the debtor will retain some form of shelter.

■EXAMPLE 21.6 Van Cleave owes Acosta $40,000. The debt is the subject of a lawsuit, and the court awards Acosta a judgment of $40,000 against Van Cleave. Van Cleave's home is valued at $50,000, and the state exemption on homesteads is $25,000. There are no outstanding mortgages or other liens. To satisfy the judgment debt, Van Cleave's family home is sold at public auction for $45,000. The proceeds of the sale are distributed as follows:

1 Van Cleave is given $25,000 as his homestead exemption.

2 Acosta is paid $20,000 toward the judgment debt, leaving a $20,000 deficiency judgment (leftover debt) that can be satisfied from any other nonexempt property (personal or real) that Van Cleave may have, if permitted by state law. **■**

Various types of personal property may also be exempt from satisfaction of judgment debts. Personal property that is most often exempt includes the following:

1 Household furniture up to a specified dollar amount.

2 Clothing and certain personal possessions, such as family pictures or a Bible or other religious text.

3 A vehicle (or vehicles) for transportation (at least up to a specified dollar amount).

4 Certain classified animals, usually livestock but including pets.

5 Equipment that the debtor uses in a business or trade, such as tools or professional instruments, up to a specified dollar amount.

BANKRUPTCY PROCEEDINGS

Bankruptcy law in the United States has two goals—to protect a debtor by giving him or her a fresh start, free from creditors' claims, and to ensure equitable treatment to creditors who are competing for a debtor's assets. Bankruptcy law is federal law, but state laws on secured transactions, liens, judgments, and exemptions also play a role in federal bankruptcy proceedings.

In 2005, Congress enacted bankruptcy reform legislation that significantly overhauled certain provisions of bankruptcy law for the first time in twenty-five years.[4] Before 2005, bankruptcy law was based on the Bankruptcy Reform Act of 1978 (called the Bankruptcy Code).

One of the major goals of the 2005 act was to require consumers to pay as many of their debts as possible instead of having those debts fully discharged in bankruptcy. Before the reforms, the vast majority of bankruptcies were filed under Chapter 7 of the Bankruptcy Code, which permits debtors, with some exceptions, to have *all* of their debts discharged in bankruptcy. Only about 20 percent of personal bankruptcies were filed under Chapter 13 of the Bankruptcy Code. As you will read later in this chapter, Chapter 13 requires the debtor to establish a repayment plan and pay off as many debts as possible over a maximum period of five years. Under the 2005 legislation, more debtors must file for bankruptcy under Chapter 13.

Bankruptcy Courts

Bankruptcy proceedings are held in federal bankruptcy courts, which are under the authority of U.S. district courts, and rulings by bankruptcy courts can be appealed to the district courts. Essentially, a bankruptcy court fulfills the role of an administrative court for the district court concerning matters in bankruptcy. The bankruptcy court holds proceedings dealing with the procedures required to administer the debtor's estate in bankruptcy (the debtor's assets, as will be discussed shortly). A bankruptcy court can conduct a jury trial if the appropriate district court has authorized it and if the parties to the bankruptcy consent to a jury trial.

Types of Bankruptcy Relief

The Bankruptcy Code is contained in Title 11 of the *United States Code* (U.S.C.) and has eight "chapters." Chapters 1, 3, and 5 of the Code include general definitional provisions and provisions governing case administration and procedures, creditors, the debtor, and the estate. These three chapters of the Code normally apply to all types of bankruptcies. There are five other chapters that set forth the different types of relief that debtors may seek. Chapter 7 provides for **liquidation** proceedings (the selling of all nonexempt assets and the distribution of the proceeds to the debtor's creditors). Chapter 9 governs the adjustment of the debts of municipalities. Chapter 11 governs reorganizations. Chapter 12 (for family farmers) and Chapter 13 (for individuals) provide for adjustment of the debts of

---

4. The full title of the act is the Bankruptcy Abuse Prevention and Consumer Protection Act of 2005, Pub. L. No. 109-8, 119 Stat. 23 (April 20, 2005).

parties with regular income.[5] A debtor (except for a municipality) need not be insolvent[6] to file for bankruptcy relief under the Bankruptcy Code. Anyone obligated to a creditor can declare bankruptcy.

Special Treatment of Consumer-Debtors

A **consumer-debtor** is a debtor whose debts result primarily from the purchase of goods for personal, family, or household use. To fully inform a consumer-debtor of the various types of relief available, the Code requires that the clerk of the court provide certain information to all consumer-debtors prior to the commencement of a bankruptcy filing. First, the clerk must give consumer-debtors written notice of the general purpose, benefits, and costs of each chapter of bankruptcy under which they may proceed. Second, the clerk must provide consumer-debtors with informational materials on the types of services available from credit counseling agencies.

In the following pages, we deal first with liquidation proceedings under Chapter 7 of the Code. We then examine the procedures required for Chapter 11 reorganizations and for Chapter 12 and Chapter 13 plans.

CHAPTER 7–LIQUIDATION

Liquidation is the most familiar type of bankruptcy proceeding and is often referred to as an *ordinary*, or *straight*, *bankruptcy*. Put simply, a debtor in a liquidation bankruptcy turns all assets over to a trustee. The trustee sells the nonexempt assets and distributes the proceeds to creditors. With certain exceptions, the remaining debts are then **discharged** (extinguished), and the debtor is relieved of the obligation to pay the debts.

Any "person"—defined as including individuals, partnerships, and corporations[7]—may be a debtor under Chapter 7. Railroads, insurance companies, banks, savings and loan associations, investment companies licensed by the Small Business Administration, and credit unions *cannot* be Chapter 7 debtors, however. Other chapters of the Code or other federal or state statutes apply to them. A husband and wife may file jointly for bankruptcy under a single petition.

---

5. There are no Chapters 2, 4, 6, 8, or 10 in Title 11. Such "gaps" are not uncommon in the *United States Code*. They occur because, when a statute is enacted, chapter numbers (or other subdivisional unit numbers) are sometimes reserved for future use. (A gap may also appear if a law has been repealed.)

6. The inability to pay debts as they become due is known as *equitable* insolvency. A *balance-sheet* insolvency, which exists when a debtor's liabilities exceed assets, is not the test. Thus, it is possible for debtors to petition voluntarily for bankruptcy even though their assets far exceed their liabilities. This situation may occur when a debtor's cash-flow problems become severe.

7. The definition of *corporation* includes unincorporated companies and associations. It also covers labor unions.

A straight bankruptcy may be commenced by the filing of either a voluntary or an involuntary **petition in bankruptcy**—the document that is filed with a bankruptcy court to initiate bankruptcy proceedings. If a debtor files the petition, then it is a *voluntary bankruptcy*. If one or more creditors file a petition to force the debtor into bankruptcy, then it is called an *involuntary bankruptcy*. We discuss both voluntary and involuntary bankruptcy proceedings under Chapter 7 in the following subsections.

Voluntary Bankruptcy

To bring a voluntary petition in bankruptcy, the debtor files official forms designated for that purpose in the bankruptcy court. The Bankruptcy Reform Act of 2005 specifies that *before* debtors can file a petition, they must receive credit counseling from an approved nonprofit agency within the 180-day period preceding the date of filing. The act provides detailed criteria for the **U.S. trustee** (a government official who performs appointment and other administrative tasks that a bankruptcy judge would otherwise have to perform) to approve nonprofit budget and counseling agencies and requires a list of approved agencies to be made publicly available. A debtor filing a Chapter 7 petition must include a certificate proving that he or she attended an individual or group briefing from an approved counseling agency within the last 180 days (roughly six months).

The Code requires a consumer-debtor who has opted for liquidation bankruptcy proceedings to confirm the accuracy of the petition's contents. The debtor must also state in the petition, at the time of filing, that he or she understands the relief available under other chapters of the Code and has chosen to proceed under Chapter 7. If an attorney is representing the consumer-debtor, the attorney must file an affidavit stating that she or he has informed the debtor of the relief available under each chapter of bankruptcy. In addition, the 2005 act requires the attorney to reasonably attempt to verify the accuracy of the consumer-debtor's petition and schedules (described below). Failure to do so is considered perjury.

Chapter 7 Schedules The voluntary petition contains the following schedules:

1 A list of both secured and unsecured creditors, their addresses, and the amount of debt owed to each.

2 A statement of the financial affairs of the debtor.

3 A list of all property owned by the debtor, including property claimed by the debtor to be exempt.

4 A listing of current income and expenses.

5 A certificate of credit counseling (as discussed previously).

6 Proof of payments received from employers within sixty days prior to the filing of the petition.

7 A statement of the amount of monthly income, itemized to show how the amount is calculated.

8 A copy of the debtor's federal income tax return for the most recent year ending immediately before the filing of the petition.

As previously noted, the official forms must be completed accurately, sworn to under oath, and signed by the debtor. To conceal assets or knowingly supply false information on these schedules is a crime under the bankruptcy laws.

Additional Information May Be Required At the request of the court, the U.S. trustee, or any party of interest, the debtor must file tax returns at the end of each tax year while the case is pending and provide copies to the court. This requirement also applies to Chapter 11 and 13 bankruptcies (discussed later in this chapter). Also, if requested by the U.S. trustee or bankruptcy trustee, the debtor must provide a photo document establishing his or her identity (such as a driver's license or passport) or other such personal identifying information.

With the exception of tax returns, failure to file the required schedules within forty-five days after the filing of the petition (unless an extension up to forty-five days is granted) will result in an automatic dismissal of the petition. The debtor has up to seven days before the date of the first creditors' meeting to provide a copy of the most current tax returns to the trustee.

When Substantial Abuse Will Be Presumed The Bankruptcy Reform Act of 2005 established a new system of "means testing"—based on the debtor's income—to determine whether a debtor's petition is presumed to be a "substantial abuse" of Chapter 7. If the debtor's family income is greater than the median family income in the state in which the petition is filed, the trustee or any party in interest (such as a creditor) can bring a motion to dismiss the Chapter 7 petition. State median incomes vary from state to state and are calculated and reported by the U.S. Bureau of the Census.

The debtor's current monthly income is calculated using the last six months' average income, less certain "allowed expenses" reflecting the basic needs of the debtor. The monthly amount is then multiplied by twelve. If the resulting income exceeds the state median income by $6,000 or more,[8] abuse is presumed, and the trustee or any creditor can file a motion to dismiss the petition. A debtor can rebut (refute) the presumption of abuse "by demonstrating special circumstances that justify additional expenses or adjustments of current monthly income for which there is no reasonable alternative." (An example might be anticipated medical costs not covered by health insurance.) These additional expenses or adjustments must be itemized and their accuracy attested to under oath by the debtor.

When Substantial Abuse Will *Not* Be Presumed If the debtor's income is below the state median (or if the debtor has successfully rebutted the means-test presumption), abuse will not be presumed. In these situations, the court may still find substantial abuse, but the creditors will not have standing (see Chapter 1) to file a motion to dismiss. Basically, this leaves intact the prior law on substantial abuse, allowing the court to consider such factors as the debtor's bad faith or circumstances indicating substantial abuse.

Can a debtor seeking relief under Chapter 7 exclude voluntary contributions to a retirement plan as a reasonably necessary expense in calculating her income? The Code does not disallow the contributions, but whether their exclusion constitutes substantial abuse requires a review of the debtor's circumstances, as in the following case.

---

8. This amount ($6,000) is the equivalent of $100 per month for five years, indicating that the debtor could pay at least $100 per month under a Chapter 13 five-year repayment plan.

CASE 21.2 **Hebbring v. U.S. Trustee**

United States Court of Appeals, Ninth Circuit, 463 F.3d 902 (2006).

FACTS In 2003, Lisa Hebbring owned a single-family home in Reno, Nevada, valued at $160,000, on which she owed $154,103. She also owned a vehicle valued at $14,000, on which she owed $18,839, and other personal property valued at $1,775. She earned $49,000 per year as a customer service representative for SBC Nevada. In June, Hebbring filed a Chapter 7 petition in a federal bankruptcy court, seeking relief from $11,124 in credit-card debt. Her petition listed monthly net income of $2,813 and expenditures of $2,897, for a deficit of $84. In calculating her income, Hebbring excluded a $232 monthly pretax deduction for a contribution to a retirement plan maintained by her employer and an $81 monthly after-tax deduction for a contribution to her own retirement savings. At

CASE 21.2–Continues next page

CASE 21.2—Continued

the time, Hebbring was thirty-three years old. The U.S. trustee assigned to oversee her case filed a motion to dismiss her petition for substantial abuse, arguing in part that the retirement savings contributions should be disallowed. According to the trustee, these and other adjustments would leave Hebbring $615 per month in disposable income, which would be enough to repay 100 percent of her credit-card debt over three years. The court dismissed her petition. She appealed to a federal district court, which affirmed the dismissal. Hebbring appealed to the U.S. Court of Appeals for the Ninth Circuit.

ISSUE Based on Hebbring's age and financial circumstances, would granting her petition in bankruptcy constitute substantial abuse?

DECISION Yes. The U.S. Court of Appeals for the Ninth Circuit affirmed the lower court's decision, "finding that Hebbring's retirement contributions are not reasonably necessary based on her age and financial circumstances, and that she is therefore capable of paying her unsecured debts."

REASON The appellate court emphasized the facts of Hebbring's situation. She was thirty-three years old, earning $49,000 per year, making mortgage payments on a house, and contributing about 8 percent of her income toward her retirement savings. "In light of these circumstances, the bankruptcy court's conclusion that Hebbring's retirement contributions are not a reasonably necessary expense is not clearly erroneous." Furthermore, based on the information that Hebbring provided on the schedules she submitted with her bankruptcy petition, even excluding her voluntary retirement plan contributions, she "has $172 per month in disposable income, sufficient to repay 56% of her unsecured [credit-card] debt over three years or 93% over five years * * * . The bankruptcy court thus did not err in finding that Hebbring is able to [pay at least] a substantial portion of the unsecured claims."

 FOR CRITICAL ANALYSIS–Ethical Consideration *Is it fair for the court to treat retirement payments differently depending on a person's age?*

Additional Grounds for Dismissal As noted, a debtor's voluntary petition for Chapter 7 relief may be dismissed for substantial abuse or for failure to provide the necessary documents (such as schedules and tax returns) within the specified time. In addition, a motion to dismiss a Chapter 7 filing might be granted in two other situations under the 2005 act. First, if the debtor has been convicted of a violent crime or a drug-trafficking offense, the victim can file a motion to dismiss the voluntary petition.[9] Second, if the debtor fails to pay postpetition domestic-support obligations (which include child and spousal support), the court may dismiss the debtor's Chapter 7 petition.

Order for Relief If the voluntary petition for bankruptcy is found to be proper, the filing of the petition will itself constitute an order for relief. (An **order for relief** is the court's grant of assistance to a debtor.) Once a consumer-debtor's voluntary petition has been filed, the clerk of the court (or other appointee) must give the trustee and creditors notice of the order for relief by mail not more than twenty days after the entry of the order.

Involuntary Bankruptcy

An involuntary bankruptcy occurs when the debtor's creditors force the debtor into bankruptcy proceedings. An involuntary case cannot be commenced against a farmer[10] or a charitable institution. For an involuntary action to be filed against other debtors, the following requirements must be met: If the debtor has twelve or more creditors, three or more of those creditors having unsecured claims totaling at least $13,475 must join in the petition. If a debtor has fewer than twelve creditors, one or more creditors having a claim of $13,475 or more may file.

If the debtor challenges the involuntary petition, a hearing will be held, and the debtor's challenge will fail if the bankruptcy court finds either of the following:

1 That the debtor is generally not paying debts as they become due.

2 That a general receiver, custodian, or assignee took possession of, or was appointed to take charge of, substantially all of the debtor's property within 120 days before the filing of the involuntary petition.

---

9. Note that the court may not dismiss a case on this ground if the debtor's bankruptcy is necessary to satisfy a claim for a domestic-support obligation.

10. The definition of *farmer* includes persons who receive more than 50 percent of their gross income from farming operations, such as tilling the soil; dairy farming; ranching; or the production or raising of crops, poultry, or livestock. Corporations and partnerships, as well as individuals, can be farmers.

If the court allows the bankruptcy to proceed, the debtor will be required to supply the same information in the bankruptcy schedules as in a voluntary bankruptcy.

An involuntary petition should not be used as an everyday debt-collection device, and the Code provides penalties for the filing of frivolous (unjustified) petitions against debtors. Judgment may be granted against the petitioning creditors for the costs and attorneys' fees incurred by the debtor in defending against an involuntary petition that is dismissed by the court. If the petition was filed in bad faith, damages can be awarded for injury to the debtor's reputation. Punitive damages may also be awarded.

Automatic Stay

The moment a petition, either voluntary or involuntary, is filed, an **automatic stay,** or suspension, of virtually all actions by creditors against the debtor or the debtor's property normally goes into effect. In other words, once a petition has been filed, creditors cannot contact the debtor by phone or mail or start any legal proceedings to recover debts or to repossess property. A secured creditor or other party in interest, however, may petition the bankruptcy court for relief from the automatic stay. If a creditor knowingly violates the automatic stay (a willful violation), any injured party, including the debtor, is entitled to recover actual damages, costs, and attorneys' fees and may be entitled to recover punitive damages as well.

Exceptions to the Automatic Stay The 2005 Bankruptcy Reform Act created several exceptions to the automatic stay. It provided an exception for domestic-support obligations, which include any debt owed to or recoverable by a spouse, a former spouse, or a child of the debtor; that child's parent or guardian; or a governmental unit. In addition, proceedings against the debtor related to divorce, child custody or visitation, domestic violence, and support enforcement are not stayed. Also excepted are investigations by a securities regulatory agency (see Chapter 27) and certain statutory liens for property taxes.

Limitations on the Automatic Stay If a creditor or other party in interest requests relief from the stay, the stay will automatically terminate sixty days after the request, unless the court grants an extension or the parties agree otherwise. Also, the automatic stay on secured debts normally will terminate thirty days after the petition is filed if the debtor had filed a bankruptcy petition that was dismissed within the prior year. Any party in interest can request the court to extend the stay by showing that the filing is in good faith.

If the debtor had two or more bankruptcy petitions dismissed during the prior year, the Code presumes bad faith, and the automatic stay does not go into effect until the court determines that the filing was made in good faith. In addition, if the petition is subsequently dismissed because the debtor failed to file the required documents within thirty days of filing, for example, the stay is terminated. Finally, the automatic stay on secured property terminates forty-five days after the creditors' meeting (to be discussed shortly) unless the debtor redeems or reaffirms certain debts (*reaffirmation* is discussed later in this chapter). In other words, the debtor cannot keep the secured property (such as a financed automobile), even if she or he continues to make payments on it, without reinstating the rights of the secured party to collect on the debt.

Property of the Estate

On the commencement of a liquidation proceeding under Chapter 7, an **estate in property** is created. The estate consists of all the debtor's interests in property currently held, wherever located, together with community property (property jointly owned by a husband and wife in certain states—see Chapter 28), property transferred in a transaction voidable by the trustee, proceeds and profits from the property of the estate, and certain after-acquired property. Interests in certain property—such as gifts, inheritances, property settlements (from divorce), and life insurance death proceeds—to which the debtor becomes entitled *within 180 days after filing* may also become part of the estate. Withholdings for employee benefit plan contributions are excluded from the estate. Generally, though, the filing of a bankruptcy petition fixes a dividing line: property acquired prior to the filing of the petition becomes property of the estate, and property acquired after the filing of the petition, except as just noted, remains the debtor's.

Creditors' Meeting and Claims

Within a reasonable time after the order of relief has been granted (not less than ten days or more than thirty days), the trustee must call a meeting of the creditors listed in the schedules filed by the debtor. The bankruptcy judge does not attend this meeting, but the debtor is required to attend and to submit to an examination under oath. At the meeting, the trustee ensures that the debtor is aware of the potential consequences of bankruptcy and of his or her ability to file under a different chapter of the Bankruptcy Code.

To be entitled to receive a portion of the debtor's estate, each creditor normally files a *proof of claim* with the bankruptcy court clerk within ninety days of the creditors' meeting.[11] The proof of claim lists the creditor's name and

---

11. This ninety-day rule applies in Chapter 12 and Chapter 13 bankruptcies as well.

address, as well as the amount that the creditor asserts is owed to the creditor by the debtor. A proof of claim is necessary if there is any dispute concerning the claim. If a creditor fails to file a proof of claim, the bankruptcy court or trustee may file the proof of claim on the creditor's behalf but is not obligated to do so.

Exemptions

The trustee takes control over the debtor's property, but an individual debtor is entitled to exempt certain property from the bankruptcy. The Bankruptcy Code exempts the following property:[12]

1 Up to $20,200 in equity in the debtor's residence and burial plot (the homestead exemption).

2 Interest in a motor vehicle up to $3,225.

3 Interest, up to $525 for a particular item, in household goods and furnishings, wearing apparel, appliances, books, animals, crops, and musical instruments (the aggregate total of all items is limited, however, to $10,775).

4 Interest in jewelry up to $1,350.

5 Interest in any other property up to $1,075, plus any unused part of the $20,200 homestead exemption up to $10,125.

6 Interest in any tools of the debtor's trade up to $2,025.

7 Any unmatured life insurance contracts owned by the debtor.

8 Certain interests in accrued dividends and interest under life insurance contracts owned by the debtor, not to exceed $10,775.

9 Professionally prescribed health aids.

10 The right to receive Social Security and certain welfare benefits, alimony and support, certain retirement funds and pensions, and education savings accounts held for specific periods of time.

11 The right to receive certain personal-injury and other awards up to $20,200.

Individual states have the power to pass legislation precluding debtors from using the federal exemptions within the state; a majority of the states have done this, as mentioned earlier in this chapter. In those states, debtors may use only state, not federal, exemptions. In the rest of the states, an individual debtor (or a husband and wife filing jointly) may choose either the exemptions provided under state law or the federal exemptions.

The Homestead Exemption

The 2005 Bankruptcy Reform Act significantly changed the law for those debtors seeking to use state homestead exemption statutes (which were discussed previously). In six states, including Florida and Texas, homestead exemptions allowed debtors petitioning for bankruptcy to shield *unlimited* amounts of equity in their homes from creditors. The Code now places limits on the amount that can be claimed as exempt in bankruptcy. Also, a debtor must have lived in a state for two years prior to filing the petition to be able to use the state homestead exemption (prior law required only six months).

In general, if the homestead was acquired within three and one-half years preceding the date of filing, the maximum equity exempted is $136,875, even if the state law would permit a higher amount. Also, if the debtor owes a debt arising from a violation of securities law or if the debtor committed certain criminal or tortious acts in the previous five years that indicate the filing was substantial abuse, the debtor may not exempt any amount of equity.

The Trustee

Promptly after the order for relief in the liquidation proceeding has been entered, a trustee is appointed. The basic duty of the trustee is to collect the debtor's available estate and reduce it to cash for distribution, preserving the interests of both the debtor and unsecured creditors. The trustee is required to promptly review all materials filed by the debtor to determine if there is substantial abuse. Within ten days after the first meeting of the creditors, the trustee must file a statement indicating whether the case is presumed to be an abuse under the means test and provide a copy to all creditors. When there is a presumption of abuse, the trustee must either file a motion to dismiss the petition (or convert it to a Chapter 13 case) or file a statement setting forth the reasons why a motion would not be appropriate. If the debtor owes a domestic-support obligation (such as child support), the trustee is required to provide written notice of the bankruptcy to the claim holder (a former spouse, for instance). (Note that these provisions are not limited to Chapter 7 bankruptcies.)

The Code gives the trustee certain powers, which must be exercised within two years of the order for relief. The trustee occupies a position *equivalent* in rights to that of certain other parties. For example, the trustee has the same rights as a creditor who could have obtained a judicial lien or levy execution on the debtor's property. This means that a trustee

---

12. The dollar amounts stated in the Bankruptcy Code are adjusted automatically every three years on April 1 based on changes in the Consumer Price Index. The adjusted amounts are rounded to the nearest $25. The amounts stated in this chapter are in accordance with those computed on April 1, 2007.

normally has priority over certain secured parties to the debtor's property. This right of a trustee, equivalent to that of a lien creditor, is known as the *strong-arm power*. A trustee also has power equivalent to that of a *bona fide purchaser* of real property from the debtor.

The Right to Possession of the Debtor's Property The trustee has the power to require persons holding the debtor's property at the time the petition is filed to deliver the property to the trustee. Usually, a trustee does not take actual physical possession of a debtor's property but instead takes constructive possession by exercising control over the property. **■EXAMPLE 21.7** A trustee needs to obtain possession of a debtor's business inventory. To effectively take (constructive) possession, the trustee could notify the debtor, change the locks on the business's doors, and hire a security guard. **■**

Avoidance Powers The trustee also has specific powers of *avoidance*—that is, the trustee can set aside a sale or other transfer of the debtor's property, taking it back as a part of the debtor's estate. These powers include any voidable rights available to the debtor, preferences, certain statutory liens, and fraudulent transfers by the debtor. Each of these powers is discussed in more detail below. Note that since the 2005 act, the trustee no longer has the power to avoid any transfer that was a bona fide payment of a domestic-support debt.

The debtor shares most of the trustee's avoidance powers. Thus, if the trustee does not take action to enforce one of the rights mentioned above, the debtor in a liquidation bankruptcy can still enforce that right.[13]

Voidable Rights A trustee steps into the shoes of the debtor. Thus, any reason that a debtor can use to obtain the return of his or her property can be used by the trustee as well. These grounds for recovery include fraud, duress, incapacity, and mutual mistake. **■EXAMPLE 21.8** Blane sells his boat to Inga. Inga gives Blane a check, knowing that she has insufficient funds in her bank account to cover the check. Inga has committed fraud. Blane has the right to avoid that transfer and recover the boat from Inga. Once an order for relief under Chapter 7 of the Code has been entered for Blane, the trustee can exercise the same right to recover the boat from Inga, and the boat becomes part of the debtor's estate. **■**

Preferences A debtor is not permitted to make a property transfer or a payment that favors—or gives a **preference** to—

one creditor over others. The trustee is allowed to recover payments made both voluntarily and involuntarily to one creditor in preference over another. If a **preferred creditor** (one who has received a preferential transfer from the debtor) has sold the property to an innocent third party, the trustee cannot recover the property from the innocent party. The preferred creditor, however, generally can be held accountable for the value of the property.

To have made a preferential payment that can be recovered, an *insolvent* debtor generally must have transferred property, for a *preexisting* debt, during the *ninety days* prior to the filing of the petition in bankruptcy. The transfer must have given the creditor more than the creditor would have received as a result of the bankruptcy proceedings. The trustee does not have to prove insolvency, as the Code provides that the debtor is presumed to be insolvent during this ninety-day period.

Preferences to Insiders. Sometimes, the creditor receiving the preference is an *insider*—an individual, a partner, a partnership, or an officer or a director of a corporation (or a relative of one of these) who has a close relationship with the debtor. In this situation, the avoidance power of the trustee is extended to transfers made within *one year* before filing; the *presumption* of insolvency is still confined to the ninety-day period, though. Therefore, the trustee must prove that the debtor was insolvent at the time of an earlier transfer.

Transfers That Do Not Constitute Preferences. Not all transfers are preferences. To be a preference, the transfer must be made in exchange for something other than current consideration. Therefore, most courts do not consider a debtor's payment for services rendered within fifteen days prior to the payment to be a preference. If a creditor receives payment in the ordinary course of business, such as payment of last month's telephone bill, the trustee in bankruptcy cannot recover the payment. To be recoverable, a preference must be a transfer for an antecedent (preexisting) debt, such as a year-old printing bill. In addition, the Code permits a consumer-debtor to transfer any property to a creditor up to a total value of $5,475, without the transfer's constituting a preference (this amount was increased from $600 to $5,000 by the 2005 act and is increased periodically under the law). Payments of domestic-support debts do not constitute a preference. Also, transfers that were made as part of an alternative repayment schedule negotiated by an approved credit counseling agency are not preferences.

Liens on Debtor's Property The trustee has the power to avoid certain statutory liens against the debtor's property, such as a lien for unpaid rent. The trustee can avoid statutory

---

13. Under a Chapter 11 bankruptcy (to be discussed later), for which no trustee other than the debtor generally exists, the debtor has the same avoidance powers as a trustee under Chapter 7. Under Chapters 12 and 13 (also to be discussed later), a trustee must be appointed.

liens that first became effective at the time the bankruptcy petition was filed or when the debtor became insolvent. The trustee can also avoid any lien against a good faith purchaser that was not perfected or enforceable on the date of the bankruptcy filing.

Fraudulent Transfers The trustee may avoid fraudulent transfers or obligations if they were made within two years of the filing of the petition or if they were made with actual intent to hinder, delay, or defraud a creditor. Transfers made for less than reasonably equivalent consideration are also vulnerable if the debtor thereby became insolvent, was left engaged in business with an unreasonably small amount of capital, or intended to incur debts that would be beyond his or her ability to pay. When a fraudulent transfer is made outside the Code's two-year limit, creditors may seek alternative relief under state laws. Some state laws allow creditors to recover for transfers made up to three years prior to the filing of a petition.

Distribution of Property

The Code provides specific rules for the distribution of the debtor's property to secured and unsecured creditors (to be discussed shortly.) If any amount remains after the priority classes of creditors have been satisfied, it is turned over to the debtor. Exhibit 21–2 illustrates graphically the collection and distribution of property in most voluntary bankruptcies.

In a bankruptcy case in which the debtor has no assets (called a "no-asset" case), creditors are notified of the debtor's petition for bankruptcy but are instructed not to file a claim because most, if not all, of these debts will be discharged.

Distribution to Secured Creditors The rights of perfected secured creditors were discussed in Chapter 20. The Code provides that a consumer-debtor, either within thirty days of filing a liquidation petition or before the date of the first meeting of the creditors (whichever is first), must file with the clerk a statement of intention with respect to the secured collateral. The statement must indicate whether the debtor will redeem the collateral (make a single payment equal to the current value of the property), reaffirm the debt (continue making payments on the debt), or surrender the property to the secured party.[14] The trustee is obligated to enforce the debtor's statement within forty-five days after the meeting of the creditors. As noted previously, failure of the debtor to redeem or reaffirm within forty-five days terminates the automatic stay.

If the collateral is surrendered to the perfected secured party, the secured creditor can enforce the security interest either by accepting the property in full satisfaction of the debt or by foreclosing on the collateral and using the proceeds to

---

14. Also, if applicable, the debtor must specify whether the collateral will be claimed as exempt property.

EXHIBIT 21–2 **Collection and Distribution of Property in Most Voluntary Bankruptcies**

This exhibit illustrates the property that might be collected in a debtor's voluntary bankruptcy and how it might be distributed to creditors. Involuntary bankruptcies and some voluntary bankruptcies could include additional types of property and other creditors.

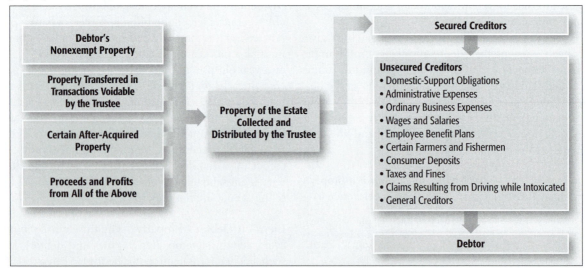

pay off the debt. Thus, the perfected secured party has priority over unsecured parties as to the proceeds from the disposition of the collateral.

Distribution to Unsecured Creditors Bankruptcy law establishes an order of priority for classes of debts owed to *unsecured* creditors, and they are paid in the order of their priority. Each class must be fully paid before the next class is entitled to any of the remaining proceeds. If there are insufficient proceeds to pay fully all the creditors in a class, the proceeds are distributed *proportionately* to the creditors in that class, and classes lower in priority receive nothing. If there is any balance remaining after all the creditors are paid, it is returned to the debtor.

The new bankruptcy law elevated domestic-support (mainly child-support) obligations to the highest priority of unsecured claims—so these are the first debts to be paid. After that, administrative expenses related to the bankruptcy (such as court costs, trustee fees, and attorneys' fees) are paid; next come any expenses that a debtor in an involuntary bankruptcy incurs in the ordinary course of business. Unpaid wages, salaries, and commissions earned within ninety days prior to the petition are paid next, followed by certain claims for contributions to employee benefit plans, claims by farmers and fishermen, consumer deposits, and certain taxes. Claims of general creditors rank last in the order of priority, which is why these unsecured creditors often receive little, if anything, in a Chapter 7 bankruptcy.

Discharge

From the debtor's point of view, the purpose of a liquidation proceeding is to obtain a fresh start through the discharge of debts.[15] As mentioned earlier, once the debtor's assets have been distributed to creditors as permitted by the Code, the

debtor's remaining debts are then discharged, meaning that the debtor is not obligated to pay them. Certain debts, however, are not dischargeable in bankruptcy. Also, certain debtors may not qualify to have all debts discharged in bankruptcy. These situations are discussed below.

Exceptions to Discharge Discharge of a debt may be denied because of the nature of the claim or the conduct of the debtor. A court will not discharge claims that are based on a debtor's willful or malicious conduct or fraud, or claims related to property or funds that the debtor obtained by false pretenses, embezzlement, or larceny. Any monetary judgment against the debtor for driving while intoxicated cannot be discharged in bankruptcy. When a debtor fails to list a creditor on the bankruptcy schedules (and thus the creditor is not notified of the bankruptcy), that creditor's claims are not dischargeable.

Claims that are not dischargeable in a liquidation bankruptcy include amounts due to the government for taxes, fines, or penalties.[16] Additionally, amounts borrowed by the debtor to pay these taxes will not be discharged. Domestic-support obligations and property settlements arising from a divorce or separation cannot be discharged. Certain student loans or educational debts are not dischargeable (unless payment of the loans imposes an undue hardship on the debtor and the debtor's dependents), nor are amounts due on a retirement account loan. Consumer debts for purchasing luxury items worth more than $550 and cash advances totaling more than $825 are generally not dischargeable.

In the following case, the court considered whether to order the discharge of a debtor's student loan obligations. What does a debtor have to prove to show "undue hardship"?

---

15. Discharges are granted under Chapter 7 only to *individuals*, not to corporations or partnerships. The latter may use Chapter 11, or they may terminate their existence under state law.

16. Taxes accruing within three years prior to bankruptcy are nondischargeable, including federal and state income taxes, employment taxes, taxes on gross receipts, property taxes, excise taxes, customs duties, and any other taxes for which the government claims the debtor is liable in some capacity. See 11 U.S.C. Sections 507(a)(8), 523(a)(1).

CASE 21.3 In re Mosley

United States Court of Appeals, Eleventh Circuit, 494 F.3d 1320 (2007).

FACTS Keldric Mosley incurred student loans while attending Georgia's Alcorn State University between 1989 and 1994. At Alcorn, Mosley joined the U.S. Army Reserve Officers' Training Corps. During training in 1993, Mosley fell from a tank and injured his hip and back. Medical problems from his injuries led him to resign his commission. He left Alcorn to live

with his mother in Atlanta from 1994 to 1999. He worked briefly for several employers, but depressed and physically limited by his injury, he was unable to keep any of the jobs. He tried to return to school but could not obtain financial aid because of the debt he had incurred at Alcorn. In 1999, a

CASE 21.3–Continues next page

CASE 21.3—Continued

federal bankruptcy court granted him a discharge under Chapter 7, but it did not include the student loans. In 2000, after a week at the Georgia Regional Hospital, a state-supported mental-health facility, Mosley was prescribed medication through the U.S. Department of Veterans Affairs for depression, back pain, and other problems. By 2004, his monthly income consisted primarily of $210 in disability benefits from the Veterans Administration. Homeless and in debt for $45,000 to Educational Credit Management Corporation, Mosley asked the bankruptcy court to reopen his case. The court granted him a discharge of his student loans on the basis of undue hardship. Educational Credit appealed to the U.S. Court of Appeals for the Eleventh Circuit.

ISSUE   Was Mosley's testimony regarding his physical and emotional problems enough to prove undue hardship, thus releasing him from his student loan obligations?

DECISION   Yes. The U.S. Court of Appeals for the Eleventh Circuit affirmed the lower court's discharge of the debtor's student loans based on undue hardship. The court found that Mosley's detailed testimony about his depression and back problems provided sufficient evidence of undue hardship in this case.

REASON   To establish undue hardship, the debtor must show that (1) he or she "cannot maintain, based on current income and expenses, a 'minimal' standard of living * * * if forced to repay the loans; (2) that additional circumstances exist indicating that this state of affairs is likely to persist for a significant portion of the repayment period of the student loans; and (3) that the debtor has made good faith efforts to repay the loans." The plaintiff, Educational Credit, claimed that the bankruptcy court was too lax in its acceptance of the debtor's testimony as evidence showing that he would remain in the same financial situation for a long period of time. Educational Credit contended that Mosley needed the opinion of a medical expert on the subject of his future recovery. The court, however, reasoned that Mosley's testimony did not purport to give a medical prognosis, but rather to relate from personal knowledge his struggles with depression, back pain, and the side effects of his medications. The court concluded that Mosley's medical problems, lack of skills, and dire living conditions made it unlikely that he would be able to hold a job and repay the loans. Mosley had made good faith efforts to repay his student loans and "would suffer undue hardship if they were excepted from [bankruptcy] discharge."

 WHAT IF THE FACTS WERE DIFFERENT?   *Suppose that Mosley relocated in a country with a lower cost of living than the United States. Should his change in circumstances be a ground for revoking the discharge of his student loans? Explain your answer.*

■

Objections to Discharge   In addition to the exceptions to discharge previously listed, a bankruptcy court may also deny the discharge of the *debtor* (as opposed to the debt). Grounds for the denial of discharge of the debtor include the following:

1 The debtor's concealment or destruction of property with the intent to hinder, delay, or defraud a creditor.

2 The debtor's fraudulent concealment or destruction of financial records.

3 The granting of a discharge to the debtor within eight years prior to the filing of the petition.

4 The debtor's failure to complete the required consumer education course (unless such a course is unavailable).

5 Proceedings in which the debtor could be found guilty of a felony. (Basically, a court may not discharge any debt until the completion of felony proceedings against the debtor.)

Revocation of Discharge   On petition by the trustee or a creditor, the bankruptcy court may, within one year, revoke the discharge decree if it is discovered that the debtor was fraudulent or dishonest during the bankruptcy proceedings. The revocation renders the discharge void, allowing creditors not satisfied by the distribution of the debtor's estate to proceed with their claims against the debtor.

Reaffirmation of Debt   An agreement to pay a debt dischargeable in bankruptcy is called a **reaffirmation agreement.** A debtor may wish to pay a debt—for example, a debt owed to a family member, physician, bank, or some other creditor—even though the debt could be discharged in bankruptcy. Also, a debtor cannot retain secured property while continuing to pay without entering into a reaffirmation agreement.

To be enforceable, reaffirmation agreements must be made before the debtor is granted a discharge. The agreement must be signed and filed with the court (along with the required disclosures, described next). Court approval is required unless the debtor is represented by an attorney during the negotiation of the reaffirmation and submits the proper documents and certifications. Even when the debtor is represented by an attorney, court approval may be required if it appears that the reaffirmation will result in undue hardship to the debtor. When court approval is required, a separate hearing will take place. The court will approve the reaffirmation only if it finds that the agreement will not result in undue hardship on the debtor and that the reaffirmation is consistent with the debtor's best interests.

Reaffirmation Disclosures To discourage creditors from engaging in abusive reaffirmation practices, the Code provides the specific language for several pages of disclosures that must be given to debtors entering reaffirmation agreements. Among other things, these disclosures explain that the debtor is not required to reaffirm any debt, but that liens on secured property, such as mortgages and cars, will remain in effect even if the debt is not reaffirmed. The reaffirmation agreement must disclose the amount of the debt reaffirmed, the rate of interest, the date payments begin, and the right to rescind.

The disclosures also caution the debtor: "Only agree to reaffirm a debt if it is in your best interest. Be sure you can afford the payments you agree to make." The original disclosure documents must be signed by the debtor, certified by the debtor's attorney, and filed with the court at the same time as the reaffirmation agreement. A reaffirmation agreement that is not accompanied by the original signed disclosures will not be effective.

CHAPTER 11–REORGANIZATION

The type of bankruptcy proceeding used most commonly by corporate debtors is the Chapter 11 *reorganization*. In a reorganization, the creditors and the debtor formulate a plan under which the debtor pays a portion of its debts and the rest of the debts are discharged. The debtor is allowed to continue in business. Although this type of bankruptcy is generally a corporate reorganization, any debtors (including individuals but excluding stockbrokers and commodities brokers) who are eligible for Chapter 7 relief are eligible for relief under Chapter 11. In 1994, Congress established a "fast-track" Chapter 11 procedure for small-business debtors whose liabilities do not exceed $2.19 million and who do not own or manage real estate. This allows bankruptcy proceedings without the appointment of committees and can save time and costs.

The same principles that govern the filing of a liquidation (Chapter 7) petition apply to reorganization (Chapter 11) proceedings. The case may be brought either voluntarily or invol-

untarily. The same guidelines govern the entry of the order for relief. The automatic-stay provision applies in reorganizations as well. The 2005 Bankruptcy Reform Act's exceptions to the automatic stay also apply to Chapter 11 proceedings, as do the new provisions regarding substantial abuse and additional grounds for dismissal (or conversion) of bankruptcy petitions. Also, the 2005 act contains specific rules and limitations for *individual* debtors who file a Chapter 11 petition. For example, an individual debtor's postpetition acquisitions and earnings become the property of the bankruptcy estate.

Under the Code, a court, after notice and a hearing, may dismiss or suspend all proceedings in a case at any time if dismissal or suspension would better serve the interests of the creditors. The Code also allows a court, after notice and a hearing, to dismiss a case under reorganization "for cause." Cause includes the absence of a reasonable likelihood of rehabilitation, the inability to effect a plan, and an unreasonable delay by the debtor that is prejudicial to (may harm the interests of) creditors.[17]

Workouts

In some instances, creditors may prefer private, negotiated adjustments of creditor-debtor relations, also known as **workouts,** to bankruptcy proceedings. Often, these out-of-court workouts are much more flexible and thus more conducive to a speedy settlement. Speed is critical because delay is one of the most costly elements in any bankruptcy proceeding. Another advantage of workouts is that they avoid the various administrative costs of bankruptcy proceedings.

Debtor in Possession

On entry of the order for relief, the debtor in Chapter 11 generally continues to operate the business as a **debtor in possession (DIP).** The court, however, may appoint a trustee (often referred to as a *receiver*) to operate the debtor's business if gross mismanagement of the business is shown or if appointing a trustee is in the best interests of the estate.

The DIP's role is similar to that of a trustee in a liquidation. The DIP is entitled to avoid preferential payments made to creditors and fraudulent transfers of assets. The DIP has the power to decide whether to cancel or assume prepetition executory contracts (those that are not yet performed) or unexpired leases.

---

17. See 11 U.S.C. Section 1112(b). Debtors are not prohibited from filing successive petitions, however. A debtor whose petition is dismissed, for example, can file a new Chapter 11 petition (which may be granted unless it is filed in bad faith).

Creditors' Committees

As soon as practicable after the entry of the order for relief, a committee of unsecured creditors is appointed. If the debtor has filed a plan accepted by the creditors, however, the trustee may decide not to call a meeting of the creditors. The committee may consult with the trustee or the DIP concerning the administration of the case or the formulation of the plan. Additional creditors' committees may be appointed to represent special interest creditors, and the court may order the trustee to change a committee's membership as needed to ensure adequate representation of the creditors.

Orders affecting the estate generally will be entered only with the consent of the committee or after a hearing in which the judge is informed of the position of the committee. As mentioned earlier, small businesses that do not own or manage real estate can avoid creditors' committees. In these cases, orders can be entered without a committee's consent.

The Reorganization Plan

A reorganization plan to rehabilitate the debtor is a plan to conserve and administer the debtor's assets in the hope of an eventual return to successful operation and solvency.

Filing the Plan   Only the debtor may file a plan within the first 120 days after the date of the order for relief. The 120-day period may be extended, but not beyond 18 months from the date of the order for relief. For a small-business debtor, the time for the debtor's filing is 180 days.

The plan must be fair and equitable and must do the following:

1 Designate classes of claims and interests.
2 Specify the treatment to be afforded the classes. (The plan must provide the same treatment for all claims in a particular class.)
3 Provide an adequate means for execution. (Individual debtors must utilize postpetition assets as necessary to execute the plan.)
4 Provide for payment of tax claims over a five-year period.

Acceptance and Confirmation of the Plan   Once the plan has been developed, it is submitted to each class of creditors for acceptance. Each class must accept the plan unless the class is not adversely affected by it. A class has accepted the plan when a majority of the creditors, representing two-thirds of the amount of the total claim, vote to approve it. Confirmation is conditioned on the debtor's certifying that all postpetition domestic-support obligations have been paid in full. For small-business debtors, if the plan meets the listed

requirements, the court must confirm the plan within forty-five days (unless this period is extended).

Even when all classes of creditors accept the plan, the court may refuse to confirm it if it is not "in the best interests of the creditors."[18] A former spouse or child of the debtor can block the plan if it does not provide for payment of her or his claims in cash. Under the reform act, if an unsecured creditor objects to the plan, specific rules apply to the value of property to be distributed under the plan. The plan can also be modified on the request of the debtor, trustee, U.S. trustee, or holder of the unsecured claim. Tax claims must be paid over a five-year period.

Even if only one class of creditors has accepted the plan, the court may still confirm the plan under the Code's so-called **cram-down provision.** In other words, the court may confirm the plan over the objections of a class of creditors. Before the court can exercise this right of cram-down confirmation, it must be demonstrated that the plan is fair and equitable, and does not discriminate unfairly against any creditors.

Discharge   The plan is binding on confirmation. The Bankruptcy Reform Act of 2005, however, provides that confirmation of a plan does not discharge an individual debtor. Individual debtors must complete the plan prior to discharge, unless the court orders otherwise. For all other debtors, the court may order discharge at any time after the plan is confirmed. The debtor is given a reorganization discharge from all claims not protected under the plan. This discharge does not apply to any claims that would be denied discharge under liquidation.

BANKRUPTCY RELIEF UNDER CHAPTER 13 AND CHAPTER 12

In addition to bankruptcy relief through liquidation (Chapter 7) and reorganization (Chapter 11), the Code also provides for individuals' repayment plans (Chapter 13) and family-farmer and family-fisherman debt adjustments (Chapter 12). We look next at the bankruptcy relief available under Chapters 12 and 13 of the Bankruptcy Code.

Individuals' Repayment Plan—Chapter 13

Chapter 13 of the Bankruptcy Code provides for the "Adjustment of Debts of an Individual with Regular Income." Individuals (not partnerships or corporations) with

---

18. The plan need not provide for full repayment to unsecured creditors. Instead, creditors receive a percentage of each dollar owed to them by the debtor.

regular income who owe fixed (liquidated, or undisputed) unsecured debts of less than $336,900 or fixed secured debts of less than $1,010,650 may take advantage of bankruptcy repayment plans. Among those eligible are salaried employees; sole proprietors; and individuals who live on welfare, Social Security, fixed pensions, or investment income. Many small-business debtors have a choice of filing under either Chapter 11 or Chapter 13. Repayment plans offer several advantages, however. One advantage is that they are less expensive and less complicated than reorganization proceedings or, for that matter, even liquidation proceedings.

Filing the Petition   A Chapter 13 repayment plan case can be initiated only by the filing of a voluntary petition by the debtor or by the conversion of a Chapter 7 petition (because of a finding of substantial abuse under the means test, for example). Certain liquidation and reorganization cases may be converted to Chapter 13 with the consent of the debtor.[19] A trustee, who will make payments under the plan, must be appointed. On the filing of a repayment plan petition, the automatic stay previously discussed takes effect. Although the stay applies to all or part of the debtor's consumer debt, it does not apply to any business debt incurred by the debtor. The automatic stay also does not apply to domestic-support obligations.

The Bankruptcy Code imposes the requirement of good faith on a debtor at both the time of the filing of the petition and the time of the filing of the plan. The Code does not define good faith—it is determined in each case through a consideration of "the totality of the circumstances." Bad faith can be cause for the dismissal of a Chapter 13 petition.

The Repayment Plan   A plan of rehabilitation by repayment must provide for the following:

1 The turning over to the trustee of such future earnings or income of the debtor as is necessary for execution of the plan.

2 Full payment through deferred cash payments of all claims entitled to priority, such as taxes.[20]

3 Identical treatment of all claims within a particular class. (The Code permits the debtor to list co-debtors, such as guarantors or sureties, as a separate class.)

Filing the Plan.   Only the debtor may file for a repayment plan. This plan may provide either for payment of all obliga-

tions in full or for payment of a lesser amount. Prior to the 2005 act, the time for repayment was usually three years unless the court approved an extension for up to five years. Today, the length of the payment plan (three or five years) is determined by the debtor's family income. If the debtor's family income is greater than the state median family income under the means test (previously discussed), the proposed plan must be for five years. The term may not exceed five years, however.

The Code requires the debtor to make "timely" payments from her or his disposable income, and the trustee must ensure that the debtor commences these payments. The debtor must begin making payments under the proposed plan within thirty days after the plan has been *filed*. Failure of the debtor to make timely payments or to begin making required payments will allow the court to convert the case to a liquidation bankruptcy or to dismiss the petition.

Confirmation of the Plan.   After the plan is filed, the court holds a confirmation hearing, at which interested parties (such as creditors) may object to the plan. The hearing must be held at least twenty days, but no more than forty-five days, after the meeting of the creditors. Confirmation of the plan is dependent on the debtor's certification that postpetition domestic-support obligations have been paid in full and that all prepetition tax returns have been filed. The court will confirm a plan with respect to each claim of a secured creditor under any of the following circumstances:

1 If the secured creditors have accepted the plan.

2 If the plan provides that secured creditors retain their liens until there is payment in full or until the debtor receives a discharge.

3 If the debtor surrenders the property securing the claims to the creditors.

Discharge   After the completion of all payments, the court grants a discharge of all debts provided for by the repayment plan. Except for allowed claims not provided for by the plan, certain long-term debts provided for by the plan, certain tax claims, payments on retirement accounts, and claims for domestic-support obligations, all other debts are dischargeable. Under prior law, a discharge of debts under a Chapter 13 repayment plan was sometimes referred to as a "superdischarge" because it allowed the discharge of fraudulently incurred debt and claims resulting from malicious or willful injury.

The 2005 act, however, deleted most of the "superdischarge" provisions, especially for debts based on fraud. Today, debts for trust fund taxes, taxes for which returns were

---

19. A Chapter 13 repayment plan may be converted to a Chapter 7 liquidation either at the request of the debtor or, under certain circumstances, "for cause" by a creditor. A Chapter 13 case may be converted to a Chapter 11 case after a hearing.
20. As with a Chapter 11 reorganization plan, full repayment of all claims is not always required.

never filed or filed late (within two years of filing), domestic-support payments, student loans, and debts related to injury or property damage caused while driving under the influence of alcohol or drugs are nondischargeable.

Family Farmers and Fishermen

In 1986, to help relieve economic pressure on small farmers, Congress created Chapter 12 of the Bankruptcy Code. In 2005, Congress extended this protection to family fishermen,[21] modified its provisions somewhat, and made it a permanent chapter in the Bankruptcy Code (previously, the statutes authorizing Chapter 12 had to be periodically renewed by Congress).

Definitions   For purposes of Chapter 12, a *family farmer* is one whose gross income is at least 50 percent farm dependent and whose debts are at least 50 percent farm related.[22] The total debt must not exceed $3,544,525. A partnership or a closely held corporation (see Chapters 24 and 25) that is at least 50 percent owned by the farm family can also qualify as a family farmer.

A *family fisherman* is defined as one whose gross income is at least 50 percent dependent on commercial fishing operations and whose debts are at least 80 percent related to commercial fishing. The total debt for a family fisherman must

---

21. Although the Code uses the terms *fishermen* and *fisherman*, Chapter 12 provisions apply equally to men and women.
22. Note that the Bankruptcy Code defines a *family farmer* and a *farmer* differently. To be a farmer, a person or business must receive 50 percent of gross income from a farming operation that the person or business owns or operates—see footnote 10.

not exceed $1,642,500. As with family farmers, a partnership or closely held corporation can also qualify.

Filing the Petition   The procedure for filing a family-farmer or family-fisherman bankruptcy plan is very similar to the procedure for filing a repayment plan under Chapter 13. The debtor must file a plan not later than ninety days after the order for relief. The filing of the petition acts as an automatic stay against creditors' and co-obligors' actions against the estate.

A farmer or fisherman who has already filed a reorganization or repayment plan may convert the plan to a Chapter 12 plan. The debtor may also convert a Chapter 12 plan to a liquidation plan.

Content and Confirmation of the Plan   The content of a plan under Chapter 12 is basically the same as that of a Chapter 13 repayment plan. The plan can be modified by the debtor but, except for cause, must be confirmed or denied within forty-five days of the filing of the plan.

Court confirmation of the plan is the same as for a repayment plan. In summary, the plan must provide for payment of secured debts at the value of the collateral. If the secured debt exceeds the value of the collateral, the remaining debt is unsecured. For unsecured debtors, the plan must be confirmed if either the value of the property to be distributed under the plan equals the amount of the claim or the plan provides that all of the debtor's disposable income to be received in a three-year period (or longer, by court approval) will be applied to making payments. Completion of payments under the plan discharges all debts provided for by the plan.

REVIEWING **Creditors' Rights and Bankruptcy**

Three months ago, Janet Hart's husband of twenty years died of cancer. Although he had medical insurance, he left Janet with outstanding medical bills of more than $50,000. Janet has worked at the local library for the past ten years, earning $1,500 per month. Since her husband's death, Janet also has received $1,500 in Social Security benefits and $1,100 in life insurance proceeds every month, giving her a monthly income of $4,300. After she pays the mortgage payment of $1,500 and the amounts due on other debts each month, Janet barely has enough left over to buy

groceries for her family (she has two teenage daughters at home). She decides to file for Chapter 7 bankruptcy, hoping for a fresh start. Using the information provided in the chapter, answer the following questions.

1 Under the Bankruptcy Code after the reform act, what must Janet do before filing a petition for relief under Chapter 7?

2 How much time does Janet have after filing the bankruptcy petition to submit the required schedules? What happens if Janet does not meet the deadline?

3 Assume that Janet files a petition under Chapter 7. Further assume that the median family income in the state in which Janet lives is $49,300. What steps would a court take to determine whether Janet's petition is presumed to be "substantial abuse" under the means test?

4 Suppose that the court determines that no presumption of substantial abuse applies in Janet's case. Nevertheless, the court finds that Janet does have the ability to pay at least a portion of the medical bills out of her disposable income. What would the court likely order in that situation?

CHAPTER SUMMARY Creditors' Rights and Bankruptcy

REMEDIES AVAILABLE TO CREDITORS

Liens
(See pages 417–419.)
	1. *Mechanic's lien*—A nonpossessory, filed lien on an owner's real estate for labor, services, or materials furnished to or made on the realty.
	
	2. *Artisan's lien*—A possessory lien on an owner's personal property for labor performed or value added.
	
	3. *Judicial liens*—
	    a. Writ of attachment—A court order authorizing the seizure of a debtor's property prior to the court's final determination of the creditor's rights to the property. Attachment is available only on the creditor's posting of a bond and strict compliance with the applicable state statutes.
	    b. Writ of execution—A court order directing the sheriff to seize (levy) and sell a debtor's nonexempt real or personal property to satisfy a court's judgment in the creditor's favor.

Garnishment (See page 419.)	A collection remedy that allows the creditor to attach a debtor's funds (such as wages owed or bank accounts) and property that are held by a third person.
Creditors' Composition Agreements (See page 419.)	A contract between a debtor and his or her creditors by which the debtor's debts are discharged by payment of a sum less than the amount that is actually owed.
Mortgage Foreclosure (See pages 419–420.)	On the debtor's default, the entire mortgage debt is due and payable, allowing the creditor to foreclose on the realty by selling it to satisfy the debt.
Suretyship and Guaranty (See pages 420–422.)	Under contract, a third person agrees to be primarily or secondarily liable for the debt owed by the principal debtor. A creditor can turn to this third person for satisfaction of the debt.

(Continued)

CHAPTER SUMMARY Creditors' Rights and Bankruptcy—Continued

LAWS ASSISTING DEBTORS

Exemptions
(See page 423.)

State laws exempt certain types of real and personal property.

1. *Exempted real property*—Each state permits a debtor to retain the family home, either in its entirety or up to a specified dollar amount, free from the claims of unsecured creditors or trustees in bankruptcy (homestead exemption).

2. *Exempted personal property*—Personal property that is most often exempt from satisfaction of judgment debts includes the following:

   a. Household furniture up to a specified dollar amount.

   b. Clothing and certain personal possessions.

   c. Transportation vehicles up to a specified dollar amount.

   d. Certain classified animals, such as livestock and pets.

   e. Equipment used in a business or trade up to a specified dollar amount.

FORMS OF BANKRUPTCY COMPARED

Issue	Chapter 7	Chapter 11	Chapters 12 and 13
Purpose	Liquidation.	Reorganization.	Adjustment.
Who Can Petition	Debtor (voluntary) or creditors (involuntary).	Debtor (voluntary) or creditors (involuntary).	Debtor (voluntary) only.
Who Can Be a Debtor	Any "person" (including partnerships and corporations) except railroads, insurance companies, banks, savings and loan institutions, investment companies licensed by the U.S. Small Business Administration, and credit unions. Farmers and charitable institutions cannot be involuntarily petitioned.	Any debtor eligible for Chapter 7 relief; railroads are also eligible.	*Chapter 12*—Any family farmer (one whose gross income is at least 50 percent farm dependent and whose debts are at least 50 percent farm related) or family fisherman (one whose gross income is at least 50 percent dependent on commercial fishing) or any partnership or closely held corporation at least 50 percent owned by a family farmer or fisherman, when total debt does not exceed $3,544,525 for a family farmer and $1,642,500 for a family fisherman. *Chapter 13*—Any individual (not partnerships or corporations) with regular income who owes fixed (liquidated) unsecured debts of less than $336,900 or fixed secured debts of less than $1,010,650.

CHAPTER SUMMARY	Creditors' Rights and Bankruptcy—Continued		
Procedure Leading to Discharge	Nonexempt property is sold with proceeds to be distributed (in order) to priority groups. Dischargeable debts are terminated.	Plan is submitted; if it is approved and followed, debts are discharged.	Plan is submitted and must be approved if the value of the property to be distributed equals the amount of the claims or if the debtor turns over disposable income for a three-year or five-year period; if the plan is followed, debts are discharged.
Advantages	On liquidation and distribution, most debts are discharged, and the debtor has an opportunity for a fresh start.	Debtor continues in business. Creditors can either accept the plan, or it can be "crammed down" on them. The plan allows for the reorganization and liquidation of debts over the plan period.	Debtor continues in business or possession of assets. If the plan is approved, most debts are discharged after the plan period.

FOR REVIEW

Answers for the even-numbered questions in this **For Review** *section can be found on this text's accompanying Web site at* **www.cengage.com/blaw/fbl**. *Select "Chapter 21" and click on "For Review."*

1 What is a prejudgment attachment? What is a writ of execution? How does a creditor use these remedies?

2 What is garnishment? When might a creditor undertake a garnishment proceeding?

3 In a bankruptcy proceeding, what constitutes the debtor's estate in property? What property is exempt from the estate under federal bankruptcy law?

4 What is the difference between an exception to discharge and an objection to discharge?

5 In a Chapter 11 reorganization, what is the role of the debtor in possession?

QUESTIONS AND CASE PROBLEMS

 ## HYPOTHETICAL SCENARIOS AND CASE PROBLEMS

21.1 Artisan's Lien. Air Ruidoso, Ltd., operated a commuter airline and air charter service between Ruidoso, New Mexico, and airports in Albuquerque and El Paso. Executive Aviation Center, Inc., provided services for airlines at the Albuquerque International Airport. When Air Ruidoso failed to pay more than $10,000 that it owed for fuel, oil, and oxygen, Executive Aviation took possession of Air Ruidoso's plane. Executive Aviation claimed that it had a lien on the plane and filed a suit in a New Mexico state court to foreclose. Do supplies such as fuel, oil, and oxygen qualify as "materials" for the purpose of creating an artisan's lien? Why or why not?

21.2 Hypothetical Question with Sample Answer. Runyan voluntarily petitions for bankruptcy. He has three major claims against his estate. One is by Calvin, a friend who holds Runyan's negotiable promissory note for $2,500; one is by Kohak, an employee who is owed three months' back wages of $4,500; and one is by the First Bank of Sunny Acres on an unsecured loan of $5,000. In addition, Martinez, an accountant retained by the trustee, is owed $500, and property taxes of $1,000 are owed to Micanopa County. Runyan's nonexempt property has been liquidated, with the proceeds totaling $5,000. Discuss fully what amount each party will receive, and why.

For a sample answer to Question 21.2, go to Appendix E at the end of this text.

21.3 Rights of the Surety. Meredith, a farmer, borrowed $5,000 from Farmer's Bank and gave the bank $4,000 in bearer bonds to hold as collateral for the loan. Meredith's neighbor, Peterson, who had known Meredith for years, signed as a surety on the note. Because of a drought, Meredith's harvest that year was only a fraction of what it normally was, and he was forced to default on his payments to Farmer's Bank. The bank did not immediately sell the bonds but instead requested $5,000 from Peterson. Peterson paid the $5,000 and then demanded that the bank give him the $4,000 in securities. Can Peterson enforce this demand? Explain.

21.4 Discharge in Bankruptcy. Between 1980 and 1987, Craig Hanson borrowed funds from Great Lakes Higher Education Corp. to finance his education at the University of Wisconsin. Hanson defaulted on the debt in 1989, and Great Lakes obtained a judgment against him for $31,583.77. Three years later, Hanson filed a bankruptcy petition under Chapter 13. Great Lakes timely filed a proof of claim in the amount of $35,531.08. Hanson's repayment plan proposed to pay $135 monthly to Great Lakes over sixty months, which in total was only 19 percent of the claim, but said nothing about discharging the remaining balance. The plan was confirmed without objection. After Hanson completed the payments under the plan, without any additional proof or argument being offered, the court granted a discharge of his student loans. In 2003, Educational Credit Management Corp. (ECMC), which had taken over Great Lakes' interest in the loans, filed a motion for relief from the discharge. What is the requirement for the discharge of a student loan obligation in bankruptcy? Did Hanson meet this requirement? Should the court grant ECMC's motion? Discuss. [*In re Hanson*, 397 F.3d 482 (7th Cir. 2005)]

21.5 Exceptions to Discharge. Between 1988 and 1992, Lorna Nys took out thirteen student loans, totaling about $30,000, to finance an associate of arts degree in drafting from the College of the Redwoods and a bachelor of arts degree from Humboldt State University (HSU) in California. In 1996, Nys began working at HSU as a drafting technician. As a "Drafter II," the highest-paying drafting position at HSU, Nys's gross income in 2002 was $40,244. She was fifty-one years old, her net monthly income was $2,299.33, and she had $2,295.05 in monthly expenses, including saving $140 for her retirement, which she planned for age sixty-five. When Educational Credit Management Corp. (ECMC) began to collect payments on Nys's student loans, she filed a Chapter 7 petition in a federal bankruptcy court, seeking a discharge of the loans. ECMC argued that Nys did not show any "additional circumstances" that would impede her ability to repay. What is the standard for the discharge of student loans under Chapter 7? Does Nys meet that standard? Why or why not? [*In re Nys*, 446 F.3d 938 (9th Cir. 2006)]

21.6 Case Problem with Sample Answer. James Stout, a professor of economics and business at Cornell College in Mount Vernon, Iowa, filed a petition in bankruptcy under Chapter 7, seeking to discharge about $95,000 in credit-card debts. At the time, Stout had been divorced for ten years and had custody of his children: Z. S., who attended college, and G. S., who was twelve years old. Stout's ex-wife did not contribute child support. According to Stout, G. S. was an "elite" ice-skater who practiced twenty hours a week and had placed between first and third at more than forty competitive events. He had decided to home school G. S., whose achievements were average for her grade level despite her frequent absences from public school. His petition showed monthly income of $4,227 and expenses of $4,806. The expenses included annual home school costs of $8,400 and annual skating expenses of $6,000. They did not include Z. S.'s college costs, such as airfare for his upcoming studies in Europe, and other items. The trustee allowed monthly expenses of $3,227—with nothing for skating—and asked the court to dismiss the petition. Can the court grant this request? Should it? If so, what might it encourage Stout to do? Explain. [*In re Stout*, 336 Bankr. 138 (N.D. Iowa 2006)]

After you have answered Problem 21.6, compare your answer with the sample answer given on the Web site that accompanies this text. Go to www.cengage.com/blaw/fbl, select "Chapter 21," and click on "Case Problem with Sample Answer."

21.7 Attachment. In 2004 and 2005, Kent Avery, on behalf of his law firm—the Law Office of Kent Avery, LLC—contracted with Marlin Broadcasting, LLC, to air commercials on WCCC-FM, 106.9 "The Rock." Avery, who was the sole member of his firm, helped to create the ads, which solicited direct contact with "defense attorney Kent Avery," featured his voice, and repeated his name and experience to make potential clients familiar with him. When WCCC was not paid for the broadcasts, Marlin filed a suit in a Connecticut state court against Avery and his firm, alleging an outstanding balance of $35,250. Pending the court's hearing of the suit, Marlin filed a request for a writ of attachment. Marlin offered in evidence the parties' contracts, the ads' transcripts, and WCCC's invoices. Avery contended that he could not be held personally liable for the cost of the ads. Marlin countered that the ads unjustly enriched Avery by conferring a personal benefit on him to Marlin's detriment. What is the purpose of attachment? What must a creditor prove to obtain a writ of attachment? Did Marlin meet this test? Explain. [*Marlin Broadcasting, LLC v. Law Office of Kent Avery, LLC*, 101 Conn.App. 638, 922 A.2d 1131 (2007)]

21.8 Discharge in Bankruptcy. Rhonda Schroeder married Gennady Shvartsshteyn (Gene) in 1997. Gene worked at Royal Courier and Air Domestic Connect in Illinois, where Melissa Winyard also worked in 1999 and 2000. During this time, Gene and Winyard had an affair. A year after leaving Royal, Winyard filed a petition in a federal bankruptcy court under Chapter 7 and was granted a discharge of her debts. Sometime later, in a letter to Schroeder, who had learned of the affair, Winyard wrote, "I never intentionally wanted any of this to happen. I never wanted to disrupt your marriage." Schroeder obtained a divorce and, in 2005, filed a suit in an Illinois state court against Winyard, alleging "alienation of affection." Schroeder claimed that there had been "mutual love and affection" in her marriage until Winyard engaged in conduct intended to alienate her husband's affection. Schroeder charged that Winyard "caused him to have sexual intercourse with her," resulting in "the destruction of the marital relationship." Winyard filed a motion for summary judgment on the ground that any liability on her part had been discharged in her bankruptcy. Is there an exception to discharge for "willful and malicious conduct"? If so, does Schroeder's claim qualify? Discuss. [*Schroeder v. Winyard*, 375 Ill.App.3d 358, 873 N.E.2d 35, 313 Ill.Dec. 740 (2 Dist. 2007)]

21.9 **A Question of Ethics.** *In January 2003, Gary Ryder and Washington Mutual Bank, F.A., executed a note in which Ryder promised to pay $2,450,000, plus interest at a rate that could vary from month to month. The amount of the first payment was $10,933. The note was to be paid in full by February 1, 2033. A mortgage on Ryder's real property at 345 Round Hill Road in Greenwich, Connecticut, in favor of the bank secured his obligations under the note. The note*

and mortgage required that he pay the taxes on the property, which he did not do in 2004 and 2005. The bank notified him that he was in default and, when he failed to act, paid $50,095.92 in taxes, penalties, interest, and fees. Other disputes arose between the parties, and Ryder filed a suit in a federal district court against the bank, alleging, in part, breach of contract. He charged, among other things, that some of his timely payments were not processed and were subjected to incorrect late fees, forcing him to make excessive payments and ultimately resulting in "non-payment by Ryder." [Ryder v. Washington Mutual Bank, F.A., 501 F.Supp.2d 311 (D.Conn. 2007)]

1 The bank filed a counterclaim, seeking to foreclose on the mortgage. What should a creditor be required to prove to foreclose on mortgaged property? What would be a debtor's most effective defense? Which party in this case is likely to prevail on the bank's counterclaim? Why?

2 The parties agreed to a settlement that released the bank from Ryder's claims and required him to pay the note by January 31, 2007. The court dismissed the suit, but when Ryder did not make the payment, the bank asked the court to reopen the case. The bank then asked for a judgment in its favor on Ryder's complaint, arguing that the settlement had "immediately" released the bank from his claims. Does this seem fair? Why or why not?

CRITICAL THINKING AND WRITING ASSIGNMENT

21.10 **Video Question.** Go to this text's Web site at **www.cengage.com/blaw/fbl** and select "Chapter 21." Click on "Video Questions" and view the video titled *The River.* Then answer the following questions.

1 In the video, a crowd (including Mel Gibson) is gathered at a farm auction in which a neighbor's (Jim Antonio's) farming goods are being sold. The people in the crowd, who are upset because they believe that the bank is selling out the farmer, begin chanting "no sale, no sale." In an effort to calm the situation, the farmer tells the crowd that "they've already foreclosed" on his farm. What does he mean?

2 Assume that the auction is a result of Chapter 7 bankruptcy proceedings. Was the farmer's petition for bankruptcy voluntary or involuntary? Explain.

3 Suppose that the farmer purchased the homestead three years prior to filing a petition in bankruptcy and that the current market value of the farm is $215,000. What is the maximum amount of equity that the farmer could claim as exempt under the 2005 Bankruptcy Reform Act?

4 Compare the results of a Chapter 12 bankruptcy as opposed to a Chapter 7 bankruptcy for the farmer in the video.

ACCESSING THE INTERNET

For updated links to resources available on the Web, as well as a variety of other materials, visit this text's Web site at

www.cengage.com/blaw/fbl

The Legal Information Institute at Cornell University offers a collection of law materials concerning debtor-creditor relationships, including federal statutes and recent Supreme Court decisions on this topic, at

topics.law.cornell.edu/wex/Debtor_and_creditor

The U.S. Department of Labor's Web site contains a page on garnishment and employees' rights in relation to garnishment proceedings at

www.dol.gov/dol/topic/wages/garnishments.htm

Another good resource for bankruptcy information is the American Bankruptcy Institute (ABI) at

www.abiworld.org

To read a brief primer on the distribution of property in a Chapter 7 bankruptcy, go to

www.lawdog.com/bkrcy/lib2a8.htm

PRACTICAL INTERNET EXERCISES

Go to this text's Web site at **www.cengage.com/blaw/fbl**, select "Chapter 21," and click on "Practical Internet Exercises." There you will find the following Internet research exercises that you can perform to learn more about the topics covered in this chapter.

PRACTICAL INTERNET EXERCISE 21-1   LEGAL PERSPECTIVE—Debtor-Creditor Relations

PRACTICAL INTERNET EXERCISE 21-2   MANAGEMENT PERSPECTIVE—Bankruptcy Alternatives

BEFORE THE TEST

Go to this text's Web site at **www.cengage.com/blaw/fbl**, select "Chapter 21," and click on "Interactive Quizzes." You will find a number of interactive questions relating to this chapter.

UNIT SIX   **EXTENDED CASE STUDY**

Central Virginia Community College v. Katz

We discussed bankruptcy law in Chapter 21. The Constitution, in Article I, grants Congress the authority to enact "uniform Laws on the subject of Bankruptcies throughout the United States." Under this clause, in the Bankruptcy Code, Congress has empowered a bankruptcy trustee to recover from a creditor a debtor's preferential transfer—a transfer of property or a payment of money made within ninety days of the filing of a bankruptcy petition. The question before the United States Supreme Court in Central Virginia Community College v. Katz,[1] the case that we examine in this extended case study, is whether a state can refuse, on an assertion of sovereign immunity, to comply with a federal bankruptcy court's order to return a debtor's preferential transfer.

CASE BACKGROUND   Wallace's Book Stores, Inc. (WBI), Wallace's Book Company (WBC), and their subsidiaries were at one time among the nation's largest suppliers of new and used textbooks and college bookstore supplies throughout North America. They provided textbook buy-back and wholesale textbook distribution services, as well as textbooks, trade books, miscellaneous course books, materials, and other goods, to colleges and universities on an open account basis.

In 2001, WBI, WBC, and sixty-seven of WBI's subsidiaries filed a petition in a federal bankruptcy court under Chapter 11 of the Bankruptcy Code. Under their "Plan of Liquidation," Bernard Katz was appointed "Liquidating Supervisor," or trustee, and was vested with a variety of responsibilities that included a duty to avoid preferential transfers.

During the ninety-day period immediately preceding the date of the petition, Central Virginia Community College and other Virginia state institutions of higher learning had

---

1. 546 U.S. 356, 126 S.Ct. 990, 163 L.Ed.2d 945 (2006). This opinion can be read online at www.findlaw.com/casecode/supreme.html. In the "Browsing" section, click on "2006 Decisions." On the resulting page, click on the name of the case to access the opinion.

received transfers that Katz sought to recover. The institutions filed a motion to dismiss this request on the basis of their sovereign immunity. The court denied the motion.

On appeal, a federal district court affirmed this decision, as did the U.S. Court of Appeals for the Sixth Circuit. The institutions appealed to the United States Supreme Court.

MAJORITY OPINION

Justice *STEVENS* delivered the opinion of the Court.

* * * *

* * * [In bankruptcy proceedings, the] term "discharge" historically had a dual meaning; it referred to both release of debts and release of the debtor from prison.

Well into the 18th century, imprisonment for debt was still ubiquitous [widespread] in * * * the American Colonies. Bankruptcy and insolvency laws remained as much concerned with ensuring full satisfaction of creditors (and, relatedly, preventing debtors' flight to parts unknown) as with securing new beginnings for debtors.

Common as imprisonment itself was, the American Colonies, and later the several States, had wildly divergent schemes for discharging debtors and their debts. At least four jurisdictions offered relief through private Acts of their legislatures. Those Acts released debtors from prison upon surrender of their property, and many coupled the release from prison with a discharge of debts. Other jurisdictions enacted general laws providing for release from prison and, in a few places, discharge of debt. Others still granted release from prison, but only in exchange for indentured servitude. Some jurisdictions provided no relief at all for the debtor. [And a debtor might be discharged in one state only to be imprisoned in another.]

* * * *

* * * The absence of extensive debate [during the Constitutional Convention] over the text of the Bankruptcy Clause * * * indicates that there was general agreement on the importance of authorizing a uniform federal response * * * .

* * * *

The text of Article I, Section 8, [clause] 4, of the Constitution * * * provides that Congress shall have the power to establish "uniform Laws on the subject of Bankruptcies throughout the United States." Although the interest in avoiding unjust imprisonment for debt and making federal discharges in bankruptcy enforceable in every State was a primary motivation for the adoption of that provision, its coverage encompasses the entire "subject of Bankruptcies."

* * * *

* * * *Those who crafted the Bankruptcy Clause would have understood it to give Congress the power to authorize courts to avoid preferential transfers and to recover the transferred property.* Petitioners do not dispute that that authority has been a core aspect of the administration of bankrupt estates since at least the 18th century. [Emphasis added.]

* * * *

Insofar as orders * * * [of] the bankruptcy courts * * * implicate States' sovereign immunity from suit, the States agreed in the plan of the [Constitutional] Convention not to assert that immunity. So much is evidenced not only by the history of the Bankruptcy Clause, * * * but also by legislation considered and enacted in the immediate wake of the Constitution's ratification.

* * * *

* * * [The Bankruptcy Act of 1800] specifically granted federal courts the authority to issue writs of *habeas corpus* effective to release debtors from state prisons.

This grant of *habeas* power is remarkable not least because it would be another 67 years, after ratification of the Fourteenth Amendment, before the writ would be made generally available to state prisoners. * * * Yet there appears to be no record of any objection to the bankruptcy legislation or its grant of *habeas* power to federal courts based on an infringement of sovereign immunity.

* * * *The Framers, in adopting the Bankruptcy Clause, plainly intended to give Congress the power to redress the rampant injustice resulting from States' refusal to respect one another's discharge orders.* As demonstrated by * * * Congress' enactment of a provision granting federal courts the authority to release debtors from state prisons, the power to enact bankruptcy legislation was understood to carry with it the power to subordinate state sovereignty * * * . [Emphasis added.]

* * * *

The judgment of the Court of Appeals for the Sixth Circuit is affirmed.

(Continued)

DISSENTING OPINION

Justice *THOMAS*, * * * dissenting.

* * * *

The majority maintains that the States' consent to suit can be ascertained from the history of the Bankruptcy Clause. But history confirms that the adoption of the Constitution merely established federal power to legislate in the area of bankruptcy law, and did not manifest an additional intention to waive the States' sovereign immunity against suit. Accordingly, I respectfully dissent.

* * * *

* * * It is inherent in the nature of sovereignty not to be amenable to the suit of an individual without [the sovereign's] consent. This * * * exemption * * * is * * * enjoyed by the government of every State in the Union.

* * * *

The majority finds a surrender of the States' immunity from suit in Article I of the Constitution, which authorizes Congress "to establish * * * uniform Laws on the subject of Bankruptcies throughout the United States." But nothing in the text of the Bankruptcy Clause suggests an abrogation or limitation of the States' sovereign immunity.

It is difficult to discern an intention to abrogate state sovereign immunity through the Bankruptcy Clause when no such intention has been found in any of the other clauses in Article I.

* * * *

For example, Article I also empowers Congress * * * to protect * * * patents. [This provision], no less than the Bankruptcy Clause, [was] motivated by the Framers' desire for nationally uniform legislation. * * * Nonetheless, we have refused, in addressing patent law, to give the need for uniformity the weight the majority today assigns it in the context of bankruptcy, instead recognizing that this need is a factor which belongs to the Article I patent-power calculus, rather than to any determination of whether a state plea of sovereign immunity deprives a patentee of property without due process of law.

QUESTIONS FOR ANALYSIS

1 **LAW.** What did the majority conclude in this case? What was the majority's reasoning in support of this conclusion?

2 **LAW.** What was the dissent's argument? On what points did the dissent base its contention?

3 **ETHICS.** From an ethical perspective, why should a trustee be allowed to recover a debtor's transfer of property or a payment of money to a creditor over the creditor's objection? What might be an ethical basis for permitting the creditor to keep the property or the money transferred?

4 **ECONOMIC DIMENSIONS.** How might the result in this case affect a state's decision to grant or deny credit to potential debtors?

5 **IMPLICATIONS FOR THE BUSINESS OWNER.** How might the holding in this case influence the decision of an individual or a business firm to conduct business with a state?

UNIT SEVEN Employment Relations

UNIT CONTENTS

CHAPTER 22
Agency Relationships

LEARNING OBJECTIVES

AFTER READING THIS CHAPTER, YOU SHOULD BE ABLE TO ANSWER THE FOLLOWING QUESTIONS:

1 What is the difference between an employee and an independent contractor?

2 How do agency relationships arise?

3 What duties do agents and principals owe to each other?

4 When is a principal liable for the agent's actions with respect to third parties? When is the agent liable?

5 What are some of the ways in which an agency relationship can be terminated?

One of the most common and important legal relationships is that of **agency.** In an agency relationship between two parties, one party, called the *agent*, agrees to represent or act for the other, called the *principal*. The principal has the right to control the agent's conduct in matters entrusted to the agent, and the agent must exercise his or her powers "for the benefit of the principal only." By using agents, a principal can conduct multiple business operations simultaneously in various locations. Thus, for example, contracts that bind the principal can be made at different places with different persons at the same time.

Agency relationships permeate the business world. Indeed, agency law is essential to the existence and operation of a corporate entity, because only through its agents can a corporation function and enter into contracts. A familiar example of an agent is a corporate officer who serves in a representative capacity for the owners of the corporation. In this capacity, the officer has the authority to bind the principal (the corporation) to a contract.

AGENCY RELATIONSHIPS

Section 1(1) of the *Restatement (Second) of Agency*[1] defines agency as "the fiduciary relation which results from the manifestation of consent by one person to another that the

other shall act in his [or her] behalf and subject to his [or her] control, and consent by the other so to act." In other words, in a principal-agent relationship, the parties have agreed that the agent will act *on behalf and instead of* the principal in negotiating and transacting business with third parties.

The term **fiduciary** is at the heart of agency law. The term can be used both as a noun and as an adjective. When used as a noun, it refers to a person having a duty created by her or his undertaking to act primarily for another's benefit in matters connected with the undertaking. When used as an adjective, as in "fiduciary relationship," it means that the relationship involves trust and confidence.

Agency relationships commonly exist between employers and employees. Agency relationships may sometimes also exist between employers and independent contractors who are hired to perform special tasks or services.

Employer-Employee Relationships

Normally, all employees who deal with third parties are deemed to be agents. A salesperson in a department store, for instance, is an agent of the store's owner (the principal) and acts on the owner's behalf. Any sale of goods made by the salesperson to a customer is binding on the principal. Similarly, most representations of fact made by the salesperson with respect to the goods sold are binding on the principal.

---

1. The *Restatement (Second) of Agency* is an authoritative summary of the law of agency and is often referred to by judges and other legal professionals.

Because employees who deal with third parties are normally deemed to be agents of their employers, agency law and employment law overlap considerably. Agency relationships, though, as will become apparent, can exist outside an employer-employee relationship and thus have a broader reach than employment law does. Additionally, agency law is based on the common law. In the employment realm, many common law doctrines have been displaced by statutory law and government regulations relating to employment relationships.

Employment laws (state and federal) apply only to the employer-employee relationship. Statutes governing Social Security, withholding taxes, workers' compensation, unemployment compensation, workplace safety, employment discrimination, and the like (see Chapter 23) are applicable only if employer-employee status exists. *These laws do not apply to an independent contractor.*

Employer–Independent Contractor Relationships

Independent contractors are not employees because, by definition, those who hire them have no control over the details of their physical performance. Section 2 of the *Restatement (Second) of Agency* defines an **independent contractor** as follows:

[An independent contractor is] a person who contracts with another to do something for him [or her] but who is not controlled by the other nor subject to the other's right to control with respect to his [or her] physical conduct in the performance of the undertaking. *He [or she] may or may not be an agent.* [Emphasis added.]

Building contractors and subcontractors are independent contractors; a property owner does not control the acts of either of these professionals. Truck drivers who own their equipment and hire themselves out on a per-job basis are independent contractors, but truck drivers who drive company trucks on a regular basis are usually employees.

The relationship between a person or firm and an independent contractor may or may not involve an agency relationship. To illustrate: An owner of real estate who hires a real estate broker to negotiate a sale of his or her property not only has contracted with an independent contractor (the real estate broker) but also has established an agency relationship for the specific purpose of assisting in the sale of the property. Another example is an insurance agent, who is both an independent contractor and an agent of the insurance company for which she or he sells policies. (Note that an insurance *broker*, in contrast, normally is an agent of the person obtaining insurance and not of the insurance company.)

Determining Employee Status

The courts are frequently asked to determine whether a particular worker is an employee or an independent contractor. How a court decides this issue can have a significant effect on the rights and liabilities of the parties. For example, employers are required to pay certain taxes, such as Social Security and unemployment taxes, for employees but not for independent contractors. (See this chapter's *Management Perspective* feature on the next page for more details on this issue.)

Criteria Used by the Courts In determining whether a worker has the status of an employee or an independent contractor, the courts often consider the following questions:

1 How much control can the employer exercise over the details of the work? (If an employer can exercise considerable control over the details of the work, this would indicate employee status. This is perhaps the most important factor weighed by the courts in determining employee status.)

2 Is the worker engaged in an occupation or business distinct from that of the employer? (If so, this points to independent-contractor status, not employee status.)

3 Is the work usually done under the employer's direction or by a specialist without supervision? (If the work is usually done under the employer's direction, this would indicate employee status.)

4 Does the employer supply the tools at the place of work? (If so, this would indicate employee status.)

5 For how long is the person employed? (If the person is employed for a long period of time, this would indicate employee status.)

6 What is the method of payment—by time period or at the completion of the job? (Payment by time period, such as once every two weeks or once a month, would indicate employee status.)

7 What degree of skill is required of the worker? (If little skill is required, this may indicate employee status.)

Sometimes, workers may benefit from having employee status—for tax purposes and to be protected under certain employment laws, for example. As mentioned earlier, federal statutes governing employment discrimination apply only when an employer-employee relationship exists.

Criteria Used by the IRS Businesspersons should be aware that the Internal Revenue Service (IRS) has established its own criteria for determining whether a worker is an independent contractor or an employee. Although the IRS once considered twenty factors in determining a worker's status,

MANAGEMENT PERSPECTIVE

Independent-Contractor Negligence

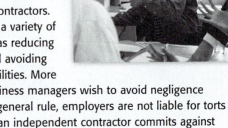

Management Faces a Legal Issue

Managers often hire independent contractors. They do so for a variety of reasons, such as reducing paperwork and avoiding certain tax liabilities. More important, business managers wish to avoid negligence lawsuits. As a general rule, employers are not liable for torts (wrongs) that an independent contractor commits against third parties. If an employer exercises significant control over the work activity of an independent contractor, however, that contractor may be considered an employee, and the employer may be held liable for the contractor's torts.

What the Courts Say

In one case, a trucking company that hired independent contractors to make deliveries was sued after a motorist was killed in a collision with one of the company's independent-contractor drivers. At trial, the trucking company prevailed. The plaintiff argued that the company had failed to investigate the background, qualifications, or experience of the driver. The appellate court, however, pointed out that an employer of an independent contractor has no control over the manner in which the work is done. The plaintiff failed to offer any proof as to why the company should have investigated the driver.[a]

In another case, a tenant whose hand was injured sued the building's owner. An independent contractor, hired by the owner to perform repair work on the outside of the building, had attempted to close the tenant's balcony door when the tenant's hand got caught, causing her injury. The appellate court ultimately held that the building's owner and

a. *Stander v. Dispoz-O-Products, Inc.*, 973 So.2d 603 (Fla.App. 2008).

its managing agent could not be held liable for the independent contractor's alleged negligence. As in the previous case, the court noted that the employer (the building's owner) had no right to control the manner in which the independent contractor did his work. The tenant suffered harm because of the independent contractor's actions, not because the premises were in disrepair.[b]

Finally, another issue that sometimes arises is a business owner's liability for injuries to employees of independent contractors that the owner has hired. In one case, two employees of an independent subcontractor suffered electrical burns while working on a construction project. They sued the business owner of the project, among others. The defendants prevailed at trial, and on appeal, the court agreed.[c]

Implications for Managers

To minimize the possibility of being held liable for an independent contractor's negligence, managers should check the qualifications of all contractors before hiring them. A thorough investigation of a contractor's background is especially important when the work may present a danger to the public (as in delivering explosives). It is also wise to require a written contract in which the contractor assumes liability for any harm caused to third parties by the contractor's negligence. Managers should insist that independent contractors carry liability insurance and ensure that the liability insurance policy is current. Additionally, business managers should refrain from doing anything that would lead a third party to believe that an independent contractor is an employee. And, of course, they cannot maintain control over an independent contractor's actions.

b. *Stagno v. 143-50 Hoover Owners Corp.*, 48 A.D.3d 548, 853 N.Y.S.2d 85 (2008).

c. *Dalton v. 933 Peachtree, LP*, 291 Ga.App. 123, 661 S.E.2d 156 (2008).

---

current guidelines focus on just one of those factors—the degree of control the business exercises over the worker.

The IRS tends to closely scrutinize a firm's classification of workers because, as mentioned, employers can avoid certain tax liabilities by hiring independent contractors instead of employees. Even when a firm classifies a worker as an independent contractor, if the IRS decides that the worker is an employee, the employer will be responsible for paying any applicable Social Security, withholding, and unemployment taxes.

■EXAMPLE 22.1 Microsoft Corporation had required a number of workers to become associated with employment agencies so that they could work for Microsoft as temporary workers. The workers sued, alleging that they were actually employees of Microsoft (rather than independent contractors) and thus entitled to participate in the company's stock option plan. The IRS determined that the workers were employees because Microsoft had exercised significant control over their work performance. A court affirmed this decision on appeal. Ultimately, Microsoft was required to pay back payroll taxes for hundreds of workers who had contractually agreed to work for Microsoft as independent contractors.[2] ▣

Employee Status and "Works for Hire" Under the Copyright Act of 1976, any copyrighted work created by an employee within the scope of her or his employment at the request of the employer is a "work for hire," and the employer owns the copyright to the work. When an employer hires an independent contractor—a freelance artist, writer, or computer programmer, for example—the independent contractor owns the copyright *unless* the parties agree in writing that the work is a "work for hire" and the work falls into one of nine specific categories, including audiovisual and other works.

■EXAMPLE 22.2 Graham marketed CD-ROM discs containing compilations of software programs that are available free to the public. Graham hired James to create a file-retrieval program that allowed users to access the software on the CDs. James built into the final version of the program a notice stating that he was the author of the program and owned the copyright. Graham removed the notice. When James sold the program to another CD-ROM publisher, Graham filed a suit claiming that James's file-retrieval program was a "work for hire" and that Graham owned the copyright to the program. The court, however, decided that James—a skilled computer programmer who controlled the manner and method of his work—was an independent contractor and not an employee for hire. Thus, James owned the copyright to the file-retrieval program.[3] ▣

HOW AGENCY RELATIONSHIPS ARE FORMED

Agency relationships normally are consensual; that is, they come about by voluntary consent and agreement between the parties. Generally, the agreement need not be in writing,[4] and consideration is not required.

A person must have contractual capacity to be a principal. Those who cannot legally enter into contracts directly should

not be allowed to do so indirectly through an agent. Any person can be an agent, though, regardless of whether he or she has the capacity to enter a contract. Because an agent derives the authority to enter into contracts from the principal and because a contract made by an agent is legally viewed as a contract of the principal, it is immaterial whether the agent personally has the legal capacity to make that contract. Thus, even a minor or a person who is legally incompetent can be appointed as an agent (but generally cannot be a principal).

An agency relationship can be created for any legal purpose. An agency relationship that is created for an illegal purpose or that is contrary to public policy is unenforceable. **■EXAMPLE 22.3** Sharp (as principal) contracts with Blesh (as agent) to sell illegal narcotics. This agency relationship is unenforceable because selling illegal narcotics is a felony and is contrary to public policy. ▣ It is also illegal for physicians and other licensed professionals to employ unlicensed agents to perform professional actions.

Generally, an agency relationship can arise in four ways: by agreement of the parties, by ratification, by estoppel, and by operation of law.

Agency by Agreement

Most agency relationships are based on an express or implied agreement that the agent will act for the principal and that the principal agrees to have the agent so act. An agency relationship can be created through a written contract or by an oral agreement. **■EXAMPLE 22.4** Reese asks Cary, a gardener, to contract with others for the care of his lawn on a regular basis. Cary agrees. In this situation, an agency relationship exists between Reese and Cary for the lawn care. ▣

An agency agreement can also be implied by conduct. **■EXAMPLE 22.5** A hotel expressly allows only Boris Koontz to park cars, but Boris has no employment contract there. The hotel's manager tells Boris when to work, as well as where and how to park the cars. The hotel's conduct amounts to a manifestation of its willingness to have Boris park its customers' cars, and Boris can infer from the hotel's conduct that he has authority to act as a parking valet. It can be inferred that Boris is an agent-employee for the hotel, his purpose being to provide valet parking services for hotel guests. ▣

Agency by Ratification

On occasion, a person who is in fact not an agent (or who is an agent acting outside the scope of her or his authority) may make a contract on behalf of another (a principal). If the principal approves or affirms that contract by word or by action, an agency relationship is created by **ratification.** Ratification involves a question of intent, and intent can be expressed by

2. *Vizcaino v. U.S. District Court for the Western District of Washington,* 173 F.3d 713 (9th Cir. 1999).

3. *Graham v. James,* 144 F.3d 229 (2d Cir. 1998); see also *Pittsburg State University/Kansas National Education Association v. Kansas Board of Regents/Pittsburg State University,* 280 Kan. 408, 122 P.3d 336 (2005).

4. There are two main exceptions to the statement that agency agreements need not be in writing: (1) Whenever agency authority empowers the agent to enter into a contract that the Statute of Frauds requires to be in writing, the agent's authority from the principal must likewise be in writing (this is called the *equal dignity rule,* to be discussed later in this chapter). (2) A power of attorney, which confers authority to an agent, must be in writing.

either words or conduct. The basic requirements for ratification will be discussed later in this chapter.

Agency by Estoppel

When a principal causes a third person to believe that another person is his or her agent, and the third person deals with the supposed agent, the principal is "estopped to deny" the agency relationship. In such a situation, the principal's actions create the *appearance* of an agency that does not in fact exist. The third person must prove that she or he *reasonably* believed that an agency relationship existed, though.[5] Facts and circumstances must show that an ordinary, prudent person familiar with business practice and custom would have been justified in concluding that the agent had authority.

■EXAMPLE 22.6 Andrew accompanies Grant, a seed sales representative, to call on a customer, Steve, the proprietor of the General Seed Store. Andrew has done independent sales work but has never signed an employment agreement with

---

[5]. These concepts also apply when a person who is in fact an agent undertakes an action that is beyond the scope of her or his authority, as will be discussed later in this chapter.

Grant. Grant boasts to Steve that he wishes he had three more assistants "just like Andrew." By making this representation, Grant creates the impression that Andrew is his agent and has authority to solicit orders. Steve has reason to believe from Grant's statements that Andrew is an agent for Grant. Steve then places seed orders with Andrew. If Grant does not correct the impression that Andrew is an agent, Grant will be bound to fill the orders just as if Andrew were really his agent. Grant's representation to Steve created the impression that Andrew was Grant's agent and had authority to solicit orders. ■

Note that the acts or declarations of a purported *agent* in and of themselves do not create an agency by estoppel. Rather, it is the deeds or statements *of the principal* that create an agency by estoppel. ■EXAMPLE 22.7 If Andrew walks into Steve's store and claims to be Grant's agent, when in fact he is not, and Grant has no knowledge of Andrew's representations, Grant will not be bound to any deal struck by Andrew and Steve. Andrew's acts and declarations alone do not create an agency by estoppel. ■

Under what other circumstances might a third party reasonably believe that an agent has the authority to act for a principal when the agent actually does not have this authority? The following case provides an illustration.

CASE 22.1 **Motorsport Marketing, Inc. v. Wiedmaier, Inc.**

Missouri Court of Appeals, Western District, 195 S.W.3d 492 (2006).
www.courts.mo.gov[a]

FACTS Wiedmaier, Inc., owns and operates Wiedmaier Truck Stop in St. Joseph, Missouri. The owners are Marsha and Jerry Wiedmaier. Their son Michael does not own an interest in the firm, but he had worked for it as a fuel truck operator. Motorsport Marketing, Inc., sells racing collectibles and memorabilia to retail outlets. In 2003, Michael faxed a credit application to Motorsport's sales manager, Lesa James. Marsha signed the form as "Secretary-Owner" of Wiedmaier; after she signed, Michael added himself to the list of owners. Motorsport approved a credit line. Michael formed Extreme Diecast, LLC, which he told Motorsport was part of Wiedmaier, and began ordering Motorsport merchandise. By early 2004, however, Michael had stopped making payments on the account, quit his job, and moved to Ohio. Patrick Rainey,

president of Motorsport, contacted Marsha. She refused to pay. Motorsport filed a suit in a Missouri state court against Wiedmaier and others to collect the unpaid amount. The court entered a judgment in favor of Motorsport, assessing liability against the defendants for the outstanding balance of $93,388.58, plus $13,406.38 in interest and $25,165.93 in attorneys' fees. The defendants appealed to a state intermediate appellate court.

ISSUE Did Motorsport reasonably believe that Michael acted as Wiedmaier's agent in ordering merchandise?

DECISION Yes. The state intermediate appellate court affirmed the judgment of the lower court, echoing the conclusion that "Michael acted as an apparent agent of Wiedmaier, Inc., in its dealings with Motorsport."

REASON The appellate court emphasized that "the credit application constituted a direct communication from Wiedmaier, Inc. (through Marsha) to Motorsport causing Motorsport to reasonably believe that Michael had authority to act for Wiedmaier, Inc." Marsha signed the application, on which Michael was listed as an owner. The defendants argued

---

a. In the "Quick Links" box, click on "Opinion & Minutes." When that page opens, click on the "Missouri Court of Appeals, Western District opinions" link. At the bottom of the next page, click on the "Search Opinions" link. In that page's "Search for" box, type "Wiedmaier" and click on "Search." In the result, click on the name of the case to access the opinion. The Missouri state courts maintain this Web site.

CASE 22.1—Continued

that Michael paid Motorsport with checks drawn on Extreme Diecast's account, which should have led Motorsport to investigate further. In response, the court pointed out that, as Motorsport was aware, "it is a common practice for a truck stop to have a separate division with a separate name to handle its diecast and other related merchandise, and that Michael represented that this is exactly what Extreme Diecast was." In good faith reliance on the credit application and Michael's representations, Motorsport extended credit to Wiedmaier and filled Michael's orders. "If the transactions executed by Michael [do] not bind Wiedmaier, Inc.,

Motorsport will suffer the loss of the balance due on the account."

 WHAT IF THE FACTS WERE DIFFERENT? *Suppose that Motorsport's sales manager had telephoned Marsha Wiedmaier rather than just faxing the credit application. Further suppose that Marsha had vouched for Michael's creditworthiness but informed Motorsport that she and her husband owned Wiedmaier and that Michael worked for them. How might the outcome of this case have been different in that situation?*

◼

Agency by Operation of Law

The courts may find an agency relationship in the absence of a formal agreement in other situations as well. This can occur in family relationships. Suppose that one spouse purchases certain basic necessaries (such as food and clothing) and charges them to the other spouse's charge account. The courts will often rule that the latter is liable to pay for the necessaries, either because of a social policy of promoting the general welfare of the spouse or because of a legal duty to supply necessaries to family members.

Agency by operation of law may also occur in emergency situations, when the agent's failure to act outside the scope of his or her authority would cause the principal substantial loss. If the agent is unable to contact the principal, the courts will often grant this emergency power. For instance, a railroad engineer may contract on behalf of her or his employer for medical care for an injured motorist hit by the train.

DUTIES OF AGENTS AND PRINCIPALS

Once the principal-agent relationship has been created, both parties have duties that govern their conduct. As discussed previously, an agency relationship is *fiduciary*—one of trust. In a fiduciary relationship, each party owes the other the duty to act with the utmost good faith. We now examine the various duties of agents and principals.

In general, for every duty of the principal, the agent has a corresponding right, and vice versa. When one party to the agency relationship violates his or her duty to the other party, the remedies available to the nonbreaching party arise out of contract and tort law. These remedies include monetary damages, termination of the agency relationship, an injunction, and required accountings.

Agent's Duties to the Principal

Generally, the agent owes the principal five duties—performance, notification, loyalty, obedience, and accounting.

Performance An implied condition in every agency contract is the agent's agreement to use reasonable diligence and skill in performing the work. When an agent fails to perform any of her or his duties, liability for breach of contract normally results. The degree of skill or care required of an agent is usually that expected of a reasonable person under similar circumstances. Generally, this is interpreted to mean ordinary care. If an agent has represented himself or herself as possessing special skills, however, the agent is expected to exercise the skills claimed. Failure to do so constitutes a breach of the agent's duty.

Not all agency relationships are based on contract. In some situations, an agent acts gratuitously—that is, not for monetary compensation. A gratuitous agent cannot be liable for breach of contract, as there is no contract; he or she is subject only to tort liability. Once a gratuitous agent has begun to act in an agency capacity, he or she has the duty to continue to perform in that capacity in an acceptable manner and is subject to the same standards of care and duty to perform as other agents.

Notification An agent is required to notify the principal of all matters that come to her or his attention concerning the subject matter of the agency. This is the *duty of notification*, or the duty to inform. **■EXAMPLE 22.8** Lang, an artist, is about to negotiate a contract to sell a series of paintings to Barber's Art Gallery for $25,000. Lang's agent learns that Barber is insolvent and will be unable to pay for the paintings. The agent has a duty to inform Lang of this fact because it is relevant to the subject matter of the agency—the sale of Lang's paintings. ◼

Generally, the law assumes that the principal knows of any information acquired by the agent that is relevant to the agency—regardless of whether the agent actually passes on this information to the principal. It is a basic tenet of agency law that notice to the agent is notice to the principal.

Loyalty   Loyalty is one of the most fundamental duties in a fiduciary relationship. Basically, the agent has the duty to act *solely for the benefit of his or her principal* and not in the interest of the agent or a third party. For example, an agent cannot represent two principals in the same transaction unless both know of the dual capacity and consent to it. The duty of loyalty also means that any information or knowledge acquired through the agency relationship is considered confidential. It would be a breach of loyalty to disclose such information either during the agency relationship or after its termination. Typical examples of confidential information are trade secrets and customer lists compiled by the principal. In short, the agent's loyalty must be undivided. The agent's actions must be strictly for the benefit of the principal and must not result in any secret profit for the agent.

Obedience   When acting on behalf of a principal, an agent has a duty to follow all lawful and clearly stated instructions of the principal. Any deviation from such instructions is a violation of this duty. During emergency situations, however, when the principal cannot be consulted, the agent may deviate from the instructions without violating this duty. Whenever instructions are not clearly stated, the agent can fulfill the duty of obedience by acting in good faith and in a manner reasonable under the circumstances.

Accounting   Unless an agent and a principal agree otherwise, the agent has the duty to keep and make available to the principal an account of all property and funds received and paid out on behalf of the principal. This includes gifts from third parties in connection with the agency. For instance, if a customer makes a gift to a salesperson for prompt deliveries by the salesperson's firm, the gift belongs to the firm, unless its policy allows otherwise. The agent has a duty to maintain separate accounts for the principal's funds and for the agent's personal funds, and the agent must not intermingle these accounts.

Principal's Duties to the Agent

The principal also owes certain duties to the agent. These duties relate to compensation, reimbursement and indemnification, cooperation, and safe working conditions.

Compensation   In general, when a principal requests certain services from an agent, the agent reasonably expects payment. The principal therefore has a duty to pay the agent for services rendered. For example, when an accountant or an attorney is asked to act as an agent, an agreement to compensate the agent for such service is implied. The principal also has a duty to pay that compensation in a timely manner. Except in a gratuitous agency relationship, in which an agent does not act in return for payment, the principal must pay the agreed-on value for an agent's services. If no amount has been expressly agreed on, the principal owes the agent the customary compensation for such services.

 **Many legal disputes arise because the principal and agent did not specify how much the agent would be paid. To avoid such disputes, always state in advance, and in writing, the amount or rate of compensation that you will pay your agents. Even when dealing with salespersons who customarily are paid a percentage of the value of the sale, it is wise to explicitly state the rate of compensation.**

■

Reimbursement and Indemnification   Whenever an agent disburses funds to fulfill the request of the principal or to pay for necessary expenses in the course of a reasonable performance of his or her agency duties, the principal has the duty to reimburse the agent for these payments. Agents cannot recover for expenses incurred through their own misconduct or negligence, though.

Subject to the terms of the agency agreement, the principal has the duty to compensate, or *indemnify*, an agent for liabilities incurred because of authorized and lawful acts and transactions. For instance, if the principal fails to perform a contract formed by the agent with a third party and the third party then sues the agent, the principal is obligated to compensate the agent for any costs incurred in defending against the lawsuit.

Additionally, the principal must indemnify (pay) the agent for the value of benefits that the agent confers on the principal. The amount of indemnification is usually specified in the agency contract. If it is not, the courts will look to the nature of the business and the type of loss to determine the amount. Note that this rule applies to acts by gratuitous agents as well. If the finder of a dog that becomes sick takes the dog to a veterinarian and pays the required fees for the veterinarian's services, the agent is entitled to be reimbursed by the owner of the dog for those fees.

Cooperation   A principal has a duty to cooperate with the agent and to assist the agent in performing her or his duties. The principal must do nothing to prevent such performance.

When a principal grants an agent an exclusive territory, for example, the principal creates an *exclusive agency* and cannot compete with the agent or appoint or allow another agent to so compete. If the principal does so, she or he will be exposed to liability for the agent's lost sales or profits. **■EXAMPLE 22.9** Akers (the principal) creates an exclusive agency by granting Johnson (the agent) an exclusive territory within which Johnson may sell Akers's products. In this situation, Akers cannot compete with Johnson within that territory—or appoint or allow another agent to so compete—because this would violate the exclusive agency. If Akers does so, he can be held liable for Johnson's lost sales or profits. ■

Safe Working Conditions Under the common law, a principal is required to provide safe working premises, equipment, and conditions for all agents and employees. The principal has a duty to inspect the working conditions and to warn agents and employees about any unsafe areas. When the agent is an employee, the employer's liability is frequently covered by state workers' compensation insurance, and federal and state statutes often require the employer to meet certain safety standards (to be discussed in Chapter 23).

AGENT'S AUTHORITY

An agent's authority to act can be either *actual* (express or implied) or *apparent*. If an agent contracts outside the scope of his or her authority, the principal may still become liable by ratifying the contract.

Express Authority

As indicated, an agent's actual authority can be express or implied. *Express authority* is authority declared in clear, direct, and definite terms. Express authority can be given orally or in writing. In most states, the **equal dignity rule** requires that if the contract being executed is or must be in writing, then the agent's authority must also be in writing. Failure to comply with the equal dignity rule can make a contract voidable *at the option of the principal*. The law regards the contract at that point as a mere offer. If the principal decides to accept the offer, acceptance must be ratified, or affirmed, in writing.

■EXAMPLE 22.10 Klee (the principal) orally asks Parkinson (the agent) to sell a ranch that Klee owns. Parkinson finds a buyer and signs a sales contract (a contract for an interest in realty must be in writing) on behalf of Klee to sell the ranch. The buyer cannot enforce the contract unless Klee subsequently ratifies Parkinson's agency status *in writing*. Once Parkinson's agency status is ratified, either party can enforce rights under the contract. ■

Modern business practice allows an exception to the equal dignity rule. An executive officer of a corporation normally is not required to obtain written authority from the corporation to conduct *ordinary* business transactions. The equal dignity rule does not apply when an agent acts in the presence of a principal or when the agent's act of signing is merely perfunctory. Thus, if Dickens (the principal) negotiates a contract but is called out of town the day it is to be signed and orally authorizes Santini to sign the contract, the oral authorization is sufficient.

Giving an agent a **power of attorney** confers express authority. The power of attorney normally is a written document and is usually notarized. (A document is notarized when a **notary public**—a public official authorized to attest to the authenticity of signatures—signs and dates the document and imprints it with his or her seal of authority.) Most states have statutory provisions for creating a power of attorney. A power of attorney can be special (permitting the agent to do specified acts only), or it can be general (permitting the agent to transact all business for the principal). Because a general power of attorney grants extensive authority to an agent to act on behalf of the principal in many ways, it should be used with great caution. Ordinarily, a power of attorney terminates on the incapacity or death of the person giving the power.[6]

Implied Authority

Actual authority may also be implied. An agent has the *implied authority* to do what is reasonably necessary to carry out express authority and accomplish the objectives of the agency. Authority can also be implied by custom or inferred from the position the agent occupies. **■EXAMPLE 22.11** Mueller is employed by Al's Supermarket to manage one of its stores. Al's has not expressly stated that Mueller has authority to contract with third persons. In this situation, though, authority to manage a business implies authority to do what is reasonably required to operate the business. This includes forming contracts to hire employees, to buy merchandise and equipment, and to advertise the products sold in the store. ■

Apparent Authority and Estoppel

Actual authority (express or implied) arises from what the principal makes clear *to the agent*. Apparent authority, in contrast, arises from what the principal causes a third party to

---

6. A *durable* power of attorney, however, continues to be effective despite the principal's incapacity. An elderly person, for example, might grant a durable power of attorney to provide for the handling of property and investments or specific health-care needs in the event that she or he becomes incompetent.

believe. An agent has **apparent authority** when the principal, by either word or action, causes a *third party* reasonably to believe that the agent has authority to act, even though the agent has no express or implied authority. If the third party changes his or her position in reliance on the principal's representations, the principal may be *estopped* (prevented) from denying that the agent had authority.

Apparent authority usually comes into existence through a principal's pattern of conduct over time. ▪**EXAMPLE 22.12** Bain is a traveling salesperson with the authority to solicit orders for a principal's goods. Because she does not carry any goods with her, she normally would not have the implied authority to collect payments from customers on behalf of the principal. Suppose that she does accept payments from Corgley Enterprises, however, and submits them to the principal's accounting department for processing. If the principal does nothing to stop Bain from continuing this practice, a pattern develops over time, and the principal confers apparent authority on Bain to accept payments from Corgley. ▪

At issue in the following case was a question of apparent authority or, as the court referred to it, "ostensible [apparent] agency."

CASE 22.2   **Ermoian v. Desert Hospital**

Court of Appeal of California, Fourth District, 152 Cal.App.4th 475, 61 Cal.Rptr.3d 754 (2007).

FACTS In 1990, Desert Hospital in California established a comprehensive perinatal services program (CPSP) to provide obstetrical care to women who were uninsured (*perinatal* is often defined as relating to the period from about the twenty-eighth week of pregnancy to around one month after birth). The CPSP was set up in an office suite across from the hospital and named "Desert Hospital Outpatient Maternity Services Clinic." The hospital contracted with a corporation controlled by Dr. Morton Gubin, which employed Dr. Masami Ogata, to provide obstetrical services. In January 1994, Jackie Shahan went to the hospital's emergency room because of cramping and other symptoms. The emergency room physician told Shahan that she was pregnant and referred her to the clinic. Shahan visited the clinic throughout her pregnancy. On May 15, Shahan's baby, Amanda Ermoian, was born with brain abnormalities that left her severely mentally retarded and unable to care for herself. Her conditions could not have been prevented, treated, or cured *in utero*. Through a guardian, Amanda filed a suit in a California state court against the hospital and others, alleging "wrongful life." She claimed that the defendants negligently failed to inform her mother of her abnormalities before her birth, depriving her mother of the opportunity to make an informed choice to terminate the pregnancy. The court ruled in the defendants' favor, holding, among other things, that the hospital was not liable because Drs. Gubin and Ogata were not its employees. Amanda appealed to a state intermediate appellate court, contending, in part, that the physicians were the hospital's "ostensible [apparent] agents."

ISSUE Did the physicians who were working at the hospital when Amanda was born have apparent authority to act for the hospital?

DECISION Yes. The state intermediate appellate court decided that, contrary to the lower court's finding, the physicians, Gubin and Ogata, were "ostensible [apparent] agents of the Hospital." The appellate court affirmed the lower court's ruling on Amanda's "wrongful life" claim, however, concluding that the physicians were not negligent in failing to advise Shahan to have an elective abortion.

REASON The court pointed out that ostensible agency (apparent agency) can be implied when a principal "by his acts has led others to believe that he has conferred authority upon an agent." Liability for an act of an ostensible agent rests on a doctrine of estoppel. The court noted that a person dealing with an agent must believe in the agent's authority. In this case, the hospital "held out the clinic and the personnel in the clinic as part of the hospital." The clinic used the same name as the hospital and labeled itself as an outpatient clinic. Moreover, personnel in the hospital's emergency room referred Shahan specifically to Dr. Gubin. When Shahan called the hospital, the receptionist told her "that she was calling the Hospital outpatient clinic which was the clinic of Dr. Gubin." The appellate court ruled that the hospital, and those associated with it, created the appearance to Shahan that the hospital was the provider of obstetrical care.

FOR CRITICAL ANALYSIS—Ethical Consideration *Does a principal have an ethical responsibility to inform an unaware third party that an apparent (ostensible) agent does not in fact have authority to act on the principal's behalf?*

▪

Ratification

Ratification occurs when the principal affirms an agent's *unauthorized* act. When ratification occurs, the principal is bound by the agent's act, and the act is treated as if it had been authorized by the principal *from the outset*. Ratification can be express or implied.

If the principal does not ratify the contract, the principal is not bound, and the third party's agreement with the agent is viewed as merely an unaccepted offer. Because the third party's agreement is an unaccepted offer, the third party can revoke the offer at any time, without liability, before the principal ratifies the contract.

The requirements for ratification can be summarized as follows:

1 The agent must have acted on behalf of an identified principal who subsequently ratifies the action.

2 The principal must know of all material facts involved in the transaction. If a principal ratifies a contract without knowing all of the facts, the principal can rescind (cancel) the contract.

3 The principal must affirm the agent's act in its entirety.

4 The principal must have the legal capacity to authorize the transaction at the time the agent engages in the act and at the time the principal ratifies. The third party must also have the legal capacity to engage in the transaction.

5 The principal's affirmation must occur before the third party withdraws from the transaction.

6 The principal must observe the same formalities when approving the act done by the agent as would have been required to authorize it initially.

LIABILITY IN AGENCY RELATIONSHIPS

Frequently, a question arises as to which party, the principal or the agent, should be held liable for contracts formed by the agent or for torts or crimes committed by the agent. We look here at these aspects of agency law.

Liability for Contracts

Liability for contracts formed by an agent depends on how the principal is classified and on whether the actions of the agent were authorized or unauthorized. Principals are classified as disclosed, partially disclosed, or undisclosed.[7]

A **disclosed principal** is a principal whose identity is known by the third party at the time the contract is made by the agent. A **partially disclosed principal** is a principal whose identity is not known by the third party, but the third party knows that the agent is or may be acting for a principal at the time the contract is made. **■EXAMPLE 22.13** Sarah has contracted with a real estate agent to sell certain property. She wishes to keep her identity a secret, but the agent makes it perfectly clear to potential buyers of the property that the agent is acting in an agency capacity. In this situation, Sarah is a partially disclosed principal. ■ An **undisclosed principal** is a principal whose identity is totally unknown by the third party, and the third party has no knowledge that the agent is acting in an agency capacity at the time the contract is made.

Authorized Acts   If an agent acts within the scope of her or his authority, normally the principal is obligated to perform the contract regardless of whether the principal was disclosed, partially disclosed, or undisclosed. Whether the agent may also be held liable under the contract, however, depends on the disclosed, partially disclosed, or undisclosed status of the principal.

Disclosed or Partially Disclosed Principal.   A disclosed or partially disclosed principal is liable to a third party for a contract made by an agent who is acting within the scope of her or his authority. If the principal is disclosed, an agent has no contractual liability for the nonperformance of the principal or the third party. If the principal is partially disclosed, in most states the agent is also treated as a party to the contract, and the third party can hold the agent liable for contractual nonperformance.[8]

Undisclosed Principal.   When neither the fact of agency nor the identity of the principal is disclosed, the undisclosed principal is bound to perform just as if the principal had been fully disclosed at the time the contract was made. The agent is also liable as a party to the contract.

When a principal's identity is undisclosed and the agent is forced to pay the third party, the agent is entitled to be indemnified (compensated) by the principal. The principal had a duty to perform, even though his or her identity was undisclosed, and failure to do so will make the principal ultimately liable. Once the undisclosed principal's identity is revealed, the third party generally can elect to hold either the principal or the agent liable on the contract. Conversely, the undisclosed principal can require the third party to fulfill the contract, *unless* (1) the undisclosed principal was expressly excluded as a party in the contract; (2) the contract is a negotiable instrument signed by the agent with no indication of signing in a representative capacity; or (3) the performance of

---

7. *Restatement (Second) of Agency*, Section 4.

8. *Restatement (Second) of Agency*, Section 321.

the agent is personal to the contract, allowing the third party to refuse the principal's performance.

Unauthorized Acts If an agent has no authority but nevertheless contracts with a third party, the principal cannot be held liable on the contract. It does not matter whether the principal was disclosed, partially disclosed, or undisclosed. The *agent* is liable, however. **■EXAMPLE 22.14** Scranton signs a contract for the purchase of a truck, purportedly acting as an agent under authority granted by Johnson. In fact, Johnson has not given Scranton any such authority. Johnson refuses to pay for the truck, claiming that Scranton had no authority to purchase it. The seller of the truck is entitled to hold Scranton liable for payment. **■**

If the principal is disclosed or partially disclosed, the agent is liable to the third party as long as the third party relied on the agency status. The agent's liability here is based on the breach of an *implied warranty of authority* (an agent impliedly warrants that he or she has the authority to enter a contract on behalf of the principal), not on breach of the contract itself.[9] If the third party knows at the time the contract is made that the agent does not have authority—or if the agent expresses to the third party *uncertainty* as to the extent of her or his authority—then the agent is not personally liable.

Liability for E-Agents Although standard agency principles once applied only to *human* agents, today these same principles are being applied to electronic agents. An electronic agent, or **e-agent,** is a semiautonomous computer program that is capable of executing specific tasks. E-agents used in e-commerce include software that can search through many databases and retrieve only information that is relevant for the user.

The Uniform Electronic Transactions Act (UETA), which was discussed in detail in Chapter 13 and has been adopted by the majority of the states, contains several provisions relating to the principal's liability for the actions of e-agents. Section 15 of the UETA states that e-agents may enter into binding agreements on behalf of their principals. Presumably, then—at least in those states that have adopted the act—the principal will be bound by the terms in a contract entered into by an e-agent. Thus, if you place an order over the Internet, the company (principal) whose system took the order via an e-agent cannot claim that it did not receive your order.

The UETA also stipulates that if an e-agent does not provide an opportunity to prevent errors at the time of the transaction, the other party to the transaction can avoid the

transaction. For instance, if an e-agent fails to provide an on-screen confirmation of a purchase or sale, the other party can avoid the effect of any errors.

Liability for Torts and Crimes

Obviously, any person, including an agent, is liable for her or his own torts and crimes. Whether a principal can also be held liable for an agent's torts and crimes depends on several factors, which we examine here.

Principal's Tortious Conduct A principal conducting an activity through an agent may be liable for harm resulting from the principal's own negligence or recklessness. Thus, a principal may be liable for giving improper instructions, authorizing the use of improper materials or tools, or establishing improper rules that resulted in the agent's committing a tort. **■EXAMPLE 22.15** Jack knows that Suki cannot drive but nevertheless tells her to use the company truck to deliver some equipment to a customer. In this situation, Jack (the principal) will be liable for his own negligence to anyone injured by Suki's negligent driving. **■**

Principal's Authorization of Agent's Tortious Conduct A principal who authorizes an agent to commit a tort may be liable to persons or property injured thereby, because the act is considered to be the principal's. **■EXAMPLE 22.16** Selkow directs his agent, Warren, to cut the corn on specific acreage, which neither of them has the right to do. The harvest is therefore a trespass (a tort), and Selkow is liable to the owner of the corn. **■**

Note also that an agent acting at the principal's direction can be liable as a *tortfeasor* (one who commits a wrong, or tort), along with the principal, for committing the tortious act even if the agent was unaware of the wrongfulness of the act. Assume in the above example that Warren, the agent, did not know that Selkow lacked the right to harvest the corn. Nevertheless, Warren can be held liable to the owner of the field for damages, along with Selkow, the principal.

Liability for Agent's Misrepresentation A principal is exposed to tort liability whenever a third person sustains a loss due to the agent's misrepresentation. The principal's liability depends on whether the agent was actually or apparently authorized to make representations and whether such representations were made within the scope of the agency. The principal is always directly responsible for an agent's misrepresentation made within the scope of the agent's authority. **■EXAMPLE 22.17** Bassett is a demonstrator for Moore's products. Moore sends Bassett to a home show to demonstrate the products and to answer questions from consumers. Moore has

---

9. The agent is not liable on the contract because the agent was never intended personally to be a party to the contract.

given Bassett authority to make statements about the products. If Bassett makes only true representations, all is fine; but if he makes false claims, Moore will be liable for any injuries or damages sustained by third parties in reliance on Bassett's false representations. ■

Liability for Agent's Negligence   Under the doctrine of *respondeat superior*,[10] the principal-employer is liable for any harm caused to a third party by an agent-employee within the scope of employment. This doctrine imposes **vicarious liability**, or indirect liability, on the employer—that is, liability without regard to the personal fault of the employer for torts committed by an employee in the course or scope of employment.[11] Third parties injured through the negligence of an employee can sue either that employee or the employer, if the employee's negligent conduct occurred while the employee was acting within the scope of employment.

Rationale Underlying the Doctrine of **Respondeat Superior.**   At early common law, a servant (employee) was

---

10. Pronounced ree-*spahn*-dee-uht soo-*peer*-ee-your. The doctrine of *respondeat superior* applies not only to employer-employee relationships but also to other principal-agent relationships in which the principal has the right of control over the agent.

11. The theory of *respondeat superior* is similar in this respect to the theory of strict liability covered in Chapter 4.

viewed as the master's (employer's) property. The master was deemed to have absolute control over the servant's acts and was held strictly liable for them no matter how carefully the master supervised the servant. The rationale for the doctrine of *respondeat superior* is based on the social duty that requires every person to manage his or her affairs, whether accomplished by the person or through agents, so as not to injure another. Liability is imposed on employers because they are deemed to be in a better financial position to bear the loss. The superior financial position carries with it the duty to be responsible for damages.

Generally, public policy requires that an injured person be afforded effective relief, and a business enterprise is usually better able to provide that relief than is an individual employee. Employers normally carry liability insurance to cover any damages awarded as a result of such lawsuits. They are also able to spread the cost of risk over the entire business enterprise.

The doctrine of *respondeat superior*, which the courts have applied for nearly two centuries, continues to have practical implications in all situations involving principal-agent (employer-employee) relationships. Today, the small-town grocer with one clerk and the multinational corporation with thousands of employees are equally subject to the doctrinal demand of "let the master respond." (Keep this principle in mind as you read through Chapter 23.)

When an agent commits a negligent act, can the agent, as well as the principal, be held liable? That was the issue in the following case.

CASE 22.3   **Warner v. Southwest Desert Images, LLC**

Court of Appeals of Arizona, 218 Ariz. 121, 180 P.3d 986 (2008).

FACTS Aegis Communications hired Southwest Desert Images (SDI) to provide landscaping services for its property. SDI employee David Hoggatt was spraying an herbicide to control weeds around the Aegis building one day when he was told that the spray was being sucked into the building by the air-conditioning system and making people sick. The building was evacuated, and employees were treated for breathing problems and itchy eyes. Aegis employee Catherine Warner, who had previously suffered two heart attacks, was taken to the hospital. It was determined that she had suffered a heart attack. She continued experiencing health complications that she blamed on exposure to the spray. Warner sued SDI and Hoggatt for negligence. The trial judge dismissed the suit against Hoggatt. The jury found SDI alone to be liable for Warner's injuries. She was awarded $3,825 in damages. She appealed the decision.

ISSUE Can Hoggatt, the employee and agent of SDI who negligently sprayed the herbicide, be held liable for damages in addition to his employer and the principal, SDI?

DECISION Yes. The appeals court held that Hoggatt should not have been dismissed from the lawsuit.

REASON The fact that Hoggatt was an agent-employee of SDI did not excuse him from liability for his negligence in spraying. The court reasoned that there was evidence that Hoggatt had ignored instructions provided by the company that sold SDI the spray. In doing so, he was negligent. An agent (Hoggatt) is not excused from responsibility for tortious conduct just because he is working for a principal (SDI). The jury found SDI completely responsible, but denied Warner the

CASE 22.3—Continues next page

CASE 22.3—Continued

right to collect from Hoggatt as a joint tortfeasor in this situation. The appeals court, however, decided that Warner should be able to collect from Hoggatt as well.

FOR CRITICAL ANALYSIS—Legal Consideration *How could SDI reduce the likelihood of similar lawsuits occurring in the future?*

∎

Determining the Scope of Employment. The key to determining whether a principal may be liable for the torts of an agent under the doctrine of *respondeat superior* is whether the torts are committed within the scope of the agency or employment. The *Restatement (Second) of Agency*, Section 229, indicates the factors that today's courts will consider in determining whether a particular act occurred within the course and scope of employment. These factors are as follows:

1 Whether the employee's act was authorized by the employer.

2 The time, place, and purpose of the act.

3 Whether the act was one commonly performed by employees on behalf of their employers.

4 The extent to which the employer's interest was advanced by the act.

5 The extent to which the private interests of the employee were involved.

6 Whether the employer furnished the means or instrumentality (for example, a truck or a machine) by which the injury was inflicted.

7 Whether the employer had reason to know that the employee would do the act in question and whether the employee had ever done it before.

8 Whether the act involved the commission of a serious crime.

The Distinction between a "Detour" and a "Frolic." A useful insight into the "scope of employment" concept may be gained from the judge's classic distinction between a "detour" and a "frolic" in the case of *Joel v. Morison.*[12] In this case, the English court held that if a servant merely took a detour from his master's business, the master will be responsible. If, however, the servant was on a "frolic of his own" and not in any way "on his master's business," the master will not be liable.

∎**EXAMPLE 22.18** Mandel, a traveling salesperson, while driving his employer's vehicle to call on a customer, decides to stop

at the post office—which is one block off his route—to mail a personal letter. As Mandel approaches the post office, he negligently runs into a parked vehicle owned by Chan. In this situation, because Mandel's detour from the employer's business is not substantial, he is still acting within the scope of employment, and the employer is liable. The result would be different, though, if Mandel had decided to pick up a few friends for cocktails in another city and in the process had negligently run into Chan's vehicle. In that circumstance, the departure from the employer's business would be substantial, and the employer normally would not be liable to Chan for damages. Mandel would be considered to have been on a "frolic" of his own. ∎

Employee Travel Time. An employee going to and from work or to and from meals is usually considered outside the scope of employment. If travel is part of a person's position, however, such as a traveling salesperson or a regional representative of a company, then travel time is normally considered within the scope of employment. Thus, the duration of the business trip, including the return trip home, is within the scope of employment unless there is a significant departure from the employer's business.

Notice of Dangerous Conditions. The employer is charged with knowledge of any dangerous conditions discovered by an employee and pertinent to the employment situation. ∎**EXAMPLE 22.19** Chad, a maintenance employee in Martin's apartment building, notices a lead pipe protruding from the ground in the building's courtyard. The employee neglects either to fix the pipe or to inform his employer of the danger. John falls on the pipe and is injured. Martin, the employer, is charged with knowledge of the dangerous condition even though Chad never actually informed him. That knowledge is imputed to the employer by virtue of the employment relationship. ∎

Liability for Agent's Intentional Torts Most intentional torts that employees commit have no relation to their employment; thus, their employers will not be held liable. Nevertheless, under the doctrine of *respondeat superior*, the employer can be liable for intentional torts of the employee that are committed within the course and scope of employment, just as the employer is liable for negligence. For

---

12. 6 Car. & P. 501, 172 Eng. Reprint 1338 (1834).

instance, an employer is liable when an employee (such as a "bouncer" at a nightclub or a security guard at a department store) commits the tort of assault and battery or false imprisonment while acting within the scope of employment.

In addition, an employer who knows or should know that an employee has a propensity for committing tortious acts is liable for the employee's acts even if they would not ordinarily be considered within the scope of employment. For example, if the employer hires a bouncer knowing that he has a history of arrests for assault and battery, the employer may be liable if the employee attacks a patron in the parking lot after hours.

An employer may also be liable for permitting an employee to engage in reckless actions that can injure others. **■EXAMPLE 22.20** An employer observes an employee smoking while filling containerized trucks with highly flammable liquids. Failure to stop the employee will cause the employer to be liable for any injuries that result if a truck explodes. ■

Liability for Independent Contractor's Torts Generally, an employer is not liable for physical harm caused to a third person by the negligent act of an independent contractor in the performance of the contract. This is because the employer does not have *the right to control* the details of an independent contractor's performance. Exceptions to this rule are made in certain situations, though, such as when unusually hazardous activities are involved. Typical examples of such activities include blasting operations, the transportation of highly volatile chemicals, and the use of poisonous gases. In these situations, an employer cannot be shielded from liability merely by using an independent contractor. Strict liability is imposed on the employer-principal as a matter of law. Also, in some states, strict liability may be imposed by statute.

Liability for Agent's Crimes An agent is liable for his or her own crimes. A principal or employer is not liable for an agent's crime even if the crime was committed within the scope of authority or employment—unless the principal participated by conspiracy or other action. In some jurisdictions, under specific statutes, a principal may be liable for an agent's violation, in the course and scope of employment, of regulations, such as those governing sanitation, prices, weights, and the sale of liquor.

HOW AGENCY RELATIONSHIPS ARE TERMINATED

Agency law is similar to contract law in that both an agency and a contract can be terminated by an act of the parties or by operation of law. Once the relationship between the principal and the agent has ended, the agent no longer has the right (*actual* authority) to bind the principal. For an agent's *apparent* authority to be terminated, though, third persons may also need to be notified that the agency has been terminated.

Termination by Act of the Parties

An agency may be terminated by act of the parties in several ways, including those discussed here.

Lapse of Time An agency agreement may specify the time period during which the agency relationship will exist. If so, the agency ends when that time period expires. For instance, if the parties agree that the agency will begin on January 1, 2009, and end on December 31, 2011, the agency is automatically terminated on December 31, 2011. If no definite time is stated, then the agency continues for a reasonable time and can be terminated at will by either party. What constitutes a "reasonable time" depends, of course, on the circumstances and the nature of the agency relationship.

Purpose Achieved An agent can be employed to accomplish a particular objective, such as the purchase of stock for a cattle rancher. In that situation, the agency automatically ends after the cattle have been purchased. If more than one agent is employed to accomplish the same purpose, such as the sale of real estate, the first agent to complete the sale automatically terminates the agency relationship for all the others.

Occurrence of a Specific Event An agency can be created to terminate on the happening of a certain event. If Posner appoints Rubik to handle her business affairs while she is away, the agency automatically terminates when Posner returns.

Mutual Agreement Recall from the chapters on contract law that parties can cancel (rescind) a contract by mutually agreeing to terminate the contractual relationship. The same holds true in agency law regardless of whether the agency contract is in writing or whether it is for a specific duration.

Termination by One Party As a general rule, either party can terminate the agency relationship (the act of termination is called *revocation* if done by the principal and *renunciation* if done by the agent). Although both parties have the *power* to terminate the agency, they may not possess the *right*. Wrongful termination can subject the canceling party to a suit for breach of contract. **■EXAMPLE 22.21** Rawlins has a one-year employment contract with Munro to act as an agent in return for $65,000. Munro has the *power* to discharge Rawlins before the contract period expires. If Munro discharges Rawlins, however, Munro can be sued for breaching the contract and will be liable to Rawlins for damages because he had no *right* to terminate the agency. ■

A special rule applies in an *agency coupled with an interest*. This type of agency is not an agency in the usual sense because it is created for the agent's benefit instead of the principal's benefit. **■EXAMPLE 22.22** Julie borrows $5,000 from Rob, giving Rob some of her jewelry and signing a letter giving Rob the power to sell the jewelry as her agent if she fails to repay the loan. After receiving the $5,000 from Rob, Julie attempts to revoke Rob's authority to sell the jewelry as her agent. Julie will not succeed in this attempt because a principal cannot revoke an agency created for the agent's benefit. ■

Notice of Termination When an agency has been terminated by act of the parties, it is the principal's duty to inform any third parties who know of the existence of the agency that it has been terminated (notice of the termination may be given by others, however). Although an agent's actual authority ends when the agency is terminated, an agent's *apparent authority* continues until the third party receives notice (from any source) that such authority has been terminated. If the principal knows that a third party has dealt with the agent, the principal is expected to notify that person *directly*. For third parties who have heard about the agency but have not yet dealt with the agent, *constructive notice* is sufficient.[13]

No particular form is required for notice of agency termination to be effective. The principal can personally notify the agent, or the agent can learn of the termination through some other means. **■EXAMPLE 22.23** Manning bids on a shipment of steel and hires Stone as an agent to arrange transportation of the shipment. When Stone learns that Manning has lost the bid, Stone's authority to make the transportation arrangement terminates. ■ If the agent's authority is written, however, it normally must be revoked in writing.

Termination by Operation of Law

Termination of an agency by operation of law occurs in the circumstances discussed here. Note that when an agency terminates by operation of law, there is no duty to notify third persons.

Death or Insanity The general rule is that the death or mental incompetence of either the principal or the agent automatically and immediately terminates the ordinary agency relationship. Knowledge of the death is not required. **■EXAMPLE 22.24** Geer sends Pyron to China to purchase a rare painting. Before Pyron makes the purchase, Geer dies. Pyron's agent status is terminated at the moment of Geer's death, even

though Pyron does not know that Geer has died. ■ Some states, however, have enacted statutes changing this common law rule to make knowledge of the principal's death a requirement for agency termination.

An agent's transactions that occur after the death of the principal are not binding on the principal's estate.[14] **■EXAMPLE 22.25** Carson is hired by Perry to collect a debt from Thomas (a third party). Perry dies, but Carson, not knowing of Perry's death, still collects the funds from Thomas. Thomas's payment to Carson is no longer legally sufficient to discharge the debt to Perry because Carson's authority to collect ended on Perry's death. If Carson absconds with the funds, Thomas is still liable for the debt to Perry's estate. ■

Impossibility When the specific subject matter of an agency is destroyed or lost, the agency terminates. **■EXAMPLE 22.26** Bullard employs Gonzalez to sell Bullard's house. Prior to any sale, the house is destroyed by fire. In this situation, Gonzalez's agency and authority to sell Bullard's house terminate. ■ Similarly, when it is impossible for the agent to perform the agency lawfully because of a change in the law, the agency terminates.

Changed Circumstances When an event occurs that has such an unusual effect on the subject matter of the agency that the agent can reasonably infer that the principal will not want the agency to continue, the agency terminates. **■EXAMPLE 22.27** Roberts hires Mullen to sell a tract of land for $20,000. Subsequently, Mullen learns that there is oil under the land and that the land is worth $1 million. The agency and Mullen's authority to sell the land for $20,000 are terminated. ■

Bankruptcy If either the principal or the agent petitions for bankruptcy, the agency is *usually* terminated. In certain circumstances, as when the agent's financial status is irrelevant to the purpose of the agency, the agency relationship may continue. Insolvency (the inability to pay debts when they become due or when the situation in which liabilities exceed assets), as distinguished from bankruptcy, does not necessarily terminate the relationship.

War When the principal's country and the agent's country are at war with each other, the agency is terminated. In this situation, the agency is automatically suspended or terminated because there is no way to enforce the legal rights and obligations of the parties.

---

13. *Constructive notice* is knowledge of a fact imputed by law to a person if he or she could have discovered the fact by proper diligence. Constructive notice is often accomplished by newspaper publication.

14. Recall from Chapter 19 that special rules apply when the agent is a bank. Banks can continue to exercise specific types of authority even after a customer has died or become mentally incompetent unless they have knowledge of the death or incompetence [Section 4–405 of the Uniform Commercial Code]. Even with knowledge of the customer's death, the bank has authority to honor checks for ten days following the customer's death in the absence of a stop-payment order.

Lynne Meyer, on her way to a business meeting and in a hurry, stopped by a Buy-Mart store for a new pair of nylons to wear to the meeting. There was a long line at one of the checkout counters, but a cashier, Valerie Watts, opened another counter and began loading the cash drawer. Meyer told Watts that she was in a hurry and asked Watts to work faster. Watts, however, only slowed her pace. At this point, Meyer hit Watts. It is not clear from the record whether Meyer hit Watts intentionally or, in an attempt to retrieve the nylons, hit her inadvertently. In response, Watts grabbed Meyer by the hair and hit her repeatedly in the back of the head, while Meyer screamed for help. Management personnel separated the two women and questioned them about the incident. Watts was immediately fired for violating the store's no-fighting policy. Meyer subsequently sued Buy-

Mart, alleging that the store was liable for the tort (assault and battery) committed by its employee. Using the information presented in the chapter, answer the following questions.

1 Under what doctrine discussed in this chapter might Buy-Mart be held liable for the tort committed by Watts?

2 What is the key factor in determining whether Buy-Mart is liable under this doctrine?

3 How is Buy-Mart's potential liability affected by whether Watts's behavior constituted an intentional tort or a tort of negligence?

4 Suppose that when Watts applied for the job at Buy-Mart, she disclosed in her application that she had previously been convicted of felony assault and battery. Nevertheless, Buy-Mart hired Watts as a cashier. How might this fact affect Buy-Mart's liability for Watts's actions?

TERMS AND CONCEPTS

agency 446
apparent authority 454
disclosed principal 455
e-agent 456
equal dignity rule 453

fiduciary 446
independent contractor 447
notary public 453
partially disclosed principal 455
power of attorney 453

ratification 449
respondeat superior 457
undisclosed principal 455
vicarious liability 457

CHAPTER SUMMARY Agency Relationships

Agency Relationships (See pages 446–449.)	In a *principal-agent* relationship, an agent acts on behalf of and instead of the principal in dealing with third parties. An employee who deals with third parties is normally an agent. An independent contractor is not an employee, and the employer has no control over the details of physical performance. An independent contractor may or may not be an agent.
How Agency Relationships Are Formed (See pages 449–451.)	Agency relationships may be formed by agreement, by ratification, by estoppel, and by operation of law.
Duties of Agents and Principals (See pages 451–453.)	1. *Duties of the agent—* a. Performance—The agent must use reasonable diligence and skill in performing her or his duties or use the special skills that the agent has represented to the principal that the agent possesses. b. Notification—The agent is required to notify the principal of all matters that come to his or her attention concerning the subject matter of the agency. c. Loyalty—The agent has a duty to act solely for the benefit of the principal and not in the interest of the agent or a third party. d. Obedience—The agent must follow all lawful and clearly stated instructions of the principal.

(Continued)

| CHAPTER SUMMARY | Agency Relationships—Continued |

Duties of Agents and Principals—Continued

e. Accounting—The agent has a duty to make available to the principal records of all property and funds received and paid out on behalf of the principal.

2. *Duties of the principal—*

a. Compensation—Except in a gratuitous agency relationship, the principal must pay the agreed-on value (or reasonable value) for an agent's services.

b. Reimbursement and indemnification—The principal must reimburse the agent for all funds disbursed at the request of the principal and for all funds the agent disburses for necessary expenses in the course of reasonable performance of his or her agency duties.

c. Cooperation—A principal must cooperate with and assist an agent in performing her or his duties.

d. Safe working conditions—A principal must provide safe working conditions for the agent-employee.

Agent's Authority
(See pages 453–455.)

1. *Express authority*—Can be oral or in writing. Authorization must be in writing if the agent is to execute a contract that must be in writing.

2. *Implied authority*—Authority customarily associated with the position of the agent or authority that is deemed necessary for the agent to carry out expressly authorized tasks.

3. *Apparent authority and estoppel*—Exists when the principal, by word or action, causes a third party reasonably to believe that an agent has authority to act, even though the agent has no express or implied authority.

4. *Ratification*—The affirmation by the principal of an agent's unauthorized action or promise. For the ratification to be effective, the principal must be aware of all material facts.

Liability in Agency Relationships
(See pages 455–459.)

1. *Liability for contracts*—If the principal's identity is disclosed or partially disclosed at the time the agent forms a contract with a third party, the principal is liable to the third party under the contract if the agent acted within the scope of his or her authority. If the principal's identity is undisclosed at the time of contract formation, the agent is personally liable to the third party, but if the agent acted within the scope of his or her authority, the principal is also bound by the contract.

2. *Liability for agent's negligence*—Under the doctrine of *respondeat superior,* the principal is liable for any harm caused to another through the agent's torts if the agent was acting within the scope of her or his employment at the time the harmful act occurred.

3. *Liability for agent's intentional torts*—Usually, employers are not liable for the intentional torts that their agents commit, *unless:*

a. The acts are committed within the scope of employment, and thus the doctrine of *respondeat superior* applies.

b. The employer allows an employee to engage in a reckless act that causes injury to another.

c. The agent's misrepresentation causes a third party to sustain damage, and the agent had either actual or apparent authority to act.

4. *Liability for independent contractor's torts*—A principal is not liable for harm caused by an independent contractor's negligence, unless hazardous activities are involved (in this situation, the principal is strictly liable for any resulting harm) or other exceptions apply.

5. *Liability for agent's crimes*—An agent is responsible for his or her own crimes, even if the crimes were committed while the agent was acting within the scope of authority or employment. A principal will be liable for an agent's crime only if the principal participated by conspiracy or other action or (in some jurisdictions) if the agent violated certain government regulations in the course of employment.

CHAPTER SUMMARY Agency Relationships—Continued

How Agency Relationships Are Terminated (See pages 459–460.)	1. *By act of the parties—* a. Lapse of time (if the parties specified a definite time for the duration of the agency when the agency was established). b. Purpose achieved. c. Occurrence of a specific event. d. Mutual rescission (requires mutual consent of principal and agent). e. Termination by act of either the principal (revocation) or the agent (renunciation). (A principal cannot revoke an agency coupled with an interest.) f. Notice to third parties is required when an agency is terminated by act of the parties. Direct notice is required for those who have previously dealt with the agency; constructive notice will suffice for all other third parties. 2. *By operation of law—* a. Death or mental incompetence of either the principal or the agent. b. Impossibility (when the purpose of the agency cannot be achieved because of an event beyond the parties' control). c. Changed circumstances (in which it would be inequitable to require that the agency be continued). d. Bankruptcy of the principal or the agent, or war between the principal's and agent's countries. e. Notice to third parties is not required when an agency is terminated by operation of law.

FOR REVIEW

Answers for the even-numbered questions in this **For Review** *section can be found on this text's accompanying Web site at* **www.cengage.com/blaw/fbl**. *Select "Chapter 22" and click on "For Review."*

1 What is the difference between an employee and an independent contractor?

2 How do agency relationships arise?

3 What duties do agents and principals owe to each other?

4 When is a principal liable for the agent's actions with respect to third parties? When is the agent liable?

5 What are some of the ways in which an agency relationship can be terminated?

QUESTIONS AND CASE PROBLEMS

HYPOTHETICAL SCENARIOS AND CASE PROBLEMS

22.1 Employee versus Independent Contractor. Stephen Hemmerling was a driver for the Happy Cab Co. Hemmerling paid certain fixed expenses and abided by a variety of rules relating to the use of the cab, the hours that could be worked, and the solicitation of fares, among other things. Rates were set by the state. Happy Cab did not withhold taxes from Hemmerling's pay. While driving the cab, Hemmerling was injured in an accident and filed a claim against Happy Cab in a Nebraska state court for workers' compensation benefits. Such benefits are not available to independent contractors. On what basis might the court hold that Hemmerling is an employee? Explain.

22.2 Hypothetical Question with Sample Answer. Paul Gett is a well-known, wealthy financial expert living in the city of Torris. Adam Wade, Gett's friend, tells Timothy Brown that he is Gett's agent for the purchase of rare coins. Wade even shows Brown a local newspaper clipping mentioning Gett's interest in coin collecting. Brown, knowing of Wade's friendship with Gett, contracts with Wade to sell a rare coin valued at $25,000 to Gett. Wade takes the coin and disappears with it. On the payment due date, Brown seeks to collect from Gett, claiming that Wade's agency made Gett liable. Gett does not deny that Wade was a friend, but he claims that Wade was never his agent. Discuss fully whether an agency was in existence at the time the contract for the rare coin was made.

For a sample answer to Question 22.2, go to Appendix E at the end of this text.

22.3 Principal's Duties to Agent. Josef Boehm was an officer and the majority shareholder of Alaska Industrial Hardware, Inc. (AIH), in Anchorage, Alaska. In August 2001, Lincolnshire Management, Inc., in New York, created AIH Acquisition Corp. to buy AIH. The three firms signed a "commitment letter" to negotiate "a definitive stock purchase agreement" (SPA). In September, Harold Snow and Ronald Braley began to work, on Boehm's behalf, with Vincent Coyle, an agent for AIH Acquisition, to produce an SPA. They exchanged many drafts and dozens of e-mails. Finally, in February 2002, Braley told Coyle that Boehm would sign the SPA "early next week." That did not occur, however, and at the end of March, after more negotiations and drafts, Boehm demanded a higher price. AIH Acquisition agreed, and following more work by the agents, another SPA was drafted. In April, the parties met in Anchorage. Boehm still refused to sign. AIH Acquisition and others filed a suit in a federal district court against AIH. Did Boehm violate any of the duties that principals owe to their agents? If so, which duty, and how was it violated? Explain. [*AIH Acquisition Corp. v. Alaska Industrial Hardware, Inc.*, __ F.Supp.2d __ (S.D.N.Y. 2004)]

22.4 Agent's Duties to the Principal. Sam and Theresa Daigle decided to build a home in Cameron Parish, Louisiana. To obtain financing, they contacted Trinity United Mortgage Co. In a meeting with Joe Diez on Trinity's behalf, on July 18, 2001, the Daigles signed a temporary loan agreement with Union Planters Bank. Diez assured them that they did not need to make payments on this loan until their house was built and that permanent financing had been secured. Because the Daigles did not make payments on the Union loan, Trinity declined to make the permanent loan. Meanwhile, Diez left Trinity's employ. On November 1, the Daigles moved into their new house. They tried to contact Diez at Trinity but were told that he was unavailable and would get back to them. Three weeks later, Diez came to the Daigles' home and had them sign documents that they believed were to secure a permanent loan but that were actually an application with Diez's new employer. Union filed a suit in a Louisiana state court against the Daigles for failing to pay on its loan. The Daigles paid Union, obtained permanent financing through another source, and filed a suit against Trinity to recover the cost. Who should have told the Daigles that Diez was no longer Trinity's agent? Could Trinity be liable to the Daigles on this basis? Explain. [*Daigle v. Trinity United Mortgage, L.L.C.*, 890 So.2d 583 (La.App. 3 Cir. 2004)]

22.5 Case Problem with Sample Answer. In July 2001, John Warren viewed a condominium in Woodland Hills, California, as a potential buyer. Hildegard Merrill was the agent for the seller. Because Warren's credit rating was poor,

Merrill told him he needed a co-borrower to obtain a mortgage at a reasonable rate. Merrill said that her daughter Charmaine would "go on title" until the loan and sale were complete if Warren would pay her $10,000. Merrill also offered to defer her commission on the sale as a loan to Warren so that he could make a 20 percent down payment on the property. He agreed to both plans. Merrill applied for and secured the mortgage in Charmaine's name alone by misrepresenting her daughter's address, business, and income. To close the sale, Merrill had Warren remove his name from the title to the property. In October, Warren moved into the condominium, repaid Merrill the amount of her deferred commission, and began paying the mortgage. Within a few months, Merrill had Warren evicted. Warren filed a suit in a California state court against Merrill and Charmaine. Who among these parties was in an agency relationship? What is the basic duty that an agent owes a principal? Was the duty breached here? Explain. [*Warren v. Merrill*, 143 Cal.App.4th 96, 49 Cal.Rptr.3d 122 (2 Dist. 2006)]

After you have answered Problem 22.5, compare your answer with the sample answer given on the Web site that accompanies this text. Go to www.cengage.com/blaw/fbl, select "Chapter 22," and click on "Case Problem with Sample Answer."

22.6 Agent's Duties to Principal. Su Ru Chen owned the Lucky Duck Fortune Cookie Factory in Everett, Massachusetts, which made Chinese-style fortune cookies for restaurants. In November 2001, Chen listed the business for sale with Bob Sun, a real estate broker, for $35,000. Sun's daughter Frances and her fiancé, Chiu Chung Chan, decided that Chan would buy the business. Acting as a broker on Chen's (the seller's) behalf, Frances asked about the Lucky Duck's finances. Chen said that each month the business sold at least 1,000 boxes of cookies at a $2,000 profit. Frances negotiated a price of $23,000, which Chan (her fiancé) paid. When Chan began to operate the Lucky Duck, it became clear that the demand for the cookies was actually about 500 boxes per month—a rate at which the business would suffer losses. Less than two months later, the factory closed. Chan filed a suit in a Massachusetts state court against Chen, alleging fraud, among other things. Chan's proof included Frances's testimony as to what Chen had said to her. Chen objected to the admission of this testimony. What is the basis for this objection? Should the court admit the testimony? Why or why not? [*Chan v. Chen*, 70 Mass.App.Ct. 79, 872 N.E.2d 1153 (2007)]

22.7 Apparent Authority. Lee Dennegar and Mark Knutson lived in Dennegar's house in Raritan, New Jersey. Dennegar paid the mortgage and other household expenses. With Dennegar's consent, Knutson managed their household's financial affairs and the "general office functions concerned with maintaining the house." Dennegar allowed Knutson to handle the mail and "to do with it as he chose." Knutson wrote checks for Dennegar to sign, although Knutson signed Dennegar's name to many of the checks with Dennegar's consent. AT&T Universal issued a credit card in Dennegar's name in 2001. Monthly statements were mailed to Dennegar's house, and payments were sometimes made on those statements. Knutson died in 2003. The unpaid charges on the card of $14,752.93 were assigned to New Century Financial Services, Inc. New Century filed a suit in a New Jersey state court against Dennegar to collect the unpaid amount. Dennegar claimed that he never applied for or used the card and knew nothing about it. Under what theory could Dennegar be liable for the charges? Explain. [*New Century Financial Services, Inc. v. Dennegar*, 394 N.J.Super. 595, 928 A.2d 48 (A.D. 2007)]

22.8 **A Question of Ethics.** *Emergency One, Inc. (EO), makes fire and rescue vehicles. Western Fire Truck, Inc., contracted with EO to be its exclusive dealer in Colorado and Wyoming through December 2003. James Costello, a Western salesperson, was authorized to order EO vehicles for his customers. Without informing Western, Costello e-mailed EO about Western's difficulties in obtaining cash to fund its operations. He asked about the viability of Western's contract and his possible employment with EO. On EO's request, and in disregard of Western's instructions, Costello sent some payments for EO vehicles directly to EO. In addition, Costello,* with EO's help, sent a competing bid to a potential Western customer. EO's representative e-mailed Costello, "You have my permission to kick [Western's] ass." In April 2002, EO terminated its contract with Western, which, after reviewing Costello's e-mail, fired Costello. Western filed a suit in a Colorado state court against Costello and EO, alleging, among other things, that Costello breached his duty as an agent and that EO aided and abetted the breach. [Western Fire Truck, Inc. v. Emergency One, Inc., 134 P.3d 570 (Colo.App. 2006)]*

1 Was there an agency relationship between Western and Costello? Western required monthly reports from its sales staff, but Costello did not report regularly. Does this indicate that Costello was *not* Western's agent? In determining whether an agency relationship exists, is the *right* to control or the *fact* of control more important? Explain.

2 Did Costello owe Western a duty? If so, what was the duty? Did Costello breach it? If so, how?

3 A Colorado state statute allows a court to award punitive damages in "circumstances of fraud, malice, or willful and wanton conduct." Did any of these circumstances exist in this case? Should punitive damages be assessed against either defendant? Why or why not?

CRITICAL THINKING AND WRITING ASSIGNMENTS

22.9 Critical Legal Thinking. What policy is served by the law that employers do not have copyright ownership in works created by independent contractors (unless there is a written "work for hire" agreement)?

22.10 **Video Question.** Go to this text's Web site at **www.cengage.com/blaw/fbl** and select "Chapter 22." Click on "Video Questions" and view the video titled *Fast Times at Ridgemont High*. Then answer the following questions.

1 Recall from the video that Brad (Judge Reinhold) is told to deliver an order of Captain Hook Fish and Chips to IBM. Is Brad an employee or an independent contractor? Why?

2 Assume that Brad is an employee and agent of Captain Hook Fish and Chips. What duties does he owe Captain Hook Fish and Chips? What duties does Captain Hook Fish and Chips, as principal, owe to Brad?

3 In the video, Brad throws part of his uniform and several bags of the food that he is supposed to deliver out of his car window while driving. If Brad is an agent-employee and his actions cause injury to a person or property, can Captain Hook Fish and Chips be held liable? Why or why not? What should Captain Hook argue to avoid liability for Brad's actions?

ACCESSING THE INTERNET

For updated links to resources available on the Web, as well as a variety of other materials, visit this text's Web site at

www.cengage.com/blaw/fbl

The Legal Information Institute at Cornell University is an excellent source for information on agency law, including court cases involving agency concepts. Go to

www.law.cornell.edu/wex/index.php/Agency

For an overview of the law of agency with references to the *Restatement (Second) of Agency,* go to Wikipedia at

en.wikipedia.org/wiki/Agency_law

PRACTICAL INTERNET EXERCISES

Go to this text's Web site at **www.cengage.com/blaw/fbl**, select "Chapter 22," and click on "Practical Internet Exercises." There you will find the following Internet research exercises that you can perform to learn more about the topics covered in this chapter.

PRACTICAL INTERNET EXERCISE 22-1 LEGAL PERSPECTIVE—Employees or Independent Contractors?

PRACTICAL INTERNET EXERCISE 22-2 MANAGEMENT PERSPECTIVE—Liability in Agency Relationships

BEFORE THE TEST

Go to this text's Web site at **www.cengage.com/blaw/fbl**, select "Chapter 22," and click on "Interactive Quizzes." You will find a number of interactive questions relating to this chapter.

CHAPTER 23
Employment and Immigration Law

AFTER READING THIS CHAPTER, YOU SHOULD BE ABLE TO ANSWER THE FOLLOWING QUESTIONS:

1 What is the employment-at-will doctrine? When and why are exceptions to this doctrine made?

2 What federal statute governs working hours and wages? What federal statutes govern labor unions and collective bargaining?

3 What federal law was enacted to protect the health and safety of employees? What are workers' compensation laws?

4 Generally, what kind of conduct is prohibited by Title VII of the Civil Rights Act of 1964, as amended?

5 What remedies are available under Title VII of the 1964 Civil Rights Act, as amended?

U ntil the early 1900s, most employer-employee relationships were governed by the common law. Today, the workplace is regulated extensively by statutes and administrative agency regulations. Recall from Chapter 1 that common law doctrines apply only to areas *not* covered by statutory law. Common law doctrines have thus been displaced to a large extent by statutory law.

In the 1930s, during the Great Depression, both state and federal governments began to regulate employment relationships. Legislation during the 1930s and subsequent decades established the right of employees to form labor unions. At the heart of labor rights is the right to unionize and bargain with management for improved working conditions, salaries, and benefits. A succession of other laws during and since the 1930s provided further protection for employees. Today's employers must comply with a myriad of laws and regulations to ensure that employee rights are protected. In this chapter, we look at the most significant laws regulating employment relationships, including those that prohibit employment discrimination.

EMPLOYMENT AT WILL

Traditionally, employment relationships have generally been governed by the common law doctrine of **employment at will**. Other common law rules governing employment relationships—including rules under contract, tort, and agency law—have already been discussed at length in previous chapters of this text.

Given that many employees (those who deal with third parties) are normally deemed agents of an employer, agency concepts are especially relevant in the employment context. The distinction under agency law between employee status and independent-contractor status is also relevant to employment relationships. Generally, the laws discussed in this chapter apply only to the employer-employee relationship; they do not apply to independent contractors.

Under the employment-at-will doctrine, either party may terminate the employment relationship at any time and for any reason, unless doing so would violate the provisions of an employment contract. Nonetheless, federal and state statutes governing employment relationships prevent the doctrine from being applied in a number of circumstances. Today, an employer is not permitted to fire an employee if to do so would violate a federal or state employment statute, such as one prohibiting employment termination for discriminatory reasons.

Exceptions to the Employment-at-Will Doctrine

Because of the harsh effects of the employment-at-will doctrine for employees, the courts have carved out various exceptions to the doctrine. These exceptions are based on contract theory, tort theory, and public policy.

Exceptions Based on Contract Theory   Some courts have held that an *implied* employment contract exists between an employer and an employee. If an employee is fired outside the terms of the implied contract, he or she may succeed in an action for breach of contract even though no written employment contract exists. **■EXAMPLE 23.1** An employer's manual or personnel bulletin states that, as a matter of policy, workers will be dismissed only for good cause. If the employee is aware of this policy and continues to work for the employer, a court may find that there is an implied contract based on the terms stated in the manual or bulletin. **■** Generally, the key consideration in determining whether an employment manual creates an implied contractual obligation is the employee's reasonable expectations.

An employer's oral promises to employees regarding discharge policy may also be considered part of an implied contract. If the employer fires a worker in a manner contrary to what was promised, a court may hold that the employer has violated the implied contract and is liable for damages. In some cases, courts have held that an implied employment contract exists even though employees agreed in writing to be employees at will.[1]

Exceptions Based on Tort Theory   In a few situations, the discharge of an employee may give rise to an action for wrongful discharge under tort theories (see Chapter 4). Abusive discharge procedures may result in a suit for intentional infliction of emotional distress or defamation. In addition, some courts have permitted workers to sue their employers under the tort theory of fraud. **■EXAMPLE 23.2** An employer induces a prospective employee to leave a lucrative job and move to another state by offering "a long-term job with a thriving business." In fact, the employer is not only having significant financial problems but is also planning a merger that will result in the elimination of the position offered to the prospective employee. If the employee takes the job in reliance on the employer's representations and is

fired shortly thereafter, the employee may be able to bring an action against the employer for fraud.[2] **■**

Exceptions Based on Public Policy   The most widespread common law exception to the employment-at-will doctrine is made on the basis of public policy. Courts may apply this exception when an employer fires a worker for reasons that violate a fundamental public policy of the jurisdiction. Generally, the courts require that the public policy involved be expressed clearly in the statutory law governing the jurisdiction. **■EXAMPLE 23.3** As you will read later in this chapter, employers with fifty or more employees are required by the Family and Medical Leave Act (FMLA) to give employees up to twelve weeks of unpaid family or medical leave per year. Mila's employer, however, has only forty employees and thus is not covered by the federal law. Nonetheless, if Mila is fired from her job because she takes three weeks of unpaid family leave to help her son through a difficult surgery, a court may deem that the employer's actions violated the public policy expressed in the FMLA. **■**

An exception may also be made for employees who "blow the whistle" on the employer's wrongdoing. **Whistleblowing** occurs when an employee tells government authorities, upper-level managers, or the press that her or his employer is engaged in some unsafe or illegal activity. Whistleblowers on occasion have been protected from wrongful discharge for reasons of public policy.[3] Normally, however, whistleblowers seek protection under statutory law. Most states have enacted so-called whistleblower statutes that protect a whistleblower from subsequent retaliation by the employer. The Whistleblower Protection Act of 1989[4] protects federal employees who blow the whistle on their employers from retaliatory actions. Whistleblower statutes sometimes also offer an incentive to disclose information by providing the whistleblower with a monetary reward. For instance, a whistleblower who has disclosed information relating to a fraud perpetrated against the U.S. government will receive between 15 and 25 percent of the proceeds if the government brings a suit against the wrongdoer.[5]

Wrongful Discharge

Whenever an employer discharges an employee in violation of an employment contract or a statute protecting employees, the employee may bring an action for **wrongful discharge.** Even if an employer's actions do not violate any provisions in

---

1. See, for example, *Kuest v. Regent Assisted Living, Inc.,* 111 Wash.App. 36, 43 P.3d 23 (2002).

2. See, for example, *Lazar v. Superior Court of Los Angeles County,* 12 Cal.4th 631, 909 P.2d 981, 49 Cal.Rptr.2d 377 (1996); and *McConkey v. AON Corp.,* 354 N.J.Super. 25, 804 A.2d 572 (A.D. 2002).

3. See, for example, *Wendeln v. The Beatrice Manor, Inc.,* 271 Neb. 373, 712 N.W.2d 226 (2006).

4. 5 U.S.C. Section 1201.

5. The False Claims Reform Act of 1986, which amended the False Claims Act of 1863, 31 U.S.C. Sections 3729–3733.

an employment contract or a statute, the employer may still be subject to liability under a common law doctrine, such as a tort theory or agency.

WAGE AND HOUR LAWS

In the 1930s, Congress enacted several laws regulating the wages and working hours of employees. In 1931, Congress passed the Davis-Bacon Act,[6] which requires contractors and subcontractors working on government construction projects to pay "prevailing wages" to their employees. In 1936, the Walsh-Healey Act[7] was passed. This act requires that a minimum wage, as well as overtime pay at 1.5 times regular pay rates, be paid to employees of manufacturers or suppliers entering into contracts with agencies of the federal government.

In 1938, Congress passed the Fair Labor Standards Act (FLSA).[8] This act extended wage-hour requirements to cover all employers engaged in interstate commerce or in the production of goods for interstate commerce, plus selected types of other businesses. We examine here the FLSA's provisions in regard to child labor, maximum hours, and minimum wages.

Child Labor

The FLSA prohibits oppressive child labor. Children under fourteen years of age are allowed to do certain types of work, such as deliver newspapers, work for their parents, and work in the entertainment and (with some exceptions) agricultural areas. Children who are fourteen or fifteen years of age are allowed to work, but not in hazardous occupations. There are also numerous restrictions on how many hours per day and per week they can work.

Working times and hours are not restricted for persons between the ages of sixteen and eighteen, but they cannot be employed in hazardous jobs or in jobs detrimental to their health and well-being. None of these restrictions apply to persons over the age of eighteen.

Wages and Hours

The FLSA provides that a **minimum wage** of a specified amount ($7.25 per hour in 2009) must be paid to employees

---

6. 40 U.S.C. Sections 276a–276a-5.
7. 41 U.S.C. Sections 35–45.
8. 29 U.S.C. Sections 201–260.

in covered industries. Congress periodically revises this minimum wage.[9] Under the FLSA, the term *wages* includes the reasonable cost of the employer in furnishing employees with board, lodging, and other facilities if they are customarily furnished by that employer.

Under the FLSA, employees who work more than forty hours per week normally must be paid 1.5 times their regular pay for all hours over forty. Note that the FLSA overtime provisions apply only after an employee has worked more than forty hours per *week*. Thus, employees who work for ten hours a day, four days per week, are not entitled to overtime pay because they do not work more than forty hours a week.

Overtime Exemptions

Certain employees—usually executive, administrative, and professional employees; outside salespersons; and computer programmers—are exempt from the FLSA's overtime provisions. Employers are not required to pay overtime wages to exempt employees. Employers can continue to pay overtime to ineligible employees if they want to do so, but they cannot waive or reduce the overtime requirements of the FLSA.

The exemptions to the overtime-pay requirement do not apply to manual laborers or to police, firefighters, licensed nurses, and other public-safety workers. White-collar workers who earn more than $100,000 per year, computer programmers, dental hygienists, and insurance adjusters are typically exempt—though they must also meet certain other criteria. An employer cannot deny overtime wages to an employee based solely on the employee's job title.[10] (Does the FLSA require employers to pay overtime wages to workers who telecommute? See this chapter's *Adapting the Law to the Online Environment* feature on page 471 for a discussion of this important issue.)

Under the overtime-pay regulations, an employee qualifies for the executive exemption if, among other requirements, his or her "primary duty" is management. This requirement was the focus of the dispute in the following case.

---

9. Note that many state and local governments also have minimum-wage laws; these laws provide for higher minimum-wage rates than required by the federal government.
10. See, for example, *In re Wal-Mart Stores, Inc.*, 395 F.3d 1177 (10th Cir. 2005); and *Martin v. Indiana Michigan Power Co.*, 381 F.3d 574 (6th Cir. 2004).

CASE 23.1 **Mims v. Starbucks Corp.**

United States District Court, Southern District of Texas, __ F.Supp.2d __ (2007).

FACTS In Starbucks Corporation's stores, baristas (coffee-making specialists) wait on customers, make drinks for

customers, serve customers, operate the cash register, clean the store, and maintain its equipment. In each store, a

CASE 23.1–Continues next page

CASE 23.1—Continued

manager supervises and motivates 6 to 30 employees, including baristas, shift supervisors, and assistant managers. The manager oversees customer service and processes employee records, payrolls, and inventory counts. He or she also develops strategies to increase revenues, control costs, and comply with corporate policies. Kevin Keevican was hired as a barista in March 2000. Keevican was promoted to shift supervisor, assistant manager, and, in November 2001, manager. During his tenure, Keevican doubled pastry sales at one store, nearly tripled revenues at another, and won sales awards at both. As a manager, Keevican worked seventy hours a week for $650 to $800, a 10 to 20 percent bonus, and fringe benefits such as paid sick leave, not available to baristas. Keevican resigned in 2004. He and other former managers, including Kathleen Mims, filed a suit in a federal district court against Starbucks, seeking unpaid overtime and other amounts. The plaintiffs admitted that they performed many managerial tasks, but argued that they spent 70 to 80 percent of their time on barista chores. Starbucks filed a motion for summary judgment.

ISSUE During their employment, was management the plaintiffs' "primary duty"?

DECISION Yes. The court issued a summary judgment in Starbucks's favor and dismissed the claims of the plaintiffs, who were exempt from the FLSA's overtime provisions as executive employees.

REASON The court held that an employee's "primary duty" is "what the employee does that is of principal value to the employer, not the collateral tasks that she may also perform, even if they consume more than half her time." The determining factors are "(1) the relative importance of managerial duties compared to other duties; (2) the frequency with which the employee makes discretionary decisions; (3) the employee's relative freedom from supervision; and (4) the relationship between the employee's salary and the wages paid to employees who perform relevant non-exempt work." In this case, the barista chores "quite obviously were of minor importance to Defendant when compared to the significant management responsibilities * * * that directly influenced the ultimate commercial and financial success or failure of the store." Also, each plaintiff was "the single highest-ranking employee in his [or her] particular store and was responsible on site for that store's day-to-day overall operations." He or she was "vested with enough discretionary power and freedom from supervision to qualify for the executive exemption." Finally, the "marked disparity in pay and benefits between Plaintiffs and the non-exempt employees is a hallmark of exempt status."

 WHAT IF THE FACTS WERE DIFFERENT? *Suppose that Keevican's job title had been "glorified barista" instead of "manager." Would the result have been different? Explain.*

■

LABOR UNIONS

In the 1930s, in addition to wage-hour laws, the government also enacted the first of several labor laws. These laws protect employees' rights to join labor unions, to bargain with management over the terms and conditions of employment, and to conduct strikes.

Federal labor laws governing union-employer relations have developed considerably since the first law was enacted in 1932. Initially, the laws were concerned with protecting the rights and interests of workers. Subsequent legislation placed some restraints on unions and granted rights to employers. We look here at four major federal statutes regulating union-employer relations.

Norris-LaGuardia Act

In 1932, Congress protected peaceful strikes, picketing, and boycotts in the Norris-LaGuardia Act.[11] The statute restricted the power of federal courts to issue injunctions against unions engaged in peaceful strikes. In effect, this act established a national policy permitting employees to organize.

National Labor Relations Act

One of the foremost statutes regulating labor is the National Labor Relations Act (NLRA) of 1935.[12] This act established

---

11. 29 U.S.C. Sections 101–110, 113–115.
12. 20 U.S.C. Section 151.

According to WorldatWork, a research organization for human resources professionals, nearly 46 million U.S. workers perform at least part of their job at home. Close to 13 million of them are full-time *telecommuters*—meaning that they work at home or off-site by means of an electronic linkup to the central workplace. The fact that employees work at a remote location does not mean that they are automatically exempt from overtime-pay requirements (or minimum-wage laws). Wage and hour laws can apply to the virtual workforce, as many businesses are finding out the unfortunate way—through litigation. Here, we examine some of the challenges employers face with overtime-pay rules when their workers telecommute.

Telecommuters and Overtime-Pay Requirements

Certain employees are exempt from the overtime-pay requirements of the Fair Labor Standards Act (FLSA). Under regulations issued in 2004, a primary duty test is to be used in classifying workers.[a] In general, workers whose primary duty involves the exercise of discretion and independent judgment are more likely to be exempt from the overtime requirements. So are those whose positions require advanced knowledge or specialized instructions, such as computer systems analysts.

Although the regulations appear detailed, they do not specifically address how these exemptions apply to telecommuters. Since the rules went into effect, telecommuters have filed a barrage of lawsuits claiming that their employers vio-lated the FLSA by failing to pay them for overtime work and to compensate them for work-related tasks.

An Increasing Number of Cases and Settlements

To date, more cases have been filed in California than in any other state. Suits are also pending in Colorado, the District of Columbia, Illinois, Missouri, New Jersey, New York, and Ohio.

Some defendants with large numbers of employees have decided to settle before their cases go to trial. Computer Sciences Corporation in El Segundo, California, for example, paid $24 million to settle a case brought by telecommuters and call-center employees,[b] and International Business Machines Corporation (IBM) settled a similar suit for $65 million.[c] Other defendants have refused to settle. Farmers Insurance Exchange went to trial but lost and faced a significant jury verdict. On appeal, however, the company prevailed.[d] In contrast, Advanced Business Integrators, Inc., had to pay nearly $50,000 in overtime compensation to a computer consultant who had spent the majority of his work time at customers' sites training their employees in the use of his employer's software.[e]

FOR CRITICAL ANALYSIS *Why might telecommuting employees sometimes accept being wrongly classified as an "executive" or a "professional" under the overtime-pay requirements and thus be exempt from overtime pay?*

a. See 29 C.F.R. Sections 541.203 and 541.400.

b. *Computer Sciences Corp.,* No. 03-08201 (C.D.Cal., settled in 2005).
c. *International Business Machines Corp.,* No. 06-00430 (N.D.Cal., settled in 2006).
d. *In re Farmers Insurance Exchange, Claims Representatives' Overtime Pay Litigation,* 481 F.3d 1119 (9th Cir. 2007).
e. *Eicher v. Advanced Business Integrators, Inc.,* 151 Cal.App.4th 1363, 61 Cal.Rptr.3d 114 (2007).

---

the rights of employees to engage in collective bargaining and to strike. The act also specifically defined a number of employer practices as unfair to labor:

1 Interference with employee efforts to form, join, or assist labor organizations or with employee efforts to engage in concerted activities for their mutual aid or protection.

2 An employer's domination of a labor organization or contribution of financial or other support to it.

3 Discrimination in the hiring or awarding of tenure to employees based on union affiliation.

4 Discrimination against employees for filing charges under the act or giving testimony under the act.

5 Refusal to bargain collectively with the duly designated representative of the employees.

To ensure that employees' rights would be protected, the NLRA established the National Labor Relations Board (NLRB). The NLRB has the authority to investigate employees' charges of unfair labor practices and to file complaints against employers in response to these charges. When violations are found, the NLRB may also issue **cease-and-desist orders**—

orders compelling employers to stop engaging in the unfair practices. Cease-and-desist orders can be enforced by a federal appellate court if necessary. Disputes over alleged unfair labor practices are first decided by the NLRB and may then be appealed to a federal court.

To be protected under the NLRA, an individual must be an employee or a job applicant (otherwise, the NLRA's ban on discrimination in regard to hiring would mean little). Additionally, the United States Supreme Court has held that individuals who are hired by a union to organize a company (union organizers) are to be considered employees of the company for NLRA purposes.[13]

Under the NLRA, employers and unions have a duty to bargain in good faith. Bargaining over certain subjects is mandatory, and a party's refusal to bargain over these subjects is an unfair labor practice that can be reported to the NLRB. **■EXAMPLE 23.4** In one case, an employer was required to bargain with the union over the use of hidden video surveillance cameras.[14] ■

Labor-Management Relations Act

The Labor-Management Relations Act (LMRA) of 1947[15] was passed to proscribe certain unfair union practices, such as the *closed shop*. A **closed shop** requires union membership by its workers as a condition of employment. Although the act made the closed shop illegal, it preserved the legality of the union shop. A **union shop** does not require membership as a prerequisite for employment but can, and usually does, require that workers join the union after a specified amount of time on the job.

The LMRA also prohibited unions from refusing to bargain with employers, engaging in certain types of picketing, and *featherbedding*—causing employers to hire more employees than necessary. The act also allowed individual states to pass their own **right-to-work laws,** which make it illegal for union membership to be required for *continued* employment in any establishment. Thus, union shops are technically illegal in the twenty-three states that have right-to-work laws.

Labor-Management Reporting and Disclosure Act

In 1959, Congress enacted the Labor-Management Reporting and Disclosure Act (LMRDA).[16] The act established an employee bill of rights and reporting requirements

for union activities. The act strictly regulates unions' internal business procedures, including union elections. For example, the LMRDA requires a union to hold regularly scheduled elections of officers using secret ballots. Ex-convicts are prohibited from holding union office. Moreover, union officials are accountable for union property and funds. Members have the right to attend and to participate in union meetings, to nominate officers, and to vote in most union proceedings.

The act also outlawed **hot-cargo agreements,** in which employers voluntarily agree with unions not to handle, use, or deal in goods produced by nonunion employees working for other employers. The act made all such boycotts (called **secondary boycotts**) illegal.

WORKER HEALTH AND SAFETY

Under the common law, employees injured on the job had to rely on tort law or contract law theories in suits they brought against their employers. Additionally, workers had some recourse under the common law governing agency relationships (discussed in Chapter 22), which imposes a duty on a principal-employer to provide a safe workplace for an agent-employee. Today, numerous state and federal statutes protect employees and their families from the risk of accidental injury, death, or disease resulting from their employment. This section discusses the primary federal statute governing health and safety in the workplace, along with state workers' compensation laws.

The Occupational Safety and Health Act

At the federal level, the primary legislation protecting employees' health and safety is the Occupational Safety and Health Act of 1970.[17] Congress passed this act in an attempt to ensure safe and healthful working conditions for practically every employee in the country. The act requires employers to meet specific standards in addition to their general duty to keep workplaces safe.

Enforcement Agencies Three federal agencies develop and enforce the standards set by the Occupational Safety and Health Act. The Occupational Safety and Health Administration (OSHA) is part of the Department of Labor and has the authority to promulgate standards, make inspections, and enforce the act. OSHA has developed safety standards governing many workplace details, such as the structural stability of ladders and the requirements for railings. OSHA also establishes standards that protect employees against exposure to substances that may be harmful to their health.

13. *National Labor Relations Board v. Town & Country Electric, Inc.,* 516 U.S. 85, 116 S.Ct. 450, 133 L.Ed.2d 371 (1995).
14. *National Steel Corp. v. National Labor Relations Board,* 324 F.3d 928 (7th Cir. 2003).
15. 29 U.S.C. Sections 141 *et seq.*
16. 29 U.S.C. Sections 401 *et seq.*
17. 29 U.S.C. Sections 553, 651–678.

The National Institute for Occupational Safety and Health is part of the Department of Health and Human Services. It conducts research on safety and health problems and recommends standards for OSHA to adopt. Finally, the Occupational Safety and Health Review Commission is an independent agency set up to handle appeals from actions taken by OSHA administrators.

Procedures and Violations OSHA compliance officers may enter and inspect facilities of any establishment covered by the Occupational Safety and Health Act. Under the act, an employer cannot discharge an employee who files a complaint or who, in good faith, refuses to work in a high-risk area if bodily harm or death might reasonably result.

Employers with eleven or more employees are required to keep occupational injury and illness records for each employee. Each record must be made available for inspection when requested by an OSHA inspector. Whenever a work-related injury or disease occurs, employers must make reports directly to OSHA. Whenever an employee is killed in a work-related accident or when five or more employees are hospitalized as a result of one accident, the employer must notify the Department of Labor within forty-eight hours. If the company fails to do so, it will be fined. Following the accident, a complete inspection of the premises is mandatory.

Criminal penalties for willful violation of the Occupational Safety and Health Act are limited. Employers may also be prosecuted under state laws, however. In other words, the act does not preempt state and local criminal laws.

State Workers' Compensation Laws

State **workers' compensation laws** establish an administrative procedure for compensating workers injured on the job. Instead of suing, an injured worker files a claim with the administrative agency or board that administers local workers' compensation claims.

Most workers' compensation statutes are similar. No state covers all employees. Typically, domestic workers, agricultural workers, temporary employees, and employees of common carriers (companies that provide transportation services to the public) are excluded, but minors are covered. Usually, the statutes allow employers to purchase insurance from a private insurer or a state fund to pay workers' compensation benefits in the event of a claim. Most states also allow employers to be self-insured—that is, employers who show an ability to pay claims do not need to buy insurance.

Requirements for Receiving Workers' Compensation In general, the right to recover benefits is predicated wholly on the existence of an employment relationship and the fact that the injury was *accidental* and *occurred on the job or in the*

course of employment, regardless of fault. Intentionally inflicted self-injury, for example, would not be considered accidental and hence would not be covered. If an employee is injured while commuting to or from work, the injury usually will not be considered to have occurred on the job or in the course of employment and hence will not be covered.

An employee must notify her or his employer promptly (usually within thirty days) of an injury. Generally, an employee must also file a workers' compensation claim with the appropriate state agency or board within a certain period (sixty days to two years) from the time the injury is first noticed, rather than from the time of the accident.

Workers' Compensation versus Litigation An employee's acceptance of workers' compensation benefits bars the employee from suing for injuries caused by the employer's negligence. By barring lawsuits for negligence, workers' compensation laws also bar employers from raising common law defenses to negligence, such as contributory negligence, assumption of risk, or injury caused by a "fellow servant" (another employee). A worker may sue an employer who *intentionally* injures the worker, however.

INCOME SECURITY

Federal and state governments participate in insurance programs designed to protect employees and their families by covering the financial impact of retirement, disability, death, hospitalization, and unemployment. The key federal law on this subject is the Social Security Act of 1935.[18]

Social Security

The Social Security Act provides for old-age (retirement), survivors, and disability insurance. The act is therefore often referred to as OASDI. Both employers and employees must "contribute" under the Federal Insurance Contributions Act (FICA)[19] to help pay for benefits that will partially make up for the employees' loss of income on retirement.

The basis for the employee's and the employer's contribution is the employee's annual wage base—the maximum amount of the employee's wages that are subject to the tax. The employer withholds the employee's FICA contribution from the employee's wages and then matches this contribution. (In 2008, employers were required to withhold 6.2 percent of each employee's wages, up to a maximum wage base of $102,000, and to match this contribution.)

Retired workers are then eligible to receive monthly payments from the Social Security Administration, which

---

18. 42 U.S.C. Sections 301–1397e.
19. 26 U.S.C. Sections 3101–3125.

administers the Social Security Act. Social Security benefits are fixed by statute but increase automatically with increases in the cost of living.

Medicare

Medicare, a federal government health-insurance program, is administered by the Social Security Administration for people sixty-five years of age and older and for some under the age of sixty-five who are disabled. It originally had two parts, one pertaining to hospital costs and the other to nonhospital medical costs, such as visits to physicians' offices. Medicare now offers additional coverage options and a prescription drug plan. People who have Medicare hospital insurance can also obtain additional federal medical insurance if they pay small monthly premiums, which increase as the cost of medical care increases.

As with Social Security contributions, both the employer and the employee "contribute" to Medicare, but unlike Social Security, there is no cap on the amount of wages subject to the Medicare tax. In 2008, both the employer and the employee were required to pay 1.45 percent of *all* wages and salaries to finance Medicare. Thus, for Social Security and Medicare together, in 2008 the employer and employee paid a combined total of 15.3 percent of the first $102,000 of income. In addition, all wages and salaries above $102,000 were taxed at a combined (employer and employee) rate of 2.9 percent for Medicare. Self-employed persons pay both the employer and the employee portions of the Social Security and Medicare taxes (15.3 percent of income up to $102,000 and 2.9 percent of income above that amount in 2008).

Private Pension Plans

The Employee Retirement Income Security Act (ERISA) of 1974[20] is the major federal act regulating employee retirement plans set up by employers to supplement Social Security benefits. This act empowers a branch of the U.S. Department of Labor to enforce its provisions governing employers who have private pension funds for their employees. ERISA created the Pension Benefit Guaranty Corporation (PBGC), an independent federal agency, to provide timely and uninterrupted payment of voluntary private pension benefits. The pension plans pay annual insurance premiums (at set rates indexed for inflation) to the PBGC, and then the PBGC pays benefits to participants. Under the Pension Protection Act of 2006,[21] the director of the PBGC is appointed by the president and confirmed by the Senate.

ERISA does not require an employer to establish a pension plan. When a plan exists, however, ERISA establishes standards for its management. A key provision of ERISA concerns vesting. **Vesting** gives an employee a legal right to receive pension benefits at some future date when he or she stops working. Before ERISA was enacted, some employees who had worked for companies for as long as thirty years received no pension benefits when their employment terminated, because those benefits had not vested. ERISA establishes complex vesting rules. Generally, however, all employee contributions to pension plans vest immediately, and employee rights to employer contributions to a plan vest after five years of employment.

In an attempt to prevent mismanagement of pension funds, ERISA has established rules on how they must be invested. Pension managers must be cautious in choosing investments and must diversify the plan's investments to minimize the risk of large losses. ERISA also contains detailed record-keeping and reporting requirements.

Unemployment Insurance

To ease the financial impact of unemployment, the United States has a system of unemployment insurance. The Federal Unemployment Tax Act (FUTA) of 1935[22] created a state-administered system that provides unemployment compensation to eligible individuals. Under this system, employers pay into a fund, and the proceeds are paid out to qualified unemployed workers. The FUTA and state laws require employers that fall under the provisions of the act to pay unemployment taxes at regular intervals.

To be eligible for unemployment compensation, a worker must be willing and able to work and be actively seeking employment. Workers who have been fired for misconduct or who have voluntarily left their jobs are not eligible for benefits. To leave a job voluntarily is to leave it without good cause.

COBRA

Federal law also provides for workers whose jobs have been terminated—and who are thus no longer eligible for group health-insurance plans—a right to continue their health-insurance coverage. The Consolidated Omnibus Budget Reconciliation Act (COBRA) of 1985[23] prohibits an employer from eliminating a worker's medical, optical, or dental insurance on the voluntary or involuntary termination of the worker's employment. Employers, with some exceptions, must comply with COBRA if they employ twenty or more workers

20. 29 U.S.C. Sections 1001 *et seq.*
21. Pub. L. No. 109-280, 120 Stat. 780.
22. 26 U.S.C. Sections 3301–3310.
23. 29 U.S.C. Sections 1161–1169.

and provide a benefit plan to those workers. An employer must inform an employee of COBRA's provisions when that worker faces termination or a reduction of hours that would affect his or her eligibility for coverage under the plan. Only workers fired for gross misconduct are excluded from protection.

A worker has sixty days (beginning with the date that the group coverage would stop) to decide whether to continue with the employer's group insurance plan. If the worker chooses to discontinue the coverage, the employer has no further obligation. If the worker chooses to continue coverage, then the employer is obligated to keep the policy active for up to eighteen months. If the worker is disabled, the employer must extend coverage up to twenty-nine months.

The coverage provided must be the same as that enjoyed by the worker prior to the termination or reduction of work. If family members were originally included, for example, COBRA prohibits their exclusion. The worker does not receive the insurance coverage for free, however. To receive continued benefits, she or he may be required to pay all of the premiums, as well as a 2 percent administrative charge. The employer is relieved of the responsibility to provide benefit coverage if the worker fails to pay the premium or if the employer completely eliminates its group benefit plan. An employer that does not comply with COBRA risks substantial penalties, such as a tax of up to 10 percent of the annual cost of the group plan or $500,000, whichever is less.

FAMILY AND MEDICAL LEAVE

In 1993, Congress passed the Family and Medical Leave Act (FMLA)[24] to allow employees to take time off from work for family or medical reasons. A majority of the states also have legislation allowing for a leave from employment for family or medical reasons, and many employers maintain private family-leave plans for their workers.

---

24. 29 U.S.C. Sections 2601, 2611–2619, 2651–2654.

Coverage and Applicability of the FMLA

The FMLA requires employers who have fifty or more employees to provide employees with up to twelve weeks of unpaid family or medical leave during any twelve-month period. The FMLA expressly covers private and public (government) employees.[25] Generally, an employee may take family leave to care for a newborn baby, an adopted child, or a foster child and take medical leave when the employee or the employee's spouse, child, or parent has a "serious health condition" requiring care. The employer must continue the worker's health-care coverage and guarantee employment in the same position or a comparable position when the employee returns to work. An important exception to the FMLA, however, allows the employer to avoid reinstating a *key employee*—defined as an employee whose pay falls within the top 10 percent of the firm's workforce. Also, the act does not apply to part-time or newly hired employees (those who have worked for less than one year).

Employees suffering from certain chronic health conditions, such as asthma, diabetes, and pregnancy, may take FMLA leave for their own incapacities that require absences of less than three days. **■EXAMPLE 23.5** Estel, an employee who has asthma, suffers from periodic episodes of illness. According to regulations issued by the Department of Labor, employees with such conditions are covered by the FMLA. Thus, Estel may take a medical leave. ■

Employees suffering from addiction to drugs and alcohol pose a special problem under the FMLA. Under what circumstances do days off resulting from the addiction, as opposed to days off for medical treatment in a medical facility, count as part of protected leave? That issue was addressed in the following case.

---

25. The United States Supreme Court affirmed that government employers could be sued for violating the FMLA in *Nevada Department of Human Resources v. Hibbs*, 538 U.S. 721, 123 S.Ct. 1972, 152 L.Ed.2d 953 (2003).

CASE 23.2   Darst v. Interstate Brands Corp.

United States Court of Appeals, Seventh Circuit, 512 F.3d 903 (2008).

FACTS Krzysztof Chalimoniuk worked for Interstate Brands Corporation (IBC) for fifteen years before he was fired for excessive absenteeism. Chalimoniuk, an alcoholic, sought treatment for his condition. He requested leave under the Family and Medical Leave Act (FMLA) from July 29 to August 14, 2000, to deal with the problem. From August 4 to 11, he was hospitalized for treatment of alcohol dependence and withdrawal. When he failed to return to work on August 15, he was fired for being absent. IBC noted that he was also absent July 29 to August 3, when he was not hospitalized, and those days were counted as improper absences because he was already over the limit for the number of days he could miss under the company's leave policy. Chalimoniuk sued,

CASE 23.2–Continues next page

contending that IBC had violated his FMLA rights. During the course of litigation, Chalimoniuk filed for bankruptcy, and his claim against IBC became part of the bankruptcy estate. Richard Darst, as trustee for the estate, continued to prosecute the claim. The district court granted summary judgment in favor of IBC. Darst appealed.

ISSUE Was Chalimoniuk entitled to FMLA leave from July 29 through August 3, before he was hospitalized for treatment of his alcoholism?

DECISION No. The appeals court affirmed the lower court's ruling. IBC had not violated Chalimoniuk's rights under the FMLA by firing him for excessive absences. FMLA leave covered the days he was receiving medical treatment, but not the days he missed work before and after treatment.

REASON Chalimoniuk was entitled to FMLA leave to obtain treatment, but not because he was incapacitated by

the alcoholism and could not, or would not, come to work. Absence from work because of an employee's use of a substance, rather than for treatment of a serious health condition caused by the substance use, does not qualify for FMLA leave. Furthermore, contrary to Chalimoniuk's assertion, IBC had the right to determine the dates during which Chalimoniuk was to receive treatment for alcoholism. This employer right is allowed unless it interferes with or denies the worker's exercise of his or her rights under the FMLA.

FOR CRITICAL ANALYSIS—Ethical Consideration *Did IBC take unfair advantage of the "letter of the law" by not granting Chalimoniuk a little more leave time given that he was, in fact, dealing with his problem? Explain your answer.*

Violations of the FMLA

An employer that violates the FMLA may be held liable for damages to compensate an employee for unpaid wages (or salary), lost benefits, denied compensation, and actual monetary losses (such as the cost of providing for care of the family member) up to an amount equivalent to the employee's wages for twelve weeks. Supervisors may also be subject to personal liability, as employers, for violations of the act. A court may require the employer to reinstate the employee in her or his job or to grant a promotion that had been denied. A successful plaintiff is entitled to court costs; attorneys' fees; and, in cases involving bad faith on the part of the employer, two times the amount of damages awarded by a judge or jury.

Employers generally are required to notify employees when an absence will be counted against leave authorized under the act. If an employer fails to provide such notice, and the employee consequently suffers an injury because he or she did not receive notice, the employer may be sanctioned.[26] **EXAMPLE 23.6** An employee, Isha Hartung, is absent from work for thirty weeks while undergoing treatment for cancer. Her employer did not inform Isha that this time off would count as FMLA leave. At the end of twelve weeks, the employer sent Isha a notice stating that she must return to work the following Monday, but she had not completed her chemotherapy and did not go back to work. In this

situation, because the employer did not notify Isha that her absence would be considered FMLA leave, a court might allow her to take additional protected time off. ■

IMMIGRATION LAW

The United States had no laws restricting immigration until the late nineteenth century. Today, the most important laws governing immigration and employment are the Immigration Reform and Control Act of 1986 (IRCA)[27] and the Immigration Act of 1990.[28] The IRCA provided amnesty to certain groups of illegal aliens then living in the United States and also established a system of sanctions against employers who hire illegal immigrants lacking work authorization. Because employers who hire illegal immigrants can face serious penalties, an understanding of the legal requirements related to immigration has become increasingly important for all businesspersons.

Immigration Reform and Control Act

The estimated 11 to 12 million illegal immigrants living in the United States today are the subject of considerable controversy. Many contend that they take jobs from U.S. citizens or hold down wages for such jobs. The IRCA was intended to

26. *Ragsdale v. Wolverine World Wide, Inc.*, 535 U.S. 81, 122 S.Ct. 1155, 152 L.Ed.2d 167 (2002).

27. 29 U.S.C. Section 1802.
28. This act amended various provisions of the Immigration and Nationality Act of 1952, 8 U.S.C. Sections 1101 *et seq.*

prevent this and made it illegal to hire, recruit, or refer for a fee someone not authorized to work in this country. The federal government—through Immigration and Customs Enforcement officers—conducts random compliance audits and engages in enforcement actions against employers who hire illegal immigrants. This section sets out the compliance requirements for employers.

I-9 Employment Verification To comply with current law, an employer must perform **I-9 verifications** for new hires, including those hired as "contractors" or "day workers" if they work under the employer's direct supervision. Form I-9, Employment Eligibility Verification, which is available from U.S. Citizenship and Immigration Services,[29] must be completed within three days of the worker's commencement of employment. The three-day period is to allow the employer to check the form's accuracy and to review and verify documents establishing the prospective worker's identity and eligibility for employment in the United States. Acceptable documents include a U.S. passport establishing the person's citizenship or a document authorizing a foreign citizen to work in the United States, such as a Permanent Resident Card or an Alien Registration Receipt Card.

The employer must attest, under penalty of perjury, that an employee produced documents establishing his or her identity and legal employability. The employee must state that he or she is a U.S. citizen or otherwise authorized to work in the United States. The employer is legally responsible for any problems with the I-9 verification process. Companies need to establish compliance procedures and keep completed I-9 forms on file for at least three years for government inspection.

The IRCA prohibits "knowing" violations, which include situations in which an employer "should have known" that the worker was unauthorized. Good faith is a defense under the statute, and employers are legally entitled to rely on a document authorizing a person to work that reasonably appears on its face to be genuine, even if it is later established to be counterfeit. Good faith is not a defense, however, to the failure to possess the proper paperwork. Moreover, if an employer subsequently learns that an employee is not authorized to work in this country, it must promptly discharge that employee or be in violation of the law.

Enforcement U.S. Immigration and Customs Enforcement (ICE) was established in 2003 as the largest investigative arm of the U.S. Department of Homeland Security. ICE has a

general inspection program that conducts random compliance audits. Other audits may occur if the agency receives a written complaint alleging an employer's violations. Government inspections include a review of an employer's file of I-9 forms. The government does not need a subpoena or a warrant to conduct such an inspection.

Administrative Actions. If an investigation reveals a possible violation, ICE will bring an administrative action and issue a Notice of Intent to Fine, which sets out the charges against the employer. The employer has a right to a hearing on the enforcement action if it files a request within thirty days. This hearing is conducted before an *administrative law judge,* and the employer has a right to counsel and to *discovery* (see Chapter 2). The typical defense in such actions is good faith or substantial compliance with the documentation provisions. As Exhibit 23–1 indicates, the federal government has increased its enforcement efforts significantly in recent years. In 2007, ICE raided and identified hundreds of illegal workers at plants owned by companies including Fresh Del Monte Produce, Jones Industrial Network, Koch Foods, and Tarrasco Steel.

Criminal Actions. ICE has increasingly sought criminal punishment for acts such as harboring an alien or illegally inducing illegal immigration. **■EXAMPLE 23.7** In 2008, an employee of

EXHIBIT 23–1 **Worksite Enforcement Arrests by U.S. Immigration and Customs Enforcement**

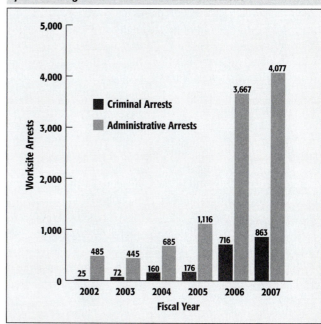

Source: U.S. Immigration and Customs Enforcement, 2008.

29. U.S. Citizenship and Immigration Services is a federal agency that is part of the U.S. Department of Homeland Security.

George's Processing, Inc., was convicted by a Missouri federal jury after an ICE raid resulted in the arrests of 136 illegal aliens at the plant. The convicted management employee was in the human resources department of the company and was involved in the hiring process. Evidence suggested that she helped applicants complete their I-9 forms knowing that they had fraudulently obtained identity documents. The potential penalty for this crime is as much as ten years in prison without parole. ▪

A possible defense to criminal charges is to show that the alleged illegal immigrant was an independent contractor rather than an employee and therefore was not subject to the I-9 requirements. Even for independent contractors, though, a party's actual knowledge that a worker was unauthorized is illegal. Ultimately, the administrative law judge reviewing the case makes a ruling and assesses penalties if he or she finds a violation. This hearing may be appealed administratively or to a federal court.

Although individuals who believe they have suffered as a result of illegal hiring may not sue an employer directly, they may bring a lawsuit under the Racketeer Influenced and Corrupt Organizations Act (RICO, which was discussed in Chapter 6).

Penalties An employer who violates the law by hiring an unauthorized alien is subject to substantial penalties. The employer may be fined up to $2,200 for each unauthorized employee for a first offense, $5,000 per employee for a second offense, and up to $11,000 for subsequent offenses. Criminal penalties including additional fines and imprisonment apply to employers who have engaged in a "pattern or practice of violations." A company may also be barred from future government contracts for violations.

In determining the penalty, ICE considers the seriousness of the violation (such as intentional falsification of documents) and the employer's past compliance. ICE regulations also provide for mitigation or aggravation of the penalty under certain circumstances, such as whether the employer cooperated in the investigation or is a small business.

Antidiscrimination Provisions The IRCA provides that it is an unfair immigration-related practice for an employer to discriminate against any individual (other than an unauthorized alien) with respect to hiring or discharging.[30] Companies must exercise reasonable care to evaluate the required I-9 documents in a fair and consistent manner. They may not require greater proof from some prospective employees or reject apparently sufficient documentation of work authorization or citizenship. The standards and procedures for evaluating an employee's discrimination claim parallel those of Title VII of the Civil Rights Act, which will be discussed later in this chapter.

The Immigration Act

Often, U.S. businesses find that they cannot hire sufficient domestic workers with specialized skills. For this reason, U.S. immigration laws have long made provisions for businesses to hire especially qualified foreign workers. The Immigration Act of 1990 placed caps on the number of visas (entry permits) that can be issued to immigrants each year.

Most temporary visas are set aside for workers who can be characterized as "persons of extraordinary ability," members of the professions holding advanced degrees, or other skilled workers and professionals. To hire these individuals, employers must submit a petition to Citizenship and Immigration Services, which determines whether the job candidate meets the legal standards. Each visa is for a specific job, and there are legal limits on the employee's ability to switch jobs once in the United States.

I-551 Alien Registration Receipts A company seeking to hire a noncitizen worker may do so if the worker is self-authorized. This means that the worker either is a lawful permanent resident or has a valid temporary Employment Authorization Document. A lawful permanent resident can prove his or her status to an employer by presenting an **I-551 Alien Registration Receipt**, known as a "green card," or a properly stamped foreign passport.

Many immigrant workers are not already self-authorized, and employers may obtain labor certification, or green cards, for those immigrants whom they wish to hire. Approximately fifty thousand new green cards are issued each year. A green card can be obtained only for a person who is being hired for a permanent, full-time position. (A separate authorization system provides for the temporary entry and hiring of nonimmigrant visa workers.)

To gain authorization for hiring a foreign worker, the employer must show that no U.S. worker is qualified, willing, and able to take the job. The employer must advertise the job opening in suitable newspapers or professional journals within six months of the hiring action. The government has detailed regulations governing this advertising requirement as well as the certification process.[31] Any U.S. applicants who meet the stated job qualifications must be interviewed for the position. The employer must also be able to show that the qualifications required for the job are a business necessity. A panel of administrative law judges rejected one company's notice for hiring kitchen supervisors because the company required that the applicants speak Spanish.[32]

---

30. 8 U.S.C. Section 1324b.

31. The most relevant regulations can be found at 20 C.F.R. Section 655 (for temporary employment) and 20 C.F.R. Section 656 (for permanent employment).

32. *In the Matter of Malnati Organization, Inc.*, 2007-INA-00035 (Bd. Alien Lab. Cert. App. 2007).

The employer must also determine from a state agency what the "prevailing wage" for the position is in the location and must offer the immigrating worker at least 100 percent of that wage. The prevailing wage rate is the average wage paid to similarly employed workers in that occupation in the area of intended employment. Fringe benefits are also considered in this calculation.

The H-1B Visa Program The most common and controversial visa program today is the H-1B visa system. Individuals with H-1B visas can stay in the United States for three to six years and work only for the sponsoring employer. The recipients of these visas include many high-tech workers, such as computer programmers and electronics specialists. Sixty-five thousand H-1B visas are set aside each year for new immigrants. In recent years, the total allotment of H1-B visas has been filled within the first few weeks of the year, leaving no slots available for the remaining eleven months. Consequently, many businesses, such as Microsoft, have lobbied Congress to expand the number of H1-B visas available to immigrants.

To obtain an H1-B visa, the potential employee must be qualified in a "specialty occupation," which is defined as involving highly specialized knowledge and the attainment of a bachelor's or higher degree or its equivalent. In one 2006 ruling, ICE found that the position of "accountant" did not qualify as a specialty occupation because the American Council for Accountancy and Taxation did not require a degree for an individual to have this credential.

Labor Certification Before an employer can submit an H-1B application, it must file a Labor Certification application on a form known as ETA 9035. The employer must agree to provide a wage level at least equal to the wages offered to other individuals with similar experience and qualifications and attest that the hiring will not adversely affect other workers similarly employed. The employer must inform U.S. workers of the intent to hire a foreign worker by posting the form. The U.S. Department of Labor reviews the applications and may reject them for incompleteness or inaccuracies.

H-2, O, L, and E Visas Other specialty temporary visas are available for other categories of employees. Workers performing agricultural labor of a seasonal nature may obtain H-2 visas. O visas provide entry for persons who have "extraordinary ability in the sciences, arts, education, business or athletics which has been demonstrated by sustained national or international acclaim." L visas allow a company's foreign managers or executives to work inside the United States. E visas permit the entry of certain foreign investors or entrepreneurs.

Immigration Reform on the Horizon

For many years, the president, members of Congress, business owners, and citizens have debated proposals for immi-

gration reform. Some proposals would allow illegal immigrants to remain legally in this country and permit many of them to eventually become citizens. At the other extreme, anti-immigration proposals would require all illegal immigrants to leave the United States and apply to return legally. At the writing of this edition, it was impossible to predict what form immigration reform would take. One thing is certain: problems with immigration will remain. The average wage differential between Mexico and the United States is more than 400 percent—larger than the differential between any other two countries that share a contiguous border. Thus, workers will have an incentive to cross the borders until economic growth in Mexico (and other Latin American countries) boosts average wage rates closer to those in the United States.

EMPLOYMENT DISCRIMINATION

Out of the 1960s civil rights movement to end racial and other forms of discrimination grew a body of law protecting employees against discrimination in the workplace. This protective legislation further eroded the employment-at-will doctrine (discussed earlier in this chapter). In the past several decades, judicial decisions, administrative agency actions, and legislation have restricted the ability of employers, as well as unions, to discriminate against workers on the basis of race, color, religion, national origin, gender, age, or disability. A class of persons defined by one or more of these criteria is known as a **protected class.**

A number of federal statutes prohibit **employment discrimination** against members of protected classes. The most important statute is Title VII of the Civil Rights Act of 1964.[33] Title VII prohibits discrimination on the basis of race, color, religion, national origin, or gender at any stage of employment. The Age Discrimination in Employment Act of 1967[34] and the Americans with Disabilities Act of 1990[35] prohibit discrimination on the basis of age and disability, respectively.

The remainder of this chapter focuses on the kinds of discrimination prohibited by these federal statutes. Note, though, that discrimination against employees on the basis of any of these criteria may also violate state human rights statutes or other state laws or public policies prohibiting discrimination.

Title VII of the Civil Rights Act of 1964

Title VII of the Civil Rights Act of 1964 and its amendments prohibit job discrimination against employees, applicants,

---

33. 42 U.S.C. Sections 2000e–2000e-17.
34. 29 U.S.C. Sections 621–634.
35. 42 U.S.C. Sections 12102–12118.

and union members on the basis of race, color, national origin, religion, or gender at any stage of employment. Title VII applies to employers with fifteen or more employees, labor unions with fifteen or more members, labor unions that operate hiring halls (to which members go regularly to be rationed jobs as they become available), employment agencies, and state and local governing units or agencies. An employer with fewer than fifteen employees is not automatically shielded from a lawsuit filed under Title VII, however.[36] A special section of the act prohibits discrimination in most federal government employment.

The Equal Employment Opportunity Commission Compliance with Title VII is monitored by the Equal Employment Opportunity Commission (EEOC). A victim of alleged discrimination, before bringing a suit against the employer, must first file a claim with the EEOC. The EEOC may investigate the dispute and attempt to obtain the parties' voluntary consent to an out-of-court settlement. If voluntary agreement cannot be reached, the EEOC may then file a suit against the employer on the employee's behalf. If the EEOC decides not to investigate the claim, the victim may bring her or his own lawsuit against the employer.

The EEOC does not investigate every claim of employment discrimination, regardless of the merits of the claim. Generally, it investigates only "priority cases," such as cases involving retaliatory discharge (firing an employee in retaliation for submitting a claim to the EEOC) and cases involving types of discrimination that are of particular concern to the EEOC.

Intentional and Unintentional Discrimination Title VII prohibits both intentional and unintentional discrimination.

Intentional Discrimination. Intentional discrimination by an employer against an employee is known as **disparate-treatment discrimination.** Because intent may sometimes be difficult to prove, courts have established certain procedures for resolving disparate-treatment cases. **■EXAMPLE 23.8** A woman applies for employment with a construction firm and is rejected. If she sues on the basis of disparate-treatment discrimination in hiring, she must show that (1) she is a member of a protected class, (2) she applied and was qualified for the job in question, (3) she was rejected by the employer, and (4) the employer continued to seek applicants for the position or filled the position with a person not in a protected class. ■

If the woman can meet these relatively easy requirements, she has made out a *prima facie* case of illegal discrimination. Making out a *prima facie* case of discrimination means that the plaintiff has met her initial burden of proof and will win in the absence of a legally acceptable employer defense. (Defenses to claims of employment discrimination will be discussed later in this chapter.) The burden then shifts to the employer-defendant, who must articulate a legal reason for not hiring the plaintiff. To prevail, the plaintiff must then show that the employer's reason is a *pretext* (not the true reason) and that discriminatory intent actually motivated the employer's decision.

Unintentional Discrimination. Employers often use interviews and testing procedures to choose from among a large number of applicants for job openings. Minimum educational requirements are also common. These practices and procedures may have an unintended discriminatory impact on a protected class. **Disparate-impact discrimination** occurs when a protected group of people is adversely affected by an employer's practices, procedures, or tests, even though they do not appear to be discriminatory. In a disparate-impact discrimination case, the complaining party must first show statistically that the employer's practices, procedures, or tests are discriminatory in effect. Once the plaintiff has made out a *prima facie* case, the burden of proof shifts to the employer to show that the practices or procedures in question were justified. There are two ways of proving that disparate-impact discrimination exists, as discussed next.

A plaintiff can prove a disparate impact by comparing the employer's workforce with the pool of qualified individuals available in the local labor market. The plaintiff must show that as a result of educational or other job requirements or hiring procedures, the percentage of nonwhites, women, or members of other protected classes in the employer's workforce does not reflect the percentage of that group in the pool of qualified applicants. If a person challenging an employment practice can show a connection between the practice and the disparity, he or she has made out a *prima facie* case and need not provide evidence of discriminatory intent.

Disparate-impact discrimination can also occur when an educational or other job requirement or hiring procedure excludes members of a protected class from an employer's workforce at a substantially higher rate than nonmembers, regardless of the racial balance in the employer's workforce. The EEOC has devised a test, called the "four-fifths rule," to determine whether an employment examination is discriminatory on its face. Under this rule, a selection rate for protected classes that is less than four-fifths, or 80 percent, of the rate for the group with the highest rate will generally be regarded as evidence of disparate impact. **■EXAMPLE 23.9** One hundred majority-group applicants take an employment test, and fifty pass the test and are hired. One hundred minority-group applicants take the test, and twenty pass the test and are hired. Because twenty is less than four-fifths (80 percent) of fifty, the test would be considered discriminatory under the EEOC guidelines. ■

---

36. See *Arbaugh v. Y&H Corp.,* 546 U.S. 500, 126 S.Ct. 1235, 163 L.Ed.2d 1097 (2006).

Discrimination Based on Race, Color, and National Origin Title VII prohibits employers from discriminating against employees or job applicants on the basis of race, color, or national origin. If an employer's standards or policies for selecting or promoting employees have a discriminatory effect on employees or job applicants in these protected classes, then a presumption of illegal discrimination arises. To avoid liability, the employer must then show that its standards or policies have a substantial, demonstrable relationship to realistic qualifications for the job in question.

■EXAMPLE 23.10 A city fires Cheng Mai, a Chinese American, who has worked in the city's planning department for two years. Mai claims that he was fired because of his national origin and presents evidence that the city's "residents only" policy has a discriminatory effect on Chinese Americans. The policy requires all city employees to become residents of the city within a reasonable time after being hired. Cheng Mai has not moved to the city but instead has continued to live with his wife and children in a nearby town that has a small population of Chinese Americans. Although residency requirements sometimes violate antidiscrimination laws, if the city can show that its residency requirement has a substantial, demonstrable relationship to realistic qualifications for the job in question, then normally it will not be illegal. ■

Note that discrimination based on race can also take the form of *reverse discrimination*, or discrimination against "majority" individuals, such as white males. **■EXAMPLE 23.11** An African American woman fired four white men from their management positions at a school district. The men filed a lawsuit for racial discrimination alleging that the woman was trying to eliminate white males from the department. The woman claimed that the terminations were part of a reorganization plan to cut costs in the department. The jury sided with the men and awarded them nearly $3 million in damages. The verdict was upheld on appeal (though the damages award was reduced slightly).[37] ■

Discrimination Based on Religion Title VII of the Civil Rights Act of 1964 also prohibits government employers, private employers, and unions from discriminating against persons because of their religion. An employer must "reasonably accommodate" the religious practices of its employees, unless to do so would cause undue hardship to the employer's business. **■EXAMPLE 23.12** If an employee's religion prohibits him from working on a certain day of the week or at a certain type of job, the employer must make a reasonable attempt to accommodate these religious requirements. Employers must reasonably accommodate an employee's religious belief even if the belief is not based on the doctrines of a traditionally recognized religion, such as Christianity or Judaism, or a denomination, such as Baptist. The only requirement is that the belief be sincerely held by the employee. ■

Discrimination Based on Gender Under Title VII, as well as under other federal acts (including those discussed here), employers are forbidden from discriminating against employees on the basis of gender. Employers are prohibited from classifying jobs as male or female and from advertising in help-wanted columns that are designated male or female unless the employer can prove that the gender of the applicant is essential to the job. Furthermore, employers cannot have separate male and female seniority lists. Generally, to succeed in a suit for gender discrimination, a plaintiff must demonstrate that gender was a determining factor in the employer's decision to hire, fire, or promote him or her. Typically, this involves looking at all of the surrounding circumstances.

The Equal Pay Act of 1963[38] prohibits employers from engaging in gender-based wage discrimination. For the act's equal pay requirements to apply, the male and female employees must work at the same establishment doing similar work. The work need not be identical, provided there is substantial equality of skill, effort, responsibility, and working conditions. To determine whether the Equal Pay Act has been violated, a court will look to the primary duties of the two jobs. It is the job content rather than the job description that controls. If a court finds that the wage differential is due to any factor other than gender, such as a seniority or merit system, then it does not violate the Equal Pay Act.

The Pregnancy Discrimination Act of 1978,[39] which amended Title VII, expanded the definition of gender discrimination to include discrimination based on pregnancy. Women affected by pregnancy, childbirth, or related medical conditions must be treated—for all employment-related purposes, including the provision of benefits under employee benefit programs—the same as other persons not so affected but similar in ability to work.

Constructive Discharge The majority of Title VII complaints involve unlawful discrimination in decisions to hire or fire employees. In some situations, however, employees who leave their jobs voluntarily can claim that they were "constructively discharged" by the employer. **Constructive discharge** occurs when the employer causes the employee's working conditions to be so intolerable that a reasonable person in the employee's position would feel compelled to quit.

The plaintiff must present objective proof of intolerable working conditions, which the employer knew or had reason to know about yet failed to correct within a reasonable time period. Courts generally also require the employee to show

---

37. *Johnston v. School District of Philadelphia,* 2006 WL 999966 (E.D.Pa. 2006).

38. 29 U.S.C. Section 206(d).
39. 42 U.S.C. Section 2000e(k).

causation—that the employer's unlawful discrimination caused the working conditions to be intolerable. Put a different way, the employee's resignation must be a foreseeable result of the employer's discriminatory action.

■EXAMPLE 23.13 Khalil's employer humiliates him by informing him in front of his co-workers that he is being demoted to an inferior position. Khalil, who was born in Iraq, is then subjected to continued insults, harassment, and derogatory remarks about his national origin by his co-workers. The employer is aware of this discriminatory treatment but does nothing to remedy the situation, despite repeated complaints from Khalil. After several months, Khalil quits his job and files a Title VII claim. In this situation, Khalil would likely have sufficient evidence to maintain an action for constructive discharge in violation of Title VII. ■ Although courts weigh the facts on a case-by-case basis, employee demotion is one of the most frequently cited reasons for a finding of constructive discharge, particularly when the employee was subjected to humiliation.

Note that constructive discharge is a theory that plaintiffs can use to establish any type of discrimination claims under Title VII, including race, color, national origin, religion, gender, pregnancy, and sexual harassment. Constructive discharge has also been successfully used in situations that involve discrimination based on age or disability (both of which will be discussed later in this chapter). Constructive discharge is most commonly asserted in cases involving sexual harassment, however.

Sexual Harassment Title VII also protects employees against **sexual harassment** in the workplace. Sexual harassment can take two forms: *quid pro quo* harassment and hostile-environment harassment. *Quid pro quo* is a Latin phrase that is often translated to mean "something in exchange for something else." *Quid pro quo* harassment occurs when sexual favors are demanded in return for job opportunities, promotions, salary increases, and the like. Hostile-environment harassment occurs when "the workplace is permeated with discriminatory intimidation, ridicule, and insult, that is sufficiently severe or pervasive to alter the conditions of the victim's employment and create an abusive working environment."[40]

Generally, the courts apply this United States Supreme Court guideline on a case-by-case basis. Typically, a single incident of sexually offensive conduct is not enough to permeate the work environment (although there have been exceptions when the conduct was particularly severe).

PREVENTING LEGAL DISPUTES

Harassment in the workplace can take many forms and be based on many characteristics (gender, race, national origin, religion, age, and disability), but sexual harassment is always based on an employee's gender. Establish written policies and review them annually. Any complaint should be taken seriously and investigated. Prompt remedial action is key, but it must not include any immediate adverse action against the complainant (such as termination). Most importantly, seek the advice of counsel as soon as a complaint arises.

■

Harassment by Supervisors. For an employer to be held liable for a supervisor's sexual harassment, the supervisor must have taken a tangible employment action against the employee. A **tangible employment action** is a significant change in employment status, such as firing or failing to promote an employee, reassigning the employee to a position with significantly different responsibilities, or effecting a significant change in employment benefits. Only a supervisor, or another person acting with the authority of the employer, can cause this sort of injury.

The United States Supreme Court has ruled that employers can sometimes be liable for a supervisor's sexual harassment even though the employer was unaware of the behavior and the employee suffered no adverse job consequences.[41] Note, however, that employers have an affirmative defense to liability if they can show the following:

1 They have taken "reasonable care to prevent and correct promptly any sexually harassing behavior" (by establishing effective harassment policies and complaint procedures, for example).

2 The employees suing for harassment failed to follow these policies and procedures.

In the context of constructive discharge cases (in which the person voluntarily leaves the job), the requirement of a tangible employment action is satisfied differently. In 2004, the United States Supreme Court clarified that the plaintiff in such cases must show that "the work environment became so intolerable that resignation was a fitting response."[42]

In 2006, the Court further clarified the requirement as applied to *retaliation* cases—which allege that an employer

---

40. *Harris v. Forklift Systems,* 510 U.S. 17, 114 S.Ct. 367, 126 L.Ed.2d 295 (1993). See also *Baker v. Via Christi Regional Medical Center,* 491 F.Supp.2d 1040 (D.Kan. 2007).

41. This was the Court's holding in two seminal cases. *Faragher v. City of Boca Raton,* 524 U.S. 775, 118 S.Ct. 2275, 141 L.Ed.2d 204 (1998); and *Burlington Industries, Inc. v. Ellerth,* 524 U.S. 742, 118 S.Ct. 2257, 141 L.Ed.2d 633 (1998).

42. *Pennsylvania State Police v. Suders,* 542 U.S. 129, 124 S.Ct. 2342, 159 L.Ed.2d 204 (2004).

has retaliated against an employee for making a discrimination claim. The Court found that an employer's retaliatory acts—such as changing the plaintiff's job duties or suspending her or him without pay—could be used as evidence of retaliatory discrimination even though there was no significant change in employment status or benefits. In retaliation claims, the plaintiff only needs to show that the employer's acts would be material to a reasonable employee.[43]

Harassment by Co-Workers and Nonemployees. Often, employees alleging harassment complain that the actions of co-workers, not supervisors, are responsible for creating a hostile working environment. In such cases, the employee may still have a cause of action against the employer. Normally, though, the employer will be held liable only if the employer knew, or should have known, about the harassment and failed to take immediate remedial action.

Employers may also be liable for harassment by *nonemployees* in certain circumstances. **■EXAMPLE 23.14** A restaurant owner or manager knows that a certain customer repeatedly harasses a waitress and permits the harassment to continue. The restaurant owner may be liable under Title VII even though the customer is not an employee of the restaurant. The issue turns on the control that the employer exerts over a nonemployee. ■

Same-Gender Harassment. The courts have also had to address the issue of whether men who are harassed by other men, or women who are harassed by other women, are protected by laws that prohibit gender-based discrimination in the workplace. For example, what if the male president of a firm demands sexual favors from a male employee? Does this action qualify as sexual harassment? For some time, the courts were widely split on this issue. The United States Supreme Court resolved the issue back in 1998 by holding that Title VII protection extends to situations in which individuals are harassed by members of the same gender.[44]

Remedies under Title VII Employer liability under Title VII may be extensive. If the plaintiff successfully proves that unlawful discrimination occurred, he or she may be awarded reinstatement, back pay, retroactive promotions, and damages. Compensatory damages are available only in cases of intentional discrimination. Punitive damages may be recovered against a private employer only if the employer acted with malice or reckless indifference to an individual's rights. The statute limits the total amount of compensatory and punitive damages that the plaintiff can recover from specific employers—ranging from $50,000 against employers with

one hundred or fewer employees to $300,000 against employers with more than five hundred employees.

Discrimination Based on Age

Age discrimination is potentially the most widespread form of discrimination, because anyone—regardless of race, color, national origin, or gender—could be a victim at some point in life. The Age Discrimination in Employment Act (ADEA) of 1967, as amended, prohibits employment discrimination on the basis of age against individuals forty years of age or older. The act also prohibits mandatory retirement for nonmanagerial workers. For the act to apply, an employer must have twenty or more employees, and the employer's business activities must affect interstate commerce. The EEOC administers the ADEA, but the act also permits private causes of action against employers for age discrimination.

Procedures under the ADEA The burden-shifting procedure under the ADEA is similar to that under Title VII. If a plaintiff can establish that she or he (1) was a member of the protected age group, (2) was qualified for the position from which she or he was discharged, and (3) was discharged under circumstances that give rise to an inference of discrimination, the plaintiff has established a *prima facie* case of unlawful age discrimination. The burden then shifts to the employer, who must articulate a legitimate reason for the discrimination. If the plaintiff can prove that the employer's reason is only a pretext (excuse) and that the plaintiff's age was a determining factor in the employer's decision, the employer will be held liable.

Whether a firing of an older worker is discriminatory or simply part of a rational business decision to prune the company's ranks is not always clear. Companies often defend a decision to discharge a worker by asserting that the worker could no longer perform his or her duties or that the worker's skills were no longer needed. The employee must prove that the discharge was motivated, at least in part, by age bias. Proof that qualified older employees are generally discharged before younger employees or that co-workers continually made unflattering age-related comments about the discharged worker may be enough.

The plaintiff need not prove that he or she was replaced by a person outside the protected class (under the age of forty years) as long as the person is younger than the plaintiff. The issue is whether age discrimination has, in fact, occurred, regardless of the age of the replacement worker. Nevertheless, the bigger the age gap, the more likely the individual is to succeed in showing age discrimination.

When an older worker who is laid off as part of a restructuring subsequently files a suit against the company for age discrimination, a court must decide what testimony concerning the company's attitudes toward workers' ages will be allowed as evidence at trial. This issue was at the heart of the following case.

43. *Burlington Northern and Santa Fe Railway Co. v. White*, 548 U.S. 53, 126 S.Ct. 2405, 165 L.Ed.2d 345 (2006).
44. *Oncale v. Sundowner Offshore Services, Inc.*, 523 U.S. 75, 118 S.Ct. 998, 140 L.Ed.2d 207 (1998).

CASE 23.3 Sprint/United Management Co. v. Mendelsohn

Supreme Court of the United States, ___ U.S. ___, 128 S.Ct. 1140, 170 L.Ed.2d 1 (2008).

FACTS Ellen Mendelsohn worked for Sprint/United Management Company (Sprint) from 1989 to 2002, when Sprint fired her during a companywide reduction in the workforce. She sued under the ADEA, alleging disparate treatment based on her age, fifty-one. Five other former Sprint employees testified that they had also suffered discrimination based on age. Three said that they heard managers make remarks belittling older workers and that age was a factor in planning who was to be fired during the restructuring. None of the five witnesses worked in the same part of the company as Mendelsohn, however, and none could testify about her supervisors. The district court excluded their testimony as to the impact on Mendelsohn because the witnesses were not "similarly situated" in the company. The appeals court held that the testimony was not *per se* irrelevant and remanded the case with instructions to admit the challenged testimony. Sprint appealed to the United States Supreme Court.

ISSUE Could the courts determine ahead of time whether or not the witnesses' testimony about the company's attitude was *per se* irrelevant and *per se* inadmissible based on factors other than the testimony itself?

DECISION No. The United States Supreme Court vacated the appellate court's decision and remanded the case to the district court so that the trial court could clarify its ruling.

REASON The Court reasoned that the trial court had gone too far in excluding the challenged testimony and that the appellate court had erred in telling the lower court to admit the testimony. The testimony is not necessarily *per se* admissible or *per se* inadmissible. According to federal rules, the relevance of such evidence is fact based and depends on many factors. The district (trial) court should study the evidence in more detail and determine if the witnesses were providing credible evidence of a discriminatory policy at Sprint that was played out through the reduction in the workforce. The courts had to assess the value of such evidence. They could not simply reject evidence that did not directly address the attitude of Mendelsohn's immediate supervisors.

FOR CRITICAL ANALYSIS—Legal Consideration *What steps should employers take to reduce the likelihood that supervisors will make negative comments about workers' ages?*

State Employees Not Covered by the ADEA Generally, the states are immune from lawsuits brought by private individuals in federal court—unless a state consents to the suit. This immunity stems from the United States Supreme Court's interpretation of the Eleventh Amendment (the text of this amendment is included in Appendix B). **■EXAMPLE 23.15** In two Florida cases, professors and librarians contended that their employers—two Florida state universities—denied them salary increases and other benefits because they were getting old and their successors could be hired at lower cost. The universities claimed that as agencies of a sovereign state, they could not be sued in federal court without the state's consent. The cases ultimately reached the United States Supreme Court, which held that the Eleventh Amendment bars private parties from suing state employers for violations of the ADEA.[45] ■

State immunity under the Eleventh Amendment is not absolute, however, as the Supreme Court explained in 2004. In some situations, such as when fundamental rights are at stake,

Congress has the power to abrogate (abolish) state immunity to private suits through legislation that unequivocally shows Congress's intent to subject states to private suits.[46] As a general rule, though, the Court has found that state employers are immune from private suits brought by employees under the ADEA (for age discrimination, as noted above), the Americans with Disabilities Act (for disability discrimination), and the Fair Labor Standards Act (which relates to wages and hours). In contrast, states are not immune from the requirements of the Family and Medical Leave Act.[47]

Federal Employees Explicitly Covered by the ADEA The ADEA includes a provision that extends its protections against age discrimination to federal government employees.[48] In 2008, the United States Supreme Court ruled that this provision encompasses not only claims of age discrimination, which are provided for in its language, but also claims of retaliation for complaining about age discrimination, which are

---

45. *Kimel v. Florida Board of Regents*, 528 U.S. 62, 120 S.Ct. 631, 145 L.Ed.2d 522 (2000).

46. *Tennessee v. Lane*, 541 U.S. 509, 124 S.Ct. 1978, 158 L.Ed.2d 820 (2004).
47. *Nevada Department of Human Resources v. Hibbs*, 538 U.S. 721, 123 S.Ct. 1972, 155 L.Ed.2d 953 (2003).
48. 29 U.S.C. Section 623a(a) (2000 ed., Supp. V).

not mentioned. The case involved a forty-five-year-old U.S. postal worker, Myrna Gómez-Pérez, who was falsely accused of misconduct and denied a transfer back to her former full-time position in retaliation for filing an age discrimination complaint. She filed an ADEA lawsuit against the Postmaster General, who argued that the section of the ADEA that applies to federal employees does not prohibit retaliation. The lower courts held in the defendant's favor. The Supreme Court reversed, ruling that the ADEA does protect federal workers from retaliation based on age-related complaints, just as it protects private-sector employees from retaliation.[49]

Discrimination Based on Disability

The Americans with Disabilities Act (ADA) of 1990 is designed to eliminate discriminatory employment practices that prevent otherwise qualified workers with disabilities from fully participating in the national labor force. Prior to 1990, the major federal law providing protection to those with disabilities was the Rehabilitation Act of 1973. That act covered only federal government employees and those employed under federally funded programs. The ADA extends federal protection against disability-based discrimination to all workplaces with fifteen or more workers (with the exception of state government employers). Basically, the ADA requires that employers "reasonably accommodate" the needs of persons with disabilities unless to do so would cause the employer to suffer an "undue hardship."

Procedures under the ADA   To prevail on a claim under the ADA, a plaintiff must show that he or she (1) has a disability, (2) is otherwise qualified for the employment in question, and (3) was excluded from the employment solely because of the disability. As in Title VII cases, a claim alleging a violation of the ADA may be commenced only after the plaintiff has pursued the claim through the EEOC. Plaintiffs may sue for many of the same remedies available under Title VII. The EEOC may decide to investigate and perhaps even sue the employer on behalf of the employee. If the EEOC decides not to sue, then the employee is entitled to sue.

Plaintiffs in lawsuits brought under the ADA may seek many of the same remedies available under Title VII. These include reinstatement, back pay, a limited amount of compensatory and punitive damages (for intentional discrimination), and certain other forms of relief. Repeat violators may be ordered to pay fines of up to $100,000.

What Is a Disability?   The ADA defines the term *disability* as "(1) a physical or mental impairment that substantially limits one or more of the major life activities of such individuals; (2) a record of such impairment; or (3) being regarded as having such an impairment."

Health conditions that have been considered disabilities under the federal law include blindness, alcoholism, heart disease, cancer, muscular dystrophy, cerebral palsy, paraplegia, diabetes, acquired immune deficiency syndrome (AIDS), testing positive for the human immunodeficiency virus (HIV), and morbid obesity (which exists when an individual's weight is two times that of a normal person's weight). The ADA excludes from coverage certain conditions, such as kleptomania (the obsessive desire to steal).

Correctable Conditions.   Although the ADA's definition of disability is broad, United States Supreme Court rulings in recent years have interpreted that definition narrowly, which has made it more difficult for employees to establish a disability under the meaning of the act. In 1999, the Court held that severe myopia (nearsightedness), which can be corrected with contact lenses, did not qualify as a disability under the ADA.[50] After that decision, when determining whether a person had a disability, the courts began focusing on how the person functioned when using corrective devices or taking medication, *not* on how the person functioned without these measures. For example, a pharmacist suffered from diabetes, which was treated with insulin. Because the medication corrected his condition, a federal court held that he was not substantially limited in major life activity and thus could not sue his employer under the ADA.[51]

In response to these limiting decisions, Congress passed the ADA Amendments Act of 2008.[52] The act was intended to reverse the Supreme Court's restrictive interpretation of the ADA. Among other things, the amendments prohibit employers from considering mitigating measures or medications when determining if an individual has a disability.

Repetitive-Stress Injuries.   In 2002, the United States Supreme Court held that carpal tunnel syndrome does not constitute a disability under the ADA. Carpal tunnel syndrome is a condition of pain and weakness in the hand caused by repetitive compression of a nerve in the wrist. The Court stated that although the employee could not perform the particular manual tasks associated with her job, the condition did not substantially limit the major life activity of performing manual tasks.[53] Thus, carpal tunnel syndrome and

---

49. *Gómez-Pérez v. Potter*, ___ U.S. ___, 128 S.Ct. 1931, ___ L.Ed.2d ___ (2008).

50. *Sutton v. United Airlines, Inc.*, 527 U.S. 471, 119 S.Ct. 2139, 144 L.Ed.2d 450 (1999).

51. *Orr v. Walmart Stores, Inc.*, 297 F.3d 720 (8th Cir. 2002).

52. Also known as the ADA Restoration Act, H.R. 3195, S.R. 3406 (September 11, 2008).

53. *Toyota Motor Manufacturing, Kentucky, Inc. v. Williams*, 534 U.S. 184, 122 S.Ct. 681, 151 L.Ed.2d 615 (2002).

other repetitive-stress injuries ordinarily do not constitute a disability under the ADA. This ruling and others holding that carpal tunnel syndrome and other repetitive-stress injuries do not constitute a disability may be affected by the passage of the 2008 ADA amendments.

Reasonable Accommodation   The ADA does not require that employers accommodate the needs of job applicants or employees with disabilities who are not otherwise qualified for the work. If a job applicant or an employee with a disability, with reasonable accommodation, can perform essential job functions, however, the employer must make the accommodation. Required modifications may include installing ramps for a wheelchair, establishing flexible working hours, creating or modifying job assignments, and creating or improving training materials and procedures.

Employers who do not accommodate the needs of persons with disabilities must demonstrate that the accommodations will cause "undue hardship." Generally, the law offers no uniform standards for identifying what is an undue hardship other than the imposition of a "significant difficulty or expense" on the employer. Usually, the courts decide whether an accommodation constitutes an undue hardship on a case-by-case basis.

Employers must modify their job-application process so that those with disabilities can compete for jobs with those who do not have disabilities. Employers are also restricted in the kinds of questions they may ask on job-application forms and during preemployment interviews. (For more on interviewing job applicants with disabilities, see this chapter's *Management Perspective* feature.) They cannot require persons with disabilities to submit to preemployment physicals unless such exams are required of all other applicants. **■EXAMPLE 23.16** When filling the position of delivery truck driver, a company cannot screen out all applicants who are unable to meet the U.S. Department of Transportation's hearing standard. To do so, the company would first have to prove that drivers who are deaf are not qualified to perform the essential job function of driving safely and pose a higher risk of accidents than drivers who are not deaf.[54] ■

Defenses to Employment Discrimination

The first line of defense for an employer charged with employment discrimination is, of course, to assert that the plaintiff has failed to meet his or her initial burden of proving that discrimination occurred. As noted, plaintiffs bringing cases under the ADA sometimes find it difficult to meet this initial burden because they must prove that their alleged dis-

abilities are disabilities covered by the ADA. Furthermore, plaintiffs in ADA cases must prove that they were otherwise qualified for the job and that their disabilities were the sole reason they were not hired or were fired.

Once a plaintiff succeeds in proving that discrimination occurred, the burden shifts to the employer to justify the discriminatory practice. Often, employers attempt to justify the discrimination by claiming that it was the result of a *business necessity, a bona fide occupational qualification,* or a *seniority system.* In some cases, as noted earlier, an effective antiharassment policy and prompt remedial action when harassment occurs may shield employers from liability under Title VII for sexual harassment.

Business Necessity   An employer may defend against a claim of disparate-impact (unintentional) discrimination by asserting that a practice that has a discriminatory effect is a **business necessity.** **■EXAMPLE 23.17** If requiring a high school diploma is shown to have a discriminatory effect, an employer might argue that a high school education is necessary for workers to perform the job at a required level of competence. If the employer can demonstrate to the court's satisfaction that a definite connection exists between a high school education and job performance, the employer normally will succeed in this business necessity defense. ■

Bona Fide Occupational Qualification   Another defense applies when discrimination against a protected class is essential to a job—that is, when a particular trait is a **bona fide occupational qualification (BFOQ).** Race, however, can never be a BFOQ. Generally, courts have restricted the BFOQ defense to instances in which the employee's gender is essential to the job. **■EXAMPLE 23.18** A women's clothing store might legitimately hire only female sales attendants if part of an attendant's job involves assisting clients in the store's dressing rooms. Similarly, the Federal Aviation Administration can legitimately impose age limits for airline pilots. ■

Seniority Systems   An employer with a history of discrimination may have no members of protected classes in upper-level positions. Even if the employer now seeks to be unbiased, it may face a lawsuit in which the plaintiff asks a court to order that minorities be promoted ahead of schedule to compensate for past discrimination. If no present intent to discriminate is shown, however, and if promotions or other job benefits are distributed according to a fair **seniority system** (in which workers with more years of service are promoted first or laid off last), the employer has a good defense against the suit. According to the Supreme Court in 2002, this defense may also apply to alleged discrimination under

---

54. *Bates v. United Parcel Service, Inc.,* 465 F.3d 1069 (9th Cir. 2006).

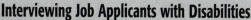

MANAGEMENT PERSPECTIVE

Interviewing Job Applicants with Disabilities

Management Faces a Legal Issue

Many employers have been held liable under the Americans with Disabilities Act (ADA) because they have asked the wrong questions when interviewing job applicants with disabilities. The Equal Employment Opportunity Commission (EEOC) has issued guidelines about which questions employers may or may not ask job applicants with disabilities. For example, an interviewer may ask a job applicant whether he or she can meet the company's attendance requirements. In contrast, the interviewer cannot ask how many days a person was sick in the previous year. An employer can ask an applicant whether he or she can do the job, but not how he or she would do the job *unless* the disability is obvious, the applicant brings up the subject during the interview, or the employer asks the question of all applicants for that particular job. After a job offer is made, the employer is allowed to ask the applicant questions concerning her or his disability, including questions about previous workers' compensation claims or the extent of, say, a drinking or drug problem.

What the Courts Say

In one case, the job applicant suffered from a hearing impairment. He alleged that the potential employer discriminated against him because of his disability when he applied for a position as an information technology specialist. At trial, one of the key issues was how the interview was conducted. The interviewer claimed that he had no concerns about the applicant's deafness. But at one point during the interview, the interviewer passed a handwritten note asking the applicant, "How do you communicate in offices where no one can sign?" The

applicant responded, "I have no problem with writing as my basic communication." The court pointed out that the interviewer did not ask this question of any other applicant. Although the applicant ultimately did not prevail at trial, the court made it clear that the interviewer should not have asked the applicant any special questions.[a]

In another case, an applicant sued the federal government after applying for the position of bank examiner. He claimed that during an interview, there was an improper inquiry about his perceived disability. In fact, the applicant had previously suffered a stroke and slurred his words when he spoke. During the interview, he was asked what was wrong with his arm and whether his disability affected his mental coherence. Ultimately, the applicant lost his case because he had lied on his résumé. Nonetheless, the defendants would have had an easier time at trial had the interviewer followed the EEOC guidelines.[b]

Implications for Managers

When preparing for job interviews, most managers should consult with an attorney who specializes in employment issues. In particular, they should review the kinds of questions typically asked of job applicants during interviews or following employment offers. Any questions that increase the risk of a lawsuit from an applicant with disabilities must be altered. All questions should be consistent with EEOC guidelines. Anyone who interviews job applicants should be informed about what questions can and cannot be asked of candidates with disabilities. Note, however, that once a job has been offered, a manager is allowed to ask the candidate for his or her medical documents in order to verify the nature of the applicant's disability.

a. *Adeyemi v. District of Columbia,* 2007 WL 1020754 (D.C.Cir. 2007).
b. *Strong v. Paulson,* 2007 WL 2859789 (7th Cir. 2007). See also *Lorah v. Tetra Tech, Inc.,* 541 F.Supp.2d 629 (D.Del. 2008).

---

the ADA. If an employee with a disability requests an accommodation (such as an assignment to a particular position) that conflicts with an employer's seniority system, the accommodation will generally not be considered "reasonable" under the act.[55]

55. *U.S. Airways, Inc. v. Barnett,* 535 U.S. 391, 122 S.Ct. 1516, 152 L.Ed.2d 589 (2002).

After-Acquired Evidence of Employee Misconduct In some situations, employers have attempted to avoid liability for employment discrimination on the basis of "after-acquired evidence"—that is, evidence that the employer discovers after a lawsuit is filed—of an employee's misconduct. **■EXAMPLE 23.19** An employer fires a worker, who then sues the employer for employment discrimination. During pretrial investigation, the employer learns that the employee made material misrepresentations on his or her employment application—misrepresentations that, had the employer known about them, would have served as a ground to fire the individual. ◼

After-acquired evidence of wrongdoing cannot be used to shield an employer entirely from liability for employment discrimination. It may, however, be used to limit the amount of damages for which the employer is liable.

AFFIRMATIVE ACTION

Federal statutes and regulations providing for equal opportunity in the workplace were designed to reduce or eliminate discriminatory practices with respect to hiring, retaining, and promoting employees. **Affirmative action** programs go a step further and attempt to "make up" for past patterns of discrimination by giving members of protected classes preferential treatment in hiring or promotion. During the 1960s, all federal and state government agencies, private companies that contract to do business with the federal government, and institutions that receive federal funding were required to implement affirmative action policies.

Title VII of the Civil Rights Act of 1964 neither requires nor prohibits affirmative action. Thus, most private firms have not been required to implement affirmative action policies, though many have chosen to do so.

Affirmative action programs have aroused much controversy over the last forty years, particularly when they have resulted in what is frequently called "reverse discrimination"—discrimination against "majority" individuals, such as white males. At issue is whether affirmative action programs, because of their inherently discriminatory nature, violate the equal protection clause of the Fourteenth Amendment to the Constitution.

Court Decision on Quota Systems

The United States Supreme Court has concluded that an affirmative action program is constitutional only if it attempts to remedy past discrimination and does not make use of quotas or preferences.[56] In other words, a program cannot require that a certain number of minority applicants be hired or admitted (into a university, for example) or give preference to a minority applicant over a nonminority applicant. Once the program has succeeded in the goal of remedying past discrimination, it must be changed or dropped.

Court Decisions on Race and Ethnicity

In 2003, the United States Supreme Court reviewed two affirmative action cases: *Gratz v. Bollinger* and *Grutter v.*

Bollinger.[57] Both cases involved admissions programs at the University of Michigan. In the *Gratz* case, two white applicants who were denied undergraduate admission to the university alleged reverse discrimination. The school's policy gave each applicant a score based on a number of factors, including grade point average, standardized test scores, and personal achievements. The system *automatically* awarded every "underrepresented" minority (African American, Hispanic, and Native American) applicant twenty points—one-fifth of the points needed to guarantee admission. The Court held that this policy violated the equal protection clause.

In contrast, in the *Grutter* case, the Court held that the University of Michigan Law School's admissions policy was constitutional. In that case, the Court concluded that "[u]niversities can, however, consider race or ethnicity more flexibly as a 'plus' factor in the context of individualized consideration of each and every applicant." The significant difference between the two admissions policies, in the Court's view, was that the law school's approach did not apply a mechanical formula giving "diversity bonuses" based on race or ethnicity.

In 2007, the United States Supreme Court ruled on two cases involving the use of racial classifications in assigning students to schools in Seattle, Washington, and Jefferson County, Kentucky. Both school districts had adopted student assignment plans that relied on race to determine which schools certain children attended. The Seattle school district plan classified children as "white" or "nonwhite" and used the racial classifications as a "tiebreaker" to determine which high school students attended. The school district in Jefferson County classified students as "black" or "other" to assign children to elementary schools. Groups of parents from the relevant public schools filed lawsuits claiming that the school districts' racial preferences violated the equal protection clause. The Court held that the school districts had failed to show that the use of racial classifications in their student assignment plans was necessary to achieve their stated goal of racial diversity.[58]

STATE STATUTES

Although the focus of this chapter has been on federal legislation, most states also have statutes that prohibit employment discrimination. Generally, the same kinds of

---

56. *Adarand Constructors, Inc. v. Peña*, 515 U.S. 200, 115 S.Ct. 2097, 132 L.Ed.2d 158 (1995).

57. 539 U.S. 244, 123 S.Ct. 2411, 156 L.Ed.2d 257 (2003); and 539 U.S. 306, 123 S.Ct. 2325, 156 L.Ed.2d 304 (2003), respectively.

58. The Court consolidated the two cases and issued only one opinion to address the issues presented by both cases. *Parents Involved in Community Schools v. Seattle School Dist. No. 1*, ___ U.S. ___, 127 S.Ct. 2738, 168 L.Ed.2d 508 (2007).

discrimination are prohibited under federal and state legislation. In addition, state statutes often provide protection for certain individuals who are not protected under federal laws. For instance, anyone over the age of eighteen is entitled to sue for age discrimination under New Jersey state law, which specifies no threshold age limit.

Furthermore, state laws prohibiting discrimination may apply to firms with fewer employees than the threshold number required under federal statutes, thus offering protection to more workers. State laws may also allow for additional

damages, such as damages for emotional distress, that are not available under federal statutes.[59] Finally, some states, including California and Washington, have passed laws that end affirmative action programs in those states or modify admissions policies at state-sponsored universities.

---

59. For a reverse discrimination case in which a former police officer was awarded nearly $80,000 in emotional distress damages based on a violation of New Jersey's law against discrimination, see *Klawitter v. City of Trenton*, 395 N.J.Super. 302, 928 A.2d 900 (2007).

REVIEWING Employment and Immigration Law

Amaani Lyle, an African American woman, took a job as a scriptwriters' assistant at Warner Brothers Television Productions working for the writers of *Friends,* a popular, adult-oriented television series. One of her essential job duties was to type detailed notes for the scriptwriters during brainstorming sessions in which they discussed jokes, dialogue, and story lines. The writers then combed through Lyle's notes after the meetings for script material. During these meetings, the three male scriptwriters told lewd and vulgar jokes and made sexually explicit comments and gestures. They often talked about their personal sexual experiences and fantasies, and some of these conversations were then used in episodes of *Friends.*

During the meetings, Lyle never complained that she found the writers' conduct offensive. After four months, she was fired because she could not type fast enough to keep up with the writers' conversations during the meetings. She filed a suit against Warner Brothers alleging sexual harassment and claiming that her termination was based on racial

discrimination. Using the information presented in the chapter, answer the following questions.

1 Would Lyle's claim of racial discrimination be for intentional (disparate treatment) or unintentional (disparate impact) discrimination? Explain.

2 Can Lyle establish a *prima facie* case of racial discrimination? Why or why not?

3 Lyle was told when she was hired that typing speed was extremely important to her position. At the time, she maintained that she could type eighty words per minute, so she was not given a typing test. It later turned out that Lyle could type only fifty words per minute. What impact might typing speed have on Lyle's lawsuit?

4 Lyle's sexual harassment claim is based on the hostile work environment created by the writers' sexually offensive conduct at meetings that she was required to attend. The writers, however, argue that their behavior was essential to the "creative process" of writing *Friends,* a show that routinely contained sexual innuendos and adult humor. Which defense discussed in the chapter might Warner Brothers assert using this argument?

TERMS AND CONCEPTS

CHAPTER SUMMARY Employment and Immigration Law

Employment at Will
(See pages 467–469.)

1. *Employment-at-will doctrine*—Under this common law doctrine, either party may terminate the employment relationship at any time and for any reason ("at will"). This doctrine is still in widespread use throughout the United States, although federal and state statutes prevent the doctrine from being applied in certain circumstances.

2. *Exceptions to the employment-at-will doctrine*—To protect employees from some of the harsh results of the employment-at-will doctrine, courts have made exceptions to the doctrine on the basis of contract theory, tort theory, and public policy. Whistleblowers have occasionally received protection under the common law for reasons of public policy. Most states have passed whistleblower statutes specifically to protect employees who "blow the whistle" on their employers from subsequent retaliation by those employers.

3. *Wrongful discharge*—Whenever an employer discharges an employee in violation of an employment contract or statutory law protecting employees, the employee may bring a suit for wrongful discharge.

Wage and Hour Laws
(See page 469.)

1. *Davis-Bacon Act (1931)*—Requires contractors and subcontractors working on federal government construction projects to pay their employees "prevailing wages."

2. *Walsh-Healey Act (1936)*—Requires that employees of firms that contract with federal agencies be paid a minimum wage and overtime pay.

3. *Fair Labor Standards Act (1938)*—Extended wage-hour requirements to cover all employers whose activities affect interstate commerce plus certain other businesses. The act has specific requirements in regard to child labor, maximum hours, and minimum wages.

Labor Unions
(See pages 469–471.)

1. *Norris-LaGuardia Act (1932)*—Protects peaceful strikes, picketing, and primary boycotts.

2. *National Labor Relations Act (1935)*—Established the rights of employees to engage in collective bargaining and to strike; also defined specific employer practices as unfair to labor. The National Labor Relations Board (NLRB) was created to administer and enforce the act.

3. *Labor-Management Relations Act (1947)*—Proscribes certain unfair union practices, such as the closed shop.

4. *Labor-Management Reporting and Disclosure Act (1959)*—Established an employee bill of rights and reporting requirements for union activities.

Worker Health and Safety
(See pages 471–472.)

1. *Occupational Safety and Health Act (1970)*—Requires employers to meet specific safety and health standards that are established and enforced by the Occupational Safety and Health Administration (OSHA).

2. *State workers' compensation laws*—Establish an administrative procedure for compensating workers who are injured in accidents that occur on the job, regardless of fault.

Income Security
(See pages 472–474.)

1. *Social Security and Medicare*—The Social Security Act of 1935 provides for old-age (retirement), survivors, and disability insurance. Both employers and employees must make contributions under the Federal Insurance Contributions Act (FICA) to help pay for benefits that will partially make up for the employees' loss of income on retirement. The Social Security Administration also administers Medicare, a health-insurance program for older or disabled persons.

2. *Private pension plans*—The federal Employee Retirement Income Security Act (ERISA) of 1974 establishes standards for the management of employer-provided pension plans.

3. *Unemployment insurance*—The Federal Unemployment Tax Act of 1935 created a system that provides unemployment compensation to eligible individuals. Covered employers are taxed to help defray the costs of unemployment compensation.

CHAPTER SUMMARY	**Employment and Immigration Law–Continued**
Income Security–Continued	4. *COBRA*—The Consolidated Omnibus Budget Reconciliation Act (COBRA) of 1985 requires employers to give employees, on termination of employment, the option of continuing their medical, optical, or dental insurance coverage for a certain period.
Family and Medical Leave (See pages 474–475.)	The Family and Medical Leave Act (FMLA) of 1993 requires employers with fifty or more employees to provide their employees (except for key employees) with up to twelve weeks of unpaid family or medical leave during any twelve-month period to care for a newborn baby, an adopted child, or a foster child; or when the employee or the employee's spouse, child, or parent has a serious health condition requiring care.
Immigration Law (See pages 475–479.)	1. *Immigration Reform and Control Act (1986)*—Prohibits employers from hiring illegal immigrants; administered by U.S. Citizenship and Immigration Services. 2. *Immigration Act (1990)*—Limits the number of legal immigrants entering the United States by capping the number of visas (entry permits) that are issued each year.
Title VII of the Civil Rights Act of 1964 (See pages 479–483.)	Title VII prohibits employment discrimination based on race, color, national origin, religion, or gender. 1. *Procedures*—Employees must file a claim with the Equal Employment Opportunity Commission (EEOC). The EEOC may sue the employer on the employee's behalf; if not, the employee may sue the employer directly. 2. *Types of discrimination*—Title VII prohibits both intentional (disparate-treatment) and unintentional (disparate-impact) discrimination. Disparate-impact discrimination occurs when an employer's practice, such as hiring only persons with a certain level of education, has the effect of discriminating against a class of persons protected by Title VII. Title VII also extends to discriminatory practices, such as various forms of sexual harassment. 3. *Remedies for discrimination under Title VII*—If a plaintiff proves that unlawful discrimination occurred, he or she may be awarded reinstatement, back pay, and retroactive promotions. Damages (both compensatory and punitive) may be awarded for intentional discrimination.
Discrimination Based on Age (See pages 483–485.)	The Age Discrimination in Employment Act (ADEA) of 1967 prohibits employment discrimination on the basis of age against individuals forty years of age or older. Procedures for bringing a case under the ADEA are similar to those for bringing a case under Title VII.
Discrimination Based on Disability (See pages 485–486.)	The Americans with Disabilities Act (ADA) of 1990 prohibits employment discrimination against persons with disabilities who are otherwise qualified to perform the essential functions of the jobs for which they apply. 1. *Procedures and remedies*—To prevail on a claim under the ADA, the plaintiff must show that she or he has a disability, is otherwise qualified for the employment in question, and was excluded from the employment solely because of the disability. Procedures under the ADA are similar to those required in Title VII cases; remedies are also similar to those under Title VII. 2. *Definition of disability*—The ADA defines the term *disability* as a physical or mental impairment that substantially limits one or more major life activities, a record of such impairment, or being regarded as having such an impairment. 3. *Reasonable accommodation*—Employers are required to reasonably accommodate the needs of persons with disabilities. Reasonable accommodations may include altering job-application procedures, modifying the physical work environment, and permitting more flexible work schedules.

(Continued)

CHAPTER SUMMARY	Employment and Immigration Law—Continued
Defenses to Employment Discrimination (See pages 486–488.)	If a plaintiff proves that employment discrimination occurred, employers may avoid liability by successfully asserting certain defenses. Employers may assert that the discrimination was required for reasons of business necessity, to meet a bona fide occupational qualification, or to maintain a legitimate seniority system. Evidence of prior employee misconduct acquired after the employee has been fired is not a defense to discrimination.
Affirmative Action (See page 488.)	Affirmative action programs attempt to "make up" for past patterns of discrimination by giving members of protected classes preferential treatment in hiring or promotion. Increasingly, such programs are being strictly scrutinized by the courts and struck down as violating the Fourteenth Amendment.
State Statutes (See pages 488–489.)	Generally, state laws also prohibit the kinds of discrimination prohibited by federal statutes. State laws may provide for more extensive protection and remedies than federal laws. Also, some states, such as California and Washington, have banned state-sponsored affirmative action programs.

FOR REVIEW

Answers for the even-numbered questions in this For Review *section can be found on this text's accompanying Web site at* **www.cengage.com/blaw/fbl**. *Select "Chapter 23" and click on "For Review."*

1 What is the employment-at-will doctrine? When and why are exceptions to this doctrine made?

2 What federal statute governs working hours and wages? What federal statutes govern labor unions and collective bargaining?

3 What federal law was enacted to protect the health and safety of employees? What are workers' compensation laws?

4 Generally, what kind of conduct is prohibited by Title VII of the Civil Rights Act of 1964, as amended?

5 What remedies are available under Title VII of the 1964 Civil Rights Act, as amended?

QUESTIONS AND CASE PROBLEMS

 HYPOTHETICAL SCENARIOS AND CASE PROBLEMS

23.1 Wage and Hour. Calzoni Boating Co. is an interstate business engaged in manufacturing and selling boats. The company has five hundred nonunion employees. Representatives of these employees are requesting a four-day, ten-hours-per-day workweek, and Calzoni is concerned that this would require paying time and a half after eight hours per day. Which federal act is Calzoni thinking of that might require this? Will the act in fact require paying time and a half for all hours worked over eight hours per day if the employees' proposal is accepted? Explain.

23.2 Hypothetical Question with Sample Answer. Denton and Carlo were employed at an appliance plant. Their job required them to do occasional maintenance work while standing on a wire mesh twenty feet above the plant floor. Other employees had fallen through the mesh; one was killed by the fall. When Denton and Carlo were asked by their supervisor to do work that would likely require them to walk on the mesh, they refused due to their fear of bodily harm or death. Because of their refusal to do the requested work, the two employees were fired from their jobs. Was their discharge wrongful? If so, under what federal employment law? To what federal agency or department should they turn for assistance?

 For a sample answer to Question 23.2, go to Appendix E at the end of this text.

23.3 Case Problem with Sample Answer. Jennifer Willis worked for Coca Cola Enterprises, Inc. (CCE), in Louisiana as a senior account manager. On a Monday in May 2003, Willis called her supervisor to tell him that she was sick and would not be able to work that day. She also said that she was pregnant, but she did not say she was sick *because* of the pregnancy. On Tuesday, she called to ask where to report to work and was told that she could not return without a doctor's release. She said that she had a doctor's appointment on "Wednesday," which her supervisor understood to be the next day. Willis meant the *following* Wednesday. More than a week later, during which time Willis did not contact CCE, she was told that she had violated CCE's "No Call/No Show" policy. Under this policy "an employee absent from work for three consecutive days without notifying the supervisor during that period will be considered to have voluntarily resigned." She was fired. Willis filed a suit in a federal district court against CCE under the Family and Medical Leave Act (FMLA). To be eligible for FMLA leave, an employee must inform an employer of the reason for the leave. Did Willis meet this requirement? Did CCE's response to Willis's absence violate the FMLA? Explain. [*Willis v. Coca Cola Enterprises, Inc.*, 445 F.3d 413 (5th Cir. 2006)]

After you have answered Problem 23.3, compare your answer with the sample answer given on the Web site that accompanies this text. Go to www.cengage.com/blaw/fbl, select "Chapter 23," and click on "Case Problem with Sample Answer."

23.4 Unemployment Insurance. Mary Garas, a chemist, sought work in Missouri through Kelly Services, Inc. Kelly is a staffing agency that places individuals in jobs of varying duration with other companies. Through Kelly, Garas worked at Merial Co. from April 2005 to February 2006. After the assignment ended, Garas asked Kelly for more work. Meanwhile, she filed a claim for unemployment benefits with the Missouri Division of Employment Security (DES). In March, Kelly recruiter Rebecca Cockrum told Garas about a temporary assignment. Garas said that she would prefer a "more stable position," but later asked Cockrum to submit her résumé. Before the employer responded, Kelly told the DES that Garas had refused suitable work. Under a state statute, a claim for unemployment benefits must be denied if "the claimant failed without good cause . . . to accept suitable work when offered the claimant . . . by an employer by whom the individual was formerly employed." The DES denied Garas's claim for benefits. She filed an appeal. Was the DES's denial right or wrong? Why? [*Garas v. Kelly Services, Inc.*, 211 S.W.3d 149 (Mo.App. E.D. 2007)]

23.5 Discrimination Based on Disability. Cerebral palsy limits Steven Bradley's use of his legs. He uses forearm crutches for short-distance walks and a wheelchair for longer distances. Standing for more than ten or fifteen minutes is difficult. With support, however, Bradley can climb stairs and get on and off a stool. His condition also restricts the use of his fourth finger to, for example, type, but it does not limit his ability to write—he completed two years of college. His grip strength is normal, and he can lift heavy objects. In 2001, Bradley applied for a "greeter" or "cashier" position at a Wal-Mart Stores, Inc., Supercenter in Richmond, Missouri. The job descriptions stated, "No experience or qualification is required." Bradley indicated that he was available for full- or part-time work from 4:00 P.M. to 10:00 P.M. any evening.

His employment history showed that he currently worked as a proofreader and that he had previously worked as an administrator. His application was rejected, according to Janet Daugherty, the personnel manager, based on his "work history" and the "direct threat" that he posed to the safety of himself and others. Bradley claimed, however, that the store refused to hire him due to his disability. What steps must Bradley follow to pursue his claim? What does he need to show to prevail? Is he likely to meet these requirements? Discuss. [*EEOC v. Wal-Mart Stores, Inc.*, 477 F.3d 561 (8th Cir. 2007)]

23.6 Hiring Illegal Aliens. Nicole Tipton and Sadik Seferi owned and operated a restaurant in Iowa. Acting on a tip from the local police, agents of Immigration and Customs Enforcement executed search warrants at the restaurant and at an apartment where some restaurant workers lived. They discovered six undocumented aliens working at the restaurant and living together. When the I-9 forms for restaurant employees were reviewed, none were found for the six aliens. They were paid in cash while regular employees were paid by check. The jury found Tipton and Seferi guilty of hiring and harboring illegal aliens. Both were given prison terms. The defendants challenged the conviction, contending that they did not violate the law because they did not know that the workers were unauthorized aliens. Was that argument credible? Why or why not? [*United States v. Tipton*, 518 F.3d 591 (8th Cir. 2008)]

23.7 Discrimination Based on Gender. The Milwaukee County Juvenile Detention Center started a new policy that required each unit of the facility to be staffed at all times by at least one officer of the same gender as the detainees housed at a unit. The purpose of the policy, administrators said, was to reduce the likelihood of sexual abuse of juveniles by officers of the other gender. Because there were many more male units in the center than female units, the policy had the effect of reducing the number of shifts available for female officers and increasing the number of shifts for men. Two female officers sued for gender discrimination. The district court held for the county, finding that the policy of assignment was based on a bona fide occupational qualification (BFOQ) and so it was not illegal gender discrimination. The female officers appealed. What would be evidence that the county had a valid BFOQ? [*Henry v. Milwaukee County*, 539 F.3d 573 (7th Cir. 2008)]

23.8 Immigration Work Status. Mohammad Hashmi, a citizen of Pakistan, entered the United States in 2002 on a student visa. Two years later, when he applied for a job at CompuCredit, he completed an I-9 form and checked the box to indicate that he was "a citizen or national of the United States." Soon after submitting that form, he married a U.S. citizen. Several months later, the federal immigration services claimed that he had misrepresented himself as a U.S. citizen. Hashmi contended that he had not misrepresented himself. At an administrative hearing, he testified that when he filled out the I-9 form he believed that he was a "national of the United

States" because he was legally in the country under a student visa and was going to marry a U.S. citizen. He requested that his immigration status be adjusted to account for the fact that he was employed and married to an American. The immigration judge rejected that request and found that Hashmi had made a false claim on the I-9 form. He ruled that Hashmi was "inadmissible" to the United States and that his legal status in the country could not be amended because of his marriage or employment. Hashmi appealed. Do you think it was reasonable for Hashmi to believe he was a U.S. national? Should his visa status be changed because of his marriage and employment? Why or why not? [*Hashmi v. Mukasey,* 533 F.3d 700 (8th Cir. 2008)]

23.9 **A Question of Ethics.** *Beverly Tull had worked for Atchison Leather Products, Inc., in Kansas for ten years when, in 1999, she began to complain of hand, wrist, and shoulder pain. Atchison recommended that she contact a certain physician, who in April 2000 diagnosed the condition as carpal tunnel syndrome "severe enough" for surgery. In August, Tull filed a claim with the state workers' compensation board. Because Atchison changed workers' compensation insurance companies every year, a dispute arose as to which company should pay Tull's claim. Fearing liability, no*

insurer would authorize treatment, and Tull was forced to delay surgery until December. The board granted her temporary total disability benefits for the subsequent six weeks that she missed work. On April 23, 2002, Berger Co. bought Atchison. The new employer adjusted Tull's work to be less demanding and stressful, but she continued to suffer pain. In July, a physician diagnosed her condition as permanent. The board granted her permanent partial disability benefits. By May 2005, the bickering over the financial responsibility for Tull's claim involved five insurers—four of which had each covered Atchison for a single year and one of which covered Berger. [Tull v. Atchison Leather Products, Inc., 37 Kan.App.2d 87, 150 P.3d 316 (2007)]

1 When an injured employee files a claim for workers' compensation, there is a proceeding to assess the injury and determine the amount of compensation. Should a dispute between insurers over the payment of the claim be resolved in the same proceeding? Why or why not?

2 The board designated April 23, 2002, as the date of Tull's injury. What is the reason for determining the date of a worker's injury? Should the board in this case have selected this date or a different date? Why?

CRITICAL THINKING AND WRITING ASSIGNMENT

23.10 **Video Question.** Go to this text's Web site at **www.cengage.com/blaw/fbl** and select "Chapter 23." Click on "Video Questions" and view the video titled *Parenthood.* Then answer the following questions.

1 In the video, Gil (Steve Martin) threatens to leave his job when he discovers that his boss is promoting another person to partner instead of him. His boss (Dennis Dugan) laughs and tells him that the threat is not realistic because if Gil leaves, he will be competing for positions with workers who are younger than he is and willing to accept lower salaries. If Gil takes his employer's advice

and stays in his current position, can he sue his boss for age discrimination based on the boss's statements? Why or why not?

2 Suppose that Gil leaves his current position and applies for a job at another firm. The prospective employer refuses to hire him based on his age. What would Gil have to prove to establish a *prima facie* case of age discrimination? Explain your answer.

3 What defenses might Gil's current employer raise if Gil sues for age discrimination?

ACCESSING THE INTERNET

For updated links to resources available on the Web, as well as a variety of other materials, visit this text's Web site at

www.cengage.com/blaw/fbl

An excellent Web site for information on employee benefits, including the full text of the Family and Medical Leave Act (FMLA), COBRA, other relevant statutes and case law, and current articles, is BenefitsLink. Go to

benefitslink.com/index.html

The Occupational Safety and Health Administration (OSHA) offers information related to workplace health and safety at

www.osha.gov

You can find the complete text of Title VII and information about the activities of the Equal Employment Opportunity Commission (EEOC) at that agency's Web site. Go to

www.eeoc.gov

PRACTICAL INTERNET EXERCISES

Go to this text's Web site at **www.cengage.com/blaw/fbl**, select "Chapter 23," and click on "Practical Internet Exercises." There you will find the following Internet research exercises that you can perform to learn more about topics covered in this chapter.

PRACTICAL INTERNET EXERCISE 23–1: LEGAL PERSPECTIVE—Americans with Disabilities

PRACTICAL INTERNET EXERCISE 23–2: MANAGEMENT PERSPECTIVE—Equal Employment Opportunity

PRACTICAL INTERNET EXERCISE 23–3: SOCIAL PERSPECTIVE—Religious and National-Origin Discrimination

BEFORE THE TEST

Go to this text's Web site at **www.cengage.com/blaw/fbl**, select "Chapter 23," and click on "Interactive Quizzes." You will find a number of interactive questions relating to this chapter.

UNIT SEVEN **EXTENDED CASE STUDY**

Batte-Holmgren v. Commissioner of Public Health

The regulation of workplace health and safety was reviewed in Chapter 23. In this extended case study, we focus on Batte-Holmgren v. Commissioner of Public Health,[1] *a case in which the plaintiffs challenged a state statute banning "indoor air pollution," or smoking, in most public establishments. The purpose of the statute was to protect employees, especially those with little choice as to where they work, from being exposed to secondhand smoke as a condition of employment.*

The plaintiffs argued that the smoking ban violated the equal protection clause of the Fourteenth Amendment to the U.S. Constitution. As explained in Chapter 1, under this clause the government must treat similarly situated persons in a similar manner. When a law limits the liberty of some persons but not others, it may violate this principle. Most laws that create classes among persons for different treatment are considered valid if there is any "rational basis" that relates the classifications to a legitimate government interest.

CASE BACKGROUND The Connecticut state legislature amended the state's General Statutes Section 19a-342 to prohibit smoking in restaurants, cafés, and other public facilities. Among the establishments exempt from the ban were most private clubs (those for which liquor permits were issued before May 1, 2003).

In July 2004, café owner Diane Batte-Holmgren and oth-

ers who owned public facilities subject to the smoking ban filed a suit in a Connecticut state court against the state's commissioner of public health and attorney general. The plaintiffs contended, among other things, that the ban violated their right to equal protection under the U.S. Constitution. They asked the court to enjoin (prevent) the enforcement of the statute, among other things. The defendants filed a motion to dismiss the complaint. The court granted the motion. The plaintiffs appealed to the Connecticut Supreme Court.

---

1. 281 Conn. 277, 914 A.2d 996 (2007).

(Continued)

MAJORITY OPINION

VERTEFEUILLE, J. [Justice]

* * * *

* * * The plaintiffs contend that the legislation violates the mandates of equal protection because it bans smoking in restaurants and cafés without banning smoking in * * * private clubs, and this unequal treatment, the plaintiffs contend, does not bear a rational relationship to a legitimate public interest. Specifically, the plaintiffs claim that, although the stated purpose of the ban was to remove secondhand smoke from workplaces, the ban was imposed on certain businesses, and not others, based on the type of liquor permit issued to the business, and this, the plaintiffs argue, bears no relationship to the nature of the workplace conditions. Because * * * private clubs are not distinguishable from restaurants and cafés in terms of their workplace conditions, the plaintiffs assert, the legislature's unequal treatment of these establishments violates equal protection principles. The plaintiffs further assert that the legal status of private clubs as "private," as opposed to "public," does not serve as a rational basis for different treatment because, the plaintiffs contend, they are as accessible to the public as are public establishments. * * *

The defendants respond that the trial court properly determined that the legislature's decision to exempt * * * private clubs from the smoking ban was supported by a rational basis. Specifically, the defendants argue that exempting private clubs from the ban is justified by the fact that such clubs are distinguishable from restaurants and cafés because state statutes provide that they are not open to the public and because the members of the club may have joined the club and paid their membership fees with the expectation that they would be able to smoke in the club facility. * * * We agree with the defendants * * * .

* * * *

We agree with the defendants that it is possible to conceive of plausible policy reasons for exempting * * * private clubs

from the smoking ban legislation. * * * Private clubs * * * hold a legal status that is different from restaurants and cafés. [State statutes] impose restrictions on private clubs to which restaurants and cafés are not subject. * * * Within the context of these legal restrictions, members of private clubs generally pay a membership fee with the expectation that they will be able to maintain their privacy and establish such conditions for the operation of the club that suit the needs and desires of the majority of the membership.

The legislature reasonably could have considered that among the conditions over which private club members may expect to exercise control is the regulation of smoking within the club facility. This consideration could have led the legislature to conclude that the imposition of a smoking ban on private clubs would upset unfairly this expectation of club members, as well as the financial investment upon which their expectation is based, and that this deprivation of the members' settled expectations would constitute an injustice that would outweigh any benefit to be derived from imposing the ban on such private facilities. *Although the legislature need not actually have been motivated by this policy consideration in order for this court to uphold the statute on that basis,* our supposition that the legislature may have been so motivated is supported by the legislature's decision to exempt from the smoking ban only those private clubs that had obtained their liquor permits prior to the effective date of the legislation. This decision to exempt existing private clubs from the smoking ban, while imposing the ban on new private clubs, is consistent with our conclusion that the legislature reasonably may have been endeavoring to protect the financial investment and settled expectations of members of private clubs. We conclude that this policy consideration constitutes a rational basis for the legislature's decision to exempt existing private clubs from the smoking ban imposed on restaurants and cafés. [Emphasis added.]

* * * *

The judgment is affirmed.

DISSENTING OPINION

SULLIVAN, C.J. [Chief Justice], dissenting.

* * * *

To the extent that the majority suggests that a statutory classification may pass constitutional muster if it promotes any legitimate state purpose, related to the statute or not, I strongly disagree. * * * Under such a standard, any legislative

classification that exempts a particular class of persons from legislation would be constitutional, because the state always has a legitimate interest in relieving its citizens of the costs and burdens of state regulation. Although it is well established that courts must give great deference to legislative classifications, it has never been suggested that we should give absolute deference to the legislature. If, for example, the legislature had determined that, in order to reduce the burdens imposed by [the smoking ban], cafés and restaurants located in towns whose names contain an even number of letters would be exempt from the statute, surely that arbitrary classification could not be saved by the fact that it promoted a legitimate public interest.

* * * *

In my view, the trial court, the defendants and the majority all have failed to articulate any ground of difference having a fair and substantial relation to the object of [the smoking ban]. Instead, they simply have begged the question by assuming that any difference between disparately treated classes justifies the disparate treatment. The defendants concede, and there is no dispute, that "the intent of [the smoking ban] was to protect employees, especially those with little choice as to where they work, from being subjected to exposure to carcinogenic secondhand smoke as a condition of their employment." I cannot conceive of any rational relationship

between this purpose and providing an exemption for establishments that purportedly were founded with the expectation that smoking would continue to be permitted there. There is no evidence in the record that private clubs have fewer employees than the establishments that are subject to the act or that their employees are somehow less susceptible to the ill effects of secondhand smoke than other employees.

Moreover, there is absolutely no evidence in the record that the members of the private clubs formed or invested in the clubs with the expectation that smoking would be allowed there or, if they did, that any such expectation was reasonable. * * * Clubs generally are subject to the same laws as other employers [and the] defendants have cited no authority for the proposition that unfounded expectations of privacy can form a constitutional basis for a legislative classification.

QUESTIONS FOR ANALYSIS

1 LAW. What did the majority conclude on the central question in this case, and what points supported this conclusion?

2 LAW. What was the dissent's analysis with regard to the question?

3 POLITICAL DIMENSIONS. To reach its conclusion, did the majority have to agree with the legislature's decision to exempt most private clubs from the smoking ban? Why or why not?

4 ECONOMIC DIMENSIONS. What are the likely economic effects of the outcome in this case? Explain.

5 IMPLICATIONS FOR EMPLOYERS. What does the ruling in this case suggest to employers who are not yet subject to the smoking ban at issue?

UNIT EIGHT Business Organizations

UNIT CONTENTS

CHAPTER 24
Sole Proprietorships, Partnerships, and Limited Liability Companies

LEARNING OBJECTIVES

AFTER READING THIS CHAPTER, YOU SHOULD BE ABLE TO ANSWER THE FOLLOWING QUESTIONS:

1 Which form of business organization is the simplest? Which form arises from an agreement between two or more persons to carry on a business for profit?

2 What are the three essential elements of a partnership?

3 What is meant by joint and several liability? Why is this often considered to be a disadvantage of the partnership form of business?

4 Why do professional groups organize as a limited liability partnership? How does this form differ from a general partnership?

5 What is a limited liability company? What are some of the advantages and disadvantages of this business form?

An entrepreneur's primary motive for undertaking a business enterprise is to make profits. An *entrepreneur* is by definition one who *initiates* and *assumes the financial risks* of a new enterprise and undertakes to provide or control its management.

One of the questions faced by any entrepreneur who wishes to start a business is what form of business organization should be chosen for the business endeavor. In making this determination, a number of factors need to be considered. Four important factors are (1) ease of creation, (2) the liability of the owners, (3) tax considerations, and (4) the need for capital. In studying this unit on business organizations, keep these factors in mind as you read about the various business organizational forms available to entrepreneurs. You might also find it helpful to refer to Exhibit 26–2 in Chapter 26, on pages 558 and 559, for a comparison of the major business forms in use today with respect to formation, liability of owners, taxation, and other factors.

Traditionally, entrepreneurs have used three major forms to structure their business enterprises—the sole proprietor-

ship, the partnership, and the corporation. In this chapter, we examine the first two of these forms. The third major traditional form—the corporation—is discussed in Chapters 25 and 26. Two relatively new forms of business enterprise—limited liability companies (LLCs) and limited liability partnerships (LLPs)—offer special advantages to businesspersons, particularly with respect to taxation and liability. We therefore look at these business forms later in this chapter.

SOLE PROPRIETORSHIPS

The simplest form of business organization is a **sole proprietorship.** In this form, the owner is the business; thus, anyone who does business without creating a separate business organization has a sole proprietorship. More than two-thirds of all U.S. businesses are sole proprietorships. They are usually small enterprises—about 99 percent of the sole proprietorships in the United States have revenues of less than $1 million per year. Sole proprietors can own and manage any type of business, ranging from an informal, home-office undertaking to a large restaurant or construction firm. Today, a number of online businesses that sell goods and services on a nationwide basis are organized as sole proprietorships.

Advantages of the Sole Proprietorship

A major advantage of the sole proprietorship is that the proprietor owns the entire business and has a right to receive all of the profits (because he or she assumes all of the risk). In addition, it is often easier and less costly to start a sole proprietorship than to start any other kind of business, as few legal formalities are involved.[1] One does not need to file any documents with the government to start a sole proprietorship (though a state business license may be required to operate certain businesses).

This type of business organization also entails more flexibility than does a partnership or a corporation. The sole proprietor is free to make any decision she or he wishes concerning the business—including whom to hire, when to take a vacation, and what kind of business to pursue, for example. In addition, the proprietor can sell or transfer all or part of the business to another party at any time and does not need approval from anyone else (as would be required from partners in a partnership or, normally, from shareholders in a corporation).

A sole proprietor pays only personal income taxes (including Social Security, or self-employment, tax) on the business's profits, which are reported as personal income on the proprietor's personal income tax return. Sole proprietors are also allowed to establish certain rertirement accounts that are tax-exempt until the funds are withdrawn.

---

1. Although starting up a sole proprietorship involves relatively few legal formalities compared with other business organizational forms, even small sole proprietorships may need to comply with certain zoning requirements, obtain appropriate licenses, and the like.

Disadvantages of the Sole Proprietorship

The major disadvantage of the sole proprietorship is that the proprietor alone bears the burden of any losses or liabilities incurred by the business enterprise. In other words, the sole proprietor has unlimited liability, or legal responsibility, for all obligations incurred in doing business. Any lawsuit against the business or its employees can lead to unlimited personal liability for the owner of a sole proprietorship. Creditors can go after the owner's personal assets to satisfy any business debts. This unlimited liability is a major factor to be considered in choosing a business form.

■EXAMPLE 24.1 Sheila Fowler operates a golf shop business as a sole proprietorship. The shop is located near one of the best golf courses in the country. A professional golfer, Dean Maheesh, is seriously injured when a display of golf clubs, which one of Fowler's employees has failed to secure, falls on him. If Maheesh sues Fowler's shop (a sole proprietorship) and wins, Fowler's personal liability could easily exceed the limits of her insurance policy. In this situation, not only might Fowler lose her business, but she could also lose her house, her car, and any other personal assets that can be attached to pay the judgment. ■

The sole proprietorship also has the disadvantage of lacking continuity on the death of the proprietor. When the owner dies, so does the business—it is automatically dissolved. Another disadvantage is that the proprietor's opportunity to raise capital is limited to personal funds and the funds of those who are willing to make loans.

The personal liability of the owner of a sole proprietorship was at issue in the following case. The case involved the federal Cable Communications Act, which prohibits a commercial establishment from broadcasting television programs to its patrons without authorization. The court had to decide whether the owner of a sole proprietorship that installed a satellite television system was personally liable for violating this act by identifying a restaurant as a "residence" for billing purposes.

CASE 24.1 **Garden City Boxing Club, Inc. v. Dominguez**

United States District Court, Northern District of Illinois, Eastern Division, __ F.Supp.2d __ (2006).

FACTS Garden City Boxing Club, Inc. (GCB), which is based in San Jose, California, owned the exclusive right to broadcast via closed-circuit television several prizefights, including the match between Oscar De La Hoya and Fernando Vargas on September 14, 2002. GCB sold the right to receive the broadcasts to bars and other commercial venues. The fee was $20 multiplied by an establishment's maximum fire code occupancy. Antenas

Enterprises in Chicago, Illinois, sells and installs satellite television systems under a contract with DISH Network. After installing a system, Antenas sends the buyer's address and other identifying information to DISH. In January 2002, Luis Garcia, an Antenas employee, identified a new customer as José Melendez at 220 Hawthorn Commons in Vernon Hills. The address was a

CASE 24.1–Continues next page

CASE 24.1–Continued

restaurant—Mundelein Burrito—but Garcia designated the account as residential. Mundelein's patrons watched the De La Hoya–Vargas match on September 14, as well as three other fights on other dates, for which the restaurant paid only the residential rate to DISH and nothing to GCB. GCB filed a suit in a federal district court against Luis Dominguez, the sole proprietor of Antenas, to collect the fee.

ISSUE Is Dominguez personally liable for the amount of Mundelein's fee?

DECISION Yes. The court issued a summary judgment in GCB's favor, holding that the plaintiff was entitled to the amount of the fee, plus damages and attorneys' fees.

REASON The court found that Mundelein was clearly a commercial establishment. "The structure of the building, an exterior identification sign, and its location in a strip mall made this obvious." Under the Cable Communications Act, "an authorized intermediary of a communication violates the Act

when it divulges communication through an electronic channel to one other than the addressee." Antenas's improper designation of Mundelein as residential allowed the unauthorized broadcast of four prizefights to the restaurant. Antenas is a sole proprietorship. A sole proprietorship has no legal identity apart from that of the individual who owns it. Furthermore, a sole proprietor is personally responsible for the acts that his or her employees commit within the scope of their employment. Dominguez owns Antenas, and Garcia is Dominguez's employee. "Accordingly, Dominguez is personally liable for the damages caused by the violation of * * * the [Cable Communications] Act."

 WHAT IF THE FACTS WERE DIFFERENT? *Suppose that the employee, Garcia, had ordered residential DISH service for the restaurant while he was at home and without Dominguez's knowledge or consent. Would this have changed the outcome of this case? Explain.*

PARTNERSHIPS

A *partnership* arises from an agreement, express or implied, between two or more persons to carry on a business for profit. Partners are co-owners of a business and have joint control over its operation and the right to share in its profits.

Partnerships are governed both by common law concepts—in particular, those relating to agency (discussed in Chapter 22)—and by statutory law. The National Conference of Commissioners on Uniform State Laws has drafted the Uniform Partnership Act (UPA), which governs the operation of partnerships *in the absence of express agreement* and has done much to reduce controversies in the law relating to partnerships. In other words, the partners are free to establish rules for their partnership that differ from those stated in the UPA. The UPA was originally set forth by the National Conference of Commissioners on Uniform State Laws in 1914 and has undergone several major revisions. Except for Louisiana, every state has adopted the UPA. The majority of states have adopted the most recent version of the UPA, which was issued in 1994 and amended in 1997 to provide limited liability for partners in a limited liability partnership. We therefore base our discussion of the UPA in this chapter on the 1997 version of the act.

Agency Concepts and Partnership Law

When two or more persons agree to do business as partners, they enter into a special relationship with one another. To an extent, their relationship is similar to an agency relationship

because each partner is deemed to be the agent of the other partners and of the partnership. The common law agency concepts that you read about in Chapter 22 thus apply—specifically, the imputation of knowledge of, and responsibility for, acts done within the scope of the partnership relationship. In their relations with one another, partners, like agents, are bound by fiduciary ties.

In one important way, however, partnership law is distinct from agency law. A partnership is based on a voluntary contract between two or more competent persons who agree to place financial capital, labor, and skill in a business with the understanding that profits and losses will be shared. In a nonpartnership agency relationship, the agent usually does not have an ownership interest in the business, nor is he or she obliged to bear a portion of the ordinary business losses.

When Does a Partnership Exist?

Conflicts commonly arise over whether a business enterprise is legally a partnership, especially in the absence of a formal, written partnership agreement. The UPA defines a **partnership** as "an association of two or more persons to carry on as co-owners a business for profit" [UPA 101(6)]. Note that under the UPA a corporation is a "person" [UPA 101(10)]. The *intent* to associate is a key element of a partnership, and a person cannot join a partnership unless all of the other partners consent [UPA 401(i)].

In resolving disputes over whether partnership status exists, courts will usually look for the following three essential elements, which are implicit in the UPA's definition of a partnership:

1 A sharing of profits and losses.

2 A joint ownership of the business.

3 An equal right to be involved in the management of the business.

Joint ownership of property, obviously, does not in and of itself create a partnership. In fact, the sharing of gross revenues and even profits from such ownership is usually not enough to create a partnership [UPA 202(c)(1), (2)]. ■**EXAMPLE 24.2** Chiang and Burke jointly own a piece of rural property. They lease the land to a farmer, with the understanding that—in lieu of set rental payments—they will receive a share of the profits from the farming operation conducted by the farmer. This arrangement normally would not make Chiang, Burke, and the farmer partners. ■

Note, though, that although the sharing of profits from ownership of property does not prove the existence of a partnership, sharing *both profits and losses* usually does. ■**EXAMPLE 24.3** Two sisters, Zoe and Cienna, buy a restaurant together, open a joint bank account from which they pay for expenses and supplies, and share the net profits that the restaurant generates. Zoe manages the restaurant and Cienna handles the bookkeeping. After eight years, Cienna stops doing the bookkeeping and does no other work for the restaurant. Zoe, who is now operating the restaurant by herself, no longer wants to share the profits with Cienna. She offers to buy her sister out, but the two cannot agree on a fair price. When Cienna files a lawsuit, a question arises as to whether the two sisters were partners in the restaurant. In this situation, a court would find that a partnership existed because the sisters shared management responsibilities, had joint accounts, and shared the profits and the losses of the restaurant equally. ■

Entity versus Aggregate Theory of Partnerships

At common law, a partnership was treated only as an aggregate of individuals and never as a separate legal entity. Thus, at common law a suit could never be brought by or against the firm in its own name; each individual partner had to sue or be sued.

Today, in contrast, a majority of the states follow the UPA and treat a partnership as an entity for most purposes. For example, a partnership usually can sue or be sued, collect judgments, and have all accounting procedures in the name of the partnership entity [UPA 201, 307(a)]. As an entity, a partnership may hold the title to real or personal property in its name rather than in the names of the individual partners. Additionally, federal procedural laws permit the partnership

to be treated as an entity in suits in federal courts and bankruptcy proceedings.

For federal income tax purposes, however, the partnership is treated as an aggregate of the individual partners rather than a separate legal entity. The partnership is a pass-through entity and not a taxpaying entity. A **pass-through entity** is a business entity that has no tax liability; the entity's income is passed through to the owners of the entity, who pay taxes on it. Thus, the income or losses the partnership incurs are "passed through" the entity framework and attributed to the partners on their individual tax returns. The partnership itself has no tax liability and is responsible only for filing an **information return** with the Internal Revenue Service. In other words, the firm itself pays no taxes. A partner's profit from the partnership (whether distributed or not) is taxed as individual income to the individual partner.

Partnership Formation

As a general rule, agreements to form a partnership can be *oral, written,* or *implied by conduct.* Some partnership agreements, however, must be in writing to be legally enforceable under the Statute of Frauds (see Chapter 10 for details). A written partnership agreement, called **articles of partnership,** can include virtually any terms that the parties wish, unless they are illegal or contrary to public policy or statute [UPA 103]. The agreement usually specifies the name and location of the business, the duration of the partnership, the purpose of the business, each partner's share of the profits, how the partnership will be managed, how assets will be distributed on dissolution, and other provisions.

The partnership agreement can specify the duration of the partnership by stating that it will continue until a certain date or the completion of a particular project. A partnership that is specifically limited in duration is called a *partnership for a term.* Generally, withdrawing from a partnership for a term prematurely (prior to the expiration date) constitutes a breach of the agreement, and the responsible partner can be held liable for any resulting losses [UPA 602(b)(2)]. If no fixed duration is specified, the partnership is a *partnership at will.*

Occasionally, persons who are not partners may nevertheless hold themselves out as partners and make representations that third parties rely on in dealing with them. In such a situation, a court may conclude that a *partnership by estoppel* exists. The law does not confer any partnership rights on these persons, but it may impose liability on them. This is also true when a partner represents, expressly or impliedly, that a nonpartner is a member of the firm [UPA 308]. ■**EXAMPLE 24.4** Sorento owns a small shop. Knowing that Midland Bank will not make a loan on his credit alone, Sorento represents that

Lukas, a financially secure businessperson, is a partner in Sorento's business. Lukas knows of Sorento's misrepresentation but fails to correct it. Midland Bank, relying on the strength of Lukas's reputation and credit, extends a loan to Sorento. Sorento will be liable to the bank for repaying the loan. Lukas could also be held liable to the bank in many states. Because Lukas has impliedly consented to the misrepresentation, she will normally be estopped (prevented) from denying that she is Sorento's partner. A court normally will treat Lukas as if she were in fact a partner in Sorento's business insofar as this loan is concerned. ■

Rights of Partners

The rights of partners in a partnership relate to the following areas: management, interest in the partnership, compensation, inspection of books, accounting, and property. In the absence of provisions to the contrary in the partnership agreement, the law imposes the rights discussed here.

Management Rights   In a general partnership, all partners have equal rights in managing the partnership [UPA 401(f)]. Unless the partners agree otherwise, each partner has one vote in management matters *regardless of the proportional size of his or her interest in the firm.* Often, in a large partnership, partners will agree to delegate daily management responsibilities to a management committee made up of one or more of the partners.

The majority rule controls decisions in ordinary matters connected with partnership business, unless otherwise specified in the agreement. Decisions that significantly affect the nature of the partnership or that are not apparently for carrying on the ordinary course of the partnership business, or business of the kind, however, require the *unanimous* consent of the partners [UPA 301(2), 401(i), (j)]. Unanimous consent is likely to be required for a decision to undertake any of the following actions:

1 To alter the essential nature of the firm's business as expressed in the partnership agreement or to alter the capital structure of the partnership.

2 To admit new partners or to enter a wholly new business.

3 To assign partnership property to a trust for the benefit of creditors.

4 To dispose of the partnership's goodwill.

5 To confess judgment against the partnership or to submit partnership claims to arbitration. (A *confession of judgment* is the act of a debtor in permitting a judgment to be entered against her or him by a creditor, for an agreed sum, without the institution of legal proceedings.)

6 To undertake any act that would make further conduct of partnership business impossible.

7 To amend the articles of the partnership agreement.

Interest in the Partnership   Each partner is entitled to the proportion of business profits and losses that is designated in the partnership agreement. If the agreement does not apportion profits (indicate how the profits will be shared), the UPA provides that profits will be shared equally. If the agreement does not apportion losses, losses will be shared in the same ratio as profits [UPA 401(b)].

■EXAMPLE 24.5 The partnership agreement for Rico and Brent provides for capital contributions of $60,000 from Rico and $40,000 from Brent, but it is silent as to how Rico and Brent will share profits or losses. In this situation, Rico and Brent will share both profits and losses equally. If their partnership agreement provided for profits to be shared in the same ratio as capital contributions, however, 60 percent of the profits would go to Rico, and 40 percent of the profits would go to Brent. If their partnership agreement was silent as to losses, losses would be shared in the same ratio as profits (60 percent and 40 percent, respectively). ■

Compensation   Devoting time, skill, and energy to partnership business is a partner's duty and generally is not a compensable service. Rather, as mentioned, a partner's income from the partnership takes the form of a distribution of profits according to the partner's share in the business. Partners can, of course, agree otherwise. For instance, the managing partner of a law firm often receives a salary in addition to her or his share of profits for performing special administrative duties, such as managing the office or personnel.

Inspection of Books   Partnership books and records must be kept at the firm's principal business office and be accessible to all partners. Each partner has the right to receive (and the corresponding duty to produce) full and complete information concerning the conduct of all aspects of partnership business [UPA 403]. Every partner is entitled to inspect all books and records on demand and to make copies of the materials.

Accounting of Partnership Assets or Profits   An accounting of partnership assets or profits is required to determine the value of each partner's share in the partnership. An accounting can be performed voluntarily, or it can be compelled by court order. Under UPA 405(b), a partner has the right to bring an action for an accounting during the term of the partnership, as well as on the firm's dissolution and winding up (discussed later in this chapter).

Property Rights   Property acquired by a partnership is the property of the partnership and not of the partners individually [UPA 203]. Partnership property includes all property that was originally contributed to the partnership and anything later purchased by the partnership or in the partnership's name (except in rare circumstances) [UPA 204]. A partner may use or possess partnership property only on behalf of the partnership [UPA 401(g)]. A partner is *not* a co-owner of partnership property and has no right to sell, mortgage, or transfer partnership property to another. (A partner can assign her or his right to a share of the partnership profits to another to satisfy a debt, however.)

Duties and Liabilities of Partners

The duties and liabilities of partners are basically derived from agency law (discussed in Chapter 22). Each partner is an agent of every other partner and acts as both a principal and an agent in any business transaction within the scope of the partnership agreement. Each partner is also a general agent of the partnership in carrying out the usual business of the firm "or business of the kind carried on by the partnership" [UPA 301(1)]. Thus, every act of a partner concerning partnership business and "business of the kind," and every contract signed by that partner in the partnership's name, bind the firm.

One significant disadvantage associated with a traditional partnership is that partners are *personally* liable for the debts of the partnership. Moreover, the liability is essentially unlimited because the acts of one partner in the ordinary course of business subject the other partners to personal liability [UPA 305]. We examine here the fiduciary duties of partners, the authority of partners, the liability of partners, and the limitations imposed on the liability of incoming partners for preexisting partnership debts.

Fiduciary Duties   The fiduciary duties a partner owes to the partnership and the other partners are the duty of loyalty and the duty of care [UPA 404(a)]. The duty of loyalty requires a partner to account to the partnership for "any property, profit, or benefit" derived by the partner from the partnership's business or the use of its property [UPA 404(b)]. A partner must also refrain from competing with the partnership in business or dealing with the firm as an adverse party. A partner's duty of care involves refraining from "grossly negligent or reckless conduct, intentional misconduct, or a knowing violation of law" [UPA 404(c)].

These duties may not be waived or eliminated in the partnership agreement, and in fulfilling them each partner must act consistently with the obligation of good faith and fair dealing, which applies to all contracts, including partnership

agreements [UPA 103(b), 404(d)]. The agreement can specify acts that the partners agree will violate a fiduciary duty.

Note that a partner may pursue his or her own interests without automatically violating these duties [UPA 404(e)]. The key is whether the partner has disclosed the interest to the other partners. For instance, a partner who owns a shopping mall may vote against a partnership proposal to open a competing mall, provided that the partner has fully disclosed her interest in the shopping mall to the other partners at the firm. A partner cannot make secret profits or put self-interest before his or her duty to the interest of the partnership, however.

Authority of Partners   Under the UPA and agency law, a partner has the authority to bind a partnership in contract. A partner may also subject the partnership to tort liability under the agency principles. When a partner is carrying on partnership business or business of the kind with third parties in the usual way, both the partner and the firm share liability.

Partners have the implied authority to perform acts that are reasonably necessary and customary to carry on the partnership's business. Their implied powers thus depend on the type of business the partnership operates. Partners in a trading partnership (a firm that has inventory and profits from buying and selling goods), for instance, have the implied authority to advertise products, hire employees, and make warranties.

Provisions of the UPA allow a partnership to attempt to limit a partner's implied powers by filing a statement of partnership authority with a state official [UPA 105, 303]. Such statements are only effective against third parties who know about the limitations.

If a partner acts within the scope of her or his authority, the partnership is legally bound to honor the partner's commitments to third parties. The partnership will not be liable, however, if the third parties know that the partner had no authority to commit the partnership. Agency concepts that we explored in Chapter 22 relating to actual (express and implied) authority, apparent authority, and ratification also apply to partnerships.

Joint Liability of Partners   Each partner in a partnership is jointly liable for the partnership's obligations. **Joint liability** means that a third party must sue all of the partners as a group, but each partner can be held liable for the full amount. Under the prior version of the UPA, which is still in effect in a few states, partners were subject to joint liability on partnership debts and contracts, but not on partnership debts arising from torts.[2] If, for instance, a third party sues a partner

---

2. Under the previous version of the UPA, the partners were subject to *joint and several liability*, which is discussed next, on debts arising from torts. States that still follow this rule include Connecticut, West Virginia, and Wyoming.

on a partnership contract, the partner has the right to demand that the other partners be sued with her or him. In fact, if the third party does not sue all of the partners, the assets of the partnership cannot be used to satisfy the judgment. Under the theory of joint liability, the partnership's assets must be exhausted before creditors can reach the partners' individual assets.[3]

Joint and Several Liability of Partners   In the majority of states, under UPA 306(a), partners are jointly and severally (separately or individually) liable for all partnership obligations, including contracts, torts, and breaches of trust. **Joint and several liability** means that a third party may sue all of the partners together (jointly) or one or more of the partners separately (severally) at his or her option. All partners in a partnership can be held liable regardless of whether the partner participated in, knew about, or ratified the conduct that gave rise to the lawsuit. Generally, under UPA 307(d), however, a creditor cannot bring an action to collect a partnership debt from the partner of a nonbankrupt partnership without first attempting to collect from the partnership or convincing a court that the attempt would be unsuccessful.

A judgment against one partner severally (separately) does not extinguish the others' liability. (Similarly, a release of one partner does not discharge the partners' several liability.) Thus, those partners not sued in the first action may be sued subsequently, unless the first action was conclusive for the partnership on the question of liability. In other words, if an action is brought against one partner and the court holds that the partnership was in no way liable, the third party cannot bring an action against another partner and succeed on the issue of the partnership's liability.

If a third party is successful in a suit against a partner or partners, she or he may collect on the judgment only against the assets of those partners named as defendants. A partner who commits a tort is required to indemnify (reimburse) the partnership for any damages it pays.

Liability of Incoming Partner   A newly admitted partner to an existing partnership normally has limited liability for whatever debts and obligations the partnership incurred prior to the new partner's admission. The new partner's liability can be satisfied only from partnership assets [UPA 306(b)]. This means that the new partner usually has no personal liability for these debts and obligations, but any capital contribution that he or she made to the partnership is subject to these debts. **■EXAMPLE 24.6** Smartclub is a partnership with four members. Alex Jaff, a newly admitted partner, contributes $100,000 to the partnership. Smartclub has about $600,000 in debt at the time Jaff joins the firm. Although Jaff's capital contribution of $100,000 can be used to satisfy Smartclub's obligations, Jaff is not personally liable for partnership debts that were incurred before he became a partner. Thus, his personal assets cannot be used to satisfy the partnership's antecedent debt. If, however, the managing partner at Smartclub borrows funds after Jaff becomes a partner, Jaff will be personally liable for those amounts. **■**

Partner's Dissociation

Dissociation occurs when a partner ceases to be associated in the carrying on of the partnership business. Although a partner always has the *power* to dissociate from the firm, he or she may not have the *right* to dissociate. Dissociation normally entitles the partner to have his or her interest purchased by the partnership and terminates his or her actual authority to act for the partnership and to participate with the partners in running the business. Otherwise, the partnership continues to do business without the dissociating partner.[4]

Events Causing Dissociation   Under UPA 601, a partner can be dissociated from a partnership in any of the following ways:

1 By the partner's voluntarily giving notice of an "express will to withdraw."

2 By the occurrence of an event agreed to in the partnership agreement.

3 By a unanimous vote of the other partners under certain circumstances, such as when a partner transfers substantially all of her or his interest in the partnership, or when it becomes unlawful to carry on partnership business with that partner.

4 By order of a court or arbitrator if the partner has engaged in wrongful conduct that affects the partnership business, breached the partnership agreement or violated a duty owed to the partnership or the other partners, or engaged in conduct that makes it "not reasonably practicable to carry on the business in partnership with the partner" [UPA 601(5)].

5 By the partner's declaring bankruptcy, assigning his or her interest in the partnership for the benefit of creditors, or becoming physically or mentally incapacitated, or by the partner's death. Note that although the bankruptcy or

---

3. For a case applying joint liability to partnerships, see *Shar's Cars, LLC v. Elder*, 97 P.3d 724 (Utah App. 2004).

4. Under the previous version of the UPA, when a partner dissociated from a partnership, the partnership was considered dissolved, its business had to be wound up, and the proceeds had to be distributed to creditors and among partners. The amendments to the UPA recognize that a partnership may not want to break up just because one partner has left the firm.

death of a partner represents that partner's "dissociation" from the partnership, it is not an *automatic* ground for the partnership's dissolution (*dissolution* will be discussed shortly).

Wrongful Dissociation As mentioned, a partner has the power to dissociate from a partnership at any time, but if she or he lacks the right to dissociate, then the dissociation is considered wrongful under the law [UPA 602]. When a partner's dissociation is in breach of the partnership agreement, for instance, it is wrongful. ■**EXAMPLE 24.7** A partnership agreement states that it is a breach of the partnership agreement for any partner to assign partnership property to a creditor without the consent of the others. If a partner, Janis, makes such an assignment, she has not only breached the agreement but has also wrongfully dissociated from the partnership. ■ Similarly, if a partner refuses to perform duties required by the partnership agreement—such as accounting for profits earned from the use of partnership property—this breach can be treated as wrongful dissociation. A partner who wrongfully dissociates is liable to the partnership and to the other partners for damages caused by the dissociation.

Effects of Dissociation Dissociation (rightful or wrongful) terminates some of the rights of the dissociated partner, requires that the partnership purchase his or her interest, and alters the liability of both parties to third parties. On a partner's dissociation, his or her right to participate in the management and conduct of the partnership business terminates [UPA 603]. The partner's duty of loyalty also ends. A partner's other fiduciary duties, including the duty of care, continue only with respect to events that occurred before dissociation, unless the partner participates in winding up the partnership's business (to be discussed shortly). ■**EXAMPLE 24.8** Debbie Pearson, a partner who leaves an accounting firm, Bubb & Pearson, can immediately compete with the firm for new clients. She must exercise care in completing ongoing client transactions, however, and must account to the firm for any fees received from the old clients based on those transactions. ■

After a partner's dissociation, his or her interest in the partnership must be purchased according to the rules in UPA 701. The *buyout price* is based on the amount that would have been distributed to the partner if the partnership were wound up on the date of dissociation. Offset against the price are amounts owed by the partner to the partnership, including any damages for the partner's wrongful dissociation.

For two years after a partner dissociates from a continuing partnership, the partnership may be bound by the acts of the dissociated partner based on apparent authority [UPA 702]. In other words, the partnership may be liable to a third party

with whom a dissociated partner enters into a transaction if the third party reasonably believed that the dissociated partner was still a partner. Similarly, a dissociated partner may be liable for partnership obligations entered into during a two-year period following dissociation [UPA 703].

Partnership Termination

The same events that cause dissociation can result in the end of the partnership if the remaining partners no longer wish to (or are unable to) continue the partnership business. The termination of a partnership is referred to as **dissolution,** which essentially means the commencement of the winding up process. **Winding up** is the actual process of collecting, liquidating, and distributing the partnership assets.[5] We discuss here the dissolution and winding up of partnership business.

Dissolution Dissolution of a partnership generally can be brought about by the acts of the partners, by the operation of law, and by judicial decree [UPA 801]. Any partnership (including one for a fixed term) can be dissolved by the partners' agreement. Similarly, if the partnership agreement states that it will dissolve on a certain event, such as a partner's death or bankruptcy, then the occurrence of that event will dissolve the partnership. A partnership for a fixed term or a particular undertaking is dissolved by operation of law at the expiration of the term or on the completion of the undertaking. Under the UPA, a court may order dissolution when it becomes obviously impractical for the firm to continue—for example, if the business can only be operated at a loss [UPA 801(5)].

Winding Up After dissolution, the partnership continues for the limited purpose of the winding up process. The partners cannot create new obligations on behalf of the partnership. They have authority only to complete transactions begun but not finished at the time of dissolution and to wind up the business of the partnership [UPA 803, 804(1)]. *Winding up* includes collecting and preserving partnership assets, discharging liabilities (paying debts), and accounting to each partner for the value of her or his interest in the partnership. Partners continue to have fiduciary duties to one another and to the firm during this process. UPA 401(h) provides that a partner is entitled to compensation for services in winding up partnership affairs (and reimbursement for expenses incurred in the process) above and apart from his or her share in the partnership profits.

---

5. Although "winding down" would seem to describe more accurately the process of settling accounts and liquidating the assets of a partnership, "winding up" has been traditionally used in English and U.S. statutory and case law to denote this final stage of a partnership's existence.

Both creditors of the partnership and creditors of the individual partners can make claims on the partnership's assets. In general, partnership creditors share proportionately with the partners' individual creditors in the assets of the partners' estates, which include their interests in the partnership. A partnership's assets are distributed according to the following priorities [UPA 807]:

1 Payment of debts, including those owed to partner and nonpartner creditors.

2 Return of capital contributions and distribution of profits to partners.

If the partnership's liabilities are greater than its assets, the partners bear the losses—in the absence of a contrary agreement—in the same proportion in which they shared the profits (rather than, for example, in proportion to their contributions to the partnership's capital).

PREVENTING LEGAL DISPUTES Before entering a partnership, agree on how the assets will be valued and divided in the event the partnership dissolves. Make express arrangements that will provide for a smooth dissolution. You and your partners can enter into a buy-sell, or buyout, agreement, which provides that one or more partners will buy out the others, should the relationship deteriorate. Agreeing beforehand on who buys what, under what circumstances, and, if possible, at what price may eliminate costly litigation later. Alternatively, the agreement may specify who will determine the value of the interest being sold and who will decide whether to buy or sell.

LIMITED LIABILITY PARTNERSHIPS

The **limited liability partnership (LLP)** is a hybrid form of business designed mostly for professionals, such as attorneys and accountants, who normally do business as partners in a partnership. In fact, nearly all the big accounting firms are LLPs. The major advantage of the LLP is that it allows a partnership to continue as a *pass-through entity* for tax purposes, but limits the personal liability of the partners.

LLPs must be formed and operated in compliance with state statutes, which often include provisions of the UPA. The appropriate form must be filed with a state agency, and the business's name must include either "Limited Liability Partnership" or "LLP" [UPA 1001, 1002]. In addition, an LLP must file an annual report with the state to remain qualified as an LLP in that state [UPA 1003]. In most states, it is relatively easy to convert a traditional partnership into an LLP because the firm's basic organizational structure remains the same. Additionally, all of the statutory and common law rules governing partnerships still apply (apart from those modified by the state's LLP statute).

Liability in an LLP

Many professionals work together using the partnership business form. Family members often do business together as partners also. As discussed previously, a major disadvantage of the general partnership is the unlimited personal liability of its owner-partners. Partners in a general partnership are also subject to joint and several (individual) liability for partnership obligations, which exposes each partner to potential liability for the malpractice of another partner.

The LLP allows professionals to avoid personal liability for the malpractice of other partners. A partner in an LLP is still liable for her or his own wrongful acts, such as negligence, however. Also liable is the partner who supervised the party who committed a wrongful act. This is generally true for all types of partners and partnerships, not just LLPs.

Although LLP statutes vary from state to state, generally each state statute limits the liability of partners in some way. For example, Delaware law protects each innocent partner from the "debts and obligations of the partnership arising from negligence, wrongful acts, or misconduct." The UPA more broadly exempts partners from personal liability for any partnership obligation, "whether arising in contract, tort, or otherwise" [UPA 306(c)].

Family Limited Liability Partnerships

A **family limited liability partnership (FLLP)** is a limited liability partnership in which the majority of the partners are persons related to each other, essentially as spouses, parents, grandparents, siblings, cousins, nephews, or nieces. A person acting in a fiduciary capacity for persons so related can also be a partner. All of the partners must be natural persons or persons acting in a fiduciary capacity for the benefit of natural persons.

Probably the most significant use of the FLLP form of business organization is in agriculture. Family-owned farms sometimes find this form to their benefit. The FLLP offers the same advantages as other LLPs with some additional advantages, such as, in Iowa, an exemption from real estate transfer taxes when partnership real estate is transferred among partners.[6]

---

6. Iowa Statutes Section 428A.2.

LIMITED PARTNERSHIPS

We now look at a business organizational form that limits the liability of *some* of its owners—the **limited partnership.** Limited partnerships originated in medieval Europe and have been in existence in the United States since the early 1800s. In many ways, limited partnerships are like the general partnerships discussed earlier in this chapter, but they differ from general partnerships in several ways. Because of this, they are sometimes referred to as *special partnerships.*

Limited partnerships consist of at least one **general partner** and one or more **limited partners.** A general partner assumes management responsibility for the partnership and so has full responsibility for the partnership and for all debts of the partnership. A limited partner contributes cash or other property and owns an interest in the firm but does not undertake any management responsibilities and is not personally liable for partnership debts beyond the amount of his or her investment. A limited partner can forfeit limited liability by taking part in the management of the business.

Until 1976, the law governing limited partnerships in all states except Louisiana was the Uniform Limited Partnership Act (ULPA). Since 1976, most states and the District of Columbia have adopted the revised version of the ULPA, known as the Revised Uniform Limited Partnership Act (RULPA). Because the RULPA is the dominant law governing limited partnerships in the United States, we will refer to the RULPA in the following discussion of limited partnerships.

Formation of the Limited Partnership

In contrast to the informal, private, and voluntary agreement that usually suffices for a general partnership, the formation of a limited partnership is formal and public. The parties must follow specific statutory requirements and file a certificate with the state. A limited partnership must have at least one general partner and one limited partner, as mentioned previously. Additionally, the partners must sign a **certificate of limited partnership,** which requires information similar to that found in articles of incorporation (see Chapter 25), such as the name, mailing address, and capital contribution of each general and limited partner. The certificate is usually open to public inspection.

Liabilities of Partners in a Limited Partnership

General partners, unlike limited partners, are personally liable to the partnership's creditors; thus, at least one general partner is necessary in a limited partnership so that someone has personal liability. This policy can be circumvented in states that allow a corporation to be the general partner in a partnership. Because the corporation has limited liability by virtue of corporate laws, if a corporation is the general partner, no one in the limited partnership has personal liability.

In contrast to the personal liability of general partners, the liability of a limited partner is limited to the capital that she or he contributes or agrees to contribute to the partnership [RULPA 502]. Limited partners enjoy limited liability so long as they do not participate in management [RULPA 303]. A limited partner who participates in management will be just as liable as a general partner to any creditor who transacts business with the limited partnership and believes, based on a limited partner's conduct, that the limited partner is a general partner [RULPA 303]. How much actual review and advisement a limited partner can engage in before being exposed to liability is an unsettled question.

Dissociation and Dissolution

A general partner has the power to voluntarily dissociate, or withdraw, from a limited partnership unless the partnership agreement specifies otherwise. A limited partner theoretically can withdraw from the partnership by giving six months' notice unless the partnership agreement specifies a term, which most do. Also, some states have passed laws prohibiting the withdrawal of limited partners.

In a limited partnership, a general partner's voluntary dissociation from the firm normally will lead to dissolution *unless* all partners agree to continue the business. Similarly, the bankruptcy, retirement, death, or mental incompetence of a general partner will cause the dissociation of that partner and the dissolution of the limited partnership unless the other members agree to continue the firm [RULPA 801]. Bankruptcy of a limited partner, however, does not dissolve the partnership unless it causes the bankruptcy of the firm. Death or an assignment of the interest of a limited partner does not dissolve a limited partnership [RULPA 702, 704, 705]. A limited partnership can be dissolved by court decree [RULPA 802].

On dissolution, creditors' claims, including those of partners who are creditors, take first priority. After that, partners and former partners receive unpaid distributions of partnership assets and, except as otherwise agreed, amounts representing returns on their contributions and amounts proportionate to their shares of the distributions [RULPA 804].

In the following case, two limited partners wanted the business of the partnership to be sold on its dissolution, while another limited partner—actor Kevin Costner—and the general partner wanted it to continue.

CASE 24.2   In re Dissolution of Midnight Star Enterprises, LP

Supreme Court of South Dakota, 2006 SD 98, 724 N.W.2d 334 (2006).

FACTS Midnight Star Enterprises, Limited Partnership, consists of a casino, bar, and restaurant in Deadwood, South Dakota. The owners are Midnight Star Enterprises, Limited (MSEL), the general partner, which owns 22 partnership units; actor Kevin Costner, a limited partner, who owns 71.5 partnership units; and Carla and Francis Caneva, limited partners, who own 3.25 partnership units each. Costner also owns MSEL and thus controls 93.5 partnership units. The Canevas were the business's managers, for which they received salaries and bonuses. When MSEL voiced concerns about the management, communication among the partners broke down. MSEL filed a petition in a South Dakota state court to dissolve the partnership. MSEL hired Paul Thorstenson, an accountant, to determine the firm's fair market value, which he calculated to be $3.1 million. The Canevas solicited a competitor's offer to buy the business for $6.2 million, which the court ruled was the appropriate amount. At the Canevas' request, the court ordered MSEL and Costner to buy the business for that price within ten days or sell it on the open market to the highest bidder. MSEL appealed to the South Dakota Supreme Court.

ISSUE Can a partner force the sale of a limited partnership when the other partners want to continue the business?

DECISION No. The South Dakota Supreme Court reversed the judgment of the lower court and remanded the case to allow MSEL and Costner to pay the Canevas the value of their 6.5 partnership units after a revaluation of the partnership.

REASON The state supreme court concluded that the partnership agreement did not require the business to be sold on the open market on the partnership's dissolution. Under the agreement, during liquidation, the firm's property could be distributed in kind among the partners if it was first offered for sale to a third party. In other words, only a decision to make an in-kind distribution of assets required that the business be offered for sale on the open market. The court also concluded that the correct value of the business was the accountant's figure, which was based on a fair market value analysis using a hypothetical buyer. This analysis provided a reasonable basis for determining value "by removing the irrationalities, strategies, and emotions" that exist in an actual offer. Besides, the partnership agreement required a "fair market value" of the assets. Finally, "since it was error for the [lower] court to value Midnight Star at $6.2 million, it was also error to force the general partners to buy the business for $6.2 million or sell the business." The state supreme court reasoned that "forced sales typically end up in economic waste." A buyout is an acceptable alternative, as long as the partners receive the fair value of their property interest. "Instead of ordering the majority partners to purchase the whole partnership for the appraised value, the majority partners should only be required to pay any interests the withdrawing partner is due."

FOR CRITICAL ANALYSIS—Ethical Consideration *Under what circumstances might a forced sale of the property of a limited partnership on its dissolution be appropriate?*

■

Limited Liability Limited Partnerships

A **limited liability limited partnership (LLLP)** is a type of limited partnership. An LLLP differs from a limited partnership in that a general partner in an LLLP has the same liability as a limited partner in a limited partnership. In other words, the liability of all partners is limited to the amount of their investments in the firm.

A few states provide expressly for LLLPs. In states that do not provide for LLLPs but do allow for limited partnerships and limited liability partnerships, a limited partnership should probably still be able to register with the state as an LLLP.

LIMITED LIABILITY COMPANIES

For many entrepreneurs and investors, the ideal business form would combine the tax advantages of the partnership form of business with the limited liability of the corporate enterprise. Although the limited partnership partially addresses these needs, the limited liability of limited partners is conditional: limited liability exists only so long as the limited partner does *not* participate in management.

This is one reason that every state has adopted legislation authorizing a form of business organization called the **limited liability company (LLC)**. The LLC is a hybrid form of business enterprise that offers the limited liability of the corporation but the tax advantages of a partnership.

Formation of an LLC

Like an LLP or LP, an LLC must be formed and operated in compliance with state law. About one-fourth of the states specifically require LLCs to have at least two owners, called **members.** In the rest of the states, although some LLC statutes are silent on this issue, one-member LLCs are usually permitted.

To form an LLC, **articles of organization** must be filed with a state agency—usually the secretary of state's office. Typically, the articles are required to set forth such information as the name of the business, its principal address, the name and address of a registered agent, the names of the owners, and information on how the LLC will be managed. The business's name must include the words "Limited Liability Company" or the initials "LLC." In addition to filing the articles of organization, a few states require that a notice of the intention to form an LLC be published in a local newspaper.

Businesspersons sometimes enter into contracts on behalf of a business organization that is not yet formed. For example, as you will read in Chapter 25, persons forming a corporation may enter into contracts during the process of incorporation but before the corporation becomes a legal entity. These contracts are referred to as preincorporation contracts. Once the corporation is formed and adopts the preincorporation contract (by means of a *novation*, discussed in Chapter 11), it can then enforce the contract terms.

In the following case, the question was whether the same principle extends to LLCs. A person in the process of forming an LLC entered into a preorganization contract under which it would be obligated to purchase the Park Plaza Hotel in Hollywood, California. Once the LLC legally existed, the owners of the hotel refused to sell the property to the LLC, claiming that the contract was unenforceable.

CASE 24.3   02 Development, LLC v. 607 South Park, LLC

Court of Appeal of California, Second District, 159 Cal.App.4th 609, 71 Cal.Rptr.3d 608 (2008).

FACTS In March 2004, 607 South Park, LLC, entered into a written agreement to sell Park Plaza Hotel to 607 Park View Associates, Ltd., for $8.7 million. The general partner of 607 Park View Associates was Creative Environments of Hollywood, Inc. In February 2005, Creative Environments assigned the rights to the hotel purchase to another company, 02 Development, LLC. At the time, 02 Development did not yet exist; it was legally created several months later. 02 Development sued 607 South Park for breach of the hotel purchase agreement. 607 South Park moved for summary judgment, arguing that no enforceable contract existed because at the time of the assignment, 02 Development did not yet legally exist. Furthermore, 607 South Park argued that 02 Development suffered no damages because it was "not ready, willing, and able to fund the purchase of the hotel." The trial court granted the motion and entered judgment in favor of 607 South Park. 02 Development appealed.

ISSUE Can 02 Development enforce a contract that had been assigned to it before the date of its legal formation?

DECISION Yes. The Court of Appeal of California reversed the judgment and directed the trial court to enter an order denying 607 South Park's motion for summary judgment.

REASON South Park's primary argument was that 02 Development did not exist at the time of the contract and was not a party to the contract. The court, however, reasoned that LLCs should be treated the same as corporations with respect to preorganization contracts. "When the assignment agreement was executed, 02 Development did not exist so it was not then a party to the agreement. But once 02 Development came into existence, it could enforce any preorganization contract made on its behalf, such as the assignment agreement, if it adopted or ratified it." 607 South Park had not argued that LLCs should be treated differently than corporations. 607 South Park had argued that 02 Development was required to present admissible evidence that it would have been financially able to close the transaction, but the court rejected this notion. "607 South Park presented no evidence that 02 Development would have been unable to arrange for the necessary funding to close the transaction on time if 607 South Park had given it the opportunity instead of repudiating a contract in advance."

 FOR CRITICAL ANALYSIS—Social Consideration *Why did the appellate court place so little emphasis on the lack of funding commitments for $8.7 million?*

Jurisdictional Requirements

One of the significant differences between LLCs and corporations has to do with federal jurisdictional requirements. Under the federal jurisdiction statute, a corporation is deemed to be a citizen of the state where it is incorporated and maintains its principal place of business. The statute does not mention the state citizenship of partnerships, LLCs, and other unincorporated associations, but the courts have tended to regard these entities as citizens of every state in which their members are citizens.

The state citizenship of an LLC may come into play when a party sues the LLC based on diversity of citizenship. Remember from Chapter 2 that when parties to a lawsuit are from different states and the amount in controversy exceeds $75,000, a federal court can exercise diversity jurisdiction. *Total* diversity of citizenship must exist, however. **■EXAMPLE 24.9** Fong, a citizen of New York, wishes to bring a suit against Skycel, an LLC formed under the laws of Connecticut. One of Skycel's members also lives in New York. Fong will not be able to bring a suit against Skycel in federal court on the basis of diversity jurisdiction because the defendant LLC is also a citizen of New York. The same would be true if Fong was bringing a suit against multiple defendants and one of the defendants lived in New York. ■

Advantages and Disadvantages of the LLC

Although the LLC offers many advantages to businesspersons, this form of business organization also has some disadvantages. We look now at some of the advantages and disadvantages of the LLC.

Advantages of the LLC A key advantage of the LLC is that the liability of members is limited to the amount of their investments. Another advantage is the flexibility of the LLC in regard to both taxation and management.

An LLC that has *two or more members* can choose to be taxed either as a partnership or as a corporation. As you will read in Chapter 25, a corporate entity must pay income taxes on its profits, and the shareholders pay personal income taxes on profits distributed as dividends. An LLC that wants to distribute profits to the members may prefer to be taxed as a partnership to avoid the "double-taxation" characteristic of the corporate entity. Unless an LLC indicates that it wishes to be taxed as a corporation, the IRS automatically taxes it as a partnership. This means that the LLC as an entity pays no taxes; rather, as in a partnership, profits are "passed through" the LLC to the members who then personally pay taxes on the profits. If an LLC's members want to reinvest the profits in the business, however, rather than distribute the profits to members, they may prefer that the LLC be taxed as a corporation. Corporate income tax rates may be lower than personal tax rates. Part of the attractiveness of the LLC is this flexibility with respect to taxation.

For federal income tax purposes, one-member LLCs are automatically taxed as sole proprietorships unless they indicate that they wish to be taxed as corporations. With respect to state taxes, most states follow the IRS rules. Still another advantage of the LLC for businesspersons is the flexibility it offers in terms of business operations and management—as will be discussed shortly. Finally, because foreign investors can participate in an LLC, the LLC form of business is attractive as a way to encourage investment.

Disadvantages of the LLC The disadvantages of the LLC are relatively few. Although initially there was uncertainty over how LLCs would be taxed, that disadvantage no longer exists. One remaining disadvantage is that state LLC statutes are not yet uniform. Until all of the states have uniform LLC laws, an LLC in one state will have to check the rules in the other states in which the firm does business to ensure that it retains its limited liability. Generally, though, most—if not all—states apply to a foreign LLC (an LLC formed in another state) the law of the state where the LLC was formed.

Still another disadvantage is the lack of case law dealing with LLCs. How the courts interpret statutes provides important guidelines for businesses. Given the relative newness of the LLC as a business form in the United States, there is not, as yet, a substantial body of case law to provide this kind of guidance.

The LLC Operating Agreement

The members of an LLC can decide how to operate the various aspects of the business by forming an **operating agreement** [ULLCA 103(a)]. Operating agreements typically contain provisions relating to management, how profits will be divided, the transfer of membership interests, whether the LLC will be dissolved on the death or departure of a member, and other important issues.

An operating agreement need not be in writing and indeed need not even be formed for an LLC to exist. Generally, though, LLC members should protect their interests by forming a written operating agreement. As with any business arrangement, disputes may arise over any number of issues. If there is no agreement covering the topic under dispute, such as how profits will be divided, the state LLC statute will govern the outcome. For example, most LLC statutes provide that if the members have not specified how profits will be divided, they will be divided equally among the members. Generally, when an issue is not covered by an operating agreement or by an LLC statute, the courts apply the principles of partnership law.

Management of an LLC

Basically, there are two options for managing an LLC. The members may decide in their operating agreement to be either a "member-managed" LLC or a "manager-managed" LLC. Most LLC statutes and the Uniform Limited Liability Company Act (ULLCA) provide that unless the articles of organization specify otherwise, an LLC is assumed to be member managed [ULLCA 203(a)(6)].

In a *member-managed* LLC, all of the members participate in management, and decisions are made by majority vote [ULLCA 404(a)]. In a *manager-managed* LLC, the members designate a group of persons to manage the firm. The management group may consist of only members, both members and nonmembers, or only nonmembers. Managers in a manager-managed LLC owe fiduciary duties to the LLC and its members, including the duty of loyalty and the duty of care [ULLCA 409(a), (h)], just as corporate directors and officers owe fiduciary duties to the corporation and its shareholders (see Chapter 26).

The members of an LLC can also set forth in their operating agreement provisions governing decision-making procedures. For instance, the agreement can include procedures for choosing or removing managers. Although most LLC statutes are silent on this issue, the ULLCA provides that members may choose and remove managers by majority vote [ULLCA 404(b)(3)].

Members may also specify in their agreement how voting rights will be apportioned. If they do not, LLC statutes in most states provide that voting rights are apportioned according to each member's capital contributions. Some states provide that, in the absence of an agreement to the contrary, each member has one vote.

Dissociation and Dissolution of an LLC

Recall that in the context of partnerships, *dissociation* occurs when a partner ceases to be associated in the carrying on of the business. The same concept applies to limited liability companies. A member of an LLC has the *power* to dissociate from the LLC at any time, but he or she may not have the *right* to dissociate. Under the ULLCA, the events that trigger a member's dissociation in an LLC are similar to the events causing a partner to be dissociated under the Uniform Partnership Act (UPA). These include voluntary withdrawal, expulsion by other members or by court order, bankruptcy, incompetence, and death. Generally, even if a member dies or otherwise dissociates from an LLC, the other members may continue to carry on LLC business, unless the operating agreement has contrary provisions.

The Effect of Dissociation When a member dissociates from an LLC, he or she loses the right to participate in management and the right to act as an agent for the LLC. His or her duty of loyalty to the LLC also terminates, and the duty of care continues only with respect to events that occurred before dissociation. Generally, the dissociated member also has a right to have his or her interest in the LLC bought out by the other members of the LLC. The LLC's operating agreement may contain provisions establishing a buyout price, but if it does not, the member's interest is usually purchased at a fair value. In states that have adopted the ULLCA, the LLC must purchase the interest at "fair" value within 120 days after the dissociation.

If the member's dissociation violates the LLC's operating agreement, it is considered legally wrongful, and the dissociated member can be held liable for damages caused by the dissociation. ■EXAMPLE 24.10 Chadwick and Barrel are members in an LLC. Chadwick manages the accounts, and Barrel, who has many connections in the community and is a skilled investor, brings in the business. If Barrel wrongfully dissociates from the LLC, the LLC's business will suffer, and Chadwick can hold Barrel liable for the loss of business resulting from her withdrawal. ■

Dissolution Regardless of whether a member's dissociation was wrongful or rightful, normally the dissociated member has no right to force the LLC to dissolve. The remaining members can opt to either continue or dissolve the business. Members can also stipulate in their operating agreement that certain events will cause dissolution, or they can agree that they have the power to dissolve the LLC by vote. As with partnerships, a court can order an LLC to be dissolved in certain circumstances, such as when the members have engaged in illegal or oppressive conduct, or when it is no longer feasible to carry on the business.

When an LLC is dissolved, any members who did not wrongfully dissociate may participate in the winding up process. To wind up the business, members must collect, liquidate, and distribute the LLC's assets. Members may preserve the assets for a reasonable time to optimize their return, and they continue to have the authority to perform reasonable acts in conjunction with winding up. In other words, the LLC will be bound by the reasonable acts of its members during the winding up process. Once all the LLC's assets have been sold, the proceeds are distributed to pay off debts to creditors first (including debts owed to members who are creditors of the LLC). The member's capital contributions are returned next, and any remaining amounts are then distributed to members in equal shares or according to their operating agreement.

SPECIAL BUSINESS FORMS

In addition to the major business organizational forms, several special forms exist. For the most part, however, they are hybrid organizations—that is, they have characteristics similar to those of partnerships or corporations or they combine features of both.

Joint Ventures, Syndicates, and Joint Stock Companies

A *joint venture* is treated much like a partnership, but it differs in that it is created in contemplation of a limited activity or a single transaction. The form of a *syndicate* or an *investment group* can vary considerably. They may exist as corporations or as general or limited partnerships. In some instances, the members merely own property jointly and have no legally recognized business arrangement. The *joint stock company* is a true hybrid of a partnership and a corporation. It is similar to a corporation in that it is a shareholder organization; because of the personal liability of its members and other characteristics, however, it is usually treated like a partnership.

Business Trusts and Cooperatives

The *business trust*, a popular form of business organization in nineteenth-century America, is somewhat similar to the corporation (see Chapter 25). Legal ownership and management of the property of the business stay with one or more of the trustees. The beneficiaries—who receive profits from the enterprise—are not personally responsible for the debts or obligations of the business trust. In some states, business trusts must pay corporate taxes. The *cooperative* is a nonprofit organization formed to provide an economic service to its members. Unincorporated cooperatives are often treated in the same way as partnerships; incorporated cooperatives, like all corporations, are subject to state corporate law.

Franchises

One can also venture into business by purchasing a franchise. About 25 percent of all retail sales and an increasing part of the gross domestic product of the United States are generated by private franchises. A **franchise** is any arrangement in which the owner of a trademark, a trade name, or a copyright has licensed others to use the trademark, trade name, or copyright in selling goods or services. A **franchisee** (a purchaser of a franchise) is generally legally independent of, but economically dependent on, the integrated business system of the **franchisor** (the seller of the franchise). In other words, the franchisee can operate as an independent businessperson but still obtain the advantages of a regional or national organization. Well-known franchises include Hilton Hotels, McDonald's, and 7-Eleven. Franchising is not so much a *form* of business organization as a way of doing business. Sole proprietorships, partnerships, and corporations can all buy and sell franchises.

REVIEWING Sole Proprietorships, Partnerships, and Limited Liability Companies

A bridge on a prominent public roadway in the city of Papagos, Arizona, was deteriorating and in need of repair. The city posted notices seeking proposals for an artistic bridge design and reconstruction. Davidson Masonry, LLC, which was owned and managed by Carl Davidson and his wife, Marilyn Rowe, submitted a bid for a decorative concrete project that incorporated artistic metalwork. They contacted Shana Lafayette, a local sculptor who specialized in large-scale metal forms, to help them design the bridge. The city selected their bridge design and awarded them the contract for a commission of $184,000. Davidson Masonry and Lafayette then entered into an agreement to work together on the bridge project. Davidson Masonry agreed to install and pay for concrete and structural work, and Lafayette agreed to install the metalwork at her expense. They agreed that overall profits would be split, with 25 percent going to Lafayette and 75 percent going to Davidson Masonry. Lafayette designed numerous metal sculptures of salmon that were incorporated into colorful decorative concrete forms designed by Rowe, while Davidson performed the structural engineering. Using the information presented in the chapter, answer the following questions.

1 Would Davidson Masonry automatically be taxed as a partnership or a corporation?

2 Is Davidson Masonry a member-managed or manager-managed LLC?

3 Suppose that during construction, Lafayette had entered into an agreement to rent space in a warehouse that was close to the bridge so that she could work on her sculptures near the site where they would eventually be installed. She entered into the contract without the knowledge or consent of Davidson Masonry. In this situation, would a court be likely to hold that Davidson Masonry was bound by the contract that Lafayette entered? Why or why not?

4 Now suppose that Rowe has an argument with her husband and wants to withdraw from being a member of Davidson Masonry. What is the term for such a withdrawal, and what effect does it have on the LLC?

TERMS AND CONCEPTS

articles of organization 511
articles of partnership 503
certificate of limited
   partnership 509
dissociation 506
dissolution 507
family limited liability
   partnership (FLLP) 508
franchise 514
franchisee 514

franchisor 514
general partner 509
information return 503
joint and several liability 506
joint liability 505
limited liability company (LLC) 510
limited liability limited
   partnership (LLLP) 510
limited liability partnership
   (LLP) 508

limited partner 509
limited partnership 509
member 511
operating agreement 512
partnership 502
pass-through entity 503
sole proprietorship 500
winding up 507

CHAPTER SUMMARY   Sole Proprietorships, Partnerships, and Limited Liability Companies

Sole Proprietorships (See pages 500–502.)	The simplest form of business organization; used by anyone who does business without creating a separate organization. The owner is the business. The owner pays personal income taxes on all profits and is personally liable for all business debts.
Partnerships (See pages 502–508.)	1. A partnership is created by agreement of the parties. 2. A partnership is treated as an entity except for limited purposes. 3. Each partner pays a proportionate share of income taxes on the net profits of the partnership, whether or not they are distributed; the partnership files only an information return with the Internal Revenue Service. 4. Each partner has an equal voice in management unless the partnership agreement provides otherwise. 5. In the absence of an agreement, partners share profits equally and share losses in the same ratio as they share profits. 6. The capital contribution of each partner is determined by agreement. 7. Partners have unlimited liability for partnership debts. 8. A partnership can be terminated by agreement or can be dissolved by action of the partners, operation of law (subsequent illegality), or court decree.
Limited Liability Partnerships (LLPs) (See page 508.)	1. *Formation*—LLPs must be formed in compliance with state statutes. Typically, an LLP is formed by professionals who normally work together as partners in a partnership. Under most state LLP statutes, it is relatively easy to convert a traditional partnership into an LLP. 2. *Liability of partners*—LLP statutes vary, but under the UPA, professionals generally can avoid personal liability for acts committed by other partners. The extent to which partners' limited liability will be recognized when the partnership does business in another state depends on

(Continued)

CHAPTER SUMMARY	Sole Proprietorships, Partnerships, and Limited Liability Companies–Continued
Limited Liability Partnerships (LLPs)– Continued	the other state's laws. Partners in an LLP continue to be liable for their own wrongful acts and for the wrongful acts of those whom they supervise. 3. *Family limited liability partnership (FLLP)*—A form of LLP in which all of the partners are family members or fiduciaries of family members; the most significant use of the FLLP is by families engaged in agricultural enterprises.
Limited Partnerships (See pages 509–510.)	1. *Formation*—A certificate of limited partnership must be filed with the secretary of state's office or other designated state official. The certificate must include information about the business, similar to the information included in a corporate charter. The partnership consists of one or more general partners and one or more limited partners. 2. *Rights and liabilities of partners*—With some exceptions, the rights of partners are the same as the rights of partners in a general partnership. General partners have unlimited liability for partnership obligations; limited partners are liable only to the extent of their contributions. 3. *Limited partners and management*—Only general partners can participate in management. Limited partners have no voice in management; if they do participate in management activities, they risk having general-partner liability. 4. *Dissociation and dissolution*—Generally, a limited partnership can be dissolved in much the same way as an ordinary partnership. A general partner has the power to voluntarily dissociate unless the parties' agreement specifies otherwise. Some states limit the power of limited partners to voluntarily withdraw from the firm. The death or assignment of interest of a limited partner does not dissolve the partnership; bankruptcy of a limited partner also will not dissolve the partnership unless it causes the bankruptcy of the firm. 5. *Limited liability limited partnerships (LLLPs)*—A special type of limited partnership in which the liability of all partners, including general partners, is limited to the amount of their investments.
Limited Liability Companies (LLCs) (See pages 510–514.)	1. *Formation*—Articles of organization must be filed with the appropriate state office—usually the office of the secretary of state—setting forth the name of the business, its principal address, the names of the owners (called *members*), and other relevant information. 2. *Advantages and disadvantages of the LLC*—Advantages of the LLC include limited liability, the option to be taxed as a partnership or as a corporation, and flexibility in deciding how the business will be managed and operated. Disadvantages relate mainly to the absence of uniformity in state LLC statutes and the lack of case law dealing with LLCs. 3. *Operating agreement*—When an LLC is formed, the members decide, in an operating agreement, how the business will be managed and what rules will apply to the organization. 4. *Management*—An LLC may be managed by members only, by some members and some nonmembers, or by nonmembers only. 5. *Dissociation and dissolution*—Members of an LLC have the power to dissociate from the LLC at any time, but they may not have the right to dissociate. Dissociation does not always result in the dissolution of an LLC; the remaining members can choose to continue the business. Dissociated members have a right to have their interest purchased by the other members. If the LLC is dissolved, the business must be wound up and the assets sold. Creditors are paid first; then members' capital investments are returned. Any remaining proceeds are distributed to members.
Special Business Forms (See page 514.)	A number of special business forms exist. Typically, they are hybrid organizations having characteristics similar to partnerships or corporations, or combining features of both. Special business forms include joint ventures, syndicates or investment groups, joint stock companies, business trusts, and cooperatives. A widely used way of conducting business is the franchise.

FOR REVIEW

Answers for the even-numbered questions in this **For Review** *section can be found on this text's accompanying Web site at* www.cengage.com/blaw/fbl. *Select "Chapter 24" and click on "For Review."*

1 Which form of business organization is the simplest? Which form arises from an agreement between two or more persons to carry on a business for profit?

2 What are the three essential elements of a partnership?

3 What is meant by joint and several liability? Why is this often considered to be a disadvantage of the partnership form of business?

4 Why do professional groups organize as a limited liability partnership? How does this form differ from a general partnership?

5 What is a limited liability company? What are some of the advantages and disadvantages of this business form?

QUESTIONS AND CASE PROBLEMS

HYPOTHETICAL SCENARIOS AND CASE PROBLEMS

24.1 Limited Liability Companies. John, Lesa, and Tabir form a limited liability company. John contributes 60 percent of the capital, and Lesa and Tabir each contribute 20 percent. Nothing is decided about how profits will be divided. John assumes that he will be entitled to 60 percent of the profits, in accordance with his contribution. Lesa and Tabir, however, assume that the profits will be divided equally. A dispute over the question arises, and ultimately a court has to decide the issue. What law will the court apply? In most states, what will result? How could this dispute have been avoided in the first place? Discuss fully.

24.2 Hypothetical Question with Sample Answer. Dorinda, Luis, and Elizabeth form a limited partnership. Dorinda is a general partner, and Luis and Elizabeth are limited partners. Consider each of the separate events below, and discuss fully which would constitute a dissolution of the limited partnership.

1 Luis assigns his partnership interest to Ashley.

2 Elizabeth is petitioned into involuntary bankruptcy.

3 Dorinda dies.

 For a sample answer to Question 24.2, go to Appendix E at the end of this text.

24.3 Partnership Formation. Daniel is the owner of a chain of shoe stores. He hires Rubya to be the manager of a new store, which is to open in Grand Rapids, Michigan. Daniel, by written contract, agrees to pay Rubya a monthly salary and 20 percent of the profits. Without Daniel's knowledge, Rubya represents himself to Classen as Daniel's partner, showing Classen the agreement to share profits. Classen extends credit to Rubya. Rubya defaults. Discuss whether Classen can hold Daniel liable as a partner.

24.4 Indications of Partnership. At least six months before the 1996 Summer Olympic Games in Atlanta, Georgia, Stafford Fontenot, Steve Turner, Mike Montelaro, Joe Sokol, and Doug Brinsmade agreed to sell Cajun food at the games and began making preparations. Calling themselves "Prairie Cajun Seafood Catering of Louisiana," on May 19 the group applied for a license with the Fulton County, Georgia, Department of Public Health–Environmental Health Services. Later, Ted Norris sold a mobile kitchen for an $8,000 check drawn on the "Prairie Cajun Seafood Catering of Louisiana" account and two promissory notes, one for $12,000 and the other for $20,000. The notes, which were dated June 12, listed only Fontenot "d/b/a Prairie Cajun Seafood" as the maker (*d/b/a* is an abbreviation for "doing business as"). On July 31, Fontenot and his friends signed a partnership agreement, which listed specific percentages of profits and losses. They drove the mobile kitchen to Atlanta, but business was "disastrous." When the notes were not paid, Norris filed a suit in a Louisiana state court against Fontenot, seeking payment. What are the elements of a partnership? Was there a partnership among Fontenot and the others? Who is liable on the notes? Explain. [*Norris v. Fontenot*, 867 So.2d 179 (La.App. 3 Cir. 2004)]

24.5 Sole Proprietorship. James Ferguson operates "Jim's 11-E Auto Sales" in Jonesborough, Tennessee, as a sole proprietorship. In 1999, Consumers Insurance Co. issued a policy to "Jim Ferguson, Jim's 11E Auto Sales" covering "Owned 'Autos' Only." *Auto* was defined to include "a land motor vehicle," which was not further explained in the policy. Coverage extended to damages caused by the owner or driver of an underinsured motor vehicle. In 2000, Ferguson bought and titled in his own name a 1976 Harley-Davidson motorcycle, intending to repair and sell the cycle through his dealership. In October 2001, while driving the motorcycle, Ferguson was struck by an auto driven by John Jenkins. Ferguson filed a suit in a Tennessee state court against Jenkins—who was underinsured with respect to Ferguson's medical bills—and Consumers. The insurer argued, among other things, that because the motorcycle was bought and titled in Ferguson's own name, and he was driving it at the time of the accident, it was his personal vehicle and thus was not covered under the dealership's policy. What is the relationship between a sole proprietor and a sole proprietorship? How might this status affect the court's decision in this case? [*Ferguson v. Jenkins*, 204 S.W.3d 779 (Tenn.App. 2006)]

24.6 Case Problem with Sample Answer. In August 2003, Tammy Duncan began working as a waitress at Bynum's Diner, which was owned by her mother, Hazel Bynum, and her stepfather, Eddie Bynum, in Valdosta, Georgia. Less than a month later, the three signed an agreement under which Eddie was to relinquish his management responsibilities, allowing Tammy to be co-manager. At the end of this six-month period, Eddie would revisit this agreement and could then extend it for another six-month period. The diner's bank account was to remain in Eddie's name. There was no provision with regard to the diner's profit, if any, and the parties did not change the business's tax information. Tammy began doing the bookkeeping, as well as waiting tables and performing other duties. On October 30, she slipped off a ladder and injured her knees. At the end of the six-month term, Tammy quit working at the diner. The Georgia State Board of Workers' Compensation determined that she had been the diner's employee and awarded her benefits under the diner's workers' compensation policy with Cypress Insurance Co. Cypress filed a suit in a Georgia state court against Tammy, arguing that she was not an employee, but a co-owner. What are the essential elements of a partnership? Was Tammy a partner in the business of the diner? Explain. [*Cypress Insurance Co. v. Duncan*, 281 Ga.App. 469, 636 S.E.2d 159 (2006)]

After you have answered Problem 24.6, compare your answer with the sample answer given on the Web site that accompanies this text. Go to **www.cengage.com/blaw/fbl**, select "Chapter 24," and click on "Case Problem with Sample Answer."

24.7 Limited Liability Companies. A "Certificate of Formation" (CF) for Grupo Dos Chiles, LLC, was filed with the Delaware secretary of state in February 2000. The CF named Jamie Rivera as the "initial member." The next month, Jamie's mother, Yolanda Martinez, and Alfred Shriver, who had a personal relationship with Martinez at the time, signed an "LLC Agreement" for Grupo, naming themselves "managing partners." Grupo's business was the operation of Dancing Peppers Cantina, a restaurant in Alexandria, Virginia. Identifying themselves as Grupo's owners, Shriver and Martinez borrowed funds from

Advanceme, Inc., a restaurant lender. In June 2003, Grupo lost its LLC status in Delaware for failing to pay state taxes, and by the end of July, Martinez and Shriver had ended their relationship. Shriver filed a suit in a Virginia state court against Martinez to wind up Grupo's affairs. Meanwhile, without consulting Shriver, Martinez paid Grupo's back taxes. Shriver filed a suit in a Delaware state court against Martinez, asking the court to dissolve the firm. What effect did the LLC agreement have on the CF? Did Martinez's unilateral act reestablish Grupo's LLC status? Should the Delaware court grant Shriver's request? Why or why not? [*In re Grupo Dos Chiles, LLC*, __ A.2d __ (Del.Ch. 2006)]

24.8 Limited Liability Companies. An LLC owned a Manhattan apartment building that was sold. The plaintiffs owned 25 percent of the membership interests in the LLC. They filed a lawsuit on behalf of the LLC—called a *derivative suit* (see Chapter 25)—claiming that those in majority control of the LLC had sold the building for less than its market value and had personally profited from the deal. The trial court dismissed the suit, holding that the plaintiffs individually could not bring a derivative suit "to redress wrongs suffered by the corporation" because such actions could not be brought for a LLC. The appellate court reversed, holding that derivative suits on behalf of LLCs are permitted. That decision was appealed. A key problem was that the state law allowing the creation of LLCs did not address the issue. How should such matters logically be resolved? Are the minority members in an LLC at the mercy of the decisions of the majority members? Explain your answer. [*Tzolis v. Wolff*, 10 N.Y.3d 100, 884 N.E.2d 1005 (2008)]

24.9 A Question of Ethics. *Blushing Brides, LLC, a publisher of wedding planning magazines in Ohio, opened an account with Gray Printing Co. in July 2000. On behalf of Blushing Brides, Louis Zacks, the firm's member-manager, signed a credit agreement that identified the firm as the "purchaser" and required payment within thirty days. Despite the agreement, Blushing Brides typically took up to six months to pay the full amount for its orders. Gray printed and shipped 10,000 copies of a 2001 issue for Blushing Brides but had not been paid when the firm ordered 15,000 copies of a 2002 issue. Gray refused to print the new order without an assurance of payment. Zacks signed a promissory note for $14,778, plus interest at 6 percent per year, payable to Gray on June 22. Gray printed the new order but by October had been paid only $7,500. Gray filed a suit in an Ohio state court against Blushing Brides and Zacks to collect the balance. [Gray Printing Co. v. Blushing Brides, LLC, __ N.E.2d __ (Ohio App.3d 2006)]*

1 Under what circumstances is a member of an LLC liable for the firm's debts? In this case, is Zacks personally liable under the credit agreement for the unpaid amount on Blushing Brides' account? Did Zacks's promissory note affect the parties' liability on the account? Explain.

2 Should a member of an LLC assume an ethical responsibility to meet the obligations of the firm? Discuss.

3 Gray shipped only 10,000 copies of the 2002 issue of Blushing Brides' magazine, waiting for the publisher to identify a destination for the other 5,000 copies. The magazine had a retail price of $4.50 per copy. Did Gray have a legal or ethical duty to "mitigate the damages" by attempting to sell or otherwise distribute these copies itself? Why or why not?

CRITICAL THINKING AND WRITING ASSIGNMENT

24.10 Critical Legal Thinking. Although a limited liability entity may be the best organizational form for most businesses, a significant number of firms may be better off as a corporation or some other form of organization. How does the fact that most of the limited liability entities are new forms for doing business affect the reasons for choosing another form of organization in which to do business? Explain.

ACCESSING THE INTERNET

For updated links to resources available on the Web, as well as a variety of other materials, visit this text's Web site at

www.cengage.com/blaw/fbl

To learn how the U.S. Small Business Administration assists in forming, financing, and operating businesses, go to

www.sbaonline.sba.gov

LLRX.com, a Web site for legal professionals, provides information on LLCs in its Web journal. Go to

www.llrx.com/features/llc.htm

You can find information on filing fees for LLCs at

www.bizcorp.com

For information on the FTC regulations on franchising, as well as state laws regulating franchising, go to

www.ftc.gov/bcp/franchise/netfran.htm

PRACTICAL INTERNET EXERCISES

Go to this text's Web site at **www.cengage.com/blaw/fbl**, select "Chapter 24," and click on "Practical Internet Exercises." There you will find the following Internet research exercises that you can perform to learn more about the topics covered in this chapter.

PRACTICAL INTERNET EXERCISE 24-1: LEGAL PERSPECTIVE—Starting a Business

PRACTICAL INTERNET EXERCISE 24-2: MANAGEMENT PERSPECTIVE—Limited Liability Companies

BEFORE THE TEST

Go to this text's Web site at **www.cengage.com/blaw/fbl**, select "Chapter 24," and click on "Interactive Quizzes." You will find a number of interactive questions relating to this chapter.

CHAPTER 25
Corporate Formation, Financing, and Termination

LEARNING OBJECTIVES

AFTER READING THIS CHAPTER, YOU SHOULD BE ABLE TO ANSWER THE FOLLOWING QUESTIONS:

1 What steps are involved in bringing a corporation into existence? Who is liable for preincorporation contracts?

2 What is the difference between a *de jure* corporation and a *de facto* corporation?

3 In what circumstances might a court disregard the corporate entity ("pierce the corporate veil") and hold the shareholders personally liable?

4 What are the steps of the merger or consolidation procedure?

5 What are the two ways in which a corporation can be voluntarily dissolved? Under what circumstances might a corporation be involuntarily dissolved by state action?

The corporation is a creature of statute—an artificial being that exists only in law. Its existence generally depends on state law, although some corporations, especially public organizations, can be created under state or federal law.

Each state has its own body of corporate law, and these laws are not entirely uniform. The Model Business Corporation Act (MBCA) is a codification of modern corporation law that has been influential in the drafting and revision of state corporation statutes. Today, the majority of state statutes are guided by the revised version of the MBCA, which is often referred to as the Revised Model Business Corporation Act (RMBCA). You should keep in mind, however, that there is considerable variation among the statutes of the states that have used the MBCA or the RMBCA as a basis for their statutes, and several states do not follow either act. Consequently, individual state corporation laws should be relied on rather than the MBCA or the RMBCA.

In this chapter, we examine the nature of the corporate form of business enterprise and the various classifications of corporations. We then discuss the formation and financing of today's corporations.

CORPORATE NATURE, CLASSIFICATION, AND POWERS

A **corporation** is a legal entity created and recognized by state law. It can consist of one or more *natural persons* (as opposed to the artificial *legal person* of the corporation) identified under a common name. A corporation can be owned by a single person, or it can have hundreds, thousands, or even millions of owners (shareholders). The corporation substitutes itself for its shareholders in conducting corporate business and in incurring liability, yet its authority to act and the liability for its actions are separate and apart from the individuals who own it.

Corporate Personnel

In a corporation, the responsibility for the overall management of the firm is entrusted to a *board of directors*, whose members are elected by the shareholders. The board of directors hires *corporate officers* and other employees to run the daily business operations of the corporation.

When an individual purchases a share of stock in a corporation, that person becomes a shareholder and thus an owner of the corporation. Unlike the members of a partnership, the body of shareholders can change constantly without affecting the continued existence of the corporation. A shareholder can sue the corporation, and the corporation can sue a shareholder. Also, under certain circumstances, a shareholder can sue on behalf of a corporation. The rights and duties of corporate personnel will be examined in detail in Chapter 26.

The shareholder form of business organization emerged in Europe at the end of the seventeenth century. These organizations, called *joint stock companies,* frequently collapsed because their organizers absconded with the funds or proved to be incompetent. Because of this history of fraud and collapse, organizations resembling corporations were initially regarded with suspicion in the United States. Although several business corporations were formed after the Revolutionary War, the corporation did not come into common use for private business until the nineteenth century.

The Constitutional Rights of Corporations

A corporation is recognized as a "person" under state and federal law, and it enjoys many of the same rights and privileges that U.S. citizens enjoy. The Bill of Rights guarantees persons certain protections, and corporations are considered persons in most instances. Accordingly, a corporation as an entity has the same right of access to the courts as a natural person and can sue or be sued. It also has a right to due process before denial of life, liberty, or property, as well as freedom from unreasonable searches and seizures (see Chapter 6 for a discussion of searches and seizures in the business context) and from double jeopardy.

Under the First Amendment, corporations are entitled to freedom of speech. As we pointed out in Chapter 1, however, commercial speech (such as advertising) and political speech (such as contributions to political causes or candidates) receive significantly less protection than noncommercial speech.

Generally, a corporation is not entitled to claim the Fifth Amendment privilege against self-incrimination. Agents or officers of the corporation therefore cannot refuse to produce corporate records on the ground that it might incriminate them.[1] Additionally, the privileges and immunities clause of the U.S. Constitution (Article IV, Section 2) does not protect

corporations.[2] This clause requires each state to treat citizens of other states equally with respect to certain rights, such as access to the courts and travel rights. The clause does not apply to corporations because corporations are legal persons only, not natural citizens.

The Limited Liability of Shareholders

One of the key advantages of the corporate form is the limited liability of its owners (shareholders). Corporate shareholders normally are not personally liable for the obligations of the corporation beyond the extent of their investments. In certain limited situations, however, the "corporate veil" can be pierced and liability for the corporation's obligations extended to shareholders—a concept that will be explained later in this chapter. Additionally, to enable the firm to obtain credit, shareholders in small companies sometimes voluntarily assume personal liability, as guarantors, for corporate obligations.

Corporate Taxation

Corporate profits are taxed by various levels of government. Corporations can do one of two things with corporate profits—retain them or pass them on to shareholders in the form of **dividends.** The corporation normally receives no tax deduction for dividends distributed to shareholders. Dividends are again taxable (except when they represent distributions of capital) as income to the shareholder receiving them. This double-taxation feature of the corporation is one of its major disadvantages.

Profits that are not distributed are retained by the corporation. These **retained earnings,** if invested properly, will yield higher corporate profits in the future and thus cause the price of the company's stock to rise. Individual shareholders can then reap the benefits of these retained earnings in the capital gains they receive when they sell their shares.

As you will read later in this chapter, the consequences of a corporation's failure to pay taxes can be severe. The state can suspend corporate status until the taxes are paid, or it can dissolve a corporation for failing to pay taxes.

Holding Companies   In recent years, some U.S. corporations have been using holding companies to reduce—or at least defer—their U.S. income taxes. At its simplest, a **holding company** (sometimes referred to as a *parent company*) is a company whose business activity consists of holding shares in another company. Typically, the holding company is established in a low-tax or no-tax offshore jurisdiction, such as

---

1. *Braswell v. United States,* 487 U.S. 99, 108 S.Ct. 2284, 101 L.Ed. 98 (1988). A court might allow an officer or employee to assert the Fifth Amendment privilege against self-incrimination in only a few circumstances. See, for example, *In re Three Grand Jury Subpoenas Duces Tecum Dated January 29, 1999,* 191 F.3d 173 (2d Cir. 1999).

2. The clause also does not protect an unincorporated association. See *W. C. M. Window Co. v. Bernardi,* 730 F.2d 486 (7th Cir. 1984).

those shown in Exhibit 25–1. Among the best known are the Cayman Islands, Dubai, Hong Kong, Luxembourg, Monaco, and Panama.

Offshore Low-Tax Jurisdictions   Sometimes, a major U.S. corporation sets up an investment holding company in a low-tax offshore environment. The corporation then transfers its cash, bonds, stocks, and other investments to the holding company. In general, any profits received by the holding company on these investments are taxed at the rate of the off-shore jurisdiction in which the company is registered, not the rates applicable to the parent company or its shareholders in their country of residence. Thus, deposits of cash, for example, may earn interest that is taxed at only a minimal rate. Once the profits are brought "onshore," though, they are taxed at the federal corporate income tax rate, and any payments received by the shareholders are also taxable at the full U.S. rates.

The use of offshore holding companies and other methods of reducing tax liability attracted criticism in 2008 when Congress reported that a study by the Government Accountability Office (GAO) found that roughly two-thirds of U.S. corporations paid no federal income taxes between 1998 and 2005. Nevertheless, it is clear that those who run corporations have a duty to minimize (legally, of course) taxes owed by the corporation and by its shareholders.

Torts and Criminal Acts

A corporation is liable for the torts committed by its agents or officers within the course and scope of their employment. This principle applies to a corporation exactly as it applies to the ordinary agency relationships discussed in Chapter 22. It follows the doctrine of *respondeat superior*.

Under modern criminal law, a corporation may be held liable for the criminal acts of its agents and employees, provided the punishment is one that can be applied to the corporation. Although corporations cannot be imprisoned, they can be fined. (Of course, corporate directors and officers can be imprisoned, and in recent years, many have faced criminal penalties for their own actions or for the actions of employees under their supervision.)

Recall from Chapter 6 that the U.S. Sentencing Commission created standardized sentencing guidelines for federal crimes. The commission created specific sentencing guidelines for crimes committed by corporate employees

EXHIBIT 25–1 Offshore Low-Tax Jurisdictions

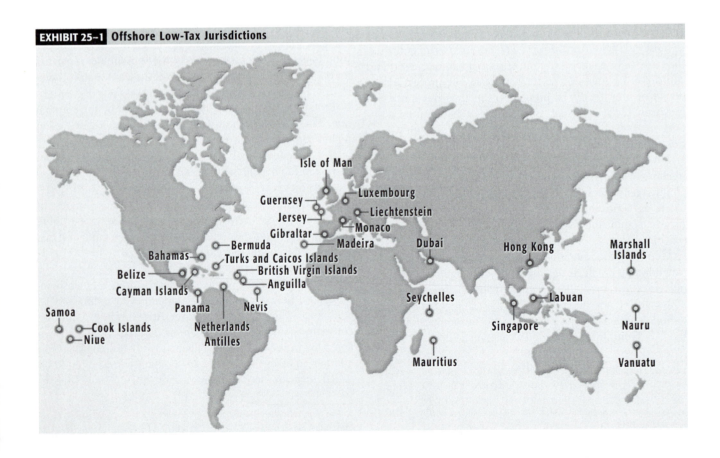

(white-collar crimes) that became effective in 2004.[3] The net effect of the guidelines has been a significant increase in criminal penalties for crimes committed by corporate person-

nel. Penalties depend on such factors as the seriousness of the offense, the amount involved, and the extent to which top company executives are implicated. Corporate lawbreakers can face fines amounting to hundreds of millions of dollars, though the guidelines allow judges to impose less severe penalties in certain circumstances.

The question in the following case was whether a corporation could be convicted for its employee's criminal negligence.

---

[3]. Note that the Sarbanes-Oxley Act of 2002, discussed in Chapter 3, stiffened the penalties for certain types of corporate crime and ordered the U.S. Sentencing Commission to revise the sentencing guidelines accordingly.

CASE 25.1 **Commonwealth v. Angelo Todesca Corp.**

Supreme Judicial Court of Massachusetts, 446 Mass. 128, 842 N.E.2d 930 (2006).
www.findlaw.com/11stategov/ma/maca.html[a]

FACTS Brian Gauthier worked as a truck driver for Angelo Todesca Corporation, a trucking and paving company. During 2000, Gauthier drove a ten-wheel tri-axle dump truck, which was designated as AT-56. Angelo's safety manual required its trucks to be equipped with back-up alarms, which were to sound automatically whenever the vehicles were in reverse gear. In November, Gauthier discovered that AT-56's alarm was missing. Angelo ordered a new alarm. Meanwhile, Gauthier continued to drive AT-56. On December 1, Angelo assigned Gauthier to haul asphalt to a work site in Centerville, Massachusetts. At the site, as Gauthier backed up AT-56 to dump its load, he struck a police officer who was directing traffic through the site and facing away from the truck. The officer died of his injuries. The commonwealth of Massachusetts charged Gauthier and Angelo in a Massachusetts state court with, among other wrongful acts, vehicular homicide. Angelo was convicted and fined $2,500. On Angelo's appeal, a state intermediate appellate court reversed Angelo's conviction. The state appealed to the Massachusetts Supreme Judicial Court, the state's highest court.

ISSUE Can a corporation be convicted for its employee's criminal negligence?

DECISION Yes. The Massachusetts Supreme Judicial Court affirmed Angelo's conviction.

a. In the "Supreme Court Opinions" section, in the "2006" row, click on "March." When that page opens, scroll to the name of the case and click on its docket number to access the opinion.

REASON The court identified three elements required to prove a corporation guilty of a criminal offense: (1) an individual commits a criminal offense; (2) at the time of commission, the individual is engaged in corporate business; and (3) the corporation vested the individual with the authority to engage in that business on its behalf. The focus in this case was on the first element, with the defendant arguing that a "corporation" could not be guilty of vehicular homicide because it cannot "operate" a vehicle. The court recognized that a corporation is not a "living person" but pointed out that it can act through its agents, which may include its employees. The court reasoned that if an employee commits a crime "while engaged in corporate business that the employee has been authorized to conduct," a corporation can be held liable for the crime. The defendant also contended that operating a truck without a back-up alarm is not a crime. The court conceded this point but explained that "the criminal conduct was Gauthier's negligent operation of the defendant's truck, resulting in the victim's death."

 WHY IS THIS CASE IMPORTANT? *Other states' courts that have considered the question at issue in this case have concluded that a corporation may be criminally liable for vehicular homicide under those states' statutes. This was the first case in which Massachusetts state courts ruled on the question under a Massachusetts statute.*

Corporate Classification

Corporations can be classified in several ways. The classification of a corporation normally depends on its location, purpose, and ownership characteristics.

Domestic, Foreign, and Alien Corporations A corporation is referred to as a **domestic corporation** by its home state (the state in which it incorporates). A corporation formed in one state but doing business in another is referred to in the second state as a **foreign corporation**. A corporation formed in another country (say, Mexico) but doing business in the United States is referred to in the United States as an **alien corporation.**

A corporation does not have an automatic right to do business in a state other than its state of incorporation. In some instances, it must obtain a *certificate of authority* in any state in which it plans to do business. Once the certificate has been issued, the corporation generally can exercise in that state all of the powers conferred on it by its home state. If a foreign corporation does business in a state without obtaining a certificate of authority, the state can impose substantial fines and sanctions on the corporation, and sometimes even on its officers, directors, or agents. Note that most state statutes specifically exempt certain activities, such as soliciting orders via the Internet, from what is considered doing business within the state. Thus, a foreign corporation normally does not need a certificate of authority to sell goods or services via the Internet or by U.S. mail.

Public and Private Corporations A public corporation is one formed by the government to meet some political or governmental purpose. Cities and towns that incorporate are common examples. In addition, many federal government organizations, such as the U.S. Postal Service, the Tennessee Valley Authority, and AMTRAK, are public corporations. Note that a public corporation is not the same as a *publicly held* corporation (often called a *public company*). A publicly held corporation is any corporation whose shares are publicly traded in securities markets, such as the New York Stock Exchange or the over-the-counter market.

In contrast to public corporations (*not* public companies), private corporations are created either wholly or in part for private benefit. Most corporations are private. Although they may serve a public purpose, as a public electric or gas utility does, they are owned by private persons rather than by the government.[4]

Nonprofit Corporations Corporations formed for purposes other than making a profit are called *nonprofit* or *not-for-profit* corporations. Private hospitals, educational institutions, charities, and religious organizations, for example, are frequently organized as nonprofit corporations. The nonprofit corporation is a convenient form of organization that allows various groups to own property and to form contracts without exposing the individual members to personal liability.

Close Corporations Most corporate enterprises in the United States fall into the category of close corporations. A **close corporation** is one whose shares are held by members of a family or by relatively few persons. Close corporations are also referred to as *closely held, family,* or *privately held* corporations. Usually, the members of the small group constituting a close corporation are personally known to one another. Because the number of shareholders is so small, there is no trading market for the shares.

In practice, a close corporation is often operated like a partnership. Some states have enacted special statutory provisions that apply to close corporations. These provisions expressly permit close corporations to depart significantly from certain formalities required by traditional corporation law.

Additionally, a provision added to the RMBCA in 1991 gives close corporations a substantial amount of flexibility in determining the rules by which they will operate [RMBCA 7.32]. If all of the shareholders of a corporation agree in writing, the corporation can operate without directors, bylaws, annual or special shareholders' or directors' meetings, stock certificates, or formal records of shareholders' or directors' decisions.[5]

Management of Close Corporations. A close corporation has a single shareholder or a closely knit group of shareholders, who usually hold the positions of directors and officers. Management of a close corporation resembles that of a sole proprietorship or a partnership. As a corporation, however, the firm must meet all specific legal requirements set forth in state statutes.

To prevent a majority shareholder from dominating a close corporation, the corporation may require that more than a simple majority of the directors approve any action taken by the board. Typically, this would apply only to extraordinary actions, such as changing the amount of dividends or dismissing an employee-shareholder, and not to ordinary business decisions.

Transfer of Shares in Close Corporations. By definition, a close corporation has a small number of shareholders. Thus, the transfer of one shareholder's shares to someone else can cause serious management problems. The other shareholders may find themselves required to share control with someone they do not know or like.

■EXAMPLE 25.1 Three brothers, Terry, Damon, and Henry Johnson, are the only shareholders of Johnson's Car Wash, Inc. Terry and Damon do not want Henry to sell his shares to

---

4. The United States Supreme Court first recognized the property rights of private corporations and clarified the distinction between public and private corporations in the landmark case *Trustees of Dartmouth College v. Woodward,* 17 U.S. (4 Wheaton) 518, 4 L.Ed. 629 (1819).

5. Shareholders cannot agree, however, to eliminate certain rights of shareholders, such as the right to inspect corporate books and records or the right to bring *derivative actions* (lawsuits on behalf of the corporation—see Chapter 26).

an unknown third person. To avoid this situation, the corporation could restrict the transferability of shares to outside persons. Shareholders could be required to offer their shares to the corporation or the other shareholders before selling them to an outside purchaser. In fact, a few states have statutes that prohibit the transfer of close corporation shares unless certain persons—including shareholders, family members, and the corporation—are first given the opportunity to purchase the shares for the same price. ■

Control of a close corporation can also be stabilized through the use of a *shareholder agreement*. A shareholder agreement can provide that when one of the original shareholders dies, her or his shares of stock in the corporation will be divided in such a way that the proportionate holdings of the survivors, and thus their proportionate control, will be maintained. Courts are generally reluctant to interfere with private agreements, including shareholder agreements.

Misappropriation of Close Corporation Finances. Sometimes, a majority shareholder in a close corporation takes advantage of her or his position to engage in misappropriation of company funds. In so doing, this shareholder clearly injures the minority shareholders. In such situations, possible remedies include many of those available to shareholders of regular corporations, including an appraisal of the minority shareholders' shares. In the following case, two wronged minority shareholders pursued an additional remedy.

CASE 25.2   **Williams v. Stanford**

District Court of Appeal of Florida, First District, 977 So.2d 722 (2008).

FACTS Two brothers, Paul and James Williams, together held 30 percent of the stock in Brown and Standard (B&S), Inc., a construction company. John Stanford owned the other 70 percent of the close corporation shares. The Williams brothers worked for B&S for five years when they became suspicious of Stanford's financial management. Stanford reported net losses for the company. The brothers asked to see the B&S books and were fired. Later, it was shown that Stanford had misappropriated at least $250,000 in B&S funds for his personal use. The Williams brothers brought a *shareholder's derivative suit* (see Chapter 26) on behalf of B&S, naming Stanford as the defendant and accusing him of breach of fiduciary duty. Before trial, Stanford resigned from B&S and closed the company. He gave the assets and liabilities of B&S to a new company he formed and owned, J. C. Stanford & Sons. He offered the Williams brothers $25,000 each for their stock in B&S. They responded with a request for $125,000 each. The trial court held that by law the Williams brothers, by making a counteroffer, gave up their rights to bring a suit against the company. Hence, the court granted summary judgment to Stanford. The Williams brothers appealed.

ISSUE If the majority shareholder in a close corporation was misappropriating and mismanaging corporate funds, can minority shareholders seek to rescind the transfer of corporate assets in addition to appraisal rights?

DECISION Yes. The appeals court reversed in favor of the Williams brothers, holding that they were entitled to a trial to determine if they could prove abuse of the company by Stanford. Although this did not follow the usual procedure for appraisal of minority shares, given the strong suspicion of fraud in this instance, the court was willing to allow for greater review.

REASON The minority shareholders claimed that their shares were worth more than the $25,000 Stanford offered. When dissenting shareholders seek more than the appraisal of their shares in the wake of dubious transactions, the courts must balance the principle that an adequate remedy should exist for the shareholder against the consideration that courts should not become bogged down in a wide range of disputes about the fairness of cash-out prices offered to minority shareholders. When shareholders point to specific acts of self-dealing or misrepresentation, they are entitled to equitable remedies beyond the normal appraisal option that dissenting shareholders must accept.

 FOR CRITICAL ANALYSIS—Ethical Consideration *Was it acceptable for the Williams brothers to demand $125,000 each for their shares? Why or why not?*

■

S Corporations   A close corporation that meets the qualifying requirements specified in Subchapter S of the Internal Revenue Code can operate as an **S corporation.** If a corporation has S corporation status, it can avoid the imposition of income taxes at the corporate level while retaining many of the advantages of a corporation, particularly limited liability.

Qualification Requirements for S Corporations.   Among the numerous requirements for S corporation status, the following are the most important:

1 The corporation must be a domestic corporation.

2 The corporation must not be a member of an affiliated group of corporations.

3 The shareholders of the corporation must be individuals, estates, or certain trusts. Partnerships and nonqualifying trusts cannot be shareholders. Corporations can be shareholders under certain circumstances.

4 The corporation must have no more than one hundred shareholders.

5 The corporation must have only one class of stock, although all shareholders do not have to have the same voting rights.

6 No shareholder of the corporation may be a nonresident alien.

Benefits of S Corporations.   At times, it is beneficial for a regular corporation to elect S corporation status. Benefits include the following:

1 When the corporation has losses, the S election allows the shareholders to use the losses to offset other taxable income.

2 When the shareholder's tax bracket is lower than the corporation's tax bracket, the S election causes the corporation's pass-through net income to be taxed in the shareholder's bracket (because it is taxed as personal income). This is particularly attractive when the corporation wants to accumulate earnings for some future business purpose.

Because of these tax benefits, many close corporations have opted for S corporation status. Today, however, the limited liability company and the limited liability partnership (both discussed in Chapter 24) offer similar advantages plus additional benefits, including more flexibility in forming and operating the business. Hence, the S corporation is losing some of its significance.

Professional Corporations   Professionals such as physicians, lawyers, dentists, and accountants can incorporate. Professional corporations are typically identified by the letters S.C. (service corporation), P.C. (professional corporation), or P.A. (professional association). In general, the laws governing professional corporations are similar to those governing ordinary business corporations, but three basic areas of liability deserve special attention.

First, some courts may, for liability purposes, regard the professional corporation as a partnership in which each partner can be held liable for any malpractice liability incurred by the others within the scope of the business. The reason for this rule is that professionals, in contrast to shareholders in other types of corporations, should not be allowed to avoid liability for their wrongful acts simply by virtue of incorporating. Second, in many states, professional persons are liable not only for their own negligent acts, but also for the misconduct of any person under their direct supervision who is rendering services on behalf of the corporation. Third, a shareholder in a professional corporation is generally protected from contractual liability and cannot be held liable for the torts—other than malpractice or a breach of duty to clients or patients— that are committed by other professionals at the firm.

Corporate Powers

When a corporation is created, the express and implied powers necessary to achieve its purpose also come into existence. The express powers of a corporation are found in its **articles of incorporation** (a document filed with the state that contains information about the corporation, including its organization and functions), in the law of the state of incorporation, and in the state and federal constitutions.

Corporate **bylaws,** which are internal rules of management adopted by the corporation at its first organizational meeting, also establish the express powers of the corporation. Because state corporation statutes frequently provide default rules that apply if the company's bylaws are silent on an issue, it is important that the bylaws set forth the specific operating rules of the corporation. In addition, after the bylaws are adopted, the corporation's board of directors will pass resolutions that also grant or restrict corporate powers.

The following order of priority is used when conflicts arise among documents involving corporations:

1 The U.S. Constitution.

2 State constitutions.

3 State statutes.

4 The articles of incorporation.

5 Bylaws.

6 Resolutions of the board of directors.

Implied Powers   Certain implied powers arise when a corporation is created. Barring express constitutional, statutory, or other prohibitions, the corporation has the implied power to perform all acts reasonably appropriate and necessary to accomplish its corporate purposes. For this reason, a corporation has the implied power to borrow funds within certain limits, to lend funds, and to extend credit to those with whom it has a legal or contractual relationship.

To borrow funds, the corporation acts through its board of directors to authorize the loan. Most often, the president or chief executive officer of the corporation will execute the necessary papers on behalf of the corporation. In so doing, corporate officers have the implied power to bind the corporation in matters directly connected with the *ordinary* business affairs of the enterprise. There is a limit to what a corporate officer can do, though. A corporate officer does not have the authority to bind the corporation to an action that will greatly affect the corporate purpose or undertaking, such as the sale of substantial corporate assets.

Ultra Vires **Doctrine** The term *ultra vires* means "beyond the powers." In corporate law, acts of a corporation that are beyond its express and implied powers are *ultra vires* acts. Most cases dealing with *ultra vires* acts have involved contracts made for unauthorized purposes. **■EXAMPLE 25.2** Suarez is the chief executive officer of SOS Plumbing, Inc. He enters a contract with Carlini for the purchase of fifty cases of brandy. It is difficult to see how this contract is reasonably related to the conduct and furtherance of the corporation's stated purpose of providing plumbing installation and services. Hence, a court would probably find such a contract to be *ultra vires*. ■

Under Section 3.04 of the RMBCA, the shareholders can seek an injunction from a court to prevent (or stop) the corporation from engaging in *ultra vires* acts. The attorney general in the state of incorporation can also bring an action to obtain an injunction against the *ultra vires* transactions or to institute dissolution proceedings against the corporation on the basis of *ultra vires* acts. The corporation or its shareholders (on behalf of the corporation) can seek damages from the officers and directors who were responsible for the *ultra vires* acts.

CORPORATE FORMATION

Up to this point, we have discussed some of the general characteristics of corporations. We now examine the process by which corporations come into existence. Incorporating a business is much simpler today than it was twenty years ago, and many states allow businesses to incorporate online via the Internet.

Note that one of the most common reasons for creating a corporation is the need for additional capital to finance expansion. Many of the Fortune 500 companies were originally sole proprietorships or partnerships before converting to a corpo-

rate entity. A sole proprietor in need of funds can seek partners who will bring capital with them. Although a partnership may be able to secure more funds from potential lenders than the sole proprietor could, the amount is still limited. When a firm wants significant growth, simply increasing the number of partners can result in so many partners that the firm can no longer operate effectively. Therefore, incorporation may be the best choice for an expanding business organization because a corporation can obtain more capital by issuing shares of stock.

Promotional Activities

In the past, preliminary steps were taken to organize and promote the business prior to incorporating. Contracts were made with investors and others on behalf of the future corporation. Today, however, due to the relative ease of forming a corporation in most states, persons incorporating their business rarely, if ever, engage in preliminary promotional activities. Nevertheless, it is important for businesspersons to understand that they are personally liable for all preincorporation contracts made with investors, accountants, or others on behalf of the future corporation. This personal liability continues until the corporation assumes the preincorporation contracts by *novation* (discussed in Chapter 11).

■EXAMPLE 25.3 Jade Sorrel contracts with an accountant, Ray Cooper, to provide tax advice for a proposed corporation, Blackstone, Inc. Cooper provides the services to Sorrel, knowing that the corporation has not yet been formed. Once Blackstone, Inc., is formed, Cooper sends an invoice to the corporation and to Sorrel personally, but the bill is not paid. Because Sorrel is personally liable for the preincorporation contract, Cooper can file a lawsuit against Sorrel for breaching the contract for accounting services. Cooper cannot seek to hold Blackstone, Inc., liable unless he has entered into a novation contract with the corporation. ■

Incorporation Procedures

Exact procedures for incorporation differ among states, but the basic steps are as follows: (1) select a state of incorporation, (2) secure the corporate name by confirming its availability, (3) prepare the articles of incorporation, and (4) file the articles of incorporation with the secretary of state accompanied by payment of the specified fees. If the articles contain all of the information required by statute, the secretary of state stamps the articles "Filed," and the corporation comes into existence. These steps are discussed in more detail in the following subsections.

Selecting the State of Incorporation The first step in the incorporation process is to select a state in which to incorporate. Because state incorporation laws differ, individuals may look for the states that offer the most advantageous tax or incorporation provisions. Another consideration is the fee that a particular state charges to incorporate, as well as the annual fees and the fees for specific transactions (such as stock transfers).

Delaware has historically had the least restrictive laws and provisions that favor corporate management. Consequently, many corporations, including a number of the largest, have incorporated there. Delaware's statutes permit firms to incorporate in that state and conduct business and locate their operating headquarters elsewhere. Most other states now permit this as well. Note, though, that closely held corporations, particularly those of a professional nature, generally incorporate in the state where their principal shareholders live and work. For reasons of convenience and cost, businesses often choose to incorporate in the state in which the corporation's business will primarily be conducted.

Securing the Corporate Name   The choice of a corporate name is subject to state approval to ensure against duplication or deception. State statutes usually require that the secretary of state run a check on the proposed name in the state of incorporation. Some states require that the persons incorporating a firm, at their own expense, run a check on the proposed name, which can often be accomplished via Internet-based services. Once cleared, a name can be reserved for a short time, for a fee, pending the completion of the articles of incorporation. All corporate statutes require the corporation name to include the word *Corporation, Incorporated, Company,* or *Limited,* or abbreviations of these terms.

A new corporation's name cannot be the same as (or deceptively similar to) the name of an existing corporation doing business within the state. The name should also be one that can be used as the business's Internet domain name. **■EXAMPLE 25.4** If an existing corporation is named Digital Synergy, Inc., you cannot choose the name Digital Synergy Company because that name is deceptively similar to the first. The state will be unlikely to allow the corporate name because it could impliedly transfer a part of the goodwill established by the first corporate user to the second corporation. In addition, you would not want to choose the name Digital Synergy Company because you would be unable to acquire an Internet domain name using the name of the business. **■**

Note that if a future firm contemplates doing business in other states—or over the Internet—those incorporating it also need to check on existing corporate names in those states as well. Otherwise, if the firm does business under a name that is the same as or deceptively similar to an existing company's name, it may be liable for trade name infringement.

PREVENTING LEGAL DISPUTES

Be cautious when choosing a corporate name. Recognize that even if a state does not require the incorporator to run a name check, doing so can help prevent future disputes. Many states provide online search capabilities, but these searches are usually limited and will only compare the proposed name to the names of active corporations within that state. Trade name disputes, however, may also arise if you use a business name that is deceptively similar to the name of a partnership or limited liability company. Disputes are even more likely to arise among online firms. Always check on the availability of a particular domain name before selecting a corporate name. It pays to be overly cautious and incur some additional cost to hire a professional to conduct a name search.

■

Preparing the Articles of Incorporation   The primary document needed to incorporate a business is the *articles of incorporation.*[6] As mentioned earlier, the articles include basic information about the corporation and serve as a primary source of authority for its future organization and business functions. The person or persons who execute (sign) the articles are called *incorporators.* Generally, the articles of incorporation *must* include the following information [RMBCA 2.02]:

1 The name of the corporation.

2 The number of shares the corporation is authorized to issue.

3 The name and address of the corporation's initial registered agent.

4 The name and address of each incorporator.

In addition, the articles *may* set forth other information, such as the names and addresses of the initial board of directors, the duration and purpose of the corporation, a par value of shares of the corporation, and any other information pertinent to the rights and duties of the corporation's shareholders and directors. Articles of incorporation vary widely depending on the size and type of corporation and the jurisdiction. Frequently, the articles do not provide much detail about the firm's operations, which are spelled out in the company's bylaws.

Shares of the Corporation.   The articles must specify the number of shares of stock authorized for issuance. For

---

6. For sample articles of incorporation, go to **www.coollawyer.com/webfront/ bizfilings/sample_articles_of_incorporation.php.**

instance, a company might state that the aggregate number of shares that the corporation has the authority to issue is five thousand. Large corporations often state a par value of each share, such as $20 per share, and specify the various types or classes of stock authorized for issuance (see the discussion of *common* and *preferred stock* later in this chapter). Sometimes, the articles set forth the capital structure of the corporation and other relevant information concerning equity, shares, and credit.

Registered Office and Agent. The corporation must indicate the location and address of its registered office within the state. Usually, the registered office is also the principal office of the corporation. The corporation must also give the name and address of a specific person who has been designated as an *agent* and who can receive legal documents (such as orders to appear in court) on behalf of the corporation.

Incorporators. Each incorporator must be listed by name and must indicate an address. The incorporators need not have any interest at all in the corporation, and sometimes signing the articles is their only duty. Many states do not have residency or age requirements for incorporators. States vary on the required number of incorporators; it can be as few as one or as many as three. Incorporators frequently participate in the first organizational meeting of the corporation.

Duration and Purpose. A corporation has perpetual existence unless stated otherwise in the articles. The owners may want to prescribe a maximum duration, however, after which the corporation must formally renew its existence.

The RMBCA does not require a specific statement of purpose to be included in the articles. A corporation can be formed for any lawful purpose. Some incorporators choose to include a general statement of purpose "to engage in any lawful act or activity," while others opt to specify the intended business activities ("to engage in the production and sale of agricultural products," for example). It is increasingly common for the articles to state that the corporation is organized for "any legal business," with no mention of specifics, to avoid the need for future amendments to the corporate articles. The trend toward general statements of corporate purpose also means that corporations today are less likely to be accused of engaging in *ultra vires* acts.

Internal Organization. The articles can describe the internal management structure of the corporation, although this is usually included in the bylaws adopted after the corporation is formed. The articles of incorporation commence the corporation; the bylaws are formed after commencement by the board of directors. Bylaws cannot conflict with

the incorporation statute or the articles of incorporation [RMBCA 2.06].

Under the RMBCA, shareholders may amend or repeal the bylaws. The board of directors may also amend or repeal the bylaws unless the articles of incorporation or provisions of the incorporation statute reserve this power to the shareholders exclusively [RMBCA 10.20]. Typical bylaw provisions describe such matters as voting requirements for shareholders, the election of the board of directors, the methods of replacing directors, and the manner and time of holding shareholders' and board meetings (these corporate activities will be discussed in Chapter 26).

Filing the Articles with the State Once the articles of incorporation have been prepared, signed, and authenticated by the incorporators, they are sent to the appropriate state official, usually the secretary of state, along with the required filing fee. In most states, as noted previously, the secretary of state then stamps the articles as "Filed" and returns a copy of the articles to the incorporators. Once this occurs, the corporation officially exists. (Note that some states issue a *certificate of incorporation*, which is similar to articles of incorporation, representing the state's authorization for the corporation to conduct business. This procedure was typical under the unrevised MBCA.)

First Organizational Meeting to Adopt Bylaws

After incorporation, the first organizational meeting must be held. If the articles of incorporation named the initial board of directors, then the directors, by majority vote, call for the meeting to adopt the bylaws and complete the company's organization. If the articles did not name the directors (as is typical), then the incorporators hold the meeting to elect the directors, adopt bylaws, and complete the routine business of incorporation (authorizing the issuance of shares and hiring employees, for example). The business transacted depends on the requirements of the state's incorporation statute, the nature of the corporation, the provisions made in the articles, and the desires of the incorporators. Adoption of bylaws—the internal rules of management for the corporation—is usually the most important function of this meeting. As mentioned earlier, the shareholders, directors, and officers must abide by the bylaws in conducting corporate business.

CORPORATE STATUS

The procedures for incorporation are very specific. If they are not followed precisely, others may be able to challenge the existence of the corporation. Errors in the incorporation procedures might become important when, for example, a third party who is attempting to enforce a contract or bring suit for a tort injury learns of them. On the basis of improper incorporation, the plaintiff could attempt to hold the would-be shareholders personally liable. Additionally, when the corporation seeks to enforce a contract against a defaulting party, that party may be able to avoid liability on the ground of a defect in the incorporation procedure.

To prevent injustice, courts will sometimes attribute corporate status to an improperly formed corporation by holding it to be a *de jure* corporation or a *de facto* corporation. Occasionally, a corporation may be held to exist by estoppel. Additionally, in certain circumstances involving abuse of the corporate form, a court may disregard the corporate entity and hold the shareholders personally liable.

De Jure and De Facto Corporations

If a corporation has substantially complied with all conditions precedent to incorporation, the corporation is said to have *de jure* (rightful and lawful) existence. In most states and under the RMBCA, the secretary of state's filing of the articles of incorporation is conclusive proof that all mandatory statutory provisions have been met [RMBCA 2.03(b)]. Because a *de jure* corporation is one that is properly formed, neither the state nor a third party can attack its existence.[7]

Sometimes, there is a defect in complying with statutory mandates—for example, the corporation failed to hold an organizational meeting. Under these circumstances, the corporation may have *de facto* (actual) status, meaning that it will be treated as a legal corporation despite the defect in its formation. A corporation with *de facto* status can be challenged only by the state, not by third parties. In other words, the shareholders of a *de facto* corporation are still protected by limited liability (provided they are unaware of the defect). The following elements are required for *de facto* status:

1 There must be a state statute under which the corporation can be validly incorporated.

2 The parties must have made a good faith attempt to comply with the statute.

3 The enterprise must already have undertaken to do business as a corporation.

Corporation by Estoppel

If a business association holds itself out to others as being a corporation but has made no attempt to incorporate, the firm normally will be estopped (prevented) from denying corporate status in a lawsuit by a third party. This usually occurs when a third party contracts with an entity that claims to be a corporation but has not filed articles of incorporation—or contracts with a person claiming to be an agent of a corporation that does not in fact exist. When the third party brings a suit naming the so-called corporation as the defendant, the association may not escape liability on the ground that no corporation exists. When justice requires, the courts treat an alleged corporation as if it were an actual corporation for the purpose of determining the rights and liabilities of its officers and directors involved in a particular situation. A corporation by estoppel is thus determined by the situation. Recognition of its corporate status does not extend beyond the resolution of the problem at hand.

Piercing the Corporate Veil

Occasionally, the owners use a corporate entity to perpetrate a fraud, circumvent the law, or in some other way accomplish an illegitimate objective. In these situations, the court will ignore the corporate structure by **piercing the corporate veil** and exposing the shareholders to personal liability. Generally, when the corporate privilege is abused for personal benefit or when the corporate business is treated so carelessly that the corporation and the controlling shareholder are no longer separate entities, the court will require the owner to assume personal liability to creditors for the corporation's debts.

In short, when the facts show that great injustice would result from the use of a corporation to avoid individual responsibility, a court of equity will look behind the corporate structure to the individual shareholder. The following are some of the factors that frequently cause the courts to pierce the corporate veil:

1 A party is tricked or misled into dealing with the corporation rather than the individual.

2 The corporation is set up never to make a profit or always to be insolvent, or it is too "thinly" capitalized—that is, it has insufficient capital at the time of formation to meet its prospective debts or other potential liabilities.

3 Statutory corporate formalities, such as holding required corporation meetings, are not followed.

4 Personal and corporate interests are **commingled** (mixed together) to such an extent that the corporation has no separate identity.

The potential for corporate assets to be used for personal benefit is especially great in a close corporation, in which the shares are held by a single person or by only a few individuals, usually family members. In such a situation, the separate

---

7. There is an exception: a few states allow state authorities, in a *quo warranto* proceeding, to bring an action against the corporation for noncompliance with a necessary condition *subsequent* to incorporation. This might occur if the corporation fails to file annual reports, for example.

status of the corporate entity and the sole shareholder (or family-member shareholders) must be carefully preserved. Certain practices invite trouble for the one-person or family-owned corporation: the commingling of corporate and personal funds, the failure to hold board of directors' meetings and record the minutes, or the shareholders' continuous personal use of corporate property (for example, vehicles).

In the following case, when a close corporation's creditors sought payment of its debts, the owners took the small value in the business for themselves, filed a bankruptcy petition for the firm, and incorporated under a new name to continue the business. Could the court recover the business assets from the new corporation for distribution to the original firm's creditors?

CASE 25.3   In re Aqua Clear Technologies, Inc.

United States Bankruptcy Court, Southern District of Florida, 361 Bankr. 567 (2007).

FACTS Harvey and Barbara Jacobson owned Aqua Clear Technologies, Inc., a small Florida business that installed and serviced home water softening systems. Barbara was Aqua's president, and Sharon, the Jacobsons' daughter, was an officer, but neither participated in the business. Although Harvey controlled the day-to-day operations, he was not an Aqua officer, director, or employee, but an independent contractor in service to the company. Aqua had no compensation agreement with the Jacobsons. Instead, whenever Harvey decided that there were sufficient funds, they took funds out of the business for their personal expenses, including the maintenance of their home and payments for their cars, health-insurance premiums, and charges on their credit cards. In December 2004, Aqua filed a bankruptcy petition in a federal bankruptcy court. Three weeks later, Harvey incorporated Discount Water Services, Inc., and continued to service water softening systems for Aqua's customers. Discount appropriated Aqua's equipment and inventory without a formal transfer and advertised Aqua's phone number as Discount's own. Kenneth Welt, Aqua's trustee, initiated a proceeding against Discount, seeking, among other things, to recover Aqua's assets. The trustee contended that Discount was Aqua's "alter ego." (An *alter ego* is the double of something—in this case, the original company.)

ISSUE Can a firm's owners file for corporate bankruptcy and then open another corporation that engages in substantially the same business with the same equipment without paying the first corporation's debts?

DECISION No. The court issued a judgment against Discount, and in the trustee's favor, for $108,732.64, which represented the amount of the claims listed in Aqua's bankruptcy schedules. The court also agreed to add the administrative expenses, and all other claims allowed against Aqua, once those amounts were determined.

REASON The bankruptcy court pointed out that Aqua—the debtor—and Discount "were in substantially the same business. They used the same telephone number. They operated from the same business location. They serviced the same geographic area and many of the same customers." Furthermore, Aqua and Discount had identical officers and directors. Consequently, "the Court may presume fraud when a transfer occurs between two corporations controlled by the same officers and directors." The court then pointed out that Aqua had sent a letter to its health insurance carrier stating that it was simply changing its name to Discount Water Services, Inc. Most of the Jacobsons' actions were designed to interfere with the collection efforts of judgment creditors. "The bottom line question is whether each entity has run its own race, or whether there has been a relay-style passing of the baton from one to the other."

 FOR CRITICAL ANALYSIS—Global Consideration *If the scope of the Jacobsons' business had been global, should the court have issued a different judgment? Explain.*

CORPORATE FINANCING

Part of the process of corporate formation involves corporate financing. Corporations are financed by the issuance and sale of corporate securities. **Securities** (stocks and bonds) evidence the right to participate in earnings and the distribution of corporate property or the obligation to pay funds.

Stocks, or *equity securities,* represent the purchase of ownership in the business firm. **Bonds** (debentures), or *debt securities,* represent the borrowing of funds by firms (and governments). Of course, not all debt is in the form of debt securities. For example, some debt is in the form of accounts payable and notes payable, which typically are short-term debts. Bonds are simply a way for the corporation to split up its long-term debt so that it can market it more easily.

Bonds

Bonds are issued by business firms and by governments at all levels as evidence of the funds they are borrowing from investors. Bonds normally have a designated *maturity date*—the date when the principal, or face, amount of the bond is returned to the investor. They are sometimes referred to as *fixed-income securities* because their owners (that is, the creditors) receive fixed-dollar interest payments, usually semiannually, during the period of time prior to maturity.

Because debt financing represents a legal obligation on the part of the corporation, various features and terms of a particular bond issue are specified in a lending agreement called a **bond indenture.** A corporate trustee, often a commercial bank trust department, represents the collective well-being of all bondholders in ensuring that the corporation meets the terms of the bond issue. The bond indenture specifies the maturity date of the bond and the pattern of interest payments until maturity. The different types of corporate bonds are described in Exhibit 25–2.

Stocks

Issuing stocks is another way that corporations can obtain financing. The ways in which stocks differ from bonds are summarized in Exhibit 25–3. Basically, as mentioned, stocks represent ownership in a business firm, whereas bonds represent borrowing by the firm.

Exhibit 25–4 on page 534 summarizes the types of stocks issued by corporations. We look now at the two major types of stock—*common stock* and *preferred stock.*

Common Stock   The true ownership of a corporation is represented by **common stock.** Common stock provides a proportionate interest in the corporation with regard to (1) control, (2) earnings, and (3) net assets. A shareholder's interest is generally in proportion to the number of shares he or she owns out of the total number of shares issued.

Voting rights in a corporation apply to the election of the firm's board of directors and to any proposed changes in the ownership structure of the firm. For example, a holder of common stock generally has the right to vote in a decision on a proposed merger, as mergers can change the proportion of ownership. State corporation law specifies the types of actions for which shareholder approval must be obtained.

Firms are not obligated to return a principal amount per share to each holder of common stock because no firm can ensure that the market price per share of its common stock will not decline over time. The issuing firm also does not have to guarantee a dividend; indeed, some corporations never pay dividends.

Holders of common stock are investors who assume a *residual* position in the overall financial structure of a business. In terms of receiving payment for their investments, they are last in line. They are entitled to the earnings that are left after preferred stockholders, bondholders, suppliers, employees, and other groups have been paid. Once those groups are paid, however, the owners of common stock may be entitled to *all* the remaining earnings as dividends. (The board of directors normally is not under any duty to declare the remaining earnings as dividends, however.)

Preferred Stock   Preferred stock is stock with *preferences.* Usually, this means that holders of preferred stock have priority over holders of common stock as to dividends and as to payment on dissolution of the corporation. Holders of preferred stock may or may not have the right to vote.

EXHIBIT 25–2	Types of Corporate Bonds
Debenture bonds	Bonds for which no specific assets of the corporation are pledged as backing. Rather, they are backed by the general credit rating of the corporation, plus any assets that can be seized if the corporation allows the debentures to go into default.
Mortgage bonds	Bonds that pledge specific property. If the corporation defaults on the bonds, the bondholders can take the property.
Convertible bonds	Bonds that can be exchanged for a specified number of shares of common stock under certain conditions.
Callable bonds	Bonds that may be called in and the principal repaid at specified times or under conditions specified in the bonds when they are issued.

EXHIBIT 25–3 How Do Stocks and Bonds Differ?

STOCKS	BONDS
1. Stocks represent ownership.	1. Bonds represent debt.
2. Stocks (common) do not have a fixed dividend rate.	2. Interest on bonds must always be paid, whether or not any profit is earned.
3. Stockholders can elect the board of directors, which controls the corporation.	3. Bondholders usually have no voice in, or control over, management of the corporation.
4. Stocks do not have a maturity date; the corporation usually does not repay the stockholder.	4. Bonds have a maturity date, when the corporation is to repay the bondholder the face value of the bond.
5. All corporations issue or offer to sell stocks. This is the usual definition of a corporation.	5. Corporations do not necessarily issue bonds.
6. Stockholders have a claim against the property and income of a corporation after all creditors' claims have been met.	6. Bondholders have a claim against the property and income of a corporation that must be met *before* the claims of stockholders.

Preferred stock is not included among the liabilities of a business because it is equity. Like other equity securities, preferred shares have no fixed maturity date on which the firm must pay them off. Although firms occasionally buy back preferred stock, they are not legally obligated to do so. Holders of preferred stock are investors who have assumed a rather cautious position in their relationship to the corporation. They have a stronger position than common shareholders with respect to dividends and claims on assets, but they will not share in the full prosperity of the firm if it grows successfully over time. This is because the value of preferred shares will not rise as rapidly as that of common shares during a period of financial success. Preferred stockholders do receive fixed dividends periodically, however, and they may benefit to some extent from changes in the market price of the shares.

The return and the risk for preferred stock lie somewhere between those for bonds and those for common stock. Preferred stock is more similar to bonds than to common stock, even though preferred stock appears in the ownership section of the firm's balance sheet. As a result, preferred stock is often categorized with corporate bonds as a fixed-income security, even though the legal status is not the same.

Venture Capital and Private Equity Capital

As discussed, corporations traditionally obtain financing through issuing and selling securities (stocks and bonds) in the capital market. In reality, however, many investors do not want to purchase stock in a business that lacks a track record, and banks are generally reluctant to extend loans to high-risk enterprises. Numerous corporations fail because they are undercapitalized. Therefore, to obtain sufficient financing, many entrepreneurs seek alternative financing.

Venture Capital Start-up businesses and high-risk enterprises often obtain venture capital financing. **Venture capital** is capital provided by professional, outside investors (*venture capitalists*, usually groups of wealthy investors and investment banks) to new business ventures. Venture capital investments are high risk—the investors must be willing to lose their invested funds—but offer the potential for well-above-average returns at some point in the future.

To obtain venture capital financing, the start-up business typically gives up a share of its ownership to the venture capitalists. In addition to funding, venture capitalists may provide managerial and technical expertise, and nearly always are given some control over the new company's decisions. Many Internet-based companies, such as Google and Amazon, were initially financed by venture capital.

Private Equity Capital In recent years, private equity firms have been playing a larger role in corporate financing. These firms obtain their capital from wealthy investors in private markets—hence, the name *private equity*. The firms use their **private equity capital** to invest in existing—often, publicly traded—corporations. Usually, they buy an entire corporation and then reorganize it. Sometimes, divisions of the purchased company are sold off to pay down debt. Ultimately, the private equity firm may sell shares in the reorganized (and perhaps more profitable) company to the

EXHIBIT 25–4 Types of Stocks

Common stock	Voting shares that represent ownership interest in a corporation. Common stock has the lowest priority with respect to payment of dividends and distribution of assets on the corporation's dissolution.
Preferred stock	Shares of stock that have priority over common-stock shares as to payment of dividends and distribution of assets on dissolution. Dividend payments are usually a fixed percentage of the face value of the share.
Cumulative preferred stock	Required dividends not paid in a given year must be paid in a subsequent year before any common-stock dividends are paid.
Participating preferred stock	Stock entitling the owner to receive the preferred-stock dividend and additional dividends if the corporation has paid dividends on common stock.
Convertible preferred stock	Stock entitling the owners to convert their shares into a specified number of common shares either in the issuing corporation or, sometimes, in another corporation.
Redeemable, or callable, preferred stock	Preferred shares issued with the express condition that the issuing corporation has the right to repurchase the shares as specified.

public in an *initial public offering* (usually called an IPO—see Chapter 27). In this way, the private equity firm can make profits by selling its shares in the company to the public. When DaimlerChrysler wanted to sell its less-than-successful Chrysler division, it sold 80 percent of it to the private equity firm Cerberus Capital Management, LP.

MERGER AND CONSOLIDATION

Sometimes, a corporation extends its operations by combining with another corporation through a merger, a consolidation, a purchase of assets, or a purchase of a controlling interest in the other corporation. The terms *merger* and *consolidation* often are used interchangeably, but they refer to two legally distinct proceedings. The rights and liabilities of the corporation, its shareholders, and its creditors are the same for both, however.

Merger

A **merger** involves the legal combination of two or more corporations in such a way that only one of the corporations continues to exist. **■EXAMPLE 25.5** Corporation A and Corporation B decide to merge. They agree that A will absorb B. Therefore, on merging, B ceases to exist as a separate entity, and A continues as the *surviving corporation*. ■ Exhibit 25–5 graphically illustrates this process.

After the merger, A is recognized as a single corporation, possessing all the rights, privileges, and powers of itself and B. It automatically acquires all of B's property and assets without the necessity of formal transfer. Additionally, A becomes liable for all of B's debts and obligations. Finally, A's articles of incorporation are deemed amended to include any changes that are stated in the *articles of merger* (a document setting forth the terms and conditions of the merger that is filed with the secretary of state).

In a merger, the surviving corporation inherits the disappearing corporation's preexisting legal rights and obligations. For example, if the disappearing corporation had a right of

EXHIBIT 25–5 Merger

Corporation A and Corporation B decide to merge. They agree that A will absorb B, so after the merger, B no longer exists as a separate entity, and A continues as the surviving corporation.

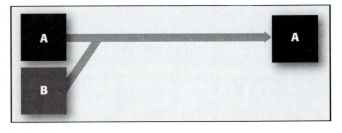

action against a third party, the surviving corporation can bring suit after the merger to recover the disappearing corporation's damages. Similarly, following a merger, a third party who had a right of action against the disappearing corporation normally will now have the right to bring an action against the successor (surviving) corporation.

Consolidation

In a **consolidation,** two or more corporations combine in such a way that each corporation ceases to exist and a new one emerges. ■**EXAMPLE 25.6** Corporation A and Corporation B consolidate to form an entirely new organization, Corporation C. In the process, A and B both terminate, and C comes into existence as an entirely new entity. Exhibit 25–6 graphically illustrates this process.

The results of a consolidation are similar to those of a merger—only one company remains—but it is an entirely new entity (the *consolidated corporation*). C is a new corporation and a single entity; A and B cease to exist. C inherits all of the rights, privileges, and powers previously held by A and B. Title to any property and assets owned by A and B passes to C without a formal transfer. C assumes liability for all debts and obligations owed by A and B. The *articles of consolidation* take the place of A's and B's original corporate articles and are thereafter regarded as C's corporate articles. ■

When a merger or a consolidation takes place, the surviving corporation or newly formed corporation will issue shares or pay some fair consideration to the shareholders of the corporation or corporations that cease to exist. True consolidations have become less common among for-profit corporations because it is often advantageous for one of the firms to survive. In contrast, nonprofit corporations and associations may prefer consolidation because it suggests a new beginning in which neither of the two initial entities is dominant.

EXHIBIT 25–6 Consolidation

Corporation A and Corporation B consolidate to form an entirely new organization, Corporation C. In the process, A and B terminate, and C comes into existence as an entirely new entity.

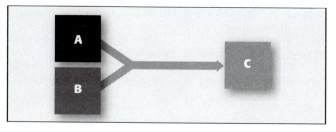

Share Exchange

In a *share exchange,* some or all of the shares of one corporation are exchanged for some or all of the shares of another corporation, but both corporations continue to exist. Share exchanges are often used to create holding companies (discussed earlier in this chapter). For example, UAL Corporation is a large holding company that owns United Airlines. If one corporation owns *all* of the shares of another corporation, it is referred to as the *parent corporation,* and the wholly owned company is the *subsidiary corporation.*

Merger, Consolidation, and Share Exchange Procedures

All states have statutes authorizing mergers, consolidations, and share exchanges for domestic (in-state) and foreign (out-of-state) corporations. The procedures vary somewhat among jurisdictions. In some states, a consolidation resulting in an entirely new corporation simply follows the initial incorporation procedures discussed earlier in this chapter, whereas other business combinations must follow the procedures outlined below.

The Revised Model Business Corporation Act (RMBCA) sets forth the following basic requirements [RMBCA 11.01–11.07]:

1 The board of directors of *each* corporation involved must adopt a plan of merger or share exchange.

2 The plan must specify any terms and conditions of the merger. It also must state the basis of valuing the shares of each merging corporation and how they will be converted into shares or other securities, cash, property, or other interests in another corporation.

3 The majority of the shareholders of *each* corporation must vote to approve the plan at a shareholders' meeting. If any class of stock is entitled to vote as a separate group, the majority of each separate voting group must approve the plan. Although RMBCA 11.04(e) requires only a simple majority of the shareholders entitled to vote once a quorum is present, frequently a corporation's articles of incorporation or bylaws require greater than a majority approval. In addition, some state statutes require the approval of two-thirds of the outstanding shares of voting stock, and others require a four-fifths approval.

4 Once approved by the directors and the shareholders of both corporations, the surviving corporation files the plan (articles of merger, consolidation, or share exchange) with the appropriate official, usually the secretary of state.

5 When state formalities are satisfied, the state issues a certificate of merger to the surviving corporation or a certificate of consolidation to the newly consolidated corporation.

Short-Form Mergers

RMBCA 11.04 provides a simplified procedure for the merger of a substantially owned subsidiary corporation into its parent corporation. Under these provisions, a **short-form merger**—also referred to as a **parent-subsidiary merger**—can be accomplished *without* the approval of the shareholders of either corporation. The short-form merger can be used only when the parent corporation owns at least 90 percent of the outstanding shares of each class of stock of the subsidiary corporation. Once the board of directors of the parent corporation approves the plan, it is filed with the state, and copies are sent to each shareholder of record in the subsidiary corporation.

Shareholder Approval

As mentioned, except in a short-form merger, the shareholders of both corporations must approve a merger or other plan of consolidation. Shareholders invest in a corporation with the expectation that the board of directors will manage the enterprise and make decisions on *ordinary* business matters. For *extraordinary* matters, normally both the board of directors and the shareholders must approve of the transaction.

Mergers and other combinations are extraordinary business matters, meaning that the board of directors must normally obtain the shareholders' approval and provide appraisal rights (discussed next). Amendments to the articles of incorporation and the dissolution of the corporation also generally require shareholder approval. Sometimes, a transaction can be structured in such a way that shareholder approval is not required, but if the shareholders challenge the transaction, a court might require shareholder approval. For this reason, the board of directors may request shareholder approval even when it might not be legally required.

Appraisal Rights

What if a shareholder disapproves of a merger or a consolidation but is outvoted by the other shareholders? The law recognizes that a dissenting shareholder should not be forced to become an unwilling shareholder in a corporation that is new or different from the one in which the shareholder originally invested. Dissenting shareholders therefore are given a statutory right to be paid the fair value of the number of shares they held on the date of the merger or consolidation. This right is referred to as the shareholder's **appraisal right.** So long as the transaction does not involve fraud or other illegal conduct, appraisal rights are the exclusive remedy for a shareholder who is dissatisfied with the price received for the stock.

Appraisal rights normally extend to regular mergers, consolidations, share exchanges, short-form mergers, and sales of substantially all of the corporate assets not in the ordinary course of business. Such rights can be particularly important in a short-form merger because the minority stockholders do not receive advance notice of the merger, the directors do not consider or approve it, and there is no vote. Appraisal rights are often the only recourse available to shareholders who object to parent-subsidiary mergers.

Each state establishes the procedures for asserting appraisal rights in that jurisdiction. Shareholders may lose their appraisal rights if they do not adhere precisely to the procedures prescribed by statute. When they lose the right to an appraisal, dissenting shareholders must go along with the transaction despite their objections.

PURCHASE OF ASSETS

When a corporation acquires all or substantially all of the assets of another corporation by direct purchase, the purchasing, or *acquiring*, corporation simply extends its ownership and control over more assets. Because no change in the legal entity occurs, the acquiring corporation usually does not need to obtain shareholder approval for the purchase.[8]

Both the U.S. Department of Justice and the Federal Trade Commission, however, have issued guidelines that significantly constrain and often prohibit mergers that could result from a purchase of assets.

Note that the corporation that is *selling* all of its assets is substantially changing its business position and perhaps its ability to carry out its corporate purposes. For that reason, the corporation whose assets are being sold must obtain approval from both its board of directors and its shareholders [RMBCA 12.02]. In most states and under RMBCA 13.02, dissenting shareholders of the selling corporation can demand appraisal rights.

Generally, a corporation that purchases the assets of another corporation is not automatically responsible for the liabilities of the selling corporation. Exceptions to this rule are made in the following circumstances:

1 When the purchasing corporation impliedly or expressly assumes the seller's liabilities.

2 When the sale transaction is actually a merger or consolidation of the two companies.[9]

---

8. Shareholder approval may be required in a few situations. If the acquiring corporation plans to pay for the assets with its own corporate stock but not enough authorized unissued shares are available, then shareholders must vote to approve an amendment to the corporate articles. Also, if the acquiring corporation is a company whose stock is traded on a national stock exchange and it will be issuing a significant number (at least 20 percent) of its outstanding shares, shareholders must approve.

9. See, for example, *New York v. National Service Industries, Inc.*, 460 F.3d 201 (2d Cir. 2006), applying New York law on *de facto* mergers.

3 When the purchasing corporation is merely a continuation of the selling corporation—that is, the buyer continues operating the seller's business in the same manner and retains the same personnel (same directors, officers, and shareholders).

4 When the sale is entered into fraudulently for the purpose of escaping liability.

In any of these situations, the acquiring corporation will be held to have assumed both the assets and the liabilities of the selling corporation.

PURCHASE OF STOCK

An alternative to the purchase of another corporation's assets is the purchase of a substantial number of the voting shares of its stock. This enables the acquiring corporation to gain control of the acquired corporation, or **target corporation.** The process of acquiring control over a corporation in this way is commonly referred to as a corporate **takeover.** The acquiring corporation deals directly with the target's shareholders by making a *tender offer.* A **tender offer** is a proposal to buy shares of stock from a target corporation's shareholders either for cash or for some type of corporate security of the acquiring company. The tender offer can be conditioned on the receipt of a specified number of outstanding shares by a certain date. As a means of inducing shareholders to accept the offer, the tender price offered generally is higher than the market price of the target's stock prior to the announcement of the tender offer. **■EXAMPLE 25.7** In the 2006 merger of AT&T and BellSouth, BellSouth shareholders received approximately $37.09 per share. This amounted to a 16 percent premium over the market price of the stock. ■ Federal securities laws strictly control the terms, duration, and circumstances under which most tender offers are made.

TERMINATION

The termination of a corporation's existence has two phases—dissolution and winding up. **Dissolution** is the legal death of the artificial "person" of the corporation. **Winding up** is the process by which corporate assets are *liquidated,* or converted into cash and distributed among creditors and shareholders according to specific rules of preference.[10]

Voluntary Dissolution

Dissolution can be brought about voluntarily by the directors and the shareholders. State incorporation statutes establish the required procedures for voluntarily dissolving a corporation. Basically, there are two possible methods: by the shareholders' unanimous vote to initiate dissolution proceedings,[11] or by a proposal of the board of directors that is submitted to the shareholders at a shareholders' meeting.

When a corporation is dissolved voluntarily, the corporation must file *articles of dissolution* with the state and notify its creditors of the dissolution. The corporation must also establish a date (at least 120 days after the date of dissolution) by which all claims against the corporation must be received [RMBCA 14.06].

Involuntary Dissolution

Because corporations are creatures of statute, the state can also dissolve a corporation in certain circumstances. The secretary of state or the state attorney general can bring an action to dissolve a corporation that has failed to pay its annual taxes or to submit required annual reports, for example [RMBCA 14.20]. A state court can also dissolve a corporation that has engaged in *ultra vires* acts or committed fraud or misrepresentation to the state during incorporation. Courts can also dissolve a corporation for mismanagement [RMBCA 14.30].

In some circumstances, a shareholder or a group of shareholders may petition a court to have the corporation dissolved. The RMBCA permits any shareholder to initiate an action for dissolution in any of the following circumstances [RMBCA 14.30]:

1 The directors are deadlocked in the management of corporate affairs, the shareholders are unable to break the deadlock, and the corporation is suffering irreparable injury as a result or is about to do so.

2 The acts of the directors or those in control of the corporation are illegal, oppressive, or fraudulent.

3 Corporate assets are being misapplied or wasted.

4 The shareholders are deadlocked in voting power and have failed, for a specified period (usually two annual meetings), to elect successors to directors whose terms have expired or would have expired with the election of successors.

As noted above, a court may dissolve a corporation if the controlling shareholders or directors have engaged in fraudulent, illegal, or oppressive conduct. **■EXAMPLE 25.8** Mt. Princeton Trout Club, Inc. (MPTC), was formed to own land

---

10. Some prefer to call this phase *liquidation,* but we use the term *winding up* to mean all acts needed to bring the legal and financial affairs of the business to an end, including liquidating the assets and distributing them among creditors and shareholders. See RMBCA 14.05.

11. Only some states allow shareholders to initiate corporation dissolution. See, for example, Delaware Code Annotated Title 8, Section 275(c).

in Colorado and provide fishing and other recreational benefits to its shareholders. The articles of incorporation prohibited MPTC from selling or leasing any of the property and assets of the corporation without the approval of a majority of the directors. Despite this provision, MPTC officers entered into leases and contracts to sell corporate property without even notifying the directors. When a shareholder, Sam Colt, petitioned for dissolution, the court dissolved MPTC based on a finding that its officers had engaged in illegal, oppressive, and fraudulent conduct.[12] ◼

---

12. *Colt v. Mt. Princeton Trout Club, Inc.*, 78 P.3d 1115 (Colo.App. 2003).

Winding Up

When dissolution takes place by voluntary action, the members of the board of directors act as trustees of the corporate assets. As trustees, they are responsible for winding up the affairs of the corporation for the benefit of corporate creditors and shareholders. This makes the board members personally liable for any breach of their fiduciary trustee duties.

When the dissolution is involuntary—or if board members do not wish to act as trustees—the court will appoint a *receiver* to wind up the corporate affairs. Courts may also appoint a receiver when shareholders or creditors can show that the board of directors should not be permitted to act as trustees of the corporate assets.

REVIEWING Corporate Formation, Financing, and Termination

William Sharp was the sole shareholder and manager of Chickasaw Club, Inc., an S corporation that operated a popular nightclub of the same name in Columbus, Georgia. Sharp maintained a corporate checking account but paid the club's employees, suppliers, and entertainers in cash out of the club's proceeds. Sharp owned the property on which the club was located. He rented it to the club but made mortgage payments out of the club's proceeds and often paid other personal expenses with Chickasaw corporate funds. At 12:45 A.M. on July 31, 2005, eighteen-year-old Aubrey Lynn Pursley, who was already intoxicated, entered the Chickasaw Club. A city ordinance prohibited individuals under the age of twenty-one from entering nightclubs, but Chickasaw employees did not check Pursley's identification to verify her age. Pursley drank more alcohol at Chickasaw and was visibly intoxicated when she left the club at 3:00 A.M. with a beer in her hand. Shortly afterward, Pursley lost control of her car, struck a tree, and was killed. Joseph Dancause, Pursley's

stepfather, filed a tort lawsuit in a Georgia state court against Chickasaw Club, Inc., and William Sharp, seeking damages. Using the information presented in the chapter, answer the following questions.

1 Under what theory might the court in this case make an exception to the limited liability of shareholders and hold Sharp personally liable for the damages? What factors would be relevant to the court's decision?

2 Suppose that Chickasaw's articles of incorporation failed to describe the corporation's purpose or management structure as required by state law. Would the court be likely to rule that Sharp is personally liable to Dancause on that basis?

3 Suppose that the club extended credit to its regular patrons in an effort to maintain a loyal clientele, although neither the articles of incorporation nor the corporate bylaws authorized this practice. Would the corporation likely have the power to engage in this activity? Explain.

4 How would the court classify the Chickasaw Club corporation—domestic or foreign, public or private?

TERMS AND CONCEPTS

alien corporation 524
appraisal right 536
articles of incorporation 526
bond 531
bond indenture 532
bylaws 526
close corporation 524
commingle 530

common stock 532
consolidation 535
corporation 520
dissolution 537
dividend 521
domestic corporation 523
foreign corporation 523
holding company 521

merger 534
parent-subsidiary merger 536
piercing the corporate veil 530
preferred stock 532
private equity capital 533
retained earnings 521
S corporation 526
securities 531

CHAPTER SUMMARY Corporate Formation, Financing, and Termination

Corporate Nature, Classification, and Powers
(See pages 520–527.)

A corporation is a legal entity distinct from its owners. Formal statutory requirements, which vary somewhat from state to state, must be followed in forming a corporation.

1. *Corporate parties*—The shareholders own the corporation. They elect a board of directors to govern the corporation. The board of directors hires corporate officers and other employees to run the daily business of the firm.

2. *Corporate taxation*—The corporation pays income tax on net profits; shareholders pay income tax on the disbursed dividends that they receive from the corporation (double-taxation feature).

3. *Torts and criminal acts*—The corporation is liable for the torts committed by its agents or officers within the course and scope of their employment (under the doctrine of *respondeat superior*). In some circumstances, a corporation can be held liable (and be fined) for the criminal acts of its agents and employees. In certain situations, corporate officers may be held personally liable for corporate crimes.

4. *Domestic, foreign, and alien corporations*—A corporation is referred to as a *domestic corporation* within its home state (the state in which it incorporates). A corporation is referred to as a *foreign corporation* by any state that is not its home state. A corporation is referred to as an *alien corporation* if it originates in another country but does business in the United States.

5. *Public and private corporations*—A public corporation is one formed by a government (for example, cities, towns, and public projects). A private corporation is one formed wholly or in part for private benefit. Most corporations are private corporations.

6. *Nonprofit corporations*—Corporations formed without a profit-making purpose (for example, charitable, educational, and religious organizations and hospitals).

7. *Close corporations*—Corporations owned by a family or a relatively small number of individuals. Transfer of shares is usually restricted, and the corporation cannot make a public offering of its securities.

8. *S corporations*—Small domestic corporations (must have no more than one hundred shareholders) that, under Subchapter S of the Internal Revenue Code, are given special tax treatment. These corporations allow shareholders to enjoy the limited legal liability of the corporate form but avoid its double-taxation feature (shareholders pay taxes on the income at personal income tax rates, and the S corporation is not taxed separately).

9. *Professional corporations*—Corporations formed by professionals (for example, doctors and lawyers) to obtain the benefits of incorporation (such as tax benefits and limited liability). In most situations, the professional corporation is treated like other corporations, but sometimes the courts will disregard the corporate form and treat the shareholders as partners.

10. *Express powers*—The express powers of a corporation are granted by the following laws and documents (listed according to their priority): federal constitution, state constitutions, state statutes, articles of incorporation, bylaws, and resolutions of the board of directors.

11. *Implied powers*—Barring express constitutional, statutory, or other prohibitions, the corporation has the implied power to do all acts reasonably appropriate and necessary to accomplish its corporate purposes.

12. *Ultra vires doctrine*—Any act of a corporation that is beyond its express or implied powers to undertake is an *ultra vires* act. The corporation (or shareholders on behalf of the corporation) may sue to enjoin or recover damages for *ultra vires* acts of corporate officers or directors.

(Continued)

CHAPTER SUMMARY	Corporate Formation, Financing, and Termination—Continued

Corporate Formation
(See pages 527–529.)
	1. *Promotional activities*—Preliminary promotional activities are rarely if ever taken today. A person who enters contracts with investors and others on behalf of the future corporation is personally liable on all preincorporation contracts. Liability remains until the corporation is formed and assumes the contract by novation.
	
	2. *Incorporation procedures*—Procedures for incorporation differ among states, but the basic steps are as follows: (a) select a state of incorporation, (b) secure the corporate name, (c) prepare the articles of incorporation, and (d) file the articles of incorporation with the secretary of state.
	  a. The articles of incorporation must include the corporate name, the number of shares of stock the corporation is authorized to issue, the registered office and agent, and the names and addresses of the incorporators.
	  b. The state's filing of the articles of incorporation (corporate charter) authorizes the corporation to conduct business.
	  c. The first organizational meeting is held after incorporation. The board of directors is elected, and other business is completed (for example, adopting bylaws and authorizing the issuance of shares).

Corporate Status (See pages 529–531.)	1. *De jure or de facto corporation*—If a corporation has been improperly incorporated, the courts will sometimes impute corporate status to the firm by holding that it is a *de jure* corporation (cannot be challenged by the state or third parties) or a *de facto* corporation (can be challenged by the state but not by third parties). 2. *Corporation by estoppel*—If a firm is neither a *de jure* nor a *de facto* corporation but represents itself to be a corporation and is sued as such by a third party, it may be held to be a corporation by estoppel. 3. *Disregarding the corporate entity*—When a corporate entity is used to perpetrate a fraud or another illegitimate purpose, courts may "pierce the corporate veil" and hold a shareholder or shareholders personally liable for a judgment against the corporation.
Corporate Financing—Bonds (See pages 531–532.)	Corporate bonds are securities representing *corporate debt*—money borrowed by a corporation. See Exhibit 25–2 on page 532 for a description of the various types of corporate bonds.
Corporate Financing—Stocks (See pages 532–534.)	Stocks are equity securities issued by a corporation that represent the purchase of ownership in the business firm. Exhibit 25–3 on page 533 describes how stocks differ from bonds, and Exhibit 25–4 on page 534 describes the various types of stocks issued by corporations, including the two main types—common stock and preferred stock. Sometimes, entrepreneurs seek alternative financing through venture capital or private equity capital.

Merger and Consolidation
(See pages 534–536.)
	1. *Merger*—The legal combination of two or more corporations, with the result that the surviving corporation acquires all the assets and obligations of the other corporation, which then ceases to exist.
	
	2. *Consolidation*—The legal combination of two or more corporations, with the result that each corporation ceases to exist and a new one emerges. The new corporation assumes all the assets and obligations of the former corporations.
	
	3. *Share exchange*—Some or all of the shares of one corporation are exchanged for some or all of the shares of another corporation, but both corporations continue to exist.
	
	4. *Procedure*—Determined by state statutes. Basic requirements are the following:
	  a. The board of directors of each corporation involved must approve the plan of merger, consolidation, or share exchange.
	  b. The shareholders of each corporation must approve the plan at a shareholders' meeting.

CHAPTER SUMMARY	Corporate Formation, Financing, and Termination–Continued
Merger and Consolidation– Continued	c. Articles of merger, consolidation, or share exchange (the plan) must be filed, usually with the secretary of state.
	d. The state issues a certificate of merger (or consolidation) to the surviving (or newly consolidated) corporation.
	5. *Short-form merger (parent-subsidiary merger)*—Possible when the parent corporation owns at least 90 percent of the outstanding shares of each class of stock of the subsidiary corporation.
	a. Shareholder approval is not required.
	b. The merger must be approved only by the board of directors of the parent corporation.
	c. A copy of the merger plan must be sent to each shareholder of record of the subsidiary corporation.
	d. The merger plan must be filed with the state.
	6. *Appraisal rights*—Rights of dissenting shareholders (given by state statute) to receive the *fair value* for their shares when a merger or consolidation takes place. If the shareholder and the corporation do not agree on the fair value, a court will determine it.
Purchase of Assets (See pages 536–537.)	A purchase of assets occurs when one corporation acquires all or substantially all of the assets of another corporation.
	1. *Acquiring corporation*—The acquiring (purchasing) corporation is not required to obtain shareholder approval; the corporation is merely increasing its assets, and no fundamental business change occurs.
	2. *Acquired corporation*—The acquired (purchased) corporation is required to obtain the approval of both its directors and its shareholders for the sale of its assets, because the sale will substantially change the corporation's business position.
Purchase of Stock (See page 537.)	By purchasing a substantial number of the voting shares of a firm (the target corporation), the acquiring corporation gains control of the acquired corporation—a process commonly referred to as a *takeover*. A takeover is typically accomplished through a *tender offer* in which the acquiring corporation seeks to purchase shares of stock directly from the target's shareholders.
Termination (See pages 537–538.)	The termination of a corporation involves the following two phases:
	1. *Dissolution*—The legal death of the artificial "person" of the corporation. Dissolution can be brought about voluntarily by the directors and shareholders or involuntarily by the state or through a court order.
	2. *Winding up (liquidation)*—The process by which corporate assets are converted into cash and distributed to creditors and shareholders according to specified rules of preference. May be supervised by members of the board of directors (when dissolution is voluntary) or by a receiver appointed by the court to wind up corporate affairs.

FOR REVIEW

Answers for the even-numbered questions in this **For Review** *section can be found on this text's accompanying Web site at* **www.cengage.com/blaw/fbl**. *Select "Chapter 25" and click on "For Review."*

1 What steps are involved in bringing a corporation into existence? Who is liable for preincorporation contracts?

2 What is the difference between a *de jure* corporation and a *de facto* corporation?

3 In what circumstances might a court disregard the corporate entity ("pierce the corporate veil") and hold the shareholders personally liable?

4 What are the steps of the merger or consolidation procedure?

5 What are two ways in which a corporation can be voluntarily dissolved? Under what circumstances might a corporation be involuntarily dissolved by state action?

QUESTIONS AND CASE PROBLEMS

HYPOTHETICAL SCENARIOS AND CASE PROBLEMS

25.1 Corporate Status. Three brothers inherited a small paper-supply business from their father, who had operated the business as a sole proprietorship. The brothers decided to incorporate under the name of Gomez Corp. and retained an attorney to draw up the necessary documents. The attorney drew up the papers and had the brothers sign them but neglected to file the articles of incorporation with the secretary of state's office. The brothers assumed that all necessary legal work had been completed, so they proceeded to do business as Gomez Corp. One day, a Gomez Corp. employee, while making a delivery to one of Gomez's customers, negligently ran a red light and caused an accident. Baxter, the driver of the other vehicle, was injured as a result and sued Gomez Corp. for damages. Baxter then learned that no state authorization had ever been issued to Gomez Corp., so he sued each of the brothers personally for damages. Can the brothers avoid personal liability for the tort of their employee? Explain.

25.2 Hypothetical Question with Sample Answer. Kora Nayenga and two business associates formed a corporation called Nayenga Corp. for the purpose of selling computer services. Kora, who owned 50 percent of the corporate shares, served as the corporation's president. Kora wished to obtain a personal loan from his bank for $250,000, but the bank required the note to be cosigned by a third party. Kora cosigned the note in the name of the corporation. Later, Kora defaulted on the note, and the bank sued the corporation for payment. The corporation asserted, as a defense, that Kora had exceeded his authority when he cosigned the note. Had he? Explain.

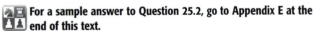
For a sample answer to Question 25.2, go to Appendix E at the end of this text.

25.3 Corporate Dissolution. Trans-System, Inc. (TSI), is an interstate trucking business. In 1994, to provide a source of well-trained drivers, TSI formed Northwestern Career Institute, Inc., a school for persons interested in obtaining a commercial driver's license. Tim Scott, who had worked for TSI since 1987, was named chief administrative officer and director. Scott, a Northwestern shareholder, disagreed with James Williams, the majority shareholder of both TSI and Northwestern, over four equipment leases between the two firms under which the sum of the payments exceeded the value of the equipment by not more than $3,000. Under four other leases, payments were $40,000 less than the value

of the equipment. Scott also disputed TSI's one-time use, for purposes unrelated to the driving school, of $125,000 borrowed by Northwestern. Scott was terminated in 1998. He filed a suit in a Washington state court against TSI, seeking, among other things, the dissolution of Northwestern on the ground that the directors of the two firms had acted in an oppressive manner and misapplied corporate assets. Should the court grant this relief? If not, what remedy might be appropriate? Discuss. [*Scott v. Trans-System, Inc.*, 148 Wash.2d 701, 64 P.3d 1 (2003)]

25.4 Case Problem with Sample Answer. Thomas Persson and Jon Nokes founded Smart Inventions, Inc., in 1991 to market household consumer products. The success of their first product, the Smart Mop, continued with later products, which were sold through infomercials and other means. Persson and Nokes were the firm's officers and equal shareholders, with Persson responsible for product development and Nokes operating the day-to-day activities. By 1998, they had become dissatisfied with each other's efforts. Nokes represented the firm as financially "dying," "in a grim state, . . . worse than ever," and offered to buy all of Persson's shares for $1.6 million. Persson accepted. On the day that they signed the agreement to transfer the shares, Smart Inventions began marketing a new product—the Tap Light, which was an instant success, generating millions of dollars in revenues. In negotiating with Persson, Nokes had intentionally kept the Tap Light a secret. Persson filed a suit in a California state court against Smart Inventions and others, asserting fraud and other claims. Under what principle might Smart Inventions be liable for Nokes's fraud? Is Smart Inventions liable in this case? Explain. [*Persson v. Smart Inventions, Inc.*, 125 Cal.App.4th 1141, 23 Cal.Rptr.3d 335 (2 Dist. 2005)]

After you have answered Problem 25.4, compare your answer with the sample answer given on the Web site that accompanies this text. Go to www.cengage.com/blaw/fbl, select "Chapter 25," and click on "Case Problem with Sample Answer."

25.5 Dissolution. Clara Mahaffey operated Mahaffey's Auto Salvage, Inc., in Dayton, Ohio, as a sole proprietorship. In 1993, Kenneth Stumpff and Mahaffey's son, Richard Harris, joined the firm. Stumpff ran the wrecker and bought the vehicles for salvage. Harris handled the day-to-day operations and the bookkeeping. They became the company's equal 50 percent shareholders on Mahaffey's death in 2002. Harris, who inherited the land on which the firm was located, increased the rent to $1,500 per month. Within two years of Mahaffey's death, and without consulting Stumpff, Harris raised the rent to $2,500. Stumpff's wife died, and he took a leave of absence, during which the company paid him $2,500 a month and provided health insurance. After two years, Harris stopped the payments, discontinued the health benefits, and fired Stumpff, threatening to call the police if he came on the premises. Stumpff withdrew $16,000 from the firm's account, leaving a balance of $113. Harris offered to buy Stumpff's interest in the business, but Stumpff refused and filed a suit in an Ohio state court against Harris. A state statute permits the dissolution of a corporation if the owners are deadlocked in its management. Should the court order the dissolution of Mahaffey's? Why or why not? [*Stumpff v. Harris*, __ N.E.2d __ (Ohio App. 2 Dist. 2006)]

25.6 Improper Incorporation. Denise Rubenstein and Christopher Mayor agreed to form Bayshore Sunrise Corp. (BSC) in New York to rent certain premises and operate a laundromat. BSC entered into a twenty-year commercial lease with Bay Shore Property Trust on April 15, 1999. Mayor signed the lease as the president of BSC. The next day—April 16—BSC's certificate of incorporation was filed with New York's secretary of state. Three years later, BSC defaulted on the lease, which resulted in its termination. Rubenstein and BSC filed a suit in a New York state court against Mayor, his brother-in-law Thomas Castellano, and Planet Laundry, Inc., claiming wrongful interference with a contractual relationship. The plaintiffs alleged that Mayor and Castellano conspired to squeeze Rubenstein out of BSC and arranged the default on the lease so that Mayor and Castellano could form and operate their own business, Planet Laundry, at the same address. The defendants argued that they could not be liable on the plaintiffs' claim because there had never been an enforceable lease—BSC lacked the capacity to enter into contracts on April 15. What theory might Rubenstein and BSC assert to refute this argument? Discuss. [*Rubenstein v. Mayor*, 41 A.D.3d 826, 839 N.Y.S.2d 170 (2 Dept. 2007)]

25.7 **A Question of Ethics.** *Mike Lyons incorporated Lyons Concrete, Inc., in Montana, but did not file its first annual report, so the state involuntarily dissolved the firm in 1996. Unaware of the dissolution, Lyons continued to do business as Lyons Concrete. In 2003, he signed a written contract with William Weimar to form and pour a certain amount of concrete on Weimar's property in Lake County for $19,810. Weimar was in a rush to complete the entire project, and he and Lyons orally agreed to additional work on a time-and-materials basis. When scheduling conflicts arose, Weimar had his own employees set some of the forms, which proved deficient. Weimar also directed Lyons to pour concrete in the rain, which undercut its quality. In mid-project, Lyons submitted an invoice for $14,389, which Weimar paid. After the work was complete, Lyons invoiced Weimar for $25,731, but he refused to pay, claiming that the $14,389 covered everything. To recover the unpaid amount, Lyons filed a mechanic's lien as "Mike Lyons d/b/a Lyons Concrete, Inc." against Weimar's property. Weimar filed a suit in a Montana state court to strike the lien, which Lyons filed a counterclaim to reassert. [Weimar v. Lyons, 338 Mont. 242, 164 P.3d 922 (2007)]*

1 Before the trial, Weimar asked for a change of venue on the ground that a sign on the courthouse lawn advertised "Lyons Concrete." How might the sign affect a trial on the parties' dispute? Should the court grant this request?

2 Weimar asked the court to dismiss the counterclaim on the ground that the state had dissolved Lyons Concrete in 1996. Lyons immediately filed new articles of incorporation for "Lyons Concrete, Inc." Under what doctrine might the court rule that Weimar could not deny the existence of Lyons Concrete? What ethical values underlie this doctrine? Should the court make this ruling?

3 At the trial, Weimar argued in part that there was no "fixed price" contract between the parties and that even if there was, the poor quality of the work, which required repairs, amounted to a breach, excusing Weimar's further performance. Should the court rule in Weimar's favor on this basis?

CRITICAL THINKING AND WRITING ASSIGNMENT

25.8 Critical Legal Thinking. What are some of the ways in which the limited liability of corporate shareholders serves the public interest? Are there any ways in which this limited liability is harmful to the public interest? Explain.

25.9 **Video Question.** Go to this text's Web site at **www.cengage.com/blaw/fbl** and select "Chapter 25." Click on "Video Questions" and view the video titled *Corporation or LLC: Which Is Better?* Then answer the following questions.

1 Compare the liability that Anna and Caleb would be exposed to as shareholders/owners of a corporation versus as members of a limited liability company (LLC).

2 How does the taxation of corporations differ from that of LLCs?

3 Given that Anna and Caleb conduct their business (Wizard Internet) over the Internet, can you think of any drawbacks to forming an LLC?

4 If you were in the position of Anna and Caleb, would you choose to create a corporation or an LLC? Why?

ACCESSING THE INTERNET

For updated links to resources available on the Web, as well as a variety of other materials, visit this text's Web site at

www.cengage.com/blaw/fbl

Cornell University's Legal Information Institute has links to state corporation (and other) statutes at

www.law.cornell.edu/topics/state_statutes.html

For information on incorporation, including a list of frequently asked questions on the topic, go to

www.bizfilings.com

For an example of one state's (Minnesota's) statute governing corporations, go to

www.revisor.leg.state.mn.us/stats/302A

PRACTICAL INTERNET EXERCISES

Go to this text's Web site at **www.cengage.com/blaw/fbl**, select "Chapter 25," and click on "Practical Internet Exercises." There you will find the following Internet research exercises that you can perform to learn more about the topics covered in this chapter.

PRACTICAL INTERNET EXERCISE 25-1 LEGAL PERSPECTIVE—Corporate Law

PRACTICAL INTERNET EXERCISE 25-2 MANAGEMENT PERSPECTIVE—Online Incorporation

PRACTICAL INTERNET EXERCISE 25-3 SOCIAL PERSPECTIVE—Mergers

BEFORE THE TEST

Go to this text's Web site at **www.cengage.com/blaw/fbl**, select "Chapter 25," and click on "Interactive Quizzes." You will find a number of interactive questions relating to this chapter.

CHAPTER 26
Corporate Directors, Officers, and Shareholders

LEARNING OBJECTIVES

AFTER READING THIS CHAPTER, YOU SHOULD BE ABLE TO ANSWER THE FOLLOWING QUESTIONS:

1 What are the duties of corporate directors and officers?

2 Directors are expected to use their best judgment in managing the corporation. What must directors do to avoid liability for honest mistakes of judgment and poor business decisions?

3 What is a voting proxy? What is cumulative voting?

4 If a group of shareholders perceives that the corporation has suffered a wrong and the directors refuse to take action, can the shareholders compel the directors to act? If so, how?

5 From what sources may dividends be paid legally? In what circumstances is a dividend illegal? What happens if a dividend is illegally paid?

A corporation is not a "natural" person but a legal fiction. No one individual shareholder or director bears sole responsibility for the corporation and its actions. Rather, a corporation joins the efforts and resources of a large number of individuals for the purpose of producing greater returns than those persons could have obtained individually.

Sometimes, actions that benefit the corporation as a whole do not coincide with the separate interests of the individuals making up the corporation. In such situations, it is important to know the rights and duties of all participants in the corporate enterprise. This chapter focuses on the rights and duties of directors, officers, and shareholders and the ways in which conflicts among them are resolved.

ROLES OF DIRECTORS AND OFFICERS

Every business corporation is governed by a board of directors. A director occupies a position of responsibility unlike that of other corporate personnel. Directors are sometimes inappropriately characterized as *agents* because they act on behalf of the corporation. No *individual* director, however, can act as an agent to bind the corporation; and as a group, directors collectively control the corporation in a way that no agent is able to control a principal. Directors are also often incorrectly characterized as *trustees* because they occupy positions of trust and control over the corporation. Unlike trustees, however, they do not own or hold title to property for the use and benefit of others.

Few legal requirements exist concerning directors' qualifications. Only a handful of states impose minimum age and residency requirements. A director may be a shareholder, but this is not necessary, unless required by statute or by the corporate articles or bylaws.

Election of Directors

Subject to statutory limitations, the number of directors is set forth in the corporation's articles or bylaws. Historically, the minimum number of directors has been three, but today many states permit fewer. Normally, the incorporators appoint the initial board of directors at the time the corporation is created, or the corporation itself names the directors in the articles. The initial board serves until the first annual shareholders' meeting. Subsequent directors are elected by a majority vote of the shareholders.

A director usually serves for a term of one year—from annual meeting to annual meeting. Most states also permit longer and staggered terms. Often, one-third of the board members are elected each year for a three-year term—a practice that provides greater management continuity.

Removal of Directors   A director can be removed *for cause*—that is, for failing to perform a required duty— either as specified in the articles or bylaws or by shareholder action. Even the board of directors itself may be given power to remove a director for cause, subject to shareholder review. In most states, a director cannot be removed without cause unless the shareholders have reserved the right to do so at the time of election. Whether shareholders should be able to remove a director without cause is part of an ongoing debate about the balance of power between a corporation and its shareholders.

Vacancies on the Board of Directors   Vacancies can occur on the board of directors if a director dies or resigns or if a new position is created through amendment of the articles or bylaws. In these situations, either the shareholders or the board itself can fill the position, depending on state law or on the provisions of the bylaws. Note, however, that even when the bylaws appear to authorize an election, a court can invalidate the election if the directors were attempting to diminish the shareholders' influence in it.

Compensation of Directors

In the past, corporate directors rarely were compensated, but today they are often paid at least nominal sums and may receive more substantial compensation in large corporations because of the time, work, effort, and especially risk involved. Most states permit the corporate articles or bylaws to authorize compensation for directors. In fact, the Revised Model Business Corporation Act (RMBCA) states that unless the articles or bylaws provide otherwise, the board of directors may set their own compensation [RMBCA 8.11]. Directors also gain through indirect benefits, such as business contacts and prestige, and other rewards, such as stock options.

In many corporations, directors are also chief corporate officers (president or chief executive officer, for example) and receive compensation in their managerial positions. A director who is also an officer of the corporation is referred to as an **inside director,** whereas a director who does not hold a management position is an **outside director.** Typically, a corporation's board of directors includes both inside and outside directors.

Board of Directors' Meetings

The board of directors conducts business by holding formal meetings with recorded minutes. The dates of regular meetings are usually established in the articles or bylaws or by board resolution, and no further notice is customarily required. Special meetings can be called, with notice sent to all directors. Today, most states allow directors to participate in board of directors' meetings from remote locations via telephone or Web conferencing, provided that all the directors can simultaneously hear each other during the meeting [RMBCA 8.20].

Unless the articles of incorporation or bylaws specify a greater number, a majority of the board of directors normally constitutes a quorum [RMBCA 8.24]. (**A quorum** is the minimum number of members of a body of officials or other group that must be present for business to be validly transacted.)

Once a quorum is present, the directors transact business and vote on issues affecting the corporation. Each director present at the meeting has one vote.[1] Ordinary matters generally require a simple majority vote; certain extraordinary issues may require a greater-than-majority vote. In other words, the affirmative vote of a majority of the directors present at a meeting binds the board of directors with regard to most decisions.

Rights of Directors

A corporate director must have certain rights to function properly in that position. The *right to participation* means that directors are entitled to participate in all board of directors' meetings and have a right to be notified of these meetings. As mentioned earlier, the dates of regular board meetings are usually preestablished and no notice of these meetings is required. If special meetings are called, however, notice is required unless waived by the director [RMBCA 8.23].

A director also has a *right of inspection*, which means that each director can access the corporation's books and records, facilities, and premises. Inspection rights are essential for directors to make informed decisions and to exercise the necessary supervision over corporate officers and employees. This right of inspection is virtually absolute and cannot be restricted (by the articles, bylaws, or any act of the board of directors).

When a director becomes involved in litigation by virtue of her or his position or actions, the director may also have a *right to indemnification* (reimbursement) for the legal costs, fees, and damages incurred. Most states allow corporations to indemnify and purchase liability insurance for corporate directors [RMBCA 8.51].

---

1. Except in Louisiana, which allows a director to vote by proxy under certain circumstances.

 **If you serve as a corporate director or officer, be aware that you may at some point become involved in litigation as a result. To protect against personal liability, make sure that the corporate bylaws explicitly give directors and officers a right to indemnification (reimbursement) for any litigation costs, as well as any judgments or settlements. Also, have the corporation purchase directors' and officers' liability insurance (D&O insurance). Having D&O insurance policies enables the corporation to avoid paying the substantial costs involved in defending a particular director or officer. Because most D&O policies have maximum coverage limits, make sure that the corporation is required to indemnify you in the event that the costs exceed the policy limits.**

Committees of the Board of Directors

When a board of directors has a large number of members and must deal with a myriad of complex business issues, meetings can become unwieldy. Therefore, the boards of large, publicly held corporations typically create committees, appoint directors to serve on individual committees, and delegate certain tasks to these committees. Committees focus on individual subjects and increase the efficiency of the board. The most common types of committees include the following:

1 *Executive committee.* The board members often elect an executive committee of directors to handle the interim management decisions between board of directors' meetings. The executive committee is limited to making decisions about ordinary business matters and conducting preliminary investigations into proposals. It cannot declare dividends, authorize the issuance of shares, amend the bylaws, or initiate any actions that require shareholder approval.

2 *Audit committee.* The audit committee is responsible for the selection, compensation, and oversight of the independent public accountants who audit the corporation's financial records. The Sarbanes-Oxley Act of 2002 requires all publicly held corporations to have an audit committee (as discussed in Chapters 27 and 31).

3 *Nominating committee.* This committee chooses the candidates for the board of directors that management wishes to submit to the shareholders in the next election. The committee cannot select directors to fill vacancies on the board, however [RMBCA 8.25].

4 *Compensation committee.* The compensation committee reviews and decides the salaries, bonuses, stock options, and other benefits that are given to the corporation's top executives. The committee may also determine the compensation of directors.

5 *Litigation committee.* This committee decides whether the corporation should pursue requests by shareholders to file a lawsuit against some party that has allegedly harmed the corporation. The committee members investigate the allegations and weigh the costs and benefits of litigation.

In addition to appointing committees, the board of directors can also delegate some of its functions to corporate officers. In doing so, the board is not relieved of its overall responsibility for directing the affairs of the corporation. Instead, corporate officers and managerial personnel are empowered to make decisions relating to ordinary, daily corporate activities within well-defined guidelines.

Corporate Officers and Executives

Officers and other executive employees are hired by the board of directors. At a minimum, most corporations have a president, one or more vice presidents, a secretary, and a treasurer. In most states, an individual can hold more than one office, such as president and secretary, and can be both an officer and a director of the corporation. In addition to carrying out the duties articulated in the bylaws, corporate and managerial officers act as agents of the corporation, and the ordinary rules of agency (discussed in Chapter 22) normally apply to their employment.

Corporate officers and other high-level managers are employees of the company, so their rights are defined by employment contracts. Regardless of the terms of an employment contract, however, the board of directors normally can remove a corporate officer at any time with or without cause—although the officer may then seek damages from the corporation for breach of contract.

The duties of corporate officers are the same as those of directors because both groups are involved in decision making and are in similar positions of control. Hence, officers and directors are viewed as having the same fiduciary duties of care and loyalty in their conduct of corporate affairs, a subject to which we now turn.

DUTIES AND LIABILITIES OF DIRECTORS AND OFFICERS

Directors and officers are deemed to be fiduciaries of the corporation because their relationship with the corporation and its shareholders is one of trust and confidence. As fiduciaries, directors and officers owe ethical—and legal—duties to the corporation and the shareholders as a whole. These fiduciary duties include the duty of care and the duty of loyalty.

Duty of Care

Directors and officers must exercise due care in performing their duties. The standard of *due care* has been variously described in judicial decisions and codified in many state corporation codes. Generally, directors and officers are required to act in good faith, to exercise the care that an ordinarily prudent person would exercise in similar circumstances, and to do what they believe is in the best interests of the corporation [RMBCA 8.30(a), 8.42(a)]. Directors and officers whose failure to exercise due care results in harm to the corporation or its shareholders can be held liable for negligence (unless the *business judgment rule* applies).

Duty to Make Informed and Reasonable Decisions Directors and officers are expected to be informed on corporate matters and to conduct a reasonable investigation of the situation before making a decision. This means that they must do what is necessary to keep adequately informed: attend meetings and presentations, ask for information from those who have it, read reports, and review other written materials. In other words, directors and officers must investigate, study, and discuss matters and evaluate alternatives before making a decision. They cannot decide on the spur of the moment without adequate research.

Although directors and officers are expected to act in accordance with their own knowledge and training, they are also normally entitled to rely on information given to them by certain other persons. Most states and Section 8.30(b) of the RMBCA allow a director to make decisions in reliance on information furnished by competent officers or employees, professionals such as attorneys and accountants, and committees of the board of directors (on which the director does not serve). The reliance must be in good faith, of course, to insulate a director from liability if the information later proves to be inaccurate or unreliable.

Duty to Exercise Reasonable Supervision Directors are also expected to exercise a reasonable amount of supervision when they delegate work to corporate officers and employees. **■EXAMPLE 26.1** Dale, a corporate bank director, fails to attend any board of directors' meetings for five years. In addition, Dale never inspects any of the corporate books or records and generally fails to supervise the efforts of the bank president and the loan committee. Meanwhile, Brennan, the bank president, who is a corporate officer, makes various improper loans and permits large overdrafts. In this situation,

Dale (the corporate director) can be held liable to the corporation for losses resulting from the unsupervised actions of the bank president and the loan committee. ■

Dissenting Directors Directors are expected to attend board of directors' meetings, and their votes should be entered into the minutes. Sometimes, an individual director disagrees with the majority's vote (which becomes an act of the board of directors). Unless a dissent is entered in the minutes, the director is presumed to have assented. If a decision later leads to the directors' being held liable for mismanagement, dissenting directors are rarely held individually liable to the corporation. For this reason, a director who is absent from a given meeting sometimes registers with the secretary of the board a dissent to actions taken at the meeting.

The Business Judgment Rule Directors and officers are expected to exercise due care and to use their best judgment in guiding corporate management, but they are not insurers of business success. Under the **business judgment rule**, a corporate director or officer will not be liable to the corporation or to its shareholders for honest mistakes of judgment and bad business decisions. Courts give significant deference to the decisions of corporate directors and officers, and consider the reasonableness of a decision at the time it was made, without the benefit of hindsight. Thus, corporate decision makers are not subjected to second-guessing by shareholders or others in the corporation.

The business judgment rule will apply as long as the director or officer (1) took reasonable steps to become informed about the matter, (2) had a rational basis for his or her decision, and (3) did not have a conflict of interest between his or her personal interest and that of the corporation. In fact, unless there is evidence of bad faith, fraud, or a clear breach of fiduciary duties, most courts will apply the rule and protect directors and officers who make bad business decisions from liability for those choices. Consequently, if there is a reasonable basis for a business decision, a court is unlikely to interfere with that decision, even if the corporation suffers as a result.

Duty of Loyalty

Loyalty can be defined as faithfulness to one's obligations and duties. In the corporate context, the duty of loyalty requires directors and officers to subordinate their personal interests to the welfare of the corporation. Among other things, this means that directors may not use corporate funds or confidential corporate information for personal advantage. They must also refrain from self-dealing. For instance, a director should not oppose a tender offer that is in the corporation's best interest simply because its acceptance may cost the director her or his position. Cases dealing with fiduciary duty may involve one or more of the following:

1 Competing with the corporation.

2 Usurping (taking personal advantage of) a corporate opportunity.

3 Having an interest that conflicts with the interest of the corporation.

4 Engaging in *insider trading* (using information that is not public to make a profit trading securities, as will be discussed in Chapter 27).

5 Authorizing a corporate transaction that is detrimental to minority shareholders.

6 Selling control over the corporation.

The following classic case illustrates the conflict that can arise between a corporate official's personal interest and his or her duty of loyalty.

CASE 26.1   **Guth v. Loft, Inc.**

LANDMARK AND CLASSIC CASES

Supreme Court of Delaware, 23 Del.Ch. 255, 5 A.2d 503 (1939).

FACTS Loft, Inc., made and sold candies, syrups, beverages, and food from its offices and plant in Long Island City, New York. Loft operated 115 retail outlets in several states and also sold its products wholesale. Charles Guth was Loft's president. Guth and his family owned Grace Company, which made syrups for soft drinks in a plant in Baltimore, Maryland. Coca-Cola Company supplied Loft with cola syrup. Unhappy with what he felt was Coca-Cola's high price, Guth entered into an agreement with Roy Megargel to acquire the trademark and formula for Pepsi-Cola and form Pepsi-Cola Corporation. Neither Guth nor Megargel could finance the new venture, however, and Grace was insolvent. Without the knowledge of Loft's board, Guth used Loft's capital, credit, facilities, and employees to further the Pepsi enterprise. At Guth's direction, Loft made the concentrate for the syrup, which was sent to Grace to add sugar and water. Loft charged Grace for the concentrate but allowed forty months' credit. Grace charged Pepsi for the syrup but also granted substantial credit. Grace sold the syrup to Pepsi's customers, including Loft, which paid on delivery or within thirty days. Loft also paid for Pepsi's advertising. Finally, losing profits at its stores as a result of switching from Coca-Cola, Loft filed a suit in a Delaware state court against Guth, Grace, and Pepsi, seeking their Pepsi stock and an accounting. The court entered a judgment in the plaintiff's favor. The defendants appealed to the Delaware Supreme Court.

ISSUE Did Guth violate his duty of loyalty to Loft by acquiring the Pepsi-Cola trademark and formula for himself without the knowledge of Loft's board of directors?

DECISION Yes. The Delaware Supreme Court upheld the judgment of the lower court. The state supreme court was "convinced that the opportunity to acquire the Pepsi-Cola

trademark and formula, goodwill and business belonged to [Loft], and that Guth, as its president, had no right to appropriate the opportunity to himself."

REASON The court pointed out that the officers and directors of a corporation stand in a fiduciary relation to that corporation and to its shareholders. Corporate officers and directors must protect the corporation's interest at all times. They must also "refrain from doing anything that works injury to the corporation." In other words, corporate officers and directors must provide undivided and unselfish loyalty to the corporation, and "that there should be no conflict between duty and self-interest." Whenever an opportunity is presented to the corporation, officers and directors with knowledge of that opportunity cannot seize it for themselves. "The corporation may elect to claim all of the benefits of the transaction for itself, and the law will impress a trust in favor of the corporation upon the property, interest, and profits required." Guth clearly created a conflict between his self-interest and his duty to Loft—the corporation of which he was president and director. Guth illegally appropriated the Pepsi-Cola opportunity for himself and thereby placed himself in a competitive position with the company for which he worked.

WHAT IF THE FACTS WERE DIFFERENT? *Suppose that Loft's board of directors had approved Pepsi-Cola's use of its personnel and equipment. Would the court's decision have been different? Discuss.*

IMPACT OF THIS CASE ON TODAY'S LAW *This early Delaware decision was one of the first to set forth a test for determining when a corporate officer or director has breached the duty of loyalty. The test has two basic parts—whether the*

CASE 26.1–Continues next page

CASE 26.1–Continued

opportunity was reasonably related to the corporation's line of business, and whether the corporation was financially able to undertake the opportunity. The court also considered whether the corporation had an interest or expectancy in the opportunity and recognized that when the corporation had "no interest or expectancy, the officer or director is entitled to treat the opportunity as his own."

RELEVANT WEB SITES *To locate information on the Web concerning the* Guth v. Loft *decision, go to this text's Web site at* **www.cengage.com/blaw/fbl**, *select "Chapter 26," and click on "URLs for Landmarks."*

■

Conflicts of Interest

Corporate directors often have many business affiliations, and a director may sit on the board of more than one corporation. Of course, directors are precluded from entering into or supporting businesses that operate in direct competition with corporations on whose boards they serve. Their fiduciary duty requires them to make a full disclosure of any potential conflicts of interest that might arise in any corporate transaction [RMBCA 8.60].

Sometimes, a corporation enters into a contract or engages in a transaction in which an officer or director has a personal interest. The director or officer must make a *full disclosure* of that interest and must abstain from voting on the proposed transaction.

■EXAMPLE 26.2 Ballo Corporation needs office space. Stephan Colson, one of its five directors, owns the building adjoining the corporation's headquarters. He negotiates a lease with Ballo for the space, making a full disclosure to Ballo and the other four directors. The lease arrangement is fair and reasonable, and it is unanimously approved by the other members of the corporation's board of directors. Under these circumstances, the contract is valid. The rule is one of reason; otherwise, directors would be prevented from ever having financial dealings with the corporations they serve. ■

State statutes set different standards for corporate contracts. Generally, though, a contract will not be voidable if it was fair and reasonable to the corporation at the time it was made, there was a full disclosure of the interest of the officers or directors involved in the transaction, and the contract was approved by a majority of the disinterested directors or shareholders [RMBCA 8.62].

Liability of Directors and Officers

Directors and officers are exposed to liability on many fronts. They can be liable for negligence in certain circumstances, as previously discussed. Corporate directors and officers may be held liable for the crimes and torts committed by themselves or by corporate employees under their supervision, as discussed in Chapters 6 and 25. Additionally, if shareholders perceive that the corporate directors are not acting in the best interests of the corporation, they may sue the directors, in what is called a *shareholder's derivative suit*, on behalf of the corporation. (This type of action will be discussed later in this chapter, in the context of shareholders' rights.) Directors and officers can also be held personally liable under a number of statutes, such as statutes enacted to protect the environment.

ROLE OF SHAREHOLDERS

The acquisition of a share of stock makes a person an owner and shareholder in a corporation. Shareholders own the corporation in the sense that they have an equitable (ownership) interest in the firm, but they have no legal title to corporate property, such as buildings and equipment, and no right to manage the firm.

Although shareholders have no right to participate in the daily management of the corporation, they have the power to choose the board of directors, which does have that responsibility. Ordinarily, corporate officers and directors owe no duty to individual shareholders unless some contract or special relationship exists between them in addition to the corporate relationship. Their duty is to act in the best interests of the corporation and its shareholder-owners as a whole. In turn, as you will read later in this chapter, controlling shareholders owe a fiduciary duty to minority shareholders. Normally, there is no legal relationship between shareholders and creditors of the corporation. Shareholders can, in fact, be creditors of the corporation and thus have the same rights of recovery against the corporation as any other creditor.

In this section, we look at the powers and voting rights of shareholders, which are generally established in the articles of incorporation and under the state's general incorporation law.

Shareholders' Powers

Shareholders must approve fundamental changes affecting the corporation before the changes can be implemented. Hence, shareholders are empowered to amend the articles of incorporation (charter) and bylaws, approve a merger or the dissolution of the corporation, and approve the sale of all or substantially all of the corporation's assets. Some of these powers are subject to prior board approval.

Members of the board of directors are elected and removed by a vote of the shareholders. The initial board of directors is either named in the articles of incorporation or chosen by the incorporators to serve until the first shareholders' meeting. From that time on, the selection and retention of directors are exclusively shareholder functions.

Directors usually serve their full terms; if the shareholders judge them unsatisfactory, they are simply not reelected. Shareholders have the inherent power, however, to remove a director from office *for cause* (breach of duty or misconduct) by a majority vote.[2] As mentioned earlier, some state statutes (and some corporate articles) even permit removal of directors without cause by the vote of a majority of the holders of outstanding shares entitled to vote.[3]

Shareholders' Meetings

Shareholders' meetings must occur at least annually. In addition, special meetings can be called to deal with urgent matters.

Notice of Meetings A corporation must notify its shareholders of the date, time, and place of an annual or special shareholders' meeting at least ten days, but not more than sixty days, before the meeting date [RMBCA 7.05].[4] (The date and time of the annual meeting can be specified in the bylaws, however.) Notices of special meetings must include a statement of the purpose of the meeting; business transacted at a special meeting is limited to that purpose.

Proxies It usually is not practical for owners of only a few shares of stock of publicly traded corporations to attend a shareholders' meeting. Therefore, the law allows stockholders to either vote in person or appoint another person as their agent to vote their shares at the meeting. The signed appointment form or electronic transmission authorizing an agent to vote the shares is called a **proxy** (from the Latin *procurare*, meaning "to manage, take care of"). Management often solic-

its proxies, but any person can solicit proxies to concentrate voting power. Proxies have been used by groups of shareholders as a device for taking over a corporation (corporate takeovers were discussed in Chapter 25). Proxies normally are revocable—that is, they can be withdrawn—unless they are specifically designated as irrevocable. Under RMBCA 7.22(c), proxies last for eleven months, unless the proxy agreement mandates a longer period.

Proxy Materials and Shareholder Proposals When shareholders want to change a company policy, they can put their idea up for a shareholder vote. They can do this by submitting a shareholder proposal to the board of directors and asking the board to include the proposal in the proxy materials that are sent to all shareholders before meetings.

The Securities and Exchange Commission (SEC), which regulates the purchase and sale of securities (see Chapter 27), has special provisions relating to proxies and shareholder proposals. SEC Rule 14a-8 provides that all shareholders who own stock worth at least $1,000 are eligible to submit proposals for inclusion in corporate proxy materials. The corporation is required to include information on whatever proposals will be considered at the shareholders' meeting along with proxy materials. Only those proposals that relate to significant policy considerations rather than ordinary business operations must be included. Under the SEC's e-proxy rules that went into effect in 2007,[5] companies may furnish proxy materials to shareholders by posting them on a Web site (see the discussion of these rules in the *Adapting the Law to the Online Environment* feature on pages 552 and 553).

Shareholder Voting

Shareholders exercise ownership control through the power of their votes. Corporate business matters are presented in the form of *resolutions*, which shareholders vote to approve or disapprove. Each shareholder is entitled to one vote per share, although the voting techniques that will be discussed shortly all enhance the power of the shareholder's vote. The articles of incorporation can exclude or limit voting rights, particularly for certain classes of shares. For example, owners of preferred shares are usually denied the right to vote [RMBCA 7.21]. If a state statute requires specific voting procedures, the corporation's articles or bylaws must be consistent with the statute.

Quorum Requirements For shareholders to conduct business at a meeting, a quorum must be present. Generally, a quorum exists when shareholders holding

---

2. A director can often demand court review of removal for cause.
3. Most states allow *cumulative voting* (which will be discussed shortly) for directors. If cumulative voting is authorized, a director may not be removed if the number of votes against removal would be sufficient to elect a director under cumulative voting. See, for example, California Corporations Code Section 303A. See also Section 8.08(c) of the RMBCA.
4. The shareholder can waive the requirement of notice by signing a waiver form [RMBCA 7.06]. A shareholder who does not receive notice but who learns of the meeting and attends without protesting the lack of notice is said to have waived notice by such conduct.

5. 17 C.F.R. Parts 240, 249, and 274.

ADAPTING THE LAW TO THE ONLINE ENVIRONMENT — Moving Company Information to the Internet

nyone who has ever owned shares in a public company knows that such companies often are required to mail voluminous paper documents that relate to proxies. Since 2007, publicly held companies can now voluntarily utilize *e-proxies*.

Notice and Access: E-Proxy Rules

New Security and Exchange Commission (SEC) rules[a] allow publicly held companies to furnish proxy materials to shareholders by posting them on a Web site and notifying the shareholders that the proxy materials are available online. This is called the "notice and access" model.

The notice and access model involves the following steps:

1 The company posts the proxy materials on its publicly accessible Web site.

a. 17 C.F.R. Parts 240, 249, and 274.

2 Subsequently, the company sends a (paper) notice to each shareholder at least forty calendar days before the date of the shareholders' meeting for which the proxy is being solicited.

3 No other materials can be sent along with the initial notice (unless the proxy is being combined with the meeting notice required by state law).

4 The notice must be written in plain English, and it must include a prominent statement of the following: the date, time, and location of the shareholders' meeting; the specific Web site at which shareholders can access the proxy materials; an explanation of how they can obtain paper copies of the proxy materials at no cost; and a clear and impartial description of each matter to be considered at the shareholders' meeting.

5 Next, the company must wait at least ten days before sending a "paper" proxy card to the shareholders. This ten-day waiting period provides shareholders with sufficient time to access the proxy materials online or to request paper copies.

6 If a shareholder requests paper proxy materials, the company must send them within three business days.

---

more than 50 percent of the outstanding shares are present. In some states, obtaining the unanimous written consent of shareholders is a permissible alternative to holding a shareholders' meeting [RMBCA 7.25].

Once a quorum is present, voting can proceed. A majority vote of the shares represented at the meeting is usually required to pass resolutions. **■EXAMPLE 26.3** Novo Pictures, Inc., has 10,000 outstanding shares of voting stock. Its articles of incorporation set the quorum at 50 percent of outstanding shares and provide that a majority vote of the shares present is necessary to pass resolutions concerning ordinary matters. Therefore, for this firm, a quorum of shareholders representing 5,000 outstanding shares must be present at a shareholders' meeting to conduct business. If exactly 5,000 shares are represented at the meeting, a vote of at least 2,501 of those shares is needed to pass a resolution. If 6,000 shares are represented, a vote of 3,001 will be required, and so on. ■

At times, more than a simple majority vote will be required either by a state statute or by the corporate articles. Extraordinary corporate matters, such as a merger, consolidation, or dissolution of the corporation (as discussed in Chapter 25), require a higher percentage of all corporate shares entitled to vote [RMBCA 7.27].

Voting Lists The corporation prepares voting lists prior to each meeting of the shareholders. Ordinarily, only persons whose names appear on the corporation's shareholder records as owners are entitled to vote.[6] The voting list contains the name and address of each shareholder as shown on the corporate records on a given cutoff, or record, date. (Under RMBCA 7.07, the record date may be as much as seventy days before the meeting.) The voting list also includes the number of voting shares held by each owner. The list is usually kept at the corporate headquarters and is available for shareholder inspection [RMBCA 7.20].

Cumulative Voting Most states permit or even require shareholders to elect directors by *cumulative voting*, a voting method designed to allow minority shareholders to be represented on the board of directors.[7] With cumulative voting, the number of board members to be elected is multiplied by the number of voting shares a shareholder owns. The result equals the number of votes the shareholder has, and this total can be cast for one or more nominees for director. All nominees stand for election at the same time. When cumulative voting is not required either by statute or under the articles,

---

6. When the legal owner is bankrupt, incompetent, deceased, or in some other way under a legal disability, his or her vote can be cast by a person designated by law to control and manage the owner's property.

7. See, for example, California Corporate Code Section 708. Under RMBCA 7.28, however, no cumulative voting rights exist unless the articles of incorporation so provide.

7 After receiving the initial paper notice, a shareholder can permanently elect to receive all future proxy materials on paper or by e-mail.

Internet Postings and Blogs

Some want the SEC to go even further in allowing information to be delivered online. On September 25, 2006, Jonathan Schwartz, the chief executive officer (CEO) of Sun Micosystems, Inc., sent a letter to the chair of the SEC arguing that the company should be able to use its Web site to disseminate information required by the SEC. Schwartz pointed out that Sun's Web site receives nearly one million hits per day and is a "tremendous vehicle for the broad delivery of timely and robust information." In his blog, Schwartz lamented that until the SEC changed its rules, companies would still be "consuming trees with press releases."

The SEC's current rule, Regulation Fair Disclosure, or Regulation FD,[b] does not allow significant information about a publicly held corporation to be distributed on the company's Web site or in its CEO's blog. Regulation FD was created in an attempt to ensure that some investors do not have more information than the general public. Under Regulation FD, when

b. 17 C.F.R. Section 243.101(e)(2).

a company gives "material nonpublic information" about its prospects to certain individuals or entities, it must disclose that information to the public. To comply with the regulation, corporate executives typically first meet with stock market analysts, either in person or by teleconference, and then hold a press conference to disseminate the information to the public. Schwartz contends that "the proliferation of the Internet supports a new policy that online communications fully satisfy Regulation FD's broad distribution requirement."[c]

So far, though, the SEC has not budged. Professor Adam Pritchard, who teaches securities law at the University of Michigan Law School, thinks that Schwartz's idea is commendable. He even suggests that a public company could just go ahead and use the corporate blog for disclosure, as nothing in the current SEC rules prohibits such use.

FOR CRITICAL ANALYSIS *Why might a company or other party choose to solicit proxies the old-fashioned way, by providing paper documents instead of Internet access, despite the added costs?*

c. Schwartz's letter is posted with a short article titled "One Small Step for the Blogosphere" at blogs.sun.com/jonathan/entry/one_small_step_for_the.

the entire board can be elected by a simple majority of shares at a shareholders' meeting.

Cumulative voting can best be understood by an example. **■EXAMPLE 26.4** A corporation has 10,000 shares issued and outstanding. One group of shareholders (the minority shareholders) holds only 3,000 shares, and the other group of shareholders (the majority shareholders) holds the other 7,000 shares. Three members of the board are to be elected. The majority shareholders' nominees are Acevedo, Barkley, and Craycik. The minority shareholders' nominee is Drake. Can Drake be elected by the minority shareholders?

If cumulative voting is allowed, the answer is yes. Together, the minority shareholders have 9,000 votes (the number of directors to be elected times the number of shares held by the minority shareholders equals 3 times 3,000, which equals

9,000 votes). All of these votes can be cast to elect Drake. The majority shareholders have 21,000 votes (3 times 7,000 equals 21,000 votes), but these votes have to be distributed among their three nominees. The principle of cumulative voting is that no matter how the majority shareholders cast their 21,000 votes, they will not be able to elect all three directors if the minority shareholders cast all of their 9,000 votes for Drake, as illustrated in Exhibit 26–1. ■

Other Voting Techniques Prior to a shareholders' meeting, a group of shareholders can agree in writing, in a *shareholder voting agreement*, to vote their shares together in a specified manner. Such agreements usually are held to be valid and enforceable. A shareholder can also appoint a voting agent and vote by proxy, as mentioned previously.

EXHIBIT 26–1 Results of Cumulative Voting

BALLOT	MAJORITY SHAREHOLDERS' VOTES			MINORITY SHAREHOLDERS' VOTES	DIRECTORS ELECTED
	Acevedo	Barkley	Craycik	Drake	
1	10,000	10,000	1,000	9,000	Acevedo/Barkley/Drake
2	9,001	9,000	2,999	9,000	Acevedo/Barkley/Drake
3	6,000	7,000	8,000	9,000	Barkley/Craycik/Drake

In the following case, corporate management was concerned about losing a proxy contest. The corporation's chief executive officer then entered into an agreement with a shareholder who would support management's candidates in return for a seat on the board of directors. A shareholder who opposed the deal filed a lawsuit claiming that this agreement was illegal and a breach of the officer's fiduciary duty.

CASE 26.2 **Portnoy v. Cryo-Cell International, Inc.**

Court of Chancery of Delaware, 940 A.2d 43 (2008).

FACTS Cryo-Cell International, Inc., a small public company, was struggling to succeed. Several of its stockholders considered mounting a proxy contest to replace the board of directors. One of those shareholders, Andrew Filipowski, used management's fear of being replaced to create a deal for himself—that is, he would be included in management's slate of directors at an upcoming stockholders' annual meeting. Another shareholder, David Portnoy, filed an opposing slate of directors. The company's chief executive officer, Mercedes Walton, created a plan that would allow management and Filipowski to win the proxy contest. This plan involved Walton as a "matchmaker" who would find stockholders willing to sell their shares to Filipowski. Walton promised Filipowski that if management's slate of directors won, Cryo-Cell's board of directors would then add another board seat that a Filipowski designee would fill. Walton's side deal, however, was not made public to the shareholders when they voted. After the election, Walton prepared to add Filipowski's designee to the board of directors. Portnoy, a dissenting shareholder, filed a lawsuit claiming that the election results should be overturned. Portnoy argued that the side agreement with Filipowski was not created in the company's best interests. Portnoy claimed that all of the dealings between Cryo-Cell and Filipowski were tainted by fiduciary misconduct and that the agreement to add Filipowski to the management slate in exchange for his support constituted an "illegal vote-buying arrangement."

ISSUE Did the CEO's promise to change the corporate bylaws and expand the number of directors after a vote constitute a breach of fiduciary duties and taint the election?

DECISION Yes. The court ruled that the incumbent board's actions and the side agreement with the company's CEO (Walton) constituted serious breaches of fiduciary duty and therefore tainted the election. The court ordered a special shareholders' meeting in order to hold a new election. The court did not, however, find the agreement to add Filipowski to the management slate of directors to be improper.

REASON The court reasoned that a mere offer of a position on a management slate should not be considered a vote-buying agreement. "When stockholders can decide for themselves whether to see the candidate who obtained a place on a management slate by way of [bargaining with management], it seems unwise to formulate a standard that involves the potential for excessive and imprecise judicial involvement." Such an arrangement is not vote-buying. Making a side agreement, in contrast, that guaranteed Filipowski's designee an additional seat on the board was quite a separate matter. Walton had promised "she and her incumbent colleagues would use their powers as directors of Cryo-Cell to increase the size of the board and to seat [Filipowski's designee]. This was therefore a promise that would not be, for the duration of the term, subject to prior approval by the electorate." Thus, it was improper.

 FOR CRITICAL ANALYSIS—Ethical Consideration *If Filipowski had promised to bring additional funding to keep Cryo-Cell from failing due to lack of capital, would the actions described in this case have been considered ethical? Explain your answer.*

RIGHTS AND LIABILITIES OF SHAREHOLDERS

As mentioned earlier, shareholders have the right to participate in elections of the board of directors and in shareholders' annual meetings. In this section, we examine additional rights of shareholders, their potential liabilities, and the duties that majority shareholders may owe to minority shareholders.

Rights of Shareholders

Shareholders possess numerous rights. A significant right—the right to vote their shares—has already been discussed. We now look at some additional rights of shareholders.

Stock Certificates A **stock certificate** is a certificate issued by a corporation that evidences ownership of a specified number of shares in the corporation. In jurisdictions that require the issuance of stock certificates, shareholders have the right to demand that the corporation issue certificates. In most states and under RMBCA 6.26, boards of directors may provide that shares of stock will be uncertificated—that is, no actual, physical stock certificates will be issued. When shares are uncertificated, the corporation may be required to send each shareholder a letter or some other form of notice that contains the same information that would normally appear on the face of stock certificates.

Stock is intangible personal property, and the ownership right exists independently of the certificate itself. If a stock certificate is lost or destroyed, ownership is not destroyed with it. A new certificate can be issued to replace one that has been lost or destroyed.[8] Notice of shareholders' meetings, dividends, and operational and financial reports are all distributed according to the recorded ownership listed in the corporation's books, not on the basis of possession of the certificate.

Preemptive Rights With **preemptive rights,** which are based on a common law concept, a shareholder receives a preference over all other purchasers to subscribe to or purchase a prorated share of a new issue of stock. In other words, a shareholder who is given preemptive rights can purchase the same percentage of the new shares being issued as she or he already holds in the company. This allows each shareholder to maintain her or his proportionate control, voting power, or financial interest in the corporation. Most statutes either (1) grant preemptive rights but allow them to be negated in the corporation's articles or (2) deny preemptive rights except to the extent that they are granted in the articles. The result is that the articles of incorporation determine the existence and scope of preemptive rights. Generally, preemptive rights apply only to additional, newly issued stock sold for cash, and the preemptive rights must be exercised within a specified time period, which is usually thirty days.

EXAMPLE 26.5 Tran Corporation authorizes and issues 1,000 shares of stock. Lebow purchases 100 shares, making her the owner of 10 percent of the company's stock. Subsequently, Tran, by vote of its shareholders, authorizes the issuance of another 1,000 shares (by amending the articles of incorpora-

tion). This increases its capital stock to a total of 2,000 shares. If preemptive rights have been provided, Lebow can purchase one additional share of the new stock being issued for each share she already owns—or 100 additional shares. Thus, she can own 200 of the 2,000 shares outstanding, and she will maintain her relative position as a shareholder. If preemptive rights are not allowed, her proportionate control and voting power may be diluted from that of a 10 percent shareholder to that of a 5 percent shareholder because of the issuance of the additional 1,000 shares. ■

Preemptive rights are most important in close corporations because each shareholder owns a relatively small number of shares but controls a substantial interest in the corporation. Without preemptive rights, it would be possible for a shareholder to lose his or her proportionate control over the firm.

Stock Warrants Usually, when preemptive rights exist and a corporation is issuing additional shares, each shareholder is given **stock warrants,** which are transferable options to acquire a given number of shares from the corporation at a stated price. Warrants are often publicly traded on securities exchanges. When the option to purchase is in effect for a short period of time, the stock warrants are usually referred to as *rights.*

Dividends As mentioned in Chapter 25, a *dividend* is a distribution of corporate profits or income *ordered by the directors* and paid to the shareholders in proportion to their respective shares in the corporation. Dividends can be paid in cash, property, stock of the corporation that is paying the dividends, or stock of other corporations.[9]

State laws vary, but each state determines the general circumstances and legal requirements under which dividends are paid. State laws also control the sources of revenue to be used; only certain funds are legally available for paying dividends. All states allow dividends to be paid from *retained earnings,* or the undistributed net profits earned by the corporation, including capital gains from the sale of fixed assets. A few states allow dividends to be issued from current *net profits* without regard to deficits in prior years. A number of states allow dividends to be paid out of any kind of *surplus.*

Illegal Dividends. Sometimes, dividends are improperly paid from an unauthorized account, or their payment causes the corporation to become insolvent. Generally, in such situations, shareholders must return illegal dividends only if they knew that the dividends were illegal when the payment was

---

8. The Uniform Commercial Code (UCC) provides that for a lost or destroyed certificate to be reissued, a shareholder normally must furnish an *indemnity bond.* An indemnity bond is a written promise to reimburse the holder for any actual or claimed loss caused by the issuer's or some other person's conduct. The bond protects the corporation against potential loss should the original certificate reappear at some future time in the hands of a bona fide purchaser [UCC 8–302, 8–405(2)].

9. On one occasion, a distillery declared and paid a "dividend" in bonded whiskey.

received. A dividend paid while the corporation is insolvent is automatically an illegal dividend, and shareholders may be required to return the payment to the corporation or its creditors. Whenever dividends are illegal or improper, the board of directors can be held personally liable for the amount of the payment. When directors can show that a shareholder knew that a dividend was illegal when it was received, however, the directors are entitled to reimbursement from the shareholder.

Directors' Failure to Declare a Dividend. When directors fail to declare a dividend, shareholders can ask a court to compel the directors to meet and to declare a dividend. To succeed, the shareholders must show that the directors have acted so unreasonably in withholding the dividend that their conduct is an abuse of their discretion.

Often, a corporation accumulates large cash reserves for a bona fide purpose, such as expansion, research, or other legitimate corporate goals. The mere fact that the firm has sufficient earnings or surplus available to pay a dividend is not enough to compel directors to distribute funds that, in the board's opinion, should not be distributed. The courts are reluctant to interfere with corporate operations and will not compel directors to declare dividends unless abuse of discretion is clearly shown.

Inspection Rights Shareholders in a corporation enjoy both common law and statutory inspection rights. The shareholder's right of inspection is limited, however, to the inspection and copying of corporate books and records for a *proper purpose*. In addition, the request must be made in advance. The shareholder can inspect in person, or an attorney, accountant, or other type of assistant can do so as the shareholder's agent. The RMBCA requires the corporation to maintain an alphabetical voting list of shareholders with addresses and number of shares owned; this list must be kept open at the annual meeting for inspection by any shareholder of record [RMBCA 7.20].

The power of inspection is fraught with potential abuses, and the corporation is allowed to protect itself from them. For example, a shareholder can properly be denied access to corporate records to prevent harassment or to protect trade secrets or other confidential corporate information. Some states require that a shareholder must have held his or her shares for a minimum period of time immediately preceding the demand to inspect or must hold a minimum number of outstanding shares. The RMBCA provides, though, that every shareholder is entitled to examine specified corporate records [RMBCA 16.02]. A shareholder who is denied the right of inspection can seek a court order to compel the inspection.

Transfer of Shares Corporate stock represents an ownership right in intangible personal property. The law generally recog-

nizes the right to transfer stock to another person unless there are valid restrictions on its transferability. Although stock certificates are negotiable and freely transferable by indorsement and delivery, transfer of stock in closely held corporations usually is restricted. These restrictions must be reasonable and may be set out in the bylaws or in a shareholder agreement. The existence of any restrictions on transferability must always be indicated on the face of the stock certificate.

When shares are transferred, a new entry is made in the corporate stock book to indicate the new owner. Until the corporation is notified and the entry is complete, all rights—including voting rights, the right to notice of shareholders' meetings, and the right to dividend distributions—remain with the current record owner.

Rights on Dissolution When a corporation is dissolved and its outstanding debts and the claims of its creditors have been satisfied, the remaining assets are distributed on a pro rata basis among the shareholders. The articles of incorporation may provide that certain classes of stock will be given priority. If no class of stock has been given preferences in the distribution of assets, all of the stockholders share the remaining assets. In some circumstances, such as when the board of directors is mishandling corporate assets or is allowing a deadlock to irreparably injure the corporation, shareholders can petition a court to have the corporation dissolved [RMBCA 1430].

The Shareholder's Derivative Suit When those in control of a corporation—the corporate directors—fail to sue in the corporate name to redress a wrong suffered by the corporation, shareholders are permitted to do so "derivatively" in what is known as a **shareholder's derivative suit.** Before a derivative suit can be brought, some wrong must have been done to the corporation, and the shareholders must have presented their complaint to the board of directors. Only if the directors fail to solve the problem or to take appropriate action can the derivative suit go forward.

The right of shareholders to bring a derivative action is especially important when the wrong suffered by the corporation results from the actions of corporate directors or officers. This is because the directors and officers would probably want to prevent any action against themselves. Nevertheless, a court will dismiss a derivative suit if the majority of directors or an independent panel determines in good faith that the lawsuit is not in the best interests of the corporation [RMBCA 7.44].

When shareholders bring a derivative suit, they are not pursuing rights or benefits for themselves personally but are acting as guardians of the corporate entity. Therefore, if the suit is successful, any damages recovered normally go into the corporation's treasury, not to the shareholders personally.

(The shareholders may be entitled to reimbursement for reasonable expenses of the lawsuit, including attorneys' fees.)

Liabilities of Shareholders

One of the hallmarks of the corporate organization is that shareholders are not personally liable for the debts of the corporation. If the corporation fails, shareholders can lose their investments, but that is generally the limit of their liability. As discussed previously, in certain instances of fraud, undercapitalization, or careless observance of corporate formalities, a court will pierce the corporate veil and hold the shareholders individually liable. These situations are the exception, however, not the rule.

A shareholder can also be personally liable in certain other rare instances. One relates to *watered stock*. Another instance is when a majority shareholder engages in oppressive conduct or attempts to exclude minority shareholders from receiving certain benefits.

When a corporation issues shares for less than their fair market value, the shares are referred to as **watered stock.**[10] Usually, the shareholder who receives watered stock must pay the difference to the corporation (the shareholder is personally liable). In some states, the shareholder who receives watered stock may be liable to creditors of the corporation for unpaid corporate debts.

---

10. The phrase *watered stock* was originally used to describe cattle that were kept thirsty during a long drive and then were allowed to drink large quantities of water just before their sale. The increased weight of the "watered stock" allowed the seller to reap a higher profit.

■EXAMPLE 26.6 During the formation of a corporation, Gomez, one of the incorporators, transfers his property, Sunset Beach, to the corporation for 10,000 shares of stock. The stock has a specific face value *(par value)* of $100 per share, and thus the total price of the 10,000 shares is $1 million. After the property is transferred and the shares are issued, Sunset Beach is carried on the corporate books at a value of $1 million. On appraisal, it is discovered that the market value of the property at the time of transfer was only $500,000. The shares issued to Gomez are therefore watered stock, and he is liable to the corporation for the difference. ■

In some instances, a majority shareholder is regarded as having a fiduciary duty to the corporation and to the minority shareholders. This occurs when a single shareholder (or a few shareholders acting in concert) owns a sufficient number of shares to exercise *de facto* (actual) control over the corporation. In these situations, majority shareholders owe a fiduciary duty to the minority shareholders. A breach of fiduciary duty can also occur when the majority shareholders of a closely held corporation use their control to exclude the minority from certain benefits of participating in the firm.

MAJOR BUSINESS FORMS COMPARED

When deciding which form of business organization to choose, businesspersons consider several factors, including ease of creation and the need for capital. Each major form of business organization offers distinct advantages and disadvantages. Exhibit 26–2 on the following two pages summarizes the essential advantages and disadvantages of each of the forms of business organization discussed in Unit 8.

EXHIBIT 26–2 Major Forms of Business Compared

CHARACTERISTIC	SOLE PROPRIETORSHIP	PARTNERSHIP	CORPORATION
Method of creation	Created at will by owner.	Created by agreement of the parties.	Authorized by the state under the state's corporation law.
Legal position	Not a separate entity; owner is the business.	Is a separate legal entity in most states.	Always a legal entity separate and distinct from its owners—a legal fiction for the purposes of owning property and being a party to litigation.
Liability	Unlimited liability.	Unlimited liability.	Limited liability of shareholders; shareholders are not liable for the debts of the corporation.
Duration	Determined by owner; automatically dissolved on owner's death.	Terminated by agreement of the partners, but can continue to do business even when a partner dissociates from the partnership.	Can have perpetual existence.
Transferability of interest	Interest can be transferred, but individual's proprietorship then ends.	Although partnership interest can be assigned, assignee does not have full rights of a partner.	Shares of stock can be transferred.
Management	Completely at owner's discretion.	Each general partner has a direct and equal voice in management unless expressly agreed otherwise in the partnership agreement.	Shareholders elect directors, who set policy and appoint officers.
Taxation	Owner pays personal taxes on business income.	Each partner pays pro rata share of income taxes on net profits, whether or not they are distributed.	Double taxation—corporation pays income tax on net profits, with no deduction for dividends, and shareholders pay income tax on disbursed dividends they receive.
Organizational fees, annual license fees, and annual reports	None or minimal.	None or minimal.	All required.
Transaction of business in other states	Generally no limitation.	Generally no limitation.[a]	Normally must qualify to do business and obtain certificate of authority.

a. A few states have enacted statutes requiring that foreign partnerships qualify to do business there.

EXHIBIT 26–2 Major Forms of Business Compared–Continued

CHARACTERISTIC	LIMITED PARTNERSHIP	LIMITED LIABILITY COMPANY	LIMITED LIABILITY PARTNERSHIP
Method of creation	Created by agreement to carry on a business for a profit. At least one party must be a general partner and the other(s) limited partner(s). Certificate of limited partnership is filed. Charter must be issued by the state.	Created by an agreement of the member-owners of the company. Articles of organization are filed. Charter must be issued by the state.	Created by agreement of the partners. A statement of qualification for the limited liability partnership is filed.
Legal position	Treated as a legal entity.	Treated as a legal entity.	Generally, treated same as a traditional partnership.
Liability	Unlimited liability of all general partners; limited partners are liable only to the extent of capital contributions.	Member-owners' liability is limited to the amount of capital contributions or investments.	Varies, but under the Uniform Partnership Act, liability of a partner for acts committed by other partners is limited.
Duration	By agreement in certificate, or by termination of the last general partner (retirement, death, and the like) or last limited partner.	Unless a single-member LLC, can have perpetual existence (same as a corporation).	Remains in existence until cancellation or revocation.
Transferability of interest	Interest can be assigned (same as traditional partnership), but if assignee becomes a member with consent of other partners, certificate must be amended.	Member interests are freely transferable.	Interest can be assigned same as in a traditional partnership.
Management	General partners have equal voice or by agreement. Limited partners may not retain limited liability if they actively participate in management.	Member-owners can fully participate in management, or can designate a group of persons to manage on behalf of the members.	Same as a traditional partnership.
Taxation	Generally taxed as a partnership.	LLC is not taxed, and members are taxed personally on profits "passed through" the LLC.	Same as a traditional partnership.
Organizational fees, annual license fees, and annual reports	Organizational fee required; usually not others.	Organizational fee required; others vary with states.	Fees are set by each state for filing statements of qualification, foreign qualification, and annual reports.
Transaction of business in other states	Generally no limitations.	Generally no limitation, but may vary depending on state.	Must file a statement of foreign qualification before doing business in another state.

REVIEWING Corporate Directors, Officers, and Shareholders

David Brock is on the board of directors of Firm Body Fitness, Inc., which owns a string of fitness clubs in New Mexico. Brock owns 15 percent of the Firm Body stock, and he is also employed as a tanning technician at one of the fitness clubs. After the January financial report showed that Firm Body's tanning division was operating at a substantial net loss, the board of directors, led by Marty Levinson, discussed terminating the tanning operations. Brock successfully convinced a majority of the board that the tanning division was necessary to market the club's overall fitness package. By April, the tanning division's financial losses had risen. The board hired a business analyst who conducted surveys and determined that the tanning operations did not significantly increase membership. A shareholder, Diego Peñada, discovered that Brock owned stock in Sunglow, Inc., the company from which Firm Body purchased its tanning equipment. Peñada notified Levinson, who privately reprimanded Brock. Shortly afterward, Brock and Mandy Vail, who owned 37 percent of Firm Body stock and also held shares of Sunglow, voted to replace Levinson on the board of directors. Using the information presented in the chapter, answer the following questions.

1 What duties did Brock, as a director, owe to Firm Body?

2 Does the fact that Brock owned shares in Sunglow establish a conflict of interest? Why or why not?

3 Suppose that Firm Body brought an action against Brock claiming that he had breached the duty of loyalty by not disclosing his interest in Sunglow to the other directors. What theory might Brock use in his defense?

4 Now suppose that Firm Body did not bring an action against Brock. What type of lawsuit might Peñada be able to bring based on these facts?

TERMS AND CONCEPTS

business judgment rule 548
inside director 546
outside director 546
preemptive rights 555

proxy 551
quorum 546
shareholder's derivative suit 556

stock certificate 555
stock warrant 555
watered stock 557

CHAPTER SUMMARY Corporate Directors, Officers, and Shareholders

Roles of Directors and Officers
(See pages 545–547.)

1. *Directors' qualifications*—Few qualifications are required; a director may be a shareholder but is not required to be.

2. *Election of directors*—The first board of directors is usually appointed by the incorporators; thereafter, directors are elected by the shareholders. Directors usually serve a one-year term, although the term can be longer, and staggered terms are permitted under most state statutes. Compensation is usually specified in the corporate articles or bylaws.

3. *Board of directors' meetings*—The board of directors conducts business by holding formal meetings with recorded minutes. The date of regular meetings is usually established in the corporate articles or bylaws; special meetings can be called, with notice sent to all directors. Quorum requirements vary from state to state; usually, a quorum is a majority of the corporate directors. Voting must usually be done in person, and in ordinary matters only a majority vote is required.

4. *Rights of directors*—Directors' rights include the rights of participation, inspection, and indemnification.

5. *Directors' committees*—A board of directors may create committees of directors and delegate various responsibilities to them. Common types of committees include an *executive committee*, which handles management decisions between board meetings; an *audit committee*, which oversees the independent audit of the company's financial records; a *nominating committee*, which chooses candidates for the board of directors; a *compensation committee*, which decides the compensation of the company's top executives; and a *litigation committee*, which determines whether the company should pursue litigation.

CHAPTER SUMMARY Corporate Directors, Officers, and Shareholders–Continued

Roles of Directors and Officers— Continued	6. *Corporate officers and executives*—Corporate officers and other executive employees are normally hired by the board of directors. As employees, corporate officers and executives have the rights defined by their employment contracts. The duties of corporate officers are the same as those of directors.
Duties and Liabilities of Directors and Officers (See pages 547–550.)	1. *Duty of care*—Directors and officers are obligated to act in good faith, to use prudent business judgment in the conduct of corporate affairs, and to act in the corporation's best interests. If a director fails to exercise this duty of care, she or he can be answerable to the corporation and to the shareholders for breaching the duty.
	2. *The business judgment rule*—This rule immunizes directors and officers from liability for a business decision as long as they took reasonable steps to become informed about the matter, had a rational basis for their decision, and did not have a conflict of interest.
	3. *Duty of loyalty*—Directors and officers have a fiduciary duty to subordinate their own interests to those of the corporation in matters relating to the corporation.
	4. *Conflicts of interest*—To fulfill their duty of loyalty, directors and officers must make a full disclosure of any potential conflicts between their personal interests and those of the corporation.
	5. *Liability of directors and officers*—Corporate directors and officers are personally liable for their own torts and crimes; additionally, they may be held personally liable for the torts and crimes committed by corporate personnel under their supervision (see Chapters 6 and 25).
Role of Shareholders (See pages 550–554.)	1. *Shareholders' powers*—Shareholders' powers include the approval of all fundamental changes affecting the corporation and the election of the board of directors.
	2. *Shareholders' meetings*—Shareholders' meetings must occur at least annually; special meetings can be called when necessary. Notice of the date, time, and place of the meeting (and its purpose, if it is specially called) must be sent to shareholders. Shareholders may vote by proxy (authorizing someone else to vote their shares) and may submit proposals to be included in the company's proxy materials sent to shareholders before meetings.
	3. *Shareholder voting*—Shareholder voting requirements and procedures are as follows:
	a. A minimum number of shareholders (a quorum—generally, more than 50 percent of shares held) must be present at a meeting for business to be conducted; resolutions are passed (usually) by simple majority vote.
	b. The corporation must prepare voting lists of shareholders of record prior to each shareholders' meeting.
	c. Cumulative voting may or may not be required or permitted. Cumulative voting gives minority shareholders a better chance to be represented on the board of directors.
	d. A shareholder voting agreement (an agreement of shareholders to vote their shares together) is usually held to be valid and enforceable.
	e. A shareholder may appoint a proxy (substitute) to vote her or his shares.
Rights and Liabilities of Shareholders (See pages 554–557.)	1. *Shareholders' rights*—In addition to voting rights, shareholders have numerous rights, which may include the following:
	a. The right to a stock certificate, preemptive rights, and the right to stock warrants (depending on the articles of incorporation).
	b. The right to obtain a dividend (at the discretion of the directors).
	c. The right to inspect the corporate records.
	d. The right to transfer shares (this right may be restricted in close corporations).
	e. The right to a share of corporate assets when the corporation is dissolved.
	f. The right to sue on behalf of the corporation (bring a shareholder's derivative suit) when the directors fail to do so.

(Continued)

CHAPTER SUMMARY Corporate Directors, Officers, and Shareholders–Continued

Rights and Liabilities of Shareholders— Continued	2. *Shareholders' liabilities and duties—*
	   a. Shareholders may be liable for the retention of illegal dividends and for the value of watered stock.
	   b. In certain situations, majority shareholders may be regarded as having a fiduciary duty to minority shareholders and will be liable if that duty is breached.

FOR REVIEW

Answers for the even-numbered questions in this **For Review** *section can be found on this text's accompanying Web site at* **www.cengage.com/blaw/fbl***. Select "Chapter 26" and click on "For Review."*

1 What are the duties of corporate directors and officers?

2 Directors are expected to use their best judgment in managing the corporation. What must directors do to avoid liability for honest mistakes of judgment and poor business decisions?

3 What is a voting proxy? What is cumulative voting?

4 If a group of shareholders perceives that the corporation has suffered a wrong and the directors refuse to take action, can the shareholders compel the directors to act? If so, how?

5 From what sources may dividends be paid legally? In what circumstances is a dividend illegal? What happens if a dividend is illegally paid?

QUESTIONS AND CASE PROBLEMS

 ## HYPOTHETICAL SCENARIOS AND CASE PROBLEMS

26.1 Voting Techniques. Algonquin Corp. has issued and has outstanding 100,000 shares of common stock. Four stockholders own 60,000 of these shares, and for the past six years they have nominated a slate of people for membership on the board, all of whom have been elected. Sergio and twenty other shareholders, owning 20,000 shares, are dissatisfied with corporate management and want a representative on the board who shares their views. Explain under what circumstances Sergio and the minority shareholders can elect their representative to the board.

26.2 Hypothetical Question with Sample Answer. Starboard, Inc., has a board of directors consisting of three members (Ellsworth, Green, and Morino) and approximately five hundred shareholders. At a regular meeting of the board, the board selects Tyson as president of the corporation by a two-to-one vote, with Ellsworth dissenting. The minutes of the meeting do not register Ellsworth's dissenting vote. Later, during an audit, it is discovered that Tyson is a former convict and has openly embezzled $500,000 from Starboard. This loss is not covered by insurance. The corporation wants to hold directors Ellsworth, Green, and Morino liable.

Ellsworth claims no liability. Discuss the personal liability of the directors to the corporation.

 For a sample answer to Question 26.2, go to Appendix E at the end of this text.

26.3 Lucia has acquired one share of common stock of a multimillion-dollar corporation with more than 500,000 shareholders. Lucia's ownership is so small that she is questioning what her rights are as a shareholder. For example, she wants to know whether owning this one share entitles her to (1) attend and vote at shareholders' meetings, (2) inspect the corporate books, and (3) receive yearly dividends. Discuss Lucia's rights in these three matters.

26.4 Inspection Rights. Craig Johnson founded Distributed Solutions, Inc. (DSI), in 1991 to make software and provide consulting services, including payroll services, for small companies. Johnson was the sole officer and director and the majority shareholder. Jeffrey Hagen was a minority shareholder. In 1993, Johnson sold DSI's payroll services to himself and a few others and set up Distributed Payroll Solutions, Inc. (DPSI). In 1996, DSI had revenues of $739,034 and assets of $541,168. DSI's revenues in 1997 were $934,532. Within a year, however, all of DSI's assets were sold, and Johnson told Hagen that he was dissolving the firm because, among other things, it conducted no business and had no prospects for future business. Hagen asked for corporate records to determine the value of DSI's stock, DSI's financial condition, and "whether unauthorized and oppressive acts had occurred in connection with the operation of the corporation which impacted the value of" the stock. When there was no response, Hagen filed a suit in an Illinois state court against DSI and Johnson, seeking an order to compel the inspection. The defendants filed a motion to dismiss, arguing that Hagen had failed to plead a proper purpose. Should the court grant Hagen's request? Discuss. [*Hagen v. Distributed Solutions, Inc.*, 328 Ill.App.3d 132, 764 N.E.2d 1141, 262 Ill.Dec. 24 (1 Dist. 2002)]

26.5 Case Problem with Sample Answer. Digital Commerce, Ltd., designed software to enable its clients to sell their products or services over the Internet. Kevin Sullivan served as a Digital vice president until 2000, when he became president. Sullivan was dissatisfied that his compensation did not include stock in Digital, but he was unable to negotiate a deal that included equity (referring to shares of ownership in the company). In May, Sullivan solicited ASR Corp.'s business for Digital while he investigated employment opportunities with ASR for himself. When ASR would not include an "equity component" in a job offer, Sullivan refused to negotiate further on Digital's behalf. A few months later, Sullivan began to form his own firm to compete with Digital, conducting organizational and marketing activities on Digital's time, including soliciting ASR's business. In August, Sullivan resigned after first having all e-mail pertaining to the new firm deleted from Digital's computers. ASR signed a contract with Sullivan's new firm and paid it $400,000 for work through October 2001. Digital filed a suit in a federal district court against Sullivan, claiming that he had usurped a corporate opportunity. Did Sullivan breach his fiduciary duty to Digital? Explain. [*In re Sullivan*, 305 Bankr. 809 (W.D.Mich. 2004)]

After you have answered Problem 26.5, compare your answer with the sample answer given on the Web site that accompanies this text. Go to www.cengage.com/blaw/fbl, select "Chapter 26," and click on "Case Problem with Sample Answer."

26.6 Fiduciary Duties and Liabilities. Harry Hoaas and Larry Griffiths were shareholders in Grand Casino, Inc., which owned and operated a casino in Watertown, South Dakota. Griffiths owned 51 percent of the stock and Hoaas 49 percent. Hoaas managed the casino, which Griffiths typically visited once a week. At the end of 1997, an accounting showed that the cash on hand was less than the amount posted in the casino's books. Later, more shortfalls were discovered. In October 1999, Griffiths did a complete audit. Hoaas was unable to account for $135,500 in missing cash. Griffiths then kept all of the casino's most recent profits, including Hoaas's $9,447.20 share, and, without telling Hoaas, sold the

casino for $100,000 and kept all of the proceeds. Hoaas filed a suit in a South Dakota state court against Griffiths, asserting, among other things, a breach of fiduciary duty. Griffiths countered with evidence of Hoaas's misappropriation of corporate cash. What duties did these parties owe each other? Did either Griffiths or Hoaas, or both of them, breach those duties? How should their dispute be resolved? How should their finances be reconciled? Explain. [*Hoaas v. Griffiths*, 2006 SD 27, 714 N.W.2d 61 (2006)]

26.7 Role of Directors. The board of a property management corporation in Oregon meets on a regular basis. In the third quarter of 2003, the company paid each of the directors $6,000. The company did not report the payments as part of payroll nor did it pay unemployment taxes on the payments. The Oregon Employment Department contended that the company owed $700 in unemployment taxes on the payments to the directors. The company protested. The administrative law judge (ALJ) for the state employment department held that the directors' fees were the same as wages for employment, so the tax payment was due. The company appealed. The court of appeals affirmed the ALJ's ruling. The company appealed to the Supreme Court of Oregon. Are payments to directors the same as wages for tax purposes? Explain. [*Necanicum Investment Co. v. Employment Department*, 345 Or. 138, 190 P.3d 368 (2008)]

26.8 A Question of Ethics. *New Orleans Paddlewheels, Inc. (NOP), is a Louisiana corporation formed in 1982. James Smith, Sr., and Warren Reuther were its only shareholders, with each holding 50 percent of the stock. NOP is part of a sprawling enterprise of tourism and hospitality companies. The positions on the board of each company were split equally between the Smith and Reuther families. At Smith's request, his son, James Smith, Jr. (JES), became involved in the businesses. In 1999, NOP's board elected JES president, in charge of day-to-day operations, and Reuther chief executive officer (CEO), in charge of marketing and development. Animosity soon developed between Reuther and JES. In 2001, JES terminated Reuther as CEO and denied him access to NOP's offices and books, literally changing the locks on the doors. At the next board meeting, deadlock ensued, with the directors voting along family lines on every issue. Complaining that the meetings were a "waste of time," JES began to run the entire enterprise by taking advantage of an unequal balance of power on the companies' executive committees. In NOP's subsequent bankruptcy proceeding, Reuther filed a motion for the appointment of a trustee to formulate a plan for the firm's reorganization, alleging misconduct by NOP's management. [In re New Orleans Paddlewheels, Inc., 350 Bankr. 667 (E.D.La. 2006)]*

1 Was Reuther legally entitled to have access to NOP's books and records? JES maintained, among other things, that NOP's books were "a mess." Was JES's denial of that access unethical? Explain.

2 How would you describe JES's attempt to gain control of NOP and the other companies? Were his actions deceptive and self-serving in the pursuit of personal gain or legitimate and reasonable in the pursuit of a business goal? Discuss.

CRITICAL THINKING AND WRITING ASSIGNMENT

26.9 Critical Legal Thinking. Do corporations benefit from shareholder's derivative suits? If so, how?

ACCESSING THE INTERNET

For updated links to resources available on the Web, as well as a variety of other materials, visit this text's Web site at

www.cengage.com/blaw/fbl

One of the best sources on the Web for information on corporations, including their directors, is the EDGAR database of the Securities and Exchange Commission (SEC) at

www.sec.gov/edgar.shtml

You can find definitions for terms used in corporate law, as well as court decisions and articles on corporate law topics, at

www.law.com

For information on the SEC's rulings, including rulings on proxy materials, go to

www.sec.gov/rules/final.shtml

PRACTICAL INTERNET EXERCISES

Go to this text's Web site at **www.cengage.com/blaw/fbl**, select "Chapter 26," and click on "Practical Internet Exercises." There you will find the following Internet research exercises that you can perform to learn more about the topics covered in this chapter.

PRACTICAL INTERNET EXERCISE 26–1 LEGAL PERSPECTIVE—Liability of Directors and Officers

PRACTICAL INTERNET EXERCISE 26–2 MANAGEMENT PERSPECTIVE—D&O Insurance

BEFORE THE TEST

Go to this text's Web site at **www.cengage.com/blaw/fbl**, select "Chapter 26," and click on "Interactive Quizzes." You will find a number of interactive questions relating to this chapter.

CHAPTER 27
Investor Protection, Insider Trading, and Corporate Governance

LEARNING OBJECTIVES

AFTER READING THIS CHAPTER, YOU SHOULD BE ABLE TO ANSWER THE FOLLOWING QUESTIONS:

1 What is meant by the term *securities?*

2 What are the two major statutes regulating the securities industry? When was the Securities and Exchange Commission created, and what are its major purposes and functions?

3 What is insider trading? Why is it prohibited?

4 What are some of the features of state securities laws?

5 What certification requirements does the Sarbanes-Oxley Act impose on corporate executives?

After the stock market crash of 1929, many members of Congress argued in favor of regulating securities markets. Basically, legislation for such regulation was enacted to provide investors with more information to help them make buying and selling decisions about **securities**—generally defined as any documents or records evidencing corporate ownership (stock) or debts (bonds)—and to prohibit deceptive, unfair, and manipulative practices. Today, the sale and transfer of securities are heavily regulated by federal and state statutes and by government agencies.

This chapter discusses the nature of federal securities regulation and its effect on the business world. We begin by looking at the federal administrative agency that regulates securities transactions. Next, we examine the major traditional laws governing securities offerings and trading. We then discuss corporate governance and the Sarbanes-Oxley Act of 2002,[1] which affects certain types of securities transactions. Finally, we look at the problem of online securities fraud.

1. 15 U.S.C. Sections 7201 *et seq.*

THE SECURITIES AND EXCHANGE COMMISSION

In 1931, the Senate passed a resolution calling for an extensive investigation of securities trading. The investigation led, ultimately, to the passage by Congress of the Securities Act of 1933, which is also known as the *truth-in-securities* bill. In the following year, Congress passed the Securities Exchange Act. This 1934 act created the Securities and Exchange Commission (SEC).

Major Responsibilities of the SEC

The SEC was created as an independent regulatory agency with the function of administering the 1933 and 1934 acts. Its major responsibilities in this respect are as follows:

1 Requiring disclosure of facts concerning offerings of securities listed on national securities exchanges and of certain securities traded over the counter (OTC).

2 Regulating the trade in securities on national and regional securities exchanges and in the OTC markets.

3 Investigating securities fraud.

4 Regulating the activities of securities brokers, dealers, and investment advisers and requiring their registration.

5 Supervising the activities of mutual funds.

6 Recommending administrative sanctions, injunctive remedies, and criminal prosecution against those who violate securities laws. (The SEC can bring enforcement actions for civil violations of federal securities laws. The Fraud Section of the Criminal Division of the Department of Justice prosecutes criminal violations.)

The SEC's Expanding Regulatory Powers

Since its creation, the SEC's regulatory functions have gradually been increased by legislation granting it authority in different areas. For example, to further curb securities fraud, the Securities Enforcement Remedies and Penny Stock Reform Act of 1990 amended existing securities laws to allow SEC administrative law judges to hear many more types of securities violation cases; the SEC's enforcement options were also greatly expanded. Additionally, the act provides that courts can prevent persons who have engaged in securities fraud from serving as officers and directors of publicly held corporations. The Securities Acts Amendments of 1990 authorized the SEC to seek sanctions against those who violate foreign securities laws.

The National Securities Markets Improvement Act of 1996 expanded the power of the SEC to exempt persons, securities, and transactions from the requirements of the securities laws. (This part of the act is also known as the Capital Markets Efficiency Act.) The act also limited the authority of the states to regulate certain securities transactions and particular investment advisory firms. The Sarbanes-Oxley Act of 2002, which will be discussed later in this chapter, further expanded the authority of the SEC by directing the agency to issue new rules relating to corporate disclosure requirements and by creating an SEC oversight board.

SECURITIES ACT OF 1933

The Securities Act of 1933[2] governs initial sales of stock by businesses. The act was designed to prohibit various forms of fraud and to stabilize the securities industry by requiring that all essential information concerning the issuance of securities be made available to the investing public. Basically, the purpose of this act is to require disclosure. The 1933 act pro-

vides that all securities transactions must be registered with the SEC or be exempt from registration requirements.

What Is a Security?

Section 2(1) of the Securities Act of 1933 contains a broad definition of securities, which generally include the following:[3]

1 Instruments and interests commonly known as securities, such as preferred and common stocks, treasury stocks, bonds, debentures, and stock warrants.

2 Any interests commonly known as securities, such as stock options, puts, calls, and other types of privilege on a security or on the right to purchase a security or a group of securities in a national security exchange.

3 Notes, instruments, or other evidence of indebtedness, including certificates of interest in a profit-sharing agreement and certificates of deposit.

4 Any fractional undivided interest in oil, gas, or other mineral rights.

5 Investment contracts, which include interests in limited partnerships and other investment schemes.

In interpreting the act, the United States Supreme Court has held that an **investment contract** is any transaction in which a person (1) invests (2) in a common enterprise (3) reasonably expecting profits (4) derived *primarily* or *substantially* from others' managerial or entrepreneurial efforts. Known as the *Howey* test, this definition continues to guide the determination of what types of contracts can be considered securities.[4]

For our purposes, it is convenient to think of securities in their most common form—stocks and bonds issued by corporations. Bear in mind, though, that securities can take many forms, including interests in whiskey, cosmetics, worms, beavers, boats, vacuum cleaners, muskrats, and cemetery lots. Almost any stake in the ownership or debt of a company can be considered a security. Investment contracts in condominiums, franchises, limited partnerships in real estate, oil or gas or other mineral rights, and farm animals accompanied by care agreements have qualified as securities.

■**EXAMPLE 27.1** Alpha Telcom sold, installed, and maintained pay-phone systems. As part of its pay-phone program, Alpha guaranteed buyers a 14 percent return on the amount of their purchase. Alpha was operating at a net loss, however, and continually borrowed funds to pay investors the fixed rate of return it had promised. Eventually, the company filed for bankruptcy, and the SEC brought an action alleging that

---

2. 15 U.S.C. Sections 77–77aa.

3. 15 U.S.C. Section 77b(1). Amendments in 1982 added stock options.
4. *SEC v. W. J. Howey Co.,* 328 U.S. 293, 66 S.Ct. 1100, 90 L.Ed. 1244 (1946).

Alpha had violated the Securities Act of 1933. In this situation, a federal court concluded that the pay-phone program was a security because it involved an investment contract.[5] ■

PREVENTING LEGAL DISPUTES **Securities are not limited to stocks and bonds but can encompass a wide variety of legal claims. The analysis hinges on the nature of the transaction rather than the instrument or substance involved. Because Congress enacted securities laws to regulate *investments,* in whatever form and by whatever name they are called, virtually any type of security that might be sold as an investment can be subject to securities laws. When in doubt about whether an investment transaction involves securities, seek the advice of a specialized attorney.**

■

Registration Statement

Section 5 of the Securities Act of 1933 broadly provides that unless a security qualifies for an exemption, that security must be *registered* before it is offered to the public. Issuing corporations must file a *registration statement* with the SEC and must provide all investors with a *prospectus.* A **prospectus** is a written disclosure document that describes the security being sold, the financial operations of the issuing corporation, and the investment or risk attaching to the security. The 1933 act requires the issuer to deliver a prospectus to investors, and issuers use this document as a selling tool. The issuer has the option of delivering the prospectus electronically via the Internet.[6] In principle, the registration statement and the prospectus supply sufficient information to enable unsophisticated investors to evaluate the financial risk involved.

Contents of the Registration Statement The registration statement must be written in plain English and fully describe the following:

1 The securities being offered for sale, including their relationship to the registrant's other capital securities.

2 The corporation's properties and business (including a financial statement certified by an independent public accounting firm).

3 The management of the corporation, including managerial compensation, stock options, pensions, and other benefits. Any interests of directors or officers in any material transactions with the corporation must be disclosed.

4 How the corporation intends to use the proceeds of the sale.

5 Any pending lawsuits or special risk factors.

All companies, both domestic and foreign, must file their registration statements electronically so that they can be posted on the SEC's electronic database, which is called EDGAR (Electronic Data Gathering, Analysis, and Retrieval). The EDGAR database includes material on initial public offerings (IPOs), proxy statements, corporations' annual reports, registration statements, and other documents that have been filed with the SEC. Investors can access the database via the Internet to obtain information for use in making investment decisions.

Registration Process The registration statement does not become effective until after it has been reviewed and approved by the SEC. The 1933 act restricts the types of activities that an issuer can engage in at each stage in the registration process. If an issuer violates the restrictions discussed here, investors can rescind their contracts to purchase the securities. During the *prefiling period* (before the registration statement is filed), the issuer cannot either sell or offer to sell the securities. No advertising of an upcoming securities offering is allowed during the prefiling period.

Waiting Period. Once the registration statement has been filed, a waiting period of at least twenty days begins during which the SEC reviews the registration statement for completeness. Typically, the SEC staff members who review the registration statement ask the registrant to make numerous changes and additions, which can extend the length of the waiting period.[7]

During the waiting period, the securities can be offered for sale but cannot be sold by the issuing corporation. Only certain types of offers are allowed. All issuers can distribute a *preliminary prospectus,* called a **red herring prospectus.**[8] A red herring prospectus contains most of the information that will be included in the final prospectus but often does not

---

5. *SEC v. Alpha Telcom, Inc.,* 187 F.Supp.2d 1250 (2002). See also *SEC v. Edwards,* 540 U.S. 389, 124 S.Ct. 892, 157 L.Ed.2d 813 (2004).

6. Basically, an electronic prospectus must meet the same requirements as a printed prospectus. The SEC has special rules that address situations in which the graphics, images, or audio files in a printed prospectus cannot be reproduced in an electronic form. 17 C.F.R. Section 232.304.

7. The SEC commonly requires a registrant to provide additional information more than once. Only after the registration statement has gone through several rounds of changes does the SEC give its approval. In these circumstances, because the process may have taken months to complete, registrants frequently request an acceleration of the twenty-day waiting period. If the SEC grants the request, registration can become effective without the issuer having to wait the full twenty days after the last round of changes.

8. The name *red herring* comes from the legend printed in red across the prospectus stating that the registration has been filed but has not become effective.

include a price. General advertising is permitted, such as a **tombstone ad,** so named because historically the format resembled a tombstone. Such ads simply tell the investor where and how to obtain a prospectus.[9]

In 2005, the SEC reformed its rules to authorize the use of a *free-writing prospectus* during this period.[10] A **free-writing prospectus** is any type of written, electronic, or graphic offer that describes the issuer or its securities and includes a legend indicating that the investor can obtain the prospectus at the SEC's Web site. The issuer normally must file the free-writing prospectus with the SEC no later than the first date it is used. Certain inexperienced issuers are required to file a *preliminary prospectus* prior to the filing of a free-writing prospectus.

Posteffective Period. Once the SEC has reviewed and approved the registration statement and the twenty-day period has elapsed, the registration is effective. The issuer can now offer and sell the securities without restrictions. If the company issued a preliminary prospectus to investors, it must provide those investors with a final prospectus either prior to or at the time they purchase the securities. The issuer can require investors to download the final prospectus from a Web site, but it must notify investors of the Internet address at which they can access the prospectus. ◼**EXAMPLE 27.2** Delphia, Inc., wants to make a public offering of its common stock. The firm files a registration statement and a prospectus with the SEC. On the same day, the company can make *offers* to sell the stock and start using a free-writing prospectus, but it cannot actually sell any of its stock. Delphia and its attorneys continue to work with the SEC and provide additional information to it for nearly six months. When the SEC finally indicates that it has all the necessary information for the registration statement to be approved, Delphia can request an acceleration of the twenty-day waiting period. Only *after* the SEC declares the registration to be effective and the waiting period has elapsed or been accelerated can Delphia sell the first shares in the issue. ◼

Exempt Securities

A number of specific securities are exempt from the registration requirements of the Securities Act of 1933. These securities—which can also generally be resold without being registered—include the following:[11]

1 Government-issued securities.

2 Bank and financial institution securities, which are regulated by banking authorities.

3 Short-term notes and drafts (negotiable instruments that have a maturity date that does not exceed nine months).

4 Securities of nonprofit, educational, and charitable organizations.

5 Securities issued by common carriers (railroads and trucking companies).

6 Any insurance, endowment, or annuity contract issued by a state-regulated insurance company.

7 Securities issued in a corporate reorganization in which one security is exchanged for another or in a bankruptcy proceeding.

8 Securities issued in stock dividends and stock splits.

Exhibit 27–1 summarizes the securities and transactions (discussed next) that are exempt from the registration requirements under the Securities Act of 1933 and SEC regulations.

Exempt Transactions

In addition to the exempt securities listed in the previous subsection, certain *transactions* are exempt from registration requirements. These transaction exemptions are very broad and can enable an issuer to avoid the high cost and complicated procedures associated with registration. Because the coverage of the exemptions overlaps somewhat, an offering may qualify for more than one. Therefore, many sales of securities occur without registration.

Regulation A Offerings Securities issued by an issuer that has offered less than $5 million in securities during any twelve-month period are exempt from registration. Under Regulation A,[12] the issuer must file with the SEC a notice of the issue and an offering circular, which must also be provided to investors before the sale. This process is much simpler and less expensive than the procedures associated with full registration. Companies are allowed to "test the waters" for potential interest before preparing the offering circular. To *test the waters* means to determine potential interest without actually selling any securities or requiring any commitment on the part of those who express interest. Small-business issuers (companies with annual revenues of less than $25 million) can also use an integrated registration and reporting system that uses simpler forms than the full registration system.

Some companies have sold their securities via the Internet using Regulation A. ◼**EXAMPLE 27.3** In 1996, the

---

9. During the waiting period, the SEC also allows *road shows*, in which a corporate executive travels around speaking to institutional investors and securities analysts, as well as electronic road shows, which are viewed via real-time communications methods, such as Webcasting.

10. See SEC Rules 164 and 433. Note also that companies that qualify as "well-known seasoned issuers" under the SEC's rules (large corporations with stock valued at $700 million or more in the hands of the public) can even use a free-writing prospectus during the prefiling period.

11. 15 U.S.C. Section 77c.

12. 17 C.F.R. Sections 230.251–230.263.

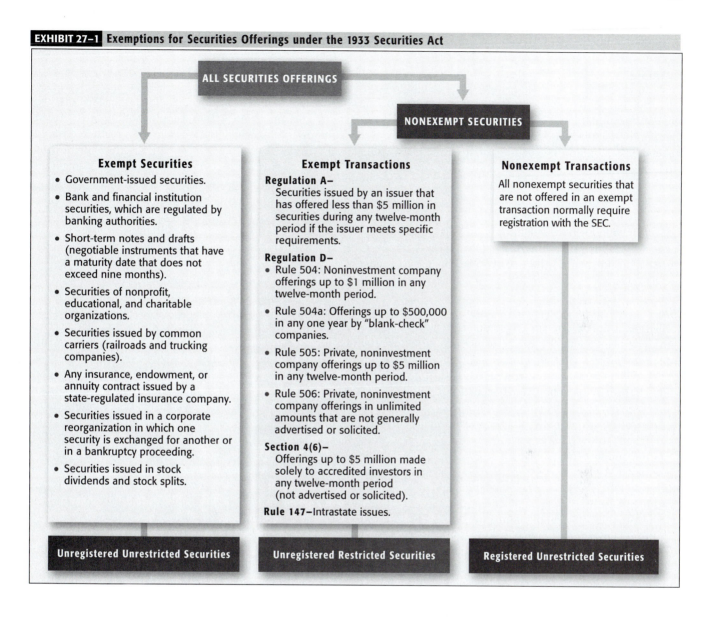

EXHIBIT 27–1 Exemptions for Securities Offerings under the 1933 Securities Act

Spring Street Brewing Company became the first company to sell securities via an online initial public offering (IPO). Spring Street raised about $1.6 million—without having to pay any commissions to brokers or underwriters. ■ Such online IPOs are particularly attractive to small companies and start-up ventures that may find it difficult to raise capital from institutional investors or through underwriters. By making the offering online under Regulation A, the company can avoid both commissions and the costly and time-consuming filings required for a traditional IPO under federal and state law.

Small Offerings—Regulation D The SEC's Regulation D contains four separate exemptions from registration requirements for limited offers (offers that either involve a small dol-

lar amount or are made in a limited manner). Regulation D provides that any of these offerings made during any twelve-month period are exempt from the registration requirements.

Rule 504. Noninvestment company offerings up to $1 million in any twelve-month period are exempt.[13] Noninvestment companies are firms that are not engaged primarily in the business of investing or trading in securities. (In contrast, an **investment company** is a firm that buys a large portfolio of securities and professionally manages it on behalf of many

---

13. 17 C.F.R. Section 230.504. Rule 504 is the exemption used by most small businesses, but that could change under new SEC Rule 1001. This rule permits, under certain circumstances, "testing the waters" for offerings of up to $5 million per transaction. These offerings can be made only to "qualified purchasers" (knowledgeable, sophisticated investors), though.

smaller shareholders/owners. A **mutual fund** is a type of investment company.)

■EXAMPLE 27.4 Zeta Enterprises is a limited partnership that develops commercial property. Zeta intends to offer $600,000 of its limited partnership interests for sale between June 1 and next May 31. The buyers will become limited partners in Zeta. Because an interest in a limited partnership meets the definition of a security (discussed earlier in this chapter), its sale is subject to the registration and prospectus requirements of the Securities Act of 1933. Under Rule 504, however, the sales of Zeta's interests are exempt from these requirements because Zeta is a noninvestment company making an offering of less than $1 million in a twelve-month period. Therefore, Zeta can sell its interests without filing a registration statement with the SEC or issuing a prospectus to any investor. ■

Rule 504a. Offerings up to $500,000 in any one year by so-called blank-check companies—companies with no specific business plans except to locate and acquire currently unknown businesses or opportunities—are exempt if no general solicitation or advertising is used; the SEC is notified of the sales; and precautions are taken against nonexempt, unregistered resales.[14] The limits on advertising and unregistered resales do not apply if the offering is made solely in states that provide for registration and disclosure and the securities are sold in compliance with those provisions.[15]

Rule 505. Private, noninvestment company offerings up to $5 million in any twelve-month period are exempt, regardless of the number of **accredited investors** (banks, insurance companies, investment companies, the issuer's executive officers and directors, and persons whose income or net worth exceeds certain limits), so long as there are no more than thirty-five unaccredited investors; no general solicitation or advertising is used; the SEC is notified of the sales; and precautions are taken against nonexempt, unregistered resales. If the sale involves *any* unaccredited investors, *all* investors must be given material information about the offering company, its business, and the securities before the sale. Unlike Rule 506 (discussed next), Rule 505 does not require that the issuer believe each unaccredited investor "has such knowledge and experience in financial and business matters that he

[or she] is capable of evaluating the merits and the risks of the prospective investment."[16]

Rule 506. Private, noninvestment company offerings in unlimited amounts that are not generally solicited or advertised are exempt if the SEC is notified of the sales and precautions are taken against nonexempt, unregistered resales. As with Rule 505, there may be no more than thirty-five unaccredited investors, but there are no limits on the number of accredited investors. If there are *any* unaccredited investors, the issuer must provide all purchasers with material information about itself, its business, and the securities before the sale.[17] In contrast to Rule 505, the issuer must believe that each unaccredited investor has sufficient knowledge or experience in financial matters to be capable of evaluating the investment's merits and risks.

This exemption is perhaps most important to firms that want to raise funds through the sale of securities without registering them. It is often referred to as the *private placement* exemption because it exempts "transactions not involving any public offering."[18] This provision applies to private offerings to a limited number of persons who are sufficiently sophisticated and able to assume the risk of the investment (and who thus have no need for federal registration protection). It also applies to private offerings to similarly situated institutional investors.

■EXAMPLE 27.5 To raise capital to expand operations, Citco decides to make a private $10 million offering of its common stock directly to two hundred accredited investors and a group of thirty highly sophisticated, but unaccredited, investors. Citco provides all of these investors with a prospectus and material information about the firm, including its most recent financial statements. As long as Citco notifies the SEC of the sale, this offering will likely qualify as an exempt transaction under Rule 506. The offering is nonpublic and not generally advertised. There are fewer than thirty-five unaccredited investors, and each of them possesses sufficient knowledge and experience to evaluate the risks involved. The issuer has provided all purchasers with the material information. Thus, Citco will *not* be required to comply with the Securities Act of 1933. ■

Small Offerings—Section 4(6) Under Section 4(6) of the Securities Act of 1933, an offer made *solely* to accredited investors is exempt if its amount is not more than $5 million. Any number of accredited investors may participate, but no unaccredited investors may do so. No general solicitation or

---

14. Precautions to be taken against nonexempt, unregistered resales include asking the investor whether he or she is buying the securities for others; before the sale, disclosing to each purchaser in writing that the securities are unregistered and thus cannot be resold, except in an exempt transaction, without first being registered; and indicating on the certificates that the securities are unregistered and restricted.

15. 17 C.F.R. Section 230.504a.

16. 17 C.F.R. Section 230.505.
17. 17 C.F.R. Section 230.506.
18. 15 U.S.C. Section 77d(2).

advertising may be used; the SEC must be notified of all sales; and precautions must be taken against nonexempt, unregistered resales. Precautions are necessary because these are *restricted* securities and may be resold only by registration or in an exempt transaction. (The securities purchased and sold by most people who deal in stock are called, in contrast, *unrestricted* securities.)

Intrastate Offerings—Rule 147 Also exempt are intrastate transactions involving purely local offerings.[19] This exemption applies to most offerings that are restricted to residents of the state in which the issuing company is organized and doing business. For nine months after the last sale, virtually no resales may be made to nonresidents, and precautions must be taken against this possibility. These offerings remain subject to applicable laws in the state of issue.

Resales Most securities can be resold without registration (although some resales may be subject to restrictions, as discussed above in connection with specific exemptions). The Securities Act of 1933 provides exemptions for resales by most persons other than issuers or underwriters. The average investor who sells shares of stock does not have to file a registration statement with the SEC. Resales of restricted securities acquired under Rule 504a, Rule 505, Rule 506, or Section 4(6), however, trigger the registration requirements unless the party selling them complies with Rule 144 or Rule 144A. These rules are sometimes referred to as "safe harbors."

Rule 144. Rule 144 exempts restricted securities from registration on resale if there is adequate current public information about the issuer, the person selling the securities has owned them for at least one year, they are sold in certain limited amounts in unsolicited brokers' transactions, and the SEC is given notice of the resale.[20] "Adequate current public information" refers to the reports that certain companies are required to file under the Securities Exchange Act of 1934. A person who has owned the securities for at least one year is subject to none of these requirements, unless the person is an affiliate. An *affiliate* is one who controls, is controlled by, or is in common control with the issuer.

Rule 144A. Securities that at the time of issue are not of the same class as securities listed on a national securities exchange or quoted in a U.S. automated interdealer quotation system may be resold under Rule 144A.[21] They may be sold only to a qualified institutional buyer (an institution, such as an insurance company or a bank that owns and invests at least $100 million in securities). The seller must take reasonable steps to ensure that the buyer knows that the seller is relying on the exemption under Rule 144A.

Violations of the 1933 Act

It is a violation of the Securities Act of 1933 to intentionally defraud investors by misrepresenting or omitting facts in a registration statement or prospectus. Liability is also imposed on those who are negligent for not discovering the fraud. Selling securities before the effective date of the registration statement or under an exemption for which the securities do not qualify results in liability.

Criminal violations are prosecuted by the U.S. Department of Justice. Violators may be fined up to $10,000, imprisoned for up to five years, or both. The SEC is authorized to seek civil sanctions against those who willfully violate the 1933 act. It can request an injunction to prevent further sales of the securities involved or ask the court to grant other relief, such as an order to a violator to refund profits. Parties who purchase securities and suffer harm as a result of false or omitted statements may also bring suits in a federal court to recover their losses and other damages.

There are three basic defenses to violations of the 1933 act. A defendant can avoid liability by proving that (1) the statement or omission was not material, (2) the plaintiff knew about the misrepresentation at the time of purchasing the stock, or (3) the defendant exercised *due diligence* in preparing the registration and reasonably believed at the time that the statements were true.

SECURITIES EXCHANGE ACT OF 1934

The Securities Exchange Act of 1934 provides for the regulation and registration of securities exchanges, brokers, dealers, and national securities associations, such as the National Association of Securities Dealers (NASD). Unlike the 1933 act, which is a one-time disclosure law, the 1934 act provides for continuous periodic disclosures by publicly held corporations to enable the SEC to regulate subsequent trading.

The Securities Exchange Act of 1934 applies to companies that have assets in excess of $10 million and five hundred or more shareholders. These corporations are referred to as Section 12 companies because they are required to register their securities under Section 12 of the 1934 act. Section 12 companies are required to file reports with the SEC annually and quarterly, and sometimes even monthly if specified events occur (such as a merger).

The act also authorizes the SEC to engage in market surveillance to deter undesirable market practices, such as fraud,

---

19. 15 U.S.C. Section 77c(a)(11); 17 C.F.R. Section 230.147.
20. 17 C.F.R. Section 230.144.
21. 17 C.F.R. Section 230.144A.

market manipulation (attempts at illegally influencing stock prices), and misrepresentation. In addition, the act provides for the SEC's regulation of proxy solicitations for voting (discussed in Chapter 26).

Section 10(b), SEC Rule 10b-5, and Insider Trading

Section 10(b) is one of the most important sections of the Securities Exchange Act of 1934. This section proscribes the use of any manipulative or deceptive device in violation of SEC rules and regulations. Among the rules that the SEC has promulgated pursuant to the 1934 act is **SEC Rule 10b-5**, which prohibits the commission of fraud in connection with the purchase or sale of any security.

Applicability of SEC Rule 10b-5 SEC Rule 10b-5 applies in virtually all cases concerning the trading of securities, whether on organized exchanges, in over-the-counter markets, or in private transactions. The rule covers just about any form of security, including notes, bonds, agreements to form a corporation, and joint-venture agreements. A firm's securities do not have to be registered under the 1933 act for the 1934 act to apply.

SEC Rule 10b-5 is applicable only when the requisites of federal jurisdiction—such as the use of stock exchange facilities, U.S. mail, or any means of interstate commerce—are present. Nevertheless, virtually every commercial transaction involves interstate contacts. In addition, the states have corporate securities laws, many of which include provisions similar to SEC Rule 10b-5.

Insider Trading One of the major goals of Section 10(b) and SEC Rule 10b-5 is to prevent so-called **insider trading**, which occurs when persons buy or sell securities on the basis of information that is not available to the public. Corporate directors, officers, and others (such as majority shareholders) often have advance inside information that can affect the future market value of the corporate stock. Obviously, if they act on this information, their positions give them a trading advantage over the general public and other shareholders. The 1934 Securities Exchange Act defines inside information and extends liability to those who take advantage of such information in their personal transactions when they know that the information is unavailable to those with whom they are dealing. Section 10(b) of the 1934 act and SEC Rule 10b-5 apply to anyone who has access to or receives information of a nonpublic nature on which trading is based—not just to corporate "insiders."

Disclosure under SEC Rule 10b-5 Any material omission or misrepresentation of material facts in connection with the purchase or sale of a security may violate not only the Securities Act of 1933 but also the antifraud provisions of Section 10(b) of the 1934 act and SEC Rule 10b-5. The key to liability (which can be civil or criminal) under Section 10(b) and SEC Rule 10b-5 is whether the insider's information is *material*.

The following are some examples of material facts calling for disclosure under SEC Rule 10b-5:

1 Fraudulent trading in the company stock by a broker-dealer.

2 A dividend change (whether up or down).

3 A contract for the sale of corporate assets.

4 A new discovery, a new process, or a new product.

5 A significant change in the firm's financial condition.

6 Potential litigation against the company.

Note that any one of these facts, by itself, is not *automatically* considered a material fact. Rather, it will be regarded as a material fact if it is significant enough to affect an investor's decision as to whether to purchase or sell the company's securities. ■**EXAMPLE 27.6** Tron, Inc., is the defendant in a class-action product liability lawsuit. Tron's attorney believes it likely that the company will ultimately be held liable for damages, resulting in a considerable loss. She advises Tron's management that the company will probably be required to pay damages as a result of the suit. If Tron wants to make a stock offering before the end of the trial, it must disclose this potential liability because these facts are significant enough to affect an investor's decision to purchase Tron's stock. ■ In the following landmark case, the court had to interpret SEC Rule 10b-5.

CASE 27.1 **SEC v. Texas Gulf Sulphur Co.**

LANDMARK AND CLASSIC CASES

United States Court of Appeals, Second Circuit, 401 F.2d 833 (1968).

FACTS In 1963, Texas Gulf Sulphur Company (TGS) drilled a hole that appeared to yield a core with an exceedingly high mineral content. TGS kept secret the results of the core sample. Officers and employees of the company made substantial purchases of TGS's stock or accepted stock options after learning of the ore discovery, even though further drilling was necessary to determine whether there was enough ore to

CASE 27.1—Continued

be mined commercially. On April 11, 1964, an unauthorized report of the mineral find appeared in the newspapers. On the following day, TGS issued a press release that played down the discovery. Later, TGS announced a strike of at least 25 million tons of ore, substantially driving up the price of TGS stock. The SEC brought suit in a federal district court against the officers and employees of TGS for violating the insider-trading prohibition of SEC Rule 10b-5. The officers and employees argued that the prohibition did not apply. They reasoned that the information on which they had traded was not material because the ore find had not been commercially proved. The court held that most of the defendants had not violated SEC Rule 10b-5, and the SEC appealed.

ISSUE Had the officers and employees of TGS violated SEC Rule 10b-5 by purchasing the stock, even though they did not know the full extent and profit potential of the mine at the time they purchased the stock?

DECISION Yes. The federal appellate court reversed the lower court's decision and remanded the case to the trial court, holding that the employees and officers had violated SEC Rule 10b-5's prohibition against insider trading.

REASON For SEC Rule 10b-5 purposes, the test of materiality is whether the information would affect the judgment of reasonable investors. Reasonable investors include speculative as well as conservative investors. "A major factor in determining whether the * * * discovery [of the ore] was a material fact is the importance attached to the drilling results by those who knew about it. * * * The timing

by those who knew of it of their stock purchases and their purchases of short-term calls [rights to buy shares at a specified price within a specified time period]—purchases in some cases by individuals who had never before purchased calls or even TGS stock—virtually compels the inference that the insiders were influenced by the drilling results. * * * We hold, therefore, that all transactions in TGS stock or calls by individuals apprised of the drilling results * * * were made in violation of Rule 10b-5."

 WHAT IF THE FACTS WERE DIFFERENT? *Suppose that further drilling revealed that there was not enough ore at this site for it to be mined commercially. Would the defendants still have been liable for violating SEC Rule 10b-5? Why or why not?*

IMPACT OF THIS CASE ON TODAY'S LAW *This case affirmed the principle that the test of whether information is "material," for SEC Rule 10b-5 purposes, is whether it would affect the judgment of reasonable investors. The corporate insiders' purchases of stock and stock options indicated that they were influenced by the drilling results and that the information about the drilling results was material. The courts continue to cite this case when applying SEC Rule 10b-5 to cases of alleged insider trading.*

RELEVANT WEB SITES *To locate information on the Web concerning* SEC v. Texas Gulf Sulphur Co., *go to this text's Web site at* **www.cengage.com/blaw/fbl**, *select "Chapter 27," and click on "URLs for Landmark Cases."*

The Private Securities Litigation Reform Act of 1995 One of the unintended effects of SEC Rule 10b-5 was to deter the disclosure of some material information, such as financial forecasts. To understand why, consider an example. **■EXAMPLE 27.7** AQT Company announces that its projected earnings for the next year will be a certain amount. The forecast turns out to be wrong. The earnings are in fact much lower, and the price of AQT's stock is affected—negatively. The shareholders then bring a class-action suit against the company, alleging that the directors violated SEC Rule 10b-5 by disclosing misleading financial information. ■

In an attempt to rectify this problem and promote disclosure, Congress passed the Private Securities Litigation Reform Act of 1995. Among other things, the act provides a "safe harbor" for publicly held companies that make forward-looking statements, such as financial forecasts. Those who make such statements are protected against liability for secu-

rities fraud as long as the statements are accompanied by "meaningful cautionary statements identifying important factors that could cause actual results to differ materially from those in the forward-looking statement."[22]

After the 1995 act was passed, a number of securities class-action suits were filed in state courts to skirt the requirements of the federal act. In response, Congress passed the Securities Litigation Uniform Standards Act of 1998 (SLUSA).[23] The act placed stringent limits on the ability of plaintiffs to bring class-action suits in state courts against firms whose securities are traded on national stock exchanges. The SLUSA not only prevents purchasers and sellers of securities from bringing class-action fraud claims

---

22. 15 U.S.C. Sections 77z-2, 78u-5.
23. Pub. L. No. 105-353. This act amended many sections of Title 15 of the *United States Code*.

under state securities laws, but also prevents investors who allege fraud from suing under state law.[24]

Outsiders and SEC Rule 10b-5   The traditional insider-trading case involves true insiders—corporate officers, directors, and majority shareholders who have access to (and trade on) inside information. Increasingly, liability under Section

10(b) of the 1934 act and SEC Rule 10b-5 is being extended to include certain "outsiders"—persons who trade on inside information acquired indirectly. Two theories have been developed under which outsiders may be held liable for insider trading: the *tipper/tippee theory* and the *misappropriation theory* (to be discussed shortly).

In the following case, the plaintiffs attempted to assert a third theory—scheme liability. Can Section 10(b) and SEC Rule 10b-5 apply to outsiders—suppliers and customers—who seemingly "aid and abet" a scheme to show inflated sales revenue figures for a publicly traded company?

---

24. See *Merrill Lynch, Pierce, Fenner & Smith, Inc. v. Dabit*, 547 U.S. 71, 126 S.Ct. 1503, 164 L.Ed.2d 179 (2006).

CASE 27.2   Stoneridge Investment Partners, LLC v. Scientific-Atlanta, Inc.

Supreme Court of the United States, ___ U.S. ___, 128 S.Ct. 761, 169 L.Ed.2d 627 (2008).
www.supremecourtus.gov/opinions/opinions.html[a]

FACTS   In 2000, the cable operator Charter Communications wanted to keep its stock price high by satisfying stock analysts' expectations about its revenue growth. When it became apparent that revenues were not growing as projected, management at Charter devised an accounting scheme that would artificially inflate its reported revenues. The scheme involved Charter's digital cable converter (set top) box suppliers, Scientific-Atlanta and Motorola. They agreed to overcharge Charter for the cable boxes in exchange for additional advertising on Charter's cable network. A group of investors, represented in this case by Stoneridge Investment Partners, sued Scientific-Atlanta and Motorola, alleging violation of Section 10(b) of the Securities Exchange Act of 1934 and of SEC Rule 10b-5. At trial, the district court dismissed the case. On appeal, the U.S. Court of Appeals for the Eighth Circuit upheld this ruling. Stoneridge then appealed to the United States Supreme Court.

ISSUE   Can Charter investors sue third-party suppliers and customers (Scientific-Atlanta and Motorola) for participating in scheme to overcharge Charter for cable boxes so that Charter could report inflated sales revenue figures?

DECISION   No. The United States Supreme Court affirmed the federal appellate court's decision that dismissed the case against Scientific-Atlanta and Motorola. Section 10(b)'s private right of action cannot be applied to a supplier or customer. Investors did not rely on Scientific-Atlanta's and Motorola's statements or representations.

REASON   The Court pointed out that Scientific-Atlanta and Motorola had no role in preparing or disseminating Charter's financial statements. The financial statements of both Scientific-Atlanta and Motorola were correct. The $20 per cable set top box that they received from Charter was offset by their agreeing to spend the equivalent of $20 per cable set top box in additional advertising. They "booked the transactions as a wash, under generally accepted accounting practices." To bring a private action under Section 10(b), the plaintiff must have relied on the defendant's deceptive acts. There has to be the "requisite causal connection between a defendant's misrepresentation and a plaintiff's injury" in order to assess liability against the defendant. But neither Scientific-Atlanta nor Motorola had a duty to disclose, and their deceptive acts were not communicated to the public. "No member of the investing public had knowledge, either actual or presumed, of [their] deceptive acts during the relevant times." As a result, Stoneridge was unable to show reliance upon any of the actions of Scientific-Atlanta and Motorola "except in an indirect chain" that the Court found too remote to justify liability.

FOR CRITICAL ANALYSIS—Ethical Consideration   As suppliers to Charter, Scientific-Atlanta and Motorola simply engaged in an accounting fiction that, as the Court pointed out, appeared on their books as a "wash." Hence, these two companies conformed to generally accepted accounting rules. Nonetheless, was their behavior ethical? Why or why not?

---

a. Click on "Opinions" and go to 2008 to find this case, which was decided on 1/15/08. Click on the case name to access the opinion.

■

Tipper/Tippee Theory. Anyone who acquires inside information as a result of a corporate insider's breach of his or her fiduciary duty can be liable under SEC Rule 10b-5. This liability extends to **tippees** (those who receive "tips" from insiders) and even remote tippees (tippees of tippees).

The key to liability under this theory is that the inside information must be obtained as a result of someone's breach of a fiduciary duty to the corporation whose shares are involved in the trading. The tippee is liable under this theory only if (1) there is a breach of a duty not to disclose inside information, (2) the disclosure is in exchange for personal benefit, and (3) the tippee knows (or should know) of this breach and benefits from it.[25]

Misappropriation Theory. Liability for insider trading may also be established under the misappropriation theory. This theory holds that an individual who wrongfully obtains (misappropriates) inside information and trades on it for her or his personal gain should be held liable because, in essence, she or he stole information rightfully belonging to another. The misappropriation theory has been controversial because it significantly extends the reach of SEC Rule 10b-5 to outsiders who ordinarily would not be deemed fiduciaries of the corporations in whose stock they trade.

Insider Reporting and Trading—Section 16(b)

Section 16(b) of the 1934 act provides for the recapture by the corporation of all profits realized by certain insiders on any purchase and sale or sale and purchase of the corporation's stock within any six-month period. It is irrelevant whether the insider actually uses inside information; *all such short-swing profits must be returned to the corporation.* In this context, insiders means officers, directors, and large stockholders of Section 12 corporations (those owning 10 percent of the class of equity securities registered under Section 12 of the 1934 act).[26] To discourage such insiders from using nonpublic information about their companies to their personal benefit in the stock market, they must file reports with the SEC concerning their ownership and trading of the corporation's securities.

Section 16(b) applies not only to stock but also to warrants, options, and securities convertible into stock. In addition, the courts have fashioned complex rules for determining profits. Note that the SEC exempts a number of transactions under Rule 16b-3.[27] For all of these reasons, corporate insiders are wise to seek specialized counsel before trading in the corporation's stock. Exhibit 27–2 compares the effects of SEC Rule 10b-5 and Section 16(b).

Proxy Statements

Section 14(a) of the Securities Exchange Act of 1934 regulates the solicitation of proxies from shareholders of Section 12 companies. The SEC regulates the content of proxy statements. As discussed in Chapter 26, a proxy statement is sent to shareholders when corporate officials are requesting authority

---

25. See, for example, *Chiarella v. United States*, 445 U.S. 222, 100 S.Ct. 1108, 63 L.Ed.2d 348 (1980); and *Dirks v. SEC*, 463 U.S. 646, 103 S.Ct. 3255, 77 L.Ed.2d 911 (1983).

26. 15 U.S.C. Section 78l. Note that Section 403 of the Sarbanes-Oxley Act of 2002 shortened the reporting deadlines specified in Section 16(b).
27. 17 C.F.R. Section 240.16b-3.

EXHIBIT 27–2 Comparison of Coverage, Application, and Liability under SEC Rule 10b–5 and Section 16(b)

AREA OF COMPARISON	SEC RULE 10b–5	SECTION 16(b)
What is the subject matter of the transaction?	Any security (does not have to be registered).	Any security (does not have to be registered).
What transactions are covered?	Purchase or sale.	Short-swing purchase and sale or short-swing sale and purchase.
Who is subject to liability?	Virtually anyone with inside information under a duty to disclose—including officers, directors, controlling shareholders, and tippees.	Officers, directors, and certain 10 percent shareholders.
Is omission or misrepresentation necessary for liability?	Yes.	No.
Are there any exempt transactions?	No.	Yes, there are a number of exemptions.
Who may bring an action?	A person transacting with an insider, the SEC, or a purchaser or seller damaged by a wrongful act.	A corporation or a shareholder by derivative action.

to vote on behalf of the shareholders in a particular election on specified issues. Whoever solicits a proxy must fully and accurately disclose in the proxy statement all of the facts that are pertinent to the matter on which the shareholders are to vote. In 2007, the SEC issued new rules allowing companies to post their proxy materials on Web sites rather than mailing the materials to shareholders (see the *Adapting the Law to the Online Environment* feature in Chapter 26 on pages 552 and 553). SEC Rule 14a-9 is similar to the antifraud provisions of SEC Rule 10b-5. Remedies for violations are extensive; they range from injunctions that prevent a vote from being taken to monetary damages.

Violations of the 1934 Act

As mentioned earlier, violations of Section 10(b) of the Securities Exchange Act of 1934 and SEC Rule 10b-5, including insider trading, may be subject to criminal or civil liability. For either criminal or civil sanctions to be imposed, however, *scienter* must exist—that is, the violator must have had an intent to defraud or knowledge of her or his misconduct (see Chapter 6). *Scienter* can be proved by showing that the defendant made false statements or wrongfully failed to disclose material facts.

Violations of Section 16(b) include the sale by insiders of stock acquired less than six months before the sale (or less than six months after the sale if selling short). These viola-

tions are subject to civil sanctions. Liability under Section 16(b) is strict liability. Thus, liability is imposed regardless of whether *scienter* or negligence existed.

Criminal Penalties For violations of Section 10(b) and Rule 10b-5, an individual may be fined up to $5 million, imprisoned for up to twenty years, or both. A partnership or a corporation may be fined up to $25 million. Under Section 807 of the Sarbanes-Oxley Act of 2002, for a *willful* violation of the 1934 act the violator may, in addition to being subject to a fine, be imprisoned for up to twenty-five years. In a criminal prosecution under the securities laws, a jury is not allowed to speculate about whether a defendant acted willfully—the prosecution must prove beyond a reasonable doubt that the defendant knew he or she was acting wrongfully.[28]

In criminal prosecutions under Sections 10(b) and 14(a), the standard for assessing the materiality of a defendant's false statements to shareholders is the perspective of the reasonable investor. The issue in the following case was whether that standard also applies to statements in documents filed with the SEC.

---

28. See, for example, *United States v. Stewart*, 305 F.Supp.2d 368 (S.D.N.Y. 2004), a case involving Martha Stewart, founder of a well-known media and homemaking empire, who was later convicted on other charges.

CASE 27.3   United States v. Berger

United States Court of Appeals, Ninth Circuit, 473 F.3d 1080 (2007).

FACTS Craig Consumer Electronics, Inc., bought car stereos, compact music centers, and small personal stereos from its offices in Hong Kong and sold the goods from its offices in California to retail stores. Richard Berger was Craig's president, chief executive officer, and board chairman. In 1994, Craig entered into a $50 million loan agreement with BT Commercial Corporation and other lenders. Under the agreement, Craig could borrow up to 85 percent of the value of its accounts receivable (the amount owed to it by retail stores) and up to 65 percent of the value of its inventory. Each business day, Craig provided the lenders with a "Borrowing Certificate" to report the amount of its accounts receivables and inventory. By 1995, Craig lacked sufficient receivables and inventory to borrow funds for its operations. To hide these facts, Berger and others falsified the certificates and also hid Craig's true financial condition in reports filed with the Securities and Exchange Commission (SEC). In 1997, owing

the banks more than $8.4 million, Craig filed for bankruptcy. Berger and others were convicted in a federal district court of criminal violations of the Securities Exchange Act of 1934 for the false statements in the reports filed with the SEC. Berger was sentenced to six months in prison, fined $1.25 million, and ordered to pay the banks $3.14 million in restitution. Berger appealed to the U.S. Court of Appeals for the Ninth Circuit.

ISSUE Should the materiality of a defendant's false statements to the SEC be judged by considering what information would be material to a reasonable investor?

DECISION Yes. The U.S. Court of Appeals for the Ninth Circuit held that the materiality of false statements in reports filed with the SEC "must be assessed from the perspective of the reasonable investor" and affirmed Berger's conviction and the restitution order. The court vacated the prison term and

CASE 27.3—Continued

fine, however, on the ground that certain factors were omitted or mistakenly applied, and it remanded the case for reconsideration of the sentence.

REASON Berger argued that the false information that he and others gave to the SEC was for the use of Craig's creditors and to obtain continued funding of the business. Specifically, Berger contended that the court "should review materiality from the perspective of the SEC" and claimed that there was insufficient evidence in this case that the falsehoods were material to the SEC. In other words, Berger argued that the falsehoods should be judged not from the reasonable investor's perspective, but only in the context of the SEC's

own regulatory decisions. The federal appellate court rejected this argument. The court reasoned, "The purpose of the 1934 Act was to benefit and protect investors, with proper agency decision making as a secondary concern." Therefore, the court concluded, "materiality should be assessed from the reasonable investor's perspective."

 FOR CRITICAL ANALYSIS—Global Consideration *Considering that Craig bought goods overseas to sell in the United States, how much blame should the court have attributed to global electronics markets for the banks' losses?*

■

Civil Sanctions The SEC can also bring suit in a federal district court against anyone violating or aiding in a violation of the 1934 act or SEC rules by purchasing or selling a security while in the possession of material nonpublic information. The violation must occur on or through the facilities of a national securities exchange or from or through a broker or dealer. The court may assess as a penalty as much as triple the profits gained or the loss avoided by the guilty party. Profit or loss is defined as "the difference between the purchase or sale price of the security and the value of that security as measured by the trading price of the security at a reasonable period of time after public dissemination of the nonpublic information."[29]

The Insider Trading and Securities Fraud Enforcement Act of 1988 enlarged the class of persons who may be subject to civil liability for insider-trading violations. This act also gave the SEC authority to award **bounty payments** (rewards given by government officials for acts beneficial to the state) to persons providing information leading to the prosecution of insider-trading violations.[30]

Private parties may also sue violators of Section 10(b) and Rule 10b-5, but normally cannot bring an action against those who "aid and abet" under these rules. A private party may obtain rescission (cancellation) of a contract to buy securities or damages to the extent of the violator's illegal profits. Those found liable have a right to seek contribution from those who share responsibility for the violations, including accountants, attorneys, and corporations. For violations of Section 16(b), a corporation can bring an action to recover the short-swing profits.

STATE SECURITIES LAWS

Today, all states have their own corporate securities laws, or "blue sky laws," that regulate the offer and sale of securities within individual state borders. (The phrase *blue sky laws* dates to a 1917 decision by the United States Supreme Court in which the Court declared that the purpose of such laws was to prevent "speculative schemes which have no more basis than so many feet of 'blue sky.'")[31] Article 8 of the Uniform Commercial Code, which has been adopted by all of the states, also imposes various requirements relating to the purchase and sale of securities.

Requirements under State Securities Laws

Despite some differences in philosophy, all state blue sky laws have certain features in common. Typically, state laws have disclosure requirements and antifraud provisions, many of which are patterned after Section 10(b) of the Securities Exchange Act of 1934 and SEC Rule 10b-5. State laws also provide for the registration or qualification of securities offered or issued for sale within the state and impose disclosure requirements. Unless an exemption from registration is applicable, issuers must register or qualify their stock with the appropriate state official, often called a *corporations commissioner.* Additionally, most state securities laws regulate securities brokers and dealers.

Concurrent Regulation

State securities laws apply mainly to intrastate transactions. Since the adoption of the 1933 and 1934 federal securities acts, the state and federal governments have regulated

---

29. The Insider Trading Sanctions Act of 1984, 15 U.S.C. Sections 78u(d)(2)(A) and (C).

30. 15 U.S.C. Section 78u-1.

31. *Hall v. Geiger-Jones Co.,* 242 U.S. 539, 37 S.Ct. 217, 61 L.Ed. 480 (1917).

securities concurrently. Issuers must comply with both federal and state securities laws, and exemptions from federal law are not exemptions from state laws.

The dual federal and state system has not always worked well, particularly during the early 1990s, when the securities markets underwent considerable expansion. In response, Congress passed the National Securities Markets Improvement Act of 1996, which eliminated some of the duplicate regulations and gave the SEC exclusive power to regulate most national securities activities. The National Conference of Commissioners on Uniform State Laws then substantially revised the Uniform Securities Act and recommended it to the states for adoption in 2002. Unlike the previous version of this law, the new act is designed to coordinate state and federal securities regulation and enforcement efforts. Thirteen states have already adopted the Uniform Securities Act, and several other states are considering adoption.[32]

CORPORATE GOVERNANCE

Corporate governance can be narrowly defined as the relationship between a corporation and its shareholders. The Organization for Economic Cooperation and Development (OECD) provides a broader definition:

> Corporate governance is the system by which business corporations are directed and controlled. The corporate governance structure specifies the distribution of rights and responsibilities among different participants in the corporation, such as the board of directors, managers, shareholders, and other stakeholders, and spells out the rules and procedures for making decisions on corporate affairs.[33]

Although this definition has no legal value, it does set the tone for the ways in which modern corporations should be governed. In other words, effective corporate governance requires more than compliance with laws and regulations. The definition and focus of corporate governance principles vary around the world.

The Need for Effective Corporate Governance

The need for effective corporate governance arises in large corporations because corporate ownership (by shareholders) is separated from corporate control (by officers and managers). In the real world, officers and managers are tempted

to advance their own interests, even when such interests conflict with those of the shareholders. The collapse of Enron Corporation and other well-publicized scandals in the corporate world in the early 2000s provide a clear illustration of the reasons for concern about managerial opportunism.

Attempts at Aligning the Interests of Officers with Those of Shareholders

Some corporations have sought to align the financial interests of their officers with those of the company's shareholders by providing the officers with **stock options,** which enable them to purchase shares of the corporation's stock at a set price. When the market price rises above that level, the officers can sell their shares for a profit. Because a stock's market price generally increases as the corporation prospers, the options give the officers a financial stake in the corporation's well-being and supposedly encourage them to work hard for the benefit of the shareholders.

Options have turned out to be an imperfect device for providing effective governance, however. Executives in some companies have been tempted to "cook" (falsify) the companies' books in order to keep share prices higher so that they could sell their stock for a profit. Executives in other corporations have experienced no losses when share prices dropped; instead, their options were "repriced" so that they did not suffer from the share price decline and could still profit from future increases above the lowered share price. Thus, although stock options theoretically can motivate officers to protect shareholder interests, stock option plans have often become a way for officers to take advantage of shareholders.

With stock options generally failing to work as planned and numerous headline-making scandals occurring within major corporations, there has been an outcry for more "outside" directors (those with no formal employment affiliation with the company). The theory is that independent directors will more closely monitor the actions of corporate officers. Hence, today we see more boards with outside directors. Note, though, that outside directors may not be truly independent of corporate officers; they may be friends or business associates of the leading officers. A study of board appointments found that the best way to increase one's probability of appointment was to "suck up" to the chief executive officer.[34]

Corporate Governance and Corporate Law

Effective corporate governance standards are designed to address problems (such as those briefly discussed above) and to motivate officers to make decisions to promote the finan-

---

32. At the time this book went to press, the Uniform Securities Act had been adopted in Georgia, Hawaii, Idaho, Indiana, Iowa, Kansas, Maine, Minnesota, Missouri, Oklahoma, South Carolina, South Dakota, Vermont, and Wisconsin, as well as in the U.S. Virgin Islands. Adoption legislation was pending in the District of Columbia, Michigan, and Washington State. You can find current information on state adoptions at **www.nccusl.org**.

33. *Governance in the 21st Century: Future Studies* (OECD, 2001).

34. Jennifer Reingold, "Suck Up and Move Fast," *Fast Company*, January 2005, p. 34.

cial interests of the company's shareholders. Generally, corporate governance entails corporate decision-making structures that monitor employees (particularly officers) to ensure that they are acting for the benefit of the shareholders. Thus, corporate governance involves, at a minimum:

1 The audited reporting of the corporation's financial progress, so that managers can be evaluated.

2 Legal protections for shareholders, so that violators of the law, who attempt to take advantage of shareholders, can be punished for misbehavior and victims can recover damages for any associated losses.

Effective corporate governance may have considerable practical significance. A study by researchers at Harvard University and the Wharton School of Business found that firms providing greater shareholder rights had higher profits, higher sales growth, higher firm value, and other economic advantages.[35] Better corporate governance in the form of greater accountability to investors may therefore offer the opportunity to increase corporations' value.

Governance and Corporation Law   Corporate governance is the essential purpose of corporation law in the United States. These statutes set up the legal framework for corporate governance. Under the corporate law of Delaware, where most major companies incorporate, all corporations must have in place certain structures of corporate governance. The key structure of corporate law is, of course, the board of directors. Directors make the most important decisions about the future of the corporation and monitor the actions of corporate officers. Directors are elected by shareholders to look out for their best interests.

The Board of Directors   Some argue that shareholder democracy is key to improving corporate governance. If shareholders could vote on major corporate decisions, shareholders could presumably have more control over the corporation. Essential to shareholder democracy is the concept of electing the board of directors, usually at the corporation's annual meeting. Under corporate law, a corporation must have a board of directors elected by the shareholders. Virtually anyone can become a director, though some organizations, such as the New York Stock Exchange, require certain standards of service for directors of their listed corporations.

Directors have the responsibility of ensuring that officers are operating wisely and in the exclusive interest of share-

holders. Directors receive reports from the officers and give them managerial directions. The board in theory controls the compensation of officers (presumably tied to performance). The reality, though, is that corporate directors devote a relatively small amount of time to monitoring officers.

Ideally, shareholders would monitor the directors' supervision of officers. As one leading board monitor commented, "Boards of directors are like subatomic particles—they behave differently when they are observed." Consequently, monitoring directors, and holding them responsible for corporate failings, can induce the directors to do a better job of monitoring officers and ensuring that the company is being managed in the interest of shareholders. Although the directors can be sued for failing to do their jobs effectively, directors are rarely held personally liable.

Importance of the Audit Committee   One crucial board committee is known as the *audit committee*. The audit committee oversees the corporation's accounting and financial reporting processes, including both internal and outside auditors. Unless the committee members have sufficient expertise and are willing to spend the time to carefully examine the corporation's bookkeeping methods, however, the audit committee may be ineffective.

The audit committee also oversees the corporation's "internal controls." These are the measures taken to ensure that reported results are accurate; they are carried out largely by the company's internal auditing staff. As an example, these controls help to determine whether a corporation's debts are collectible. If the debts are not collectible, it is up to the audit committee to make sure that the corporation's financial officers do not simply pretend that payment will eventually be made.

The Role of the Compensation Committee   Another important committee of the board of directors is the *compensation committee*. This committee monitors and determines the compensation to be paid to the company's officers. As part of this process, it is responsible for assessing the officers' performance and for designing a compensation system that will better align the officers' interests with those of shareholders.

The Sarbanes-Oxley Act of 2002

As discussed in Chapter 3, in 2002, following a series of corporate scandals, Congress passed the Sarbanes-Oxley Act. The act separately addresses certain issues relating to corporate governance. Generally, the act attempts to increase corporate accountability by imposing strict disclosure requirements and harsh penalties for violations of securities

---

35. Paul A. Gompers, Joy L. Ishii, and Andrew Metrick, "Corporate Governance and Equity Prices," *Quarterly Journal of Economics*, Vol. 118 (2003), p. 107.

laws. Among other things, the act requires chief corporate executives to take responsibility for the accuracy of financial statements and reports that are filed with the SEC. Chief executive officers and chief financial officers must personally certify that the statements and reports are accurate and complete.

Additionally, the new rules require that certain financial and stock-transaction reports must be filed with the SEC earlier than was required under the previous rules. The act also mandates SEC oversight over a new entity, called the Public Company Accounting Oversight Board, which regulates and oversees public accounting firms. Other provisions of the act created new private civil actions and expanded the SEC's remedies in administrative and civil actions. Some of the act's key provisions relating to corporate accountability are highlighted in Exhibit 27–3.

More Internal Controls and Accountability The Sarbanes-Oxley Act includes some traditional securities law provisions but also introduces direct *federal* corporate governance requirements for public companies (companies whose shares are traded in the public securities markets). The law addresses many of the corporate governance procedures just discussed and creates new requirements in an attempt to make the system work more effectively. The requirements deal with independent monitoring of company officers by both the board of directors and auditors.

Sections 302 and 404 of Sarbanes-Oxley require high-level managers (the most senior officers) to establish and maintain an effective system of internal controls. Moreover, senior management must reassess the system's effectiveness on an annual basis. Some companies already had strong and effective internal control systems in place before the passage

---

EXHIBIT 27–3 **Some Key Provisions of the Sarbanes-Oxley Act of 2002 Relating to Corporate Accountability**

Certification Requirements—Under Section 906 of the Sarbanes-Oxley Act, the chief executive officers (CEOs) and chief financial officers (CFOs) of most major companies listed on public stock exchanges must certify financial statements that are filed with the SEC. CEOs and CFOs have to certify that virtually all filed financial reports "fully comply" with SEC requirements and that all of the information reported "fairly represents in all material respects, the financial conditions and results of operations of the issuer."

Under Section 302 of the act, CEOs and CFOs of reporting companies are required to certify that a signing officer reviewed each quarterly and annual filing with the SEC and that it contains no untrue statements of material fact. Also, the signing officer or officers must certify that they have established an internal control system to identify all material information and that any deficiencies in the system were disclosed to the auditors.

Loans to Directors and Officers—Section 402 prohibits any reporting company, as well as any private company that is filing an initial public offering, from making personal loans to directors and executive officers (with a few limited exceptions, such as for certain consumer and housing loans).

Protection for Whistleblowers—Section 806 protects "whistleblowers"—employees who report ("blow the whistle" on) securities violations by their employers—from being fired or in any way discriminated against by their employers.

Blackout Periods—Section 306 prohibits certain types of securities transactions during "blackout periods"—periods during which the issuer's ability to purchase, sell, or otherwise transfer funds in individual account plans (such as pension funds) is suspended.

Enhanced Penalties for—

• *Violations of Section 906 Certification Requirements*—A CEO or CFO who certifies a financial report or statement filed with the SEC knowing that the report or statement does not fulfill all of the requirements of Section 906 will be subject to criminal penalties of up to $1 million in fines, ten years in prison, or both. *Willful* violators of the certification requirements may be subject to $5 million in fines, twenty years in prison, or both.

• *Violations of the Securities Exchange Act of 1934*—Penalties for securities fraud under the 1934 act were also increased (as discussed earlier in this chapter). Individual violators may be fined up to $5 million, imprisoned for up to twenty years, or both. *Willful* violators may be imprisoned for up to twenty-five years in addition to being fined.

• *Destruction or Alteration of Documents*—Anyone who alters, destroys, or conceals documents or otherwise obstructs any official proceeding will be subject to fines, imprisonment for up to twenty years, or both.

• *Other Forms of White-Collar Crime*—The act stiffened the penalties for certain criminal violations, such as federal mail and wire fraud, and ordered the U.S. Sentencing Commission to revise the sentencing guidelines for white-collar crimes (see Chapter 6).

Statute of Limitations for Securities Fraud—Section 804 provides that a private right of action for securities fraud may be brought no later than two years after the discovery of the violation or five years after the violation, whichever is earlier.

of the act, but others had to take expensive steps to bring their internal controls up to the new federal standard. These include "disclosure controls and procedures" to ensure that company financial reports are accurate and timely. Assessment must involve documenting financial results and accounting policies before reporting the results. Hundreds of companies have reported that they have identified and corrected shortcomings in their internal control systems.

Certification and Monitoring Requirements As Exhibit 27–3 indicates, Section 906 requires that chief executive officers and chief financial officers certify the accuracy of the information in the corporate financial statements. This requirement makes officers directly accountable for their companies' financial reporting and avoids any "ignorance defense" if shortcomings are later discovered.

Another requirement is aimed at improving directors' monitoring of officers' activities. All members of the corporate audit committee for public companies must be outside directors. The New York Stock Exchange has a similar rule that also extends to the board's compensation committee. The audit committee must have a written charter that sets out its duties and provides for performance appraisal. At least one "financial expert" must serve on the audit committee, which must hold executive meetings without company officers being present. The audit committee must establish procedures for "whistleblowers" to report violations. In addition to reviewing the internal controls, the committee also monitors the actions of the outside auditor.

ONLINE SECURITIES FRAUD

A major problem facing the SEC today is how to enforce the antifraud provisions of the securities laws in the online environment. In 1999, in the first cases involving illegal online securities offerings, the SEC filed suit against three individuals for illegally offering securities on an Internet auction site.[36] In essence, all three indicated that their companies would go public soon and attempted to sell unregistered securities via the Web auction site. All of these actions were in violation of Sections 5, 17(a)(1), and 17(a)(3) of the 1933 Securities Act. Since then, the SEC has brought a variety of Internet-related fraud cases, including cases involving investment scams and the manipulation of stock prices in Internet chat rooms. The SEC regularly issues interpretive releases to explain how securities laws apply in the online environment and revises its rules to address new issues that arise in the Internet context.

---

36. *In re Davis*, SEC Administrative File No. 3-10080 (October 20, 1999); *In re Haas*, SEC Administrative File No. 3-10081 (October 20, 1999); and *In re Sitaras*, SEC Administrative File No. 3-10082 (October 20, 1999).

Investment Scams

An ongoing problem is how to curb online investment scams. One fraudulent investment scheme involved twenty thousand investors, who lost, in all, more than $3 million. Some cases have involved false claims about the earnings potential of home business programs, such as the claim that one could "earn $4,000 or more each month." Others have concerned claims of "guaranteed credit repair."

Using Chat Rooms to Manipulate Stock Prices

"Pumping and dumping" occurs when a person who has purchased a particular stock heavily promotes (pumps up) that stock—thereby creating a great demand for it and driving up its price—and then sells (dumps) it. The practice of pumping up a stock and then dumping it is quite old. In the online world, however, the process can occur much more quickly and efficiently.

■EXAMPLE 27.8 Jonathan Lebed, a fifteen-year-old from New Jersey, became the first minor charged with securities fraud. The SEC charged that Lebed bought thinly traded stocks. After purchasing a stock, he would flood stock-related chat rooms with messages touting the stock's virtues. He used numerous false names so no one would know that a single person was posting the messages. He would say that the stock was the most "undervalued stock in history" and that its price would jump by 1,000 percent very soon. When other investors bought the stock, the price went up quickly, and he sold. The SEC forced the teenager to repay almost $300,000 in gains, plus interest. ■ The SEC has been bringing an increasing number of cases against those who manipulate stock prices in this way. Many of these online investment scams are perpetrated through mass e-mails (spam), online newsletters, and chat rooms.

Hacking into Online Stock Accounts

The last few years have seen the emergence of a new form of pumping and dumping stock that involves hackers who break into existing online stock accounts and make unauthorized transfers. Millions of people buy and sell investments through online brokerage companies such as TD Ameritrade. Sophisticated hackers have learned to use online investing to their advantage.

By installing keystroke-monitoring software on computer terminals in public places, hackers can gain access to online account information. They simply wait for a person to access his or her online account and then monitor the next several dozen keystrokes to determine the customer's account number and password. Once they have this information, they can access the account and liquidate existing stock holdings. The hackers then use the customer's funds to purchase thinly traded, microcap securities, also known as *penny stocks*. The goal is to boost the price of a stock that the hacker has already purchased at a lower price. When the stock price goes up, the hacker sells all the stock and wires the funds to either an offshore account or a dummy corporation, making it difficult for the SEC to trace the transactions and prosecute the offender.

REVIEWING Investor Protection, Insider Trading, and Corporate Governance

Dale Emerson served as the chief financial officer for Reliant Electric Company, a distributor of electricity serving portions of Montana and North Dakota. Reliant was in the final stages of planning a takeover of Dakota Gasworks, Inc., a natural gas distributor that operated solely within North Dakota. Emerson went on a weekend fishing trip with his uncle, Ernest Wallace. Emerson mentioned to Wallace that he had been putting in a lot of extra hours at the office planning a takeover of Dakota Gasworks. On returning from the fishing trip, Wallace met with a broker from Chambers Investments and purchased $20,000 of Reliant stock. Three weeks later, Reliant made a tender offer to Dakota Gasworks stockholders and purchased 57 percent of Dakota Gasworks stock. Over the next two weeks, the price of Reliant stock rose 72 percent before leveling out. Wallace then sold his Reliant stock for a gross profit of $14,400. Using the information presented in the chapter, answer the following questions.

1 Would registration with the SEC be required for Dakota Gasworks securities? Why or why not?

2 Did Emerson violate Section 10(b) of the Securities Exchange Act of 1934 and SEC Rule 10b-5? Why or why not?

3 What theory or theories might a court use to hold Wallace liable for insider trading?

4 Under the Sarbanes-Oxley Act of 2002, who would be required to certify the accuracy of financial statements filed with the SEC?

TERMS AND CONCEPTS

accredited investors 570
bounty payment 577
corporate governance 578
free-writing prospectus 568
insider trading 572

investment company 569
investment contract 566
mutual fund 570
prospectus 567
red herring prospectus 567

SEC Rule 10b-5 572
security 565
stock options 578
tippee 575
tombstone ad 568

CHAPTER SUMMARY Investor Protection, Insider Trading, and Corporate Governance

Securities Act of 1933 (See pages 566–571.)	Prohibits fraud and stabilizes the securities industry by requiring disclosure of all essential information relating to the issuance of securities to the investing public.
	1. *Registration requirements*—Securities, unless exempt, must be registered with the SEC before being offered to the public. The *registration statement* must include detailed financial information about the issuing corporation; the intended use of the proceeds of the securities being issued; and certain disclosures, such as interests of directors or officers and pending lawsuits.
	2. *Prospectus*—The issuer must provide investors with a *prospectus* that describes the security being sold, the issuing corporation, and the risk attaching to the security.
	3. *Exemptions*—The SEC has exempted certain offerings from the requirements of the Securities Act of 1933. Exemptions may be determined on the basis of the size of the issue, whether the

CHAPTER SUMMARY	Investor Protection, Insider Trading, and Corporate Governance–Continued
Securities Act of 1933—Continued	offering is private or public, and whether advertising is involved. Exemptions are summarized in Exhibit 27–1 on page 569.

Securities Exchange Act of 1934 (See pages 571–577.)	Provides for the regulation and registration of securities exchanges, brokers, dealers, and national securities associations (such as the NASD). Maintains a continuous disclosure system for all corporations with securities on the securities exchanges and for those companies that have assets in excess of $10 million and five hundred or more shareholders (Section 12 companies).
	
	1. *SEC Rule 10b-5 [under Section 10(b) of the 1934 act]*—
	  a. Applies in virtually all cases concerning the trading of securities—a firm's securities do not have to be registered under the 1933 act for the 1934 act to apply.
	  b. Applies only when the requisites of federal jurisdiction (such as use of the mails, stock exchange facilities, or any facility of interstate commerce) are present.
	  c. Applies to insider trading by corporate officers, directors, majority shareholders, and any persons receiving inside information (information not available to the investing public) who base their trading on this information.
	  d. Liability for violations can be civil or criminal.
	  e. May be violated by failing to disclose "material facts" that must be disclosed under this rule.
	  f. Liability may be based on the tipper/tippee or the misappropriation theory.
	
	2. *Insider trading [under Section 16(b) of the 1934 act]*—To prevent corporate officers and directors from taking advantage of inside information, the 1934 act requires officers, directors, and shareholders owning 10 percent or more of the issued stock of a corporation to turn over to the corporation all short-term profits (called *short-swing profits*) realized from the purchase and sale or sale and purchase of corporate stock within any six-month period.
	
	3. *Proxies [under Section 14(a) of the 1934 act]*—The SEC regulates the content of proxy statements sent to shareholders by corporate managers of Section 12 companies who are requesting authority to vote on behalf of the shareholders in a particular election on specified issues. Section 14(a) is essentially a disclosure law, with provisions similar to the antifraud provisions of SEC Rule 10b-5.

State Securities Laws (See pages 577–578.)	All states have corporate securities laws (*blue sky laws*) that regulate the offer and sale of securities within state borders. States regulate securities concurrently with the federal government. The Uniform Securities Act of 2002, which has been adopted by thirteen states and is being considered by several others, is designed to promote coordination and reduce duplication between state and federal securities regulation.
Corporate Governance (See pages 578–581.)	1. *Definition*—Corporate governance is the system by which business corporations are governed, including policies and procedures for making decisions on corporate affairs. 2. *The need for corporate governance*—Corporate governance is necessary in large corporations because corporate ownership (by the shareholders) is separated from corporate control (by officers and managers). This separation of corporate ownership and control can often result in conflicting interests. Corporate governance standards address such issues. 3. *Sarbanes-Oxley Act of 2002*—This act attempts to increase corporate accountability by imposing strict disclosure requirements and harsh penalties for violations of securities laws.
Online Securities Fraud (See pages 581–582.)	A major problem facing the SEC today is how to enforce the antifraud provisions of the securities laws in the online environment. Internet-related forms of securities fraud include investment scams and the manipulation of stock prices in online chat rooms.

FOR REVIEW

Answers for the even-numbered questions in this **For Review** *section can be found on this text's accompanying Web site at* **www.cengage.com/blaw/fbl**. *Select "Chapter 27" and click on "For Review."*

1 What is meant by the term *securities*?

2 What are the two major statutes regulating the securities industry? When was the Securities and Exchange Commission created, and what are its major purposes and functions?

3 What is insider trading? Why is it prohibited?

4 What are some of the features of state securities laws?

5 What certification requirements does the Sarbanes-Oxley Act impose on corporate executives?

QUESTIONS AND CASE PROBLEMS

HYPOTHETICAL SCENARIOS AND CASE PROBLEMS

27.1 **Registration Requirements.** Langley Brothers, Inc., a corporation incorporated and doing business in Kansas, decides to sell common stock worth $1 million to the public. The stock will be sold only within the state of Kansas. Joseph Langley, the chairman of the board, says the offering need not be registered with the Securities and Exchange Commission. His brother, Harry, disagrees. Who is right? Explain.

27.2 **Hypothetical Question with Sample Answer.** Huron Corp. has 300,000 common shares outstanding. The owners of these outstanding shares live in several different states. Huron has decided to split the 300,000 shares two for one. Will Huron Corp. have to file a registration statement and prospectus on the 300,000 new shares to be issued as a result of the split? Explain.

 For a sample answer to Question 27.2, go to Appendix E at the end of this text.

27.3 **Securities Laws.** Scott Ginsburg was chief executive officer (CEO) of Evergreen Media Corp., which owned and operated radio stations. In 1996, Evergreen became interested in acquiring EZ Communications, Inc., which also owned radio stations. To initiate negotiations, Ginsburg met with EZ's CEO, Alan Box, on Friday, July 12. Two days later, Scott phoned his brother Mark, who, on Monday, bought 3,800 shares of EZ stock. Mark discussed the deal with their father, Jordan, who bought 20,000 EZ shares on Thursday. On July 25, the day before the EZ bid was due, Scott phoned his parents' home, and Mark bought another 3,200 EZ shares. The same routine was followed over the next few days, with Scott periodically phoning Mark or Jordan, both of whom continued to buy EZ shares. Evergreen's bid was refused, but on August 5, EZ announced its merger with another company. The price of EZ stock rose 30 percent, increasing the value of Mark and Jordan's shares by $664,024 and $412,875, respectively. The Securities and Exchange Commission (SEC) filed a civil suit in a federal district court against Scott. What was the most

likely allegation? What is required to impose sanctions for this offense? Should the court hold Scott liable? Why or why not? [*SEC v. Ginsburg*, 362 F.3d 1292 (11th Cir. 2004)]

27.4 **Case Problem with Sample Answer.** In 1997, WTS Transnational, Inc., required financing to develop a prototype of an unpatented fingerprint-verification system. At the time, WTS had no revenue, $655,000 in liabilities, and only $10,000 in assets. Thomas Cavanagh and Frank Nicolois, who operated an investment banking company called U.S. Milestone (USM), arranged the financing using Curbstone Acquisition Corp. Curbstone had no assets but had registered approximately 3.5 million shares of stock with the Securities and Exchange Commission (SEC). Under the terms of the deal, Curbstone acquired WTS, and the resulting entity was named Electro-Optical Systems Corp. (EOSC). New EOSC shares were issued to all of the WTS shareholders. Only Cavanagh and others affiliated with USM could sell EOSC stock to the public, however. Over the next few months, these individuals issued false press releases, made small deceptive purchases of EOSC shares at high prices, distributed hundreds of thousands of shares to friends and relatives, and sold their own shares at inflated prices through third party companies they owned. When the SEC began to investigate, the share price fell to its actual value, and innocent investors lost over $15 million. Were any securities laws violated in this case? If so, what might be an appropriate remedy? [*SEC v. Cavanagh*, 445 F.3d 105 (2d Cir. 2006)]

After you have answered Problem 27.4, compare your answer with the sample answer given on the Web site that accompanies this text. Go to www.cengage.com/blaw/fbl, select "Chapter 27," and click on "Case Problem with Sample Answer."

27.5 **Securities Trading.** Between 1994 and 1998, Richard Svoboda, a credit officer for NationsBank N.A., in Dallas, Texas, evaluated and approved his employer's extensions of credit to clients. These responsibilities gave Svoboda access to nonpublic information about the clients' earnings, performance, acquisitions, and business plans in confidential memos, e-mail, credit applications, and other sources. Svoboda devised a scheme with Michael Robles, an independent accountant, to use this information to trade securities. Pursuant to their scheme, Robles traded in the securities of more than twenty different companies and profited by more than $1 million. Svoboda also executed trades for his own profit of more than $200,000, despite their agreement that Robles would do all of the trading. Aware that their scheme violated NationsBank's policy, they attempted to conduct their trades to avoid suspicion. When NationsBank questioned Svoboda about his actions, he lied, refused to cooperate, and was fired. Did Svoboda or Robles commit any crimes? Are they subject to civil liability? If so, who could file a suit and on what ground? What are the possible sanctions? What might be a defense? How should a court rule? Discuss. [*SEC v. Svoboda*, 409 F.Supp.2d 331 (S.D.N.Y. 2006)]

27.6 Duty to Disclose. Orphan Medical, Inc., is a pharmaceutical company that focuses on treating central nervous system disorders. Its major product was the drug Xyrem. In 2004, Orphan merged with a company called Jazz at a stock price of $10.75 per share. Before the merger was completed, a phase of testing of Xyrem was completed that indicated the Food and Drug Administration (FDA) would allow the drug to go to the next stage of testing, which was required for the drug to possibly be marketed more widely. If that happened, the value of the drug would increase significantly, and consequently, so would the stock price. Little Gem Life Sciences, LLC, was an Orphan shareholder that received $10.75 per share at the time of the merger. Little Gem sued, claiming violations of federal securities laws, because shareholders were not told during the merger process that the current stage of FDA tests had been successful. Little Gem claimed that had the information been made public, the Orphan stock price would have been higher. The district court dismissed the suit, holding that it did not meet the standards required by the Private Securities Litigation Reform Act. Little Gem appealed. Did Orphan's directors have a duty to reveal all relevant drug-testing information to shareholders?

Explain your answer. [*Little Gem Life Sciences, LLC v. Orphan Medical, Inc.*, 537 F.3d 913 (8th Cir. 2008)]

27.7 **A Question of Ethics.** *Melvin Lyttle told John Montana and Paul Knight about a "Trading Program" that purportedly would buy and sell securities in deals that were fully insured, as well as monitored and controlled by the Federal Reserve Bank. Without checking the details or even verifying whether the Program existed, Montana and Knight, with Lyttle's help, began to sell interests in the Program to investors. For a minimum investment of $1 million, the investors were promised extraordinary rates of return—from 10 percent to as much as 100 percent per week—without risk. They were told, among other things, that the Program would "utilize banks that can ensure full bank integrity of The Transaction whose undertaking[s] are in complete harmony with international banking rules and protocol and who [sic] guarantee maximum security of a Funder's Capital Placement Amount." Nothing was required but the investors' funds and their silence—the Program was to be kept secret. Over a four-month period in 1999, Montana raised approximately $23 million from twenty-two investors. The promised gains did not accrue, however. Instead, Montana, Lyttle, and Knight depleted investors' funds in high-risk trades or spent the funds on themselves. [SEC v. Montana, 464 F.Supp.2d 772 (S.D.Ind. 2006)]*

1 The Securities and Exchange Commission (SEC) filed a suit in a federal district court against Montana and the others, seeking an injunction, civil penalties, and disgorgement of profits with interest. The SEC alleged, among other things, violations of Section 10(b) of the Securities Exchange Act of 1934 and SEC Rule 10b-5. What is required to establish a violation of these laws? Describe how and why the facts in this case meet, or fail to meet, these requirements.

2 It is often remarked, "There's a sucker born every minute!" Does that phrase describe the Program's investors? Ultimately, about half of the investors recouped the amount they invested. Should the others be considered at least partly responsible for their own losses? Why or why not?

CRITICAL THINKING AND WRITING ASSIGNMENTS

27.8 Critical Legal Thinking. Do you think that the tipper/tippee and misappropriation theories extend liability under SEC Rule 10b-5 too far? Why or why not?

27.9 Critical Thinking and Writing Assignment for Business. Insider trading, as you learned, is illegal. Not everyone agrees that it should be, though. A small group of legal scholars believe that insider trading should be completely legal. They argue that insider trading, if more widespread, would cause stock prices to almost instantly adjust to new information. They further argue that "insiders," if able to make

profits from insider trading, would therefore accept lower salaries and benefits.

1 Why is insider trading illegal in the first place? Who is supposed to be protected and why?

2 What is wrong with the argument advanced by the legal scholars who want insider trading made legal? Or, are they right? Explain your answer.

27.10 **Video Question.** Go to this text's Web site at **www.cengage.com/blaw/fbl** and select "Chapter 27." Click on "Video Questions" and view the video titled *Mergers and Acquisitions*. Then answer the following questions.

1 Analyze whether the purchase of Onyx Advertising is a material fact that the Quigley Co. had a duty to disclose under SEC Rule 10b-5.

2 Does it matter whether Quigley personally knew about or authorized the company spokesperson's statements? Why or why not?

3 Who else might be able to bring a suit against the Quigley Co. for insider trading under SEC Rule 10b-5?

ACCESSING THE INTERNET

For updated links to resources available on the Web, as well as a variety of other materials, visit this text's Web site at

www.cengage.com/blaw/fbl

To access the EDGAR database of the Securities and Exchange Commission (SEC), go to

www.sec.gov/edgar.shtml

The Center for Corporate Law of the University of Cincinnati College of Law maintains the *Securities Lawyer's Deskbook* online. The *Deskbook* contains the basic federal securities laws and regulations and links to the principal SEC forms under those laws and regulations. Go to

www.law.uc.edu/CCL

For information on investor protection and securities fraud, including answers to frequently asked questions about securities fraud, go to

www.securitieslaw.com

PRACTICAL INTERNET EXERCISES

Go to this text's Web site at **www.cengage.com/blaw/fbl**, select "Chapter 27," and click on "Practical Internet Exercises." There you will find the following Internet research exercises that you can perform to learn more about the topics covered in this chapter.

PRACTICAL INTERNET EXERCISE 27-1   LEGAL PERSPECTIVE—Electronic Delivery

PRACTICAL INTERNET EXERCISE 27-2   MANAGEMENT PERSPECTIVE—The SEC's Role

BEFORE THE TEST

Go to this text's Web site at **www.cengage.com/blaw/fbl**, select "Chapter 27," and click on "Interactive Quizzes." You will find a number of interactive questions relating to this chapter.

United States v. Bhagat

Violations of the securities laws discussed in Chapter 27 may constitute crimes. As explained in Chapter 6 on criminal law and procedure, an indictment formally charges a defendant with a crime. An indictment must refer to the evidence on which a charge is based to allow the accused party to defend against it. Nevertheless, for some purposes, a court may admit evidence not mentioned in an indictment without affecting the legitimacy of a subsequent conviction. For example, such evidence might be admitted to contradict a defendant's testimony. In this extended case study, we examine United States v. Bhagat,[1] *a case in which the defendant was charged with criminal violations of securities laws. During the trial, the prosecution asked questions that, in the defendant's view, suggested a basis for conviction supported by evidence not mentioned in the indictment.*

CASE BACKGROUND

On Sunday, March 5, 2000, Microsoft Corporation awarded Nvidia Corporation a multimillion-dollar contract to develop the X-Box. Late that night, Nvidia sent a companywide e-mail to tell its employees about the contract. The next morning, also via e-mail, Nvidia advised the employees that the X-Box deal should be kept confidential, that they should not buy Nvidia stock for several days, and that they should cancel any open or outstanding orders for the stock.

Twenty minutes after the last e-mail was sent, Atul Bhagat, a Nvidia engineer, bought one thousand shares of Nvidia stock—the largest purchase of the stock that he had made in three years. Rumors about the X-Box contract

began circulating the next day, and the price of Nvidia stock rose sharply. Three days later, the news was made public and the price skyrocketed. Another four days later, Bhagat sold his shares, reaping a substantial profit.

The government indicted Bhagat in a federal district court for criminal violations of securities laws. Among other things, he was charged with insider trading, based solely on Nvidia's e-mail to its employees. After a jury convicted Bhagat, he appealed to the U.S. Court of Appeals for the Ninth Circuit. The most hotly contested issue was whether the government had adequately proved that Bhagat knew of the X-Box contract before he purchased the stock.

1. 436 F.3d 1140 (9th Cir. 2006).

MAJORITY OPINION

RAWLINSON, Circuit Judge:
* * * *

The principal theory of the prosecution during the trial was that Bhagat knew about the contract from reading his own e-mail. During cross-examination, however, the prosecutor also questioned Bhagat about conversations among his co-workers that he had heard that morning concerning the X-Box contract. This line of questioning set the stage for what the parties refer to as the "office 'abuzz' theory."
* * * *

During closing arguments, the government referenced the "office abuzz" theory in passing, stating that the jury should consider the fact that the office was "abuzz" with the news of the X-Box contract, and that Bhagat had to walk through the office to reach his cubicle. The government also repeatedly informed the jury that in order to find Bhagat guilty, the government would have to prove that he read the company-wide e-mails prior to purchasing the stock.
* * * *

Bhagat contends that the government's reference to the "office abuzz" theory introduced an alternative theory by which the jury could infer Bhagat's knowledge of the X-Box contract

prior to the stock transaction. The government counters that it invoked the "office abuzz" theory for the limited purpose of impeaching [calling into question] Bhagat's credibility when he testified that he had not heard anyone mention the X-Box contract upon entering the office on Monday morning.

The government's conduct throughout the trial is consistent with its contention. The government repeatedly informed the jury that conviction should be based upon a determination that Bhagat had read the companywide e-mails prior to executing his trades. It was only during cross-examination, after Bhagat denied reading the pertinent e-mails, that the government questioned Bhagat about whether he had heard any office chatter regarding the X-Box contract.
* * * *

* * * The record in this case reflects that the reference to the "office abuzz" theory was not intended to and did not amend the indictment. The facts presented were not distinctly different from those in the indictment. Neither was the crime charged in the indictment * * * substantially altered at trial. That being so, no constructive amendment [the court will not legally construe or interpret the theory as an amendment] of the indictment occurred. Rather, the evidence was admitted for impeachment purposes * * * .
* * * *

(Continued)

A material variance exists if a materially different set of facts from those alleged in the indictment is presented at trial, and if that variance affects the defendant's substantial rights. [Emphasis added.]

* * * *

No [such] situation exists in this case. At all times, the pertinent fact was that Bhagat was aware of the e-mails notifying employees of the X-Box contract award. * * * The record does not support a claim of variance.

* * * *

To convict Bhagat of insider trading, the government was required to prove that he traded stock on the basis of material, nonpublic information.

The government offered significant evidence to support the jury's conclusion that Bhagat was aware of the confidential X-Box information before he executed his trades. The X-Box e-mails were sent prior to his purchase. The e-mails were found on his computer. Bhagat was at his office for several hours prior to executing his trade, which provided him the opportunity to read the e-mails. Finally, Bhagat took virtually no action to divest himself of the stock, or to inform his company that he had violated the company's trading blackout. * * *

* * * *

The government's use of the "office abuzz" theory did not constructively amend the indictment or create a material variance between the facts alleged in the indictment and the evidence presented at trial.

CONVICTION AFFIRMED * * * .

DISSENTING OPINION

TASHIMA, Circuit Judge, dissenting.

* * * *

The government's initial theory, consistent with the indictment, was that Defendant read the e-mails when he arrived at work * * * Monday morning, but there is no direct evidence that he did so. Defendant denied that he read the e-mails before placing his buy order and testified that he did not read them until 1:00 P.M., approximately 40 minutes after he made his purchase.

During its cross-examination of Defendant, the government pursued what the parties refer to as the "office abuzz" theory. The government's questioning of Defendant suggested that because of the open cubicle configuration of the office, Defendant could not help but overhear conversations among his co-workers regarding the exciting news of the X-Box contract—that the office was "abuzz" with the news. Defendant denied that he overheard any X-Box office conversation. The district court overruled Defendant's objection that the government should not be allowed to argue the "office abuzz" theory because "there is no evidence in the record the company was abuzz with the news," as indeed there was not, as a basis of liability.

* * * *

This "office abuzz" theory of liability as to how Defendant acquired insider information, an essential element of the charged crime, is factually distinct from the theory charged in the indictment, that Defendant acquired the insider information through reading the companywide e-mails. Because it is a new, uncharged theory, Defendant had no notice of it and no opportunity to defend against it, to rebut it with his own evidence.

* * * *

* * * One of the primary purposes of an indictment is to inform a defendant of what he is accused of doing in violation of the criminal law, so that he can prepare his defense. * * * This purpose was not served here. * * * Accordingly, I would conclude that the variance here affected Defendant's substantial rights and, thus, requires reversal.

QUESTIONS FOR ANALYSIS

1 **LAW.** What did the majority rule with respect to the dispute in this case? On what rationale did the majority base this ruling?

2 **LAW.** What was the dissent's position on the issue before the court? What were the dissent's reasons in support of its position?

3 **ETHICS.** When a case is tried before a jury, the jury determines the credibility of the witnesses, resolves conflicts in the evidence, and draws reasonable inferences from the facts. Is it appropriate for a prosecutor, as in this case, or a defendant to suggest an inference for the jury to make? Explain.

4 **SOCIAL DIMENSIONS.** Suppose that a corporate insider, without revealing any material, nonpublic information, advises a friend to buy stock in the company. Can the insider legitimately share the profit on the stock's sale? Why or why not?

5 **IMPLICATIONS FOR THE INVENTOR.** What does the outcome of this case suggest for the employee who wants to buy stock in her or his employer's firm on the basis of a potentially profitable development?

UNIT NINE Property and Its Protection

UNIT CONTENTS

Personal Property and Bailments

Property consists of the legally protected rights and interests a person has in anything with an ascertainable value that is subject to ownership. Property would have little value (and the word would have little meaning) if the law did not define the right to use it, to sell or dispose of it, and to prevent trespass on it.

Property is divided into real property and personal property. **Real property** (sometimes called *realty* or *real estate*) means the land and everything permanently attached to it. Everything else is **personal property** (sometimes referred to in case law as *personalty* or **chattel**). Personal property can be tangible or intangible. *Tangible* personal property, such as a television set or a car, has physical substance. *Intangible* personal property represents some set of rights and interests but has no real physical existence. Stocks and bonds, patents, and copyrights are examples of intangible personal property.

In the first part of this chapter, we look at the ways in which title to property is held; the methods of acquiring ownership of personal property; and issues relating to mislaid, lost, and abandoned personal property. In the second part of the chap-

ter, we examine bailment relationships. A *bailment* is created when personal property is temporarily delivered into the care of another without a transfer of title, such as when you take an item of clothing to the dry cleaner. This is the distinguishing characteristic of a bailment compared with a sale or a gift—there is no passage of title and no intent to transfer title.

PROPERTY OWNERSHIP

Property ownership[1] can be viewed as a bundle of rights, including the right to possess property and to dispose of it—by sale, gift, lease, or other means.

Fee Simple

An individual who holds the entire bundle of rights to property is said to be the owner in **fee simple.** The owner in fee simple is entitled to use, possess, or dispose of the property as he or she

---

1. The principles discussed in this section apply equally to real property ownership (to be discussed in Chapter 29).

chooses during his or her lifetime, and on this owner's death, the interests in the property descend to his or her heirs. We will return to this form of property ownership in Chapter 29, in the context of ownership rights in real property.

Concurrent Ownership

Persons who share ownership rights simultaneously in a particular piece of property are said to be *concurrent* owners. There are two principal types of **concurrent ownership:** *tenancy in common* and *joint tenancy.* Other types of concurrent ownership include *tenancy by the entirety* and *community property.*

Tenancy in Common The term **tenancy in common** refers to a form of co-ownership in which each of two or more persons owns an *undivided* interest in the property. The interest is undivided because each tenant has rights in the *whole* property. ■**EXAMPLE 28.1** Rosa and Chad own a rare stamp collection together as tenants in common. This does not mean that Rosa owns some particular stamps and Chad others. Rather, it means that Rosa and Chad each have rights in the *entire* collection. (If Rosa owned some of the stamps and Chad owned others, then the interest would be divided.) ■

On the death of a tenant in common, that tenant's interest in the property passes to her or his heirs. ■**EXAMPLE 28.2** Should Rosa die before Chad, a one-half interest in the stamp collection will become the property of Rosa's heirs. If Rosa sells her interest to Fred before she dies, Fred and Chad will be co-owners as tenants in common. If Fred dies, his interest in the personal property will pass to his heirs, and they in turn will own the property with Chad as tenants in common. ■

Joint Tenancy In a **joint tenancy,** each of two or more persons owns an undivided interest in the property, and a deceased joint tenant's interest passes to the surviving joint tenant or tenants. The rights of a surviving joint tenant to inherit a deceased joint tenant's ownership interest—which are referred to as *survivorship rights*—distinguish the joint tenancy from the tenancy in common. A joint tenancy can be terminated before a joint tenant's death by gift or by sale; in this situation, the person who receives the property as a gift or who purchases the property becomes a tenant in common, not a joint tenant. ■**EXAMPLE 28.3** If, in the preceding example, Rosa and Chad held their stamp collection in a joint tenancy and if Rosa died before Chad, the entire collection would become the property of Chad; Rosa's heirs would receive absolutely no interest in the collection. If Rosa, while living, sold her interest to Fred, however, the sale would terminate the joint tenancy, and Fred and Chad would become owners as tenants in common. ■

Generally, it is presumed that a co-tenancy is a tenancy in common unless there is a clear intention to establish a joint tenancy. Thus, language such as "to Jerrold and Eva as joint tenants with right of survivorship, and not as tenants in common" would be necessary to create a joint tenancy.

Tenancy by the Entirety A **tenancy by the entirety** is a less common form of ownership that can be created by a conveyance (transfer) of real property to a husband and wife. It differs from a joint tenancy only by the fact that neither spouse can make a separate lifetime transfer of his or her interest without the consent of the other spouse. In some states where statutes give the wife the right to convey her property, this form of concurrent ownership has been effectively abolished. A divorce, either spouse's death, or mutual agreement will terminate a tenancy by the entirety.

Community Property A married couple is allowed to own property as **community property** in only a limited number of states.[2] If property is held as community property, each spouse technically owns an undivided one-half interest in property acquired during the marriage. Generally, community property does not include property acquired prior to the marriage or property acquired by gift or inheritance as separate property during the marriage. After a divorce, community property is divided equally in some states and according to the discretion of the court in other states.

ACQUIRING OWNERSHIP OF PERSONAL PROPERTY

The most common way of acquiring personal property is by purchasing it. We have already discussed the purchase and sale of personal property (goods) in Chapters 14 through 17. Often, property is acquired by will or inheritance, a topic we will cover in Chapter 30. Here we look at additional ways in which ownership of personal property can be acquired, including acquisition by possession, production, gift, accession, and confusion.

Possession

One example of acquiring ownership by possession is the capture of wild animals. Wild animals belong to no one in their natural state, and the first person to take possession of a wild animal normally owns it. The killing of a wild animal amounts to assuming ownership of it. Merely being in hot pursuit does not give title, however. This basic rule has two exceptions. First, any wild animals captured by a trespasser are the property of the landowner, not the trespasser. Second, if wild animals are captured or killed in violation of wild-game

---

2. These states include Alaska, Arizona, California, Idaho, Louisiana, Nevada, New Mexico, Texas, Washington, and Wisconsin. Puerto Rico allows property to be owned as community property as well.

statutes, the state, and not the capturer, obtains title to the animals.

Those who find lost or abandoned property can also acquire ownership rights through mere possession of the property, as will be discussed later in the chapter. (Ownership rights in real property can also be acquired through possession, such as *adverse possession*—see Chapter 29.)

Production

Production—the fruits of labor—is another means of acquiring ownership of personal property. For instance, writers, inventors, and manufacturers all produce personal property and thereby acquire title to it. (In some situations, though, as when a researcher is hired to invent a new product or technique, the researcher-producer may not own what is produced—see Chapter 22.)

Gifts

A **gift** is another fairly common means of acquiring and transferring ownership of real and personal property. A gift is essentially a voluntary transfer of property ownership for which no consideration is given. As discussed in Chapter 8, the presence of consideration is what distinguishes a contract from a gift.

To be an effective gift, three requirements must be met: (1) donative intent on the part of the *donor* (the one giving the gift); (2) delivery; and (3) acceptance by the *donee* (the one receiving the gift). We examine each of these requirements here, as well as the requirements of a gift made in contemplation of imminent death. Until these three requirements are met, no effective gift has been made. **■EXAMPLE 28.4** Suppose that your aunt tells you that she *intends* to give you a new Mercedes-Benz for your next birthday. This is simply a promise to make a gift. It is not considered a gift until the Mercedes-Benz is delivered and accepted. **■**

Donative Intent When a gift is challenged in court, the court will determine whether donative intent exists by looking at the language of the donor and the surrounding circumstances. **■EXAMPLE 28.5** A court might question donative intent when a person gives a gift to his enemy. Similarly, when a person has given away a large portion of her assets,

the court will scrutinize the transaction closely to determine the mental capacity of the donor and ascertain whether fraud or duress was involved. **■**

Delivery The gift must be delivered to the donee. Delivery is obvious in most cases, but some objects cannot be relinquished physically. Then the question of delivery depends on the surrounding circumstances.

Constructive Delivery. When the object itself cannot be physically delivered, a symbolic, or constructive, delivery will be sufficient. **Constructive delivery** does not confer actual possession of the object in question, only the right to take actual possession. Thus, *constructive delivery* is a general term used to describe an action that the law holds to be the equivalent of real delivery. **■EXAMPLE 28.6** Suppose that you want to make a gift of various rare coins that you have stored in a safe-deposit box at your bank. You certainly cannot deliver the box itself to the donee, and you do not want to take the coins out of the bank. In this situation, you can simply deliver the key to the box to the donee and authorize the donee's access to the box and its contents. This action constitutes a constructive delivery of the contents of the box. **■**

The delivery of intangible property—such as stocks, bonds, insurance policies, and contracts, for example—must always be accomplished by symbolic, or constructive, delivery. This is because the documents represent rights and are not, in themselves, the true property.

Relinquishing Dominion and Control. An effective delivery also requires giving up complete control and **dominion** (ownership rights) over the subject matter of the gift. The outcome of disputes often turns on whether control has actually been relinquished. The Internal Revenue Service scrutinizes transactions between relatives when one claims to have given income-producing property to the other. A relative who does not relinquish complete control over a piece of property will have to pay taxes on the income from that property, as opposed to the family member who received the "gift."

In the following classic case, the court focused on the requirement that a donor must relinquish complete control and dominion over property given to the donee before a gift can be effectively delivered.

CASE 28.1   **In re Estate of Piper**

LANDMARK AND CLASSIC CASES

Missouri Court of Appeals, 676 S.W.2d 897 (1984).

FACTS Gladys Piper died intestate (without a will) in 1982. At her death, she owned miscellaneous personal property worth $5,000 and had in her purse $200 in cash and two diamond rings, known as the Andy Piper rings. The contents of her purse were taken by her niece Wanda Brown,

CASE 28.1—Continued

allegedly to preserve them for the estate. Clara Kauffmann, a friend of Piper's, filed a claim against the estate for $4,800. From October 1974 until Piper's death, Kauffmann had taken Piper to the doctor, beauty shop, and grocery store; had written her checks to pay her bills; and had helped her care for her home. Kauffmann maintained that Piper had promised to pay her for these services and had given her the diamond rings as a gift. A Missouri state trial court denied her request for payment; the court found that her services had been voluntary. Kauffmann then filed a petition for delivery of personal property—the rings—which was granted by the trial court. Brown, other heirs, and the administrator of Piper's estate appealed.

ISSUE Had Gladys Piper made an effective gift of the rings to Clara Kauffmann?

DECISION No. The state appellate court reversed the judgment of the trial court on the ground that Piper had never delivered the rings to Kauffmann.

REASON Kauffmann claimed that the rings belonged to her by reason of a "consummated gift long prior to the death of Gladys Piper." Two witnesses testified for Kauffmann at the trial that Piper had told them the rings belonged to Kauffmann but that she was going to wear them until she died. The appellate court found "no evidence of any actual delivery." The court held that the essentials of a gift are (1) a present intention to make a gift on the part of the donor, (2) a delivery of the property by the donor to the donee, and (3) an acceptance by the donee.

The evidence in the case showed only an intent to make a gift. Because there was no delivery—either actual or constructive—a valid gift was not made. For Piper to have made a gift, her intention would have to have been executed by the complete and unconditional delivery of the property or the delivery of a proper written instrument evidencing the gift. As this did not occur, the court found that there had been no gift.

WHAT IF THE FACTS WERE DIFFERENT? *Suppose that Gladys Piper had told Clara Kauffmann that she was giving the rings to Kauffmann but wished to keep them in her possession for a few more days. Would this have affected the court's decision in this case? Why or why not?*

IMPACT OF THIS CASE ON TODAY'S LAW *This case clearly illustrates the delivery requirement when making a gift. Assuming that Piper did, indeed, intend for Kauffmann to have the rings, it was unfortunate that Kauffmann had no right to receive them after Piper's death. Yet the alternative could lead to perhaps even more unfairness. The policy behind the delivery requirement is to protect alleged donors and their heirs from fraudulent claims based solely on parol evidence. If not for this policy, an alleged donee could easily claim that a gift was made when, in fact, it was not.*

RELEVANT WEB SITES *To locate information on the Web concerning the Piper decision, go to this text's Web site at **www.cengage.com/blaw/fbl**, select "Chapter 28," and click on "URLs for Landmarks."*

■

Acceptance The final requirement of a valid gift is acceptance by the donee. This rarely presents any problem, as most donees readily accept their gifts. The courts generally assume acceptance unless the circumstances indicate otherwise.

Gifts *Inter Vivos* and Gifts *Causa Mortis* A gift made during one's lifetime is termed a **gift *inter vivos***. Gifts *causa mortis* (so-called *deathbed gifts*), in contrast, are made in contemplation of imminent death. A gift *causa mortis* does not become absolute until the donor dies from the contemplated illness, and it is automatically revoked if the donor recovers from the illness. Moreover, the donee must survive to take the gift. To be effective, a gift *causa mortis* must also meet the three requirements discussed earlier—donative intent, delivery, and acceptance by the donee.

■**EXAMPLE 28.7** Yang is to be operated on for a cancerous tumor. Before the operation, he delivers an envelope to a close business associate. The envelope contains a letter say-

ing, "I realize my days are numbered, and I want to give you this check for $1 million in the event of my death from this operation." The business associate cashes the check. The surgeon performs the operation and removes the tumor. Yang recovers fully. Several months later, Yang dies from a heart attack that is totally unrelated to the operation. If Yang's personal representative (the party charged with administering Yang's estate) tries to recover the $1 million, normally she will succeed. The gift *causa mortis* is automatically revoked if the donor recovers. The *specific event* that was contemplated in making the gift was death from a particular operation. Because Yang's death was not the result of this event, the gift is revoked, and the $1 million passes to Yang's estate. ■

Accession

Accession means "something added." Accession occurs when someone adds value to an item of personal property by the use of either labor or materials. Generally, there is no dispute about who owns the property after the accession occurs, especially when the accession is accomplished with the owner's consent. **■EXAMPLE 28.8** A Corvette-customizing specialist comes to Hoshi's house. Hoshi has all the materials necessary to customize the car. The specialist uses them to add a unique bumper to Hoshi's Corvette. Hoshi simply pays the customizer for the value of the labor, retaining title to the property. **■**

When accession occurs without the owner's permission, the courts tend to favor the owner over the improver—the one who improves the property—provided that the accession was wrongful and undertaken in bad faith. This is true even if the accession increased the value of the property substantially. In addition, many courts will deny the improver (wrongdoer) any compensation for the value added. **■EXAMPLE 28.9** Patti steals a car and puts expensive new tires on it. Obviously, a car thief will not be compensated for the value of the new tires if the rightful owner recovers the car. **■**

If the accession is performed in good faith, however, even without the owner's consent, ownership of the improved item most often depends on whether the accession has increased the value of the property or changed its identity. The greater the increase in value, the more likely that ownership will pass to the improver. If ownership does pass, the improver must compensate the original owner for the value of the property prior to the accession. If the increase in value is not sufficient for ownership to pass to the improver, most courts will require the owner to compensate the improver for the value added.

Confusion

Confusion is the commingling (mixing together) of goods so that one person's personal property cannot be distinguished from another's. Confusion frequently occurs when the goods are *fungible. Fungible goods* are goods consisting of identical particles, such as grain or oil. For instance, if two farmers put their number 2–grade winter wheat into the same storage bin, confusion will occur and the farmers become tenants in common.

When goods are confused due to a wrongful and willful act and the wrongdoer is unable to prove what percentage of the confused goods belongs to him or her, then the innocent party ordinarily acquires title to the whole. If confusion occurs as a result of agreement, an honest mistake, or the act of some third party, the owners share ownership as tenants in common and will share any loss in proportion to their ownership interests in the property. **■EXAMPLE 28.10** Five farmers in a small Iowa community enter a cooperative arrangement. Each fall, the farmers harvest the same amount of number 2–grade yellow corn and

store it in silos that are held by the cooperative. Each farmer thus owns one-fifth of the total corn in the silos. If one farmer harvests and stores more corn than the others in the cooperative silos and wants to claim a greater ownership interest, that farmer must keep careful records. Otherwise, the courts will presume that each farmer has an equal interest in the corn. **■**

MISLAID, LOST, AND ABANDONED PROPERTY

As already mentioned, one of the methods of acquiring ownership of property is to possess it. Simply finding something and holding on to it, however, does not necessarily give the finder any legal rights in the property. Different rules apply, depending on whether the property was mislaid, lost, or abandoned.

Mislaid Property

Property that has voluntarily been placed somewhere by the owner and then inadvertently forgotten is **mislaid property.** **■EXAMPLE 28.11** Suppose that you go to a movie theater. While paying for popcorn at the concession stand, you set your iPhone on the counter and then leave it there. The iPhone is mislaid property, and the theater owner is entrusted with the duty of reasonable care for it. **■** When mislaid property is found, the finder does not obtain title to it. Instead, the owner of the place where the property was mislaid becomes the caretaker of the property because the true owner is highly likely to return.[3]

Lost Property

Property that is involuntarily left and forgotten is **lost property.** A finder of the property can claim title to the property against the whole world *except the true owner.*[4] If the true owner demands that the lost property be returned, the finder must return it. If a third party attempts to take possession of lost property from a finder, the third party cannot assert a better title than the finder.

■EXAMPLE 28.12 Khalia works in a large library at night. As she crosses the courtyard on her way home, she finds a piece of gold jewelry set with stones that look like precious stones to her. She takes it to a jeweler to have it appraised. While pretending to weigh the jewelry, the jeweler's employee removes several of the stones. If Khalia brings an action to

---

3. The finder of mislaid property is an involuntary bailee (to be discussed later in this chapter).
4. The landmark case establishing this rule is *Armory v. Delamirie,* 93 Eng.Rep. 664 (King's Bench 1722); see also *Payne v. TK Atuo Wholesalers,* 98 Conn.App. 533, 911 A.2d 747 (2006).

recover the stones from the jeweler, she normally will win because she found lost property and holds valid title against everyone *except the true owner.* Because the property was lost, rather than mislaid, the finder is the caretaker of the jewelry, and the finder acquires title good against the whole world (except the true owner). ■

When a finder knows who the true owner of the property is and fails to return it to that person, the finder is guilty of the tort of *conversion* (the wrongful taking of another's property—see Chapter 4). Many states require the finder to make a reasonably diligent search to locate the true owner of lost property. Many states also have *estray statutes,* which encourage and facilitate the return of property to its true owner and then reward the finder for honesty if the property remains unclaimed. These laws provide an incentive for finders to report their discoveries by making it possible for them, after the passage of a specified period of time, to acquire legal title to the property they have found.

Abandoned Property

Property that has been discarded by the true owner, with no intention of reclaiming title to it, is **abandoned property.** Someone who finds abandoned property acquires title to it, and such title is good against the whole world, *including the original owner.* The owner of lost property who eventually gives up any further attempt to find it is frequently held to have abandoned the property. If a person finds abandoned property while trespassing on the property of another, title vests in the owner of the land, not in the finder.

■EXAMPLE 28.13 Aleka is driving with the windows down in her car. Somewhere along her route, a valuable scarf blows out the window. She retraces her route and searches for the scarf but cannot find it. She finally gives up her search and proceeds to her destination five hundred miles away. Six months later, Frye, a hitchhiker, finds the scarf. Frye has acquired title, which is good even against Aleka. By completely giving up her search, Aleka abandoned the scarf just as effectively as if she had intentionally discarded it. ■

BAILMENTS

A **bailment** is formed by the delivery of personal property, without transfer of title, by one person, called a **bailor,** to another, called a **bailee,** usually under an agreement for a particular purpose—for example, to loan, lease, store, repair, or transport the property. On completion of the purpose, the bailee is obligated to return the bailed property in the same or better condition to the bailor or a third person or to dispose of it as directed.

Bailments are usually created by agreement, but not necessarily by contract, because in many bailments not all of the elements of a contract (such as mutual assent and consideration) are present. **■EXAMPLE 28.14** If you lend your bicycle to a friend, a bailment is created, but not by contract, because there is no consideration. Many commercial bailments, such as the delivery of clothing to the cleaners for dry cleaning, are based on contract, though. ■

PREVENTING LEGAL DISPUTES **The law of bailments applies to many routine transactions that occur daily in the business community. When a transaction involves a bailment, whether you realize it or not, you are subject to the obligations and duties that arise from the bailment relationship. Consequently, knowing how bailment relationships are created, and what rights, duties, and liabilities flow from ordinary bailments, is critical in avoiding legal disputes. Also important is understanding that bailees can limit the dollar amount of their liability by contract.**

■

Elements of a Bailment

Not all transactions involving the delivery of property from one person to another create a bailment. For such a transfer to become a bailment, the following three elements must be present:

1 Personal property.

2 Delivery of possession (without title).

3 Agreement that the property will be returned to the bailor or otherwise disposed of according to its owner's directions.

Personal Property Requirement Only personal property is bailable; there can be no bailment of persons. Although a bailment of your luggage is created when it is transported by an airline, as a passenger you are not the subject of a bailment. Additionally, you cannot bail realty; thus, leasing your house to a tenant does not create a bailment. Although bailments commonly involve *tangible* items—jewelry, cattle, automobiles, and the like—*intangible* personal property, such as promissory notes and shares of corporate stock, may also be bailed.

Delivery of Possession *Delivery of possession* means the transfer of possession of the property to the bailee. For delivery to occur, the bailee must be given exclusive possession and control over the property, and the bailee must *knowingly* accept the personal property.[5] In other words, the bailee must *intend* to exercise control over it.

If either delivery of possession or knowing acceptance is lacking, there is no bailment relationship. **■EXAMPLE 28.15** Kim takes a friend out to dinner at an expensive restaurant. When they enter the restaurant, Kim's friend checks her coat. In the pocket of the coat is a $20,000 diamond necklace. The bailee, by accepting the coat, does not knowingly also accept the necklace. Thus, a bailment of the coat exists—because the restaurant has exclusive possession and control over the coat and knowingly accepted it—but not a bailment of the necklace. ■

Physical versus Constructive Delivery. Either *physical* or *constructive* delivery will result in the bailee's exclusive possession of and control over the property. As discussed earlier in the context of gifts, constructive delivery is a substitute, or symbolic, delivery. What is delivered to the bailee is not the actual property bailed (such as a car) but something so related to the property (such as the car keys) that the requirement of delivery is satisfied.

Involuntary Bailments. In certain situations, a bailment is found despite the apparent lack of the requisite elements of control and knowledge. One example of such a situation occurs when the bailee acquires the property accidentally or by mistake—as in finding someone else's lost or mislaid property. A bailment is created even though the bailor did not voluntarily deliver the property to the bailee. Such bailments are called *constructive* or *involuntary* bailments. **■EXAMPLE 28.16** Several corporate managers attend a meeting at the law firm of Jacobs & Matheson. One of the managers, Kyle Gustafson, inadvertently leaves his briefcase at the firm after the meeting. In this situation, a court could find that an involuntary bailment was created even though Gustafson did not voluntarily deliver the briefcase and the law firm did not intentionally accept it. If an involuntary bailment existed, the firm would be responsible for taking care of the briefcase and returning it to Gustafson. ■

Bailment Agreement A bailment agreement, or contract, can be express or implied. Although a written agreement is not required for bailments of less than one year (that is, the Statute of Frauds does not apply—see Chapter 10), it is a good idea to have one, especially when valuable property is involved.

The bailment agreement expressly or impliedly provides for the return of the bailed property to the bailor or to a third

---

5. We are dealing here with *voluntary bailments*. This does not apply to *involuntary bailments*.

person, or for disposal of the property by the bailee. The agreement presupposes that the bailee will return the identical goods originally given by the bailor. In certain types of bailments, though, such as bailments of fungible goods, the property returned need only be equivalent property. **■EXAMPLE 28.17** Holman stores his grain (fungible goods) in Joe's Warehouse, creating a bailment. At the end of the storage period, the warehouse is not obligated to return to Holman exactly the same grain that he stored. As long as the warehouse returns grain of the same *type*, *grade*, and *quantity*, the warehouse—the bailee—has performed its obligation. ■

Ordinary Bailments

Bailments are either *ordinary* or *special (extraordinary)*. There are three types of ordinary bailments. They are distinguished according to *which party receives a benefit from the bailment*. This factor will dictate the rights and liabilities of the parties, and the courts may use it to determine the standard of care required of the bailee in possession of the personal property. The three types of ordinary bailments are as follows:

1 *Bailment for the sole benefit of the bailor.* This is a gratuitous bailment (a bailment without consideration) for the convenience and benefit of the bailor. **■EXAMPLE 28.18** Allen asks his friend, Sumi, to store his car in her garage while he is away. If Sumi agrees to do so, then it is a gratuitous bailment because the bailment of the car is for the sole benefit of the bailor (Allen). ■

2 *Bailment for the sole benefit of the bailee.* This type of bailment typically occurs when one person lends an item to another person (the bailee) solely for the bailee's convenience and benefit. **■EXAMPLE 28.19** Allen asks to borrow Sumi's boat so that he can go sailing over the weekend. The bailment of the boat is for Allen's (the bailee's) sole benefit. ■

3 *Bailment for the mutual benefit of the bailee and the bailor.* This is the most common kind of bailment and involves some form of compensation for storing items or holding property while it is being serviced. It is a contractual bailment and may be referred to as a *bailment for hire* or a *commercial bailment.* **■EXAMPLE 28.20** Allen leaves his car at a service station for an oil change. Because the service station will be paid to change Allen's oil, this is a mutual-benefit bailment. ■ Many lease arrangements in which the lease involves goods (leases were discussed in Chapters 14 through 17) also fall into this category of bailment once the lessee takes possession.

Rights of the Bailee Certain rights are implicit in the bailment agreement. Generally, the bailee has the right to take possession, to utilize the property for accomplishing the purpose of the bailment, to receive some form of compensation, and to limit her or his liability for the bailed goods. These rights of the bailee are present (with some limitations) in varying degrees in all bailment transactions.

Right of Possession. A hallmark of the bailment agreement is that the bailee acquires the *right to control and possess the property temporarily.* The bailee's right of possession permits the bailee to recover damages from any third person for damage or loss of the property. If the property is stolen, the bailee has a legal right to regain possession of it or to obtain damages from any third person who has wrongfully interfered with the bailee's possessory rights. The bailee's right to regain possession of the property or to obtain damages is important because, as you will read shortly, a bailee is liable to the bailor for any loss or damage to bailed property resulting from the bailee's negligence.

Right to Use Bailed Property. Depending on the type of bailment and the terms of the bailment agreement, a bailee may also have a right to use the bailed property. When no provision is made, the extent of use depends on how necessary it is for the goods to be at the bailee's disposal for the ordinary purpose of the bailment to be carried out. **■EXAMPLE 28.21** If you borrow a friend's car to drive to the airport, you, as the bailee, would obviously be expected to use the car. In a bailment involving the long-term storage of a car, however, the bailee is not expected to use the car because the ordinary purpose of a storage bailment does not include use of the property. **■**

Right of Compensation. Except in a gratuitous bailment, a bailee has a right to be compensated as provided for in the bailment agreement, to be reimbursed for costs and services rendered in the keeping of the bailed property, or both. Even in a gratuitous bailment, a bailee has a right to be reimbursed or compensated for costs incurred in the keeping of the bailed property. **■EXAMPLE 28.22** Margo loses her pet dog, and Justine finds it. Justine takes Margo's dog to her home and feeds it. Even though she takes good care of the dog, it becomes ill, and she takes it to a veterinarian. Justine pays the bill for the veterinarian's services and the medicine. Justine normally will be entitled to be reimbursed by Margo for all reasonable costs incurred in the keeping of Margo's dog. **■**

To enforce the right of compensation, the bailee has a right to place a *possessory lien* (which entitles a creditor to retain possession of the debtor's goods until a debt is paid) on the specific bailed property until he or she has been fully compensated. This type of lien, sometimes referred to as an *artisan's lien* or a *bailee's lien*, was discussed in Chapter 21.

Right to Limit Liability. In ordinary bailments, bailees have the right to limit their liability as long as the limitations are called to the attention of the bailor and are not against public policy. It is essential that the bailor be informed of the limitation in some way. Even when the bailor knows of the limitation, certain types of disclaimers of liability have been considered to be against public policy and therefore illegal. The courts carefully scrutinize *exculpatory clauses*, or clauses that limit a person's liability for her or his own wrongful acts, and in bailments they are often held to be illegal. This is particularly true in bailments for the mutual benefit of the bailor and the bailee. **■EXAMPLE 28.23** A receipt from a parking garage expressly disclaims liability for any damage to parked cars, regardless of the cause. Because the bailee has attempted to exclude liability for the bailee's own negligence, including the parking attendant's negligence, the clause will likely be deemed unenforceable because it is against public policy. **■**

Duties of the Bailee The bailee has two basic responsibilities: (1) to take appropriate care of the property and (2) to surrender the property to the bailor or dispose of it in accordance with the bailor's instructions at the end of the bailment.

The Duty of Care. The bailee must exercise reasonable care in preserving the bailed property. What constitutes reasonable care in a bailment situation normally depends on the nature and specific circumstances of the bailment. Traditionally, the courts have determined the appropriate standard of care on the basis of the type of bailment involved. In a bailment for the sole benefit of the bailor, for example, the bailee need exercise only a slight degree of care. In a bailment for the sole benefit of the bailee, however, the bailee must exercise great care. In a mutual-benefit bailment, courts normally impose a reasonable standard of care—that is, the bailee must exercise the degree of care that a reasonable and prudent person would exercise in the same circumstances. Exhibit 28–1 illustrates these concepts. A bailee's failure to exercise appropriate care in handling the bailor's property results in tort liability.

Duty to Return Bailed Property. At the end of the bailment, the bailee normally must hand over the original property to either the bailor or someone the bailor designates or

EXHIBIT 28–1 Degree of Care Required of a Bailee

Bailment for the Sole Benefit of the Bailor	Mutual-Benefit Bailment	Bailment for the Sole Benefit of the Bailee
	DEGREE OF CARE	
SLIGHT	REASONABLE	GREAT

otherwise dispose of it as directed. This is usually a *contractual* duty arising from the bailment agreement (contract). Failure to give up possession at the time the bailment ends is a breach of contract and could result in the tort of conversion or an action based on bailee negligence. If the bailed property has been lost or is returned damaged, a court will presume that the bailee was negligent. The bailee's obligation is excused, however, if the goods or chattels were destroyed, lost, or stolen through no fault of the bailee (or claimed by a third party with a superior claim).

Because the bailee has a duty to return the bailed goods to the bailor, a bailee may be liable if the goods being held or delivered are given to the wrong person. Hence, a bailee must be satisfied that a person (other than the bailor) to whom the goods are being delivered is the actual owner or has authority from the owner to take possession of the goods. Should the bailee deliver in error, then the bailee may be liable for conversion or misdelivery.

Duties of the Bailor   It goes without saying that the duties of a bailor are essentially the same as the rights of a bailee. Obviously, a bailor has a duty to compensate the bailee either as agreed or as reimbursement for costs incurred by the bailee in keeping the bailed property. A bailor also has an all-encompassing duty to provide the bailee with goods or chattels that are free from known defects that could cause injury to the bailee.

Bailor's Duty to Reveal Defects.   The bailor's duty to reveal defects to the bailee translates into two rules:

1 In a *mutual-benefit bailment*, the bailor must notify the bailee of all known defects and any hidden defects that the bailor knows of or could have discovered with reasonable diligence and proper inspection.

2 In a *bailment for the sole benefit of the bailee*, the bailor must notify the bailee of any known defects.

The bailor's duty to reveal defects is based on a negligence theory of tort law. A bailor who fails to give the appropriate notice is liable to the bailee and to any other person who might reasonably be expected to come into contact with the defective article.

■**EXAMPLE 28.24** Rentco (the bailor) rents a tractor to Hal Iverson. Unknown to Rentco (but *discoverable* by reasonable inspection), the brake mechanism on the tractor is defective at the time the bailment is made. Iverson uses the defective tractor without knowledge of the brake problem and is injured along with two other field workers when the tractor rolls out of control. Because this is a mutual-benefit bailment, Rentco has a *duty* to notify Iverson of the discoverable brake defect. Rentco's failure to fulfill this duty is the *proximate cause* (discussed in Chapter 4) of injuries to farm workers who might be expected to use, or have contact with, the tractor. Therefore, Rentco is liable under a negligence theory for the injuries sustained by Iverson and the two others. ■

Warranty Liability for Defective Goods.   A bailor can also incur *warranty liability* based on contract law (see Chapter 17) for injuries resulting from the bailment of defective articles. Property leased by a bailor must be *fit for the intended purpose of the bailment*. Warranties of fitness arise by law in sales contracts and leases, and judges have extended these warranties to situations in which the bailees are compensated for the bailment (such as when one leaves a car with a parking attendant). Article 2A of the Uniform Commercial Code (UCC) extends the implied warranties of merchantability and fitness for a particular purpose to bailments whenever the bailments include rights to use the bailed goods.[6]

Special Types of Bailments

Although many bailments are the ordinary bailments that we have just discussed, a business is also likely to engage in some special types of bailment transactions. These include bailments in which the bailee's duty of care is *extraordinary*—that is, the bailee's liability for loss or damage to the property is absolute—as is generally true in bailments involving common carriers and innkeepers. Warehouse companies have the same duty of care as ordinary bailees, but, like carriers, they are subject to extensive regulation under federal and state laws, including Article 7 of the UCC.

Common Carriers   *Common carriers* are publicly licensed to provide transportation services to the general public. They are distinguished from private carriers, which operate transportation facilities for a select clientele. A private carrier is not required to provide service to every person or company making a request. A common carrier, however, must arrange carriage for all who apply, within certain limitations.[7]

The delivery of goods to a common carrier creates a bailment relationship between the shipper (bailor) and the common carrier (bailee). Unlike ordinary bailees, the common carrier is held to a standard of care based on *strict liability*, rather than reasonable care, in protecting the bailed personal property. This means that the common carrier is absolutely liable, regardless of due care, for all loss or damage to goods except damage caused by one of the following common law exceptions: (1) an act of

---

6. UCC 2A–212, 2A–213.

7. A common carrier is not required to take any and all property anywhere in all instances. Public regulatory agencies govern common carriers, and carriers can be restricted to geographic areas. They can also be limited to carrying certain kinds of goods or to providing only special types of transportation equipment.

God, (2) an act of a public enemy, (3) an order of a public authority, (4) an act of the shipper, or (5) the inherent nature of the goods.

Common carriers cannot contract away their liability for damaged goods. Subject to government regulations, however, they are permitted to limit their dollar liability to an amount stated on the shipment contract or rate filing.[8] This point is illustrated in the following case.

---

8. Federal laws require common carriers to offer shippers the opportunity to obtain higher dollar limits for loss by paying a higher fee for the transport.

CASE 28.2   Treiber & Straub, Inc. v. United Parcel Service, Inc.

United States Court of Appeals, Seventh Circuit, 474 F.3d 379 (2007).

FACTS Michael Straub is the president of Treiber & Straub, Inc., a fine-jewelry store in Wisconsin. To return a diamond ring to Norman Silverman Company, a wholesaler in California, Straub chose United Parcel Service, Inc. (UPS), and, through **www.ups.com**, arranged to ship the ring via "Next Day Air." To ship a package using the Web site, a customer has to click on two on-screen boxes to agree to "My UPS Terms and Conditions." Among these terms, UPS and its insurer, UPS Capital Insurance Agency, Inc., limit their liability and the amount of insurance coverage on packages to $50,000. UPS refuses to ship items of "unusual value"—those worth more than $50,000—and the carrier and its insurer disclaim liability *entirely* for such items. The ring was worth $105,000. Undeterred, Straub opted for the maximum coverage and indicated on the air bill that the value was "$50,000 or less." UPS lost the ring. Treiber & Straub reimbursed the wholesaler for the full loss and filed a suit in a federal district court against UPS and its insurer to recover $50,000 under the insurance policy. The court issued a summary judgment in the defendants' favor based on the disclaimer. The plaintiff appealed to the U.S. Court of Appeals for the Seventh Circuit, arguing, among other things, that the disclaimer was "literally buried among all the other extensive terms and conditions on the vast UPS Web site."

ISSUE Was the carrier's disclaimer enforceable?

DECISION Yes. The U.S. Court of Appeals for the Seventh Circuit affirmed the judgment of the lower court. The appellate court held that the carrier's disclaimer was prominent enough.

REASON The court examined the relevant pages on the UPS Web site. On those pages, UPS initially limits its liability to $100 but offers customers an opportunity to buy insurance for coverage up to $50,000. If a customer wants to ship a package with a value of more than $50,000, UPS refuses to accept it or to insure it. UPS does not explain all of the details about these limits on a single page, but the court ruled that this "does not call for a different result in light of everything else that was available to the shipper." The limitation and the disclaimer are repeated several times on the Web site. This ensures "clear and reasonable notice" of the terms, to which a customer has to click twice in agreement to arrange a shipment. Further, the court reasoned that if UPS accepted packages with values greater than $50,000 but insured them for no more than that amount, "it would distort the mix of claims it is insuring, skewing it toward the high-value end, necessitating a significant change in premiums. The risk of theft would also increase for packages with higher declared values." The court also pointed out that in this case, "by indicating on the air bill the insured value (of $50,000 or less) rather than the actual value" of the ring, "Treiber [& Straub] effectively breached the shipping contract."

WHAT IF THE FACTS WERE DIFFERENT?
If Straub had claimed that he had not read the terms, would the result in this case have been different? Why or why not?

■

Warehouse Companies *Warehousing* is the business of providing storage of property for compensation.[9] Like ordinary bailees, warehouse companies are liable for loss or damage to property resulting from *negligence*. A warehouse company, however, is a professional bailee and is therefore expected to exercise a high degree of care to protect and preserve the goods. A warehouse company can limit the dollar amount of its liability, but the bailor must be given the option of paying an increased storage rate for an increase in the liability limit.

Unlike ordinary bailees, a warehouse company can issue *documents of title*—in particular, *warehouse receipts*—and is

---

9. UCC 7–102(h) defines the person engaged in the storing of goods for hire as a "warehouseman."

subject to extensive government regulation, including Article 7 of the UCC.[10] A warehouse receipt describes the bailed property and the terms of the bailment contract. It can be negotiable or nonnegotiable, depending on how it is written. It is negotiable if its terms provide that the warehouse company will deliver the goods "to the bearer" of the receipt or "to the order of" a person named on the receipt.[11] The warehouse receipt represents the goods (that is, it indicates title) and hence has value and utility in financing commercial transactions.

■EXAMPLE 28.25 Ossip delivers 6,500 cases of canned corn to Chaney, the owner of a warehouse. Chaney issues a negotiable warehouse receipt payable "to bearer" and gives it to Ossip. Ossip sells and delivers the warehouse receipt to Better Foods, Inc. Better Foods is now the owner of the corn and has the right to obtain the cases by simply presenting the warehouse receipt to Chaney. ■

---

10. A *document of title* is defined in UCC 1–201(15) as any "document which in the regular course of business or financing is treated as adequately evidencing that the person in possession of it is entitled to receive, hold, and dispose of the document and the goods it covers." A *warehouse receipt* is a document of title issued by a person engaged in the business of storing goods for hire.

11. UCC 7–104.

Innkeepers At common law, innkeepers and hotel owners were strictly liable for the loss of any cash or property that guests brought into their rooms. Today, only those who provide lodging to the public for compensation as a *regular* business are covered under this rule of strict liability. Moreover, the rule applies only to those who are guests, as opposed to lodgers, who are persons that permanently reside at the hotel or inn.

In many states, innkeepers can avoid strict liability for loss of guests' cash and valuables by (1) providing a safe in which to keep them and (2) notifying guests that a safe is available. In addition, statutes often limit the liability of innkeepers with regard to articles that are not kept in the safe and may limit the availability of damages in the absence of innkeeper negligence. Most statutes require that the innkeeper post these limitations or otherwise notify the guest. Such postings, or notices, are frequently found on the doors of the rooms in motels and hotels.

■EXAMPLE 28.26 Joyce stays for a night at the Harbor Hotel. When she returns from eating breakfast in the hotel restaurant, she discovers that her suitcase has been stolen and sees that the lock on the door between her room and the room next door is broken. Joyce claims that the hotel is liable for her loss. Because the hotel was not negligent, however, normally it is not liable under state law. ■

REVIEWING Personal Property and Bailments

Vanessa Denai owned forty acres of land in rural Louisiana with a 1,600-square-foot house on it and a metal barn near the house. Denai later met Lance Finney, who had been seeking a small plot of rural property to rent. After several meetings, Denai invited Finney to live in a corner of her property in exchange for Finney's assistance in cutting wood and tending her property. Denai agreed to store Finney's sailboat in her barn. With Denai's consent, Finney constructed a concrete and oak foundation on Denai's property and purchased a 190-square-foot dome from Dome Baja for $3,395. The dome was shipped by Doty Express, a transportation company licensed to serve the public. When it arrived, Finney installed the dome frame and fabric exterior so that the dome was detachable from the foundation. A year after Finney installed the dome, Denai wrote Finney a note stating, "I've decided to give you four acres of land surrounding your dome as drawn on this map." This gift violated no local land-use restrictions. Using the information presented in the chapter, answer the following questions.

1 Is the dome real property or personal property? Explain.

2 Is Denai's gift of land to Finney a testamentary gift, a gift *causa mortis,* or a gift *inter vivos*?

3 What type of bailment relationship was created when Denai agreed to store Finney's boat? What degree of care was Denai required to exercise in storing the boat?

4 What standard of care applied to the shipment of the dome by Doty Express?

TERMS AND CONCEPTS

abandoned property 595	bailment 595	community property 591
accession 593	bailor 595	concurrent ownership 591
bailee 595	chattel 590	confusion 594

CHAPTER SUMMARY	Personal Property and Bailments

PERSONAL PROPERTY

Definition of Personal Property (See page 590.)	Personal property (also referred to as personalty or chattel) includes all property not classified as real property (realty). Personal property can be tangible (such as a TV or a car) or intangible (such as stocks or bonds).
Property Ownership (See pages 590–591.)	Having the fullest ownership rights in property is called *fee simple* ownership. There are various ways of co-owning property, including *tenancy in common, joint tenancy, tenancy by the entirety,* and *community property.*
Acquiring Ownership of Personal Property (See pages 591–594.)	The most common means of acquiring ownership in personal property is by purchasing it (see Chapters 14 through 17). Personal property is also often acquired by will or inheritance (see Chapter 30). The following are additional methods of acquiring personal property:

1. *Possession*—Ownership may be acquired by possession if no other person has ownership title (for example, capturing wild animals or finding abandoned property).

2. *Production*—Any product or item produced by an individual (with minor exceptions) becomes the property of that individual.

3. *Gift*—A gift is effective when the following conditions exist:

   a. There is evidence of *intent* to make a gift of the property in question.

   b. The gift is *delivered* (physically or constructively) to the donee.

   c. The gift is *accepted* by the donee.

4. *Accession*—When someone adds value to an item of personal property by the use of labor or materials, the added value generally becomes the property of the owner of the original property (includes accessions made in bad faith or wrongfully). Good faith accessions that substantially increase the property's value or change the identity of the property may cause title to pass to the improver.

5. *Confusion*—If a person wrongfully and willfully commingles fungible goods with those of another in order to render them indistinguishable, the innocent party acquires title to the whole. Otherwise, the owners become tenants in common of the commingled goods.

Mislaid, Lost, and Abandoned Property (See pages 594–595.)	1. *Mislaid property*—Property that is placed somewhere voluntarily by the owner and then inadvertently forgotten. A finder of mislaid property will not acquire title to the goods, and the owner of the place where the property was mislaid becomes a caretaker of the mislaid property.

2. *Lost property*—Property that is involuntarily left and forgotten. A finder of lost property can claim title to the property against the whole world *except the true owner.*

3. *Abandoned property*—Property that has been discarded by the true owner, who has no intention of claiming title to the property in the future. A finder of abandoned property can claim title to it against the whole world, *including the original owner.*

(Continued)

CHAPTER SUMMARY	Personal Property and Bailments–Continued
	BAILMENTS

Elements of a Bailment (See pages 595–596.)	1. *Personal property*—Bailments involve only personal property. 2. *Delivery of possession*—For an effective bailment to exist, the bailee (the one receiving the property) must be given exclusive possession and control over the property, and in a voluntary bailment, the bailee must knowingly accept the personal property. 3. *The bailment agreement*—Expressly or impliedly provides for the return of the bailed property to the bailor or a third party, or for the disposal of the bailed property by the bailee.

Ordinary Bailments (See pages 596–598.)	1. *Types of bailments*—
	  a. Bailment for the sole benefit of the bailor—A gratuitous bailment undertaken for the sole benefit of the bailor (for example, as a favor to the bailor).
	  b. Bailment for the sole benefit of the bailee—A gratuitous loan of an article to a person (the bailee) solely for the bailee's benefit.
	  c. Mutual-benefit (contractual) bailment—The most common kind of bailment; involves compensation between the bailee and bailor for the service provided.
	
	2. *Rights of a bailee (duties of a bailor)*—
	  a. The right of possession—Allows actions against third persons who damage or convert the bailed property and allows actions against the bailor for wrongful breach of the bailment.
	  b. The right to be compensated and reimbursed for expenses—In the event of nonpayment, the bailee has the right to place a possessory (bailee's) lien on the bailed property.
	  c. The right to limit liability—An ordinary bailee can limit his or her liability for loss or damage, provided proper notice is given and the limitation is not against public policy. In special bailments, limitations on liability for negligence or on types of losses usually are not allowed, but limitations on the monetary amount of liability are permitted.
	
	3. *Duties of a bailee (rights of a bailor)*—
	  a. A bailee must exercise appropriate care over property entrusted to her or him. What constitutes appropriate care normally depends on the nature and circumstances of the bailment.
	  b. Bailed goods in a bailee's possession must be either returned to the bailor or disposed of according to the bailor's directions. A bailee's failure to return the bailed property creates a presumption of negligence and constitutes a breach of contract or the tort of conversion of goods.

Special Types of Bailments (See pages 598–600.)	1. *Common carriers*—Carriers that are publicly licensed to provide transportation services to the general public. A common carrier is held to a standard of care based on *strict liability* unless the bailed property is lost or destroyed due to (a) an act of God, (b) an act of a public enemy, (c) an order of a public authority, (d) an act of the shipper, or (e) the inherent nature of the goods. 2. *Warehouse companies*—Professional bailees that differ from ordinary bailees in that they (a) can issue documents of title (warehouse receipts) and (b) are subject to state and federal statutes, including Article 7 of the UCC (as are common carriers). They must exercise a high degree of care over the bailed property and are liable for loss of or damage to property if they fail to do so. 3. *Innkeepers (hotel operators)*—Those who provide lodging to the public for compensation as a *regular* business. The common law strict liability standard to which innkeepers were once held is limited today by state statutes, which vary from state to state.

FOR REVIEW

Answers for the even-numbered questions in this **For Review** *section can be found on this text's accompanying Web site at* **www.cengage.com/blaw/fbl**. *Select "Chapter 28" and click on "For Review."*

1 What is real property? What is personal property?

2 What does it mean to own property in fee simple? What is the difference between a joint tenancy and a tenancy in common?

3 What are the three elements necessary for an effective gift? How else can property be acquired?

4 What are the three elements of a bailment?

5 What are the basic rights and duties of a bailee? What are the rights and duties of a bailor?

QUESTIONS AND CASE PROBLEMS

 ## HYPOTHETICAL SCENARIOS AND CASE PROBLEMS

28.1 Duties of the Bailee. Discuss the standard of care traditionally required of the bailee for the bailed property in each of the following situations, and determine whether the bailee breached that duty.

   1 Ricardo borrows Steve's lawn mower because his own lawn mower needs repair. Ricardo mows his front yard. To mow the backyard, he needs to move some hoses and lawn furniture. He leaves the mower in front of his house while doing so. When he returns to the front yard, he discovers that the mower has been stolen.

   2 Alicia owns a valuable speedboat. She is going on vacation and asks her neighbor, Maureen, to store the boat in one stall of Maureen's double garage. Maureen consents, and the boat is moved into the garage. Maureen needs some grocery items for dinner and drives to the store. She leaves the garage door open while she is gone, as is her custom, and the speedboat is stolen during that time.

28.2 Gifts. Jaspal has a severe heart attack and is taken to the hospital. He is aware that he is not expected to live. Because he is a bachelor with no close relatives nearby, Jaspal gives his car keys to his close friend, Friedrich, telling Friedrich that he is expected to die and that the car is Friedrich's. Jaspal survives the heart attack, but two months later he dies from pneumonia. Sam, Jaspal's uncle and the executor of his estate, wants Friedrich to return the car. Friedrich refuses, claiming that the car was given to him by Jaspal as a gift. Discuss whether Friedrich will be required to return the car to Jaspal's estate.

28.3 Hypothetical Question with Sample Answer. Curtis is an executive on a business trip to the West Coast. He has driven his car on this trip and checks into the Hotel Ritz. The hotel has a guarded underground parking lot. Curtis gives his car keys to the parking lot attendant but fails to notify the attendant that his wife's $10,000 fur coat is in a box in the trunk. The next day, on checking out, he discovers that his car has been stolen. Curtis wants to hold the hotel liable for both the car and the coat. Discuss the probable success of his claim.

 For a sample answer to Question 28.3, go to Appendix E at the end of this text.

28.4 Gratuitous Bailments. Raul, David, and Javier immigrated to the United States from Colima, Mexico, to find jobs and help their families. When they learned that a mutual friend, Francisco, planned to travel to Colima, they asked him to deliver various sums, totaling more than $25,000, to their families. During customs inspections at the border, Francisco told U.S. customs officials that he was not carrying more than $10,000, when, in fact, he carried more than $35,000. The government seized the cash and arrested Francisco. Raul, David, and Javier requested the government to return their cash, arguing that Francisco was a gratuitous bailee and that they still retained title. Are they right? Explain fully.

28.5 Found Property. A. D. Lock owned Lock Hospitality, Inc., which in turn owned the Best Western Motel in Conway, Arkansas. Joe Terry and David Stocks were preparing the motel for renovation. As they were removing the ceiling tiles in room 118, with Lock present in the room, they noticed a dusty cardboard box near the heating and air-supply vent where it had apparently been concealed. Terry climbed a ladder to reach the box, opened it, and handed it to Stocks. The box was filled with more than $38,000 in old currency. Lock took possession of the box and its contents. Terry and Stocks filed a suit in an Arkansas state court against Lock and his corporation to obtain the cash. Should the cash be characterized as lost, mislaid, or abandoned property? To whom should the court award it? Explain. [*Terry v. Lock,* 343 Ark. 452, 37 S.W.3d 202 (2001)]

28.6 Case Problem with Sample Answer. Vincent Slavin was a partner at Cantor Fitzgerald Securities in the World Trade

Center (WTC) in New York City. In 1998, Slavin and Anna Baez became engaged and began living together. They placed both of their names on three accounts at Chase Manhattan Bank according to the bank's terms, which provided that "accounts with multiple owners are joint, payable to either owner or the survivor." Slavin arranged for the direct deposit of his salary and commissions into one of the accounts. On September 11, 2001, Slavin died when two planes piloted by terrorists crashed into the WTC towers, causing their collapse. At the time, the balance in the three accounts was $656,944.36. On September 14, Cantor Fitzgerald deposited an additional $58,264.73 into the direct-deposit account. Baez soon withdrew the entire amount from all of the accounts. Mary Jelnek, Slavin's mother, filed a suit in a New York state court against Baez to determine the ownership of the funds that had been in the accounts. In what form of ownership were the accounts held? Who is entitled to which of the funds and why? [*In re Jelnek*, 3 Misc.3d 725, 777 N.Y.S.2d 871 (2004)]

 After you have answered Problem 28.6, compare your answer with the sample answer given on the Web site that accompanies this text. Go to **www.cengage.com/blaw/fbl**, select "Chapter 28," and click on "Case Problem with Sample Answer."

28.7 Concurrent Ownership. In July 2003, Chester Dellinger and his son Michael opened a joint bank account with Advancial Federal Credit Union in Dallas, Texas. Both of them signed the "Account Application," which designated Chester as a "member" and Michael as a "joint owner." Both of them received a copy of the "Account Agreement, Disclosures and Privacy Policy," which provided that "a multiple party account includes rights of survivorship." Chester died in February 2005. His will designated Michael as the executor of the estate, most of which was to be divided equally between Michael and his brother, Joseph, Chester's other son. Michael determined the value of the estate to be about $117,000. He did not include the Advancial account balance, which was about $234,000. Joseph filed a suit in a Texas state court against Michael, contending that the funds in the Advancial account should

be included in the estate. Michael filed a motion for summary judgment. Who owned the Advancial account when Chester was alive? Who owned it after he died? What should the court rule? Explain. [*In re Estate of Dellinger*, 224 S.W.3d 434 (Tex.App.—Dallas 2007)]

28.8 **A Question of Ethics.** *Marcella Lashmett was engaged in the business of farming in Illinois. Her daughter Christine Montgomery was also a farmer. Christine often borrowed Marcella's farm equipment. More than once, Christine used the equipment as a trade-in on the purchase of new equipment titled in Christine's name alone. After each transaction, Christine paid Marcella an agreed-to sum of money, and Marcella filed a gift tax return. Marcella died on December 19, 1999. Her heirs included Christine and Marcella's other daughter, Cheryl Thomas. Marcella's will gave whatever farm equipment remained on her death to Christine. If Christine chose to sell or trade any of the items, however, the proceeds were to be split equally with Cheryl. The will designated Christine to handle the disposition of the estate, but she did nothing. Eventually, Cheryl filed a petition with an Illinois state court, which appointed her to administer the will. Cheryl then filed a suit against her sister to discover what assets their mother had owned. [In re Estate of Lashmett, 369 Ill.App.3d 1013, 874 N.E.2d 65 (4 Dist. 2007)]*

1 Cheryl learned that three months before Marcella's death, Christine had used Marcella's tractor as a trade-in on the purchase of a new tractor. The trade-in credit had been $55,296.28. Marcella had been paid nothing, and no gift tax return had been filed. Christine claimed, among other things, that the old tractor had been a gift. What is a "gift"? What are the elements of a gift? What do the facts suggest on this claim? Discuss.

2 Christine also claimed that she had tried to pay Marcella $20,000 on the trade-in of the tractor but that her mother had refused to accept it. Christine showed a check made out to Marcella for that amount and marked "void." Would you rule in Christine's favor on this claim? Why or why not?

 ## CRITICAL THINKING AND WRITING ASSIGNMENTS

28.9 Critical Legal Thinking. Suppose that a certificate of deposit (CD) owned by two joint tenants (with the right of survivorship) is given by one of the joint tenants as security for a loan (without the other joint tenant's knowledge). Further suppose that the joint tenant dies after defaulting on the loan. Who has superior rights in the CD, the creditor or the other surviving joint tenant?

28.10 **Video Question.** Go to this text's Web site at **www.cengage.com/blaw/fbl** and select "Chapter 28."

Click on "Video Questions" and view the video titled *Personal Property and Bailments*. Then answer the following questions.

1 What type of bailment is discussed in the video?

2 What were Vinny's duties with regard to the rug-cleaning machine? What standard of care should apply?

3 Did Vinny exercise the appropriate degree of care? Why or why not? How would a court decide this issue?

ACCESSING THE INTERNET

For updated links to resources available on the Web, as well as a variety of other materials, visit this text's Web site at

www.cengage.com/blaw/fbl

To learn whether a married person has ownership rights in a gift received by his or her spouse, go to the Web page of the Scott Law Firm at

www.scottlawfirm.com/property.htm

For a discussion of the origins of the term *bailment* and how bailment relationships have been defined, go to

www.lectlaw.com/def/b005.htm

Cornell Law School's Legal Information Institute offers a hypertext version of Article 7 of the Uniform Commercial Code, which pertains to warehouse receipts, bills of lading, and other documents of title, at

www.law.cornell.edu/ucc/7/overview.html

PRACTICAL INTERNET EXERCISES

Go to this text's Web site at **www.cengage.com/blaw/fbl**, select "Chapter 28," and click on "Practical Internet Exercises." There you will find the following Internet research exercises that you can perform to learn more about the topics covered in this chapter.

PRACTICAL INTERNET EXERCISE 28–1 LEGAL PERSPECTIVE—Lost Property

PRACTICAL INTERNET EXERCISE 28–2 MANAGEMENT PERSPECTIVE—Bailments

BEFORE THE TEST

Go to this text's Web site at **www.cengage.com/blaw/fbl**, select "Chapter 28," and click on "Interactive Quizzes." You will find a number of interactive questions relating to this chapter.

CHAPTER 29
Real Property and Landlord-Tenant Law

From earliest times, property has provided a means for survival. Primitive peoples lived off the fruits of the land, eating the vegetation and wildlife. Later, as the wildlife was domesticated and the vegetation cultivated, property provided pasturage and farmland. In the twelfth and thirteenth centuries in Europe, the power of feudal lords was determined by the amount of land they held—the more land, the more powerful they were. After the age of feudalism passed, property continued to be an indicator of family wealth and social position. In the Western world, an individual's right to his or her property has become one of the "most sacred of all the rights of citizenship."

In this chapter, we first examine the nature of real property. We then look at the various ways in which real property can be owned and at how ownership rights in real property are transferred from one person to another. We conclude the chapter with a discussion of leased property and landlord-tenant relationships.

THE NATURE OF REAL PROPERTY

Real property consists of land and the buildings, plants, and trees that are on it. Real property also includes subsurface and airspace rights, as well as personal property that has become permanently attached to real property. Whereas personal property is movable, real property—also called *real estate* or *realty*—is immovable.

Land

Land includes the soil on the surface of the earth and the natural or artificial structures that are attached to it. It further includes all the waters contained on or under the surface and much, but not necessarily all, of the airspace above it. The exterior boundaries of land extend down to the center of the earth and up to the farthest reaches of the atmosphere (subject to certain qualifications).

Airspace and Subsurface Rights

The owner of real property has rights to the airspace above the land, as well as to the soil and minerals underneath it. Limitations on either airspace rights or subsurface rights normally have to be indicated on the document that transfers title at the time of purchase. When no such limitations, or *encumbrances*, are noted, a purchaser can normally expect to have an unlimited right to possession of the property.

Airspace Rights Disputes concerning airspace rights may involve the right of commercial and private planes to fly over property and the right of individuals and governments to seed clouds and produce rain artificially. Flights over private land normally do not violate property rights unless the flights are so low and so frequent that they directly interfere with the owner's enjoyment and use of the land. Leaning walls or buildings and projecting eave spouts or roofs may also violate the airspace rights of an adjoining property owner.

Subsurface Rights In many states, land ownership may be separated, in that the surface of a piece of land and the subsurface may have different owners. Subsurface rights can be extremely valuable, as these rights include the ownership of minerals, oil, and natural gas. Subsurface rights would be of little value, however, if the owner could not use the surface to exercise those rights. Hence, a subsurface owner will have a right (called a *profit*, to be discussed later in this chapter) to go onto the surface of the land to, for example, discover and mine minerals.

When the ownership is separated into surface and subsurface rights, each owner can pass title to what she or he owns without the consent of the other owner. Of course, conflicts can arise between a surface owner's use and the subsurface owner's need to extract minerals, oil, or natural gas. One party's interest may become subservient (secondary) to the other party's interest either by statute or case law. At common law and generally today, if the owners of the subsurface rights excavate (dig), they are absolutely liable if their excavation causes the surface to collapse. Depending on the circumstances, the excavators may also be liable for any damage to structures on the land. Many states have statutes that extend excavators' liability to include damage to structures on the property. Typically, these statutes provide precise requirements for excavations of various depths.

Plant Life and Vegetation

Plant life, both natural and cultivated, is also considered to be real property. In many instances, the natural vegetation, such as trees, adds greatly to the value of the realty. When a parcel of land is sold and the land has growing crops on it, the sale includes the crops, unless otherwise specified in the sales contract. When crops are sold by themselves, however, they are considered to be personal property or goods. Consequently, the sale of crops is a sale of goods and thus is governed by the Uniform Commercial Code (UCC) rather than by real property law (see Chapters 14 through 17).

Fixtures

Certain personal property can become so closely associated with the real property to which it is attached that the law views it as real property. Such property is known as a **fixture**—a thing *affixed* to realty, meaning that it is attached to the real property

by roots; embedded in it; permanently situated on it; or permanently attached by means of cement, plaster, bolts, nails, or screws. The fixture can be physically attached to real property, be attached to another fixture, or even be without any actual physical attachment to the land (such as a statue). As long as the owner intends the property to be a fixture, normally it will be a fixture.

Fixtures are included in the sale of land if the sales contract does not provide otherwise. The sale of a house includes the land and the house and the garage on the land, as well as the cabinets, plumbing, and windows. Because these are permanently affixed to the property, they are considered to be a part of it. Certain items, such as drapes and window-unit air conditioners, are difficult to classify. Thus, a contract for the sale of a house or commercial realty should indicate which items of this sort are included in the sale.

■**EXAMPLE 29.1** A farm had an eight-tower center-pivot irrigation system, bolted to a cement slab and connected to an underground well. The bank held a mortgage note on the farm secured by "all buildings, improvements, and fixtures." The farm's owners had also used the property as security for other loans, but the contracts for those loans did not specifically mention fixtures or the irrigation system. Later, the farmers filed for bankruptcy, and a dispute arose between the bank and another creditor over the irrigation system. A court held that the irrigation system was a fixture because it was firmly attached to the land and integral to the farm's operation. Therefore, the bank's security interest had priority over that of the other creditor.[1] ■

PREVENTING LEGAL DISPUTES

When real property is being sold, transferred, or subjected to a security interest, make sure that any contract specifically lists which fixtures are to be included. Without such a list, you and the other party may have very different ideas as to what is being transferred with the real property (or included as collateral for a loan). It is much simpler and less expensive to itemize fixtures in a contract than to engage in litigation.

■

OWNERSHIP INTERESTS IN REAL PROPERTY

Ownership of property is an abstract concept that cannot exist independently of the legal system. No one can actually possess or *hold* a piece of land, the airspace above it, the earth

---

1. *In re Sand & Sage Farm & Ranch, Inc.*, 266 Bankr. 507 (D.Kans. 2001).

below it, and all the water contained on it. The legal system therefore recognizes certain rights and duties that constitute ownership interests in real property.

Recall from Chapter 28 that property ownership is often viewed as a bundle of rights. One who possesses the entire bundle of rights is said to hold the property in *fee simple*, which is the most complete form of ownership. When only some of the rights in the bundle are transferred to another person, the effect is to limit the ownership rights of both the transferor of the rights and the recipient.

Ownership in Fee Simple

In a **fee simple absolute,** the owner has the greatest aggregation of rights, privileges, and power possible. The owner can give the property away or dispose of the property by *deed* (the instrument used to transfer property, as will be discussed later

in this chapter) or by will. When there is no will, the fee simple passes to the owner's legal heirs on her or his death. A fee simple is potentially infinite in duration and is assigned forever to a person and her or his heirs without limitation or condition. The owner has the rights of *exclusive* possession and use of the property.

The rights that accompany a fee simple include the right to use the land for whatever purpose the owner sees fit. Of course, other laws, including applicable zoning, noise, and environmental laws, may limit the owner's ability to use the property in certain ways.

In the following case, the court had to decide whether the noise—rock and roll music, conversation, and clacking pool balls—coming from a local bar (called a "saloon" during the days of cowboys in the United States) unreasonably interfered with a neighboring property owner's rights.

CASE 29.1   **Biglane v. Under the Hill Corp.**

Mississippi Supreme Court, 949 So.2d 9 (2007).
www.mssc.state.ms.us[a]

FACTS In 1967, Nancy and James Biglane bought and refurbished a building at 27 Silver Street in Natchez, Mississippi, and opened the lower portion as a gift shop. In 1973, Andre Farish and Paul O'Malley bought the building next door, at 25 Silver Street, and opened the Natchez Under the Hill Saloon (the Saloon). Later, the Biglanes converted the upper floors of their building into an apartment and moved into it. Even though the Biglanes installed insulated walls and windows, located their bedroom on the side of the building away from the Saloon, and placed the air-conditioning unit on the side nearest the Saloon, the noise from the Saloon kept them awake at night. During the summer, the Saloon, which had no air-conditioning, opened its windows and doors, and live music echoed up and down the street. After the Biglanes complained about the noise, the Saloon installed thicker windows, replaced the loudest band, and asked the other bands to keep their output below a certain level of decibels. Still dissatisfied, the Biglanes filed a suit in a Mississippi state court against the Saloon. The court enjoined the defendant from opening doors or windows when music was playing and ordered it to prevent its patrons from loitering in the street. Both parties appealed to the Mississippi Supreme Court.

ISSUE Did the Saloon's noise unreasonably interfere with the Biglanes' property rights?

DECISION Yes. The Mississippi Supreme Court affirmed the lower court's injunction: "One landowner may not use his land so as to unreasonably annoy, inconvenience, or harm others."

REASON The state supreme court pointed out that an owner may be subject to liability when the owner's conduct is "an invasion of another's interest in the private use and enjoyment of land and that invasion is * * * intentional and unreasonable." Reasonable use of property does not include "obnoxious noises, which in turn result in a material injury to owners of property in the vicinity, causing them to suffer substantial annoyance, inconvenience, and discomfort." An owner does not have to be driven from his or her property. The interference can be sufficient if "the enjoyment of life and property is rendered materially uncomfortable and annoying." Each case is to be decided on its own facts, including the location of the property and the surrounding circumstances. Here, the court balanced the interests of the Biglanes and the Saloon "in a quest for an equitable remedy that allowed the couple to enjoy their private apartment * * * while protecting a popular business and tourist attraction from over-regulation."

FOR CRITICAL ANALYSIS—Ethical Consideration *At one point in their dispute, the Biglanes blocked off two parking lots that served the Saloon. Was this an unreasonable interference with the Saloon's rights? Explain.*

---

a. Click on the "Decisions Search" link. On the next page, click on "Natural Language." When that page opens, in the query box, type "2005-CA-01751-SCT" and click on "Search." In the result, click on the first item in the list that includes that number to access the opinion. The Mississippi Supreme Court maintains this Web site.

■

Life Estates

A **life estate** is an estate that lasts for the life of some specified individual. A **conveyance,** or transfer of real property, "to A for his life" creates a life estate. In a life estate, the life tenant's ownership rights cease to exist on the life tenant's death.[2] The life tenant has the right to use the land, provided that he or she commits no waste (injury to the land). In other words, the life tenant cannot use the land in a manner that would adversely affect its value. The life tenant is entitled to any rents generated by the land and can harvest crops from the land. If mines and oil wells are already on the land, the life tenant can extract minerals and oil and is entitled to the royalties, but he or she cannot exploit the land by creating new wells or mines.

The life tenant can create liens, *easements* (discussed below), and leases, but none can extend beyond the life of the tenant. In addition, with few exceptions, the owner of a life estate has an exclusive right to possession during her or his life.

Along with these rights, the life tenant also has some duties—to keep the property in repair and to pay property taxes. In short, the owner of the life estate has the same rights as a fee simple owner except that the life tenant must maintain the value of the property during her or his tenancy.

Nonpossessory Interests

In contrast to the types of property interests just described, some interests in land do not include any rights to possess the property. These interests, known as **nonpossessory interests,** include easements, profits, and licenses.

An **easement** is the right of a person to make limited use of another person's real property without taking anything from the property. An easement, for instance, can be the right to walk or drive across another's property. In contrast, a **profit**[3] is the right to go onto land owned by another and take away some part of the land itself or some product of the land. **■EXAMPLE 29.2** Akmed owns Sandy View. Akmed gives Carmen the right to go there to remove all the sand and gravel that she needs for her cement business. Carmen has a profit. **■**

Easements and profits can be classified as either *appurtenant* or *in gross.* Because easements and profits are similar and the same rules apply to both, we discuss them together.

---

2. Because a life tenant's rights in the property cease at death, life estates are frequently used to avoid probate proceedings—see Chapter 30. The person who owns the property deeds it to the person who would eventually inherit the property and reserves a life estate for herself or himself. That way, the property owner can live there until death, and the property then passes to the intended heir without the need for legal proceedings.
3. The term *profit,* as used here, does not refer to the "profits" made by a business firm. Rather, it means a gain or an advantage.

Easement or Profit Appurtenant An easement or profit *appurtenant* arises when the owner of one piece of land has a right to go onto (or remove things from) an adjacent piece of land owned by another. The land that is benefited by the easement is called the *dominant estate,* and the land that is burdened is called the *servient estate.* Because easements appurtenant are intended to *benefit the land,* they run with the land when it is transferred. **■EXAMPLE 29.3** Acosta has a right to drive his car across Green's land, which is adjacent to Acosta's land. This right-of-way over Green's property is an easement appurtenant to Acosta's property and can be used only by Acosta. If Acosta sells his land, the easement runs with the land to benefit the new owner. **■**

Easement or Profit in Gross In an easement or profit *in gross,* the right to use or take things from another's land is given to one who does not own an adjacent tract of land. These easements are intended to *benefit a particular person or business,* not a particular piece of land, and cannot be transferred. **■EXAMPLE 29.4** Avery owns a parcel of land with a marble quarry. Avery conveys to Classic Stone Corporation the right to come onto her land and remove up to five hundred pounds of marble per day. Classic Stone owns a profit in gross and cannot transfer this right to another. **■** Similarly, when a utility company is granted an easement to run its power lines across another's property, it obtains an easement in gross.

Creation of an Easement or Profit Most easements and profits are created by an express grant in a contract, deed, or will. This allows the parties to include terms defining the extent and length of time of use. In some situations, an easement or profit can also be created without an express agreement.

An easement or profit may arise by *implication* when the circumstances surrounding the division of a parcel of property imply its existence. **■EXAMPLE 29.5** Barrow divides a parcel of land that has only one well for drinking water. If Barrow conveys the half without a well to Jarad, a profit by implication arises because Jarad needs drinking water. **■**

An easement may also be created by *necessity.* An easement by necessity does not require a division of property for its existence. A person who rents an apartment, for example, has an easement by necessity in the private road leading up to it. An easement arises by *prescription* when one person exercises an easement, such as a right-of-way, on another person's land without the landowner's consent, and the use is apparent and continues for the length of time required by the applicable statute of limitations. (In much the same way, title to property may be obtained by *adverse possession,* as will be discussed later in this chapter.)

Termination of an Easement or Profit An easement or profit can be terminated or extinguished in several ways. The simplest way is to deed it back to the owner of the land that is burdened by it. Another way is to abandon it and create evidence of intent to relinquish the right to use it. Mere nonuse will not extinguish an easement or profit *unless the nonuse is accompanied by an overt act showing the intent to abandon.* Also, if the owner of an easement or profit becomes the owner of the property burdened by it, then it is merged into the property.

License In the context of real property, a **license** is the revocable right of a person to come onto another person's land. It is a personal privilege that arises from the consent of the owner of the land and can be revoked by the owner. A ticket to attend a movie at a theater is an example of a license. **■EXAMPLE 29.6** A Broadway theater owner issues Alena a ticket to see a play. If Alena is refused entry into the theater because she is improperly dressed, she has no right to force her way into the theater. The ticket is only a revocable license, not a conveyance of an interest in property. **■**

In essence, a license grants a person the authority to enter the land of another and perform a specified act or series of acts without obtaining any permanent interest in the land. What happens when a person with a license exceeds the authority granted and undertakes an action that is not permitted? That was the central issue in the following case.

CASE 29.2 **Roman Catholic Church of Our Lady of Sorrows v. Prince Realty Management, LLC**

New York Supreme Court, Appellate Division, 47 A.D.3d 909, 850 N.Y.S.2d 569 (2008).

FACTS The Roman Catholic Church of Our Lady of Sorrows (the Church) and Prince Realty Management, LLC (Prince), own adjoining property in Queens County, New York. In 2005, the parties entered into an agreement by which the Church granted Prince a three-month license to use a three-foot strip of its property immediately adjacent to Prince's property. The license specifically authorized Prince to remove an existing chainlink fence on the licensed strip and to "put up plywood panels surrounding the construction site, including the [licensed strip]." The license also required that Prince restore the boundary line between the properties with a new brick fence. The purpose of the license was to allow Prince to erect a temporary plywood fence in order to protect Prince's property during the construction of a new building. During the license's term, Prince installed structures consisting of steel piles and beams on the licensed property. The Church objected to these structures and repeatedly demanded that they be removed. The Church commenced an action to recover damages for breach of the license. The trial court concluded that the Church had made a *prima facie* case showing that structures were placed on its property by the defendant in violation of the license and that Prince had failed to dispute the plaintiff's claim that it had violated the agreement. Prince appealed.

ISSUE Does a license that conveys the right to construct a temporary plywood fence on a three-foot strip of land during a construction project also convey the right to install steel piles and beams on the property?

DECISION No. The state appellate court held that the license did not permit the adjoining property owner to install structures consisting of steel piles and beams on the licensed strip of property. The court found that by exceeding the authority granted in the license, the defendant's actions constituted trespass.

REASON The reviewing court pointed out that "a license, within the context of real property law, grants the licensee a revocable non-assignable privilege to do one or more acts upon the land of a licensor, without granting possession of any interest herein. A license is the authority to do a particular act or series of acts upon another's land, which would amount to a trespass without such permission." The evidence was clear that the license allowed only for temporary structures. The defendant nonetheless installed structures consisting of steel piles and beams on the licensed property. "The plaintiff * * * established as a matter of law that the defendant's installation of these structures constituted a trespass regardless of whether they were subsequently removed."

FOR CRITICAL ANALYSIS—Legal Consideration *The Church sued for damages. What would be an appropriate calculation of those damages?*

■

TRANSFER OF OWNERSHIP

Ownership of real property can pass from one person to another in several ways. Commonly, ownership interests in land are transferred by sale, and the terms of the transfer are specified in a real estate sales contract. Often, real estate brokers or agents who are licensed by the state assist the buyers and sellers during the sales transaction. (For a discussion of some issues involving online advertising by real estate professionals, see this chapter's *Adapting the Law to the Online Environment* feature on the following page.) Real property ownership can also be transferred by gift, by will or inheritance, by possession, or by *eminent domain*. When ownership rights in real property are transferred, the type of interest being transferred and the conditions of the transfer normally are set forth in a *deed* executed by the person who is conveying the property.

Deeds

Possession and title to land are passed from person to person by means of a **deed**—the instrument of conveyance of real property. A deed is a writing signed by an owner of real property that transfers title to another. Deeds must meet certain requirements, but unlike a contract, a deed does not have to be supported by legally sufficient consideration. Gifts of real property are common, and they require deeds even though there is no consideration for the gift. To be valid, a deed must include the following:

1 The names of the *grantor* (the giver or seller) and the *grantee* (the donee or buyer).

2 Words evidencing an intent to convey the property (for example, "I hereby bargain, sell, grant, or give").

3 A legally sufficient description of the land.

4 The grantor's (and usually her or his spouse's) signature.

5 Delivery of the deed.

Warranty Deeds   Different types of deeds provide different degrees of protection against defects of title. A **warranty deed** makes the greatest number of warranties and thus provides the greatest protection against defects of title. In most states, special language is required to create a general warranty deed.

Warranty deeds commonly include a number of *covenants*, or promises, that the grantor makes to the grantee. These covenants include a covenant that the grantor has the title to, and the power to convey, the property; a covenant of quiet enjoyment (a warranty that the buyer will not be disturbed in her or his possession of the land); and a covenant that transfer of the property is made without knowledge of adverse claims of third parties. Generally, the warranty deed makes the grantor liable for all defects of title by the grantor and previous titleholders.

■EXAMPLE 29.7 Julio sells a two-acre lot by warranty deed. Subsequently, a third person appears, shows that she has better title than Julio had, and forces the buyer off the property. Here, the covenant of quiet enjoyment has been breached, and the buyer can sue Julio to recover the purchase price of the land plus any other damages incurred as a result. ■

Special Warranty Deeds   In contrast to a warranty deed, a **special warranty deed,** which is also referred to as a *limited warranty deed,* warrants only that the grantor or seller held good title during his or her ownership of the property. In other words, the grantor is not warranting that there were no defects of title when the property was held by previous owners.

If the special warranty deed discloses all liens or other encumbrances, the seller will not be liable to the buyer if a third person subsequently interferes with the buyer's ownership. If the third person's claim arises out of, or is related to, some act of the seller, however, the seller will be liable to the buyer for damages.

Implied Warranties in the Sale of New Homes   Today, most states imply a warranty—the *implied warranty of habitability* (to be discussed later in this chapter in the context of leases)—in the sale of new homes. The seller of a new house warrants that it will be fit for human habitation even if the deed or contract of sale does not include such a warranty. Essentially, the seller is warranting that the house is in reasonable working order and is of reasonably sound construction. Thus, under this warranty, the seller of a new home is in effect a guarantor of its fitness. In some states, the warranty protects not only the first purchaser but any subsequent purchaser as well.

In most jurisdictions, courts impose on sellers a duty to disclose any known defect that materially affects the value of the property and that the buyer could not reasonably discover. Failure to disclose such a material defect gives the buyer a right to *rescind* (cancel) the real estate sales contract and sue for damages based on fraud or misrepresentation.

Quitclaim Deeds   A **quitclaim deed** offers the least amount of protection against defects in the title. Basically, a quitclaim deed conveys to the grantee whatever interest the grantor had; so, if the grantor had no interest, then the grantee receives no interest. Naturally, if the grantor had a defective title or no title at all, a conveyance by warranty deed or special warranty deed would not cure the defects. Such deeds, however, will give the buyer a cause of action to sue the seller.

Potential Problems When Real Estate Is Advertised Online

The Internet has transformed the real estate business, just as it has transformed other industries. Today's real estate professionals market properties—and themselves—online. Given that the Internet knows no physical borders, what happens when an online advertisement reaches people outside the state in which the real estate professional is licensed? Is this illegal? Can the agent be sued for fraud if the ad contains misrepresentations?

State Licensing Statutes and Advertising

Every state requires anyone who sells or offers to sell real property in that state to obtain a license. To be licensed, a person normally must pass a state examination and pay a fee and then must take continuing education courses periodically (every year or two) to maintain the license. Usually, a person must also be licensed to list real property for sale or to negotiate the purchase, sale, lease, or exchange of real property or a business opportunity involving real property.[a]

State laws can differ on the exact activities that require a real estate license, though. Consider, for example, the problems faced by Stroman Realty, Inc., a licensed Realtor® in Texas. (The term *Realtor* is "a registered collective membership mark that identifies a real estate professional who is a member of the National Association of Realtors.") Stroman's business focuses on reselling time shares (which allow the owner to use the property for a specified interval of time per year) on the secondary market. The company used a computerized service to match potential buyers with properties and maintained a Web site where buyers could view available times shares. Stroman advertised its time-share resale services both in print and via the Internet and frequently engaged in transactions involving parties in multiple states.

After a complaint from an Illinois resident, the Illinois agency in charge of enforcing licensing requirements sent Stroman a cease-and-desist letter. The agency stated that Stroman had engaged in activities in Illinois that required a real estate license, and it ordered the company to stop these activities. Stroman filed a lawsuit asking a federal district court to stay (suspend) the administrative action, arguing that Illinois licensing law was unconstitutional and violated the dormant commerce clause (see Chapter 1). The court, however, refused to exercise jurisdiction on the constitutionality issue and dismissed Stroman's complaint. The court noted that the regulation of the real estate profession is an important state interest and that Illinois was merely enforcing its Licensing Act when it took action against Stroman.[b]

Actions for Misrepresentations (Fraud)

Suppose that a real estate agent, either inadvertently or intentionally, makes a misstatement online about some important aspect of real property that is for sale. Someone, relying on the statements, responds to the ad and eventually contracts to buy the property, only to discover later that the ad misrepresented it. What remedies does the buyer have? In this situation, the buyer can complain to the state authority that granted the agent's license, and the state may even revoke the license for such conduct. If the buyer wants to obtain damages or cancel the contract, however, he or she will have to sue the agent for fraud (see Chapter 4). At this point, jurisdictional problems may arise.

If the real estate agent and the buyer are located in different states and the Internet ad was the agent's only contact with the buyer's state, the buyer may have to travel to the agent's state to file the suit. Courts have reached different conclusions on the type of Internet advertising that permits a court to have jurisdiction over an out-of-state advertiser. In addition, courts may sometimes refuse to exercise jurisdiction over an out-of-state defendant even if they could do so (as the court did in the case just discussed involving Stroman Realty). Thus, people who are deceived when buying real property from an online ad and wish to sue the perpetrator of the fraud may be in a precarious position depending on the state where they live.

FOR CRITICAL ANALYSIS *Do you think that the federal government should regulate the advertising of real property on the Internet to protect consumers from potential fraud? If so, what kind of regulations would be appropriate, and how might they be enforced?*

---

a. See, for example, California Business and Professions Code Section 10131 and 26 Vermont Statutes Annotated Sections 2211–2212.

b. *Stroman Realty, Inc. v. Grillo,* 438 F.Supp.2d 929 (N.D.Ill. 2006); see also *Quilles v. Benden,* 2007 WL 1099477 (N.D.Ill. 2007).

A quitclaim deed can and often does serve as a release of the grantor's interest in a particular parcel of property. **■EXAMPLE 29.8** After ten years of marriage, Sandi and Jim are getting a divorce. During the marriage, Sandi purchased a parcel of waterfront property next to her grandparents' home in Louisiana. Jim helped make some improvements to the property, but he is not sure what ownership interests, if any, he has in the property because Sandi used her own funds (acquired before the marriage) to purchase the lot. Jim agrees to quitclaim the property to Sandi as part of the divorce settlement, releasing any interest he might have in that piece of property. ■

Recording Statutes Every jurisdiction has **recording statutes,** which allow deeds to be recorded for a fee. The grantee normally pays this fee because he or she is the one who will be protected by recording the deed.

Recording a deed gives notice to the public that a certain person is now the owner of a particular parcel of real estate. Thus, prospective buyers can check the public records to see whether there have been earlier transactions creating interests or rights in specific parcels of real property. Putting everyone on notice as to the identity of the true owner is intended to prevent the previous owners from fraudulently conveying the land to other purchasers. Deeds are recorded in the county where the property is located. Many state statutes require that the grantor sign the deed in the presence of two witnesses before it can be recorded.

Will or Inheritance

Property that is transferred on an owner's death is passed either by will or by state inheritance laws. If the owner of land dies with a will, the land passes in accordance with the terms of the will. If the owner dies without a will, state inheritance statutes prescribe how and to whom the property will pass. Transfers of property by will or inheritance are examined in detail in Chapter 30.

Adverse Possession

Adverse possession is a means of obtaining title to land without delivery of a deed. Essentially, when one person possesses the property of another for a certain statutory period of time (three to thirty years, with ten years being most common), that person, called the *adverse possessor,* acquires title to the land and cannot be removed from it by the original owner. The adverse possessor may ultimately obtain a perfect title just as if there had been a conveyance by deed.

For property to be held adversely, four elements must be satisfied:

1 Possession must be *actual and exclusive*; that is, the possessor must take sole physical occupancy of the property.

2 The possession must be *open, visible, and notorious,* not secret or clandestine. The possessor must occupy the land for all the world to see.

3 Possession must be *continuous and peaceable for the required period of time.* This requirement means that the possessor must not be interrupted in the occupancy by the true owner or by the courts.

4 Possession must be *hostile and adverse.* In other words, the possessor must claim the property as against the whole world. He or she cannot be living on the property with the permission of the owner.

There are a number of public-policy reasons for the adverse possession doctrine. These include society's interest in resolving boundary disputes, in determining title when title to property is in question, and in ensuring that real property remains in the stream of commerce. More fundamentally, policies behind the doctrine include rewarding possessors for putting land to productive use and punishing owners who sit on their rights too long and do not take action when they see adverse possession.

Eminent Domain

Even ownership in real property in fee simple absolute is limited by a superior ownership. Just as in medieval England the king was the ultimate landowner, so in the United States the government has an ultimate ownership right in all land. This right, known as **eminent domain,** is sometimes referred to as the *condemnation power* of government to take land for public use. It gives the government the right to acquire possession of real property in the manner directed by the U.S. Constitution and the laws of the state whenever the public interest requires it. Property may be taken only for public use, not for private benefit.

■EXAMPLE 29.9 When a new public highway is to be built, the government must decide where to build it and how much land to condemn. After the government determines that a particular parcel of land is necessary for public use, it will first offer to buy the property. If the owner refuses the offer, the government brings a judicial (**condemnation**) proceeding to obtain title to the land. Then, in another proceeding, the court determines the *fair value* of the land, which is usually approximately equal to its market value. ■

When the government takes land owned by a private party for public use, it is referred to as a **taking,** and the government must compensate the private party. Under the so-called *takings clause* of the Fifth Amendment to the U.S.

Constitution, the government may not take private property for public use without "just compensation." State constitutions contain similar provisions.

In 2005, the United States Supreme Court ruled that the power of eminent domain can be used to further economic development.[4] Since that decision, a number of state legislatures have passed laws limiting the power of the government to use eminent domain, particularly for urban redevelopment projects that benefit private developers.

LEASEHOLD ESTATES

A **leasehold estate** is created when a real property owner or lessor (landlord) agrees to convey the right to possess and use the property to a lessee (tenant) for a certain period of time. In every leasehold estate, the tenant has a *qualified* right to exclusive possession (qualified by the landlord's right to enter on the premises to assure that the tenant is not causing damage to the property). The *temporary* nature of possession, under a lease, is what distinguishes a tenant from a purchaser, who acquires title to the property. The tenant can use the land—for example, by harvesting crops—but cannot injure it by such activities as cutting down timber for sale or extracting oil.

The respective rights and duties of the landlord and tenant that arise under a lease agreement will be discussed shortly. Here, we look at the types of leasehold estates, or tenancies, that can be created when real property is leased.

Fixed-Term Tenancy or Tenancy for Years

A **fixed-term tenancy**, also called a *tenancy for years*, is created by an express contract by which property is leased for a specified period of time, such as a day, a month, a year, or a period of years. Signing a one-year lease to occupy an apartment, for instance, creates a fixed-term tenancy. Note that the term need not be specified by date and can be conditioned on the occurrence of an event, such as leasing a cabin for the summer or an apartment during Mardi Gras. At the end of the period specified in the lease, the lease ends (without notice), and possession of the apartment returns to the lessor. If the tenant dies during the period of the lease, the lease interest passes to the tenant's heirs as personal property. Often, leases include renewal or extension provisions.

Periodic Tenancy

A **periodic tenancy** is created by a lease that does not specify how long it is to last but does specify that rent is to be paid at certain intervals. This type of tenancy is automatically

renewed for another rental period unless properly terminated. **■EXAMPLE 29.10** Kayla enters a lease with Capital Properties. The lease states, "Rent is due on the tenth day of every month." This provision creates a periodic tenancy from month to month. ■ This type of tenancy can also extend from week to week or from year to year.

Under the common law, to terminate a periodic tenancy, the landlord or tenant must give at least one period's notice to the other party. If the tenancy extends from month to month, for example, one month's notice must be given prior to the last month's rent payment. State statutes may require a different period for notice of termination in a periodic tenancy, however.

Tenancy at Will

When a leasehold interest is created in which either party can terminate the tenancy without notice, it is called a **tenancy at will.** This type of tenancy can arise if a landlord rents certain property to a tenant "for as long as both agree" or allows a person to live on the premises without paying rent. Tenancy at will is rare in today's world because most state statutes require a landlord to provide some period of notice to terminate a tenancy (as previously noted). States may also require a landowner to have sufficient cause (reason) to end a residential tenancy. Certain events, such as the death of either party or the voluntary commission of waste by the tenant, automatically terminate a tenancy at will.

Tenancy at Sufferance

The mere possession of land without right is called a **tenancy at sufferance.** A tenancy at sufferance is not a true tenancy because it is created when a tenant *wrongfully* retains possession of property. Whenever a tenancy for years or a periodic tenancy ends and the tenant continues to retain possession of the premises without the owner's permission, a tenancy at sufferance is created.

LANDLORD-TENANT RELATIONSHIPS

In the past several decades, landlord-tenant relationships have become much more complex, as has the law governing them. Generally, the law has come to apply contract doctrines, such as those relating to implied warranties and unconscionability, to the landlord-tenant relationship. Increasingly, landlord-tenant relationships have become subject to specific state and local statutes and ordinances as well. In 1972, in an effort to create more uniformity in the law governing landlord-tenant relationships, the National Conference of Commissioners on Uniform State Laws issued

---

4. *Kelo v. City of New London, Connecticut,* 545 U.S. 469, 125 S.Ct. 2655, 162 L.Ed.2d 439 (2005).

the Uniform Residential Landlord and Tenant Act (URLTA). Twenty-one states have adopted variations of the URLTA. We look now at how a landlord-tenant relationship is created and at the respective rights and duties of landlords and tenants.

A landlord-tenant relationship is established by a lease contract. A lease may be oral or written. In most states, statutes mandate that leases be in writing for some tenancies (such as those exceeding one year). Generally, to ensure the validity of a lease agreement, it should be in writing and do the following:

1 Express an intent to establish the relationship.

2 Provide for the transfer of the property's possession to the tenant at the beginning of the term.

3 Provide for the landlord's *reversionary* (future) interest, which entitles the property owner to retake possession at the end of the term.

4 Describe the property—for example, give its street address.

5 Indicate the length of the term, the amount of the rent, and how and when it is to be paid.

State or local law often dictates permissible lease terms. For example, a statute or ordinance might prohibit the leasing of a structure that is in a certain physical condition or is not in compliance with local building codes. Similarly, a statute may prohibit the leasing of property for a particular purpose, such as gambling. Thus, if a landlord and tenant intend that the leased premises be used only to house an illegal betting operation, their lease is unenforceable.

A property owner cannot legally discriminate against prospective tenants on the basis of race, color, national origin, religion, gender, or disability. In addition, a tenant cannot legally promise to do something counter to laws prohibiting discrimination. A commercial tenant, for example, cannot legally promise to do business only with members of a particular race. The public policy underlying these prohibitions is to treat all people equally.

Rights and Duties

The rights and duties of landlords and tenants generally pertain to four broad areas of concern—the possession, use, maintenance, and, of course, rent of leased property.

Possession A landlord is obligated to give a tenant possession of the property that the tenant has agreed to lease. After obtaining possession, the tenant retains the property exclusively until the lease expires, unless the lease states otherwise.

The covenant of quiet enjoyment mentioned previously also applies to leased premises. Under this covenant, the

landlord promises that during the lease term, neither the landlord nor anyone having a superior title to the property will disturb the tenant's use and enjoyment of the property. This covenant forms the essence of the landlord-tenant relationship, and if it is breached, the tenant can terminate the lease and sue for damages.

If the landlord deprives the tenant of possession of the leased property or interferes with the tenant's use or enjoyment of it, an **eviction** occurs. An eviction occurs, for instance, when the landlord changes the lock and refuses to give the tenant a new key. A **constructive eviction** occurs when the landlord wrongfully performs or fails to perform any of the duties the lease requires, thereby making the tenant's further use and enjoyment of the property exceedingly difficult or impossible. Examples of constructive eviction include a landlord's failure to provide heat in the winter, light, or other essential utilities.

Use and Maintenance of the Premises If the parties do not limit by agreement the uses to which the property may be put, the tenant may make any use of it, as long as the use is legal and reasonably relates to the purpose for which the property is adapted or ordinarily used and does not injure the landlord's interest.

The tenant is responsible for any damage to the premises that he or she causes, intentionally or negligently, and may be held liable for the cost of returning the property to the physical condition it was in at the lease's inception. Also, the tenant is not entitled to substantially interfere with others' quiet enjoyment of their property rights. Unless the parties have agreed otherwise, the tenant is not responsible for ordinary wear and tear and the property's consequent depreciation in value.

In some jurisdictions, landlords of residential property are required by statute to maintain the premises in good repair. Landlords must also comply with any applicable state statutes and city ordinances regarding maintenance and repair of buildings.

Implied Warranty of Habitability The **implied warranty of habitability** requires a landlord who leases residential property to ensure that the premises are habitable—that is, in a condition that is safe and suitable for people to live there. Also, the landlord must make repairs to maintain the premises in that condition for the lease's duration. Generally, this warranty applies to major, or *substantial*, physical defects that the landlord knows or should know about and has had a reasonable time to repair—for example, a large hole in the roof.

Rent *Rent* is the tenant's payment to the landlord for the tenant's occupancy or use of the landlord's real property. Usually, the tenant must pay the rent even if she or he refuses to occupy the property or moves out, as long as the refusal or the move is unjustified and the lease is in force. Under the common law, if the leased premises were destroyed by fire or flood, the tenant still had to pay rent. Today, however, most state's statutes provide that if an apartment building burns down, tenants are not required to continue to pay rent.

In some situations, such as when a landlord breaches the implied warranty of habitability, a tenant may be allowed to withhold rent as a remedy. When rent withholding is authorized under a statute, the tenant must usually put the amount withheld into an *escrow account.* This account is held in the name of the depositor (the tenant) and an *escrow agent* (usually the court or a government agency), and the funds are returnable to the depositor if the third person (the landlord) fails to make the premises habitable.

Transferring Rights to Leased Property

Either the landlord or the tenant may wish to transfer her or his rights to the leased property during the term of the lease. If the landlord transfers complete title to the leased property, the tenant becomes the tenant of the new owner. The new owner may collect subsequent rent but must abide by the terms of the existing lease agreement.

The tenant's transfer of his or her entire interest in the leased property to a third person is an *assignment of the lease.* Many leases require that the assignment have the landlord's written consent. An assignment that lacks consent can be avoided (nullified) by the landlord. State statutes may specify that the landlord may not unreasonably withhold such consent, though. Also, a landlord who knowingly accepts rent from the assignee may be held to have waived the consent requirement. When an assignment is valid, the assignee acquires all of the tenant's rights under the lease. But an assignment does not release the assigning tenant from the obligation to pay rent should the assignee default.

The tenant's transfer of all or part of the premises for a period shorter than the lease term is a **sublease.** The same restrictions that apply to an assignment of the tenant's interest in leased property apply to a sublease. If the landlord's consent is required, a sublease without such permission is ineffective. Also, a sublease does not release the tenant from her or his obligations under the lease any more than an assignment does.

REVIEWING **Real Property and Landlord-Tenant Law**

Vern Shoepke purchased a two-story home from Walter and Eliza Bruster in the town of Roche, Maine. The warranty deed did not specify what covenants would be included in the conveyance. The property was adjacent to a public park that included a popular Frisbee golf course. (Frisbee golf is a sport similar to golf but using Frisbees.) Wayakichi Creek ran along the north end of the park and along Shoepke's property. The deed allowed Roche citizens the right to walk across a five-foot-wide section of the lot beside Wayakichi Creek as part of a two-mile public trail system. Teenagers regularly threw Frisbee golf discs from the walking path behind Shoepke's property over his yard to the adjacent park. Shoepke habitually shouted and cursed at the teenagers, demanding that they not throw objects over his yard. Two months after moving into his Roche home, Shoepke leased the second floor to Lauren Slater for nine months. (The lease agreement did not specify that Shoepke's consent would be required to sublease the second floor.) After three months of tenancy, Slater sublet the second floor to a local artist, Javier Indalecio. Over the remaining six months, Indalecio's use of oil paints damaged the carpeting in Shoepke's home. Using the information presented in the chapter, answer the following questions.

1 What is the term for the right of Roche citizens to walk across Shoepke's land on the trail?

2 In the warranty deed that was used in the property transfer from the Brusters to Shoepke, what covenants would be inferred by most courts?

3 Can Shoepke hold Slater financially responsible for the damage to the carpeting caused by Indalecio?

TERMS AND CONCEPTS

adverse possession 613
condemnation 613
constructive eviction 615
conveyance 609
deed 611

easement 609
eminent domain 613
eviction 615
fee simple absolute 608
fixed-term tenancy 614

fixture 607
implied warranty
  of habitability 615
leasehold estate 614
license 610

CHAPTER SUMMARY	Real Property and Landlord-Tenant Law
The Nature of Real Property (See pages 606–607.)	Real property (also called real estate or realty) is immovable. It includes land, subsurface and airspace rights, plant life and vegetation, and fixtures.
Ownership Interests in Real Property (See pages 607–610.)	1. *Fee simple absolute*—The most complete form of ownership. 2. *Life estate*—An estate that lasts for the life of a specified individual, during which time the individual is entitled to possess, use, and benefit from the estate; the life tenant's ownership rights in the life estate cease to exist on her or his death. 3. *Nonpossessory interest*—An interest that involves the right to use real property but not to possess it. Easements, profits, and licenses are nonpossessory interests.
Transfer of Ownership (See pages 611–614.)	1. *By deed*—When real property is sold or transferred as a gift, title to the property is conveyed by means of a deed. A deed must meet specific legal requirements. A *warranty deed* warrants the most extensive protection against defects of title. A *quitclaim deed* conveys to the grantee only whatever interest the grantor had in the property. A deed may be recorded in the manner prescribed by *recording statutes* in the appropriate jurisdiction to give third parties notice of the owner's interest. 2. *By will or inheritance*—If the owner dies after having made a valid will, the land passes as specified in the will. If the owner dies without having made a will, the heirs inherit according to state inheritance statutes. 3. *By adverse possession*—When a person possesses the property of another for a statutory period of time (three to thirty years, with ten years being the most common), that person acquires title to the property, provided the possession is actual and exclusive, open and visible, continuous and peaceable, and hostile and adverse (without the permission of the owner). 4. *By eminent domain*—The government can take land for public use, with just compensation, when the public interest requires the taking.
Leasehold Estates (See page 614.)	A leasehold estate is an interest in real property that is held for only a limited period of time, as specified in the lease agreement. Types of tenancies relating to leased property include the following: 1. *Fixed-term tenancy*—Tenancy for a period of time stated by express contract. 2. *Periodic tenancy*—Tenancy for a period determined by the frequency of rent payments; automatically renewed unless proper notice is given. 3. *Tenancy at will*—Tenancy for as long as both parties agree; no notice of termination is required. 4. *Tenancy at sufferance*—Possession of land without legal right.
Landlord-Tenant Relationships (See pages 614–616.)	1. *Lease agreement*—The landlord-tenant relationship is created by a lease agreement. State or local laws may dictate whether the lease must be in writing and what lease terms are permissible. 2. *Rights and duties*—The rights and duties that arise under a lease agreement generally pertain to the following areas: a. Possession—The tenant has an exclusive right to possess the leased premises, which must be available to the tenant at the agreed-on time. Under the covenant of quiet enjoyment,

(Continued)

CHAPTER SUMMARY Real Property and Landlord-Tenant Law—Continued

Landlord-Tenant Relationships— Continued	the landlord promises that during the lease term neither the landlord nor anyone having superior title to the property will disturb the tenant's use and enjoyment of the property.

b. Use and maintenance of the premises—Unless the parties agree otherwise, the tenant may make any legal use of the property. The tenant is responsible for any damage that he or she causes. The landlord must comply with laws that set specific standards for the maintenance of real property. The implied warranty of habitability requires that a landlord furnish and maintain residential premises in a habitable condition (that is, in a condition safe and suitable for human life).

c. Rent—The tenant must pay the rent as long as the lease is in force, unless the tenant justifiably refuses to occupy the property or withholds the rent because of the landlord's failure to maintain the premises properly.

3. *Transferring rights to leased property—*

a. If the landlord transfers complete title to the leased property, the tenant becomes the tenant of the new owner. The new owner may then collect the rent but must abide by the existing lease.

b. Generally, in the absence of an agreement to the contrary, tenants may assign their rights (but not their duties) under a lease contract to a third person. Tenants may also sublease leased property to a third person, but the original tenant is not relieved of any obligations to the landlord under the lease. In either situation, the landlord's consent may be required, but statutes may prohibit the landlord from unreasonably withholding such consent.

FOR REVIEW

Answers for the even-numbered questions in this **For Review** *section can be found on this text's accompanying Web site at* **www.cengage.com/blaw/fbl**. *Select "Chapter 29" and click on "For Review."*

1 What can a person who holds property in fee simple absolute do with the property?

2 What are the requirements for acquiring property by adverse possession?

3 What limitations may be imposed on the rights of property owners?

4 What is a leasehold estate? What types of leasehold estates, or tenancies, can be created when real property is leased?

5 What are the respective duties of the landlord and tenant concerning the use and maintenance of leased property? Is the tenant responsible for all damage that he or she causes?

QUESTIONS AND CASE PROBLEMS

 HYPOTHETICAL SCENARIOS AND CASE PROBLEMS

29.1 Property Ownership. Twenty-two years ago, Lorenz was a wanderer. At that time, he decided to settle down on an unoccupied, three-acre parcel of land that he did not own. People in the area told him that they had no idea who owned the property. Lorenz built a house on the land, got married, and raised three children while living there. He fenced in the land, installed a gate with a sign above it that read "Lorenz's Homestead," and removed trespassers. Lorenz is now confronted by Joe Reese, who has a deed in his name as owner of the property. Reese, claiming owner-ship of the land, orders Lorenz and his family off the prop-erty. Discuss who has the better "title" to the property.

29.2 Hypothetical Question with Sample Answer. Wiley and Gemma are neighbors. Wiley's lot is extremely large, and his present and future use of it will not involve the entire area. Gemma wants to build a single-car garage and driveway along the present lot boundary. Because the placement of her exist-ing structures makes it impossible for her to comply with an ordinance requiring buildings to be set back fifteen feet from an adjoining property line, Gemma cannot build the garage. Gemma contracts to purchase ten feet of Wiley's property along their boundary line for $3,000. Wiley is willing to sell but will give Gemma only a quitclaim deed, whereas Gemma wants a warranty deed. Discuss the differences between these deeds as they would affect the rights of the parties if the title to this ten feet of land later proves to be defective.

For a sample answer to Question 29.2, go to Appendix E at the end of this text.

29.3 Landlord's Responsibilities. Sarah has rented a house from Frank. The house is only two years old, but the roof leaks every time it rains. The water that has accumulated in the attic has caused plaster to fall off ceilings in the upstairs bedrooms, and one ceiling has started to sag. Sarah has complained to Frank and asked him to have the roof repaired. Frank says that he has caulked the roof, but the roof still leaks. Frank claims that because Sarah has sole control of the leased premises, she has the duty to repair the roof. Sarah insists that the repair of the roof is Frank's responsibility. Discuss fully who is responsible for repairing the roof and, if the responsibility belongs to Frank, what remedies are available to Sarah.

29.4 Adverse Possession. In 1972, Ted Pafundi bought a quarry in West Pawlet, Vermont, from his neighbor, Marguerite Scott. The deed vaguely described the eastern boundary of the quarry as "the westerly boundary of the lands of" the neighboring property owners. Pafundi quarried green slate from the west wall until his death in 1979, when his son Gary began to work the east wall until *his* death in 1989. Gary's daughter Connie then took over operations. All of the Pafundis used the floor of the quarry as their base of operations. In 1992, N.A.S. Holdings, Inc., bought the neighboring property. A survey revealed that virtually the entire quarry was within the boundaries of N.A.S.'s property and that twenty years earlier, Ted had actually bought only a small strip of land on the west side. When N.A.S. attempted to begin quarrying, Connie blocked the access. N.A.S. filed a suit in a Vermont state court against Connie, seeking to establish title. Connie argued that she had title to the quarry through adverse possession under a state statute with a possessory period of fifteen years. What are the elements to acquire title by adverse possession? Are they satisfied in this case? In whose favor should the court rule, and why? [*N.A.S. Holdings, Inc. v. Pafundi*, 169 Vt. 437, 736 A.2d 780 (1999)]

29.5 Commercial Lease Terms. Metropolitan Life Insurance Co. leased space in its Trail Plaza Shopping Center in Florida to Winn-Dixie Stores, Inc., to operate a supermarket. Under the lease, the landlord agreed not to permit "any [other] property located within the shopping center to be used for or occupied by any business dealing in or which shall keep in stock or sell for off-premises consumption any staple or fancy groceries" in more than "500 square feet of sales area." In 1999, Metropolitan leased 22,000 square feet of

space in Trail Plaza to 99 Cent Stuff–Trail Plaza, LLC, under a lease that prohibited it from selling "groceries" in more than 500 square feet of "sales area." Shortly after 99 Cent Stuff opened, it began selling food and other products, including soap, matches, and paper napkins. Alleging that these sales violated the parties' leases, Winn-Dixie filed a suit in a Florida state court against 99 Cent Stuff and others. The defendants argued, among other things, that the groceries provision covered only food and that the 500-square-foot restriction included only shelf space, not store aisles. How should these lease terms be interpreted? Should the court grant an injunction in Winn-Dixie's favor? Explain. [*Winn-Dixie Stores, Inc. v. 99 Cent Stuff–Trail Plaza, LLC*, 811 So.2d 719 (Fla.App. 3 Dist. 2002)]

29.6 Easements. The Wallens family owned a cabin on Lummi Island in the state of Washington. A driveway ran from the cabin across their property to South Nugent Road. In 1952, Floyd Massey bought the adjacent lot and built a cabin. To gain access to his property, he used a bulldozer to extend the driveway, without the Wallenses' permission but also without their objection. In 1975, the Wallenses sold their property to Wright Fish Co. Massey continued to use and maintain the driveway without permission or objection. In 1984, Massey sold his property to Robert Drake. Drake and his employees continued to use and maintain the driveway without permission or objection, although Drake knew it was located largely on Wright's property. In 1997, Wright sold its lot to Robert Smersh. The next year, Smersh told Drake to stop using the driveway. Drake filed a suit in a Washington state court against Smersh, claiming an easement by prescription (which is created by meeting the same requirements as adverse possession). Does Drake's use of the driveway meet all of the requirements? What should the court rule? Explain. [*Drake v. Smersh*, 122 Wash.App. 147, 89 P.3d 726 (Div. 1 2004)]

29.7 Case Problem with Sample Answer. The Hope Partnership for Education, a religious organization, proposed to build a private independent middle school in a blighted neighborhood in Philadelphia, Pennsylvania. In 2002, the Hope Partnership asked the Redevelopment Authority of the City of Philadelphia to acquire specific land for the project and sell it to the Hope Partnership for a nominal price. The land included a house at 1839 North Eighth Street owned by Mary Smith, whose daughter Veronica lived there with her family. The Authority offered Smith $12,000 for the house and initiated a taking of the property. Smith filed a suit in a Pennsylvania state court against the Authority, admitting that the house was a "substandard structure in a blighted area," but arguing that the taking was unconstitutional because its beneficiary was private. The Authority asserted that only the public purpose of the taking should be considered, not the status of the property's developer. On what basis can a government entity use the power of eminent domain to take property? What are the limits to this power? How should the court rule? Why? [*In re*

Redevelopment Authority of City of Philadelphia, 588 Pa. 789, 906 A.2d 1197 (2006)]

 After you have answered Problem 29.7, compare your answer with the sample answer given on the Web site that accompanies this text. Go to www.cengage.com/blaw/fbl, select "Chapter 29," and click on "Case Problem with Sample Answer."

29.8 Ownership in Fee Simple. Thomas and Teresa Cline built a house on a 76-acre parcel of real estate next to Roy Berg's home and property in Augusta County, Virginia. The homes were about 1,800 feet apart but in view of each other. After several disagreements between the parties, Berg equipped an 11-foot tripod with motion sensors and floodlights that intermittently illuminated the Clines' home. Berg also installed surveillance cameras that tracked some of the movement on the Clines' property. The cameras transmitted on an open frequency, which could be received by any television within range. The Clines asked Berg to turn off, or at least redirect, the lights. When he refused, they erected a fence for 200 feet along the parties' common property line. The 32-foot-high fence consisted of 20 utility poles spaced 10 feet apart with plastic wrap stretched between the poles. This effectively blocked the lights and cameras. Berg filed a suit against the Clines in a Virginia state court, complaining that the fence interfered unreasonably with his use and enjoyment of his property. He asked the court to order the Clines to take the fence down. What are the limits on an owner's use of property? How should the court rule in this case? Why? [*Cline v. Berg*, 273 Va. 142, 639 S.E.2d 231 (2007)]

29.9 **A Question of Ethics.** *In 1999, Stephen and Linda Kailin bought the Monona Center, a mall in Madison, Wisconsin, from Perry Armstrong for $760,000. The contract provided, "Seller represents to Buyer that as of the date of acceptance Seller had no notice or knowledge of conditions affecting the Property or transaction" other than certain items disclosed at the time of the offer. Armstrong told the Kailins about the Center's eight tenants, their lease expiration dates, and the monthly and annual rent due under each lease. One of the lessees, Ring's All-American Karate, occupied about a third of the Center's space under a five-year lease. Because of Ring's financial difficulties, Armstrong had agreed to reduce its rent for nine months in 1997. By the time of the sale to the Kailins, Ring owed $13,910 in unpaid rent, but Armstrong did not tell the Kailins, who did not ask. Ring continued to fail to pay rent and finally vacated the Center. The Kailins filed a suit in a Wisconsin state court against Armstrong and others, alleging, among other things, misrepresentation. [Kailin v. Armstrong, 252 Wis.2d 676, 643 N.W.2d 132 (2002)]*

1 Did Armstrong have a duty to disclose Ring's delinquency and default to the Kailins? Explain.

2 What obligation, if any, did Ring have to the Kailins or Armstrong after failing to pay the rent and eventually defaulting on the lease? Why?

 **CRITICAL THINKING AND WRITING ASSIGNMENT**

29.10 Critical Thinking and Writing Assignment for Business. Garza Construction Co. erects a silo (a grain storage facility) on Reeve's ranch. Garza also lends Reeve funds to pay for the silo under an agreement providing that the silo is not to become part of the land until Reeve completes the loan payments. Before the silo is paid for, Metropolitan State Bank, the mortgage holder on Reeve's land, forecloses on the property. Metropolitan contends that the silo is a fixture to the realty and that the bank is therefore entitled to the proceeds from its sale. Garza argues that the silo is personal property and that the proceeds should therefore go to Garza. Is the silo a fixture? Why or why not?

For information on Veterans Administration home loans, go to

www.homeloans.va.gov

Tenant Net is an advocacy Web site focusing on New York City and the state of New York. To view this site, go to

www.tenant.net

PRACTICAL INTERNET EXERCISES

Go to this text's Web site at **www.cengage.com/blaw/fbl**, select "Chapter 29," and click on "Practical Internet Exercises." There you will find the following Internet research exercises that you can perform to learn more about the topics covered in this chapter.

PRACTICAL INTERNET EXERCISE 29–1 LEGAL PERSPECTIVE—Eminent Domain

PRACTICAL INTERNET EXERCISE 29–2 MANAGEMENT PERSPECTIVE—Fair Housing

PRACTICAL INTERNET EXERCISE 29–3 SOCIAL PERSPECTIVE—The Rights of Tenants

BEFORE THE TEST

Go to this text's Web site at **www.cengage.com/blaw/fbl**, select "Chapter 29," and click on "Interactive Quizzes." You will find a number of interactive questions relating to this chapter.

CHAPTER 30
Insurance, Wills, and Trusts

LEARNING OBJECTIVES

AFTER READING THIS CHAPTER, YOU SHOULD BE ABLE TO ANSWER THE FOLLOWING QUESTIONS:

1 What is an insurable interest? When must an insurable interest exist—at the time the insurance policy is obtained, at the time the loss occurs, or both?

2 Is an insurance broker the agent of the insurance applicant or the agent of the insurer?

3 What are the basic requirements for executing a will? How may a will be revoked?

4 What is the difference between a *per stirpes* distribution and a *per capita* distribution of an estate to the grandchildren of the deceased?

5 What are the four essential elements of a trust? What is the difference between an express trust and an implied trust?

Most individuals insure both real and personal property (as well as their lives). By insuring our property, we protect ourselves against damage and loss. The first part of this chapter focuses on insurance, which is a foremost concern of all property owners. We then examine how property is transferred on the death of its owner. Certainly, the laws of succession of property are a necessary corollary to the concept of private ownership of property. Our laws require that on death, title to the property of a decedent (one who has recently died) must be delivered in full somewhere. In this chapter, we see that this can be done by will, through trusts, or through state laws prescribing distribution of property among heirs or next of kin.

INSURANCE

Many precautions may be taken to protect against the hazards of life. For instance, an individual may wear a seat belt to protect against injuries from automobile accidents or install smoke detectors to guard against injury from fire. Of course, no one can predict whether an accident or a fire will ever occur, but individuals and businesses must establish plans to protect their personal and financial interests should some event threaten to undermine their security.

Insurance is a contract by which the insurance company (the insurer) promises to pay a certain amount or give some-

thing of value to another (either the insured or the beneficiary) in the event that the insured is injured, dies, or sustains damage to her or his property as a result of particular, stated contingencies. Basically, insurance is an arrangement for *transferring and allocating risk*. In many instances, **risk** can be described as a prediction concerning potential loss based on known and unknown factors. Insurance, however, involves much more than a game of chance.

Risk management normally involves the transfer of certain risks from the individual to the insurance company by a contractual agreement. The insurance contract and its provisions will be examined shortly. First, however, we look at the different types of insurance that can be obtained, insurance terminology, and the concept of insurable interest.

Classifications of Insurance

Insurance is classified according to the nature of the risk involved. For instance, fire insurance, casualty insurance, life insurance, and title insurance apply to different types of risk. Furthermore, policies of these types protect different persons and interests. This is reasonable because the types of losses that are expected and that are foreseeable or unforeseeable vary with the nature of the activity. Exhibit 30–1 on pages 624 and 625 presents a list of insurance classifications.

Insurance Terminology

An insurance contract is called a **policy;** the consideration paid to the insurer is called a **premium;** and the insurance company is sometimes called an **underwriter.** The parties to an insurance policy are the *insurer* (the insurance company) and the *insured* (the person covered by its provisions or the holder of the policy).

Insurance contracts are usually obtained through an *agent,* who ordinarily works for the insurance company, or through a *broker,* who is ordinarily an *independent contractor.* When a broker deals with an applicant for insurance, the broker is, in effect, the applicant's agent and not an agent of the insurance company. In contrast, an insurance agent is an agent of the insurance company, not of the applicant. As a general rule, the insurance company is bound by the acts of its insurance agents when they act within the agency relationship (discussed in Chapter 22). In most situations, state law determines the status of all parties writing or obtaining insurance.

Insurable Interest

A person can insure anything in which she or he has an **insurable interest.** Without this insurable interest, there is no enforceable contract, and a transaction to purchase insurance coverage would have to be treated as a wager. In regard to real and personal property, an insurable interest exists when the insured derives a pecuniary benefit (a benefit consisting of or relating to money) from the preservation and continued existence of the property. Put another way, one has an insurable interest in property when one would sustain a financial loss from its destruction. In regard to life insurance, a person must have a reasonable expectation of benefit from the continued life of another in order to have an insurable interest in that person's life. The benefit may be pecuniary (as with so-called *key-person insurance,* which insures the lives of important employees, usually in small companies), or it may be founded on the relationship between the parties (by blood or affinity).

For property insurance, the insurable interest must exist at the time the loss occurs but need not exist when the policy is purchased. In contrast, for life insurance, the insurable interest must exist at the time the policy is obtained. The existence of an insurable interest is a primary concern in determining liability under an insurance policy.

The Insurance Contract

An insurance contract is governed by the general principles of contract law, although the insurance industry is heavily regulated by each state. Several aspects of the insurance contract will be treated here, including the application for insurance,

the date when the contract takes effect, and some of the important provisions typically found in insurance contracts. In addition, we will also discuss the cancellation of an insurance policy and defenses that insurance companies can raise against payment on a policy.

Application The filled-in application form for insurance is usually attached to the policy and made a part of the insurance contract. Thus, an insurance applicant is bound by any false statements that appear in the application (subject to certain exceptions). Because the insurance company evaluates the risk factors based on the information included in the insurance application, misstatements or misrepresentations can void a policy, especially if the insurance company can show that it would not have extended insurance if it had known the true facts.

Effective Date The effective date of an insurance contract—that is, the date on which the insurance coverage begins—is important. In some instances, the insurance applicant is not protected until a formal written policy is issued. In other situations, the applicant is protected between the time the application is received and the time the insurance company either accepts or rejects it. Four facts should be kept in mind:

1 A broker is merely the agent of an applicant. Therefore, until the broker obtains a policy, the applicant normally is not insured.

2 A person who seeks insurance from an insurance company's agent will usually be protected from the moment the application is made, provided that some form of premium has been paid. Between the time the application is received and either rejected or accepted, the applicant is covered (possibly subject to passing a physical examination). Usually, the agent will write a memorandum, or **binder,** indicating that a policy is pending and stating its essential terms.

3 If the parties agree that the policy will be issued and delivered at a later time, the contract is not effective until the policy is issued and delivered or sent to the applicant, depending on the agreement. Thus, any loss sustained between the time of application and the delivery of the policy is not covered.

4 The parties may agree that a life insurance policy will be binding at the time the insured pays the first premium, or the policy may be expressly contingent on the applicant's passing a physical examination. If the applicant pays the premium and passes the examination, the policy coverage is continuously in effect. If the applicant pays the premium but dies before having the physical examination,

EXHIBIT 30–1 **Insurance Classifications**

TYPE OF INSURANCE	COVERAGE
Accident	Covers expenses, losses, and suffering incurred by the insured because of accidents causing physical injury and any consequent disability; sometimes includes a specified payment to heirs of the insured if death results from an accident.
All-risk	Covers all losses that the insured may incur except those that are specifically excluded. Typical exclusions are war, pollution, earthquakes, and floods.
Automobile	May cover damage to automobiles resulting from specified hazards or occurrences (such as fire, vandalism, theft, or collision); normally provides protection against liability for personal injuries and property damage resulting from the operation of the vehicle.
Casualty	Protects against losses incurred by the insured as a result of being held liable for personal injuries or property damage sustained by others.
Credit	Pays to a creditor the balance of a debt on the disability, death, insolvency, or bankruptcy of the debtor; often offered by lending institutions.
Decreasing-term life	Provides life insurance; requires uniform payments over the life (term) of the policy, but with a decreasing face value (amount of coverage).
Employer's liability	Insures employers against liability for injuries or losses sustained by employees during the course of their employment; covers claims not covered under workers' compensation insurance.
Fidelity or guaranty	Provides indemnity against losses in trade or losses caused by the dishonesty of employees, the insolvency of debtors, or breaches of contract.
Fire	Covers losses incurred by the insured as a result of fire.
Floater	Covers movable property, as long as the property is within the territorial boundaries specified in the contract.
Group	Provides individual life, medical, or disability insurance coverage but is obtainable through a group of persons, usually employees. The policy premium is paid either entirely by the employer or partially by the employer and partially by the employee.

then in order to collect, the applicant's estate must show that the applicant *would have passed* the examination had he or she not died.

Coinsurance Clauses   Often, when taking out fire insurance policies, property owners insure their property for less than full value because most fires do not result in a total loss. To encourage owners to insure their property for an amount as close to full value as possible, fire insurance policies commonly include a coinsurance clause. Typically, a *coinsurance clause* provides that if the owner insures the property up to a specified percentage—usually 80 percent—of its value, she or he will recover any loss up to the face amount of the policy. If the insurance is for less than the fixed percentage, the owner is responsible for a proportionate share of the loss.

Coinsurance applies only in instances of partial loss. The amount of the recovery is calculated by using the following formula.

$$\text{Loss} \times \left(\frac{\text{Amount of Insurance Coverage}}{\text{Coinsurance Percentage} \times \text{Property Value}} \right) = \text{Amount of Recovery}$$

■ EXAMPLE 30.1 If the owner of property valued at $200,000 takes out a policy in the amount of $100,000 and suffers a loss of $80,000, the recovery will be $50,000. The owner will be responsible for (coinsure) the balance of the loss, or $30,000.

$$\$80,000 \times \left(\frac{\$100,000}{0.8 \times \$200,000} \right) = \$50,000$$

If the owner had taken out a policy in the amount of 80 percent of the value of the property, or $160,000, then according to the same formula, the owner would have recovered the full amount of the loss (the face amount of the policy). ■

Other Provisions and Clauses   Some other important provisions and clauses contained in insurance contracts are listed and defined in Exhibit 30–2 on page 626. The courts are aware that most people do not have the special training necessary to understand the intricate terminology used in insurance policies. Thus, the words used in an insurance contract have their ordinary meanings. They are interpreted by the courts in light of the nature of the coverage involved.

EXHIBIT 30–1 Insurance Classifications—Continued

TYPE OF INSURANCE	COVERAGE
Health	Covers expenses incurred by the insured as a result of physical injury or illness and other expenses relating to health and life maintenance.
Homeowners'	Protects homeowners against some or all risks of loss to their residences and the residences' contents or liability arising from the use of the property.
Key-person	Protects a business in the event of the death or disability of a key employee.
Liability	Protects against liability imposed on the insured as a result of injuries to the person or property of another.
Life	Covers the death of the policyholder. On the death of the insured, the insurer pays the amount specified in the policy to the insured's beneficiary.
Major medical	Protects the insured against major hospital, medical, or surgical expenses.
Malpractice	Protects professionals (physicians, lawyers, and others) against malpractice claims brought against them by their patients or clients; a form of liability insurance.
Marine	Covers movable property (including ships, freight, and cargo) against certain perils or navigation risks during a specific voyage or time period.
Mortgage	Covers a mortgage loan. The insurer pays the balance of the mortgage to the creditor on the death or disability of the debtor.
No-fault auto	Covers personal injuries and (sometimes) property damage resulting from automobile accidents. The insured submits his or her claims to his or her own insurance company, regardless of who was at fault. A person may sue the party at fault or that party's insurer only when an accident results in serious medical injury and consequent high medical costs. Governed by state "no-fault" statutes.
Term life	Provides life insurance for a specified period of time (term) with no cash surrender value; usually renewable.
Title	Protects against any defects in title to real property and any losses incurred as a result of existing claims against or liens on the property at the time of purchase.

Ambiguities Are Interpreted against Insurance Companies When there is an ambiguity in the policy, the provision generally is interpreted against the insurance company. The courts dislike vague language or unclear terms and will resolve any doubts in favor of the insured.[1] Also, when it is unclear whether an insurance contract actually exists because the written policy has not been delivered, the uncertainty normally is resolved against the insurance company. The court presumes that the policy is in effect unless the company can show otherwise. Similarly, an insurer must make sure that the insured is adequately notified of any change in coverage under an existing policy.

Cancellation The insured can cancel a policy at any time, and the insurer can cancel under certain circumstances. When an insurance company can cancel its insurance contract, the policy or a state statute usually requires that the insurer give advance written notice of the cancellation to the insured. The same requirement applies when only part of a policy is can-

celed. Any premium paid in advance may be refundable on the policy's cancellation. The insured may also be entitled to a life insurance policy's cash surrender value.

The insurer may cancel an insurance policy for various reasons, depending on the type of insurance. For example, automobile insurance can be canceled for nonpayment of premiums or suspension of the insured's driver's license. Property insurance can be canceled for nonpayment of premiums or for other reasons, including the insured's fraud or misrepresentation, conviction for a crime that increases the hazard insured against, or gross negligence that increases the risk assumed by the insurer. Life and health policies can be canceled because of false statements made by the insured in the application, but the cancellation must take place before the effective date of an incontestability clause. An insurer cannot cancel—or refuse to renew—a policy for discriminatory reasons or other reasons that violate public policy, or because the insured has appeared as a witness in a case against the company.

Good Faith Obligations Both parties to an insurance contract are responsible for the obligations they assume under the

1. See, for example, *Cary v. Omaha Life Insurance Co.*, 108 P.3d 288 (Colo. 2005).

EXHIBIT 30–2 **Insurance Contract Provisions and Clauses**

Antilapse clause	An antilapse clause provides that the policy will not automatically lapse if no payment is made on the date due. Ordinarily, under such a provision, the insured has a *grace period* of thirty or thirty-one days within which to pay an overdue premium before the policy is canceled.
Appraisal clause	Insurance policies frequently provide that if the parties cannot agree on the amount of a loss covered under the policy or the value of the property lost, an appraisal, or estimate, by an impartial and qualified third party can be demanded.
Arbitration clause	Many insurance policies include clauses that call for arbitration of disputes that may arise between the insurer and the insured concerning the settlement of claims.
Incontestability clause	An incontestability clause provides that after a policy has been in force for a specified length of time—usually two or three years—the insurer cannot contest statements made in the application.
Multiple insurance	Many insurance policies include a clause providing that if the insured has multiple insurance policies that cover the same property and the amount of coverage exceeds the loss, the loss will be shared proportionately by the insurance companies.

contract (contract law was discussed in Chapters 7 through 13). In addition, both the insured and the insurer have an implied duty to act in good faith.

Good faith requires the party who is applying for insurance to reveal everything necessary for the insurer to evaluate the risk. In other words, the applicant must disclose all material facts, including all facts that an insurer would consider in determining whether to charge a higher premium or to refuse to issue a policy altogether. Many insurance companies today require that an applicant give the company permission to access other information, such as private medical records and credit ratings, for the purpose of evaluating the risk.

Once the insurer has accepted the risk, and some event occurs that gives rise to a claim, the insurer has a duty to inves-

tigate to determine the facts. When a policy provides insurance against third party claims, the insurer is obligated to make reasonable efforts to settle such a claim. If a settlement cannot be reached, then regardless of the claim's merit, the insurer has a *duty to defend* any suit against the insured. The insurer also owes a *duty to pay* any legitimate claims up to the face amount of the policy.

An insurer has a duty to provide or pay an attorney to defend its insured when a complaint against the insured alleges facts that could, if proved, impose liability on the insured within the policy's coverage. In the following case, the question was whether a policy covered a dentist's potential liability arising from a practical joke that he played on an employee while performing a dental procedure.

CASE 30.1 **Woo v. Fireman's Fund Insurance Co.**

Supreme Court of Washington, 161 Wash.2d 43, 164 P.3d 454 (2007).

FACTS Tina Alberts worked for Robert Woo as a dental surgical assistant. Her family also raised potbellied pigs, and she often talked about them at work. Sometimes, Woo mentioned the pigs, intending to encourage a "friendly working environment." Alberts interpreted the comments as offensive. Alberts asked Woo to replace two of her teeth with implants. The procedure required the installation of temporary partial bridges called "flippers." While Alberts was anesthetized, Woo installed a set of flippers shaped like boar tusks, as a joke, and took photos. Before Alberts regained consciousness, he inserted the normal flippers. A month later, Woo's staff gave Alberts the photos at a gathering to celebrate her birthday. Stunned, Alberts refused to return to work. Woo tried to apologize.

Alberts filed a suit in a Washington state court against him, alleging battery and other torts. He asked Fireman's Fund Insurance Company to defend him, claiming coverage under his policy. The insurer refused. Woo settled the suit with Alberts for $250,000 and filed a suit against Fireman's, claiming that it had breached its duty to defend him. The court awarded him $750,000 in damages, plus the amount of the settlement and attorneys' fees and costs. A state intermediate appellate court reversed the award. Woo appealed to the Washington Supreme Court.

ISSUE Did the insurance company have an obligation to defend a customer-dentist who, as a practical joke, temporarily installed a set of boar-tusk flippers into his

CASE 30.1—Continued

patient-employee's mouth during a routine dental procedure?

DECISION Yes. The Washington Supreme Court reversed the decision of the lower court. The court held that Fireman's had a duty to defend Woo under the professional liability provision of his policy.

REASON The court reasoned that the Fireman's professional liability provision in its policy stated that it would defend any claim brought against the insured "even if the allegations of the claim are groundless, false or fraudulent." Furthermore, the policy defines *dental services* as "all services which are performed in the practice of the dentistry profession as defined in the business and professional codes

of the state where [the dentist is licensed]." Washington State law defined the practice of dentistry quite broadly, and Woo's practical joke took place while Woo was conducting his dental practice. Therefore, the court concluded that the insertion of boar-tusk flippers in Alberts's mouth conceivably fell within the policy's broad definition of the practice of dentistry. The insertion of boar-tusk flippers was also intertwined with Woo's dental practice because it involved an interaction with an employee.

 FOR CRITICAL ANALYSIS—Legal Consideration *In determining if an insurer has a duty to defend an insured, should a court ask whether the insured had a "reasonable expectation" of coverage? Explain.*

■

Bad Faith Actions Although the law of insurance generally follows contract law, most states now recognize a "bad faith" tort action against insurers. Thus, if an insurer in bad faith denies coverage of a claim, the insured may recover in tort in an amount exceeding the policy's coverage limits and may even recover millions of dollars in punitive damages. Some courts have held insurers liable for bad faith refusals to settle claims for reasonable amounts within the policy limits.

Defenses against Payment An insurance company can raise any of the defenses that would be valid in an ordinary action on a contract, as well as some defenses that do not apply in ordinary contract actions. If the insurance company can show that the policy was procured by fraud or misrepresentation, it may have a valid defense for not paying on a claim. (The insurance company may also have the right to disaffirm or rescind an insurance contract.) An absolute defense exists if the insurer can show that the insured lacked an insurable interest—thus rendering the policy void from the beginning. Improper actions, such as those that are against public policy or that are otherwise illegal, can also give the insurance company a defense against the payment of a claim or allow it to rescind the contract.

An insurance company can be prevented from asserting some defenses that are normally available, however. **■EXAMPLE 30.2** Farmers' Co-op Insurance Company tells an insured, Berta Rydell, that information requested on a form is optional, but she provides it anyway. The company cannot use the information to avoid its contractual obligation under the insurance contract. Similarly, an insurance company normally cannot escape payment on the death of an insured on

the ground that the person's age was stated incorrectly on the application. ■

WILLS

Private ownership of property leads logically to both the protection of that property by insurance coverage while the owner is alive and the transfer of that property on the death of the owner to those designated in the owner's will. A **will** is the final declaration of how a person desires to have her or his property disposed of after death. It is a formal instrument that must follow exactly the requirements of state law to be effective. A will is referred to as a *testamentary disposition* of property, and one who dies after having made a valid will is said to have died **testate**. A will can serve other purposes besides the distribution of property. It can appoint a guardian for minor children or incapacitated adults. It can also appoint a personal representative to settle the affairs of the deceased.

A person who dies without having created a valid will is said to have died **intestate**. In this situation, state **intestacy laws** prescribe the distribution of the property among heirs or next of kin. If no heirs or kin can be found, title to the property will be transferred to the state.

Terminology of Wills

A person who makes out a will is known as a **testator** (from the Latin *testari*, "to make a will"). The court responsible for administering any legal problems surrounding a will is called a *probate court*, as mentioned in Chapter 2. When a person dies, a personal representative administers the estate and settles finally all of the decedent's (deceased person's) affairs. An **executor** is a personal representative named in the will; an **administrator** is a personal representative appointed by the court for a decedent who dies without a will. The court will also appoint an administrator if the will does not name an executor or if the named person lacks the capacity to serve as an executor.

A gift of real estate by will is generally called a **devise**, and a gift of personal property by will is called a **bequest,** or **legacy.** The recipient of a gift by will is a **devisee** or a **legatee**, depending on whether the gift was a devise or a legacy.

Types of Gifts

Gifts by will can be specific, general, or residuary. A *specific* devise or bequest (legacy) describes particular property (such as "Eastwood Estate" or "my gold pocket watch") that can be distinguished from all the rest of the testator's property. A *general* devise or bequest (legacy) uses less restrictive terminology. For example, "I devise all my lands" is a general devise. A general bequest often specifies a sum of money instead of a particular item of property, such as a watch or an automobile. For example, "I give to my nephew, Carleton, $30,000" is a general bequest.

If the assets of an estate are insufficient to pay in full all general bequests provided for in the will, an *abatement* takes

place, meaning the legatees receive reduced benefits. **■EXAMPLE 30.3** Yusuf's will leaves "$15,000 each to my children, Tamara and Kwame." On Yusuf's death, only $10,000 is available to honor these bequests. By abatement, each child will receive $5,000. ■ If bequests are more complicated, abatement may be more complex. The testator's intent, as expressed in the will, controls.

Sometimes, a will provides that any assets remaining after the estate's debts have been paid and specific gifts have been made—called the *residuary* (or *residuum*)—are to be distributed in a specific way, such as to the testator's spouse or descendants. Such a clause, called a *residuary clause*, is often used when the exact amount to be distributed cannot be determined until all of the other gifts and payouts have been made. If the testator has not indicated what party or parties should receive the residuary of the estate, the residuary passes according to state laws of intestacy.

A testator's disposition of his or her property passes all of the property that he or she was entitled to dispose of at the time of death. The corollary principle is that property a testator does not own at the time of death is not subject to transfer by will. These principles were applied in the following case involving a residuary clause.

CASE 30.2 **Shaw Family Archives, Ltd. v. CMG Worldwide, Inc.**

United States District Court, Southern District of New York, 486 F.Supp.2d 309 (2007).

FACTS The actress Marilyn Monroe, a New York resident, died in California on August 5, 1962. Her will gave her estate's residuary assets to Lee Strasberg and two other beneficiaries. Lee died in 1982. On the death of Aaron Frosch (the executor of Monroe's estate), Lee's widow, Anna, was appointed administrator. In 2001, the residuary assets were transferred to Marilyn Monroe, LLC (MMLLC), which Anna formed to manage those assets. During Monroe's life, photographer Sam Shaw took photos of her. After his death, the photos descended to the Shaw Family Archives (SFA). With Bradford Licensing Associates, SFA maintained a Web site through which they licensed Monroe's picture, image, and likeness for commercial use. In 2006, T-shirts that bore her picture and SFA's inscription on the label were offered for sale in Indiana. MMLLC asserted that under Indiana's Right of Publicity Act (which creates a right of publicity that survives for one hundred years after a person's death), it owned a right of publicity bequeathed by the residuary clause of Monroe's will and that SFA had violated this right. SFA and others filed a suit

in a federal district court against MMLLC and CMG Worldwide, Inc., contending that MMLLC did not own such a right. Both parties filed motions for summary judgment.

ISSUE Did the residuary clause in Marilyn Monroe's will transfer a "right of publicity" to MMLLC that was not recognized by statute until many years after her death?

DECISION No. The court issued a summary judgment in SFA's favor, holding that MMLLC had not become the owner of a right of publicity in Marilyn Monroe's name, likeness, and persona through her will.

REASON The court concluded that in 1962, when Marilyn Monroe died, inheritable after-death publicity rights were not recognized in California, Indiana, or New York. "To this day New York law does not recognize any common law right of publicity and limits its statutory publicity rights to living persons." California did not pass its inheritable after-death publicity rights law until twenty-two years following Monroe's death. Indiana did so only in 1994. "Thus, at the time of her

CASE 30.2—Continued

death * * * Ms. Monroe did not have any postmortem right of publicity under the law of any relevant state. As a result, any publicity rights she enjoyed during her lifetime were extinguished at her death by operation of law." California and New York were the only two states in which Monroe could have conceivably been domiciled. Neither state at that time permitted a "testator to dispose by will of a property she does not own at the time of her death."

 FOR CRITICAL ANALYSIS—Technological Consideration *Did SFA and Bradford's online offer of licenses for the commercial use of Monroe's image have any effect on the court's decision in this case? Why or why not?*

■

Requirements for a Valid Will

A will must comply with certain statutory formalities designed to ensure that the testator understood his or her actions at the time the will was made. These formalities are intended to help prevent fraud. Unless they are followed, the will is declared void, and the decedent's property is distributed according to the laws of intestacy of that state. Although the required formalities vary among jurisdictions, most states uphold certain basic requirements for executing a will. In 1969, to promote more uniformity among the states, the National Conference of Commissioners on Uniform State Laws issued the Uniform Probate Code (UPC). Almost half of the states have adopted at least some of its provisions. We now look at the basic requirements for a valid will, including references to the UPC when appropriate.

Testamentary Capacity and Intent For a will to be valid, the testator must have testamentary capacity—that is, the testator must be of legal age and sound mind *at the time the will is made.* The legal age for executing a will varies, but in most states and under the UPC, the minimum age is eighteen years [UPC 2–501]. Thus, the will of a twenty-one-year-old decedent written when the person was sixteen is invalid if, under state law, the legal age for executing a will is eighteen.

The "Sound-Mind" Requirement. The concept of "being of sound mind" refers to the testator's ability to formulate and to comprehend a personal plan for the disposition of property. Generally, a testator must (1) intend the document to be his or her last will and testament, (2) comprehend the kind and character of the property being distributed, and (3) comprehend and remember the "natural objects of his or her bounty" (usually, family members and persons for whom the testator has affection).

Intent. A valid will is one that represents the maker's intention to transfer and distribute her or his property. When it can be shown that the decedent's plan of distribution was the result of fraud or of undue influence, the will is declared invalid. The court may sometimes infer undue influence if the testator ignored blood relatives and named as a beneficiary a nonrelative who was in constant close contact with the testator and in a position to influence the making of the will. **■EXAMPLE 30.4** Frieda is a nurse who was responsible for caring for Juana, the testator, for the last few years of her life. After Juana's death, her family discovered that her will named Frieda as a beneficiary and excluded all family members. If Juana's family challenges the validity of the will on the basis of undue influence, the court might well infer that Frieda unduly influenced Juana and declare the will invalid. ■

Writing Requirements Generally, a will must be in writing. The writing itself can be informal as long as it substantially complies with the statutory requirements. In some states, a will can be handwritten in crayon or ink. It can be written on a sheet or scrap of paper, on a paper bag, or on a piece of cloth. A will that is completely in the handwriting of the testator is called a **holographic will** (sometimes referred to as an *olographic will*).

In some instances, oral wills are found valid. A **nuncupative will** is an oral will made before witnesses. Most states do not permit such wills. Where authorized by statute, such wills are generally valid only if made during the last illness of the testator and are therefore sometimes referred to as *deathbed wills.* Normally, only personal property can be transferred by a nuncupative will. Statutes frequently permit military personnel to make nuncupative wills when on active duty.

Signature Requirements It is a fundamental requirement that the testator's signature appear, generally at the end of the will. Each jurisdiction dictates by statute and court decision what constitutes a signature. Initials, an X or other mark, and words such as "Mom" have all been upheld as valid when it was shown that the testators *intended* them to be signatures.

Witness Requirements A will normally must be attested (sworn to) by two, and sometimes three, witnesses. The number of witnesses, their qualifications, and the manner in which the witnessing must be done are generally set out in a statute. A witness can be required to be disinterested—that is, not a beneficiary under the will. The UPC, however, provides that a will is valid even if it is attested by an interested witness [UPC 2–505]. There are no age requirements for witnesses, but they must be mentally competent.

The purpose of witnesses is to verify that the testator actually executed (signed) the will and had the requisite intent and capacity at the time. A witness does not have to read the contents of the will. Usually, the testator and all witnesses must sign in the sight or the presence of one another, but there are exceptions.[2] The UPC does not require all parties to sign in the presence of one another and deems it sufficient if the testator acknowledges her or his signature to the witnesses [UPC 2–502].

Publication Requirements A will is *published* by an oral declaration by the maker to the witnesses that the document they are about to sign is his or her "last will and testament." Publication is becoming an unnecessary formality in most states, and it is not required under the UPC.

Revocation of Wills

An executed will is revocable by the maker at any time during the maker's lifetime. The maker may revoke a will by a physical act, such as tearing up the will, or by a subsequent writing. Wills can also be revoked by operation of law. Revocation can be partial or complete, and it must follow certain strict formalities.

Revocation by a Physical Act of the Maker A testator may revoke a will by intentionally burning, tearing, canceling, obliterating, or otherwise destroying it, or by having someone else do so in the presence of the maker and at the maker's direction.[3] When a state statute prescribes the specific methods for revoking a will by physical act, only those methods can be used to revoke the will. In some states, partial revocation by physical act of the maker is recognized. Thus, those portions of a will lined out or torn away are dropped, and the remaining parts of the will are valid. At no time, however, can a provision be crossed out and an additional or substitute provision written in. Such altered portions require reexecution (re-signing) and reattestation (rewitnessing).

Revocation by a Subsequent Writing A will may also be wholly or partially revoked by a **codicil,** a written instrument

separate from the will that amends or revokes provisions in the will. A codicil eliminates the necessity of redrafting an entire will merely to add to it or amend it. A codicil can also be used to revoke an entire will. The codicil must be executed with the same formalities required for a will, and it must refer expressly to the will. In effect, it updates a will because the will is "incorporated by reference" into the codicil.

A new will (second will) can be executed that may or may not revoke the first or a prior will, depending on the language used. To revoke a prior will, the second will must use language specifically revoking other wills, such as, "This will hereby revokes all prior wills." If the second will is otherwise valid and properly executed, it will revoke all prior wills. If the express *declaration of revocation* is missing, then both wills are read together. If any of the dispositions made in the second will are inconsistent with the prior will, the second will controls.

Revocation by Operation of Law Revocation by *operation of law* occurs when marriage, divorce or annulment, or the birth of a child takes place after a will has been executed. In most states, when a testator marries after executing a will that does not include the new spouse, on the testator's death the spouse can still receive the amount he or she would have taken had the testator died intestate—that is, without a will (how an intestate's property is distributed under state laws will be discussed shortly). In effect, the will is revoked to the point of providing the spouse with an intestate share. The rest of the estate is passed under the will [UPC 2–301, 2–508]. If, however, the new spouse is otherwise provided for in the will (or by transfer of property outside the will), he or she will not be given an intestate amount.

At common law and under the UPC, divorce does not necessarily revoke the entire will. A divorce or an annulment occurring after a will has been executed will revoke those dispositions of property made under the will to the former spouse [UPC 2–508].

If a child is born after a will has been executed and if it appears that the deceased parent would have made a provision for the child, the child is entitled to receive whatever portion of the estate she or he is allowed under state laws providing for the distribution of an intestate's property. Most state laws allow a child to receive some portion of a parent's estate if no provision is made in the parent's will, unless it appears from the terms of the will that the testator intended to disinherit the child. Under the UPC, the rule is the same.

Probate Procedures

Laws governing wills come into play when a will is probated. To **probate** a will means to establish its validity and to carry the administration of the estate through a court process. Like the requirements for wills, probate laws vary from state to

---

2. See, for example, *Slack v. Truitt*, 368 Md. 2, 791 A.2d 129 (2002).
3. The destruction cannot be inadvertent. The maker's intent to revoke must be shown. Consequently, when a will has been burned or torn accidentally, the maker should normally have a new document created to avoid any suggestion that the maker intended to revoke the will.

state. Typically, though, probate procedures depend on the size of the decedent's estate.

Informal Probate   For smaller estates, most state statutes provide for the distribution of assets without formal probate proceedings. Faster and less expensive methods are then used. Property can be transferred by *affidavit* (a written statement taken before a person who has authority to affirm it), and problems or questions can be handled during an administrative hearing. Some state statutes allow title to cars, savings and checking accounts, and certain other property to be transferred simply by filling out forms.

A majority of states also provide for *family settlement agreements*, which are private agreements among the beneficiaries. Once a will is admitted to probate, the family members can agree to settle among themselves the distribution of the decedent's assets. Although a family settlement agreement speeds the settlement process, a court order is still needed to protect the estate from future creditors and to clear title to the assets involved. The use of these and other types of summary procedures in estate administration can save time and expenses.

Formal Probate   For larger estates, formal probate proceedings normally are undertaken, and the probate court supervises every aspect of the settlement of the decedent's estate. Additionally, in some situations—such as when a guardian for minor children or for an incompetent person must be appointed and a trust has been created to protect the minor or the incompetent person—more formal probate procedures cannot be avoided. Formal probate proceedings may take several months to complete, and as a result, a sizable portion of the decedent's assets (as much as 10 percent) may go toward payment of court costs and fees charged by attorneys and personal representatives (regardless of whether the person is the executor named in the will or an administrator appointed by the court).

Property Transfers outside the Probate Process   In the ordinary situation, a person can employ various **will substitutes** to avoid the cost of probate—for example, *living trusts* (discussed later in this chapter), life insurance policies or individual retirement accounts (IRAs) with named beneficiaries, or joint-tenancy arrangements. Not all alternatives to formal probate administration are suitable to every estate, however.

PREVENTING LEGAL DISPUTES   For most people, estate planning involves not only ensuring that, after they die, their property goes to the intended recipients, but also avoiding probate and maximizing their estates. To this end, many choose to set up a living trust, arrange for a joint tenancy, or name beneficiaries of an IRA or an insurance policy. If you use these will substitutes, though, you should be aware that a court will not apply the same principles in reviewing a transfer outside the probate process as it would apply to a testamentary transfer. Therefore, any such arrangements must be carefully drafted by your attorney and must comply with all legal requirements. To avoid disputes between beneficiaries after your death, make sure that your words and actions in such property transfers are clear and represent the final expression of your intent.

◼

Intestacy Laws

As mentioned, state intestacy laws determine how property will be distributed when a person dies intestate (without a valid will). These statutes are also known as *statutes of descent and distribution*. Intestacy laws attempt to carry out the likely intent and wishes of the decedent. These laws assume that deceased persons would have intended that their natural heirs (spouses, children, grandchildren, or other family members) inherit their property. Therefore, intestacy statutes set out rules and priorities under which these heirs inherit the property. If no heirs exist, the state will assume ownership of the property. The rules of descent vary widely from state to state.

Surviving Spouse and Children   Usually, state statutes provide that first the debts of the decedent must be satisfied out of the estate; then the remaining assets pass to the surviving spouse and to the children. A surviving spouse usually receives only a share of the estate—one-half if there is also a surviving child and one-third if there are two or more children. Only if no children or grandchildren survive the decedent will a surviving spouse succeed to the entire estate.

◼**EXAMPLE 30.5** Allen dies intestate and is survived by his wife, Beth, and his children, Duane and Tara. Allen's property passes according to intestacy laws. After his outstanding debts are paid, Beth will receive the homestead (either in fee simple or as a life estate) and ordinarily a one-third interest in all other property. The remaining real and personal property will pass to Duane and Tara in equal portions. ◼ Under most state intestacy laws and under the UPC, in-laws do not share in an estate. If a child dies before his or her parents, the child's spouse will not receive an inheritance on the parents' death. For example, if Duane died before his father (Allen), Duane's spouse would not inherit Duane's share of Allen's estate.

When there is no surviving spouse or child, the order of inheritance is grandchildren, then brothers and sisters, and, in some states, parents of the decedent. These relatives are usually called *lineal descendants*. If there are no lineal descendants, then *collateral heirs*—nieces, nephews, aunts, and uncles of the decedent—make up the next group to share. If there are no survivors in any of these groups, most statutes provide for the property to be distributed among the next of kin of the collateral heirs.

Stepchildren, Adopted Children, and Illegitimate Children   Under intestacy laws, stepchildren are not considered kin. Legally adopted children, however, are recognized as lawful heirs of their adoptive parents. Statutes vary from state to state in regard to the inheritance rights of illegitimate children. Generally, an illegitimate child is treated as the child of the mother and can inherit from her and her relatives. The child is usually not regarded as the legal child of the father with the right of inheritance unless paternity was established through some legal proceeding prior to the father's death.[4]

Distribution to Grandchildren   Usually, a will provides for how the decedent's estate will be distributed to descendants of deceased children—that is, to the decedent's grandchildren. If a will does not include such a provision—or if a person dies intestate—the question arises as to what share the grandchildren of the decedent will receive. Each state designates one of two methods of distributing the assets of intestate decedents.

One method of dividing an intestate's estate is *per stirpes.* Under this method, within a class or group of distributees (for example, grandchildren), the children of any one descendant take the share that their deceased parent *would have been* entitled to inherit. ■**EXAMPLE 30.6** Michael, a widower, has two children, Scott and Jonathan. Scott has two children (Becky and Holly), and Jonathan has one child (Paul). Scott and Jonathan die before their father, and then Michael dies. If Michael's estate is distributed *per stirpes*, Becky and Holly each receive one-fourth of the estate (dividing Scott's one-half share). Paul receives one-half of the estate (taking Jonathan's one-half share). ■

An estate may also be distributed on a *per capita* basis, which means that each person in a class or group takes an equal share of the estate. If Michael's estate is distributed *per capita*, Becky, Holly, and Paul each receive a one-third share.

TRUSTS

A **trust** is any arrangement through which property is transferred from one person to a trustee to be administered for the transferor's or another party's benefit. It can also be defined as

a right of property, real or personal, held by one party for the benefit of another. A trust can be created for any purpose that is not illegal or against public policy. Its essential elements are as follows:

1 A designated beneficiary.

2 A designated trustee.

3 A fund sufficiently identified to enable title to pass to the trustee.

4 Actual delivery by the settlor or grantor (the person creating the trust) to the trustee with the intention of passing title.

Numerous types of trusts can be established. In this section, we look at some of the major types of trusts and their characteristics.

Express Trusts

An express trust is created or declared in explicit terms, usually in writing. There are numerous types of express trusts, each with its own special characteristics.

Living Trusts   A living trust—or *inter vivos* **trust** (*inter vivos* is Latin for "between or among the living")—is a trust created by a grantor during her or his lifetime. Living trusts have become a popular estate-planning option because at the grantor's death, assets held in a living trust can pass to the heirs without going through probate. Note, however, that living trusts do not shelter assets from estate taxes, and the grantor may still have to pay income taxes on trust earnings—depending on whether the trust is revocable or irrevocable.

Revocable Living Trusts.   Living trusts can be revocable or irrevocable. In a *revocable* living trust, which is the most common type, the grantor retains control over the trust property during her or his lifetime. The grantor deeds the property to the trustee but retains the power to amend, alter, or revoke the trust during her or his lifetime. The grantor may also serve as a trustee or co-trustee, and can arrange to receive income earned by the trust assets during her or his lifetime. Because the grantor is in control of the funds, she or he is required to pay income taxes on the trust earnings. Unless the trust is revoked, the principal of the trust is transferred to the trust beneficiary on the grantor's death.
   ■**EXAMPLE 30.7** James Cortez owns and operates a large farm. After his wife dies, James decides to create a living trust for the benefit of his three children, Alicia, Emma, and Jayden. He contacts his attorney, who prepares the documents creating the trust, executes a deed conveying the farm to the trust, and transfers the farm's bank accounts into the name of the trust. The trust designates James as the trustee

---

4. For a landmark case regarding the rights of illegitimate children, see *Trimble v. Gordon*, 430 U.S. 762, 97 S.Ct. 1459, 52 L.Ed.2d 31 (1977).

and names his son Jayden as the *successor trustee*, who will take over the management of the trust when James dies or becomes incapacitated. James is the beneficiary during his lifetime and will receive an income from the trust (hence, he is called the *income beneficiary*). On James's death, the farm will pass to his three children without having to go through probate (the children are referred to as *remainder beneficiaries*). By holding the property in a revocable living trust, James still has control over the farm and accounts: he can make changes to the trust or end the trust at any time during his life. After his death, the trust becomes irrevocable, and Jayden, as trustee, must manage and distribute the trust property according to the trust's terms. This trust arrangement is illustrated in Exhibit 30–3. ▣

Irrevocable Living Trusts. In an *irrevocable* living trust, in contrast, the grantor permanently gives up control over the property to the trustee. The grantor executes a trust deed, and legal title to the trust property passes to the named trustee. The trustee has a duty to administer the property as directed by the grantor for the benefit and in the interest of the beneficiaries. The trustee must preserve the trust property; make it productive; and, if required by the terms of the trust agreement, pay income to the beneficiaries, all in accordance with the terms of the trust. Because the grantor has, in effect, given over the property for the benefit of the beneficiaries, he or she is no longer responsible for paying income taxes on the trust earnings.

Testamentary Trusts A **testamentary trust** is created as part of a will and comes into existence on the settlor's death. Although a testamentary trust has a trustee who maintains legal title to the trust property, the trustee's actions are subject to judicial approval. This trustee can be named in the will or be appointed by the court. Thus, a testamentary trust does not fail because a trustee has not been named in the will. The legal responsibilities of the trustee are the same as in an *inter vivos* trust. If the will setting up a testamentary trust is invalid, the trust will also be invalid. The property that was supposed to be in the trust will then pass according to intestacy laws, not according to the terms of the trust.

Charitable Trusts A **charitable trust** is an express trust designed for the benefit of a segment of the public or the public in general. It differs from other types of trusts in that the identities of the beneficiaries are uncertain and it can be established to last indefinitely. Usually, to be deemed a charitable trust, a trust must be created for charitable, educational, religious, or scientific purposes.

Spendthrift Trusts A **spendthrift trust** is created to provide for the maintenance of a beneficiary by preventing him or her from being careless with the bestowed funds. Unlike beneficiaries in other trusts, the beneficiary in a spendthrift trust is not permitted to transfer or assign his or her right to the trust's principal or future payments from the trust (*assignments* were discussed in Chapter 11). Essentially, the beneficiary can draw only a certain portion of the total amount to which he or she is entitled at any one time. The majority of states allow spendthrift trust provisions that prohibit creditors from attaching such trusts.

Totten Trusts A **Totten trust**[5] is created when one person deposits funds in her or his own name with instructions that on the settlor's death, whatever is in that account should go to a specific beneficiary. This trust is revocable at will until the depositor dies or completes the gift during her or his lifetime (by delivering the funds to the intended beneficiary, for example). The beneficiary has no access to the funds until the depositor's death, when the beneficiary obtains property rights to the balance on hand.

Implied Trusts

Sometimes, a trust will be imposed (implied) by law, even in the absence of an express trust. Implied trusts include resulting trusts and constructive trusts.

A **resulting trust** arises from the conduct of the parties. Here, the trust results, or is created, when circumstances raise an inference that the party holding legal title to the

5. This type of trust derives its unusual name from *In re Totten*, 179 N.Y. 112, 71 N.E. 748 (1904).

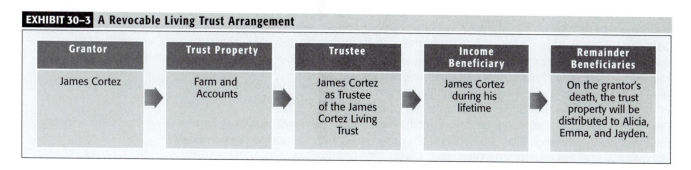

EXHIBIT 30–3 A Revocable Living Trust Arrangement

Grantor	Trust Property	Trustee	Income Beneficiary	Remainder Beneficiaries
James Cortez	Farm and Accounts	James Cortez as Trustee of the James Cortez Living Trust	James Cortez during his lifetime	On the grantor's death, the trust property will be distributed to Alicia, Emma, and Jayden.

property does so for the benefit of another. **■EXAMPLE 30.8** Garrison wants to put land that she owns on the market for sale. Because she is going out of the country for two years and will not be able to deed the property to a buyer during that period, Garrison conveys the property to her good friend Oswald. Oswald can then attempt to sell the property while Garrison is gone. Because Garrison intended neither to sell nor to give the land to Oswald, he will hold the property in trust (a resulting trust) for Garrison's benefit. On Garrison's return, Oswald will be required either to deed back the property to Garrison or, if it has been sold, to turn over the proceeds (held in trust) to her.■

A **constructive trust** is an equitable trust imposed by a court in the interests of fairness and justice. In a constructive trust, the owner is declared to be a trustee for the parties who are, in equity, actually entitled to the benefits that flow from the trust. If someone wrongfully holds legal title to property—because the property was obtained through fraud or in breach of a legal duty, for example—a court may impose a constructive trust.

The Trustee

The *trustee* is the person holding the trust property. Anyone legally capable of holding title to, and dealing in, property can be a trustee. If the settlor of a trust fails to name a trustee, or if a named trustee cannot or will not serve, the trust does not fail—an appropriate court can appoint a trustee. When a settlor creates a trust, he or she may prescribe the trustee's powers and performance. State law governs in the absence of specific terms in the trust.

A trustee must act with honesty, good faith, and prudence in administering the trust and must exercise a high degree of loyalty toward the trust beneficiary. The general standard of care is the degree of care a prudent person would exercise in his or her personal affairs.[6] The duty of loyalty requires that the trustee act in the exclusive interest of the beneficiary.

Among specific duties, a trustee must keep clear and accurate accounts of the trust's administration and furnish complete and correct information to the beneficiary. A trustee must keep trust assets separate from her or his own assets. A trustee has a duty to pay to an income beneficiary the net income of the trust assets at reasonable intervals. A trustee also has a duty to distribute the risk of loss from investments by reasonable diversification and to dispose of assets that do not represent prudent investments. Depending on the particular circumstances, prudent investment choices might include federal, state, or municipal bonds; corporate bonds; and shares of preferred or common stock.

---

6. Revised Uniform Principal and Income Act, Section 2(a)(3); *Restatement (Third) of Trusts (Prudent Investor Rule)*, Section 227. This rule is in force in the majority of states by statute and in a small number of states under the common law.

REVIEWING Insurance, Wills, and Trusts

In June 2009, Bernard Ramish set up a $48,000 trust fund through West Plains Credit Union to provide tuition for his nephew, Nathan Covacek, to attend Tri-State Polytechnic Institute. The trust was established under Ramish's control and went into effect that August. In December, Ramish suffered a brain aneurysm that caused frequent, severe headaches but no other symptoms. In August 2010, Ramish developed heat stroke and collapsed on the golf course at La Prima Country Club. After recuperating at the clubhouse, Ramish quickly wrote his will on the back of a wine list. It stated, "My last will and testament: Upon my death, I give all of my personal property to my friend Bernard Eshom and my home to Lizzie Johansen." He signed the will at the bottom in the presence of five men in the La Prima clubhouse, and all five men signed as witnesses. A week later,

Ramish suffered a second aneurysm and died in his sleep. He was survived by his mother, Dorris Ramish; his nephew, Nathan Covacek; his son-in-law, Bruce Lupin; and his granddaughter, Tori Lupin. Using the information presented in the chapter, answer the following questions.

1 Does Ramish's testament on the back of the wine list meet the requirements for a valid will?

2 Suppose that after Ramish's first aneurysm in 2009, Covacek contacted an insurance company to obtain a life insurance policy on Ramish's life. Would Covacek have had an insurable interest in his uncle's life? Why or why not?

3 What would the order of inheritance have been if Ramish had died intestate?

4 What will most likely happen to the trust fund established for Covacek on Ramish's death?

TERMS AND CONCEPTS

administrator 628
bequest 628
binder 623
charitable trust 633
codicil 630
constructive trust 634
devise 628
devisee 628
executor 628
holographic will 629
insurable interest 623
insurance 622

inter vivos trust 632
intestacy laws 627
intestate 627
legacy 628
legatee 628
nuncupative will 629
per capita 632
per stirpes 632
policy 623
premium 623
probate 630
resulting trust 633

risk 622
risk management 622
spendthrift trust 633
testamentary trust 633
testate 627
testator 627
Totten trust 633
trust 632
underwriter 623
will 627
will substitutes 631

CHAPTER SUMMARY — Insurance, Wills, and Trusts

INSURANCE

Classifications (See page 622.)	See Exhibit 30–1 on pages 624 and 625.
Terminology (See page 623.)	1. *Policy*—The insurance contract. 2. *Premium*—The consideration paid to the insurer for a policy. 3. *Underwriter*—The insurance company. 4. *Parties*—Include the insurer (the insurance company), the insured (the person covered by insurance), an agent (a representative of the insurance company) or a broker (ordinarily an independent contractor), and a beneficiary (a person to receive proceeds under the policy).
Insurable Interest (See page 623.)	An insurable interest exists whenever an individual or entity benefits from the preservation of the health or life of the insured or the property to be insured. For life insurance, an insurable interest must exist at the time the policy is issued. For property insurance, an insurable interest must exist at the time of the loss.
The Insurance Contract (See pages 623–627.)	1. *Laws governing*—The general principles of contract law are applied; the insurance industry is also heavily regulated by the states. 2. *Application*—An insurance applicant is bound by any false statements that appear in the application (subject to certain exceptions), which is part of the insurance contract. Misstatements or misrepresentations may be grounds for voiding the policy. 3. *Effective date*—Coverage on an insurance policy can begin when a *binder* (a written memorandum indicating that a formal policy is pending and stating its essential terms) is written; when the policy is issued; at the time of contract formation; or depending on the terms of the contract, when certain conditions are met. 4. *Provisions and clauses*—See Exhibit 30–2 on page 626. Words will be given their ordinary meanings, and any ambiguity in the policy will be interpreted against the insurance company. 5. *Defenses against payment to the insured*—Defenses include misrepresentation or fraud by the applicant.

WILLS

Terminology (See pages 627–629.)	1. *Intestate*—One who dies without a valid will.

(Continued)

CHAPTER SUMMARY	Insurance, Wills, and Trusts–Continued
Terminology–Continued	2. *Testator*–A person who makes out a will.
	3. *Personal representative*–A person appointed in a will or by a court to settle the affairs of a decedent. A personal representative named in the will is an *executor;* a personal representative appointed by the court for an intestate decedent is an *administrator.*
	4. *Devise*–A gift of real estate by will; may be general or specific. The recipient of a devise is a *devisee.*
	5. *Bequest, or legacy*–A gift of personal property by will; may be general or specific. The recipient of a bequest (legacy) is a *legatee.*
Requirements for a Valid Will (See pages 629–630.)	1. The testator must have testamentary capacity (be of legal age and sound mind at the time the will is made).
	2. A will must be in writing (except for nuncupative wills). A holographic will is completely in the handwriting of the testator.
	3. A will must be signed by the testator; what constitutes a signature varies from jurisdiction to jurisdiction.
	4. A nonholographic will (an attested will) must be witnessed in the manner prescribed by state statute.
	5. A will may have to be *published*–that is, the testator may be required to announce to witnesses that this is his or her "last will and testament"; not required under the Uniform Probate Code.
Revocation of Wills (See page 630.)	1. *By physical act of the maker*–Tearing up, canceling, obliterating, or deliberately destroying part or all of a will.
	2. *By subsequent writing*–
	a. Codicil–A formal, separate document to amend or revoke an existing will.
	b. Second will or new will–A new, properly executed will expressly revoking the existing will.
	3. *By operation of law*–
	a. Marriage–Generally revokes part of a will written before the marriage.
	b. Divorce or annulment–Revokes dispositions of property made under a will to a former spouse.
	c. Subsequently born child–It is *implied* that the child is entitled to receive the portion of the estate granted under intestacy distribution laws.
Probate Procedures (See pages 630–631.)	To probate a will means to establish its validity and to carry the administration of the estate through a court process. Probate laws vary from state to state. Probate procedures may be informal or formal, depending on the size of the estate and other factors, such as whether a guardian for minor children must be appointed.
Intestacy Laws (See pages 631–632.)	1. Intestacy laws vary widely from state to state. Usually, the law provides that the surviving spouse and children inherit the property of the decedent (after the decedent's debts are paid). The spouse usually inherits the entire estate if there are no children, one-half of the estate if there is one child, and one-third of the estate if there are two or more children.
	2. If there is no surviving spouse or child, then, in order, lineal descendants (grandchildren, brothers and sisters, and–in some states–parents of the decedent) inherit. If there are no lineal descendants, then collateral heirs (nieces, nephews, aunts, and uncles of the decedent) inherit.
	<div align="center">**TRUSTS**</div>
Definition (See page 632.)	A trust is any arrangement through which property is transferred from one person to a trustee to be administered for another party's benefit. The essential elements of a trust are (1) a designated

CHAPTER SUMMARY	Insurance, Wills, and Trusts–Continued
Definition—Continued	beneficiary, (2) a designated trustee, (3) a fund sufficiently identified to enable title to pass to the trustee, and (4) actual delivery to the trustee with the intention of passing title.
Express Trusts (See pages 632–633.)	Express trusts are created by explicit terms, usually in writing, and include the following: 1. *Living (inter vivos) trust*—A trust created by a grantor during her or his lifetime. 2. *Testamentary trust*—A trust that is created by will and comes into existence on the death of the grantor. 3. *Charitable trust*—A trust designed for the benefit of a public group or the public in general. 4. *Spendthrift trust*—A trust created to provide for the maintenance of a beneficiary and to protect him or her from spending all the funds to which he or she is entitled. The beneficiary is allowed to withdraw only a certain amount at any one time. 5. *Totten trust*—A trust created when one person deposits funds in his or her own name as a trustee for another.
Implied Trusts (See pages 633–634.)	Implied trusts, which are imposed by law in the interests of fairness and justice, include the following: 1. *Resulting trust*—Arises from the conduct of the parties when an *apparent intention* to create a trust is present. 2. *Constructive trust*—Arises by operation of law when a person wrongfully takes title to property. A court may require the owner to hold the property in trust for those who, in equity, are entitled to enjoy its benefits.

FOR REVIEW

Answers for the even-numbered questions in this **For Review** *section can be found on this text's accompanying Web site at* **www.cengage.com/blaw/fbl**. *Select "Chapter 30" and click on "For Review."*

1 What is an insurable interest? When must an insurable interest exist—at the time the insurance policy is obtained, at the time the loss occurs, or both?

2 Is an insurance broker the agent of the insurance applicant or the agent of the insurer?

3 What are the basic requirements for executing a will? How may a will be revoked?

4 What is the difference between a *per stirpes* distribution and a *per capita* distribution of an estate to the grandchildren of the deceased?

5 What are the four essential elements of a trust? What is the difference between an express trust and an implied trust?

QUESTIONS AND CASE PROBLEMS

HYPOTHETICAL SCENARIOS AND CASE PROBLEMS

30.1 Timing of Insurance Coverage. On October 10, Joleen Vora applied for a $50,000 life insurance policy with Magnum Life Insurance Co.; she named her husband, Jay, as the beneficiary. Joleen paid the insurance company the first year's policy premium on making the application. Two days later, before she had a chance to take the physical examination required by the insurance company and before the policy was issued, Joleen was killed in an automobile accident. Jay submitted a claim to the insurance company for the $50,000. Can Jay collect? Explain.

30.2 Hypothetical Question with Sample Answer. Benjamin is a widower who has two married children, Edward and Patricia. Patricia has two children, Perry and Paul. Edward has no children. Benjamin dies, and his typewritten will leaves all his property equally to his children, Edward and Patricia, and provides that should a child predecease him, the grandchildren are to take *per stirpes*. The will was witnessed by Patricia and by Benjamin's lawyer and was signed by Benjamin in their presence. Patricia has predeceased Benjamin. Edward claims the will is invalid.

1 Discuss whether the will is valid.

2 Discuss the distribution of Benjamin's estate if the will is invalid.

3 Discuss the distribution of Benjamin's estate if the will is valid.

For a sample answer to Question 30.2, go to Appendix E at the end of this text.

30.3 Cancellation of Insurance Policy. James Mitchell bought a building in Los Angeles, California, in February 2000 and applied to United National Insurance Co. for a fire insurance policy. The application stated, among other things, that the building measured 3,420 square feet, it was to be used as a video production studio, the business would generate $300,000 in revenue, and the building had no uncorrected fire code violations. In fact, the building measured less than 2,000 square feet; it was used to film only one music video over a two-day period; the business generated only $6,500 in revenue; and the city had cited the building for combustible debris, excessive weeds, broken windows, missing doors, damaged walls, and other problems. In November, Mitchell met Carl Robinson, who represented himself as a business consultant. Mitchell gave Robinson the keys to the property to show it to a prospective buyer. On November 22, Robinson set fire to the building and was killed in the blaze. Mitchell filed a claim for the loss. United denied the claim and rescinded the policy. Mitchell filed a suit in a California state court against United. Can an insurer cancel a policy? If so, on what ground might United have justifiably canceled Mitchell's policy? What might Mitchell argue to oppose a cancellation? What should the court rule? Explain. [*Mitchell v. United National Insurance Co.*, 127 Cal.App.4th 457, 25 Cal.Rptr.3d 627 (2 Dist. 2005)]

30.4 Case Problem with Sample Answer. Richard Vanderbrook's home in New Orleans, Louisiana, was insured through Unitrin Preferred Insurance Co. His policy excluded coverage for, among other things, "[f]lood, surface water, waves, tidal water, overflow of a body of water, or spray from any of these, whether or not driven by wind." The policy did not define the term *flood*. In August 2005, Hurricane Katrina struck along the coast of the Gulf of Mexico, devastating portions of Louisiana. In New Orleans, some of the most significant damage occurred when the levees along three canals—the 17th Street Canal, the Industrial Canal, and the London Avenue Canal—ruptured and water submerged about 80 percent of the city, including Vanderbrook's home. He filed a claim for the loss, but Unitrin refused to pay.

Vanderbrook and others whose policies contained similar exclusions asked a federal district court to order their insurers to pay. They contended that their losses were due to the negligent design, construction, and maintenance of the levees and that the policies did not clearly exclude coverage for an inundation of water induced by negligence. On what does a decision in this case hinge? What reasoning supports a ruling in the plaintiffs' favor? In the defendants' favor? [*In re Katrina Canal Breaches Litigation*, 495 F.3d 191 (5th Cir. 2007)]

After you have answered Problem 30.4, compare your answer with the sample answer given on the Web site that accompanies this text. Go to www.cengage.com/blaw/fbl, select "Chapter 30," and click on "Case Problem with Sample Answer."

30.5 Wills. James Lillard's first wife had a child whom James adopted when he married the child's mother. James fathered other children with her until they divorced in the early 1970s. In 1975, James married his second wife. During this marriage, each spouse's biological children remained the other's stepchildren, because neither spouse adopted the other's children. James's second wife died in 2002, and he was diagnosed with terminal cancer in January 2004. In February, he executed a will that divided his property equally among all of his children and stepchildren. By October, James was living with his children, who managed his finances and administered his prescribed drugs, which impaired him mentally and physically. A hospice worker noted that on October 5 James had difficulty completing sentences and was forgetful. A visitor two days later described him as "morphined up." On this same day, he tore his first will in half and executed a new will that left most of his property to his children. James died on October 19. His children submitted the second will to a Georgia state court for probate. His stepchildren objected, alleging, among other things, that at the time of its execution, James lacked testamentary capacity. His children responded that the first will had been validly revoked. Which will should be declared valid? Why? [*Lillard v. Owens*, 281 Ga. 619, 641 S.E.2d 511 (2007)]

30.6 Insurance Coverage. PAJ, Inc., a jewelry company, had a commercial general liability (CGL) policy from Hanover Insurance Company. It covered, among other things, liability for advertising injury. The policy required PAJ to notify Hanover of any claim or suit against PAJ "as soon as practicable." Yurman Designs sued PAJ for copyright infringement because of the design of a particular jewelry line. Unaware that the CGL policy applied to this matter, PAJ did not notify Hanover of the suit until four to six months after litigation began. Hanover contended that the late notification violated the terms of the policy, so the policy did not apply to this incident. PAJ sued Hanover, seeking a declaration that it was obligated to defend and indemnify PAJ. The trial court held for Hanover, as did the appeals court. PAJ appealed to the Supreme Court of Texas. Does Hanover have an obligation to provide PAJ assistance, or did

PAJ violate the insurance contract? [*PAJ, Inc. v. Hanover Insurance Co.*, 243 S.W.3d 630 (Sup.Ct. Tex. 2008)]

30.7 **A Question of Ethics.** *Vickie Lynn Smith, an actress and model also known as Anna Nicole Smith, met J. Howard Marshall II in 1991. During their courtship, J. Howard lavished gifts and large sums of money on Anna Nicole, and they married on June 27, 1994. J. Howard died on August 4, 1995. According to Anna Nicole, J. Howard intended to provide for her financial security through a trust, but under the terms of his will, all of his assets were transferred to a trust for the benefit of E. Pierce Marshall, one of J. Howard's sons. While J. Howard's estate was subject to probate proceedings in a Texas state court, Anna Nicole filed for bankruptcy in a federal bankruptcy court. Pierce filed a claim in the bankruptcy proceeding, alleging that Anna Nicole had defamed him when her lawyers told the media that Pierce had engaged in forgery and fraud to gain control of his father's assets. Anna Nicole filed a counterclaim, alleging that Pierce prevented the transfer of his father's assets to a trust for her by, among other things, imprisoning J. Howard against his wishes, surrounding him* with security guards to prevent contact with her, and transferring property against his wishes. [*Marshall v. Marshall*, 547 U.S. 293, 126 S.Ct. 1735, 164 L.Ed.2d 480 (2006)]

1 What is the purpose underlying the requirements for a valid will? Which of these requirements might be at issue in this case? How should it apply here? Why?

2 State courts generally have jurisdiction over the probate of a will and the administration of an estate. Does the Texas state court thus have the sole authority to adjudicate all of the claims in this case? Why or why not?

3 How should Pierce's claim against Anna Nicole and her counterclaim be resolved?

4 Anna Nicole executed her will in 2001. The beneficiary—Daniel, her son, who was not J. Howard's child—died in 2006, shortly after Anna Nicole gave birth to a daughter, Dannielynn. In 2007, before executing a new will, Anna Nicole died. What happens if a will's beneficiary dies before the testator? What happens if a child is born after a will is executed?

CRITICAL THINKING AND WRITING ASSIGNMENTS

30.8 Critical Legal Thinking. Statistics show that the extent of risk assumed by insurance companies varies depending on the gender of the insured. Many people contend that laws prohibiting gender-based insurance rates are thus fundamentally unfair. Why might gender discrimination be fair when it comes to insurance premiums when it is clearly unfair (and illegal) in housing or employment?

30.9 **Video Question.** Go to this text's Web site at **www.cengage.com/blaw/fbl** and select "Chapter 30." Click on "Video Questions" and view the video titled *Double Indemnity*. Then answer the following questions.

1 Recall from the video that Mrs. Dietrichson (Barbara Stanwyck) is attempting to take out an "accident insurance" policy (similar to life insurance) on her husband without his knowledge. Does Mrs. Dietrichson have an insurable interest in the life of her husband? Why or why not?

2 Why would Walter (Fred MacMurray), the insurance agent, refuse to sell Mrs. Dietrichson an insurance policy covering her husband's life without her husband's knowledge?

ACCESSING THE INTERNET

For updated links to resources available on the Web, as well as a variety of other materials, visit this text's Web site at

www.cengage.com/blaw/fbl

The Web site of the Insurance Information Institute provides a wealth of news and information on insurance-related issues, including statistical data, a glossary of insurance terms, and various PowerPoint presentations. Go to

www.iii.org

To find the wills of many famous people, including Benjamin Franklin and Elvis Presley, go to

www.geocities.com/Athens/Acropolis/6537/wills.htm

You can find the Uniform Probate Code, as well as links to various state probate statutes, at Cornell University's Legal Information Institute. Go to

www.law.cornell.edu/uniform/probate.html

The American Academy of Estate Planning Attorneys offers information about various estate-planning tools on its Web site at

www.aaepa.com

PRACTICAL INTERNET EXERCISES

Go to this text's Web site at **www.cengage.com/blaw/fbl**, select "Chapter 30," and click on "Practical Internet Exercises." There you will find the following Internet research exercises that you can perform to learn more about the topics covered in this chapter.

PRACTICAL INTERNET EXERCISE 30-1 SOCIAL PERSPECTIVE—Disappearing Decisions

PRACTICAL INTERNET EXERCISE 30-2 LEGAL PERSPECTIVE—Wills and Trusts

PRACTICAL INTERNET EXERCISE 30-3 MANAGEMENT PERSPECTIVE—Risk Management in Cyberspace

BEFORE THE TEST

Go to this text's Web site at **www.cengage.com/blaw/fbl**, select "Chapter 30," and click on "Interactive Quizzes." You will find a number of interactive questions relating to this chapter.

UNIT NINE **EXTENDED CASE STUDY**

In re Estate of Robertson

Types of real property ownership and the various rights of the owners were discussed in Chapter 29. In a fee simple absolute, the owner has the most rights with respect to the property and can dispose of it in any way. A life estate is an interest in land that lasts only for the life of some specified individual. As explained in Chapter 30, a transfer of real property by will is a devise. With a trust, property is transferred from one person to a trustee to be administered for a third party's benefit. A testamentary trust is created by will to come into existence on the death of its grantor, or settlor (the party whose will creates the trust).

Many limitations and conditions may be imposed on the duration of an owner's interest in real estate, the owner's use of the property, or the owner's transfer of his or her rights in it. The courts will not enforce some conditions, however. For example, a restraint of marriage is universally acknowledged to be an invalid condition of ownership. Thus, if a testator attempted to limit the duration of ownership of a gift of real property by will to the period during which the recipient remained unmarried, the courts would refuse to enforce the devise because its receipt was conditioned on the devisee's never marrying.

In this extended case study, we review **In re Estate of Robertson,**[1] *a case in which a trustee filed a "Petition to Determine Heirs and Disposition of Residential Property" of a testamentary trust. The trustee contended that the beneficiary had violated a valid restraint of marriage set out in the will that had created the trust.*

CASE BACKGROUND Julianna Robertson was married to Lynn Robertson. She was also the mother of James, Bret, and Melissa Nye, and the sole owner of a residence at 320

Blair Pike in Peru, Indiana. Julianna died on January 10, 2002. Her will provided as follows:

> I hereby give and devise my real estate . . . more commonly known as 320 Blair Pike, Peru, Indiana, IN TRUST to James Lewis Nye, as Trustee, for the following uses and purposes, to-wit:

---

1. 859 N.E.2d 772 (Ind.App. 2007).

a) The Trustee shall allow my husband, Lynn D. Robertson, if he survives me, to continue to live at said real estate as if he had been devised a life estate in said real estate, or until he remarries or allows any female companion to live with him who is not a blood relative. . . .

b) Upon the death of my husband, or upon any prior termination of his interest, I devise said real estate to my children, James Louis Nye, Bret Alan Nye, and Melissa Ann Nye, equally, . . . and this Trust shall terminate."

Following Julianna's death, Lynn remarried. James filed a petition with an Indiana state court to probate Julianna's will. The court ruled that the will gave Lynn a life estate in the property at 320 Blair Pike and that the provision limiting his rights to the property if he remarried was an invalid condition in "restraint of marriage." The court voided the condition but upheld the life estate. James appealed these rulings to a state intermediate appellate court.

MAJORITY OPINION

SULLIVAN, Judge.

* * * *

* * * The prohibition of conditions in restraint of marriage as a general matter is not restricted to testamentary transfers. Indeed, such conditions arising in contracts are also void as a matter of public policy. As even Nye explains in his brief, *it is a matter of public policy for society to protect the institution of marriage* * * * . [Emphasis added.]

* * * *

Nye's * * * argument is that the disputed provision in the will making Robertson trust beneficiary of 320 Blair Pike "until he remarries * * * " is a valid limitation rather than an invalid condition. * * *

* * * *

Words of limitation mark the period which is to determine the estate; but words of condition render the estate liable to be defeated in the intermediate time, if the event expressed in the condition arises before the determination of the estate, or completion of the period described by the limitation. The one specifies the utmost time of continuance, and the other marks some event, which, if it takes place in the course of that time, will defeat the estate.

* * * *

* * * [Thus] the provision making Robertson trust beneficiary of 320 Blair Pike "as if he had been devised a life estate in said real estate, or until he remarries" is an invalid condition in restraint of marriage rather than any sort of valid limitation. * * * The determination of whether a provision in restraint of

marriage is a void condition or a valid limitation turns upon the term such provision intends to cover. In [previous cases], the provisions granting property rights for the period of time "as/so long as she remains my widow" were construed to be valid limitations because they were the only available reference point for purposes of determining the length of time such property rights were intended by the testator to last. Such limitations served as "measuring sticks," signaling the period of time the testator intended for the rights to last, rather than as conditions which could operate to divest a beneficiary of property upon the happening of some subsequent event.

Here * * * the "measuring stick" for Robertson's right to 320 Blair Pike was not such period of time until he remarried or cohabited with a female companion, but instead was his lifetime. In providing for Robertson, as beneficiary of her testamentary trust, to continue to live at 320 Blair Pike "as if he had been devised a life estate," it is apparent that Julianna intended Robertson's tenure at 320 Blair Pike to last the entirety of his life, and that such tenure would subsequently be cut short if he were to remarry. Such provision is therefore a void condition in restraint of marriage, not a valid limitation upon the term of the devise.

* * * *

Having found that the testamentary trust provision at issue making Robertson lifetime beneficiary of 320 Blair Pike "until he remarries" to be a void condition in restraint of marriage, we affirm the trial court's order voiding this condition. Accordingly, we conclude, as the trial court did, that Robertson maintains a life interest in the property at 320 Blair Pike subject to the remaining terms of the testamentary trust.

The judgment of the trial court is affirmed.

DISSENTING OPINION

ROBB, Judge, dissenting.

I dissent because the majority's analysis of Nye's * * * argument appears to elevate form over substance * * * .

I acknowledge Indiana's recognition of the difference between conditions and limitations, as well as the importance of classifying language in an instrument transferring property as either a limitation, marking the period that determines an

(Continued)

estate, or a condition, rendering an estate liable to defeat. However, the distinction is only drawn where it is logical to do so, which is not presently the case. Here, the clause "or until he remarries" is a restraint of marriage, and void in light of public policy against such restraints. Regardless of how the instrument is worded, or whether the restrictive language is classified as a condition or a limitation, Lynn gets only a life estate. The language of the bequest allowing Lynn "to Continue to live at said real estate as if he had been devised a life estate in said real estate, or until he remarries" makes it clear he does not receive an interest in fee simple. No matter whether he receives a life estate unless he remarries (void as a condition), or whether he may live on the property so long as he does not remarry (a permitted limitation), the

"measuring stick" is the life of Lynn, and in either case his interest in the property is shortened by remarriage. Thus, either language produces the same result.

Clearly then, under the present circumstances, it should make no difference whether this language is classified as a condition or a limitation because the substance of the clause acts as a restraint of marriage. In other words, the intent behind the use of such a clause—whether to penalize remarriage or to demarcate the period of time an estate shall exist—cannot alter the consequential disincentive to remarry. Under the present circumstances, either both versions of the provision are a restraint on marriage, or neither one is. But having two interpretations here, one considered acceptable and the other invalid, makes no sense.

QUESTIONS FOR ANALYSIS

1   LAW. How does the majority respond to the trustee's argument in this case? What is the majority's reasoning?

2   LAW. How does the dissent analyze the majority's distinction between conditions and limitations?

3   ECONOMIC DIMENSIONS. Does the majority's ruling make real property more alienable (available for transfer), or is the dissent's position more favorable for the real estate market? Why?

4   SOCIAL DIMENSIONS. Why is a restraint on marriage considered to be against public policy?

5   IMPLICATIONS FOR THE GRANTOR. What does the interpretation of the language in the will at the center of this case suggest to grantors who wish to impose certain restrictions on their beneficiaries?

UNIT CONTENTS

CHAPTER 31
Liability of Accountants and Other Professionals

LEARNING OBJECTIVES

AFTER READING THIS CHAPTER, YOU SHOULD BE ABLE TO ANSWER THE FOLLOWING QUESTIONS:

1 Under what common law theories may professionals be liable to clients?

2 What are the rules concerning an auditor's liability to third parties?

3 How might an accountant violate federal securities laws?

4 What crimes might an accountant commit under the Internal Revenue Code?

5 What constrains professionals to keep communications with their clients confidential?

n the past decade or so, accountants, attorneys, physicians, and other professionals have found themselves increasingly subject to liability. This more extensive liability has resulted in large part from a greater public awareness of the fact that professionals are required to deliver competent services and are obligated to adhere to standards of performance commonly accepted within their professions.

Certainly, the dizzying collapse of Enron Corporation and the failure of other major companies, including WorldCom, Inc., in the early 2000s called attention to the importance of abiding by professional accounting standards. Arthur Andersen, LLP, one of the world's leading public accounting firms, ended up being indicted on criminal charges for its role in thwarting the government's investigation into Enron's accounting practices.[1] As a result, Arthur Andersen ceased to exist and roughly 85,000 employees lost their jobs. Moreover, under the Sarbanes-Oxley Act of 2002, which Congress passed in response to these events, public

accounting firms throughout the nation will feel the effects for years to come. Among other things, the act imposed stricter regulation and oversight on the public accounting industry.

Considering the many potential sources of legal liability that may be imposed on them, accountants, attorneys, and other professionals should be very aware of their legal obligations. In the first part of this chapter, we look at the potential common law liability of professionals and then examine the potential liability of accountants under securities laws and the Internal Revenue Code. The chapter concludes with a brief examination of the relationship of professionals, particularly accountants and attorneys, with their clients.

POTENTIAL COMMON LAW LIABILITY TO CLIENTS

Under the common law, professionals may be liable to clients for breach of contract, negligence, or fraud.

Liability for Breach of Contract

Accountants and other professionals face liability for any breach of contract under the common law. A professional owes a duty to his or her client to honor the terms of the contract

---

1. Although Arthur Andersen, LLP, was subsequently convicted in a federal district court on the charge of obstructing justice, the United States Supreme Court reversed and remanded the case in 2005 due to erroneous jury instructions. *Arthur Andersen, LLP v. United States,* 544 U.S. 696, 125 S.Ct. 2129, 161 L.Ed.2d 1008 (2005).

and to perform the contract within the stated time period. If the professional fails to perform as agreed in the contract, then he or she has breached the contract, and the client has the right to recover damages from the professional. A professional may be held liable for expenses incurred by the client in securing another professional to provide the contracted-for services, for penalties imposed on the client for failure to meet time deadlines, and for any other reasonable and foreseeable monetary losses that arise from the professional's breach.

Liability for Negligence

Accountants and other professionals may also be held liable under the common law for negligence in the performance of their services. The elements that must be proved to establish negligence on the part of a professional are as follows:

1 A duty of care existed.

2 That duty of care was breached.

3 The plaintiff suffered an injury.

4 The injury was proximately caused by the defendant's breach of the duty of care.

All professionals are subject to standards of conduct established by codes of professional ethics, by state statutes, and by judicial decisions. They are also governed by the contracts they enter into with their clients. In their performance of contracts, professionals must exercise the established standards of care, knowledge, and judgment generally accepted by members of their professional group. We look below at the duty of care owed by two groups of professionals that frequently perform services for business firms: accountants and attorneys.

Accountant's Duty of Care Accountants play a major role in a business's financial system. Accountants have the necessary expertise and experience in establishing and maintaining accurate financial records to design, control, and audit record-keeping systems; to prepare reliable statements that reflect an individual's or a business's financial status; and to give tax advice and prepare tax returns.

GAAP and GAAS. In performing their services, accountants must comply with **generally accepted accounting principles (GAAP)** and **generally accepted auditing standards (GAAS).** The Financial Accounting Standards Board (FASB, usually pronounced "faz-bee") determines what accounting conventions, rules, and procedures constitute GAAP at a given point in time. GAAS are standards concerning an auditor's professional qualities and the judgment that he or she exercises in performing an audit and report. GAAS are established by the American Institute of Certified Public Accountants. As long as

an accountant conforms to generally accepted accounting principles and acts in good faith, he or she normally will not be held liable to the client for incorrect judgment.

As a general rule, an accountant is not required to discover every impropriety, **defalcation**[2] (embezzlement), or fraud in her or his client's books. If, however, the impropriety, defalcation, or fraud has gone undiscovered because of the accountant's negligence or failure to perform an express or implied duty, the accountant will be liable for any resulting losses suffered by the client. Therefore, an accountant who uncovers suspicious financial transactions and fails to investigate the matter fully or to inform the client of the discovery can be held liable to the client for the resulting loss.

A violation of GAAP and GAAS will be considered *prima facie* evidence of negligence on the part of the accountant. Compliance with GAAP and GAAS, however, does not *necessarily* relieve an accountant from potential legal liability. An accountant may be held to a higher standard of conduct established by state statute and by judicial decisions.

Audits, Qualified Opinions, and Disclaimers. One of the most important tasks that an accountant may perform for a business is an audit. An *audit* is a systematic inspection, by analyses and tests, of a business's financial records. The purpose of an audit is to provide the auditor with evidence to support an opinion on the reliability of the business's financial statements. A normal audit is not intended to uncover fraud or other misconduct. Nevertheless, an accountant may be liable for failing to detect misconduct if a normal audit would have revealed it. Also, if the auditor agreed to examine the records for evidence of fraud or other obvious misconduct and then failed to detect it, he or she may be liable. After performing an audit, the auditor issues an opinion letter stating whether, in his or her opinion, the financial statements fairly present the business's financial position.

In issuing an opinion letter, an auditor may qualify the opinion or include a disclaimer. An opinion that disclaims any liability for false or misleading financial statements is too general, however. A qualified opinion or a disclaimer must be specific and identify the reason for the qualification or disclaimer. For example, an auditor of a corporation might qualify the opinion by stating that there is uncertainty about how a lawsuit against the firm will be resolved. In that situation, the auditor will not be liable if the outcome of the suit is bad for the firm. The auditor could still be liable, however, for failing to discover other problems that an audit in compliance with GAAS and GAAP would have revealed. In a

---

2. This term, pronounced deh-ful-*kay*-shun, is derived from the Latin *de* ("off") and *falx* ("sickle"—a tool for cutting grain or tall grass). In law, the term refers to the act of a defaulter or of an embezzler. As used here, it means embezzlement.

disclaimer, the auditor is basically stating that she or he does not have sufficient information to issue an opinion. Again, the auditor must identify what the problem is and what information is lacking.

Unaudited Financial Statements. Sometimes, accountants are hired to prepare unaudited financial statements. (A financial statement is considered unaudited if incomplete auditing procedures have been used in its preparation or if insufficient procedures have been used to justify an opinion.) Accountants may be subject to liability for failing, in accordance with standard accounting procedures, to designate a balance sheet as "unaudited." An accountant will also be held liable for failure to disclose to a client the facts or circumstances that give reason to believe that misstatements have been made or that a fraud has been committed.

Defenses to Negligence. As this discussion has described, an accountant may be held liable to a client for losses resulting from the accountant's negligence in performing various accounting services. An accountant facing a cause of action for damages based on negligence, however, has several possible defenses, including the following:

1 That the accountant was not negligent.

2 That if the accountant was negligent, this negligence was not the proximate cause of the client's losses.[3]

---

3. See, for example, *Oregon Steel Mills, Inc. v. Coopers & Lybrand, LLP,* 336 Or. 329, 83 P.3d 322 (2004).

3 That the client was also negligent (depending on whether state law allows contributory negligence or comparative negligence as a defense—see Chapter 4).

Attorney's Duty of Care The conduct of attorneys is governed by rules established by each state and by the American Bar Association's Model Rules of Professional Conduct. All attorneys owe a duty to provide competent and diligent representation. Attorneys are required to be familiar with well-settled principles of law applicable to a case and to find law that can be discovered through a reasonable amount of research. The lawyer must also investigate and discover facts that could materially affect the client's legal rights.

Standard of Care. In judging an attorney's performance, the standard used will normally be that of a reasonably competent general practitioner of ordinary skill, experience, and capacity. If an attorney holds himself or herself out as having expertise in a special area of law (for example, intellectual property), then the attorney's standard of care in that area is higher than for attorneys without such expertise.

Misconduct. Generally, a state's rules of professional conduct for attorneys provide that committing a criminal act that reflects adversely on the person's "honesty or trustworthiness, or fitness as a lawyer in other respects" is professional misconduct. The rules often further provide that a lawyer should not engage in conduct involving "dishonesty, fraud, deceit, or misrepresentation." Such rules were in force in Wisconsin when the events in the following case took place.

CASE 31.1 **In re Disciplinary Proceedings against Inglimo**

Supreme Court of Wisconsin, 2007 WI 126, 305 Wis.2d 71, 740 N.W.2d 125 (2007).

FACTS A little more than a decade after Michael Inglimo was admitted to the practice of law in Wisconsin, he started occasionally using marijuana with one of his clients. Inglimo represented this client in a criminal case in 2000 and 2001. He was under the influence of drugs during that trial and was not prepared for it. Later, he wrote checks from bank accounts that he maintained in trust for his clients to purchase a car for himself. He also maintained personal funds in these trust accounts and did not keep a running balance of receipts, disbursements, and the amount remaining in the trust account for each client. He did not record the deposits in the trust account checkbook register. In 2003, he was convicted for misdemeanor possession of marijuana. The state Office of Legal Regulation (OLR) filed a complaint against him. A

referee concluded that he had violated the state's rules of professional conduct for attorneys and recommended that he be suspended from the practice of law for eighteen months. Both Inglimo and the OLR appealed to the Wisconsin Supreme Court.

ISSUE Is an eighteen-month suspension from the practice of law appropriate discipline for an attorney who used drugs and failed to keep his clients' funds in a separate trust account?

DECISION No. The state's highest court concluded that a three-year suspension was necessary to protect the public. It agreed with the OLR that the referee's recommendation of an eighteen-month suspension was too lenient.

REASON The court stated that "an eighteen-month suspension in the current case, given the number and nature of ethical violations, would unduly depreciate the seriousness of attorney Inglimo's professional misconduct." The reviewing court was unimpressed with Inglimo's contention that he had removed "from his life both controlled substances and the persons who connected him to that lifestyle." Unconvinced, the court stated that "a substantial period of suspension is necessary in this case to impress upon attorney Inglimo and

other lawyers in this state the seriousness of the professional misconduct at issue here and to protect the public from similar misconduct in the future."

FOR CRITICAL ANALYSIS—Ethical Consideration *Should an attorney's misbehavior be considered a violation of the rules of professional conduct even if he or she is not convicted of a crime? Discuss.*

Liability for Malpractice. When an attorney fails to exercise reasonable care and professional judgment, she or he breaches the duty of care and can be held liable for **malpractice** (professional negligence). In malpractice cases—as in all cases involving allegations of negligence—the plaintiff must prove that the attorney's breach of the duty of care actually caused the plaintiff to suffer some injury. ■EXAMPLE 31.1 Attorney Colette Boehmer allows the statute of limitations to lapse on the claim of Sufi Carn, her client. Boehmer can be held liable for malpractice because Carn can no longer file a cause of action in this case and has lost a potential award of damages. ■

Liability for Fraud

Recall from Chapter 10 that fraud, or misrepresentation, involves the following elements:

1 A misrepresentation of a material fact has occurred.
2 There is an intent to deceive.
3 The innocent party has justifiably relied on the misrepresentation.
4 For damages, the innocent party must have been injured.

A professional may be held liable for *actual* fraud when he or she intentionally misstates a material fact to mislead his or her client and the client justifiably relies on the misstated fact to his or her injury. A material fact is one that a reasonable person would consider important in deciding whether to act.

In contrast, a professional may be held liable for *constructive* fraud whether or not he or she acted with fraudulent intent. Constructive fraud may be found when an accountant is grossly negligent in performing his or her duties. ■EXAMPLE 31.2 Paula, an accountant, is conducting an audit of National Computing Company (NCC). Paula accepts the explanations of Ron, an NCC officer, regarding certain financial irregularities, despite evidence that contradicts those explanations and indicates that the irregularities may be

illegal. Paula's conduct could be characterized as an intentional failure to perform a duty in reckless disregard of the consequences of such failure. This would constitute gross negligence and could be held to be constructive fraud. ■ Both actual and constructive fraud may potentially lead to an accountant or other professional being held liable to a client for losses resulting from the fraud.

Limiting Professionals' Liability

Accountants and other professionals can limit their liability to some extent by disclaiming it. Depending on the circumstances, a disclaimer that does not meet certain requirements will not be effective, however; and in some situations, a disclaimer may not be effective at all.

Professionals may be able to limit their liability for the misconduct of other professionals with whom they work by organizing the business as a professional corporation (P.C.) or a limited liability partnership (LLP). In some states, a professional who is a member of a P.C. is not personally liable for a co-member's misconduct unless she or he participated in it or supervised the member who acted wrongly. The innocent professional is liable only to the extent of his or her interest in the assets of the firm. This is also true for professionals who are partners in an LLP. P.C.s were discussed in more detail in Chapter 25. LLPs were covered in Chapter 24.

POTENTIAL LIABILITY TO THIRD PARTIES

Traditionally, an accountant or other professional did not owe any duty to a third person with whom she or he had no direct contractual relationship—that is, to any person not in *privity of contract* with the professional. A professional's duty was only to her or his client. Violations of statutory laws, fraud, and other intentional or reckless acts of wrongdoing were the only exceptions to this general rule.

Today, numerous third parties—including investors, shareholders, creditors, corporate managers and directors, regulatory agencies, and others—rely on professional opinions, such as those of auditors, when making decisions. In view of this extensive reliance, many courts have all but abandoned the privity requirement in regard to accountants' liability to third parties.

In this section, we focus primarily on the potential liability of auditors to third parties. Understanding an auditor's common law liability to third parties is critical because often, when a business fails, its independent auditor (accountant) may be one of the few potentially solvent defendants. The majority of courts now hold that auditors can be held liable to third parties for negligence, but the standard for the imposition of this liability varies. There are generally three different views of accountants' liability to third parties, each of which we discuss next.

The *Ultramares* Rule

The traditional rule regarding an accountant's liability to third parties was enunciated by Chief Judge Benjamin Cardozo in *Ultramares Corp. v. Touche*, a case decided in 1931.[4] In *Ultramares*, Fred Stern & Company hired the public accounting firm of Touche, Niven & Company to review Stern's financial records and prepare a balance sheet for the year ending December 31, 1923.[5] Touche prepared the balance sheet and supplied Stern with thirty-two certified copies. According to the certified balance sheet, Stern had a net worth (assets less liabilities) of $1,070,715.26. In reality, however, Stern was insolvent—the company's records had been falsified by Stern's insiders to reflect a positive net worth. In reliance on the certified balance sheets, a lender, Ultramares Corporation, loaned substantial amounts to Stern. After Stern was declared bankrupt, Ultramares brought an action against Touche for negligence in an attempt to recover damages.

The Requirement of Privity The New York Court of Appeals (that state's highest court) refused to impose liability on the accountants and concluded that they owed a duty of care only to those persons for whose "primary benefit" the statements were intended. In this case, Stern was the only person for whose primary benefit the statements were intended. The court held that in the absence of privity or a relationship "so close as to approach that of privity," a party could not recover from an accountant. The court's requirement of privity has since been referred to as the *Ultramares* rule, or the New York rule.

Modified to Allow Near Privity The *Ultramares* rule was restated and somewhat modified in a 1985 New York case, *Credit Alliance Corp. v. Arthur Andersen & Co.*[6] In that case, the court held that if a third party has a sufficiently close relationship or nexus (link or connection) with an accountant, then the *Ultramares* privity requirement may be satisfied even if no accountant-client relationship is established. The rule enunciated in *Credit Alliance* is often referred to as the "near privity" rule. Only a minority of states have adopted this rule of accountants' liability to third parties.

The *Restatement* Rule

The *Ultramares* rule has been severely criticized. Auditors perform much of their work for use by persons who are not parties to the contract; thus, it is asserted that they owe a duty to these third parties. Consequently, there has been an erosion of the *Ultramares* rule, and accountants have increasingly been exposed to potential liability to third parties. The majority of courts have adopted the position taken by the *Restatement (Second) of Torts*. Under the *Restatement*, accountants are subject to liability for negligence not only to their clients but also to foreseen, or known, users—and users within a foreseen class of users—of their reports or financial statements.

Under Section 552(2) of the *Restatement (Second) of Torts*, an accountant's liability extends to:

1 Persons for whose benefit and guidance the accountant intends to supply the information or knows that the recipient intends to supply it, and

2 Persons whom the accountant intends the information to influence or knows that the recipient so intends.

■**EXAMPLE 31.3** Steve, an accountant, prepares a financial statement for Tech Software, Inc., a client, knowing that the client will submit that statement to First National Bank to secure a loan. If Steve makes negligent misstatements or omissions in the statement, the bank may hold Steve liable because he knew that the bank would rely on his work product when deciding whether to make the loan. ■

Liability to Reasonably Foreseeable Users

A small minority of courts hold accountants liable to any users whose reliance on an accountant's statements or reports was *reasonably foreseeable*. This standard has been criticized as extending liability too far and exposing accountants to massive liability.

---

4. 255 N.Y. 170, 174 N.E. 441 (1931).

5. Banks, creditors, stockholders, purchasers, or sellers often rely on a balance sheet as a basis for making decisions relating to a company's business.

6. 65 N.Y.2d 536, 483 N.E.2d 110 (1985). A "relationship sufficiently intimate to be equated with privity" is sufficient for a third party to sue another's accountant for negligence.

The majority of the courts have concluded that the *Restatement*'s approach is the more reasonable one because it allows accountants to control their exposure to liability. Liability is "fixed by the accountants' particular knowledge at the moment the audit is published," not by the foreseeability of the harm that might occur to a third party after the report is released.

Liability of Attorneys to Third Parties

Like accountants, attorneys may be held liable under the common law to third parties who rely on legal opinions to their detriment. Generally, an attorney is not liable to a non-client unless there is fraud (or malicious conduct) by the attorney. The liability principles stated in Section 552 of the *Restatement (Second) of Torts*, however, may apply to attorneys just as they may apply to accountants.

THE SARBANES-OXLEY ACT OF 2002

As previously mentioned, Congress enacted the Sarbanes-Oxley Act in 2002. The act imposes a number of strict requirements on both domestic and foreign public accounting firms that provide auditing services to companies ("issuers") whose securities are sold to public investors. The act defines the term *issuer* as a company that has securities that are registered under Section 12 of the Securities Exchange Act of 1934, that is required to file reports under Section 15(d) of the 1934 act, or that files—or has filed—a registration statement that has not yet become effective under the Securities Act of 1933.

The Public Company Accounting Oversight Board

Among other things, the Sarbanes-Oxley Act increased the degree of government oversight over public accounting practices by creating the Public Company Accounting Oversight Board, which reports to the Securities and Exchange Commission. The board consists of a chair and four other members. As discussed in Chapter 27, the purpose of the board is to oversee the audit of public companies that are subject to securities laws. The goal is to protect public investors and to ensure that public accounting firms comply with the provisions of the Sarbanes-Oxley Act.

Applicability to Public Accounting Firms

Titles I and II of the act set forth the key provisions relating to the duties of the oversight board and the requirements relating to *public accounting firms*—defined by the act as firms and associated persons that are "engaged in the practice of public

accounting or preparing or issuing audit reports." These provisions are summarized in Exhibit 31–1 on the following page. (Provisions relating to corporate fraud and the responsibilities of corporate officers and directors were described in Chapter 27 and listed in Exhibit 27–3 on page 580.)

Requirements for Maintaining Working Papers

Performing an audit for a client involves an accumulation of **working papers**—the various documents used and developed during the audit. These include notes, computations, memoranda, copies, and other papers that make up the work product of an accountant's services to a client. Under case law, which in this instance has been codified in a number of states, working papers remain the accountant's property. It is important for accountants to retain such records in the event that they need to defend against lawsuits for negligence or other actions in which their competence is challenged. The client also has a right to access an accountant's working papers because they reflect the client's financial situation. On a client's request, an accountant must return to the client any of the client's records or journals, and failure to do so may result in liability.

Section 802(a)(1) of the Sarbanes-Oxley Act provides that accountants must maintain working papers relating to an audit or review for five years—subsequently increased to seven years—from the end of the fiscal period in which the audit or review was concluded. A knowing violation of this requirement will subject the accountant to a fine, imprisonment for up to ten years, or both.

POTENTIAL STATUTORY LIABILITY OF ACCOUNTANTS

Both civil and criminal liability may be imposed on accountants under the Securities Act of 1933, the Securities Exchange Act of 1934, and the Private Securities Litigation Reform Act of 1995.[7]

Liability under the Securities Act of 1933

The Securities Act of 1933 requires registration statements to be filed with the Securities and Exchange Commission (SEC) prior to an offering of securities (see Chapter 27).[8] Accountants frequently prepare and certify (attest to the

---

7. Civil and criminal liability may also be imposed on accountants and other professionals under other statutes, including the Racketeer Influenced and Corrupt Organizations Act (RICO). RICO was discussed in Chapter 6.
8. Many securities and transactions are expressly exempted from the 1933 act.

EXHIBIT 31–1 Key Provisions of the Sarbanes-Oxley Act of 2002 Relating to Public Accounting Firms

AUDITOR INDEPENDENCE

To help ensure that auditors remain independent of the firms that they audit, Title II of the Sarbanes-Oxley Act does the following:

- Makes it unlawful for Registered Public Accounting Firms (RPAFs) to perform both audit and nonaudit services for the same company at the same time. Nonaudit services include the following:

    1. Bookkeeping or other services related to the accounting records or financial statements of the audit client.

    2. Financial information systems design and implementation.

    3. Appraisal or valuation services.

    4. Fairness opinions.

    5. Management functions.

    6. Broker or dealer, investment adviser, or investment banking services.

- Requires preapproval for most auditing services from the issuer's (the corporation's) audit committee.

- Requires audit partner rotation by prohibiting RPAFs from providing audit services to an issuer if either the lead audit partner or the audit partner responsible for reviewing the audit has provided such services to that corporation in each of the prior five years.

- Requires RPAFs to make timely reports to the audit committees of the corporations. The report must indicate all critical accounting policies and practices to be used; all alternative treatments of financial information within generally accepted accounting principles that have been discussed with the corporation's management officials, the ramifications of the use of such alternative treatments, and the treatment preferred by the auditor; and other material written communications between the auditor and the corporation's management.

- Makes it unlawful for an RPAF to provide auditing services to an issuer if the corporation's chief executive officer, chief financial officer, chief accounting officer, or controller was previously employed by the auditor and participated in any capacity in the audit of the corporation during the one-year period preceding the date that the audit began.

DOCUMENT RETENTION AND DESTRUCTION

- The Sarbanes-Oxley Act provides that anyone who destroys, alters, or falsifies records with the intent to obstruct or influence a federal investigation or in relation to bankruptcy proceedings can be criminally prosecuted and sentenced to a fine, imprisonment for up to twenty years, or both.

- The act also requires accountants who audit or review publicly traded companies to retain all working papers related to the audit or review for a period of five years (now amended to seven years). Violators can be sentenced to a fine, imprisonment for up to ten years, or both.

---

accuracy of) the issuer's financial statements that are included in the registration statement.

Liability under Section 11 Section 11 of the Securities Act of 1933 imposes civil liability on accountants for misstatements and omissions of material facts in registration statements. An accountant may be liable if he or she prepared any financial statements included in the registration statement that "contained an untrue statement of a material fact or omitted to state a material fact required to be stated therein or necessary to make the statements therein not misleading."[9]

Under Section 11, an accountant's liability for a misstatement or omission of a material fact in a registration statement extends to anyone who acquires a security covered by the registration statement. A purchaser of a security need only demonstrate that she or he has suffered a loss on the security. Proof of reliance on the materially false statement or misleading omission ordinarily is not required. Nor is there a requirement of privity between the accountant and the security purchasers.

The Due Diligence Standard. Section 11 imposes a duty on accountants to use **due diligence** in preparing the financial statements included in the filed registration statements. After a purchaser has proved a loss on the security, the accountant has the burden of showing that he or she exercised due diligence in preparing the financial statements. To avoid liability, the accountant must show that he or she had, "after reasonable investigation, reasonable grounds to believe and did believe, at the time such part of the registration statement became effective, that the statements therein were true and that there was no omission of a material fact required to

---

9. 15 U.S.C. Section 77k(a).

be stated therein or necessary to make the statements therein not misleading."[10] Failure to follow GAAP and GAAS is also proof of a lack of due diligence.

In particular, the due diligence standard places a burden on accountants to verify information furnished by a corporation's officers and directors. The burden of proving due diligence requires an accountant to demonstrate that she or he is free from negligence or fraud. Merely asking questions is not always sufficient to satisfy the requirement. Accountants can be held liable for failing to detect danger signals in documents furnished by corporate officers that, under GAAS, require further investigation under the circumstances.[11]

 When "danger signals" exist, you must investigate the situation further. Remember that persons other than accountants, such as corporate directors, can also be liable for failing to perform due diligence. Courts are more likely to impose liability when someone has ignored warning signs that suggest accounting errors or misstatements. To avoid liability, always investigate financial statements that appear "too good to be true." Compare recent financial statements with earlier ones, read minutes of shareholders' and directors' meetings, and inspect changes in material contracts, bad debts, and newly discovered liabilities. Know what is required to meet due diligence standards in the particular jurisdiction and conduct yourself in a manner that is above reproach.

◼

Defenses to Liability. Besides proving that he or she has acted with due diligence, an accountant can raise the following defenses to Section 11 liability:

1 There were no misstatements or omissions.

2 The misstatements or omissions were not of material facts.

3 The misstatements or omissions had no causal connection to the plaintiff's loss.

4 The plaintiff purchaser invested in the securities knowing of the misstatements or omissions.

Liability under Section 12(2) Section 12(2) of the Securities Act of 1933 imposes civil liability for fraud in rela-

tion to offerings or sales of securities.[12] Liability is based on communication to an investor, whether orally or in the written prospectus (see Chapter 25), of an untrue statement or omission of a material fact.

Penalties and Sanctions for Violations Those who purchase securities and suffer harm as a result of a false or omitted statement, or some other violation, may bring a suit in a federal court to recover their losses and other damages. The U.S. Department of Justice brings criminal actions against those who commit willful violations. The penalties include fines up to $10,000, imprisonment up to five years, or both. The SEC is authorized to seek an injunction against a willful violator to prevent further violations. The SEC can also ask a court to grant other relief, such as an order to a violator to refund profits derived from an illegal transaction.

Liability under the Securities Exchange Act of 1934

Under Sections 18 and 10(b) of the Securities Exchange Act of 1934 and SEC Rule 10b-5, an accountant may be found liable for fraud. A plaintiff has a substantially heavier burden of proof under the 1934 act than under the 1933 act, because under the 1934 act an accountant does not have to prove due diligence to escape liability.

Liability under Section 18 Section 18 of the 1934 act imposes civil liability on an accountant who makes or causes to be made in any application, report, or document a statement that at the time and in light of the circumstances was false or misleading with respect to any material fact.[13]

Section 18 liability is narrow in that it applies only to applications, reports, documents, and registration statements filed with the SEC. This remedy is further limited in that it applies only to sellers and purchasers. Under Section 18, a seller or purchaser must prove one of the following:

1 That the false or misleading statement affected the price of the security.

2 That the purchaser or seller relied on the false or misleading statement in making the purchase or sale and was not aware of the inaccuracy of the statement.

An accountant will not be liable for violating Section 18 if he or she acted in good faith in preparing the financial statement. To demonstrate good faith, an accountant must show that he or she had no knowledge that the financial statement

10. 15 U.S.C. Section 77k(b)(3).
11. See *In re Cardinal Health, Inc. Securities Litigations,* 426 F.Supp.2d 688 (S.D. Ohio 2006); and *In re WorldCom, Inc. Securities Litigation,* 352 F.Supp.2d 472 (S.D.N.Y. 2005).

12. 15 U.S.C. Section 77l.
13. 15 U.S.C. Section 78r(a).

was false and misleading. Acting in good faith also requires that the accountant lacked any intent to deceive, manipulate, defraud, or seek unfair advantage over another party. (Note that "mere" negligence in preparing a financial statement does not lead to liability under the 1934 act. This differs from the 1933 act, under which an accountant is liable for *all* negligent acts.)

In addition to the good faith defense, accountants can escape liability by proving that the buyer or seller knew the financial statement was false and misleading. Sellers and purchasers must bring a cause of action "within one year after the discovery of the facts constituting the cause of action and within three years after such cause of action accrued."[14] A court also has the discretion to assess reasonable costs, including attorneys' fees, against accountants who violate this section.

Liability under Section 10(b) and Rule 10b-5 Accountants additionally face potential legal liability under the antifraud provisions contained in the Securities Exchange Act of 1934 and SEC Rule 10b-5. The scope of these antifraud provisions is very broad and allows private parties to bring civil actions against violators.

Section 10(b) makes it unlawful for any person, including accountants, to use, in connection with the purchase or sale of any security, any manipulative or deceptive device or contrivance in contravention of SEC rules and regulations.[15] Rule 10b-5 further makes it unlawful for any person, by use of any means or instrumentality of interstate commerce, to do the following:

1 To employ any device, scheme, or artifice (pretense) to defraud.

2 To make any untrue statement of a material fact or to omit to state a material fact necessary to make the statements made, in light of the circumstances, not misleading.

3 To engage in any act, practice, or course of business that operates or would operate as a fraud or deceit on any person in connection with the purchase or sale of any security.[16]

Accountants may be held liable only to sellers or purchasers under Section 10(b) and Rule 10b-5. Privity is not necessary for a recovery. An accountant may be found liable not only for fraudulent misstatements of material facts in written material filed with the SEC, but also for any fraudulent oral statements or omissions made in connection with the purchase or sale of any security.

For a plaintiff to succeed in recovering damages under these antifraud provisions, however, she or he must prove intent (*scienter*) to commit the fraudulent or deceptive act. Ordinary negligence is not enough.

Do accountants have a duty to correct misstatements that they discover in *previous* financial statements that they prepared? What if they know that potential investors are relying on those statements? Those were the questions in the following case.

---

14. 15 U.S.C. Section 78r(c).
15. 15 U.S.C. Section 78j(b).

---

16. 17 C.F.R. Section 240.10b-5.

CASE 31.2 ◼ **Overton v. Todman & Co., CPAs**

United States Court of Appeals, Second Circuit, 478 F.3d 479 (2007).

FACTS From 1999 through 2002, Todman & Company, CPAs, a professional corporation, audited the financial statements of Direct Brokerage, Inc. (DBI), a broker-dealer in New York registered with the Securities and Exchange Commission (SEC). Each year, Todman issued an unqualified opinion that DBI's financial statements were accurate. DBI filed its statements and Todman's opinions with the SEC. Despite the certifications of accuracy, Todman made significant errors that concealed DBI's largest liability—its payroll taxes—in the 1999 and 2000 audits. The errors came to light in 2003 when the New York State Division of Taxation subpoenaed DBI's payroll records, and it became clear that the company had not filed or paid its payroll taxes for 1999 or 2000. This put DBI in a precarious financial position, owing the state more than $3 million in unpaid taxes, interest, and penalties. To meet its needs, DBI sought outside investors, including David Overton, who relied on DBI's statements and Todman's opinion for 2002 to invest in DBI. When DBI collapsed under the weight of its liabilities in 2004, Overton and others filed a suit in a federal district court against Todman, asserting in part, fraud under Section 10(b) and Rule 10b-5. The court dismissed the complaint. The plaintiffs appealed to the U.S. Court of Appeals for the Second Circuit.

ISSUE Is an accountant who certifies a financial statement that contains a misstatement, later learns of the misstatement,

CASE 31.2–Continued

knows that potential investors are relying on it, and fails to correct it liable for securities fraud?

DECISION Yes. The U.S. Court of Appeals for the Second Circuit held that an accountant is liable in these circumstances under Section 10(b) and Rule 10b-5. The court vacated the lower court's dismissal and remanded the case "for further proceedings consistent with this opinion."

REASON The appellate court pointed out that "[a]ny person or entity," including an accountant, "who employs a manipulative device or makes a material misstatement (or omission) on which a purchaser or seller of securities relies may be liable as a primary violator under [Section] 10b-5, assuming all of the requirements for primary liability under Rule 10b-5 are met." To be liable, one of the requirements is a "duty to speak." Such a duty arises "when one party has information that the other party is entitled to know because of a fiduciary or other similar relation of trust and confidence between them." When an

accountant issues a certified opinion, it creates the required special relationship with investors. Thus, accountants have a duty to take reasonable steps to correct misstatements that they discover in previous financial statements on which they know the public is relying. Silence in this situation can constitute a false or misleading statement under Section 10(b) and Rule 10b-5. The court cited Section 10(b), which covers "any person," as well as a United States Supreme Court decision that "labeled a critical element under [Section] 10(b) and Rule 10b-5: reliance by potential investors on the accountant's omission"[a] and other authorities.

WHAT IF THE FACTS WERE DIFFERENT?
If Todman had conducted an audit for DBI but had not issued a certified opinion about DBI's financial statements, would the result in this case have been the same? Explain.

a. *Central Bank of Denver v. First Interstate Bank of Denver,* 511 U.S. 164, 114 S.Ct. 1439, 128 L.Ed.2d 119 (1994).

The Private Securities Litigation Reform Act of 1995

The Private Securities Litigation Reform Act of 1995 changed the potential liability of accountants and other professionals in securities fraud cases.[17] Among other things, the act imposed a statutory obligation on accountants to use adequate procedures in an audit to detect any illegal acts of the company being audited. If something illegal is detected, the auditor must disclose it to the company's board of directors, the audit committee, or the SEC, depending on the circumstances.[18]

In terms of liability, the 1995 act provides that in most situations, a party is liable only for the proportion of damages for which he or she is responsible.[19] An accountant who does not participate in, and is unaware of, illegal conduct may not liable for the entire loss caused by the illegality. **EXAMPLE 31.4** Nina, an accountant, helped the president and owner of Midstate Trucking Company draft financial statements that misrepresented the firm's financial condition, but Nina did not participate in, and was not aware of the fraud. Nina might be held liable, but the amount of her liability could be proportionately less than the entire loss. ■

If an accountant knowingly aids and abets a primary violator, the SEC can seek an injunction or monetary damages. **EXAMPLE 31.5** Smith & Jones, an accounting firm, performs an audit for Belco Sales that is so inadequate as to constitute gross negligence. Belco uses the materials provided by Smith & Jones as part of a scheme to defraud investors. When the scheme is uncovered, the SEC can bring an action against Smith & Jones for aiding and abetting on the ground that the firm knew or should have known of the material misrepresentations that were in its audit and on which investors were likely to rely. ■

POTENTIAL CRIMINAL LIABILITY

An accountant may be found criminally liable for violations of the Securities Act of 1933, the Securities Exchange Act of 1934, the Internal Revenue Code, and both state and federal criminal codes. Under both the 1933 act and the 1934 act, accountants may be subject to criminal penalties for *willful* violations—imprisonment for up to ten years and/or a fine of up to $10,000 under the 1933 act and up to $100,000 under the 1934 act. Under the Sarbanes-Oxley Act of 2002, for a securities filing that is accompanied by an accountant's false or misleading certified audit statement, the accountant may be fined up to $5 million, imprisoned for up to twenty years, or both.

---

17. Some parties attempted to bypass the new law by filing their suits in state, rather than federal, courts. Congress acted to block such suits by passing the Securities Litigation Uniform Standards Act of 1998.
18. 15 U.S.C. Section 78j-1.
19. 15 U.S.C. Section 78u-4(g).

The Internal Revenue Code makes aiding or assisting in the preparation of a false tax return a felony punishable by a fine of $100,000 ($500,000 in the case of a corporation) and imprisonment for up to three years.[20] This provision applies to anyone who prepares tax returns for others for compensation, and not just to accountants.[21] A penalty of $250 per tax return is levied on tax preparers for negligent understatement of the client's tax liability. For willful understatement of tax liability or reckless or intentional disregard of rules or regulations, a penalty of $1,000 is imposed.[22]

A tax preparer may also be subject to penalties for failing to furnish the taxpayer with a copy of the return, failing to sign the return, or failing to furnish the appropriate tax identification numbers.[23] In addition, those who prepare tax returns for others may be fined $1,000 per document for aiding and abetting another's understatement of tax liability (the penalty is increased to $10,000 in corporate cases).[24] The tax preparer's liability is limited to one penalty per taxpayer per tax year.

In most states, criminal penalties may be imposed for such actions as knowingly certifying false or fraudulent reports; falsifying, altering, or destroying books of account; and obtaining property or credit through the use of false financial statements.

CONFIDENTIALITY AND PRIVILEGE

Professionals are restrained by the ethical tenets of their professions to keep all communications with their clients confidential.

---

20. 26 U.S.C. Section 7206(2).
21. 26 U.S.C. Section 7701(a)(36).
22. 26 U.S.C. Section 6694.
23. 26 U.S.C. Section 6695.
24. 26 U.S.C. Section 6701.

Attorney-Client Relationships

The confidentiality of attorney-client communications is protected by law, which confers a privilege on such communications. This privilege is granted because of the need for full disclosure to the attorney of the facts of a client's case. To encourage frankness, confidential attorney-client communications relating to representation are normally held in strictest confidence and protected by law. The attorney and her or his employees may not discuss the client's case with anyone—even under court order—without the client's permission. The client holds the privilege, and only the client may waive it—by disclosing privileged information to someone outside the privilege, for example.

Note, however, that since the Sarbanes-Oxley Act, the SEC has implemented new rules requiring attorneys who become aware that a client has violated securities laws to report the violation to the SEC. Reporting a client's misconduct could be a breach of the attorney-client privilege and has caused much controversy in the legal community.

Accountant-Client Relationships

In a few states, accountant-client communications are privileged by state statute. In these states, accountant-client communications may not be revealed even in court or in court-sanctioned proceedings without the client's permission. The majority of states, however, abide by the common law, which provides that, if a court so orders, an accountant must disclose information about his or her client to the court. Physicians and other professionals may similarly be compelled to disclose in court information given to them in confidence by patients or clients.

Communications between professionals and their clients—other than those between an attorney and her or his client—are not privileged under federal law. In cases involving federal law, state-provided rights to confidentiality of accountant-client communications are not recognized. Thus, in those cases, in response to a court order, an accountant must provide the information sought.

REVIEWING Liability of Accountants and Other Professionals

Superior Wholesale Corporation planned to purchase Regal Furniture, Inc., and wished to determine Regal's net worth. Superior hired Lynette Shuebke, of the accounting firm Shuebke Delgado, to review an audit that had been prepared by Norman Chase, the accountant for Regal.

Shuebke advised Superior that Chase had performed a high-quality audit and that Regal's inventory on the audit dates was stated fairly on the general ledger. As a result of these representations, Superior went forward with its purchase of Regal. After the purchase, Superior discovered that the audit by Chase had been materially inaccurate and misleading, primarily because the inventory had been grossly overstated on the balance sheet. Later, a former Regal employee who had begun working for Superior exposed an e-mail exchange between Chase and former Regal chief executive officer Buddy Gantry. The exchange revealed that Chase had cooperated in overstating the inventory and understating Regal's tax liability. Using the information presented in the chapter, answer the following questions.

1 If Shuebke's review was conducted in good faith and conformed to generally accepted accounting principles, could Superior hold Shuebke Delgado liable for negligently failing to detect material omissions in Chase's audit? Why or why not?

2 According to the rule adopted by the majority of courts to determine accountants' liability to third parties, could Chase have been liable to Superior?

3 Generally, what requirements must be met before Superior can recover damages under Section 10(b) of the Securities Exchange Act of 1934 and SEC Rule 10b-5? Could Superior meet these requirements?

4 Suppose that a court determined that Chase had aided Regal in willfully understating its tax liability. What is the maximum penalty that could be imposed on Chase?

TERMS AND CONCEPTS

defalcation 645
due diligence 650
generally accepted accounting
   principles (GAAP) 645

generally accepted auditing
   standards (GAAS) 645

malpractice 647
working papers 649

CHAPTER SUMMARY   Liability of Accountants and Other Professionals

COMMON LAW LIABILITY

Potential Common Law Liability to Clients
(See pages 644–647.)

1. *Breach of contract*—An accountant or other professional who fails to perform according to his or her contractual obligations can be held liable for breach of contract and resulting damages.

2. *Negligence*—An accountant or other professional, in performance of her or his duties, must use the care, knowledge, and judgment generally used by professionals in the same or similar circumstances. Failure to do so is negligence. An accountant's violation of generally accepted accounting principles and generally accepted auditing standards is *prima facie* evidence of negligence. An accountant who reveals confidential information or the contents of working papers without the client's permission or a court order can be held liable for malpractice.

3. *Fraud*—Actual intent to misrepresent a material fact to a client, when the client relies on the misrepresentation, is fraud. Gross negligence in performance of duties is constructive fraud.

Potential Liability to Third Parties
(See pages 647–649.)

An accountant may be liable for negligence to any third person the accountant knows or should have known will benefit from the accountant's work. The standard for imposing this liability varies, but generally courts follow one of the following rules:

1. *Ultramares rule*—Liability will be imposed only if the accountant is in privity, or near privity, with the third party.

2. *Restatement rule*—Liability will be imposed only if the third party's reliance is foreseen, or known, or if the third party is among a class of foreseen, or known, users. The majority of courts follow this rule.

3. *"Reasonably foreseeable user" rule*—Liability will be imposed if the third party's use was reasonably foreseeable.

STATUTORY LIABILITY

The Sarbanes–Oxley Act of 2002
(See page 649.)

1. *Purpose*—The purpose of this act was to impose requirements on public accounting firms that provide auditing services to companies whose securities are sold to public investors.

2. *Government oversight*—Among other things, the act created the Public Company Accounting Oversight Board to provide government oversight over public accounting practices.

(Continued)

CHAPTER SUMMARY	Liability of Accountants and Other Professionals—Continued
The Sarbanes–Oxley Act of 2002—Continued	3. *Working papers*—The act requires accountants to maintain working papers relating to an audit or review for seven years from the end of the fiscal period in which the audit or review was concluded. 4. *Other requirements*—See Exhibit 31–1 on page 650.
Securities Act of 1933, Section 11 (See pages 649–651.)	An accountant who makes a false statement or omits a material fact in audited financial statements required for registration of securities under the law may be liable to anyone who acquires securities covered by the registration statement. The accountant's defense is basically the use of due diligence and the reasonable belief that the work was complete and correct. The burden of proof is on the accountant. Willful violations of this act may be subject to criminal penalties.
Securities Act of 1933, Section 12(2) (See page 651.)	In some jurisdictions, an accountant may be liable for aiding and abetting the seller or offeror of securities when a prospectus or communication presented to an investor contained an untrue statement or omission of a material fact. To be liable, the accountant must have known, or at least should have known, that an untrue statement or omission of material fact existed in the offer to sell the security.
Securities Exchange Act of 1934, Sections 10(b) and 18 (See pages 651–653.)	Accountants are held liable for false and misleading applications, reports, and documents required under the act. The burden is on the plaintiff, and the accountant has numerous defenses, including good faith and lack of knowledge that what was submitted was false. Willful violations of this act may be subject to criminal penalties.
Potential Criminal Liability (See pages 653–654.)	1. Aiding or assisting in the preparation of a false tax return is a felony. Aiding and abetting an individual's understatement of tax liability is a separate crime. 2. Tax preparers who negligently or willfully understate a client's tax liability or who recklessly or intentionally disregard Internal Revenue rules or regulations are subject to criminal penalties. 3. Tax preparers who fail to provide a taxpayer with a copy of the return, fail to sign the return, or fail to furnish the appropriate tax identification numbers may also be subject to criminal penalties.

FOR REVIEW

Answers for the even-numbered questions in this **For Review** *section can be found on this text's accompanying Web site at* **www.cengage.com/blaw/fbl**. *Select "Chapter 31" and click on "For Review."*

1 Under what common law theories may professionals be liable to clients?

2 What are the rules concerning an auditor's liability to third parties?

3 How might an accountant violate federal securities laws?

4 What crimes might an accountant commit under the Internal Revenue Code?

5 What constrains professionals to keep communications with their clients confidential?

QUESTIONS AND CASE PROBLEMS

HYPOTHETICAL SCENARIOS AND CASE PROBLEMS

31.1 The *Ultramares* Rule. Larkin, Inc., retains Howard Perkins to manage its books and prepare its financial statements. Perkins, a certified public accountant, lives in Indiana and practices there. After twenty years, Perkins has become a bit bored with generally accepted accounting principles and has adopted more creative accounting methods. Now, though, Perkins has a problem, as he is being sued by Molly Tucker, one of Larkin's creditors. Tucker alleges that Perkins either knew or should have known that Larkin's financial statements would be distributed to various individuals. Furthermore, she asserts that these financial statements were negligently prepared and seriously inaccurate. What are the consequences of Perkins's failure to follow generally accepted accounting principles? Under the traditional *Ultramares* rule, can Tucker recover damages from Perkins? Explain.

31.2 Hypothetical Question with Sample Answer. The accounting firm of Goldman, Walters, Johnson & Co. prepared financial statements for Lucy's Fashions, Inc. After reviewing the various financial statements, Happydays State Bank agreed to loan Lucy's Fashions $35,000 for expansion. When Lucy's Fashions declared bankruptcy under Chapter 11 six months later, Happydays State Bank promptly filed an action against Goldman, Walters, Johnson & Co., alleging negligent preparation of financial statements. Assuming that the court has abandoned the *Ultramares* approach, what is the result? What are the policy reasons for holding accountants liable to third parties with whom they are not in privity?

For a sample answer to Question 31.2, go to Appendix E at the end of this text.

31.3 Accountant's Liability under Rule 10b-5. In early 1995, Bennett, Inc., offered a substantial number of new common shares to the public. Harvey Helms had a long-standing interest in Bennett because his grandfather had once been president of the company. On receiving a prospectus prepared and distributed by Bennett, Helms was dismayed by the pessimism it embodied. Helms decided to delay purchasing stock in the company. Later, Helms asserted that the prospectus prepared by the accountants was overly pessimistic and contained materially misleading statements. Discuss fully how successful Helms would be in bringing a cause of action under Rule 10b-5 against the accountants of Bennett, Inc.

31.4 Accountant's Liability under the Private Securities Litigation Reform Act. Solucorp Industries, Ltd., a corporation headquartered in New York, develops and markets products for use in environmental clean-ups. Solucorp's financial statements for the six months ending December 31, 1997, recognized $1.09 million in license fees payable by Smart International, Ltd. The fees comprised about 50 percent of Solucorp's revenue for the period. At the time, however, the parties had a license agreement only "in principle," and Smart had made only one payment of $150,000. Glenn Ohlhauser, an accountant asked to audit the statements, objected to the inclusion of the fees. In February 1998, Solucorp showed Ohlhauser a license agreement backdated to September 1997 but refused to provide any financial information about Smart. Ohlhauser issued an unqualified opinion on the 1997 statements, which were included with forms filed with the Securities and Exchange Commission (SEC). The SEC sued Ohlhauser. What might be the basis in the Private Securities Litigation Reform Act for the SEC's suit? What might be

Ohlhauser's defense? Discuss. [*Securities and Exchange Commission v. Solucorp Industries, Ltd.*, 197 F.Supp.2d 4 (S.D.N.Y. 2002)]

31.5 Case Problem with Sample Answer. In October 1993, Marilyn Greenen, a licensed certified public accountant (CPA), began working at the Port of Vancouver, Washington (the Port), as an account manager. She was not directly engaged in public accounting at the Port, but she oversaw the preparation of financial statements and supervised employees with accounting duties. At the start of her employment, she enrolled her husband for benefits under the Port's medical plan. Her marriage was dissolved in November, but she did not notify the Port of the change. In May 1998 and April 1999, the Port confronted her about the divorce, but she did not update her insurance information. After she was terminated, she reimbursed the Port for the additional premiums it had paid for unauthorized coverage for her former spouse. The Washington State Board of Accountancy imposed sanctions on Greenen for "dishonesty and misleading representations" while, in the words of an applicable state statute, "representing oneself as a CPA." Greenen asked a Washington state court to review the case. What might be an appropriate sanction in this case? What might be Greenen's best argument against the board's action? On what reasoning might the court uphold the decision? [*Greenen v. Washington State Board of Accountancy*, 824 Wash.App. 126, 110 P.3d 224 (Div. 2 2005)]

After you have answered Problem 31.5, compare your answer with the sample answer given on the Web site that accompanies this text. Go to www.cengage.com/blaw/fbl, select "Chapter 31," and click on "Case Problem with Sample Answer."

31.6 Confidentiality and Privilege. Napster, Inc., offered a service that allowed its users to browse digital music files on other users' computers and download selections for free. Music industry principals filed a suit in a federal district court against Napster, alleging copyright infringement. The court ordered Napster to remove from its service files that were identified as infringing. Napster failed to comply and was shut down in July 2001. In October, Bertelsmann AG, a German corporation, loaned Napster $85 million to fund its anticipated transition to a licensed digital music distribution system. The terms allowed Napster to spend the loan on "general, administrative and overhead expenses." In an e-mail, Hank Barry, Napster's chief executive officer, referred to a "side deal" under which Napster could use up to $10 million of the loan to pay litigation expenses. Napster failed to launch the new system before declaring bankruptcy in June 2002. Some of the plaintiffs filed a suit in a federal district court against Bertelsmann, charging that by its loan, it prolonged Napster's infringement. The plaintiffs asked the court to order the disclosure of all attorney-client communications related to the loan. What principle could Bertelsmann assert to protect these communications?

What is the purpose of this protection? Should this principle protect a client who consults an attorney for advice that will help the client commit fraud? Should the court grant the plaintiffs' request? Discuss. [*In re Napster, Inc. Copyright Litigation*, 479 F.3d 1078 (9th Cir. 2007)]

31.7 Accountant's Liability for Audit. A West Virginia bank ran its asset value from $100 million to $1 billion over seven years by aggressively marketing subprime loans. The Office of the Comptroller of the Currency, a federal regulator, audited the bank and discovered that the books had been "cooked" (falsified) for several years, and that the bank was insolvent. The comptroller closed the bank and brought criminal charges against its managers. The comptroller fined Grant Thornton, the bank's accounting firm, $300,000 for recklessly failing to meet Generally Accepted Auditing Standards during the years it audited the bank. The comptroller claimed that Thornton violated federal law by "participating in . . . unsafe and unsound banking practice." Thornton appealed, contending that it was not involved in bank operations to that extent based on its audit function. What would be the key to determining if the accounting firm could be held liable for that violation of federal law? [*Grant Thornton, LLP v. Office of the Comptroller of the Currency*, 514 F.3d 1328 (D.C.Cir. 2008)]

31.8 **A Question of Ethics.** *Portland Shellfish Co. processes live shellfish in Maine. As one of the firm's two owners, Frank Wetmore held 300 voting and 150 nonvoting shares of the stock. Donna Holden held the other 300 voting shares. Donna's husband, Jeff, managed the company's daily operations, including production, procurement, and sales. The board of directors consisted of Frank and Jeff. In 2001, disagreements arose over the company's management. The Holdens invoked the "Shareholders' Agreement," which provided that "[i]n the event of a deadlock, the directors shall hire an accountant at [MacDonald, Page, Schatz, Fletcher & Co., LLC] to deter-*

mine the value of the outstanding shares. . . . [E]ach shareholder shall have the right to buy out the other shareholder(s)' interest." MacDonald Page estimated the stock's "fair market value" to be $1.09 million. Donna offered to buy Frank's shares at a price equal to his proportionate share. Frank countered by offering $1.25 million for Donna's shares. Donna rejected Frank's offer and insisted that he sell his shares to her or she would sue. In the face of this threat, Frank sold his shares to Donna for $750,705. Believing the stock to be worth more than twice MacDonald Page's estimate, Frank filed a suit in a federal district court against the accountant. [Wetmore v. MacDonald, Page, Schatz, Fletcher & Co., LLC, 476 F.3d 1 (1st Cir. 2007)]

1 Frank claimed that in valuing the stock, the accountant disregarded "commonly accepted and reliable methods of valuation in favor of less reliable methods." He alleged negligence, among other things. MacDonald Page filed a motion to dismiss the complaint. What are the elements that establish negligence? Which is the most critical element in this case?

2 MacDonald Page evaluated the company's stock by identifying its "fair market value," defined as "[t]he price at which the property would change hands between a willing buyer and a willing seller, neither being under a compulsion to buy or sell and both having reasonable knowledge of relevant facts." The accountant knew that the shareholders would use its estimate to determine the price that one would pay to the other. Under these circumstances, was Frank's injury foreseeable? Explain.

3 What factor might have influenced Frank to sell his shares to Donna even if he thought that MacDonald Page's "fair market value" figure was less than half what it should have been? Does this factor represent an unfair, or unethical, advantage? Why or why not?

CRITICAL THINKING AND WRITING ASSIGNMENTS

31.9 Critical Legal Thinking. In cases involving third parties who have suffered losses in reliance on negligent misrepresentation in accountants' financial reports, the courts apply different standards to assess liability. Some courts impose liability only when there is privity between the accountant and the party who seeks recovery. Other courts impose liability under a foreseeability rule. What do you see as the implications of imposing liability on accountants for losses suffered by third parties on the basis of foreseeability rather than privity?

31.10 Video Question. Go to this text's Web site at **www.cengage.com/blaw/fbl** and select "Chapter 31." Click on "Video Questions" and view the video titled *Accountant's Liability*. Then answer the following questions.

1 Should Ray prepare a financial statement that values a list of assets provided by the advertising firm without verifying that the firm actually owns these assets?

2 Discuss whether Ray is in privity with the company interested in buying Laura's advertising firm.

3 Under the *Ultramares* rule, to whom does Ray owe a duty?

4 Assume that Laura did not tell Ray that she intended to give the financial statement to the potential acquirer. Would this fact change Ray's liability under the *Ultramares* rule? Explain.

ACCESSING THE INTERNET

For updated links to resources available on the Web, as well as a variety of other materials, visit this text's Web site at

www.cengage.com/blaw/fbl

The Web site for the Financial Accounting Standards Board can be found at

www.fasb.org

For information on the accounting profession, including links to the Sarbanes-Oxley Act of 2002 and articles on its impact on the accounting profession, go to the Web site of the American Institute of Certified Public Accountants at

www.aicpa.org

Federal tax forms and federal tax information are available from the Internal Revenue Service at its Web site, which can be found at

www.irs.gov

Paul R. Rice, a law professor at American University's Washington College of Law, maintains a Web site containing a large number of articles on attorney-client privilege. Go to

www.acprivilege.com

PRACTICAL INTERNET EXERCISES

Go to this text's Web site at **www.cengage.com/blaw/fbl**, select "Chapter 31," and click on "Practical Internet Exercises." There you will find the following Internet research exercises that you can perform to learn more about the topics covered in this chapter.

PRACTICAL INTERNET EXERCISE 31-1   LEGAL PERSPECTIVE—The Sarbanes-Oxley Act of 2002

PRACTICAL INTERNET EXERCISE 31-2   MANAGEMENT PERSPECTIVE—Avoiding Legal Liability

BEFORE THE TEST

Go to this text's Web site at **www.cengage.com/blaw/fbl**, select "Chapter 31," and click on "Interactive Quizzes." You will find a number of interactive questions relating to this chapter.

CHAPTER 32
International Law in a Global Economy

AFTER READING THIS CHAPTER, YOU SHOULD BE ABLE TO ANSWER THE FOLLOWING QUESTIONS:

1 What is the principle of comity, and why do courts deciding disputes involving a foreign law or judicial decree apply this principle?

2 What is the act of state doctrine? In what circumstances is this doctrine applied?

3 Under the Foreign Sovereign Immunities Act of 1976, on what bases might a foreign state be considered subject to the jurisdiction of U.S. courts?

4 What types of provisions, or clauses, are often included in international sales contracts?

5 Do U.S. laws prohibiting employment discrimination apply in all circumstances to U.S. employees working for U.S. employers abroad?

International business transactions are not unique to the modern world. Indeed, people have always found that they can benefit from exchanging goods with others. What is new in our day is the dramatic growth in world trade and the emergence of a global business community. Because the exchange of goods, services, and ideas on a global level is now routine, students of business law and the legal environment should be familiar with the laws pertaining to international business transactions.

Laws affecting the international legal environment of business include both international law and national law. **International law** can be defined as a body of law—formed as a result of international customs, treaties, and organizations—that governs relations among or between nations. International law may be public, creating standards for the nations themselves; or it may be private, establishing international standards for private transactions that cross national borders. **National law** is the law of a particular nation, such as Brazil, Germany, Japan, or the United States.

In this chapter, we examine how both international law and national law frame business operations in the international context. We also look at some selected areas relating to business activities in a global context, including international sales contracts, civil dispute resolution, letters of credit, and

investment protection. We conclude the chapter with a discussion of the application of certain U.S. laws in a transnational setting.

INTERNATIONAL LAW— SOURCES AND PRINCIPLES

The major difference between international law and national law is that government authorities can enforce national law. What government, however, can enforce international law? By definition, a *nation* is a sovereign entity—which means that there is no higher authority to which that nation must submit. If a nation violates an international law and persuasive tactics fail, other countries or international organizations have no recourse except to take coercive actions—from severance of diplomatic relations and boycotts to, as a last resort, war—against the violating nation.

In essence, international law is the result of centuries-old attempts to reconcile the traditional need of each country to be the final authority over its own affairs with the desire of nations to benefit economically from trade and harmonious relations with one another. Sovereign nations can, and do, voluntarily agree to be governed in certain respects by international law for the purpose of facilitating international trade and commerce, as well as civilized discourse. As a result, a body of international law has evolved. In this section, we examine the primary sources and characteristics of that body of law, as well as some important legal principles and doctrines that have been developed over time to facilitate dealings among nations.

Sources of International Law

Basically, there are three sources of international law: international customs, treaties and international agreements, and international organizations and conferences. We look at each of these sources here.

International Customs   One important source of international law consists of the international customs that have evolved among nations in their relations with one another. Article 38(1) of the Statute of the International Court of Justice refers to an international custom as "evidence of a general practice accepted as law." The legal principles and doctrines that you will read about shortly are rooted in international customs and traditions that have evolved over time in the international arena.

Treaties and International Agreements   Treaties and other explicit agreements between or among foreign nations provide another important source of international law. A **treaty** is an agreement or contract between two or more nations that must be authorized and ratified by the supreme power of each nation. Under Article II, Section 2, of the U.S. Constitution, the president has the power "by and with the Advice and Consent of the Senate, to make Treaties, provided two-thirds of the Senators present concur."

A *bilateral* agreement, as the term implies, is an agreement formed by two nations to govern their commercial exchanges or other relations with one another. A *multilateral* agreement is formed by several nations. For example, regional trade associations such as the European Union (EU, which will be discussed later in this chapter) are the result of multilateral trade agreements. Other regional trade associations that have been created through multilateral agreements include the Association of Southeast Asian Nations (ASEAN) and the Andean Common Market (ANCOM).

International Organizations   In international law, the term **international organization** generally refers to an organization composed mainly of officials of member nations and usually established by treaty. The United States is a member of more than one hundred multilateral and bilateral organizations, including at least twenty through the United Nations. These organizations adopt resolutions, declarations, and other types of standards that often require nations to behave in a particular manner. The General Assembly of the United Nations, for example, has adopted numerous nonbinding resolutions and declarations that embody principles of international law. Disputes with respect to these resolutions and declarations may be brought before the International Court of Justice. That court, however, normally has authority to settle legal disputes only when nations voluntarily submit to its jurisdiction.

The United Nations Commission on International Trade Law has made considerable progress in establishing uniformity in international law as it relates to trade and commerce. One of the commission's most significant creations to date is the 1980 Convention on Contracts for the International Sale of Goods (CISG). As discussed in Chapter 14, the CISG is similar to Article 2 of the Uniform Commercial Code in that it is designed to settle disputes between parties to sales contracts. It spells out the duties of international buyers and sellers that will apply if the parties have not agreed otherwise in their contracts.

Common Law and Civil Law Systems

Companies operating in foreign nations are subject to the laws of those nations. In addition, international disputes often are resolved through the court systems of foreign nations. Therefore, businesspersons should understand that legal systems around the globe generally are divided into *common law* and *civil law* systems. As discussed in Chapter 1, in a common law system, the courts independently develop the rules governing certain areas of law, such as torts and contracts. These common law rules apply to all areas not covered by statutory law. Although the common law doctrine of *stare decisis* obligates judges to follow precedential decisions in their jurisdictions, courts may modify or even overturn precedents when deemed necessary.

In contrast to common law countries, most of the European nations, as well as nations in Latin America, Africa, and Asia, base their legal systems on Roman civil law, or "code law." The term *civil law*, as used here, refers not to civil as opposed to criminal law but to *codified* law—an ordered grouping of legal principles enacted into law by a legislature or other governing body. In a **civil law system,** the only official source of law is a statutory code. Courts interpret the code and apply the rules to individual cases, but courts may not depart from the code and develop their own laws. In theory, the law code sets forth all of the principles needed for the legal system. Trial procedures also differ in civil law systems. Unlike judges in common law systems, judges in civil systems often actively question witnesses. (See Exhibit 1–3 on page 10 for a list of nations that use civil law systems and common law systems.)

International Principles and Doctrines

Over time, a number of legal principles and doctrines have evolved and have been employed—to a greater or lesser extent—by the courts of various nations to resolve or reduce conflicts that involve a foreign element. The three important legal principles and doctrines discussed in the following subsections are based primarily on courtesy and respect and are applied in the interests of maintaining harmonious relations among nations.

The Principle of Comity   Under what is known as the principle of **comity,** one nation will defer to and give effect to the laws and judicial decrees of another country, as long as those laws and judicial decrees are consistent with the law and public policy of the accommodating nation.

■EXAMPLE 32.1 A Swedish seller and a U.S. buyer have formed a contract, which the buyer breaches. The seller sues the buyer in a Swedish court, which awards damages. The buyer's assets, however, are in the United States and cannot be reached unless the judgment is enforced by a U.S. court of law. In this situation, if a U.S. court determines that the procedures and laws applied in the Swedish court were consistent with U.S. national law and policy, that court will likely defer to (and enforce) the foreign court's judgment. ■

One way to understand the principle of comity (and the *act of state doctrine,* which will be discussed shortly) is to consider the relationships among the states in our federal form of government. Each state honors (gives "full faith and credit" to) the contracts, property deeds, wills, and other legal obligations formed in other states, as well as judicial decisions with respect to such obligations. On a worldwide basis, nations similarly attempt to honor judgments rendered in other countries when it is feasible to do so. Of course, in the United States the states are constitutionally required to honor other states' actions, whereas internationally, nations are not *required* to honor the actions of other nations.

The Act of State Doctrine   The **act of state doctrine** is a judicially created doctrine that provides that the judicial branch of one country will not examine the validity of public acts committed by a recognized foreign government within its own territory. The act of state doctrine can have important consequences for individuals and firms doing business with, and investing in, other countries. For example, this doctrine is frequently employed in situations involving expropriation or confiscation. **Expropriation** occurs when a government seizes a privately owned business or privately owned goods for a proper public purpose and awards just compensation. When a government seizes private property for an illegal purpose or without just compensation, the taking is referred to as

a **confiscation.** The line between these two forms of taking is sometimes blurred because of differing interpretations of what is illegal and what constitutes just compensation.

■EXAMPLE 32.2 Flaherty, Inc., a U.S. company, owns a mine in Brazil. The government of Brazil seizes the mine for public use and claims that the profits that Flaherty realized from the mine in preceding years constitute just compensation. Flaherty disagrees, but the act of state doctrine may prevent the company's recovery in a U.S. court. ■ Note that in a case alleging that a foreign government has wrongfully taken the plaintiff's property, the defendant government has the burden of proving that the taking was an expropriation, not a confiscation.

When applicable, both the act of state doctrine and the doctrine of *sovereign immunity* (to be discussed next) tend to immunize (protect) foreign governments from the jurisdiction of U.S. courts. This means that firms or individuals who own property overseas often have diminished legal protection against government actions in the countries in which they operate.

The Doctrine of Sovereign Immunity   When certain conditions are satisfied, the doctrine of **sovereign immunity** immunizes foreign nations from the jurisdiction of U.S. courts. In 1976, Congress codified this rule in the Foreign Sovereign Immunities Act (FSIA).[1] The FSIA exclusively governs the circumstances in which an action may be brought in the United States against a foreign nation, including attempts to attach a foreign nation's property. Because the law is jurisdictional in nature, a plaintiff has the burden of showing that a defendant is not entitled to sovereign immunity.

Section 1605 of the FSIA sets forth the major exceptions to the jurisdictional immunity of a foreign state. A foreign state is not immune from the jurisdiction of U.S. courts in the following situations:

1 When the foreign state has waived its immunity either explicitly or by implication.

2 When the foreign state has engaged in commercial activity within the United States or in commercial activity outside the United States that has "a direct effect in the United States."[2]

3 When the foreign state has committed a tort in the United States or has violated certain international laws.

In applying the FSIA, questions frequently arise as to whether an entity is a "foreign state" and what constitutes a

---

1. 28 U.S.C. Section 1602–1611.
2. See, for example, *Keller v. Central Bank of Nigeria,* 277 F.3d 811 (6th Cir. 2002), in which the court held that failure to pay promised funds to a Cleveland account was an action having a direct effect in the United States.

"commercial activity." Under Section 1603 of the FSIA, a *foreign state* includes both a political subdivision of a foreign state and an instrumentality (department or agency of any branch of a government) of a foreign state. Section 1603 broadly defines a *commercial activity* as a commercial activity that is carried out by a foreign state within the United States, but it does not describe the particulars of what constitutes a commercial activity. Thus, the courts are left to decide whether a particular activity is governmental or commercial in nature.

DOING BUSINESS INTERNATIONALLY

A U.S. domestic firm can engage in international business transactions in a number of ways. The simplest way is to seek out foreign markets for domestically produced products or services. In other words, U.S. firms can **export** their goods and services to markets abroad. Alternatively, a U.S. firm can establish foreign production facilities so as to be closer to the foreign market or markets in which its products are sold. The advantages may include lower labor costs, fewer government regulations, and lower taxes and trade barriers. A domestic firm can also obtain revenues by licensing its technology to an existing foreign company or by selling franchises to overseas entities.

Exporting

Exporting can take two forms: direct exporting and indirect exporting. In *direct exporting*, a U.S. company signs a sales contract with a foreign purchaser that provides for the conditions of shipment and payment for the goods. (How payments are made in international transactions will be discussed later in this chapter.) If sufficient business develops in a foreign country, a U.S. corporation may set up a specialized marketing organization in that foreign market by appointing a foreign agent or a foreign distributor. This is called *indirect exporting*.

When a U.S. firm desires to limit its involvement in an international market, it will typically establish an *agency relationship* with a foreign firm (*agency* was discussed in Chapter 22). The foreign firm then acts as the U.S. firm's agent and can enter contracts in the foreign location on behalf of the principal (the U.S. company).

When a substantial market exists in a foreign country, a U.S. firm may wish to appoint a distributor located in that country. The U.S. firm and the distributor enter into a **distribution agreement,** which is a contract between the seller and the distributor setting out the terms and conditions of the distributorship. These terms and conditions—for example, price, currency of payment, availability of supplies, and method of payment—primarily involve contract law. Disputes concerning distribution agreements may involve jurisdictional or other

issues (will be discussed in detail later in this chapter). In addition, in some instances an **exclusive distributorship**—in which the distributor agrees to distribute only the seller's goods—has raised antitrust problems.

Manufacturing Abroad

An alternative to direct or indirect exporting is the establishment of foreign manufacturing facilities. Typically, U.S. firms establish manufacturing plants abroad if they believe that doing so will reduce their costs—particularly for labor, shipping, and raw materials—and enable them to compete more effectively in foreign markets. Foreign firms have done the same in the United States. Sony, Nissan, and other Japanese manufacturers have established U.S. plants to avoid import duties that the U.S. Congress may impose on Japanese products entering this country.

A U.S. firm can manufacture goods in other countries in several ways. They include licensing, franchising, and investing in a wholly owned subsidiary or a joint venture.

Licensing A U.S. firm can obtain business from abroad by licensing a foreign manufacturing company to use its copyrighted, patented, or trademarked intellectual property or trade secrets. Like any other licensing agreement, a licensing agreement with a foreign-based firm calls for a payment of royalties on some basis—such as so many cents per unit produced or a certain percentage of profits from units sold in a particular geographic territory.

In some circumstances, even in the absence of a patent, a firm may be able to license the "know-how" associated with a particular manufacturing process—for example, a plant design or a secret formula. The foreign firm that agrees to sign the licensing agreement further agrees to keep the know-how confidential and to pay royalties. **■EXAMPLE 32.3** The Coca-Cola Bottling Company licenses firms worldwide to use (and keep confidential) its secret formula for the syrup used in its soft drink. In return, the foreign firms licensed to make the syrup pay Coca-Cola a percentage of the income earned from the sale of the soft drink. ■

The licensing of intellectual property rights benefits all parties to the transaction. The firm that receives the license can take advantage of an established reputation for quality. The firm that grants the license receives income from the foreign sales of its products and also establishes a global reputation. Additionally, once a firm's trademark is known worldwide, the firm may experience increased demand for other products it manufactures or sells—obviously an important consideration.

Franchising Franchising is a well-known form of licensing. Recall from Chapter 24 that in a franchise arrangement the owner of a trademark, trade name, or copyright (the franchisor) licenses another (the franchisee) to use the trademark, trade name, or copyright under certain conditions or limitations in the selling of goods or services. In return, the franchisee pays a fee, which is usually based on a percentage of gross or net sales. Examples of international franchises include Holiday Inn and Hertz.

Investing in a Wholly Owned Subsidiary or a Joint Venture Another way to expand into a foreign market is to establish a wholly owned subsidiary firm in a foreign country. When a wholly owned subsidiary is established, the parent company, which remains in the United States, retains complete ownership of all the facilities in the foreign country, as well as complete authority and control over all phases of the operation. A U.S. firm can also expand into international markets through a joint venture. In a joint venture, the U.S. company owns only part of the operation; the rest is owned either by local owners in the foreign country or by another foreign entity. All of the firms involved in a joint venture share responsibilities, as well as profits and liabilities.

REGULATION OF SPECIFIC BUSINESS ACTIVITIES

Doing business abroad can affect the economies, foreign policies, domestic policies, and other national interests of the countries involved. For this reason, nations impose laws to restrict or facilitate international business. Controls may also be imposed by international agreements. We discuss here how different types of international activities are regulated.

Investing

Firms that invest in foreign nations face the risk that the foreign government may take possession of the investment property. Expropriation, as already mentioned, occurs when property is taken and the owner is paid just compensation for what is taken. Expropriation does not violate generally observed principles of international law. Such principles are normally violated, however, when a government confiscates property without compensation (or without adequate compensation). Few remedies are available for confiscation of property by a foreign government. Claims are often resolved by lump-sum settlements after negotiations between the United States and the taking nation.

To counter the deterrent effect that the possibility of confiscation may have on potential investors, many countries guarantee that foreign investors will be compensated if their property is taken. A guaranty can take the form of national constitutional or statutory laws or provisions in international treaties. As further protection for foreign investments, some

countries provide insurance for their citizens' investments abroad.

Export Controls

The U.S. Constitution provides in Article I, Section 9, that "No Tax or Duty shall be laid on Articles exported from any State." Thus, Congress cannot impose any export taxes. Congress can, however, use a variety of other devices to control exports. Congress may set export quotas on various items, such as grain being sold abroad. Under the Export Administration Act of 1979,[3] the flow of technologically advanced products and technical data can be restricted. In recent years, the U.S. Department of Commerce has made a controversial attempt to restrict the export of encryption software.

While restricting certain exports, the United States (and other nations) also uses devices such as export incentives and subsidies to stimulate other exports and thereby aid domestic businesses. The Revenue Act of 1971,[4] for instance, gave tax benefits to firms marketing their products overseas through certain foreign sales corporations by exempting income produced by the exports. Under the Export Trading Company Act of 1982,[5] U.S. banks are encouraged to invest in export trading companies, which are formed when exporting firms join together to export a line of goods. The Export-Import Bank of the United States provides financial assistance, consisting primarily of credit guaranties given to commercial banks that in turn lend funds to U.S. exporting companies.

Import Controls

All nations have restrictions on imports, and the United States is no exception. Restrictions include strict prohibitions, quotas, and tariffs. Under the Trading with the Enemy Act of 1917,[6] for instance, no goods may be imported from nations that have been designated enemies of the United States. Other laws prohibit the importation of illegal drugs, books that urge insurrection against the United States, and agricultural products that pose dangers to domestic crops or animals.

Importing goods that infringe U.S. patents is also prohibited. The International Trade Commission (ITC) investigates allegations that imported goods infringe U.S. patents and imposes penalties if necessary. In the following case, a party fined more than $13.5 million for importing certain disposable cameras appealed to the U.S. Court of Appeals for the Federal Circuit.

---

3. 50 U.S.C. Sections 2401–2420.
4. 26 U.S.C. Sections 991–994.
5. 15 U.S.C. Sections 4001, 4003.
6. 12 U.S.C. Section 95a.

CASE 32.1 Fuji Photo Film Co. v. International Trade Commission

United States Court of Appeals, Federal Circuit, 474 F.3d 1281 (2007).

FACTS Fuji Photo Film Company owns fifteen U.S. patents for "lens-fitted film packages" (LFFPs), popularly known as disposable cameras. An LFFP consists of a plastic shell preloaded with film. To develop the film, a consumer gives the LFFP to a film processor and receives back the negatives and prints, but not the shell. Fuji makes and sells LFFPs. Jazz Photo Corporation collected used LFFP shells in the United States, shipped them abroad to have new film inserted, and then imported them back into the United States for sale. The International Trade Commission (ITC) determined that Jazz's resale of shells originally sold outside the United States infringed Fuji's patents. In 1999, the ITC issued a cease-and-desist order to stop the imports. While the order was being disputed at the ITC and in the courts, between August 2001 and December 2003 Jazz imported and sold 27 million refurbished LFFPs. Fuji complained to the ITC, which fined Jazz more than $13.5 million. Jack Benun, Jazz's chief operating officer, appealed to the U.S. Court of Appeals for the Federal Circuit.

ISSUE Did Jazz violate the cease-and-desist order?

DECISION Yes. The U.S. Court of Appeals for the Federal Circuit affirmed this part of the ITC's decision. The court held, among other things, that "substantial evidence supports the finding that the majority of the cameras were first sold abroad."

REASON The court explained that to determine Jazz's violations of Fuji's patents, the ITC had used identifying numbers printed on Fuji's LFFPs and Fuji's production and shipping databases to pinpoint where Jazz's refurbished LFFPs were first sold. Against this evidence, Benun asserted that Jazz utilized its own "informed compliance program" to track the LFFP shells from their collection to their sale. Benun argued that this tracking system ensured that only shells collected from the United States were refurbished for sale here. The court reasoned, however, that this tracking program would ensure "at most" only that Jazz refurbished LFFPs collected from the United States, not that Jazz refurbished LFFPs first sold here. Besides, Jazz's tracking program was "too incomplete and disorganized to be credible." Because "there was no suggestion that the incomplete and disorganized nature of the program was due to Fuji's actions, this ground alone was sufficient to justify a conclusion that Benun" did not prove the refurbished LFFPs had been sold first in the United States.

FOR CRITICAL ANALYSIS—Global Consideration How does prohibiting the importing of goods that infringe U.S. patents protect those patents outside the United States?

Quotas and Tariffs Limits on the amounts of goods that can be imported are known as **quotas.** At one time, the United States had legal quotas on the number of automobiles that could be imported from Japan. Today, Japan "voluntarily" restricts the number of automobiles exported to the United States. **Tariffs** are taxes on imports. A tariff is usually a percentage of the value of the import, but it can be a flat rate per unit (for example, per barrel of oil). Tariffs raise the prices of goods, causing some consumers to purchase more domestically manufactured goods and less imported goods.

Dumping The United States has specific laws directed at what it sees as unfair international trade practices. **Dumping,** for example, is the sale of imported goods at "less than fair value." "Fair value" is usually determined by the price of those goods in the exporting country. Foreign firms that engage in dumping in the United States hope to undersell U.S. businesses to obtain a larger share of the U.S. market. To

prevent this, an extra tariff—known as an *antidumping duty*—may be assessed on the imports.

Minimizing Trade Barriers Restrictions on imports are also known as *trade barriers.* The elimination of trade barriers is sometimes seen as essential to the world's economic well-being. Most of the world's leading trading nations are members of the World Trade Organization (WTO), which was established in 1995. To minimize trade barriers among nations, each member country of the WTO is required to grant **normal trade relations (NTR) status** (formerly known as *most-favored-nation status*) to other member countries. This means each member is obligated to treat other members at least as well as it treats the country that receives its most favorable treatment with regard to imports or exports.

Various regional trade agreements and associations also help to minimize trade barriers between nations. The European Union (EU), for example, is working to minimize or remove barriers to trade among its member countries. The EU is a single integrated trading unit made up of twenty-seven European nations. Another important regional trade agreement is the North American Free Trade Agreement (NAFTA). NAFTA, which became effective on January 1, 1994, created a regional trading unit consisting of Canada, Mexico, and the United States. The primary goal of NAFTA is to eliminate tariffs among these three countries on substantially all goods over a period of fifteen to twenty years.

A more recent trade agreement is the Central America–Dominican Republic–United States Free Trade Agreement (CAFTA-DR), which was signed into law by President George W. Bush in 2005. This agreement was formed by Costa Rica, the Dominican Republic, El Salvador, Guatemala, Honduras, Nicaragua, and the United States. The purpose of the agreement was to reduce trade tariffs and improve market access among all of the signatory nations, including the United States. As of 2009, legislatures from all seven countries had approved the CAFTA-DR, despite significant opposition in certain nations, including Costa Rica, where nationwide strikes erupted in response to legislation adopting the treaty.

Bribing Foreign Officials

Giving cash or in-kind benefits to foreign government officials to obtain business contracts and other favors is often considered normal practice. To reduce such bribery by representatives of U.S. corporations, Congress enacted the Foreign Corrupt Practices Act in 1977.[7] This act and its implications for American businesspersons engaged in international business transactions were discussed in Chapter 6.

COMMERCIAL CONTRACTS IN AN INTERNATIONAL SETTING

Like all commercial contracts, an international contract should be in writing. Unlike domestic contracts, however, language and legal differences among nations can create special problems for parties to international contracts when disputes arise. It is possible to avoid these problems by including in a contract special provisions designating the official language of the contract, the legal forum (court or place) in which disputes under the contract will be settled, and the substantive law that will be applied in settling any disputes. Parties to international contracts should also indicate in their contracts what acts or events will excuse the parties from performance under the contract and whether disputes under the contract will be arbitrated or litigated.

---

7. 15 U.S.C. Sections 78m–78ff.

Choice of Language

A deal struck between a U.S. company and a company in another country normally involves two languages. Typically, many phrases in one language are not readily translatable into another. Consequently, the complex contractual terms involved may not be understood by one party in the other party's language. To make sure that no disputes arise out of this language problem, an international sales contract should have a **choice-of-language clause** designating the official language by which the contract will be interpreted in the event of disagreement.

PREVENTING LEGAL DISPUTES **When entering into international contracts, always determine whether the foreign nation has any applicable language requirements. In France, for instance, certain legal documents, such as the prospectuses used in securities offerings, must be written in French. In addition, contracts with any state or local authority in France, instruction manuals, and warranties for goods and services offered for sale in France must also be written in French. To avoid disputes, know the law of the jurisdiction before you enter into any agreements in that nation. Remember that certain legal terms or phrases in documents may not easily translate from one language to another. Finding out that a nation has language requirements may influence your decision whether to enter into a contract in that location and will definitely affect your decision whether to include a choice-of-law clause (to be discussed shortly).**

■

Choice of Forum

When parties from several countries are involved, litigation may be pursued in courts in different nations. There are no universally accepted rules as to which court has jurisdiction over particular subject matter or parties to a dispute. Consequently, parties to an international transaction should always include in the contract a **forum-selection clause** indicating what court, jurisdiction, or tribunal will decide any disputes arising under the contract. It is especially important to indicate the specific court that will have jurisdiction. The forum does not necessarily have to be within the geographic boundaries of the home nation of either party.

■EXAMPLE 32.4 Garware Polyester, Ltd., based in Mumbai, India, develops and makes plastics and high-tech polyester film. Intermax Trading Corporation, based in New York, acted as Garware's North American sales agent and sold its products on a commission basis. Garware and Intermax had executed a series of agency agreements under which the courts of Mumbai (Bombay), India, would have exclusive jurisdiction over any disputes relating to their agreement. When Intermax fell behind in its payments to Garware, Garware filed a lawsuit in a U.S. court to collect the balance due, claiming that the forum-selection clause did not apply to sales of warehoused goods. The court, however, sided with Intermax. Because the forum-selection clause was valid and enforceable, Garware had to bring its complaints against Intermax in a court in India.[8] ■

Choice of Law

A contractual provision designating the applicable law—such as the law of Germany or the United Kingdom or California—is called a **choice-of-law clause.** Every international contract typically includes a choice-of-law clause. At common law (and in European civil law systems), parties are allowed to choose the law that will govern their contractual relationship, provided that the law chosen is the law of a jurisdiction that has a substantial relationship to the parties and to the international business transaction.

Under Section 1–105 of the Uniform Commercial Code, parties may choose the law that will govern the contract as long as the choice is "reasonable." Article 6 of the United Nations Convention on Contracts for the International Sale of Goods (discussed in Chapter 14), however, imposes no limitation on the parties' choice of what law will govern the contract. The 1986 Hague Convention on the Law Applicable to Contracts for the International Sale of Goods—often referred to as the Choice-of-Law Convention—allows unlimited autonomy in the choice of law. The Hague Convention indicates that whenever a contract does not specify a choice of law, the governing law is that of the country in which the *seller's* place of business is located.

Force Majeure Clause

Every contract, particularly those involving international transactions, should have a *force majeure* **clause.** *Force majeure* is a French term meaning "impossible or irresistible force"—sometimes loosely identified as "an act of God." In international business contracts, *force majeure* clauses commonly stipulate that in addition to acts of God, a number of other eventualities (such as government orders or embargoes, for example) may excuse a party from liability for nonperformance.

---

8. *Garware Polyester, Ltd. v. Intermax Trading Corp.*, ___ F.Supp.2d ___ (S.D.N.Y. 2001).

Civil Dispute Resolution

International contracts frequently include arbitration clauses. By means of such clauses, the parties agree in advance to be bound by the decision of a specified third party in the event of a dispute, as discussed in Chapter 2. The United Nations Convention on the Recognition and Enforcement of Foreign Arbitral Awards (often referred to as the New York Convention) assists in the enforcement of arbitration clauses, as do provisions in specific treaties among nations. The New York Convention has been implemented in nearly one hundred countries, including the United States.

If a sales contract does not include an arbitration clause, litigation may occur. If the contract contains forum-selection and choice-of-law clauses, the lawsuit will be heard by a court in the specified forum and decided according to that forum's law. If no forum and choice of law have been specified, however, legal proceedings will be more complex and attended by much more uncertainty. For instance, litigation may take place in two or more countries, with each country applying its own choice-of-law rules to determine the substantive law that will be applied to the particular transactions. Even if a plaintiff wins a favorable judgment in a lawsuit litigated in the plaintiff's country, there is no way to predict whether courts in the defendant's country will enforce the judgment.

PAYMENT METHODS FOR INTERNATIONAL TRANSACTIONS

Currency differences between nations and the geographic distance between parties to international sales contracts add a degree of complexity to international sales that does not exist in the domestic market. Because international contracts involve greater financial risks, special care should be taken in drafting these contracts to specify both the currency in which payment is to be made and the method of payment.

Monetary Systems

Although our national currency, the U.S. dollar, is one of the primary forms of international currency, any U.S. firm undertaking business transactions abroad must be prepared to deal with one or more other currencies. After all, just as a U.S. firm wants to be paid in U.S. dollars for goods and services sold abroad, so, too, does a Japanese firm want to be paid in Japanese yen for goods and services sold outside Japan. Both firms therefore must rely on the convertibility of currencies.

Currencies are convertible when they can be freely exchanged one for the other at some specified market rate in a **foreign exchange market.** Foreign exchange markets make up a worldwide system for the buying and selling of foreign currencies. At any point in time, the foreign exchange rate is set by the forces of supply and demand in unrestricted foreign exchange markets. The foreign exchange rate is simply the price of a unit of one country's currency in terms of another country's currency. For example, if today's exchange rate is one hundred Japanese yen for one dollar, that means that anybody with one hundred yen can obtain one dollar, and vice versa.

Frequently, a U.S. company can rely on its domestic bank to take care of all international transfers of funds. Commercial banks often transfer funds internationally through their **correspondent banks** in other countries. ∎EXAMPLE 32.5 A customer of Citibank wishes to pay a bill in euros to a company in Paris. Citibank can draw a bank check payable in euros on its account in Crédit Agricole, a Paris correspondent bank, and then send the check to the French company to which its customer owes the funds. Alternatively, Citibank's customer can request a wire transfer of the funds to the French company. Citibank instructs Crédit Agricole by wire to pay the necessary amount in euros. ∎

The Clearinghouse Interbank Payment System (CHIPS) handles about 90 percent of both national and international interbank transfers of U.S. funds. In addition, the Society for Worldwide International Financial Telecommunications (SWIFT) is a communication system that provides banks with messages concerning international transactions.

Letters of Credit

Because buyers and sellers engaged in international business transactions are frequently separated by thousands of miles, special precautions are often taken to ensure performance under the contract. Sellers want to avoid delivering goods for which they might not be paid. Buyers desire the assurance that sellers will not be paid until there is evidence that the goods have been shipped. Thus, **letters of credit** are frequently used to facilitate international business transactions.

In a simple letter-of-credit transaction, the *issuer* (a bank) agrees to issue a letter of credit and to ascertain whether the *beneficiary* (seller) performs certain acts. In return, the *account party* (buyer) promises to reimburse the issuer for the amount paid to the beneficiary. The issuer is bound to pay the beneficiary (seller) when the beneficiary has complied with the terms and conditions of the letter of credit. Typically, the letter of credit will require that the beneficiary deliver a *bill of lading* to the issuing bank to prove that shipment has been made.

The basic principle behind letters of credit is that payment is made against the documents presented by the beneficiary and not against the facts that the documents purport to reflect. Thus, in a letter-of-credit transaction, the issuer does not police the underlying contract; a letter of credit is independent of the underlying contract between the buyer and the seller. Moreover, the use of a letter of credit protects both buyers and sellers.

U.S. LAWS IN A GLOBAL CONTEXT

The internationalization of business raises questions about the extraterritorial application of a nation's laws—that is, the effect of the country's laws outside its boundaries. To what extent do U.S. domestic laws apply to other nations' businesses? To what extent do U.S. domestic laws apply to U.S. firms doing business abroad? Here, we discuss international tort claims and laws prohibiting employment discrimination.

International Tort Claims

The international application of tort liability is growing in significance and controversy. An increasing number of U.S. plaintiffs are suing foreign (or U.S.) entities for torts that these entities have allegedly committed overseas. Often, these cases involve human rights violations by foreign governments. The Alien Tort Claims Act (ATCA),[9] adopted in 1789, allows even foreign citizens to bring civil suits in U.S. courts for injuries caused by violations of the law of nations or a treaty of the United States.

Since 1980, plaintiffs have increasingly used the ATCA to bring actions against companies operating in other countries. ATCA actions have been brought against companies doing business in nations such as Colombia, Ecuador, Egypt, Guatemala, India, Indonesia, Nigeria, and Saudi Arabia. Some of these cases have involved alleged environmental destruction. In addition, mineral companies in Southeast Asia have been sued for collaborating with oppressive government regimes.

The following case involved claims against "hundreds" of corporations that allegedly "aided and abetted" the government of South Africa in maintaining its apartheid (racially discriminatory) regime.

---

9. 28 U.S.C. Section 1350.

CASE 32.2 Khulumani v. Barclay National Bank, Ltd.

United States Court of Appeals, Second Circuit, 504 F.3d 254 (2007).

FACTS The Khulumani plaintiffs, along with other plaintiff groups, filed class-action claims on behalf of victims of apartheid-related atrocities, human rights violations, crimes against humanity, and unfair and discriminatory forced-labor practices. The plaintiffs brought this action under the Alien Tort Claims Act (ATCA) against more than fifty corporate defendants and others. These corporations included Bank of America, Barclay National Bank, Citigroup, Credit Suisse Group, General Electric, and IBM. The plaintiffs filed separate actions in multiple federal district courts. All of the actions were transferred to a federal district court in the Southern District of New York. The defendants filed motions to dismiss. The district court held that the plaintiffs had failed to establish subject-matter jurisdiction under the ATCA. The court dismissed the plaintiffs' complaints in their entirety. The plaintiffs appealed to the U.S. Court of Appeals for the Second Circuit.

ISSUE Can the plaintiffs bring a claim against U.S. and foreign companies under the ATCA for "aiding and abetting" human rights violations?

DECISION Yes. The U.S. Court of Appeals for the Second Circuit vacated the district court's dismissal of the plaintiffs' claims and remanded the case for further proceedings.

According to the reviewing court, a plaintiff may plead a theory of aiding and abetting liability under the ATCA.

REASON The court stated that the district court "erred in holding that aiding and abetting violations of a customary international law cannot provide a basis for ATCA jurisdiction." The court reasoned that the United States Supreme Court has instructed courts in this nation to exercise caution and carefully evaluate international norms and potential adverse foreign policy consequences in deciding whether to hear ATCA claims. Thus, "the determination whether a norm is sufficiently definite to support a cause of action should (indeed, inevitably must) involve an element of judgment about the practical consequences of making that cause available to litigants in the federal courts." The court rejected the defendants' argument that an adjudication of the case by the U.S. court "would offend amicable working relationships with a foreign country."

FOR CRITICAL ANALYSIS—Ethical Consideration *Should the companies cited as defendants in this case have refused all business dealings with South Africa during the era of apartheid when that country's white government severely limited the rights of the majority black African population?*

Antidiscrimination Laws

As explained in Chapter 23, federal laws in the United States prohibit discrimination on the basis of race, color, national origin, religion, gender, age, and disability. These laws, as they affect employment relationships, generally apply extraterritorially. Since 1984, for example, the Age Discrimination in Employment Act of 1967 has covered U.S. employees working abroad for U.S. employers. The Americans with Disabilities Act of 1990, which requires employers to accommodate the needs of workers with disabilities, also applies to U.S. nationals working abroad for U.S. firms.

For some time, it was uncertain whether the major U.S. law regulating discriminatory practices in the workplace, Title VII of the Civil Rights Act of 1964, applied extraterritorially. The Civil Rights Act of 1991 addressed this issue. The act provides that Title VII applies extraterritorially to all U.S. employees working for U.S. employers abroad. Generally, U.S. employers must abide by U.S. discrimination laws unless to do so would violate the laws of the country where their workplaces are located. This "foreign laws exception" allows employers to avoid being subjected to conflicting laws.

REVIEWING International Law in a Global Economy

Robco, Inc., was a Florida arms dealer. The armed forces of Honduras contracted to purchase weapons

from Robco over a six-year period. After the government was replaced and a democracy installed, the Honduran government sought to reduce the size of its military, and its relationship with Robco deteriorated. Honduras refused to honor the contract by purchasing the inventory of arms, which

Robco could sell only at a much lower price. Robco filed a suit in a federal district court in the United States to recover damages for this breach of contract by the government of Honduras. Using the information provided in the chapter, answer the following questions.

1 Should the Foreign Sovereign Immunities Act (FSIA) preclude this lawsuit? Why or why not?

2 Does the act of state doctrine bar Robco from seeking to enforce the contract? Explain.

3 Suppose that prior to this lawsuit, the new government of Honduras had enacted a law making it illegal to purchase weapons from foreign arms dealers. What doctrine might lead a U.S. court to dismiss Robco's case in that situation?

4 Now suppose that the U.S. court hears the case and awards damages to Robco, but the government of Honduras has no assets in the United States that can be used to satisfy the judgment. Under which doctrine might Robco be able to collect the damages by asking another nation's court to enforce the U.S. judgment?

TERMS AND CONCEPTS

act of state doctrine 662
choice-of-language clause 666
choice-of-law clause 667
civil law system 661
comity 662
confiscation 662
correspondent bank 668
distribution agreement 663
dumping 665

exclusive distributorship 663
export 663
expropriation 662
force majeure clause 667
foreign exchange market 667
forum-selection clause 666
international law 660
international organization 661

letter of credit 668
national law 660
normal trade relations
   (NTR) status 665
quota 665
sovereign immunity 662
tariff 665
treaty 661

CHAPTER SUMMARY   International Law in a Global Economy

International Law—Sources and Principles (See pages 660–663.)	1. *Sources*—The three main sources of international law are international customs, treaties and international agreements, and international organizations and conferences.
	
	2. *Principles and doctrines*—
	
	   a. *The principle of comity*—Under this principle, nations give effect to the laws and judicial decrees of other nations for reasons of courtesy and international harmony.
	   b. *The act of state doctrine*—A doctrine under which U.S. courts avoid passing judgment on the validity of public acts committed by a recognized foreign government within its own territory.
	   c. *The doctrine of sovereign immunity*—When certain conditions are satisfied, foreign nations are immune from U.S. jurisdiction under the Foreign Sovereign Immunities Act of 1976. Exceptions are made (1) when a foreign state has "waived its immunity either explicitly or by implication" or (2) when the action is taken "in connection with a commercial activity carried on in the United States by the foreign state."

Doing Business Internationally (See pages 663–664.)	Ways in which U.S. domestic firms engage in international business transactions include (a) exporting, which may involve foreign agents or distributors, and (b) manufacturing abroad through licensing arrangements, franchising operations, wholly owned subsidiaries, or joint ventures.
Regulation of Specific Business Activities (See pages 664–666.)	In the interests of their economies, foreign policies, domestic policies, or other national priorities, nations impose laws that restrict or facilitate international business. Such laws regulate foreign investments, exporting, and importing. The World Trade Organization attempts to minimize trade barriers among nations, as do regional trade agreements and associations, including the European Union and the North American Free Trade Agreement.

CHAPTER SUMMARY	**International Law in a Global Economy—Continued**
Commercial Contracts in an International Setting (See pages 666–667.)	International business contracts often include choice-of-language, forum-selection, and choice-of-law clauses to reduce the uncertainties associated with interpreting the language of the agreement and dealing with legal differences. Most domestic and international contracts include *force majeure* clauses. They commonly stipulate that certain events, such as floods, fire, accidents, labor strikes, and government orders, may excuse a party from liability for nonperformance of the contract. Arbitration clauses are also frequently found in international contracts.
Payment Methods for International Transactions (See pages 667–668.)	1. *Currency conversion*—Because nations have different monetary systems, payment on international contracts requires currency conversion at a rate specified in a foreign exchange market. 2. *Correspondent banking*—Correspondent banks facilitate the transfer of funds from a buyer in one country to a seller in another. 3. *Letters of credit*—Letters of credit facilitate international transactions by ensuring payment to sellers and assuring buyers that payment will not be made until the sellers have complied with the terms of the letters of credit. Typically, compliance occurs when a bill of lading is delivered to the issuing bank.
U.S. Laws in a Global Context (See pages 668–669.)	1. *International tort claims*—U.S. plaintiffs may bring claims against U.S. or foreign entities for torts allegedly committed overseas. The Alien Tort Claims Act of 1789 allows even foreign citizens to bring civil suits in U.S. courts for injuries caused by violations of the law of nations or a U.S. treaty. 2. *Antidiscrimination laws*—The major U.S. laws prohibiting employment discrimination, including Title VII of the Civil Rights Act of 1964, the Age Discrimination in Employment Act of 1967, and the Americans with Disabilities Act of 1990, cover U.S. employees working abroad for U.S. firms—*unless* applying the U.S. laws would violate the laws of the host country.

FOR REVIEW

Answers for the even-numbered questions in this **For Review** *section can be found on this text's accompanying Web site at* **www.cengage.com/blaw/fbl**. *Select "Chapter 32" and click on "For Review."*

1 What is the principle of comity, and why do courts deciding disputes involving a foreign law or judicial decree apply this principle?

2 What is the act of state doctrine? In what circumstances is this doctrine applied?

3 Under the Foreign Sovereign Immunities Act of 1976, on what bases might a foreign state be considered subject to the jurisdiction of U.S. courts?

4 What types of provisions, or clauses, are often included in international sales contracts?

5 Do U.S. laws prohibiting employment discrimination apply in all circumstances to U.S. employees working for U.S. employers abroad?

QUESTIONS AND CASE PROBLEMS

HYPOTHETICAL SCENARIOS AND CASE PROBLEMS

32.1 Letters of Credit. The Swiss Credit Bank issued a letter of credit in favor of Antex Industries to cover the sale of 92,000 electronic integrated circuits manufactured by Electronic Arrays. The letter of credit specified that the chips would be transported to Tokyo by ship. Antex shipped the circuits by air. Payment on the letter of credit was dishonored because the shipment by air did not fulfill the precise terms of the letter of credit. Should a court compel payment? Explain.

32.2 Hypothetical Question with Sample Answer. As China and other nations move toward free enterprise, they must develop a new set of business laws. What kind of business law system would you adopt, a civil law system or a common law system? What kind of business regulations would you impose?

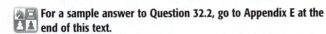 **For a sample answer to Question 32.2, go to Appendix E at the end of this text.**

32.3 Import Controls. DaimlerChrysler Corp. made and marketed motor vehicles. DaimlerChrysler assembled the 1993 and 1994 model years of its trucks at plants in Mexico. Assembly involved sheet metal components sent from the United States. DaimlerChrysler subjected some of the parts to a complicated treatment process, which included applying coats of paint to prevent corrosion, impart color, and protect the finish. Under U.S. law, goods that are assembled abroad using U.S.-made parts can be imported tariff free. A U.S. *statute* provides that painting is "incidental" to assembly and does not affect the status of the goods. A U.S. *regulation*, however, states that "painting primarily intended to enhance the appearance of an article or to impart distinctive features or characteristics" is not incidental. The U.S. Customs Service levied a tariff on the trucks. DaimlerChrysler filed a suit in the U.S. Court of International Trade, challenging the levy. Should the court rule in DaimlerChrysler's favor? Why or why not? [*DaimlerChrysler Corp. v. United States*, 361 F.3d 1378 (Fed.Cir. 2004)]

32.4 Comity. E&L Consulting, Ltd., is a U.S. corporation that sells lumber products in New Jersey, New York, and Pennsylvania. Doman Industries, Ltd., is a Canadian corporation that also sells lumber products, including green hem-fir, a durable product used for homebuilding. Doman supplies more than 95 percent of the green hem-fir for sale in the northeastern United States. In 1990, Doman contracted to sell green hem-fir through E&L, which received monthly payments plus commissions. In 1998, Sherwood Lumber Corp., a New York firm and an E&L competitor, approached E&L about a merger. The negotiations were unsuccessful. According to E&L, Sherwood and Doman then conspired to monopolize the U.S. green hem-fir market. When Doman terminated its contract with E&L, the latter filed a suit in a federal district court against Doman, alleging violations of U.S. antitrust law. Doman filed for bankruptcy in a Canadian court and asked the U.S. court to dismiss E&L's suit under the principle of comity, among other things. What is the "principle of comity"? On what basis would it apply in this case? What would be the likely result? Discuss. [*E&L Consulting, Ltd. v. Doman Industries, Ltd.*, 360 F.Supp.2d 465 (E.D.N.Y. 2005)]

32.5 Dumping. A newspaper printing press system is more than one hundred feet long, stands four or five stories tall, and

weighs 2 million pounds. Only about ten of the systems are sold each year in the United States. Because of the size and cost, a newspaper may update its system, rather than replace it, by buying "additions." By the 1990s, Goss International Corp. was the only domestic maker of the equipment and represented the entire U.S. market. Tokyo Kikai Seisakusho (TKSC), a Japanese corporation, makes the systems in Japan. In the 1990s, TKSC began to compete in the U.S. market, forcing Goss to cut its prices below cost. TKSC's tactics included offering its customers "secret" rebates on prices that were ultimately substantially less than the products' actual market value in Japan. According to TKSC office memos, the goal was to "win completely this survival game" against Goss, the "enemy." Goss filed a suit in a federal district court against TKSC and others, alleging illegal dumping. At what point does a foreign firm's attempt to compete with a domestic manufacturer in the United States become illegal dumping? Was that point reached in this case? Discuss. [*Goss International Corp. v. Man Roland Druckmaschinen Aktiengesellschaft*, 434 F.3d 1081 (8th Cir. 2006)]

32.6 Case Problem with Sample Answer. Jan Voda, M.D., a resident of Oklahoma City, Oklahoma, owns three U.S. patents related to guiding catheters for use in interventional cardiology, as well as corresponding foreign patents issued by the European Patent Office, Canada, France, Germany, and Great Britain. Voda filed a suit in a federal district court against Cordis Corp., a U.S. firm, alleging infringement of the U.S. patents under U.S. patent law and of the corresponding foreign patents under the patent law of the various foreign countries. Cordis admitted, "[T]he XB catheters have been sold domestically and internationally since 1994. The XB catheters were manufactured in Miami Lakes, Florida, from 1993 to 2001 and have been manufactured in Juarez, Mexico, since 2001." Cordis argued, however, that Voda could not assert infringement claims under foreign patent law because the court did not have jurisdiction over such claims. Which of the important international legal principles discussed in this chapter would be most likely to apply in this case? How should the court apply it? Explain. [*Voda v. Cordis Corp.*, 476 F.3d 887 (Fed.Cir. 2007)]

After you have answered Problem 32.6, compare your answer with the sample answer given on the Web site that accompanies this text. Go to www.cengage.com/blaw/fbl, select "Chapter 32," and click on "Case Problem with Sample Answer."

32.7 Sovereign Immunity. When Ferdinand Marcos was president of the Republic of the Philippines, he put assets into a company called Arelma. Its holdings are in New York. A group of plaintiffs, Pimentel, joined a class-action lawsuit in a U.S. district court for human rights violations by Marcos. They won a judgment of $2 billion and sought to attach the assets of Arelma to help pay the judgment. At the same time, the Philippines established a commission to recover property wrongfully taken by Marcos. A court in the

Philippines was determining whether Marcos's property, including Arelma, should be forfeited to the republic or to other parties. The government of the Philippines, in opposition to the Pimentel judgment, moved to dismiss the U.S. court proceedings. The district court refused, and the U.S. Court of Appeals for the Ninth Circuit agreed that Pimentel should take the assets. The Republic of the Philippines appealed. What are the key international legal issues? [*Republic of the Philippines v. Pimentel*, ___ U.S. ___, 128 S.Ct. 2180, 171 L.Ed 131 (2008)

32.8 **A Question of Ethics.** *On December 21, 1988, Pan Am Flight 103 exploded 31,000 feet in the air over Lockerbie, Scotland, killing all 259 passengers and crew on board and 11 people on the ground. Among those killed was Roger Hurst, a U.S. citizen. An investigation determined that a portable radio–cassette player packed in a brown Samsonite suitcase smuggled onto the plane was the source of the explosion. The explosive device was constructed with a digital timer specially made for, and bought by, Libya. Abdel Basset Ali Al-Megrahi, a Libyan government official and an employee of the Libyan Arab Airline (LAA), was convicted by the Scottish High Court of Justiciary on criminal charges that he planned and executed the bombing in association*

with members of the Jamahiriya Security Organization (JSO) (an agency of the Libyan government that performs security and intelligence functions) or the Libyan military. Members of the victims' families filed a suit in a U.S. federal district court against the JSO, the LAA, Al-Megrahi, and others. The plaintiffs claimed violations of U.S. federal law, including the Anti-Terrorism Act, and state law, including the intentional infliction of emotional distress. [Hurst v. Socialist People's Libyan Arab Jamahiriya, 474 F.Supp.2d 19 (D.D.C. 2007)]

1 Under what doctrine, codified in which federal statute, might the defendants claim to be immune from the jurisdiction of a U.S. court? Should this law include an exception for "state-sponsored terrorism"? Why or why not?

2 The defendants agreed to pay $2.7 billion, or $10 million per victim, to settle all claims for "compensatory death damages." The families of eleven victims, including Hurst, were excluded from the settlement because they were "not wrongful death beneficiaries under applicable state law." These plaintiffs continued the suit. The defendants filed a motion to dismiss. Should the motion be granted on the ground that the settlement bars the plaintiffs' claims? Explain.

CRITICAL THINKING AND WRITING ASSIGNMENT

32.9 **Video Question.** Go to this text's Web site at **www.cengage.com/blaw/fbl** and select "Chapter 32." Click on "Video Questions" and view the video titled *International: Letter of Credit.* Then answer the following questions.

1 Do banks always require the same documents to be presented in letter-of-credit transactions? If not, who dictates what documents will be required in the letter of credit?

2 At what point does the seller receive payment in a letter-of-credit transaction?

3 What assurances does a letter of credit provide to the buyer and the seller involved in the transaction?

ACCESSING THE INTERNET

For updated links to resources available on the Web, as well as a variety of other materials, visit this text's Web site at

www.cengage.com/blaw/fbl

FindLaw's Web site includes an extensive array of links to international doctrines, treaties, and the laws of other nations. Go to

www.findlaw.com/12international

For information on the legal requirements of doing business abroad, a good source is the Internet Law Library's collection of laws of other nations. Go to

www.lawguru.com/ilawlib/index.html

PRACTICAL INTERNET EXERCISES

Go to this text's Web site at **www.cengage.com/blaw/fbl**, select "Chapter 32," and click on "Practical Internet Exercises." There you will find the following Internet research exercises that you can perform to learn more about the topics covered in this chapter.

PRACTICAL INTERNET EXERCISE 32–1 LEGAL PERSPECTIVE—The World Trade Organization

PRACTICAL INTERNET EXERCISE 32–2 MANAGEMENT PERSPECTIVE—Overseas Business Opportunities

BEFORE THE TEST

Go to this text's Web site at **www.cengage.com/blaw/fbl**, select "Chapter 32," and click on "Interactive Quizzes." You will find a number of interactive questions relating to this chapter.

UNIT TEN **EXTENDED CASE STUDY**

Dole Food Co. v. Patrickson

Chapter 32 discusses the Foreign Sovereign Immunities Act of 1976 (FSIA). Under the FSIA, foreign states, or nations, can claim certain rights in suits against them in U.S. courts, including in some circumstances immunity from the litigation. A corporate entity that is an "instrumentality" of a foreign state, as defined in the FSIA, may also avail itself of some of these rights. (Corporations and their characteristics were covered in Chapters 25 and 26.) In this extended case study, we review **Dole Food Co. v. Patrickson,**[1] *a case focusing on this definition. The specific question was whether a corporate subsidiary can claim to be an instrumentality of a foreign state if the state does not own a majority of the shares of the subsidiary's stock, but does own a majority of the shares of the corporate parent.*

CASE BACKGROUND   In 1851, Dole Food Company was founded in Hawaii. Dole is the world's largest producer and seller of fresh fruit, fresh vegetables, and fresh-cut flowers and markets a growing line of packaged foods. The firm does business in more than 90 countries, employing globally more than 33,000 full-time permanent employees and 24,000 full-time seasonal or temporary employees.

In 1997, Gerardo Patrickson and other farmworkers who worked in banana fields in Costa Rica, Ecuador, Guatemala, and Panama filed a suit in a Hawaii state court against Dole and others, seeking damages for injuries from exposure to dibromochloropropane, a chemical used as an agricultural pesticide. Dole impleaded[2] two Israeli firms—Dead Sea Bromine Company and Bromine Compounds, Ltd. (the Dead Sea companies)—that allegedly made the pesticides.

The Dead Sea companies asked a U.S. district court to hear the suit on the ground that they were instrumentalities of a foreign state as defined in the FSIA. The court denied this request, but held that it had jurisdiction on other grounds and dismissed the suit. The workers appealed to the U.S. Court of Appeals for the Ninth Circuit, which reversed the dismissal but agreed that the Dead Sea companies were not instrumentalities of a foreign state as defined in the FSIA. The Dead Sea companies appealed to the United States Supreme Court.

---

1. 538 U.S. 468, 123 S.Ct. 1655, 155 L.Ed.2d 843 (2004). This opinion may be accessed online at **www.law.cornell.edu/supct/search/index.html**. Enter "Dole Food Company" in the "Search" box, and select "All Decisions." Scroll to the name of the case and click on it to access the opinion.

2. To *implead* is to bring a new party into a suit between others, with the allegation that the new party is liable for part of the claim to the party that impleaded it.

MAJORITY OPINION

Justice *KENNEDY*, delivered the opinion of the Court.

* * * *

The State of Israel did not have direct ownership of shares in either of the Dead Sea Companies at any time pertinent to this suit. Rather, these companies were, at various times, separated from the State of Israel by one or more intermediate corporate tiers. For example, from 1984–1985, Israel wholly owned a company called Israeli Chemicals, Ltd.; which owned a majority of shares in another company called Dead Sea Works, Ltd.; which owned a majority of shares in Dead Sea Bromine Co., Ltd.; which owned a majority of shares in Bromine Compounds, Ltd.

* * * *

* * * The Dead Sea Companies urge us to ignore corporate formalities and use the colloquial [everyday] sense of that term. They ask whether, in common parlance, Israel would be said to own the Dead Sea Companies. *We reject this analysis. In issues of corporate law, structure often matters.* It is evident from the [FSIA's] text that Congress was aware of settled principles of corporate law and legislated within that context. The language of [Section] 1603(b)(2) refers to ownership of "shares," showing that *Congress intended statutory coverage to turn on formal corporate ownership.* Likewise, [Section] 1603(b)(1), another component of the definition of instrumentality, refers to a "separate legal person, corporate or otherwise." * * * [Emphasis added.]

A basic tenet [rule] of American corporate law is that the corporation and its shareholders are distinct entities. An individual shareholder, by virtue of his ownership of shares, does not own the corporation's assets and, as a result, does not own subsidiary corporations in which the corporation holds an interest. A corporate parent which owns the shares of a subsidiary does not, for that reason alone, own or have legal title to the assets of the subsidiary; and, it follows with even greater force, *the parent does not own or have legal title to the subsidiaries of the subsidiary.* The fact that the shareholder is a foreign state does not change the analysis. [Emphasis added.]

Applying these principles, it follows that Israel did not own a majority of shares in the Dead Sea Companies. The State of Israel owned a majority of shares, at various times, in companies one or more corporate tiers above the Dead Sea Companies, but at no time did Israel own a majority of shares in the Dead Sea Companies. Those companies were subsidiaries of other corporations.

* * * *

The Dead Sea Companies say that the State of Israel exercised considerable control over their operations, notwithstanding Israel's indirect relationship to those companies. They appear to think that, in determining instrumentality status under the Act, control may be substituted for an ownership interest. Control and ownership, however, are distinct concepts. The terms of [Section] 1603(b)(2) are explicit and straightforward. Majority ownership by a foreign state, not control, is the benchmark of instrumentality status.

* * * *

The judgment of the Court of Appeals * * * is affirmed * * * .

DISSENTING OPINION

Justice *BREYER*, * * * dissenting * * * .

* * * Unlike the majority, I believe that the statutory phrase "other ownership interest * * * owned by a foreign state" covers a Foreign Nation's legal interest in a Corporate Subsidiary, where that interest consists of the Foreign Nation's ownership of a Corporate Parent that owns the shares of the Subsidiary.

* * * *

As far as [the FSIA] is concerned, decisions about how to incorporate, how to structure corporate entities, or whether to act through a single corporate layer or through several corporate layers are matters purely of form, not of substance. The need for federal court determination of a sovereign immunity claim is no less important where subsidiaries are involved. The need for [the FSIA's] protections is no less compelling. The risk of adverse foreign policy consequences is no less great.

That is why I doubt the majority's claim that its reading of the text of the FSIA is "[t]he better reading," leading to "[t]he better rule." The majority's rule is not better for a foreign nation, say, Mexico or Honduras, which may use a tiered corporate structure to manage and control important areas of national interest, such as natural resources, and, as a result, will find its ability to use the [U.S.] federal courts to adjudicate matters of national importance and potential sensitivity restricted. Congress is most unlikely to characterize as "better" a rule tied to legal formalities that undercuts its basic jurisdictional objectives. And working lawyers will now have to factor into complex corporate restructuring equations * * *

(Continued)

a risk that the government might lose its previously available access to federal court.

Given these consequences, from what perspective can the Court's unnecessarily technical reading of this part of the statute produce a "better rule"? To hold, as the Court does today, that for purposes of the FSIA "other ownership interest" does not include the interest that a Foreign Nation has in a tiered Corporate Subsidiary would be not merely to depart from the primary rule that words are to be taken in their ordinary sense, but to narrow the operation of the statute to an extent that would seriously imperil the accomplishment of its purpose.

QUESTIONS FOR ANALYSIS

1 LAW. What did the majority rule in this case, and why?

2 LAW. Why did the dissent disagree with the majority's ruling?

3 SOCIAL CONSIDERATION. Why did the majority conclude that "[m]ajority ownership by a foreign state, not control, is the benchmark of instrumentality status"?

4 ETHICAL DIMENSIONS. Under what circumstances might a court "pierce the corporate veil" to hold a corporation's owner liable? Should the United States Supreme Court have applied these principles in this case to hold that the Dead Sea companies were instrumentalities of the state under the FSIA? Why or why not?

5 IMPLICATIONS FOR THE INVESTOR. How might the holding in this case affect investments in foreign "instrumentalities"?

APPENDIX A
How to Brief Cases and Analyze Case Problems

How to Brief Cases

To fully understand the law with respect to business, you need to be able to read and understand court decisions. To make this task easier, you can use a method of case analysis that is called *briefing*. There is a fairly standard procedure that you can follow when you "brief" any court case. You must first read the case opinion carefully. When you feel you understand the case, you can prepare a brief of it.

Although the format of the brief may vary, typically it will present the essentials of the case under headings such as those listed below.

1 **Citation.** Give the full citation for the case, including the name of the case, the date it was decided, and the court that decided it.

2 **Facts.** Briefly indicate (a) the reasons for the lawsuit; (b) the identity and arguments of the plaintiff(s) and defendant(s), respectively; and (c) the lower court's decision—if appropriate.

3 **Issue.** Concisely phrase, in the form of a question, the essential issue before the court. (If more than one issue is involved, you may have two—or even more—questions here.)

4 **Decision.** Indicate here—with a "yes" or "no," if possible—the court's answer to the question (or questions) in the *Issue* section above.

5 **Reason.** Summarize as briefly as possible the reasons given by the court for its decision (or decisions) and the case or statutory law relied on by the court in arriving at its decision.

An Example of a Brief Sample Court Case

As an example of the format used in briefing cases, we present here a briefed version of the sample court case that was presented in Exhibit 1A–3 on pages 31 and 32.

BERGER v. CITY OF SEATTLE
United States Court of Appeals,
Ninth Circuit, 2008.
512 F.3d 582.

FACTS The Seattle Center is an entertainment "zone" in downtown Seattle, Washington, that attracts nearly ten million tourists each year. The center encompasses theaters, arenas, museums, exhibition halls, conference rooms, outdoor stadiums, and restaurants, and features street performers. Under the authority of the city, the center's director issued rules in 2002 to address safety concerns and other matters. Among other things, street performers were required

to obtain permits and wear badges. After members of the public filed numerous complaints of threatening behavior by street performer and balloon artist Michael Berger, Seattle Center staff cited Berger for several rules violations. He filed a suit in a federal district court against the city and others, alleging, in part, that the rules violated his free speech rights under the First Amendment to the U.S. Constitution. The court issued a judgment in the plaintiff's favor. The city appealed to the U.S. Court of Appeals for the Ninth Circuit.

ISSUE Did the rules issued by the Seattle Center under the city's authority meet the requirements for valid restrictions on speech under the First Amendment?

DECISION Yes. The U.S. Court of Appeals for the Ninth Circuit reversed the decision of the lower court and remanded the case for further proceedings. "Such content neutral and narrowly tailored rules * * * must be upheld."

REASON The court concluded first that the rules requiring permits and badges were "content neutral." Time, place, and manner restrictions do not violate the First Amendment if they burden all expression equally and do not allow officials to treat different messages differently. In this case, the rules met this test and thus did not discriminate based on content. The court also concluded that the rules were "narrowly tailored" to "promote a substantial government interest that would be achieved less effectively" otherwise. With the rules, the city was trying to "reduce territorial disputes among performers, deter patron harassment, and facilitate the identification and apprehension of offending performers." This was pursuant to the valid governmental objective of protecting the safety and convenience of the other performers and the public generally. The public's complaints about Berger and others showed that unregulated street performances posed a threat to these interests. The court was "satisfied that the city's permit scheme was designed to further valid governmental objectives."

Review of Sample Court Case

Here, we provide a review of the briefed version to indicate the kind of information that is contained in each section.

CITATION The name of the case is *Berger v. City of Seattle*. Berger is the plaintiff; the City of Seattle is the defendant. The U.S. Court of Appeals for the Ninth Circuit decided this case in 2008. The citation states that this case can be found in volume 512 of the *Federal Reporter, Third Series*, on page 582.

FACTS The *Facts* section identifies the plaintiff and the defendant, describes the events leading up to this suit, the allegations made by the plaintiff in the initial suit, and (because this case is an appellate court decision) the lower court's ruling and the party appealing. The party appealing's argument on appeal is also sometimes included here.

ISSUE The *Issue* section presents the central issue (or issues) decided by the court. In this case, the U.S. Court of Appeals for the Ninth Circuit considered whether certain rules imposed on street performers by local government authorities satisfied the requirements for valid restrictions on speech under the First Amendment to the U.S. Constitution.

DECISION The *Decision* section includes the court's decision on the issues before it. The decision reflects the opinion of the judge or justice hearing the case. Decisions by appellate courts are frequently phrased in reference to the lower court's decision. In other words, the appellate court may "affirm" the lower court's ruling or "reverse" it. Here, the court determined that Seattle's rules were "content neutral" and "narrowly tailored" to "promote a substantial government interest that would otherwise be achieved less effectively." The court found in favor of the city and reversed the lower court's ruling in the plaintiff's (Berger's) favor.

REASON The *Reason* section includes references to the relevant laws and legal principles that the court applied in coming to its conclusion in the case. The relevant law in the *Berger* case included the requirements under the First Amendment for evaluating the purpose and effect of government regulation with respect to expression. This section also explains the court's application of the law to the facts in this case.

Analyzing Case Problems

In addition to learning how to brief cases, students of business law and the legal environment also find it helpful to know how to analyze case problems. Part of the study of business law and the legal environment usually involves analyzing case problems, such as those included in this text at the end of each chapter.

For each case problem in this book, we provide the relevant background and facts of the lawsuit and the issue before the court. When you are assigned one of these problems, your job will be to determine how the court should decide the issue, and why. In other words, you will need to engage in legal analysis and reasoning. Here, we offer some suggestions on how to make this task less daunting. We begin by presenting a sample problem:

> While Janet Lawson, a famous pianist, was shopping in Quality Market, she slipped and fell on a wet floor in one of the aisles. The floor had recently been mopped by one of the store's employees, but there were no signs warning customers that the floor in that area was wet. As a result of the fall, Lawson injured her right arm and was unable to perform piano concerts for the next six months. Had she been able to perform the scheduled concerts, she would have earned approximately $60,000 over that period of time. Lawson sued Quality Market for this amount, plus another $10,000 in medical expenses. She claimed

that the store's failure to warn customers of the wet floor constituted negligence and therefore the market was liable for her injuries. Will the court agree with Lawson? Discuss.

Understand the Facts

This may sound obvious, but before you can analyze or apply the relevant law to a specific set of facts, you must clearly understand those facts. In other words, you should read through the case problem carefully—more than once, if necessary—to make sure you understand the identity of the plaintiff(s) and defendant(s) in the case and the progression of events that led to the lawsuit.

In the sample case problem just given, the identity of the parties is fairly obvious. Janet Lawson is the one bringing the suit; therefore, she is the plaintiff. Quality Market, against whom she is bringing the suit, is the defendant. Some of the case problems you may work on have multiple plaintiffs or defendants. Often, it is helpful to use abbreviations for the parties. To indicate a reference to a plaintiff, for example, the *pi* symbol—π—is often used, and a defendant is denoted by a *delta*—Δ—a triangle.

The events leading to the lawsuit are also fairly straightforward. Lawson slipped and fell on a wet floor, and she contends that Quality Market should be liable for her injuries because it was negligent in not posting a sign warning customers of the wet floor.

When you are working on case problems, realize that the facts should be accepted as they are given. For example, in our sample problem, it should be accepted that the floor was wet and that there was no sign. In other words, avoid making conjectures, such as "Maybe the floor wasn't too wet," or "Maybe an employee was getting a sign to put up," or "Maybe someone stole the sign." Questioning the facts as they are presented only adds confusion to your analysis.

Legal Analysis and Reasoning

Once you understand the facts given in the case problem, you can begin to analyze the case. Recall from Chapter 1 that the IRAC method is a helpful tool to use in the legal analysis and reasoning process. IRAC is an acronym for **I**ssue, **R**ule, **A**pplication, **C**onclusion. Applying this method to our sample problem would involve the following steps:

1 First, you need to decide what legal **issue** is involved in the case. In our sample case, the basic issue is whether Quality Market's failure to warn customers of the wet floor constituted negligence. As discussed in Chapter 4 negligence is a *tort*—a civil wrong. In a tort lawsuit, the plaintiff seeks to be compensated for another's wrongful act. A defendant will be deemed negligent if he or she breached a duty of care owed to the plaintiff and the breach of that duty caused the plaintiff to suffer harm.

2 Once you have identified the issue, the next step is to determine what **rule of law** applies to the issue. To make this determination, you will want to review carefully the text of the chapter in which the relevant rule of law for the problem appears. Our sample case problem involves the tort of negligence, which is covered in Chapter 4. The applicable rule of law is the tort law principle that business owners owe a duty to exercise reasonable care to protect their customers *(business invitees)*. Reasonable care, in this

context, includes either removing—or warning customers of—*foreseeable* risks about which the owner *knew* or *should have known.* Business owners need not warn customers of "open and obvious" risks, however. If a business owner breaches this duty of care (fails to exercise the appropriate degree of care toward customers), and the breach of duty causes a customer to be injured, the business owner will be liable to the customer for the customer's injuries.

3 The next—and usually the most difficult—step in analyzing case problems is the **application** of the relevant rule of law to the specific facts of the case you are studying. In our sample problem, applying the tort law principle just discussed presents few difficulties. An employee of the store had mopped the floor in the aisle where Lawson slipped and fell, but no sign was present indicating that the floor was wet. That a customer might fall on a wet floor is clearly a foreseeable risk. Therefore, the failure to warn customers about the wet floor was a breach of the duty of care owed by the business owner to the store's customers.

4 Once you have completed Step 3 in the IRAC method, you should be ready to draw your **conclusion.** In our sample problem, Quality Market is liable to Lawson for her injuries, because the market's breach of its duty of care caused Lawson's injuries.

The fact patterns in the case problems presented in this text are not always as simple as those presented in our sample problem. Often, for example, a case has more than one plaintiff or defendant. A case may also involve more than one issue and have more than one applicable rule of law. Furthermore, in some case problems the facts may indicate that the general rule of law should not apply. For example, suppose that a store employee advised Lawson not to walk on the floor in the aisle because it was wet, but Lawson decided to walk on it anyway. This fact could alter the outcome of the case because the store could then raise the defense of *assumption of risk* (see Chapter 4). Nonetheless, a careful review of the chapter should always provide you with the knowledge you need to analyze the problem thoroughly and arrive at accurate conclusions.

APPENDIX B
The Constitution of the United States

PREAMBLE

We the People of the United States, in Order to form a more perfect Union, establish Justice, insure domestic Tranquility, provide for the common defence, promote the general Welfare, and secure the Blessings of Liberty to ourselves and our Posterity, do ordain and establish this Constitution for the United States of America.

ARTICLE I

Section 1. All legislative Powers herein granted shall be vested in a Congress of the United States, which shall consist of a Senate and House of Representatives.

Section 2. The House of Representatives shall be composed of Members chosen every second Year by the People of the several States, and the Electors in each State shall have the Qualifications requisite for Electors of the most numerous Branch of the State Legislature.

No Person shall be a Representative who shall not have attained to the Age of twenty five Years, and been seven Years a Citizen of the United States, and who shall not, when elected, be an Inhabitant of that State in which he shall be chosen.

Representatives and direct Taxes shall be apportioned among the several States which may be included within this Union, according to their respective Numbers, which shall be determined by adding to the whole Number of free Persons, including those bound to Service for a Term of Years, and excluding Indians not taxed, three fifths of all other Persons. The actual Enumeration shall be made within three Years after the first Meeting of the Congress of the United States, and within every subsequent Term of ten Years, in such Manner as they shall by Law direct. The Number of Representatives shall not exceed one for every thirty Thousand, but each State shall have at Least one Representative; and until such enumeration shall be made, the State of New Hampshire shall be entitled to chuse three, Massachusetts eight, Rhode Island and Providence Plantations one, Connecticut five, New York six, New Jersey four, Pennsylvania eight, Delaware one, Maryland six, Virginia ten, North Carolina five, South Carolina five, and Georgia three.

When vacancies happen in the Representation from any State, the Executive Authority thereof shall issue Writs of Election to fill such Vacancies.

The House of Representatives shall chuse their Speaker and other Officers; and shall have the sole Power of Impeachment.

Section 3. The Senate of the United States shall be composed of two Senators from each State, chosen by the Legislature thereof, for six Years; and each Senator shall have one Vote.

Immediately after they shall be assembled in Consequence of the first Election, they shall be divided as equally as may be into three Classes. The Seats of the Senators of the first Class shall be vacated at the Expiration of the second Year, of the second Class at the Expiration of the fourth Year, and of the third Class at the Expiration of the sixth Year, so that one third may be chosen every second Year; and if Vacancies happen by Resignation, or otherwise, during the Recess of the Legislature of any State, the Executive thereof may make temporary Appointments until the next Meeting of the Legislature, which shall then fill such Vacancies.

No Person shall be a Senator who shall not have attained to the Age of thirty Years, and been nine Years a Citizen of the United States, and who shall not, when elected, be an Inhabitant of that State for which he shall be chosen.

The Vice President of the United States shall be President of the Senate, but shall have no Vote, unless they be equally divided.

The Senate shall chuse their other Officers, and also a President pro tempore, in the Absence of the Vice President, or when he shall exercise the Office of President of the United States.

The Senate shall have the sole Power to try all Impeachments. When sitting for that Purpose, they shall be on Oath or Affirmation. When the President of the United States is tried, the Chief Justice shall preside: And no Person shall be convicted without the Concurrence of two thirds of the Members present.

Judgment in Cases of Impeachment shall not extend further than to removal from Office, and disqualification to hold and enjoy any Office of honor, Trust, or Profit under the United States: but the Party convicted shall nevertheless be liable and subject to Indictment, Trial, Judgment, and Punishment, according to Law.

Section 4. The Times, Places and Manner of holding Elections for Senators and Representatives, shall be prescribed in each State by the Legislature thereof; but the Congress may at any time by Law make or alter such Regulations, except as to the Places of chusing Senators.

The Congress shall assemble at least once in every Year, and such Meeting shall be on the first Monday in December, unless they shall by Law appoint a different Day.

Section 5. Each House shall be the Judge of the Elections, Returns, and Qualifications of its own Members, and a Majority of each shall constitute a Quorum to do Business; but a smaller Number may adjourn from day to day, and may be authorized to compel the Attendance of absent Members, in such Manner, and under such Penalties as each House may provide.

Each House may determine the Rules of its Proceedings, punish its Members for disorderly Behavior, and, with the Concurrence of two thirds, expel a Member.

Each House shall keep a Journal of its Proceedings, and from time to time publish the same, excepting such Parts as may in their Judgment require Secrecy; and the Yeas and Nays of the Members of either House on any question shall, at the Desire of one fifth of those Present, be entered on the Journal.

Neither House, during the Session of Congress, shall, without the Consent of the other, adjourn for more than three days, nor to any other Place than that in which the two Houses shall be sitting.

Section 6. The Senators and Representatives shall receive a Compensation for their Services, to be ascertained by Law, and paid out of the Treasury of the United States. They shall in all Cases, except Treason, Felony and Breach of the Peace, be privileged from Arrest during their Attendance at the Session of their respective Houses, and in going to and returning from the same; and for any Speech or Debate in either House, they shall not be questioned in any other Place.

No Senator or Representative shall, during the Time for which he was elected, be appointed to any civil Office under the Authority of the United States, which shall have been created, or the Emoluments whereof shall have been increased during such time; and no Person holding any Office under the United States, shall be a Member of either House during his Continuance in Office.

Section 7. All Bills for raising Revenue shall originate in the House of Representatives; but the Senate may propose or concur with Amendments as on other Bills.

Every Bill which shall have passed the House of Representatives and the Senate, shall, before it become a Law, be presented to the President of the United States; If he approve he shall sign it, but if not he shall return it, with his Objections to the House in which it shall have originated, who shall enter the Objections at large on their Journal, and proceed to reconsider it. If after such Reconsideration two thirds of that House shall agree to pass the Bill, it shall be sent together with the Objections, to the other House, by which it shall likewise be reconsidered, and if approved by two thirds of that House, it shall become a Law. But in all such Cases the Votes of both Houses shall be determined by Yeas and Nays, and the Names of the Persons voting for and against the Bill shall be entered on the Journal of each House respectively. If any Bill shall not be returned by the President within ten Days (Sundays excepted) after it shall have been presented to him, the Same shall be a Law, in like Manner as if he had signed it, unless the Congress by their Adjournment prevent its Return in which Case it shall not be a Law.

Every Order, Resolution, or Vote, to which the Concurrence of the Senate and House of Representatives may be necessary (except on a question of Adjournment) shall be presented to the President of the United States; and before the Same shall take Effect, shall be approved by him, or being disapproved by him, shall be repassed by two thirds of the Senate and House of Representatives, according to the Rules and Limitations prescribed in the Case of a Bill.

Section 8. The Congress shall have Power To lay and collect Taxes, Duties, Imposts and Excises, to pay the Debts and provide for the common Defence and general Welfare of the United States; but all Duties, Imposts and Excises shall be uniform throughout the United States;

To borrow Money on the credit of the United States;

To regulate Commerce with foreign Nations, and among the several States, and with the Indian Tribes;

To establish an uniform Rule of Naturalization, and uniform Laws on the subject of Bankruptcies throughout the United States;

To coin Money, regulate the Value thereof, and of foreign Coin, and fix the Standard of Weights and Measures;

To provide for the Punishment of counterfeiting the Securities and current Coin of the United States;

To establish Post Offices and post Roads;

To promote the Progress of Science and useful Arts, by securing for limited Times to Authors and Inventors the exclusive Right to their respective Writings and Discoveries;

To constitute Tribunals inferior to the supreme Court;

To define and punish Piracies and Felonies committed on the high Seas, and Offenses against the Law of Nations;

To declare War, grant Letters of Marque and Reprisal, and make Rules concerning Captures on Land and Water;

To raise and support Armies, but no Appropriation of Money to that Use shall be for a longer Term than two Years;

To provide and maintain a Navy;

To make Rules for the Government and Regulation of the land and naval Forces;

To provide for calling forth the Militia to execute the Laws of the Union, suppress Insurrections and repel Invasions;

To provide for organizing, arming, and disciplining, the Militia, and for governing such Part of them as may be employed in the Service of the United States, reserving to the States respectively, the Appointment of the Officers, and the Authority of training the Militia according to the discipline prescribed by Congress;

To exercise exclusive Legislation in all Cases whatsoever, over such District (not exceeding ten Miles square) as may, by Cession of particular States, and the Acceptance of Congress, become the Seat of the Government of the United States, and to exercise like Authority over all Places purchased by the Consent of the Legislature of the State in which the Same shall be, for the Erection of Forts, Magazines, Arsenals, dock-Yards, and other needful Buildings;—And

To make all Laws which shall be necessary and proper for carrying into Execution the foregoing Powers, and all other Powers vested by this Constitution in the Government of the United States, or in any Department or Officer thereof.

Section 9. The Migration or Importation of such Persons as any of the States now existing shall think proper to admit, shall not be prohibited by the Congress prior to the Year one thousand eight hundred and eight, but a Tax or duty may be imposed on such Importation, not exceeding ten dollars for each Person.

The privilege of the Writ of Habeas Corpus shall not be suspended, unless when in Cases of Rebellion or Invasion the public Safety may require it.

No Bill of Attainder or ex post facto Law shall be passed.

No Capitation, or other direct, Tax shall be laid, unless in Proportion to the Census or Enumeration herein before directed to be taken.

No Tax or Duty shall be laid on Articles exported from any State.

No Preference shall be given by any Regulation of Commerce or Revenue to the Ports of one State over those of another: nor shall

Vessels bound to, or from, one State be obliged to enter, clear, or pay Duties in another.

No Money shall be drawn from the Treasury, but in Consequence of Appropriations made by Law; and a regular Statement and Account of the Receipts and Expenditures of all public Money shall be published from time to time.

No Title of Nobility shall be granted by the United States: And no Person holding any Office of Profit or Trust under them, shall, without the Consent of the Congress, accept of any present, Emolument, Office, or Title, of any kind whatever, from any King, Prince, or foreign State.

Section 10. No State shall enter into any Treaty, Alliance, or Confederation; grant Letters of Marque and Reprisal; coin Money; emit Bills of Credit; make any Thing but gold and silver Coin a Tender in Payment of Debts; pass any Bill of Attainder, ex post facto Law, or Law impairing the Obligation of Contracts, or grant any Title of Nobility.

No State shall, without the Consent of the Congress, lay any Imposts or Duties on Imports or Exports, except what may be absolutely necessary for executing its inspection Laws: and the net Produce of all Duties and Imposts, laid by any State on Imports or Exports, shall be for the Use of the Treasury of the United States; and all such Laws shall be subject to the Revision and Controul of the Congress.

No State shall, without the Consent of Congress, lay any Duty of Tonnage, keep Troops, or Ships of War in time of Peace, enter into any Agreement or Compact with another State, or with a foreign Power, or engage in War, unless actually invaded, or in such imminent Danger as will not admit of delay.

ARTICLE II

Section 1. The executive Power shall be vested in a President of the United States of America. He shall hold his Office during the Term of four Years, and, together with the Vice President, chosen for the same Term, be elected, as follows:

Each State shall appoint, in such Manner as the Legislature thereof may direct, a Number of Electors, equal to the whole Number of Senators and Representatives to which the State may be entitled in the Congress; but no Senator or Representative, or Person holding an Office of Trust or Profit under the United States, shall be appointed an Elector.

The Electors shall meet in their respective States, and vote by Ballot for two Persons, of whom one at least shall not be an Inhabitant of the same State with themselves. And they shall make a List of all the Persons voted for, and of the Number of Votes for each; which List they shall sign and certify, and transmit sealed to the Seat of the Government of the United States, directed to the President of the Senate. The President of the Senate shall, in the Presence of the Senate and House of Representatives, open all the Certificates, and the Votes shall then be counted. The Person having the greatest Number of Votes shall be the President, if such Number be a Majority of the whole Number of Electors appointed; and if there be more than one who have such Majority, and have an equal Number of Votes, then the House of Representatives shall immediately chuse by Ballot one of them for President; and if no Person have a Majority, then from the five highest on the List the said House shall in like Manner chuse the President. But in chusing the President, the Votes shall be taken by States, the

Representation from each State having one Vote; A quorum for this Purpose shall consist of a Member or Members from two thirds of the States, and a Majority of all the States shall be necessary to a Choice. In every Case, after the Choice of the President, the Person having the greater Number of Votes of the Electors shall be the Vice President. But if there should remain two or more who have equal Votes, the Senate shall chuse from them by Ballot the Vice President.

The Congress may determine the Time of chusing the Electors, and the Day on which they shall give their Votes; which Day shall be the same throughout the United States.

No person except a natural born Citizen, or a Citizen of the United States, at the time of the Adoption of this Constitution, shall be eligible to the Office of President; neither shall any Person be eligible to that Office who shall not have attained to the Age of thirty five Years, and been fourteen Years a Resident within the United States.

In Case of the Removal of the President from Office, or of his Death, Resignation or Inability to discharge the Powers and Duties of the said Office, the same shall devolve on the Vice President, and the Congress may by Law provide for the Case of Removal, Death, Resignation or Inability, both of the President and Vice President, declaring what Officer shall then act as President, and such Officer shall act accordingly, until the Disability be removed, or a President shall be elected.

The President shall, at stated Times, receive for his Services, a Compensation, which shall neither be increased nor diminished during the Period for which he shall have been elected, and he shall not receive within that Period any other Emolument from the United States, or any of them.

Before he enter on the Execution of his Office, he shall take the following Oath or Affirmation: "I do solemnly swear (or affirm) that I will faithfully execute the Office of President of the United States, and will to the best of my Ability, preserve, protect and defend the Constitution of the United States."

Section 2. The President shall be Commander in Chief of the Army and Navy of the United States, and of the Militia of the several States, when called into the actual Service of the United States; he may require the Opinion, in writing, of the principal Officer in each of the executive Departments, upon any Subject relating to the Duties of their respective Offices, and he shall have Power to grant Reprieves and Pardons for Offenses against the United States, except in Cases of Impeachment.

He shall have Power, by and with the Advice and Consent of the Senate to make Treaties, provided two thirds of the Senators present concur; and he shall nominate, and by and with the Advice and Consent of the Senate, shall appoint Ambassadors, other public Ministers and Consuls, Judges of the supreme Court, and all other Officers of the United States, whose Appointments are not herein otherwise provided for, and which shall be established by Law; but the Congress may by Law vest the Appointment of such inferior Officers, as they think proper, in the President alone, in the Courts of Law, or in the Heads of Departments.

The President shall have Power to fill up all Vacancies that may happen during the Recess of the Senate, by granting Commissions which shall expire at the End of their next Session.

Section 3. He shall from time to time give to the Congress Information of the State of the Union, and recommend to their

Consideration such Measures as he shall judge necessary and expedient; he may, on extraordinary Occasions, convene both Houses, or either of them, and in Case of Disagreement between them, with Respect to the Time of Adjournment, he may adjourn them to such Time as he shall think proper; he shall receive Ambassadors and other public Ministers; he shall take Care that the Laws be faithfully executed, and shall Commission all the Officers of the United States.

Section 4. The President, Vice President and all civil Officers of the United States, shall be removed from Office on Impeachment for, and Conviction of, Treason, Bribery, or other high Crimes and Misdemeanors.

ARTICLE III

Section 1. The judicial Power of the United States, shall be vested in one supreme Court, and in such inferior Courts as the Congress may from time to time ordain and establish. The Judges, both of the supreme and inferior Courts, shall hold their Offices during good Behaviour, and shall, at stated Times, receive for their Services a Compensation, which shall not be diminished during their Continuance in Office.

Section 2. The judicial Power shall extend to all Cases, in Law and Equity, arising under this Constitution, the Laws of the United States, and Treaties made, or which shall be made, under their Authority;—to all Cases affecting Ambassadors, other public Ministers and Consuls;—to all Cases of admiralty and maritime Jurisdiction;—to Controversies to which the United States shall be a Party;—to Controversies between two or more States;—between a State and Citizens of another State;—between Citizens of different States;—between Citizens of the same State claiming Lands under Grants of different States, and between a State, or the Citizens thereof, and foreign States, Citizens or Subjects.

In all Cases affecting Ambassadors, other public Ministers and Consuls, and those in which a State shall be a Party, the supreme Court shall have original Jurisdiction. In all the other Cases before mentioned, the supreme Court shall have appellate Jurisdiction, both as to Law and Fact, with such Exceptions, and under such Regulations as the Congress shall make.

The Trial of all Crimes, except in Cases of Impeachment, shall be by Jury; and such Trial shall be held in the State where the said Crimes shall have been committed; but when not committed within any State, the Trial shall be at such Place or Places as the Congress may by Law have directed.

Section 3. Treason against the United States, shall consist only in levying War against them, or, in adhering to their Enemies, giving them Aid and Comfort. No Person shall be convicted of Treason unless on the Testimony of two Witnesses to the same overt Act, or on Confession in open Court.

The Congress shall have Power to declare the Punishment of Treason, but no Attainder of Treason shall work Corruption of Blood, or Forfeiture except during the Life of the Person attainted.

ARTICLE IV

Section 1. Full Faith and Credit shall be given in each State to the public Acts, Records, and judicial Proceedings of every other State. And the Congress may by general Laws prescribe the Manner in which such Acts, Records and Proceedings shall be proved, and the Effect thereof.

Section 2. The Citizens of each State shall be entitled to all Privileges and Immunities of Citizens in the several States.

A Person charged in any State with Treason, Felony, or other Crime, who shall flee from Justice, and be found in another State, shall on Demand of the executive Authority of the State from which he fled, be delivered up, to be removed to the State having Jurisdiction of the Crime.

No Person held to Service or Labour in one State, under the Laws thereof, escaping into another, shall, in Consequence of any Law or Regulation therein, be discharged from such Service or Labour, but shall be delivered up on Claim of the Party to whom such Service or Labour may be due.

Section 3. New States may be admitted by the Congress into this Union; but no new State shall be formed or erected within the Jurisdiction of any other State; nor any State be formed by the Junction of two or more States, or Parts of States, without the Consent of the Legislatures of the States concerned as well as of the Congress.

The Congress shall have Power to dispose of and make all needful Rules and Regulations respecting the Territory or other Property belonging to the United States; and nothing in this Constitution shall be so construed as to Prejudice any Claims of the United States, or of any particular State.

Section 4. The United States shall guarantee to every State in this Union a Republican Form of Government, and shall protect each of them against Invasion; and on Application of the Legislature, or of the Executive (when the Legislature cannot be convened) against domestic Violence.

ARTICLE V

The Congress, whenever two thirds of both Houses shall deem it necessary, shall propose Amendments to this Constitution, or, on the Application of the Legislatures of two thirds of the several States, shall call a Convention for proposing Amendments, which, in either Case, shall be valid to all Intents and Purposes, as part of this Constitution, when ratified by the Legislatures of three fourths of the several States, or by Conventions in three fourths thereof, as the one or the other Mode of Ratification may be proposed by the Congress; Provided that no Amendment which may be made prior to the Year One thousand eight hundred and eight shall in any Manner affect the first and fourth Clauses in the Ninth Section of the first Article; and that no State, without its Consent, shall be deprived of its equal Suffrage in the Senate.

ARTICLE VI

All Debts contracted and Engagements entered into, before the Adoption of this Constitution shall be as valid against the United States under this Constitution, as under the Confederation.

This Constitution, and the Laws of the United States which shall be made in Pursuance thereof; and all Treaties made, or which shall be made, under the Authority of the United States, shall be the supreme Law of the Land; and the Judges in every State shall be bound thereby, any Thing in the Constitution or Laws of any State to the Contrary notwithstanding.

The Senators and Representatives before mentioned, and the Members of the several State Legislatures, and all executive and judicial Officers, both of the United States and of the several States, shall be bound by Oath or Affirmation, to support this Constitution; but no religious Test shall ever be required as a Qualification to any Office or public Trust under the United States.

ARTICLE VII

The Ratification of the Conventions of nine States shall be sufficient for the Establishment of this Constitution between the States so ratifying the Same.

AMENDMENT I [1791]

Congress shall make no law respecting an establishment of religion, or prohibiting the free exercise thereof; or abridging the freedom of speech, or of the press; or the right of the people peaceably to assembly, and to petition the Government for a redress of grievances.

AMENDMENT II [1791]

A well regulated Militia, being necessary to the security of a free State, the right of the people to keep and bear Arms, shall not be infringed.

AMENDMENT III [1791]

No Soldier shall, in time of peace be quartered in any house, without the consent of the Owner, nor in time of war, but in a manner to be prescribed by law.

AMENDMENT IV [1791]

The right of the people to be secure in their persons, houses, papers, and effects, against unreasonable searches and seizures, shall not be violated, and no Warrants shall issue, but upon probable cause, supported by Oath or affirmation, and particularly describing the place to be searched, and the persons or things to be seized.

AMENDMENT V [1791]

No person shall be held to answer for a capital, or otherwise infamous crime, unless on a presentment or indictment of a Grand Jury, except in cases arising in the land or naval forces, or in the Militia, when in actual service in time of War or public danger; nor shall any person be subject for the same offence to be twice put in jeopardy of life or limb; nor shall be compelled in any criminal case to be a witness against himself, nor be deprived of life, liberty, or property, without due process of law; nor shall private property be taken for public use, without just compensation.

AMENDMENT VI [1791]

In all criminal prosecutions, the accused shall enjoy the right to a speedy and public trial, by an impartial jury of the State and district wherein the crime shall have been committed, which district shall have been previously ascertained by law, and to be informed of the nature and cause of the accusation; to be confronted with the witnesses against him; to have compulsory process for obtaining witnesses in his favor, and to have the Assistance of Counsel for his defence.

AMENDMENT VII [1791]

In Suits at common law, where the value in controversy shall exceed twenty dollars, the right of trial by jury shall be preserved, and no fact tried by jury, shall be otherwise re-examined in any Court of the United States, than according to the rules of the common law.

AMENDMENT VIII [1791]

Excessive bail shall not be required, nor excessive fines imposed, nor cruel and unusual punishments inflicted.

AMENDMENT IX [1791]

The enumeration in the Constitution, of certain rights, shall not be construed to deny or disparage others retained by the people.

AMENDMENT X [1791]

The powers not delegated to the United States by the Constitution, nor prohibited by it to the States, are reserved to the States respectively, or to the people.

AMENDMENT XI [1798]

The Judicial power of the United States shall not be construed to extend to any suit in law or equity, commenced or prosecuted against one of the United States by Citizens of another State, or by Citizens or Subjects of any Foreign State.

AMENDMENT XII [1804]

The Electors shall meet in their respective states, and vote by ballot for President and Vice-President, one of whom, at least, shall not be an inhabitant of the same state with themselves; they shall name in their ballots the person voted for as President, and in distinct ballots the person voted for as Vice-President, and they shall make distinct lists of all persons voted for as President, and of all persons voted for as Vice-President, and of the number of votes for each, which lists they shall sign and certify, and transmit sealed to the seat of the government of the United States, directed to the President of the Senate;—The President of the Senate shall, in the presence of the Senate and House of Representatives, open all the certificates and the votes shall then be counted;—The person having the greatest number of votes for President, shall be the President, if such number be a majority of the whole number of Electors appointed; and if no person have such majority, then from the persons having the highest numbers not exceeding three on the list of those voted for as President, the House of Representatives shall choose immediately, by ballot, the President. But in choosing the President, the votes shall be taken by states, the representation from each state having one vote; a quorum for this purpose shall consist of a member or members from two-thirds of the states, and a majority of all states shall be necessary to a choice. And if the House of Representatives shall not choose a President whenever the right of choice shall devolve upon them, before the fourth day of March next following, then the Vice-President shall act as President, as in the case of the death or other constitutional disability of the President.—The person having the greatest number of votes as Vice-President, shall be the Vice-President, if such number be a majority of the whole number of Electors appointed, and if no person have a majority, then from the two highest numbers on the list, the Senate shall choose the Vice-President; a quorum for the purpose shall consist of two-thirds of the whole number of Senators, and a majority of the whole number shall be necessary to a choice. But no person constitutionally ineligible to the office of President shall be eligible to that of Vice-President of the United States.

AMENDMENT XIII [1865]

Section 1. Neither slavery nor involuntary servitude, except as a punishment for crime whereof the party shall have been duly convicted, shall exist within the United States, or any place subject to their jurisdiction.

Section 2. Congress shall have power to enforce this article by appropriate legislation.

AMENDMENT XIV [1868]

Section 1. All persons born or naturalized in the United States, and subject to the jurisdiction thereof, are citizens of the United States and of the State wherein they reside. No State shall make or enforce any law which shall abridge the privileges or immunities of citizens of the United States; nor shall any State deprive any person of life, liberty, or property, without due process of law; nor deny to any person within its jurisdiction the equal protection of the laws.

Section 2. Representatives shall be apportioned among the several States according to their respective numbers, counting the whole number of persons in each State, excluding Indians not taxed. But when the right to vote at any election for the choice of electors for President and Vice President of the United States, Representatives in Congress, the Executive and Judicial officers of a State, or the members of the Legislature thereof, is denied to any of the male inhabitants of such State, being twenty-one years of age, and citizens of the United States, or in any way abridged, except for participation in rebellion, or other crime, the basis of representation therein shall be reduced in the proportion which the number of such male citizens shall bear to the whole number of male citizens twenty-one years of age in such State.

Section 3. No person shall be a Senator or Representative in Congress, or elector of President and Vice President, or hold any office, civil or military, under the United States, or under any State, who having previously taken an oath, as a member of Congress, or as an officer of the United States, or as a member of any State legislature, or as an executive or judicial officer of any State, to support the Constitution of the United States, shall have engaged in insurrection or rebellion against the same, or given aid or comfort to the enemies thereof. But Congress may by a vote of two-thirds of each House, remove such disability.

Section 4. The validity of the public debt of the United States, authorized by law, including debts incurred for payment of pensions and bounties for services in suppressing insurrection or rebellion, shall not be questioned. But neither the United States nor any State shall assume or pay any debt or obligation incurred in aid of insurrection or rebellion against the United States, or any claim for the loss or emancipation of any slave; but all such debts, obligations and claims shall be held illegal and void.

Section 5. The Congress shall have power to enforce, by appropriate legislation, the provisions of this article.

AMENDMENT XV [1870]

Section 1. The right of citizens of the United States to vote shall not be denied or abridged by the United States or by any State on account of race, color, or previous condition of servitude.

Section 2. The Congress shall have power to enforce this article by appropriate legislation.

AMENDMENT XVI [1913]

The Congress shall have power to lay and collect taxes on incomes, from whatever source derived, without apportionment among the several States, and without regard to any census or enumeration.

AMENDMENT XVII [1913]

Section 1. The Senate of the United States shall be composed of two Senators from each State, elected by the people thereof, for six years; and each Senator shall have one vote. The electors in each State shall have the qualifications requisite for electors of the most numerous branch of the State legislatures.

Section 2. When vacancies happen in the representation of any State in the Senate, the executive authority of such State shall issue writs of election to fill such vacancies: *Provided,* That the legislature of any State may empower the executive thereof to make temporary appointments until the people fill the vacancies by election as the legislature may direct.

Section 3. This amendment shall not be so construed as to affect the election or term of any Senator chosen before it becomes valid as part of the Constitution.

AMENDMENT XVIII [1919]

Section 1. After one year from the ratification of this article the manufacture, sale, or transportation of intoxicating liquors within, the importation thereof into, or the exportation thereof from the United States and all territory subject to the jurisdiction thereof for beverage purposes is hereby prohibited.

Section 2. The Congress and the several States shall have concurrent power to enforce this article by appropriate legislation.

Section 3. This article shall be inoperative unless it shall have been ratified as an amendment to the Constitution by the legislatures of the several States, as provided in the Constitution, within seven years from the date of the submission hereof to the States by the Congress.

AMENDMENT XIX [1920]

Section 1. The right of citizens of the United States to vote shall not be denied or abridged by the United States or by any State on account of sex.

Section 2. Congress shall have power to enforce this article by appropriate legislation.

AMENDMENT XX [1933]

Section 1. The terms of the President and Vice President shall end at noon on the 20th day of January, and the terms of Senators and Representatives at noon on the 3d day of January, of the years in which such terms would have ended if this article had not been ratified; and the terms of their successors shall then begin.

Section 2. The Congress shall assemble at least once in every year, and such meeting shall begin at noon on the 3d day of January, unless they shall by law appoint a different day.

Section 3. If, at the time fixed for the beginning of the term of the President, the President elect shall have died, the Vice President elect shall become President. If the President shall not have been chosen before the time fixed for the beginning of his term, or if the President elect shall have failed to qualify, then the Vice President elect shall act as President until a President shall have qualified; and the Congress may by law provide for the case wherein neither a President elect nor a Vice President elect shall have qualified, declaring who shall then act as President, or the manner in which one who is to act shall be selected, and such person shall act accordingly until a President or Vice President shall have qualified.

Section 4. The Congress may by law provide for the case of the death of any of the persons from whom the House of Representatives may choose a President whenever the right of choice shall have devolved upon them, and for the case of the death of any of the persons from whom the Senate may choose a Vice President whenever the right of choice shall have devolved upon them.

Section 5. Sections 1 and 2 shall take effect on the 15th day of October following the ratification of this article.

Section 6. This article shall be inoperative unless it shall have been ratified as an amendment to the Constitution by the legislatures of three-fourths of the several States within seven years from the date of its submission.

AMENDMENT XXI [1933]

Section 1. The eighteenth article of amendment to the Constitution of the United States is hereby repealed.

Section 2. The transportation or importation into any State, Territory, or possession of the United States for delivery or use therein of intoxicating liquors, in violation of the laws thereof, is hereby prohibited.

Section 3. This article shall be inoperative unless it shall have been ratified as an amendment to the Constitution by conventions in the several States, as provided in the Constitution, within seven years from the date of the submission hereof to the States by the Congress.

AMENDMENT XXII [1951]

Section 1. No person shall be elected to the office of the President more than twice, and no person who has held the office of President, or acted as President, for more than two years of a term to which some other person was elected President shall be elected to the office of President more than once. But this Article shall not apply to any person holding the office of President when this Article was proposed by the Congress, and shall not prevent any person who may be holding the office of President, or acting as President, during the term within which this Article becomes operative from holding the office of President or acting as President during the remainder of such term.

Section 2. This article shall be inoperative unless it shall have been ratified as an amendment to the Constitution by the legislatures of three-fourths of the several States within seven years from the date of its submission to the States by the Congress.

AMENDMENT XXIII [1961]

Section 1. The District constituting the seat of Government of the United States shall appoint in such manner as the Congress may direct:

A number of electors of President and Vice President equal to the whole number of Senators and Representatives in Congress to which the District would be entitled if it were a State, but in no event more than the least populous state; they shall be in addition to those appointed by the states, but they shall be considered, for the purposes of the election of President and Vice President, to be electors appointed by a state; and they shall meet in the District and perform such duties as provided by the twelfth article of amendment.

Section 2. The Congress shall have power to enforce this article by appropriate legislation.

AMENDMENT XXIV [1964]

Section 1. The right of citizens of the United States to vote in any primary or other election for President or Vice President, for electors for President or Vice President, or for Senator or Representative in Congress, shall not be denied or abridged by the United States, or any State by reason of failure to pay any poll tax or other tax.

Section 2. The Congress shall have power to enforce this article by appropriate legislation.

AMENDMENT XXV [1967]

Section 1. In case of the removal of the President from office or of his death or resignation, the Vice President shall become President.

Section 2. Whenever there is a vacancy in the office of the Vice President, the President shall nominate a Vice President who shall take office upon confirmation by a majority vote of both Houses of Congress.

Section 3. Whenever the President transmits to the President pro tempore of the Senate and the Speaker of the House of Representatives his written declaration that he is unable to discharge the powers and duties of his office, and until he transmits to them a written declaration to the contrary, such powers and duties shall be discharged by the Vice President as Acting President.

Section 4. Whenever the Vice President and a majority of either the principal officers of the executive departments or of such other body as Congress may by law provide, transmit to the President pro tempore of the Senate and the Speaker of the House of Representatives their written declaration that the President is unable to discharge the powers and duties of his office, the Vice President shall immediately assume the powers and duties of the office as Acting President.

Thereafter, when the President transmits to the President pro tempore of the Senate and the Speaker of the House of Representatives his written declaration that no inability exists, he shall resume the powers and duties of his office unless the Vice President and a majority of either the principal officers of the executive department or of such other body as Congress may by law provide, transmit within four days to the President pro tempore of the Senate and the Speaker of the House of Representatives their written declaration that the President is unable to discharge the powers and duties of his office. Thereupon Congress shall decide the issue, assembling within forty-eight hours for that purpose if not in session. If the Congress, within twenty-one days after receipt of the latter written declaration, or, if Congress is not in session, within twenty-one days after Congress is required to assemble, determines by two-thirds vote of both Houses that the President is unable to discharge the powers and duties of his office, the Vice President shall continue to discharge the same as Acting President; otherwise, the President shall resume the powers and duties of his office.

AMENDMENT XXVI [1971]

Section 1. The right of citizens of the United States, who are eighteen years of age or older, to vote shall not be denied or abridged by the United States or by any State on account of age.

Section 2. The Congress shall have power to enforce this article by appropriate legislation.

AMENDMENT XXVII [1992]

No law, varying the compensation for the services of the Senators and Representatives, shall take effect, until an election of Representatives shall have intervened.

APPENDIX C
The Uniform Commercial Code (Excerpts)

(Adopted in fifty-two jurisdictions: all fifty States, although Louisiana has adopted only Articles 1, 3, 4, 7, 8, and 9; the District of Columbia; and the Virgin Islands.)

The Uniform Commercial Code consists of the following articles:

1. General Provisions
2. Sales
2A. Leases
3. Negotiable Instruments
4. Bank Deposits and Collections
4A. Funds Transfers
5. Letters of Credit
6. Repealer of Article 6—Bulk Transfers and [Revised] Article 6 —Bulk Sales
7. Warehouse Receipts, Bills of Lading and Other Documents of Title
8. Investment Securities
9. Secured Transactions
10. Effective Date and Repealer
11. Effective Date and Transition Provisions

Article 1
GENERAL PROVISIONS

Part 1 General Provisions

§ 1–101. Short Titles.

(a) This [Act] may be cited as Uniform Commercial Code.

(b) This article may be cited as Uniform Commercial Code-Uniform Provisions.

§ 1–102. Scope of Article.

This article applies to a transaction to the extent that it is governed by another article of [the Uniform Commercial Code].

§ 1–103. Construction of [Uniform Commercial Code] to Promote Its Purpose and Policies; Applicability of Supplemental Principles of Law.

(a) [The Uniform Commercial Code] must be liberally construed and applied to promote its underlying purposes and policies, which are:

(1) to simplify, clarify, and modernize the law governing commercial transactions;

(2) to permit the continued expansion of commercial practices through custom, usage, and agreement of the parties; and

(3) to make uniform the law among the various jurisdictions.

(b) Unless displaced by the particular provisions of [the Uniform Commercial Code], the principles of law and equity, including the law merchant and the law relative to capacity to contract, principal and agent, estoppel, fraud, misrepresentation, duress, coercion, mistake, bankruptcy, and other validating or invalidating cause, supplement its provisions.

§ 1–104. Construction Against Implicit Repeal.

This Act being a general act intended as a unified coverage of its subject matter, no part of it shall be deemed to be impliedly repealed by subsequent legislation if such construction can reasonably be avoided.

§ 1–105. Severability.

If any provision or clause of [the Uniform Commercial Code] or its application to any person or circumstance is held invalid, the invalidity does not affect other provisions or applications of [the Uniform Commercial Code] which can be given effect without the invalid provision or application, and to this end the provisions of [the Uniform Commercial Code] are severable.

§ 1–106. Use of Singular and Plural; Gender.

In [the Uniform Commercial Code], unless the statutory context otherwise requires:

(1) words in the singular number include the plural, and those in the plural include the singular; and

(2) words of any gender also refer to any other gender.

§ 1–107. Section Captions.

Section captions are part of [the Uniform Commercial Code].

§ 1–108. Relation to Electronic Signatures in Global and National Commerce Act.

This article modifies, limits, and supersedes the Federal Electronic Signatures in Global and National Commerce Act, 15 U.S.C. Sections 7001 *et seq.*, except that nothing in this article modifies, limits, or supersedes section 7001(c) of that act or authorizes electronic delivery of any of the notices described in section 7003(b) of that Act.

Part 2 General Definitions and Principles of Interpretation

§ 1–201. General Definitions.

Subject to additional definitions contained in the subsequent Articles of this Act which are applicable to specific Articles or Parts thereof, and unless the context otherwise requires, in this Act:

(1) "Action", in the sense of a judicial proceeding, includes recoupment, counterclaim, set-off, suit in equity, and any other proceedings in which rights are determined.

(2) "Aggrieved party" means a party entitled to resort to a remedy.

(3) "Agreement", as distinguished from "contract", means the bargain of the parties in fact, as found in their language or by implication from other circumstances, including course of performance, course of dealing, or usage of trade as provided in Section 1-303.

(4) "Bank" means a person engaged in the business of banking and includes a savings bank, savings and loan association, credit union, and trust company.

(5) "Bearer" means a person in control of a negotiable electronic document of title or a person in possession of a negotiable instrument, negotiable tangible document of title, or certificated security that is payable to bearer or indorsed in blank.

(6) "Bill of lading" means a document of title evidencing the receipt of goods for shipment issued by a person engaged in the business of directly or indirectly transporting or forwarding goods. The term does not include a warehouse receipt.

(7) "Branch" includes a separately incorporated foreign branch of a bank.

(8) "Burden of establishing" a fact means the burden of persuading the trier of fact that the existence of the fact is more probable than its nonexistence.

(9) "Buyer in ordinary course of business" means a person that buys goods in good faith, without knowledge that the sale violates the rights of another person in the goods, and in the ordinary course from a person, other than a pawnbroker, in the business of selling goods of that kind. A person buys goods in the ordinary course if the sale to the person comports with the usual or customary practices in the kind of business in which the seller is engaged or with the seller's own usual or customary practices. A person that sells oil, gas, or other minerals at the wellhead or minehead is a person in the business of selling goods of that kind. A buyer in ordinary course of business may buy for cash, by exchange of other property, or on secured or unsecured credit, and may acquire goods or documents of title under a pre-existing contract for sale. Only a buyer that takes possession of the goods or has a right to recover the goods from the seller under Article 2 may be a buyer in ordinary course of business. A person that acquires goods in a transfer in bulk or as security for or in total or partial satisfaction of a money debt is not a buyer in ordinary course of business.

(10) "Conspicuous", with reference to a term, means so written, displayed, or presented that a reasonable person against which it is to operate ought to have noticed it. Whether a term is "conspicuous" or not is a decision for the court. Conspicuous terms include the following:

(A) a heading in capitals equal to or greater in size than the surrounding text, or in contrasting type, font, or color to the surrounding text of the same or lesser size; and

(B) language in the body of a record or display in larger type than the surrounding text, or in contrasting type, font, or color to the surrounding text of the same size, or set off from surrounding text of the same size by symbols or other marks that call attention to the language.

(11) "Consumer" means an individual who enters into a transaction primarily for personal, family, or household purposes.

(12) "Contract", as distinguished from "agreement", means the total legal obligation that results from the parties' agreement as determined by [the Uniform Commercial Code] as supplemented by any other laws.

(13) "Creditor" includes a general creditor, a secured creditor, a lien creditor and any representative of creditors, including an assignee for the benefit of creditors, a trustee in bankruptcy, a receiver in equity and an executor or administrator of an insolvent debtor's or assignor's estate.

(14) "Defendant" includes a person in the position of defendant in a counterclaim, cross-action, or third-party claim.

(15) "Delivery" with respect to an electronic document of title means voluntary transfer of control and with respect to an instrument, a tangible document of title, or chattel paper means voluntary transfer of possession.

(16) "Document of title" means a record (i) that in regular course of business or financing is treated as adequately evidencing that the person in possession or control of the record is entitled to receive, control, hold, and dispose of the record and the goods the record covers and (ii) that purports to be issued by or addressed to a bailee and to cover goods in the bailee's possession which are either identified or are fungible portions of an identified mass. The term includes a bill of lading, transport document, dock warrant, dock receipt, warehouse receipt, and order for delivery of goods. An electronic document of title means a document of title evidenced by a record consisting of information stored in an electronic medium. A tangible document of title means a document of title evidenced by a record consisting of information that is inscribed on a tangible medium.

(17) "Fault" means a default, breach, or wrongful act or omission.

(18) "Fungible goods" means:

(A) goods of which any unit, by nature or usage of trade, is the equivalent of any other like unit; or

(B) goods that by agreement are treated as equivalent.

(19) "Genuine" means free of forgery or counterfeiting.

(20) "Good faith," except as otherwise provided in Article 5, means honesty in fact and the observance of reasonable commercial standards of fair dealing.

(21) "Holder" means:

(A) the person in possession of a negotiable instrument that is payable either to bearer or to an identified person that is the person in possession;

(B) the person in possession of a negotiable tangible document of title if the goods are deliverable either to bearer or to the order of the person in possession; or

(C) the person in control of a negotiable electronic document of title.

(22) "Insolvency proceeding" includes an assignment for the benefit of creditors or other proceeding intended to liquidate or rehabilitate the estate of the person involved.

(23) "Insolvent" means:

(A) having generally ceased to pay debts in the ordinary course of business other than as a result of bona fide dispute;

(B) being unable to pay debts as they become due; or

(C) being insolvent within the meaning of federal bankruptcy law.

(24) "Money" means a medium of exchange currently authorized or adopted by a domestic or foreign government. The term includes a monetary unit of account established by an intergovernmental organization or by agreement between two or more countries.

(25) "Organization" means a person other than an individual.

(26) "Party", as distinguished from "third party", means a person that has engaged in a transaction or made an agreement subject to [the Uniform Commercial Code].

(27) "Person" means an individual, corporation, business trust, estate, trust, partnership, limited liability company, association, joint venture, government, governmental subdivision, agency, or instrumentality, public corporation, or any other legal or commercial entity.

(28) "Present value" means the amount as of a date certain of one or more sums payable in the future, discounted to the date certain by use of either an interest rate specified by the parties if that rate is not manifestly unreasonable at the time the transaction is entered into or, if an interest rate is not so specified, a commercially reasonable rate that takes into account the facts and circumstances at the time the transaction is entered into.

(29) "Purchase" means taking by sale, lease, discount, negotiation, mortgage, pledge, lien, security interest, issue or reissue, gift, or any other voluntary transaction creating an interest in property.

(30) "Purchaser" means a person that takes by purchase.

(31) "Record" means information that is inscribed on a tangible medium or that is stored in an electronic or other medium and is retrievable in perceivable form.

(32) "Remedy" means any remedial right to which an aggrieved party is entitled with or without resort to a tribunal.

(33) "Representative" means a person empowered to act for another, including an agent, an officer of a corporation or association, and a trustee, executor, or administrator of an estate.

(34) "Right" includes remedy.

(35) "Security interest" means an interest in personal property or fixtures which secures payment or performance of an obligation. "Security interest" includes any interest of a consignor and a buyer of accounts, chattel paper, a payment intangible, or a promissory note in a transaction that is subject to Article 9. "Security interest" does not include the special property interest of a buyer of goods on identifica-

tion of those goods to a contract for sale under Section 2-401, but a buyer may also acquire a "security interest" by complying with Article 9. Except as otherwise provided in Section 2-505, the right of a seller or lessor of goods under Article 2 or 2A to retain or acquire possession of the goods is not a "security interest", but a seller or lessor may also acquire a "security interest" by complying with Article 9. The retention or reservation of title by a seller of goods notwithstanding shipment or delivery to the buyer under Section 2-401 is limited in effect to a reservation of a "security interest." Whether a transaction in the form of a lease creates a "security interest" is determined pursuant to Section 1-203.

(36) "Send" in connection with a writing, record, or notice means:

(A) to deposit in the mail or deliver for transmission by any other usual means of communication with postage or cost of transmission provided for and properly addressed and, in the case of an instrument, to an address specified thereon or otherwise agreed, or if there be none to any address reasonable under the circumstances; or

(B) in any other way to cause to be received any record or notice within the time it would have arrived if properly sent.

(37) "Signed" includes using any symbol executed or adopted with present intention to adopt or accept a writing.

(38) "State" means a State of the United States, the District of Columbia, Puerto Rico, the United States Virgin Islands, or any territory or insular possession subject to the jurisdiction of the United States.

(39) "Surety" includes a guarantor or other secondary obligor.

(40) "Term" means a portion of an agreement that relates to a particular matter.

(41) "Unauthorized signature" means a signature made without actual, implied, or apparent authority. The term includes a forgery.

(42) "Warehouse receipt" means a document of title issued by a person engaged in the business of storing goods for hire.

(43) "Writing" includes printing, typewriting, or any other intentional reduction to tangible form. "Written" has a corresponding meaning.

As amended in 2003.

* * * *

§ 1-205. Reasonable Time; Seasonableness.

(a) Whether a time for taking an action required by [the Uniform Commercial Code] is reasonable depends on the nature, purpose, and circumstances of the action.

(b) An action is taken seasonably if it is taken at or within the time agreed or, if no time is agreed, at or within a reasonable time.

* * * *

Part 3 Territorial Applicability and General Rules

* * * *

§ 1-303. Course of Performance, Course of Dealing, and Usage of Trade.

(a) A "course of performance" is a sequence of conduct between the parties to a particular transaction that exists if:

(1) the agreement of the parties with respect to the transaction involves repeated occasions for performance by a party; and

(2) the other party, with knowledge of the nature of the performance and opportunity for objection to it, accepts the performance or acquiesces in it without objection.

(b) A "course of dealing" is a sequence of conduct concerning previous transactions between the parties to a particular transaction that is fairly to be regarded as establishing a common basis of understanding for interpreting their expressions and other conduct.

(c) A "usage of trade" is any practice or method of dealing having such regularity of observance in a place, vocation, or trade as to justify an expectation that it will be observed with respect to the transaction in question. The existence and scope of such a usage must be proved as facts. If it is established that such a usage is embodied in a trade code or similar record, the interpretation of the record is a question of law.

(d) A course of performance or course of dealing between the parties or usage of trade in the vocation or trade in which they are engaged or of which they are or should be aware is relevant in ascertaining the meaning of the parties' agreement, may give particular meaning to specific terms of the agreement, and may supplement or qualify the terms of the agreement. A usage of trade applicable in the place in which part of the performance under the agreement is to occur may be so utilized as to that part of the performance.

(e) Except as otherwise provided in subsection (f), the express terms of an agreement and any applicable course of performance, course of dealing, or usage of trade must be construed whenever reasonable as consistent with each other. If such a construction is unreasonable:

(1) express terms prevail over course of performance, course of dealing, and usage of trade;

(2) course of performance prevails over course of dealing and usage of trade; and

(3) course of dealing prevails over usage of trade.

(f) Subject to Section 2-209 and Section 2A-208, a course of performance is relevant to show a waiver or modification of any term inconsistent with the course of performance.

(g) Evidence of a relevant usage of trade offered by one party is not admissible unless that party has given the other party notice that the court finds sufficient to prevent unfair surprise to the other party.

§ 1–304. Obligation of Good Faith.

Every contract or duty within [the Uniform Commercial Code] imposes an obligation of good faith in its performance and enforcement.

* * * *

§ 1–309. Option to Accelerate at Will.

A term providing that one party or that party's successor in interest may accelerate payment or performance or require collateral or additional collateral "at will" or when the party "deems itself insecure," or words of similar import, means that the party has power to do so only if that party in good faith believes that the prospect of payment or performance is impaired. The burden of establishing lack of good faith is on the party against which the power has been exercised.

§ 1–310. Subordinated Obligations.

An obligation may be issued as subordinated to performance of another obligation of the person obligated, or a creditor may subordinate its right to performance of an obligation by agreement with either the person obligated or another creditor of the person obligated. Subordination does not create a security interest as against either the common debtor or a subordinated creditor.

Article 2
SALES

Part 1 Short Title, General Construction and Subject Matter

§ 2–101. Short Title.

This Article shall be known and may be cited as Uniform Commercial Code—Sales.

§ 2–102. Scope; Certain Security and Other Transactions Excluded From This Article.

Unless the context otherwise requires, this Article applies to transactions in goods; it does not apply to any transaction which although in the form of an unconditional contract to sell or present sale is intended to operate only as a security transaction nor does this Article impair or repeal any statute regulating sales to consumers, farmers or other specified classes of buyers.

§ 2–103. Definitions and Index of Definitions.

(1) In this Article unless the context otherwise requires

(a) "Buyer" means a person who buys or contracts to buy goods.

(b) "Good faith" in the case of a merchant means honesty in fact and the observance of reasonable commercial standards of fair dealing in the trade.

(c) "Receipt" of goods means taking physical possession of them.

(d) "Seller" means a person who sells or contracts to sell goods.

(2) Other definitions applying to this Article or to specified Parts thereof, and the sections in which they appear are:

"Acceptance". Section 2–606.
"Banker's credit". Section 2–325.
"Between merchants". Section 2–104.
"Cancellation". Section 2–106(4).
"Commercial unit". Section 2–105.
"Confirmed credit". Section 2–325.
"Conforming to contract". Section 2–106.
"Contract for sale". Section 2–106.
"Cover". Section 2–712.
"Entrusting". Section 2–403.
"Financing agency". Section 2–104.
"Future goods". Section 2–105.
"Goods". Section 2–105.
"Identification". Section 2–501.
"Installment contract". Section 2–612.
"Letter of Credit". Section 2–325.
"Lot". Section 2–105.

"Merchant". Section 2–104.

"Overseas". Section 2–323.

"Person in position of seller". Section 2–707.

"Present sale". Section 2–106.

"Sale". Section 2–106.

"Sale on approval". Section 2–326.

"Sale or return". Section 2–326.

"Termination". Section 2–106.

(3) The following definitions in other Articles apply to this Article:

"Check". Section 3–104.

"Consignee". Section 7–102.

"Consignor". Section 7–102.

"Consumer goods". Section 9–109.

"Dishonor". Section 3–507.

"Draft". Section 3–104.

(4) In addition Article 1 contains general definitions and principles of construction and interpretation applicable throughout this Article.

As amended in 1994 and 1999.

§ 2–104. Definitions: "Merchant"; "Between Merchants"; "Financing Agency".

(1) "Merchant" means a person who deals in goods of the kind or otherwise by his occupation holds himself out as having knowledge or skill peculiar to the practices or goods involved in the transaction or to whom such knowledge or skill may be attributed by his employment of an agent or broker or other intermediary who by his occupation holds himself out as having such knowledge or skill.

(2) "Financing agency" means a bank, finance company or other person who in the ordinary course of business makes advances against goods or documents of title or who by arrangement with either the seller or the buyer intervenes in ordinary course to make or collect payment due or claimed under the contract for sale, as by purchasing or paying the seller's draft or making advances against it or by merely taking it for collection whether or not documents of title accompany the draft. "Financing agency" includes also a bank or other person who similarly intervenes between persons who are in the position of seller and buyer in respect to the goods (Section 2–707).

(3) "Between merchants" means in any transaction with respect to which both parties are chargeable with the knowledge or skill of merchants.

§ 2–105. Definitions: Transferability; "Goods"; "Future" Goods; "Lot"; "Commercial Unit".

(1) "Goods" means all things (including specially manufactured goods) which are movable at the time of identification to the contract for sale other than the money in which the price is to be paid, investment securities (Article 8) and things in action. "Goods" also includes the unborn young of animals and growing crops and other identified things attached to realty as described in the section on goods to be severed from realty (Section 2–107).

(2) Goods must be both existing and identified before any interest in them can pass. Goods which are not both existing and identified are "future" goods. A purported present sale of future goods or of any interest therein operates as a contract to sell.

(3) There may be a sale of a part interest in existing identified goods.

(4) An undivided share in an identified bulk of fungible goods is sufficiently identified to be sold although the quantity of the bulk is not determined. Any agreed proportion of such a bulk or any quantity thereof agreed upon by number, weight or other measure may to the extent of the seller's interest in the bulk be sold to the buyer who then becomes an owner in common.

(5) "Lot" means a parcel or a single article which is the subject matter of a separate sale or delivery, whether or not it is sufficient to perform the contract.

(6) "Commercial unit" means such a unit of goods as by commercial usage is a single whole for purposes of sale and division of which materially impairs its character or value on the market or in use. A commercial unit may be a single article (as a machine) or a set of articles (as a suite of furniture or an assortment of sizes) or a quantity (as a bale, gross, or carload) or any other unit treated in use or in the relevant market as a single whole.

§ 2–106. Definitions: "Contract"; "Agreement"; "Contract for Sale"; "Sale"; "Present Sale"; "Conforming" to Contract; "Termination"; "Cancellation".

(1) In this Article unless the context otherwise requires "contract" and "agreement" are limited to those relating to the present or future sale of goods. "Contract for sale" includes both a present sale of goods and a contract to sell goods at a future time. A "sale" consists in the passing of title from the seller to the buyer for a price (Section 2–401). A "present sale" means a sale which is accomplished by the making of the contract.

(2) Goods or conduct including any part of a performance are "conforming" or conform to the contract when they are in accordance with the obligations under the contract.

(3) "Termination" occurs when either party pursuant to a power created by agreement or law puts an end to the contract otherwise than for its breach. On "termination" all obligations which are still executory on both sides are discharged but any right based on prior breach or performance survives.

(4) "Cancellation" occurs when either party puts an end to the contract for breach by the other and its effect is the same as that of "termination" except that the cancelling party also retains any remedy for breach of the whole contract or any unperformed balance.

§ 2–107. Goods to Be Severed From Realty: Recording.

(1) A contract for the sale of minerals or the like (including oil and gas) or a structure or its materials to be removed from realty is a contract for the sale of goods within this Article if they are to be severed by the seller but until severance a purported present sale thereof which is not effective as a transfer of an interest in land is effective only as a contract to sell.

(2) A contract for the sale apart from the land of growing crops or other things attached to realty and capable of severance without material harm thereto but not described in subsection (1) or of timber to be cut is a contract for the sale of goods within this Article whether the subject matter is to be severed by the buyer or by the seller even though it forms part of the realty at the time of contracting, and the parties can by identification effect a present sale before severance.

(3) The provisions of this section are subject to any third party rights provided by the law relating to realty records, and the contract for sale may be executed and recorded as a document transferring

an interest in land and shall then constitute notice to third parties of the buyer's rights under the contract for sale.

As amended in 1972.

Part 2 Form, Formation and Readjustment of Contract

§ 2–201. Formal Requirements; Statute of Frauds.

(1) Except as otherwise provided in this section a contract for the sale of goods for the price of $500 or more is not enforceable by way of action or defense unless there is some writing sufficient to indicate that a contract for sale has been made between the parties and signed by the party against whom enforcement is sought or by his authorized agent or broker. A writing is not insufficient because it omits or incorrectly states a term agreed upon but the contract is not enforceable under this paragraph beyond the quantity of goods shown in such writing.

(2) Between merchants if within a reasonable time a writing in confirmation of the contract and sufficient against the sender is received and the party receiving it has reason to know its contents, its satisfies the requirements of subsection (1) against such party unless written notice of objection to its contents is given within ten days after it is received.

(3) A contract which does not satisfy the requirements of subsection (1) but which is valid in other respects is enforceable

(a) if the goods are to be specially manufactured for the buyer and are not suitable for sale to others in the ordinary course of the seller's business and the seller, before notice of repudiation is received and under circumstances which reasonably indicate that the goods are for the buyer, has made either a substantial beginning of their manufacture or commitments for their procurement; or

(b) if the party against whom enforcement is sought admits in his pleading, testimony or otherwise in court that a contract for sale was made, but the contract is not enforceable under this provision beyond the quantity of goods admitted; or

(c) with respect to goods for which payment has been made and accepted or which have been received and accepted (Sec. 2–606).

§ 2–202. Final Written Expression: Parol or Extrinsic Evidence.

Terms with respect to which the confirmatory memoranda of the parties agree or which are otherwise set forth in a writing intended by the parties as a final expression of their agreement with respect to such terms as are included therein may not be contradicted by evidence of any prior agreement or of a contemporaneous oral agreement but may be explained or supplemented

(a) by course of dealing or usage of trade (Section 1–205) or by course of performance (Section 2–208); and

(b) by evidence of consistent additional terms unless the court finds the writing to have been intended also as a complete and exclusive statement of the terms of the agreement.

§ 2–203. Seals Inoperative.

The affixing of a seal to a writing evidencing a contract for sale or an offer to buy or sell goods does not constitute the writing a sealed instrument and the law with respect to sealed instruments does not apply to such a contract or offer.

§ 2–204. Formation in General.

(1) A contract for sale of goods may be made in any manner sufficient to show agreement, including conduct by both parties which recognizes the existence of such a contract.

(2) An agreement sufficient to constitute a contract for sale may be found even though the moment of its making is undetermined.

(3) Even though one or more terms are left open a contract for sale does not fail for indefiniteness if the parties have intended to make a contract and there is a reasonably certain basis for giving an appropriate remedy.

§ 2–205. Firm Offers.

An offer by a merchant to buy or sell goods in a signed writing which by its terms gives assurance that it will be held open is not revocable, for lack of consideration, during the time stated or if no time is stated for a reasonable time, but in no event may such period of irrevocability exceed three months; but any such term of assurance on a form supplied by the offeree must be separately signed by the offeror.

§ 2–206. Offer and Acceptance in Formation of Contract.

(1) Unless other unambiguously indicated by the language or circumstances

(a) an offer to make a contract shall be construed as inviting acceptance in any manner and by any medium reasonable in the circumstances;

(b) an order or other offer to buy goods for prompt or current shipment shall be construed as inviting acceptance either by a prompt promise to ship or by the prompt or current shipment of conforming or nonconforming goods, but such a shipment of non-conforming goods does not constitute an acceptance if the seller seasonably notifies the buyer that the shipment is offered only as an accommodation to the buyer.

(2) Where the beginning of a requested performance is a reasonable mode of acceptance an offeror who is not notified of acceptance within a reasonable time may treat the offer as having lapsed before acceptance.

§ 2–207. Additional Terms in Acceptance or Confirmation.

(1) A definite and seasonable expression of acceptance or a written confirmation which is sent within a reasonable time operates as an acceptance even though it states terms additional to or different from those offered or agreed upon, unless acceptance is expressly made conditional on assent to the additional or different terms.

(2) The additional terms are to be construed as proposals for addition to the contract. Between merchants such terms become part of the contract unless:

(a) the offer expressly limits acceptance to the terms of the offer;

(b) they materially alter it; or

(c) notification of objection to them has already been given or is given within a reasonable time after notice of them is received.

(3) Conduct by both parties which recognizes the existence of a contract is sufficient to establish a contract for sale although the

writings of the parties do not otherwise establish a contract. In such case the terms of the particular contract consist of those terms on which the writings of the parties agree, together with any supplementary terms incorporated under any other provisions of this Act.

§ 2–208. Course of Performance or Practical Construction.

(1) Where the contract for sale involves repeated occasions for performance by either party with knowledge of the nature of the performance and opportunity for objection to it by the other, any course of performance accepted or acquiesced in without objection shall be relevant to determine the meaning of the agreement.

(2) The express terms of the agreement and any such course of performance, as well as any course of dealing and usage of trade, shall be construed whenever reasonable as consistent with each other; but when such construction is unreasonable, express terms shall control course of performance and course of performance shall control both course of dealing and usage of trade (Section 1–205).

(3) Subject to the provisions of the next section on modification and waiver, such course of performance shall be relevant to show a waiver or modification of any term inconsistent with such course of performance.

§ 2–209. Modification, Rescission and Waiver.

(1) An agreement modifying a contract within this Article needs no consideration to be binding.

(2) A signed agreement which excludes modification or rescission except by a signed writing cannot be otherwise modified or rescinded, but except as between merchants such a requirement on a form supplied by the merchant must be separately signed by the other party.

(3) The requirements of the statute of frauds section of this Article (Section 2–201) must be satisfied if the contract as modified is within its provisions.

(4) Although an attempt at modification or rescission does not satisfy the requirements of subsection (2) or (3) it can operate as a waiver.

(5) A party who has made a waiver affecting an executory portion of the contract may retract the waiver by reasonable notification received by the other party that strict performance will be required of any term waived, unless the retraction would be unjust in view of a material change of position in reliance on the waiver.

§ 2–210. Delegation of Performance; Assignment of Rights.

(1) A party may perform his duty through a delegate unless otherwise agreed or unless the other party has a substantial interest in having his original promisor perform or control the acts required by the contract. No delegation of performance relieves the party delegating of any duty to perform or any liability for breach.

(2) Except as otherwise provided in Section 9–406, unless otherwise agreed, all rights of either seller or buyer can be assigned except where the assignment would materially change the duty of the other party, or increase materially the burden or risk imposed on him by his contract, or impair materially his chance of obtaining return performance. A right to damages for breach of the whole contract or a right arising out of the assignor's due performance of his entire obligation can be assigned despite agreement otherwise.

(3) The creation, attachment, perfection, or enforcement of a security interest in the seller's interest under a contract is not a transfer that materially changes the duty of or increases materially the burden or risk imposed on the buyer or impairs materially the buyer's chance of obtaining return performance within the purview of subsection (2) unless, and then only to the extent that, enforcement actually results in a delegation of material performance of the seller. Even in that event, the creation, attachment, perfection, and enforcement of the security interest remain effective, but (i) the seller is liable to the buyer for damages caused by the delegation to the extent that the damages could not reasonably by prevented by the buyer, and (ii) a court having jurisdiction may grant other appropriate relief, including cancellation of the contract for sale or an injunction against enforcement of the security interest or consummation of the enforcement.

(4) Unless the circumstances indicate the contrary a prohibition of assignment of "the contract" is to be construed as barring only the delegation to the assignee of the assignor's performance.

(5) An assignment of "the contract" or of "all my rights under the contract" or an assignment in similar general terms is an assignment of rights and unless the language or the circumstances (as in an assignment for security) indicate the contrary, it is a delegation of performance of the duties of the assignor and its acceptance by the assignee constitutes a promise by him to perform those duties. This promise is enforceable by either the assignor or the other party to the original contract.

(6) The other party may treat any assignment which delegates performance as creating reasonable grounds for insecurity and may without prejudice to his rights against the assignor demand assurances from the assignee (Section 2–609).

As amended in 1999.

Part 3 General Obligation and Construction of Contract

§ 2–301. General Obligations of Parties.

The obligation of the seller is to transfer and deliver and that of the buyer is to accept and pay in accordance with the contract.

§ 2–302. Unconscionable Contract or Clause.

(1) If the court as a matter of law finds the contract or any clause of the contract to have been unconscionable at the time it was made the court may refuse to enforce the contract, or it may enforce the remainder of the contract without the unconscionable clause, or it may so limit the application of any unconscionable clause as to avoid any unconscionable result.

(2) When it is claimed or appears to the court that the contract or any clause thereof may be unconscionable the parties shall be afforded a reasonable opportunity to present evidence as to its commercial setting, purpose and effect to aid the court in making the determination.

§ 2–303. Allocations or Division of Risks.

Where this Article allocates a risk or a burden as between the parties "unless otherwise agreed", the agreement may not only shift the allocation but may also divide the risk or burden.

§ 2–304. Price Payable in Money, Goods, Realty, or Otherwise.

(1) The price can be made payable in money or otherwise. If it is payable in whole or in part in goods each party is a seller of the goods which he is to transfer.

(2) Even though all or part of the price is payable in an interest in realty the transfer of the goods and the seller's obligations with reference to them are subject to this Article, but not the transfer of the interest in realty or the transferor's obligations in connection therewith.

§ 2–305. Open Price Term.

(1) The parties if they so intend can conclude a contract for sale even though the price is not settled. In such a case the price is a reasonable price at the time for delivery if

(a) nothing is said as to price; or

(b) the price is left to be agreed by the parties and they fail to agree; or

(c) the price is to be fixed in terms of some agreed market or other standard as set or recorded by a third person or agency and it is not so set or recorded.

(2) A price to be fixed by the seller or by the buyer means a price for him to fix in good faith.

(3) When a price left to be fixed otherwise than by agreement of the parties fails to be fixed through fault of one party the other may at his option treat the contract as cancelled or himself fix a reasonable price.

(4) Where, however, the parties intend not to be bound unless the price be fixed or agreed and it is not fixed or agreed there is no contract. In such a case the buyer must return any goods already received or if unable so to do must pay their reasonable value at the time of delivery and the seller must return any portion of the price paid on account.

§ 2–306. Output, Requirements and Exclusive Dealings.

(1) A term which measures the quantity by the output of the seller or the requirements of the buyer means such actual output or requirements as may occur in good faith, except that no quantity unreasonably disproportionate to any stated estimate or in the absence of a stated estimate to any normal or otherwise comparable prior output or requirements may be tendered or demanded.

(2) A lawful agreement by either the seller or the buyer for exclusive dealing in the kind of goods concerned imposes unless otherwise agreed an obligation by the seller to use best efforts to supply the goods and by the buyer to use best efforts to promote their sale.

§ 2–307. Delivery in Single Lot or Several Lots.

Unless otherwise agreed all goods called for by a contract for sale must be tendered in a single delivery and payment is due only on such tender but where the circumstances give either party the right to make or demand delivery in lots the price if it can be apportioned may be demanded for each lot.

§ 2–308. Absence of Specified Place for Delivery.

Unless otherwise agreed

(a) the place for delivery of goods is the seller's place of business or if he has none his residence; but

(b) in a contract for sale of identified goods which to the knowledge of the parties at the time of contracting are in some other place, that place is the place for their delivery; and

(c) documents of title may be delivered through customary banking channels.

§ 2–309. Absence of Specific Time Provisions; Notice of Termination.

(1) The time for shipment or delivery or any other action under a contract if not provided in this Article or agreed upon shall be a reasonable time.

(2) Where the contract provides for successive performances but is indefinite in duration it is valid for a reasonable time but unless otherwise agreed may be terminated at any time by either party.

(3) Termination of a contract by one party except on the happening of an agreed event requires that reasonable notification be received by the other party and an agreement dispensing with notification is invalid if its operation would be unconscionable.

§ 2–310. Open Time for Payment or Running of Credit; Authority to Ship Under Reservation.

Unless otherwise agreed

(a) payment is due at the time and place at which the buyer is to receive the goods even though the place of shipment is the place of delivery; and

(b) if the seller is authorized to send the goods he may ship them under reservation, and may tender the documents of title, but the buyer may inspect the goods after their arrival before payment is due unless such inspection is inconsistent with the terms of the contract (Section 2–513); and

(c) if delivery is authorized and made by way of documents of title otherwise than by subsection (b) then payment is due at the time and place at which the buyer is to receive the documents regardless of where the goods are to be received; and

(d) where the seller is required or authorized to ship the goods on credit the credit period runs from the time of shipment but post-dating the invoice or delaying its dispatch will correspondingly delay the starting of the credit period.

§ 2–311. Options and Cooperation Respecting Performance.

(1) An agreement for sale which is otherwise sufficiently definite (subsection (3) of Section 2–204) to be a contract is not made invalid by the fact that it leaves particulars of performance to be specified by one of the parties. Any such specification must be made in good faith and within limits set by commercial reasonableness.

(2) Unless otherwise agreed specifications relating to assortment of the goods are at the buyer's option and except as otherwise provided in subsections (1)(c) and (3) of Section 2–319 specifications or arrangements relating to shipment are at the seller's option.

(3) Where such specification would materially affect the other party's performance but is not seasonably made or where one party's cooperation is necessary to the agreed performance of the other but is not seasonably forthcoming, the other party in addition to all other remedies

(a) is excused for any resulting delay in his own performance; and

(b) may also either proceed to perform in any reasonable manner or after the time for a material part of his own performance treat the failure to specify or to cooperate as a breach by failure to deliver or accept the goods.

§ 2–312. Warranty of Title and Against Infringement; Buyer's Obligation Against Infringement.

(1) Subject to subsection (2) there is in a contract for sale a warranty by the seller that

(a) the title conveyed shall be good, and its transfer rightful; and

(b) the goods shall be delivered free from any security interest or other lien or encumbrance of which the buyer at the time of contracting has no knowledge.

(2) A warranty under subsection (1) will be excluded or modified only by specific language or by circumstances which give the buyer reason to know that the person selling does not claim title in himself or that he is purporting to sell only such right or title as he or a third person may have.

(3) Unless otherwise agreed a seller who is a merchant regularly dealing in goods of the kind warrants that the goods shall be delivered free of the rightful claim of any third person by way of infringement or the like but a buyer who furnishes specifications to the seller must hold the seller harmless against any such claim which arises out of compliance with the specifications.

§ 2–313. Express Warranties by Affirmation, Promise, Description, Sample.

(1) Express warranties by the seller are created as follows:

(a) Any affirmation of fact or promise made by the seller to the buyer which relates to the goods and becomes part of the basis of the bargain creates an express warranty that the goods shall conform to the affirmation or promise.

(b) Any description of the goods which is made part of the basis of the bargain creates an express warranty that the goods shall conform to the description.

(c) Any sample or model which is made part of the basis of the bargain creates an express warranty that the whole of the goods shall conform to the sample or model.

(2) It is not necessary to the creation of an express warranty that the seller use formal words such as "warrant" or "guarantee" or that he have a specific intention to make a warranty, but an affirmation merely of the value of the goods or a statement purporting to be merely the seller's opinion or commendation of the goods does not create a warranty.

§ 2–314. Implied Warranty: Merchantability; Usage of Trade.

(1) Unless excluded or modified (Section 2–316), a warranty that the goods shall be merchantable is implied in a contract for their sale if the seller is a merchant with respect to goods of that kind. Under this section the serving for value of food or drink to be consumed either on the premises or elsewhere is a sale.

(2) Goods to be merchantable must be at least such as

(a) pass without objection in the trade under the contract description; and

(b) in the case of fungible goods, are of fair average quality within the description; and

(c) are fit for the ordinary purposes for which such goods are used; and

(d) run, within the variations permitted by the agreement, of even kind, quality and quantity within each unit and among all units involved; and

(e) are adequately contained, packaged, and labeled as the agreement may require; and

(f) conform to the promises or affirmations of fact made on the container or label if any.

(3) Unless excluded or modified (Section 2–316) other implied warranties may arise from course of dealing or usage of trade.

§ 2–315. Implied Warranty: Fitness for Particular Purpose.

Where the seller at the time of contracting has reason to know any particular purpose for which the goods are required and that the buyer is relying on the seller's skill or judgment to select or furnish suitable goods, there is unless excluded or modified under the next section an implied warranty that the goods shall be fit for such purpose.

§ 2–316. Exclusion or Modification of Warranties.

(1) Words or conduct relevant to the creation of an express warranty and words or conduct tending to negate or limit warranty shall be construed wherever reasonable as consistent with each other; but subject to the provisions of this Article on parol or extrinsic evidence (Section 2–202) negation or limitation is inoperative to the extent that such construction is unreasonable.

(2) Subject to subsection (3), to exclude or modify the implied warranty of merchantability or any part of it the language must mention merchantability and in case of a writing must be conspicuous, and to exclude or modify any implied warranty of fitness the exclusion must be by a writing and conspicuous. Language to exclude all implied warranties of fitness is sufficient if it states, for example, that "There are no warranties which extend beyond the description on the face hereof."

(3) Notwithstanding subsection (2)

(a) unless the circumstances indicate otherwise, all implied warranties are excluded by expressions like "as is", "with all faults" or other language which in common understanding calls the buyer's attention to the exclusion of warranties and makes plain that there is no implied warranty; and

(b) when the buyer before entering into the contract has examined the goods or the sample or model as fully as he desired or has refused to examine the goods there is no implied warranty with regard to defects which an examination ought in the circumstances to have revealed to him; and

(c) an implied warranty can also be excluded or modified by course of dealing or course of performance or usage of trade.

(4) Remedies for breach of warranty can be limited in accordance with the provisions of this Article on liquidation or limitation of damages and on contractual modification of remedy (Sections 2–718 and 2–719).

§ 2–317. Cumulation and Conflict of Warranties Express or Implied.

Warranties whether express or implied shall be construed as consistent with each other and as cumulative, but if such construction is unreasonable the intention of the parties shall determine which warranty is dominant. In ascertaining that intention the following rules apply:

(a) Exact or technical specifications displace an inconsistent sample or model or general language of description.

(b) A sample from an existing bulk displaces inconsistent general language of description.

(c) Express warranties displace inconsistent implied warranties other than an implied warranty of fitness for a particular purpose.

§ 2–318. Third Party Beneficiaries of Warranties Express or Implied.

Note: If this Act is introduced in the Congress of the United States this section should be omitted. (States to select one alternative.)

Alternative A

A seller's warranty whether express or implied extends to any natural person who is in the family or household of his buyer or who is a guest in his home if it is reasonable to expect that such person may use, consume or be affected by the goods and who is injured in person by breach of the warranty. A seller may not exclude or limit the operation of this section.

Alternative B

A seller's warranty whether express or implied extends to any natural person who may reasonably be expected to use, consume or be affected by the goods and who is injured in person by breach of the warranty. A seller may not exclude or limit the operation of this section.

Alternative C

A seller's warranty whether express or implied extends to any person who may reasonably be expected to use, consume or be affected by the goods and who is injured by breach of the warranty. A seller may not exclude or limit the operation of this section with respect to injury to the person of an individual to whom the warranty extends. As amended 1966.

§ 2–319. F.O.B. and F.A.S. Terms.

(1) Unless otherwise agreed the term F.O.B. (which means "free on board") at a named place, even though used only in connection with the stated price, is a delivery term under which

(a) when the term is F.O.B. the place of shipment, the seller must at that place ship the goods in the manner provided in this Article (Section 2–504) and bear the expense and risk of putting them into the possession of the carrier; or

(b) when the term is F.O.B. the place of destination, the seller must at his own expense and risk transport the goods to that place and there tender delivery of them in the manner provided in this Article (Section 2–503);

(c) when under either (a) or (b) the term is also F.O.B. vessel, car or other vehicle, the seller must in addition at his own expense and risk load the goods on board. If the term is F.O.B. vessel the buyer must name the vessel and in an appropriate case the seller must comply with the provisions of this Article on the form of bill of lading (Section 2–323).

(2) Unless otherwise agreed the term F.A.S. vessel (which means "free alongside") at a named port, even though used only in connection with the stated price, is a delivery term under which the seller must

(a) at his own expense and risk deliver the goods alongside the vessel in the manner usual in that port or on a dock designated and provided by the buyer; and

(b) obtain and tender a receipt for the goods in exchange for which the carrier is under a duty to issue a bill of lading.

(3) Unless otherwise agreed in any case falling within subsection (1)(a) or (c) or subsection (2) the buyer must seasonably give any needed instructions for making delivery, including when the term is F.A.S. or F.O.B. the loading berth of the vessel and in an appropriate case its name and sailing date. The seller may treat the failure of needed instructions as a failure of cooperation under this Article (Section 2–311). He may also at his option move the goods in any reasonable manner preparatory to delivery or shipment.

(4) Under the term F.O.B. vessel or F.A.S. unless otherwise agreed the buyer must make payment against tender of the required documents and the seller may not tender nor the buyer demand delivery of the goods in substitution for the documents.

§ 2–320. C.I.F. and C. & F. Terms.

(1) The term C.I.F. means that the price includes in a lump sum the cost of the goods and the insurance and freight to the named destination. The term C. & F. or C.F. means that the price so includes cost and freight to the named destination.

(2) Unless otherwise agreed and even though used only in connection with the stated price and destination, the term C.I.F. destination or its equivalent requires the seller at his own expense and risk to

(a) put the goods into the possession of a carrier at the port for shipment and obtain a negotiable bill or bills of lading covering the entire transportation to the named destination; and

(b) load the goods and obtain a receipt from the carrier (which may be contained in the bill of lading) showing that the freight has been paid or provided for; and

(c) obtain a policy or certificate of insurance, including any war risk insurance, of a kind and on terms then current at the port of shipment in the usual amount, in the currency of the contract, shown to cover the same goods covered by the bill of lading and providing for payment of loss to the order of the buyer or for the account of whom it may concern; but the seller may add to the price the amount of the premium for any such war risk insurance; and

(d) prepare an invoice of the goods and procure any other documents required to effect shipment or to comply with the contract; and

(e) forward and tender with commercial promptness all the documents in due form and with any indorsement necessary to perfect the buyer's rights.

(3) Unless otherwise agreed the term C. & F. or its equivalent has the same effect and imposes upon the seller the same obligations and risks as a C.I.F. term except the obligation as to insurance.

(4) Under the term C.I.F. or C. & F. unless otherwise agreed the buyer must make payment against tender of the required documents and the seller may not tender nor the buyer demand delivery of the goods in substitution for the documents.

§ 2–321. C.I.F. or C. & F.: "Net Landed Weights"; "Payment on Arrival"; Warranty of Condition on Arrival.

Under a contract containing a term C.I.F. or C. & F.

(1) Where the price is based on or is to be adjusted according to "net landed weights", "delivered weights", "out turn" quantity or quality or the like, unless otherwise agreed the seller must reasonably estimate the price. The payment due on tender of the documents called for by the contract is the amount so estimated, but after final adjustment of the price a settlement must be made with commercial promptness.

(2) An agreement described in subsection (1) or any warranty of quality or condition of the goods on arrival places upon the seller the risk of ordinary deterioration, shrinkage and the like in transportation but has no effect on the place or time of identification to the contract for sale or delivery or on the passing of the risk of loss.

(3) Unless otherwise agreed where the contract provides for payment on or after arrival of the goods the seller must before payment allow such preliminary inspection as is feasible; but if the goods are lost delivery of the documents and payment are due when the goods should have arrived.

§ 2–322. Delivery "Ex-Ship".

(1) Unless otherwise agreed a term for delivery of goods "ex-ship" (which means from the carrying vessel) or in equivalent language is not restricted to a particular ship and requires delivery from a ship which has reached a place at the named port of destination where goods of the kind are usually discharged.

(2) Under such a term unless otherwise agreed

(a) the seller must discharge all liens arising out of the carriage and furnish the buyer with a direction which puts the carrier under a duty to deliver the goods; and

(b) the risk of loss does not pass to the buyer until the goods leave the ship's tackle or are otherwise properly unloaded.

§ 2–323. Form of Bill of Lading Required in Overseas Shipment; "Overseas".

(1) Where the contract contemplates overseas shipment and contains a term C.I.F. or C. & F. or F.O.B. vessel, the seller unless otherwise agreed must obtain a negotiable bill of lading stating that the goods have been loaded on board or, in the case of a term C.I.F. or C. & F., received for shipment.

(2) Where in a case within subsection (1) a bill of lading has been issued in a set of parts, unless otherwise agreed if the documents are not to be sent from abroad the buyer may demand tender of the full set; otherwise only one part of the bill of lading need be tendered. Even if the agreement expressly requires a full set

(a) due tender of a single part is acceptable within the provisions of this Article on cure of improper delivery (subsection (1) of Section 2–508); and

(b) even though the full set is demanded, if the documents are sent from abroad the person tendering an incomplete set may nevertheless require payment upon furnishing an indemnity which the buyer in good faith deems adequate.

(3) A shipment by water or by air or a contract contemplating such shipment is "overseas" insofar as by usage of trade or agreement it is subject to the commercial, financing or shipping practices characteristic of international deep water commerce.

§ 2–324. "No Arrival, No Sale" Term.

Under a term "no arrival, no sale" or terms of like meaning, unless otherwise agreed,

(a) the seller must properly ship conforming goods and if they arrive by any means he must tender them on arrival but he assumes no obligation that the goods will arrive unless he has caused the non-arrival; and

(b) where without fault of the seller the goods are in part lost or have so deteriorated as no longer to conform to the contract or arrive after the contract time, the buyer may proceed as if there had been casualty to identified goods (Section 2–613).

§ 2–325. "Letter of Credit" Term; "Confirmed Credit".

(1) Failure of the buyer seasonably to furnish an agreed letter of credit is a breach of the contract for sale.

(2) The delivery to seller of a proper letter of credit suspends the buyer's obligation to pay. If the letter of credit is dishonored, the seller may on seasonable notification to the buyer require payment directly from him.

(3) Unless otherwise agreed the term "letter of credit" or "banker's credit" in a contract for sale means an irrevocable credit issued by a financing agency of good repute and, where the shipment is overseas, of good international repute. The term "confirmed credit" means that the credit must also carry the direct obligation of such an agency which does business in the seller's financial market.

§ 2–326. Sale on Approval and Sale or Return; Rights of Creditors.

(1) Unless otherwise agreed, if delivered goods may be returned by the buyer even though they conform to the contract, the transaction is

(a) a "sale on approval" if the goods are delivered primarily for use, and

(b) a "sale or return" if the goods are delivered primarily for resale.

(2) Goods held on approval are not subject to the claims of the buyer's creditors until acceptance; goods held on sale or return are subject to such claims while in the buyer's possession.

(3) Any "or return" term of a contract for sale is to be treated as a separate contract for sale within the statute of frauds section of this Article (Section 2–201) and as contradicting the sale aspect of the contract within the provisions of this Article on parol or extrinsic evidence (Section 2–202).

As amended in 1999.

§ 2–327. Special Incidents of Sale on Approval and Sale or Return.

(1) Under a sale on approval unless otherwise agreed

(a) although the goods are identified to the contract the risk of loss and the title do not pass to the buyer until acceptance; and

(b) use of the goods consistent with the purpose of trial is not acceptance but failure seasonably to notify the seller of election to return the goods is acceptance, and if the goods conform to the contract acceptance of any part is acceptance of the whole; and

(c) after due notification of election to return, the return is at the seller's risk and expense but a merchant buyer must follow any reasonable instructions.

(2) Under a sale or return unless otherwise agreed

(a) the option to return extends to the whole or any commercial unit of the goods while in substantially their original condition, but must be exercised seasonably; and

(b) the return is at the buyer's risk and expense.

§ 2–328. Sale by Auction.

(1) In a sale by auction if goods are put up in lots each lot is the subject of a separate sale.

(2) A sale by auction is complete when the auctioneer so announces by the fall of the hammer or in other customary manner. Where a bid is made while the hammer is falling in acceptance of a prior bid the auctioneer may in his discretion reopen the bidding or declare the goods sold under the bid on which the hammer was falling.

(3) Such a sale is with reserve unless the goods are in explicit terms put up without reserve. In an auction with reserve the auctioneer may withdraw the goods at any time until he announces completion of the sale. In an auction without reserve, after the auctioneer calls for bids on an article or lot, that article or lot cannot be withdrawn unless no bid is made within a reasonable time. In either case a bidder may retract his bid until the auctioneer's announcement of completion of the sale, but a bidder's retraction does not revive any previous bid.

(4) If the auctioneer knowingly receives a bid on the seller's behalf or the seller makes or procures such as bid, and notice has not been given that liberty for such bidding is reserved, the buyer may at his option avoid the sale or take the goods at the price of the last good faith bid prior to the completion of the sale. This subsection shall not apply to any bid at a forced sale.

Part 4 Title, Creditors and Good Faith Purchasers

§ 2–401. Passing of Title; Reservation for Security; Limited Application of This Section.

Each provision of this Article with regard to the rights, obligations and remedies of the seller, the buyer, purchasers or other third parties applies irrespective of title to the goods except where the provision refers to such title. Insofar as situations are not covered by the other provisions of this Article and matters concerning title became material the following rules apply:

(1) Title to goods cannot pass under a contract for sale prior to their identification to the contract (Section 2–501), and unless otherwise explicitly agreed the buyer acquires by their identification a special property as limited by this Act. Any retention or reservation by the seller of the title (property) in goods shipped or delivered to the buyer is limited in effect to a reservation of a security interest. Subject to these provisions and to the provisions of the Article on Secured Transactions (Article 9), title to goods passes from the seller to the buyer in any manner and on any conditions explicitly agreed on by the parties.

(2) Unless otherwise explicitly agreed title passes to the buyer at the time and place at which the seller completes his performance with reference to the physical delivery of the goods, despite any reservation of a security interest and even though a document of title is to be delivered at a different time or place; and in particular and despite any reservation of a security interest by the bill of lading

    (a) if the contract requires or authorizes the seller to send the goods to the buyer but does not require him to deliver them at destination, title passes to the buyer at the time and place of shipment; but

    (b) if the contract requires delivery at destination, title passes on tender there.

(3) Unless otherwise explicitly agreed where delivery is to be made without moving the goods,

    (a) if the seller is to deliver a document of title, title passes at the time when and the place where he delivers such documents; or

    (b) if the goods are at the time of contracting already identified and no documents are to be delivered, title passes at the time and place of contracting.

(4) A rejection or other refusal by the buyer to receive or retain the goods, whether or not justified, or a justified revocation of acceptance revests title to the goods in the seller. Such revesting occurs by operation of law and is not a "sale".

§ 2–402. Rights of Seller's Creditors Against Sold Goods.

(1) Except as provided in subsections (2) and (3), rights of unsecured creditors of the seller with respect to goods which have been identified to a contract for sale are subject to the buyer's rights to recover the goods under this Article (Sections 2–502 and 2–716).

(2) A creditor of the seller may treat a sale or an identification of goods to a contract for sale as void if as against him a retention of possession by the seller is fraudulent under any rule of law of the state where the goods are situated, except that retention of possession in good faith and current course of trade by a merchant-seller for a commercially reasonable time after a sale or identification is not fraudulent.

(3) Nothing in this Article shall be deemed to impair the rights of creditors of the seller

    (a) under the provisions of the Article on Secured Transactions (Article 9); or

    (b) where identification to the contract or delivery is made not in current course of trade but in satisfaction of or as security for a pre-existing claim for money, security or the like and is made under circumstances which under any rule of law of the state where the goods are situated would apart from this Article constitute the transaction a fraudulent transfer or voidable preference.

§ 2–403. Power to Transfer; Good Faith Purchase of Goods; "Entrusting".

(1) A purchaser of goods acquires all title which his transferor had or had power to transfer except that a purchaser of a limited interest acquires rights only to the extent of the interest purchased. A person with voidable title has power to transfer a good title to a good faith purchaser for value. When goods have been delivered under a transaction of purchase the purchaser has such power even though

    (a) the transferor was deceived as to the identity of the purchaser, or

    (b) the delivery was in exchange for a check which is later dishonored, or

    (c) it was agreed that the transaction was to be a "cash sale", or

    (d) the delivery was procured through fraud punishable as larcenous under the criminal law.

(2) Any entrusting of possession of goods to a merchant who deals in goods of that kind gives him power to transfer all rights of the entruster to a buyer in ordinary course of business.

(3) "Entrusting" includes any delivery and any acquiescence in retention of possession regardless of any condition expressed between the parties to the delivery or acquiescence and regardless of whether the procurement of the entrusting or the possessor's disposition of the goods have been such as to be larcenous under the criminal law.

(4) The rights of other purchasers of goods and of lien creditors are governed by the Articles on Secured Transactions (Article 9), Bulk Transfers (Article 6) and Documents of Title (Article 7).

As amended in 1988.

Part 5 Performance

§ 2–501. Insurable Interest in Goods; Manner of Identification of Goods.

(1) The buyer obtains a special property and an insurable interest in goods by identification of existing goods as goods to which the contract refers even though the goods so identified are nonconforming and he has an option to return or reject them. Such identification can be made at any time and in any manner explicitly agreed to by the parties. In the absence of explicit agreement identification occurs

(a) when the contract is made if it is for the sale of goods already existing and identified;

(b) if the contract is for the sale of future goods other than those described in paragraph (c), when goods are shipped, marked or otherwise designated by the seller as goods to which the contract refers;

(c) when the crops are planted or otherwise become growing crops or the young are conceived if the contract is for the sale of unborn young to be born within twelve months after contracting or for the sale of crops to be harvested within twelve months or the next normal harvest season after contracting whichever is longer.

(2) The seller retains an insurable interest in goods so long as title to or any security interest in the goods remains in him and where the identification is by the seller alone he may until default or insolvency or notification to the buyer that the identification is final substitute other goods for those identified.

(3) Nothing in this section impairs any insurable interest recognized under any other statute or rule of law.

§ 2–502. Buyer's Right to Goods on Seller's Insolvency.

(1) Subject to subsections (2) and (3) and even though the goods have not been shipped a buyer who has paid a part or all of the price of goods in which he has a special property under the provisions of the immediately preceding section may on making and keeping good a tender of any unpaid portion of their price recover them from the seller if:

(a) in the case of goods bought for personal, family, or household purposes, the seller repudiates or fails to deliver as required by the contract; or

(b) in all cases, the seller becomes insolvent within ten days after receipt of the first installment on their price.

(2) The buyer's right to recover the goods under subsection (1)(a) vests upon acquisition of a special property, even if the seller had not then repudiated or failed to deliver.

(3) If the identification creating his special property has been made by the buyer he acquires the right to recover the goods only if they conform to the contract for sale.

As amended in 1999.

§ 2–503. Manner of Seller's Tender of Delivery.

(1) Tender of delivery requires that the seller put and hold conforming goods at the buyer's disposition and give the buyer any notification reasonably necessary to enable him to take delivery. The manner, time and place for tender are determined by the agreement and this Article, and in particular

(a) tender must be at a reasonable hour, and if it is of goods they must be kept available for the period reasonably necessary to enable the buyer to take possession; but

(b) unless otherwise agreed the buyer must furnish facilities reasonably suited to the receipt of the goods.

(2) Where the case is within the next section respecting shipment tender requires that the seller comply with its provisions.

(3) Where the seller is required to deliver at a particular destination tender requires that he comply with subsection (1) and also in any appropriate case tender documents as described in subsections (4) and (5) of this section.

(4) Where goods are in the possession of a bailee and are to be delivered without being moved

(a) tender requires that the seller either tender a negotiable document of title covering such goods or procure acknowledgment by the bailee of the buyer's right to possession of the goods; but

(b) tender to the buyer of a non-negotiable document of title or of a written direction to the bailee to deliver is sufficient tender unless the buyer seasonably objects, and receipt by the bailee of notification of the buyer's rights fixes those rights as against the bailee and all third persons; but risk of loss of the goods and of any failure by the bailee to honor the non-negotiable document of title or to obey the direction remains on the seller until the buyer has had a reasonable time to present the document or direction, and a refusal by the bailee to honor the document or to obey the direction defeats the tender.

(5) Where the contract requires the seller to deliver documents

(a) he must tender all such documents in correct form, except as provided in this Article with respect to bills of lading in a set (subsection (2) of Section 2–323); and

(b) tender through customary banking channels is sufficient and dishonor of a draft accompanying the documents constitutes non-acceptance or rejection.

§ 2–504. Shipment by Seller.

Where the seller is required or authorized to send the goods to the buyer and the contract does not require him to deliver them at a particular destination, then unless otherwise agreed he must

(a) put the goods in the possession of such a carrier and make such a contract for their transportation as may be reasonable having regard to the nature of the goods and other circumstances of the case; and

(b) obtain and promptly deliver or tender in due form any document necessary to enable the buyer to obtain possession of the goods or otherwise required by the agreement or by usage of trade; and

(c) promptly notify the buyer of the shipment.

Failure to notify the buyer under paragraph (c) or to make a proper contract under paragraph (a) is a ground for rejection only if material delay or loss ensues.

§ 2–505. Seller's Shipment under Reservation.

(1) Where the seller has identified goods to the contract by or before shipment:

(a) his procurement of a negotiable bill of lading to his own order or otherwise reserves in him a security interest in the goods. His procurement of the bill to the order of a financing agency or of the buyer indicates in addition only the seller's expectation of transferring that interest to the person named.

(b) a non-negotiable bill of lading to himself or his nominee reserves possession of the goods as security but except in a case of conditional delivery (subsection (2) of Section 2–507) a non-negotiable bill of lading naming the buyer as consignee reserves no security interest even though the seller retains possession of the bill of lading.

(2) When shipment by the seller with reservation of a security interest is in violation of the contract for sale it constitutes an improper contract for transportation within the preceding section but impairs neither the rights given to the buyer by shipment and identification of the goods to the contract nor the seller's powers as a holder of a negotiable document.

§ 2–506. Rights of Financing Agency.

(1) A financing agency by paying or purchasing for value a draft which relates to a shipment of goods acquires to the extent of the payment or purchase and in addition to its own rights under the draft and any document of title securing it any rights of the shipper in the goods including the right to stop delivery and the shipper's right to have the draft honored by the buyer.

(2) The right to reimbursement of a financing agency which has in good faith honored or purchased the draft under commitment to or authority from the buyer is not impaired by subsequent discovery of defects with reference to any relevant document which was apparently regular on its face.

§ 2–507. Effect of Seller's Tender; Delivery on Condition.

(1) Tender of delivery is a condition to the buyer's duty to accept the goods and, unless otherwise agreed, to his duty to pay for them. Tender entitles the seller to acceptance of the goods and to payment according to the contract.

(2) Where payment is due and demanded on the delivery to the buyer of goods or documents of title, his right as against the seller to retain or dispose of them is conditional upon his making the payment due.

§ 2–508. Cure by Seller of Improper Tender or Delivery; Replacement.

(1) Where any tender or delivery by the seller is rejected because non-conforming and the time for performance has not yet expired, the seller may seasonably notify the buyer of his intention to cure and may then within the contract time make a conforming delivery.

(2) Where the buyer rejects a non-conforming tender which the seller had reasonable grounds to believe would be acceptable with or without money allowance the seller may if he seasonably notifies the buyer have a further reasonable time to substitute a conforming tender.

§ 2–509. Risk of Loss in the Absence of Breach.

(1) Where the contract requires or authorizes the seller to ship the goods by carrier

(a) if it does not require him to deliver them at a particular destination, the risk of loss passes to the buyer when the goods are duly delivered to the carrier even though the shipment is under reservation (Section 2–505); but

(b) if it does require him to deliver them at a particular destination and the goods are there duly tendered while in the possession of the carrier, the risk of loss passes to the buyer when the goods are there duly so tendered as to enable the buyer to take delivery.

(2) Where the goods are held by a bailee to be delivered without being moved, the risk of loss passes to the buyer

(a) on his receipt of a negotiable document of title covering the goods; or

(b) on acknowledgment by the bailee of the buyer's right to possession of the goods; or

(c) after his receipt of a non-negotiable document of title or other written direction to deliver, as provided in subsection (4)(b) of Section 2–503.

(3) In any case not within subsection (1) or (2), the risk of loss passes to the buyer on his receipt of the goods if the seller is a merchant; otherwise the risk passes to the buyer on tender of delivery.

(4) The provisions of this section are subject to contrary agreement of the parties and to the provisions of this Article on sale on approval (Section 2–327) and on effect of breach on risk of loss (Section 2–510).

§ 2–510. Effect of Breach on Risk of Loss.

(1) Where a tender or delivery of goods so fails to conform to the contract as to give a right of rejection the risk of their loss remains on the seller until cure or acceptance.

(2) Where the buyer rightfully revokes acceptance he may to the extent of any deficiency in his effective insurance coverage treat the risk of loss as having rested on the seller from the beginning.

(3) Where the buyer as to conforming goods already identified to the contract for sale repudiates or is otherwise in breach before risk of their loss has passed to him, the seller may to the extent of any deficiency in his effective insurance coverage treat the risk of loss as resting on the buyer for a commercially reasonable time.

§ 2–511. Tender of Payment by Buyer; Payment by Check.

(1) Unless otherwise agreed tender of payment is a condition to the seller's duty to tender and complete any delivery.

(2) Tender of payment is sufficient when made by any means or in any manner current in the ordinary course of business unless the

seller demands payment in legal tender and gives any extension of time reasonably necessary to procure it.

(3) Subject to the provisions of this Act on the effect of an instrument on an obligation (Section 3–310), payment by check is conditional and is defeated as between the parties by dishonor of the check on due presentment.

As amended in 1994.

§ 2–512. Payment by Buyer Before Inspection.

(1) Where the contract requires payment before inspection nonconformity of the goods does not excuse the buyer from so making payment unless

(a) the non-conformity appears without inspection; or

(b) despite tender of the required documents the circumstances would justify injunction against honor under this Act (Section 5–109(b)).

(2) Payment pursuant to subsection (1) does not constitute an acceptance of goods or impair the buyer's right to inspect or any of his remedies.

As amended in 1995.

§ 2–513. Buyer's Right to Inspection of Goods.

(1) Unless otherwise agreed and subject to subsection (3), where goods are tendered or delivered or identified to the contract for sale, the buyer has a right before payment or acceptance to inspect them at any reasonable place and time and in any reasonable manner. When the seller is required or authorized to send the goods to the buyer, the inspection may be after their arrival.

(2) Expenses of inspection must be borne by the buyer but may be recovered from the seller if the goods do not conform and are rejected.

(3) Unless otherwise agreed and subject to the provisions of this Article on C.I.F. contracts (subsection (3) of Section 2–321), the buyer is not entitled to inspect the goods before payment of the price when the contract provides

(a) for delivery "C.O.D." or on other like terms; or

(b) for payment against documents of title, except where such payment is due only after the goods are to become available for inspection.

(4) A place or method of inspection fixed by the parties is presumed to be exclusive but unless otherwise expressly agreed it does not postpone identification or shift the place for delivery or for passing the risk of loss. If compliance becomes impossible, inspection shall be as provided in this section unless the place or method fixed was clearly intended as an indispensable condition failure of which avoids the contract.

§ 2–514. When Documents Deliverable on Acceptance; When on Payment.

Unless otherwise agreed documents against which a draft is drawn are to be delivered to the drawee on acceptance of the draft if it is payable more than three days after presentment; otherwise, only on payment.

§ 2–515. Preserving Evidence of Goods in Dispute.

In furtherance of the adjustment of any claim or dispute

(a) either party on reasonable notification to the other and for the purpose of ascertaining the facts and preserving evidence has the right to inspect, test and sample the goods including such of them as may be in the possession or control of the other; and

(b) the parties may agree to a third party inspection or survey to determine the conformity or condition of the goods and may agree that the findings shall be binding upon them in any subsequent litigation or adjustment.

Part 6 Breach, Repudiation and Excuse

§ 2–601. Buyer's Rights on Improper Delivery.

Subject to the provisions of this Article on breach in installment contracts (Section 2–612) and unless otherwise agreed under the sections on contractual limitations of remedy (Sections 2–718 and 2–719), if the goods or the tender of delivery fail in any respect to conform to the contract, the buyer may

(a) reject the whole; or

(b) accept the whole; or

(c) accept any commercial unit or units and reject the rest.

§ 2–602. Manner and Effect of Rightful Rejection.

(1) Rejection of goods must be within a reasonable time after their delivery or tender. It is ineffective unless the buyer seasonably notifies the seller.

(2) Subject to the provisions of the two following sections on rejected goods (Sections 2–603 and 2–604),

(a) after rejection any exercise of ownership by the buyer with respect to any commercial unit is wrongful as against the seller; and

(b) if the buyer has before rejection taken physical possession of goods in which he does not have a security interest under the provisions of this Article (subsection (3) of Section 2–711), he is under a duty after rejection to hold them with reasonable care at the seller's disposition for a time sufficient to permit the seller to remove them; but

(c) the buyer has no further obligations with regard to goods rightfully rejected.

(3) The seller's rights with respect to goods wrongfully rejected are governed by the provisions of this Article on Seller's remedies in general (Section 2–703).

§ 2–603. Merchant Buyer's Duties as to Rightfully Rejected Goods.

(1) Subject to any security interest in the buyer (subsection (3) of Section 2–711), when the seller has no agent or place of business at the market of rejection a merchant buyer is under a duty after rejection of goods in his possession or control to follow any reasonable instructions received from the seller with respect to the goods and in the absence of such instructions to make reasonable efforts to sell them for the seller's account if they are perishable or threaten to decline in value speedily. Instructions are not reasonable if on demand indemnity for expenses is not forthcoming.

(2) When the buyer sells goods under subsection (1), he is entitled to reimbursement from the seller or out of the proceeds for reasonable expenses of caring for and selling them, and if the expenses include no selling commission then to such commission as is usual

in the trade or if there is none to a reasonable sum not exceeding ten per cent on the gross proceeds.

(3) In complying with this section the buyer is held only to good faith and good faith conduct hereunder is neither acceptance nor conversion nor the basis of an action for damages.

§ 2–604. Buyer's Options as to Salvage of Rightfully Rejected Goods.

Subject to the provisions of the immediately preceding section on perishables if the seller gives no instructions within a reasonable time after notification of rejection the buyer may store the rejected goods for the seller's account or reship them to him or resell them for the seller's account with reimbursement as provided in the preceding section. Such action is not acceptance or conversion.

§ 2–605. Waiver of Buyer's Objections by Failure to Particularize.

(1) The buyer's failure to state in connection with rejection a particular defect which is ascertainable by reasonable inspection precludes him from relying on the unstated defect to justify rejection or to establish breach

(a) where the seller could have cured it if stated seasonably; or

(b) between merchants when the seller has after rejection made a request in writing for a full and final written statement of all defects on which the buyer proposes to rely.

(2) Payment against documents made without reservation of rights precludes recovery of the payment for defects apparent on the face of the documents.

§ 2–606. What Constitutes Acceptance of Goods.

(1) Acceptance of goods occurs when the buyer

(a) after a reasonable opportunity to inspect the goods signifies to the seller that the goods are conforming or that he will take or retain them in spite of their nonconformity; or

(b) fails to make an effective rejection (subsection (1) of Section 2–602), but such acceptance does not occur until the buyer has had a reasonable opportunity to inspect them; or

(c) does any act inconsistent with the seller's ownership; but if such act is wrongful as against the seller it is an acceptance only if ratified by him.

(2) Acceptance of a part of any commercial unit is acceptance of that entire unit.

§ 2–607. Effect of Acceptance; Notice of Breach; Burden of Establishing Breach After Acceptance; Notice of Claim or Litigation to Person Answerable Over.

(1) The buyer must pay at the contract rate for any goods accepted.

(2) Acceptance of goods by the buyer precludes rejection of the goods accepted and if made with knowledge of a non-conformity cannot be revoked because of it unless the acceptance was on the reasonable assumption that the non-conformity would be seasonably cured but acceptance does not of itself impair any other remedy provided by this Article for non-conformity.

(3) Where a tender has been accepted

(a) the buyer must within a reasonable time after he discovers or should have discovered any breach notify the seller of breach or be barred from any remedy; and

(b) if the claim is one for infringement or the like (subsection (3) of Section 2–312) and the buyer is sued as a result of such a breach he must so notify the seller within a reasonable time after he receives notice of the litigation or be barred from any remedy over for liability established by the litigation.

(4) The burden is on the buyer to establish any breach with respect to the goods accepted.

(5) Where the buyer is sued for breach of a warranty or other obligation for which his seller is answerable over

(a) he may give his seller written notice of the litigation. If the notice states that the seller may come in and defend and that if the seller does not do so he will be bound in any action against him by his buyer by any determination of fact common to the two litigations, then unless the seller after seasonable receipt of the notice does come in and defend he is so bound.

(b) if the claim is one for infringement or the like (subsection (3) of Section 2–312) the original seller may demand in writing that his buyer turn over to him control of the litigation including settlement or else be barred from any remedy over and if he also agrees to bear all expense and to satisfy any adverse judgment, then unless the buyer after seasonable receipt of the demand does turn over control the buyer is so barred.

(6) The provisions of subsections (3), (4) and (5) apply to any obligation of a buyer to hold the seller harmless against infringement or the like (subsection (3) of Section 2–312).

§ 2–608. Revocation of Acceptance in Whole or in Part.

(1) The buyer may revoke his acceptance of a lot or commercial unit whose non-conformity substantially impairs its value to him if he has accepted it

(a) on the reasonable assumption that its nonconformity would be cured and it has not been seasonably cured; or

(b) without discovery of such non-conformity if his acceptance was reasonably induced either by the difficulty of discovery before acceptance or by the seller's assurances.

(2) Revocation of acceptance must occur within a reasonable time after the buyer discovers or should have discovered the ground for it and before any substantial change in condition of the goods which is not caused by their own defects. It is not effective until the buyer notifies the seller of it.

(3) A buyer who so revokes has the same rights and duties with regard to the goods involved as if he had rejected them.

§ 2–609. Right to Adequate Assurance of Performance.

(1) A contract for sale imposes an obligation on each party that the other's expectation of receiving due performance will not be impaired. When reasonable grounds for insecurity arise with respect to the performance of either party the other may in writing demand adequate assurance of due performance and until he receives such assurance may if commercially reasonable suspend any performance for which he has not already received the agreed return.

(2) Between merchants the reasonableness of grounds for insecurity and the adequacy of any assurance offered shall be determined according to commercial standards.

(3) Acceptance of any improper delivery or payment does not prejudice the party's right to demand adequate assurance of future performance.

(4) After receipt of a justified demand failure to provide within a reasonable time not exceeding thirty days such assurance of due performance as is adequate under the circumstances of the particular case is a repudiation of the contract.

§ 2–610. Anticipatory Repudiation.

When either party repudiates the contract with respect to a performance not yet due the loss of which will substantially impair the value of the contract to the other, the aggrieved party may

(a) for a commercially reasonable time await performance by the repudiating party; or

(b) resort to any remedy for breach (Section 2–703 or Section 2–711), even though he has notified the repudiating party that he would await the latter's performance and has urged retraction; and

(c) in either case suspend his own performance or proceed in accordance with the provisions of this Article on the seller's right to identify goods to the contract notwithstanding breach or to salvage unfinished goods (Section 2–704).

§ 2–611. Retraction of Anticipatory Repudiation.

(1) Until the repudiating party's next performance is due he can retract his repudiation unless the aggrieved party has since the repudiation cancelled or materially changed his position or otherwise indicated that he considers the repudiation final.

(2) Retraction may be by any method which clearly indicates to the aggrieved party that the repudiating party intends to perform, but must include any assurance justifiably demanded under the provisions of this Article (Section 2–609).

(3) Retraction reinstates the repudiating party's rights under the contract with due excuse and allowance to the aggrieved party for any delay occasioned by the repudiation.

§ 2–612. "Installment Contract"; Breach.

(1) An "installment contract" is one which requires or authorizes the delivery of goods in separate lots to be separately accepted, even though the contract contains a clause "each delivery is a separate contract" or its equivalent.

(2) The buyer may reject any installment which is non-conforming if the non-conformity substantially impairs the value of that installment and cannot be cured or if the non-conformity is a defect in the required documents; but if the non-conformity does not fall within subsection (3) and the seller gives adequate assurance of its cure the buyer must accept that installment.

(3) Whenever non-conformity or default with respect to one or more installments substantially impairs the value of the whole contract there is a breach of the whole. But the aggrieved party reinstates the contract if he accepts a non-conforming installment without seasonably notifying of cancellation or if he brings an action with respect only to past installments or demands performance as to future installments.

§ 2–613. Casualty to Identified Goods.

Where the contract requires for its performance goods identified when the contract is made, and the goods suffer casualty without fault of either party before the risk of loss passes to the buyer, or in a proper case under a "no arrival, no sale" term (Section 2–324) then

(a) if the loss is total the contract is avoided; and

(b) if the loss is partial or the goods have so deteriorated as no longer to conform to the contract the buyer may nevertheless demand inspection and at his option either treat the contract as voided or accept the goods with due allowance from the contract price for the deterioration or the deficiency in quantity but without further right against the seller.

§ 2–614. Substituted Performance.

(1) Where without fault of either party the agreed berthing, loading, or unloading facilities fail or an agreed type of carrier becomes unavailable or the agreed manner of delivery otherwise becomes commercially impracticable but a commercially reasonable substitute is available, such substitute performance must be tendered and accepted.

(2) If the agreed means or manner of payment fails because of domestic or foreign governmental regulation, the seller may withhold or stop delivery unless the buyer provides a means or manner of payment which is commercially a substantial equivalent. If delivery has already been taken, payment by the means or in the manner provided by the regulation discharges the buyer's obligation unless the regulation is discriminatory, oppressive or predatory.

§ 2–615. Excuse by Failure of Presupposed Conditions.

Except so far as a seller may have assumed a greater obligation and subject to the preceding section on substituted performance:

(a) Delay in delivery or non-delivery in whole or in part by a seller who complies with paragraphs (b) and (c) is not a breach of his duty under a contract for sale if performance as agreed has been made impracticable by the occurrence of a contingency the nonoccurrence of which was a basic assumption on which the contract was made or by compliance in good faith with any applicable foreign or domestic governmental regulation or order whether or not it later proves to be invalid.

(b) Where the causes mentioned in paragraph (a) affect only a part of the seller's capacity to perform, he must allocate production and deliveries among his customers but may at his option include regular customers not then under contract as well as his own requirements for further manufacture. He may so allocate in any manner which is fair and reasonable.

(c) The seller must notify the buyer seasonably that there will be delay or non-delivery and, when allocation is required under paragraph (b), of the estimated quota thus made available for the buyer.

§ 2–616. Procedure on Notice Claiming Excuse.

(1) Where the buyer receives notification of a material or indefinite delay or an allocation justified under the preceding section he may by written notification to the seller as to any delivery concerned, and where the prospective deficiency substantially impairs the value of the whole contract under the provisions of this Article relating to breach of installment contracts (Section 2–612), then also as to the whole,

(a) terminate and thereby discharge any unexecuted portion of the contract; or

(b) modify the contract by agreeing to take his available quota in substitution.

(2) If after receipt of such notification from the seller the buyer fails so to modify the contract within a reasonable time not exceeding thirty days the contract lapses with respect to any deliveries affected.

(3) The provisions of this section may not be negated by agreement except in so far as the seller has assumed a greater obligation under the preceding section.

Part 7 Remedies

§ 2–701. Remedies for Breach of Collateral Contracts Not Impaired.

Remedies for breach of any obligation or promise collateral or ancillary to a contract for sale are not impaired by the provisions of this Article.

§ 2–702. Seller's Remedies on Discovery of Buyer's Insolvency.

(1) Where the seller discovers the buyer to be insolvent he may refuse delivery except for cash including payment for all goods theretofore delivered under the contract, and stop delivery under this Article (Section 2–705).

(2) Where the seller discovers that the buyer has received goods on credit while insolvent he may reclaim the goods upon demand made within ten days after the receipt, but if misrepresentation of solvency has been made to the particular seller in writing within three months before delivery the ten day limitation does not apply. Except as provided in this subsection the seller may not base a right to reclaim goods on the buyer's fraudulent or innocent misrepresentation of solvency or of intent to pay.

(3) The seller's right to reclaim under subsection (2) is subject to the rights of a buyer in ordinary course or other good faith purchaser under this Article (Section 2–403). Successful reclamation of goods excludes all other remedies with respect to them.

§ 2–703. Seller's Remedies in General.

Where the buyer wrongfully rejects or revokes acceptance of goods or fails to make a payment due on or before delivery or repudiates with respect to a part or the whole, then with respect to any goods directly affected and, if the breach is of the whole contract (Section 2–612), then also with respect to the whole undelivered balance, the aggrieved seller may

(a) withhold delivery of such goods;

(b) stop delivery by any bailee as hereafter provided (Section 2–705);

(c) proceed under the next section respecting goods still unidentified to the contract;

(d) resell and recover damages as hereafter provided (Section 2–706);

(e) recover damages for non-acceptance (Section 2–708) or in a proper case the price (Section 2–709);

(f) cancel.

§ 2–704. Seller's Right to Identify Goods to the Contract Notwithstanding Breach or to Salvage Unfinished Goods.

(1) An aggrieved seller under the preceding section may

(a) identify to the contract conforming goods not already identified if at the time he learned of the breach they are in his possession or control;

(b) treat as the subject of resale goods which have demonstrably been intended for the particular contract even though those goods are unfinished.

(2) Where the goods are unfinished an aggrieved seller may in the exercise of reasonable commercial judgment for the purposes of avoiding loss and of effective realization either complete the manufacture and wholly identify the goods to the contract or cease manufacture and resell for scrap or salvage value or proceed in any other reasonable manner.

§ 2–705. Seller's Stoppage of Delivery in Transit or Otherwise.

(1) The seller may stop delivery of goods in the possession of a carrier or other bailee when he discovers the buyer to be insolvent (Section 2–702) and may stop delivery of carload, truckload, planeload or larger shipments of express or freight when the buyer repudiates or fails to make a payment due before delivery or if for any other reason the seller has a right to withhold or reclaim the goods.

(2) As against such buyer the seller may stop delivery until

(a) receipt of the goods by the buyer; or

(b) acknowledgment to the buyer by any bailee of the goods except a carrier that the bailee holds the goods for the buyer; or

(c) such acknowledgment to the buyer by a carrier by reshipment or as warehouseman; or

(d) negotiation to the buyer of any negotiable document of title covering the goods.

(3) (a) To stop delivery the seller must so notify as to enable the bailee by reasonable diligence to prevent delivery of the goods.

(b) After such notification the bailee must hold and deliver the goods according to the directions of the seller but the seller is liable to the bailee for any ensuing charges or damages.

(c) If a negotiable document of title has been issued for goods the bailee is not obliged to obey a notification to stop until surrender of the document.

(d) A carrier who has issued a non-negotiable bill of lading is not obliged to obey a notification to stop received from a person other than the consignor.

§ 2–706. Seller's Resale Including Contract for Resale.

(1) Under the conditions stated in Section 2–703 on seller's remedies, the seller may resell the goods concerned or the undelivered balance thereof. Where the resale is made in good faith and in a commercially reasonable manner the seller may recover the difference between the resale price and the contract price together with any incidental damages allowed under the provisions of this Article (Section 2–710), but less expenses saved in consequence of the buyer's breach.

(2) Except as otherwise provided in subsection (3) or unless otherwise agreed resale may be at public or private sale including sale by way of one or more contracts to sell or of identification to an existing contract of the seller. Sale may be as a unit or in parcels and at any time and place and on any terms but every aspect of the sale including the method, manner, time, place and terms must be commercially reasonable. The resale must be reasonably identified as referring to the broken contract, but it is not necessary that the goods be in existence or that any or all of them have been identified to the contract before the breach.

(3) Where the resale is at private sale the seller must give the buyer reasonable notification of his intention to resell.

(4) Where the resale is at public sale

(a) only identified goods can be sold except where there is a recognized market for a public sale of futures in goods of the kind; and

(b) it must be made at a usual place or market for public sale if one is reasonably available and except in the case of goods which are perishable or threaten to decline in value speedily the seller must give the buyer reasonable notice of the time and place of the resale; and

(c) if the goods are not to be within the view of those attending the sale the notification of sale must state the place where the goods are located and provide for their reasonable inspection by prospective bidders; and

(d) the seller may buy.

(5) A purchaser who buys in good faith at a resale takes the goods free of any rights of the original buyer even though the seller fails to comply with one or more of the requirements of this section.

(6) The seller is not accountable to the buyer for any profit made on any resale. A person in the position of a seller (Section 2–707) or a buyer who has rightfully rejected or justifiably revoked acceptance must account for any excess over the amount of his security interest, as hereinafter defined (subsection (3) of Section 2–711).

§ 2–707. "Person in the Position of a Seller".

(1) A "person in the position of a seller" includes as against a principal an agent who has paid or become responsible for the price of goods on behalf of his principal or anyone who otherwise holds a security interest or other right in goods similar to that of a seller.

(2) A person in the position of a seller may as provided in this Article withhold or stop delivery (Section 2–705) and resell (Section 2–706) and recover incidental damages (Section 2–710).

§ 2–708. Seller's Damages for Non-Acceptance or Repudiation.

(1) Subject to subsection (2) and to the provisions of this Article with respect to proof of market price (Section 2–723), the measure of damages for non-acceptance or repudiation by the buyer is the difference between the market price at the time and place for tender and the unpaid contract price together with any incidental damages provided in this Article (Section 2–710), but less expenses saved in consequence of the buyer's breach.

(2) If the measure of damages provided in subsection (1) is inadequate to put the seller in as good a position as performance would have done then the measure of damages is the profit (including reasonable overhead) which the seller would have made from full performance by the buyer, together with any incidental damages provided in this Article (Section 2–710), due allowance for costs reasonably incurred and due credit for payments or proceeds of resale.

§ 2–709. Action for the Price.

(1) When the buyer fails to pay the price as it becomes due the seller may recover, together with any incidental damages under the next section, the price

(a) of goods accepted or of conforming goods lost or damaged within a commercially reasonable time after risk of their loss has passed to the buyer; and

(b) of goods identified to the contract if the seller is unable after reasonable effort to resell them at a reasonable price or the circumstances reasonably indicate that such effort will be unavailing.

(2) Where the seller sues for the price he must hold for the buyer any goods which have been identified to the contract and are still in his control except that if resale becomes possible he may resell them at any time prior to the collection of the judgment. The net proceeds of any such resale must be credited to the buyer and payment of the judgment entitles him to any goods not resold.

(3) After the buyer has wrongfully rejected or revoked acceptance of the goods or has failed to make a payment due or has repudiated (Section 2–610), a seller who is held not entitled to the price under this section shall nevertheless be awarded damages for non-acceptance under the preceding section.

§ 2–710. Seller's Incidental Damages.

Incidental damages to an aggrieved seller include any commercially reasonable charges, expenses or commissions incurred in stopping delivery, in the transportation, care and custody of goods after the buyer's breach, in connection with return or resale of the goods or otherwise resulting from the breach.

§ 2–711. Buyer's Remedies in General; Buyer's Security Interest in Rejected Goods.

(1) Where the seller fails to make delivery or repudiates or the buyer rightfully rejects or justifiably revokes acceptance then with respect to any goods involved, and with respect to the whole if the breach goes to the whole contract (Section 2–612), the buyer may cancel and whether or not he has done so may in addition to recovering so much of the price as has been paid

(a) "cover" and have damages under the next section as to all the goods affected whether or not they have been identified to the contract; or

(b) recover damages for non-delivery as provided in this Article (Section 2–713).

(2) Where the seller fails to deliver or repudiates the buyer may also

(a) if the goods have been identified recover them as provided in this Article (Section 2–502); or

(b) in a proper case obtain specific performance or replevy the goods as provided in this Article (Section 2–716).

(3) On rightful rejection or justifiable revocation of acceptance a buyer has a security interest in goods in his possession or control for any payments made on their price and any expenses reasonably incurred in their inspection, receipt, transportation, care and custody and may hold such goods and resell them in like manner as an aggrieved seller (Section 2–706).

§ 2–712. "Cover"; Buyer's Procurement of Substitute Goods.

(1) After a breach within the preceding section the buyer may "cover" by making in good faith and without unreasonable delay any reasonable purchase of or contract to purchase goods in substitution for those due from the seller.

(2) The buyer may recover from the seller as damages the difference between the cost of cover and the contract price together with any incidental or consequential damages as hereinafter defined (Section 2–715), but less expenses saved in consequence of the seller's breach.

(3) Failure of the buyer to effect cover within this section does not bar him from any other remedy.

§ 2–713. Buyer's Damages for Non-Delivery or Repudiation.

(1) Subject to the provisions of this Article with respect to proof of market price (Section 2–723), the measure of damages for non-delivery or repudiation by the seller is the difference between the market price at the time when the buyer learned of the breach and the contract price together with any incidental and consequential damages provided in this Article (Section 2–715), but less expenses saved in consequence of the seller's breach.

(2) Market price is to be determined as of the place for tender or, in cases of rejection after arrival or revocation of acceptance, as of the place of arrival.

§ 2–714. Buyer's Damages for Breach in Regard to Accepted Goods.

(1) Where the buyer has accepted goods and given notification (subsection (3) of Section 2–607) he may recover as damages for any non-conformity of tender the loss resulting in the ordinary course of events from the seller's breach as determined in any manner which is reasonable.

(2) The measure of damages for breach of warranty is the difference at the time and place of acceptance between the value of the goods accepted and the value they would have had if they had been as warranted, unless special circumstances show proximate damages of a different amount.

(3) In a proper case any incidental and consequential damages under the next section may also be recovered.

§ 2–715. Buyer's Incidental and Consequential Damages.

(1) Incidental damages resulting from the seller's breach include expenses reasonably incurred in inspection, receipt, transportation and care and custody of goods rightfully rejected, any commercially reasonable charges, expenses or commissions in connection with effecting cover and any other reasonable expense incident to the delay or other breach.

(2) Consequential damages resulting from the seller's breach include

(a) any loss resulting from general or particular requirements and needs of which the seller at the time of contracting had reason to know and which could not reasonably be prevented by cover or otherwise; and

(b) injury to person or property proximately resulting from any breach of warranty.

§ 2–716. Buyer's Right to Specific Performance or Replevin.

(1) Specific performance may be decreed where the goods are unique or in other proper circumstances.

(2) The decree for specific performance may include such terms and conditions as to payment of the price, damages, or other relief as the court may deem just.

(3) The buyer has a right of replevin for goods identified to the contract if after reasonable effort he is unable to effect cover for such goods or the circumstances reasonably indicate that such effort will be unavailing or if the goods have been shipped under reservation and satisfaction of the security interest in them has been made or tendered. In the case of goods bought for personal, family, or household purposes, the buyer's right of replevin vests upon acquisition of a special property, even if the seller had not then repudiated or failed to deliver. As amended in 1999.

§ 2–717. Deduction of Damages From the Price.

The buyer on notifying the seller of his intention to do so may deduct all or any part of the damages resulting from any breach of the contract from any part of the price still due under the same contract.

§ 2–718. Liquidation or Limitation of Damages; Deposits.

(1) Damages for breach by either party may be liquidated in the agreement but only at an amount which is reasonable in the light of the anticipated or actual harm caused by the breach, the difficulties of proof of loss, and the inconvenience or nonfeasibility of otherwise obtaining an adequate remedy. A term fixing unreasonably large liquidated damages is void as a penalty.

(2) Where the seller justifiably withholds delivery of goods because of the buyer's breach, the buyer is entitled to restitution of any amount by which the sum of his payments exceeds

(a) the amount to which the seller is entitled by virtue of terms liquidating the seller's damages in accordance with subsection (1), or

(b) in the absence of such terms, twenty per cent of the value of the total performance for which the buyer is obligated under the contract or $500, whichever is smaller.

(3) The buyer's right to restitution under subsection (2) is subject to offset to the extent that the seller establishes

(a) a right to recover damages under the provisions of this Article other than subsection (1), and

(b) the amount or value of any benefits received by the buyer directly or indirectly by reason of the contract.

(4) Where a seller has received payment in goods their reasonable value or the proceeds of their resale shall be treated as payments for the purposes of subsection (2); but if the seller has notice of the buyer's breach before reselling goods received in part performance, his resale is subject to the conditions laid down in this Article on resale by an aggrieved seller (Section 2–706).

§ 2–719. Contractual Modification or Limitation of Remedy.

(1) Subject to the provisions of subsections (2) and (3) of this section and of the preceding section on liquidation and limitation of damages,

(a) the agreement may provide for remedies in addition to or in substitution for those provided in this Article and may limit or alter the measure of damages recoverable under this Article, as by limiting the buyer's remedies to return of the goods and repayment of the price or to repair and replacement of nonconforming goods or parts; and

(b) resort to a remedy as provided is optional unless the remedy is expressly agreed to be exclusive, in which case it is the sole remedy.

(2) Where circumstances cause an exclusive or limited remedy to fail of its essential purpose, remedy may be had as provided in this Act.

(3) Consequential damages may be limited or excluded unless the limitation or exclusion is unconscionable. Limitation of consequential damages for injury to the person in the case of consumer goods is prima facie unconscionable but limitation of damages where the loss is commercial is not.

§ 2–720. Effect of "Cancellation" or "Rescission" on Claims for Antecedent Breach.

Unless the contrary intention clearly appears, expressions of "cancellation" or "rescission" of the contract or the like shall not be construed as a renunciation or discharge of any claim in damages for an antecedent breach.

§ 2–721. Remedies for Fraud.

Remedies for material misrepresentation or fraud include all remedies available under this Article for non-fraudulent breach. Neither rescission or a claim for rescission of the contract for sale nor rejection or return of the goods shall bar or be deemed inconsistent with a claim for damages or other remedy.

§ 2–722. Who Can Sue Third Parties for Injury to Goods.

Where a third party so deals with goods which have been identified to a contract for sale as to cause actionable injury to a party to that contract

(a) a right of action against the third party is in either party to the contract for sale who has title to or a security interest or a special property or an insurable interest in the goods; and if the goods have been destroyed or converted a right of action is also in the party who either bore the risk of loss under the contract for sale or has since the injury assumed that risk as against the other;

(b) if at the time of the injury the party plaintiff did not bear the risk of loss as against the other party to the contract for sale and there is no arrangement between them for disposition of the recovery, his suit or settlement is, subject to his own interest, as a fiduciary for the other party to the contract;

(c) either party may with the consent of the other sue for the benefit of whom it may concern.

§ 2–723. Proof of Market Price: Time and Place.

(1) If an action based on anticipatory repudiation comes to trial before the time for performance with respect to some or all of the goods, any damages based on market price (Section 2–708 or Section 2–713) shall be determined according to the price of such goods prevailing at the time when the aggrieved party learned of the repudiation.

(2) If evidence of a price prevailing at the times or places described in this Article is not readily available the price prevailing within any reasonable time before or after the time described or at any other place which in commercial judgment or under usage of trade would serve as a reasonable substitute for the one described may be used, making any proper allowance for the cost of transporting the goods to or from such other place.

(3) Evidence of a relevant price prevailing at a time or place other than the one described in this Article offered by one party is not admissible unless and until he has given the other party such notice as the court finds sufficient to prevent unfair surprise.

§ 2–724. Admissibility of Market Quotations.

Whenever the prevailing price or value of any goods regularly bought and sold in any established commodity market is in issue, reports in official publications or trade journals or in newspapers or periodicals of general circulation published as the reports of such market shall be admissible in evidence. The circumstances of the preparation of such a report may be shown to affect its weight but not its admissibility.

§ 2–725. Statute of Limitations in Contracts for Sale.

(1) An action for breach of any contract for sale must be commenced within four years after the cause of action has accrued. By the original agreement the parties may reduce the period of limitation to not less than one year but may not extend it.

(2) A cause of action accrues when the breach occurs, regardless of the aggrieved party's lack of knowledge of the breach. A breach of warranty occurs when tender of delivery is made, except that where a warranty explicitly extends to future performance of the goods and discovery of the breach must await the time of such performance the cause of action accrues when the breach is or should have been discovered.

(3) Where an action commenced within the time limited by subsection (1) is so terminated as to leave available a remedy by another action for the same breach such other action may be commenced after the expiration of the time limited and within six months after the termination of the first action unless the termination resulted from voluntary discontinuance or from dismissal for failure or neglect to prosecute.

(4) This section does not alter the law on tolling of the statute of limitations nor does it apply to causes of action which have accrued before this Act becomes effective.

Article 2A
LEASES

Part 1 General Provisions

§ 2A–101. Short Title.

This Article shall be known and may be cited as the Uniform Commercial Code—Leases.

§ 2A–102. Scope.

This Article applies to any transaction, regardless of form, that creates a lease.

§ 2A–103. Definitions and Index of Definitions.

(1) In this Article unless the context otherwise requires:

(a) "Buyer in ordinary course of business" means a person who in good faith and without knowledge that the sale to him [or her] is in violation of the ownership rights or security interest or leasehold interest of a third party in the goods buys in ordinary course from a person in the business of selling goods of that kind but does not include a pawnbroker. "Buying" may be for cash or by exchange of other property or on secured or unsecured credit and includes receiving goods or documents of title under a pre-existing contract for sale but does not include a transfer in bulk or as security for or in total or partial satisfaction of a money debt.

(b) "Cancellation" occurs when either party puts an end to the lease contract for default by the other party.

(c) "Commercial unit" means such a unit of goods as by commercial usage is a single whole for purposes of lease and division of which materially impairs its character or value on the market or in use. A commercial unit may be a single article, as a machine, or a set of articles, as a suite of furniture or a line of machinery, or a quantity, as a gross or carload, or any other unit treated in use or in the relevant market as a single whole.

(d) "Conforming" goods or performance under a lease contract means goods or performance that are in accordance with the obligations under the lease contract.

(e) "Consumer lease" means a lease that a lessor regularly engaged in the business of leasing or selling makes to a lessee who is an individual and who takes under the lease primarily for a personal, family, or household purpose [, if the total payments to be made under the lease contract, excluding payments for options to renew or buy, do not exceed $_____].

(f) "Fault" means wrongful act, omission, breach, or default.

(g) "Finance lease" means a lease with respect to which:

(i) the lessor does not select, manufacture or supply the goods;

(ii) the lessor acquires the goods or the right to possession and use of the goods in connection with the lease; and

(iii) one of the following occurs:

(A) the lessee receives a copy of the contract by which the lessor acquired the goods or the right to possession and use of the goods before signing the lease contract;

(B) the lessee's approval of the contract by which the lessor acquired the goods or the right to possession and use of the goods is a condition to effectiveness of the lease contract;

(C) the lessee, before signing the lease contract, receives an accurate and complete statement designating the promises and warranties, and any disclaimers of warranties, limitations or modifications of remedies, or liquidated damages, including those of a third party, such as the manufacturer of the goods, provided to the lessor by the person supplying the goods in connection with or as part of the contract by which the lessor acquired the goods or the right to possession and use of the goods; or

(D) if the lease is not a consumer lease, the lessor, before the lessee signs the lease contract, informs the lessee in writing (a) of the identity of the person supplying the goods to the lessor, unless the lessee has selected that person and directed the lessor to acquire the goods or the right to possession and use of the goods from that person, (b) that the lessee is entitled under this Article to any promises and warranties, including those of any third party, provided to the lessor by the person supplying the goods in connection with or as part of the contract by which the lessor acquired the goods or the right to possession and use of the goods, and (c) that the lessee may communicate with the person supplying the goods to the lessor and receive an accurate and complete statement of those promises and warranties, including any disclaimers and limitations of them or of remedies.

(h) "Goods" means all things that are movable at the time of identification to the lease contract, or are fixtures (Section 2A–309), but the term does not include money, documents, instruments, accounts, chattel paper, general intangibles, or minerals or the like, including oil and gas, before extraction. The term also includes the unborn young of animals.

(i) "Installment lease contract" means a lease contract that authorizes or requires the delivery of goods in separate lots to be separately accepted, even though the lease contract contains a clause "each delivery is a separate lease" or its equivalent.

(j) "Lease" means a transfer of the right to possession and use of goods for a term in return for consideration, but a sale, including a sale on approval or a sale or return, or retention or creation of a security interest is not a lease. Unless the context clearly indicates otherwise, the term includes a sublease.

(k) "Lease agreement" means the bargain, with respect to the lease, of the lessor and the lessee in fact as found in their language or by implication from other circumstances including course of dealing or usage of trade or course of performance as provided in this Article. Unless the context clearly indicates otherwise, the term includes a sublease agreement.

(l) "Lease contract" means the total legal obligation that results from the lease agreement as affected by this Article and any other applicable rules of law. Unless the context clearly indicates otherwise, the term includes a sublease contract.

(m) "Leasehold interest" means the interest of the lessor or the lessee under a lease contract.

(n) "Lessee" means a person who acquires the right to possession and use of goods under a lease. Unless the context clearly indicates otherwise, the term includes a sublessee.

(o) "Lessee in ordinary course of business" means a person who in good faith and without knowledge that the lease to him [or her] is in violation of the ownership rights or security interest or leasehold interest of a third party in the goods, leases in ordinary course from a person in the business of selling or leasing goods of that kind but does not include a pawnbroker. "Leasing" may be for cash or by exchange of other property or on secured or unsecured credit and includes receiving goods or documents of title under a pre-existing lease contract but does not include a transfer in bulk or as security for or in total or partial satisfaction of a money debt.

(p) "Lessor" means a person who transfers the right to possession and use of goods under a lease. Unless the context clearly indicates otherwise, the term includes a sublessor.

(q) "Lessor's residual interest" means the lessor's interest in the goods after expiration, termination, or cancellation of the lease contract.

(r) "Lien" means a charge against or interest in goods to secure payment of a debt or performance of an obligation, but the term does not include a security interest.

(s) "Lot" means a parcel or a single article that is the subject matter of a separate lease or delivery, whether or not it is sufficient to perform the lease contract.

(t) "Merchant lessee" means a lessee that is a merchant with respect to goods of the kind subject to the lease.

(u) "Present value" means the amount as of a date certain of one or more sums payable in the future, discounted to the date certain. The discount is determined by the interest rate specified by the parties if the rate was not manifestly unreasonable at the time the transaction was entered into; otherwise, the discount is determined by a commercially reasonable rate that takes into account the facts and circumstances of each case at the time the transaction was entered into.

(v) "Purchase" includes taking by sale, lease, mortgage, security interest, pledge, gift, or any other voluntary transaction creating an interest in goods.

(w) "Sublease" means a lease of goods the right to possession and use of which was acquired by the lessor as a lessee under an existing lease.

(x) "Supplier" means a person from whom a lessor buys or leases goods to be leased under a finance lease.

(y) "Supply contract" means a contract under which a lessor buys or leases goods to be leased.

(z) "Termination" occurs when either party pursuant to a power created by agreement or law puts an end to the lease contract otherwise than for default.

(2) Other definitions applying to this Article and the sections in which they appear are:

"Accessions". Section 2A–310(1).
"Construction mortgage". Section 2A–309(1)(d).
"Encumbrance". Section 2A–309(1)(e).
"Fixtures". Section 2A–309(1)(a).
"Fixture filing". Section 2A–309(1)(b).
"Purchase money lease". Section 2A–309(1)(c).

(3) The following definitions in other Articles apply to this Article:

"Accounts". Section 9–106.
"Between merchants". Section 2–104(3).
"Buyer". Section 2–103(1)(a).
"Chattel paper". Section 9–105(1)(b).
"Consumer goods". Section 9–109(1).
"Document". Section 9–105(1)(f).
"Entrusting". Section 2–403(3).
"General intangibles". Section 9–106.
"Good faith". Section 2–103(1)(b).
"Instrument". Section 9–105(1)(i).
"Merchant". Section 2–104(1).
"Mortgage". Section 9–105(1)(j).
"Pursuant to commitment". Section 9–105(1)(k).
"Receipt". Section 2–103(1)(c).
"Sale". Section 2–106(1).
"Sale on approval". Section 2–326.
"Sale or return". Section 2–326.
"Seller". Section 2–103(1)(d).

(4) In addition Article 1 contains general definitions and principles of construction and interpretation applicable throughout this Article.

As amended in 1990 and 1999.

§ 2A–104. Leases Subject to Other Law.

(1) A lease, although subject to this Article, is also subject to any applicable:

(a) certificate of title statute of this State: (list any certificate of title statutes covering automobiles, trailers, mobile homes, boats, farm tractors, and the like);

(b) certificate of title statute of another jurisdiction (Section 2A–105); or

(c) consumer protection statute of this State, or final consumer protection decision of a court of this State existing on the effective date of this Article.

(2) In case of conflict between this Article, other than Sections 2A–105, 2A–304(3), and 2A–305(3), and a statute or decision referred to in subsection (1), the statute or decision controls.

(3) Failure to comply with an applicable law has only the effect specified therein.

As amended in 1990.

§ 2A–105. Territorial Application of Article to Goods Covered by Certificate of Title.

Subject to the provisions of Sections 2A–304(3) and 2A–305(3), with respect to goods covered by a certificate of title issued under a statute of this State or of another jurisdiction, compliance and the effect of compliance or noncompliance with a certificate of title statute are governed by the law (including the conflict of laws rules) of the jurisdiction issuing the certificate until the earlier of (a) surrender of the certificate, or (b) four months after the goods are removed from that jurisdiction and thereafter until a new certificate of title is issued by another jurisdiction.

§ 2A–106. Limitation on Power of Parties to Consumer Lease to Choose Applicable Law and Judicial Forum.

(1) If the law chosen by the parties to a consumer lease is that of a jurisdiction other than a jurisdiction in which the lessee resides at the time the lease agreement becomes enforceable or within 30 days thereafter or in which the goods are to be used, the choice is not enforceable.

(2) If the judicial forum chosen by the parties to a consumer lease is a forum that would not otherwise have jurisdiction over the lessee, the choice is not enforceable.

§ 2A–107. Waiver or Renunciation of Claim or Right After Default.

Any claim or right arising out of an alleged default or breach of warranty may be discharged in whole or in part without consideration by a written waiver or renunciation signed and delivered by the aggrieved party.

§ 2A–108. Unconscionability.

(1) If the court as a matter of law finds a lease contract or any clause of a lease contract to have been unconscionable at the time it was made the court may refuse to enforce the lease contract, or it may enforce the remainder of the lease contract without the unconscionable clause, or it may so limit the application of any unconscionable clause as to avoid any unconscionable result.

(2) With respect to a consumer lease, if the court as a matter of law finds that a lease contract or any clause of a lease contract has been induced by unconscionable conduct or that unconscionable conduct has occurred in the collection of a claim arising from a lease contract, the court may grant appropriate relief.

(3) Before making a finding of unconscionability under subsection (1) or (2), the court, on its own motion or that of a party, shall afford the parties a reasonable opportunity to present evidence as to the setting, purpose, and effect of the lease contract or clause thereof, or of the conduct.

(4) In an action in which the lessee claims unconscionability with respect to a consumer lease:

(a) If the court finds unconscionability under subsection (1) or (2), the court shall award reasonable attorney's fees to the lessee.

(b) If the court does not find unconscionability and the lessee claiming unconscionability has brought or maintained an action he [or she] knew to be groundless, the court shall award reasonable attorney's fees to the party against whom the claim is made.

(c) In determining attorney's fees, the amount of the recovery on behalf of the claimant under subsections (1) and (2) is not controlling.

§ 2A–109. Option to Accelerate at Will.

(1) A term providing that one party or his [or her] successor in interest may accelerate payment or performance or require collateral or additional collateral "at will" or "when he [or she] deems himself [or herself] insecure" or in words of similar import must be construed to mean that he [or she] has power to do so only if he [or she] in good faith believes that the prospect of payment or performance is impaired.

(2) With respect to a consumer lease, the burden of establishing good faith under subsection (1) is on the party who exercised the power; otherwise the burden of establishing lack of good faith is on the party against whom the power has been exercised.

Part 2 Formation and Construction of Lease Contract

§ 2A–201. Statute of Frauds.

(1) A lease contract is not enforceable by way of action or defense unless:

(a) the total payments to be made under the lease contract, excluding payments for options to renew or buy, are less than $1,000; or

(b) there is a writing, signed by the party against whom enforcement is sought or by that party's authorized agent, sufficient to indicate that a lease contract has been made between the parties and to describe the goods leased and the lease term.

(2) Any description of leased goods or of the lease term is sufficient and satisfies subsection (1)(b), whether or not it is specific, if it reasonably identifies what is described.

(3) A writing is not insufficient because it omits or incorrectly states a term agreed upon, but the lease contract is not enforceable under subsection (1)(b) beyond the lease term and the quantity of goods shown in the writing.

(4) A lease contract that does not satisfy the requirements of subsection (1), but which is valid in other respects, is enforceable:

(a) if the goods are to be specially manufactured or obtained for the lessee and are not suitable for lease or sale to others in the ordinary course of the lessor's business, and the lessor, before notice of repudiation is received and under circumstances that reasonably indicate that the goods are for the lessee, has made either a substantial beginning of their manufacture or commitments for their procurement;

(b) if the party against whom enforcement is sought admits in that party's pleading, testimony or otherwise in court that a lease contract was made, but the lease contract is not enforceable under this provision beyond the quantity of goods admitted; or

(c) with respect to goods that have been received and accepted by the lessee.

(5) The lease term under a lease contract referred to in subsection (4) is:

(a) if there is a writing signed by the party against whom enforcement is sought or by that party's authorized agent specifying the lease term, the term so specified;

(b) if the party against whom enforcement is sought admits in that party's pleading, testimony, or otherwise in court a lease term, the term so admitted; or

(c) a reasonable lease term.

§ 2A–202. Final Written Expression: Parol or Extrinsic Evidence.

Terms with respect to which the confirmatory memoranda of the parties agree or which are otherwise set forth in a writing intended by the parties as a final expression of their agreement with respect to such terms as are included therein may not be contradicted by evidence of any prior agreement or of a contemporaneous oral agreement but may be explained or supplemented:

(a) by course of dealing or usage of trade or by course of performance; and

(b) by evidence of consistent additional terms unless the court finds the writing to have been intended also as a complete and exclusive statement of the terms of the agreement.

§ 2A–203. Seals Inoperative.

The affixing of a seal to a writing evidencing a lease contract or an offer to enter into a lease contract does not render the writing a sealed instrument and the law with respect to sealed instruments does not apply to the lease contract or offer.

§ 2A–204. Formation in General.

(1) A lease contract may be made in any manner sufficient to show agreement, including conduct by both parties which recognizes the existence of a lease contract.

(2) An agreement sufficient to constitute a lease contract may be found although the moment of its making is undetermined.

(3) Although one or more terms are left open, a lease contract does not fail for indefiniteness if the parties have intended to make a lease contract and there is a reasonably certain basis for giving an appropriate remedy.

§ 2A–205. Firm Offers.

An offer by a merchant to lease goods to or from another person in a signed writing that by its terms gives assurance it will be held open is not revocable, for lack of consideration, during the time stated or, if no time is stated, for a reasonable time, but in no event may the period of irrevocability exceed 3 months. Any such term of assurance on a form supplied by the offeree must be separately signed by the offeror.

§ 2A–206. Offer and Acceptance in Formation of Lease Contract.

(1) Unless otherwise unambiguously indicated by the language or circumstances, an offer to make a lease contract must be construed as inviting acceptance in any manner and by any medium reasonable in the circumstances.

(2) If the beginning of a requested performance is a reasonable mode of acceptance, an offeror who is not notified of acceptance within a reasonable time may treat the offer as having lapsed before acceptance.

§ 2A–207. Course of Performance or Practical Construction.

(1) If a lease contract involves repeated occasions for performance by either party with knowledge of the nature of the performance and opportunity for objection to it by the other, any course of performance accepted or acquiesced in without objection is relevant to determine the meaning of the lease agreement.

(2) The express terms of a lease agreement and any course of performance, as well as any course of dealing and usage of trade, must be construed whenever reasonable as consistent with each other; but if that construction is unreasonable, express terms control course of performance, course of performance controls both course of dealing and usage of trade, and course of dealing controls usage of trade.

(3) Subject to the provisions of Section 2A–208 on modification and waiver, course of performance is relevant to show a waiver or modification of any term inconsistent with the course of performance.

§ 2A–208. Modification, Rescission and Waiver.

(1) An agreement modifying a lease contract needs no consideration to be binding.

(2) A signed lease agreement that excludes modification or rescission except by a signed writing may not be otherwise modified or rescinded, but, except as between merchants, such a requirement on a form supplied by a merchant must be separately signed by the other party.

(3) Although an attempt at modification or rescission does not satisfy the requirements of subsection (2), it may operate as a waiver.

(4) A party who has made a waiver affecting an executory portion of a lease contract may retract the waiver by reasonable notification received by the other party that strict performance will be required of any term waived, unless the retraction would be unjust in view of a material change of position in reliance on the waiver.

§ 2A–209. Lessee under Finance Lease as Beneficiary of Supply Contract.

(1) The benefit of the supplier's promises to the lessor under the supply contract and of all warranties, whether express or implied, including those of any third party provided in connection with or as part of the supply contract, extends to the lessee to the extent of the lessee's leasehold interest under a finance lease related to the supply contract, but is subject to the terms warranty and of the supply contract and all defenses or claims arising therefrom.

(2) The extension of the benefit of supplier's promises and of warranties to the lessee (Section 2A–209(1)) does not: (i) modify the rights and obligations of the parties to the supply contract, whether arising therefrom or otherwise, or (ii) impose any duty or liability under the supply contract on the lessee.

(3) Any modification or rescission of the supply contract by the supplier and the lessor is effective between the supplier and the lessee unless, before the modification or rescission, the supplier has received notice that the lessee has entered into a finance lease related to the supply contract. If the modification or rescission is effective between the supplier and the lessee, the lessor is deemed to have assumed, in addition to the obligations of the lessor to the lessee under the lease contract, promises of the supplier to the lessor and warranties that were so modified or rescinded as they existed and were available to the lessee before modification or rescission.

(4) In addition to the extension of the benefit of the supplier's promises and of warranties to the lessee under subsection (1), the lessee retains all rights that the lessee may have against the supplier which arise from an agreement between the lessee and the supplier or under other law. As amended in 1990.

§ 2A–210. Express Warranties.

(1) Express warranties by the lessor are created as follows:

(a) Any affirmation of fact or promise made by the lessor to the lessee which relates to the goods and becomes part of the basis of the bargain creates an express warranty that the goods will conform to the affirmation or promise.

(b) Any description of the goods which is made part of the basis of the bargain creates an express warranty that the goods will conform to the description.

(c) Any sample or model that is made part of the basis of the bargain creates an express warranty that the whole of the goods will conform to the sample or model.

(2) It is not necessary to the creation of an express warranty that the lessor use formal words, such as "warrant" or "guarantee," or that the lessor have a specific intention to make a warranty, but an affirmation merely of the value of the goods or a statement purporting to be merely the lessor's opinion or commendation of the goods does not create a warranty.

§ 2A–211. Warranties Against Interference and Against Infringement; Lessee's Obligation Against Infringement.

(1) There is in a lease contract a warranty that for the lease term no person holds a claim to or interest in the goods that arose from an act or omission of the lessor, other than a claim by way of infringement or the like, which will interfere with the lessee's enjoyment of its leasehold interest.

(2) Except in a finance lease there is in a lease contract by a lessor who is a merchant regularly dealing in goods of the kind a warranty that the goods are delivered free of the rightful claim of any person by way of infringement or the like.

(3) A lessee who furnishes specifications to a lessor or a supplier shall hold the lessor and the supplier harmless against any claim by way of infringement or the like that arises out of compliance with the specifications.

§ 2A–212. Implied Warranty of Merchantability.

(1) Except in a finance lease, a warranty that the goods will be merchantable is implied in a lease contract if the lessor is a merchant with respect to goods of that kind.

(2) Goods to be merchantable must be at least such as

(a) pass without objection in the trade under the description in the lease agreement;

(b) in the case of fungible goods, are of fair average quality within the description;

(c) are fit for the ordinary purposes for which goods of that type are used;

(d) run, within the variation permitted by the lease agreement, of even kind, quality, and quantity within each unit and among all units involved;

(e) are adequately contained, packaged, and labeled as the lease agreement may require; and

(f) conform to any promises or affirmations of fact made on the container or label.

(3) Other implied warranties may arise from course of dealing or usage of trade.

§ 2A–213. Implied Warranty of Fitness for Particular Purpose.

Except in a finance of lease, if the lessor at the time the lease contract is made has reason to know of any particular purpose for which the goods are required and that the lessee is relying on the lessor's skill or judgment to select or furnish suitable goods, there is in the lease contract an implied warranty that the goods will be fit for that purpose.

§ 2A–214. Exclusion or Modification of Warranties.

(1) Words or conduct relevant to the creation of an express warranty and words or conduct tending to negate or limit a warranty must be construed wherever reasonable as consistent with each other; but, subject to the provisions of Section 2A–202 on parol or extrinsic evidence, negation or limitation is inoperative to the extent that the construction is unreasonable.

(2) Subject to subsection (3), to exclude or modify the implied warranty of merchantability or any part of it the language must mention "merchantability", be by a writing, and be conspicuous. Subject to subsection (3), to exclude or modify any implied warranty of fitness the exclusion must be by a writing and be conspicuous. Language to exclude all implied warranties of fitness is sufficient if it is in writing, is conspicuous and states, for example, "There is no warranty that the goods will be fit for a particular purpose".

(3) Notwithstanding subsection (2), but subject to subsection (4),

(a) unless the circumstances indicate otherwise, all implied warranties are excluded by expressions like "as is" or "with all faults" or by other language that in common understanding calls the lessee's attention to the exclusion of warranties and makes plain that there is no implied warranty, if in writing and conspicuous;

(b) if the lessee before entering into the lease contract has examined the goods or the sample or model as fully as desired or has refused to examine the goods, there is no implied warranty with regard to defects that an examination ought in the circumstances to have revealed; and

(c) an implied warranty may also be excluded or modified by course of dealing, course of performance, or usage of trade.

(4) To exclude or modify a warranty against interference or against infringement (Section 2A–211) or any part of it, the language must be specific, be by a writing, and be conspicuous, unless the circumstances, including course of performance, course of dealing, or usage of trade, give the lessee reason to know that the goods are being leased subject to a claim or interest of any person.

§ 2A–215. Cumulation and Conflict of Warranties Express or Implied.

Warranties, whether express or implied, must be construed as consistent with each other and as cumulative, but if that construction is unreasonable, the intention of the parties determines which warranty is dominant. In ascertaining that intention the following rules apply:

(a) Exact or technical specifications displace an inconsistent sample or model or general language of description.

(b) A sample from an existing bulk displaces inconsistent general language of description.

(c) Express warranties displace inconsistent implied warranties other than an implied warranty of fitness for a particular purpose.

§ 2A–216. Third-Party Beneficiaries of Express and Implied Warranties.

Alternative A

A warranty to or for the benefit of a lessee under this Article, whether express or implied, extends to any natural person who is in the family or household of the lessee or who is a guest in the lessee's home if it is reasonable to expect that such person may use, consume, or be affected by the goods and who is injured in person by breach of the warranty. This section does not displace principles of law and equity that extend a warranty to or for the benefit of a lessee to other persons. The operation of this section may not be excluded, modified, or limited, but an exclusion, modification, or limitation of the warranty, including any with respect to rights and remedies, effective against the lessee is also effective against any beneficiary designated under this section.

Alternative B

A warranty to or for the benefit of a lessee under this Article, whether express or implied, extends to any natural person who may reasonably be expected to use, consume, or be affected by the goods and who is injured in person by breach of the warranty. This section does not displace principles of law and equity that extend a warranty to or for the benefit of a lessee to other persons. The operation of this section may not be excluded, modified, or limited, but an exclusion, modification, or limitation of the warranty, including any with respect to rights and remedies, effective against the lessee is also effective against the beneficiary designated under this section.

Alternative C

A warranty to or for the benefit of a lessee under this Article, whether express or implied, extends to any person who may reasonably be expected to use, consume, or be affected by the goods and who is injured by breach of the warranty. The operation of this section may not be excluded, modified, or limited with respect to injury to the person of an individual to whom the warranty extends, but an exclusion, modification, or limitation of the warranty, including any with respect to rights and remedies, effective against the lessee is also effective against the beneficiary designated under this section.

§ 2A–217. Identification.

Identification of goods as goods to which a lease contract refers may be made at any time and in any manner explicitly agreed to by the parties. In the absence of explicit agreement, identification occurs:

(a) when the lease contract is made if the lease contract is for a lease of goods that are existing and identified;

(b) when the goods are shipped, marked, or otherwise designated by the lessor as goods to which the lease contract refers, if the lease contract is for a lease of goods that are not existing and identified; or

(c) when the young are conceived, if the lease contract is for a lease of unborn young of animals.

§ 2A–218. Insurance and Proceeds.

(1) A lessee obtains an insurable interest when existing goods are identified to the lease contract even though the goods identified are nonconforming and the lessee has an option to reject them.

(2) If a lessee has an insurable interest only by reason of the lessor's identification of the goods, the lessor, until default or insolvency or notification to the lessee that identification is final, may substitute other goods for those identified.

(3) Notwithstanding a lessee's insurable interest under subsections (1) and (2), the lessor retains an insurable interest until an option to buy has been exercised by the lessee and risk of loss has passed to the lessee.

(4) Nothing in this section impairs any insurable interest recognized under any other statute or rule of law.

(5) The parties by agreement may determine that one or more parties have an obligation to obtain and pay for insurance covering the goods and by agreement may determine the beneficiary of the proceeds of the insurance.

§ 2A–219. Risk of Loss.

(1) Except in the case of a finance lease, risk of loss is retained by the lessor and does not pass to the lessee. In the case of a finance lease, risk of loss passes to the lessee.

(2) Subject to the provisions of this Article on the effect of default on risk of loss (Section 2A–220), if risk of loss is to pass to the lessee and the time of passage is not stated, the following rules apply:

(a) If the lease contract requires or authorizes the goods to be shipped by carrier

(i) and it does not require delivery at a particular destination, the risk of loss passes to the lessee when the goods are duly delivered to the carrier; but

(ii) if it does require delivery at a particular destination and the goods are there duly tendered while in the possession of the carrier, the risk of loss passes to the lessee when the goods are there duly so tendered as to enable the lessee to take delivery.

(b) If the goods are held by a bailee to be delivered without being moved, the risk of loss passes to the lessee on acknowledgment by the bailee of the lessee's right to possession of the goods.

(c) In any case not within subsection (a) or (b), the risk of loss passes to the lessee on the lessee's receipt of the goods if the lessor, or, in the case of a finance lease, the supplier, is a merchant; otherwise the risk passes to the lessee on tender of delivery.

§ 2A–220. Effect of Default on Risk of Loss.

(1) Where risk of loss is to pass to the lessee and the time of passage is not stated:

(a) If a tender or delivery of goods so fails to conform to the lease contract as to give a right of rejection, the risk of their loss remains with the lessor, or, in the case of a finance lease, the supplier, until cure or acceptance.

(b) If the lessee rightfully revokes acceptance, he [or she], to the extent of any deficiency in his [or her] effective insurance coverage, may treat the risk of loss as having remained with the lessor from the beginning.

(2) Whether or not risk of loss is to pass to the lessee, if the lessee as to conforming goods already identified to a lease contract repudiates or is otherwise in default under the lease contract, the lessor, or, in the case of a finance lease, the supplier, to the extent of any deficiency in his [or her] effective insurance coverage may treat the risk of loss as resting on the lessee for a commercially reasonable time.

§ 2A–221. Casualty to Identified Goods.

If a lease contract requires goods identified when the lease contract is made, and the goods suffer casualty without fault of the lessee, the lessor or the supplier before delivery, or the goods suffer casualty before risk of loss passes to the lessee pursuant to the lease agreement or Section 2A–219, then:

(a) if the loss is total, the lease contract is avoided; and

(b) if the loss is partial or the goods have so deteriorated as to no longer conform to the lease contract, the lessee may nevertheless demand inspection and at his [or her] option either treat the lease contract as avoided or, except in a finance lease that is not a consumer lease, accept the goods with due allowance from the rent payable for the balance of the lease term for the deterioration or the deficiency in quantity but without further right against the lessor.

Part 3 Effect of Lease Contract

§ 2A–301. Enforceability of Lease Contract.

Except as otherwise provided in this Article, a lease contract is effective and enforceable according to its terms between the parties, against purchasers of the goods and against creditors of the parties.

§ 2A–302. Title to and Possession of Goods.

Except as otherwise provided in this Article, each provision of this Article applies whether the lessor or a third party has title to the goods, and whether the lessor, the lessee, or a third party has possession of the goods, notwithstanding any statute or rule of law that possession or the absence of possession is fraudulent.

§ 2A–303. Alienability of Party's Interest Under Lease Contract or of Lessor's Residual Interest in Goods; Delegation of Performance; Transfer of Rights.

(1) As used in this section, "creation of a security interest" includes the sale of a lease contract that is subject to Article 9, Secured Transactions, by reason of Section 9–109(a)(3).

(2) Except as provided in subsections (3) and Section 9–407, a provision in a lease agreement which (i) prohibits the voluntary or involuntary transfer, including a transfer by sale, sublease, creation or enforcement of a security interest, or attachment, levy, or other judicial process, of an interest of a party under the lease contract or of the lessor's residual interest in the goods, or (ii) makes such a transfer an event of default, gives rise to the rights and remedies provided in subsection (4), but a transfer that is prohibited or is an event of default under the lease agreement is otherwise effective.

(3) A provision in a lease agreement which (i) prohibits a transfer of a right to damages for default with respect to the whole lease contract or of a right to payment arising out of the transferor's due performance of the transferor's entire obligation, or (ii) makes such a transfer an event of default, is not enforceable, and such a transfer is not a transfer that materially impairs the propsect of obtaining return performance by, materially changes the duty of, or materially increases the burden or risk imposed on, the other party to the lease contract within the purview of subsection (4).

(4) Subject to subsection (3) and Section 9–407:

(a) if a transfer is made which is made an event of default under a lease agreement, the party to the lease contract not making the transfer, unless that party waives the default or otherwise agrees, has the rights and remedies described in Section 2A–501(2);

(b) if paragraph (a) is not applicable and if a transfer is made that (i) is prohibited under a lease agreement or (ii) materially impairs the prospect of obtaining return performance by, materially changes the duty of, or materially increases the burden or risk imposed on, the other party to the lease contract, unless the party not making the transfer agrees at any time to the transfer in the lease contract or otherwise, then, except as limited by contract, (i) the transferor is liable to the party not making the transfer for damages caused by the transfer to the extent that the damages could not reasonably be prevented by the party not making the transfer and (ii) a court having jurisdiction may grant other appropriate relief, including cancellation of the lease contract or an injunction against the transfer.

(5) A transfer of "the lease" or of "all my rights under the lease", or a transfer in similar general terms, is a transfer of rights and, unless the language or the circumstances, as in a transfer for security, indicate the contrary, the transfer is a delegation of duties by the transferor to the transferee. Acceptance by the transferee constitutes a promise by the transferee to perform those duties. The promise is enforceable by either the transferor or the other party to the lease contract.

(6) Unless otherwise agreed by the lessor and the lessee, a delegation of performance does not relieve the transferor as against the other party of any duty to perform or of any liability for default.

(7) In a consumer lease, to prohibit the transfer of an interest of a party under the lease contract or to make a transfer an event of default, the language must be specific, by a writing, and conspicuous.

As amended in 1990 and 1999.

§ 2A–304. Subsequent Lease of Goods by Lessor.

(1) Subject to Section 2A–303, a subsequent lessee from a lessor of goods under an existing lease contract obtains, to the extent of the leasehold interest transferred, the leasehold interest in the goods that the lessor had or had power to transfer, and except as provided in subsection (2) and Section 2A–527(4), takes subject to the existing lease contract. A lessor with voidable title has power to transfer a good leasehold interest to a good faith subsequent lessee for value, but only to the extent set forth in the preceding sentence. If goods have been delivered under a transaction of purchase the lessor has that power even though:

(a) the lessor's transferor was deceived as to the identity of the lessor;

(b) the delivery was in exchange for a check which is later dishonored;

(c) it was agreed that the transaction was to be a "cash sale"; or

(d) the delivery was procured through fraud punishable as larcenous under the criminal law.

(2) A subsequent lessee in the ordinary course of business from a lessor who is a merchant dealing in goods of that kind to whom the goods were entrusted by the existing lessee of that lessor before the interest of the subsequent lessee became enforceable against that lessor obtains, to the extent of the leasehold interest transferred, all of that lessor's and the existing lessee's rights to the goods, and takes free of the existing lease contract.

(3) A subsequent lessee from the lessor of goods that are subject to an existing lease contract and are covered by a certificate of title issued under a statute of this State or of another jurisdiction takes no greater rights than those provided both by this section and by the certificate of title statute.

As amended in 1990.

§ 2A–305. Sale or Sublease of Goods by Lessee.

(1) Subject to the provisions of Section 2A–303, a buyer or sublessee from the lessee of goods under an existing lease contract obtains, to the extent of the interest transferred, the leasehold interest in the goods that the lessee had or had power to transfer, and except as provided in subsection (2) and Section 2A–511(4), takes subject to the existing lease contract. A lessee with a voidable leasehold interest has power to transfer a good leasehold interest to a good faith buyer for value or a good faith sublessee for value, but only to the extent set forth in the preceding sentence. When goods have been delivered under a transaction of lease the lessee has that power even though:

(a) the lessor was deceived as to the identity of the lessee;

(b) the delivery was in exchange for a check which is later dishonored; or

(c) the delivery was procured through fraud punishable as larcenous under the criminal law.

(2) A buyer in the ordinary course of business or a sublessee in the ordinary course of business from a lessee who is a merchant dealing in goods of that kind to whom the goods were entrusted by the lessor obtains, to the extent of the interest transferred, all of the lessor's and lessee's rights to the goods, and takes free of the existing lease contract.

(3) A buyer or sublessee from the lessee of goods that are subject to an existing lease contract and are covered by a certificate of title issued under a statute of this State or of another jurisdiction takes no greater rights than those provided both by this section and by the certificate of title statute.

§ 2A–306. Priority of Certain Liens Arising by Operation of Law.

If a person in the ordinary course of his [or her] business furnishes services or materials with respect to goods subject to a lease contract, a lien upon those goods in the possession of that person given by statute or rule of law for those materials or services takes priority over any interest of the lessor or lessee under the lease contract or this Article unless the lien is created by statute and the statute provides otherwise or unless the lien is created by rule of law and the rule of law provides otherwise.

§ 2A–307. Priority of Liens Arising by Attachment or Levy on, Security Interests in, and Other Claims to Goods.

(1) Except as otherwise provided in Section 2A–306, a creditor of a lessee takes subject to the lease contract.

(2) Except as otherwise provided in subsection (3) and in Sections 2A–306 and 2A–308, a creditor of a lessor takes subject to the lease contract unless the creditor holds a lien that attached to the goods before the lease contract became enforceable.

(3) Except as otherwise provided in Sections 9–317, 9–321, and 9–323, a lessee takes a leasehold interest subject to a security interest held by a creditor of the lessor.

As amended in 1990 and 1999.

§ 2A–308. Special Rights of Creditors.

(1) A creditor of a lessor in possession of goods subject to a lease contract may treat the lease contract as void if as against the creditor retention of possession by the lessor is fraudulent under any statute or rule of law, but retention of possession in good faith and current course of trade by the lessor for a commercially reasonable time after the lease contract becomes enforceable is not fraudulent.

(2) Nothing in this Article impairs the rights of creditors of a lessor if the lease contract (a) becomes enforceable, not in current course of trade but in satisfaction of or as security for a pre-existing claim for money, security, or the like, and (b) is made under circumstances which under any statute or rule of law apart from this Article would constitute the transaction a fraudulent transfer or voidable preference.

(3) A creditor of a seller may treat a sale or an identification of goods to a contract for sale as void if as against the creditor retention of possession by the seller is fraudulent under any statute or rule of law, but retention of possession of the goods pursuant to a lease contract entered into by the seller as lessee and the buyer as lessor in connection with the sale or identification of the goods is not fraudulent if the buyer bought for value and in good faith.

§ 2A–309. Lessor's and Lessee's Rights When Goods Become Fixtures.

(1) In this section:

(a) goods are "fixtures" when they become so related to particular real estate that an interest in them arises under real estate law;

(b) a "fixture filing" is the filing, in the office where a mortgage on the real estate would be filed or recorded, of a financing statement covering goods that are or are to become fixtures and conforming to the requirements of Section 9–502(a) and (b);

(c) a lease is a "purchase money lease" unless the lessee has possession or use of the goods or the right to possession or use of the goods before the lease agreement is enforceable;

(d) a mortgage is a "construction mortgage" to the extent it secures an obligation incurred for the construction of an improvement on land including the acquisition cost of the land, if the recorded writing so indicates; and

(e) "encumbrance" includes real estate mortgages and other liens on real estate and all other rights in real estate that are not ownership interests.

(2) Under this Article a lease may be of goods that are fixtures or may continue in goods that become fixtures, but no lease exists under this Article of ordinary building materials incorporated into an improvement on land.

(3) This Article does not prevent creation of a lease of fixtures pursuant to real estate law.

(4) The perfected interest of a lessor of fixtures has priority over a conflicting interest of an encumbrancer or owner of the real estate if:

(a) the lease is a purchase money lease, the conflicting interest of the encumbrancer or owner arises before the goods become fixtures, the interest of the lessor is perfected by a fixture filing before the goods become fixtures or within ten days thereafter, and the lessee has an interest of record in the real estate or is in possession of the real estate; or

(b) the interest of the lessor is perfected by a fixture filing before the interest of the encumbrancer or owner is of record, the lessor's interest has priority over any conflicting interest of a predecessor in title of the encumbrancer or owner, and the lessee has an interest of record in the real estate or is in possession of the real estate.

(5) The interest of a lessor of fixtures, whether or not perfected, has priority over the conflicting interest of an encumbrancer or owner of the real estate if:

(a) the fixtures are readily removable factory or office machines, readily removable equipment that is not primarily used or leased for use in the operation of the real estate, or readily removable replacements of domestic appliances that are goods subject to a consumer lease, and before the goods become fixtures the lease contract is enforceable; or

(b) the conflicting interest is a lien on the real estate obtained by legal or equitable proceedings after the lease contract is enforceable; or

(c) the encumbrancer or owner has consented in writing to the lease or has disclaimed an interest in the goods as fixtures; or

(d) the lessee has a right to remove the goods as against the encumbrancer or owner. If the lessee's right to remove terminates, the priority of the interest of the lessor continues for a reasonable time.

(6) Notwithstanding paragraph (4)(a) but otherwise subject to subsections (4) and (5), the interest of a lessor of fixtures, including the lessor's residual interest, is subordinate to the conflicting interest of an encumbrancer of the real estate under a construction mortgage recorded before the goods become fixtures if the goods become fixtures before the completion of the construction. To the extent given to refinance a construction mortgage, the conflicting interest of an encumbrancer of the real estate under a mortgage has this priority to the same extent as the encumbrancer of the real estate under the construction mortgage.

(7) In cases not within the preceding subsections, priority between the interest of a lessor of fixtures, including the lessor's residual interest, and the conflicting interest of an encumbrancer or owner of the real estate who is not the lessee is determined by the priority rules governing conflicting interests in real estate.

(8) If the interest of a lessor of fixtures, including the lessor's residual interest, has priority over all conflicting interests of all owners and encumbrancers of the real estate, the lessor or the lessee may (i) on default, expiration, termination, or cancellation of the lease agreement but subject to the agreement and this Article, or (ii) if necessary to enforce other rights and remedies of the lessor or lessee under this Article, remove the goods from the real estate, free and clear of all conflicting interests of all owners and encumbrancers of the real estate, but the lessor or lessee must reimburse any encum-

brancer or owner of the real estate who is not the lessee and who has not otherwise agreed for the cost of repair of any physical injury, but not for any diminution in value of the real estate caused by the absence of the goods removed or by any necessity of replacing them. A person entitled to reimbursement may refuse permission to remove until the party seeking removal gives adequate security for the performance of this obligation.

(9) Even though the lease agreement does not create a security interest, the interest of a lessor of fixtures, including the lessor's residual interest, is perfected by filing a financing statement as a fixture filing for leased goods that are or are to become fixtures in accordance with the relevant provisions of the Article on Secured Transactions (Article 9).

As amended in 1990 and 1999.

§ 2A–310. Lessor's and Lessee's Rights When Goods Become Accessions.

(1) Goods are "accessions" when they are installed in or affixed to other goods.

(2) The interest of a lessor or a lessee under a lease contract entered into before the goods became accessions is superior to all interests in the whole except as stated in subsection (4).

(3) The interest of a lessor or a lessee under a lease contract entered into at the time or after the goods became accessions is superior to all subsequently acquired interests in the whole except as stated in subsection (4) but is subordinate to interests in the whole existing at the time the lease contract was made unless the holders of such interests in the whole have in writing consented to the lease or disclaimed an interest in the goods as part of the whole.

(4) The interest of a lessor or a lessee under a lease contract described in subsection (2) or (3) is subordinate to the interest of

    (a) a buyer in the ordinary course of business or a lessee in the ordinary course of business of any interest in the whole acquired after the goods became accessions; or

    (b) a creditor with a security interest in the whole perfected before the lease contract was made to the extent that the creditor makes subsequent advances without knowledge of the lease contract.

(5) When under subsections (2) or (3) and (4) a lessor or a lessee of accessions holds an interest that is superior to all interests in the whole, the lessor or the lessee may (a) on default, expiration, termination, or cancellation of the lease contract by the other party but subject to the provisions of the lease contract and this Article, or (b) if necessary to enforce his [or her] other rights and remedies under this Article, remove the goods from the whole, free and clear of all interests in the whole, but he [or she] must reimburse any holder of an interest in the whole who is not the lessee and who has not otherwise agreed for the cost of repair of any physical injury but not for any diminution in value of the whole caused by the absence of the goods removed or by any necessity for replacing them. A person entitled to reimbursement may refuse permission to remove until the party seeking removal gives adequate security for the performance of this obligation.

§ 2A–311. Priority Subject to Subordination.

Nothing in this Article prevents subordination by agreement by any person entitled to priority.

As added in 1990.

Part 4 Performance of Lease Contract: Repudiated, Substituted and Excused

§ 2A–401. Insecurity: Adequate Assurance of Performance.

(1) A lease contract imposes an obligation on each party that the other's expectation of receiving due performance will not be impaired.

(2) If reasonable grounds for insecurity arise with respect to the performance of either party, the insecure party may demand in writing adequate assurance of due performance. Until the insecure party receives that assurance, if commercially reasonable the insecure party may suspend any performance for which he [or she] has not already received the agreed return.

(3) A repudiation of the lease contract occurs if assurance of due performance adequate under the circumstances of the particular case is not provided to the insecure party within a reasonable time, not to exceed 30 days after receipt of a demand by the other party.

(4) Between merchants, the reasonableness of grounds for insecurity and the adequacy of any assurance offered must be determined according to commercial standards.

(5) Acceptance of any nonconforming delivery or payment does not prejudice the aggrieved party's right to demand adequate assurance of future performance.

§ 2A–402. Anticipatory Repudiation.

If either party repudiates a lease contract with respect to a performance not yet due under the lease contract, the loss of which performance will substantially impair the value of the lease contract to the other, the aggrieved party may:

    (a) for a commercially reasonable time, await retraction of repudiation and performance by the repudiating party;

    (b) make demand pursuant to Section 2A–401 and await assurance of future performance adequate under the circumstances of the particular case; or

    (c) resort to any right or remedy upon default under the lease contract or this Article, even though the aggrieved party has notified the repudiating party that the aggrieved party would await the repudiating party's performance and assurance and has urged retraction. In addition, whether or not the aggrieved party is pursuing one of the foregoing remedies, the aggrieved party may suspend performance or, if the aggrieved party is the lessor, proceed in accordance with the provisions of this Article on the lessor's right to identify goods to the lease contract notwithstanding default or to salvage unfinished goods (Section 2A–524).

§ 2A–403. Retraction of Anticipatory Repudiation.

(1) Until the repudiating party's next performance is due, the repudiating party can retract the repudiation unless, since the repudiation, the aggrieved party has cancelled the lease contract or materially changed the aggrieved party's position or otherwise indicated that the aggrieved party considers the repudiation final.

(2) Retraction may be by any method that clearly indicates to the aggrieved party that the repudiating party intends to perform under the lease contract and includes any assurance demanded under Section 2A–401.

(3) Retraction reinstates a repudiating party's rights under a lease contract with due excuse and allowance to the aggrieved party for any delay occasioned by the repudiation.

§ 2A–404. Substituted Performance.

(1) If without fault of the lessee, the lessor and the supplier, the agreed berthing, loading, or unloading facilities fail or the agreed type of carrier becomes unavailable or the agreed manner of delivery otherwise becomes commercially impracticable, but a commercially reasonable substitute is available, the substitute performance must be tendered and accepted.

(2) If the agreed means or manner of payment fails because of domestic or foreign governmental regulation:

(a) the lessor may withhold or stop delivery or cause the supplier to withhold or stop delivery unless the lessee provides a means or manner of payment that is commercially a substantial equivalent; and

(b) if delivery has already been taken, payment by the means or in the manner provided by the regulation discharges the lessee's obligation unless the regulation is discriminatory, oppressive, or predatory.

§ 2A–405. Excused Performance.

Subject to Section 2A–404 on substituted performance, the following rules apply:

(a) Delay in delivery or nondelivery in whole or in part by a lessor or a supplier who complies with paragraphs (b) and (c) is not a default under the lease contract if performance as agreed has been made impracticable by the occurrence of a contingency the nonoccurrence of which was a basic assumption on which the lease contract was made or by compliance in good faith with any applicable foreign or domestic governmental regulation or order, whether or not the regulation or order later proves to be invalid.

(b) If the causes mentioned in paragraph (a) affect only part of the lessor's or the supplier's capacity to perform, he [or she] shall allocate production and deliveries among his [or her] customers but at his [or her] option may include regular customers not then under contract for sale or lease as well as his [or her] own requirements for further manufacture. He [or she] may so allocate in any manner that is fair and reasonable.

(c) The lessor seasonably shall notify the lessee and in the case of a finance lease the supplier seasonably shall notify the lessor and the lessee, if known, that there will be delay or nondelivery and, if allocation is required under paragraph (b), of the estimated quota thus made available for the lessee.

§ 2A–406. Procedure on Excused Performance.

(1) If the lessee receives notification of a material or indefinite delay or an allocation justified under Section 2A–405, the lessee may by written notification to the lessor as to any goods involved, and with respect to all of the goods if under an installment lease contract the value of the whole lease contract is substantially impaired (Section 2A–510):

(a) terminate the lease contract (Section 2A–505(2)); or

(b) except in a finance lease that is not a consumer lease, modify the lease contract by accepting the available quota in substitution, with due allowance from the rent payable for the balance of the lease term for the deficiency but without further right against the lessor.

(2) If, after receipt of a notification from the lessor under Section 2A–405, the lessee fails so to modify the lease agreement within a reasonable time not exceeding 30 days, the lease contract lapses with respect to any deliveries affected.

§ 2A–407. Irrevocable Promises: Finance Leases.

(1) In the case of a finance lease that is not a consumer lease the lessee's promises under the lease contract become irrevocable and independent upon the lessee's acceptance of the goods.

(2) A promise that has become irrevocable and independent under subsection (1):

(a) is effective and enforceable between the parties, and by or against third parties including assignees of the parties, and

(b) is not subject to cancellation, termination, modification, repudiation, excuse, or substitution without the consent of the party to whom the promise runs.

(3) This section does not affect the validity under any other law of a covenant in any lease contract making the lessee's promises irrevocable and independent upon the lessee's acceptance of the goods.

As amended in 1990.

Part 5 Default

A. In General

§ 2A–501. Default: Procedure.

(1) Whether the lessor or the lessee is in default under a lease contract is determined by the lease agreement and this Article.

(2) If the lessor or the lessee is in default under the lease contract, the party seeking enforcement has rights and remedies as provided in this Article and, except as limited by this Article, as provided in the lease agreement.

(3) If the lessor or the lessee is in default under the lease contract, the party seeking enforcement may reduce the party's claim to judgment, or otherwise enforce the lease contract by self-help or any available judicial procedure or nonjudicial procedure, including administrative proceeding, arbitration, or the like, in accordance with this Article.

(4) Except as otherwise provided in Section 1–106(1) or this Article or the lease agreement, the rights and remedies referred to in subsections (2) and (3) are cumulative.

(5) If the lease agreement covers both real property and goods, the party seeking enforcement may proceed under this Part as to the goods, or under other applicable law as to both the real property and the goods in accordance with that party's rights and remedies in respect of the real property, in which case this Part does not apply.

As amended in 1990.

§ 2A–502. Notice After Default.

Except as otherwise provided in this Article or the lease agreement, the lessor or lessee in default under the lease contract is not entitled to notice of default or notice of enforcement from the other party to the lease agreement.

§ 2A–503. Modification or Impairment of Rights and Remedies.

(1) Except as otherwise provided in this Article, the lease agreement may include rights and remedies for default in addition to or in substitution for those provided in this Article and may limit or alter the measure of damages recoverable under this Article.

(2) Resort to a remedy provided under this Article or in the lease agreement is optional unless the remedy is expressly agreed to be exclusive. If circumstances cause an exclusive or limited remedy to fail of its essential purpose, or provision for an exclusive remedy is unconscionable, remedy may be had as provided in this Article.

(3) Consequential damages may be liquidated under Section 2A–504, or may otherwise be limited, altered, or excluded unless the limitation, alteration, or exclusion is unconscionable. Limitation, alteration, or exclusion of consequential damages for injury to the person in the case of consumer goods is prima facie unconscionable but limitation, alteration, or exclusion of damages where the loss is commercial is not prima facie unconscionable.

(4) Rights and remedies on default by the lessor or the lessee with respect to any obligation or promise collateral or ancillary to the lease contract are not impaired by this Article.

As amended in 1990.

§ 2A–504. Liquidation of Damages.

(1) Damages payable by either party for default, or any other act or omission, including indemnity for loss or diminution of anticipated tax benefits or loss or damage to lessor's residual interest, may be liquidated in the lease agreement but only at an amount or by a formula that is reasonable in light of the then anticipated harm caused by the default or other act or omission.

(2) If the lease agreement provides for liquidation of damages, and such provision does not comply with subsection (1), or such provision is an exclusive or limited remedy that circumstances cause to fail of its essential purpose, remedy may be had as provided in this Article.

(3) If the lessor justifiably withholds or stops delivery of goods because of the lessee's default or insolvency (Section 2A–525 or 2A–526), the lessee is entitled to restitution of any amount by which the sum of his [or her] payments exceeds:

    (a) the amount to which the lessor is entitled by virtue of terms liquidating the lessor's damages in accordance with subsection (1); or

    (b) in the absence of those terms, 20 percent of the then present value of the total rent the lessee was obligated to pay for the balance of the lease term, or, in the case of a consumer lease, the lesser of such amount or $500.

(4) A lessee's right to restitution under subsection (3) is subject to offset to the extent the lessor establishes:

    (a) a right to recover damages under the provisions of this Article other than subsection (1); and

    (b) the amount or value of any benefits received by the lessee directly or indirectly by reason of the lease contract.

§ 2A–505. Cancellation and Termination and Effect of Cancellation, Termination, Rescission, or Fraud on Rights and Remedies.

(1) On cancellation of the lease contract, all obligations that are still executory on both sides are discharged, but any right based on prior default or performance survives, and the cancelling party also retains any remedy for default of the whole lease contract or any unperformed balance.

(2) On termination of the lease contract, all obligations that are still executory on both sides are discharged but any right based on prior default or performance survives.

(3) Unless the contrary intention clearly appears, expressions of "cancellation," "rescission," or the like of the lease contract may not be construed as a renunciation or discharge of any claim in damages for an antecedent default.

(4) Rights and remedies for material misrepresentation or fraud include all rights and remedies available under this Article for default.

(5) Neither rescission nor a claim for rescission of the lease contract nor rejection or return of the goods may bar or be deemed inconsistent with a claim for damages or other right or remedy.

§ 2A–506. Statute of Limitations.

(1) An action for default under a lease contract, including breach of warranty or indemnity, must be commenced within 4 years after the cause of action accrued. By the original lease contract the parties may reduce the period of limitation to not less than one year.

(2) A cause of action for default accrues when the act or omission on which the default or breach of warranty is based is or should have been discovered by the aggrieved party, or when the default occurs, whichever is later. A cause of action for indemnity accrues when the act or omission on which the claim for indemnity is based is or should have been discovered by the indemnified party, whichever is later.

(3) If an action commenced within the time limited by subsection (1) is so terminated as to leave available a remedy by another action for the same default or breach of warranty or indemnity, the other action may be commenced after the expiration of the time limited and within 6 months after the termination of the first action unless the termination resulted from voluntary discontinuance or from dismissal for failure or neglect to prosecute.

(4) This section does not alter the law on tolling of the statute of limitations nor does it apply to causes of action that have accrued before this Article becomes effective.

§ 2A–507. Proof of Market Rent: Time and Place.

(1) Damages based on market rent (Section 2A–519 or 2A–528) are determined according to the rent for the use of the goods concerned for a lease term identical to the remaining lease term of the original lease agreement and prevailing at the times specified in Sections 2A–519 and 2A–528.

(2) If evidence of rent for the use of the goods concerned for a lease term identical to the remaining lease term of the original lease agreement and prevailing at the times or places described in this Article is not readily available, the rent prevailing within any reasonable time before or after the time described or at any other place or for a different lease term which in commercial judgment or under usage of trade would serve as a reasonable substitute for the one described may be used, making any proper allowance for the difference, including the cost of transporting the goods to or from the other place.

(3) Evidence of a relevant rent prevailing at a time or place or for a lease term other than the one described in this Article offered by one

party is not admissible unless and until he [or she] has given the other party notice the court finds sufficient to prevent unfair surprise.

(4) If the prevailing rent or value of any goods regularly leased in any established market is in issue, reports in official publications or trade journals or in newspapers or periodicals of general circulation published as the reports of that market are admissible in evidence. The circumstances of the preparation of the report may be shown to affect its weight but not its admissibility.

As amended in 1990.

B. Default by Lessor

§ 2A–508. Lessee's Remedies.

(1) If a lessor fails to deliver the goods in conformity to the lease contract (Section 2A–509) or repudiates the lease contract (Section 2A–402), or a lessee rightfully rejects the goods (Section 2A–509) or justifiably revokes acceptance of the goods (Section 2A–517), then with respect to any goods involved, and with respect to all of the goods if under an installment lease contract the value of the whole lease contract is substantially impaired (Section 2A–510), the lessor is in default under the lease contract and the lessee may:

(a) cancel the lease contract (Section 2A–505(1));

(b) recover so much of the rent and security as has been paid and is just under the circumstances;

(c) cover and recover damages as to all goods affected whether or not they have been identified to the lease contract (Sections 2A–518 and 2A–520), or recover damages for nondelivery (Sections 2A–519 and 2A–520);

(d) exercise any other rights or pursue any other remedies provided in the lease contract.

(2) If a lessor fails to deliver the goods in conformity to the lease contract or repudiates the lease contract, the lessee may also:

(a) if the goods have been identified, recover them (Section 2A–522); or

(b) in a proper case, obtain specific performance or replevy the goods (Section 2A–521).

(3) If a lessor is otherwise in default under a lease contract, the lessee may exercise the rights and pursue the remedies provided in the lease contract, which may include a right to cancel the lease, and in Section 2A–519(3).

(4) If a lessor has breached a warranty, whether express or implied, the lessee may recover damages (Section 2A–519(4)).

(5) On rightful rejection or justifiable revocation of acceptance, a lessee has a security interest in goods in the lessee's possession or control for any rent and security that has been paid and any expenses reasonably incurred in their inspection, receipt, transportation, and care and custody and may hold those goods and dispose of them in good faith and in a commercially reasonable manner, subject to Section 2A–527(5).

(6) Subject to the provisions of Section 2A–407, a lessee, on notifying the lessor of the lessee's intention to do so, may deduct all or any part of the damages resulting from any default under the lease contract from any part of the rent still due under the same lease contract.

As amended in 1990.

§ 2A–509. Lessee's Rights on Improper Delivery; Rightful Rejection.

(1) Subject to the provisions of Section 2A–510 on default in installment lease contracts, if the goods or the tender or delivery fail in any respect to conform to the lease contract, the lessee may reject or accept the goods or accept any commercial unit or units and reject the rest of the goods.

(2) Rejection of goods is ineffective unless it is within a reasonable time after tender or delivery of the goods and the lessee seasonably notifies the lessor.

§ 2A–510. Installment Lease Contracts: Rejection and Default.

(1) Under an installment lease contract a lessee may reject any delivery that is nonconforming if the nonconformity substantially impairs the value of that delivery and cannot be cured or the nonconformity is a defect in the required documents; but if the nonconformity does not fall within subsection (2) and the lessor or the supplier gives adequate assurance of its cure, the lessee must accept that delivery.

(2) Whenever nonconformity or default with respect to one or more deliveries substantially impairs the value of the installment lease contract as a whole there is a default with respect to the whole. But, the aggrieved party reinstates the installment lease contract as a whole if the aggrieved party accepts a nonconforming delivery without seasonably notifying of cancellation or brings an action with respect only to past deliveries or demands performance as to future deliveries.

§ 2A–511. Merchant Lessee's Duties as to Rightfully Rejected Goods.

(1) Subject to any security interest of a lessee (Section 2A–508(5)), if a lessor or a supplier has no agent or place of business at the market of rejection, a merchant lessee, after rejection of goods in his [or her] possession or control, shall follow any reasonable instructions received from the lessor or the supplier with respect to the goods. In the absence of those instructions, a merchant lessee shall make reasonable efforts to sell, lease, or otherwise dispose of the goods for the lessor's account if they threaten to decline in value speedily. Instructions are not reasonable if on demand indemnity for expenses is not forthcoming.

(2) If a merchant lessee (subsection (1)) or any other lessee (Section 2A–512) disposes of goods, he [or she] is entitled to reimbursement either from the lessor or the supplier or out of the proceeds for reasonable expenses of caring for and disposing of the goods and, if the expenses include no disposition commission, to such commission as is usual in the trade, or if there is none, to a reasonable sum not exceeding 10 percent of the gross proceeds.

(3) In complying with this section or Section 2A–512, the lessee is held only to good faith. Good faith conduct hereunder is neither acceptance or conversion nor the basis of an action for damages.

(4) A purchaser who purchases in good faith from a lessee pursuant to this section or Section 2A–512 takes the goods free of any rights of the lessor and the supplier even though the lessee fails to comply with one or more of the requirements of this Article.

§ 2A–512. Lessee's Duties as to Rightfully Rejected Goods.

(1) Except as otherwise provided with respect to goods that threaten to decline in value speedily (Section 2A–511) and subject to any security interest of a lessee (Section 2A–508(5)):

(a) the lessee, after rejection of goods in the lessee's possession, shall hold them with reasonable care at the lessor's or the supplier's disposition for a reasonable time after the lessee's seasonable notification of rejection;

(b) if the lessor or the supplier gives no instructions within a reasonable time after notification of rejection, the lessee may store the rejected goods for the lessor's or the supplier's account or ship them to the lessor or the supplier or dispose of them for the lessor's or the supplier's account with reimbursement in the manner provided in Section 2A–511; but

(c) the lessee has no further obligations with regard to goods rightfully rejected.

(2) Action by the lessee pursuant to subsection (1) is not acceptance or conversion.

§ 2A–513. Cure by Lessor of Improper Tender or Delivery; Replacement.

(1) If any tender or delivery by the lessor or the supplier is rejected because nonconforming and the time for performance has not yet expired, the lessor or the supplier may seasonably notify the lessee of the lessor's or the supplier's intention to cure and may then make a conforming delivery within the time provided in the lease contract.

(2) If the lessee rejects a nonconforming tender that the lessor or the supplier had reasonable grounds to believe would be acceptable with or without money allowance, the lessor or the supplier may have a further reasonable time to substitute a conforming tender if he [or she] seasonably notifies the lessee.

§ 2A–514. Waiver of Lessee's Objections.

(1) In rejecting goods, a lessee's failure to state a particular defect that is ascertainable by reasonable inspection precludes the lessee from relying on the defect to justify rejection or to establish default:

(a) if, stated seasonably, the lessor or the supplier could have cured it (Section 2A–513); or

(b) between merchants if the lessor or the supplier after rejection has made a request in writing for a full and final written statement of all defects on which the lessee proposes to rely.

(2) A lessee's failure to reserve rights when paying rent or other consideration against documents precludes recovery of the payment for defects apparent on the face of the documents.

§ 2A–515. Acceptance of Goods.

(1) Acceptance of goods occurs after the lessee has had a reasonable opportunity to inspect the goods and

(a) the lessee signifies or acts with respect to the goods in a manner that signifies to the lessor or the supplier that the goods are conforming or that the lessee will take or retain them in spite of their nonconformity; or

(b) the lessee fails to make an effective rejection of the goods (Section 2A–509(2)).

(2) Acceptance of a part of any commercial unit is acceptance of that entire unit.

§ 2A–516. Effect of Acceptance of Goods; Notice of Default; Burden of Establishing Default after Acceptance; Notice of Claim or Litigation to Person Answerable Over.

(1) A lessee must pay rent for any goods accepted in accordance with the lease contract, with due allowance for goods rightfully rejected or not delivered.

(2) A lessee's acceptance of goods precludes rejection of the goods accepted. In the case of a finance lease, if made with knowledge of a nonconformity, acceptance cannot be revoked because of it. In any other case, if made with knowledge of a nonconformity, acceptance cannot be revoked because of it unless the acceptance was on the reasonable assumption that the nonconformity would be seasonably cured. Acceptance does not of itself impair any other remedy provided by this Article or the lease agreement for nonconformity.

(3) If a tender has been accepted:

(a) within a reasonable time after the lessee discovers or should have discovered any default, the lessee shall notify the lessor and the supplier, if any, or be barred from any remedy against the party notified;

(b) except in the case of a consumer lease, within a reasonable time after the lessee receives notice of litigation for infringement or the like (Section 2A–211) the lessee shall notify the lessor or be barred from any remedy over for liability established by the litigation; and

(c) the burden is on the lessee to establish any default.

(4) If a lessee is sued for breach of a warranty or other obligation for which a lessor or a supplier is answerable over the following apply:

(a) The lessee may give the lessor or the supplier, or both, written notice of the litigation. If the notice states that the person notified may come in and defend and that if the person notified does not do so that person will be bound in any action against that person by the lessee by any determination of fact common to the two litigations, then unless the person notified after seasonable receipt of the notice does come in and defend that person is so bound.

(b) The lessor or the supplier may demand in writing that the lessee turn over control of the litigation including settlement if the claim is one for infringement or the like (Section 2A–211) or else be barred from any remedy over. If the demand states that the lessor or the supplier agrees to bear all expense and to satisfy any adverse judgment, then unless the lessee after seasonable receipt of the demand does turn over control the lessee is so barred.

(5) Subsections (3) and (4) apply to any obligation of a lessee to hold the lessor or the supplier harmless against infringement or the like (Section 2A–211).

As amended in 1990.

§ 2A–517. Revocation of Acceptance of Goods.

(1) A lessee may revoke acceptance of a lot or commercial unit whose nonconformity substantially impairs its value to the lessee if the lessee has accepted it:

(a) except in the case of a finance lease, on the reasonable assumption that its nonconformity would be cured and it has not been seasonably cured; or

(b) without discovery of the nonconformity if the lessee's acceptance was reasonably induced either by the lessor's assurances or, except in the case of a finance lease, by the difficulty of discovery before acceptance.

(2) Except in the case of a finance lease that is not a consumer lease, a lessee may revoke acceptance of a lot or commercial unit if the lessor defaults under the lease contract and the default substantially impairs the value of that lot or commercial unit to the lessee.

(3) If the lease agreement so provides, the lessee may revoke acceptance of a lot or commercial unit because of other defaults by the lessor.

(4) Revocation of acceptance must occur within a reasonable time after the lessee discovers or should have discovered the ground for it and before any substantial change in condition of the goods which is not caused by the nonconformity. Revocation is not effective until the lessee notifies the lessor.

(5) A lessee who so revokes has the same rights and duties with regard to the goods involved as if the lessee had rejected them.

As amended in 1990.

§ 2A–518. Cover; Substitute Goods.

(1) After a default by a lessor under the lease contract of the type described in Section 2A–508(1), or, if agreed, after other default by the lessor, the lessee may cover by making any purchase or lease of or contract to purchase or lease goods in substitution for those due from the lessor.

(2) Except as otherwise provided with respect to damages liquidated in the lease agreement (Section 2A–504) or otherwise determined pursuant to agreement of the parties (Sections 1–102(3) and 2A–503), if a lessee's cover is by lease agreement substantially similar to the original lease agreement and the new lease agreement is made in good faith and in a commercially reasonable manner, the lessee may recover from the lessor as damages (i) the present value, as of the date of the commencement of the term of the new lease agreement, of the rent under the new lease agreement applicable to that period of the new lease term which is comparable to the then remaining term of the original lease agreement minus the present value as of the same date of the total rent for the then remaining lease term of the original lease agreement, and (ii) any incidental or consequential damages, less expenses saved in consequence of the lessor's default.

(3) If a lessee's cover is by lease agreement that for any reason does not qualify for treatment under subsection (2), or is by purchase or otherwise, the lessee may recover from the lessor as if the lessee had elected not to cover and Section 2A–519 governs.

As amended in 1990.

§ 2A–519. Lessee's Damages for Non-Delivery, Repudiation, Default, and Breach of Warranty in Regard to Accepted Goods.

(1) Except as otherwise provided with respect to damages liquidated in the lease agreement (Section 2A–504) or otherwise determined pursuant to agreement of the parties (Sections 1–102(3) and 2A–503), if a lessee elects not to cover or a lessee elects to cover and the cover is by lease agreement that for any reason does not qualify for treatment under Section 2A–518(2), or is by purchase or otherwise, the measure of damages for non-delivery or repudiation by the lessor or for rejection or revocation of acceptance by the lessee is the present value, as of the date of the default, of the then market rent minus the present value as of the same date of the original rent, computed for the remaining lease term of the original lease agreement, together with incidental and consequential damages, less expenses saved in consequence of the lessor's default.

(2) Market rent is to be determined as of the place for tender or, in cases of rejection after arrival or revocation of acceptance, as of the place of arrival.

(3) Except as otherwise agreed, if the lessee has accepted goods and given notification (Section 2A–516(3)), the measure of damages for non-conforming tender or delivery or other default by a lessor is the loss resulting in the ordinary course of events from the lessor's default as determined in any manner that is reasonable together with incidental and consequential damages, less expenses saved in consequence of the lessor's default.

(4) Except as otherwise agreed, the measure of damages for breach of warranty is the present value at the time and place of acceptance of the difference between the value of the use of the goods accepted and the value if they had been as warranted for the lease term, unless special circumstances show proximate damages of a different amount, together with incidental and consequential damages, less expenses saved in consequence of the lessor's default or breach of warranty.

As amended in 1990.

§ 2A–520. Lessee's Incidental and Consequential Damages.

(1) Incidental damages resulting from a lessor's default include expenses reasonably incurred in inspection, receipt, transportation, and care and custody of goods rightfully rejected or goods the acceptance of which is justifiably revoked, any commercially reasonable charges, expenses or commissions in connection with effecting cover, and any other reasonable expense incident to the default.

(2) Consequential damages resulting from a lessor's default include:

(a) any loss resulting from general or particular requirements and needs of which the lessor at the time of contracting had reason to know and which could not reasonably be prevented by cover or otherwise; and

(b) injury to person or property proximately resulting from any breach of warranty.

§ 2A–521. Lessee's Right to Specific Performance or Replevin.

(1) Specific performance may be decreed if the goods are unique or in other proper circumstances.

(2) A decree for specific performance may include any terms and conditions as to payment of the rent, damages, or other relief that the court deems just.

(3) A lessee has a right of replevin, detinue, sequestration, claim and delivery, or the like for goods identified to the lease contract if after reasonable effort the lessee is unable to effect cover for those goods or the circumstances reasonably indicate that the effort will be unavailing.

§ 2A–522. Lessee's Right to Goods on Lessor's Insolvency.

(1) Subject to subsection (2) and even though the goods have not been shipped, a lessee who has paid a part or all of the rent and security for goods identified to a lease contract (Section 2A–217) on making and keeping good a tender of any unpaid portion of the rent and security due under the lease contract may recover the goods identified from the lessor if the lessor becomes insolvent within 10 days after receipt of the first installment of rent and security.

(2) A lessee acquires the right to recover goods identified to a lease contract only if they conform to the lease contract.

C. Default by Lessee

§ 2A–523. Lessor's Remedies.

(1) If a lessee wrongfully rejects or revokes acceptance of goods or fails to make a payment when due or repudiates with respect to a part or the whole, then, with respect to any goods involved, and with respect to all of the goods if under an installment lease contract the value of the whole lease contract is substantially impaired (Section 2A–510), the lessee is in default under the lease contract and the lessor may:

(a) cancel the lease contract (Section 2A–505(1));

(b) proceed respecting goods not identified to the lease contract (Section 2A–524);

(c) withhold delivery of the goods and take possession of goods previously delivered (Section 2A–525);

(d) stop delivery of the goods by any bailee (Section 2A–526);

(e) dispose of the goods and recover damages (Section 2A–527), or retain the goods and recover damages (Section 2A–528), or in a proper case recover rent (Section 2A–529)

(f) exercise any other rights or pursue any other remedies provided in the lease contract.

(2) If a lessor does not fully exercise a right or obtain a remedy to which the lessor is entitled under subsection (1), the lessor may recover the loss resulting in the ordinary course of events from the lessee's default as determined in any reasonable manner, together with incidental damages, less expenses saved in consequence of the lessee's default.

(3) If a lessee is otherwise in default under a lease contract, the lessor may exercise the rights and pursue the remedies provided in the lease contract, which may include a right to cancel the lease. In addition, unless otherwise provided in the lease contract:

(a) if the default substantially impairs the value of the lease contract to the lessor, the lessor may exercise the rights and pursue the remedies provided in subsections (1) or (2); or

(b) if the default does not substantially impair the value of the lease contract to the lessor, the lessor may recover as provided in subsection (2).

As amended in 1990.

§ 2A–524. Lessor's Right to Identify Goods to Lease Contract.

(1) After default by the lessee under the lease contract of the type described in Section 2A–523(1) or 2A–523(3)(a) or, if agreed, after other default by the lessee, the lessor may:

(a) identify to the lease contract conforming goods not already identified if at the time the lessor learned of the default they were in the lessor's or the supplier's possession or control; and

(b) dispose of goods (Section 2A–527(1)) that demonstrably have been intended for the particular lease contract even though those goods are unfinished.

(2) If the goods are unfinished, in the exercise of reasonable commercial judgment for the purposes of avoiding loss and of effective realization, an aggrieved lessor or the supplier may either complete manufacture and wholly identify the goods to the lease contract or cease manufacture and lease, sell, or otherwise dispose of the goods for scrap or salvage value or proceed in any other reasonable manner.

As amended in 1990.

§ 2A–525. Lessor's Right to Possession of Goods.

(1) If a lessor discovers the lessee to be insolvent, the lessor may refuse to deliver the goods.

(2) After a default by the lessee under the lease contract of the type described in Section 2A–523(1) or 2A–523(3)(a) or, if agreed, after other default by the lessee, the lessor has the right to take possession of the goods. If the lease contract so provides, the lessor may require the lessee to assemble the goods and make them available to the lessor at a place to be designated by the lessor which is reasonably convenient to both parties. Without removal, the lessor may render unusable any goods employed in trade or business, and may dispose of goods on the lessee's premises (Section 2A–527).

(3) The lessor may proceed under subsection (2) without judicial process if that can be done without breach of the peace or the lessor may proceed by action.

As amended in 1990.

§ 2A–526. Lessor's Stoppage of Delivery in Transit or Otherwise.

(1) A lessor may stop delivery of goods in the possession of a carrier or other bailee if the lessor discovers the lessee to be insolvent and may stop delivery of carload, truckload, planeload, or larger shipments of express or freight if the lessee repudiates or fails to make a payment due before delivery, whether for rent, security or otherwise under the lease contract, or for any other reason the lessor has a right to withhold or take possession of the goods.

(2) In pursuing its remedies under subsection (1), the lessor may stop delivery until

(a) receipt of the goods by the lessee;

(b) acknowledgment to the lessee by any bailee of the goods, except a carrier, that the bailee holds the goods for the lessee; or

(c) such an acknowledgment to the lessee by a carrier via reshipment or as warehouseman.

(3) (a) To stop delivery, a lessor shall so notify as to enable the bailee by reasonable diligence to prevent delivery of the goods.

(b) After notification, the bailee shall hold and deliver the goods according to the directions of the lessor, but the lessor is liable to the bailee for any ensuing charges or damages.

(c) A carrier who has issued a nonnegotiable bill of lading is not obliged to obey a notification to stop received from a person other than the consignor.

§ 2A–527. Lessor's Rights to Dispose of Goods.

(1) After a default by a lessee under the lease contract of the type described in Section 2A–523(1) or 2A–523(3)(a) or after the lessor refuses to deliver or takes possession of goods (Section 2A–525 or 2A–526), or, if agreed, after other default by a lessee, the lessor may dispose of the goods concerned or the undelivered balance thereof by lease, sale, or otherwise.

(2) Except as otherwise provided with respect to damages liquidated in the lease agreement (Section 2A–504) or otherwise determined pursuant to agreement of the parties (Sections 1–102(3) and

2A–503), if the disposition is by lease agreement substantially similar to the original lease agreement and the new lease agreement is made in good faith and in a commercially reasonable manner, the lessor may recover from the lessee as damages (i) accrued and unpaid rent as of the date of the commencement of the term of the new lease agreement, (ii) the present value, as of the same date, of the total rent for the then remaining lease term of the original lease agreement minus the present value, as of the same date, of the rent under the new lease agreement applicable to that period of the new lease term which is comparable to the then remaining term of the original lease agreement, and (iii) any incidental damages allowed under Section 2A–530, less expenses saved in consequence of the lessee's default.

(3) If the lessor's disposition is by lease agreement that for any reason does not qualify for treatment under subsection (2), or is by sale or otherwise, the lessor may recover from the lessee as if the lessor had elected not to dispose of the goods and Section 2A–528 governs.

(4) A subsequent buyer or lessee who buys or leases from the lessor in good faith for value as a result of a disposition under this section takes the goods free of the original lease contract and any rights of the original lessee even though the lessor fails to comply with one or more of the requirements of this Article.

(5) The lessor is not accountable to the lessee for any profit made on any disposition. A lessee who has rightfully rejected or justifiably revoked acceptance shall account to the lessor for any excess over the amount of the lessee's security interest (Section 2A–508(5)).

As amended in 1990.

§ 2A–528. Lessor's Damages for Non-acceptance, Failure to Pay, Repudiation, or Other Default.

(1) Except as otherwise provided with respect to damages liquidated in the lease agreement (Section 2A–504) or otherwise determined pursuant to agreement of the parties (Section 1–102(3) and 2A–503), if a lessor elects to retain the goods or a lessor elects to dispose of the goods and the disposition is by lease agreement that for any reason does not qualify for treatment under Section 2A–527(2), or is by sale or otherwise, the lessor may recover from the lessee as damages for a default of the type described in Section 2A–523(1) or 2A–523(3)(a), or if agreed, for other default of the lessee, (i) accrued and unpaid rent as of the date of the default if the lessee has never taken possession of the goods, or, if the lessee has taken possession of the goods, as of the date the lessor repossesses the goods or an earlier date on which the lessee makes a tender of the goods to the lessor, (ii) the present value as of the date determined under clause (i) of the total rent for the then remaining lease term of the original lease agreement minus the present value as of the same date of the market rent as the place where the goods are located computed for the same lease term, and (iii) any incidental damages allowed under Section 2A–530, less expenses saved in consequence of the lessee's default.

(2) If the measure of damages provided in subsection (1) is inadequate to put a lessor in as good a position as performance would have, the measure of damages is the present value of the profit, including reasonable overhead, the lessor would have made from full performance by the lessee, together with any incidental damages allowed under Section 2A–530, due allowance for costs reasonably incurred and due credit for payments or proceeds of disposition.

As amended in 1990.

§ 2A–529. Lessor's Action for the Rent.

(1) After default by the lessee under the lease contract of the type described in Section 2A–523(1) or 2A–523(3)(a) or, if agreed, after other default by the lessee, if the lessor complies with subsection (2), the lessor may recover from the lessee as damages:

(a) for goods accepted by the lessee and not repossessed by or tendered to the lessor, and for conforming goods lost or damaged within a commercially reasonable time after risk of loss passes to the lessee (Section 2A–219), (i) accrued and unpaid rent as of the date of entry of judgment in favor of the lessor (ii) the present value as of the same date of the rent for the then remaining lease term of the lease agreement, and (iii) any incidental damages allowed under Section 2A–530, less expenses saved in consequence of the lessee's default; and

(b) for goods identified to the lease contract if the lessor is unable after reasonable effort to dispose of them at a reasonable price or the circumstances reasonably indicate that effort will be unavailing, (i) accrued and unpaid rent as of the date of entry of judgment in favor of the lessor, (ii) the present value as of the same date of the rent for the then remaining lease term of the lease agreement, and (iii) any incidental damages allowed under Section 2A–530, less expenses saved in consequence of the lessee's default.

(2) Except as provided in subsection (3), the lessor shall hold for the lessee for the remaining lease term of the lease agreement any goods that have been identified to the lease contract and are in the lessor's control.

(3) The lessor may dispose of the goods at any time before collection of the judgment for damages obtained pursuant to subsection (1). If the disposition is before the end of the remaining lease term of the lease agreement, the lessor's recovery against the lessee for damages is governed by Section 2A–527 or Section 2A–528, and the lessor will cause an appropriate credit to be provided against a judgment for damages to the extent that the amount of the judgment exceeds the recovery available pursuant to Section 2A–527 or 2A–528.

(4) Payment of the judgment for damages obtained pursuant to subsection (1) entitles the lessee to the use and possession of the goods not then disposed of for the remaining lease term of and in accordance with the lease agreement.

(5) After default by the lessee under the lease contract of the type described in Section 2A–523(1) or Section 2A–523(3)(a) or, if agreed, after other default by the lessee, a lessor who is held not entitled to rent under this section must nevertheless be awarded damages for non-acceptance under Sections 2A–527 and 2A–528.

As amended in 1990.

§ 2A–530. Lessor's Incidental Damages.

Incidental damages to an aggrieved lessor include any commercially reasonable charges, expenses, or commissions incurred in stopping delivery, in the transportation, care and custody of goods after the lessee's default, in connection with return or disposition of the goods, or otherwise resulting from the default.

§ 2A–531. Standing to Sue Third Parties for Injury to Goods.

(1) If a third party so deals with goods that have been identified to a lease contract as to cause actionable injury to a party to the lease contract (a) the lessor has a right of action against the third party,

and (b) the lessee also has a right of action against the third party if the lessee:

(i) has a security interest in the goods;

(ii) has an insurable interest in the goods; or

(iii) bears the risk of loss under the lease contract or has since the injury assumed that risk as against the lessor and the goods have been converted or destroyed.

(2) If at the time of the injury the party plaintiff did not bear the risk of loss as against the other party to the lease contract and there is no arrangement between them for disposition of the recovery, his [or her] suit or settlement, subject to his [or her] own interest, is as a fiduciary for the other party to the lease contract.

(3) Either party with the consent of the other may sue for the benefit of whom it may concern.

§ 2A–532. Lessor's Rights to Residual Interest.

In addition to any other recovery permitted by this Article or other law, the lessor may recover from the lessee an amount that will fully compensate the lessor for any loss of or damage to the lessor's residual interest in the goods caused by the default of the lessee.

As added in 1990.

Revised Article 3
NEGOTIABLE INSTRUMENTS

Part 1 General Provisions and Definitions

§ 3–101. Short Title.

This Article may be cited as Uniform Commercial Code–Negotiable Instruments.

§ 3–102. Subject Matter.

(a) This Article applies to negotiable instruments. It does not apply to money, to payment orders governed by Article 4A, or to securities governed by Article 8.

(b) If there is conflict between this Article and Article 4 or 9, Articles 4 and 9 govern.

(c) Regulations of the Board of Governors of the Federal Reserve System and operating circulars of the Federal Reserve Banks supersede any inconsistent provision of this Article to the extent of the inconsistency.

§ 3–103. Definitions.

(a) In this Article:

(1) "Acceptor" means a drawee who has accepted a draft.

(2) "Drawee" means a person ordered in a draft to make payment.

(3) "Drawer" means a person who signs or is identified in a draft as a person ordering payment.

(4) "Good faith" means honesty in fact and the observance of reasonable commercial standards of fair dealing.

(5) "Maker" means a person who signs or is identified in a note as a person undertaking to pay.

(6) "Order" means a written instruction to pay money signed by the person giving the instruction. The instruction may be addressed to any person, including the person giving the instruction, or to one or more persons jointly or in the alternative but not in succession. An authorization to pay is not an order unless the person authorized to pay is also instructed to pay.

(7) "Ordinary care" in the case of a person engaged in business means observance of reasonable commercial standards, prevailing in the area in which the person is located, with respect to the business in which the person is engaged. In the case of a bank that takes an instrument for processing for collection or payment by automated means, reasonable commercial standards do not require the bank to examine the instrument if the failure to examine does not violate the bank's prescribed procedures and the bank's procedures do not vary unreasonably from general banking usage not disapproved by this Article or Article 4.

(8) "Party" means a party to an instrument.

(9) "Promise" means a written undertaking to pay money signed by the person undertaking to pay. An acknowledgment of an obligation by the obligor is not a promise unless the obligor also undertakes to pay the obligation.

(10) "Prove" with respect to a fact means to meet the burden of establishing the fact (Section 1–201(8)).

(11) "Remitter" means a person who purchases an instrument from its issuer if the instrument is payable to an identified person other than the purchaser.

(b) [Other definitions' section references deleted.]

(c) [Other definitions' section references deleted.]

(d) In addition, Article 1 contains general definitions and principles of construction and interpretation applicable throughout this Article.

§ 3–104. Negotiable Instrument.

(a) Except as provided in subsections (c) and (d), "negotiable instrument" means an unconditional promise or order to pay a fixed amount of money, with or without interest or other charges described in the promise or order, if it:

(1) is payable to bearer or to order at the time it is issued or first comes into possession of a holder;

(2) is payable on demand or at a definite time; and

(3) does not state any other undertaking or instruction by the person promising or ordering payment to do any act in addition to the payment of money, but the promise or order may contain (i) an undertaking or power to give, maintain, or protect collateral to secure payment, (ii) an authorization or power to the holder to confess judgment or realize on or dispose of collateral, or (iii) a waiver of the benefit of any law intended for the advantage or protection of an obligor.

(b) "Instrument" means a negotiable instrument.

(c) An order that meets all of the requirements of subsection (a), except paragraph (1), and otherwise falls within the definition of "check" in subsection (f) is a negotiable instrument and a check.

(d) A promise or order other than a check is not an instrument if, at the time it is issued or first comes into possession of a holder, it contains a conspicuous statement, however expressed, to the effect that the promise or order is not negotiable or is not an instrument governed by this Article.

(e) An instrument is a "note" if it is a promise and is a "draft" if it is an order. If an instrument falls within the definition of both "note" and "draft," a person entitled to enforce the instrument may treat it as either.

(f) "Check" means (i) a draft, other than a documentary draft, payable on demand and drawn on a bank or (ii) a cashier's check or teller's check. An instrument may be a check even though it is described on its face by another term, such as "money order."

(g) "Cashier's check" means a draft with respect to which the drawer and drawee are the same bank or branches of the same bank.

(h) "Teller's check" means a draft drawn by a bank (i) on another bank, or (ii) payable at or through a bank.

(i) "Traveler's check" means an instrument that (i) is payable on demand, (ii) is drawn on or payable at or through a bank, (iii) is designated by the term "traveler's check" or by a substantially similar term, and (iv) requires, as a condition to payment, a countersignature by a person whose specimen signature appears on the instrument.

(j) "Certificate of deposit" means an instrument containing an acknowledgment by a bank that a sum of money has been received by the bank and a promise by the bank to repay the sum of money. A certificate of deposit is a note of the bank.

§ 3–105. Issue of Instrument.

(a) "Issue" means the first delivery of an instrument by the maker or drawer, whether to a holder or nonholder, for the purpose of giving rights on the instrument to any person.

(b) An unissued instrument, or an unissued incomplete instrument that is completed, is binding on the maker or drawer, but nonissuance is a defense. An instrument that is conditionally issued or is issued for a special purpose is binding on the maker or drawer, but failure of the condition or special purpose to be fulfilled is a defense.

(c) "Issuer" applies to issued and unissued instruments and means a maker or drawer of an instrument.

§ 3–106. Unconditional Promise or Order.

(a) Except as provided in this section, for the purposes of Section 3–104(a), a promise or order is unconditional unless it states (i) an express condition to payment, (ii) that the promise or order is subject to or governed by another writing, or (iii) that rights or obligations with respect to the promise or order are stated in another writing. A reference to another writing does not of itself make the promise or order conditional.

(b) A promise or order is not made conditional (i) by a reference to another writing for a statement of rights with respect to collateral, prepayment, or acceleration, or (ii) because payment is limited to resort to a particular fund or source.

(c) If a promise or order requires, as a condition to payment, a countersignature by a person whose specimen signature appears on the promise or order, the condition does not make the promise or order conditional for the purposes of Section 3–104(a). If the person whose specimen signature appears on an instrument fails to countersign the instrument, the failure to countersign is a defense to the obligation of the issuer, but the failure does not prevent a transferee of the instrument from becoming a holder of the instrument.

(d) If a promise or order at the time it is issued or first comes into possession of a holder contains a statement, required by applicable statutory or administrative law, to the effect that the rights of a holder or transferee are subject to claims or defenses that the issuer could assert against the original payee, the promise or order is not thereby made conditional for the purposes of Section 3–104(a); but if the promise or order is an instrument, there cannot be a holder in due course of the instrument.

§ 3–107. Instrument Payable in Foreign Money.

Unless the instrument otherwise provides, an instrument that states the amount payable in foreign money may be paid in the foreign money or in an equivalent amount in dollars calculated by using the current bank-offered spot rate at the place of payment for the purchase of dollars on the day on which the instrument is paid.

§ 3–108. Payable on Demand or at Definite Time.

(a) A promise or order is "payable on demand" if it (i) states that it is payable on demand or at sight, or otherwise indicates that it is payable at the will of the holder, or (ii) does not state any time of payment.

(b) A promise or order is "payable at a definite time" if it is payable on elapse of a definite period of time after sight or acceptance or at a fixed date or dates or at a time or times readily ascertainable at the time the promise or order is issued, subject to rights of (i) prepayment, (ii) acceleration, (iii) extension at the option of the holder, or (iv) extension to a further definite time at the option of the maker or acceptor or automatically upon or after a specified act or event.

(c) If an instrument, payable at a fixed date, is also payable upon demand made before the fixed date, the instrument is payable on demand until the fixed date and, if demand for payment is not made before that date, becomes payable at a definite time on the fixed date.

§ 3–109. Payable to Bearer or to Order.

(a) A promise or order is payable to bearer if it:

(1) states that it is payable to bearer or to the order of bearer or otherwise indicates that the person in possession of the promise or order is entitled to payment;

(2) does not state a payee; or

(3) states that it is payable to or to the order of cash or otherwise indicates that it is not payable to an identified person.

(b) A promise or order that is not payable to bearer is payable to order if it is payable (i) to the order of an identified person or (ii) to an identified person or order. A promise or order that is payable to order is payable to the identified person.

(c) An instrument payable to bearer may become payable to an identified person if it is specially indorsed pursuant to Section 3–205(a). An instrument payable to an identified person may become payable to bearer if it is indorsed in blank pursuant to Section 3–205(b).

§ 3–110. Identification of Person to Whom Instrument Is Payable.

(a) The person to whom an instrument is initially payable is determined by the intent of the person, whether or not authorized, signing as, or in the name or behalf of, the issuer of the instrument. The instrument is payable to the person intended by the signer even if that person is identified in the instrument by a name or other identification that is not that of the intended person. If more than one person signs in the name or behalf of the issuer of an instrument and all the signers do not intend the same person as payee, the instrument is payable to any person intended by one or more of the signers.

(b) If the signature of the issuer of an instrument is made by automated means, such as a check-writing machine, the payee of the instrument is determined by the intent of the person who supplied the name or identification of the payee, whether or not authorized to do so.

(c) A person to whom an instrument is payable may be identified in any way, including by name, identifying number, office, or account number. For the purpose of determining the holder of an instrument, the following rules apply:

(1) If an instrument is payable to an account and the account is identified only by number, the instrument is payable to the person to whom the account is payable. If an instrument is payable to an account identified by number and by the name of a person, the instrument is payable to the named person, whether or not that person is the owner of the account identified by number.

(2) If an instrument is payable to:

(i) a trust, an estate, or a person described as trustee or representative of a trust or estate, the instrument is payable to the trustee, the representative, or a successor of either, whether or not the beneficiary or estate is also named;

(ii) a person described as agent or similar representative of a named or identified person, the instrument is payable to the represented person, the representative, or a successor of the representative;

(iii) a fund or organization that is not a legal entity, the instrument is payable to a representative of the members of the fund or organization; or

(iv) an office or to a person described as holding an office, the instrument is payable to the named person, the incumbent of the office, or a successor to the incumbent.

(d) If an instrument is payable to two or more persons alternatively, it is payable to any of them and may be negotiated, discharged, or enforced by any or all of them in possession of the instrument. If an instrument is payable to two or more persons not alternatively, it is payable to all of them and may be negotiated, discharged, or enforced only by all of them. If an instrument payable to two or more persons is ambiguous as to whether it is payable to the persons alternatively, the instrument is payable to the persons alternatively.

§ 3–111. Place of Payment.

Except as otherwise provided for items in Article 4, an instrument is payable at the place of payment stated in the instrument. If no place of payment is stated, an instrument is payable at the address of the drawee or maker stated in the instrument. If no address is stated, the place of payment is the place of business of the drawee or maker. If a drawee or maker has more than one place of business, the place of payment is any place of business of the drawee or maker chosen by the person entitled to enforce the instrument. If the drawee or maker has no place of business, the place of payment is the residence of the drawee or maker.

§ 3–112. Interest.

(a) Unless otherwise provided in the instrument, (i) an instrument is not payable with interest, and (ii) interest on an interest-bearing instrument is payable from the date of the instrument.

(b) Interest may be stated in an instrument as a fixed or variable amount of money or it may be expressed as a fixed or variable rate or rates. The amount or rate of interest may be stated or described in the instrument in any manner and may require reference to information not contained in the instrument. If an instrument provides for interest, but the amount of interest payable cannot be ascertained from the description, interest is payable at the judgment rate in effect at the place of payment of the instrument and at the time interest first accrues.

§ 3–113. Date of Instrument.

(a) An instrument may be antedated or postdated. The date stated determines the time of payment if the instrument is payable at a fixed period after date. Except as provided in Section 4–401(c), an instrument payable on demand is not payable before the date of the instrument.

(b) If an instrument is undated, its date is the date of its issue or, in the case of an unissued instrument, the date it first comes into possession of a holder.

§ 3–114. Contradictory Terms of Instrument.

If an instrument contains contradictory terms, typewritten terms prevail over printed terms, handwritten terms prevail over both, and words prevail over numbers.

§ 3–115. Incomplete Instrument.

(a) "Incomplete instrument" means a signed writing, whether or not issued by the signer, the contents of which show at the time of signing that it is incomplete but that the signer intended it to be completed by the addition of words or numbers.

(b) Subject to subsection (c), if an incomplete instrument is an instrument under Section 3–104, it may be enforced according to its terms if it is not completed, or according to its terms as augmented by completion. If an incomplete instrument is not an instrument under Section 3–104, but, after completion, the requirements of Section 3–104 are met, the instrument may be enforced according to its terms as augmented by completion.

(c) If words or numbers are added to an incomplete instrument without authority of the signer, there is an alteration of the incomplete instrument under Section 3–407.

(d) The burden of establishing that words or numbers were added to an incomplete instrument without authority of the signer is on the person asserting the lack of authority.

§ 3–116. Joint and Several Liability; Contribution.

(a) Except as otherwise provided in the instrument, two or more persons who have the same liability on an instrument as makers, drawers, acceptors, indorsers who indorse as joint payees, or anomalous indorsers are jointly and severally liable in the capacity in which they sign.

(b) Except as provided in Section 3–419(e) or by agreement of the affected parties, a party having joint and several liability who pays the instrument is entitled to receive from any party having the same joint and several liability contribution in accordance with applicable law.

(c) Discharge of one party having joint and several liability by a person entitled to enforce the instrument does not affect the right under subsection (b) of a party having the same joint and several liability to receive contribution from the party discharged.

§ 3–117. Other Agreements Affecting Instrument.

Subject to applicable law regarding exclusion of proof of contemporaneous or previous agreements, the obligation of a party to an instrument to pay the instrument may be modified, supplemented, or nullified by a separate agreement of the obligor and a person entitled to enforce the instrument, if the instrument is issued or the obligation is incurred in reliance on the agreement or as part of the same transaction giving rise to the agreement. To the extent an obligation is modified, supplemented, or nullified by an agreement under this section, the agreement is a defense to the obligation.

§ 3–118. Statute of Limitations.

(a) Except as provided in subsection (e), an action to enforce the obligation of a party to pay a note payable at a definite time must be commenced within six years after the due date or dates stated in the note or, if a due date is accelerated, within six years after the accelerated due date.

(b) Except as provided in subsection (d) or (e), if demand for payment is made to the maker of a note payable on demand, an action to enforce the obligation of a party to pay the note must be commenced within six years after the demand. If no demand for payment is made to the maker, an action to enforce the note is barred if neither principal nor interest on the note has been paid for a continuous period of 10 years.

(c) Except as provided in subsection (d), an action to enforce the obligation of a party to an unaccepted draft to pay the draft must be commenced within three years after dishonor of the draft or 10 years after the date of the draft, whichever period expires first.

(d) An action to enforce the obligation of the acceptor of a certified check or the issuer of a teller's check, cashier's check, or traveler's check must be commenced within three years after demand for payment is made to the acceptor or issuer, as the case may be.

(e) An action to enforce the obligation of a party to a certificate of deposit to pay the instrument must be commenced within six years after demand for payment is made to the maker, but if the instrument states a due date and the maker is not required to pay before that date, the six-year period begins when a demand for payment is in effect and the due date has passed.

(f) An action to enforce the obligation of a party to pay an accepted draft, other than a certified check, must be commenced (i) within six years after the due date or dates stated in the draft or acceptance if the obligation of the acceptor is payable at a definite time, or (ii) within six years after the date of the acceptance if the obligation of the acceptor is payable on demand.

(g) Unless governed by other law regarding claims for indemnity or contribution, an action (i) for conversion of an instrument, for money had and received, or like action based on conversion, (ii) for breach of warranty, or (iii) to enforce an obligation, duty, or right arising under this Article and not governed by this section must be commenced within three years after the [cause of action] accrues.

§ 3–119. Notice of Right to Defend Action.

In an action for breach of an obligation for which a third person is answerable over pursuant to this Article or Article 4, the defendant may give the third person written notice of the litigation, and the person notified may then give similar notice to any other person who is answerable over. If the notice states (i) that the person notified may come in and defend and (ii) that failure to do so will bind the person notified in an action later brought by the person giving the notice as to any determination of fact common to the two litigations, the person notified is so bound unless after seasonable receipt of the notice the person notified does come in and defend.

Part 2 Negotiation, Transfer, and Indorsement

§ 3–201. Negotiation.

(a) "Negotiation" means a transfer of possession, whether voluntary or involuntary, of an instrument by a person other than the issuer to a person who thereby becomes its holder.

(b) Except for negotiation by a remitter, if an instrument is payable to an identified person, negotiation requires transfer of possession of the instrument and its indorsement by the holder. If an instrument is payable to bearer, it may be negotiated by transfer of possession alone.

§ 3–202. Negotiation Subject to Rescission.

(a) Negotiation is effective even if obtained (i) from an infant, a corporation exceeding its powers, or a person without capacity, (ii) by fraud, duress, or mistake, or (iii) in breach of duty or as part of an illegal transaction.

(b) To the extent permitted by other law, negotiation may be rescinded or may be subject to other remedies, but those remedies may not be asserted against a subsequent holder in due course or a person paying the instrument in good faith and without knowledge of facts that are a basis for rescission or other remedy.

§ 3–203. Transfer of Instrument; Rights Acquired by Transfer.

(a) An instrument is transferred when it is delivered by a person other than its issuer for the purpose of giving to the person receiving delivery the right to enforce the instrument.

(b) Transfer of an instrument, whether or not the transfer is a negotiation, vests in the transferee any right of the transferor to enforce the instrument, including any right as a holder in due course, but the transferee cannot acquire rights of a holder in due course by a transfer, directly or indirectly, from a holder in due course if the transferee engaged in fraud or illegality affecting the instrument.

(c) Unless otherwise agreed, if an instrument is transferred for value and the transferee does not become a holder because of lack of indorsement by the transferor, the transferee has a specifically enforceable right to the unqualified indorsement of the transferor, but negotiation of the instrument does not occur until the indorsement is made.

(d) If a transferor purports to transfer less than the entire instrument, negotiation of the instrument does not occur. The transferee obtains no rights under this Article and has only the rights of a partial assignee.

§ 3–204. Indorsement.

(a) "Indorsement" means a signature, other than that of a signer as maker, drawer, or acceptor, that alone or accompanied by other words is made on an instrument for the purpose of (i) negotiating the instrument, (ii) restricting payment of the instrument, or (iii) incurring indorser's liability on the instrument, but regardless of the intent of the signer, a signature and its accompanying words is an indorsement unless the accompanying words, terms of the instrument, place of the signature, or other circumstances unambiguously indicate that the signature was made for a purpose other than indorsement. For the purpose of determining whether a signature is made on an instrument, a paper affixed to the instrument is a part of the instrument.

(b) "Indorser" means a person who makes an indorsement.

(c) For the purpose of determining whether the transferee of an instrument is a holder, an indorsement that transfers a security interest in the instrument is effective as an unqualified indorsement of the instrument.

(d) If an instrument is payable to a holder under a name that is not the name of the holder, indorsement may be made by the holder in the name stated in the instrument or in the holder's name or both, but signature in both names may be required by a person paying or taking the instrument for value or collection.

§ 3–205. Special Indorsement; Blank Indorsement; Anomalous Indorsement.

(a) If an indorsement is made by the holder of an instrument, whether payable to an identified person or payable to bearer, and the indorsement identifies a person to whom it makes the instrument payable, it is a "special indorsement." When specially indorsed, an instrument becomes payable to the identified person and may be negotiated only by the indorsement of that person. The principles stated in Section 3–110 apply to special indorsements.

(b) If an indorsement is made by the holder of an instrument and it is not a special indorsement, it is a "blank indorsement." When indorsed in blank, an instrument becomes payable to bearer and may be negotiated by transfer of possession alone until specially indorsed.

(c) The holder may convert a blank indorsement that consists only of a signature into a special indorsement by writing, above the signature of the indorser, words identifying the person to whom the instrument is made payable.

(d) "Anomalous indorsement" means an indorsement made by a person who is not the holder of the instrument. An anomalous indorsement does not affect the manner in which the instrument may be negotiated.

§ 3–206. Restrictive Indorsement.

(a) An indorsement limiting payment to a particular person or otherwise prohibiting further transfer or negotiation of the instrument is not effective to prevent further transfer or negotiation of the instrument.

(b) An indorsement stating a condition to the right of the indorsee to receive payment does not affect the right of the indorsee to enforce the instrument. A person paying the instrument or taking it for value or collection may disregard the condition, and the rights and liabilities of that person are not affected by whether the condition has been fulfilled.

(c) If an instrument bears an indorsement (i) described in Section 4–201(b), or (ii) in blank or to a particular bank using the words "for deposit," "for collection," or other words indicating a purpose of having the instrument collected by a bank for the indorser or for a particular account, the following rules apply:

(1) A person, other than a bank, who purchases the instrument when so indorsed converts the instrument unless the amount paid

for the instrument is received by the indorser or applied consistently with the indorsement.

(2) A depositary bank that purchases the instrument or takes it for collection when so indorsed converts the instrument unless the amount paid by the bank with respect to the instrument is received by the indorser or applied consistently with the indorsement.

(3) A payor bank that is also the depositary bank or that takes the instrument for immediate payment over the counter from a person other than a collecting bank converts the instrument unless the proceeds of the instrument are received by the indorser or applied consistently with the indorsement.

(4) Except as otherwise provided in paragraph (3), a payor bank or intermediary bank may disregard the indorsement and is not liable if the proceeds of the instrument are not received by the indorser or applied consistently with the indorsement.

(d) Except for an indorsement covered by subsection (c), if an instrument bears an indorsement using words to the effect that payment is to be made to the indorsee as agent, trustee, or other fiduciary for the benefit of the indorser or another person, the following rules apply:

(1) Unless there is notice of breach of fiduciary duty as provided in Section 3–307, a person who purchases the instrument from the indorsee or takes the instrument from the indorsee for collection or payment may pay the proceeds of payment or the value given for the instrument to the indorsee without regard to whether the indorsee violates a fiduciary duty to the indorser.

(2) A subsequent transferee of the instrument or person who pays the instrument is neither given notice nor otherwise affected by the restriction in the indorsement unless the transferee or payor knows that the fiduciary dealt with the instrument or its proceeds in breach of fiduciary duty.

(e) The presence on an instrument of an indorsement to which this section applies does not prevent a purchaser of the instrument from becoming a holder in due course of the instrument unless the purchaser is a converter under subsection (c) or has notice or knowledge of breach of fiduciary duty as stated in subsection (d).

(f) In an action to enforce the obligation of a party to pay the instrument, the obligor has a defense if payment would violate an indorsement to which this section applies and the payment is not permitted by this section.

§ 3–207. Reacquisition.

Reacquisition of an instrument occurs if it is transferred to a former holder, by negotiation or otherwise. A former holder who reacquires the instrument may cancel indorsements made after the reacquirer first became a holder of the instrument. If the cancellation causes the instrument to be payable to the reacquirer or to bearer, the reacquirer may negotiate the instrument. An indorser whose indorsement is canceled is discharged, and the discharge is effective against any subsequent holder.

Part 3 Enforcement of Instruments

§ 3–301. Person Entitled to Enforce Instrument.

"Person entitled to enforce" an instrument means (i) the holder of the instrument, (ii) a nonholder in possession of the instrument who has the rights of a holder, or (iii) a person not in possession of the instrument who is entitled to enforce the instrument pursuant to Section 3–309 or 3–418(d). A person may be a person entitled to enforce the instrument even though the person is not the owner of the instrument or is in wrongful possession of the instrument.

§ 3–302. Holder in Due Course.

(a) Subject to subsection (c) and Section 3–106(d), "holder in due course" means the holder of an instrument if:

(1) the instrument when issued or negotiated to the holder does not bear such apparent evidence of forgery or alteration or is not otherwise so irregular or incomplete as to call into question its authenticity; and

(2) the holder took the instrument (i) for value, (ii) in good faith, (iii) without notice that the instrument is overdue or has been dishonored or that there is an uncured default with respect to payment of another instrument issued as part of the same series, (iv) without notice that the instrument contains an unauthorized signature or has been altered, (v) without notice of any claim to the instrument described in Section 3–306, and (vi) without notice that any party has a defense or claim in recoupment described in Section 3–305(a).

(b) Notice of discharge of a party, other than discharge in an insolvency proceeding, is not notice of a defense under subsection (a), but discharge is effective against a person who became a holder in due course with notice of the discharge. Public filing or recording of a document does not of itself constitute notice of a defense, claim in recoupment, or claim to the instrument.

(c) Except to the extent a transferor or predecessor in interest has rights as a holder in due course, a person does not acquire rights of a holder in due course of an instrument taken (i) by legal process or by purchase in an execution, bankruptcy, or creditor's sale or similar proceeding, (ii) by purchase as part of a bulk transaction not in ordinary course of business of the transferor, or (iii) as the successor in interest to an estate or other organization.

(d) If, under Section 3–303(a)(1), the promise of performance that is the consideration for an instrument has been partially performed, the holder may assert rights as a holder in due course of the instrument only to the fraction of the amount payable under the instrument equal to the value of the partial performance divided by the value of the promised performance.

(e) If (i) the person entitled to enforce an instrument has only a security interest in the instrument and (ii) the person obliged to pay the instrument has a defense, claim in recoupment, or claim to the instrument that may be asserted against the person who granted the security interest, the person entitled to enforce the instrument may assert rights as a holder in due course only to an amount payable under the instrument which, at the time of enforcement of the instrument, does not exceed the amount of the unpaid obligation secured.

(f) To be effective, notice must be received at a time and in a manner that gives a reasonable opportunity to act on it.

(g) This section is subject to any law limiting status as a holder in due course in particular classes of transactions.

§ 3–303. Value and Consideration.

(a) An instrument is issued or transferred for value if:

(1) the instrument is issued or transferred for a promise of performance, to the extent the promise has been performed;

(2) the transferee acquires a security interest or other lien in the instrument other than a lien obtained by judicial proceeding;

(3) the instrument is issued or transferred as payment of, or as security for, an antecedent claim against any person, whether or not the claim is due;

(4) the instrument is issued or transferred in exchange for a negotiable instrument; or

(5) the instrument is issued or transferred in exchange for the incurring of an irrevocable obligation to a third party by the person taking the instrument.

(b) "Consideration" means any consideration sufficient to support a simple contract. The drawer or maker of an instrument has a defense if the instrument is issued without consideration. If an instrument is issued for a promise of performance, the issuer has a defense to the extent performance of the promise is due and the promise has not been performed. If an instrument is issued for value as stated in subsection (a), the instrument is also issued for consideration.

§ 3–304. Overdue Instrument.

(a) An instrument payable on demand becomes overdue at the earliest of the following times:

(1) on the day after the day demand for payment is duly made;

(2) if the instrument is a check, 90 days after its date; or

(3) if the instrument is not a check, when the instrument has been outstanding for a period of time after its date which is unreasonably long under the circumstances of the particular case in light of the nature of the instrument and usage of the trade.

(b) With respect to an instrument payable at a definite time the following rules apply:

(1) If the principal is payable in installments and a due date has not been accelerated, the instrument becomes overdue upon default under the instrument for nonpayment of an installment, and the instrument remains overdue until the default is cured.

(2) If the principal is not payable in installments and the due date has not been accelerated, the instrument becomes overdue on the day after the due date.

(3) If a due date with respect to principal has been accelerated, the instrument becomes overdue on the day after the accelerated due date.

(c) Unless the due date of principal has been accelerated, an instrument does not become overdue if there is default in payment of interest but no default in payment of principal.

§ 3–305. Defenses and Claims in Recoupment.

(a) Except as stated in subsection (b), the right to enforce the obligation of a party to pay an instrument is subject to the following:

(1) a defense of the obligor based on (i) infancy of the obligor to the extent it is a defense to a simple contract, (ii) duress, lack of legal capacity, or illegality of the transaction which, under other law, nullifies the obligation of the obligor, (iii) fraud that induced the obligor to sign the instrument with neither knowl-

edge nor reasonable opportunity to learn of its character or its essential terms, or (iv) discharge of the obligor in insolvency proceedings;

(2) a defense of the obligor stated in another section of this Article or a defense of the obligor that would be available if the person entitled to enforce the instrument were enforcing a right to payment under a simple contract; and

(3) a claim in recoupment of the obligor against the original payee of the instrument if the claim arose from the transaction that gave rise to the instrument; but the claim of the obligor may be asserted against a transferee of the instrument only to reduce the amount owing on the instrument at the time the action is brought.

(b) The right of a holder in due course to enforce the obligation of a party to pay the instrument is subject to defenses of the obligor stated in subsection (a)(1), but is not subject to defenses of the obligor stated in subsection (a)(2) or claims in recoupment stated in subsection (a)(3) against a person other than the holder.

(c) Except as stated in subsection (d), in an action to enforce the obligation of a party to pay the instrument, the obligor may not assert against the person entitled to enforce the instrument a defense, claim in recoupment, or claim to the instrument (Section 3–306) of another person, but the other person's claim to the instrument may be asserted by the obligor if the other person is joined in the action and personally asserts the claim against the person entitled to enforce the instrument. An obligor is not obliged to pay the instrument if the person seeking enforcement of the instrument does not have rights of a holder in due course and the obligor proves that the instrument is a lost or stolen instrument.

(d) In an action to enforce the obligation of an accommodation party to pay an instrument, the accommodation party may assert against the person entitled to enforce the instrument any defense or claim in recoupment under subsection (a) that the accommodated party could assert against the person entitled to enforce the instrument, except the defenses of discharge in insolvency proceedings, infancy, and lack of legal capacity.

§ 3–306. Claims to an Instrument.

A person taking an instrument, other than a person having rights of a holder in due course, is subject to a claim of a property or possessory right in the instrument or its proceeds, including a claim to rescind a negotiation and to recover the instrument or its proceeds. A person having rights of a holder in due course takes free of the claim to the instrument.

§ 3–307. Notice of Breach of Fiduciary Duty.

(a) In this section:

(1) "Fiduciary" means an agent, trustee, partner, corporate officer or director, or other representative owing a fiduciary duty with respect to an instrument.

(2) "Represented person" means the principal, beneficiary, partnership, corporation, or other person to whom the duty stated in paragraph (1) is owed.

(b) If (i) an instrument is taken from a fiduciary for payment or collection or for value, (ii) the taker has knowledge of the fiduciary status of the fiduciary, and (iii) the represented person makes a claim

to the instrument or its proceeds on the basis that the transaction of the fiduciary is a breach of fiduciary duty, the following rules apply:

(1) Notice of breach of fiduciary duty by the fiduciary is notice of the claim of the represented person.

(2) In the case of an instrument payable to the represented person or the fiduciary as such, the taker has notice of the breach of fiduciary duty if the instrument is (i) taken in payment of or as security for a debt known by the taker to be the personal debt of the fiduciary, (ii) taken in a transaction known by the taker to be for the personal benefit of the fiduciary, or (iii) deposited to an account other than an account of the fiduciary, as such, or an account of the represented person.

(3) If an instrument is issued by the represented person or the fiduciary as such, and made payable to the fiduciary personally, the taker does not have notice of the breach of fiduciary duty unless the taker knows of the breach of fiduciary duty.

(4) If an instrument is issued by the represented person or the fiduciary as such, to the taker as payee, the taker has notice of the breach of fiduciary duty if the instrument is (i) taken in payment of or as security for a debt known by the taker to be the personal debt of the fiduciary, (ii) taken in a transaction known by the taker to be for the personal benefit of the fiduciary, or (iii) deposited to an account other than an account of the fiduciary, as such, or an account of the represented person.

§ 3–308. Proof of Signatures and Status as Holder in Due Course.

(a) In an action with respect to an instrument, the authenticity of, and authority to make, each signature on the instrument is admitted unless specifically denied in the pleadings. If the validity of a signature is denied in the pleadings, the burden of establishing validity is on the person claiming validity, but the signature is presumed to be authentic and authorized unless the action is to enforce the liability of the purported signer and the signer is dead or incompetent at the time of trial of the issue of validity of the signature. If an action to enforce the instrument is brought against a person as the undisclosed principal of a person who signed the instrument as a party to the instrument, the plaintiff has the burden of establishing that the defendant is liable on the instrument as a represented person under Section 3–402(a).

(b) If the validity of signatures is admitted or proved and there is compliance with subsection (a), a plaintiff producing the instrument is entitled to payment if the plaintiff proves entitlement to enforce the instrument under Section 3–301, unless the defendant proves a defense or claim in recoupment. If a defense or claim in recoupment is proved, the right to payment of the plaintiff is subject to the defense or claim, except to the extent the plaintiff proves that the plaintiff has rights of a holder in due course which are not subject to the defense or claim.

§ 3–309. Enforcement of Lost, Destroyed, or Stolen Instrument.

(a) A person not in possession of an instrument is entitled to enforce the instrument if (i) the person was in possession of the instrument and entitled to enforce it when loss of possession occurred, (ii) the loss of possession was not the result of a transfer by the person or a lawful seizure, and (iii) the person cannot reasonably obtain possession of the instrument because the instrument was destroyed, its whereabouts cannot be determined, or it is in the wrongful possession of an unknown person or a person that cannot be found or is not amenable to service of process.

(b) A person seeking enforcement of an instrument under subsection (a) must prove the terms of the instrument and the person's right to enforce the instrument. If that proof is made, Section 3–308 applies to the case as if the person seeking enforcement had produced the instrument. The court may not enter judgment in favor of the person seeking enforcement unless it finds that the person required to pay the instrument is adequately protected against loss that might occur by reason of a claim by another person to enforce the instrument. Adequate protection may be provided by any reasonable means.

§ 3–310. Effect of Instrument on Obligation for Which Taken.

(a) Unless otherwise agreed, if a certified check, cashier's check, or teller's check is taken for an obligation, the obligation is discharged to the same extent discharge would result if an amount of money equal to the amount of the instrument were taken in payment of the obligation. Discharge of the obligation does not affect any liability that the obligor may have as an indorser of the instrument.

(b) Unless otherwise agreed and except as provided in subsection (a), if a note or an uncertified check is taken for an obligation, the obligation is suspended to the same extent the obligation would be discharged if an amount of money equal to the amount of the instrument were taken, and the following rules apply:

(1) In the case of an uncertified check, suspension of the obligation continues until dishonor of the check or until it is paid or certified. Payment or certification of the check results in discharge of the obligation to the extent of the amount of the check.

(2) In the case of a note, suspension of the obligation continues until dishonor of the note or until it is paid. Payment of the note results in discharge of the obligation to the extent of the payment.

(3) Except as provided in paragraph (4), if the check or note is dishonored and the obligee of the obligation for which the instrument was taken is the person entitled to enforce the instrument, the obligee may enforce either the instrument or the obligation. In the case of an instrument of a third person which is negotiated to the obligee by the obligor, discharge of the obligor on the instrument also discharges the obligation.

(4) If the person entitled to enforce the instrument taken for an obligation is a person other than the obligee, the obligee may not enforce the obligation to the extent the obligation is suspended. If the obligee is the person entitled to enforce the instrument but no longer has possession of it because it was lost, stolen, or destroyed, the obligation may not be enforced to the extent of the amount payable on the instrument, and to that extent the obligee's rights against the obligor are limited to enforcement of the instrument.

(c) If an instrument other than one described in subsection (a) or (b) is taken for an obligation, the effect is (i) that stated in subsection (a) if the instrument is one on which a bank is liable as maker or acceptor, or (ii) that stated in subsection (b) in any other case.

§ 3–311. Accord and Satisfaction by Use of Instrument.

(a) If a person against whom a claim is asserted proves that (i) that person in good faith tendered an instrument to the claimant as full satisfaction of the claim, (ii) the amount of the claim was unliq-

uidated or subject to a bona fide dispute, and (iii) the claimant obtained payment of the instrument, the following subsections apply.

(b) Unless subsection (c) applies, the claim is discharged if the person against whom the claim is asserted proves that the instrument or an accompanying written communication contained a conspicuous statement to the effect that the instrument was tendered as full satisfaction of the claim.

(c) Subject to subsection (d), a claim is not discharged under subsection (b) if either of the following applies:

(1) The claimant, if an organization, proves that (i) within a reasonable time before the tender, the claimant sent a conspicuous statement to the person against whom the claim is asserted that communications concerning disputed debts, including an instrument tendered as full satisfaction of a debt, are to be sent to a designated person, office, or place, and (ii) the instrument or accompanying communication was not received by that designated person, office, or place.

(2) The claimant, whether or not an organization, proves that within 90 days after payment of the instrument, the claimant tendered repayment of the amount of the instrument to the person against whom the claim is asserted. This paragraph does not apply if the claimant is an organization that sent a statement complying with paragraph (1)(i).

(d) A claim is discharged if the person against whom the claim is asserted proves that within a reasonable time before collection of the instrument was initiated, the claimant, or an agent of the claimant having direct responsibility with respect to the disputed obligation, knew that the instrument was tendered in full satisfaction of the claim.

§ 3–312. Lost, Destroyed, or Stolen Cashier's Check, Teller's Check, or Certified Check.

(a) In this section:

(1) "Check" means a cashier's check, teller's check, or certified check.

(2) "Claimant" means a person who claims the right to receive the amount of a cashier's check, teller's check, or certified check that was lost, destroyed, or stolen.

(3) "Declaration of loss" means a written statement, made under penalty of perjury, to the effect that (i) the declarer lost possession of a check, (ii) the declarer is the drawer or payee of the check, in the case of a certified check, or the remitter or payee of the check, in the case of a cashier's check or teller's check, (iii) the loss of possession was not the result of a transfer by the declarer or a lawful seizure, and (iv) the declarer cannot reasonably obtain possession of the check because the check was destroyed, its whereabouts cannot be determined, or it is in the wrongful possession of an unknown person or a person that cannot be found or is not amenable to service of process.

(4) "Obligated bank" means the issuer of a cashier's check or teller's check or the acceptor of a certified check.

(b) A claimant may assert a claim to the amount of a check by a communication to the obligated bank describing the check with reasonable certainty and requesting payment of the amount of the check, if (i) the claimant is the drawer or payee of a certified check or the remitter or payee of a cashier's check or teller's check, (ii) the communication contains or is accompanied by a declaration of loss of the claimant with respect to the check, (iii) the communication is received at a time and in a manner affording the bank a reasonable time to act on it before the check is paid, and (iv) the claimant provides reasonable identification if requested by the obligated bank. Delivery of a declaration of loss is a warranty of the truth of the statements made in the declaration. If a claim is asserted in compliance with this subsection, the following rules apply:

(1) The claim becomes enforceable at the later of (i) the time the claim is asserted, or (ii) the 90th day following the date of the check, in the case of a cashier's check or teller's check, or the 90th day following the date of the acceptance, in the case of a certified check.

(2) Until the claim becomes enforceable, it has no legal effect and the obligated bank may pay the check or, in the case of a teller's check, may permit the drawee to pay the check. Payment to a person entitled to enforce the check discharges all liability of the obligated bank with respect to the check.

(3) If the claim becomes enforceable before the check is presented for payment, the obligated bank is not obliged to pay the check.

(4) When the claim becomes enforceable, the obligated bank becomes obliged to pay the amount of the check to the claimant if payment of the check has not been made to a person entitled to enforce the check. Subject to Section 4–302(a)(1), payment to the claimant discharges all liability of the obligated bank with respect to the check.

(c) If the obligated bank pays the amount of a check to a claimant under subsection (b)(4) and the check is presented for payment by a person having rights of a holder in due course, the claimant is obliged to (i) refund the payment to the obligated bank if the check is paid, or (ii) pay the amount of the check to the person having rights of a holder in due course if the check is dishonored.

(d) If a claimant has the right to assert a claim under subsection (b) and is also a person entitled to enforce a cashier's check, teller's check, or certified check which is lost, destroyed, or stolen, the claimant may assert rights with respect to the check either under this section or Section 3–309.

Added in 1991.

Part 4 Liability of Parties

§ 3–401. Signature.

(a) A person is not liable on an instrument unless (i) the person signed the instrument, or (ii) the person is represented by an agent or representative who signed the instrument and the signature is binding on the represented person under Section 3–402.

(b) A signature may be made (i) manually or by means of a device or machine, and (ii) by the use of any name, including a trade or assumed name, or by a word, mark, or symbol executed or adopted by a person with present intention to authenticate a writing.

§ 3–402. Signature by Representative.

(a) If a person acting, or purporting to act, as a representative signs an instrument by signing either the name of the represented person or

the name of the signer, the represented person is bound by the signature to the same extent the represented person would be bound if the signature were on a simple contract. If the represented person is bound, the signature of the representative is the "authorized signature of the represented person" and the represented person is liable on the instrument, whether or not identified in the instrument.

(b) If a representative signs the name of the representative to an instrument and the signature is an authorized signature of the represented person, the following rules apply:

(1) If the form of the signature shows unambiguously that the signature is made on behalf of the represented person who is identified in the instrument, the representative is not liable on the instrument.

(2) Subject to subsection (c), if (i) the form of the signature does not show unambiguously that the signature is made in a representative capacity or (ii) the represented person is not identified in the instrument, the representative is liable on the instrument to a holder in due course that took the instrument without notice that the representative was not intended to be liable on the instrument. With respect to any other person, the representative is liable on the instrument unless the representative proves that the original parties did not intend the representative to be liable on the instrument.

(c) If a representative signs the name of the representative as drawer of a check without indication of the representative status and the check is payable from an account of the represented person who is identified on the check, the signer is not liable on the check if the signature is an authorized signature of the represented person.

§ 3–403. Unauthorized Signature.

(a) Unless otherwise provided in this Article or Article 4, an unauthorized signature is ineffective except as the signature of the unauthorized signer in favor of a person who in good faith pays the instrument or takes it for value. An unauthorized signature may be ratified for all purposes of this Article.

(b) If the signature of more than one person is required to constitute the authorized signature of an organization, the signature of the organization is unauthorized if one of the required signatures is lacking.

(c) The civil or criminal liability of a person who makes an unauthorized signature is not affected by any provision of this Article which makes the unauthorized signature effective for the purposes of this Article.

§ 3–404. Impostors; Fictitious Payees.

(a) If an impostor, by use of the mails or otherwise, induces the issuer of an instrument to issue the instrument to the impostor, or to a person acting in concert with the impostor, by impersonating the payee of the instrument or a person authorized to act for the payee, an indorsement of the instrument by any person in the name of the payee is effective as the indorsement of the payee in favor of a person who, in good faith, pays the instrument or takes it for value or for collection.

(b) If (i) a person whose intent determines to whom an instrument is payable (Section 3–110(a) or (b)) does not intend the person identified as payee to have any interest in the instrument, or (ii) the person identified as payee of an instrument is a fictitious person, the following rules apply until the instrument is negotiated by special indorsement:

(1) Any person in possession of the instrument is its holder.

(2) An indorsement by any person in the name of the payee stated in the instrument is effective as the indorsement of the payee in favor of a person who, in good faith, pays the instrument or takes it for value or for collection.

(c) Under subsection (a) or (b), an indorsement is made in the name of a payee if (i) it is made in a name substantially similar to that of the payee or (ii) the instrument, whether or not indorsed, is deposited in a depositary bank to an account in a name substantially similar to that of the payee.

(d) With respect to an instrument to which subsection (a) or (b) applies, if a person paying the instrument or taking it for value or for collection fails to exercise ordinary care in paying or taking the instrument and that failure substantially contributes to loss resulting from payment of the instrument, the person bearing the loss may recover from the person failing to exercise ordinary care to the extent the failure to exercise ordinary care contributed to the loss.

§ 3–405. Employer's Responsibility for Fraudulent Indorsement by Employee.

(a) In this section:

(1) "Employee" includes an independent contractor and employee of an independent contractor retained by the employer.

(2) "Fraudulent indorsement" means (i) in the case of an instrument payable to the employer, a forged indorsement purporting to be that of the employer, or (ii) in the case of an instrument with respect to which the employer is the issuer, a forged indorsement purporting to be that of the person identified as payee.

(3) "Responsibility" with respect to instruments means authority (i) to sign or indorse instruments on behalf of the employer, (ii) to process instruments received by the employer for bookkeeping purposes, for deposit to an account, or for other disposition, (iii) to prepare or process instruments for issue in the name of the employer, (iv) to supply information determining the names or addresses of payees of instruments to be issued in the name of the employer, (v) to control the disposition of instruments to be issued in the name of the employer, or (vi) to act otherwise with respect to instruments in a responsible capacity. "Responsibility" does not include authority that merely allows an employee to have access to instruments or blank or incomplete instrument forms that are being stored or transported or are part of incoming or outgoing mail, or similar access.

(b) For the purpose of determining the rights and liabilities of a person who, in good faith, pays an instrument or takes it for value or for collection, if an employer entrusted an employee with responsibility with respect to the instrument and the employee or a person acting in concert with the employee makes a fraudulent indorsement of the instrument, the indorsement is effective as the indorsement of the person to whom the instrument is payable if it is made in the name of that person. If the person paying the instrument or taking it for value or for collection fails to exercise ordinary care in paying or taking the instrument and that failure substantially contributes to loss resulting from the fraud, the person bearing the loss may recover

from the person failing to exercise ordinary care to the extent the failure to exercise ordinary care contributed to the loss.

(c) Under subsection (b), an indorsement is made in the name of the person to whom an instrument is payable if (i) it is made in a name substantially similar to the name of that person or (ii) the instrument, whether or not indorsed, is deposited in a depositary bank to an account in a name substantially similar to the name of that person.

§ 3–406. Negligence Contributing to Forged Signature or Alteration of Instrument.

(a) A person whose failure to exercise ordinary care substantially contributes to an alteration of an instrument or to the making of a forged signature on an instrument is precluded from asserting the alteration or the forgery against a person who, in good faith, pays the instrument or takes it for value or for collection.

(b) Under subsection (a), if the person asserting the preclusion fails to exercise ordinary care in paying or taking the instrument and that failure substantially contributes to loss, the loss is allocated between the person precluded and the person asserting the preclusion according to the extent to which the failure of each to exercise ordinary care contributed to the loss.

(c) Under subsection (a), the burden of proving failure to exercise ordinary care is on the person asserting the preclusion. Under subsection (b), the burden of proving failure to exercise ordinary care is on the person precluded.

§ 3–407. Alteration.

(a) "Alteration" means (i) an unauthorized change in an instrument that purports to modify in any respect the obligation of a party, or (ii) an unauthorized addition of words or numbers or other change to an incomplete instrument relating to the obligation of a party.

(b) Except as provided in subsection (c), an alteration fraudulently made discharges a party whose obligation is affected by the alteration unless that party assents or is precluded from asserting the alteration. No other alteration discharges a party, and the instrument may be enforced according to its original terms.

(c) A payor bank or drawee paying a fraudulently altered instrument or a person taking it for value, in good faith and without notice of the alteration, may enforce rights with respect to the instrument (i) according to its original terms, or (ii) in the case of an incomplete instrument altered by unauthorized completion, according to its terms as completed.

§ 3–408. Drawee Not Liable on Unaccepted Draft.

A check or other draft does not of itself operate as an assignment of funds in the hands of the drawee available for its payment, and the drawee is not liable on the instrument until the drawee accepts it.

§ 3–409. Acceptance of Draft; Certified Check.

(a) "Acceptance" means the drawee's signed agreement to pay a draft as presented. It must be written on the draft and may consist of the drawee's signature alone. Acceptance may be made at any time and becomes effective when notification pursuant to instructions is given or the accepted draft is delivered for the purpose of giving rights on the acceptance to any person.

(b) A draft may be accepted although it has not been signed by the drawer, is otherwise incomplete, is overdue, or has been dishonored.

(c) If a draft is payable at a fixed period after sight and the acceptor fails to date the acceptance, the holder may complete the acceptance by supplying a date in good faith.

(d) "Certified check" means a check accepted by the bank on which it is drawn. Acceptance may be made as stated in subsection (a) or by a writing on the check which indicates that the check is certified. The drawee of a check has no obligation to certify the check, and refusal to certify is not dishonor of the check.

§ 3–410. Acceptance Varying Draft.

(a) If the terms of a drawee's acceptance vary from the terms of the draft as presented, the holder may refuse the acceptance and treat the draft as dishonored. In that case, the drawee may cancel the acceptance.

(b) The terms of a draft are not varied by an acceptance to pay at a particular bank or place in the United States, unless the acceptance states that the draft is to be paid only at that bank or place.

(c) If the holder assents to an acceptance varying the terms of a draft, the obligation of each drawer and indorser that does not expressly assent to the acceptance is discharged.

§ 3–411. Refusal to Pay Cashier's Checks, Teller's Checks, and Certified Checks.

(a) In this section, "obligated bank" means the acceptor of a certified check or the issuer of a cashier's check or teller's check bought from the issuer.

(b) If the obligated bank wrongfully (i) refuses to pay a cashier's check or certified check, (ii) stops payment of a teller's check, or (iii) refuses to pay a dishonored teller's check, the person asserting the right to enforce the check is entitled to compensation for expenses and loss of interest resulting from the nonpayment and may recover consequential damages if the obligated bank refuses to pay after receiving notice of particular circumstances giving rise to the damages.

(c) Expenses or consequential damages under subsection (b) are not recoverable if the refusal of the obligated bank to pay occurs because (i) the bank suspends payments, (ii) the obligated bank asserts a claim or defense of the bank that it has reasonable grounds to believe is available against the person entitled to enforce the instrument, (iii) the obligated bank has a reasonable doubt whether the person demanding payment is the person entitled to enforce the instrument, or (iv) payment is prohibited by law.

§ 3–412. Obligation of Issuer of Note or Cashier's Check.

The issuer of a note or cashier's check or other draft drawn on the drawer is obliged to pay the instrument (i) according to its terms at the time it was issued or, if not issued, at the time it first came into possession of a holder, or (ii) if the issuer signed an incomplete instrument, according to its terms when completed, to the extent stated in Sections 3–115 and 3–407. The obligation is owed to a person entitled to enforce the instrument or to an indorser who paid the instrument under Section 3–415.

§ 3–413. Obligation of Acceptor.

(a) The acceptor of a draft is obliged to pay the draft (i) according to its terms at the time it was accepted, even though the acceptance

states that the draft is payable "as originally drawn" or equivalent terms, (ii) if the acceptance varies the terms of the draft, according to the terms of the draft as varied, or (iii) if the acceptance is of a draft that is an incomplete instrument, according to its terms when completed, to the extent stated in Sections 3–115 and 3–407. The obligation is owed to a person entitled to enforce the draft or to the drawer or an indorser who paid the draft under Section 3–414 or 3–415.

(b) If the certification of a check or other acceptance of a draft states the amount certified or accepted, the obligation of the acceptor is that amount. If (i) the certification or acceptance does not state an amount, (ii) the amount of the instrument is subsequently raised, and (iii) the instrument is then negotiated to a holder in due course, the obligation of the acceptor is the amount of the instrument at the time it was taken by the holder in due course.

§ 3–414. Obligation of Drawer.

(a) This section does not apply to cashier's checks or other drafts drawn on the drawer.

(b) If an unaccepted draft is dishonored, the drawer is obliged to pay the draft (i) according to its terms at the time it was issued or, if not issued, at the time it first came into possession of a holder, or (ii) if the drawer signed an incomplete instrument, according to its terms when completed, to the extent stated in Sections 3–115 and 3–407. The obligation is owed to a person entitled to enforce the draft or to an indorser who paid the draft under Section 3–415.

(c) If a draft is accepted by a bank, the drawer is discharged, regardless of when or by whom acceptance was obtained.

(d) If a draft is accepted and the acceptor is not a bank, the obligation of the drawer to pay the draft if the draft is dishonored by the acceptor is the same as the obligation of an indorser under Section 3–415(a) and (c).

(e) If a draft states that it is drawn "without recourse" or otherwise disclaims liability of the drawer to pay the draft, the drawer is not liable under subsection (b) to pay the draft if the draft is not a check. A disclaimer of the liability stated in subsection (b) is not effective if the draft is a check.

(f) If (i) a check is not presented for payment or given to a depositary bank for collection within 30 days after its date, (ii) the drawee suspends payments after expiration of the 30-day period without paying the check, and (iii) because of the suspension of payments, the drawer is deprived of funds maintained with the drawee to cover payment of the check, the drawer to the extent deprived of funds may discharge its obligation to pay the check by assigning to the person entitled to enforce the check the rights of the drawer against the drawee with respect to the funds.

§ 3–415. Obligation of Indorser.

(a) Subject to subsections (b), (c), and (d) and to Section 3–419(d), if an instrument is dishonored, an indorser is obliged to pay the amount due on the instrument (i) according to the terms of the instrument at the time it was indorsed, or (ii) if the indorser indorsed an incomplete instrument, according to its terms when completed, to the extent stated in Sections 3–115 and 3–407. The obligation of the indorser is owed to a person entitled to enforce the instrument or to a subsequent indorser who paid the instrument under this section.

(b) If an indorsement states that it is made "without recourse" or otherwise disclaims liability of the indorser, the indorser is not liable under subsection (a) to pay the instrument.

(c) If notice of dishonor of an instrument is required by Section 3–503 and notice of dishonor complying with that section is not given to an indorser, the liability of the indorser under subsection (a) is discharged.

(d) If a draft is accepted by a bank after an indorsement is made, the liability of the indorser under subsection (a) is discharged.

(e) If an indorser of a check is liable under subsection (a) and the check is not presented for payment, or given to a depositary bank for collection, within 30 days after the day the indorsement was made, the liability of the indorser under subsection (a) is discharged.

As amended in 1993.

§ 3–416. Transfer Warranties.

(a) A person who transfers an instrument for consideration warrants to the transferee and, if the transfer is by indorsement, to any subsequent transferee that:

(1) the warrantor is a person entitled to enforce the instrument;

(2) all signatures on the instrument are authentic and authorized;

(3) the instrument has not been altered;

(4) the instrument is not subject to a defense or claim in recoupment of any party which can be asserted against the warrantor; and

(5) the warrantor has no knowledge of any insolvency proceeding commenced with respect to the maker or acceptor or, in the case of an unaccepted draft, the drawer.

(b) A person to whom the warranties under subsection (a) are made and who took the instrument in good faith may recover from the warrantor as damages for breach of warranty an amount equal to the loss suffered as a result of the breach, but not more than the amount of the instrument plus expenses and loss of interest incurred as a result of the breach.

(c) The warranties stated in subsection (a) cannot be disclaimed with respect to checks. Unless notice of a claim for breach of warranty is given to the warrantor within 30 days after the claimant has reason to know of the breach and the identity of the warrantor, the liability of the warrantor under subsection (b) is discharged to the extent of any loss caused by the delay in giving notice of the claim.

(d) A [cause of action] for breach of warranty under this section accrues when the claimant has reason to know of the breach.

§ 3–417. Presentment Warranties.

(a) If an unaccepted draft is presented to the drawee for payment or acceptance and the drawee pays or accepts the draft, (i) the person obtaining payment or acceptance, at the time of presentment, and (ii) a previous transferor of the draft, at the time of transfer, warrant to the drawee making payment or accepting the draft in good faith that:

(1) the warrantor is, or was, at the time the warrantor transferred the draft, a person entitled to enforce the draft or authorized to obtain payment or acceptance of the draft on behalf of a person entitled to enforce the draft;

(2) the draft has not been altered; and

(3) the warrantor has no knowledge that the signature of the drawer of the draft is unauthorized.

(b) A drawee making payment may recover from any warrantor damages for breach of warranty equal to the amount paid by the drawee less the amount the drawee received or is entitled to receive from the drawer because of the payment. In addition, the drawee is entitled to compensation for expenses and loss of interest resulting from the breach. The right of the drawee to recover damages under this subsection is not affected by any failure of the drawee to exercise ordinary care in making payment. If the drawee accepts the draft, breach of warranty is a defense to the obligation of the acceptor. If the acceptor makes payment with respect to the draft, the acceptor is entitled to recover from any warrantor for breach of warranty the amounts stated in this subsection.

(c) If a drawee asserts a claim for breach of warranty under subsection (a) based on an unauthorized indorsement of the draft or an alteration of the draft, the warrantor may defend by proving that the indorsement is effective under Section 3–404 or 3–405 or the drawer is precluded under Section 3–406 or 4–406 from asserting against the drawee the unauthorized indorsement or alteration.

(d) If (i) a dishonored draft is presented for payment to the drawer or an indorser or (ii) any other instrument is presented for payment to a party obliged to pay the instrument, and (iii) payment is received, the following rules apply:

(1) The person obtaining payment and a prior transferor of the instrument warrant to the person making payment in good faith that the warrantor is, or was, at the time the warrantor transferred the instrument, a person entitled to enforce the instrument or authorized to obtain payment on behalf of a person entitled to enforce the instrument.

(2) The person making payment may recover from any warrantor for breach of warranty an amount equal to the amount paid plus expenses and loss of interest resulting from the breach.

(e) The warranties stated in subsections (a) and (d) cannot be disclaimed with respect to checks. Unless notice of a claim for breach of warranty is given to the warrantor within 30 days after the claimant has reason to know of the breach and the identity of the warrantor, the liability of the warrantor under subsection (b) or (d) is discharged to the extent of any loss caused by the delay in giving notice of the claim.

(f) A [cause of action] for breach of warranty under this section accrues when the claimant has reason to know of the breach.

§ 3–418. Payment or Acceptance by Mistake.

(a) Except as provided in subsection (c), if the drawee of a draft pays or accepts the draft and the drawee acted on the mistaken belief that (i) payment of the draft had not been stopped pursuant to Section 4–403 or (ii) the signature of the drawer of the draft was authorized, the drawee may recover the amount of the draft from the person to whom or for whose benefit payment was made or, in the case of acceptance, may revoke the acceptance. Rights of the drawee under this subsection are not affected by failure of the drawee to exercise ordinary care in paying or accepting the draft.

(b) Except as provided in subsection (c), if an instrument has been paid or accepted by mistake and the case is not covered by subsection (a), the person paying or accepting may, to the extent permitted by the law governing mistake and restitution, (i) recover the payment from the person to whom or for whose benefit payment was made or (ii) in the case of acceptance, may revoke the acceptance.

(c) The remedies provided by subsection (a) or (b) may not be asserted against a person who took the instrument in good faith and for value or who in good faith changed position in reliance on the payment or acceptance. This subsection does not limit remedies provided by Section 3–417 or 4–407.

(d) Notwithstanding Section 4–215, if an instrument is paid or accepted by mistake and the payor or acceptor recovers payment or revokes acceptance under subsection (a) or (b), the instrument is deemed not to have been paid or accepted and is treated as dishonored, and the person from whom payment is recovered has rights as a person entitled to enforce the dishonored instrument.

§ 3–419. Instruments Signed for Accommodation.

(a) If an instrument is issued for value given for the benefit of a party to the instrument ("accommodated party") and another party to the instrument ("accommodation party") signs the instrument for the purpose of incurring liability on the instrument without being a direct beneficiary of the value given for the instrument, the instrument is signed by the accommodation party "for accommodation."

(b) An accommodation party may sign the instrument as maker, drawer, acceptor, or indorser and, subject to subsection (d), is obliged to pay the instrument in the capacity in which the accommodation party signs. The obligation of an accommodation party may be enforced notwithstanding any statute of frauds and whether or not the accommodation party receives consideration for the accommodation.

(c) A person signing an instrument is presumed to be an accommodation party and there is notice that the instrument is signed for accommodation if the signature is an anomalous indorsement or is accompanied by words indicating that the signer is acting as surety or guarantor with respect to the obligation of another party to the instrument. Except as provided in Section 3–605, the obligation of an accommodation party to pay the instrument is not affected by the fact that the person enforcing the obligation had notice when the instrument was taken by that person that the accommodation party signed the instrument for accommodation.

(d) If the signature of a party to an instrument is accompanied by words indicating unambiguously that the party is guaranteeing collection rather than payment of the obligation of another party to the instrument, the signer is obliged to pay the amount due on the instrument to a person entitled to enforce the instrument only if (i) execution of judgment against the other party has been returned unsatisfied, (ii) the other party is insolvent or in an insolvency proceeding, (iii) the other party cannot be served with process, or (iv) it is otherwise apparent that payment cannot be obtained from the other party.

(e) An accommodation party who pays the instrument is entitled to reimbursement from the accommodated party and is entitled to enforce the instrument against the accommodated party. An accommodated party who pays the instrument has no right of recourse against, and is not entitled to contribution from, an accommodation party.

§ 3–420. Conversion of Instrument.

(a) The law applicable to conversion of personal property applies to instruments. An instrument is also converted if it is taken by transfer, other than a negotiation, from a person not entitled to enforce the instrument or a bank makes or obtains payment with respect to the instrument for a person not entitled to enforce the instrument or receive payment. An action for conversion of an instrument may not be brought by (i) the issuer or acceptor of the instrument or (ii) a payee or indorsee who did not receive delivery of the instrument either directly or through delivery to an agent or a co-payee.

(b) In an action under subsection (a), the measure of liability is presumed to be the amount payable on the instrument, but recovery may not exceed the amount of the plaintiff's interest in the instrument.

(c) A representative, other than a depositary bank, who has in good faith dealt with an instrument or its proceeds on behalf of one who was not the person entitled to enforce the instrument is not liable in conversion to that person beyond the amount of any proceeds that it has not paid out.

Part 5 Dishonor

§ 3–501. Presentment.

(a) "Presentment" means a demand made by or on behalf of a person entitled to enforce an instrument (i) to pay the instrument made to the drawee or a party obliged to pay the instrument or, in the case of a note or accepted draft payable at a bank, to the bank, or (ii) to accept a draft made to the drawee.

(b) The following rules are subject to Article 4, agreement of the parties, and clearing-house rules and the like:

(1) Presentment may be made at the place of payment of the instrument and must be made at the place of payment if the instrument is payable at a bank in the United States; may be made by any commercially reasonable means, including an oral, written, or electronic communication; is effective when the demand for payment or acceptance is received by the person to whom presentment is made; and is effective if made to any one of two or more makers, acceptors, drawees, or other payors.

(2) Upon demand of the person to whom presentment is made, the person making presentment must (i) exhibit the instrument, (ii) give reasonable identification and, if presentment is made on behalf of another person, reasonable evidence of authority to do so, and (. . .) sign a receipt on the instrument for any payment made or surrender the instrument if full payment is made.

(3) Without dishonoring the instrument, the party to whom presentment is made may (i) return the instrument for lack of a necessary indorsement, or (ii) refuse payment or acceptance for failure of the presentment to comply with the terms of the instrument, an agreement of the parties, or other applicable law or rule.

(4) The party to whom presentment is made may treat presentment as occurring on the next business day after the day of presentment if the party to whom presentment is made has established a cut-off hour not earlier than 2 P.M. for the receipt and processing of instruments presented for payment or acceptance and presentment is made after the cut-off hour.

§ 3–502. Dishonor.

(a) Dishonor of a note is governed by the following rules:

(1) If the note is payable on demand, the note is dishonored if presentment is duly made to the maker and the note is not paid on the day of presentment.

(2) If the note is not payable on demand and is payable at or through a bank or the terms of the note require presentment, the note is dishonored if presentment is duly made and the note is not paid on the day it becomes payable or the day of presentment, whichever is later.

(3) If the note is not payable on demand and paragraph (2) does not apply, the note is dishonored if it is not paid on the day it becomes payable.

(b) Dishonor of an unaccepted draft other than a documentary draft is governed by the following rules:

(1) If a check is duly presented for payment to the payor bank otherwise than for immediate payment over the counter, the check is dishonored if the payor bank makes timely return of the check or sends timely notice of dishonor or nonpayment under Section 4–301 or 4–302, or becomes accountable for the amount of the check under Section 4–302.

(2) If a draft is payable on demand and paragraph (1) does not apply, the draft is dishonored if presentment for payment is duly made to the drawee and the draft is not paid on the day of presentment.

(3) If a draft is payable on a date stated in the draft, the draft is dishonored if (i) presentment for payment is duly made to the drawee and payment is not made on the day the draft becomes payable or the day of presentment, whichever is later, or (ii) presentment for acceptance is duly made before the day the draft becomes payable and the draft is not accepted on the day of presentment.

(4) If a draft is payable on elapse of a period of time after sight or acceptance, the draft is dishonored if presentment for acceptance is duly made and the draft is not accepted on the day of presentment.

(c) Dishonor of an unaccepted documentary draft occurs according to the rules stated in subsection (b)(2), (3), and (4), except that payment or acceptance may be delayed without dishonor until no later than the close of the third business day of the drawee following the day on which payment or acceptance is required by those paragraphs.

(d) Dishonor of an accepted draft is governed by the following rules:

(1) If the draft is payable on demand, the draft is dishonored if presentment for payment is duly made to the acceptor and the draft is not paid on the day of presentment.

(2) If the draft is not payable on demand, the draft is dishonored if presentment for payment is duly made to the acceptor and payment is not made on the day it becomes payable or the day of presentment, whichever is later.

(e) In any case in which presentment is otherwise required for dishonor under this section and presentment is excused under Section 3–504, dishonor occurs without presentment if the instrument is not duly accepted or paid.

(f) If a draft is dishonored because timely acceptance of the draft was not made and the person entitled to demand acceptance consents to a late acceptance, from the time of acceptance the draft is treated as never having been dishonored.

§ 3–503. Notice of Dishonor.

(a) The obligation of an indorser stated in Section 3–415(a) and the obligation of a drawer stated in Section 3–414(d) may not be enforced unless (i) the indorser or drawer is given notice of dishonor of the instrument complying with this section or (ii) notice of dishonor is excused under Section 3–504(b).

(b) Notice of dishonor may be given by any person; may be given by any commercially reasonable means, including an oral, written, or electronic communication; and is sufficient if it reasonably identifies the instrument and indicates that the instrument has been dishonored or has not been paid or accepted. Return of an instrument given to a bank for collection is sufficient notice of dishonor.

(c) Subject to Section 3–504(c), with respect to an instrument taken for collection by a collecting bank, notice of dishonor must be given (i) by the bank before midnight of the next banking day following the banking day on which the bank receives notice of dishonor of the instrument, or (ii) by any other person within 30 days following the day on which the person receives notice of dishonor. With respect to any other instrument, notice of dishonor must be given within 30 days following the day on which dishonor occurs.

§ 3–504. Excused Presentment and Notice of Dishonor.

(a) Presentment for payment or acceptance of an instrument is excused if (i) the person entitled to present the instrument cannot with reasonable diligence make presentment, (ii) the maker or acceptor has repudiated an obligation to pay the instrument or is dead or in insolvency proceedings, (iii) by the terms of the instrument presentment is not necessary to enforce the obligation of indorsers or the drawer, (iv) the drawer or indorser whose obligation is being enforced has waived presentment or otherwise has no reason to expect or right to require that the instrument be paid or accepted, or (v) the drawer instructed the drawee not to pay or accept the draft or the drawee was not obligated to the drawer to pay the draft.

(b) Notice of dishonor is excused if (i) by the terms of the instrument notice of dishonor is not necessary to enforce the obligation of a party to pay the instrument, or (ii) the party whose obligation is being enforced waived notice of dishonor. A waiver of presentment is also a waiver of notice of dishonor.

(c) Delay in giving notice of dishonor is excused if the delay was caused by circumstances beyond the control of the person giving the notice and the person giving the notice exercised reasonable diligence after the cause of the delay ceased to operate.

§ 3–505. Evidence of Dishonor.

(a) The following are admissible as evidence and create a presumption of dishonor and of any notice of dishonor stated:

(1) a document regular in form as provided in subsection (b) which purports to be a protest;

(2) a purported stamp or writing of the drawee, payor bank, or presenting bank on or accompanying the instrument stating that acceptance or payment has been refused unless reasons for

the refusal are stated and the reasons are not consistent with dishonor;

(3) a book or record of the drawee, payor bank, or collecting bank, kept in the usual course of business which shows dishonor, even if there is no evidence of who made the entry.

(b) A protest is a certificate of dishonor made by a United States consul or vice consul, or a notary public or other person authorized to administer oaths by the law of the place where dishonor occurs. It may be made upon information satisfactory to that person. The protest must identify the instrument and certify either that presentment has been made or, if not made, the reason why it was not made, and that the instrument has been dishonored by nonacceptance or nonpayment. The protest may also certify that notice of dishonor has been given to some or all parties.

Part 6 Discharge and Payment

§ 3–601. Discharge and Effect of Discharge.

(a) The obligation of a party to pay the instrument is discharged as stated in this Article or by an act or agreement with the party which would discharge an obligation to pay money under a simple contract.

(b) Discharge of the obligation of a party is not effective against a person acquiring rights of a holder in due course of the instrument without notice of the discharge.

§ 3–602. Payment.

(a) Subject to subsection (b), an instrument is paid to the extent payment is made (i) by or on behalf of a party obliged to pay the instrument, and (ii) to a person entitled to enforce the instrument. To the extent of the payment, the obligation of the party obliged to pay the instrument is discharged even though payment is made with knowledge of a claim to the instrument under Section 3–306 by another person.

(b) The obligation of a party to pay the instrument is not discharged under subsection (a) if:

(1) a claim to the instrument under Section 3–306 is enforceable against the party receiving payment and (i) payment is made with knowledge by the payor that payment is prohibited by injunction or similar process of a court of competent jurisdiction, or (ii) in the case of an instrument other than a cashier's check, teller's check, or certified check, the party making payment accepted, from the person having a claim to the instrument, indemnity against loss resulting from refusal to pay the person entitled to enforce the instrument; or

(2) the person making payment knows that the instrument is a stolen instrument and pays a person it knows is in wrongful possession of the instrument.

§ 3–603. Tender of Payment.

(a) If tender of payment of an obligation to pay an instrument is made to a person entitled to enforce the instrument, the effect of tender is governed by principles of law applicable to tender of payment under a simple contract.

(b) If tender of payment of an obligation to pay an instrument is made to a person entitled to enforce the instrument and the tender is refused, there is discharge, to the extent of the amount of the tender, of the obligation of an indorser or accommodation party having a right of recourse with respect to the obligation to which the tender relates.

(c) If tender of payment of an amount due on an instrument is made to a person entitled to enforce the instrument, the obligation of the obligor to pay interest after the due date on the amount tendered is discharged. If presentment is required with respect to an instrument and the obligor is able and ready to pay on the due date at every place of payment stated in the instrument, the obligor is deemed to have made tender of payment on the due date to the person entitled to enforce the instrument.

§ 3–604. Discharge by Cancellation or Renunciation.

(a) A person entitled to enforce an instrument, with or without consideration, may discharge the obligation of a party to pay the instrument (i) by an intentional voluntary act, such as surrender of the instrument to the party, destruction, mutilation, or cancellation of the instrument, cancellation or striking out of the party's signature, or the addition of words to the instrument indicating discharge, or (ii) by agreeing not to sue or otherwise renouncing rights against the party by a signed writing.

(b) Cancellation or striking out of an indorsement pursuant to subsection (a) does not affect the status and rights of a party derived from the indorsement.

§ 3–605. Discharge of Indorsers and Accommodation Parties.

(a) In this section, the term "indorser" includes a drawer having the obligation described in Section 3–414(d).

(b) Discharge, under Section 3–604, of the obligation of a party to pay an instrument does not discharge the obligation of an indorser or accommodation party having a right of recourse against the discharged party.

(c) If a person entitled to enforce an instrument agrees, with or without consideration, to an extension of the due date of the obligation of a party to pay the instrument, the extension discharges an indorser or accommodation party having a right of recourse against the party whose obligation is extended to the extent the indorser or accommodation party proves that the extension caused loss to the indorser or accommodation party with respect to the right of recourse.

(d) If a person entitled to enforce an instrument agrees, with or without consideration, to a material modification of the obligation of a party other than an extension of the due date, the modification discharges the obligation of an indorser or accommodation party having a right of recourse against the person whose obligation is modified to the extent the modification causes loss to the indorser or accommodation party with respect to the right of recourse. The loss suffered by the indorser or accommodation party as a result of the modification is equal to the amount of the right of recourse unless the person enforcing the instrument proves that no loss was caused by the modification or that the loss caused by the modification was an amount less than the amount of the right of recourse.

(e) If the obligation of a party to pay an instrument is secured by an interest in collateral and a person entitled to enforce the instrument impairs the value of the interest in collateral, the obligation of an indorser or accommodation party having a right of recourse against the obligor is discharged to the extent of the impairment. The value of an interest in collateral is impaired to the extent (i) the value of the interest is reduced to an amount less than the amount of the right of recourse of the party asserting discharge, or (ii) the reduction in value of the interest causes an increase in the amount by which the amount of the right of recourse exceeds the value of the interest. The burden of proving impairment is on the party asserting discharge.

(f) If the obligation of a party is secured by an interest in collateral not provided by an accommodation party and a person entitled to enforce the instrument impairs the value of the interest in collateral, the obligation of any party who is jointly and severally liable with respect to the secured obligation is discharged to the extent the impairment causes the party asserting discharge to pay more than that party would have been obliged to pay, taking into account rights of contribution, if impairment had not occurred. If the party asserting discharge is an accommodation party not entitled to discharge under subsection (e), the party is deemed to have a right to contribution based on joint and several liability rather than a right to reimbursement. The burden of proving impairment is on the party asserting discharge.

(g) Under subsection (e) or (f), impairing value of an interest in collateral includes (i) failure to obtain or maintain perfection or recordation of the interest in collateral, (ii) release of collateral without substitution of collateral of equal value, (iii) failure to perform a duty to preserve the value of collateral owed, under Article 9 or other law, to a debtor or surety or other person secondarily liable, or (iv) failure to comply with applicable law in disposing of collateral.

(h) An accommodation party is not discharged under subsection (c), (d), or (e) unless the person entitled to enforce the instrument knows of the accommodation or has notice under Section 3–419(c) that the instrument was signed for accommodation.

(i) A party is not discharged under this section if (i) the party asserting discharge consents to the event or conduct that is the basis of the discharge, or (ii) the instrument or a separate agreement of the party provides for waiver of discharge under this section either specifically or by general language indicating that parties waive defenses based on suretyship or impairment of collateral.

ADDENDUM TO REVISED ARTICLE 3

Notes to Legislative Counsel

1. If revised Article 3 is adopted in your state, the reference in Section 2–511 to Section 3–802 should be changed to Section 3–310.

2. If revised Article 3 is adopted in your state and the Uniform Fiduciaries Act is also in effect in your state, you may want to consider amending Uniform Fiduciaries Act § 9 to conform to Section 3–307(b)(2)(iii) and (4)(iii). See Official Comment 3 to Section 3–307.

Revised Article 4
BANK DEPOSITS AND COLLECTIONS

Part 1 General Provisions and Definitions

§ 4–101. Short Title.

This Article may be cited as Uniform Commercial Code—Bank Deposits and Collections.

As amended in 1990.

§ 4–102. Applicability.

(a) To the extent that items within this Article are also within Articles 3 and 8, they are subject to those Articles. If there is conflict, this Article governs Article 3, but Article 8 governs this Article.

(b) The liability of a bank for action or non-action with respect to an item handled by it for purposes of presentment, payment, or collection is governed by the law of the place where the bank is located. In the case of action or non-action by or at a branch or separate office of a bank, its liability is governed by the law of the place where the branch or separate office is located.

§ 4–103. Variation by Agreement; Measure of Damages; Action Constituting Ordinary Care.

(a) The effect of the provisions of this Article may be varied by agreement, but the parties to the agreement cannot disclaim a bank's responsibility for its lack of good faith or failure to exercise ordinary care or limit the measure of damages for the lack or failure. However, the parties may determine by agreement the standards by which the bank's responsibility is to be measured if those standards are not manifestly unreasonable.

(b) Federal Reserve regulations and operating circulars, clearinghouse rules, and the like have the effect of agreements under subsection (a), whether or not specifically assented to by all parties interested in items handled.

(c) Action or non-action approved by this Article or pursuant to Federal Reserve regulations or operating circulars is the exercise of ordinary care and, in the absence of special instructions, action or non-action consistent with clearing-house rules and the like or with a general banking usage not disapproved by this Article, is prima facie the exercise of ordinary care.

(d) The specification or approval of certain procedures by this Article is not disapproval of other procedures that may be reasonable under the circumstances.

(e) The measure of damages for failure to exercise ordinary care in handling an item is the amount of the item reduced by an amount that could not have been realized by the exercise of ordinary care. If there is also bad faith it includes any other damages the party suffered as a proximate consequence.

As amended in 1990.

§ 4–104. Definitions and Index of Definitions.

(a) In this Article, unless the context otherwise requires:

(1) "Account" means any deposit or credit account with a bank, including a demand, time, savings, passbook, share draft, or like account, other than an account evidenced by a certificate of deposit;

(2) "Afternoon" means the period of a day between noon and midnight;

(3) "Banking day" means the part of a day on which a bank is open to the public for carrying on substantially all of its banking functions;

(4) "Clearing house" means an association of banks or other payors regularly clearing items;

(5) "Customer" means a person having an account with a bank or for whom a bank has agreed to collect items, including a bank that maintains an account at another bank;

(6) "Documentary draft" means a draft to be presented for acceptance or payment if specified documents, certificated securities (Section 8–102) or instructions for uncertificated securities (Section 8–102), or other certificates, statements, or the like are to be received by the drawee or other payor before acceptance or payment of the draft;

(7) "Draft" means a draft as defined in Section 3–104 or an item, other than an instrument, that is an order;

(8) "Drawee" means a person ordered in a draft to make payment;

(9) "Item" means an instrument or a promise or order to pay money handled by a bank for collection or payment. The term does not include a payment order governed by Article 4A or a credit or debit card slip;

(10) "Midnight deadline" with respect to a bank is midnight on its next banking day following the banking day on which it receives the relevant item or notice or from which the time for taking action commences to run, whichever is later;

(11) "Settle" means to pay in cash, by clearing-house settlement, in a charge or credit or by remittance, or otherwise as agreed. A settlement may be either provisional or final;

(12) "Suspends payments" with respect to a bank means that it has been closed by order of the supervisory authorities, that a public officer has been appointed to take it over, or that it ceases or refuses to make payments in the ordinary course of business.

(b) [Other definitions' section references deleted.]

(c) [Other definitions' section references deleted.]

(d) In addition, Article 1 contains general definitions and principles of construction and interpretation applicable throughout this Article.

§ 4–105. "Bank"; "Depositary Bank"; "Payor Bank"; "Intermediary Bank"; "Collecting Bank"; "Presenting Bank".

In this Article:

(1) "Bank" means a person engaged in the business of banking, including a savings bank, savings and loan association, credit union, or trust company;

(2) "Depositary bank" means the first bank to take an item even though it is also the payor bank, unless the item is presented for immediate payment over the counter;

(3) "Payor bank" means a bank that is the drawee of a draft;

(4) "Intermediary bank" means a bank to which an item is transferred in course of collection except the depositary or payor bank;

(5) "Collecting bank" means a bank handling an item for collection except the payor bank;

(6) "Presenting bank" means a bank presenting an item except a payor bank.

§ 4–106. Payable Through or Payable at Bank: Collecting Bank.

(a) If an item states that it is "payable through" a bank identified in the item, (i) the item designates the bank as a collecting bank and does not by itself authorize the bank to pay the item, and (ii) the item may be presented for payment only by or through the bank.

Alternative A

(b) If an item states that it is "payable at" a bank identified in the item, the item is equivalent to a draft drawn on the bank.

Alternative B

(b) If an item states that it is "payable at" a bank identified in the item, (i) the item designates the bank as a collecting bank and does not by itself authorize the bank to pay the item, and (ii) the item may be presented for payment only by or through the bank.

(c) If a draft names a nonbank drawee and it is unclear whether a bank named in the draft is a co-drawee or a collecting bank, the bank is a collecting bank.

As added in 1990.

§ 4–107. Separate Office of Bank.

A branch or separate office of a bank is a separate bank for the purpose of computing the time within which and determining the place at or to which action may be taken or notices or orders shall be given under this Article and under Article 3.

As amended in 1962 and 1990.

§ 4–108. Time of Receipt of Items.

(a) For the purpose of allowing time to process items, prove balances, and make the necessary entries on its books to determine its position for the day, a bank may fix an afternoon hour of 2 P.M. or later as a cutoff hour for the handling of money and items and the making of entries on its books.

(b) An item or deposit of money received on any day after a cutoff hour so fixed or after the close of the banking day may be treated as being received at the opening of the next banking day.

As amended in 1990.

§ 4–109. Delays.

(a) Unless otherwise instructed, a collecting bank in a good faith effort to secure payment of a specific item drawn on a payor other than a bank, and with or without the approval of any person involved, may waive, modify, or extend time limits imposed or permitted by this [act] for a period not exceeding two additional banking days without discharge of drawers or indorsers or liability to its transferor or a prior party.

(b) Delay by a collecting bank or payor bank beyond time limits prescribed or permitted by this [act] or by instructions is excused if (i) the delay is caused by interruption of communication or computer facilities, suspension of payments by another bank, war, emergency conditions, failure of equipment, or other circumstances beyond the control of the bank, and (ii) the bank exercises such diligence as the circumstances require.

§ 4–110. Electronic Presentment.

(a) "Agreement for electronic presentment" means an agreement, clearing-house rule, or Federal Reserve regulation or operating circular, providing that presentment of an item may be made by transmission of an image of an item or information describing the item ("presentment notice") rather than delivery of the item itself. The agreement may provide for procedures governing retention, presentment, payment, dishonor, and other matters concerning items subject to the agreement.

(b) Presentment of an item pursuant to an agreement for presentment is made when the presentment notice is received.

(c) If presentment is made by presentment notice, a reference to "item" or "check" in this Article means the presentment notice unless the context otherwise indicates.

As added in 1990.

§ 4–111. Statute of Limitations.

An action to enforce an obligation, duty, or right arising under this Article must be commenced within three years after the [cause of action] accrues.

As added in 1990.

Part 2 Collection of Items: Depositary and Collecting Banks

§ 4–201. Status of Collecting Bank as Agent and Provisional Status of Credits; Applicability of Article; Item Indorsed "Pay Any Bank".

(a) Unless a contrary intent clearly appears and before the time that a settlement given by a collecting bank for an item is or becomes final, the bank, with respect to an item, is an agent or sub-agent of the owner of the item and any settlement given for the item is provisional. This provision applies regardless of the form of indorsement or lack of indorsement and even though credit given for the item is subject to immediate withdrawal as of right or is in fact withdrawn; but the continuance of ownership of an item by its owner and any rights of the owner to proceeds of the item are subject to rights of a collecting bank, such as those resulting from outstanding advances on the item and rights of recoupment or setoff. If an item is handled by banks for purposes of presentment, payment, collection, or return, the relevant provisions of this Article apply even though action of the parties clearly establishes that a particular bank has purchased the item and is the owner of it.

(b) After an item has been indorsed with the words "pay any bank" or the like, only a bank may acquire the rights of a holder until the item has been:

(1) returned to the customer initiating collection; or

(2) specially indorsed by a bank to a person who is not a bank.

As amended in 1990.

§ 4–202. Responsibility for Collection or Return; When Action Timely.

(a) A collecting bank must exercise ordinary care in:

(1) presenting an item or sending it for presentment;

(2) sending notice of dishonor or nonpayment or returning an item other than a documentary draft to the bank's transferor after learning that the item has not been paid or accepted, as the case may be;

(3) settling for an item when the bank receives final settlement; and

(4) notifying its transferor of any loss or delay in transit within a reasonable time after discovery thereof.

(b) A collecting bank exercises ordinary care under subsection (a) by taking proper action before its midnight deadline following

receipt of an item, notice, or settlement. Taking proper action within a reasonably longer time may constitute the exercise of ordinary care, but the bank has the burden of establishing timeliness.

(c) Subject to subsection (a)(1), a bank is not liable for the insolvency, neglect, misconduct, mistake, or default of another bank or person or for loss or destruction of an item in the possession of others or in transit.

As amended in 1990.

§ 4–203. Effect of Instructions.

Subject to Article 3 concerning conversion of instruments (Section 3–420) and restrictive indorsements (Section 3–206), only a collecting bank's transferor can give instructions that affect the bank or constitute notice to it, and a collecting bank is not liable to prior parties for any action taken pursuant to the instructions or in accordance with any agreement with its transferor.

§ 4–204. Methods of Sending and Presenting; Sending Directly to Payor Bank.

(a) A collecting bank shall send items by a reasonably prompt method, taking into consideration relevant instructions, the nature of the item, the number of those items on hand, the cost of collection involved, and the method generally used by it or others to present those items.

(b) A collecting bank may send:

(1) an item directly to the payor bank;

(2) an item to a nonbank payor if authorized by its transferor; and

(3) an item other than documentary drafts to a nonbank payor, if authorized by Federal Reserve regulation or operating circular, clearing-house rule, or the like.

(c) Presentment may be made by a presenting bank at a place where the payor bank or other payor has requested that presentment be made.

As amended in 1990.

§ 4–205. Depositary Bank Holder of Unindorsed Item.

If a customer delivers an item to a depositary bank for collection:

(1) the depositary bank becomes a holder of the item at the time it receives the item for collection if the customer at the time of delivery was a holder of the item, whether or not the customer indorses the item, and, if the bank satisfies the other requirements of Section 3–302, it is a holder in due course; and

(2) the depositary bank warrants to collecting banks, the payor bank or other payor, and the drawer that the amount of the item was paid to the customer or deposited to the customer's account.

As amended in 1990.

§ 4–206. Transfer Between Banks.

Any agreed method that identifies the transferor bank is sufficient for the item's further transfer to another bank.

As amended in 1990.

§ 4–207. Transfer Warranties.

(a) A customer or collecting bank that transfers an item and receives a settlement or other consideration warrants to the transferee and to any subsequent collecting bank that:

(1) the warrantor is a person entitled to enforce the item;

(2) all signatures on the item are authentic and authorized;

(3) the item has not been altered;

(4) the item is not subject to a defense or claim in recoupment (Section 3–305(a)) of any party that can be asserted against the warrantor; and

(5) the warrantor has no knowledge of any insolvency proceeding commenced with respect to the maker or acceptor or, in the case of an unaccepted draft, the drawer.

(b) If an item is dishonored, a customer or collecting bank transferring the item and receiving settlement or other consideration is obliged to pay the amount due on the item (i) according to the terms of the item at the time it was transferred, or (ii) if the transfer was of an incomplete item, according to its terms when completed as stated in Sections 3–115 and 3–407. The obligation of a transferor is owed to the transferee and to any subsequent collecting bank that takes the item in good faith. A transferor cannot disclaim its obligation under this subsection by an indorsement stating that it is made "without recourse" or otherwise disclaiming liability.

(c) A person to whom the warranties under subsection (a) are made and who took the item in good faith may recover from the warrantor as damages for breach of warranty an amount equal to the loss suffered as a result of the breach, but not more than the amount of the item plus expenses and loss of interest incurred as a result of the breach.

(d) The warranties stated in subsection (a) cannot be disclaimed with respect to checks. Unless notice of a claim for breach of warranty is given to the warrantor within 30 days after the claimant has reason to know of the breach and the identity of the warrantor, the warrantor is discharged to the extent of any loss caused by the delay in giving notice of the claim.

(e) A cause of action for breach of warranty under this section accrues when the claimant has reason to know of the breach.

As amended in 1990.

§ 4–208. Presentment Warranties.

(a) If an unaccepted draft is presented to the drawee for payment or acceptance and the drawee pays or accepts the draft, (i) the person obtaining payment or acceptance, at the time of presentment, and (ii) a previous transferor of the draft, at the time of transfer, warrant to the drawee that pays or accepts the draft in good faith that:

(1) the warrantor is, or was, at the time the warrantor transferred the draft, a person entitled to enforce the draft or authorized to obtain payment or acceptance of the draft on behalf of a person entitled to enforce the draft;

(2) the draft has not been altered; and

(3) the warrantor has no knowledge that the signature of the purported drawer of the draft is unauthorized.

(b) A drawee making payment may recover from a warrantor damages for breach of warranty equal to the amount paid by the drawee less the amount the drawee received or is entitled to receive from the drawer because of the payment. In addition, the drawee is entitled to compensation for expenses and loss of interest resulting from the breach. The right of the drawee to recover damages under this subsection is not affected by any failure of the drawee to exercise ordinary care in making payment. If the drawee accepts the draft (i) breach of warranty is a defense to the obligation of the acceptor, and

(ii) if the acceptor makes payment with respect to the draft, the acceptor is entitled to recover from a warrantor for breach of warranty the amounts stated in this subsection.

(c) If a drawee asserts a claim for breach of warranty under subsection (a) based on an unauthorized indorsement of the draft or an alteration of the draft, the warrantor may defend by proving that the indorsement is effective under Section 3–404 or 3–405 or the drawer is precluded under Section 3–406 or 4–406 from asserting against the drawee the unauthorized indorsement or alteration.

(d) If (i) a dishonored draft is presented for payment to the drawer or an indorser or (ii) any other item is presented for payment to a party obliged to pay the item, and the item is paid, the person obtaining payment and a prior transferor of the item warrant to the person making payment in good faith that the warrantor is, or was, at the time the warrantor transferred the item, a person entitled to enforce the item or authorized to obtain payment on behalf of a person entitled to enforce the item. The person making payment may recover from any warrantor for breach of warranty an amount equal to the amount paid plus expenses and loss of interest resulting from the breach.

(e) The warranties stated in subsections (a) and (d) cannot be disclaimed with respect to checks. Unless notice of a claim for breach of warranty is given to the warrantor within 30 days after the claimant has reason to know of the breach and the identity of the warrantor, the warrantor is discharged to the extent of any loss caused by the delay in giving notice of the claim.

(f) A cause of action for breach of warranty under this section accrues when the claimant has reason to know of the breach.

As amended in 1990.

§ 4–209. Encoding and Retention Warranties.

(a) A person who encodes information on or with respect to an item after issue warrants to any subsequent collecting bank and to the payor bank or other payor that the information is correctly encoded. If the customer of a depositary bank encodes, that bank also makes the warranty.

(b) A person who undertakes to retain an item pursuant to an agreement for electronic presentment warrants to any subsequent collecting bank and to the payor bank or other payor that retention and presentment of the item comply with the agreement. If a customer of a depositary bank undertakes to retain an item, that bank also makes this warranty.

(c) A person to whom warranties are made under this section and who took the item in good faith may recover from the warrantor as damages for breach of warranty an amount equal to the loss suffered as a result of the breach, plus expenses and loss of interest incurred as a result of the breach.

As added in 1990.

§ 4–210. Security Interest of Collecting Bank in Items, Accompanying Documents and Proceeds.

(a) A collecting bank has a security interest in an item and any accompanying documents or the proceeds of either:

(1) in case of an item deposited in an account, to the extent to which credit given for the item has been withdrawn or applied;

(2) in case of an item for which it has given credit available for withdrawal as of right, to the extent of the credit given, whether

or not the credit is drawn upon or there is a right of charge-back; or

(3) if it makes an advance on or against the item.

(b) If credit given for several items received at one time or pursuant to a single agreement is withdrawn or applied in part, the security interest remains upon all the items, any accompanying documents or the proceeds of either. For the purpose of this section, credits first given are first withdrawn.

(c) Receipt by a collecting bank of a final settlement for an item is a realization on its security interest in the item, accompanying documents, and proceeds. So long as the bank does not receive final settlement for the item or give up possession of the item or accompanying documents for purposes other than collection, the security interest continues to that extent and is subject to Article 9, but:

(1) no security agreement is necessary to make the security interest enforceable (Section 9–203(1)(a));

(2) no filing is required to perfect the security interest; and

(3) the security interest has priority over conflicting perfected security interests in the item, accompanying documents, or proceeds.

As amended in 1990 and 1999.

§ 4–211. When Bank Gives Value for Purposes of Holder in Due Course.

For purposes of determining its status as a holder in due course, a bank has given value to the extent it has a security interest in an item, if the bank otherwise complies with the requirements of Section 3–302 on what constitutes a holder in due course.

As amended in 1990.

§ 4–212. Presentment by Notice of Item Not Payable by, Through, or at Bank; Liability of Drawer or Indorser.

(a) Unless otherwise instructed, a collecting bank may present an item not payable by, through, or at a bank by sending to the party to accept or pay a written notice that the bank holds the item for acceptance or payment. The notice must be sent in time to be received on or before the day when presentment is due and the bank must meet any requirement of the party to accept or pay under Section 3–501 by the close of the bank's next banking day after it knows of the requirement.

(b) If presentment is made by notice and payment, acceptance, or request for compliance with a requirement under Section 3–501 is not received by the close of business on the day after maturity or, in the case of demand items, by the close of business on the third banking day after notice was sent, the presenting bank may treat the item as dishonored and charge any drawer or indorser by sending it notice of the facts.

As amended in 1990.

§ 4–213. Medium and Time of Settlement by Bank.

(a) With respect to settlement by a bank, the medium and time of settlement may be prescribed by Federal Reserve regulations or circulars, clearing-house rules, and the like, or agreement. In the absence of such prescription:

(1) the medium of settlement is cash or credit to an account in a Federal Reserve bank of or specified by the person to receive settlement; and

(2) the time of settlement is:

(i) with respect to tender of settlement by cash, a cashier's check, or teller's check, when the cash or check is sent or delivered;

(ii) with respect to tender of settlement by credit in an account in a Federal Reserve Bank, when the credit is made;

(iii) with respect to tender of settlement by a credit or debit to an account in a bank, when the credit or debit is made or, in the case of tender of settlement by authority to charge an account, when the authority is sent or delivered; or

(iv) with respect to tender of settlement by a funds transfer, when payment is made pursuant to Section 4A–406(a) to the person receiving settlement.

(b) If the tender of settlement is not by a medium authorized by subsection (a) or the time of settlement is not fixed by subsection (a), no settlement occurs until the tender of settlement is accepted by the person receiving settlement.

(c) If settlement for an item is made by cashier's check or teller's check and the person receiving settlement, before its midnight deadline:

(1) presents or forwards the check for collection, settlement is final when the check is finally paid; or

(2) fails to present or forward the check for collection, settlement is final at the midnight deadline of the person receiving settlement.

(d) If settlement for an item is made by giving authority to charge the account of the bank giving settlement in the bank receiving settlement, settlement is final when the charge is made by the bank receiving settlement if there are funds available in the account for the amount of the item.

As amended in 1990.

§ 4–214. Right of Charge-Back or Refund; Liability of Collecting Bank: Return of Item.

(a) If a collecting bank has made provisional settlement with its customer for an item and fails by reason of dishonor, suspension of payments by a bank, or otherwise to receive settlement for the item which is or becomes final, the bank may revoke the settlement given by it, charge back the amount of any credit given for the item to its customer's account, or obtain refund from its customer, whether or not it is able to return the item, if by its midnight deadline or within a longer reasonable time after it learns the facts it returns the item or sends notification of the facts. If the return or notice is delayed beyond the bank's midnight deadline or a longer reasonable time after it learns the facts, the bank may revoke the settlement, charge back the credit, or obtain refund from its customer, but it is liable for any loss resulting from the delay. These rights to revoke, charge back, and obtain refund terminate if and when a settlement for the item received by the bank is or becomes final.

(b) A collecting bank returns an item when it is sent or delivered to the bank's customer or transferor or pursuant to its instructions.

(c) A depositary bank that is also the payor may charge back the amount of an item to its customer's account or obtain refund in accordance with the section governing return of an item received by a payor bank for credit on its books (Section 4–301).

(d) The right to charge back is not affected by:

(1) previous use of a credit given for the item; or

(2) failure by any bank to exercise ordinary care with respect to the item, but a bank so failing remains liable.

(e) A failure to charge back or claim refund does not affect other rights of the bank against the customer or any other party.

(f) If credit is given in dollars as the equivalent of the value of an item payable in foreign money, the dollar amount of any charge-back or refund must be calculated on the basis of the bank-offered spot rate for the foreign money prevailing on the day when the person entitled to the charge-back or refund learns that it will not receive payment in ordinary course.

As amended in 1990.

§ 4–215. Final Payment of Item by Payor Bank; When Provisional Debits and Credits Become Final; When Certain Credits Become Available for Withdrawal.

(a) An item is finally paid by a payor bank when the bank has first done any of the following:

(1) paid the item in cash;

(2) settled for the item without having a right to revoke the settlement under statute, clearing-house rule, or agreement; or

(3) made a provisional settlement for the item and failed to revoke the settlement in the time and manner permitted by statute, clearing-house rule, or agreement.

(b) If provisional settlement for an item does not become final, the item is not finally paid.

(c) If provisional settlement for an item between the presenting and payor banks is made through a clearing house or by debits or credits in an account between them, then to the extent that provisional debits or credits for the item are entered in accounts between the presenting and payor banks or between the presenting and successive prior collecting banks seriatim, they become final upon final payment of the item by the payor bank.

(d) If a collecting bank receives a settlement for an item which is or becomes final, the bank is accountable to its customer for the amount of the item and any provisional credit given for the item in an account with its customer becomes final.

(e) Subject to (i) applicable law stating a time for availability of funds and (ii) any right of the bank to apply the credit to an obligation of the customer, credit given by a bank for an item in a customer's account becomes available for withdrawal as of right:

(1) if the bank has received a provisional settlement for the item, when the settlement becomes final and the bank has had a reasonable time to receive return of the item and the item has not been received within that time;

(2) if the bank is both the depositary bank and the payor bank, and the item is finally paid, at the opening of the bank's second banking day following receipt of the item.

(f) Subject to applicable law stating a time for availability of funds and any right of a bank to apply a deposit to an obligation of the depositor, a deposit of money becomes available for withdrawal as of right at the opening of the bank's next banking day after receipt of the deposit.

As amended in 1990.

§ 4– 216. Insolvency and Preference.

(a) If an item is in or comes into the possession of a payor or collecting bank that suspends payment and the item has not been finally paid, the item must be returned by the receiver, trustee, or agent in charge of the closed bank to the presenting bank or the closed bank's customer.

(b) If a payor bank finally pays an item and suspends payments without making a settlement for the item with its customer or the presenting bank which settlement is or becomes final, the owner of the item has a preferred claim against the payor bank.

(c) If a payor bank gives or a collecting bank gives or receives a provisional settlement for an item and thereafter suspends payments, the suspension does not prevent or interfere with the settlement's becoming final if the finality occurs automatically upon the lapse of certain time or the happening of certain events.

(d) If a collecting bank receives from subsequent parties settlement for an item, which settlement is or becomes final and the bank suspends payments without making a settlement for the item with its customer which settlement is or becomes final, the owner of the item has a preferred claim against the collecting bank.

As amended in 1990.

Part 3 Collection of Items: Payor Banks

§ 4–301. Deferred Posting; Recovery of Payment by Return of Items; Time of Dishonor; Return of Items by Payor Bank.

(a) If a payor bank settles for a demand item other than a documentary draft presented otherwise than for immediate payment over the counter before midnight of the banking day of receipt, the payor bank may revoke the settlement and recover the settlement if, before it has made final payment and before its midnight deadline, it

(1) returns the item; or

(2) sends written notice of dishonor or nonpayment if the item is unavailable for return.

(b) If a demand item is received by a payor bank for credit on its books, it may return the item or send notice of dishonor and may revoke any credit given or recover the amount thereof withdrawn by its customer, if it acts within the time limit and in the manner specified in subsection (a).

(c) Unless previous notice of dishonor has been sent, an item is dishonored at the time when for purposes of dishonor it is returned or notice sent in accordance with this section.

(d) An item is returned:

(1) as to an item presented through a clearing house, when it is delivered to the presenting or last collecting bank or to the clearing house or is sent or delivered in accordance with clearing-house rules; or

(2) in all other cases, when it is sent or delivered to the bank's customer or transferor or pursuant to instructions.

As amended in 1990.

§ 4–302. Payor Bank's Responsibility for Late Return of Item.

(a) If an item is presented to and received by a payor bank, the bank is accountable for the amount of:

(1) a demand item, other than a documentary draft, whether properly payable or not, if the bank, in any case in which it is not also the depositary bank, retains the item beyond midnight of the banking day of receipt without settling for it or, whether or not it is also the depositary bank, does not pay or return the item or send notice of dishonor until after its midnight deadline; or

(2) any other properly payable item unless, within the time allowed for acceptance or payment of that item, the bank either accepts or pays the item or returns it and accompanying documents.

(b) The liability of a payor bank to pay an item pursuant to subsection (a) is subject to defenses based on breach of a presentment warranty (Section 4–208) or proof that the person seeking enforcement of the liability presented or transferred the item for the purpose of defrauding the payor bank.

As amended in 1990.

§ 4–303. When Items Subject to Notice, Stop-Payment Order, Legal Process, or Setoff; Order in Which Items May Be Charged or Certified.

(a) Any knowledge, notice, or stop-payment order received by, legal process served upon, or setoff exercised by a payor bank comes too late to terminate, suspend, or modify the bank's right or duty to pay an item or to charge its customer's account for the item if the knowledge, notice, stop-payment order, or legal process is received or served and a reasonable time for the bank to act thereon expires or the setoff is exercised after the earliest of the following:

(1) the bank accepts or certifies the item;

(2) the bank pays the item in cash;

(3) the bank settles for the item without having a right to revoke the settlement under statute, clearing-house rule, or agreement;

(4) the bank becomes accountable for the amount of the item under Section 4–302 dealing with the payor bank's responsibility for late return of items; or

(5) with respect to checks, a cutoff hour no earlier than one hour after the opening of the next banking day after the banking day on which the bank received the check and no later than the close of that next banking day or, if no cutoff hour is fixed, the close of the next banking day after the banking day on which the bank received the check.

(b) Subject to subsection (a), items may be accepted, paid, certified, or charged to the indicated account of its customer in any order.

As amended in 1990.

Part 4 Relationship Between Payor Bank and Its Customer

§ 4–401. When Bank May Charge Customer's Account.

(a) A bank may charge against the account of a customer an item that is properly payable from the account even though the charge creates an overdraft. An item is properly payable if it is authorized by the customer and is in accordance with any agreement between the customer and bank.

(b) A customer is not liable for the amount of an overdraft if the customer neither signed the item nor benefited from the proceeds of the item.

(c) A bank may charge against the account of a customer a check that is otherwise properly payable from the account, even though payment was made before the date of the check, unless the customer has given notice to the bank of the postdating describing the check with reasonable certainty. The notice is effective for the period stated in Section 4–403(b) for stop-payment orders, and must be received at such time and in such manner as to afford the bank a reasonable opportunity to act on it before the bank takes any action with respect to the check described in Section 4–303. If a bank charges against the account of a customer a check before the date stated in the notice of postdating, the bank is liable for damages for the loss resulting from its act. The loss may include damages for dishonor of subsequent items under Section 4–402.

(d) A bank that in good faith makes payment to a holder may charge the indicated account of its customer according to:

(1) the original terms of the altered item; or

(2) the terms of the completed item, even though the bank knows the item has been completed unless the bank has notice that the completion was improper.

As amended in 1990.

§ 4–402. Bank's Liability to Customer for Wrongful Dishonor; Time of Determining Insufficiency of Account.

(a) Except as otherwise provided in this Article, a payor bank wrongfully dishonors an item if it dishonors an item that is properly payable, but a bank may dishonor an item that would create an overdraft unless it has agreed to pay the overdraft.

(b) A payor bank is liable to its customer for damages proximately caused by the wrongful dishonor of an item. Liability is limited to actual damages proved and may include damages for an arrest or prosecution of the customer or other consequential damages. Whether any consequential damages are proximately caused by the wrongful dishonor is a question of fact to be determined in each case.

(c) A payor bank's determination of the customer's account balance on which a decision to dishonor for insufficiency of available funds is based may be made at any time between the time the item is received by the payor bank and the time that the payor bank returns the item or gives notice in lieu of return, and no more than one determination need be made. If, at the election of the payor bank, a subsequent balance determination is made for the purpose of reevaluating the bank's decision to dishonor the item, the account balance at that time is determinative of whether a dishonor for insufficiency of available funds is wrongful.

As amended in 1990.

§ 4–403. Customer's Right to Stop Payment; Burden of Proof of Loss.

(a) A customer or any person authorized to draw on the account if there is more than one person may stop payment of any item drawn on the customer's account or close the account by an order to the bank describing the item or account with reasonable certainty received at a time and in a manner that affords the bank a reasonable opportunity to act on it before any action by the bank with respect to the item described in Section 4–303. If the signature of more than one person is required to draw on an account, any of these persons may stop payment or close the account.

(b) A stop-payment order is effective for six months, but it lapses after 14 calendar days if the original order was oral and was not confirmed in writing within that period. A stop-payment order may be renewed for additional six-month periods by a writing given to the bank within a period during which the stop-payment order is effective.

(c) The burden of establishing the fact and amount of loss resulting from the payment of an item contrary to a stop-payment order or order to close an account is on the customer. The loss from payment of an item contrary to a stop-payment order may include damages for dishonor of subsequent items under Section 4–402.

As amended in 1990.

§ 4–404. Bank Not Obliged to Pay Check More Than Six Months Old.

A bank is under no obligation to a customer having a checking account to pay a check, other than a certified check, which is presented more than six months after its date, but it may charge its customer's account for a payment made thereafter in good faith.

§ 4–405. Death or Incompetence of Customer.

(a) A payor or collecting bank's authority to accept, pay, or collect an item or to account for proceeds of its collection, if otherwise effective, is not rendered ineffective by incompetence of a customer of either bank existing at the time the item is issued or its collection is undertaken if the bank does not know of an adjudication of incompetence. Neither death nor incompetence of a customer revokes the authority to accept, pay, collect, or account until the bank knows of the fact of death or of an adjudication of incompetence and has reasonable opportunity to act on it.

(b) Even with knowledge, a bank may for 10 days after the date of death pay or certify checks drawn on or before the date unless ordered to stop payment by a person claiming an interest in the account.

As amended in 1990.

§ 4–406. Customer's Duty to Discover and Report Unauthorized Signature or Alteration.

(a) A bank that sends or makes available to a customer a statement of account showing payment of items for the account shall either return or make available to the customer the items paid or provide information in the statement of account sufficient to allow the customer reasonably to identify the items paid. The statement of account provides sufficient information if the item is described by item number, amount, and date of payment.

(b) If the items are not returned to the customer, the person retaining the items shall either retain the items or, if the items are destroyed, maintain the capacity to furnish legible copies of the items until the expiration of seven years after receipt of the items. A customer may request an item from the bank that paid the item, and that bank must provide in a reasonable time either the item or, if the item has been destroyed or is not otherwise obtainable, a legible copy of the item.

(c) If a bank sends or makes available a statement of account or items pursuant to subsection (a), the customer must exercise reasonable promptness in examining the statement or the items to determine whether any payment was not authorized because of an alteration of an item or because a purported signature by or on behalf of the customer was not authorized. If, based on the statement or items provided, the customer should reasonably have dis-

covered the unauthorized payment, the customer must promptly notify the bank of the relevant facts.

(d) If the bank proves that the customer failed, with respect to an item, to comply with the duties imposed on the customer by subsection (c), the customer is precluded from asserting against the bank:

(1) the customer's unauthorized signature or any alteration on the item, if the bank also proves that it suffered a loss by reason of the failure; and

(2) the customer's unauthorized signature or alteration by the same wrongdoer on any other item paid in good faith by the bank if the payment was made before the bank received notice from the customer of the unauthorized signature or alteration and after the customer had been afforded a reasonable period of time, not exceeding 30 days, in which to examine the item or statement of account and notify the bank.

(e) If subsection (d) applies and the customer proves that the bank failed to exercise ordinary care in paying the item and that the failure substantially contributed to loss, the loss is allocated between the customer precluded and the bank asserting the preclusion according to the extent to which the failure of the customer to comply with subsection (c) and the failure of the bank to exercise ordinary care contributed to the loss. If the customer proves that the bank did not pay the item in good faith, the preclusion under subsection (d) does not apply.

(f) Without regard to care or lack of care of either the customer or the bank, a customer who does not within one year after the statement or items are made available to the customer (subsection (a)) discover and report the customer's unauthorized signature on or any alteration on the item is precluded from asserting against the bank the unauthorized signature or alteration. If there is a preclusion under this subsection, the payor bank may not recover for breach or warranty under Section 4–208 with respect to the unauthorized signature or alteration to which the preclusion applies.

As amended in 1990.

§ 4–407. Payor Bank's Right to Subrogation on Improper Payment.

If a payor has paid an item over the order of the drawer or maker to stop payment, or after an account has been closed, or otherwise under circumstances giving a basis for objection by the drawer or maker, to prevent unjust enrichment and only to the extent necessary to prevent loss to the bank by reason of its payment of the item, the payor bank is subrogated to the rights

(1) of any holder in due course on the item against the drawer or maker;

(2) of the payee or any other holder of the item against the drawer or maker either on the item or under the transaction out of which the item arose; and

(3) of the drawer or maker against the payee or any other holder of the item with respect to the transaction out of which the item arose.

As amended in 1990.

Part 5 Collection of Documentary Drafts

§ 4–501. Handling of Documentary Drafts; Duty to Send for Presentment and to Notify Customer of Dishonor.

A bank that takes a documentary draft for collection shall present or send the draft and accompanying documents for presentment and, upon learning that the draft has not been paid or accepted in due course, shall seasonably notify its customer of the fact even though it may have discounted or bought the draft or extended credit available for withdrawal as of right.

As amended in 1990.

§ 4–502. Presentment of "On Arrival" Drafts.

If a draft or the relevant instructions require presentment "on arrival", "when goods arrive" or the like, the collecting bank need not present until in its judgment a reasonable time for arrival of the goods has expired. Refusal to pay or accept because the goods have not arrived is not dishonor; the bank must notify its transferor of the refusal but need not present the draft again until it is instructed to do so or learns of the arrival of the goods.

§ 4–503. Responsibility of Presenting Bank for Documents and Goods; Report of Reasons for Dishonor; Referee in Case of Need.

Unless otherwise instructed and except as provided in Article 5, a bank presenting a documentary draft:

(1) must deliver the documents to the drawee on acceptance of the draft if it is payable more than three days after presentment, otherwise, only on payment; and

(2) upon dishonor, either in the case of presentment for acceptance or presentment for payment, may seek and follow instructions from any referee in case of need designated in the draft or, if the presenting bank does not choose to utilize the referee's services, it must use diligence and good faith to ascertain the reason for dishonor, must notify its transferor of the dishonor and of the results of its effort to ascertain the reasons therefor, and must request instructions.

However, the presenting bank is under no obligation with respect to goods represented by the documents except to follow any reasonable instructions seasonably received; it has a right to reimbursement for any expense incurred in following instructions and to prepayment of or indemnity for those expenses.

As amended in 1990.

§ 4–504. Privilege of Presenting Bank to Deal With Goods; Security Interest for Expenses.

(a) A presenting bank that, following the dishonor of a documentary draft, has seasonably requested instructions but does not receive them within a reasonable time may store, sell, or otherwise deal with the goods in any reasonable manner.

(b) For its reasonable expenses incurred by action under subsection (a) the presenting bank has a lien upon the goods or their proceeds, which may be foreclosed in the same manner as an unpaid seller's lien.

As amended in 1990.

Article 4A
FUNDS TRANSFERS

Part 1 Subject Matter and Definitions

§ 4A–101. Short Title.

This Article may be cited as Uniform Commercial Code—Funds Transfers.

§ 4A–102. Subject Matter.

Except as otherwise provided in Section 4A–108, this Article applies to funds transfers defined in Section 4A–104.

§ 4A–103. Payment Order–Definitions.

(a) In this Article:

(1) "Payment order" means an instruction of a sender to a receiving bank, transmitted orally, electronically, or in writing, to pay, or to cause another bank to pay, a fixed or determinable amount of money to a beneficiary if:

(i) the instruction does not state a condition to payment to the beneficiary other than time of payment,

(ii) the receiving bank is to be reimbursed by debiting an account of, or otherwise receiving payment from, the sender, and

(iii) the instruction is transmitted by the sender directly to the receiving bank or to an agent, funds-transfer system, or communication system for transmittal to the receiving bank.

(2) "Beneficiary" means the person to be paid by the beneficiary's bank.

(3) "Beneficiary's bank" means the bank identified in a payment order in which an account of the beneficiary is to be credited pursuant to the order or which otherwise is to make payment to the beneficiary if the order does not provide for payment to an account.

(4) "Receiving bank" means the bank to which the sender's instruction is addressed.

(5) "Sender" means the person giving the instruction to the receiving bank.

(b) If an instruction complying with subsection (a)(1) is to make more than one payment to a beneficiary, the instruction is a separate payment order with respect to each payment.

(c) A payment order is issued when it is sent to the receiving bank.

§ 4A–104. Funds Transfer–Definitions.

In this Article:

(a) "Funds transfer" means the series of transactions, beginning with the originator's payment order, made for the purpose of making payment to the beneficiary of the order. The term includes any payment order issued by the originator's bank or an intermediary bank intended to carry out the originator's payment order. A funds transfer is completed by acceptance by the beneficiary's bank of a payment order for the benefit of the beneficiary of the originator's payment order.

(b) "Intermediary bank" means a receiving bank other than the originator's bank or the beneficiary's bank.

(c) "Originator" means the sender of the first payment order in a funds transfer.

(d) "Originator's bank" means (i) the receiving bank to which the payment order of the originator is issued if the originator is not a bank, or (ii) the originator if the originator is a bank.

§ 4A–105. Other Definitions.

(a) In this Article:

(1) "Authorized account" means a deposit account of a customer in a bank designated by the customer as a source of

payment of payment orders issued by the customer to the bank. If a customer does not so designate an account, any account of the customer is an authorized account if payment of a payment order from that account is not inconsistent with a restriction on the use of that account.

(2) "Bank" means a person engaged in the business of banking and includes a savings bank, savings and loan association, credit union, and trust company. A branch or separate office of a bank is a separate bank for purposes of this Article.

(3) "Customer" means a person, including a bank, having an account with a bank or from whom a bank has agreed to receive payment orders.

(4) "Funds-transfer business day" of a receiving bank means the part of a day during which the receiving bank is open for the receipt, processing, and transmittal of payment orders and cancellations and amendments of payment orders.

(5) "Funds-transfer system" means a wire transfer network, automated clearing house, or other communication system of a clearing house or other association of banks through which a payment order by a bank may be transmitted to the bank to which the order is addressed.

(6) "Good faith" means honesty in fact and the observance of reasonable commercial standards of fair dealing.

(7) "Prove" with respect to a fact means to meet the burden of establishing the fact (Section 1–201(8)).

(b) Other definitions applying to this Article and the sections in which they appear are:

"Acceptance"	Section 4A–209
"Beneficiary"	Section 4A–103
"Beneficiary's bank"	Section 4A–103
"Executed"	Section 4A–301
"Execution date"	Section 4A–301
"Funds transfer"	Section 4A–104
"Funds-transfer system rule"	Section 4A–501
"Intermediary bank"	Section 4A–104
"Originator"	Section 4A–104
"Originator's bank"	Section 4A–104
"Payment by beneficiary's bank to beneficiary"	Section 4A–405
"Payment by originator to beneficiary"	Section 4A–406
"Payment by sender to receiving bank"	Section 4A–403
"Payment date"	Section 4A–401
"Payment order"	Section 4A–103
"Receiving bank"	Section 4A–103
"Security procedure"	Section 4A–201
"Sender"	Section 4A–103

(c) The following definitions in Article 4 apply to this Article:

"Clearing house"	Section 4–104
"Item"	Section 4–104
"Suspends payments"	Section 4–104

(d) In addition, Article 1 contains general definitions and principles of construction and interpretation applicable throughout this Article.

§ 4A–106. Time Payment Order Is Received.

(a) The time of receipt of a payment order or communication cancelling or amending a payment order is determined by the rules applicable to receipt of a notice stated in Section 1–201(27). A receiving bank may fix a cut-off time or times on a funds-transfer business day for the receipt and processing of payment orders and communications cancelling or amending payment orders. Different cut-off times may apply to payment orders, cancellations, or amendments, or to different categories of payment orders, cancellations, or amendments. A cut-off time may apply to senders generally or different cut-off times may apply to different senders or categories of payment orders. If a payment order or communication cancelling or amending a payment order is received after the close of a funds-transfer business day or after the appropriate cut-off time on a funds-transfer business day, the receiving bank may treat the payment order or communication as received at the opening of the next funds-transfer business day.

(b) If this Article refers to an execution date or payment date or states a day on which a receiving bank is required to take action, and the date or day does not fall on a funds-transfer business day, the next day that is a funds-transfer business day is treated as the date or day stated, unless the contrary is stated in this Article.

§ 4A–107. Federal Reserve Regulations and Operating Circulars.

Regulations of the Board of Governors of the Federal Reserve System and operating circulars of the Federal Reserve Banks supersede any inconsistent provision of this Article to the extent of the inconsistency.

§ 4A–108. Exclusion of Consumer Transactions Governed by Federal Law.

This Article does not apply to a funds transfer any part of which is governed by the Electronic Fund Transfer Act of 1978 (Title XX, Public Law 95–630, 92 Stat. 3728, 15 U.S.C. § 1693 et seq.) as amended from time to time.

Part 2 Issue and Acceptance of Payment Order

§ 4A–201. Security Procedure.

"Security procedure" means a procedure established by agreement of a customer and a receiving bank for the purpose of (i) verifying that a payment order or communication amending or cancelling a payment order is that of the customer, or (ii) detecting error in the transmission or the content of the payment order or communication. A security procedure may require the use of algorithms or other codes, identifying words or numbers, encryption, callback procedures, or similar security devices. Comparison of a signature on a payment order or communication with an authorized specimen signature of the customer is not by itself a security procedure.

§ 4A–202. Authorized and Verified Payment Orders.

(a) A payment order received by the receiving bank is the authorized order of the person identified as sender if that person authorized the order or is otherwise bound by it under the law of agency.

(b) If a bank and its customer have agreed that the authenticity of payment orders issued to the bank in the name of the customer as sender will be verified pursuant to a security procedure, a payment order received by the receiving bank is effective as the order of the customer, whether or not authorized, if (i) the security procedure is a commercially reasonable method of providing security against unauthorized payment orders, and (ii) the bank proves that it accepted the payment order in good faith and in compliance with the security procedure and any written agreement or instruction of the customer restricting acceptance of payment orders issued in the name of the customer. The bank is not required to follow an instruction that violates a written agreement with the customer or notice of which is not received at a time and in a manner affording the bank a reasonable opportunity to act on it before the payment order is accepted.

(c) Commercial reasonableness of a security procedure is a question of law to be determined by considering the wishes of the customer expressed to the bank, the circumstances of the customer known to the bank, including the size, type, and frequency of payment orders normally issued by the customer to the bank, alternative security procedures offered to the customer, and security procedures in general use by customers and receiving banks similarly situated. A security procedure is deemed to be commercially reasonable if (i) the security procedure was chosen by the customer after the bank offered, and the customer refused, a security procedure that was commercially reasonable for that customer, and (ii) the customer expressly agreed in writing to be bound by any payment order, whether or not authorized, issued in its name and accepted by the bank in compliance with the security procedure chosen by the customer.

(d) The term "sender" in this Article includes the customer in whose name a payment order is issued if the order is the authorized order of the customer under subsection (a), or it is effective as the order of the customer under subsection (b).

(e) This section applies to amendments and cancellations of payment orders to the same extent it applies to payment orders.

(f) Except as provided in this section and in Section 4A–203(a)(1), rights and obligations arising under this section or Section 4A–203 may not be varied by agreement.

§ 4A–203. Unenforceability of Certain Verified Payment Orders.

(a) If an accepted payment order is not, under Section 4A–202(a), an authorized order of a customer identified as sender, but is effective as an order of the customer pursuant to Section 4A–202(b), the following rules apply:

(1) By express written agreement, the receiving bank may limit the extent to which it is entitled to enforce or retain payment of the payment order.

(2) The receiving bank is not entitled to enforce or retain payment of the payment order if the customer proves that the order was not caused, directly or indirectly, by a person (i) entrusted at any time with duties to act for the customer with respect to payment orders or the security procedure, or (ii) who obtained access to transmitting facilities of the customer or who obtained, from a source controlled by the customer and without authority of the receiving bank, information facilitating breach of the security procedure, regardless of how the information was obtained or whether the customer was at fault. Information includes any access device, computer software, or the like.

(b) This section applies to amendments of payment orders to the same extent it applies to payment orders.

§ 4A–204. Refund of Payment and Duty of Customer to Report with Respect to Unauthorized Payment Order.

(a) If a receiving bank accepts a payment order issued in the name of its customer as sender which is (i) not authorized and not effective as the order of the customer under Section 4A–202, or (ii) not enforceable, in whole or in part, against the customer under Section 4A–203, the bank shall refund any payment of the payment order received from the customer to the extent the bank is not entitled to enforce payment and shall pay interest on the refundable amount calculated from the date the bank received payment to the date of the refund. However, the customer is not entitled to interest from the bank on the amount to be refunded if the customer fails to exercise ordinary care to determine that the order was not authorized by the customer and to notify the bank of the relevant facts within a reasonable time not exceeding 90 days after the date the customer received notification from the bank that the order was accepted or that the customer's account was debited with respect to the order. The bank is not entitled to any recovery from the customer on account of a failure by the customer to give notification as stated in this section.

(b) Reasonable time under subsection (a) may be fixed by agreement as stated in Section 1–204(1), but the obligation of a receiving bank to refund payment as stated in subsection (a) may not otherwise be varied by agreement.

§ 4A–205. Erroneous Payment Orders.

(a) If an accepted payment order was transmitted pursuant to a security procedure for the detection of error and the payment order (i) erroneously instructed payment to a beneficiary not intended by the sender, (ii) erroneously instructed payment in an amount greater than the amount intended by the sender, or (iii) was an erroneously transmitted duplicate of a payment order previously sent by the sender, the following rules apply:

(1) If the sender proves that the sender or a person acting on behalf of the sender pursuant to Section 4A–206 complied with the security procedure and that the error would have been detected if the receiving bank had also complied, the sender is not obliged to pay the order to the extent stated in paragraphs (2) and (3).

(2) If the funds transfer is completed on the basis of an erroneous payment order described in clause (i) or (iii) of subsection (a), the sender is not obliged to pay the order and the receiving bank is entitled to recover from the beneficiary any amount paid to the beneficiary to the extent allowed by the law governing mistake and restitution.

(3) If the funds transfer is completed on the basis of a payment order described in clause (ii) of subsection (a), the sender is not obliged to pay the order to the extent the amount received by the beneficiary is greater than the amount intended by the sender. In that case, the receiving bank is entitled to recover from the beneficiary the excess amount received to the extent allowed by the law governing mistake and restitution.

(b) If (i) the sender of an erroneous payment order described in subsection (a) is not obliged to pay all or part of the order, and (ii) the sender receives notification from the receiving bank that the order was accepted by the bank or that the sender's account was debited with respect to the order, the sender has a duty to exercise ordinary care, on the basis of information available to the sender, to discover the error with respect to the order and to advise the bank of the relevant facts within a reasonable time, not exceeding 90 days, after the bank's notification was received by the sender. If the bank proves that the sender failed to perform that duty, the sender is liable to the bank for the loss the bank proves it incurred as a result of the failure, but the liability of the sender may not exceed the amount of the sender's order.

(c) This section applies to amendments to payment orders to the same extent it applies to payment orders.

§ 4A–206. Transmission of Payment Order through Funds-Transfer or Other Communication System.

(a) If a payment order addressed to a receiving bank is transmitted to a funds-transfer system or other third party communication system for transmittal to the bank, the system is deemed to be an agent of the sender for the purpose of transmitting the payment order to the bank. If there is a discrepancy between the terms of the payment order transmitted to the system and the terms of the payment order transmitted by the system to the bank, the terms of the payment order of the sender are those transmitted by the system. This section does not apply to a funds-transfer system of the Federal Reserve Banks.

(b) This section applies to cancellations and amendments to payment orders to the same extent it applies to payment orders.

§ 4A–207. Misdescription of Beneficiary.

(a) Subject to subsection (b), if, in a payment order received by the beneficiary's bank, the name, bank account number, or other identification of the beneficiary refers to a nonexistent or unidentifiable person or account, no person has rights as a beneficiary of the order and acceptance of the order cannot occur.

(b) If a payment order received by the beneficiary's bank identifies the beneficiary both by name and by an identifying or bank account number and the name and number identify different persons, the following rules apply:

(1) Except as otherwise provided in subsection (c), if the beneficiary's bank does not know that the name and number refer to different persons, it may rely on the number as the proper identification of the beneficiary of the order. The beneficiary's bank need not determine whether the name and number refer to the same person.

(2) If the beneficiary's bank pays the person identified by name or knows that the name and number identify different persons, no person has rights as beneficiary except the person paid by the beneficiary's bank if that person was entitled to receive payment from the originator of the funds transfer. If no person has rights as beneficiary, acceptance of the order cannot occur.

(c) If (i) a payment order described in subsection (b) is accepted, (ii) the originator's payment order described the beneficiary inconsistently by name and number, and (iii) the beneficiary's bank pays the person identified by number as permitted by subsection (b)(1), the following rules apply:

(1) If the originator is a bank, the originator is obliged to pay its order.

(2) If the originator is not a bank and proves that the person identified by number was not entitled to receive payment from the originator, the originator is not obliged to pay its order unless the originator's bank proves that the originator, before acceptance of the originator's order, had notice that payment of a payment order issued by the originator might be made by the beneficiary's bank on the basis of an identifying or bank account number even if it identifies a person different from the named beneficiary. Proof of notice may be made by any admissible evidence. The originator's bank satisfies the burden of proof if it proves that the originator, before the payment order was accepted, signed a writing stating the information to which the notice relates.

(d) In a case governed by subsection (b)(1), if the beneficiary's bank rightfully pays the person identified by number and that person was not entitled to receive payment from the originator, the amount paid may be recovered from that person to the extent allowed by the law governing mistake and restitution as follows:

(1) If the originator is obliged to pay its payment order as stated in subsection (c), the originator has the right to recover.

(2) If the originator is not a bank and is not obliged to pay its payment order, the originator's bank has the right to recover.

§ 4A–208. Misdescription of Intermediary Bank or Beneficiary's Bank.

(a) This subsection applies to a payment order identifying an intermediary bank or the beneficiary's bank only by an identifying number.

(1) The receiving bank may rely on the number as the proper identification of the intermediary or beneficiary's bank and need not determine whether the number identifies a bank.

(2) The sender is obliged to compensate the receiving bank for any loss and expenses incurred by the receiving bank as a result of its reliance on the number in executing or attempting to execute the order.

(b) This subsection applies to a payment order identifying an intermediary bank or the beneficiary's bank both by name and an identifying number if the name and number identify different persons.

(1) If the sender is a bank, the receiving bank may rely on the number as the proper identification of the intermediary or beneficiary's bank if the receiving bank, when it executes the sender's order, does not know that the name and number identify different persons. The receiving bank need not determine whether the name and number refer to the same person or whether the number refers to a bank. The sender is obliged to compensate the receiving bank for any loss and expenses incurred by the receiving bank as a result of its reliance on the number in executing or attempting to execute the order.

(2) If the sender is not a bank and the receiving bank proves that the sender, before the payment order was accepted, had notice that the receiving bank might rely on the number as the proper identification of the intermediary or beneficiary's bank even if it identifies a person different from the bank identified by name, the rights and obligations of the sender and the receiving bank are governed by subsection (b)(1), as though the sender were a bank. Proof of notice may be made by any admissible evidence. The receiving bank satisfies the burden of proof if it proves that the sender, before the payment order was

accepted, signed a writing stating the information to which the notice relates.

(3) Regardless of whether the sender is a bank, the receiving bank may rely on the name as the proper identification of the intermediary or beneficiary's bank if the receiving bank, at the time it executes the sender's order, does not know that the name and number identify different persons. The receiving bank need not determine whether the name and number refer to the same person.

(4) If the receiving bank knows that the name and number identify different persons, reliance on either the name or the number in executing the sender's payment order is a breach of the obligation stated in Section 4A–302(a)(1).

§ 4A–209. Acceptance of Payment Order.

(a) Subject to subsection (d), a receiving bank other than the beneficiary's bank accepts a payment order when it executes the order.

(b) Subject to subsections (c) and (d), a beneficiary's bank accepts a payment order at the earliest of the following times:

(1) When the bank (i) pays the beneficiary as stated in Section 4A–405(a) or 4A–405(b), or (ii) notifies the beneficiary of receipt of the order or that the account of the beneficiary has been credited with respect to the order unless the notice indicates that the bank is rejecting the order or that funds with respect to the order may not be withdrawn or used until receipt of payment from the sender of the order;

(2) When the bank receives payment of the entire amount of the sender's order pursuant to Section 4A–403(a)(1) or 4A–403(a)(2); or

(3) The opening of the next funds-transfer business day of the bank following the payment date of the order if, at that time, the amount of the sender's order is fully covered by a withdrawable credit balance in an authorized account of the sender or the bank has otherwise received full payment from the sender, unless the order was rejected before that time or is rejected within (i) one hour after that time, or (ii) one hour after the opening of the next business day of the sender following the payment date if that time is later. If notice of rejection is received by the sender after the payment date and the authorized account of the sender does not bear interest, the bank is obliged to pay interest to the sender on the amount of the order for the number of days elapsing after the payment date to the day the sender receives notice or learns that the order was not accepted, counting that day as an elapsed day. If the withdrawable credit balance during that period falls below the amount of the order, the amount of interest payable is reduced accordingly.

(c) Acceptance of a payment order cannot occur before the order is received by the receiving bank. Acceptance does not occur under subsection (b)(2) or (b)(3) if the beneficiary of the payment order does not have an account with the receiving bank, the account has been closed, or the receiving bank is not permitted by law to receive credits for the beneficiary's account.

(d) A payment order issued to the originator's bank cannot be accepted until the payment date if the bank is the beneficiary's bank, or the execution date if the bank is not the beneficiary's bank. If the originator's bank executes the originator's payment order before the execution date or pays the beneficiary of the originator's payment order before the payment date and the payment order is subsequently cancelled pursuant to Section 4A–211(b), the bank may recover from the beneficiary any payment received to the extent allowed by the law governing mistake and restitution.

§ 4A–210. Rejection of Payment Order.

(a) A payment order is rejected by the receiving bank by a notice of rejection transmitted to the sender orally, electronically, or in writing. A notice of rejection need not use any particular words and is sufficient if it indicates that the receiving bank is rejecting the order or will not execute or pay the order. Rejection is effective when the notice is given if transmission is by a means that is reasonable in the circumstances. If notice of rejection is given by a means that is not reasonable, rejection is effective when the notice is received. If an agreement of the sender and receiving bank establishes the means to be used to reject a payment order, (i) any means complying with the agreement is reasonable and (ii) any means not complying is not reasonable unless no significant delay in receipt of the notice resulted from the use of the noncomplying means.

(b) This subsection applies if a receiving bank other than the beneficiary's bank fails to execute a payment order despite the existence on the execution date of a withdrawable credit balance in an authorized account of the sender sufficient to cover the order. If the sender does not receive notice of rejection of the order on the execution date and the authorized account of the sender does not bear interest, the bank is obliged to pay interest to the sender on the amount of the order for the number of days elapsing after the execution date to the earlier of the day the order is cancelled pursuant to Section 4A–211(d) or the day the sender receives notice or learns that the order was not executed, counting the final day of the period as an elapsed day. If the withdrawable credit balance during that period falls below the amount of the order, the amount of interest is reduced accordingly.

(c) If a receiving bank suspends payments, all unaccepted payment orders issued to it are are deemed rejected at the time the bank suspends payments.

(d) Acceptance of a payment order precludes a later rejection of the order. Rejection of a payment order precludes a later acceptance of the order.

§ 4A–211. Cancellation and Amendment of Payment Order.

(a) A communication of the sender of a payment order cancelling or amending the order may be transmitted to the receiving bank orally, electronically, or in writing. If a security procedure is in effect between the sender and the receiving bank, the communication is not effective to cancel or amend the order unless the communication is verified pursuant to the security procedure or the bank agrees to the cancellation or amendment.

(b) Subject to subsection (a), a communication by the sender cancelling or amending a payment order is effective to cancel or amend the order if notice of the communication is received at a time and in a manner affording the receiving bank a reasonable opportunity to act on the communication before the bank accepts the payment order.

(c) After a payment order has been accepted, cancellation or amendment of the order is not effective unless the receiving bank agrees or a funds-transfer system rule allows cancellation or amendment without agreement of the bank.

(1) With respect to a payment order accepted by a receiving bank other than the beneficiary's bank, cancellation or amendment is not effective unless a conforming cancellation or amendment of the payment order issued by the receiving bank is also made.

(2) With respect to a payment order accepted by the beneficiary's bank, cancellation or amendment is not effective unless the order was issued in execution of an unauthorized payment order, or because of a mistake by a sender in the funds transfer which resulted in the issuance of a payment order (i) that is a duplicate of a payment order previously issued by the sender, (ii) that orders payment to a beneficiary not entitled to receive payment from the originator, or (iii) that orders payment in an amount greater than the amount the beneficiary was entitled to receive from the originator. If the payment order is cancelled or amended, the beneficiary's bank is entitled to recover from the beneficiary any amount paid to the beneficiary to the extent allowed by the law governing mistake and restitution.

(d) An unaccepted payment order is cancelled by operation of law at the close of the fifth funds-transfer business day of the receiving bank after the execution date or payment date of the order.

(e) A cancelled payment order cannot be accepted. If an accepted payment order is cancelled, the acceptance is nullified and no person has any right or obligation based on the acceptance. Amendment of a payment order is deemed to be cancellation of the original order at the time of amendment and issue of a new payment order in the amended form at the same time.

(f) Unless otherwise provided in an agreement of the parties or in a funds-transfer system rule, if the receiving bank, after accepting a payment order, agrees to cancellation or amendment of the order by the sender or is bound by a funds-transfer system rule allowing cancellation or amendment without the bank's agreement, the sender, whether or not cancellation or amendment is effective, is liable to the bank for any loss and expenses, including reasonable attorney's fees, incurred by the bank as a result of the cancellation or amendment or attempted cancellation or amendment.

(g) A payment order is not revoked by the death or legal incapacity of the sender unless the receiving bank knows of the death or of an adjudication of incapacity by a court of competent jurisdiction and has reasonable opportunity to act before acceptance of the order.

(h) A funds-transfer system rule is not effective to the extent it conflicts with subsection (c)(2).

§ 4A–212. Liability and Duty of Receiving Bank Regarding Unaccepted Payment Order.

If a receiving bank fails to accept a payment order that it is obliged by express agreement to accept, the bank is liable for breach of the agreement to the extent provided in the agreement or in this Article, but does not otherwise have any duty to accept a payment order or, before acceptance, to take any action, or refrain from taking action, with respect to the order except as provided in this Article or by express agreement. Liability based on acceptance arises only when acceptance occurs as stated in Section 4A–209, and liability is limited to that provided in this Article. A receiving bank is not the agent of the sender or beneficiary of the payment order it accepts, or of any other party to the

funds transfer, and the bank owes no duty to any party to the funds transfer except as provided in this Article or by express agreement.

Part 3 Execution of Sender's Payment Order by Receiving Bank

§ 4A–301. Execution and Execution Date.

(a) A payment order is "executed" by the receiving bank when it issues a payment order intended to carry out the payment order received by the bank. A payment order received by the beneficiary's bank can be accepted but cannot be executed.

(b) "Execution date" of a payment order means the day on which the receiving bank may properly issue a payment order in execution of the sender's order. The execution date may be determined by instruction of the sender but cannot be earlier than the day the order is received and, unless otherwise determined, is the day the order is received. If the sender's instruction states a payment date, the execution date is the payment date or an earlier date on which execution is reasonably necessary to allow payment to the beneficiary on the payment date.

§ 4A–302. Obligations of Receiving Bank in Execution of Payment Order.

(a) Except as provided in subsections (b) through (d), if the receiving bank accepts a payment order pursuant to Section 4A–209(a), the bank has the following obligations in executing the order:

(1) The receiving bank is obliged to issue, on the execution date, a payment order complying with the sender's order and to follow the sender's instructions concerning (i) any intermediary bank or funds-transfer system to be used in carrying out the funds transfer, or (ii) the means by which payment orders are to be transmitted in the funds transfer. If the originator's bank issues a payment order to an intermediary bank, the originator's bank is obliged to instruct the intermediary bank according to the instruction of the originator. An intermediary bank in the funds transfer is similarly bound by an instruction given to it by the sender of the payment order it accepts.

(2) If the sender's instruction states that the funds transfer is to be carried out telephonically or by wire transfer or otherwise indicates that the funds transfer is to be carried out by the most expeditious means, the receiving bank is obliged to transmit its payment order by the most expeditious available means, and to instruct any intermediary bank accordingly. If a sender's instruction states a payment date, the receiving bank is obliged to transmit its payment order at a time and by means reasonably necessary to allow payment to the beneficiary on the payment date or as soon thereafter as is feasible.

(b) Unless otherwise instructed, a receiving bank executing a payment order may (i) use any funds-transfer system if use of that system is reasonable in the circumstances, and (ii) issue a payment order to the beneficiary's bank or to an intermediary bank through which a payment order conforming to the sender's order can expeditiously be issued to the beneficiary's bank if the receiving bank exercises ordinary care in the selection of the intermediary bank. A receiving bank is not required to follow an instruction of the sender designating a funds-transfer system to be used in carrying out the funds transfer if the receiving bank, in good faith, determines that it is not feasible to follow the instruction or that following the instruction would unduly delay completion of the funds transfer.

(c) Unless subsection (a)(2) applies or the receiving bank is otherwise instructed, the bank may execute a payment order by transmitting its payment order by first class mail or by any means reasonable in the circumstances. If the receiving bank is instructed to execute the sender's order by transmitting its payment order by a particular means, the receiving bank may issue its payment order by the means stated or by any means as expeditious as the means stated.

(d) Unless instructed by the sender, (i) the receiving bank may not obtain payment of its charges for services and expenses in connection with the execution of the sender's order by issuing a payment order in an amount equal to the amount of the sender's order less the amount of the charges, and (ii) may not instruct a subsequent receiving bank to obtain payment of its charges in the same manner.

§ 4A–303. Erroneous Execution of Payment Order.

(a) A receiving bank that (i) executes the payment order of the sender by issuing a payment order in an amount greater than the amount of the sender's order, or (ii) issues a payment order in execution of the sender's order and then issues a duplicate order, is entitled to payment of the amount of the sender's order under Section 4A–402(c) if that subsection is otherwise satisfied. The bank is entitled to recover from the beneficiary of the erroneous order the excess payment received to the extent allowed by the law governing mistake and restitution.

(b) A receiving bank that executes the payment order of the sender by issuing a payment order in an amount less than the amount of the sender's order is entitled to payment of the amount of the sender's order under Section 4A–402(c) if (i) that subsection is otherwise satisfied and (ii) the bank corrects its mistake by issuing an additional payment order for the benefit of the beneficiary of the sender's order. If the error is not corrected, the issuer of the erroneous order is entitled to receive or retain payment from the sender of the order it accepted only to the extent of the amount of the erroneous order. This subsection does not apply if the receiving bank executes the sender's payment order by issuing a payment order in an amount less than the amount of the sender's order for the purpose of obtaining payment of its charges for services and expenses pursuant to instruction of the sender.

(c) If a receiving bank executes the payment order of the sender by issuing a payment order to a beneficiary different from the beneficiary of the sender's order and the funds transfer is completed on the basis of that error, the sender of the payment order that was erroneously executed and all previous senders in the funds transfer are not obliged to pay the payment orders they issued. The issuer of the erroneous order is entitled to recover from the beneficiary of the order the payment received to the extent allowed by the law governing mistake and restitution.

§ 4A–304. Duty of Sender to Report Erroneously Executed Payment Order.

If the sender of a payment order that is erroneously executed as stated in Section 4A–303 receives notification from the receiving bank that the order was executed or that the sender's account was debited with respect to the order, the sender has a duty to exercise ordinary care to determine, on the basis of information available to the sender, that the order was erroneously executed and to notify the bank of the relevant facts within a reasonable time not exceed-

ing 90 days after the notification from the bank was received by the sender. If the sender fails to perform that duty, the bank is not obliged to pay interest on any amount refundable to the sender under Section 4A–402(d) for the period before the bank learns of the execution error. The bank is not entitled to any recovery from the sender on account of a failure by the sender to perform the duty stated in this section.

§ 4A–305. Liability for Late or Improper Execution or Failure to Execute Payment Order.

(a) If a funds transfer is completed but execution of a payment order by the receiving bank in breach of Section 4A–302 results in delay in payment to the beneficiary, the bank is obliged to pay interest to either the originator or the beneficiary of the funds transfer for the period of delay caused by the improper execution. Except as provided in subsection (c), additional damages are not recoverable.

(b) If execution of a payment order by a receiving bank in breach of Section 4A–302 results in (i) noncompletion of the funds transfer, (ii) failure to use an intermediary bank designated by the originator, or (iii) issuance of a payment order that does not comply with the terms of the payment order of the originator, the bank is liable to the originator for its expenses in the funds transfer and for incidental expenses and interest losses, to the extent not covered by subsection (a), resulting from the improper execution. Except as provided in subsection (c), additional damages are not recoverable.

(c) In addition to the amounts payable under subsections (a) and (b), damages, including consequential damages, are recoverable to the extent provided in an express written agreement of the receiving bank.

(d) If a receiving bank fails to execute a payment order it was obliged by express agreement to execute, the receiving bank is liable to the sender for its expenses in the transaction and for incidental expenses and interest losses resulting from the failure to execute. Additional damages, including consequential damages, are recoverable to the extent provided in an express written agreement of the receiving bank, but are not otherwise recoverable.

(e) Reasonable attorney's fees are recoverable if demand for compensation under subsection (a) or (b) is made and refused before an action is brought on the claim. If a claim is made for breach of an agreement under subsection (d) and the agreement does not provide for damages, reasonable attorney's fees are recoverable if demand for compensation under subsection (d) is made and refused before an action is brought on the claim.

(f) Except as stated in this section, the liability of a receiving bank under subsections (a) and (b) may not be varied by agreement.

Part 4 Payment

§ 4A–401. Payment Date.

"Payment date" of a payment order means the day on which the amount of the order is payable to the beneficiary by the beneficiary's bank. The payment date may be determined by instruction of the sender but cannot be earlier than the day the order is received by the beneficiary's bank and, unless otherwise determined, is the day the order is received by the beneficiary's bank.

§ 4A–402. Obligation of Sender to Pay Receiving Bank.

(a) This section is subject to Sections 4A–205 and 4A–207.

(b) With respect to a payment order issued to the beneficiary's bank, acceptance of the order by the bank obliges the sender to pay the bank the amount of the order, but payment is not due until the payment date of the order.

(c) This subsection is subject to subsection (e) and to Section 4A–303. With respect to a payment order issued to a receiving bank other than the beneficiary's bank, acceptance of the order by the receiving bank obliges the sender to pay the bank the amount of the sender's order. Payment by the sender is not due until the execution date of the sender's order. The obligation of that sender to pay its payment order is excused if the funds transfer is not completed by acceptance by the beneficiary's bank of a payment order instructing payment to the beneficiary of that sender's payment order.

(d) If the sender of a payment order pays the order and was not obliged to pay all or part of the amount paid, the bank receiving payment is obliged to refund payment to the extent the sender was not obliged to pay. Except as provided in Sections 4A–204 and 4A–304, interest is payable on the refundable amount from the date of payment.

(e) If a funds transfer is not completed as stated in subsection (c) and an intermediary bank is obliged to refund payment as stated in subsection (d) but is unable to do so because not permitted by applicable law or because the bank suspends payments, a sender in the funds transfer that executed a payment order in compliance with an instruction, as stated in Section 4A–302(a)(1), to route the funds transfer through that intermediary bank is entitled to receive or retain payment from the sender of the payment order that it accepted. The first sender in the funds transfer that issued an instruction requiring routing through that intermediary bank is subrogated to the right of the bank that paid the intermediary bank to refund as stated in subsection (d).

(f) The right of the sender of a payment order to be excused from the obligation to pay the order as stated in subsection (c) or to receive refund under subsection (d) may not be varied by agreement.

§ 4A–403. Payment by Sender to Receiving Bank.

(a) Payment of the sender's obligation under Section 4A–402 to pay the receiving bank occurs as follows:

> (1) If the sender is a bank, payment occurs when the receiving bank receives final settlement of the obligation through a Federal Reserve Bank or through a funds-transfer system.

> (2) If the sender is a bank and the sender (i) credited an account of the receiving bank with the sender, or (ii) caused an account of the receiving bank in another bank to be credited, payment occurs when the credit is withdrawn or, if not withdrawn, at midnight of the day on which the credit is withdrawable and the receiving bank learns of that fact.

> (3) If the receiving bank debits an account of the sender with the receiving bank, payment occurs when the debit is made to the extent the debit is covered by a withdrawable credit balance in the account.

(b) If the sender and receiving bank are members of a funds-transfer system that nets obligations multilaterally among participants, the receiving bank receives final settlement when settlement is complete in accordance with the rules of the system. The obligation of the sender to pay the amount of a payment order transmitted through the funds-transfer system may be satisfied, to the extent permitted by the rules of the system, by setting off and applying against the sender's obligation the right of the sender to receive payment from the receiving bank of the amount of any other payment order transmitted to the sender by the receiving bank through the funds-transfer system. The aggregate balance of obligations owed by each sender to each receiving bank in the funds-transfer system may be satisfied, to the extent permitted by the rules of the system, by setting off and applying against that balance the aggregate balance of obligations owed to the sender by other members of the system. The aggregate balance is determined after the right of setoff stated in the second sentence of this subsection has been exercised.

(c) If two banks transmit payment orders to each other under an agreement that settlement of the obligations of each bank to the other under Section 4A–402 will be made at the end of the day or other period, the total amount owed with respect to all orders transmitted by one bank shall be set off against the total amount owed with respect to all orders transmitted by the other bank. To the extent of the setoff, each bank has made payment to the other.

(d) In a case not covered by subsection (a), the time when payment of the sender's obligation under Section 4A–402(b) or 4A–402(c) occurs is governed by applicable principles of law that determine when an obligation is satisfied.

§ 4A–404. Obligation of Beneficiary's Bank to Pay and Give Notice to Beneficiary.

(a) Subject to Sections 4A–211(e), 4A–405(d), and 4A–405(e), if a beneficiary's bank accepts a payment order, the bank is obliged to pay the amount of the order to the beneficiary of the order. Payment is due on the payment date of the order, but if acceptance occurs on the payment date after the close of the funds-transfer business day of the bank, payment is due on the next funds-transfer business day. If the bank refuses to pay after demand by the beneficiary and receipt of notice of particular circumstances that will give rise to consequential damages as a result of nonpayment, the beneficiary may recover damages resulting from the refusal to pay to the extent the bank had notice of the damages, unless the bank proves that it did not pay because of a reasonable doubt concerning the right of the beneficiary to payment.

(b) If a payment order accepted by the beneficiary's bank instructs payment to an account of the beneficiary, the bank is obliged to notify the beneficiary of receipt of the order before midnight of the next funds-transfer business day following the payment date. If the payment order does not instruct payment to an account of the beneficiary, the bank is required to notify the beneficiary only if notice is required by the order. Notice may be given by first class mail or any other means reasonable in the circumstances. If the bank fails to give the required notice, the bank is obliged to pay interest to the beneficiary on the amount of the payment order from the day notice should have been given until the day the beneficiary learned of receipt of the payment order by the bank. No other damages are recoverable. Reasonable attorney's fees are also recoverable if demand for interest is made and refused before an action is brought on the claim.

(c) The right of a beneficiary to receive payment and damages as stated in subsection (a) may not be varied by agreement or a funds-transfer system rule. The right of a beneficiary to be notified as stated in subsection (b) may be varied by agreement of the beneficiary or by a funds-transfer system rule if the beneficiary is notified of the rule before initiation of the funds transfer.

§ 4A–405. Payment by Beneficiary's Bank to Beneficiary.

(a) If the beneficiary's bank credits an account of the beneficiary of a payment order, payment of the bank's obligation under Section 4A–404(a) occurs when and to the extent (i) the beneficiary is notified of the right to withdraw the credit, (ii) the bank lawfully applies the credit to a debt of the beneficiary, or (iii) funds with respect to the order are otherwise made available to the beneficiary by the bank.

(b) If the beneficiary's bank does not credit an account of the beneficiary of a payment order, the time when payment of the bank's obligation under Section 4A–404(a) occurs is governed by principles of law that determine when an obligation is satisfied.

(c) Except as stated in subsections (d) and (e), if the beneficiary's bank pays the beneficiary of a payment order under a condition to payment or agreement of the beneficiary giving the bank the right to recover payment from the beneficiary if the bank does not receive payment of the order, the condition to payment or agreement is not enforceable.

(d) A funds-transfer system rule may provide that payments made to beneficiaries of funds transfers made through the system are provisional until receipt of payment by the beneficiary's bank of the payment order it accepted. A beneficiary's bank that makes a payment that is provisional under the rule is entitled to refund from the beneficiary if (i) the rule requires that both the beneficiary and the originator be given notice of the provisional nature of the payment before the funds transfer is initiated, (ii) the beneficiary, the beneficiary's bank, and the originator's bank agreed to be bound by the rule, and (iii) the beneficiary's bank did not receive payment of the payment order that it accepted. If the beneficiary is obliged to refund payment to the beneficiary's bank, acceptance of the payment order by the beneficiary's bank is nullified and no payment by the originator of the funds transfer to the beneficiary occurs under Section 4A–406.

(e) This subsection applies to a funds transfer that includes a payment order transmitted over a funds-transfer system that (i) nets obligations multilaterally among participants, and (ii) has in effect a loss-sharing agreement among participants for the purpose of providing funds necessary to complete settlement of the obligations of one or more participants that do not meet their settlement obligations. If the beneficiary's bank in the funds transfer accepts a payment order and the system fails to complete settlement pursuant to its rules with respect to any payment order in the funds transfer, (i) the acceptance by the beneficiary's bank is nullified and no person has any right or obligation based on the acceptance, (ii) the beneficiary's bank is entitled to recover payment from the beneficiary, (iii) no payment by the originator to the beneficiary occurs under Section 4A–406, and (iv) subject to Section 4A–402(e), each sender in the funds transfer is excused from its obligation to pay its payment order under Section 4A–402(c) because the funds transfer has not been completed.

§ 4A–406. Payment by Originator to Beneficiary; Discharge of Underlying Obligation.

(a) Subject to Sections 4A–211(e), 4A–405(d), and 4A–405(e), the originator of a funds transfer pays the beneficiary of the originator's payment order (i) at the time a payment order for the benefit of the beneficiary is accepted by the beneficiary's bank in the funds transfer and (ii) in an amount equal to the amount of the order accepted by the beneficiary's bank, but not more than the amount of the originator's order.

(b) If payment under subsection (a) is made to satisfy an obligation, the obligation is discharged to the same extent discharge would result from payment to the beneficiary of the same amount in money, unless (i) the payment under subsection (a) was made by a means prohibited by the contract of the beneficiary with respect to the obligation, (ii) the beneficiary, within a reasonable time after receiving notice of receipt of the order by the beneficiary's bank, notified the originator of the beneficiary's refusal of the payment, (iii) funds with respect to the order were not withdrawn by the beneficiary or applied to a debt of the beneficiary, and (iv) the beneficiary would suffer a loss that could reasonably have been avoided if payment had been made by a means complying with the contract. If payment by the originator does not result in discharge under this section, the originator is subrogated to the rights of the beneficiary to receive payment from the beneficiary's bank under Section 4A–404(a).

(c) For the purpose of determining whether discharge of an obligation occurs under subsection (b), if the beneficiary's bank accepts a payment order in an amount equal to the amount of the originator's payment order less charges of one or more receiving banks in the funds transfer, payment to the beneficiary is deemed to be in the amount of the originator's order unless upon demand by the beneficiary the originator does not pay the beneficiary the amount of the deducted charges.

(d) Rights of the originator or of the beneficiary of a funds transfer under this section may be varied only by agreement of the originator and the beneficiary.

Part 5 Miscellaneous Provisions

§ 4A–501. Variation by Agreement and Effect of Funds-Transfer System Rule.

(a) Except as otherwise provided in this Article, the rights and obligations of a party to a funds transfer may be varied by agreement of the affected party.

(b) "Funds-transfer system rule" means a rule of an association of banks (i) governing transmission of payment orders by means of a funds-transfer system of the association or rights and obligations with respect to those orders, or (ii) to the extent the rule governs rights and obligations between banks that are parties to a funds transfer in which a Federal Reserve Bank, acting as an intermediary bank, sends a payment order to the beneficiary's bank. Except as otherwise provided in this Article, a funds-transfer system rule governing rights and obligations between participating banks using the system may be effective even if the rule conflicts with this Article and indirectly affects another party to the funds transfer who does not consent to the rule. A funds-transfer system rule may also govern rights and obligations of parties other than participating banks using the system to the extent stated in Sections 4A–404(c), 4A–405(d), and 4A–507(c).

§ 4A–502. Creditor Process Served on Receiving Bank; Setoff by Beneficiary's Bank.

(a) As used in this section, "creditor process" means levy, attachment, garnishment, notice of lien, sequestration, or similar process issued by or on behalf of a creditor or other claimant with respect to an account.

(b) This subsection applies to creditor process with respect to an authorized account of the sender of a payment order if the creditor process is served on the receiving bank. For the purpose of determining rights with respect to the creditor process, if the receiving bank accepts the payment order the balance in the authorized account is deemed to be reduced by the amount of the payment order to the extent the bank did not otherwise receive payment of the order, unless the creditor process is served at a time and in a manner affording the bank a reasonable opportunity to act on it before the bank accepts the payment order.

(c) If a beneficiary's bank has received a payment order for payment to the beneficiary's account in the bank, the following rules apply:

(1) The bank may credit the beneficiary's account. The amount credited may be set off against an obligation owed by the beneficiary to the bank or may be applied to satisfy creditor process served on the bank with respect to the account.

(2) The bank may credit the beneficiary's account and allow withdrawal of the amount credited unless creditor process with respect to the account is served at a time and in a manner affording the bank a reasonable opportunity to act to prevent withdrawal.

(3) If creditor process with respect to the beneficiary's account has been served and the bank has had a reasonable opportunity to act on it, the bank may not reject the payment order except for a reason unrelated to the service of process.

(d) Creditor process with respect to a payment by the originator to the beneficiary pursuant to a funds transfer may be served only on the beneficiary's bank with respect to the debt owed by that bank to the beneficiary. Any other bank served with the creditor process is not obliged to act with respect to the process.

§ 4A–503. Injunction or Restraining Order with Respect to Funds Transfer.

For proper cause and in compliance with applicable law, a court may restrain (i) a person from issuing a payment order to initiate a funds transfer, (ii) an originator's bank from executing the payment order of the originator, or (iii) the beneficiary's bank from releasing funds to the beneficiary or the beneficiary from withdrawing the funds. A court may not otherwise restrain a person from issuing a payment order, paying or receiving payment of a payment order, or otherwise acting with respect to a funds transfer.

§ 4A–504. Order in Which Items and Payment Orders May Be Charged to Account; Order of Withdrawals from Account.

(a) If a receiving bank has received more than one payment order of the sender or one or more payment orders and other items that are payable from the sender's account, the bank may charge the sender's account with respect to the various orders and items in any sequence.

(b) In determining whether a credit to an account has been withdrawn by the holder of the account or applied to a debt of the holder of the account, credits first made to the account are first withdrawn or applied.

§ 4A–505. Preclusion of Objection to Debit of Customer's Account.

If a receiving bank has received payment from its customer with respect to a payment order issued in the name of the customer as sender and accepted by the bank, and the customer received notification reasonably identifying the order, the customer is precluded from asserting that the bank is not entitled to retain the payment unless the customer notifies the bank of the customer's objection to the payment within one year after the notification was received by the customer.

§ 4A–506. Rate of Interest.

(a) If, under this Article, a receiving bank is obliged to pay interest with respect to a payment order issued to the bank, the amount payable may be determined (i) by agreement of the sender and receiving bank, or (ii) by a funds-transfer system rule if the payment order is transmitted through a funds-transfer system.

(b) If the amount of interest is not determined by an agreement or rule as stated in subsection (a), the amount is calculated by multiplying the applicable Federal Funds rate by the amount on which interest is payable, and then multiplying the product by the number of days for which interest is payable. The applicable Federal Funds rate is the average of the Federal Funds rates published by the Federal Reserve Bank of New York for each of the days for which interest is payable divided by 360. The Federal Funds rate for any day on which a published rate is not available is the same as the published rate for the next preceding day for which there is a published rate. If a receiving bank that accepted a payment order is required to refund payment to the sender of the order because the funds transfer was not completed, but the failure to complete was not due to any fault by the bank, the interest payable is reduced by a percentage equal to the reserve requirement on deposits of the receiving bank.

§ 4A–507. Choice of Law.

(a) The following rules apply unless the affected parties otherwise agree or subsection (c) applies:

(1) The rights and obligations between the sender of a payment order and the receiving bank are governed by the law of the jurisdiction in which the receiving bank is located.

(2) The rights and obligations between the beneficiary's bank and the beneficiary are governed by the law of the jurisdiction in which the beneficiary's bank is located.

(3) The issue of when payment is made pursuant to a funds transfer by the originator to the beneficiary is governed by the law of the jurisdiction in which the beneficiary's bank is located.

(b) If the parties described in each paragraph of subsection (a) have made an agreement selecting the law of a particular jurisdiction to govern rights and obligations between each other, the law of that jurisdiction governs those rights and obligations, whether or not the payment order or the funds transfer bears a reasonable relation to that jurisdiction.

(c) A funds-transfer system rule may select the law of a particular jurisdiction to govern (i) rights and obligations between participating banks with respect to payment orders transmitted or processed through the system, or (ii) the rights and obligations of some or all parties to a funds transfer any part of which is carried out by means of the system. A choice of law made pursuant to clause (i) is binding on participating banks. A choice of law made pursuant to clause (ii) is binding on the originator, other sender, or a receiving bank having notice that the funds-transfer system might be used in the funds transfer and of the choice of law by the system when the originator, other sender, or receiving bank issued or accepted a payment order. The beneficiary of a funds transfer is bound by the choice of law if, when the funds transfer is initiated, the beneficiary has notice that the funds-transfer system might be used in the funds transfer and of the choice of law by the system. The law of a jurisdiction selected pursuant to this subsection may govern, whether or not that law bears a reasonable relation to the matter in issue.

(d) In the event of inconsistency between an agreement under subsection (b) and a choice-of-law rule under subsection (c), the agreement under subsection (b) prevails.

(e) If a funds transfer is made by use of more than one funds-transfer system and there is inconsistency between choice-of-law rules of the systems, the matter in issue is governed by the law of the selected jurisdiction that has the most significant relationship to the matter in issue.

Revised Article 9
SECURED TRANSACTIONS

Part 1 General Provisions

[Subpart 1. Short Title, Definitions, and General Concepts]

§ 9–101. Short Title.

This article may be cited as Uniform Commercial Code—Secured Transactions.

§ 9–102. Definitions and Index of Definitions.

(a) In this article:

(1) "Accession" means goods that are physically united with other goods in such a manner that the identity of the original goods is not lost.

(2) "Account", except as used in "account for", means a right to payment of a monetary obligation, whether or not earned by performance, (i) for property that has been or is to be sold, leased, licensed, assigned, or otherwise disposed of, (ii) for services rendered or to be rendered, (iii) for a policy of insurance issued or to be issued, (iv) for a secondary obligation incurred or to be incurred, (v) for energy provided or to be provided, (vi) for the use or hire of a vessel under a charter or other contract, (vii) arising out of the use of a credit or charge card or information contained on or for use with the card, or (viii) as winnings in a lottery or other game of chance operated or sponsored by a State, governmental unit of a State, or person licensed or authorized to operate the game by a State or governmental unit of a State. The term includes health-care insurance receivables. The term does not include (i) rights to payment evidenced by chattel paper or an instrument, (ii) commercial tort claims, (iii) deposit accounts, (iv) investment property, (v) letter-of-credit rights or letters of credit, or (vi) rights to payment for money or funds advanced or sold, other than rights arising out of the use of a credit or charge card or information contained on or for use with the card.

(3) "Account debtor" means a person obligated on an account, chattel paper, or general intangible. The term does not include

persons obligated to pay a negotiable instrument, even if the instrument constitutes part of chattel paper.

(4) "Accounting", except as used in "accounting for", means a record:

(A) authenticated by a secured party;

(B) indicating the aggregate unpaid secured obligations as of a date not more than 35 days earlier or 35 days later than the date of the record; and

(C) identifying the components of the obligations in reasonable detail.

(5) "Agricultural lien" means an interest, other than a security interest, in farm products:

(A) which secures payment or performance of an obligation for:

(i) goods or services furnished in connection with a debtor's farming operation; or

(ii) rent on real property leased by a debtor in connection with its farming operation;

(B) which is created by statute in favor of a person that:

(i) in the ordinary course of its business furnished goods or services to a debtor in connection with a debtor's farming operation; or

(ii) leased real property to a debtor in connection with the debtor's farming operation; and

(C) whose effectiveness does not depend on the person's possession of the personal property.

(6) "As-extracted collateral" means:

(A) oil, gas, or other minerals that are subject to a security interest that:

(i) is created by a debtor having an interest in the minerals before extraction; and

(ii) attaches to the minerals as extracted; or

(B) accounts arising out of the sale at the wellhead or minehead of oil, gas, or other minerals in which the debtor had an interest before extraction.

(7) "Authenticate" means:

(A) to sign; or

(B) to execute or otherwise adopt a symbol, or encrypt or similarly process a record in whole or in part, with the present intent of the authenticating person to identify the person and adopt or accept a record.

(8) "Bank" means an organization that is engaged in the business of banking. The term includes savings banks, savings and loan associations, credit unions, and trust companies.

(9) "Cash proceeds" means proceeds that are money, checks, deposit accounts, or the like.

(10) "Certificate of title" means a certificate of title with respect to which a statute provides for the security interest in question to be indicated on the certificate as a condition or result of the security interest's obtaining priority over the rights of a lien creditor with respect to the collateral.

(11) "Chattel paper" means a record or records that evidence both a monetary obligation and a security interest in specific goods, a

security interest in specific goods and software used in the goods, a security interest in specific goods and license of software used in the goods, a lease of specific goods, or a lease of specific goods and license of software used in the goods. In this paragraph, "monetary obligation" means a monetary obligation secured by the goods or owed under a lease of the goods and includes a monetary obligation with respect to software used in the goods. The term does not include (i) charters or other contracts involving the use or hire of a vessel or (ii) records that evidence a right to payment arising out of the use of a credit or charge card or information contained on or for use with the card. If a transaction is evidenced by records that include an instrument or series of instruments, the group of records taken together constitutes chattel paper.

(12) "Collateral" means the property subject to a security interest or agricultural lien. The term includes:

(A) proceeds to which a security interest attaches;

(B) accounts, chattel paper, payment intangibles, and promissory notes that have been sold; and

(C) goods that are the subject of a consignment.

(13) "Commercial tort claim" means a claim arising in tort with respect to which:

(A) the claimant is an organization; or

(B) the claimant is an individual and the claim:

(i) arose in the course of the claimant's business or profession; and

(ii) does not include damages arising out of personal injury to or the death of an individual.

(14) "Commodity account" means an account maintained by a commodity intermediary in which a commodity contract is carried for a commodity customer.

(15) "Commodity contract" means a commodity futures contract, an option on a commodity futures contract, a commodity option, or another contract if the contract or option is:

(A) traded on or subject to the rules of a board of trade that has been designated as a contract market for such a contract pursuant to federal commodities laws; or

(B) traded on a foreign commodity board of trade, exchange, or market, and is carried on the books of a commodity intermediary for a commodity customer.

(16) "Commodity customer" means a person for which a commodity intermediary carries a commodity contract on its books.

(17) "Commodity intermediary" means a person that:

(A) is registered as a futures commission merchant under federal commodities law; or

(B) in the ordinary course of its business provides clearance or settlement services for a board of trade that has been designated as a contract market pursuant to federal commodities law.

(18) "Communicate" means:

(A) to send a written or other tangible record;

(B) to transmit a record by any means agreed upon by the persons sending and receiving the record; or

(C) in the case of transmission of a record to or by a filing office, to transmit a record by any means prescribed by filing-office rule.

(19) "Consignee" means a merchant to which goods are delivered in a consignment.

(20) "Consignment" means a transaction, regardless of its form, in which a person delivers goods to a merchant for the purpose of sale and:

(A) the merchant:

(i) deals in goods of that kind under a name other than the name of the person making delivery;

(ii) is not an auctioneer; and

(iii) is not generally known by its creditors to be substantially engaged in selling the goods of others;

(B) with respect to each delivery, the aggregate value of the goods is $1,000 or more at the time of delivery;

(C) the goods are not consumer goods immediately before delivery; and

(D) the transaction does not create a security interest that secures an obligation.

(21) "Consignor" means a person that delivers goods to a consignee in a consignment.

(22) "Consumer debtor" means a debtor in a consumer transaction.

(23) "Consumer goods" means goods that are used or bought for use primarily for personal, family, or household purposes.

(24) "Consumer-goods transaction" means a consumer transaction in which:

(A) an individual incurs an obligation primarily for personal, family, or household purposes; and

(B) a security interest in consumer goods secures the obligation.

(25) "Consumer obligor" means an obligor who is an individual and who incurred the obligation as part of a transaction entered into primarily for personal, family, or household purposes.

(26) "Consumer transaction" means a transaction in which (i) an individual incurs an obligation primarily for personal, family, or household purposes, (ii) a security interest secures the obligation, and (iii) the collateral is held or acquired primarily for personal, family, or household purposes. The term includes consumer-goods transactions.

(27) "Continuation statement" means an amendment of a financing statement which:

(A) identifies, by its file number, the initial financing statement to which it relates; and

(B) indicates that it is a continuation statement for, or that it is filed to continue the effectiveness of, the identified financing statement.

(28) "Debtor" means:

(A) a person having an interest, other than a security interest or other lien, in the collateral, whether or not the person is an obligor;

(B) a seller of accounts, chattel paper, payment intangibles, or promissory notes; or

(C) a consignee.

(29) "Deposit account" means a demand, time, savings, passbook, or similar account maintained with a bank. The term does not include investment property or accounts evidenced by an instrument.

(30) "Document" means a document of title or a receipt of the type described in Section 7–201(2).

(31) "Electronic chattel paper" means chattel paper evidenced by a record or records consisting of information stored in an electronic medium.

(32) "Encumbrance" means a right, other than an ownership interest, in real property. The term includes mortgages and other liens on real property.

(33) "Equipment" means goods other than inventory, farm products, or consumer goods.

(34) "Farm products" means goods, other than standing timber, with respect to which the debtor is engaged in a farming operation and which are:

(A) crops grown, growing, or to be grown, including:

(i) crops produced on trees, vines, and bushes; and

(ii) aquatic goods produced in aquacultural operations;

(B) livestock, born or unborn, including aquatic goods produced in aquacultural operations;

(C) supplies used or produced in a farming operation; or

(D) products of crops or livestock in their unmanufactured states.

(35) "Farming operation" means raising, cultivating, propagating, fattening, grazing, or any other farming, livestock, or aquacultural operation.

(36) "File number" means the number assigned to an initial financing statement pursuant to Section 9–519(a).

(37) "Filing office" means an office designated in Section 9–501 as the place to file a financing statement.

(38) "Filing-office rule" means a rule adopted pursuant to Section 9–526.

(39) "Financing statement" means a record or records composed of an initial financing statement and any filed record relating to the initial financing statement.

(40) "Fixture filing" means the filing of a financing statement covering goods that are or are to become fixtures and satisfying Section 9–502(a) and (b). The term includes the filing of a financing statement covering goods of a transmitting utility which are or are to become fixtures.

(41) "Fixtures" means goods that have become so related to particular real property that an interest in them arises under real property law.

(42) "General intangible" means any personal property, including things in action, other than accounts, chattel paper, commercial tort claims, deposit accounts, documents, goods, instruments, investment property, letter-of-credit rights, letters of credit, money, and oil, gas, or other minerals before extraction. The term includes payment intangibles and software.

(43) "Good faith" means honesty in fact and the observance of reasonable commercial standards of fair dealing.

(44) "Goods" means all things that are movable when a security interest attaches. The term includes (i) fixtures, (ii) standing timber that is to be cut and removed under a conveyance or contract for sale, (iii) the unborn young of animals, (iv) crops grown, growing, or to be grown, even if the crops are produced on trees, vines, or bushes, and (v) manufactured homes. The term also includes a computer program embedded in goods and any supporting information provided in connection with a transaction relating to the program if (i) the program is associated with the goods in such a manner that it customarily is considered part of the goods, or (ii) by becoming the owner of the goods, a person acquires a right to use the program in connection with the goods. The term does not include a computer program embedded in goods that consist solely of the medium in which the program is embedded. The term also does not include accounts, chattel paper, commercial tort claims, deposit accounts, documents, general intangibles, instruments, investment property, letter-of-credit rights, letters of credit, money, or oil, gas, or other minerals before extraction.

(45) "Governmental unit" means a subdivision, agency, department, county, parish, municipality, or other unit of the government of the United States, a State, or a foreign country. The term includes an organization having a separate corporate existence if the organization is eligible to issue debt on which interest is exempt from income taxation under the laws of the United States.

(46) "Health-care-insurance receivable" means an interest in or claim under a policy of insurance which is a right to payment of a monetary obligation for health-care goods or services provided.

(47) "Instrument" means a negotiable instrument or any other writing that evidences a right to the payment of a monetary obligation, is not itself a security agreement or lease, and is of a type that in ordinary course of business is transferred by delivery with any necessary indorsement or assignment. The term does not include (i) investment property, (ii) letters of credit, or (iii) writings that evidence a right to payment arising out of the use of a credit or charge card or information contained on or for use with the card.

(48) "Inventory" means goods, other than farm products, which:

(A) are leased by a person as lessor;

(B) are held by a person for sale or lease or to be furnished under a contract of service;

(C) are furnished by a person under a contract of service; or

(D) consist of raw materials, work in process, or materials used or consumed in a business.

(49) "Investment property" means a security, whether certificated or uncertificated, security entitlement, securities account, commodity contract, or commodity account.

(50) "Jurisdiction of organization", with respect to a registered organization, means the jurisdiction under whose law the organization is organized.

(51) "Letter-of-credit right" means a right to payment or performance under a letter of credit, whether or not the beneficiary has demanded or is at the time entitled to demand payment or performance. The term does not include the right of a beneficiary to demand payment or performance under a letter of credit.

(52) "Lien creditor" means:

(A) a creditor that has acquired a lien on the property involved by attachment, levy, or the like;

(B) an assignee for benefit of creditors from the time of assignment;

(C) a trustee in bankruptcy from the date of the filing of the petition; or

(D) a receiver in equity from the time of appointment.

(53) "Manufactured home" means a structure, transportable in one or more sections, which, in the traveling mode, is eight body feet or more in width or 40 body feet or more in length, or, when erected on site, is 320 or more square feet, and which is built on a permanent chassis and designed to be used as a dwelling with or without a permanent foundation when connected to the required utilities, and includes the plumbing, heating, air-conditioning, and electrical systems contained therein. The term includes any structure that meets all of the requirements of this paragraph except the size requirements and with respect to which the manufacturer voluntarily files a certification required by the United States Secretary of Housing and Urban Development and complies with the standards established under Title 42 of the United States Code.

(54) "Manufactured-home transaction" means a secured transaction:

(A) that creates a purchase-money security interest in a manufactured home, other than a manufactured home held as inventory; or

(B) in which a manufactured home, other than a manufactured home held as inventory, is the primary collateral.

(55) "Mortgage" means a consensual interest in real property, including fixtures, which secures payment or performance of an obligation.

(56) "New debtor" means a person that becomes bound as debtor under Section 9–203(d) by a security agreement previously entered into by another person.

(57) "New value" means (i) money, (ii) money's worth in property, services, or new credit, or (iii) release by a transferee of an interest in property previously transferred to the transferee. The term does not include an obligation substituted for another obligation.

(58) "Noncash proceeds" means proceeds other than cash proceeds.

(59) "Obligor" means a person that, with respect to an obligation secured by a security interest in or an agricultural lien on the collateral, (i) owes payment or other performance of the obligation, (ii) has provided property other than the collateral to secure payment or other performance of the obligation, or (iii) is otherwise accountable in whole or in part for payment or other performance of the obligation. The term does not include issuers or nominated persons under a letter of credit.

(60) "Original debtor", except as used in Section 9–310(c), means a person that, as debtor, entered into a security agreement to which a new debtor has become bound under Section 9–203(d).

(61) "Payment intangible" means a general intangible under which the account debtor's principal obligation is a monetary obligation.

(62) "Person related to", with respect to an individual, means:

(A) the spouse of the individual;

(B) a brother, brother-in-law, sister, or sister-in-law of the individual;

(C) an ancestor or lineal descendant of the individual or the individual's spouse; or

(D) any other relative, by blood or marriage, of the individual or the individual's spouse who shares the same home with the individual.

(63) "Person related to", with respect to an organization, means:

(A) a person directly or indirectly controlling, controlled by, or under common control with the organization;

(B) an officer or director of, or a person performing similar functions with respect to, the organization;

(C) an officer or director of, or a person performing similar functions with respect to, a person described in subparagraph (A);

(D) the spouse of an individual described in subparagraph (A), (B), or (C); or

(E) an individual who is related by blood or marriage to an individual described in subparagraph (A), (B), (C), or (D) and shares the same home with the individual.

(64) "Proceeds", except as used in Section 9–609(b), means the following property:

(A) whatever is acquired upon the sale, lease, license, exchange, or other disposition of collateral;

(B) whatever is collected on, or distributed on account of, collateral;

(C) rights arising out of collateral;

(D) to the extent of the value of collateral, claims arising out of the loss, nonconformity, or interference with the use of, defects or infringement of rights in, or damage to, the collateral; or

(E) to the extent of the value of collateral and to the extent payable to the debtor or the secured party, insurance payable by reason of the loss or nonconformity of, defects or infringement of rights in, or damage to, the collateral.

(65) "Promissory note" means an instrument that evidences a promise to pay a monetary obligation, does not evidence an order to pay, and does not contain an acknowledgment by a bank that the bank has received for deposit a sum of money or funds.

(66) "Proposal" means a record authenticated by a secured party which includes the terms on which the secured party is willing to accept collateral in full or partial satisfaction of the obligation it secures pursuant to Sections 9–620, 9–621, and 9–622.

(67) "Public-finance transaction" means a secured transaction in connection with which:

(A) debt securities are issued;

(B) all or a portion of the securities issued have an initial stated maturity of at least 20 years; and

(C) the debtor, obligor, secured party, account debtor or other person obligated on collateral, assignor or assignee of a secured obligation, or assignor or assignee of a security interest is a State or a governmental unit of a State.

(68) "Pursuant to commitment", with respect to an advance made or other value given by a secured party, means pursuant to the secured party's obligation, whether or not a subsequent event of default or other event not within the secured party's control has relieved or may relieve the secured party from its obligation.

(69) "Record", except as used in "for record", "of record", "record or legal title", and "record owner", means information that is inscribed on a tangible medium or which is stored in an electronic or other medium and is retrievable in perceivable form.

(70) "Registered organization" means an organization organized solely under the law of a single State or the United States and as to which the State or the United States must maintain a public record showing the organization to have been organized.

(71) "Secondary obligor" means an obligor to the extent that:

(A) the obligor's obligation is secondary; or

(B) the obligor has a right of recourse with respect to an obligation secured by collateral against the debtor, another obligor, or property of either.

(72) "Secured party" means:

(A) a person in whose favor a security interest is created or provided for under a security agreement, whether or not any obligation to be secured is outstanding;

(B) a person that holds an agricultural lien;

(C) a consignor;

(D) a person to which accounts, chattel paper, payment intangibles, or promissory notes have been sold;

(E) a trustee, indenture trustee, agent, collateral agent, or other representative in whose favor a security interest or agricultural lien is created or provided for; or

(F) a person that holds a security interest arising under Section 2–401, 2–505, 2–711(3), 2A–508(5), 4–210, or 5–118.

(73) "Security agreement" means an agreement that creates or provides for a security interest.

(74) "Send", in connection with a record or notification, means:

(A) to deposit in the mail, deliver for transmission, or transmit by any other usual means of communication, with postage or cost of transmission provided for, addressed to any address reasonable under the circumstances; or

(B) to cause the record or notification to be received within the time that it would have been received if properly sent under subparagraph (A).

(75) "Software" means a computer program and any supporting information provided in connection with a transaction relating to the program. The term does not include a computer program that is included in the definition of goods.

(76) "State" means a State of the United States, the District of Columbia, Puerto Rico, the United States Virgin Islands, or any territory or insular possession subject to the jurisdiction of the United States.

(77) "Supporting obligation" means a letter-of-credit right or secondary obligation that supports the payment or performance of an account, chattel paper, a document, a general intangible, an instrument, or investment property.

(78) "Tangible chattel paper" means chattel paper evidenced by a record or records consisting of information that is inscribed on a tangible medium.

(79) "Termination statement" means an amendment of a financing statement which:

(A) identifies, by its file number, the initial financing statement to which it relates; and

(B) indicates either that it is a termination statement or that the identified financing statement is no longer effective.

(80) "Transmitting utility" means a person primarily engaged in the business of:

(A) operating a railroad, subway, street railway, or trolley bus;

(B) transmitting communications electrically, electromagnetically, or by light;

(C) transmitting goods by pipeline or sewer; or

(D) transmitting or producing and transmitting electricity, steam, gas, or water.

(b) The following definitions in other articles apply to this article:

"Applicant."	Section 5–102
"Beneficiary."	Section 5–102
"Broker."	Section 8–102
"Certificated security."	Section 8–102
"Check."	Section 3–104
"Clearing corporation."	Section 8–102
"Contract for sale."	Section 2–106
"Customer."	Section 4–104
"Entitlement holder."	Section 8–102
"Financial asset."	Section 8–102
"Holder in due course."	Section 3–302
"Issuer" (with respect to a letter of credit or letter-of-credit right).	Section 5–102
"Issuer" (with respect to a security).	Section 8–201
"Lease."	Section 2A–103
"Lease agreement."	Section 2A–103
"Lease contract."	Section 2A–103
"Leasehold interest."	Section 2A–103
"Lessee."	Section 2A–103
"Lessee in ordinary course of business."	Section 2A–103
"Lessor."	Section 2A–103
"Lessor's residual interest."	Section 2A–103
"Letter of credit."	Section 5–102
"Merchant."	Section 2–104
"Negotiable instrument."	Section 3–104
"Nominated person."	Section 5–102

(c) Article 1 contains general definitions and principles of construction and interpretation applicable throughout this article.

Amended in 1999 and 2000.

§ 9–103. Purchase-Money Security Interest; Application of Payments; Burden of Establishing.

(a) In this section:

(1) "purchase-money collateral" means goods or software that secures a purchase-money obligation incurred with respect to that collateral; and

(2) "purchase-money obligation" means an obligation of an obligor incurred as all or part of the price of the collateral or for value given to enable the debtor to acquire rights in or the use of the collateral if the value is in fact so used.

(b) A security interest in goods is a purchase-money security interest:

(1) to the extent that the goods are purchase-money collateral with respect to that security interest;

(2) if the security interest is in inventory that is or was purchase-money collateral, also to the extent that the security interest secures a purchase-money obligation incurred with respect to other inventory in which the secured party holds or held a purchase-money security interest; and

(3) also to the extent that the security interest secures a purchase-money obligation incurred with respect to software in which the secured party holds or held a purchase-money security interest.

(c) A security interest in software is a purchase-money security interest to the extent that the security interest also secures a purchase-money obligation incurred with respect to goods in which the secured party holds or held a purchase-money security interest if:

(1) the debtor acquired its interest in the software in an integrated transaction in which it acquired an interest in the goods; and

(2) the debtor acquired its interest in the software for the principal purpose of using the software in the goods.

(d) The security interest of a consignor in goods that are the subject of a consignment is a purchase-money security interest in inventory.

(e) In a transaction other than a consumer-goods transaction, if the extent to which a security interest is a purchase-money security interest depends on the application of a payment to a particular obligation, the payment must be applied:

(1) in accordance with any reasonable method of application to which the parties agree;

(2) in the absence of the parties' agreement to a reasonable method, in accordance with any intention of the obligor manifested at or before the time of payment; or

(3) in the absence of an agreement to a reasonable method and a timely manifestation of the obligor's intention, in the following order:

(A) to obligations that are not secured; and

(B) if more than one obligation is secured, to obligations secured by purchase-money security interests in the order in which those obligations were incurred.

(f) In a transaction other than a consumer-goods transaction, a purchase-money security interest does not lose its status as such, even if:

(1) the purchase-money collateral also secures an obligation that is not a purchase-money obligation;

(2) collateral that is not purchase-money collateral also secures the purchase-money obligation; or

(3) the purchase-money obligation has been renewed, refinanced, consolidated, or restructured.

(g) In a transaction other than a consumer-goods transaction, a secured party claiming a purchase-money security interest has the burden of establishing the extent to which the security interest is a purchase-money security interest.

(h) The limitation of the rules in subsections (e), (f), and (g) to transactions other than consumer-goods transactions is intended to leave to the court the determination of the proper rules in consumer-goods transactions. The court may not infer from that limitation the nature of the proper rule in consumer-goods transactions and may continue to apply established approaches.

§ 9–104. Control of Deposit Account.

(a) A secured party has control of a deposit account if:

(1) the secured party is the bank with which the deposit account is maintained;

(2) the debtor, secured party, and bank have agreed in an authenticated record that the bank will comply with instructions originated by the secured party directing disposition of the funds in the deposit account without further consent by the debtor; or

(3) the secured party becomes the bank's customer with respect to the deposit account.

(b) A secured party that has satisfied subsection (a) has control, even if the debtor retains the right to direct the disposition of funds from the deposit account.

§ 9–105. Control of Electronic Chattel Paper.

A secured party has control of electronic chattel paper if the record or records comprising the chattel paper are created, stored, and assigned in such a manner that:

(1) a single authoritative copy of the record or records exists which is unique, identifiable and, except as otherwise provided in paragraphs (4), (5), and (6), unalterable;

(2) the authoritative copy identifies the secured party as the assignee of the record or records;

(3) the authoritative copy is communicated to and maintained by the secured party or its designated custodian;

(4) copies or revisions that add or change an identified assignee of the authoritative copy can be made only with the participation of the secured party;

(5) each copy of the authoritative copy and any copy of a copy is readily identifiable as a copy that is not the authoritative copy; and

(6) any revision of the authoritative copy is readily identifiable as an authorized or unauthorized revision.

§ 9–106. Control of Investment Property.

(a) A person has control of a certificated security, uncertificated security, or security entitlement as provided in Section 8–106.

(b) A secured party has control of a commodity contract if:

(1) the secured party is the commodity intermediary with which the commodity contract is carried; or

(2) the commodity customer, secured party, and commodity intermediary have agreed that the commodity intermediary will apply any value distributed on account of the commodity contract as directed by the secured party without further consent by the commodity customer.

(c) A secured party having control of all security entitlements or commodity contracts carried in a securities account or commodity account has control over the securities account or commodity account.

§ 9–107. Control of Letter-of-Credit Right.

A secured party has control of a letter-of-credit right to the extent of any right to payment or performance by the issuer or any nominated person if the issuer or nominated person has consented to an assignment of proceeds of the letter of credit under Section 5–114(c) or otherwise applicable law or practice.

§ 9–108. Sufficiency of Description.

(a) Except as otherwise provided in subsections (c), (d), and (e), a description of personal or real property is sufficient, whether or not it is specific, if it reasonably identifies what is described.

(b) Except as otherwise provided in subsection (d), a description of collateral reasonably identifies the collateral if it identifies the collateral by:

(1) specific listing;

(2) category;

(3) except as otherwise provided in subsection (e), a type of collateral defined in [the Uniform Commercial Code];

(4) quantity;

(5) computational or allocational formula or procedure; or

(6) except as otherwise provided in subsection (c), any other method, if the identity of the collateral is objectively determinable.

(c) A description of collateral as "all the debtor's assets" or "all the debtor's personal property" or using words of similar import does not reasonably identify the collateral.

(d) Except as otherwise provided in subsection (e), a description of a security entitlement, securities account, or commodity account is sufficient if it describes:

(1) the collateral by those terms or as investment property; or

(2) the underlying financial asset or commodity contract.

(e) A description only by type of collateral defined in [the Uniform Commercial Code] is an insufficient description of:

(1) a commercial tort claim; or

(2) in a consumer transaction, consumer goods, a security entitlement, a securities account, or a commodity account.

[Subpart 2. Applicability of Article]

§ 9–109. Scope.

(a) Except as otherwise provided in subsections (c) and (d), this article applies to:

(1) a transaction, regardless of its form, that creates a security interest in personal property or fixtures by contract;

(2) an agricultural lien;

(3) a sale of accounts, chattel paper, payment intangibles, or promissory notes;

(4) a consignment;

(5) a security interest arising under Section 2–401, 2–505, 2–711(3), or 2A–508(5), as provided in Section 9–110; and

(6) a security interest arising under Section 4–210 or 5–118.

(b) The application of this article to a security interest in a secured obligation is not affected by the fact that the obligation is itself secured by a transaction or interest to which this article does not apply.

(c) This article does not apply to the extent that:

(1) a statute, regulation, or treaty of the United States preempts this article;

(2) another statute of this State expressly governs the creation, perfection, priority, or enforcement of a security interest created by this State or a governmental unit of this State;

(3) a statute of another State, a foreign country, or a governmental unit of another State or a foreign country, other than a statute generally applicable to security interests, expressly governs creation, perfection, priority, or enforcement of a security interest created by the State, country, or governmental unit; or

(4) the rights of a transferee beneficiary or nominated person under a letter of credit are independent and superior under Section 5–114.

(d) This article does not apply to:

(1) a landlord's lien, other than an agricultural lien;

(2) a lien, other than an agricultural lien, given by statute or other rule of law for services or materials, but Section 9–333 applies with respect to priority of the lien;

(3) an assignment of a claim for wages, salary, or other compensation of an employee;

(4) a sale of accounts, chattel paper, payment intangibles, or promissory notes as part of a sale of the business out of which they arose;

(5) an assignment of accounts, chattel paper, payment intangibles, or promissory notes which is for the purpose of collection only;

(6) an assignment of a right to payment under a contract to an assignee that is also obligated to perform under the contract;

(7) an assignment of a single account, payment intangible, or promissory note to an assignee in full or partial satisfaction of a preexisting indebtedness;

(8) a transfer of an interest in or an assignment of a claim under a policy of insurance, other than an assignment by or to a health-care provider of a health-care-insurance receivable and any subsequent assignment of the right to payment, but Sections 9–315 and 9–322 apply with respect to proceeds and priorities in proceeds;

(9) an assignment of a right represented by a judgment, other than a judgment taken on a right to payment that was collateral;

(10) a right of recoupment or set-off, but:

(A) Section 9–340 applies with respect to the effectiveness of rights of recoupment or set-off against deposit accounts; and

(B) Section 9–404 applies with respect to defenses or claims of an account debtor;

(11) the creation or transfer of an interest in or lien on real property, including a lease or rents thereunder, except to the extent that provision is made for:

(A) liens on real property in Sections 9–203 and 9–308;

(B) fixtures in Section 9–334;

(C) fixture filings in Sections 9–501, 9–502, 9–512, 9–516, and 9–519; and

(D) security agreements covering personal and real property in Section 9–604;

(12) an assignment of a claim arising in tort, other than a commercial tort claim, but Sections 9–315 and 9–322 apply with respect to proceeds and priorities in proceeds; or

(13) an assignment of a deposit account in a consumer transaction, but Sections 9–315 and 9–322 apply with respect to proceeds and priorities in proceeds.

§ 9–110. Security Interests Arising under Article 2 or 2A.

A security interest arising under Section 2–401, 2–505, 2–711(3), or 2A–508(5) is subject to this article. However, until the debtor obtains possession of the goods:

(1) the security interest is enforceable, even if Section 9–203(b)(3) has not been satisfied;

(2) filing is not required to perfect the security interest;

(3) the rights of the secured party after default by the debtor are governed by Article 2 or 2A; and

(4) the security interest has priority over a conflicting security interest created by the debtor.

Part 2 Effectiveness of Security Agreement; Attachment of Security Interest; Rights of Parties to Security Agreement
[Subpart 1. Effectiveness and Attachment]

§ 9–201. General Effectiveness of Security Agreement.

(a) Except as otherwise provided in [the Uniform Commercial Code], a security agreement is effective according to its terms between the parties, against purchasers of the collateral, and against creditors.

(b) A transaction subject to this article is subject to any applicable rule of law which establishes a different rule for consumers and

[insert reference to (i) any other statute or regulation that regulates the rates, charges, agreements, and practices for loans, credit sales, or other extensions of credit and (ii) any consumer-protection statute or regulation].

(c) In case of conflict between this article and a rule of law, statute, or regulation described in subsection (b), the rule of law, statute, or regulation controls. Failure to comply with a statute or regulation described in subsection (b) has only the effect the statute or regulation specifies.

(d) This article does not:

(1) validate any rate, charge, agreement, or practice that violates a rule of law, statute, or regulation described in subsection (b); or

(2) extend the application of the rule of law, statute, or regulation to a transaction not otherwise subject to it.

§ 9–202. Title to Collateral Immaterial.

Except as otherwise provided with respect to consignments or sales of accounts, chattel paper, payment intangibles, or promissory notes, the provisions of this article with regard to rights and obligations apply whether title to collateral is in the secured party or the debtor.

§ 9–203. Attachment and Enforceability of Security Interest; Proceeds; Supporting Obligations; Formal Requisites.

(a) A security interest attaches to collateral when it becomes enforceable against the debtor with respect to the collateral, unless an agreement expressly postpones the time of attachment.

(b) Except as otherwise provided in subsections (c) through (i), a security interest is enforceable against the debtor and third parties with respect to the collateral only if:

(1) value has been given;

(2) the debtor has rights in the collateral or the power to transfer rights in the collateral to a secured party; and

(3) one of the following conditions is met:

(A) the debtor has authenticated a security agreement that provides a description of the collateral and, if the security interest covers timber to be cut, a description of the land concerned;

(B) the collateral is not a certificated security and is in the possession of the secured party under Section 9–313 pursuant to the debtor's security agreement;

(C) the collateral is a certificated security in registered form and the security certificate has been delivered to the secured party under Section 8–301 pursuant to the debtor's security agreement; or

(D) the collateral is deposit accounts, electronic chattel paper, investment property, or letter-of-credit rights, and the secured party has control under Section 9–104, 9–105, 9–106, or 9–107 pursuant to the debtor's security agreement.

(c) Subsection (b) is subject to Section 4–210 on the security interest of a collecting bank, Section 5–118 on the security interest of a letter-of-credit issuer or nominated person, Section 9–110 on a security interest arising under Article 2 or 2A, and Section 9–206 on security interests in investment property.

(d) A person becomes bound as debtor by a security agreement entered into by another person if, by operation of law other than this article or by contract:

(1) the security agreement becomes effective to create a security interest in the person's property; or

(2) the person becomes generally obligated for the obligations of the other person, including the obligation secured under the security agreement, and acquires or succeeds to all or substantially all of the assets of the other person.

(e) If a new debtor becomes bound as debtor by a security agreement entered into by another person:

(1) the agreement satisfies subsection (b)(3) with respect to existing or after-acquired property of the new debtor to the extent the property is described in the agreement; and

(2) another agreement is not necessary to make a security interest in the property enforceable.

(f) The attachment of a security interest in collateral gives the secured party the rights to proceeds provided by Section 9–315 and is also attachment of a security interest in a supporting obligation for the collateral.

(g) The attachment of a security interest in a right to payment or performance secured by a security interest or other lien on personal or real property is also attachment of a security interest in the security interest, mortgage, or other lien.

(h) The attachment of a security interest in a securities account is also attachment of a security interest in the security entitlements carried in the securities account.

(i) The attachment of a security interest in a commodity account is also attachment of a security interest in the commodity contracts carried in the commodity account.

§ 9–204. After-Acquired Property; Future Advances.

(a) Except as otherwise provided in subsection (b), a security agreement may create or provide for a security interest in after-acquired collateral.

(b) A security interest does not attach under a term constituting an after-acquired property clause to:

(1) consumer goods, other than an accession when given as additional security, unless the debtor acquires rights in them within 10 days after the secured party gives value; or

(2) a commercial tort claim.

(c) A security agreement may provide that collateral secures, or that accounts, chattel paper, payment intangibles, or promissory notes are sold in connection with, future advances or other value, whether or not the advances or value are given pursuant to commitment.

§ 9–205. Use or Disposition of Collateral Permissible.

(a) A security interest is not invalid or fraudulent against creditors solely because:

(1) the debtor has the right or ability to:

(A) use, commingle, or dispose of all or part of the collateral, including returned or repossessed goods;

(B) collect, compromise, enforce, or otherwise deal with collateral;

(C) accept the return of collateral or make repossessions; or

(D) use, commingle, or dispose of proceeds; or

(2) the secured party fails to require the debtor to account for proceeds or replace collateral.

(b) This section does not relax the requirements of possession if attachment, perfection, or enforcement of a security interest depends upon possession of the collateral by the secured party.

§ 9–206. Security Interest Arising in Purchase or Delivery of Financial Asset.

(a) A security interest in favor of a securities intermediary attaches to a person's security entitlement if:

(1) the person buys a financial asset through the securities intermediary in a transaction in which the person is obligated to pay the purchase price to the securities intermediary at the time of the purchase; and

(2) the securities intermediary credits the financial asset to the buyer's securities account before the buyer pays the securities intermediary.

(b) The security interest described in subsection (a) secures the person's obligation to pay for the financial asset.

(c) A security interest in favor of a person that delivers a certificated security or other financial asset represented by a writing attaches to the security or other financial asset if:

(1) the security or other financial asset:

(A) in the ordinary course of business is transferred by delivery with any necessary indorsement or assignment; and

(B) is delivered under an agreement between persons in the business of dealing with such securities or financial assets; and

(2) the agreement calls for delivery against payment.

(d) The security interest described in subsection (c) secures the obligation to make payment for the delivery.

[Subpart 2. Rights and Duties]

§ 9–207. Rights and Duties of Secured Party Having Possession or Control of Collateral.

(a) Except as otherwise provided in subsection (d), a secured party shall use reasonable care in the custody and preservation of collateral in the secured party's possession. In the case of chattel paper or an instrument, reasonable care includes taking necessary steps to preserve rights against prior parties unless otherwise agreed.

(b) Except as otherwise provided in subsection (d), if a secured party has possession of collateral:

(1) reasonable expenses, including the cost of insurance and payment of taxes or other charges, incurred in the custody, preservation, use, or operation of the collateral are chargeable to the debtor and are secured by the collateral;

(2) the risk of accidental loss or damage is on the debtor to the extent of a deficiency in any effective insurance coverage;

(3) the secured party shall keep the collateral identifiable, but fungible collateral may be commingled; and

(4) the secured party may use or operate the collateral:

(A) for the purpose of preserving the collateral or its value;

(B) as permitted by an order of a court having competent jurisdiction; or

(C) except in the case of consumer goods, in the manner and to the extent agreed by the debtor.

(c) Except as otherwise provided in subsection (d), a secured party having possession of collateral or control of collateral under Section 9–104, 9–105, 9–106, or 9–107:

(1) may hold as additional security any proceeds, except money or funds, received from the collateral;

(2) shall apply money or funds received from the collateral to reduce the secured obligation, unless remitted to the debtor; and

(3) may create a security interest in the collateral.

(d) If the secured party is a buyer of accounts, chattel paper, payment intangibles, or promissory notes or a consignor:

(1) subsection (a) does not apply unless the secured party is entitled under an agreement:

(A) to charge back uncollected collateral; or

(B) otherwise to full or limited recourse against the debtor or a secondary obligor based on the nonpayment or other default of an account debtor or other obligor on the collateral; and

(2) subsections (b) and (c) do not apply.

§ 9–208. Additional Duties of Secured Party Having Control of Collateral.

(a) This section applies to cases in which there is no outstanding secured obligation and the secured party is not committed to make advances, incur obligations, or otherwise give value.

(b) Within 10 days after receiving an authenticated demand by the debtor:

(1) a secured party having control of a deposit account under Section 9–104(a)(2) shall send to the bank with which the deposit account is maintained an authenticated statement that releases the bank from any further obligation to comply with instructions originated by the secured party;

(2) a secured party having control of a deposit account under Section 9–104(a)(3) shall:

(A) pay the debtor the balance on deposit in the deposit account; or

(B) transfer the balance on deposit into a deposit account in the debtor's name;

(3) a secured party, other than a buyer, having control of electronic chattel paper under Section 9–105 shall:

(A) communicate the authoritative copy of the electronic chattel paper to the debtor or its designated custodian;

(B) if the debtor designates a custodian that is the designated custodian with which the authoritative copy of the electronic chattel paper is maintained for the secured party, communicate to the custodian an authenticated record releasing the designated custodian from any further obligation to comply with instructions originated by the secured party and instructing the custodian to comply with instructions originated by the debtor; and

(C) take appropriate action to enable the debtor or its designated custodian to make copies of or revisions to the authoritative copy which add or change an identified assignee of the authoritative copy without the consent of the secured party;

(4) a secured party having control of investment property under Section 8–106(d)(2) or 9–106(b) shall send to the securities intermediary or commodity intermediary with which the security entitlement or commodity contract is maintained an authenticated

record that releases the securities intermediary or commodity intermediary from any further obligation to comply with entitlement orders or directions originated by the secured party; and

(5) a secured party having control of a letter-of-credit right under Section 9–107 shall send to each person having an unfulfilled obligation to pay or deliver proceeds of the letter of credit to the secured party an authenticated release from any further obligation to pay or deliver proceeds of the letter of credit to the secured party.

§ 9–209. Duties of Secured Party If Account Debtor Has Been Notified of Assignment.

(a) Except as otherwise provided in subsection (c), this section applies if:

(1) there is no outstanding secured obligation; and

(2) the secured party is not committed to make advances, incur obligations, or otherwise give value.

(b) Within 10 days after receiving an authenticated demand by the debtor, a secured party shall send to an account debtor that has received notification of an assignment to the secured party as assignee under Section 9–406(a) an authenticated record that releases the account debtor from any further obligation to the secured party.

(c) This section does not apply to an assignment constituting the sale of an account, chattel paper, or payment intangible.

§ 9–210. Request for Accounting; Request Regarding List of Collateral or Statement of Account.

(a) In this section:

(1) "Request" means a record of a type described in paragraph (2), (3), or (4).

(2) "Request for an accounting" means a record authenticated by a debtor requesting that the recipient provide an accounting of the unpaid obligations secured by collateral and reasonably identifying the transaction or relationship that is the subject of the request.

(3) "Request regarding a list of collateral" means a record authenticated by a debtor requesting that the recipient approve or correct a list of what the debtor believes to be the collateral securing an obligation and reasonably identifying the transaction or relationship that is the subject of the request.

(4) "Request regarding a statement of account" means a record authenticated by a debtor requesting that the recipient approve or correct a statement indicating what the debtor believes to be the aggregate amount of unpaid obligations secured by collateral as of a specified date and reasonably identifying the transaction or relationship that is the subject of the request.

(b) Subject to subsections (c), (d), (e), and (f), a secured party, other than a buyer of accounts, chattel paper, payment intangibles, or promissory notes or a consignor, shall comply with a request within 14 days after receipt:

(1) in the case of a request for an accounting, by authenticating and sending to the debtor an accounting; and

(2) in the case of a request regarding a list of collateral or a request regarding a statement of account, by authenticating and sending to the debtor an approval or correction.

(c) A secured party that claims a security interest in all of a particular type of collateral owned by the debtor may comply with a request regarding a list of collateral by sending to the debtor an authenticated record including a statement to that effect within 14 days after receipt.

(d) A person that receives a request regarding a list of collateral, claims no interest in the collateral when it receives the request, and claimed an interest in the collateral at an earlier time shall comply with the request within 14 days after receipt by sending to the debtor an authenticated record:

(1) disclaiming any interest in the collateral; and

(2) if known to the recipient, providing the name and mailing address of any assignee of or successor to the recipient's interest in the collateral.

(e) A person that receives a request for an accounting or a request regarding a statement of account, claims no interest in the obligations when it receives the request, and claimed an interest in the obligations at an earlier time shall comply with the request within 14 days after receipt by sending to the debtor an authenticated record:

(1) disclaiming any interest in the obligations; and

(2) if known to the recipient, providing the name and mailing address of any assignee of or successor to the recipient's interest in the obligations.

(f) A debtor is entitled without charge to one response to a request under this section during any six-month period. The secured party may require payment of a charge not exceeding $25 for each additional response.

As amended in 1999.

Part 3 Perfection and Priority

[Subpart 1. Law Governing Perfection and Priority]

§ 9–301. Law Governing Perfection and Priority of Security Interests.

Except as otherwise provided in Sections 9–303 through 9–306, the following rules determine the law governing perfection, the effect of perfection or nonperfection, and the priority of a security interest in collateral:

(1) Except as otherwise provided in this section, while a debtor is located in a jurisdiction, the local law of that jurisdiction governs perfection, the effect of perfection or nonperfection, and the priority of a security interest in collateral.

(2) While collateral is located in a jurisdiction, the local law of that jurisdiction governs perfection, the effect of perfection or nonperfection, and the priority of a possessory security interest in that collateral.

(3) Except as otherwise provided in paragraph (4), while negotiable documents, goods, instruments, money, or tangible chattel paper is located in a jurisdiction, the local law of that jurisdiction governs:

(A) perfection of a security interest in the goods by filing a fixture filing;

(B) perfection of a security interest in timber to be cut; and

(C) the effect of perfection or nonperfection and the priority of a nonpossessory security interest in the collateral.

(4) The local law of the jurisdiction in which the wellhead or minehead is located governs perfection, the effect of perfection or nonperfection, and the priority of a security interest in as-extracted collateral.

§ 9–302. Law Governing Perfection and Priority of Agricultural Liens.

While farm products are located in a jurisdiction, the local law of that jurisdiction governs perfection, the effect of perfection or nonperfection, and the priority of an agricultural lien on the farm products.

§ 9–303. Law Governing Perfection and Priority of Security Interests in Goods Covered by a Certificate of Title.

(a) This section applies to goods covered by a certificate of title, even if there is no other relationship between the jurisdiction under whose certificate of title the goods are covered and the goods or the debtor.

(b) Goods become covered by a certificate of title when a valid application for the certificate of title and the applicable fee are delivered to the appropriate authority. Goods cease to be covered by a certificate of title at the earlier of the time the certificate of title ceases to be effective under the law of the issuing jurisdiction or the time the goods become covered subsequently by a certificate of title issued by another jurisdiction.

(c) The local law of the jurisdiction under whose certificate of title the goods are covered governs perfection, the effect of perfection or nonperfection, and the priority of a security interest in goods covered by a certificate of title from the time the goods become covered by the certificate of title until the goods cease to be covered by the certificate of title.

§ 9–304. Law Governing Perfection and Priority of Security Interests in Deposit Accounts.

(a) The local law of a bank's jurisdiction governs perfection, the effect of perfection or nonperfection, and the priority of a security interest in a deposit account maintained with that bank.

(b) The following rules determine a bank's jurisdiction for purposes of this part:

(1) If an agreement between the bank and the debtor governing the deposit account expressly provides that a particular jurisdiction is the bank's jurisdiction for purposes of this part, this article, or [the Uniform Commercial Code], that jurisdiction is the bank's jurisdiction.

(2) If paragraph (1) does not apply and an agreement between the bank and its customer governing the deposit account expressly provides that the agreement is governed by the law of a particular jurisdiction, that jurisdiction is the bank's jurisdiction.

(3) If neither paragraph (1) nor paragraph (2) applies and an agreement between the bank and its customer governing the deposit account expressly provides that the deposit account is maintained at an office in a particular jurisdiction, that jurisdiction is the bank's jurisdiction.

(4) If none of the preceding paragraphs applies, the bank's jurisdiction is the jurisdiction in which the office identified in an account statement as the office serving the customer's account is located.

(5) If none of the preceding paragraphs applies, the bank's jurisdiction is the jurisdiction in which the chief executive office of the bank is located.

§ 9–305. Law Governing Perfection and Priority of Security Interests in Investment Property.

(a) Except as otherwise provided in subsection (c), the following rules apply:

(1) While a security certificate is located in a jurisdiction, the local law of that jurisdiction governs perfection, the effect of perfection or nonperfection, and the priority of a security interest in the certificated security represented thereby.

(2) The local law of the issuer's jurisdiction as specified in Section 8–110(d) governs perfection, the effect of perfection or nonperfection, and the priority of a security interest in an uncertificated security.

(3) The local law of the securities intermediary's jurisdiction as specified in Section 8–110(e) governs perfection, the effect of perfection or nonperfection, and the priority of a security interest in a security entitlement or securities account.

(4) The local law of the commodity intermediary's jurisdiction governs perfection, the effect of perfection or nonperfection, and the priority of a security interest in a commodity contract or commodity account.

(b) The following rules determine a commodity intermediary's jurisdiction for purposes of this part:

(1) If an agreement between the commodity intermediary and commodity customer governing the commodity account expressly provides that a particular jurisdiction is the commodity intermediary's jurisdiction for purposes of this part, this article, or [the Uniform Commercial Code], that jurisdiction is the commodity intermediary's jurisdiction.

(2) If paragraph (1) does not apply and an agreement between the commodity intermediary and commodity customer governing the commodity account expressly provides that the agreement is governed by the law of a particular jurisdiction, that jurisdiction is the commodity intermediary's jurisdiction.

(3) If neither paragraph (1) nor paragraph (2) applies and an agreement between the commodity intermediary and commodity customer governing the commodity account expressly provides that the commodity account is maintained at an office in a particular jurisdiction, that jurisdiction is the commodity intermediary's jurisdiction.

(4) If none of the preceding paragraphs applies, the commodity intermediary's jurisdiction is the jurisdiction in which the office identified in an account statement as the office serving the commodity customer's account is located.

(5) If none of the preceding paragraphs applies, the commodity intermediary's jurisdiction is the jurisdiction in which the chief executive office of the commodity intermediary is located.

(c) The local law of the jurisdiction in which the debtor is located governs:

(1) perfection of a security interest in investment property by filing;

(2) automatic perfection of a security interest in investment property created by a broker or securities intermediary; and

(3) automatic perfection of a security interest in a commodity contract or commodity account created by a commodity intermediary.

§ 9–306. Law Governing Perfection and Priority of Security Interests in Letter-of-Credit Rights.

(a) Subject to subsection (c), the local law of the issuer's jurisdiction or a nominated person's jurisdiction governs perfection, the effect of perfection or nonperfection, and the priority of a security interest in a letter-of-credit right if the issuer's jurisdiction or nominated person's jurisdiction is a State.

(b) For purposes of this part, an issuer's jurisdiction or nominated person's jurisdiction is the jurisdiction whose law governs the liability of the issuer or nominated person with respect to the letter-of-credit right as provided in Section 5–116.

(c) This section does not apply to a security interest that is perfected only under Section 9–308(d).

§ 9–307. Location of Debtor.

(a) In this section, "place of business" means a place where a debtor conducts its affairs.

(b) Except as otherwise provided in this section, the following rules determine a debtor's location:

(1) A debtor who is an individual is located at the individual's principal residence.

(2) A debtor that is an organization and has only one place of business is located at its place of business.

(3) A debtor that is an organization and has more than one place of business is located at its chief executive office.

(c) Subsection (b) applies only if a debtor's residence, place of business, or chief executive office, as applicable, is located in a jurisdiction whose law generally requires information concerning the existence of a nonpossessory security interest to be made generally available in a filing, recording, or registration system as a condition or result of the security interest's obtaining priority over the rights of a lien creditor with respect to the collateral. If subsection (b) does not apply, the debtor is located in the District of Columbia.

(d) A person that ceases to exist, have a residence, or have a place of business continues to be located in the jurisdiction specified by subsections (b) and (c).

(e) A registered organization that is organized under the law of a State is located in that State.

(f) Except as otherwise provided in subsection (i), a registered organization that is organized under the law of the United States and a branch or agency of a bank that is not organized under the law of the United States or a State are located:

(1) in the State that the law of the United States designates, if the law designates a State of location;

(2) in the State that the registered organization, branch, or agency designates, if the law of the United States authorizes the registered organization, branch, or agency to designate its State of location; or

(3) in the District of Columbia, if neither paragraph (1) nor paragraph (2) applies.

(g) A registered organization continues to be located in the jurisdiction specified by subsection (e) or (f) notwithstanding:

(1) the suspension, revocation, forfeiture, or lapse of the registered organization's status as such in its jurisdiction of organization; or

(2) the dissolution, winding up, or cancellation of the existence of the registered organization.

(h) The United States is located in the District of Columbia.

(i) A branch or agency of a bank that is not organized under the law of the United States or a State is located in the State in which the branch or agency is licensed, if all branches and agencies of the bank are licensed in only one State.

(j) A foreign air carrier under the Federal Aviation Act of 1958, as amended, is located at the designated office of the agent upon which service of process may be made on behalf of the carrier.

(k) This section applies only for purposes of this part.

[Subpart 2. Perfection]

§ 9–308. When Security Interest or Agricultural Lien Is Perfected; Continuity of Perfection.

(a) Except as otherwise provided in this section and Section 9–309, a security interest is perfected if it has attached and all of the applicable requirements for perfection in Sections 9–310 through 9–316 have been satisfied. A security interest is perfected when it attaches if the applicable requirements are satisfied before the security interest attaches.

(b) An agricultural lien is perfected if it has become effective and all of the applicable requirements for perfection in Section 9–310 have been satisfied. An agricultural lien is perfected when it becomes effective if the applicable requirements are satisfied before the agricultural lien becomes effective.

(c) A security interest or agricultural lien is perfected continuously if it is originally perfected by one method under this article and is later perfected by another method under this article, without an intermediate period when it was unperfected.

(d) Perfection of a security interest in collateral also perfects a security interest in a supporting obligation for the collateral.

(e) Perfection of a security interest in a right to payment or performance also perfects a security interest in a security interest, mortgage, or other lien on personal or real property securing the right.

(f) Perfection of a security interest in a securities account also perfects a security interest in the security entitlements carried in the securities account.

(g) Perfection of a security interest in a commodity account also perfects a security interest in the commodity contracts carried in the commodity account.

Legislative Note: Any statute conflicting with subsection (e) must be made expressly subject to that subsection.

§ 9–309. Security Interest Perfected upon Attachment.

The following security interests are perfected when they attach:

(1) a purchase-money security interest in consumer goods, except as otherwise provided in Section 9–311(b) with respect to consumer goods that are subject to a statute or treaty described in Section 9–311(a);

(2) an assignment of accounts or payment intangibles which does not by itself or in conjunction with other assignments to the same assignee transfer a significant part of the assignor's outstanding accounts or payment intangibles;

(3) a sale of a payment intangible;

(4) a sale of a promissory note;

(5) a security interest created by the assignment of a health-care-insurance receivable to the provider of the health-care goods or services;

(6) a security interest arising under Section 2–401, 2–505, 2–711(3), or 2A–508(5), until the debtor obtains possession of the collateral;

(7) a security interest of a collecting bank arising under Section 4–210;

(8) a security interest of an issuer or nominated person arising under Section 5–118;

(9) a security interest arising in the delivery of a financial asset under Section 9–206(c);

(10) a security interest in investment property created by a broker or securities intermediary;

(11) a security interest in a commodity contract or a commodity account created by a commodity intermediary;

(12) an assignment for the benefit of all creditors of the transferor and subsequent transfers by the assignee thereunder; and

(13) a security interest created by an assignment of a beneficial interest in a decedent's estate; and

(14) a sale by an individual of an account that is a right to payment of winnings in a lottery or other game of chance.

§ 9–310. When Filing Required to Perfect Security Interest or Agricultural Lien; Security Interests and Agricultural Liens to Which Filing Provisions Do Not Apply.

(a) Except as otherwise provided in subsection (b) and Section 9–312(b), a financing statement must be filed to perfect all security interests and agricultural liens.

(b) The filing of a financing statement is not necessary to perfect a security interest:

(1) that is perfected under Section 9–308(d), (e), (f), or (g);

(2) that is perfected under Section 9–309 when it attaches;

(3) in property subject to a statute, regulation, or treaty described in Section 9–311(a);

(4) in goods in possession of a bailee which is perfected under Section 9–312(d)(1) or (2);

(5) in certificated securities, documents, goods, or instruments which is perfected without filing or possession under Section 9–312(e), (f), or (g);

(6) in collateral in the secured party's possession under Section 9–313;

(7) in a certificated security which is perfected by delivery of the security certificate to the secured party under Section 9–313;

(8) in deposit accounts, electronic chattel paper, investment property, or letter-of-credit rights which is perfected by control under Section 9–314;

(9) in proceeds which is perfected under Section 9–315; or

(10) that is perfected under Section 9–316.

(c) If a secured party assigns a perfected security interest or agricultural lien, a filing under this article is not required to continue the perfected status of the security interest against creditors of and transferees from the original debtor.

§ 9–311. Perfection of Security Interests in Property Subject to Certain Statutes, Regulations, and Treaties.

(a) Except as otherwise provided in subsection (d), the filing of a financing statement is not necessary or effective to perfect a security interest in property subject to:

(1) a statute, regulation, or treaty of the United States whose requirements for a security interest's obtaining priority over the rights of a lien creditor with respect to the property preempt Section 9–310(a);

(2) [list any certificate-of-title statute covering automobiles, trailers, mobile homes, boats, farm tractors, or the like, which provides for a security interest to be indicated on the certificate as a condition or result of perfection, and any non-Uniform Commercial Code central filing statute]; or

(3) a certificate-of-title statute of another jurisdiction which provides for a security interest to be indicated on the certificate as a condition or result of the security interest's obtaining priority over the rights of a lien creditor with respect to the property.

(b) Compliance with the requirements of a statute, regulation, or treaty described in subsection (a) for obtaining priority over the rights of a lien creditor is equivalent to the filing of a financing statement under this article. Except as otherwise provided in subsection (d) and Sections 9–313 and 9–316(d) and (e) for goods covered by a certificate of title, a security interest in property subject to a statute, regulation, or treaty described in subsection (a) may be perfected only by compliance with those requirements, and a security interest so perfected remains perfected notwithstanding a change in the use or transfer of possession of the collateral.

(c) Except as otherwise provided in subsection (d) and Section 9–316(d) and (e), duration and renewal of perfection of a security interest perfected by compliance with the requirements prescribed by a statute, regulation, or treaty described in subsection (a) are governed by the statute, regulation, or treaty. In other respects, the security interest is subject to this article.

(d) During any period in which collateral subject to a statute specified in subsection (a)(2) is inventory held for sale or lease by a person or leased by that person as lessor and that person is in the business of selling goods of that kind, this section does not apply to a security interest in that collateral created by that person.

Legislative Note: This Article contemplates that perfection of a security interest in goods covered by a certificate of title occurs upon receipt by

appropriate State officials of a properly tendered application for a certificate of title on which the security interest is to be indicated, without a relation back to an earlier time. States whose certificate-of-title statutes provide for perfection at a different time or contain a relation-back provision should amend the statutes accordingly.

§ 9–312. Perfection of Security Interests in Chattel Paper, Deposit Accounts, Documents, Goods Covered by Documents, Instruments, Investment Property, Letter-of-Credit Rights, and Money; Perfection by Permissive Filing; Temporary Perfection without Filing or Transfer of Possession.

(a) A security interest in chattel paper, negotiable documents, instruments, or investment property may be perfected by filing.

(b) Except as otherwise provided in Section 9–315(c) and (d) for proceeds:

(1) a security interest in a deposit account may be perfected only by control under Section 9–314;

(2) and except as otherwise provided in Section 9–308(d), a security interest in a letter-of-credit right may be perfected only by control under Section 9–314; and

(3) a security interest in money may be perfected only by the secured party's taking possession under Section 9–313.

(c) While goods are in the possession of a bailee that has issued a negotiable document covering the goods:

(1) a security interest in the goods may be perfected by perfecting a security interest in the document; and

(2) a security interest perfected in the document has priority over any security interest that becomes perfected in the goods by another method during that time.

(d) While goods are in the possession of a bailee that has issued a nonnegotiable document covering the goods, a security interest in the goods may be perfected by:

(1) issuance of a document in the name of the secured party;

(2) the bailee's receipt of notification of the secured party's interest; or

(3) filing as to the goods.

(e) A security interest in certificated securities, negotiable documents, or instruments is perfected without filing or the taking of possession for a period of 20 days from the time it attaches to the extent that it arises for new value given under an authenticated security agreement.

(f) A perfected security interest in a negotiable document or goods in possession of a bailee, other than one that has issued a negotiable document for the goods, remains perfected for 20 days without filing if the secured party makes available to the debtor the goods or documents representing the goods for the purpose of:

(1) ultimate sale or exchange; or

(2) loading, unloading, storing, shipping, transshipping, manufacturing, processing, or otherwise dealing with them in a manner preliminary to their sale or exchange.

(g) A perfected security interest in a certificated security or instrument remains perfected for 20 days without filing if the secured party delivers the security certificate or instrument to the debtor for the purpose of:

(1) ultimate sale or exchange; or

(2) presentation, collection, enforcement, renewal, or registration of transfer.

(h) After the 20-day period specified in subsection (e), (f), or (g) expires, perfection depends upon compliance with this article.

§ 9–313. When Possession by or Delivery to Secured Party Perfects Security Interest without Filing.

(a) Except as otherwise provided in subsection (b), a secured party may perfect a security interest in negotiable documents, goods, instruments, money, or tangible chattel paper by taking possession of the collateral. A secured party may perfect a security interest in certificated securities by taking delivery of the certificated securities under Section 8–301.

(b) With respect to goods covered by a certificate of title issued by this State, a secured party may perfect a security interest in the goods by taking possession of the goods only in the circumstances described in Section 9–316(d).

(c) With respect to collateral other than certificated securities and goods covered by a document, a secured party takes possession of collateral in the possession of a person other than the debtor, the secured party, or a lessee of the collateral from the debtor in the ordinary course of the debtor's business, when:

(1) the person in possession authenticates a record acknowledging that it holds possession of the collateral for the secured party's benefit; or

(2) the person takes possession of the collateral after having authenticated a record acknowledging that it will hold possession of collateral for the secured party's benefit.

(d) If perfection of a security interest depends upon possession of the collateral by a secured party, perfection occurs no earlier than the time the secured party takes possession and continues only while the secured party retains possession.

(e) A security interest in a certificated security in registered form is perfected by delivery when delivery of the certificated security occurs under Section 8–301 and remains perfected by delivery until the debtor obtains possession of the security certificate.

(f) A person in possession of collateral is not required to acknowledge that it holds possession for a secured party's benefit.

(g) If a person acknowledges that it holds possession for the secured party's benefit:

(1) the acknowledgment is effective under subsection (c) or Section 8–301(a), even if the acknowledgment violates the rights of a debtor; and

(2) unless the person otherwise agrees or law other than this article otherwise provides, the person does not owe any duty to the secured party and is not required to confirm the acknowledgment to another person.

(h) A secured party having possession of collateral does not relinquish possession by delivering the collateral to a person other than the debtor or a lessee of the collateral from the debtor in the ordinary course of the debtor's business if the person was instructed before the delivery or is instructed contemporaneously with the delivery:

(1) to hold possession of the collateral for the secured party's benefit; or

(2) to redeliver the collateral to the secured party.

(i) A secured party does not relinquish possession, even if a delivery under subsection (h) violates the rights of a debtor. A person to which collateral is delivered under subsection (h) does not owe any duty to the secured party and is not required to confirm the delivery to another person unless the person otherwise agrees or law other than this article otherwise provides.

§ 9–314. Perfection by Control.

(a) A security interest in investment property, deposit accounts, letter-of-credit rights, or electronic chattel paper may be perfected by control of the collateral under Section 9–104, 9–105, 9–106, or 9–107.

(b) A security interest in deposit accounts, electronic chattel paper, or letter-of-credit rights is perfected by control under Section 9–104, 9–105, or 9–107 when the secured party obtains control and remains perfected by control only while the secured party retains control.

(c) A security interest in investment property is perfected by control under Section 9–106 from the time the secured party obtains control and remains perfected by control until:

(1) the secured party does not have control; and

(2) one of the following occurs:

(A) if the collateral is a certificated security, the debtor has or acquires possession of the security certificate;

(B) if the collateral is an uncertificated security, the issuer has registered or registers the debtor as the registered owner; or

(C) if the collateral is a security entitlement, the debtor is or becomes the entitlement holder.

§ 9–315. Secured Party's Rights on Disposition of Collateral and in Proceeds.

(a) Except as otherwise provided in this article and in Section 2–403(2):

(1) a security interest or agricultural lien continues in collateral notwithstanding sale, lease, license, exchange, or other disposition thereof unless the secured party authorized the disposition free of the security interest or agricultural lien; and

(2) a security interest attaches to any identifiable proceeds of collateral.

(b) Proceeds that are commingled with other property are identifiable proceeds:

(1) if the proceeds are goods, to the extent provided by Section 9–336; and

(2) if the proceeds are not goods, to the extent that the secured party identifies the proceeds by a method of tracing, including application of equitable principles, that is permitted under law other than this article with respect to commingled property of the type involved.

(c) A security interest in proceeds is a perfected security interest if the security interest in the original collateral was perfected.

(d) A perfected security interest in proceeds becomes unperfected on the 21st day after the security interest attaches to the proceeds unless:

(1) the following conditions are satisfied:

(A) a filed financing statement covers the original collateral;

(B) the proceeds are collateral in which a security interest may be perfected by filing in the office in which the financing statement has been filed; and

(C) the proceeds are not acquired with cash proceeds;

(2) the proceeds are identifiable cash proceeds; or

(3) the security interest in the proceeds is perfected other than under subsection (c) when the security interest attaches to the proceeds or within 20 days thereafter.

(e) If a filed financing statement covers the original collateral, a security interest in proceeds which remains perfected under subsection (d)(1) becomes unperfected at the later of:

(1) when the effectiveness of the filed financing statement lapses under Section 9–515 or is terminated under Section 9–513; or

(2) the 21st day after the security interest attaches to the proceeds.

§ 9–316. Continued Perfection of Security Interest Following Change in Governing Law.

(a) A security interest perfected pursuant to the law of the jurisdiction designated in Section 9–301(1) or 9–305(c) remains perfected until the earliest of:

(1) the time perfection would have ceased under the law of that jurisdiction;

(2) the expiration of four months after a change of the debtor's location to another jurisdiction; or

(3) the expiration of one year after a transfer of collateral to a person that thereby becomes a debtor and is located in another jurisdiction.

(b) If a security interest described in subsection (a) becomes perfected under the law of the other jurisdiction before the earliest time or event described in that subsection, it remains perfected thereafter. If the security interest does not become perfected under the law of the other jurisdiction before the earliest time or event, it becomes unperfected and is deemed never to have been perfected as against a purchaser of the collateral for value.

(c) A possessory security interest in collateral, other than goods covered by a certificate of title and as-extracted collateral consisting of goods, remains continuously perfected if:

(1) the collateral is located in one jurisdiction and subject to a security interest perfected under the law of that jurisdiction;

(2) thereafter the collateral is brought into another jurisdiction; and

(3) upon entry into the other jurisdiction, the security interest is perfected under the law of the other jurisdiction.

(d) Except as otherwise provided in subsection (e), a security interest in goods covered by a certificate of title which is perfected by any method under the law of another jurisdiction when the goods become covered by a certificate of title from this State remains perfected until the security interest would have become unperfected under the law of the other jurisdiction had the goods not become so covered.

(e) A security interest described in subsection (d) becomes unperfected as against a purchaser of the goods for value and is deemed never to have been perfected as against a purchaser of the goods for value if the applicable requirements for perfection under Section 9–311(b) or 9–313 are not satisfied before the earlier of:

(1) the time the security interest would have become unperfected under the law of the other jurisdiction had the goods not become covered by a certificate of title from this State; or

(2) the expiration of four months after the goods had become so covered.

(f) A security interest in deposit accounts, letter-of-credit rights, or investment property which is perfected under the law of the bank's jurisdiction, the issuer's jurisdiction, a nominated person's jurisdiction, the securities intermediary's jurisdiction, or the commodity intermediary's jurisdiction, as applicable, remains perfected until the earlier of:

(1) the time the security interest would have become unperfected under the law of that jurisdiction; or

(2) the expiration of four months after a change of the applicable jurisdiction to another jurisdiction.

(g) If a security interest described in subsection (f) becomes perfected under the law of the other jurisdiction before the earlier of the time or the end of the period described in that subsection, it remains perfected thereafter. If the security interest does not become perfected under the law of the other jurisdiction before the earlier of that time or the end of that period, it becomes unperfected and is deemed never to have been perfected as against a purchaser of the collateral for value.

[Subpart 3. Priority]

§ 9–317. Interests That Take Priority over or Take Free of Security Interest or Agricultural Lien.

(a) A security interest or agricultural lien is subordinate to the rights of:

(1) a person entitled to priority under Section 9–322; and

(2) except as otherwise provided in subsection (e), a person that becomes a lien creditor before the earlier of the time:

(A) the security interest or agricultural lien is perfected; or

(B) one of the conditions specified in Section 9–203(b)(3) is met and a financing statement covering the collateral is filed.

(b) Except as otherwise provided in subsection (e), a buyer, other than a secured party, of tangible chattel paper, documents, goods, instruments, or a security certificate takes free of a security interest or agricultural lien if the buyer gives value and receives delivery of the collateral without knowledge of the security interest or agricultural lien and before it is perfected.

(c) Except as otherwise provided in subsection (e), a lessee of goods takes free of a security interest or agricultural lien if the lessee gives value and receives delivery of the collateral without knowledge of the security interest or agricultural lien and before it is perfected.

(d) A licensee of a general intangible or a buyer, other than a secured party, of accounts, electronic chattel paper, general intangibles, or investment property other than a certificated security takes free of a security interest if the licensee or buyer gives value without knowledge of the security interest and before it is perfected.

(e) Except as otherwise provided in Sections 9–320 and 9–321, if a person files a financing statement with respect to a purchase-money security interest before or within 20 days after the debtor receives delivery of the collateral, the security interest takes priority over the rights of a buyer, lessee, or lien creditor which arise between the time the security interest attaches and the time of filing.

As amended in 2000.

§ 9–318. No Interest Retained in Right to Payment That Is Sold; Rights and Title of Seller of Account or Chattel Paper with Respect to Creditors and Purchasers.

(a) A debtor that has sold an account, chattel paper, payment intangible, or promissory note does not retain a legal or equitable interest in the collateral sold.

(b) For purposes of determining the rights of creditors of, and purchasers for value of an account or chattel paper from, a debtor that has sold an account or chattel paper, while the buyer's security interest is unperfected, the debtor is deemed to have rights and title to the account or chattel paper identical to those the debtor sold.

§ 9–319. Rights and Title of Consignee with Respect to Creditors and Purchasers.

(a) Except as otherwise provided in subsection (b), for purposes of determining the rights of creditors of, and purchasers for value of goods from, a consignee, while the goods are in the possession of the consignee, the consignee is deemed to have rights and title to the goods identical to those the consignor had or had power to transfer.

(b) For purposes of determining the rights of a creditor of a consignee, law other than this article determines the rights and title of a consignee while goods are in the consignee's possession if, under this part, a perfected security interest held by the consignor would have priority over the rights of the creditor.

§ 9–320. Buyer of Goods.

(a) Except as otherwise provided in subsection (e), a buyer in ordinary course of business, other than a person buying farm products from a person engaged in farming operations, takes free of a security interest created by the buyer's seller, even if the security interest is perfected and the buyer knows of its existence.

(b) Except as otherwise provided in subsection (e), a buyer of goods from a person who used or bought the goods for use primarily for personal, family, or household purposes takes free of a security interest, even if perfected, if the buyer buys:

(1) without knowledge of the security interest;

(2) for value;

(3) primarily for the buyer's personal, family, or household purposes; and

(4) before the filing of a financing statement covering the goods.

(c) To the extent that it affects the priority of a security interest over a buyer of goods under subsection (b), the period of effectiveness of a filing made in the jurisdiction in which the seller is located is governed by Section 9–316(a) and (b).

(d) A buyer in ordinary course of business buying oil, gas, or other minerals at the wellhead or minehead or after extraction takes free of an interest arising out of an encumbrance.

(e) Subsections (a) and (b) do not affect a security interest in goods in the possession of the secured party under Section 9–313.

§ 9–321. Licensee of General Intangible and Lessee of Goods in Ordinary Course of Business.

(a) In this section, "licensee in ordinary course of business" means a person that becomes a licensee of a general intangible in good faith, without knowledge that the license violates the rights of another person in the general intangible, and in the ordinary course from a person in the business of licensing general intangibles of that kind. A person becomes a licensee in the ordinary course if the license to the person comports with the usual or customary practices in the kind of business in which the licensor is engaged or with the licensor's own usual or customary practices.

(b) A licensee in ordinary course of business takes its rights under a nonexclusive license free of a security interest in the general intangible created by the licensor, even if the security interest is perfected and the licensee knows of its existence.

(c) A lessee in ordinary course of business takes its leasehold interest free of a security interest in the goods created by the lessor, even if the security interest is perfected and the lessee knows of its existence.

§ 9–322. Priorities among Conflicting Security Interests in and Agricultural Liens on Same Collateral.

(a) Except as otherwise provided in this section, priority among conflicting security interests and agricultural liens in the same collateral is determined according to the following rules:

(1) Conflicting perfected security interests and agricultural liens rank according to priority in time of filing or perfection. Priority dates from the earlier of the time a filing covering the collateral is first made or the security interest or agricultural lien is first perfected, if there is no period thereafter when there is neither filing nor perfection.

(2) A perfected security interest or agricultural lien has priority over a conflicting unperfected security interest or agricultural lien.

(3) The first security interest or agricultural lien to attach or become effective has priority if conflicting security interests and agricultural liens are unperfected.

(b) For the purposes of subsection (a)(1):

(1) the time of filing or perfection as to a security interest in collateral is also the time of filing or perfection as to a security interest in proceeds; and

(2) the time of filing or perfection as to a security interest in collateral supported by a supporting obligation is also the time of filing or perfection as to a security interest in the supporting obligation.

(c) Except as otherwise provided in subsection (f), a security interest in collateral which qualifies for priority over a conflicting security interest under Section 9–327, 9–328, 9–329, 9–330, or 9–331 also has priority over a conflicting security interest in:

(1) any supporting obligation for the collateral; and

(2) proceeds of the collateral if:

(A) the security interest in proceeds is perfected;

(B) the proceeds are cash proceeds or of the same type as the collateral; and

(C) in the case of proceeds that are proceeds of proceeds, all intervening proceeds are cash proceeds, proceeds of the same type as the collateral, or an account relating to the collateral.

(d) Subject to subsection (e) and except as otherwise provided in subsection (f), if a security interest in chattel paper, deposit accounts, negotiable documents, instruments, investment property, or letter-of-credit rights is perfected by a method other than filing, conflicting perfected security interests in proceeds of the collateral rank according to priority in time of filing.

(e) Subsection (d) applies only if the proceeds of the collateral are not cash proceeds, chattel paper, negotiable documents, instruments, investment property, or letter-of-credit rights.

(f) Subsections (a) through (e) are subject to:

(1) subsection (g) and the other provisions of this part;

(2) Section 4–210 with respect to a security interest of a collecting bank;

(3) Section 5–118 with respect to a security interest of an issuer or nominated person; and

(4) Section 9–110 with respect to a security interest arising under Article 2 or 2A.

(g) A perfected agricultural lien on collateral has priority over a conflicting security interest in or agricultural lien on the same collateral if the statute creating the agricultural lien so provides.

§ 9–323. Future Advances.

(a) Except as otherwise provided in subsection (c), for purposes of determining the priority of a perfected security interest under Section 9–322(a)(1), perfection of the security interest dates from the time an advance is made to the extent that the security interest secures an advance that:

(1) is made while the security interest is perfected only:

(A) under Section 9–309 when it attaches; or

(B) temporarily under Section 9–312(e), (f), or (g); and

(2) is not made pursuant to a commitment entered into before or while the security interest is perfected by a method other than under Section 9–309 or 9–312(e), (f), or (g).

(b) Except as otherwise provided in subsection (c), a security interest is subordinate to the rights of a person that becomes a lien creditor to the extent that the security interest secures an advance made more than 45 days after the person becomes a lien creditor unless the advance is made:

(1) without knowledge of the lien; or

(2) pursuant to a commitment entered into without knowledge of the lien.

(c) Subsections (a) and (b) do not apply to a security interest held by a secured party that is a buyer of accounts, chattel paper, payment intangibles, or promissory notes or a consignor.

(d) Except as otherwise provided in subsection (e), a buyer of goods other than a buyer in ordinary course of business takes free of a security interest to the extent that it secures advances made after the earlier of:

(1) the time the secured party acquires knowledge of the buyer's purchase; or

(2) 45 days after the purchase.

(e) Subsection (d) does not apply if the advance is made pursuant to a commitment entered into without knowledge of the buyer's purchase and before the expiration of the 45-day period.

(f) Except as otherwise provided in subsection (g), a lessee of goods, other than a lessee in ordinary course of business, takes the leasehold interest free of a security interest to the extent that it secures advances made after the earlier of:

(1) the time the secured party acquires knowledge of the lease; or

(2) 45 days after the lease contract becomes enforceable.

(g) Subsection (f) does not apply if the advance is made pursuant to a commitment entered into without knowledge of the lease and before the expiration of the 45-day period.

As amended in 1999.

§ 9–324. Priority of Purchase-Money Security Interests.

(a) Except as otherwise provided in subsection (g), a perfected purchase-money security interest in goods other than inventory or livestock has priority over a conflicting security interest in the same goods, and, except as otherwise provided in Section 9–327, a perfected security interest in its identifiable proceeds also has priority, if the purchase-money security interest is perfected when the debtor receives possession of the collateral or within 20 days thereafter.

(b) Subject to subsection (c) and except as otherwise provided in subsection (g), a perfected purchase-money security interest in inventory has priority over a conflicting security interest in the same inventory, has priority over a conflicting security interest in chattel paper or an instrument constituting proceeds of the inventory and in proceeds of the chattel paper, if so provided in Section 9–330, and, except as otherwise provided in Section 9–327, also has priority in identifiable cash proceeds of the inventory to the extent the identifiable cash proceeds are received on or before the delivery of the inventory to a buyer, if:

(1) the purchase-money security interest is perfected when the debtor receives possession of the inventory;

(2) the purchase-money secured party sends an authenticated notification to the holder of the conflicting security interest;

(3) the holder of the conflicting security interest receives the notification within five years before the debtor receives possession of the inventory; and

(4) the notification states that the person sending the notification has or expects to acquire a purchase-money security interest in inventory of the debtor and describes the inventory.

(c) Subsections (b)(2) through (4) apply only if the holder of the conflicting security interest had filed a financing statement covering the same types of inventory:

(1) if the purchase-money security interest is perfected by filing, before the date of the filing; or

(2) if the purchase-money security interest is temporarily perfected without filing or possession under Section 9–312(f), before the beginning of the 20-day period thereunder.

(d) Subject to subsection (e) and except as otherwise provided in subsection (g), a perfected purchase-money security interest in livestock that are farm products has priority over a conflicting security interest in the same livestock, and, except as otherwise provided in Section 9–327, a perfected security interest in their identifiable proceeds and identifiable products in their unmanufactured states also has priority, if:

(1) the purchase-money security interest is perfected when the debtor receives possession of the livestock;

(2) the purchase-money secured party sends an authenticated notification to the holder of the conflicting security interest;

(3) the holder of the conflicting security interest receives the notification within six months before the debtor receives possession of the livestock; and

(4) the notification states that the person sending the notification has or expects to acquire a purchase-money security interest in livestock of the debtor and describes the livestock.

(e) Subsections (d)(2) through (4) apply only if the holder of the conflicting security interest had filed a financing statement covering the same types of livestock:

(1) if the purchase-money security interest is perfected by filing, before the date of the filing; or

(2) if the purchase-money security interest is temporarily perfected without filing or possession under Section 9–312(f), before the beginning of the 20-day period thereunder.

(f) Except as otherwise provided in subsection (g), a perfected purchase-money security interest in software has priority over a conflicting security interest in the same collateral, and, except as otherwise provided in Section 9–327, a perfected security interest in its identifiable proceeds also has priority, to the extent that the purchase-money security interest in the goods in which the software was acquired for use has priority in the goods and proceeds of the goods under this section.

(g) If more than one security interest qualifies for priority in the same collateral under subsection (a), (b), (d), or (f):

(1) a security interest securing an obligation incurred as all or part of the price of the collateral has priority over a security interest securing an obligation incurred for value given to enable the debtor to acquire rights in or the use of collateral; and

(2) in all other cases, Section 9–322(a) applies to the qualifying security interests.

§ 9–325. Priority of Security Interests in Transferred Collateral.

(a) Except as otherwise provided in subsection (b), a security interest created by a debtor is subordinate to a security interest in the same collateral created by another person if:

(1) the debtor acquired the collateral subject to the security interest created by the other person;

(2) the security interest created by the other person was perfected when the debtor acquired the collateral; and

(3) there is no period thereafter when the security interest is unperfected.

(b) Subsection (a) subordinates a security interest only if the security interest:

(1) otherwise would have priority solely under Section 9–322(a) or 9–324; or

(2) arose solely under Section 2–711(3) or 2A–508(5).

§ 9–326. Priority of Security Interests Created by New Debtor.

(a) Subject to subsection (b), a security interest created by a new debtor which is perfected by a filed financing statement that is effective solely under Section 9–508 in collateral in which a new debtor has or acquires rights is subordinate to a security interest in the same collateral which is perfected other than by a filed financing statement that is effective solely under Section 9–508.

(b) The other provisions of this part determine the priority among conflicting security interests in the same collateral perfected by filed financing statements that are effective solely under Section 9–508. However, if the security agreements to which a new debtor became bound as debtor were not entered into by the same original debtor, the conflicting security interests rank according to priority in time of the new debtor's having become bound.

§ 9–327. Priority of Security Interests in Deposit Account.

The following rules govern priority among conflicting security interests in the same deposit account:

(1) A security interest held by a secured party having control of the deposit account under Section 9–104 has priority over a conflicting security interest held by a secured party that does not have control.

(2) Except as otherwise provided in paragraphs (3) and (4), security interests perfected by control under Section 9–314 rank according to priority in time of obtaining control.

(3) Except as otherwise provided in paragraph (4), a security interest held by the bank with which the deposit account is maintained has priority over a conflicting security interest held by another secured party.

(4) A security interest perfected by control under Section 9–104(a)(3) has priority over a security interest held by the bank with which the deposit account is maintained.

§ 9–328. Priority of Security Interests in Investment Property.

The following rules govern priority among conflicting security interests in the same investment property:

(1) A security interest held by a secured party having control of investment property under Section 9–106 has priority over a security interest held by a secured party that does not have control of the investment property.

(2) Except as otherwise provided in paragraphs (3) and (4), conflicting security interests held by secured parties each of which has control under Section 9–106 rank according to priority in time of:

(A) if the collateral is a security, obtaining control;

(B) if the collateral is a security entitlement carried in a securities account and:

(i) if the secured party obtained control under Section 8–106(d)(1), the secured party's becoming the person for which the securities account is maintained;

(ii) if the secured party obtained control under Section 8–106(d)(2), the securities intermediary's agreement to comply with the secured party's entitlement orders with respect to security entitlements carried or to be carried in the securities account; or

(iii) if the secured party obtained control through another person under Section 8–106(d)(3), the time on which priority would be based under this paragraph if the other person were the secured party; or

(C) if the collateral is a commodity contract carried with a commodity intermediary, the satisfaction of the requirement for control specified in Section 9–106(b)(2) with respect to commodity contracts carried or to be carried with the commodity intermediary.

(3) A security interest held by a securities intermediary in a security entitlement or a securities account maintained with the securities intermediary has priority over a conflicting security interest held by another secured party.

(4) A security interest held by a commodity intermediary in a commodity contract or a commodity account maintained with the commodity intermediary has priority over a conflicting security interest held by another secured party.

(5) A security interest in a certificated security in registered form which is perfected by taking delivery under Section 9–313(a) and not by control under Section 9–314 has priority over a conflicting security interest perfected by a method other than control.

(6) Conflicting security interests created by a broker, securities intermediary, or commodity intermediary which are perfected without control under Section 9–106 rank equally.

(7) In all other cases, priority among conflicting security interests in investment property is governed by Sections 9–322 and 9–323.

§ 9–329. Priority of Security Interests in Letter-of-Credit Right.

The following rules govern priority among conflicting security interests in the same letter-of-credit right:

(1) A security interest held by a secured party having control of the letter-of-credit right under Section 9–107 has priority to the extent of its control over a conflicting security interest held by a secured party that does not have control.

(2) Security interests perfected by control under Section 9–314 rank according to priority in time of obtaining control.

§ 9–330. Priority of Purchaser of Chattel Paper or Instrument.

(a) A purchaser of chattel paper has priority over a security interest in the chattel paper which is claimed merely as proceeds of inventory subject to a security interest if:

   (1) in good faith and in the ordinary course of the purchaser's business, the purchaser gives new value and takes possession of the chattel paper or obtains control of the chattel paper under Section 9–105; and

   (2) the chattel paper does not indicate that it has been assigned to an identified assignee other than the purchaser.

(b) A purchaser of chattel paper has priority over a security interest in the chattel paper which is claimed other than merely as proceeds of inventory subject to a security interest if the purchaser gives new value and takes possession of the chattel paper or obtains control of the chattel paper under Section 9–105 in good faith, in the ordinary course of the purchaser's business, and without knowledge that the purchase violates the rights of the secured party.

(c) Except as otherwise provided in Section 9–327, a purchaser having priority in chattel paper under subsection (a) or (b) also has priority in proceeds of the chattel paper to the extent that:

   (1) Section 9–322 provides for priority in the proceeds; or

   (2) the proceeds consist of the specific goods covered by the chattel paper or cash proceeds of the specific goods, even if the purchaser's security interest in the proceeds is unperfected.

(d) Except as otherwise provided in Section 9–331(a), a purchaser of an instrument has priority over a security interest in the instru-

ment perfected by a method other than possession if the purchaser gives value and takes possession of the instrument in good faith and without knowledge that the purchase violates the rights of the secured party.

(e) For purposes of subsections (a) and (b), the holder of a purchase-money security interest in inventory gives new value for chattel paper constituting proceeds of the inventory.

(f) For purposes of subsections (b) and (d), if chattel paper or an instrument indicates that it has been assigned to an identified secured party other than the purchaser, a purchaser of the chattel paper or instrument has knowledge that the purchase violates the rights of the secured party.

§ 9–331. Priority of Rights of Purchasers of Instruments, Documents, and Securities under Other Articles; Priority of Interests in Financial Assets and Security Entitlements under Article 8.

(a) This article does not limit the rights of a holder in due course of a negotiable instrument, a holder to which a negotiable document of title has been duly negotiated, or a protected purchaser of a security. These holders or purchasers take priority over an earlier security interest, even if perfected, to the extent provided in Articles 3, 7, and 8.

(b) This article does not limit the rights of or impose liability on a person to the extent that the person is protected against the assertion of a claim under Article 8.

(c) Filing under this article does not constitute notice of a claim or defense to the holders, or purchasers, or persons described in subsections (a) and (b).

§ 9–332. Transfer of Money; Transfer of Funds from Deposit Account.

(a) A transferee of money takes the money free of a security interest unless the transferee acts in collusion with the debtor in violating the rights of the secured party.

(b) A transferee of funds from a deposit account takes the funds free of a security interest in the deposit account unless the transferee acts in collusion with the debtor in violating the rights of the secured party.

§ 9–333. Priority of Certain Liens Arising by Operation of Law.

(a) In this section, "possessory lien" means an interest, other than a security interest or an agricultural lien:

   (1) which secures payment or performance of an obligation for services or materials furnished with respect to goods by a person in the ordinary course of the person's business;

   (2) which is created by statute or rule of law in favor of the person; and

   (3) whose effectiveness depends on the person's possession of the goods.

(b) A possessory lien on goods has priority over a security interest in the goods unless the lien is created by a statute that expressly provides otherwise.

§ 9–334. Priority of Security Interests in Fixtures and Crops.

(a) A security interest under this article may be created in goods that are fixtures or may continue in goods that become fixtures. A security interest does not exist under this article in ordinary building materials incorporated into an improvement on land.

(b) This article does not prevent creation of an encumbrance upon fixtures under real property law.

(c) In cases not governed by subsections (d) through (h), a security interest in fixtures is subordinate to a conflicting interest of an encumbrancer or owner of the related real property other than the debtor.

(d) Except as otherwise provided in subsection (h), a perfected security interest in fixtures has priority over a conflicting interest of an encumbrancer or owner of the real property if the debtor has an interest of record in or is in possession of the real property and:

(1) the security interest is a purchase-money security interest;

(2) the interest of the encumbrancer or owner arises before the goods become fixtures; and

(3) the security interest is perfected by a fixture filing before the goods become fixtures or within 20 days thereafter.

(e) A perfected security interest in fixtures has priority over a conflicting interest of an encumbrancer or owner of the real property if:

(1) the debtor has an interest of record in the real property or is in possession of the real property and the security interest:

(A) is perfected by a fixture filing before the interest of the encumbrancer or owner is of record; and

(B) has priority over any conflicting interest of a predecessor in title of the encumbrancer or owner;

(2) before the goods become fixtures, the security interest is perfected by any method permitted by this article and the fixtures are readily removable:

(A) factory or office machines;

(B) equipment that is not primarily used or leased for use in the operation of the real property; or

(C) replacements of domestic appliances that are consumer goods;

(3) the conflicting interest is a lien on the real property obtained by legal or equitable proceedings after the security interest was perfected by any method permitted by this article; or

(4) the security interest is:

(A) created in a manufactured home in a manufactured-home transaction; and

(B) perfected pursuant to a statute described in Section 9–311(a)(2).

(f) A security interest in fixtures, whether or not perfected, has priority over a conflicting interest of an encumbrancer or owner of the real property if:

(1) the encumbrancer or owner has, in an authenticated record, consented to the security interest or disclaimed an interest in the goods as fixtures; or

(2) the debtor has a right to remove the goods as against the encumbrancer or owner.

(g) The priority of the security interest under paragraph (f)(2) continues for a reasonable time if the debtor's right to remove the goods as against the encumbrancer or owner terminates.

(h) A mortgage is a construction mortgage to the extent that it secures an obligation incurred for the construction of an improvement on land, including the acquisition cost of the land, if a recorded record of the mortgage so indicates. Except as otherwise provided in subsections (e) and (f), a security interest in fixtures is subordinate to a construction mortgage if a record of the mortgage is recorded before the goods become fixtures and the goods become fixtures before the completion of the construction. A mortgage has this priority to the same extent as a construction mortgage to the extent that it is given to refinance a construction mortgage.

(i) A perfected security interest in crops growing on real property has priority over a conflicting interest of an encumbrancer or owner of the real property if the debtor has an interest of record in or is in possession of the real property.

(j) Subsection (i) prevails over any inconsistent provisions of the following statutes:

[List here any statutes containing provisions inconsistent with subsection (i).]

Legislative Note: States that amend statutes to remove provisions inconsistent with subsection (i) need not enact subsection (j).

§ 9–335. Accessions.

(a) A security interest may be created in an accession and continues in collateral that becomes an accession.

(b) If a security interest is perfected when the collateral becomes an accession, the security interest remains perfected in the collateral.

(c) Except as otherwise provided in subsection (d), the other provisions of this part determine the priority of a security interest in an accession.

(d) A security interest in an accession is subordinate to a security interest in the whole which is perfected by compliance with the requirements of a certificate-of-title statute under Section 9–311(b).

(e) After default, subject to Part 6, a secured party may remove an accession from other goods if the security interest in the accession has priority over the claims of every person having an interest in the whole.

(f) A secured party that removes an accession from other goods under subsection (e) shall promptly reimburse any holder of a security interest or other lien on, or owner of, the whole or of the other goods, other than the debtor, for the cost of repair of any physical injury to the whole or the other goods. The secured party need not reimburse the holder or owner for any diminution in value of the whole or the other goods caused by the absence of the accession removed or by any necessity for replacing it. A person entitled to reimbursement may refuse permission to remove until the secured party gives adequate assurance for the performance of the obligation to reimburse.

§ 9–336. Commingled Goods.

(a) In this section, "commingled goods" means goods that are physically united with other goods in such a manner that their identity is lost in a product or mass.

(b) A security interest does not exist in commingled goods as such. However, a security interest may attach to a product or mass that results when goods become commingled goods.

(c) If collateral becomes commingled goods, a security interest attaches to the product or mass.

(d) If a security interest in collateral is perfected before the collateral becomes commingled goods, the security interest that attaches to the product or mass under subsection (c) is perfected.

(e) Except as otherwise provided in subsection (f), the other provisions of this part determine the priority of a security interest that attaches to the product or mass under subsection (c).

(f) If more than one security interest attaches to the product or mass under subsection (c), the following rules determine priority:

(1) A security interest that is perfected under subsection (d) has priority over a security interest that is unperfected at the time the collateral becomes commingled goods.

(2) If more than one security interest is perfected under subsection (d), the security interests rank equally in proportion to the value of the collateral at the time it became commingled goods.

§ 9–337. Priority of Security Interests in Goods Covered by Certificate of Title.

If, while a security interest in goods is perfected by any method under the law of another jurisdiction, this State issues a certificate of title that does not show that the goods are subject to the security interest or contain a statement that they may be subject to security interests not shown on the certificate:

(1) a buyer of the goods, other than a person in the business of selling goods of that kind, takes free of the security interest if the buyer gives value and receives delivery of the goods after issuance of the certificate and without knowledge of the security interest; and

(2) the security interest is subordinate to a conflicting security interest in the goods that attaches, and is perfected under Section 9–311(b), after issuance of the certificate and without the conflicting secured party's knowledge of the security interest.

§ 9–338. Priority of Security Interest or Agricultural Lien Perfected by Filed Financing Statement Providing Certain Incorrect Information.

If a security interest or agricultural lien is perfected by a filed financing statement providing information described in Section 9–516(b)(5) which is incorrect at the time the financing statement is filed:

(1) the security interest or agricultural lien is subordinate to a conflicting perfected security interest in the collateral to the extent that the holder of the conflicting security interest gives value in reasonable reliance upon the incorrect information; and

(2) a purchaser, other than a secured party, of the collateral takes free of the security interest or agricultural lien to the extent that, in reasonable reliance upon the incorrect information, the purchaser gives value and, in the case of chattel paper, documents, goods, instruments, or a security certificate, receives delivery of the collateral.

§ 9–339. Priority Subject to Subordination.

This article does not preclude subordination by agreement by a person entitled to priority.

[Subpart 4. Rights of Bank]

§ 9–340. Effectiveness of Right of Recoupment or Set-Off against Deposit Account.

(a) Except as otherwise provided in subsection (c), a bank with which a deposit account is maintained may exercise any right of recoupment or set-off against a secured party that holds a security interest in the deposit account.

(b) Except as otherwise provided in subsection (c), the application of this article to a security interest in a deposit account does not affect a right of recoupment or set-off of the secured party as to a deposit account maintained with the secured party.

(c) The exercise by a bank of a set-off against a deposit account is ineffective against a secured party that holds a security interest in the deposit account which is perfected by control under Section 9–104(a)(3), if the set-off is based on a claim against the debtor.

§ 9–341. Bank's Rights and Duties with Respect to Deposit Account.

Except as otherwise provided in Section 9–340(c), and unless the bank otherwise agrees in an authenticated record, a bank's rights and duties with respect to a deposit account maintained with the bank are not terminated, suspended, or modified by:

(1) the creation, attachment, or perfection of a security interest in the deposit account;

(2) the bank's knowledge of the security interest; or

(3) the bank's receipt of instructions from the secured party.

§ 9–342. Bank's Right to Refuse to Enter into or Disclose Existence of Control Agreement.

This article does not require a bank to enter into an agreement of the kind described in Section 9–104(a)(2), even if its customer so requests or directs. A bank that has entered into such an agreement is not required to confirm the existence of the agreement to another person unless requested to do so by its customer.

Part 4   Rights of Third Parties

§ 9–401. Alienability of Debtor's Rights.

(a) Except as otherwise provided in subsection (b) and Sections 9–406, 9–407, 9–408, and 9–409, whether a debtor's rights in collateral may be voluntarily or involuntarily transferred is governed by law other than this article.

(b) An agreement between the debtor and secured party which prohibits a transfer of the debtor's rights in collateral or makes the transfer a default does not prevent the transfer from taking effect.

§ 9–402. Secured Party Not Obligated on Contract of Debtor or in Tort.

The existence of a security interest, agricultural lien, or authority given to a debtor to dispose of or use collateral, without more, does not subject a secured party to liability in contract or tort for the debtor's acts or omissions.

§ 9–403. Agreement Not to Assert Defenses against Assignee.

(a) In this section, "value" has the meaning provided in Section 3–303(a).

(b) Except as otherwise provided in this section, an agreement between an account debtor and an assignor not to assert against an assignee any claim or defense that the account debtor may have against the assignor is enforceable by an assignee that takes an assignment:

(1) for value;

(2) in good faith;

(3) without notice of a claim of a property or possessory right to the property assigned; and

(4) without notice of a defense or claim in recoupment of the type that may be asserted against a person entitled to enforce a negotiable instrument under Section 3–305(a).

(c) Subsection (b) does not apply to defenses of a type that may be asserted against a holder in due course of a negotiable instrument under Section 3–305(b).

(d) In a consumer transaction, if a record evidences the account debtor's obligation, law other than this article requires that the record include a statement to the effect that the rights of an assignee are subject to claims or defenses that the account debtor could assert against the original obligee, and the record does not include such a statement:

(1) the record has the same effect as if the record included such a statement; and

(2) the account debtor may assert against an assignee those claims and defenses that would have been available if the record included such a statement.

(e) This section is subject to law other than this article which establishes a different rule for an account debtor who is an individual and who incurred the obligation primarily for personal, family, or household purposes.

(f) Except as otherwise provided in subsection (d), this section does not displace law other than this article which gives effect to an agreement by an account debtor not to assert a claim or defense against an assignee.

§ 9–404. Rights Acquired by Assignee; Claims and Defenses against Assignee.

(a) Unless an account debtor has made an enforceable agreement not to assert defenses or claims, and subject to subsections (b) through (e), the rights of an assignee are subject to:

(1) all terms of the agreement between the account debtor and assignor and any defense or claim in recoupment arising from the transaction that gave rise to the contract; and

(2) any other defense or claim of the account debtor against the assignor which accrues before the account debtor receives a notification of the assignment authenticated by the assignor or the assignee.

(b) Subject to subsection (c) and except as otherwise provided in subsection (d), the claim of an account debtor against an assignor may be asserted against an assignee under subsection (a) only to reduce the amount the account debtor owes.

(c) This section is subject to law other than this article which establishes a different rule for an account debtor who is an individual and who incurred the obligation primarily for personal, family, or household purposes.

(d) In a consumer transaction, if a record evidences the account debtor's obligation, law other than this article requires that the record include a statement to the effect that the account debtor's recovery against an assignee with respect to claims and defenses against the assignor may not exceed amounts paid by the account debtor under the record, and the record does not include such a statement, the extent to which a claim of an account debtor against the assignor may

be asserted against an assignee is determined as if the record included such a statement.

(e) This section does not apply to an assignment of a health-care-insurance receivable.

§ 9–405. Modification of Assigned Contract.

(a) A modification of or substitution for an assigned contract is effective against an assignee if made in good faith. The assignee acquires corresponding rights under the modified or substituted contract. The assignment may provide that the modification or substitution is a breach of contract by the assignor. This subsection is subject to subsections (b) through (d).

(b) Subsection (a) applies to the extent that:

(1) the right to payment or a part thereof under an assigned contract has not been fully earned by performance; or

(2) the right to payment or a part thereof has been fully earned by performance and the account debtor has not received notification of the assignment under Section 9–406(a).

(c) This section is subject to law other than this article which establishes a different rule for an account debtor who is an individual and who incurred the obligation primarily for personal, family, or household purposes.

(d) This section does not apply to an assignment of a health-care-insurance receivable.

§ 9–406. Discharge of Account Debtor; Notification of Assignment; Identification and Proof of Assignment; Restrictions on Assignment of Accounts, Chattel Paper, Payment Intangibles, and Promissory Notes Ineffective.

(a) Subject to subsections (b) through (i), an account debtor on an account, chattel paper, or a payment intangible may discharge its obligation by paying the assignor until, but not after, the account debtor receives a notification, authenticated by the assignor or the assignee, that the amount due or to become due has been assigned and that payment is to be made to the assignee. After receipt of the notification, the account debtor may discharge its obligation by paying the assignee and may not discharge the obligation by paying the assignor.

(b) Subject to subsection (h), notification is ineffective under subsection (a):

(1) if it does not reasonably identify the rights assigned;

(2) to the extent that an agreement between an account debtor and a seller of a payment intangible limits the account debtor's duty to pay a person other than the seller and the limitation is effective under law other than this article; or

(3) at the option of an account debtor, if the notification notifies the account debtor to make less than the full amount of any installment or other periodic payment to the assignee, even if:

(A) only a portion of the account, chattel paper, or payment intangible has been assigned to that assignee;

(B) a portion has been assigned to another assignee; or

(C) the account debtor knows that the assignment to that assignee is limited.

(c) Subject to subsection (h), if requested by the account debtor, an assignee shall seasonably furnish reasonable proof that the assignment has been made. Unless the assignee complies, the account debtor may discharge its obligation by paying the assignor, even if the account debtor has received a notification under subsection (a).

(d) Except as otherwise provided in subsection (e) and Sections 2A–303 and 9–407, and subject to subsection (h), a term in an agreement between an account debtor and an assignor or in a promissory note is ineffective to the extent that it:

(1) prohibits, restricts, or requires the consent of the account debtor or person obligated on the promissory note to the assignment or transfer of, or the creation, attachment, perfection, or enforcement of a security interest in, the account, chattel paper, payment intangible, or promissory note; or

(2) provides that the assignment or transfer or the creation, attachment, perfection, or enforcement of the security interest may give rise to a default, breach, right of recoupment, claim, defense, termination, right of termination, or remedy under the account, chattel paper, payment intangible, or promissory note.

(e) Subsection (d) does not apply to the sale of a payment intangible or promissory note.

(f) Except as otherwise provided in Sections 2A–303 and 9–407 and subject to subsections (h) and (i), a rule of law, statute, or regulation that prohibits, restricts, or requires the consent of a government, governmental body or official, or account debtor to the assignment or transfer of, or creation of a security interest in, an account or chattel paper is ineffective to the extent that the rule of law, statute, or regulation:

(1) prohibits, restricts, or requires the consent of the government, governmental body or official, or account debtor to the assignment or transfer of, or the creation, attachment, perfection, or enforcement of a security interest in the account or chattel paper; or

(2) provides that the assignment or transfer or the creation, attachment, perfection, or enforcement of the security interest may give rise to a default, breach, right of recoupment, claim, defense, termination, right of termination, or remedy under the account or chattel paper.

(g) Subject to subsection (h), an account debtor may not waive or vary its option under subsection (b)(3).

(h) This section is subject to law other than this article which establishes a different rule for an account debtor who is an individual and who incurred the obligation primarily for personal, family, or household purposes.

(i) This section does not apply to an assignment of a health-care-insurance receivable.

(j) This section prevails over any inconsistent provisions of the following statutes, rules, and regulations:

[List here any statutes, rules, and regulations containing provisions inconsistent with this section.]

Legislative Note: States that amend statutes, rules, and regulations to remove provisions inconsistent with this section need not enact subsection (j).

As amended in 1999 and 2000.

§ 9–407. Restrictions on Creation or Enforcement of Security Interest in Leasehold Interest or in Lessor's Residual Interest.

(a) Except as otherwise provided in subsection (b), a term in a lease agreement is ineffective to the extent that it:

(1) prohibits, restricts, or requires the consent of a party to the lease to the assignment or transfer of, or the creation, attachment, perfection, or enforcement of a security interest in an interest of a party under the lease contract or in the lessor's residual interest in the goods; or

(2) provides that the assignment or transfer or the creation, attachment, perfection, or enforcement of the security interest may give rise to a default, breach, right of recoupment, claim, defense, termination, right of termination, or remedy under the lease.

(b) Except as otherwise provided in Section 2A–303(7), a term described in subsection (a)(2) is effective to the extent that there is:

(1) a transfer by the lessee of the lessee's right of possession or use of the goods in violation of the term; or

(2) a delegation of a material performance of either party to the lease contract in violation of the term.

(c) The creation, attachment, perfection, or enforcement of a security interest in the lessor's interest under the lease contract or the lessor's residual interest in the goods is not a transfer that materially impairs the lessee's prospect of obtaining return performance or materially changes the duty of or materially increases the burden or risk imposed on the lessee within the purview of Section 2A–303(4) unless, and then only to the extent that, enforcement actually results in a delegation of material performance of the lessor.

As amended in 1999.

§ 9–408. Restrictions on Assignment of Promissory Notes, Health-Care-Insurance Receivables, and Certain General Intangibles Ineffective.

(a) Except as otherwise provided in subsection (b), a term in a promissory note or in an agreement between an account debtor and a debtor which relates to a health-care-insurance receivable or a general intangible, including a contract, permit, license, or franchise, and which term prohibits, restricts, or requires the consent of the person obligated on the promissory note or the account debtor to, the assignment or transfer of, or creation, attachment, or perfection of a security interest in, the promissory note, health-care-insurance receivable, or general intangible, is ineffective to the extent that the term:

(1) would impair the creation, attachment, or perfection of a security interest; or

(2) provides that the assignment or transfer or the creation, attachment, or perfection of the security interest may give rise to a default, breach, right of recoupment, claim, defense, termination, right of termination, or remedy under the promissory note, health-care-insurance receivable, or general intangible.

(b) Subsection (a) applies to a security interest in a payment intangible or promissory note only if the security interest arises out of a sale of the payment intangible or promissory note.

(c) A rule of law, statute, or regulation that prohibits, restricts, or requires the consent of a government, governmental body or official, person obligated on a promissory note, or account debtor to the assignment or transfer of, or creation of a security interest in, a promissory note, health-care-insurance receivable, or general intangible, including a contract, permit, license, or franchise between an account debtor and a debtor, is ineffective to the extent that the rule of law, statute, or regulation:

(1) would impair the creation, attachment, or perfection of a security interest; or

(2) provides that the assignment or transfer or the creation, attachment, or perfection of the security interest may give rise to

a default, breach, right of recoupment, claim, defense, termination, right of termination, or remedy under the promissory note, health-care-insurance receivable, or general intangible.

(d) To the extent that a term in a promissory note or in an agreement between an account debtor and a debtor which relates to a health-care-insurance receivable or general intangible or a rule of law, statute, or regulation described in subsection (c) would be effective under law other than this article but is ineffective under subsection (a) or (c), the creation, attachment, or perfection of a security interest in the promissory note, health-care-insurance receivable, or general intangible:

(1) is not enforceable against the person obligated on the promissory note or the account debtor;

(2) does not impose a duty or obligation on the person obligated on the promissory note or the account debtor;

(3) does not require the person obligated on the promissory note or the account debtor to recognize the security interest, pay or render performance to the secured party, or accept payment or performance from the secured party;

(4) does not entitle the secured party to use or assign the debtor's rights under the promissory note, health-care-insurance receivable, or general intangible, including any related information or materials furnished to the debtor in the transaction giving rise to the promissory note, health-care-insurance receivable, or general intangible;

(5) does not entitle the secured party to use, assign, possess, or have access to any trade secrets or confidential information of the person obligated on the promissory note or the account debtor; and

(6) does not entitle the secured party to enforce the security interest in the promissory note, health-care-insurance receivable, or general intangible.

(e) This section prevails over any inconsistent provisions of the following statutes, rules, and regulations:

[List here any statutes, rules, and regulations containing provisions inconsistent with this section.]

Legislative Note: States that amend statutes, rules, and regulations to remove provisions inconsistent with this section need not enact subsection (e).

As amended in 1999.

§ 9–409. Restrictions on Assignment of Letter-of-Credit Rights Ineffective.

(a) A term in a letter of credit or a rule of law, statute, regulation, custom, or practice applicable to the letter of credit which prohibits, restricts, or requires the consent of an applicant, issuer, or nominated person to a beneficiary's assignment of or creation of a security interest in a letter-of-credit right is ineffective to the extent that the term or rule of law, statute, regulation, custom, or practice:

(1) would impair the creation, attachment, or perfection of a security interest in the letter-of-credit right; or

(2) provides that the assignment or the creation, attachment, or perfection of the security interest may give rise to a default, breach, right of recoupment, claim, defense, termination, right of termination, or remedy under the letter-of-credit right.

(b) To the extent that a term in a letter of credit is ineffective under subsection (a) but would be effective under law other than this article or a custom or practice applicable to the letter of credit, to the transfer of a right to draw or otherwise demand performance under the letter of credit, or to the assignment of a right to proceeds of the letter of credit, the creation, attachment, or perfection of a security interest in the letter-of-credit right:

(1) is not enforceable against the applicant, issuer, nominated person, or transferee beneficiary;

(2) imposes no duties or obligations on the applicant, issuer, nominated person, or transferee beneficiary; and

(3) does not require the applicant, issuer, nominated person, or transferee beneficiary to recognize the security interest, pay or render performance to the secured party, or accept payment or other performance from the secured party.

As amended in 1999.

Part 5 Filing

[Subpart 1. Filing Office; Contents and Effectiveness of Financing Statement]

§ 9–501. Filing Office.

(a) Except as otherwise provided in subsection (b), if the local law of this State governs perfection of a security interest or agricultural lien, the office in which to file a financing statement to perfect the security interest or agricultural lien is:

(1) the office designated for the filing or recording of a record of a mortgage on the related real property, if:

(A) the collateral is as-extracted collateral or timber to be cut; or

(B) the financing statement is filed as a fixture filing and the collateral is goods that are or are to become fixtures; or

(2) the office of [ ] [or any office duly authorized by [ ]], in all other cases, including a case in which the collateral is goods that are or are to become fixtures and the financing statement is not filed as a fixture filing.

(b) The office in which to file a financing statement to perfect a security interest in collateral, including fixtures, of a transmitting utility is the office of [ ]. The financing statement also constitutes a fixture filing as to the collateral indicated in the financing statement which is or is to become fixtures.

Legislative Note: The State should designate the filing office where the brackets appear. The filing office may be that of a governmental official (e.g., the Secretary of State) or a private party that maintains the State's filing system.

§ 9–502. Contents of Financing Statement; Record of Mortgage as Financing Statement; Time of Filing Financing Statement.

(a) Subject to subsection (b), a financing statement is sufficient only if it:

(1) provides the name of the debtor;

(2) provides the name of the secured party or a representative of the secured party; and

(3) indicates the collateral covered by the financing statement.

(b) Except as otherwise provided in Section 9–501(b), to be sufficient, a financing statement that covers as-extracted collateral or timber to be cut, or which is filed as a fixture filing and covers goods that are or are to become fixtures, must satisfy subsection (a) and also:

(1) indicate that it covers this type of collateral;

(2) indicate that it is to be filed [for record] in the real property records;

(3) provide a description of the real property to which the collateral is related [sufficient to give constructive notice of a mortgage under the law of this State if the description were contained in a record of the mortgage of the real property]; and

(4) if the debtor does not have an interest of record in the real property, provide the name of a record owner.

(c) A record of a mortgage is effective, from the date of recording, as a financing statement filed as a fixture filing or as a financing statement covering as-extracted collateral or timber to be cut only if:

(1) the record indicates the goods or accounts that it covers;

(2) the goods are or are to become fixtures related to the real property described in the record or the collateral is related to the real property described in the record and is as-extracted collateral or timber to be cut;

(3) the record satisfies the requirements for a financing statement in this section other than an indication that it is to be filed in the real property records; and

(4) the record is [duly] recorded.

(d) A financing statement may be filed before a security agreement is made or a security interest otherwise attaches.

Legislative Note: Language in brackets is optional. Where the State has any special recording system for real property other than the usual grantor-grantee index (as, for instance, a tract system or a title registration or Torrens system) local adaptations of subsection (b) and Section 9–519(d) and (e) may be necessary. See, e.g., Mass. Gen. Laws Chapter 106, Section 9–410.

§ 9–503. Name of Debtor and Secured Party.

(a) A financing statement sufficiently provides the name of the debtor:

(1) if the debtor is a registered organization, only if the financing statement provides the name of the debtor indicated on the public record of the debtor's jurisdiction of organization which shows the debtor to have been organized;

(2) if the debtor is a decedent's estate, only if the financing statement provides the name of the decedent and indicates that the debtor is an estate;

(3) if the debtor is a trust or a trustee acting with respect to property held in trust, only if the financing statement:

(A) provides the name specified for the trust in its organic documents or, if no name is specified, provides the name of the settlor and additional information sufficient to distinguish the debtor from other trusts having one or more of the same settlors; and

(B) indicates, in the debtor's name or otherwise, that the debtor is a trust or is a trustee acting with respect to property held in trust; and

(4) in other cases:

(A) if the debtor has a name, only if it provides the individual or organizational name of the debtor; and

(B) if the debtor does not have a name, only if it provides the names of the partners, members, associates, or other persons comprising the debtor.

(b) A financing statement that provides the name of the debtor in accordance with subsection (a) is not rendered ineffective by the absence of:

(1) a trade name or other name of the debtor; or

(2) unless required under subsection (a)(4)(B), names of partners, members, associates, or other persons comprising the debtor.

(c) A financing statement that provides only the debtor's trade name does not sufficiently provide the name of the debtor.

(d) Failure to indicate the representative capacity of a secured party or representative of a secured party does not affect the sufficiency of a financing statement.

(e) A financing statement may provide the name of more than one debtor and the name of more than one secured party.

§ 9–504. Indication of Collateral.

A financing statement sufficiently indicates the collateral that it covers if the financing statement provides:

(1) a description of the collateral pursuant to Section 9–108; or

(2) an indication that the financing statement covers all assets or all personal property.

As amended in 1999.

§ 9–505. Filing and Compliance with Other Statutes and Treaties for Consignments, Leases, Other Bailments, and Other Transactions.

(a) A consignor, lessor, or other bailor of goods, a licensor, or a buyer of a payment intangible or promissory note may file a financing statement, or may comply with a statute or treaty described in Section 9–311(a), using the terms "consignor", "consignee", "lessor", "lessee", "bailor", "bailee", "licensor", "licensee", "owner", "registered owner", "buyer", "seller", or words of similar import, instead of the terms "secured party" and "debtor".

(b) This part applies to the filing of a financing statement under subsection (a) and, as appropriate, to compliance that is equivalent to filing a financing statement under Section 9–311(b), but the filing or compliance is not of itself a factor in determining whether the collateral secures an obligation. If it is determined for another reason that the collateral secures an obligation, a security interest held by the consignor, lessor, bailor, licensor, owner, or buyer which attaches to the collateral is perfected by the filing or compliance.

§ 9–506. Effect of Errors or Omissions.

(a) A financing statement substantially satisfying the requirements of this part is effective, even if it has minor errors or omissions, unless the errors or omissions make the financing statement seriously misleading.

(b) Except as otherwise provided in subsection (c), a financing statement that fails sufficiently to provide the name of the debtor in accordance with Section 9–503(a) is seriously misleading.

(c) If a search of the records of the filing office under the debtor's correct name, using the filing office's standard search logic, if any, would disclose a financing statement that fails sufficiently to provide the name of the debtor in accordance with Section 9–503(a), the name provided does not make the financing statement seriously misleading.

(d) For purposes of Section 9–508(b), the "debtor's correct name" in subsection (c) means the correct name of the new debtor.

§ 9–507. Effect of Certain Events on Effectiveness of Financing Statement.

(a) A filed financing statement remains effective with respect to collateral that is sold, exchanged, leased, licensed, or otherwise disposed of and in which a security interest or agricultural lien continues, even if the secured party knows of or consents to the disposition.

(b) Except as otherwise provided in subsection (c) and Section 9–508, a financing statement is not rendered ineffective if, after the financing statement is filed, the information provided in the financing statement becomes seriously misleading under Section 9–506.

(c) If a debtor so changes its name that a filed financing statement becomes seriously misleading under Section 9–506:

(1) the financing statement is effective to perfect a security interest in collateral acquired by the debtor before, or within four months after, the change; and

(2) the financing statement is not effective to perfect a security interest in collateral acquired by the debtor more than four months after the change, unless an amendment to the financing statement which renders the financing statement not seriously misleading is filed within four months after the change.

§ 9–508. Effectiveness of Financing Statement If New Debtor Becomes Bound by Security Agreement.

(a) Except as otherwise provided in this section, a filed financing statement naming an original debtor is effective to perfect a security interest in collateral in which a new debtor has or acquires rights to the extent that the financing statement would have been effective had the original debtor acquired rights in the collateral.

(b) If the difference between the name of the original debtor and that of the new debtor causes a filed financing statement that is effective under subsection (a) to be seriously misleading under Section 9–506:

(1) the financing statement is effective to perfect a security interest in collateral acquired by the new debtor before, and within four months after, the new debtor becomes bound under Section 9B–203(d); and

(2) the financing statement is not effective to perfect a security interest in collateral acquired by the new debtor more than four months after the new debtor becomes bound under Section 9–203(d) unless an initial financing statement providing the name of the new debtor is filed before the expiration of that time.

(c) This section does not apply to collateral as to which a filed financing statement remains effective against the new debtor under Section 9–507(a).

§ 9–509. Persons Entitled to File a Record.

(a) A person may file an initial financing statement, amendment that adds collateral covered by a financing statement, or amendment that adds a debtor to a financing statement only if:

(1) the debtor authorizes the filing in an authenticated record or pursuant to subsection (b) or (c); or

(2) the person holds an agricultural lien that has become effective at the time of filing and the financing statement covers only collateral in which the person holds an agricultural lien.

(b) By authenticating or becoming bound as debtor by a security agreement, a debtor or new debtor authorizes the filing of an initial financing statement, and an amendment, covering:

(1) the collateral described in the security agreement; and

(2) property that becomes collateral under Section 9–315(a)(2), whether or not the security agreement expressly covers proceeds.

(c) By acquiring collateral in which a security interest or agricultural lien continues under Section 9–315(a)(1), a debtor authorizes the filing of an initial financing statement, and an amendment, covering the collateral and property that becomes collateral under Section 9–315(a)(2).

(d) A person may file an amendment other than an amendment that adds collateral covered by a financing statement or an amendment that adds a debtor to a financing statement only if:

(1) the secured party of record authorizes the filing; or

(2) the amendment is a termination statement for a financing statement as to which the secured party of record has failed to file or send a termination statement as required by Section 9–513(a) or (c), the debtor authorizes the filing, and the termination statement indicates that the debtor authorized it to be filed.

(e) If there is more than one secured party of record for a financing statement, each secured party of record may authorize the filing of an amendment under subsection (d).

As amended in 2000.

§ 9–510. Effectiveness of Filed Record.

(a) A filed record is effective only to the extent that it was filed by a person that may file it under Section 9–509.

(b) A record authorized by one secured party of record does not affect the financing statement with respect to another secured party of record.

(c) A continuation statement that is not filed within the six-month period prescribed by Section 9–515(d) is ineffective.

§ 9–511. Secured Party of Record.

(a) A secured party of record with respect to a financing statement is a person whose name is provided as the name of the secured party or a representative of the secured party in an initial financing statement that has been filed. If an initial financing statement is filed under Section 9–514(a), the assignee named in the initial financing statement is the secured party of record with respect to the financing statement.

(b) If an amendment of a financing statement which provides the name of a person as a secured party or a representative of a secured party is filed, the person named in the amendment is a secured party of record. If an amendment is filed under Section 9–514(b), the assignee named in the amendment is a secured party of record.

(c) A person remains a secured party of record until the filing of an amendment of the financing statement which deletes the person.

§ 9–512. Amendment of Financing Statement.

[Alternative A]

(a) Subject to Section 9–509, a person may add or delete collateral covered by, continue or terminate the effectiveness of, or, subject to subsection (e), otherwise amend the information provided in, a financing statement by filing an amendment that:

(1) identifies, by its file number, the initial financing statement to which the amendment relates; and

(2) if the amendment relates to an initial financing statement filed [or recorded] in a filing office described in Section 9–501(a)(1), provides the information specified in Section 9–502(b).

[Alternative B]

(a) Subject to Section 9–509, a person may add or delete collateral covered by, continue or terminate the effectiveness of, or, subject to subsection (e), otherwise amend the information provided in, a financing statement by filing an amendment that:

(1) identifies, by its file number, the initial financing statement to which the amendment relates; and

(2) if the amendment relates to an initial financing statement filed [or recorded] in a filing office described in Section 9–501(a)(1), provides the date [and time] that the initial financing statement was filed [or recorded] and the information specified in Section 9–502(b).

[End of Alternatives]

(b) Except as otherwise provided in Section 9–515, the filing of an amendment does not extend the period of effectiveness of the financing statement.

(c) A financing statement that is amended by an amendment that adds collateral is effective as to the added collateral only from the date of the filing of the amendment.

(d) A financing statement that is amended by an amendment that adds a debtor is effective as to the added debtor only from the date of the filing of the amendment.

(e) An amendment is ineffective to the extent it:

(1) purports to delete all debtors and fails to provide the name of a debtor to be covered by the financing statement; or

(2) purports to delete all secured parties of record and fails to provide the name of a new secured party of record.

Legislative Note: States whose real-estate filing offices require additional information in amendments and cannot search their records by both the name of the debtor and the file number should enact Alternative B to Sections 9–512(a), 9–518(b), 9–519(f), and 9–522(a).

§ 9–513. Termination Statement.

(a) A secured party shall cause the secured party of record for a financing statement to file a termination statement for the financing statement if the financing statement covers consumer goods and:

(1) there is no obligation secured by the collateral covered by the financing statement and no commitment to make an advance, incur an obligation, or otherwise give value; or

(2) the debtor did not authorize the filing of the initial financing statement.

(b) To comply with subsection (a), a secured party shall cause the secured party of record to file the termination statement:

(1) within one month after there is no obligation secured by the collateral covered by the financing statement and no commitment to make an advance, incur an obligation, or otherwise give value; or

(2) if earlier, within 20 days after the secured party receives an authenticated demand from a debtor.

(c) In cases not governed by subsection (a), within 20 days after a secured party receives an authenticated demand from a debtor, the secured party shall cause the secured party of record for a financing statement to send to the debtor a termination statement for the financing statement or file the termination statement in the filing office if:

(1) except in the case of a financing statement covering accounts or chattel paper that has been sold or goods that are the subject of a consignment, there is no obligation secured by the collateral covered by the financing statement and no commitment to make an advance, incur an obligation, or otherwise give value;

(2) the financing statement covers accounts or chattel paper that has been sold but as to which the account debtor or other person obligated has discharged its obligation;

(3) the financing statement covers goods that were the subject of a consignment to the debtor but are not in the debtor's possession; or

(4) the debtor did not authorize the filing of the initial financing statement.

(d) Except as otherwise provided in Section 9–510, upon the filing of a termination statement with the filing office, the financing statement to which the termination statement relates ceases to be effective. Except as otherwise provided in Section 9–510, for purposes of Sections 9–519(g), 9–522(a), and 9–523(c), the filing with the filing office of a termination statement relating to a financing statement that indicates that the debtor is a transmitting utility also causes the effectiveness of the financing statement to lapse.

As amended in 2000.

§ 9–514. Assignment of Powers of Secured Party of Record.

(a) Except as otherwise provided in subsection (c), an initial financing statement may reflect an assignment of all of the secured party's power to authorize an amendment to the financing statement by providing the name and mailing address of the assignee as the name and address of the secured party.

(b) Except as otherwise provided in subsection (c), a secured party of record may assign of record all or part of its power to authorize an amendment to a financing statement by filing in the filing office an amendment of the financing statement which:

(1) identifies, by its file number, the initial financing statement to which it relates;

(2) provides the name of the assignor; and

(3) provides the name and mailing address of the assignee.

(c) An assignment of record of a security interest in a fixture covered by a record of a mortgage which is effective as a financing statement filed as a fixture filing under Section 9–502(c) may be made only by an assignment of record of the mortgage in the manner provided by law of this State other than [the Uniform Commercial Code].

§ 9–515. Duration and Effectiveness of Financing Statement; Effect of Lapsed Financing Statement.

(a) Except as otherwise provided in subsections (b), (e), (f), and (g), a filed financing statement is effective for a period of five years after the date of filing.

(b) Except as otherwise provided in subsections (e), (f), and (g), an initial financing statement filed in connection with a public-finance transaction or manufactured-home transaction is effective for a period of 30 years after the date of filing if it indicates that it is filed in connection with a public-finance transaction or manufactured-home transaction.

(c) The effectiveness of a filed financing statement lapses on the expiration of the period of its effectiveness unless before the lapse a continuation statement is filed pursuant to subsection (d). Upon lapse, a financing statement ceases to be effective and any security interest or agricultural lien that was perfected by the financing statement becomes unperfected, unless the security interest is perfected otherwise. If the security interest or agricultural lien becomes unperfected upon lapse, it is deemed never to have been perfected as against a purchaser of the collateral for value.

(d) A continuation statement may be filed only within six months before the expiration of the five-year period specified in subsection (a) or the 30-year period specified in subsection (b), whichever is applicable.

(e) Except as otherwise provided in Section 9–510, upon timely filing of a continuation statement, the effectiveness of the initial financing statement continues for a period of five years commencing on the day on which the financing statement would have become ineffective in the absence of the filing. Upon the expiration of the five-year period, the financing statement lapses in the same manner as provided in subsection (c), unless, before the lapse, another continuation statement is filed pursuant to subsection (d). Succeeding continuation statements may be filed in the same manner to continue the effectiveness of the initial financing statement.

(f) If a debtor is a transmitting utility and a filed financing statement so indicates, the financing statement is effective until a termination statement is filed.

(g) A record of a mortgage that is effective as a financing statement filed as a fixture filing under Section 9–502(c) remains effective as a financing statement filed as a fixture filing until the mortgage is released or satisfied of record or its effectiveness otherwise terminates as to the real property.

§ 9–516. What Constitutes Filing; Effectiveness of Filing.

(a) Except as otherwise provided in subsection (b), communication of a record to a filing office and tender of the filing fee or acceptance of the record by the filing office constitutes filing.

(b) Filing does not occur with respect to a record that a filing office refuses to accept because:

(1) the record is not communicated by a method or medium of communication authorized by the filing office;

(2) an amount equal to or greater than the applicable filing fee is not tendered;

(3) the filing office is unable to index the record because:

(A) in the case of an initial financing statement, the record does not provide a name for the debtor;

(B) in the case of an amendment or correction statement, the record:

(i) does not identify the initial financing statement as required by Section 9–512 or 9–518, as applicable; or

(ii) identifies an initial financing statement whose effectiveness has lapsed under Section 9–515;

(C) in the case of an initial financing statement that provides the name of a debtor identified as an individual or an amendment that provides a name of a debtor identified as an individual which was not previously provided in the financing statement to which the record relates, the record does not identify the debtor's last name; or

(D) in the case of a record filed [or recorded] in the filing office described in Section 9–501(a)(1), the record does not provide a sufficient description of the real property to which it relates;

(4) in the case of an initial financing statement or an amendment that adds a secured party of record, the record does not provide a name and mailing address for the secured party of record;

(5) in the case of an initial financing statement or an amendment that provides a name of a debtor which was not previously provided in the financing statement to which the amendment relates, the record does not:

(A) provide a mailing address for the debtor;

(B) indicate whether the debtor is an individual or an organization; or

(C) if the financing statement indicates that the debtor is an organization, provide:

(i) a type of organization for the debtor;

(ii) a jurisdiction of organization for the debtor; or

(iii) an organizational identification number for the debtor or indicate that the debtor has none;

(6) in the case of an assignment reflected in an initial financing statement under Section 9–514(a) or an amendment filed under Section 9–514(b), the record does not provide a name and mailing address for the assignee; or

(7) in the case of a continuation statement, the record is not filed within the six-month period prescribed by Section 9–515(d).

(c) For purposes of subsection (b):

(1) a record does not provide information if the filing office is unable to read or decipher the information; and

(2) a record that does not indicate that it is an amendment or identify an initial financing statement to which it relates, as required by Section 9–512, 9–514, or 9–518, is an initial financing statement.

(d) A record that is communicated to the filing office with tender of the filing fee, but which the filing office refuses to accept for a reason other than one set forth in subsection (b), is effective as a filed record except as against a purchaser of the collateral which gives value in reasonable reliance upon the absence of the record from the files.

§ 9–517. Effect of Indexing Errors.

The failure of the filing office to index a record correctly does not affect the effectiveness of the filed record.

§ 9–518. Claim Concerning Inaccurate or Wrongfully Filed Record.

(a) A person may file in the filing office a correction statement with respect to a record indexed there under the person's name if the person believes that the record is inaccurate or was wrongfully filed.

[Alternative A]

(b) A correction statement must:

(1) identify the record to which it relates by the file number assigned to the initial financing statement to which the record relates;

(2) indicate that it is a correction statement; and

(3) provide the basis for the person's belief that the record is inaccurate and indicate the manner in which the person believes the record should be amended to cure any inaccuracy or provide the basis for the person's belief that the record was wrongfully filed.

[Alternative B]

(b) A correction statement must:

(1) identify the record to which it relates by:

(A) the file number assigned to the initial financing statement to which the record relates; and

(B) if the correction statement relates to a record filed [or recorded] in a filing office described in Section 9–501(a)(1), the date [and time] that the initial financing statement was filed [or recorded] and the information specified in Section 9–502(b);

(2) indicate that it is a correction statement; and

(3) provide the basis for the person's belief that the record is inaccurate and indicate the manner in which the person believes the record should be amended to cure any inaccuracy or provide the basis for the person's belief that the record was wrongfully filed.

[End of Alternatives]

(c) The filing of a correction statement does not affect the effectiveness of an initial financing statement or other filed record.

Legislative Note: States whose real-estate filing offices require additional information in amendments and cannot search their records by both the name of the debtor and the file number should enact Alternative B to Sections 9–512(a), 9–518(b), 9–519(f), and 9–522(a).

[Subpart 2. Duties and Operation of Filing Office]

§ 9–519. Numbering, Maintaining, and Indexing Records; Communicating Information Provided in Records.

(a) For each record filed in a filing office, the filing office shall:

(1) assign a unique number to the filed record;

(2) create a record that bears the number assigned to the filed record and the date and time of filing;

(3) maintain the filed record for public inspection; and

(4) index the filed record in accordance with subsections (c), (d), and (e).

(b) A file number [assigned after January 1, 2002,] must include a digit that:

(1) is mathematically derived from or related to the other digits of the file number; and

(2) aids the filing office in determining whether a number communicated as the file number includes a single-digit or transpositional error.

(c) Except as otherwise provided in subsections (d) and (e), the filing office shall:

(1) index an initial financing statement according to the name of the debtor and index all filed records relating to the initial financing statement in a manner that associates with one another an initial financing statement and all filed records relating to the initial financing statement; and

(2) index a record that provides a name of a debtor which was not previously provided in the financing statement to which the record relates also according to the name that was not previously provided.

(d) If a financing statement is filed as a fixture filing or covers as-extracted collateral or timber to be cut, [it must be filed for record and] the filing office shall index it:

(1) under the names of the debtor and of each owner of record shown on the financing statement as if they were the mortgagors under a mortgage of the real property described; and

(2) to the extent that the law of this State provides for indexing of records of mortgages under the name of the mortgagee, under the name of the secured party as if the secured party were the mortgagee thereunder, or, if indexing is by description, as if the financing statement were a record of a mortgage of the real property described.

(e) If a financing statement is filed as a fixture filing or covers as-extracted collateral or timber to be cut, the filing office shall index an assignment filed under Section 9–514(a) or an amendment filed under Section 9–514(b):

(1) under the name of the assignor as grantor; and

(2) to the extent that the law of this State provides for indexing a record of the assignment of a mortgage under the name of the assignee, under the name of the assignee.

[Alternative A]

(f) The filing office shall maintain a capability:

(1) to retrieve a record by the name of the debtor and by the file number assigned to the initial financing statement to which the record relates; and

(2) to associate and retrieve with one another an initial financing statement and each filed record relating to the initial financing statement.

[Alternative B]

(f) The filing office shall maintain a capability:

(1) to retrieve a record by the name of the debtor and:

(A) if the filing office is described in Section 9–501(a)(1), by the file number assigned to the initial financing statement to which the record relates and the date [and time] that the record was filed [or recorded]; or

    (B) if the filing office is described in Section 9–501(a)(2), by the file number assigned to the initial financing statement to which the record relates; and

(2) to associate and retrieve with one another an initial financing statement and each filed record relating to the initial financing statement.

[End of Alternatives]

(g) The filing office may not remove a debtor's name from the index until one year after the effectiveness of a financing statement naming the debtor lapses under Section 9–515 with respect to all secured parties of record.

(h) The filing office shall perform the acts required by subsections (a) through (e) at the time and in the manner prescribed by filing-office rule, but not later than two business days after the filing office receives the record in question.

[(i) Subsection[s] [(b)] [and] [(h)] do[es] not apply to a filing office described in Section 9–501(a)(1).]

Legislative Notes:

1. States whose filing offices currently assign file numbers that include a verification number, commonly known as a "check digit," or can implement this requirement before the effective date of this Article should omit the bracketed language in subsection (b).

2. In States in which writings will not appear in the real property records and indices unless actually recorded the bracketed language in subsection (d) should be used.

3. States whose real-estate filing offices require additional information in amendments and cannot search their records by both the name of the debtor and the file number should enact Alternative B to Sections 9–512(a), 9–518(b), 9–519(f), and 9–522(a).

4. A State that elects not to require real-estate filing offices to comply with either or both of subsections (b) and (h) may adopt an applicable variation of subsection (i) and add "Except as otherwise provided in subsection (i)," to the appropriate subsection or subsections.

§ 9–520. Acceptance and Refusal to Accept Record.

(a) A filing office shall refuse to accept a record for filing for a reason set forth in Section 9–516(b) and may refuse to accept a record for filing only for a reason set forth in Section 9–516(b).

(b) If a filing office refuses to accept a record for filing, it shall communicate to the person that presented the record the fact of and reason for the refusal and the date and time the record would have been filed had the filing office accepted it. The communication must be made at the time and in the manner prescribed by filing-office rule but [, in the case of a filing office described in Section 9–501(a)(2),] in no event more than two business days after the filing office receives the record.

(c) A filed financing statement satisfying Section 9–502(a) and (b) is effective, even if the filing office is required to refuse to accept it for filing under subsection (a). However, Section 9–338 applies to a filed financing statement providing information described in Section 9–516(b)(5) which is incorrect at the time the financing statement is filed.

(d) If a record communicated to a filing office provides information that relates to more than one debtor, this part applies as to each debtor separately.

Legislative Note: A State that elects not to require real-property filing offices to comply with subsection (b) should include the bracketed language.

§ 9–521. Uniform Form of Written Financing Statement and Amendment.

(a) A filing office that accepts written records may not refuse to accept a written initial financing statement in the following form and format except for a reason set forth in Section 9–516(b):

[NATIONAL UCC FINANCING STATEMENT (FORM UCC1)(REV. 7/29/98)]

[NATIONAL UCC FINANCING STATEMENT ADDENDUM (FORM UCC1Ad)(REV. 07/29/98)]

(b) A filing office that accepts written records may not refuse to accept a written record in the following form and format except for a reason set forth in Section 9–516(b):

[NATIONAL UCC FINANCING STATEMENT AMENDMENT (FORM UCC3)(REV. 07/29/98)]

[NATIONAL UCC FINANCING STATEMENT AMENDMENT ADDENDUM (FORM UCC3Ad)(REV. 07/29/98)]

§ 9–522. Maintenance and Destruction of Records.

[Alternative A]

(a) The filing office shall maintain a record of the information provided in a filed financing statement for at least one year after the effectiveness of the financing statement has lapsed under Section 9–515 with respect to all secured parties of record. The record must be retrievable by using the name of the debtor and by using the file number assigned to the initial financing statement to which the record relates.

[Alternative B]

(a) The filing office shall maintain a record of the information provided in a filed financing statement for at least one year after the effectiveness of the financing statement has lapsed under Section 9–515 with respect to all secured parties of record. The record must be retrievable by using the name of the debtor and:

    (1) if the record was filed [or recorded] in the filing office described in Section 9–501(a)(1), by using the file number assigned to the initial financing statement to which the record relates and the date [and time] that the record was filed [or recorded]; or

    (2) if the record was filed in the filing office described in Section 9–501(a)(2), by using the file number assigned to the initial financing statement to which the record relates.

[End of Alternatives]

(b) Except to the extent that a statute governing disposition of public records provides otherwise, the filing office immediately may destroy any written record evidencing a financing statement. However, if the filing office destroys a written record, it shall maintain another record of the financing statement which complies with subsection (a).

Legislative Note: States whose real-estate filing offices require additional information in amendments and cannot search their records by both the name of the debtor and the file number should enact Alternative B to Sections 9–512(a), 9–518(b), 9–519(f), and 9–522(a).

§ 9–523. Information from Filing Office; Sale or License of Records.

(a) If a person that files a written record requests an acknowledgment of the filing, the filing office shall send to the person an image of the record showing the number assigned to the record pursuant to Section 9–519(a)(1) and the date and time of the filing of the record. However, if the person furnishes a copy of the record to the filing office, the filing office may instead:

(1) note upon the copy the number assigned to the record pursuant to Section 9–519(a)(1) and the date and time of the filing of the record; and

(2) send the copy to the person.

(b) If a person files a record other than a written record, the filing office shall communicate to the person an acknowledgment that provides:

(1) the information in the record;

(2) the number assigned to the record pursuant to Section 9–519(a)(1); and

(3) the date and time of the filing of the record.

(c) The filing office shall communicate or otherwise make available in a record the following information to any person that requests it:

(1) whether there is on file on a date and time specified by the filing office, but not a date earlier than three business days before the filing office receives the request, any financing statement that:

(A) designates a particular debtor [or, if the request so states, designates a particular debtor at the address specified in the request];

(B) has not lapsed under Section 9–515 with respect to all secured parties of record; and

(C) if the request so states, has lapsed under Section 9–515 and a record of which is maintained by the filing office under Section 9–522(a);

(2) the date and time of filing of each financing statement; and

(3) the information provided in each financing statement.

(d) In complying with its duty under subsection (c), the filing office may communicate information in any medium. However, if requested, the filing office shall communicate information by issuing [its written certificate] [a record that can be admitted into evidence in the courts of this State without extrinsic evidence of its authenticity].

(e) The filing office shall perform the acts required by subsections (a) through (d) at the time and in the manner prescribed by filing-office rule, but not later than two business days after the filing office receives the request.

(f) At least weekly, the [insert appropriate official or governmental agency] [filing office] shall offer to sell or license to the public on a nonexclusive basis, in bulk, copies of all records filed in it under this part, in every medium from time to time available to the filing office.

Legislative Notes:

1. States whose filing office does not offer the additional service of responding to search requests limited to a particular address should omit the bracketed language in subsection (c)(1)(A).

2. A State that elects not to require real-estate filing offices to comply with either or both of subsections (e) and (f) should specify in the appropriate subsection(s) only the filing office described in Section 9–501(a)(2).

§ 9–524. Delay by Filing Office.

Delay by the filing office beyond a time limit prescribed by this part is excused if:

(1) the delay is caused by interruption of communication or computer facilities, war, emergency conditions, failure of equipment, or other circumstances beyond control of the filing office; and

(2) the filing office exercises reasonable diligence under the circumstances.

§ 9–525. Fees.

(a) Except as otherwise provided in subsection (e), the fee for filing and indexing a record under this part, other than an initial financing statement of the kind described in subsection (b), is [the amount specified in subsection (c), if applicable, plus]:

(1) $[X] if the record is communicated in writing and consists of one or two pages;

(2) $[2X] if the record is communicated in writing and consists of more than two pages; and

(3) $[½X] if the record is communicated by another medium authorized by filing-office rule.

(b) Except as otherwise provided in subsection (e), the fee for filing and indexing an initial financing statement of the following kind is [the amount specified in subsection (c), if applicable, plus]:

(1) $_____ if the financing statement indicates that it is filed in connection with a public-finance transaction;

(2) $_____ if the financing statement indicates that it is filed in connection with a manufactured-home transaction.

[Alternative A]

(c) The number of names required to be indexed does not affect the amount of the fee in subsections (a) and (b).

[Alternative B]

(c) Except as otherwise provided in subsection (e), if a record is communicated in writing, the fee for each name more than two required to be indexed is $_____.

[End of Alternatives]

(d) The fee for responding to a request for information from the filing office, including for [issuing a certificate showing] [communicating] whether there is on file any financing statement naming a particular debtor, is:

(1) $_____ if the request is communicated in writing; and

(2) $_____ if the request is communicated by another medium authorized by filing-office rule.

(e) This section does not require a fee with respect to a record of a mortgage which is effective as a financing statement filed as a fixture filing or as a financing statement covering as-extracted collateral or timber to be cut under Section 9–502(c). However, the recording and satisfaction fees that otherwise would be applicable to the record of the mortgage apply.

Legislative Notes:

1. To preserve uniformity, a State that places the provisions of this section together with statutes setting fees for other services should do so without modification.

2. A State should enact subsection (c), Alternative A, and omit the bracketed language in subsections (a) and (b) unless its indexing system entails a substantial additional cost when indexing additional names.

As amended in 2000.

§ 9–526. Filing-Office Rules.

(a) The [insert appropriate governmental official or agency] shall adopt and publish rules to implement this article. The filing-office rules must be[:

(1)] consistent with this article[; and

(2) adopted and published in accordance with the [insert any applicable state administrative procedure act]].

(b) To keep the filing-office rules and practices of the filing office in harmony with the rules and practices of filing offices in other jurisdictions that enact substantially this part, and to keep the technology used by the filing office compatible with the technology used by filing offices in other jurisdictions that enact substantially this part, the [insert appropriate governmental official or agency], so far as is consistent with the purposes, policies, and provisions of this article, in adopting, amending, and repealing filing-office rules, shall:

(1) consult with filing offices in other jurisdictions that enact substantially this part; and

(2) consult the most recent version of the Model Rules promulgated by the International Association of Corporate Administrators or any successor organization; and

(3) take into consideration the rules and practices of, and the technology used by, filing offices in other jurisdictions that enact substantially this part.

§ 9–527. Duty to Report.

The [insert appropriate governmental official or agency] shall report [annually on or before _____] to the [Governor and Legislature] on the operation of the filing office. The report must contain a statement of the extent to which:

(1) the filing-office rules are not in harmony with the rules of filing offices in other jurisdictions that enact substantially this part and the reasons for these variations; and

(2) the filing-office rules are not in harmony with the most recent version of the Model Rules promulgated by the International Association of Corporate Administrators, or any successor organization, and the reasons for these variations.

Part 6 Default

[Subpart 1. Default and Enforcement of Security Interest]

§ 9–601. Rights after Default; Judicial Enforcement; Consignor or Buyer of Accounts, Chattel Paper, Payment Intangibles, or Promissory Notes.

(a) After default, a secured party has the rights provided in this part and, except as otherwise provided in Section 9–602, those provided by agreement of the parties. A secured party:

(1) may reduce a claim to judgment, foreclose, or otherwise enforce the claim, security interest, or agricultural lien by any available judicial procedure; and

(2) if the collateral is documents, may proceed either as to the documents or as to the goods they cover.

(b) A secured party in possession of collateral or control of collateral under Section 9–104, 9–105, 9–106, or 9–107 has the rights and duties provided in Section 9–207.

(c) The rights under subsections (a) and (b) are cumulative and may be exercised simultaneously.

(d) Except as otherwise provided in subsection (g) and Section 9–605, after default, a debtor and an obligor have the rights provided in this part and by agreement of the parties.

(e) If a secured party has reduced its claim to judgment, the lien of any levy that may be made upon the collateral by virtue of an execution based upon the judgment relates back to the earliest of:

(1) the date of perfection of the security interest or agricultural lien in the collateral;

(2) the date of filing a financing statement covering the collateral; or

(3) any date specified in a statute under which the agricultural lien was created.

(f) A sale pursuant to an execution is a foreclosure of the security interest or agricultural lien by judicial procedure within the meaning of this section. A secured party may purchase at the sale and thereafter hold the collateral free of any other requirements of this article.

(g) Except as otherwise provided in Section 9–607(c), this part imposes no duties upon a secured party that is a consignor or is a buyer of accounts, chattel paper, payment intangibles, or promissory notes.

§ 9–602. Waiver and Variance of Rights and Duties.

Except as otherwise provided in Section 9–624, to the extent that they give rights to a debtor or obligor and impose duties on a secured party, the debtor or obligor may not waive or vary the rules stated in the following listed sections:

(1) Section 9–207(b)(4)(C), which deals with use and operation of the collateral by the secured party;

(2) Section 9–210, which deals with requests for an accounting and requests concerning a list of collateral and statement of account;

(3) Section 9–607(c), which deals with collection and enforcement of collateral;

(4) Sections 9–608(a) and 9–615(c) to the extent that they deal with application or payment of noncash proceeds of collection, enforcement, or disposition;

(5) Sections 9–608(a) and 9–615(d) to the extent that they require accounting for or payment of surplus proceeds of collateral;

(6) Section 9–609 to the extent that it imposes upon a secured party that takes possession of collateral without judicial process the duty to do so without breach of the peace;

(7) Sections 9–610(b), 9–611, 9–613, and 9–614, which deal with disposition of collateral;

(8) Section 9–615(f), which deals with calculation of a deficiency or surplus when a disposition is made to the secured party, a person related to the secured party, or a secondary obligor;

(9) Section 9–616, which deals with explanation of the calculation of a surplus or deficiency;

(10) Sections 9–620, 9–621, and 9–622, which deal with acceptance of collateral in satisfaction of obligation;

(11) Section 9–623, which deals with redemption of collateral;

(12) Section 9–624, which deals with permissible waivers; and

(13) Sections 9–625 and 9–626, which deal with the secured party's liability for failure to comply with this article.

§ 9–603. Agreement on Standards Concerning Rights and Duties.

(a) The parties may determine by agreement the standards measuring the fulfillment of the rights of a debtor or obligor and the duties of a secured party under a rule stated in Section 9–602 if the standards are not manifestly unreasonable.

(b) Subsection (a) does not apply to the duty under Section 9–609 to refrain from breaching the peace.

§ 9–604. Procedure If Security Agreement Covers Real Property or Fixtures.

(a) If a security agreement covers both personal and real property, a secured party may proceed:

(1) under this part as to the personal property without prejudicing any rights with respect to the real property; or

(2) as to both the personal property and the real property in accordance with the rights with respect to the real property, in which case the other provisions of this part do not apply.

(b) Subject to subsection (c), if a security agreement covers goods that are or become fixtures, a secured party may proceed:

(1) under this part; or

(2) in accordance with the rights with respect to real property, in which case the other provisions of this part do not apply.

(c) Subject to the other provisions of this part, if a secured party holding a security interest in fixtures has priority over all owners and encumbrancers of the real property, the secured party, after default, may remove the collateral from the real property.

(d) A secured party that removes collateral shall promptly reimburse any encumbrancer or owner of the real property, other than the debtor, for the cost of repair of any physical injury caused by the removal. The secured party need not reimburse the encumbrancer or owner for any diminution in value of the real property caused by the absence of the goods removed or by any necessity of replacing them. A person entitled to reimbursement may refuse permission to remove until the secured party gives adequate assurance for the performance of the obligation to reimburse.

§ 9–605. Unknown Debtor or Secondary Obligor.

A secured party does not owe a duty based on its status as secured party:

(1) to a person that is a debtor or obligor, unless the secured party knows:

(A) that the person is a debtor or obligor;

(B) the identity of the person; and

(C) how to communicate with the person; or

(2) to a secured party or lienholder that has filed a financing statement against a person, unless the secured party knows:

(A) that the person is a debtor; and

(B) the identity of the person.

§ 9–606. Time of Default for Agricultural Lien.

For purposes of this part, a default occurs in connection with an agricultural lien at the time the secured party becomes entitled to enforce the lien in accordance with the statute under which it was created.

§ 9–607. Collection and Enforcement by Secured Party.

(a) If so agreed, and in any event after default, a secured party:

(1) may notify an account debtor or other person obligated on collateral to make payment or otherwise render performance to or for the benefit of the secured party;

(2) may take any proceeds to which the secured party is entitled under Section 9–315;

(3) may enforce the obligations of an account debtor or other person obligated on collateral and exercise the rights of the debtor with respect to the obligation of the account debtor or other person obligated on collateral to make payment or otherwise render performance to the debtor, and with respect to any property that secures the obligations of the account debtor or other person obligated on the collateral;

(4) if it holds a security interest in a deposit account perfected by control under Section 9–104(a)(1), may apply the balance of the deposit account to the obligation secured by the deposit account; and

(5) if it holds a security interest in a deposit account perfected by control under Section 9–104(a)(2) or (3), may instruct the bank to pay the balance of the deposit account to or for the benefit of the secured party.

(b) If necessary to enable a secured party to exercise under subsection (a)(3) the right of a debtor to enforce a mortgage nonjudicially, the secured party may record in the office in which a record of the mortgage is recorded:

(1) a copy of the security agreement that creates or provides for a security interest in the obligation secured by the mortgage; and

(2) the secured party's sworn affidavit in recordable form stating that:

(A) a default has occurred; and

(B) the secured party is entitled to enforce the mortgage nonjudicially.

(c) A secured party shall proceed in a commercially reasonable manner if the secured party:

(1) undertakes to collect from or enforce an obligation of an account debtor or other person obligated on collateral; and

(2) is entitled to charge back uncollected collateral or otherwise to full or limited recourse against the debtor or a secondary obligor.

(d) A secured party may deduct from the collections made pursuant to subsection (c) reasonable expenses of collection and enforcement, including reasonable attorney's fees and legal expenses incurred by the secured party.

(e) This section does not determine whether an account debtor, bank, or other person obligated on collateral owes a duty to a secured party.

As amended in 2000.

§ 9–608. Application of Proceeds of Collection or Enforcement; Liability for Deficiency and Right to Surplus.

(a) If a security interest or agricultural lien secures payment or performance of an obligation, the following rules apply:

(1) A secured party shall apply or pay over for application the cash proceeds of collection or enforcement under Section 9–607 in the following order to:

(A) the reasonable expenses of collection and enforcement and, to the extent provided for by agreement and not prohibited by law, reasonable attorney's fees and legal expenses incurred by the secured party;

(B) the satisfaction of obligations secured by the security interest or agricultural lien under which the collection or enforcement is made; and

(C) the satisfaction of obligations secured by any subordinate security interest in or other lien on the collateral subject to the security interest or agricultural lien under which the collection or enforcement is made if the secured party receives an authenticated demand for proceeds before distribution of the proceeds is completed.

(2) If requested by a secured party, a holder of a subordinate security interest or other lien shall furnish reasonable proof of the interest or lien within a reasonable time. Unless the holder complies, the secured party need not comply with the holder's demand under paragraph (1)(C).

(3) A secured party need not apply or pay over for application noncash proceeds of collection and enforcement under Section 9–607 unless the failure to do so would be commercially unreasonable. A secured party that applies or pays over for application noncash proceeds shall do so in a commercially reasonable manner.

(4) A secured party shall account to and pay a debtor for any surplus, and the obligor is liable for any deficiency.

(b) If the underlying transaction is a sale of accounts, chattel paper, payment intangibles, or promissory notes, the debtor is not entitled to any surplus, and the obligor is not liable for any deficiency.

As amended in 2000.

§ 9–609. Secured Party's Right to Take Possession after Default.

(a) After default, a secured party:

(1) may take possession of the collateral; and

(2) without removal, may render equipment unusable and dispose of collateral on a debtor's premises under Section 9–610.

(b) A secured party may proceed under subsection (a):

(1) pursuant to judicial process; or

(2) without judicial process, if it proceeds without breach of the peace.

(c) If so agreed, and in any event after default, a secured party may require the debtor to assemble the collateral and make it available to the secured party at a place to be designated by the secured party which is reasonably convenient to both parties.

§ 9–610. Disposition of Collateral after Default.

(a) After default, a secured party may sell, lease, license, or otherwise dispose of any or all of the collateral in its present condition or following any commercially reasonable preparation or processing.

(b) Every aspect of a disposition of collateral, including the method, manner, time, place, and other terms, must be commercially reasonable. If commercially reasonable, a secured party may dispose of collateral by public or private proceedings, by one or more contracts, as a unit or in parcels, and at any time and place and on any terms.

(c) A secured party may purchase collateral:

(1) at a public disposition; or

(2) at a private disposition only if the collateral is of a kind that is customarily sold on a recognized market or the subject of widely distributed standard price quotations.

(d) A contract for sale, lease, license, or other disposition includes the warranties relating to title, possession, quiet enjoyment, and the like which by operation of law accompany a voluntary disposition of property of the kind subject to the contract.

(e) A secured party may disclaim or modify warranties under subsection (d):

(1) in a manner that would be effective to disclaim or modify the warranties in a voluntary disposition of property of the kind subject to the contract of disposition; or

(2) by communicating to the purchaser a record evidencing the contract for disposition and including an express disclaimer or modification of the warranties.

(f) A record is sufficient to disclaim warranties under subsection (e) if it indicates "There is no warranty relating to title, possession, quiet enjoyment, or the like in this disposition" or uses words of similar import.

§ 9–611. Notification before Disposition of Collateral.

(a) In this section, "notification date" means the earlier of the date on which:

(1) a secured party sends to the debtor and any secondary obligor an authenticated notification of disposition; or
(2) the debtor and any secondary obligor waive the right to notification.

(b) Except as otherwise provided in subsection (d), a secured party that disposes of collateral under Section 9–610 shall send to the persons specified in subsection (c) a reasonable authenticated notification of disposition.

(c) To comply with subsection (b), the secured party shall send an authenticated notification of disposition to:

(1) the debtor;

(2) any secondary obligor; and

(3) if the collateral is other than consumer goods:

(A) any other person from which the secured party has received, before the notification date, an authenticated notification of a claim of an interest in the collateral;

(B) any other secured party or lienholder that, 10 days before the notification date, held a security interest in or other lien on the collateral perfected by the filing of a financing statement that:

  (i) identified the collateral;

  (ii) was indexed under the debtor's name as of that date; and

  (iii) was filed in the office in which to file a financing statement against the debtor covering the collateral as of that date; and

(C) any other secured party that, 10 days before the notification date, held a security interest in the collateral perfected by compliance with a statute, regulation, or treaty described in Section 9–311(a).

(d) Subsection (b) does not apply if the collateral is perishable or threatens to decline speedily in value or is of a type customarily sold on a recognized market.

(e) A secured party complies with the requirement for notification prescribed by subsection (c)(3)(B) if:

(1) not later than 20 days or earlier than 30 days before the notification date, the secured party requests, in a commercially reasonable manner, information concerning financing statements indexed under the debtor's name in the office indicated in subsection (c)(3)(B); and

(2) before the notification date, the secured party:

  (A) did not receive a response to the request for information; or

  (B) received a response to the request for information and sent an authenticated notification of disposition to each secured party or other lienholder named in that response whose financing statement covered the collateral.

§ 9–612. Timeliness of Notification before Disposition of Collateral.

(a) Except as otherwise provided in subsection (b), whether a notification is sent within a reasonable time is a question of fact.

(b) In a transaction other than a consumer transaction, a notification of disposition sent after default and 10 days or more before the earliest time of disposition set forth in the notification is sent within a reasonable time before the disposition.

§ 9–613. Contents and Form of Notification before Disposition of Collateral: General.

Except in a consumer-goods transaction, the following rules apply:

(1) The contents of a notification of disposition are sufficient if the notification:

  (A) describes the debtor and the secured party;

  (B) describes the collateral that is the subject of the intended disposition;

  (C) states the method of intended disposition;

  (D) states that the debtor is entitled to an accounting of the unpaid indebtedness and states the charge, if any, for an accounting; and

  (E) states the time and place of a public disposition or the time after which any other disposition is to be made.

(2) Whether the contents of a notification that lacks any of the information specified in paragraph (1) are nevertheless sufficient is a question of fact.

(3) The contents of a notification providing substantially the information specified in paragraph (1) are sufficient, even if the notification includes:

  (A) information not specified by that paragraph; or

  (B) minor errors that are not seriously misleading.

(4) A particular phrasing of the notification is not required.

(5) The following form of notification and the form appearing in Section 9–614(3), when completed, each provides sufficient information:

NOTIFICATION OF DISPOSITION OF COLLATERAL

To: [*Name of debtor, obligor, or other person to which the notification is sent*]

From: [*Name, address, and telephone number of secured party*]

Name of Debtor(s): [*Include only if debtor(s) are not an addressee*]

  [*For a public disposition:*]

  We will sell [*or lease or license, as applicable*] the [*describe collateral*] [*to the highest qualified bidder*] in public as follows:

  Day and Date: _____

  Time: _____

  Place: _____

  [*For a private disposition:*]

  We will sell [*or lease or license, as applicable*] the [*describe collateral*] privately sometime after [*day and date*].

You are entitled to an accounting of the unpaid indebtedness secured by the property that we intend to sell [*or lease or license, as applicable*] [*for a charge of $_____*]. You may request an accounting by calling us at [*telephone number*].

[End of Form]

As amended in 2000.

§ 9–614. Contents and Form of Notification before Disposition of Collateral: Consumer-Goods Transaction.

In a consumer-goods transaction, the following rules apply:

(1) A notification of disposition must provide the following information:

  (A) the information specified in Section 9–613(1);

  (B) a description of any liability for a deficiency of the person to which the notification is sent;

  (C) a telephone number from which the amount that must be paid to the secured party to redeem the collateral under Section 9–623 is available; and

  (D) a telephone number or mailing address from which additional information concerning the disposition and the obligation secured is available.

(2) A particular phrasing of the notification is not required.

(3) The following form of notification, when completed, provides sufficient information:

  [*Name and address of secured party*]

  [*Date*]

NOTICE OF OUR PLAN TO SELL PROPERTY

[*Name and address of any obligor who is also a debtor*]

Subject: [*Identification of Transaction*]

We have your [*describe collateral*], because you broke promises in our agreement.

[*For a public disposition:*]

We will sell [*describe collateral*] at public sale. A sale could include a lease or license. The sale will be held as follows:

Date: _____

Time: _____

Place: _____

You may attend the sale and bring bidders if you want.

[*For a private disposition:*]

We will sell [*describe collateral*] at private sale sometime after [*date*]. A sale could include a lease or license.

The money that we get from the sale (after paying our costs) will reduce the amount you owe. If we get less money than you owe, you [*will or will not, as applicable*] still owe us the difference. If we get more money than you owe, you will get the extra money, unless we must pay it to someone else.

You can get the property back at any time before we sell it by paying us the full amount you owe (not just the past due payments), including our expenses. To learn the exact amount you must pay, call us at [*telephone number*].

If you want us to explain to you in writing how we have figured the amount that you owe us, you may call us at [*telephone number*] [or write us at [*secured party's address*]] and request a written explanation. [We will charge you $_____ for the explanation if we sent you another written explanation of the amount you owe us within the last six months.]

If you need more information about the sale call us at [*telephone number*] [or write us at [*secured party's address*]].

We are sending this notice to the following other people who have an interest in [*describe collateral*] or who owe money under your agreement:

[*Names of all other debtors and obligors, if any*]

[End of Form]

(4) A notification in the form of paragraph (3) is sufficient, even if additional information appears at the end of the form.

(5) A notification in the form of paragraph (3) is sufficient, even if it includes errors in information not required by paragraph (1), unless the error is misleading with respect to rights arising under this article.

(6) If a notification under this section is not in the form of paragraph (3), law other than this article determines the effect of including information not required by paragraph (1).

§ 9–615. Application of Proceeds of Disposition; Liability for Deficiency and Right to Surplus.

(a) A secured party shall apply or pay over for application the cash proceeds of disposition under Section 9–610 in the following order to:

(1) the reasonable expenses of retaking, holding, preparing for disposition, processing, and disposing, and, to the extent provided for by agreement and not prohibited by law, reasonable attorney's fees and legal expenses incurred by the secured party;

(2) the satisfaction of obligations secured by the security interest or agricultural lien under which the disposition is made;

(3) the satisfaction of obligations secured by any subordinate security interest in or other subordinate lien on the collateral if:

(A) the secured party receives from the holder of the subordinate security interest or other lien an authenticated demand for proceeds before distribution of the proceeds is completed; and

(B) in a case in which a consignor has an interest in the collateral, the subordinate security interest or other lien is senior to the interest of the consignor; and

(4) a secured party that is a consignor of the collateral if the secured party receives from the consignor an authenticated demand for proceeds before distribution of the proceeds is completed.

(b) If requested by a secured party, a holder of a subordinate security interest or other lien shall furnish reasonable proof of the interest or lien within a reasonable time. Unless the holder does so, the secured party need not comply with the holder's demand under subsection (a)(3).

(c) A secured party need not apply or pay over for application noncash proceeds of disposition under Section 9–610 unless the failure to do so would be commercially unreasonable. A secured party that applies or pays over for application noncash proceeds shall do so in a commercially reasonable manner.

(d) If the security interest under which a disposition is made secures payment or performance of an obligation, after making the payments and applications required by subsection (a) and permitted by subsection (c):

(1) unless subsection (a)(4) requires the secured party to apply or pay over cash proceeds to a consignor, the secured party shall account to and pay a debtor for any surplus; and

(2) the obligor is liable for any deficiency.

(e) If the underlying transaction is a sale of accounts, chattel paper, payment intangibles, or promissory notes:

(1) the debtor is not entitled to any surplus; and

(2) the obligor is not liable for any deficiency.

(f) The surplus or deficiency following a disposition is calculated based on the amount of proceeds that would have been realized in a disposition complying with this part to a transferee other than the secured party, a person related to the secured party, or a secondary obligor if:

(1) the transferee in the disposition is the secured party, a person related to the secured party, or a secondary obligor; and

(2) the amount of proceeds of the disposition is significantly below the range of proceeds that a complying disposition to a person other than the secured party, a person related to the secured party, or a secondary obligor would have brought.

(g) A secured party that receives cash proceeds of a disposition in good faith and without knowledge that the receipt violates the rights of the holder of a security interest or other lien that is not subordinate to the security interest or agricultural lien under which the disposition is made:

(1) takes the cash proceeds free of the security interest or other lien;

(2) is not obligated to apply the proceeds of the disposition to the satisfaction of obligations secured by the security interest or other lien; and

(3) is not obligated to account to or pay the holder of the security interest or other lien for any surplus.

As amended in 2000.

§ 9–616. Explanation of Calculation of Surplus or Deficiency.

(a) In this section:

(1) "Explanation" means a writing that:

(A) states the amount of the surplus or deficiency;

(B) provides an explanation in accordance with subsection (c) of how the secured party calculated the surplus or deficiency;

(C) states, if applicable, that future debits, credits, charges, including additional credit service charges or interest, rebates, and expenses may affect the amount of the surplus or deficiency; and

(D) provides a telephone number or mailing address from which additional information concerning the transaction is available.

(2) "Request" means a record:

(A) authenticated by a debtor or consumer obligor;

(B) requesting that the recipient provide an explanation; and

(C) sent after disposition of the collateral under Section 9–610.

(b) In a consumer-goods transaction in which the debtor is entitled to a surplus or a consumer obligor is liable for a deficiency under Section 9–615, the secured party shall:

(1) send an explanation to the debtor or consumer obligor, as applicable, after the disposition and:

(A) before or when the secured party accounts to the debtor and pays any surplus or first makes written demand on the consumer obligor after the disposition for payment of the deficiency; and

(B) within 14 days after receipt of a request; or

(2) in the case of a consumer obligor who is liable for a deficiency, within 14 days after receipt of a request, send to the consumer obligor a record waiving the secured party's right to a deficiency.

(c) To comply with subsection (a)(1)(B), a writing must provide the following information in the following order:

(1) the aggregate amount of obligations secured by the security interest under which the disposition was made, and, if the amount reflects a rebate of unearned interest or credit service charge, an indication of that fact, calculated as of a specified date:

(A) if the secured party takes or receives possession of the collateral after default, not more than 35 days before the secured party takes or receives possession; or

(B) if the secured party takes or receives possession of the collateral before default or does not take possession of the collateral, not more than 35 days before the disposition;

(2) the amount of proceeds of the disposition;

(3) the aggregate amount of the obligations after deducting the amount of proceeds;

(4) the amount, in the aggregate or by type, and types of expenses, including expenses of retaking, holding, preparing for disposition, processing, and disposing of the collateral, and attorney's fees secured by the collateral which are known to the secured party and relate to the current disposition;

(5) the amount, in the aggregate or by type, and types of credits, including rebates of interest or credit service charges, to which the obligor is known to be entitled and which are not reflected in the amount in paragraph (1); and

(6) the amount of the surplus or deficiency.

(d) A particular phrasing of the explanation is not required. An explanation complying substantially with the requirements of subsection (a) is sufficient, even if it includes minor errors that are not seriously misleading.

(e) A debtor or consumer obligor is entitled without charge to one response to a request under this section during any six-month period in which the secured party did not send to the debtor or consumer obligor an explanation pursuant to subsection (b)(1). The secured party may require payment of a charge not exceeding $25 for each additional response.

§ 9–617. Rights of Transferee of Collateral.

(a) A secured party's disposition of collateral after default:

(1) transfers to a transferee for value all of the debtor's rights in the collateral;

(2) discharges the security interest under which the disposition is made; and

(3) discharges any subordinate security interest or other subordinate lien [other than liens created under [cite acts or statutes providing for liens, if any, that are not to be discharged]].

(b) A transferee that acts in good faith takes free of the rights and interests described in subsection (a), even if the secured party fails to comply with this article or the requirements of any judicial proceeding.

(c) If a transferee does not take free of the rights and interests described in subsection (a), the transferee takes the collateral subject to:

(1) the debtor's rights in the collateral;

(2) the security interest or agricultural lien under which the disposition is made; and

(3) any other security interest or other lien.

§ 9–618. Rights and Duties of Certain Secondary Obligors.

(a) A secondary obligor acquires the rights and becomes obligated to perform the duties of the secured party after the secondary obligor:

(1) receives an assignment of a secured obligation from the secured party;

(2) receives a transfer of collateral from the secured party and agrees to accept the rights and assume the duties of the secured party; or

(3) is subrogated to the rights of a secured party with respect to collateral.

(b) An assignment, transfer, or subrogation described in subsection (a):

(1) is not a disposition of collateral under Section 9–610; and

(2) relieves the secured party of further duties under this article.

§ 9–619. Transfer of Record or Legal Title.

(a) In this section, "transfer statement" means a record authenticated by a secured party stating:

(1) that the debtor has defaulted in connection with an obligation secured by specified collateral;

(2) that the secured party has exercised its post-default remedies with respect to the collateral;

(3) that, by reason of the exercise, a transferee has acquired the rights of the debtor in the collateral; and

(4) the name and mailing address of the secured party, debtor, and transferee.

(b) A transfer statement entitles the transferee to the transfer of record of all rights of the debtor in the collateral specified in the statement in any official filing, recording, registration, or certificate-of-title system covering the collateral. If a transfer statement is presented with the applicable fee and request form to the official or office responsible for maintaining the system, the official or office shall:

(1) accept the transfer statement;

(2) promptly amend its records to reflect the transfer; and

(3) if applicable, issue a new appropriate certificate of title in the name of the transferee.

(c) A transfer of the record or legal title to collateral to a secured party under subsection (b) or otherwise is not of itself a disposition of collateral under this article and does not of itself relieve the secured party of its duties under this article.

§ 9–620. Acceptance of Collateral in Full or Partial Satisfaction of Obligation; Compulsory Disposition of Collateral.

(a) Except as otherwise provided in subsection (g), a secured party may accept collateral in full or partial satisfaction of the obligation it secures only if:

(1) the debtor consents to the acceptance under subsection (c);

(2) the secured party does not receive, within the time set forth in subsection (d), a notification of objection to the proposal authenticated by:

(A) a person to which the secured party was required to send a proposal under Section 9–621; or

(B) any other person, other than the debtor, holding an interest in the collateral subordinate to the security interest that is the subject of the proposal;

(3) if the collateral is consumer goods, the collateral is not in the possession of the debtor when the debtor consents to the acceptance; and

(4) subsection (e) does not require the secured party to dispose of the collateral or the debtor waives the requirement pursuant to Section 9–624.

(b) A purported or apparent acceptance of collateral under this section is ineffective unless:

(1) the secured party consents to the acceptance in an authenticated record or sends a proposal to the debtor; and

(2) the conditions of subsection (a) are met.

(c) For purposes of this section:

(1) a debtor consents to an acceptance of collateral in partial satisfaction of the obligation it secures only if the debtor agrees to the terms of the acceptance in a record authenticated after default; and

(2) a debtor consents to an acceptance of collateral in full satisfaction of the obligation it secures only if the debtor agrees to the terms of the acceptance in a record authenticated after default or the secured party:

(A) sends to the debtor after default a proposal that is unconditional or subject only to a condition that collateral not in the possession of the secured party be preserved or maintained;

(B) in the proposal, proposes to accept collateral in full satisfaction of the obligation it secures; and

(C) does not receive a notification of objection authenticated by the debtor within 20 days after the proposal is sent.

(d) To be effective under subsection (a)(2), a notification of objection must be received by the secured party:

(1) in the case of a person to which the proposal was sent pursuant to Section 9–621, within 20 days after notification was sent to that person; and

(2) in other cases:

(A) within 20 days after the last notification was sent pursuant to Section 9–621; or

(B) if a notification was not sent, before the debtor consents to the acceptance under subsection (c).

(e) A secured party that has taken possession of collateral shall dispose of the collateral pursuant to Section 9–610 within the time specified in subsection (f) if:

(1) 60 percent of the cash price has been paid in the case of a purchase-money security interest in consumer goods; or

(2) 60 percent of the principal amount of the obligation secured has been paid in the case of a non-purchase-money security interest in consumer goods.

(f) To comply with subsection (e), the secured party shall dispose of the collateral:

(1) within 90 days after taking possession; or

(2) within any longer period to which the debtor and all secondary obligors have agreed in an agreement to that effect entered into and authenticated after default.

(g) In a consumer transaction, a secured party may not accept collateral in partial satisfaction of the obligation it secures.

§ 9–621. Notification of Proposal to Accept Collateral.

(a) A secured party that desires to accept collateral in full or partial satisfaction of the obligation it secures shall send its proposal to:

(1) any person from which the secured party has received, before the debtor consented to the acceptance, an authenticated notification of a claim of an interest in the collateral;

(2) any other secured party or lienholder that, 10 days before the debtor consented to the acceptance, held a security interest in or other lien on the collateral perfected by the filing of a financing statement that:

(A) identified the collateral;

(B) was indexed under the debtor's name as of that date; and

(C) was filed in the office or offices in which to file a financing statement against the debtor covering the collateral as of that date; and

(3) any other secured party that, 10 days before the debtor consented to the acceptance, held a security interest in the collateral perfected by compliance with a statute, regulation, or treaty described in Section 9–311(a).

(b) A secured party that desires to accept collateral in partial satisfaction of the obligation it secures shall send its proposal to any secondary obligor in addition to the persons described in subsection (a).

§ 9–622. Effect of Acceptance of Collateral.

(a) A secured party's acceptance of collateral in full or partial satisfaction of the obligation it secures:

(1) discharges the obligation to the extent consented to by the debtor;

(2) transfers to the secured party all of a debtor's rights in the collateral;

(3) discharges the security interest or agricultural lien that is the subject of the debtor's consent and any subordinate security interest or other subordinate lien; and

(4) terminates any other subordinate interest.

(b) A subordinate interest is discharged or terminated under subsection (a), even if the secured party fails to comply with this article.

§ 9–623. Right to Redeem Collateral.

(a) A debtor, any secondary obligor, or any other secured party or lienholder may redeem collateral.

(b) To redeem collateral, a person shall tender:

(1) fulfillment of all obligations secured by the collateral; and

(2) the reasonable expenses and attorney's fees described in Section 9–615(a)(1).

(c) A redemption may occur at any time before a secured party:

(1) has collected collateral under Section 9–607;

(2) has disposed of collateral or entered into a contract for its disposition under Section 9–610; or

(3) has accepted collateral in full or partial satisfaction of the obligation it secures under Section 9–622.

§ 9–624. Waiver.

(a) A debtor or secondary obligor may waive the right to notification of disposition of collateral under Section 9–611 only by an agreement to that effect entered into and authenticated after default.

(b) A debtor may waive the right to require disposition of collateral under Section 9–620(e) only by an agreement to that effect entered into and authenticated after default.

(c) Except in a consumer-goods transaction, a debtor or secondary obligor may waive the right to redeem collateral under Section 9–623 only by an agreement to that effect entered into and authenticated after default.

[Subpart 2. Noncompliance with Article]

§ 9–625. Remedies for Secured Party's Failure to Comply with Article.

(a) If it is established that a secured party is not proceeding in accordance with this article, a court may order or restrain collection, enforcement, or disposition of collateral on appropriate terms and conditions.

(b) Subject to subsections (c), (d), and (f), a person is liable for damages in the amount of any loss caused by a failure to comply with this article. Loss caused by a failure to comply may include loss resulting from the debtor's inability to obtain, or increased costs of, alternative financing.

(c) Except as otherwise provided in Section 9–628:

(1) a person that, at the time of the failure, was a debtor, was an obligor, or held a security interest in or other lien on the collateral may recover damages under subsection (b) for its loss; and

(2) if the collateral is consumer goods, a person that was a debtor or a secondary obligor at the time a secured party failed to comply with this part may recover for that failure in any event an amount not less than the credit service charge plus 10 percent of the principal amount of the obligation or the time-price differential plus 10 percent of the cash price.

(d) A debtor whose deficiency is eliminated under Section 9–626 may recover damages for the loss of any surplus. However, a debtor or secondary obligor whose deficiency is eliminated or reduced under Section 9–626 may not otherwise recover under subsection (b) for noncompliance with the provisions of this part relating to collection, enforcement, disposition, or acceptance.

(e) In addition to any damages recoverable under subsection (b), the debtor, consumer obligor, or person named as a debtor in a filed record, as applicable, may recover $500 in each case from a person that:

(1) fails to comply with Section 9–208;

(2) fails to comply with Section 9–209;

(3) files a record that the person is not entitled to file under Section 9–509(a);

(4) fails to cause the secured party of record to file or send a termination statement as required by Section 9–513(a) or (c);

(5) fails to comply with Section 9–616(b)(1) and whose failure is part of a pattern, or consistent with a practice, of noncompliance; or

(6) fails to comply with Section 9–616(b)(2).

(f) A debtor or consumer obligor may recover damages under subsection (b) and, in addition, $500 in each case from a person that, without reasonable cause, fails to comply with a request under Section 9–210. A recipient of a request under Section 9–210 which never claimed an interest in the collateral or obligations that are the subject of a request under that section has a reasonable excuse for failure to comply with the request within the meaning of this subsection.

(g) If a secured party fails to comply with a request regarding a list of collateral or a statement of account under Section 9–210, the secured party may claim a security interest only as shown in the list or statement included in the request as against a person that is reasonably misled by the failure.

As amended in 2000.

§ 9–626. Action in Which Deficiency or Surplus Is in Issue.

(a) In an action arising from a transaction, other than a consumer transaction, in which the amount of a deficiency or surplus is in issue, the following rules apply:

(1) A secured party need not prove compliance with the provisions of this part relating to collection, enforcement, disposition, or acceptance unless the debtor or a secondary obligor places the secured party's compliance in issue.

(2) If the secured party's compliance is placed in issue, the secured party has the burden of establishing that the collection, enforcement, disposition, or acceptance was conducted in accordance with this part.

(3) Except as otherwise provided in Section 9–628, if a secured party fails to prove that the collection, enforcement, disposition, or acceptance was conducted in accordance with the provisions of this part relating to collection, enforcement, disposition, or acceptance, the liability of a debtor or a secondary obligor for a deficiency is limited to an amount by which the sum of the secured obligation, expenses, and attorney's fees exceeds the greater of:

(A) the proceeds of the collection, enforcement, disposition, or acceptance; or

(B) the amount of proceeds that would have been realized had the noncomplying secured party proceeded in accordance with the provisions of this part relating to collection, enforcement, disposition, or acceptance.

(4) For purposes of paragraph (3)(B), the amount of proceeds that would have been realized is equal to the sum of the secured obligation, expenses, and attorney's fees unless the secured party proves that the amount is less than that sum.

(5) If a deficiency or surplus is calculated under Section 9–615(f), the debtor or obligor has the burden of establishing that the amount of proceeds of the disposition is significantly below the range of prices that a complying disposition to a person other than the secured party, a person related to the secured party, or a secondary obligor would have brought.

(b) The limitation of the rules in subsection (a) to transactions other than consumer transactions is intended to leave to the court the determination of the proper rules in consumer transactions. The court may not infer from that limitation the nature of the proper rule in consumer transactions and may continue to apply established approaches.

§ 9–627. Determination of Whether Conduct Was Commercially Reasonable.

(a) The fact that a greater amount could have been obtained by a collection, enforcement, disposition, or acceptance at a different time or in a different method from that selected by the secured party is not of itself sufficient to preclude the secured party from establishing that the collection, enforcement, disposition, or acceptance was made in a commercially reasonable manner.

(b) A disposition of collateral is made in a commercially reasonable manner if the disposition is made:

(1) in the usual manner on any recognized market;

(2) at the price current in any recognized market at the time of the disposition; or

(3) otherwise in conformity with reasonable commercial practices among dealers in the type of property that was the subject of the disposition.

(c) A collection, enforcement, disposition, or acceptance is commercially reasonable if it has been approved:

(1) in a judicial proceeding;

(2) by a bona fide creditors' committee;

(3) by a representative of creditors; or

(4) by an assignee for the benefit of creditors.

(d) Approval under subsection (c) need not be obtained, and lack of approval does not mean that the collection, enforcement, disposition, or acceptance is not commercially reasonable.

§ 9–628. Nonliability and Limitation on Liability of Secured Party; Liability of Secondary Obligor.

(a) Unless a secured party knows that a person is a debtor or obligor, knows the identity of the person, and knows how to communicate with the person:

(1) the secured party is not liable to the person, or to a secured party or lienholder that has filed a financing statement against the person, for failure to comply with this article; and

(2) the secured party's failure to comply with this article does not affect the liability of the person for a deficiency.

(b) A secured party is not liable because of its status as secured party:

(1) to a person that is a debtor or obligor, unless the secured party knows:

(A) that the person is a debtor or obligor;

(B) the identity of the person; and

(C) how to communicate with the person; or

(2) to a secured party or lienholder that has filed a financing statement against a person, unless the secured party knows:

(A) that the person is a debtor; and

(B) the identity of the person.

(c) A secured party is not liable to any person, and a person's liability for a deficiency is not affected, because of any act or omission arising out of the secured party's reasonable belief that a transaction is not a consumer-goods transaction or a consumer transaction or that goods are not consumer goods, if the secured party's belief is based on its reasonable reliance on:

(1) a debtor's representation concerning the purpose for which collateral was to be used, acquired, or held; or

(2) an obligor's representation concerning the purpose for which a secured obligation was incurred.

(d) A secured party is not liable to any person under Section 9–625(c)(2) for its failure to comply with Section 9–616.

(e) A secured party is not liable under Section 9–625(c)(2) more than once with respect to any one secured obligation.

Part 7 Transition

§ 9–701. Effective Date.

This [Act] takes effect on July 1, 2001.

§ 9–702. Savings Clause.

(a) Except as otherwise provided in this part, this [Act] applies to a transaction or lien within its scope, even if the transaction or lien was entered into or created before this [Act] takes effect.

(b) Except as otherwise provided in subsection (c) and Sections 9–703 through 9–709:

(1) transactions and liens that were not governed by [former Article 9], were validly entered into or created before this [Act] takes effect, and would be subject to this [Act] if they had been entered into or created after this [Act] takes effect, and the rights, duties, and interests flowing from those transactions and liens remain valid after this [Act] takes effect; and

(2) the transactions and liens may be terminated, completed, consummated, and enforced as required or permitted by this [Act] or by the law that otherwise would apply if this [Act] had not taken effect.

(c) This [Act] does not affect an action, case, or proceeding commenced before this [Act] takes effect.

As amended in 2000.

§ 9–703. Security Interest Perfected before Effective Date.

(a) A security interest that is enforceable immediately before this [Act] takes effect and would have priority over the rights of a person that becomes a lien creditor at that time is a perfected security interest under this [Act] if, when this [Act] takes effect, the applicable requirements for enforceability and perfection under this [Act] are satisfied without further action.

(b) Except as otherwise provided in Section 9–705, if, immediately before this [Act] takes effect, a security interest is enforceable and would have priority over the rights of a person that becomes a lien creditor at that time, but the applicable requirements for enforceability or perfection under this [Act] are not satisfied when this [Act] takes effect, the security interest:

(1) is a perfected security interest for one year after this [Act] takes effect;

(2) remains enforceable thereafter only if the security interest becomes enforceable under Section 9–203 before the year expires; and

(3) remains perfected thereafter only if the applicable requirements for perfection under this [Act] are satisfied before the year expires.

§ 9–704. Security Interest Unperfected before Effective Date.

A security interest that is enforceable immediately before this [Act] takes effect but which would be subordinate to the rights of a person that becomes a lien creditor at that time:

(1) remains an enforceable security interest for one year after this [Act] takes effect;

(2) remains enforceable thereafter if the security interest becomes enforceable under Section 9–203 when this [Act] takes effect or within one year thereafter; and

(3) becomes perfected:

(A) without further action, when this [Act] takes effect if the applicable requirements for perfection under this [Act] are satisfied before or at that time; or

(B) when the applicable requirements for perfection are satisfied if the requirements are satisfied after that time.

§ 9–705. Effectiveness of Action Taken before Effective Date.

(a) If action, other than the filing of a financing statement, is taken before this [Act] takes effect and the action would have resulted in priority of a security interest over the rights of a person that becomes a lien creditor had the security interest become enforceable before this [Act] takes effect, the action is effective to perfect a security interest that attaches under this [Act] within one year after this [Act] takes effect. An attached security interest becomes unperfected one year after this [Act] takes effect unless the security interest becomes a perfected security interest under this [Act] before the expiration of that period.

(b) The filing of a financing statement before this [Act] takes effect is effective to perfect a security interest to the extent the filing would satisfy the applicable requirements for perfection under this [Act].

(c) This [Act] does not render ineffective an effective financing statement that, before this [Act] takes effect, is filed and satisfies the applicable requirements for perfection under the law of the jurisdiction governing perfection as provided in [former Section 9–103]. However, except as otherwise provided in subsections (d) and (e) and Section 9–706, the financing statement ceases to be effective at the earlier of:

(1) the time the financing statement would have ceased to be effective under the law of the jurisdiction in which it is filed; or

(2) June 30, 2006.

(d) The filing of a continuation statement after this [Act] takes effect does not continue the effectiveness of the financing statement filed before this [Act] takes effect. However, upon the timely filing of a continuation statement after this [Act] takes effect and in accordance with the law of the jurisdiction governing perfection as provided in Part 3, the effectiveness of a financing statement filed in the same office in that jurisdiction before this [Act] takes effect continues for the period provided by the law of that jurisdiction.

(e) Subsection (c)(2) applies to a financing statement that, before this [Act] takes effect, is filed against a transmitting utility and satisfies the applicable requirements for perfection under the law of the jurisdiction governing perfection as provided in [former Section 9–103] only to the extent that Part 3 provides that the law of a jurisdiction other than the jurisdiction in which the financing statement is filed governs perfection of a security interest in collateral covered by the financing statement.

(f) A financing statement that includes a financing statement filed before this [Act] takes effect and a continuation statement filed after this [Act] takes effect is effective only to the extent that it satisfies the requirements of Part 5 for an initial financing statement.

§ 9–706. When Initial Financing Statement Suffices to Continue Effectiveness of Financing Statement.

(a) The filing of an initial financing statement in the office specified in Section 9–501 continues the effectiveness of a financing statement filed before this [Act] takes effect if:

(1) the filing of an initial financing statement in that office would be effective to perfect a security interest under this [Act];

(2) the pre-effective-date financing statement was filed in an office in another State or another office in this State; and

(3) the initial financing statement satisfies subsection (c).

(b) The filing of an initial financing statement under subsection (a) continues the effectiveness of the pre-effective-date financing statement:

(1) if the initial financing statement is filed before this [Act] takes effect, for the period provided in [former Section 9–403] with respect to a financing statement; and

(2) if the initial financing statement is filed after this [Act] takes effect, for the period provided in Section 9–515 with respect to an initial financing statement.

(c) To be effective for purposes of subsection (a), an initial financing statement must:

(1) satisfy the requirements of Part 5 for an initial financing statement;

(2) identify the pre-effective-date financing statement by indicating the office in which the financing statement was filed and providing the dates of filing and file numbers, if any, of the financing statement and of the most recent continuation statement filed with respect to the financing statement; and

(3) indicate that the pre-effective-date financing statement remains effective.

§ 9–707. Amendment of Pre-Effective-Date Financing Statement.

(a) In this section, "Pre-effective-date financing statement" means a financing statement filed before this [Act] takes effect.

(b) After this [Act] takes effect, a person may add or delete collateral covered by, continue or terminate the effectiveness of, or otherwise amend the information provided in, a pre-effective-date financing statement only in accordance with the law of the jurisdiction governing perfection as provided in Part 3. However, the effectiveness of a pre-effective-date financing statement also may be terminated in accordance with the law of the jurisdiction in which the financing statement is filed.

(c) Except as otherwise provided in subsection (d), if the law of this State governs perfection of a security interest, the information in a pre-effective-date financing statement may be amended after this [Act] takes effect only if:

(1) the pre-effective-date financing statement and an amendment are filed in the office specified in Section 9–501;

(2) an amendment is filed in the office specified in Section 9–501 concurrently with, or after the filing in that office of, an initial financing statement that satisfies Section 9–706(c); or

(3) an initial financing statement that provides the information as amended and satisfies Section 9–706(c) is filed in the office specified in Section 9–501.

(d) If the law of this State governs perfection of a security interest, the effectiveness of a pre-effective-date financing statement may be continued only under Section 9–705(d) and (f) or 9–706.

(e) Whether or not the law of this State governs perfection of a security interest, the effectiveness of a pre-effective-date financing statement filed in this State may be terminated after this [Act] takes effect by filing a termination statement in the office in which the pre-effective-date financing statement is filed, unless an initial financing statement that satisfies Section 9–706(c) has been filed in the office specified by the law of the jurisdiction governing perfection as provided in Part 3 as the office in which to file a financing statement.

As amended in 2000.

§ 9–708. Persons Entitled to File Initial Financing Statement or Continuation Statement.

A person may file an initial financing statement or a continuation statement under this part if:

(1) the secured party of record authorizes the filing; and

(2) the filing is necessary under this part:

(A) to continue the effectiveness of a financing statement filed before this [Act] takes effect; or

(B) to perfect or continue the perfection of a security interest.

As amended in 2000.

§ 9–709. Priority.

(a) This [Act] determines the priority of conflicting claims to collateral. However, if the relative priorities of the claims were established before this [Act] takes effect, [former Article 9] determines priority.

(b) For purposes of Section 9–322(a), the priority of a security interest that becomes enforceable under Section 9–203 of this [Act] dates from the time this [Act] takes effect if the security interest is perfected under this [Act] by the filing of a financing statement before this [Act] takes effect which would not have been effective to perfect the security interest under [former Article 9]. This subsection does not apply to conflicting security interests each of which is perfected by the filing of such a financing statement.

As amended in 2000.

APPENDIX D
The Sarbanes-Oxley Act of 2002 (Excerpts and Explanatory Comments)

Note: The author's explanatory comments appear in italics following the excerpt from each section.

SECTION 302
Corporate responsibility for financial reports[1]

(a) Regulations required

The Commission shall, by rule, require, for each company filing periodic reports under section 13(a) or 15(d) of the Securities Exchange Act of 1934 (15 U.S.C. 78m, 78o(d)), that the principal executive officer or officers and the principal financial officer or officers, or persons performing similar functions, certify in each annual or quarterly report filed or submitted under either such section of such Act that—

(1) the signing officer has reviewed the report;

(2) based on the officer's knowledge, the report does not contain any untrue statement of a material fact or omit to state a material fact necessary in order to make the statements made, in light of the circumstances under which such statements were made, not misleading;

(3) based on such officer's knowledge, the financial statements, and other financial information included in the report, fairly present in all material respects the financial condition and results of operations of the issuer as of, and for, the periods presented in the report;

(4) the signing officers—

(A) are responsible for establishing and maintaining internal controls;

(B) have designed such internal controls to ensure that material information relating to the issuer and its consolidated subsidiaries is made known to such officers by others within those entities, particularly during the period in which the periodic reports are being prepared;

(C) have evaluated the effectiveness of the issuer's internal controls as of a date within 90 days prior to the report; and

(D) have presented in the report their conclusions about the effectiveness of their internal controls based on their evaluation as of that date;

(5) the signing officers have disclosed to the issuer's auditors and the audit committee of the board of directors (or persons fulfilling the equivalent function)—

(A) all significant deficiencies in the design or operation of internal controls which could adversely affect the issuer's ability to record, process, summarize, and report financial data and have identified for the issuer's auditors any material weaknesses in internal controls; and

(B) any fraud, whether or not material, that involves management or other employees who have a significant role in the issuer's internal controls; and

(6) the signing officers have indicated in the report whether or not there were significant changes in internal controls or in other factors that could significantly affect internal controls subsequent to the date of their evaluation, including any corrective actions with regard to significant deficiencies and material weaknesses.

(b) Foreign reincorporations have no effect

Nothing in this section shall be interpreted or applied in any way to allow any issuer to lessen the legal force of the statement required under this section, by an issuer having reincorporated or having engaged in any other transaction that resulted in the transfer of the corporate domicile or offices of the issuer from inside the United States to outside of the United States.

(c) Deadline

The rules required by subsection (a) of this section shall be effective not later than 30 days after July 30, 2002.

* * * *

EXPLANATORY COMMENTS: *Section 302 requires the chief executive officer (CEO) and chief financial officer (CFO) of each public company to certify that they have reviewed the company's quarterly and annual reports to be filed with the Securities and Exchange Commission (SEC). The CEO and CFO must certify that, based on their knowledge, the reports do not contain any untrue statement of a material fact or any half-truth that would make the report misleading, and that the information contained in the reports fairly presents the company's financial condition.*

In addition, this section also requires the CEO and CFO to certify that they have created and designed an internal control system for their company and have recently evaluated that system to ensure that it is effectively providing them with relevant and accurate financial information. If the signing officers have found any significant deficiencies or weaknesses in the company's system or have discovered any evidence of fraud, they must have reported the situation, and any corrective actions they have taken, to the auditors and the audit committee.

---

1. This section of the Sarbanes-Oxley Act is codified at 15 U.S.C. Section 7241.

SECTION 306

Insider trades during pension fund blackout periods[2]

(a) Prohibition of insider trading during pension fund blackout periods

(1) In general

Except to the extent otherwise provided by rule of the Commission pursuant to paragraph (3), it shall be unlawful for any director or executive officer of an issuer of any equity security (other than an exempted security), directly or indirectly, to purchase, sell, or otherwise acquire or transfer any equity security of the issuer (other than an exempted security) during any blackout period with respect to such equity security if such director or officer acquires such equity security in connection with his or her service or employment as a director or executive officer.

(2) Remedy

(A) In general

Any profit realized by a director or executive officer referred to in paragraph (1) from any purchase, sale, or other acquisition or transfer in violation of this subsection shall inure to and be recoverable by the issuer, irrespective of any intention on the part of such director or executive officer in entering into the transaction.

(B) Actions to recover profits

An action to recover profits in accordance with this subsection may be instituted at law or in equity in any court of competent jurisdiction by the issuer, or by the owner of any security of the issuer in the name and in behalf of the issuer if the issuer fails or refuses to bring such action within 60 days after the date of request, or fails diligently to prosecute the action thereafter, except that no such suit shall be brought more than 2 years after the date on which such profit was realized.

(3) Rulemaking authorized

The Commission shall, in consultation with the Secretary of Labor, issue rules to clarify the application of this subsection and to prevent evasion thereof. Such rules shall provide for the application of the requirements of paragraph (1) with respect to entities treated as a single employer with respect to an issuer under section 414(b), (c), (m), or (o) of Title 26 to the extent necessary to clarify the application of such requirements and to prevent evasion thereof. Such rules may also provide for appropriate exceptions from the requirements of this subsection, including exceptions for purchases pursuant to an automatic dividend reinvestment program or purchases or sales made pursuant to an advance election.

(4) Blackout period

For purposes of this subsection, the term "blackout period", with respect to the equity securities of any issuer—

(A) means any period of more than 3 consecutive business days during which the ability of not fewer than 50 percent of the participants or beneficiaries under all individual account plans maintained by the issuer to purchase, sell, or otherwise acquire

or transfer an interest in any equity of such issuer held in such an individual account plan is temporarily suspended by the issuer or by a fiduciary of the plan; and

(B) does not include, under regulations which shall be prescribed by the Commission—

(i) a regularly scheduled period in which the participants and beneficiaries may not purchase, sell, or otherwise acquire or transfer an interest in any equity of such issuer, if such period is—

(I) incorporated into the individual account plan; and

(II) timely disclosed to employees before becoming participants under the individual account plan or as a subsequent amendment to the plan; or

(ii) any suspension described in subparagraph (A) that is imposed solely in connection with persons becoming participants or beneficiaries, or ceasing to be participants or beneficiaries, in an individual account plan by reason of a corporate merger, acquisition, divestiture, or similar transaction involving the plan or plan sponsor.

(5) Individual account plan

For purposes of this subsection, the term "individual account plan" has the meaning provided in section 1002(34) of Title 29, except that such term shall not include a one-participant retirement plan (within the meaning of section 1021(i)(8)(B) of Title 29).

(6) Notice to directors, executive officers, and the Commission

In any case in which a director or executive officer is subject to the requirements of this subsection in connection with a blackout period (as defined in paragraph (4)) with respect to any equity securities, the issuer of such equity securities shall timely notify such director or officer and the Securities and Exchange Commission of such blackout period.

* * * *

EXPLANATORY COMMENTS: *Corporate pension funds typically prohibit employees from trading shares of the corporation during periods when the pension fund is undergoing significant change. Prior to 2002, however, these blackout periods did not affect the corporation's executives, who frequently received shares of the corporate stock as part of their compensation. During the collapse of Enron, for example, its pension plan was scheduled to change administrators at a time when Enron's stock price was falling. Enron's employees therefore could not sell their shares while the price was dropping, but its executives could and did sell their stock, consequently avoiding some of the losses. Section 306 was Congress's solution to the basic unfairness of this situation. This section of the act required the SEC to issue rules that prohibit any director or executive officer from trading during pension fund blackout periods. (The SEC later issued these rules, entitled Regulation Blackout Trading Restriction, or Reg BTR.) Section 306 also provided shareholders with a right to file a shareholder's derivative suit against officers and directors who have profited from trading during these blackout periods (provided that the corporation has failed to bring a suit). The officer or director can be forced to return to the corporation any profits received, regardless of whether the director or officer acted with bad intent.*

---

2. Codified at 15 U.S.C. Section 7244.

SECTION 402

Periodical and other reports[3]

* * * *

(i) Accuracy of financial reports

Each financial report that contains financial statements, and that is required to be prepared in accordance with (or reconciled to) generally accepted accounting principles under this chapter and filed with the Commission shall reflect all material correcting adjustments that have been identified by a registered public accounting firm in accordance with generally accepted accounting principles and the rules and regulations of the Commission.

(j) Off-balance sheet transactions

Not later than 180 days after July 30, 2002, the Commission shall issue final rules providing that each annual and quarterly financial report required to be filed with the Commission shall disclose all material off-balance sheet transactions, arrangements, obligations (including contingent obligations), and other relationships of the issuer with unconsolidated entities or other persons, that may have a material current or future effect on financial condition, changes in financial condition, results of operations, liquidity, capital expenditures, capital resources, or significant components of revenues or expenses.

(k) Prohibition on personal loans to executives

(1) In general

It shall be unlawful for any issuer (as defined in section 7201 of this title), directly or indirectly, including through any subsidiary, to extend or maintain credit, to arrange for the extension of credit, or to renew an extension of credit, in the form of a personal loan to or for any director or executive officer (or equivalent thereof) of that issuer. An extension of credit maintained by the issuer on July 30, 2002, shall not be subject to the provisions of this subsection, provided that there is no material modification to any term of any such extension of credit or any renewal of any such extension of credit on or after July 30, 2002.

(2) Limitation

Paragraph (1) does not preclude any home improvement and manufactured home loans (as that term is defined in section 1464 of Title 12), consumer credit (as defined in section 1602 of this title), or any extension of credit under an open end credit plan (as defined in section 1602 of this title), or a charge card (as defined in section 1637(c)(4)(e) of this title), or any extension of credit by a broker or dealer registered under section 78o of this title to an employee of that broker or dealer to buy, trade, or carry securities, that is permitted under rules or regulations of the Board of Governors of the Federal Reserve System pursuant to section 78g of this title (other than an extension of credit that would be used to purchase the stock of that issuer), that is—

(A) made or provided in the ordinary course of the consumer credit business of such issuer;

(B) of a type that is generally made available by such issuer to the public; and

(C) made by such issuer on market terms, or terms that are no more favorable than those offered by the issuer to the general public for such extensions of credit.

(3) Rule of construction for certain loans

Paragraph (1) does not apply to any loan made or maintained by an insured depository institution (as defined in section 1813 of Title 12), if the loan is subject to the insider lending restrictions of section 375b of Title 12.

(l) Real time issuer disclosures

Each issuer reporting under subsection (a) of this section or section 78o(d) of this title shall disclose to the public on a rapid and current basis such additional information concerning material changes in the financial condition or operations of the issuer, in plain English, which may include trend and qualitative information and graphic presentations, as the Commission determines, by rule, is necessary or useful for the protection of investors and in the public interest.

EXPLANATORY COMMENTS: *Corporate executives during the Enron era typically received extremely large salaries, significant bonuses, and abundant stock options, even when the companies for which they worked were suffering. Executives were also routinely given personal loans from corporate funds, many of which were never paid back. The average large company during that period loaned almost $1 million a year to top executives, and some companies, including Tyco International and Adelphia Communications Corporation, loaned hundreds of millions of dollars to their executives every year. Section 402 amended the 1934 Securities Exchange Act to prohibit public companies from making personal loans to executive officers and directors. There are a few exceptions to this prohibition, such as home-improvement loans made in the ordinary course of business. Note also that while loans are forbidden, outright gifts are not. A corporation is free to give gifts to its executives, including cash, provided that these gifts are disclosed on its financial reports. The idea is that corporate directors will be deterred from making substantial gifts to their executives by the disclosure requirement—particularly if the corporation's financial condition is questionable—because making such gifts could be perceived as abusing their authority.*

SECTION 403

Directors, officers, and principal stockholders[4]

(a) Disclosures required

(1) Directors, officers, and principal stockholders required to file

Every person who is directly or indirectly the beneficial owner of more than 10 percent of any class of any equity security (other than an exempted security) which is registered pursuant to section 78l of this title, or who is a director or an officer of the issuer of such security, shall file the statements required by this subsection with the Commission (and, if such security is registered on a national securities exchange, also with the exchange).

(2) Time of filing

The statements required by this subsection shall be filed—

---

3. This section of the Sarbanes-Oxley Act amended some of the provisions of the 1934 Securities Exchange Act and added the paragraphs reproduced here at 15 U.S.C. Section 78m.

4. This section of the Sarbanes-Oxley Act amended the disclosure provisions of the 1934 Securities Exchange Act, at 15 U.S.C. Section 78p.

(A) at the time of the registration of such security on a national securities exchange or by the effective date of a registration statement filed pursuant to section 78l(g) of this title;

(B) within 10 days after he or she becomes such beneficial owner, director, or officer;

(C) if there has been a change in such ownership, or if such person shall have purchased or sold a security-based swap agreement (as defined in section 206(b) of the Gramm-Leach-Bliley Act (15 U.S.C. 78c note)) involving such equity security, before the end of the second business day following the day on which the subject transaction has been executed, or at such other time as the Commission shall establish, by rule, in any case in which the Commission determines that such 2-day period is not feasible.

(3) Contents of statements

A statement filed—

(A) under subparagraph (A) or (B) of paragraph (2) shall contain a statement of the amount of all equity securities of such issuer of which the filing person is the beneficial owner; and

(B) under subparagraph (C) of such paragraph shall indicate ownership by the filing person at the date of filing, any such changes in such ownership, and such purchases and sales of the security-based swap agreements as have occurred since the most recent such filing under such subparagraph.

(4) Electronic filing and availability

Beginning not later than 1 year after July 30, 2002—

(A) a statement filed under subparagraph (C) of paragraph (2) shall be filed electronically;

(B) the Commission shall provide each such statement on a publicly accessible Internet site not later than the end of the business day following that filing; and

(C) the issuer (if the issuer maintains a corporate website) shall provide that statement on that corporate website, not later than the end of the business day following that filing.

*   *   *   *

EXPLANATORY COMMENTS: *This section dramatically shortens the time period provided in the Securities Exchange Act of 1934 for disclosing transactions by insiders. The prior law stated that most transactions had to be reported within ten days of the beginning of the following month, although certain transactions did not have to be reported until the following fiscal year (within the first forty-five days). Because some of the insider trading that occurred during the Enron fiasco did not have to be disclosed (and was therefore not discovered) until long after the transactions, Congress added this section to reduce the time period for making disclosures. Under Section 403, most transactions by insiders must be electronically filed with the SEC within two business days. Also, any company that maintains a Web site must post these SEC filings on its site by the end of the next business day. Congress enacted this section in the belief that if insiders are required to file reports of their transactions promptly with the SEC, companies will do more to police themselves and prevent insider trading.*

SECTION 404

Management assessment of internal controls[5]

(a) Rules required

The Commission shall prescribe rules requiring each annual report required by section 78m(a) or 78o(d) of this title to contain an internal control report, which shall—

(1) state the responsibility of management for establishing and maintaining an adequate internal control structure and procedures for financial reporting; and

(2) contain an assessment, as of the end of the most recent fiscal year of the issuer, of the effectiveness of the internal control structure and procedures of the issuer for financial reporting.

(b) Internal control evaluation and reporting

With respect to the internal control assessment required by subsection (a) of this section, each registered public accounting firm that prepares or issues the audit report for the issuer shall attest to, and report on, the assessment made by the management of the issuer. An attestation made under this subsection shall be made in accordance with standards for attestation engagements issued or adopted by the Board. Any such attestation shall not be the subject of a separate engagement.

*   *   *   *

EXPLANATORY COMMENTS: *This section was enacted to prevent corporate executives from claiming they were ignorant of significant errors in their companies' financial reports. For instance, several CEOs testified before Congress that they simply had no idea that the corporations' financial statements were off by billions of dollars. Congress therefore passed Section 404, which requires each annual report to contain a description and assessment of the company's internal control structure and financial reporting procedures. The section also requires that an audit be conducted of the internal control assessment, as well as the financial statements contained in the report. This section goes hand in hand with Section 302 (which, as discussed previously, requires various certifications attesting to the accuracy of the information in financial reports).*

Section 404 has been one of the more controversial and expensive provisions in the Sarbanes-Oxley Act because it requires companies to assess their own internal financial controls to make sure that their financial statements are reliable and accurate. A corporation might need to set up a disclosure committee and a coordinator, establish codes of conduct for accounting and financial personnel, create documentation procedures, provide training, and outline the individuals who are responsible for performing each of the procedures. Companies that were already well managed have not experienced substantial difficulty complying with this section. Other companies, however, have spent millions of dollars setting up, documenting, and evaluating their internal financial control systems. Although initially creating the internal financial control system is a one-time-only expense, the costs of maintaining and evaluating it are ongoing. Some corporations that spent considerable sums complying with Section 404 have been able to offset these costs by discovering and correcting inefficiencies or frauds within their systems. Nevertheless, it is unlikely that any corporation will find compliance with this section to be inexpensive.

---

5. Codified at 15 U.S.C. Section 7262.

SECTION 802(a)

Destruction, alteration, or falsification of records in Federal investigations and bankruptcy[6]

Whoever knowingly alters, destroys, mutilates, conceals, covers up, falsifies, or makes a false entry in any record, document, or tangible object with the intent to impede, obstruct, or influence the investigation or proper administration of any matter within the jurisdiction of any department or agency of the United States or any case filed under title 11, or in relation to or contemplation of any such matter or case, shall be fined under this title, imprisoned not more than 20 years, or both.

Destruction of corporate audit records[7]

(a) (1) Any accountant who conducts an audit of an issuer of securities to which section 10A(a) of the Securities Exchange Act of 1934 (15 U.S.C. 78j-1(a)) applies, shall maintain all audit or review workpapers for a period of 5 years from the end of the fiscal period in which the audit or review was concluded.

(2) The Securities and Exchange Commission shall promulgate, within 180 days, after adequate notice and an opportunity for comment, such rules and regulations, as are reasonably necessary, relating to the retention of relevant records such as workpapers, documents that form the basis of an audit or review, memoranda, correspondence, communications, other documents, and records (including electronic records) which are created, sent, or received in connection with an audit or review and contain conclusions, opinions, analyses, or financial data relating to such an audit or review, which is conducted by any accountant who conducts an audit of an issuer of securities to which section 10A(a) of the Securities Exchange Act of 1934 (15 U.S.C. 78j-1(a)) applies. The Commission may, from time to time, amend or supplement the rules and regulations that it is required to promulgate under this section, after adequate notice and an opportunity for comment, in order to ensure that such rules and regulations adequately comport with the purposes of this section.

(b) Whoever knowingly and willfully violates subsection (a)(1), or any rule or regulation promulgated by the Securities and Exchange Commission under subsection (a)(2), shall be fined under this title, imprisoned not more than 10 years, or both.

(c) Nothing in this section shall be deemed to diminish or relieve any person of any other duty or obligation imposed by Federal or State law or regulation to maintain, or refrain from destroying, any document.

* * * *

EXPLANATORY COMMENTS: *Section 802(a) enacted two new statutes that punish those who alter or destroy documents. The first statute is not specifically limited to securities fraud cases. It provides that anyone who alters, destroys, or falsifies records in federal investigations or bankruptcy may be criminally prosecuted and sentenced to a fine or to up to twenty years in prison, or both. The second statute requires auditors of public companies to keep all audit or review working papers for five years but expressly allows the SEC to amend or supplement these requirements as it sees fit. The SEC has, in fact,*

amended this section by issuing a rule that requires auditors who audit reporting companies to retain working papers for seven years from the conclusion of the review. Section 802(a) further provides that anyone who knowingly and willfully violates this statute is subject to criminal prosecution and can be sentenced to a fine, imprisoned for up to ten years, or both if convicted.

This portion of the Sarbanes-Oxley Act implicitly recognizes that persons who are under investigation often are tempted to respond by destroying or falsifying documents that might prove their complicity in wrongdoing. The severity of the punishment should provide a strong incentive for these individuals to resist the temptation.

SECTION 804

Time limitations on the commencement of civil actions arising under Acts of Congress[8]

(a) Except as otherwise provided by law, a civil action arising under an Act of Congress enacted after the date of the enactment of this section may not be commenced later than 4 years after the cause of action accrues.

(b) Notwithstanding subsection (a), a private right of action that involves a claim of fraud, deceit, manipulation, or contrivance in contravention of a regulatory requirement concerning the securities laws, as defined in section 3(a)(47) of the Securities Exchange Act of 1934 (15 U.S.C. 78c(a)(47)), may be brought not later than the earlier of—

(1) 2 years after the discovery of the facts constituting the violation; or

(2) 5 years after such violation.

* * * *

EXPLANATORY COMMENTS: *Prior to the enactment of this section, Section 10(b) of the Securities Exchange Act of 1934 had no express statute of limitations. The courts generally required plaintiffs to have filed suit within one year from the date that they should (using due diligence) have discovered that a fraud had been committed but no later than three years after the fraud occurred. Section 804 extends this period by specifying that plaintiffs must file a lawsuit within two years after they discover (or should have discovered) a fraud but no later than five years after the fraud's occurrence. This provision has prevented the courts from dismissing numerous securities fraud lawsuits.*

SECTION 806

Civil action to protect against retaliation in fraud cases[9]

(a) Whistleblower protection for employees of publicly traded companies.—

No company with a class of securities registered under section 12 of the Securities Exchange Act of 1934 (15 U.S.C. 78l), or that is required to file reports under section 15(d) of the Securities Exchange Act of 1934 (15 U.S.C. 78o(d)), or any officer, employee, contractor, subcontractor, or agent of such company, may discharge, demote, suspend, threaten, harass, or in any other manner discriminate against an

---

6. Codified at 15 U.S.C. Section 1519.
7. Codified at 15 U.S.C. Section 1520.

8. Codified at 28 U.S.C. Section 1658.
9. Codified at 18 U.S.C. Section 1514A.

employee in the terms and conditions of employment because of any lawful act done by the employee—

(1) to provide information, cause information to be provided, or otherwise assist in an investigation regarding any conduct which the employee reasonably believes constitutes a violation of section 1341, 1343, 1344, or 1348, any rule or regulation of the Securities and Exchange Commission, or any provision of Federal law relating to fraud against shareholders, when the information or assistance is provided to or the investigation is conducted by—

(A) a Federal regulatory or law enforcement agency;

(B) any Member of Congress or any committee of Congress; or

(C) a person with supervisory authority over the employee (or such other person working for the employer who has the authority to investigate, discover, or terminate misconduct); or

(2) to file, cause to be filed, testify, participate in, or otherwise assist in a proceeding filed or about to be filed (with any knowledge of the employer) relating to an alleged violation of section 1341, 1343, 1344, or 1348, any rule or regulation of the Securities and Exchange Commission, or any provision of Federal law relating to fraud against shareholders.

(b) Enforcement action.—

(1) In general.—A person who alleges discharge or other discrimination by any person in violation of subsection (a) may seek relief under subsection (c), by—

(A) filing a complaint with the Secretary of Labor; or

(B) if the Secretary has not issued a final decision within 180 days of the filing of the complaint and there is no showing that such delay is due to the bad faith of the claimant, bringing an action at law or equity for de novo review in the appropriate district court of the United States, which shall have jurisdiction over such an action without regard to the amount in controversy.

(2) Procedure.—

(A) In general.—An action under paragraph (1)(A) shall be governed under the rules and procedures set forth in section 42121(b) of title 49, United States Code.

(B) Exception.—Notification made under section 42121(b)(1) of title 49, United States Code, shall be made to the person named in the complaint and to the employer.

(C) Burdens of proof.—An action brought under paragraph (1)(B) shall be governed by the legal burdens of proof set forth in section 42121(b) of title 49, United States Code.

(D) Statute of limitations.—An action under paragraph (1) shall be commenced not later than 90 days after the date on which the violation occurs.

(c) Remedies.—

(1) In general.—An employee prevailing in any action under subsection (b)(1) shall be entitled to all relief necessary to make the employee whole.

(2) Compensatory damages.—Relief for any action under paragraph (1) shall include—

(A) reinstatement with the same seniority status that the employee would have had, but for the discrimination;

(B) the amount of back pay, with interest; and

(C) compensation for any special damages sustained as a result of the discrimination, including litigation costs, expert witness fees, and reasonable attorney fees.

(d) Rights retained by employee.—Nothing in this section shall be deemed to diminish the rights, privileges, or remedies of any employee under any Federal or State law, or under any collective bargaining agreement.

EXPLANATORY COMMENTS: *Section 806 is one of several provisions that were included in the Sarbanes-Oxley Act to encourage and protect whistleblowers—that is, employees who report their employer's alleged violations of securities law to the authorities. This section applies to employees, agents, and independent contractors who work for publicly traded companies or testify about such a company during an investigation. It sets up an administrative procedure at the U.S. Department of Labor for individuals who claim that their employer retaliated against them (fired or demoted them, for example) for blowing the whistle on the employer's wrongful conduct. It also allows the award of civil damages—including back pay, reinstatement, special damages, attorneys' fees, and court costs—to employees who prove that they suffered retaliation. Since this provision was enacted, whistleblowers have filed numerous complaints with the U.S. Department of Labor under this section.*

SECTION 807

Securities fraud[10]

Whoever knowingly executes, or attempts to execute, a scheme or artifice—

(1) to defraud any person in connection with any security of an issuer with a class of securities registered under section 12 of the Securities Exchange Act of 1934 (15 U.S.C. 78l) or that is required to file reports under section 15(d) of the Securities Exchange Act of 1934 (15 U.S.C. 78o(d)); or

(2) to obtain, by means of false or fraudulent pretenses, representations, or promises, any money or property in connection with the purchase or sale of any security of an issuer with a class of securities registered under section 12 of the Securities Exchange Act of 1934 (15 U.S.C. 78l) or that is required to file reports under section 15(d) of the Securities Exchange Act of 1934 (15 U.S.C. 78o(d)); shall be fined under this title, or imprisoned not more than 25 years, or both.

* * * *

EXPLANATORY COMMENTS: *Section 807 adds a new provision to the federal criminal code that addresses securities fraud. Prior to 2002, federal securities law had already made it a crime—under Section 10(b) of the Securities Exchange Act of 1934 and SEC Rule 10b-5, both of which are discussed in Chapter 27—to intentionally defraud someone in connection with a purchase or sale of securities, but the offense was not listed in the federal criminal code. Also, paragraph 2 of Section 807 goes beyond what is prohibited under securities law by making it a crime to obtain by means of false or fraudulent pretenses any money or property from the purchase or sale of securities. This new provision allows violators to be punished by up to twenty-five years in prison, a fine, or both.*

---

10. Codified at 18 U.S.C. Section 1348.

SECTION 906

Failure of corporate officers to certify financial reports[11]

(a) Certification of periodic financial reports.—Each periodic report containing financial statements filed by an issuer with the Securities Exchange Commission pursuant to section 13(a) or 15(d) of the Securities Exchange Act of 1934 (15 U.S.C. 78m(a) or 78o(d)) shall be accompanied by a written statement by the chief executive officer and chief financial officer (or equivalent thereof) of the issuer.

(b) Content.—The statement required under subsection (a) shall certify that the periodic report containing the financial statements fully complies with the requirements of section 13(a) or 15(d) of the Securities Exchange Act of 1934 (15 U.S.C. 78m or 78o(d)) and that information contained in the periodic report fairly presents, in all material respects, the financial condition and results of operations of the issuer.

(c) Criminal penalties.—Whoever—

(1) certifies any statement as set forth in subsections (a) and (b) of this section knowing that the periodic report accompanying the statement does not comport with all the requirements set forth in this section shall be fined not more than $1,000,000 or imprisoned not more than 10 years, or both; or

(2) willfully certifies any statement as set forth in subsections (a) and (b) of this section knowing that the periodic report accompanying the statement does not comport with all the requirements set forth in this section shall be fined not more than $5,000,000, or imprisoned not more than 20 years, or both.

EXPLANATORY COMMENTS: *As previously discussed, under Section 302 a corporation's CEO and CFO are required to certify that they believe the quarterly and annual reports their company files with the SEC are accurate and fairly present the company's financial condition. Section 906 adds "teeth" to these requirements by authorizing criminal penalties for those officers who intentionally certify inaccurate SEC filings. Knowing violations of the requirements are punishable by a fine of up to $1 million, ten years' imprisonment, or both. Willful violators may be fined up to $5 million, sentenced to up to twenty years' imprisonment, or both. Although the difference between a knowing and a willful violation is not entirely clear, the section is obviously intended to remind corporate officers of the serious consequences of certifying inaccurate reports to the SEC.*

11. Codified at 18 U.S.C. Section 1350.

APPENDIX E
Sample Answers for End-of-Chapter Hypothetical Questions with Sample Answers

1.2A HYPOTHETICAL QUESTION WITH SAMPLE ANSWER

1. The U.S. Constitution—The U.S. Constitution is the supreme law of the land. A law in violation of the Constitution, no matter what its source, will be declared unconstitutional and will not be enforced.

2. The federal statute—Under the U.S. Constitution, when there is a conflict between federal law and state law, federal law prevails.

3. The state statute—State statutes are enacted by state legislatures. Areas not covered by state statutory law are governed by state case law.

4. The U.S. Constitution—State constitutions are supreme within their respective borders unless they conflict with the U.S. Constitution, which is the supreme law of the land.

5. The federal administrative regulation—Under the U.S. Constitution, when there is a conflict between federal law and state law, federal law prevails.

2.2A HYPOTHETICAL QUESTION WITH SAMPLE ANSWER

Marya can bring suit in all three courts. The trucking firm did business in Florida, and the accident occurred there. Thus, the state of Florida would have jurisdiction over the defendant. Because the firm was headquartered in Georgia and had its principal place of business in that state, Marya could also sue in a Georgia court. Finally, because the amount in controversy exceeds $75,000, the suit could be brought in federal court on the basis of diversity of citizenship.

3.2A HYPOTHETICAL QUESTION WITH SAMPLE ANSWER

This question essentially asks whether good behavior can ever be unethical. The answer to this question depends on which approach to ethical reasoning you are using. Under the outcome-based approach of utilitarianism, it is simply not possible for selfish motives to be unethical if they result in good conduct. A good outcome is moral regardless of the nature of the action itself or the reason for the action. Under a duty-based approach, motive would be more relevant in assessing whether a firm's conduct was ethical. You would need to analyze the firm's conduct in terms of religious truths or to determine whether human beings were being treated with the inherent dignity that they deserve. Although a good motive would not justify a bad act to a religious ethicist, in this situation the actions were good and the motive was questionable (because the firm was simply seeking to increase its profit). Nevertheless, unless one's religion prohibited making a profit, the firm's actions would likely not be considered unethical. Applying Kantian ethics would require you to evaluate the firm's actions in light of what would happen if everyone in society acted that way (categorical imperative). Here, because the conduct was good, it would be positive for soci-

ety if every firm acted that way. Hence, the profit-seeking motive would be irrelevant in a Kantian analysis. In a debate between motive and conduct, then, conduct is almost always given greater weight in evaluating ethics.

4.2A HYPOTHETICAL QUESTION WITH SAMPLE ANSWER

The correct answer is (2). The *Restatement (Second) of Torts* defines negligence as "conduct that falls below the standard established by law for the protection of others against unreasonable risk of harm." The standard established by law is that of a reasonable person acting with due care in the circumstances. Mary was well aware that the medication she took would make her drowsy, and her failure to observe due care (that is, refrain from driving) under the circumstances was negligent. Answer (1) is incorrect because Mary had no reason to believe the golf club was defective, and she could not have prevented the injury by the exercise of due care.

5.2A HYPOTHETICAL QUESTION WITH SAMPLE ANSWER

1. Making a photocopy of an article in a scholarly journal "for purposes such as . . . scholarship, or research, is not an infringement of copyright" under Section 107 of the Copyright Act.

2. This is an example of trademark infringement. Whenever a trademark is copied to a substantial degree or used in its entirety by one who is not entitled to its use, the trademark has been infringed.

3. This is the most likely example of copyright infringement. Generally, determining whether the reproduction of copyrighted material constitutes copyright infringement is made on a case-by-case basis under the "fair use" doctrine, as expressed in Section 107 of the Copyright Act. Courts look at such factors as the "purpose and character" of a use, such as whether it is "of a commercial nature;" "the amount and substantiality of the portion used in relation to the copyrighted work as a whole;" and "the effect of the use on the potential market" for the copied work. In this question, the DVD store owner is copying copyright-protected works in their entirety for commercial purposes, thereby affecting the market for the works.

4. Recording a television program "for purposes such as . . . teaching . . . is not an infringement of copyright" under Section 107 of the Copyright Act.

6.2A HYPOTHETICAL QUESTION WITH SAMPLE ANSWER

1. Sarah has wrongfully taken and carried away the personal property of another with the intent to permanently deprive the owner of such property. She has committed the crime of larceny.

A-132

2. Sarah has unlawfully and forcibly taken the personal property of another. She has committed the crime of robbery.

3. Sarah has broken and entered a dwelling with the intent to commit a felony. She has committed the crime of burglary. (Most states have dispensed with the requirement that the act take place at night.)

Note the basic differences: Burglary requires breaking and entering into a building without the use of force against a person. Robbery does not involve any breaking and entering, but force is required. Larceny is the taking of personal property without force and without breaking and entering into a building. Generally, because force is used, robbery is considered the most serious of these crimes and carries the most severe penalties. Larceny involves no force or threat to human life; therefore, it carries the least severe penalty of the three. Burglary, because it involves breaking and entering, frequently where people live, carries a lesser penalty than robbery but a greater penalty than larceny.

7.2A HYPOTHETICAL QUESTION WITH SAMPLE ANSWER

According to the question, Janine was apparently unconscious or otherwise unable to agree to a contract for the nursing services she received while she was in the hospital. As you read in the chapter, however, sometimes the law will create a fictional contract in order to prevent one party from unjustly receiving a benefit at the expense of another. This is known as a quasi contract and provides a basis for Nursing Services to recover the value of the services it provided while Janine was in the hospital. As for the at-home services that were provided to Janine, because Janine was aware that those services were being provided for her, Nursing Services can recover for those services under an implied-in-fact contract. Under this type of contract, the conduct of the parties creates and defines the terms. Janine's acceptance of the services constitutes her agreement to form a contract, and she will probably be required to pay Nursing Services in full.

8.2A HYPOTHETICAL QUESTION WITH SAMPLE ANSWER

1. Death of either the offeror or the offeree prior to acceptance automatically terminates a revocable offer. The basic legal reason is that the offer is personal to the parties and cannot be passed on to others, not even to the estate of the deceased. This rule applies even if the other party is unaware of the death. Thus, Cherneck's offer terminates on Cherneck's death, and Bollow's later acceptance does not constitute a contract.

2. An offer is automatically terminated by the destruction of the specific subject matter of the offer prior to acceptance. Thus, Bollow's acceptance after the fire does not constitute a contract.

3. When the offer is irrevocable, under an option contract, death of the offeror does not terminate the option contract, and the offeree can accept the offer to sell the equipment, binding the offeror's estate to performance. Performance is not personal to Cherneck, as the estate can transfer title to the equipment. Knowledge of the death is immaterial to the offeree's right of acceptance. Thus, Bollow can hold Cherneck's estate to a contract for the purchase of the equipment.

4. When the offer is irrevocable, under an option contract, death of the offeree also does not terminate the offer. Because the option is a

separate contract, the contract survives and passes to the offeree's estate, which can exercise the option by acceptance within the option period. Thus, acceptance by Bollow's estate binds Cherneck to a contract for the sale of the equipment.

9.2A HYPOTHETICAL QUESTION WITH SAMPLE ANSWER

Contracts in restraint of trade are usually illegal and unenforceable. An exception to this rule applies to a covenant not to compete that is ancillary to certain types of business contracts in which some fair protection is deemed appropriate (such as in the sale of a business). The covenant, however, must be reasonable in terms of time and area to be legally enforceable. If either term is excessive, the court can declare that the restraint goes beyond what is necessary for reasonable protection. In this event, the court can either declare the covenant illegal or it can reform the covenant to make the terms of time and area reasonable and then enforce it. Suppose the court declares the covenant illegal and unenforceable. Because the covenant is ancillary and severable from the primary contract, the primary contract is not affected by such a ruling. In the case of Hotel Lux, the primary contract concerns employment; the covenant is ancillary and desirable for the protection of the hotel. The time period of one year may be considered reasonable for a chef with an international reputation. The reasonableness of the three-state area restriction may be questioned, however. If it is found to be reasonable, the covenant probably will be enforced. If it is not found to be reasonable, the court could declare the entire covenant illegal, allowing Perlee to be employed by any restaurant or hotel, including one in direct competition with Hotel Lux. Alternatively, the court could reform the covenant, making its terms reasonable for protecting Hotel Lux's normal customer market area.

10.2A HYPOTHETICAL QUESTION WITH SAMPLE ANSWER

In this situation, Gemma becomes what is known as a *guarantor* on the loan. That is, she guarantees the hardware store that she will pay for the mower if her brother fails to do so. This kind of collateral promise, in which the guarantor states that he or she will become responsible *only* if the primary party does not perform, must be in writing to be enforceable. There is an exception, however. If the main purpose in accepting secondary liability is to secure a personal benefit—for example, if Gemma's brother bought the mower for her—the contract need not be in writing. The assumption is that a court can infer from the circumstances of the case whether the main purpose was to secure a personal benefit and thus, in effect, to answer for the guarantor's own debt.

11.3A. HYPOTHETICAL QUESTION WITH SAMPLE ANSWER

As a general rule any right(s) flowing from a contract can be assigned. There are, however, exceptions, such as when the contract expressly and specifically prohibits or limits the right of assignment. Because of the principle of freedom of contract, this type of prohibition is enforced—unless it is deemed contrary to public policy. For example, courts have held that a prohibition clause against assignment that restrains the alienation of property is invalid by virtue of being against public policy. Authorities differ on how a case like Aron's should be decided. Some courts would enforce the prohibition completely, holding that Aron's assignment to Erica is completely ineffective without the landlord's consent. Others would permit the assignment to be effective, with the landlord's remedies limited to the normal contract remedies ensuing from Aron's breach.

12.2A HYPOTHETICAL QUESTION WITH SAMPLE ANSWER

Generally, the equitable remedy of specific performance will be granted only if two criteria are met: monetary damages (under the circumstances) must be inadequate as a remedy, and the subject matter of the contract must be unique.

1. In the sale of land, the buyer's contract is for a specific piece of real property. The land under contract is unique, because no two pieces of real property have the same legal description. In addition, monetary damages would not compensate a buyer adequately, as the same land cannot be purchased elsewhere. Specific performance is an appropriate remedy.

2. The basic criteria for specific performance do not apply well to personal service contracts. If the identical service contracted for is readily available from others, the service is not unique and monetary damages for nonperformance are adequate. If, however, the services are so personal that only the contracted party can perform them, the contract meets the test of uniqueness; but the courts will refuse to decree specific performance based on either of two theories. First, the enforcement of specific performance requires involuntary servitude (prohibited by the Thirteenth Amendment to the U. S. Constitution). Second, it is impractical to attempt to force meaningful performance by someone against his or her will. In the case of Marita and Horace, specific performance is not an appropriate remedy.

3. A rare coin is unique, and monetary damages for breach are inadequate, as Juan cannot obtain a substantially identical substitute in the market. This is a typical case where specific performance is an appropriate remedy.

4. The key fact for consideration here is that this is a closely held corporation. Therefore, the stock is not available in the market, and the shares become unique. The uniqueness of these shares is enhanced by the fact that if Cary sells his 4 percent of the shares to De Valle, De Valle will have a controlling voice in the corporation. Because of this, monetary damages for De Valle are totally inadequate as a remedy. Specific performance is an appropriate remedy.

13.2A HYPOTHETICAL QUESTION WITH SAMPLE ANSWER

Anne has entered into an enforceable contract to subscribe to *E-Commerce Weekly*. In this problem, the offer to deliver, via e-mail, the newsletter was presented by the offeror with a statement of how to accept—by clicking on the "SUBSCRIBE" button. Consideration was in the promise to deliver the newsletter and at the price that the subscriber agreed to pay. The offeree had an opportunity to read the terms of the subscription agreement before making the contract. Whether or not she actually read those terms does not matter.

14.2A HYPOTHETICAL QUESTION WITH SAMPLE ANSWER

The entire answer falls under UCC 2–206(1)(b), because the situation deals with a buyer's order to buy goods for prompt shipment. The law is that such an order or offer invites acceptance by a prompt *promise* to ship conforming goods. If the promise (acceptance) is sent by a medium reasonable under the circumstances, the acceptance is effective when sent. Therefore, a contract was formed on October 8, and it required Fulsom to ship one hundred model Color-X television sets. Fulsom's shipment is nonconforming, and Salinger is correct in claiming that Fulsom is in breach. Fulsom's claim would be valid if Fulsom had not sent its promise of shipment. The Code provides that shipment of nonconforming goods constitutes an acceptance *unless* the seller seasonably notifies the buyer that such shipment is sent only as an accommodation. Thus, had a contract not been formed on October 8, the nonconforming shipment on the 28th would not be treated as an acceptance, and no contract would be in existence to breach.

15.2A HYPOTHETICAL QUESTION WITH SAMPLE ANSWER

1. In a destination contract, the risk of loss passes to the buyer when the goods are tendered to the buyer at the specified destination—in this case, San Francisco.

2. In a shipment contract, if the seller is required or authorized to ship goods by carrier, but the contract specifies no locale, the risk of loss passes to the buyer when the goods are duly delivered to the carrier.

3. If the seller is a merchant, risk of loss to goods held by the seller passes to the buyer when the buyer actually takes physical possession of the goods. If the seller is not a merchant, the risk of loss to goods held by the seller passes to the buyer on tender of delivery.

4. When a bailee is holding goods for a person who has contracted to sell them and the goods are to be delivered without being moved, risk of loss passes to the buyer when (1) the buyer receives a negotiable document of title for the goods, (2) the bailee acknowledges the buyer's right to possess the goods, or (3) the buyer receives a nonnegotiable document of title and has had a reasonable time to present the document to the bailee and demand the goods. (If the bailee refuses to honor the document, the risk of loss remains with the seller.) If the goods are to be delivered by being moved, but the contract does not specify whether it is a destination or a shipment contract, it is presumed to be a shipment contract. If no locale is specified in the contract, risk of loss passes to the buyer when the seller delivers the goods to the carrier.

16.2A HYPOTHETICAL QUESTION WITH SAMPLE ANSWER

No. Cummings had not breached the sales contract because the C.O.D. shipment had deprived him of his absolute right, in the absence of agreement, to inspect the goods before accepting them. Had Cummings requested or agreed to the C.O.D. method of shipment, the result would have been different. Because he had not agreed to the C.O.D. shipment, he was fully within his rights to refuse to accept the goods because he could not inspect them prior to acceptance. In this case, it was the seller who had breached the contract by shipping the goods C.O.D. without Cummings's consent.

17.2A HYPOTHETICAL QUESTION WITH SAMPLE ANSWER

Yes. To disclaim the implied warranty of fitness for a particular purpose, the disclaimer must be in writing and be conspicuous. Although the implied warranty of merchantability can be disclaimed orally, if the disclaimer is in writing it must be conspicuously written. This means that the disclaimer must—either by different color or type size or some other technique—stand out from the context in which it is printed so as to readily alert the reader of the document of the disclaimer. In this case, the disclaimer was printed in the same size and color of type as the rest of the contract and was not conspicuous. If this was the only warranty disclaimer, it is not effective and Tandy can recover.

18.2A HYPOTHETICAL QUESTION WITH SAMPLE ANSWER

No. Material alteration of a negotiable instrument may be a real defense against payment on the instrument. As against a holder in due course, the raising of the amount (material alteration) is only a defense as to the altered amount, and the HDC can recover according to the original tenor of the instrument [UCC 3–407(b)]. In this case, however, Williams materially contributed to the alteration by his negligence in writing the check in pencil. Thus, the defense of material alteration was not available to him, and Williams is liable to Boz for the $10,000 [UCC 3–406]. If Williams had written the check in ink, and Stein had altered the amount in such a clever fashion that Boz could take the check without notice and become an HDC, then Williams would have a real defense against paying $10,000. In the latter case, Boz, as an HDC, could collect only $1,000, the original amount of the check.

19.2A HYPOTHETICAL QUESTION WITH SAMPLE ANSWER

Under the Home Mortgage Disclosure Act (HMDA) and the Community Reinvestment Act of 1977, which were passed to prevent discrimination in lending practices, a bank is required to define its market area. This area must be established contiguous to the bank's branch offices. It must be mapped using the existing boundaries of the counties or the standard metropolitan areas (SMAs) in which the offices are located. A bank must delineate the community served, and annually review this delineation. The issue here is how a successful Internet-only bank could delineate its community. Does an Internet bank have a physically limited market area or serve a physically distinct community? Will the Federal Reserve Board, the government agency charged with enforcing this law, allow a bank to describe its market area as a "cybercommunity"?

20.2A HYPOTHETICAL QUESTION WITH SAMPLE ANSWER

Mendez has a security interest in Arabian Knight and is a perfected secured party. He has met all the necessary criteria listed under UCC 9–203 to be a secured creditor. Mendez has given value of $5,000 and has taken possession of the collateral, Arabian Knight, owned by Marsh (who has rights in the collateral). Thus, he has a security interest even though Marsh did not sign a security agreement. Once a security interest attaches, a transfer of possession of the collateral to the secured party can perfect the party's security interest without a filing [UCC 9–310(b)(6); 9–313]. Thus, a security interest was created and perfected at the time Marsh transferred Arabian Knight to Mendez as security for the loan.

21.2A. HYPOTHETICAL QUESTION WITH SAMPLE ANSWER

The Bankruptcy Code establishes a payment priority of claims from the debtor's estate. Each class of debt in this priority list must be fully paid before the next class in priority is entitled to any of the proceeds. If insufficient funds remain to pay an entire class, the proceeds are

distributed on a pro rata basis to each creditor within that class. The order of priority for claims listed in this problem is as follows:

1. Administrative bankruptcy costs (Martinez)—$500.
2. Claims for back wages, limited to $4,300 per claimant, provided wages were earned within ninety days of petition (Kohak)—$4,300.
3. Taxes and penalties due and owing (Micanopy County)—$1,000.
4. General creditors, $10,000 (First Bank of Sunny Acres—$5,000; Calvin—$2,500; balance of Kohak wages owed—$2,500).

Because the amount remaining after paying (a), (b), and (c) is only $1,200, the general creditors will share on a pro rata basis. First Bank of Sunny Acres will receive $600 ($5,000/$10,000 × $1,200 = $600), and Calvin and Kohak will each receive $300 ($2,500/$10,000 × $1,200 = $300).

22.2A HYPOTHETICAL QUESTION WITH SAMPLE ANSWER

Agency is usually a consensual relationship in that the principal and agent agree that the agent will have the authority to act for the principal, binding the principal to any contract with a third party. If no agency in fact exists, the purported agent's contracts with third parties are not binding on the principal. In this case, no agency by agreement was created. Brown may claim that an agency by estoppel was created; however, this argument will fail. Agency by estoppel is applicable only when a *principal* causes a third person to believe that another person is the principal's agent. Then the third party's actions in dealing with the agent are in reliance upon the principal's words or actions and the third party's reasonable belief that the agent has authority. This is said to estop the principal from claiming that in fact no agency existed. Acts and declarations of the *agent*, however, do not in and of themselves create an agency by estoppel, because such actions should not reasonably lead a third person to believe that the purported agent has authority. In this case, Wade's declarations and allegations alone led Brown to believe that Wade was an agent. Gett's actions were not involved. It is not reasonable to believe that someone is an agent solely because he or she is a friend of the principal. Therefore, Brown cannot hold Gett liable unless Gett ratifies Wade's contract—which is unlikely, as Wade has disappeared with the rare coin.

23.2A HYPOTHETICAL QUESTION WITH SAMPLE ANSWER

The Occupational Safety and Health Act (OSHA) requires employers to provide safe working conditions for employees. The act prohibits employers from discharging or discriminating against any employee who refuses to work when the employee believes in good faith that he or she will risk death or great bodily harm by undertaking the employment activity. Denton and Carlo had sufficient reason to believe that the maintenance job required of them by their employer involved great risk, and therefore, under OSHA, their discharge was wrongful. Denton and Carlo can turn to the Occupational Safety and Health Administration, which is part of the U.S. Department of Labor, for assistance.

24.2A. QUESTION WITH SAMPLE ANSWER

1. A limited partner's interest is assignable. In fact, assignment allows the assignee to become a substituted limited partner with the consent of the remaining partners. The assignment, however, does not dissolve the limited partnership.

2. Bankruptcy of the limited partnership itself causes dissolution, but bankruptcy of one of the limited partners does not dissolve the partnership unless it causes the bankruptcy of the firm.

3. The retirement, death, or insanity of a general partner dissolves the partnership unless the business can be continued by the remaining general partners. Because Dorinda was the only general partner, her death dissolves the limited partnership.

25.2A HYPOTHETICAL QUESTION WITH SAMPLE ANSWER

It could be argued that Kora exceeded his authority when he co-signed the note on behalf of the corporation. The board of directors of a corporation delegates the authority to transact all ordinary business of the corporation to the president. If cosigning a note for a personal loan is not "ordinary business of the corporation," then the board, as principal, must ratify the act. There is no indication in the question that the board did so in this case.

26.2A HYPOTHETICAL QUESTION WITH SAMPLE ANSWER

Directors are personally answerable to the corporation and the shareholders for breach of their duty to exercise reasonable care in conducting the affairs of the corporation. Reasonable care is defined as being the degree of care that a reasonably prudent person would use in the conduct of personal business affairs. When directors delegate the running of the corporate affairs to officers, the directors are expected to use reasonable care in the selection and supervision of such officers. Failure to do so will make the directors liable for negligence or mismanagement. A director who dissents to an action by the board is not personally liable for losses resulting from that action. Unless the dissent is entered into the board meeting minutes, however, the director is presumed to have assented. Therefore, the first issue in the case of Starboard, Inc., is whether the board members failed to use reasonable care in the selection of the president, Tyson. If so, and particularly if the board failed to provide a reasonable amount of supervision (and openly embezzled funds indicate that failure), the directors will be personally liable. This liability will include Ellsworth unless she can prove that she dissented and that she tried to reasonably supervise Tyson. Considering the facts in this case, it is questionable that Ellsworth could prove this.

27.2A HYPOTHETICAL QUESTION WITH SAMPLE ANSWER

No. Under federal securities law, a stock split is exempt from registration requirements. This is because no *sale* of stock is involved. The existing shares are merely being split, and no consideration is received by the corporation for the additional shares created.

28.3A HYPOTHETICAL QUESTION WITH SAMPLE ANSWER

For Curtis to recover against the hotel, he must first prove that a bailment relationship was created between himself and the hotel as to the car or the fur coat, or both. For a bailment to exist, there must be a delivery of the personal property that gives the bailee exclusive possession of the property, and the bailee must knowingly accept the bailed property. If either element is lacking, there is no bailment relationship and no liability on the part of the bailee hotel. The facts clearly indicate that the bailee hotel took exclusive possession and control of Curtis's car, and it knowingly accepted the car when the attendant took the car from Curtis and parked it in the underground guarded garage, retaining the keys. Thus, a bailment was created as to the car, and, because a mutual benefit bailment was created, the hotel owes Curtis the duty to exercise reasonable care over the property and to return the bailed car at the end of the bailment. Failure to return the car creates a presumption of negligence (lack of reasonable care), and unless the hotel can rebut this presumption, the hotel is liable to Curtis for the loss of the car. As to the fur coat, the hotel neither knew nor expected that the trunk contained an expensive fur coat. Thus, although the hotel knowingly took exclusive possession of the car, the hotel did not do so with the fur coat. (But for a regular coat and other items likely to be in the car, the hotel would be liable.) Because no bailment of the expensive fur coat was created, the hotel has no liability for its loss.

29.2A HYPOTHETICAL QUESTION WITH SAMPLE ANSWER

Wiley understandably wants a general warranty deed, as this type of deed will give him the most extensive protection against any defects of title claimed against the property transferred. The general warranty would have Gemma warranting the following covenants:

1. Covenant of seisin and right to convey—a warranty that the seller has good title and power to convey.

2. Covenant against encumbrances—a guaranty by the seller that, unless stated, there are no outstanding encumbrances or liens against the property conveyed.

3. Covenant of quiet possession—a warranty that the grantee's possession will not be disturbed by others claiming a prior legal right. Gemma, however, is conveying only ten feet along a property line that may not even be accurately surveyed. Gemma therefore does not wish to make these warranties. Consequently, she is offering a quitclaim deed, which does not convey any warranties but conveys only whatever interest, if any, the grantor owns. Although title is passed by the quitclaim deed, the quality of the title is not warranted. Because Wiley really needs the property, it appears that he has three choices: he can accept the quitclaim deed; he can increase his offer price to obtain the general warranty deed he wants; or he can offer to have a title search made, which should satisfy both parties.

30.2A HYPOTHETICAL QUESTION WITH SAMPLE ANSWER

1. In most states, for a will to be valid, it must be in writing, signed by the testator, and witnessed (attested to) according to the statutes of the state. In some states the testator is also required to publish (declare) that the document is his or her last will and testament. (Such is not required under the Uniform Probate Code.) In the case of Benjamin, the will is unquestionably written (typewritten) and signed by the testator. The only problem is with the witnesses. Some states require three witnesses, and some invalidate a will if a named beneficiary is also a witness. The Uniform Probate Code provides that a will is valid even if attested to by an interested witness. Therefore, whether the will is valid depends on the state laws dealing with witness qualifications.

2. If the will is declared invalid, Benjamin's estate will pass in accordance with the state's intestacy laws. These statutes provide for distribution of an estate when there is no valid will. The intent of the statutes is to distribute the estate in the way that the deceased person would have wished. Generally, the estate is divided between a surviving spouse and all surviving children. Because Benjamin is a widower, if his only surviving child is Edward, the entire estate will go to Edward, and Benjamin's grandchildren, Perry and Paul, will receive nothing from the estate.

3. If the will is valid, the estate will be divided between Benjamin's two children, Patricia and Edward. Should either or both predecease Benjamin, leaving children (Benjamin's grandchildren), the grandchildren take *per stirpes* the share that would have gone to their parent. In this case Edward, as a surviving child of Benjamin, would receive one-half of the estate, and Perry and Paul, as grandchildren, would each receive *per stirpes* one-fourth of the estate (one-half of the share that would have gone to their deceased mother, Patricia).

31.2A Hypothetical Question with Sample Answer

Assuming that the circuit court has abandoned the *Ultramares* rule, it is likely that the accounting firm of Goldman, Walters, Johnson & Co. will be held liable to Happydays State Bank for negligent preparation of financial statements. This hypothetical scenario is partially derived from *Citizens State Bank v. Timm, Schmidt & Co.* In *Citizens State Bank* the Supreme Court of Wisconsin enunciated various policy reasons for holding accountants liable to third parties even in the absence of privity. The court suggested that this potential liability would make accountants more careful in the preparation of financial statements. Moreover, in some situations the accountants may be the only solvent defendants, and hence, unless liability is imposed on accountants, third parties who reasonably rely on financial statements may go unprotected. The court further asserted that accountants, rather than third parties, are in better positions to spread the risks. If third parties such as banks have to absorb the costs of bad loans made as a result of negligently prepared financial statements, then the cost of credit to the public in general will increase.

In contrast, the court suggests that accountants are in a better position to spread the risk by purchasing liability insurance.

32.2A Hypothetical Question with Sample Answer

Each system has its advantages and its disadvantages. In a common law system, the courts independently develop the rules governing certain areas of law, such as torts and contracts. This judge-made law exists in addition to the laws passed by a legislature. Judges must follow precedential decisions in their jurisdictions, but courts may modify or even overturn precedents when deemed necessary. Also, if there is no case law to guide a court, the court may create a new rule of law. In a civil law system, the only official source of law is a statutory code. Courts are required to interpret the code and apply the rules to individual cases, but courts may not depart from the code and develop their own laws. In theory, the law code will set forth all the principles needed for the legal system. Common law and civil law systems are not wholly distinct. For example, the United States has a common law system, but crimes are defined by statute as in civil law systems. Civil law systems may allow considerable room for judges to develop law: law codes cannot be so precise as to address every contested issue, so the judiciary must interpret the codes. There are also significant differences among common law countries. The judges of different common law nations have produced differing common law principles. The roles of judges and lawyers under the different systems should be taken into account. Among other factors that should be considered in establishing a business law system and in deciding what regulations to impose are the goals that the system and its regulations are intended to achieve and the expectations of those to whom both will apply, including foreign and domestic investors.

Glossary

A

abandoned property ■ Property with which the owner has voluntarily parted, with no intention of recovering it.

acceleration clause ■ A clause that allows a payee or other holder of a time instrument to demand payment of the entire amount due, with interest, if a certain event occurs, such as a default in the payment of an installment when due.

acceptance ■ In contract law, a voluntary act by the offeree that shows assent, or agreement, to the terms of an offer; may consist of words or conduct. In negotiable instruments law, the drawee's signed agreement to pay a draft when it is presented.

acceptor ■ A drawee that is legally obligated to pay an instrument when it is presented later for payment.

accession ■ Occurs when an individual adds value to personal property by the use of either labor or materials. In some situations, a person may acquire ownership rights in another's property through accession.

accommodation party ■ A person who signs an instrument for the purpose of lending her or his name as credit to another party on the instrument.

accord and satisfaction ■ A common means of settling a disputed claim, whereby a debtor offers to pay a lesser amount than the creditor purports is owed. The creditor's acceptance of the offer creates an accord (agreement), and when the accord is executed, satisfaction occurs.

accredited investors ■ In the context of securities offerings, "sophisticated" investors, such as banks, insurance companies, investment companies, the issuer's executive officers and directors, and persons whose income or net worth exceeds certain limits.

act of state doctrine ■ A doctrine providing that the judicial branch of one country will not examine the validity of public acts committed by a recognized foreign government within its own territory.

actionable ■ Capable of serving as the basis of a lawsuit. An actionable claim can be pursued in a lawsuit or other court action.

actual malice ■ The deliberate intent to cause harm, which exists when a person makes a statement either knowing that it is false or showing a reckless disregard for whether it is true. In defamation law, a statement made about a public figure normally must be made with actual malice for the plaintiff to recover damages.

actus reus ■ A guilty (prohibited) act. The commission of a prohibited act is one of the two essential elements required for criminal liability, the other element being the intent to commit a crime.

adhesion contract ■ A "standard-form" contract, such as that between a large retailer and a consumer, in which the stronger party dictates the terms.

adjudicate ■ The act of rendering a judicial decision. In an administrative process, the proceeding in which an administrative law judge hears and decides on issues that arise when an administrative agency charges a person or a firm with violating a law or regulation enforced by the agency.

administrative agency ■ A federal or state government agency established to perform a specific function. Administrative agencies are authorized by legislative acts to make and enforce rules in order to administer and enforce the acts.

administrative law ■ The body of law created by administrative agencies (in the form of rules, regulations, orders, and decisions) in order to carry out their duties and responsibilities.

administrative process ■ The procedure used by administrative agencies in the administration of law.

administrator ■ One who is appointed by a court to handle the probate (disposition) of a person's estate if that person dies intestate (without a valid will) or if the executor named in the will cannot serve.

adverse possession ■ The acquisition of title to real property by occupying it openly, without the consent of the owner, for a period of time specified by a state statute. The occupation must be actual, open, notorious, exclusive, and in opposition to all others, including the owner.

affirmative action ■ Job-hiring policies that give special consideration to members of protected classes in an effort to overcome present effects of past discrimination.

after-acquired property ■ Property that is acquired by the debtor after the execution of a security agreement.

agency ■ A relationship between two parties in which one party (the agent) agrees to represent or act for the other (the principal).

agent ■ A person who agrees to represent or act for another, called the principal.

agreement ■ A meeting of two or more minds in regard to the terms of a contract; usually broken down into two events—an offer by one party to form a contract and an acceptance of the offer by the person to whom the offer is made.

alien corporation ■ A designation in the United States for a corporation formed in another country but doing business in the United States.

alienation ■ The process of transferring land out of one's possession (thus "alienating" the land from oneself).

allonge ■ A piece of paper firmly attached to a negotiable instrument, on which transferees can make indorsements if there is no room left on the instrument itself.

alternative dispute resolution (ADR) ■ The resolution of disputes in ways other than those involved in the traditional judicial process. Negotiation, mediation, and arbitration are forms of ADR.

answer ■ Procedurally, a defendant's response to the plaintiff's complaint.

anticipatory repudiation ■ An assertion or action by a party indicating that he or she will not perform an obligation that the party is contractually obligated to perform at a future time.

apparent authority ■ Authority that is only apparent, not real. In agency law, a person may be deemed to have had the power to act as an agent for another party if the other party's manifestations to a third party led the third party to believe that an agency existed when, in fact, it did not.

appraisal right ■ The right of a dissenting shareholder, who objects to an extraordinary transaction of the corporation (such as a merger or a consolidation), to have his or her shares appraised and to be paid the fair value of those shares by the corporation.

appropriation ■ In tort law, the use by one person of another person's name, likeness, or other identifying characteristic without permission and for the benefit of the user.

arbitration ■ The settling of a dispute by submitting it to a disinterested third party (other than a court), who renders a decision that is (most often) legally binding.

arbitration clause ■ A clause in a contract that provides that, in the event of a dispute, the parties will submit the dispute to arbitration rather than litigate the dispute in court.

arson ■ The intentional burning of another's dwelling. Some statutes have expanded this to include any real property regardless of ownership and the destruction of property by other means—for example, by explosion.

articles of incorporation ■ The document filed with the appropriate governmental agency, usually the secretary of state, when a business is incorporated. State statutes usually prescribe what kind of information must be contained in the articles of incorporation.

articles of organization ■ The document filed with a designated state official by which a limited liability company is formed.

articles of partnership ■ A written agreement that sets forth each partner's rights and obligations with respect to the partnership.

artisan's lien ■ A possessory lien given to a person who has made improvements and added value to another person's personal property as security for payment for services performed.

assault ■ Any word or action intended to make another person fearful of immediate physical harm; a reasonably believable threat.

assignee ■ A party to whom the rights under a contract are transferred, or assigned.

assignment ■ The act of transferring to another all or part of one's rights arising under a contract.

assignor ■ A party who transfers (assigns) his or her rights under a contract to another party (called the *assignee*).

assumption of risk ■ A doctrine under which a plaintiff may not recover for injuries or damage suffered from risks he or she knows of and has voluntarily assumed.

attachment ■ In a secured transaction, the process by which a secured creditor's interest "attaches" to the property of another (collateral) and the creditor's security interest becomes enforceable. In the context of judicial liens, a court-ordered seizure and taking into custody of property prior to the securing of a judgment for a past-due debt.

automatic stay ■ In bankruptcy proceedings, the suspension of virtually all litigation and other action by creditors against the debtor or the debtor's property. The stay is effective the moment the debtor files a petition in bankruptcy.

award ■ In litigation, the amount of monetary compensation awarded to a plaintiff in a civil lawsuit as damages. In the context of alternative dispute resolution, the decision rendered by an arbitrator.

 B

backdating ■ The practice of marketing a document with a date that precedes the actual date. Persons who backdate stock options are picking a date when the stock was trading at a lower price than the date of the options grant.

bailee ■ One to whom goods are entrusted by a bailor.

bailment ■ A situation in which the personal property of one person (a bailor) is entrusted to another (a bailee), who is obligated to return the bailed property to the bailor or dispose of it as directed.

bailor ■ One who entrusts goods to a bailee.

bankruptcy court ■ A federal court of limited jurisdiction that handles only bankruptcy proceedings, which are governed by federal bankruptcy law.

battery ■ The unprivileged, intentional touching of another.

bearer ■ A person in possession of an instrument payable to bearer or indorsed in blank.

bearer instrument ■ Any instrument that is not payable to a specific person, including instruments payable to the bearer or to "cash."

bequest ■ A gift of personal property by will (from the verb *to bequeath*).

beyond a reasonable doubt ■ The standard of proof used in criminal cases. If there is any reasonable doubt that a criminal defendant committed the crime with which she or he has been charged, then the verdict must be "not guilty."

bilateral contract ■ A type of contract that arises when a promise is given in exchange for a return promise.

bilateral mistake ■ A mistake that occurs when both parties to a contract are mistaken about the same material fact and the mistake is one that a reasonable person would make; either party can rescind the contract.

Bill of Rights ■ The first ten amendments to the U.S. Constitution.

binder ■ A written, temporary insurance policy.

binding authority ■ Any source of law that a court must follow when deciding a case.

blank indorsement ■ An indorsement that specifies no particular indorsee and can consist of a mere signature. An order instrument that is indorsed in blank becomes a bearer instrument.

blue laws ■ State or local laws that prohibit the performance of certain types of commercial activities on Sunday.

blue sky laws ■ State laws that regulate the offering and sale of securities.

bona fide occupational qualification (BFOQ) ■ Identifiable characteristics reasonably necessary to the normal operation of a particular business. These characteristics can include gender, national origin, and religion, but not race.

bond ■ A certificate that evidences a corporate (or government) debt. It is a security that involves no ownership interest in the issuing entity.

bond indenture ■ A contract between the issuer of a bond and the bondholder.

bounty payment ■ A reward (payment) given to a person or persons who perform a certain service, such as informing legal authorities of illegal actions.

breach ■ The failure to perform a legal obligation.

breach of contract ■ The failure, without legal excuse, of a promisor to perform the obligations of a contract.

brief ■ A formal legal document prepared by a party's attorney and submitted to an appellate court when a case is appealed, which outlines the facts and issues of the case that are in dispute.

browse-wrap terms ■ Terms and conditions of use that are presented to an Internet user at the time certain products, such as software, are being downloaded but that need not be agreed to (by clicking "I agree," for example) before the user is able to install or use the product.

burglary ■ The unlawful entry or breaking into a building with the intent to commit a felony (or any crime, in some states).

business ethics ■ Ethics in a business context; a consensus as to what constitutes right or wrong behavior in the world of business and the application of moral principles to situations that arise in a business setting.

business invitee ■ A person, such as a customer or a client, who is invited onto business premises by the owner of those premises for business purposes.

business judgment rule ■ A rule that immunizes corporate management from liability for actions that result in corporate losses or damages if the actions are undertaken in good faith and are within both the power of the corporation and the authority of management to make.

business necessity ■ A defense to allegations of employment discrimination in which the employer demonstrates that an employment practice that discriminates against members of a protected class is related to job performance.

business tort ■ Wrongful interference with another's business rights.

business trust ■ A form of business organization in which investors (trust beneficiaries) transfer cash or property to trustees in exchange for trust certificates that represent their investment shares. The certificate holders share in the trust's profits but have limited liability.

bylaws ■ A set of governing rules adopted by a corporation or other association.

case law ■ The rules of law announced in court decisions. Case law includes the aggregate of reported cases that interpret judicial precedents, statutes, regulations, and constitutional provisions.

cashier's check ■ A check drawn by a bank on itself.

categorical imperative ■ A concept developed by the philosopher Immanuel Kant as an ethical guideline for behavior. In deciding whether an action is right or wrong, or desirable or undesirable, a person should evaluate the action in terms of what would happen if everybody else in the same situation, or category, acted the same way.

causation in fact ■ An act or omission without which an event would not have occurred.

certificate of deposit (CD) ■ A note issued by a bank in which the bank acknowledges the receipt of funds from a party and promises to repay that amount, with interest, to the party on a certain date.

certificate of limited partnership ■ The basic document filed with a designated state official by which a limited partnership is formed.

certification mark ■ A mark used by one or more persons, other than the owner, to certify the region, materials, mode of manufacture, quality, or other characteristic of specific goods or services.

certified check ■ A check that has been accepted in writing by the bank on which it is drawn. Essentially, the bank, by certifying (accepting) the check, promises to pay the check at the time the check is presented.

charitable trust ■ A trust in which the property held by the trustee must be used for a charitable purpose, such as the advancement of health, education, or religion.

chattel ■ All forms of personal property.

check ■ A draft drawn by a drawer ordering the drawee bank or financial institution to pay a certain amount of money to the holder on demand.

choice-of-language clause ■ A clause in a contract designating the official language by which the contract will be interpreted in the event of a future disagreement over the contract's terms.

choice-of-law clause ■ A clause in a contract designating the law (such as the law of a particular state or nation) that will govern the contract.

citation ■ A reference to a publication in which a legal authority—such as a statute or a court decision—or other source can be found.

civil law ■ The branch of law dealing with the definition and enforcement of all private or public rights, as opposed to criminal matters.

civil law system ■ A system of law derived from that of the Roman Empire and based on a code rather than case law; the predominant system of law in the nations of continental Europe and the nations that were once their colonies.

clearinghouse ■ A system or place where banks exchange checks and drafts drawn on each other and settle daily balances.

click-on agreement ■ An agreement that arises when a buyer, engaging in a transaction on a computer, indicates assent to be bound by the terms of an offer by clicking on a button that says, for example, "I agree"; sometimes referred to as a *click-on license* or a *click-wrap agreement*.

close corporation ■ A corporation whose shareholders are limited to a small group of persons, often including only family members.

closed shop ■ A firm that requires union membership by its workers as a condition of employment. The closed shop was made illegal by the Labor-Management Relations Act of 1947.

codicil ■ A written supplement or modification to a will. A codicil must be executed with the same formalities as a will.

collateral ■ Under Article 9 of the UCC, the property subject to a security interest, including accounts and chattel paper that have been sold.

collateral promise ■ A secondary promise that is ancillary (subsidiary) to a principal transaction or primary contractual relationship, such as a promise made by one person to pay the debts of another if the latter fails to perform. A collateral promise normally must be in writing to be enforceable.

collecting bank ■ Any bank handling an item for collection, except the payor bank.

collective mark ■ A mark used by members of a cooperative, association, union, or other organization to certify the region, materials, mode of manufacture, quality, or other characteristic of specific goods or services.

comity ■ The principle by which one nation defers to and gives effect to the laws and judicial decrees of another nation. This recognition is based primarily on respect.

commerce clause ■ The provision in Article I, Section 8, of the U.S. Constitution that gives Congress the power to regulate interstate commerce.

commercial impracticability ■ A doctrine under which a party may be excused from performing a contract when (1) a contingency occurs, (2) the contingency's occurrence makes performance impracticable, and (3) the nonoccurrence of the contingency was a basic assumption on which the contract was made.

commingle ■ To put funds or goods together into one mass so that they are so mixed that they no longer have separate identities. In corporate law, if personal and corporate interests are commingled to the extent that the corporation has no separate identity, a court may "pierce the corporate veil" and expose the shareholders to personal liability.

common law ■ The body of law developed from custom or judicial decisions in English and U.S. courts, not attributable to a legislature.

common stock ■ Shares of ownership in a corporation that give the owner of the stock a proportionate interest in the corporation with regard to control, earnings, and net assets. Shares of common stock are lowest in priority with respect to payment of dividends and distribution of the corporation's assets on dissolution.

community property ■ A form of concurrent ownership of property in which each spouse technically owns an undivided one-half interest in property acquired during the marriage.

comparative negligence ■ A rule followed by most states in tort cases that reduces the plaintiff's recovery in proportion to the plaintiff's degree of fault, rather than barring recovery completely.

compensatory damages ■ A monetary award equivalent to the actual value of injuries or damage sustained by the aggrieved party.

complaint ■ The pleading made by a plaintiff alleging wrongdoing on the part of the defendant; the document that, when filed with a court, initiates a lawsuit.

computer crime ■ Any act that is directed against computers and computer parts, that uses computers as instruments of crime, or that involves computers and constitutes abuse.

concurrent conditions ■ Conditions that must occur or be performed at the same time; they are mutually dependent. No obligations arise until these conditions are simultaneously performed.

concurrent ownership ■ Joint ownership.

condemnation ■ The process of taking private property for public use through the government's power of eminent domain.

condition ■ A qualification, provision, or clause in a contractual agreement, the occurrence or nonoccurrence of which creates, suspends, or terminates the obligations of the contracting parties.

condition precedent ■ In a contractual agreement, a condition that must be met before a party's promise becomes absolute.

condition subsequent ■ A condition in a contract that, if not fulfilled, operates to terminate a party's absolute promise to perform.

confession of judgment ■ The act or agreement of a debtor in permitting a judgment to be entered against him or her by a creditor, for an agreed sum, without the institution of legal proceedings.

confiscation ■ A government's taking of a privately owned business or personal property without a proper public purpose or an award of just compensation.

conforming goods ■ Goods that conform to contract specifications.

confusion ■ The mixing together of goods belonging to two or more owners so that the separately owned goods cannot be identified.

consent ■ Voluntary agreement to a proposition or an act of another; a concurrence of wills.

consequential damages ■ Special damages that compensate for a loss that does not directly or immediately result from the breach (for example, lost profits). For the plaintiff to collect consequential damages, they must have been reasonably foreseeable at the time the breach or injury occurred.

consideration ■ Generally, the value given in return for a promise; involves two elements—the giving of something of legally sufficient value and a bargained-for exchange. The consideration must result in a detriment to the promisee or a benefit to the promisor.

consignment ■ A transaction in which an owner of goods (the consignor) delivers the goods to another (the consignee) for the consignee to sell. The consignee pays the consignor only for the goods that are sold by the consignee.

consolidation ■ A contractual and statutory process in which two or more corporations join to become a completely new corporation. The original corporations cease to exist, and the new corporation acquires all their assets and liabilities.

constitutional law ■ The body of law derived from the U.S. Constitution and the constitutions of the various states.

constructive delivery ■ An act equivalent to the actual, physical delivery of property that cannot be physically delivered because of difficulty or impossibility. For example, the transfer of a key to a safe constructively delivers the contents of the safe.

constructive discharge ■ A termination of employment brought about by making the employee's working conditions so intolerable that the employee reasonably feels compelled to leave.

constructive eviction ■ A form of eviction that occurs when a landlord fails to perform adequately any of the duties (such as providing heat in the winter) required by the lease, thereby making the tenant's further use and enjoyment of the property exceedingly difficult or impossible.

constructive trust ■ An equitable trust that is imposed in the interests of fairness and justice when someone wrongfully holds legal title to property. A court may require the owner to hold the property in trust for the person or persons who should rightfully own the property.

consumer-debtor ■ An individual whose debts are primarily consumer debts (debts for purchases made primarily for personal, family, or household use).

continuation statement ■ A statement that, if filed within six months prior to the expiration date of the original financing statement, continues the perfection of the original security interest for another five years. The perfection of a security interest can be continued in the same manner indefinitely.

contract ■ An agreement that can be enforced in court; formed by two or more competent parties who agree, for consideration, to perform or to refrain from performing some legal act now or in the future.

contractual capacity ■ The threshold mental capacity required by the law for a party who enters into a contract to be bound by that contract.

contributory negligence ■ A rule in tort law that completely bars the plaintiff from recovering any damages if the damage suffered is partly the plaintiff's own fault; used in a minority of states.

conversion ■ Wrongfully taking or retaining possession of an individual's personal property and placing it in the service of another.

conveyance ■ The transfer of title to land from one person to another by deed; a document (such as a deed) by which an interest in land is transferred from one person to another.

"cooling-off" laws ■ Laws that allow buyers a period of time, such as three days, in which to cancel door-to-door sales contracts.

copyright ■ The exclusive right of an author or originator of a literary or artistic production (including computer programs) to publish, print, or sell that production for a statutory period of time.

corporate governance ■ A set of policies or procedures affecting the way a corporation is directed or controlled.

corporate social responsibility ■ The idea that corporations can and should act ethically and be accountable to society for their actions.

corporation ■ A legal entity formed in compliance with statutory requirements that is distinct from its shareholder-owners.

correspondent bank ■ A bank in which another bank has an account (and vice versa) for the purpose of facilitating fund transfers.

cost-benefit analysis ■ A decision-making technique that involves weighing the costs of a given action against the benefits of that action.

co-surety ■ A joint surety; a person who assumes liability jointly with another surety for the payment of an obligation.

counterclaim ■ A claim made by a defendant in a civil lawsuit against the plaintiff. In effect, the defendant is suing the plaintiff.

counteroffer ■ An offeree's response to an offer in which the offeree rejects the original offer and at the same time makes a new offer.

course of dealing ■ Prior conduct between the parties to a contract that establishes a common basis for their understanding.

covenant not to compete ■ A contractual promise of one party to refrain from conducting business similar to that of another party for a certain period of time and within a specified geographic area. Courts commonly enforce such covenants if they are reasonable in terms of time and geographic area and are part of, or supplemental to, a contract for the sale of a business or an employment contract.

covenant not to sue ■ An agreement to substitute a contractual obligation for some other type of legal action based on a valid claim.

cover ■ Under the UCC, a remedy that allows the buyer or lessee, on the seller's or lessor's breach, to purchase goods from another seller or lessor and substitute them for the goods due under the contract. If the cost of cover exceeds the cost of the contract goods, the buyer or lessee can recover the difference, plus incidental and consequential damages.

cram-down provision ■ A provision of the Bankruptcy Code that allows a court to confirm a debtor's Chapter 11 reorganization plan even though only one class of creditors has accepted it.

creditors' composition agreement ■ An agreement formed between a debtor and his or her creditors in which the creditors agree to accept a lesser sum than that owed by the debtor in full satisfaction of the debt.

crime ■ A wrong against society proclaimed in a statute and, if committed, punishable by society through fines and/or imprisonment—and, in some cases, death.

criminal law ■ Law that defines and governs actions that constitute crimes. Generally, criminal law has to do with wrongful actions committed against society for which society demands redress.

cross-collateralization ■ The use of an asset that is not the subject of a loan to collateralize that loan.

cure ■ The right of a party who tenders nonconforming performance to correct that performance within the contract period [UCC 2–508(1)].

cyber crime ■ A crime that occurs online, in the virtual community of the Internet, as opposed to the physical world.

cyber mark ■ A trademark in cyberspace.

cyber tort ■ A tort committed in cyberspace.

cyberlaw ■ An informal term used to refer to all laws governing electronic communications and transactions, particularly those conducted via the Internet.

cybernotary ■ A legally recognized authority that can certify the validity of digital signatures.

cybersquatting ■ The act of registering a domain name that is the same as, or confusingly similar to, the trademark of another and then offering to sell that domain name back to the trademark owner.

cyberterrorist ■ A hacker whose purpose is to exploit a target computer for a serious impact, such as corrupting a program to sabotage a business.

 D

damages ■ Money sought as a remedy for a breach of contract or a tortious action.

debtor ■ Under Article 9 of the UCC, any party who owes payment or performance of a secured obligation, whether or not the party actually owns or has rights in the collateral.

debtor in possession (DIP) ■ In Chapter 11 bankruptcy proceedings, a debtor who is allowed to continue in possession of the estate in property (the business) and to continue business operations.

deed ■ A document by which title to property (usually real property) is passed.

defalcation ■ Embezzlement; the misappropriation of funds by a party, such as a corporate officer or public official, in a fiduciary relationship with another.

defamation ■ Anything published or publicly spoken that causes injury to another's good name, reputation, or character.

default ■ Failure to observe a promise or discharge an obligation; commonly used to refer to failure to pay a debt when it is due.

default judgment ■ A judgment entered by a court against a defendant who has failed to appear in court to answer or defend against the plaintiff's claim.

defendant ■ One against whom a lawsuit is brought; the accused person in a criminal proceeding.

defense ■ A reason offered and alleged by a defendant in an action or suit as to why the plaintiff should not recover or establish what she or he seeks.

deficiency judgment ■ A judgment against a debtor for the amount of a debt remaining unpaid after the collateral has been repossessed and sold.

delegatee ■ A party to whom contractual obligations are transferred, or delegated.

delegation of duties ■ The act of transferring to another all or part of one's duties arising under a contract.

delegator ■ A party who transfers (delegates) her or his obligations under a contract to another party (called the *delegatee*).

depositary bank ■ The first bank to receive a check for payment.

deposition ■ The testimony of a party to a lawsuit or a witness taken under oath before a trial.

destination contract ■ A contract for the sale of goods in which the seller is required or authorized to ship the goods by carrier and tender delivery of the goods at a particular destination. The seller assumes liability for any losses or damage to the goods until they are tendered at the destination specified in the contract.

devise ■ As a noun, a gift of real property by will; as a verb, to make a gift of real property by will.

devisee ■ One designated in a will to receive a gift of real property.

digital cash ■ Funds contained on computer software, in the form of secure programs stored on microchips and on other computer devices.

disaffirmance ■ The legal avoidance, or setting aside, of a contractual obligation.

discharge ■ The termination of an obligation. In contract law, discharge occurs when the parties have fully performed their contractual obligations or when other events occur that release the parties from performance. In bankruptcy proceedings, discharge is the

extinction of the debtor's dischargeable debts, thereby relieving the debtor of the obligation to pay the debts.

disclosed principal ■ A principal whose identity is known to a third party at the time the agent makes a contract with the third party.

discovery ■ A phase in the litigation process during which the opposing parties may obtain information from each other and from third parties prior to trial.

dishonor ■ A negotiable instrument is dishonored when payment or acceptance of the instrument, whichever is required, is refused even though the instrument is presented in a timely and proper manner.

disparagement of property ■ An economically injurious falsehood made about another's product or property; a general term for torts that are more specifically referred to as slander of quality or slander of title.

disparate-impact discrimination ■ A form of employment discrimination that results from certain employer practices or procedures that, although not discriminatory on their face, have a discriminatory effect.

disparate-treatment discrimination ■ A form of employment discrimination that results when an employer intentionally discriminates against employees who are members of protected classes.

dissociation ■ The severance of the relationship between a partner and a partnership when the partner ceases to be associated with the carrying on of the partnership business.

dissolution ■ The formal disbanding of a partnership or a corporation. It can take place by (1) acts of the partners or, in a corporation, acts of the shareholders and board of directors; (2) the subsequent illegality of the firm's business; (3) the expiration of a time period stated in a partnership agreement or a certificate of incorporation; or (4) judicial decree.

distributed network ■ A network that can be used by persons located (distributed) around the country or the globe to share computer files.

distribution agreement ■ A contract between a seller and a distributor of the seller's products setting out the terms and conditions of the distributorship.

diversity of citizenship ■ Under Article III, Section 2, of the U.S. Constitution, a basis for federal district court jurisdiction over a lawsuit between (1) citizens of different states, (2) a foreign country and citizens of a state or of different states, or (3) citizens of a state.

dividend ■ A distribution to corporate shareholders of corporate profits or income, disbursed in proportion to the number of shares held.

docket ■ The list of cases entered on a court's calendar and thus scheduled to be heard by the court.

document of title ■ A paper exchanged in the regular course of business that evidences the right to possession of goods (for example, a bill of lading or a warehouse receipt).

domain name ■ The last part of an Internet address, such as "westlaw.edu." The top level (the part of the name to the right of the period) indicates the type of entity that operates the site ("edu" is an abbreviation for "educational"). The second level (the part of the name to the left of the period) is chosen by the entity.

domestic corporation ■ In a given state, a corporation that does business in, and is organized under the law of, that state.

dominion ■ Ownership rights in property, including the right to possess and control the property.

double jeopardy ■ A situation occurring when a person is tried twice for the same criminal offense; prohibited by the Fifth Amendment to the Constitution.

draft ■ Any instrument drawn on a drawee that orders the drawee to pay a certain sum of money, usually to a third party (the payee), on demand or at a definite future time.

dram shop act ■ A state statute that imposes liability on the owners of bars and taverns, as well as those who serve alcoholic drinks to the public, for injuries resulting from accidents caused by intoxicated persons when the sellers or servers of alcoholic drinks contributed to the intoxication.

drawee ■ The party that is ordered to pay a draft or check. With a check, a bank or a financial institution is always the drawee.

drawer ■ The party that initiates a draft (such as a check), thereby ordering the drawee to pay.

due diligence ■ A required standard of care that certain professionals, such as accountants, must meet to avoid liability for securities violations.

due process clause ■ The provisions in the Fifth and Fourteenth Amendments to the Constitution that guarantee that no person shall be deprived of life, liberty, or property without due process of law. Similar clauses are found in most state constitutions.

dumping ■ The selling of goods in a foreign country at a price below the price charged for the same goods in the domestic market.

duress ■ Unlawful pressure brought to bear on a person, causing the person to perform an act that she or he would not otherwise perform.

duty of care ■ The duty of all persons, as established by tort law, to exercise a reasonable amount of care in their dealings with others. Failure to exercise due care, which is normally determined by the reasonable person standard, constitutes the tort of negligence.

E

e-agent ■ A computer program that by electronic or other automated means can independently initiate an action or respond to electronic messages or data without review by an individual.

easement ■ A nonpossessory right to use another's property in a manner established by either express or implied agreement.

e-contract ■ A contract that is formed electronically.

e-evidence ■ Evidence that consists of computer-generated or electronically recorded information, including e-mail, voice mail, spreadsheets, word-processing documents, and other data.

electronic fund transfer (EFT) ■ A transfer of funds with the use of an electronic terminal, a telephone, a computer, or magnetic tape.

emancipation ■ In regard to minors, the act of being freed from parental control; occurs when a child's parent or legal guardian relinquishes the legal right to exercise control over the child or when a minor leaves home to support himself or herself.

embezzlement ■ The fraudulent appropriation of funds or other property by a person to whom the funds or property has been entrusted.

eminent domain ■ The power of a government to take land from private citizens for public use on the payment of just compensation.

e-money ■ Prepaid funds recorded on a computer or a card (such as a smart card or a stored-value card).

employment at will ■ A common law doctrine under which either party may terminate an employment relationship at any time for any reason, unless a contract specifies otherwise.

employment contract ■ A contract between an employer and an employee in which the terms and conditions of employment are stated.

employment discrimination ■ Treating employees or job applicants unequally on the basis of race, color, national origin, religion, gender, age, or disability; prohibited by federal statutes.

enabling legislation ■ A statute enacted by Congress that authorizes the creation of an administrative agency and specifies the name, composition, purpose, and powers of the agency being created.

entrapment ■ In criminal law, a defense in which the defendant claims that he or she was induced by a public official—usually an undercover agent or police officer—to commit a crime that he or she would otherwise not have committed.

entrepreneur ■ One who initiates and assumes the financial risk of a new business enterprise and undertakes to provide or control its management.

entrustment rule ■ The transfer of goods to a merchant who deals in goods of that kind and who may transfer those goods and all rights to them to a buyer in the ordinary course of business [UCC 2–403(2)].

e-signature ■ As defined by the Uniform Electronic Transactions Act, "an electronic sound, symbol, or process attached to or logically associated with a record and executed or adopted by a person with the intent to sign the record."

establishment clause ■ The provision in the First Amendment to the Constitution that prohibits the government from establishing any state-sponsored religion or enacting any law that promotes religion or favors one religion over another.

estate in property ■ In bankruptcy proceedings, all of the debtor's interests in property currently held, wherever located, together with certain jointly owned property, property transferred in transactions voidable by the trustee, proceeds and profits from the property of the estate, and certain property interests to which the debtor becomes entitled within 180 days after filing for bankruptcy.

estopped ■ Barred, impeded, or precluded.

estray statute ■ A statute defining finders' rights in property when the true owners are unknown.

ethical reasoning ■ A reasoning process in which an individual links his or her moral convictions or ethical standards to the particular situation at hand.

ethics ■ Moral principles and values applied to social behavior.

eviction ■ A landlord's act of depriving a tenant of possession of the leased premises.

exclusionary rule ■ In criminal procedure, a rule under which any evidence that is obtained in violation of the accused's constitutional rights guaranteed by the Fourth, Fifth, and Sixth Amendments, as well as any evidence derived from illegally obtained evidence, will not be admissible in court.

exclusive distributorship ■ A distributorship in which the seller and the distributor of the seller's products agree that the distributor will distribute only the seller's products.

exclusive jurisdiction ■ Jurisdiction that exists when a case can be heard only in a particular court or type of court.

exculpatory clause ■ A clause that releases a contractual party from liability in the event of monetary or physical injury, no matter who is at fault.

executed contract ■ A contract that has been completely performed by both parties.

execution ■ An action to carry into effect the directions in a court decree or judgment.

executive agency ■ An administrative agency within the executive branch of government. At the federal level, executive agencies are those within the cabinet departments.

executor ■ A person appointed by a testator in a will to see that her or his will is administered appropriately.

executory contract ■ A contract that has not as yet been fully performed.

export ■ The goods and services that domestic firms sell to buyers located in other countries.

express contract ■ A contract in which the terms of the agreement are stated in words, oral or written.

express warranty ■ A seller's or lessor's oral or written promise or affirmation of fact, ancillary to an underlying sales or lease agreement, as to the quality, description, or performance of the goods being sold or leased.

expropriation ■ The seizure by a government of a privately owned business or personal property for a proper public purpose and with just compensation.

extension clause ■ A clause in a time instrument that allows the instrument's date of maturity to be extended into the future.

F

family limited liability partnership (FLLP) ■ A type of limited liability partnership owned by family members or fiduciaries of family members.

federal question ■ A question that pertains to the U.S. Constitution, acts of Congress, or treaties. A federal question provides a basis for federal jurisdiction.

Federal Reserve System ■ A network of twelve district banks and related branches located around the country and headed by the Federal Reserve Board of Governors. Most banks in the United States have Federal Reserve accounts.

fee simple ■ An absolute form of property ownership entitling the property owner to use, possess, or dispose of the property as he or she chooses during his or her lifetime. On death, the interest in the property descends to the owner's heirs.

fee simple absolute ■ An ownership interest in land in which the owner has the greatest possible aggregation of rights, privileges, and power. Ownership in fee simple absolute is limited absolutely to a person and her or his heirs.

felony ■ A crime—such as arson, murder, rape, or robbery—that carries the most severe sanctions, ranging from one year in a state or federal prison to the death penalty.

fictitious payee ■ A payee on a negotiable instrument whom the maker or drawer does not intend to have an interest in the instrument. Indorsements by fictitious payees are treated as authorized indorsements under Article 3 of the UCC.

fiduciary ■ As a noun, a person having a duty created by his or her undertaking to act primarily for another's benefit in matters connected with the undertaking. As an adjective, a relationship founded on trust and confidence.

filtering software ■ A computer program that is designed to block access to certain Web sites based on their content. The software blocks the retrieval of a site whose URL or key words are on a list within the program.

financing statement ■ A document prepared by a secured creditor and filed with the appropriate state or local official, to give notice to the public that the creditor has a security interest in collateral belonging to the debtor named in the statement. Financing statement's must contain the names and addresses of both the debtor and the secured party and must describe the collateral.

firm offer ■ An offer (by a merchant) that is irrevocable without the necessity of consideration for a stated period of time or, if no definite period is stated, for a reasonable time (neither period to exceed three months). A firm offer by a merchant must be in writing and must be signed by the offeror.

fixed-term tenancy ■ A type of tenancy under which property is leased for a specified period of time, such as a month, a year, or a period of years; also called a *tenancy for years*.

fixture ■ A thing that was once personal property but has become attached to real property in such a way that it takes on the characteristics of real property and becomes part of that real property.

floating lien ■ A security interest in proceeds, after-acquired property, or collateral subject to future advances by the secured party (or all three); a security interest in collateral that is retained even when the collateral changes in character, classification, or location.

forbearance ■ The act of refraining from an action that one has a legal right to undertake.

***force majeure* clause** ■ A provision in a contract stipulating that certain unforeseen events—such as war, political upheavals, or acts of God—will excuse a party from liability for nonperformance of contractual obligations.

foreign corporation ■ In a given state, a corporation that does business in the state without being incorporated therein.

foreign exchange market ■ A worldwide system in which foreign currencies are bought and sold.

forgery ■ The fraudulent making or altering of any writing in a way that changes the legal rights and liabilities of another.

formal contract ■ A contract that by law requires a specific form, such as being executed under seal, for its validity.

forum-selection clause ■ A provision in a contract designating the court, jurisdiction, or tribunal that will decide any disputes arising under the contract.

franchise ■ Any arrangement in which the owner of a trademark, trade name, or copyright licenses another to use that trademark, trade name, or copyright in the selling of goods or services.

franchisee ■ One receiving a license to use another's (the franchisor's) trademark, trade name, or copyright in the sale of goods and services.

franchisor ■ One licensing another (the franchisee) to use the owner's trademark, trade name, or copyright in the selling of goods or services.

fraudulent misrepresentation ■ Any misrepresentation, either by misstatement or by omission of a material fact, knowingly made with the intention of deceiving another and on which a reasonable person would and does rely to his or her detriment.

free exercise clause ■ The provision in the First Amendment to the Constitution that prohibits the government from interfering with people's religious practices or forms of worship.

free-writing prospectus ■ Any type of written, electronic, or graphic offer that describes the issuing corporation or its securities and includes a legend indicating that the investor may obtain the prospectus at the SEC's Web site.

frustration of purpose ■ A court-created doctrine under which a party to a contract will be relieved of her or his duty to perform when the objective purpose for performance no longer exists (due to reasons beyond that party's control).

fungible goods ■ Goods that are alike by physical nature, by agreement, or by trade usage (for example, wheat, oil, and wine that are identical in type and quality). When owners of fungible goods hold the goods as tenants in common, title and risk can pass without actually separating the goods being sold from the mass of fungible goods.

garnishment ■ A legal process used by a creditor to collect a debt by seizing property of the debtor (such as wages) that is being held by a third party (such as the debtor's employer).

general partner ■ In a limited partnership, a partner who assumes responsibility for the management of the partnership and liability for all partnership debts.

generally accepted accounting principles (GAAP) ■ The conventions, rules, and procedures that define accepted accounting practices at a particular time. The source of the principles is the Financial Accounting Standards Board.

generally accepted auditing standards (GAAS) ■ Standards concerning an auditor's professional qualities and the judgment exercised by him or her in the performance of an audit and report. The source of the standards is the American Institute of Certified Public Accountants.

gift ■ Any voluntary transfer of property made without consideration, past or present.

gift *causa mortis* ■ A gift made in contemplation of death. If the donor does not die of that ailment, the gift is revoked.

gift *inter vivos* ■ A gift made during one's lifetime and not in contemplation of imminent death, in contrast to a gift *causa mortis*.

good faith purchaser ■ A purchaser who buys without notice of any circumstance that would cause a person of ordinary prudence to inquire as to whether the seller has valid title to the goods being sold.

good Samaritan statute ■ A state statute stipulating that persons who provide emergency services to, or rescue, someone in peril cannot be sued for negligence, unless they act recklessly, thereby causing further harm.

grand jury ■ A group of citizens called to decide, after hearing the state's evidence, whether a reasonable basis (probable cause) exists for believing that a crime has been committed and that a trial ought to be held.

guarantor ■ A person who agrees to satisfy the debt of another (the debtor) only after the principal debtor defaults. Thus, a guarantor's liability is secondary.

H

hacker ■ A person who uses one computer to break into another. Professional computer programmers refer to such persons as "crackers."

holder ■ Any person in possession of an instrument drawn, issued, or indorsed to him or her, to his or her order, to bearer, or in blank.

holder in due course (HDC) ■ A holder who acquires a negotiable instrument for value; in good faith; and without notice that the instrument is overdue, that it has been dishonored, that any person has a defense against it or a claim to it, or that the instrument contains unauthorized signatures, has been altered, or is so irregular or incomplete as to call into question its authenticity.

holding company ■ A company whose business activity is holding shares in another company.

holographic will ■ A will written entirely in the signer's handwriting and usually not witnessed.

homestead exemption ■ A law permitting a debtor to retain the family home, either in its entirety or up to a specified dollar amount, free from the claims of unsecured creditors or trustees in bankruptcy.

hot-cargo agreement ■ An agreement in which employers voluntarily agree with unions not to handle, use, or deal in other employers' goods that were not produced by union employees; a type of secondary boycott explicitly prohibited by the Labor-Management Reporting and Disclosure Act of 1959.

I-9 verification ■ All employers must verify the employment eligibility and identity of any worker hired in the United States. To comply with the law, employers must complete an I-9 Employment Eligibility Verification Form for all new hires within three business days.

I-551 Alien Registration Receipt ■ A document that provides proof that a foreign-born individual is lawfully admitted for permanent residence in the United States; commonly referred to as a "green card." Persons seeking employment can prove to prospective employers that they are legally within the U.S. by showing this receipt.

identification ■ In a sale of goods, the express designation of the goods provided for in the contract.

identity theft ■ The act of stealing another's identifying information—such as a name, date of birth, or Social Security number—and using that information to access the victim's financial resources.

implied warranty ■ A warranty that arises by law because of the circumstances of a sale, rather than by the seller's express promise.

implied warranty of fitness for a particular purpose ■ A warranty that goods sold or leased are fit for a particular purpose. The warranty arises when any seller or lessor knows the particular purpose for which a buyer or lessee will use the goods and knows that the buyer or lessee is relying on the skill and judgment of the seller or lessor to select suitable goods.

implied warranty of habitability ■ An implied promise by a landlord that rented residential premises are fit for human habitation—that is, in a condition that is safe and suitable for people to live there.

implied warranty of merchantability ■ A warranty that goods being sold or leased are reasonably fit for the general purpose for which they are sold or leased, are properly packaged and labeled, and are of proper quality. The warranty automatically arises in every sale or lease of goods made by a merchant who deals in goods of the kind sold or leased.

implied-in-fact contract ■ A contract formed in whole or in part from the conduct of the parties (as opposed to an express contract).

impossibility of performance ■ A doctrine under which a party to a contract is relieved of her or his duty to perform when performance becomes objectively impossible or totally impracticable (through no fault of either party).

imposter ■ One who, by use of the mails, Internet, telephone, or personal appearance, induces a maker or drawer to issue an instrument in the name of an impersonated payee. Indorsements by imposters are treated as authorized indorsements under Article 3 of the UCC.

incidental beneficiary ■ A third party who incidentally benefits from a contract but whose benefit was not the reason the contract was formed. An incidental beneficiary has no rights in a contract and cannot sue to have the contract enforced.

incidental damages ■ Damages awarded to compensate for reasonable expenses that are directly incurred because of a breach of contract—such as the cost of obtaining performance from another source.

independent contractor ■ One who works for, and receives payment from, an employer but whose working conditions and methods are not controlled by the employer. An independent contractor is not an employee but may be an agent.

independent regulatory agency ■ An administrative agency that is not considered part of the government's executive branch and is not subject to the authority of the president. Independent agency officials cannot be removed without cause.

indictment ■ A charge by a grand jury that a named person has committed a crime.

indorsee ■ The person to whom a negotiable instrument is transferred by indorsement.

indorsement ■ A signature placed on an instrument for the purpose of transferring one's ownership rights in the instrument.

indorser ■ A person who transfers an instrument by signing (indorsing) it and delivering it to another person.

informal contract ■ A contract that does not require a specified form or formality to be valid.

information ■ A formal accusation or complaint (without an indictment) issued in certain types of actions (usually criminal actions involving lesser crimes) by a government prosecutor.

information return ■ A tax return submitted by a partnership that only reports the income and losses earned by the business. The partnership as an entity does not pay taxes on the income received by the partnership. A partner's profit from the partnership (whether distributed or not) is taxed as individual income to the individual partner.

inside director ■ A person on the board of directors who is also an officer of the corporation.

insider trading ■ The purchase or sale of securities on the basis of *inside information* (information that has not been made available to the public).

insolvent ■ Under the UCC, a term describing a person who ceases to pay "his [or her] debts in the ordinary course of business or cannot pay his [or her] debts as they become due or is insolvent within the meaning of federal bankruptcy law" [UCC 1–201(23)].

installment contract ■ Under the UCC, a contract that requires or authorizes delivery in two or more separate lots to be accepted and paid for separately.

insurable interest ■ In regard to the sale or lease of goods, a property interest in the goods that is sufficiently substantial to permit a party to insure against damage to the goods. In the context of insurance, an interest either in a person's life or well-being that is sufficiently substantial to justify insuring against injury to (or death of) the person.

insurance ■ A contract in which, for a stipulated consideration, one party agrees to compensate the other for loss on a specific subject by a specified peril.

intangible property ■ Property that cannot be seen or touched but exists only conceptually, such as corporate stocks and bonds, patents and copyrights, and ordinary contract rights. Article 2 of the UCC does not govern intangible property.

intellectual property ■ Property resulting from intellectual, creative processes.

intended beneficiary ■ A third party for whose benefit a contract is formed. An intended beneficiary can sue the promisor if such a contract is breached.

intentional tort ■ A wrongful act knowingly committed.

inter vivos **trust** ■ A trust created by the grantor (settlor) and effective during the grantor's lifetime; a trust not established by a will.

intermediary bank ■ Any bank to which an item is transferred in the course of collection, except the depositary or payor bank.

international law ■ The law that governs relations among nations. National laws, customs, treaties, and international conferences and organizations are generally considered to be the most important sources of international law.

international organization ■ In international law, a term that generally refers to an organization composed mainly of nations and usually established by treaty. The United States is a member of more than one hundred multilateral and bilateral organizations, including at least twenty through the United Nations.

interrogatories ■ A series of written questions for which written answers are prepared by a party to a lawsuit, usually with the assistance of the party's attorney, and then signed under oath.

intestacy laws ■ State statutes that specify how property will be distributed when a person dies intestate (without a valid will); also called *statutes of descent and distribution.*

intestate ■ As a noun, one who has died without having created a valid will; as an adjective, the state of having died without a will.

investment company ■ A company that acts on behalf of many smaller shareholders/owners by buying a large portfolio of securities and professionally managing that portfolio.

investment contract ■ In securities law, a transaction in which a person invests in a common enterprise reasonably expecting profits that are derived primarily from the efforts of others.

J

joint and several liability ■ In partnership law, a doctrine under which a plaintiff may sue, and collect a judgment from, all of the partners together (jointly) or one or more of the partners separately (severally, or individually). This is true even if one of the partners sued did not participate in, ratify, or know about whatever it was that gave rise to the cause of action.

joint tenancy ■ The joint ownership of property by two or more co-owners in which each co-owner owns an undivided portion of the property. On the death of one of the joint tenants, his or her interest automatically passes to the surviving joint tenant(s).

judicial review ■ The process by which a court decides on the constitutionality of legislative enactments and actions of the executive branch.

junior lienholder ■ A party that holds a lien that is subordinate to one or more other liens on the same property.

jurisdiction ■ The authority of a court to hear and decide a specific case.

jurisprudence ■ The science or philosophy of law.

justiciable controversy ■ A controversy that is not hypothetical or academic but real and substantial; a requirement that must be satisfied before a court will hear a case.

L

larceny ■ The wrongful taking and carrying away of another person's personal property with the intent to permanently deprive the owner of the property. Some states classify larceny as either grand or petit, depending on the property's value.

law ■ A body of enforceable rules governing relationships among individuals and between individuals and their society.

lease ■ Under Article 2A of the UCC, a transfer of the right to possess and use goods for a period of time in exchange for payment.

lease agreement ■ In regard to the lease of goods, an agreement in which one person (the lessor) agrees to transfer the right to the possession and use of property to another person (the lessee) in exchange for rental payments.

leasehold estate ■ An estate in realty held by a tenant under a lease. In every leasehold estate, the tenant has a qualified right to possess and/or use the land.

legacy ■ A gift of personal property under a will.

legatee ■ One designated in a will to receive a gift of personal property.

lessee ■ A person who acquires the right to the possession and use of another's goods in exchange for rental payments.

lessor ■ A person who transfers the right to the possession and use of goods to another in exchange for rental payments.

letter of credit ■ A written instrument, usually issued by a bank on behalf of a customer or other person, in which the issuer promises to honor drafts or other demands for payment by third persons in accordance with the terms of the instrument.

levy ■ The obtaining of funds by legal process through the seizure and sale of nonsecured property, usually done after a writ of execution has been issued.

libel ■ Defamation in writing or other form having the quality of permanence (such as a digital recording).

license ■ A revocable right or privilege of a person to come onto another person's land. In the context of intellectual property law, an agreement permitting the use of a trademark, copyright, patent, or trade secret for certain limited purposes.

lien ■ An encumbrance on a property to satisfy a debt or protect a claim for payment of a debt.

life estate ■ An interest in land that exists only for the duration of the life of some person, usually the holder of the estate.

limited liability company (LLC) ■ A hybrid form of business enterprise that offers the limited liability of a corporation and the tax advantages of a partnership.

limited liability limited partnership (LLLP) ■ A type of limited partnership in which the liability of all of the partners, including general partners, is limited to the amount of their investments.

limited liability partnership (LLP) ■ A hybrid form of business organization that is used mainly by professionals who normally do business in a partnership. Like a partnership, an LLP is a pass-through entity for tax purposes, but the personal liability of the partners is limited.

limited partner ■ In a limited partnership, a partner who contributes capital to the partnership but has no right to participate in the management and operation of the business. The limited partner assumes no liability for partnership debts beyond the capital contributed.

limited partnership ■ A partnership consisting of one or more general partners (who manage the business and are liable to the full extent of their personal assets for debts of the partnership) and one or more limited partners (who contribute only assets and are liable only up to the extent of their contributions).

liquidated damages ■ An amount, stipulated in a contract, that the parties to the contract believe to be a reasonable estimation of the damages that will occur in the event of a breach.

liquidated debt ■ A debt for which the amount has been ascertained, fixed, agreed on, settled, or exactly determined. If the amount of the debt is in dispute, the debt is considered unliquidated.

liquidation ■ The sale of all of the nonexempt assets of a debtor and the distribution of the proceeds to the debtor's creditors. Chapter 7 of the Bankruptcy Code provides for liquidation bankruptcy proceedings.

litigation ■ The process of resolving a dispute through the court system.

long arm statute ■ A state statute that permits a state to obtain personal jurisdiction over nonresident defendants. A defendant must have certain "minimum contacts" with that state for the statute to apply.

lost property ■ Property with which the owner has involuntarily parted and then cannot find or recover.

M

mailbox rule ■ A rule providing that an acceptance of an offer becomes effective on dispatch (on being placed in an official mailbox), if mail is, expressly or impliedly, an authorized means of communication of acceptance to the offeror.

maker ■ One who promises to pay a fixed amount of money to the holder of a promissory note or a certificate of deposit (CD).

malpractice ■ Professional misconduct or unreasonable lack of skill. The failure of a professional to use the degree of care common to the average reputable members of the profession or to apply the skills and learning the professional claims to possess, resulting in injury, loss, or damage to those relying on the professional.

market-share liability ■ A theory of sharing liability among all firms that manufactured and distributed a particular product during a certain period of time. This form of liability sharing is used only in some jurisdictions and only when the true source of the harmful product in unidentifiable.

mechanic's lien ■ A statutory lien on the real property of another, created to ensure payment for work performed and materials furnished in the repair or improvement of real property, such as a building.

mediation ■ A method of settling disputes outside of court by using the services of a neutral third party, who acts as a communicating agent between the parties and assists them in negotiating a settlement.

member ■ The term used to designate a person who has an ownership interest in a limited liability company.

mens rea ■ Mental state, or intent. A wrongful mental state is as necessary as a wrongful act to establish criminal liability. What constitutes a mental state varies according to the wrongful action. Thus, for murder, the *mens rea* is the intent to take a life.

merchant ■ A person who is engaged in the purchase and sale of goods. Under the UCC, a person who deals in goods of the kind involved in the sales contract or who holds herself or himself out as having skill or knowledge peculiar to the practices or goods being purchased or sold [UCC 2–104].

merger ■ A contractual and statutory process in which one corporation (the surviving corporation) acquires all of the assets and liabilities of another corporation (the merged corporation). The shareholders of the merged corporation either are paid for their shares or receive shares in the surviving corporation.

meta tag ■ A key word in a document that can serve as an index reference to the document. On the Web, search engines return results based, in part, on the tags in Web documents.

minimum wage ■ The lowest wage, either by government regulation or union contract, that an employer may pay an hourly worker.

mirror image rule ■ A common law rule that requires that the terms of the offeree's acceptance adhere exactly to the terms of the offeror's offer for a valid contract to be formed.

misdemeanor ■ A lesser crime than a felony, punishable by a fine or incarceration in jail for up to one year.

mislaid property ■ Property with which the owner has voluntarily parted and then cannot find or recover.

mitigation of damages ■ A rule requiring a plaintiff to do whatever is reasonable to minimize the damages caused by the defendant.

money laundering ■ Falsely reporting income that has been obtained through criminal activity as income obtained through a legitimate business enterprise—in effect, "laundering" the "dirty money."

moral minimum ■ The minimum degree of ethical behavior expected of a business firm, which is usually defined as compliance with the law.

mortgage ■ A written instrument giving a creditor an interest in (lien on) the debtor's real property as security for payment of a debt.

mortgagee ■ Under a mortgage agreement, the creditor who takes a security interest in the debtor's property.

mortgagor ■ Under a mortgage agreement, the debtor who gives the creditor a security interest in the debtor's property in return for a mortgage loan.

motion for a directed verdict ■ In a jury trial, a motion for the judge to take the decision out of the hands of the jury and to direct a verdict for the party who filed the motion on the ground that the other party has not produced sufficient evidence to support her or his claim.

motion for a new trial ■ A motion asserting that the trial was so fundamentally flawed (because of error, newly discovered evidence, prejudice, or another reason) that a new trial is necessary to prevent a miscarriage of justice.

motion for judgment *n.o.v.* ■ A motion requesting the court to grant judgment in favor of the party making the motion on the ground that the jury's verdict against him or her was unreasonable and erroneous.

motion for judgment on the pleadings ■ A motion by either party to a lawsuit at the close of the pleadings requesting the court to decide the issue solely on the pleadings without proceeding to trial. The motion will be granted only if no facts are in dispute.

motion for summary judgment ■ A motion requesting the court to enter a judgment without proceeding to trial. The motion can be based on evidence outside the pleadings and will be granted only if no facts are in dispute.

motion to dismiss ■ A pleading in which a defendant asserts that the plaintiff's claim fails to state a cause of action (that is, has no basis in law) or that there are other grounds on which a suit should be dismissed. Although the defendant normally is the party requesting a dismissal, either the plaintiff or the court can also make a motion to dismiss the case.

mutual fund ■ A specific type of investment company that continually buys or sells to investors shares of ownership in a portfolio.

N

national law ■ Law that pertains to a particular nation (as opposed to international law).

necessaries ■ Necessities required for life, such as food, shelter, clothing, and medical attention; may include whatever is believed to be necessary to maintain a person's standard of living or financial and social status.

negligence ■ The failure to exercise the standard of care that a reasonable person would exercise in similar circumstances.

negligence *per se* ■ An action or failure to act in violation of a statutory requirement.

negotiable instrument ■ A signed writing (record) that contains an unconditional promise or order to pay an exact sum on demand or at an exact future time to a specific person or order, or to bearer.

negotiation ■ A process in which parties attempt to settle their dispute informally, with or without attorneys to represent them. In the context of negotiable instruments, the transfer of an instrument in such form that the transferee (the person to whom the instrument is transferred) becomes a holder.

nominal damages ■ A small monetary award (often one dollar) granted to a plaintiff when no actual damage was suffered.

nonpossessory interest ■ In the context of real property, an interest in land that does not include any right to possess the property.

normal trade relations (NTR) status ■ A status granted in an international treaty by a provision stating that the citizens of the contracting nations may enjoy the privileges accorded by either party to citizens of its NTR nations. Generally, this status is designed to establish equality of international treatment.

notary public ■ A public official authorized to attest to the authenticity of signatures.

novation ■ The substitution, by agreement, of a new contract for an old one, with the rights under the old one being terminated. Typically, novation involves the substitution of a new person who is responsible for the contract and the removal of an original party's rights and duties under the contract.

nuncupative will ■ An oral will (often called a *deathbed will*) made before witnesses; usually limited to transfers of personal property.

O

objective theory of contracts ■ A theory under which the intent to form a contract will be judged by outward, objective facts (what the party said when entering into the contract, how the party acted or appeared, and the circumstances surrounding the transaction) as interpreted by a reasonable person, rather than by the party's own secret, subjective intentions.

obligee ■ One to whom an obligation is owed.

obligor ■ One who owes an obligation to another.

offer ■ A promise or commitment to perform or refrain from performing some specified act in the future.

offeree ■ A person to whom an offer is made.

offeror ■ A person who makes an offer.

online dispute resolution (ODR) ■ The resolution of disputes with the assistance of organizations that offer dispute-resolution services via the Internet.

operating agreement ■ In a limited liability company, an agreement in which the members set forth the details of how the business will be managed and operated. State statutes typically give the members wide latitude in deciding for themselves the rules that will govern their organization.

option contract ■ A contract under which the offeror cannot revoke the offer for a stipulated time period. During this period, the offeree can accept or reject the offer without fear that the offer will be made to another person. The offeree must give consideration for the option (the irrevocable offer) to be enforceable.

order for relief ■ A court's grant of assistance to a complainant. In bankruptcy proceedings, the order relieves the debtor of the immediate obligation to pay the debts listed in the bankruptcy petition.

order instrument ■ A negotiable instrument that is payable "to the order of an identified person" or "to an identified person or order."

ordinance ■ A regulation enacted by a city or county legislative body that becomes part of that state's statutory law.

output contract ■ An agreement in which a seller agrees to sell and a buyer agrees to buy all or up to a stated amount of what the seller produces.

outside director ■ A person on the board of directors who does not hold a management position at the corporation.

overdraft ■ A check that is paid by the bank when the checking account on which the check is written contains insufficient funds to cover the check.

P

parol evidence rule ■ A rule under which a court will not receive into evidence the parties' prior negotiations, prior agreements, or contemporaneous oral agreements if that evidence contradicts or varies the terms of the parties' written contract.

parent-subsidiary merger ■ A merger of companies in which one company (the parent corporation) owns most of the stock of the other (the subsidiary corporation). A parent-subsidiary merger (short-form merger) can use a simplified procedure when the parent corporation owns at least 90 percent of the outstanding shares of each class of stock of the subsidiary corporation.

partially disclosed principal ■ A principal whose identity is unknown by a third party, but the third party knows that the agent is or may be acting for a principal at the time the agent and the third party form a contract.

partnering agreement ■ An agreement between a seller and a buyer who frequently do business with each other concerning the terms and conditions that will apply to all subsequently formed electronic contracts.

partnership ■ An agreement by two or more persons to carry on, as co-owners, a business for profit.

pass-through entity ■ A business entity that has no tax liability. The entity's income is passed through to the owners, and the owners pay taxes on the income.

past consideration ■ An act that takes place before the contract is made and that ordinarily, by itself, cannot be consideration for a later promise to pay for the act.

patent ■ A government grant that gives an inventor the exclusive right or privilege to make, use, or sell his or her invention for a limited time period.

payee ■ A person to whom an instrument is made payable.

payor bank ■ The bank on which a check is drawn (the drawee bank).

peer-to-peer (P2P) networking ■ The sharing of resources (such as files, hard drives, and processing styles) among multiple computers without necessarily requiring a central network server.

penalty ■ A contractual clause that states that a certain amount of monetary damages will be paid in the event of a future default or breach of contract. The damages are a punishment for a default and not a measure of compensation for the contract's breach. The agreement as to the penalty amount will not be enforced, and recovery will be limited to actual damages.

per capita ■ A Latin term meaning "per person." In the law governing estate distribution, a method of distributing the property of an intestate's estate so that each heir in a certain class (such as grandchildren) receives an equal share.

per stirpes ■ A Latin term meaning "by the roots." In estate law, a method of distributing an intestate's estate so that each heir in a certain class (such as grandchildren) takes the share to which her or his deceased ancestor (such as a mother or father) would have been entitled.

perfection ■ The legal process by which secured parties protect themselves against the claims of third parties who may wish to have their debts satisfied out of the same collateral; usually accomplished by filing a financing statement with the appropriate government official.

performance ■ In contract law, the fulfillment of one's duties arising under a contract with another; the normal way of discharging one's contractual obligations.

periodic tenancy ■ A lease interest in land for an indefinite period involving payment of rent at fixed intervals, such as week to week, month to month, or year to year.

personal defenses ■ Defenses that can be used to avoid payment to an ordinary holder of a negotiable instrument but not a holder in due course (HDC) or a holder with the rights of an HDC.

personal property ■ Property that is movable; any property that is not real property.

persuasive authority ■ Any legal authority or source of law that a court may look to for guidance but on which it need not rely in making its decision. Persuasive authorities include cases from other jurisdictions and secondary sources of law.

petition in bankruptcy ■ The document that is filed with a bankruptcy court to initiate bankruptcy proceedings. The official forms required for a petition in bankruptcy must be completed accurately, sworn to under oath, and signed by the debtor.

petty offense ■ In criminal law, the least serious kind of criminal offense, such as a traffic or building-code violation.

piercing the corporate veil ■ An action in which a court disregards the corporate entity and holds the shareholders personally liable for corporate debts and obligations. ■

plaintiff ■ One who initiates a lawsuit.

plea bargaining ■ The process by which a criminal defendant and the prosecutor in a criminal case work out a mutually satisfactory disposition of the case, subject to court approval; usually involves the defendant's pleading guilty to a lesser offense in return for a lighter sentence.

pleadings ■ Statements made by the plaintiff and the defendant in a lawsuit that detail the facts, charges, and defenses involved in the litigation. The complaint and answer are part of the pleadings.

pledge ■ A common law security device (retained in Article 9 of the UCC) in which personal property is transferred into the possession of the creditor as security for the payment of a debt and retained by the creditor until the debt is paid.

policy ■ In insurance law, a contract between the insurer and the insured in which, for a stipulated consideration, the insurer agrees to compensate the insured for loss on a specific subject by a specified peril.

power of attorney ■ A written document, which is usually notarized, authorizing another to act as one's agent; can be special (permitting the agent to do specified acts only) or general (permitting the agent to transact all business for the principal).

precedent ■ A court decision that furnishes an example or authority for deciding subsequent cases involving identical or similar facts.

predatory behavior ■ Business behavior that is undertaken with the intention of unlawfully driving competitors out of the market.

predominant-factor test ■ A test courts use to determine whether a contract is primarily for the sale of goods or for the sale of services.

preemption ■ A doctrine under which certain federal laws preempt, or take precedence over, conflicting state or local laws.

preemptive rights ■ Rights held by shareholders that entitle them to purchase newly issued shares of a corporation's stock, equal in percentage to shares already held, before the stock is offered to any outside buyers. Preemptive rights enable shareholders to maintain their proportionate ownership and voice in the corporation.

preference ■ In bankruptcy proceedings, property transfers or payments made by the debtor that favor (give preference to) one creditor over others. The bankruptcy trustee is allowed to recover payments made both voluntarily and involuntarily to one creditor in preference over another.

preferred creditor ■ In the context of bankruptcy, a creditor who has received a preferential transfer from a debtor.

preferred stock ■ Classes of stock that have priority over common stock as to both payment of dividends and distribution of assets on the corporation's dissolution.

premium ■ In insurance law, the price paid by the insured for insurance protection for a specified period of time.

prenuptial agreement ■ An agreement made before marriage that defines each partner's ownership rights in the other partner's property. Prenuptial agreements must be in writing to be enforceable.

presentment ■ The act of presenting an instrument to the party liable on the instrument to collect payment. Presentment also occurs when a person presents an instrument to a drawee for a required acceptance.

presentment warranties ■ Implied warranties, made by any person who presents an instrument for payment or acceptance, that (1) the person obtaining payment or acceptance is entitled to enforce the instrument or is authorized to obtain payment or acceptance on behalf of a person who is entitled to enforce the instrument, (2) the instrument has not been altered, and (3) the person obtaining payment or acceptance has no knowledge that the signature of the drawer of the instrument is unauthorized.

prima facie **case** ■ A case in which the plaintiff has produced sufficient evidence of his or her claim that the case can go to a jury; a case in which the evidence compels a decision for the plaintiff if the defendant produces no affirmative defense or evidence to disprove the plaintiff's assertion.

primary source of law ■ A document that establishes the law on a particular issue, such as a constitution, a statute, an administrative rule, or a court decision.

principal ■ In agency law, a person who agrees to have another, called the agent, act on her or his behalf.

principle of rights ■ The principle that human beings have certain fundamental rights (to life, freedom, and the pursuit of happiness, for example). Those who adhere to this "rights theory" believe that a key factor in determining whether a business decision is ethical is how that decision affects the rights of various groups. These groups include the firm's owners, its employees, the consumers of its products or services, its suppliers, the community in which it does business, and society as a whole.

private equity capital ■ A financing method by which a company sells equity in an existing business to a private or institutional investor.

privilege ■ A legal right, exemption, or immunity granted to a person or a class of persons. In the context of defamation, an absolute privilege immunizes the person making the statements from a lawsuit, regardless of whether the statements were malicious.

privity of contract ■ The relationship that exists between the promisor and the promisee of a contract.

probable cause ■ Reasonable grounds for believing that a person should be arrested or searched.

probate ■ The process of proving and validating a will and settling all matters pertaining to an estate.

probate court ■ A state court of limited jurisdiction that conducts proceedings relating to the settlement of a deceased person's estate.

procedural law ■ Law that establishes the methods of enforcing the rights established by substantive law.

proceeds ■ Under Article 9 of the UCC, whatever is received when collateral is sold or otherwise disposed of, such as by exchange.

product liability ■ The legal liability of manufacturers, sellers, and lessors of goods to consumers, users, and bystanders for injuries or damages that are caused by the goods.

profit ■ In real property law, the right to enter onto and remove things from the property of another (for example, the right to enter onto a person's land and remove sand and gravel).

promise ■ An assertion that something either will or will not happen in the future.

promisee ■ A person to whom a promise is made.

promisor ■ A person who makes a promise.

promissory estoppel ■ A doctrine that applies when a promisor makes a clear and definite promise on which the promisee justifiably relies. Such a promise is binding if justice will be better served by the enforcement of the promise.

promissory note ■ A written promise made by one person (the maker) to pay a fixed amount of money to another person (the payee or a subsequent holder) on demand or on a specified date.

property ■ Legally protected rights and interests in anything with an ascertainable value that is subject to ownership.

prospectus ■ A written document, required by securities laws, that describes the security being sold, the financial operations of the issuing corporation, and the investment or risk attaching to the security. It is designed to provide sufficient information to enable investors to evaluate the risk involved in purchasing the security.

protected class ■ A group of persons protected by specific laws because of the group's defining characteristics. Under laws prohibiting employment discrimination, these characteristics include race, color, religion, national origin, gender, age, and disability.

proximate cause ■ Legal cause; exists when the connection between an act and an injury is strong enough to justify imposing liability.

proxy ■ In corporation law, a written agreement between a stockholder and another under which the shareholder authorizes the other to vote the stockholder's shares in a certain manner.

puffery ■ A salesperson's often exaggerated claims concerning the quality of property offered for sale. Such claims involve opinions rather than facts and are not considered to be legally binding promises or warranties.

punitive damages ■ Monetary damages that may be awarded to a plaintiff to punish the defendant and deter future similar conduct.

purchase-money security interest (PMSI) ■ A security interest that arises when a seller or lender extends credit for part or all of the purchase price of goods purchased by a buyer.

 Q

qualified indorsement ■ An indorsement on a negotiable instrument in which the indorser disclaims any contract liability on the instrument. The notation "without recourse" is commonly used to create a qualified indorsement.

quasi contract ■ A fictional contract imposed on the parties by a court in the interests of fairness and justice; usually imposed to avoid the unjust enrichment of one party at the expense of another.

question of fact ■ In a lawsuit, an issue that involves only disputed facts, and not what the law is on a given point. Questions of fact are decided by the jury in a jury trial (by the judge if there is no jury).

question of law ■ In a lawsuit, an issue involving the application or interpretation of a law. Only a judge, not a jury, can rule on questions of law.

quitclaim deed ■ A deed intended to pass any title, interest, or claim that the grantor may have in the property without warranting that such title is valid. A quitclaim deed offers the least amount of protection against defects in the title.

quorum ■ The number of members of a decision making body that must be present before business may be transacted.

quota ■ A set limit on the amount of goods that can be imported.

ratification ■ The act of accepting and giving legal force to an obligation that previously was not enforceable.

reaffirmation agreement ■ An agreement between a debtor and a creditor in which the debtor voluntarily agrees to pay, or reaffirm, a debt dischargeable in bankruptcy. To be enforceable, the agreement must be made before the debtor is granted a discharge.

real property ■ Land and everything attached to it, such as trees and buildings.

reasonable person standard ■ The standard of behavior expected of a hypothetical "reasonable person"; the standard against which negligence is measured and that must be observed to avoid liability for negligence.

record ■ According to the Uniform Electronic Transactions Act, information that is either inscribed on a tangible medium or stored in an electronic or other medium and is retrievable.

recording statutes ■ Statutes that allow deeds, mortgages, and other real property transactions to be recorded so as to provide notice to future purchasers or creditors of an existing claim on the property.

red herring prospectus ■ A preliminary prospectus that can be distributed to potential investors after the registration statement (for a securities offering) has been filed with the Securities and Exchange Commission. The name derives from the red legend printed across the prospectus stating that the registration has been filed but has not become effective.

reformation ■ A court-ordered correction of a written contract so that it reflects the true intentions of the parties.

Regulation E ■ A set of rules issued by the Federal Reserve System's Board of Governors to protect users of elecronic fund transfer systems.

release ■ A contract in which one party forfeits the right to pursue a legal claim against the other party.

remedy ■ The relief given to an innocent party to enforce a right or compensate for the violation of a right.

replevin ■ An action to recover identified goods in the hands of a party who is wrongfully withholding them from the other party. Under the UCC, this remedy is usually available only if the buyer or lessee is unable to cover.

reply ■ Procedurally, a plaintiff's response to a defendant's answer.

requirements contract ■ An agreement in which a buyer agrees to purchase and the seller agrees to sell all or up to a stated amount of what the buyer needs or requires.

res ipsa loquitur ■ A doctrine under which negligence may be inferred simply because an event occurred, if it is the type of event that would not occur in the absence of negligence. Literally, the term means "the facts speak for themselves."

rescission ■ A remedy whereby a contract is canceled and the parties are returned to the positions they occupied before the contract was made; may be effected through the mutual consent of the parties, by the parties' conduct, or by court decree.

respondeat superior ■ Latin for "let the master respond." A doctrine under which a principal or an employer is held liable for the wrongful acts committed by agents or employees while acting within the course and scope of their agency or employment.

restitution ■ An equitable remedy under which a person is restored to his or her original position prior to loss or injury, or placed in the position he or she would have been in had the breach not occurred.

restrictive indorsement ■ Any indorsement on a negotiable instrument that requires the indorsee to comply with certain instructions regarding the funds involved. A restrictive indorsement does not prohibit the further negotiation of the instrument.

resulting trust ■ An implied trust arising from the conduct of the parties. A trust in which a party holds the actual legal title to another's property but only for that person's benefit.

retained earnings ■ The portion of a corporation's profits that has not been paid out as dividends to shareholders.

revocation ■ In contract law, the withdrawal of an offer by an offeror. Unless the offer is irrevocable, it can be revoked at any time prior to acceptance without liability.

right of contribution ■ The right of a co-surety who pays more than her or his proportionate share on a debtor's default to recover the excess paid from other co-sureties.

right of reimbursement ■ The legal right of a person to be restored, repaid, or indemnified for costs, expenses, or losses incurred or expended on behalf of another.

right of subrogation ■ The right of a person to stand in the place of (be substituted for) another, giving the substituted party the same legal rights that the original party had.

right-to-work law ■ A state law providing that employees may not be required to join a union as a condition of retaining employment.

risk ■ A prediction concerning potential loss based on known and unknown factors.

risk management ■ Planning that is undertaken to protect one's interest should some event threaten to undermine its security. In the context of insurance, risk management involves transferring certain risks from the insured to the insurance company.

robbery ■ The act of forcefully and unlawfully taking personal property of any value from another. Force or intimidation is usually necessary for an act of theft to be considered robbery.

rule of four ■ A rule of the United States Supreme Court under which the Court will not issue a writ of *certiorari* unless at least four justices approve of the decision to issue the writ.

S corporation ■ A close business corporation that has met certain requirements set out in the Internal Revenue Code and thus qualifies for special income tax treatment. Essentially, an S corporation is taxed the same as a partnership, but its owners enjoy the privilege of limited liability.

sale ■ The passing of title to property from the seller to the buyer for a price.

sale on approval ■ A type of conditional sale in which the buyer may take the goods on a trial basis. The sale becomes absolute only when the buyer approves of (or is satisfied with) the goods being sold.

sale or return ■ A type of conditional sale in which title and possession pass from the seller to the buyer, but the buyer retains the option to return the goods during a specified period even though the goods conform to the contract.

sales contract ■ A contract for the sale of goods under which the ownership of goods is transferred from a seller to a buyer for a price.

scienter ■ Knowledge by the misrepresenting party that material facts have been falsely represented or omitted with an intent to deceive.

search warrant ■ An order granted by a public authority, such as a judge, that authorizes law enforcement personnel to search a particular premise or property.

seasonably ■ Within a specified time period or, if no period is specified, within a reasonable time.

SEC Rule 10b-5 ■ A rule of the Securities and Exchange Commission that makes it unlawful, in connection with the purchase or sale of any security, to make any untrue statement of a material fact or to omit a material fact if such omission causes the statement to be misleading.

secondary boycott ■ A union's refusal to work for, purchase from, or handle the products of a secondary employer, with whom the union has no dispute, in order to force that employer to stop doing business with the primary employer, with whom the union has a labor dispute.

secondary source of law ■ A publication that summarizes or interprets the law, such as a legal encyclopedia, a legal treatise, or an article in a law review.

secured party ■ A lender, seller, or any other person in whose favor there is a security interest, including a person to whom accounts or chattel paper have been sold.

secured transaction ■ Any transaction in which the payment of a debt is guaranteed, or secured, by personal property owned by the debtor or in which the debtor has a legal interest.

securities ■ Generally, stock certificates, bonds, notes, debentures, warrants, or other documents given as evidence of an ownership interest in a corporation or as a promise of repayment by a corporation.

security ■ Generally, a stock certificate, bond, note, debenture, warrant, or other document or record evidencing an ownership interest in a corporation or a promise to repay a corporation's debt.

security agreement ■ An agreement that creates or provides for a security interest between the debtor and a secured party.

security interest ■ Any interest in personal property or fixtures that secures payment or performance of an obligation.

self-defense ■ The legally recognized privilege to protect oneself or one's property against injury by another. The privilege of self-defense usually applies only to acts that are reasonably necessary to protect oneself, one's property, or another person.

self-incrimination ■ The giving of testimony that may subject the testifier to criminal prosecution. The Fifth Amendment to the Constitution protects against self-incrimination by providing that no person "shall be compelled in any criminal case to be a witness against himself."

seniority system ■ In regard to employment relationships, a system in which those who have worked longest for the employer are first in line for promotions, salary increases, and other benefits. They are also the last to be laid off if the workforce must be reduced.

service mark ■ A mark used in the sale or the advertising of services to distinguish the services of one person from those of others. Titles, character names, and other distinctive features of radio and television programs may be registered as service marks.

sexual harassment ■ In the employment context, the demanding of sexual favors in return for job promotions or other benefits, or language or conduct that is so sexually offensive that it creates a hostile working environment.

shareholder's derivative suit ■ A suit brought by a shareholder to enforce a corporate cause of action against a third person.

shelter principle ■ The principle that the holder of a negotiable instrument who cannot qualify as a holder in due course (HDC), but who derives his or her title through an HDC, acquires the rights of an HDC.

shipment contract ■ A contract for the sale of goods in which the seller is required or authorized to ship the goods by carrier. The seller assumes liability for any losses or damage to the goods until they are delivered to the carrier.

short-form (parent-subsidiary) merger ■ A merger of companies in which one company (the parent corporation) owns at least 90 percent of the outstanding shares of each class of stock of the other corporation (the subsidiary corporation). The merger can be accomplished without the approval of the shareholders of either corporation.

shrink-wrap agreement ■ An agreement whose terms are expressed in a document located inside a box in which goods (usually software) are packaged; sometimes called a *shrink-wrap license*.

signature ■ Under the UCC, "any symbol executed or adopted by a party with a present intention to authenticate a writing."

slander ■ Defamation in oral form.

slander of quality (trade libel) ■ The publication of false information about another's product, alleging that it is not what its seller claims.

slander of title ■ The publication of a statement that denies or casts doubt on another's legal ownership of any property, causing financial loss to that property's owner.

small claims court ■ A special court in which parties may litigate small claims (such as $5,000 or less). Attorneys are not required in small claims courts and, in some states, are not allowed to represent the parties.

smart card ■ A card containing a microprocessor that permits storage of funds via security programming, can communicate with other computers, and does not require online authorization for fund transfers.

sole proprietorship ■ The simplest form of business organization, in which the owner is the business. The owner reports business income on his or her personal income tax return and is legally responsible for all debts and obligations incurred by the business.

sovereign immunity ■ A doctrine that immunizes foreign nations from the jurisdiction of U.S. courts when certain conditions are satisfied.

spam ■ Bulk, unsolicited ("junk") e-mail.

special indorsement ■ An indorsement on an instrument that indicates the specific person to whom the indorser intends to make the instrument payable; that is, it names the indorsee.

special warranty deed ■ A deed in which the grantor warrants only that the grantor or seller held good title during his or her ownership of the property and does not warrant that there were no defects of title when the property was held by previous owners.

specific performance ■ An equitable remedy requiring exactly the performance that was specified; usually granted only when monetary damages would be an inadequate remedy and the subject matter of the contract is unique.

spendthrift trust ■ A trust created to protect the beneficiary from spending all the funds to which she or he is entitled. Only a certain portion of the total amount is given to the beneficiary at any one time, and most states prohibit creditors from attaching assets of the trust.

stale check ■ A check, other than a certified check, that is presented for payment more than six months after its date.

standing to sue ■ The requirement that an individual must have a sufficient stake in a controversy before he or she can bring a lawsuit. The plaintiff must demonstrate that he or she has been either injured or threatened with injury.

stare decisis ■ A common law doctrine under which judges are obligated to follow the precedents established in prior decisions.

Statute of Frauds ■ A state statute under which certain types of contracts must be in writing to be enforceable.

statute of limitations ■ A federal or state statute setting the maximum time period during which a certain action can be brought or certain rights enforced.

statutory law ■ The body of law enacted by legislative bodies (as opposed to constitutional law, administrative law, or case law).

stock ■ An equity (ownership) interest in a corporation, measured in units of shares.

stock certificate ■ A certificate issued by a corporation evidencing the ownership of a specified number of shares in the corporation.

stock options ■ An agreement that grants the owner the option to buy a given number of shares of stock, usually within a set time period.

stock warrant ■ A certificate that grants the owner the option to buy a given number of shares of stock, usually within a set time period.

stop-payment order ■ An order by a bank customer to his or her bank not to pay or certify a certain check.

stored-value card ■ A card bearing a magnetic strip that holds magnetically encoded data, providing access to stored funds.

strict liability ■ Liability regardless of fault. In tort law, strict liability is imposed on a manufacturer or seller that introduces into commerce a good that is unreasonably dangerous when in a defective condition.

sublease ■ A lease executed by the lessee of real estate to a third person, conveying the same interest that the lessee enjoys but for a shorter term than that held by the lessee.

substantive law ■ Law that defines, describes, regulates, and creates legal rights and obligations.

summary jury trial (SJT) ■ A method of settling disputes, used in many federal courts, in which a trial is held, but the jury's verdict is not binding. The verdict acts only as a guide to both sides in reaching an agreement during the mandatory negotiations that immediately follow the summary jury trial.

summons ■ A document informing a defendant that a legal action has been commenced against him or her and that the defendant must appear in court on a certain date to answer the plaintiff's complaint.

surety ■ A person, such as a cosigner on a note, who agrees to be primarily responsible for the debt of another.

suretyship ■ An express contract in which a third party to a debtor-creditor relationship (the surety) promises to be primarily responsible for the debtor's obligation.

symbolic speech ■ Nonverbal expressions of beliefs. Symbolic speech, which includes gestures, movements, and articles of clothing, is given substantial protection by the courts.

takeover ■ The acquisition of control over a corporation through the purchase of a substantial number of the voting shares of the corporation.

taking ■ The taking of private property by the government for public use. The government may not take private property for public use without "just compensation."

tangible property ■ Property that has physical existence and can be distinguished by the senses of touch or sight. A car is tangible property; a patent right is intangible property.

target corporation ■ The corporation to be acquired in a corporate takeover; a corporation whose shareholders receive a tender offer.

tariff ■ A tax on imported goods.

tenancy at sufferance ■ A type of tenancy under which a tenant who, after rightfully being in possession of leased premises, continues (wrongfully) to occupy the property after the lease has terminated. The tenant has no rights to possess the property and occupies it only because the person entitled to evict the tenant has not done so.

tenancy at will ■ A type of tenancy that either party can terminate without notice; usually arises when a tenant who has been under a tenancy for years retains possession, with the landlord's consent, after the tenancy for years has terminated.

tenancy in common ■ Co-ownership of property in which each party owns an undivided interest that passes to her or his heirs at death.

tender ■ An unconditional offer to perform an obligation by a person who is ready, willing, and able to do so.

tender of delivery ■ Under the Uniform Commercial Code, a seller's or lessor's act of placing conforming goods at the disposal of the buyer or lessee and giving the buyer or lessor whatever notification is reasonably necessary to enable the buyer or lessee to take delivery.

tender offer ■ An offer to purchase made by one company directly to the shareholders of another (target) company; sometimes referred to as a *takeover bid.*

testamentary trust ■ A trust that is created by will and therefore does not take effect until the death of the testator.

testate ■ Having left a will at death.

testator ■ One who makes and executes a will.

third party beneficiary ■ One for whose benefit a promise is made in a contract but who is not a party to the contract.

tippee ■ A person who receives inside information.

tombstone ad ■ An advertisement, historically in a format resembling a tombstone, of a securities offering. The ad tells potential investors where and how they may obtain a prospectus.

tort ■ A civil wrong not arising from a breach of contract; a breach of a legal duty that proximately causes harm or injury to another.

tortfeasor ■ One who commits a tort.

Totten trust ■ A trust created by the deposit of a person's own funds in his or her own name as a trustee for another. It is a tentative trust, revocable at will until the depositor dies or completes the gift in his or her lifetime by some unequivocal act or declaration.

trade dress ■ The image and overall appearance of a product—for example, the distinctive decor, menu, layout, and style of service of a particular restaurant. Basically, trade dress is subject to the same protection as trademarks.

trade libel ■ The publication of false information about another's product, alleging it is not what its seller claims; also referred to as *slander of quality.*

trade name ■ A term that is used to indicate part or all of a business's name and that is directly related to the business's reputation and goodwill. Trade names are protected under the common law (and under trademark law, if the name is the same as the firm's trademarked product).

trade secrets ■ Information or processes that give a business an advantage over competitors that do not know the information or processes.

trademark ■ A distinctive mark, motto, device, or emblem that a manufacturer stamps, prints, or otherwise affixes to the goods it produces so that they may be identified on the market and their origins made known. Once a trademark is established (under the common law or through registration), the owner is entitled to its exclusive use.

transfer warranties ■ Implied warranties, made by any person who transfers an instrument for consideration to subsequent transferees and holders who take the instrument in good faith, that (1) the transferor is entitled to enforce the instrument; (2) all signatures are authentic and authorized; (3) the instrument has not been altered; (4) the instrument is not subject to a defense or claim of any party that can be asserted against the transferor; and (5) the transferor has no knowledge of any insolvency proceedings against the maker, the acceptor, or the drawer of the instrument.

traveler's check ■ A check that is payable on demand, drawn on or payable through a financial institution (bank), and designated as a traveler's check.

treaty ■ An agreement formed between two or more independent nations.

trespass to land ■ The entry onto, above, or below the surface of land owned by another without the owner's permission or legal authorization.

trespass to personal property ■ The unlawful taking or harming of another's personal property; interference with another's right to the exclusive possession of his or her personal property.

trust ■ An arrangement in which title to property is held by one person (a trustee) for the benefit of another (a beneficiary).

trust indorsement ■ An indorsement for the benefit of the indorser or a third person; also known as an *agency indorsement.* The indorsement results in legal title vesting in the original indorsee.

U.S. trustee ■ A government official who performs certain administrative tasks that a bankruptcy judge would otherwise have to perform.

ultra vires ■ A Latin term meaning "beyond the powers"; in corporate law, acts of a corporation that are beyond its express and implied powers to undertake.

unconscionable contract (or unconscionable clause) ■ A contract or clause that is void on the basis of public policy because one party, as a result of disproportionate bargaining power, is forced to accept terms that are unfairly burdensome and that unfairly benefit the dominating party.

underwriter ■ In insurance law, the insurer, or the one assuming a risk in return for the payment of a premium.

undisclosed principal ■ A principal whose identity is unknown by a third person, and the third person has no knowledge that the agent is acting for a principal at the time the agent and the third person form a contract.

unenforceable contract ■ A valid contract rendered unenforceable by some statute or law.

uniform law ■ A model law created by the National Conference of Commissioners on Uniform State Laws and/or the American Law Institute for the states to consider adopting. If the state adopts the law, it becomes statutory law in that state. Each state has the option of adopting or rejecting all or part of a uniform law.

unilateral contract ■ A contract that results when an offer can only be accepted by the offeree's performance.

unilateral mistake ■ A mistake that occurs when only one party to a contract is mistaken about a material fact.

union shop ■ A firm that requires all workers, once employed, to become union members within a specified period of time as a condition of their continued employment.

universal defenses ■ Defenses that are valid against all holders of a negotiable instrument, including holders in due course (HDCs) and holders with the rights of HDCs.

unreasonably dangerous product ■ In product liability law, a product that is defective to the point of threatening a consumer's health and safety. A product will be considered unreasonably dangerous if it is dangerous beyond the expectation of the ordinary consumer or if a less dangerous alternative was economically feasible for the manufacturer, but the manufacturer failed to produce it.

usage of trade ■ Any practice or method of dealing having such regularity of observance in a place, vocation, or trade as to justify an expectation that it will be observed with respect to the transaction in question.

usury ■ Charging an illegal rate of interest.

utilitarianism ■ An approach to ethical reasoning that evaluates behavior in light of the consequences of that behavior for those who will be affected by it, rather than on the basis of any absolute ethical or moral values. In utilitarian reasoning, a "good" decision is one that results in the greatest good for the greatest number of people affected by the decision.

valid contract ■ A contract that results when the elements necessary for contract formation (agreement, consideration, legal purpose, and contractual capacity) are present.

venture capital ■ Capital (funds and other assets) provided by professional, outside investors (*venture capitalists*, usually groups of wealthy investors and investment banks) to start new business ventures.

venue ■ The geographic district in which a legal action is tried and from which the jury is selected.

vesting ■ The creation of an absolute or unconditional right or power.

vicarious liability ■ Legal responsibility placed on one person for the acts of another; indirect liability imposed on a supervisory party (such as an employer) for the actions of a subordinate (such as an employee) because of the relationship between the two parties.

void contract ■ A contract having no legal force or binding effect.

voidable contract ■ A contract that may be legally avoided (canceled, or annulled) at the option of one or both of the parties.

voir dire ■ An old French phrase meaning "to speak the truth." In legal terms, it refers to the process in which the attorneys question prospective jurors to learn about their backgrounds, attitudes, biases, and other characteristics that may affect their ability to serve as impartial jurors.

warranty deed ■ A deed in which the grantor assures (warrants to) the grantee that the grantor has title to the property conveyed in the deed, that there are no encumbrances on the property other than what the grantor has represented, and that the grantee will enjoy quiet possession of the property; a deed that provides the greatest amount of protection for the grantee.

watered stock ■ Shares of stock issued by a corporation for which the corporation receives, as payment, less than the stated value of the shares.

whistleblowing ■ An employee's disclosure to government authorities, upper-level managers, or the press that the employer is engaged in unsafe or illegal activities.

white-collar crime ■ Nonviolent crime committed by individuals or corporations to obtain a personal or business advantage.

will ■ An instrument directing what is to be done with the testator's property on his or her death, made by the testator and revocable during his or her lifetime. No interests in the testator's property pass until the testator dies.

will substitutes ■ Various documents that attempt to dispose of an estate in the same or similar manner as a will, such as trusts or life insurance plans.

winding up ■ The second of two stages in the termination of a partnership or corporation. Once the firm is dissolved, it continues to exist legally until the process of winding up all business affairs (collecting and distributing the firm's assets) is complete.

workers' compensation laws ■ State statutes establishing an administrative procedure for compensating workers' injuries that arise out of—or in the course of—their employment, regardless of fault.

working papers ■ The various documents used and developed by an accountant during an audit, such as notes and computations, that make up the work product of an accountant's services to a client.

workout ■ An out-of-court agreement between a debtor and creditors in which the parties work out a payment plan or schedule under which the debtor's debts can be discharged.

writ of attachment ■ A court's order, issued prior to a trial to collect a debt, directing the sheriff or other public officer to seize nonexempt property of the debtor. If the creditor prevails at trial, the seized property can be sold to satisfy the judgment.

writ of *certiorari* ■ A writ from a higher court asking the lower court for the record of a case.

writ of execution ■ A court's order, issued after a judgment has been entered against a debtor, directing the sheriff to seize (levy) and sell any of the debtor's nonexempt real or personal property. The proceeds of the sale are used to pay off the judgment, accrued interest, and costs of the sale; any surplus is paid to the debtor.

wrongful discharge ■ An employer's termination of an employee's employment in violation of the law.

Table of Cases

Index

Manager-managed LLCs, 513
Manufacturing. *See also* Product
    liability
  abroad, 663–664
  defects, 332
Marijuana, medical, 12
Market-share liability, 334
Marriage
  promises made in consideration of,
    211
  will revocation, 630
Mechanic's liens, 417–418
Mediation
  as ADR option, 49–50
  advantage of, 50
  binding, 52
  online service providers, 54
Mediation-arbitration (med-arb), 52
Medical Device Amendments (MDA)
    (1976), 335
Medicare, 474
Meetings
  board of directors, 546
  of shareholders, 551
Member (LLCs), 511, 513
Member-managed LLCs, 513
Mens rea, 126
Mental incapacity. *See* Mental
    incompetence
Mental incompetence
  of agents or principals, 460
  of bank customers, 377
  and contractual capacity, 185, 188
  as defense to negotiable instrument
    liability, 365
  insanity defense, 133–134
  of offeror of offeree, offer termination
    by, 173
  of partner, 506–507
Mental state, 126–127
Merchantability, implied warranty of,
    325, 329
Merchantable food, 326
Merchantable goods, 325
Merchants
  both parties as, 279
  defined, 274–275
  firm offer by, 277–278
  written confirmation between, 281
Merck & Company, 62
Mergers, 534–536, 551
Meta tags, 107
Mill, John Stuart, 65
Minimum wage, 469
Minimum-contacts standard, 34
Mini-trials, 52
Minors

age of majority and, 185
contractual capacity, 185–187
emancipation, 185
Miranda Rule, 138–139
Mirror image rule, 173
Misappropriation of funds, 525
Misappropriation theory, 575
Misconduct, 646
Misdemeanors, 132
Mislaid property, 594
Misrepresentation
  of age, 186–187
  by agent, 456–457
  by conduct, 206–207
  fraudulent, 87, 205–208
  of law, 207
  product liability based on, 331
  by professionals, 647
  by realtors, 612
  by silence, 207
Mistakes
  bilateral (mutual), 204
  contracts, 203–204
  as defense to criminal liability, 134
  of fact, 134, 203–204
  unilateral, 204
Misuse, product, 335
Mitigation of damages, 244
M'Naghten test, 134
Model Business Corporation Act
    (MBCA), 520
Model Penal Code, 126–127, 135
Monetary systems, 667–668
Money, defined, 351
Money damages. *See* Damages
Money laundering, 132
Moral minimum, 67
Mortgage bonds, 532
Mortgage notes, 349
Mortgagee, 419
Mortgages, 419–420
Mortgagor, 419
Most-favored-nation status, 665
Motion(s)
  to compel discovery, 43
  for directed verdict, 46
  to dismiss, 42, 43
  for judgment as matter of law, 46
  for judgment *n.o.v.*, 46
  for judgment on the pleadings, 42, 43
  to make more definite and certain,
    43
  for new trial, 46
  posttrial, 46
  pretrial, 42
  to strike, 43
  for summary judgment, 42, 43

MP3 players, 113–115
Music industry, copyright issues,
    113–115
Mutual (bilateral) mistakes, 204
Mutual funds, 570

N

Names, corporate, 528
Nation, defined, 660
National Arbitration and Mediation
    (NAM), 54
National Conference of
    Commissioners on Uniform State
    Laws (NCCUSL), 4–5, 261, 347,
    502, 578, 614–615, 629
National Information Infrastructure
    Protection Act (1996), 143
National Institute for Occupational
    Safety and Health, 473
National Labor Relations Act (NLRA)
    (1935), 470–472
National Labor Relations Board
    (NLRB), 471
National law, 9–10, 660
National origin, discrimination based
    on, 481
National Reporter System (West), 25,
    26
National Securities Markets
    Improvement Act (1996), 566, 578
Necessaries, 187
Negligence
  of agent, 457–458
  of bank, 378–379
  of bank customer, 377–380
  causation, 92
  comparative, 93, 335–336
  contributory, 93
  criminal, 126–127
  damages, 92
  "danger invites rescue" doctrine, 93
  defenses to, 92–93, 646
  dram shop acts, 94
  duty of care, 90–91
  Good Samaritan statutes, 94
  of independent contractors, 448
  injury requirement, 91
  per se, 93
  product liability, 330
  of professionals, 645–647
  res ipsa loquitur, 93
  as unintentional tort, 82
Negligent misrepresentation, 87
Negotiable instruments, 346–395
  cancellation, 366
  checks. *See* Checks